THE OXFORD HANDBOOK OF

COMPUTATIONAL LINGUISTICS

THE OXFORD HANDBOOK OF

COMPUTATIONAL
LINGUISTICS

Edited by

RUSLAN MITKOV

OXFORD

UNIVERSITY PRESS

OXFORD

UNIVERSITY PRESS

Great Clarendon Street, Oxford OX2 6DP

Oxford University Press is a department of the University of Oxford.
It furthers the University's objective of excellence in research, scholarship,
and education by publishing worldwide in

Oxford New York

Auckland Bangkok Buenos Aires Cape Town Chennai
Dar es Salaam Delhi Hong Kong Istanbul Karachi Kolkata
Kuala Lumpur Madrid Melbourne Mexico City Mumbai
Nairobi São Paulo Shanghai Taipei Tokyo Toronto

Oxford is a registered trade mark of Oxford University Press
in the UK and in certain other countries

Published in the United States
by Oxford University Press Inc., New York

© editorial matter and organization Ruslan Mitkov 2003
© chapters their several authors 2003

British Library Cataloguing in Publication Data

Data available

Library of Congress Cataloging in Publication Data

Data available

ISBN 0-19-823882-7

1 3 5 7 9 10 8 6 4 2

Typeset in Minion
by Peter Kahrel, Lancaster
Printed in Great Britain
on acid-free paper by
Biddles Ltd., Guildford & King's Lynn

Contents

Preface   ix
RUSLAN MITKOV

Abbreviations   xi

Introduction   xvii
MARTIN KAY

PART I FUNDAMENTALS

1. Phonology   3
STEVEN BIRD

2. Morphology   25
HARALD TROST

3. Lexicography   48
PATRICK HANKS

4. Syntax   70
RONALD M. KAPLAN

5. Semantics   91
SHALOM LAPPIN

6. Discourse   112
ALLAN RAMSAY

7. Pragmatics and Dialogue   136
GEOFFREY LEECH AND MARTIN WEISSER

8. Formal Grammars and Languages   157
    CARLOS MARTÍN-VIDE

9. Complexity   178
    BOB CARPENTER

PART II PROCESSES, METHODS, AND RESOURCES

10. Text Segmentation   201
    ANDREI MIKHEEV

11. Part-of-Speech Tagging   219
    ATRO VOUTILAINEN

12. Parsing   233
    JOHN CARROLL

13. Word–Sense Disambiguation   249
    MARK STEVENSON AND YORICK WILKS

14. Anaphora Resolution   266
    RUSLAN MITKOV

15. Natural Language Generation   284
    JOHN BATEMAN AND MICHAEL ZOCK

16. Speech Recognition   305
    LORI LAMEL AND JEAN-LUC GAUVAIN

17. Text-to-Speech Synthesis   323
    THIERRY DUTOIT AND YANNIS STYLIANOU

18. Finite-State Technology   339
    LAURI KARTTUNEN

19. Statistical Methods   358
    CHRISTER SAMUELSSON

20. Machine Learning   376
     RAYMOND J. MOONEY

21. Lexical Knowledge Acquisition   395
     YUJI MATSUMOTO

22. Evaluation   414
     LYNETTE HIRSCHMAN AND INDERJEET MANI

23. Sublanguages and Controlled Languages   430
     RICHARD I. KITTREDGE

24. Corpus Linguistics   448
     TONY McENERY

25. Ontologies   464
     PIEK VOSSEN

26. Tree-Adjoining Grammars   483
     ARAVIND K. JOSHI

PART III APPLICATIONS

27. Machine Translation: General Overview   501
     JOHN HUTCHINS

28. Machine Translation: Latest Developments   512
     HAROLD SOMERS

29. Information Retrieval   529
     EVELYNE TZOUKERMANN, JUDITH L. KLAVANS,
     AND TOMEK STRZALKOWSKI

30. Information Extraction   545
     RALPH GRISHMAN

31. Question Answering   560
     SANDA HARABAGIU AND DAN MOLDOVAN

32. Text Summarization   583
    EDUARD HOVY

33. Term Extraction and Automatic Indexing   599
    CHRISTIAN JACQUEMIN AND DIDIER BOURIGAULT

34. Text Data Mining   616
    MARTI A. HEARST

35. Natural Language Interaction   629
    ION ANDROUTSOPOULOS AND MARIA ARETOULAKI

36. Natural Language in Multimodal and Multimedia Systems   650
    ELISABETH ANDRÉ

37. Natural Language Processing in Computer-Assisted
    Language Learning   670
    JOHN NERBONNE

38. Multilingual On-Line Natural Language Processing   699
    GREGORY GREFENSTETTE AND FRÉDÉRIQUE SEGOND

    Notes on Contributors   717
    Glossary   727
    Index of Authors   761
    Subject Index   775

PREFACE

Computational Linguistics is an interdisciplinary field concerned with the processing of language by computers. Since machine translation began to emerge some
fifty years ago (see Martin Kay's introduction below), Computational Linguistics
has grown and developed exponentially. It has expanded theoretically through the
development of computational and formal models of language. In the process it has
vastly increased the range and usefulness of its applications. At a time of continuing
and vigorous growth the *Oxford Handbook of Computational Linguistics* provides
a much-needed reference and guide. It aims to be of use to everyone interested in
the subject, including students wanting to familiarize themselves with its key areas,
researchers in other areas in search of an appropriate model or method, and those
already working in the field who want to discover the latest developments in areas
adjacent to their own.

The *Handbook* is structured in three parts which reflect a natural progression from
theory to applications.

Part I introduces the fundamentals: it considers, from a computational perspective,
the main areas of linguistics such as phonology, morphology, lexicography, syntax,
semantics, discourse, pragmatics, and dialogue. It also looks at central issues in mathematical linguistics such as formal grammars and languages, and complexity.

Part II is devoted to the basic stages, tasks, methods, and resources in and required
for automatic language processing. It examines text segmentation, part-of-speech
tagging, parsing, word–sense disambiguation, anaphora resolution, natural language
generation, speech recognition, text-to-speech synthesis, finite state technology,
statistical methods, machine learning, lexical knowledge acquisition, evaluation, sublanguages, controlled languages, corpora, ontologies, and tree-adjoining grammars.

Part III describes the main real-world applications based on Computational
Linguistics techniques, including machine translation, information retrieval, information extraction, question answering, text summarization, term extraction, text
data mining, natural language interfaces, spoken dialogue systems, multimodal/
multimedia systems, computer-aided language learning, and multilingual on-line
language processing.

Those who are relatively new to Computational Linguistics may find it helpful to
familiarize themselves with the preliminaries in Part I before going on to subjects in
Parts II and III. Reading Chapter 4 on syntax, for example, should help the reader to
understand the account of parsing in Chapter 12.

To make the book as coherent and useful as possible I encouraged the authors to adopt a consistent structure and style of presentation. I also added numerous cross-references and, with the help of the authors, compiled a glossary. This latter will, I hope, be useful for students and others getting to know the field.

The diverse readership for whom the *Handbook* is intended includes university researchers, teachers, and students; researchers in industry; company directors; software engineers; computer scientists; linguists and language specialists; and translators. In sum the book is for all those who are drawn to this endlessly fascinating and rewarding field.

I thank all the contributors to the *Handbook* for the high quality of their input and their cooperation. I am particularly indebted to Eduard Hovy, Lauri Karttunen, John Hutchins, and Yorick Wilks for their helpful comments and to Patrick Hanks for his dedicated assistance in compiling the glossary. I thank John Davey, OUP's linguistics editor, for his help and encouragement. I acknowledge gratefully the support received from the University of Wolverhampton. Finally, I would like to express gratitude to my late mother Penka Georgieva Moldovanska for her kind words and moral support at the beginning of this challenging editorial project.

Ruslan Mitkov
March 2002

ABBREVIATIONS

ACL	Association for Computational Linguistics
AECMA	Association Européenne des Constructeurs de Matériel Aéro-spatiale (European Association of Aerospace Industries)
AFL	abstract family of languages
AI	artificial intelligence
ALPAC	Automatic Language Processing Advisory Committee
API	application programming interface
ATIS	Air Travel Information Systems
ATN	augmented transition network
AVM	attribute-value matrix
BNN	Broadcast News Navigator
CA	conversational analysis
CAI	computer-aided instruction
CALL	computer-assisted language learning
CART	classification and regressions tree
CAT	computer-aided (or computer-assisted) translation
CCG	Combinatory Categorial Grammar
CDNS	Columbia Digital News System
CF	context-free
CFG	context-free grammar
CG	Constraint Grammar
CIDE	*Cambridge International Dictionary of English*
CKY	Cocke–Kasami–Younger
CL	controlled language
CLAW	controlled language applications workshop
CLEF	Cross-Language Evaluation Forum
CLIR	cross-language information retrieval
CNF	Chomsky normal form
COBUILD	Collins Birmingham University International Language Database
COLLINS	*Collins English Dictionary*
COMPUTERM	International Workshop on Computational Terminology
COP	Constituent Object Parser
CP	cooperative principle

CS	context-sensitive
CSG	context-sensitive grammar
DAMSL	Dialog Act Markup in Several Layers
DARPA	Defense Advanced Research Projects Agency
DCG	definite clause grammar
DFA	deterministic finite automaton
DFM	Derivation Final Model
DLT	Distributed Language Translation (MT system)
DM	data mining
DNF	disjunctive normal form
DOBJ	direct object
DP	dynamic programming
DPDA	Deterministic Pushdown Dutomaton
DRI	Discourse Resource Initiative
DRS	discourse representation structure
DRT	Discourse Representation Theory
EAGLES	Expert Advisory Group on Language Engineering Standards
EBMT	example-based machine translation
EC	European Community
ECI	European Corpus Initiative
EDA	Exploratory Data Analysis
EDL	extended domain of locality
EDR	Electronic Dictionary Research (Institute)
ELDA	European Language Resources Distribution Agency
ELRA	European Language Resources Association
EM	Expectation Maximization
ENGCG	English Constraint Grammar
EPDA	embedded pushdown automaton
EUROPHRAS	European Society for Phraseology
FA	finite automaton
FACS	facial action coding system
FAPs	facial animation parameters
FAQ	frequently asked questions
FoG	Forecast Generator (Environment Canada's bilingual text generator for meteorological sublanguages)
FRD	factoring recursion from the domain of dependencies
FSA	finite-state automaton
FUF	Functional Unification Formalism
GNF	Greibach normal form
GPSG	Generalized Phrase Structure Grammar
GQ	generalized quantifier
HCRC	Human Communication Research Centre

HLT	Human Language Technology
HMM	hidden Markov model
HPKB	high performance knowledge bases
HPSG	Head-Driven Phrase Structure Grammar
ICALL	Intelligent Computer-Assisted Language Learning
ICT	Information and Communication Technology
IE	information extraction
IL	Intensional Logic
ILP	Inductive Logic Programming
IPA	International Phonetic Alphabet
IPFP	Iterative Proportional Fitting Procedure
IR	information retrieval
ISO	International Organization for Standardization
ISOBJ	'is the OBJect of'
IST	Information Society technology
IV	intransitive verb
KBMT	knowledge-based machine translation
KDD	Knowledge Discovery in Databases
KIF	knowledge interchange format
KNF	Kuroda normal form
KNN	K Nearest Neighbor
KPML	Komet-Penman MultiLingual resource development environment
KWIC	key-word in context
LCS	Lexical Conceptual Structure
LDC	Linguistic Data Consortium
LDOCE	*Longman Dictionary of Contemporary English*
LFG	Lexical Functional Grammar
LIN	linear grammar
LINDI	Linking Information for Novel Discovery and Insight
LLIN	left-linear grammar
LM	language model
LMI	linguistically motivated indexing
LPC	linear predictive coding
LREC	Language Resources and Evaluation Conference
LSI	Latent Semantic Indexing
LTAG	Lexicalized Tree-Adjoining Grammar
LTS	letter-to-sound
LVCSR	large vocabulary continuous speech recognition
MAHT	machine-aided human translation
MAP	maximum a posteriori
MATE	Multilevel Annotation Tools Engineering
MBROLA	multiband resynthesis overlap add

MC-LTAG	multi-component Lexicalized Tree-Adjoining Grammar
MCS	mildly context-sensitive language
MC-TAG	Multi-Component Tree-Adjoining Grammar
MDL	Minimal Description Length
ME	maximum entropy
MFC	Mel frequency cepstral
MFCC	Mel Frequency Cepstral Coefficients
ML	machine learning
MLLR	maximum likelihood linear regression
MMR	Maximum Marginal Relevance
MRD	machine-readable dictionary
MRL	meaning representation language
MT	machine translation
MTM	Meaning-Text Model
MUC	Message Understanding Conference
N	noun
NEC	Nippon Electric Company
NER	named entity recognition
NFA	non-deterministic finite automaton
NIML	non-indigenous minority language
NIST	National Institute of Standards and Technology (USA)
NL	natural language
NLG	natural language generation
NLI	natural language interface
NLP	natural language processing
NODE	*New Oxford Dictionary of English*
NP	noun phrase
NP	non-deterministic polynomial
NPDA	non-deterministic pushdown automaton
+Nsg	singular noun
OALD	*Oxford Advanced Learners' Dictionary*
OALDCE	*Oxford Advanced Learner's Dictionary of Current English*
OCR	Optical Character Recognition
OED	*Oxford English Dictionary*
OOV	out-of-vocabulary
OPP	optimum position policy
OT	Optimality Theory
P	probability
P	(deterministic) polynomial
PARC	Palo Alto Research Center
PaT-Nets	parallel transition networks
PCFG	Probabilistic Context-Free Grammar

PCM	Parallel Correspondence Model
PDA	pushdown automaton
PDF	probability density function
PLP	Perceptual Linear Prediction
PNF	Penttonen normal form
POS	part of speech
QA	question answering
RAGS	Reference Architecture for Generation Systems
RE	Recursively Enumerable language
REG	regular grammar
RLIN	right-linear grammar
RST	rhetorical structure theory
RTN	recursive transition network
S	sentence
SAT	speaker adaptive training
SBD	sentence boundary disambiguation
SDC	Systems Development Corporation
SDS	spoken dialogue system
SFG	systemic functional grammar
SGML	Standard Generalized Markup Language
SIGGEN	Special Interest Group on Generation
SIGPHON	ACL Special Interest Group in Computational Phonology
SL	source language
SLT	spoken language translation
SNOMED	Systematized Nomenclature of Medicine
Sp	speaker
SUBJ	subject
SURGE	Systemic Unification Realization Grammar for English
SUSY	Saarbrücker Übersetzungssystem (MT system)
TAG	tree-adjoining grammar
TDM	text data mining
TD-PSOLA	time-domain pitch-synchronous-overlap-add
TDT	topic detection and tracking
TEFL	Teaching English as a Foreign Language
TEI	Text-Encoding Initiative
TELRI	Trans-European Language Resources Infrastructure
TESL	Teaching English as a Second Language
TF*IDF	term frequency and inverse document frequency
TIDES	Translingual Information Detection, Extraction, and Summarization
TL	target language
TM	translation memory
TMR	text-meaning representation

TREC	Text Retrieval Conference
TRINDI	Task Oriented Instructional Dialogue
TSA	tree-structure analysis
TTS	text-to-speech
UMLS	Unified Medical Language System
URL	universal resource locator
+Vb	verb
VP	verb phrase
+VpastT	verb past participle
WFST	well-formed substring table
WOZ	Wizard of Oz
WSD	word-sense disambiguation
WSJ	*Wall Street Journal*
WWW	World Wide Web
XDOD	Xerox Document On Demand
XIFSP	Xerox Incremental Finite State Processing
XML	eXtensible Markup Language
XRCE	Xerox Research Centre Europe

INTRODUCTION

MARTIN KAY

Computational Linguistics is about as robust a field of intellectual endeavour as one could find, with its books, journals, conferences, professorial chairs, societies, associations and the like. But, of course, it was not always so. Computational Linguistics crept into existence shyly, almost furtively. When shall we say it all began? Perhaps in 1949, when Warren Weaver wrote his famous memorandum suggesting that translation by machine might be possible. The first conference on machine translation took place at MIT in 1952 and the first journal, *Mechanical Translation*, began in 1954. However, the phrase 'Computational Linguistics' started to appear only in the mid-1960s. The journal changed its name to *Mechanical Translation and Computational Linguistics* in 1965 but the words 'and Computational Linguistics' appeared in very small type. This change coincided with the adoption of the journal by the Association for Machine Translation and Computational Linguistics, which was formed in 1962.

The term 'Computational Linguistics' was probably coined by David Hays during the time that he was a member of the Automatic Language Processing Advisory Committee of the National Academy of Sciences. The publication of this committee's final report, generally known as the ALPAC report, certainly constituted one of the most dramatic moments in the history of the field—proposing, as it did, that machine translation be abandoned as a short-term engineering goal in favour of more fundamental scientific research in language and language processing. Hays saw this coming and realized that, if the money that had been flowing into machine translation could be diverted into a new field of enquiry, the most pressing requirement was for the field to be given a name. The name took hold. Redirection of the funds did not.

Progression from machine translation to Computational Linguistics occurred in 1974 when *Machine Translation and Computational Linguistics* was replaced by the *American Journal of Computational Linguistics*, which appeared initially only in microfiche form. In 1980, this became *Computational Linguistics*, which is still alive and vigorous today.

By the 1980s, machine translation began to look practical again, at least to some people and for some purposes and, in 1986, the circle was completed with the publication of the first issue of *Computers and Translation*, renamed *Machine Translation* in 1988. The *International Journal of Machine Translation* followed in 1991.

Warren Weaver's vision of machine translation came from his war-time experience as a cryptographer and he considered the problem to be one of treating textual
material, by fundamentally statistical techniques. But the founders of Computational
Linguistics were mostly linguists, not statisticians, and they saw the potential of the
computer less in the possibility of deriving a characterization of the translation relation from emergent properties of parallel corpora, than in carrying out exactly, and
with great speed, the minutely specified rules that they would write. Chomsky's *Syntactic Structures* (1957) served to solidify the notion of grammar as a deductive system which therefore seemed eminently suited to computer applications. The fact that
Chomsky himself saw little value in such an enterprise, or that the particular scheme
of axioms and rules that he advocated was ill suited to the automatic analysis of text,
did nothing to diminish the attractiveness of the general idea.

Computational Linguistics thus came to be an exercise in creating and implementing the formal systems that were increasingly seen as constituting the core of linguistic theory. If any single event marks the birth of the field, it is surely the proposal by
John Cocke in 1960 of the scheme for deriving all analyses of a string with a grammar of binary context-free rules that we now know as the Cocke–Kasami–Younger
algorithm. It soon became clear that more powerful formalisms would be required
to meet the specific needs of human language, and more general chart parsers, augmented transition networks, unification grammars, and many other formal and computational devices were created.

There were two principal motivations for this activity. One was theoretical and
came from the growing perception that the pursuit of computational goals could
give rise to important advances in linguistic theory. Requiring that a formal system
be implementable helped to ensure its internal consistency and revealed its formal
complexity properties. The results are to be seen most clearly in syntactic formalisms
such as Generalized Phrase Structure Grammar, Lexical Functional Grammar, and
Head Driven Phrase Structure as well as in application of finite-state methods to
phonology and morphology.

The second motivation, which had existed from the beginning, came from the
desire to create a technology, based on sound scientific principles, to support a large
and expanding list of practical requirements for translation, information extraction, summarization, grammar checking, and the like. In none of these enterprises
is success achievable by linguistic methods alone. To varying extents, each involves
language not just as a formal system, but as a means of encoding and conveying
information about something outside, something which, for want of a better term,
we may loosely call 'the world'. Much of the robustness of language comes from the
imprecision and ambiguity which allow people to use it in a casual manner. But
this works only because people are able to restore missing information and resolve
ambiguities on the basis of what makes sense in a larger context provided not only
by the surrounding words but by the world outside. If there is any field that should
be responsible for the construction of comprehensive, general models of the world, it

is presumably artificial intelligence, but the task is clearly a great deal more daunting even than building comprehensive linguistic models, and success has been limited.

As a result, Computational Linguistics has gained a reputation for not measuring up to the challenges of technology, and this in turn has given rise to much frustration and misunderstanding both within and outside the community of computational linguists. There is, of course, much that still remains to be done by computational linguists, but very little of the responsibility for the apparently poor showing of the field belongs to them. As I have said, a significant reason for this is the lack of a broader technological environment in which Computational Linguistics can thrive. Lacking an artificial intelligence in which to embed their technology, linguists have been forced to seek a surrogate, however imperfect, and many think they have found it in what is generally known as 'statistical natural language processing'.

Roughly speaking, statistical NLP associates probabilities with the alternatives encountered in the course of analysing an utterance or a text and accepts the most probable outcome as the correct one. In 'the boy saw the girl with the telescope', the phrase 'with the telescope' is more likely to modify 'saw' than 'the girl', let us say, because 'telescope' has often been observed in situations which, like this one, represent it as an instrument for seeing. This is an undeniable fact about seeing and telescopes, but it is not a fact about English. Not surprisingly, words that name phenomena that are closely related in the world, or our perception of it, frequently occur close to one another so that crisp facts about the world are reflected in somewhat fuzzier facts about texts.

There is much room for debate in this view. The more fundamentalist of its proponents claim that the only hope for constructing useful systems for processing natural language is to learn them entirely from primary data as children do. If the analogy is good, and if Chomsky is right, this implies that the systems must be strongly predisposed towards certain kinds of languages because the primary data provides no negative examples and the information that it contains occurs, in any case, in too weak dilution to support the construction of sufficiently robust models without strong initial constraints.

If, as I have suggested, text processing depends on knowledge of the world as well as knowledge of language, then the proponents of radical statistical NLP face a stronger challenge than Chomsky's language learner because they must also construct this knowledge of the world entirely on the basis of what they read about it, and in no way on the basis of direct experience. The question that remains wide open is: Just how much of the knowledge of these two kinds that is required for NLP is derivable, even in principle, from emergent properties of text? The work done over the next few years should do much to clarify the issue and thus to suggest the direction that the field will follow thereafter.

This book stands on its own in the sense that it will not only bring people working in the field up to date on what is going on in parallel specialities to their own, but also introduce outsiders to the aims, methods, and achievements of computational linguists. The chapters of Part I have the same titles that one might expect to find in an introductory text on general linguistics. With the exception of the last, they correspond to the various levels of abstraction on which linguists work, from individual sounds to structures that span whole texts or dialogues, to the interface between meaning and the objective world, and the making of dictionaries. The difference, of course, is that they concentrate on the opportunities for computational exploration that each of these domains opens up, and on the problems that must be solved in each of them before they can contribute to the creation of linguistic technology.

I have suggested that requiring a formal system to be implementable led linguists to attend to the formal complexity properties of their theories. The last chapter of Part I provides an introduction to the mathematical notion of complexity and explores the crucial role that it plays in Computational Linguistics.

Part II of the book gives a chapter to each of the areas that have turned out to be the principal centres of activity in the field. For these purposes, Computational Linguistics is construed very broadly. On the one hand, it treats speech recognition and text-to-speech synthesis, the fundamentals of which are more often studied in departments of electrical engineering than linguistics and on the other, it contains a chapter entitled 'Corpora', an activity in which students of language use large collections of text or recorded speech as sources of evidence in their investigations. Part III is devoted to applications—starting, as is only fitting, with a pair of chapters on machine translation followed by a discussion of some topics that are at the centre of attention in the field at the present.

It is clear from the table of contents alone that, during the half century in which the field, if not the name, of Computational Linguistics has existed, it has come to cover a very wide territory, enriching virtually every part of theoretical linguistics with a computational and a technological component. However, it has been only poorly supplied with textbooks or comprehensive reference works. This book should go a long way towards meeting the second need.

PART I

FUNDAMENTALS

CHAPTER 1

PHONOLOGY

STEVEN BIRD

ABSTRACT

Phonology is the systematic study of the sounds used in language, and their composition into syllables, words, and phrases. **Computational phonology** is the application of formal and computational techniques to the representation and processing of phonological information. This chapter will present the fundamentals of descriptive phonology along with a brief overview of computational phonology.

1.1 PHONOLOGICAL CONTRAST, THE PHONEME, AND DISTINCTIVE FEATURES

There is no limit to the number of distinct sounds that can be produced by the human vocal apparatus. However, this infinite variety is harnessed by human languages into **sound systems** consisting of a few dozen language-specific categories, or **phonemes**. An example of an English phoneme is t. English has a variety of t-like sounds, such as the aspirated t^h of *ten*, the unreleased $t^{\urcorner}$ of *net*, and the flapped Γ of *water* (in some dialects). In English, these distinctions are not used to differentiate words, and so we do not find pairs of English words which are identical but for their use of t^h versus $t^{\urcorner}$. (By comparison, in some other languages, such as Icelandic and Bengali, aspiration is contrastive.) Nevertheless, since these sounds (or *phones*, or **segments**) are phonetically similar, and since they occur in *complementary distribution* (i.e. disjoint contexts) and cannot differentiate words in English, they are all said to be **allophones** of the English phoneme *t*.

Of course, setting up a few allophonic variants for each of a finite set of phonemes does not account for the infinite variety of sounds mentioned above. If one were to record multiple instances of the same utterance by the single speaker, many small variations could be observed in loudness, pitch, rate, vowel quality, and so on. These variations arise because speech is a motor activity involving coordination of many independent articulators, and perfect repetition of any utterance is simply impossible. Similar variations occur between different speakers, since one person's vocal apparatus is different from the next person's (and this is how we can distinguish people's voices). So 10 people saying *ten* 10 times each will produce 100 distinct acoustic records for the *t* sound. This diversity of tokens associated with a single type is sometimes referred to as *free variation*.

Above, the notion of phonetic similarity was used. The primary way to judge the similarity of phones is in terms of their *place* and *manner* of articulation. The consonant chart of the International Phonetic Alphabet (IPA) tabulates phones in this way,

	Bilabial	Labiodental	Dental	Alveolar	Postalveolar	Retroflex	Palatal	Velar	Uvular	Pharyngeal	Glottal
Plosive	p b			t d		ʈ ɖ	c ɟ	k ɡ	q ɢ		ʔ
Nasal	m	ɱ		n		ɳ	ɲ	ŋ	ɴ		
Trill	ʙ			r					ʀ		
Tap or Flap				ɾ		ɽ					
Fricative	ɸ β	f v	θ ð	s z	ʃ ʒ	ʂ ʐ	ç ʝ	x ɣ	χ ʁ	ħ ʕ	h ɦ
Lateral fricative				ɬ ɮ							
Approximant		ʋ		ɹ		ɻ	j	ɰ			
Lateral approximant				l		ɭ	ʎ	ʟ			

Fig. 1.1 Pulmonic Consonants from the International Phonetic Alphabet

as shown in Fig. 1.1. The IPA provides symbols for all sounds that are contrastive in at least one language.

The major axes of this chart are for place of articulation (horizontal), which is the location in the oral cavity of the primary constriction, and manner of articulation (vertical), the nature and degree of that constriction. Many cells of the chart contain two consonants, one *voiced* and the other *unvoiced*. These complementary properties are usually expressed as opposite values of a *binary feature* [±voiced].

A more elaborate model of the similarity of phones is provided by the theory of **distinctive features**. Two phones are considered more similar to the extent that they agree on the value of their features. A set of distinctive features and their values for five different phones is shown in (1.1). (Note that many of the features have an extended technical definition, for which it is necessary to consult a textbook.)

(1.1)

	t	z	m	l	i
anterior	+	+	+	+	−
coronal	+	+	−	+	−
labial	−	−	+	−	−
distributed	−	−	−	−	−
consonantal	+	+	+	+	−
sonorant	−	−	+	+	+
voiced	−	+	+	+	+
approximant	−	−	−	+	+
continuant	−	+	−	+	+
lateral	−	−	−	+	−
nasal	−	−	+	−	−
strident	−	+	−	−	−

Statements about the distribution of phonological information, usually expressed with rules or constraints, often apply to particular subsets of phones. Instead of listing these sets, it is virtually always simpler to list two or three feature values which pick out the required set. For example [+labial, −continuant] picks out *b*, *p*, and *m*, shown in the top left corner of Fig. 1.1. Sets of phones which can be picked out in this way are called **natural classes**, and phonological analyses can be evaluated in terms of their reliance on natural classes. How can we express these analyses? The rest of this chapter discusses some key approaches to this question.

Unfortunately, as with any introductory chapter like this one, it will not be possible to cover many important topics of interest to phonologists, such as acquisition, diachrony, orthography, universals, sign language phonology, the phonology/syntax interface, systems of intonation and stress, and many others besides. However, numerous bibliographic references are supplied at the end of the chapter, and readers may wish to consult these other works.

1.2 EARLY GENERATIVE PHONOLOGY

Some key concepts of phonology are best introduced by way of simple examples involving real data. We begin with some data from Russian in (1.2). The example shows some nouns, in nominative and dative cases, transcribed using the International Phonetic Alphabet. Note that x is the symbol for a voiceless velar fricative (e.g. the *ch* of Scottish *loch*).

(1.2)	*Nominative*	*Dative*	*Gloss*
	xlep	xlebu	'bread'
	grop	grobu	'coffin'
	sat	sadu	'garden'
	prut	prudu	'pond'
	rok	rogu	'horn'
	ras	razu	'time'

Observe that the dative form involves suffixation of *-u*, and a change to the final consonant of the nominative form. In (1.2) we see four changes: *p* becomes *b*, *t* becomes *d*, *k* becomes *g*, and *s* becomes *z*.

Where they differ is in their *voicing*; for example, *b* is a *voiced* version of *p*, since *b* involves periodic vibration of the vocal folds, while *p* does not. The same applies to the other pairs of sounds. Now we see that the changes we observed in (1.2) are actually quite systematic. Such systematic patterns are called **alternations**, and this particular one is known as a **voicing alternation**. We can formulate this alternation using a *phonological rule* as follows:

$$(1.3) \quad \begin{bmatrix} C \\ voiced \end{bmatrix} \rightarrow [\text{+voiced}] \, / \, \underline{\quad} V$$

A consonant becomes voiced in the presence of a following vowel

Rule (1.3) uses the format of early generative phonology. In this notation, C represents any consonant and V represents any vowel. The rule says that, if a voiceless consonant appears in the *phonological environment* '___ V' (i.e. preceding a vowel), then the consonant becomes voiced. By default, vowels have the feature [+voiced]), and so we can make the observation that the consonant *assimilates* the voicing feature of the following vowel.

One way to see if our analysis generalizes is to check for any nominative forms that end in a voiced consonant. We expect this consonant to stay the same in the dative form. However, it turns out that we do not find any nominative forms ending in a voiced consonant. Rather, we see the pattern in example (1.4). (Note that č is an alternative symbol for IPA ʧ.)

(1.4) | Nominative | Dative | Gloss |
|---|---|---|
| čerep | čerepu | 'skull' |
| xolop | xolopu | 'bondman' |
| trup | trupu | 'corpse' |
| cvet | cvetu | 'colour' |
| les | lesu | 'forest' |
| porok | poroku | 'vice' |

For these words, the voiceless consonants of the nominative form are unchanged in the dative form, contrary to our rule (1.3). These cannot be treated as exceptions, since this second pattern is quite pervasive. A solution is to construct an artificial form which is the dative word form minus the *-u* suffix. We will call this the **underlying form** of the word. Example (1.5) illustrates this for two cases:

(1.5) | Underlying | Nominative | Dative | Gloss |
|---|---|---|---|
| prud | prut | prudu | 'pond' |
| cvet | cvet | cvetu | 'colour' |

Now we can account for the dative form simply by suffixing the *-u*. We account for the nominative form with the following *devoicing rule*:

(1.6)
$$\begin{bmatrix} C \\ +voiced \end{bmatrix} \rightarrow [\ voiced] / \underline{\quad} \#$$

A consonant becomes devoiced word finally

This rule states that a voiced consonant is devoiced (i.e. [+voiced] becomes [–voiced]) if the consonant is followed by a word boundary (symbolized by #). It solves a problem with rule (1.3) which only accounts for half of the data. Rule (1.6) is called a *neutralization* rule, because the *voicing contrast* of the underlying form is removed in the nominative form. Now the analysis accounts for all the nominative and dative forms. Typically, rules like (1.6) can simultaneously employ several of the distinctive features from (1.1).

Observe that our analysis involves a certain degree of abstractness. We have constructed a new level of representation and drawn inferences about the underlying forms by inspecting the observed surface forms.

To conclude the development so far, we have seen a simple kind of phonological representation (namely sequences of alphabetic symbols, where each stands for a bundle of distinctive features), a distinction between levels of representation, and rules which account for the relationship between the representations on various levels. One way or another, most of phonology is concerned about these three things: representations, levels, and rules.

Finally, let us consider the plural forms shown in example (1.7). The plural morpheme is either *-a* or *-y*.

(1.7)

Singular	Plural	Gloss
xlep	xleba	'bread'
grop	groby	'coffin'
čerep	čerepa	'skull'
xolop	xolopy	'bondman'
trup	trupy	'corpse'
sat	sady	'garden'
prut	prudy	'pond'
cvet	cveta	'colour'
ras	razy	'time'
les	lesa	'forest'
rok	roga	'horn'
porok	poroky	'vice'

The phonological environment of the suffix provides us with no way of predicting which allomorph is chosen. One solution would be to enrich the underlying form once more (for example, we could include the plural suffix in the underlying form, and then have rules to delete it in all cases but the plural). A better approach in this case is to distinguish two *morphological classes*, one for nouns taking the *-y* plural, and one for nouns taking the *-a* plural. This information would then be an idiosyncratic property of each lexical item, and a morphological rule would be responsible for the choice between the *-y* and *-a* **allomorphs**. A full account of these data, then, must involve phonological, morphological, and lexical modules of a grammar.

As another example, let us consider the vowels of Turkish. These vowels are tabulated below, along with a decomposition into distinctive features: [high], [back], and [round]. The features [high] and [back] relate to the position of the tongue body in the oral cavity. The feature [round] relates to the rounding of the lips, as in the English *w* sound.[1]

(1.8)

	u	o	ü	ö	ı	a	i	e
high	+	–	+	–	+	–	+	–
back	+	+	–	–	+	+	–	–
round	+	+	+	+	–	–	–	–

Consider the following Turkish words, paying particular attention to the four versions of the possessive suffix. Note that similar data are discussed in Chapter 2.

(1.9)

ip	'rope'	ipin	'rope's'
kız	'girl'	kızın	'girl's'
yüz	'face'	yüzün	'face's'
pul	'stamp'	pulun	'stamp's'
el	'hand'	elin	'hand's'

---

[1] Note that there is a distinction made in the Turkish alphabet between the dotted *i* and the dotless *ı*. This *ı* is a high, back, unrounded vowel that does not occur in English.

çan	'bell'	çanın	'bell's'
köy	'village'	köyün	'village's'
son	'end'	sonun	'end's'

The possessive suffix has the forms *in, ın, ün,* and *un.* In terms of the distinctive feature chart in (1.8), we can observe that the suffix vowel is always [+high]. The other features of the suffix vowel are copied from the stem vowel. This copying is called **vowel harmony.** Let us see how this behaviour can be expressed using a phonological rule. To do this, we assume that the vowel of the possessive affix is only specified as [+high] and is underspecified for its other features. In the following rule, *C* denotes any consonant, and the Greek letter variables range over the + and – values of the feature.

$$(1.10) \quad \begin{bmatrix} V \\ +\text{high} \end{bmatrix} \rightarrow \begin{bmatrix} \alpha\text{back} \\ \beta\text{round} \end{bmatrix} \bigg/ \begin{bmatrix} \alpha\text{back} \\ \beta\text{round} \end{bmatrix} C^* \underline{\quad}$$

A high vowel assimilates to the backness and rounding of the preceding vowel

So long as the stem vowel is specified for the properties [high] and [back], this rule will make sure that they are copied onto the affix vowel. However, there is nothing in the rule formalism to stop the variables being used in inappropriate ways (e.g. α back → α round). So we can see that the rule formalism does not permit us to express the notion that certain features are shared by more than one segment. Instead, we would like to be able to represent the sharing explicitly, as follows, where ±H abbreviates [±high], an underspecified vowel position:

(1.11)

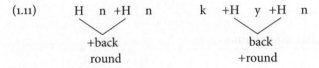

The lines of this diagram indicate that the backness and roundness properties are shared by both vowels in a word. A single vowel property (or type) is manifested on two separate vowels (tokens).

Entities like [+back, –round] that function over extended regions are often referred to as **prosodies**, and this kind of picture is sometimes called a *non-linear* representation. Many phonological models use non-linear representations of one sort or another. Here we shall consider one particular model, namely **autosegmental phonology**, since it is the most widely used non-linear model. The term comes from 'autonomous + segment', and refers to the autonomous nature of segments (or certain groups of features) once they have been liberated from one-dimensional strings.

1.3 Autosegmental Phonology

In autosegmental phonology, diagrams like those we saw above are known as *charts*. A chart consists of two or more *tiers*, along with some *association lines* drawn between the autosegments on those tiers. The *no-crossing constraint* is a stipulation that association lines are not allowed to cross, ensuring that association lines can be interpreted as asserting some kind of temporal overlap or inclusion. *Autosegmental rules* are procedures for converting one representation into another, by adding or removing association lines and autosegments. A rule for Turkish vowel harmony is shown below on the left in (1.12), where V denotes any vowel, and the dashed line indicates that a new association is created. This rule applies to the representation in the middle, to yield the one on the right.

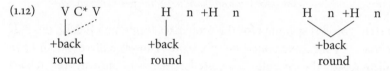

(1.12)

In order to fully appreciate the power of autosegmental phonology, we will use it to analyse some data from an African tone language. Consider the data in Table 1.1. Twelve nouns are listed down the left side, and the isolation form and five contextual

Table 1.1 Tone Data from Chakosi (Ghana)

Word form	A. ___ isolation	B. i ___ 'his ...'	C. am goro ___ 'your (pl) brother's ...'	D. ___ kũ 'one ...'	E. am ___ wo dɔ 'your (pl) ... is there'	F. jiine ___ ni 'that ...'
1. baka 'tree'	– ‾	‥‾ –	˙‥‥ – –	– ‾‥	˙‥ – – ‥	‥ – ‾ – ‥
2. saka 'comb'	– ˥	‥‾ –	˙‥‥ – ˥	– ‾‥	˙‥ – – ‥	‥ – ‾ – ‥
3. buri 'duck'	– ‾	‥ – –	˙‥ – – ‾	– – ‥		‥ – – ‥
4. siri 'goat'	– ˥	‥ – ˥	˙‥ – – ˥	– – ‥	˙‥ – – – ‥	‥ – – ‥
5. gado 'bed'	– –	‥ – –	˙‥ – –	– – ‥		‥ – – ‥
6. gɔrɔ 'brother'	– –	‥ ‾ –		– – – ‥	˙‥ – – ‥	
7. ca 'dog'	˩	‥ –	˙‥‥ ˩	– ‥	˙ ‥ – ‥	– ‥
8. ni 'mother'	–	‥ –	˙‥ – –	‾ ‥		‥ – ‥
9. jɔkɔrɔ 'chain'	– – ‾	‥ – ‾	˙‥‥ – – ‾	– – ‾ ‥	˙‥ – – – ‥	‥ – ‾ – ‥
10. tokoro 'window'	– – –	‥ – – –	˙‥ – – –	– – – ‥	˙‥ – – – ‥	‥ – – – ‥
11. bulali 'iron'	– – ‾ ‥	‥ – ‾ ‥	˙‥ – – ‾ ‥	– – ‾ ‥	˙‥ – – ‥	‥ – – ‥
12. misini 'needle'	– ‾ –	‥ – ‾ –	˙‥ – ‾ ‥	– – – ‥	˙‥ – ‾ ‥	‥ – – – ‥

forms are provided across the table. The line segments indicate voice pitch (the fundamental frequency of the voice); dotted lines are for the syllables of the context words, and full lines are for the syllables of the target word, as it is pronounced in this context. At first glace these data seem bewildering in their complexity. However, we will see how autosegmental analysis reveals the simple underlying structure of the data.

Looking across the table, observe that the contextual forms of a given noun are quite variable. For example *bulali* appears as ‾‾_, ‾‾_, ‾‾‾, and ‾‾‾.

We could begin the analysis by identifying all the levels (here there are five), assigning a name or number to each, and looking for patterns. However, this approach does not capture the relative nature of tone, where _‾_ is not distinguished from ‾‾_. Instead, our approach just has to be sensitive to differences between adjacent tones. So these distinct tone sequences could be represented identically as +1, −2, since we go up a small amount from the first to the second tone (+1), and then down a larger amount −2. In autosegmental analysis, we treat *contour tones* as being made up of two or more *level tones* compressed into the space of a single syllable. Therefore, we can treat _‿ as another instance of +1, −2. Given our autosegmental perspective, a sequence of two or more identical tones corresponds to a single spread tone. This means that we can collapse sequences of like tones to a single tone.[2] When we retranscribe our data in this way, some interesting patterns emerge.

First, by observing the raw frequency of these intertone intervals, we see that −2 and +1 are by far the most common, occurring 63 and 39 times respectively. A −1 difference occurs 8 times, while a +2 difference is very rare (only occurring 3 times, and only in phrase-final contour tones). This patterning is characteristic of a *terrace tone language*. In analysing such a language, phonologists typically propose an inventory of just two tones, H (high) and L (low), where these might be represented featurally as [±hi]. In such a model, the tone sequence HL corresponds to ‾_, a pitch difference of −2.

In terrace tone languages, an H tone does not achieve its former level after an L tone, so HLH is *phonetically realized* as ‾_‾, (instead of ‾_‾). This kind of H-lowering is called **automatic downstep**. A pitch difference of +1 corresponds to an LH tone sequence. With this model, we already account for the prevalence of the −2 and +1 intervals. What about −1 and +2?

As we will see later, the −1 difference arises when the middle tone of ‾_‾ (HLH) is deleted, leaving just ‾‾. In this situation we write H!H, where the exclamation mark indicates the lowering of the following H due to a deleted (or *floating* low tone). This kind of H-lowering is called **conditioned downstep**. The rare +2 difference only occurs for an LH contour; we can assume that automatic downstep only applies when a LH sequence is linked to two separate syllables (_‾) and not when the sequence is linked to a single syllable (‿).

---

[2] This assumption cannot be maintained in more sophisticated approaches involving lexical and prosodic domains. However, it is a very useful simplifying assumption for the purposes of this presentation.

To summarize these conventions, we associate the pitch differences to tone sequences as shown in (1.13). Syllable boundaries are marked with a dot.

(1.13) *Interval*   −2   −1   +1   +2
        Pitches   ‾ _   ‾ _   _ ‾   ⌐
        Tones   H.L   H.!H   L.H   LH

Now we are in a position to provide tonal transcriptions for the forms in Table 1.1. Example (1.14) gives the transcriptions for the forms involving *bulali*. Tones corresponding to the noun are underlined.

(1.14) *Transcriptions of* bulali *'iron'*

bulali	'iron'	‾ ‾ _	L.<u>H.L</u>
i bulali	'his iron'	··· ‾ _	H.<u>H.!H.L</u>
am goro bulali	'your (pl) brother's iron'	··· ··· ‾ ‾ _	HL.L.L.<u>L.H.L</u>
bulali kū	'one iron'	‾ ‾ ‾ ···	L.<u>H.H</u>.L
am bulali wo dɔ	'your (pl) iron is there'	··· ‾ ‾ ‾ ···	HL.<u>L.H.H</u>.!H.L
jiine bulali ni	'that iron'	··· ‾ ‾ ‾ ···	L.H.<u>H.!H.H</u>.L

Looking down the right-hand column of (1.14) at the underlined tones, observe again the diversity of surface forms corresponding to the single lexical item. An autosegmental analysis is able to account for all this variation with a single spreading rule.

(1.15) *High tone spread*

σ σ σ
| ⤳ ⧸
H L

A high tone spreads to the following (non-final) syllable, delinking the low tone

Rule (1.15) applies to any sequence of three syllables (σ) where the first is linked to an H tone and the second is linked to an L tone. The rule spreads H to the right, delinking the L. Crucially, the L itself is not deleted, but remains as a *floating tone*, and continues to influence surface tone as downstep. Example (1.16) shows the application of the H spread rule to forms involving *bulali*. The first row of autosegmental diagrams shows the underlying forms, where *bulali* is assigned an LHL **tone melody**. In the second row, we see the result of applying H spread. Following standard practice, the floating low tones are circled. Where a floating L appears between two H tones, it gives rise to downstep. The final assignment of tones to syllables and the position of the downsteps are shown in the last row of the table.

Example (1.16) shows the power of autosegmental phonology—together with suitable underlying forms and appropriate principles of phonetic interpretation—in analysing complex patterns with simple rules. Space precludes a full analysis of the data; interested readers can try hypothesizing underlying forms for the other words, along with new rules, to account for the rest of the data in Table 1.1.

The preceding discussion of segmental and autosegmental phonology highlights the multi-linear organization of phonological representations, which derives from

(1.16) B. his iron   D. one iron   E. your (pl) iron   F. that iron

        i bu la li   bu la li ku   am bu la li wo dɔ   jii ni bu la li ni
        H L H L   L H L L   H L L H L H L   L H L H L L

        i bu la li   bu la li ku   am bu la li wo dɔ   jii ni bu la li ni
        H Ⓛ H L   L H Ⓛ L   H L L H Ⓛ H L   L H Ⓛ H Ⓛ L

        i bu la li   bu la li ku   am bu la li wo dɔ   jii ni bu la li ni
        H H !H L   L H H L   HL L H H !H L   L H H !H H L

the temporal nature of the speech stream. Phonological representations are also organized hierarchically. We already know that phonological information comprises words, and words, phrases. This is one kind of hierarchical organization of phonological information. But phonological analysis has also demonstrated the need for other kinds of hierarchy, such as the **prosodic hierarchy**, which builds structure involving syllables, feet, and intonational phrases above the segment level, and **feature geometry**, which involves hierarchical organization beneath the level of the segment. Phonological rules and constraints can refer to the prosodic hierarchy in order to account for the observed *distribution* of phonological information across the linear sequence of segments. Feature geometry serves the dual purpose of accounting for the inventory of contrastive sounds available to a language, and for the alternations we can observe. Here we will consider just one level of phonological hierarchy, namely the syllable.

1.4 SYLLABLE STRUCTURE

Syllables are a fundamental organizational unit in phonology. In many languages, phonological alternations are sensitive to syllable structure. For example, *t* has several allophones in English, and the choice of allophone depends on phonological context. For example, in many English dialects, *t* is pronounced as the flap [ɾ] between vowels, as in *water*. Two other variants are shown in (1.17), where the phonetic transcription is given in brackets, and syllable boundaries are marked with a dot.

(1.17)   a. atlas [ætʔ.ləs]
          b. cactus [kæk.tʰəs]

Native English syllables cannot begin with *tl*, and so the *t* of *atlas* is syllabified with the preceding vowel. Syllable final *t* is regularly glottalized or unreleased in English, while syllable initial *t* is regularly aspirated. Thus we have a natural explanation for the patterning of these allophones in terms of syllable structure.

Other evidence for the syllable comes from loanwords. When words are borrowed into one language from another, they must be adjusted so as to conform to the legal sound patterns (or **phonotactics**) of the host language. For example, consider the following borrowings from English into Dschang, a language of Cameroon (Bird 1999).

(1.18) afruwa *flower*, akalatusi *eucalyptus*, alɛsa *razor*, alɔba *rubber*, aplɛŋɛ *blanket*, asəkuu *school*, cɛɛn *chain*, dəək *debt*, kapinda *carpenter*, kɛsiŋ *kitchen*, kuum *comb*, laam *lamp*, lɛsi *rice*, luum *room*, mbasəku *bicycle*, mbrusi *brush*, mbərəək *brick*, mɛta *mat*, mɛtərasi *mattress*, ŋglasi *glass*, ɲjakasi *jackass*, mɛtisi *match*, nubatisi *rheumatism*, pɔkɛ *pocket*, ŋgalɛ *garden*, səsa *scissors*, tɛwɛlɛ *towel*, wasi *watch*, ziiŋ *zinc*

In Dschang, the **syllable canon** is much more restricted than in English. Consider the patterning of *t*. This segment is illegal in syllable-final position. In technical language, we would say that alveolars are not *licensed* in the syllable coda. In mɛta *mat*, a vowel is inserted, making the *t* into the initial segment of the next syllable. For dəək *debt*, the place of articulation of the *t* is changed to velar, making it a legal syllable-final consonant. For aplɛŋɛ *blanket*, the final *t* is deleted. Many other adjustments can be seen in (1.18), and most of them can be explained with reference to syllable structure.

A third source of evidence for syllable structure comes from morphology. In Ulwa, a Nicaraguan language, the position of the possessive *infix* is sensitive to syllable structure. The Ulwa syllable canon is (C)V(V|C)(C), and any **intervocalic** consonant (i.e. consonant between two vowels) is syllabified with the following syllable, a universal principle known as **onset maximization**. Consider the Ulwa data in (1.19).

(1.19)

Word	Possessive	Gloss	Word	Possessive	Gloss
baa	baa.**ka**	'excrement'	bi.lam	bi.lam.**ka**	'fish'
dii.muih	dii.**ka**.muih	'snake'	gaad	gaad.**ka**	'god'
ii.bin	ii.**ka**.bin	'heaven'	ii.li.lih	ii.**ka**.li.lih	'shark'
ka h.ma	kah.**ka**.ma	'iguana'	ka.pak	ka.pak.**ka**	'manner'
lii.ma	lii.**ka**.ma	'lemon'	mis.tu	mis.**ka**.tu	'cat'
on.yan	on.**ka**.yan	'onion'	pau.mak	pau.**ka**.mak	'tomato'
sik.bilh	sik.**ka**.bilh	'horsefly'	taim	taim.**ka**	'time'
ta i.tai	tai.**ka**.tai	'grey squirrel'	uu.mak	uu.**ka**.mak	'window'
wa i.ku	wai.**ka**.ku	'moon, month'	wa.sa.la	wa.sa.**ka**.la	'possum'

Observe that the infix appears at a syllable boundary, and so we can already state that the infix position is sensitive to syllable structure. Any analysis of the infix position must take **syllable weight** into consideration. Syllables having a single short vowel and no following consonants are defined to be **light**. (The presence of onset consonants is irrelevant to syllable weight.) All other syllables, i.e. those which have two vowels, or a single long vowel, or a final consonant, are defined to be **heavy**; e.g. *kah*, *kaa*, *muih*, *bilh, ii, on.* Two common phonological representations for this syllable structure are the onset-rhyme model, and the moraic model. Representations for the syllables just listed are shown in (1.20). In these diagrams, σ denotes a syllable, O onset, R rhyme, N nucleus, C coda, and μ *mora* (the traditional, minimal unit of syllable weight).

(1.20) *a.   The onset-rhyme model of syllable structure*

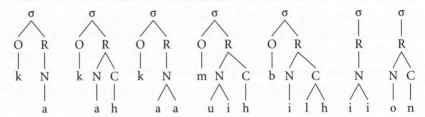

    b.   The moraic model of syllable structure

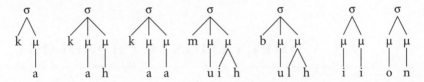

In the onset-rhyme model (1.20*a*), consonants coming before the first vowel are linked to the onset node, and the rest of the material comes under the rhyme node.[3] A rhyme contains an obligatory nucleus and an optional coda. In this model, a syllable is said to be heavy if and only if its rhyme or its nucleus are branching.

In the moraic mode (1.20*b*), any consonants that appear before the first vowel are linked directly to the syllable node. The first vowel is linked to its own mora node (symbolized by μ), and any remaining material is linked to the second mora node. A syllable is said to be heavy if and only if it has more than one mora.

These are just two of several ways that have been proposed for representing syllable structure. The syllables constituting a word can be linked to higher levels of structure, such as the *foot* and the *prosodic word*. For now, it is sufficient to know that such higher levels exist, and that we have a way to represent the binary distinction of syllable weight.

Now we can return to the Ulwa data, from example (1.19). A relatively standard way to account for the infix position is to stipulate that the first light syllable, if present, is actually invisible to the rules which assign syllables to higher levels; such syllables are said to be **extra-metrical**. They are a sort of 'upbeat' to the word, and are often associated with the preceding word in continuous speech. Given these general principles

---

[3] Two syllables usually have to agree on the material in their rhyme constituents in order for them to be considered rhyming, hence the name.

concerning hierarchical structure, we can simply state that the Ulwa possessive affix is infixed after the first syllable.[4]

In the foregoing discussion, I hope to have revealed many interesting issues which are confronted by phonological analysis, without delving too deeply into the abstract theoretical constructs which phonologists have proposed. Theories differ enormously in their organization of phonological information and the ways in which they permit this information to be subjected to rules and constraints, and the way the information is used in a lexicon and an overarching grammatical framework. Some of these theoretical frameworks include: lexical phonology, underspecification phonology, government phonology, declarative phonology, and optimality theory. For more information about these, please see section 1.5.3 for literature references.

1.5 COMPUTATIONAL PHONOLOGY

When phonological information is treated as a string of atomic symbols, it is immediately amenable to processing using existing models. A particularly successful example is the work on finite-state transducers (see Chapter 18). However, phonologists abandoned linear representations in the 1970s, and so we will consider some computational models that have been proposed for multi-linear, hierarchical, phonological representations. It turns out that these pose some interesting challenges.

Early models of generative phonology, like that of the Sound Pattern of English (SPE), were sufficiently explicit that they could be implemented directly. A necessary first step in implementing many of the more recent theoretical models is to formalize them, and to discover the intended semantics of some subtle, graphical notations. A practical approach to this problem has been to try to express phonological information using existing, well-understood computational models. The principal models are finite-state devices and attribute-value matrices.

1.5.1 Finite-state models of non-linear phonology

Finite-state machines cannot process structured data, only strings, so special methods are required for these devices to process complex phonological representations. All approaches involve a many-to-one mapping from the parallel layers of representa-

---

[4] A better analysis of the Ulwa infixation data involves reference to **metrical feet**, phonological units above the level of the syllable. This is beyond the scope of the current chapter, however.

tion to a single machine. There are essentially three places where this many-to-one mapping can be situated. The first approach is to employ multi-tape machines (Kay 1987). Each tier is represented as a string, and the set of strings is processed simultaneously by a single machine. The second approach is to map the multiple layers into a single string, and to process that with a conventional single-tape machine (Kornai 1995). The third approach is to encode each layer itself as a finite-state machine, and to combine the machines using automaton intersection (Bird and Ellison 1994).

This work demonstrates how representations can be compiled into a form that can be directly manipulated by finite-state machines. Independently of this, we also need to provide a means for phonological generalizations (such as rules and constraints) to be given a finite-state interpretation. This problem is well studied for the linear case, and compilers exist that will take a rule formatted somewhat like the SPE style and produce an equivalent finite-state transducer. Whole constellations of ordered rules or optimality-theoretic constraints can also be compiled in this way. However, the compilation of rules and constraints involving autosegmental structures is still largely unaddressed.

The finite-state approaches emphasize the temporal (or left-to-right) ordering of phonological representations. In contrast, attribute-value models emphasize the hierarchical nature of phonological representations.

1.5.2 Attribute-value matrices

The success of attribute-value matrices (AVMs) as a convenient formal representation for constraint-based approaches to syntax (see Chapter 3), and concerns about the formal properties of non-linear phonological information, led some researchers to apply AVMs to phonology. Hierarchical structures can be represented using AVM nesting, as shown in (1.21a), and autosegmental diagrams can be encoded using AVM indices, as shown in (1.21b).

(1.21) $a.$
$$\begin{bmatrix} \text{onset} & \langle k \rangle \\ \text{rhyme} & \begin{bmatrix} \text{nucleus} & \langle u, i \rangle \\ \text{coda} & \langle h \rangle \end{bmatrix} \end{bmatrix}$$

$b.$
$$\begin{bmatrix} \text{syllable} & \langle i_{\boxed{1}}, bu_{\boxed{2}}, la_{\boxed{3}}, li_{\boxed{4}} \rangle \\ \text{tone} & \langle H_{\boxed{5}}, L_{\boxed{6}}, H_{\boxed{7}}, L_{\boxed{8}} \rangle \\ \text{associations} & \{ \langle \boxed{1}, \boxed{5} \rangle, \langle \boxed{2}, \boxed{5} \rangle, \langle \boxed{3}, \boxed{7} \rangle, \langle \boxed{4}, \boxed{8} \rangle \} \end{bmatrix}$$

AVMs permit re-entrancy by virtue of the numbered indices, and so parts of a hierarchical structure can be shared. For example, (1.22a) illustrates a consonant shared between two adjacent syllables, for the word *cousin* (this kind of double affiliation is called **ambisyllabicity**). Example (1.22*b*) illustrates shared structure within a single syllable *full*, to represent the **coarticulation** of the onset consonant with the vowel.

(1.22) *a.*

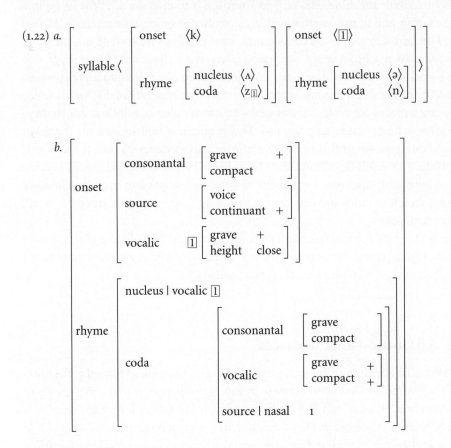

b.

Given such flexible and extensible representations, rules and constraints can manipulate and enrich the phonological information. Computational implementations of these AVM models have been used in speech synthesis systems.

1.5.3 Computational tools for phonological research

Once a phonological model is implemented, it ought to be possible to use the implementation to evaluate theories against data sets. A phonologist's workbench should help people to 'debug' their analyses and spot errors before going to press with an analysis. Developing such tools is much more difficult than it might appear.

First, there is no agreed method for modelling non-linear representations, and each proposal has shortcomings. Second, processing data sets presents its own set of problems, having to do with tokenization, symbols which are ambiguous as to their featural decomposition, symbols marked as uncertain or optional, and so on. Third, some innocuous-looking rules and constraints may be surprisingly difficult to model, and it might only be possible to approximate the desired behaviour. Additionally, certain universal principles and tendencies may be hard to express in a formal manner. A final, pervasive problem is that symbolic transcriptions may fail to adequately reflect linguistically significant acoustic differences in the speech signal.

Nevertheless, whether the phonologist is sorting data, or generating helpful tabulations, or gathering statistics, or searching for a (counter-)example, or verifying the transcriptions used in a manuscript, the principal challenge remains a computational one. Recently, new directed-graph models (e.g. Emu, MATE, Annotation Graphs) appear to provide good solutions to the first two problems, while new advances on finite-state models of phonology are addressing the third problem. Therefore, we have grounds for confidence that there will be significant advances on these problems in the near future.

FURTHER READING AND RELEVANT RESOURCES

The phonology community is served by an excellent journal *Phonology*, published by Cambridge University Press. Useful textbooks and collections include: Katamba (1989); Frost and Katz (1992); Kenstowicz (1994); Goldsmith (1995); Clark and Yallop (1995); Gussenhoven and Jacobs (1998); Goldsmith (1999); Roca, Johnson, and Roca (1999); Jurafsky and Martin (2000); Harrington and Cassidy (1999). Oxford University Press publishes a series *The Phonology of the World's Languages*, including monographs on Armenian (Vaux 1998), Dutch (Booij 1995), English (Hammond 1999), German (Wiese 1996), Hungarian (Siptár and Törkenczy 2000), Kimatuumbi (Odden 1996), Norwegian (Kristoffersen 1996), Portuguese (Mateus and Andrade 2000), and Slovak (Rubach 1993). An important survey of phonological variation is the *Atlas of North American English* (Labov et al. 2001).

Phonology is the oldest discipline in linguistics and has a rich history. Some historically important works include: Joos (1957); Pike (1947); Firth (1952); Bloch (1948); Hockett (1955); Chomsky and Halle (1968). The most comprehensive history of phonology is Anderson (1985).

Useful resources for phonetics include: Catford (1988); Laver (1994); Ladefoged and Maddieson (1996); Stevens (1999); International Phonetic Association (1999); Ladefoged (2000); Handke (2001), and the homepage of the International Phonetic Association http://www.arts.gla.ac.uk/IPA/ipa.html. The phonology/phonetics interface is an area of vigorous research, and the main focus of the *Laboratory Phonology* series published by Cambridge University Press: Kingston and Beckman (1991); Docherty and Ladd (1992); Keating (1994); Connell and Arvaniti (1995); Broe and Pierrehumbert (2000). Two interesting essays on the relationship between phonetics and phonology are Pierrehumbert (1990); Fleming (2000).

Important works on the syllable, stress, intonation, and tone include the following: Pike and Pike (1947); Liberman and Prince (1977); Burzio (1994); Hayes (1994); Blevins (1995); Ladd (1996); Hirst and Di Cristo (1998); Hyman and Kisseberth (1998); van der Hulst and Ritter (1999). Studies of partial specification and redundancy include: Archangeli (1988); Broe (1993); Archangeli and Pulleyblank (1994).

Attribute-value and directed graph models for phonological representations and constraints are described in the following papers and monographs: Bird and Klein (1994); Bird (1995); Coleman (1998); Scobbie (1998); Bird and Liberman (2001); Cassidy and Harrington (2001).

The last decade has seen two major developments in phonology, both falling outside the scope of this limited chapter. On the theoretical side, Alan Prince, Paul Smolensky, John McCarthy, and many others have developed a model of constraint interaction called *Optimality Theory* (OT) (Archangeli and Langendoen 1997; Kager 1999; Tesar and Smolensky 2000). The Rutgers Optimality Archive houses an extensive collection of OT papers (http://ruccs.rutgers.edu/roa.html). On the computational side, the Association for Computational Linguistics (ACL) has a special interest group in computational phonology (SIGPHON) with a homepage at http://www.cogsci.ed.ac.uk/sigphon/. The organization has held five meetings to date, with proceedings published by the ACL and many papers available on-line from the SIGPHON site: Bird (1994b); Sproat (1996); Coleman (1997); Ellison (1998); Eisner et al. (2000). Another collection of papers was published as a special issue of the journal *Computational Linguistics* in 1994 (Bird 1994a). Several Ph.D. theses on computational phonology have appeared: Bird (1995); Kornai (1995); Tesar (1995); Carson-Berndsen (1997); Walther (1997); Boersma (1998); Wareham (1999); Kiraz (2000). Key contributions to computational OT include the proceedings of the fourth and fifth SIGPHON meetings and Ellison (1994); Tesar (1995); Eisner (1997); Karttunen (1998).

The sources of data published in this chapter are as follows: Russian (Kenstowicz and Kisseberth 1979); Chakosi (Ghana: Language Data Series, MS); Ulwa (Sproat 1992).

Acknowledgements

I am grateful to D. Robert Ladd and Eugene Buckley for comments on an earlier version of this chapter, and to James Roberts for furnishing me with the Chakosi data.

REFERENCES

Anderson, S. R. 1985. *Phonology in the Twentieth Century: Theories of Rules and Theories of Representations*. Chicago: University of Chicago Press.

Archangeli, D. 1988. 'Aspects of underspecification theory'. *Phonology*, 5, 183–207.

——and Langendoen, D. T. (eds.). 1997. *Optimality Theory: An Overview*. Oxford: Blackwell.

——and D. Pulleyblank. 1994. *Grounded Phonology*. Cambridge, Mass.: MIT Press.

Bird, S. (ed.). 1994a. *Computational Linguistics: Special Issue on Computational Phonology*, 20(3).

——(ed.). 1994b. *Proceedings of the 1st Meeting of the Association for Computational Linguistics Special Interest Group in Computational Phonology (ACL '94)* (Las Cruces, N. Mex.).

——1995. *Computational Phonology: A Constraint-Based Approach*. Studies in Natural Language Processing. Cambridge: Cambridge University Press.

——1999. 'Dschang syllable structure'. In H. van der Hulst and N. Ritter (eds.), *The Syllable: Views and Facts*, Studies in Generative Grammar, Berlin: Mouton de Gruyter, 447–76.

——and T. M. Ellison. 1994. 'One level phonology: autosegmental representations and rules as finite automata'. *Computational Linguistics*, 20, 55–90.

——and E. Klein. 1994. 'Phonological analysis in typed feature systems'. *Computational Linguistics*, 20, 455–91.

——and M. Liberman. 2001. 'A formal framework for linguistic annotation'. *Speech Communication*, 33, 23–60.

Blevins, J. 1995. 'The syllable in phonological theory'. In J. A. Goldsmith (ed.), *The Handbook of Phonological Theory*. Cambridge, Mass.: Blackwell, 206–44.

Bloch, B. 1948. 'A set of postulates for phonemic analysis'. *Language*, 24, 3–46.

Boersma, P. 1998. *Functional phonology: formalizing the interactions between articulatory and perceptual drives*. Ph.D. thesis, University of Amsterdam.

Booij, G. 1995. *The Phonology of Dutch*. The Phonology of the World's Languages. Oxford: Clarendon Press.

Broe, M. 1993. 'Specification theory: the treatment of redundancy in generative phonology'. Ph.D. thesis, University of Edinburgh.

——and J. Pierrehumbert (eds.). 2000. *Papers in Laboratory Phonology*, v: *Language Acquisition and the Lexicon*. Cambridge: Cambridge University Press.

Burzio, L. 1994. *Principles of English Stress*. Cambridge: Cambridge University Press.

Carson-Berndsen, J. 1997. *Time Map Phonology: Finite State Models and Event Logics in Speech Recognition*. Text, Speech and Language Technology 5. Dordrecht: Kluwer.

Cassidy, S. and J. Harrington. 2001. 'Multi-level annotation of speech: an overview of the Emu speech database management system'. *Speech Communication*, 33, 61–77.

Catford, J. C. 1988. *Practical Introduction to Phonetics*. Oxford: Clarendon Press.

Chomsky, N. and M. Halle. 1968. *The Sound Pattern of English*. New York: Harper and Row.

Clark, J. and C. Yallop. 1995. *An Introduction to Phonetics and Phonology*. Oxford: Blackwell.

Coleman, J. (ed.). 1997. *Proceedings of the 3rd Meeting of the Association for Computational Linguistics Special Interest Group in Computational Phonology (ACL '97)* (Madrid).

——1998. *Phonological Representations: Their Names, Forms and Powers*. Cambridge Studies in Linguistics. Cambridge: Cambridge University Press.

Connell, B. and A. Arvaniti. 1995. *Papers in Laboratory Phonology*, iv: *Phonology and Phonetic Evidence*. Cambridge: Cambridge University Press.

Docherty, G. J. and D. R. Ladd (eds.). 1992. *Papers in Laboratory Phonology* ii: *Gesture, Segment, Prosody*. Cambridge: Cambridge University Press.

Eisner, J. 1997. 'Efficient generation in primitive optimality theory'. *Proceedings of the 35th Annual Meeting of the Association for Computational Linguistics (ACL '97)* (Madrid), 313–20.

——L. Karttunen, and A. Thériault (eds.). 2000. *Proceedings of the 5th Meeting of the Association for Computational Linguistics Special Interest Group in Computational Phonology (ACL 2000)* (Luxembourg).

Ellison, T. M. 1994. 'Phonological derivation in optimality theory'. *Proceedings of the 15th International Conference on Computational Linguistics (COLING '94)* (Kyoto), 1007–13.

——(ed.). 1998. *Proceedings of the 4th Meeting of the Association for Computational Linguistics Special Interest Group in Computational Phonology* (Quebec).

Firth, J. R. 1957. 'Sounds and prosodies'. In *Papers in Linguistics 1934–1951*. London: Clarendon Press, 121–38. First pub. 1948.

Fleming, E. 2000. 'Scalar and categorical phenomena in a unified model of phonetics and phonology'. *Phonology*, 1, 7–44.

Frost, R. and L. Katz (eds.). 1992. *Orthography, Phonology, Morphology and Meaning*. Advances in Psychology 94. Amsterdam: North-Holland.

Goldsmith, J. A. (ed.). 1995. *The Handbook of Phonological Theory*. Cambridge, Mass.: Blackwell.

——(ed.). 1999. *Phonological Theory: The Essential Readings*. Cambridge, Mass.: Blackwell.

Gussenhoven, C. and H. Jacobs. 1998. *Understanding Phonology*. London: Edward Arnold.

Hammond, M. 1999. *The Phonology of English: A Prosodic Optimality-Theoretic Approach*. Oxford: Clarendon Press.

Handke, J. 2001. *The Mouton Interactive Introduction to Phonetics and Phonology*. Berlin: Mouton de Gruyter.

Harrington, J. and S. Cassidy. 1999. *Techniques in Speech Acoustics*. Dordrecht: Kluwer.

Hayes, B. 1994. *Metrical Stress Theory: Principles and Case Studies*. Chicago: University of Chicago Press.

Hirst, D. and A. Di Cristo (eds.). 1998. *Intonation Systems: A Survey of Twenty Languages*. Cambridge: Cambridge University Press.

Hockett, C. F. 1955. *A Manual of Phonology*. Baltimore: Waverly Press.

Hyman, L. M. and C. Kisseberth (eds.). 1998. *Theoretical Aspects of Bantu Tone*. Stanford, Calif.: CSLI Publications.

International Phonetic Association 1999. *Handbook of the International Phonetic Association: A Guide to the Use of the International Phonetic Alphabet*. Cambridge: Cambridge University Press.

Joos, M. (ed.). 1957. *Readings in Linguistics*, i: *The Development of Descriptive Linguistics in America, 1925–56*. Chicago: University of Chicago Press.

Jurafsky, D. and J. H. Martin. 2000. *Speech and Language Processing: An Introduction to Natural Language Processing, Computational Linguistics, and Speech Recognition*. Prentice Hall.

Kager, R. 1999. *Optimality Theory*. Cambridge: Cambridge University Press.

Karttunen, L. 1998. *The proper treatment of optimality in computational phonology*. http://xxx.lanl.gov/abs/cmp-lg/9804002.

Katamba, F. 1989. *An Introduction to Phonology*. Reading, Mass: Addison Wesley.

Kay, M. 1987. 'Nonconcatenative finite-state morphology'. *Proceedings of the 3rd Meeting of the European Chapter of the Association for Computational Linguistics (ACL '87)* (Copenhagen), 2–10.

Keating, P. A. 1994. *Papers in Laboratory Phonology*, iii: *Phonological Structure and Phonetic Form*. Cambridge: Cambridge University Press.

Kenstowicz, M. 1994. *Phonology in Generative Grammar*. Oxford: Blackwell.

——and C. Kisseberth. 1979. *Generative Phonology: Description and Theory*. New York: Academic Press.

Kingston, J. and M. E. Beckman (eds.). 1991. *Papers in Laboratory Phonology*, i: *Between the Grammar and the Physics of Speech*. Cambridge: Cambridge University Press.

Kiraz, G. 2000. *Computational Approach to Non-linear Morphology*. Studies in Natural Language Processing. Cambridge: Cambridge University Press.

Kornai, A. 1995. *Formal Phonology*. New York: Garland Publishing.

Kristoffersen, G. 1996. *The Phonology of Norwegian*. The Phonology of the World's Languages. Oxford: Clarendon Press.

Labov, W., S. Ash, and C. Boberg. 2001. *Atlas of North American English*. Berlin: Mouton de Gruyter.

Ladd, D. R. 1996. *Intonational Phonology*. Cambridge: Cambridge University Press.

Ladefoged, P. 2000. *Vowels and Consonants: An Introduction to the Sounds of Languages*. Cambridge, Mass.: Blackwell.

——and I. Maddieson. 1996. *The Sounds of the World's Languages*. Cambridge, Mass.: Blackwell.

Laver, J. 1994. *Principles of Phonetics*. Cambridge Textbooks in Linguistics. Cambridge: Cambridge University Press.

Liberman, M. Y. and A. S. Prince. 1977. 'On stress and linguistic rhythm'. *Linguistic Inquiry*, 8, 249–336.

Mateus, H. and E. d'Andrade. 2000. *The Phonology of Portuguese*. The Phonology of the World's Languages. Oxford: Clarendon Press.

Odden, D. 1996. *The Phonology and Morphology of Kimatuumbi*. The Phonology of the World's Languages. Oxford: Clarendon Press.

Pierrehumbert, J. 1990. 'Phonological and phonetic representation'. *Journal of Phonetics*, 18, 375–94.

Pike, K. L. 1947. *Phonemics: A Technique for Reducing Language to Writing*. Ann Arbor: University of Michigan Press.

——and E. V. Pike. 1947. 'Immediate constituents of Mazateco syllables'. *International Journal of American Linguistics*, 13, 78–91.

Roca, I., W. Johnson, and A. Roca. 1999. *A Course in Phonology*. Cambridge, Mass.: Blackwell.

Rubach, J. 1993. *The Lexical Phonology of Slovak*. Oxford: Clarendon Press.

Scobbie, J. 1998. *Attribute-Value Phonology*. New York: Garland Publishing.

Siptár, P. and M. Törkenczy. 2000. *The Phonology of Hungarian*. The Phonology of the World's Languages. Oxford: Clarendon Press.

Sproat, R. 1992. *Morphology and Computation*. Natural Language Processing. Cambridge, Mass.: MIT Press.

——(ed.). 1996. *Computational Phonology in Speech Technology: Proceedings of the 2nd Meeting of the Association for Computational Linguistics Special Interest Group in Computational Phonology (ACL '96)*. (Santa Cruz).

Stevens, K. N. 1999. *Acoustic Phonetics*. Cambridge, Mass.: MIT Press.

Tesar, B. 1995. *Computational optimality theory*. Ph.D. thesis, Rutgers University.

——and P. Smolensky. 2000. *Learnability in Optimality Theory*. Cambridge, Mass.: MIT Press.

van der Hulst, H. and N. Ritter (eds.). 1999. *The Syllable: Views and Facts.* Studies in Generative Grammar. Berlin: Mouton de Gruyter.

Vaux, B. 1998. *The Phonology of Armenian.* The Phonology of the World's Languages. Oxford: Clarendon Press.

Walther, M. 1997. *Declarative prosodic morphology: constraint-based analyses and computational models of Finnish and Tigrinya.* Ph.D. thesis, Heinrich-Heine-Universität, Düsseldorf (in German).

Wareham, T. 1999. *Systematic parameterized complexity analysis in computational phonology.* Ph.D. thesis, University of Victoria.

Wiese, R. 1996. *The Phonology of German.* The Phonology of the World's Languages. Oxford: Clarendon Press.

CHAPTER 2

MORPHOLOGY

HARALD TROST

ABSTRACT

Computational morphology deals with the processing of words in both their graphemic, i.e. written, and their phonemic, i.e. spoken form. It has a wide range of practical applications. Probably every one of you has already come across some of them. Ever used spelling correction? Or automated hyphenation? This is computational morphology at work. These tasks may seem simple to a human but they pose hard problems to a computer program. This chapter will provide you with insights into why this is so and what techniques are available to tackle these tasks.

2.1 LINGUISTIC BACKGROUND

Natural languages have intricate systems to create words and word forms from smaller units in a systematic way. The part of linguistics concerned with these phenomena is morphology. This chapter starts with a quick overview of this fascinating field. The account given will be mostly pre-theoretic and purely descriptive. Readers interested in morphological theory should consult the Further Reading section.

What is morphology all about? A simple answer is that morphology deals with words. In formal language words are just arbitrary strings denoting constants or variables. Nobody cares about a morphology of formal languages. In contrast, human languages contain some hundreds of thousands of words, each describing some particular feature of our world. Continuously new words are integrated while others are drifting out of use. This infinity of words is produced from a finite collection of smaller units. The task of morphology is to find and describe the mechanisms behind this process.

The basic building blocks are **morphemes**, defined as the smallest unit in language to which a meaning may be assigned or, alternatively, as the minimal unit of grammatical analysis. Morphemes are abstract entities expressing basic features, either semantic concepts like *door*, *blue*, or *take* which are called **roots** or abstract features like *past* or *plural*.

Their realization as part of a word is called **morph**. Often, there is a one-to-one relation, e.g. the morpheme *door* is realized as the morph *door*. With *take*, on the other hand, we find the morphs *take* and *took*. In such a case we speak of **allomorphs**. Plural in English is usually expressed by the morph *-s*. There are exceptions though: in *oxen* plural is expressed through the morph *-en*, in *men* by stem vowel alteration. All these different forms are allomorphs of the plural morpheme.

Free morphs may form a word on their own, e.g. the morph *door*. Such words are **monomorphemic**, i.e. they consist of a single morph. **Bound** morphs occur only in combination with other forms. All affixes are bound morphs. For example, the word *doors* consists of the free morph *door* and the bound morph *-s*. Words may also consist of free morphs only, e.g. *tearoom*, or bound morphs only, e.g. *exclude*.

Every language typically contains some 10,000 morphs. This is a magnitude below the number of words. Strict rules govern the combination of these morphs to form words (cf. section 2.5). This way of structuring the lexicon makes the cognitive load of remembering so many words much easier.

2.2 WHAT IS A WORD?

Surprisingly, there is no straight answer to this question. One can easily spot 'words' in a text because they are separated from each other by blanks or punctuation. However, if you record ordinary speech you will find out that there are no obvious breaks. On the other hand, we could isolate units occurring—in different combinations—over and over again. Therefore, the notion of 'word' makes sense. How can we define it?

From a syntactic point of view, 'words' are the units that make up sentences. Words are grouped according to their function in the sentential structure. Morphology, on the other hand, is concerned with the inner structure of 'words'. It tries to uncover the rules that govern the formation of words from smaller units. We notice that words that convey the same meaning look different depending on their syntactic context. Take, e.g., the words *degrade*, *degrades*, *degrading*, and *degraded*. We can think of those as different forms of the same 'word'. The part that carries the meaning is the **base form**. In our example this is the form *degrade*. All other forms are produced by combination with additional morphs. All the different forms of a word together are called its **paradigm**.

In English, the base form always coincides with a specific word form, e.g. degrade is also present tense, active voice, non-third person singular. In other languages we find a slightly different situation. Italian marks nouns for gender and number. Different affixes are used to signal masculine and feminine on the one hand and singular and plural on the other hand.

(2.1)   *Singular*   *Plural*
    Masculine pomodor<u>o</u>   pomodor<u>i</u>   'tomato'
    Feminine   cipoll<u>a</u>   cipoll<u>e</u>   'onion'

We must assume that the base form is what is left over after removing the respective suffixes, i.e. *pomodor-* and *cipoll-*. Such base forms are called **stems**.

Base forms are not necessarily atomic. By comparing *degrade* to *downgrade*, *retro-grade*, and *upgrade* on the one hand and *decompose*, *decrease*, and *deport* on the other hand, we notice that *degrade* is composed of the morphs *de-* and *grade*. The morpheme carrying the central meaning of the word is often called the **root**. Roots may combine with affixes or other roots (cf. section 2.3.2) to form new base forms.

In phonology 'words' define the range for certain phonological processes. Often the phonological word is identical with the morphological word but sometimes boundaries differ. A good example for such a discrepancy is cliticization (cf. section 2.5.2).

2.3 FUNCTIONS OF MORPHOLOGY

How much and what sort of information is expressed by morphology differs widely between languages. Information that is expressed by syntax in one language is expressed morphologically in another one. For example, *English* uses an auxiliary verb construction, *Spanish* a suffix to express the future tense.

(2.2) I speak—hablo
       I will speak—hablaré

Also, some type of information may be present in one language while missing in another one. For example, many languages mark nouns for plural. Japanese does not.

(2.3)   book—hon
      books—hon

The means for encoding information vary widely. Most common is the use of different types of affixes. Traditionally, linguists discriminate between the following types of languages:

- **Isolating languages** (e.g. Mandarin Chinese): there are no bound forms, e.g. no affixes. The only morphological operation is composition.
- **Agglutinative languages** (e.g. Ugro-Finnic and Turkic languages): all bound forms are affixes, i.e. are added to a stem like beads on a string. Every affix represents a distinct morphological feature. Every feature is expressed by exactly one affix.
- **Inflectional languages** (e.g. Indo-European languages): distinct features are merged into a single bound form (portmanteau morph). The same underlying feature may be expressed differently, depending on the paradigm.
- **Polysynthetic languages** (e.g. Inuit languages): these languages express more structural information morphologically than other languages, e.g. verb arguments are incorporated into the verb.

Real languages rarely fall cleanly into one of the above classes, e.g. even Mandarin has a few suffixes. Moreover, this classification mixes the aspect of what is expressed morphologically and the means for expressing it.

2.3.1 Inflection

Inflection is required in particular syntactic contexts. It does not change the part-of-speech category but the grammatical function. The different forms of a word produced by inflection form its **paradigm**. Inflection is *complete*, i.e. with rare exceptions all the forms of its paradigm exist for a specific word. Regarding inflection, words can be categorized in three classes:

- **Particles** or non-inflecting words: they occur in just one form. In English, prepositions, adverbs, conjunctions, and articles are particles;
- **Verbs** or words following conjugation;
- **Nominals** or words following declination, i.e. nouns, adjectives, and pronouns.

Conjugation is mainly concerned with defining tense, aspect, and agreement (e.g. person and number). Take for example the *German* verb 'lesen' (to read):

(2.4)

	Present				Past			
	Indicative		*Subjunctive*		*Indicative*		*Subjunctive*	
	Sing.	*Plural*	*Sing.*	*Plural*	*Sing.*	*Plural*	*Sing.*	*Plural*
1st person	lese	lesen	lese	lesen	las	lasen	läse	läsen
2nd person	liest	lest	lesest	leset	last	last	läsest	läset
3rd person	liest	lesen	lese	lesen	las	lasen	läse	läsen
Participle	lesend				gelesen			
Imperative	lies	lest						
Infinitive	lesen							

Declination marks various agreement features like *number* (singular, plural, dual, etc.), *case* (as governed by verbs and prepositions, or to mark various kinds of semantic relations), *gender* (male, female, neuter), and *comparison*.

2.3.2 Derivation and compounding

Derivation and compounding are processes that create *new words*. They have nothing to do with morphosyntax but are a means to extend our lexicon in an economic and principled way.

In **derivation**, a new word—usually of a different part-of-speech category—is produced by adding a bound morph to a base form. Derivation is incomplete, i.e. a derivational morph cannot be applied to all words of the appropriate class. For example, in German the very productive derivational suffix *-bar* can be applied to most but not all verbs to produce adjectives:

(2.5) essen   'eat'   —   ess<u>bar</u>   'eatable'
      absehen   'conceive'   —   abseh<u>bar</u>   'conceivable'
      sehen   'see'   —   *seh<u>bar</u>   'visible'

Application of a derivational morph may be restricted to a certain subclass. For example, the English derivational suffix *-ity* combines with stems of Latin origin only, while the Germanic suffix *-ness* applies to a wider range:

(2.6) rare   —   rar<u>ity</u>   —   rare<u>ness</u>
      red   —   *redd<u>ity</u>   —   red<u>ness</u>
      grave   —   grav<u>ity</u>   —   grave<u>ness</u>
      weird   —   *weird<u>ity</u>   —   weird<u>ness</u>

Derivation can be applied recursively, i.e. words that are already the product of derivation can undergo the process again. That way a potentially infinite number of words can be produced. Take, for example, the following chain of derivations:

(2.7) hospital—hospital<u>ize</u>—hospitaliz<u>ation</u>—<u>pseudo</u>hospitalization

Semantic interpretation of the derived word is often difficult. While a derivational suffix can usually be given a unique semantic meaning, many of the derived words may still resist compositional interpretation.

While inflectional and derivational morphology are mediated by the attachment of a bound morph, **compounding** is the joining of two or more base forms to form a new word as in *state monopoly, bedtime*, or *red wine*. In some cases parts are joined by a linking morph (usually the remnant of case marking) as in *bull's eye* or German *Liebeslied* (love-song).

The last part of a compound usually defines its morphosyntactic properties. Semantic interpretation is even more difficult than with derivation. Almost any semantic relationship may hold between the components of a compound:

(2.8) Wienerschnitzel   'cutlet Vienna style'
      Schweineschnitzel 'pork cutlet'
      Kinderschnitzel   'cutlet for children'

The boundary between derivation and compounding is fuzzy. Historically, most derivational suffixes developed from words frequently used in compounding. An obvious example is the *-ful* suffix as in *hopeful, wishful, thankful*.

Phrases and compounds cannot always be distinguished. The English expression *red wine* in its written form could be both. In spoken language the stress pattern differs: *red wíne* vs. *réd wine*. In German phrases are morphologically marked, while compounds are not: *roter Wein* vs. *Rotwein*. For verb compounds the situation is similar to English: *zu Hause bleiben* vs. *zuhausebleiben*.

2.4 WHAT CONSTITUTES A MORPH?

Every word form must at the core contain a root which can (must) then be complemented with additional morphs. How are these morphs realized? Obviously, a morph must somehow be recognizable in the phonetic or orthographic pattern constituting the word. The most common type of morph is a continuous sequence of phonemes. All roots and most affixes are of this form. A complex word then consists of a sequence of concatenated morphs. Agglutinative languages function almost exclusively this way. But there are surprisingly many other possibilities.

2.4.1 Affixation

An **affix** is a bound morph that is realized as a sequence of phonemes (or graphemes).

By far the most common types of affixes are prefixes and suffixes. Many languages have only these two types of affixes. Among them is English (at least under standard morphological analyses).

A **prefix** is an affix that is attached in front of a stem. An example is the English negative marker *un-* attached to adjectives:

(2.9)   common   <u>un</u>common

A **suffix** is an affix that is attached after a stem, e.g. the English plural marker *-s*:

(2.10) shoe   shoe<u>s</u>

Across languages suffixation is far more frequent than prefixation. Also, certain kinds of morphological information are never expressed via prefixes, e.g. nominal case marking. Many computational systems for morphological analysis and generation assume a model of morphology based on prefixation and suffixation only.

A **circumfix** is the combination of a prefix and a suffix which together express some feature. From a computational point of view a circumfix can be viewed as really two affixes applied one after the other.

In *German*, the circumfixes *ge—t* and *ge—n* form the past participle of verbs:

(2.11) sag*en* 'to say' <u>ge</u>sag<u>t</u>   'said'
        lauf*en* 'to run' <u>ge</u>lauf<u>en</u> 'run'

An **infix** is an affix where the placement is defined in terms of some phonological condition(s). These might result in the infix appearing within the root to which it is affixed. In *Bontoc* (Philippines) the infix *-um-* turns adjectives and nouns into verbs (Fromkin and Rodman 1997: 129). The infix attaches after the initial consonant:

(2.12) /fikas/   'strong' /f<u>um</u>ikas/   'to be strong'
        /kilad/   'red'   /k<u>um</u>ilad/   'to be red'
        /fusul/   'enemy'   /f<u>um</u>usul/   'to be an enemy'

Reduplication is a border case of affixation. The form of the affix is a function of the stem to which it is attached, i.e. it copies (some portion of) the stem. Reduplication may be complete or partial. In the latter case it may be prefixal, infixal, or suffixal. Reduplication can include phonological alteration on the copy or the original.

In *Javanese* **complete reduplication** expresses the *habitual-repetitive*. If the second vowel is non-/a/, the first vowel in the copy is made non-low and the second becomes /a/. When the second vowel is /a/, the copy remains unchanged while in the original the /a/ is changed to /ɛ/ (Kiparsky 1987):

(2.13) /adʊs/   'take a bath' /<u>odas</u>adʊs/
        /bali/   'return'   /<u>bola</u>bali/
        /bozən/ 'tired of'   /<u>bozan</u>bozən/
        /ɛlɛq/   'return'   /<u>elaq</u>ɛlɛq/
        /dolan/ 'recreate'   /<u>dolan</u>dolɛn/
        /udan/   'horse'   /<u>udan</u>udɛn/

Partial reduplication is more common. In *Yidiɲ* (Australia) **prefixal reduplication** by copying the 'minimal word' is used for plural marking (Nash 1980).

(2.14)   /mulari/   'initiated man'   /mula̱mulari/
         /gindalba/   'lizard'   /ginda̱lgindalba/

In *Amharic* (Ethiopia) **infixal reduplication** is used to express the *frequentative* (Rose 2001).

(2.15)   /kətəfə/   'chop'   /ki̱tatəfə/   'chop a lot'
         /k'əbələ/   'decrease'   /k'i̱babələ/   'decrease greatly'
         /wək'ət'ə/   'fight'   /wik'̱ak'ət'ə/   'fight a lot'
         /lak'ət'ə/   'mix'   /li̱k'ak'ət'ə/   'mix a lot'

From a computational point of view one property of reduplication is especially important: since reduplication involves copying it cannot—at least in the general case—completely be described with the use of finite-state methods.

2.4.2 Non-concatenative phenomena

Semitic languages (at least according to standard analyses) exhibit a very peculiar type of morphology, often called **root-and-template morphology**. A so-called root, consisting of two to four consonants, conveys the basic semantic meaning. A vowel pattern marks information about voice and aspect. A derivational template gives the class of the word. *Arabic* verb stems are constructed this way. The root *ktb* (write) produces—among others—the following stems:

(2.16) *Template*   *Vowel pattern*
                        A (active)   *UI (passive)*

CVCVC	katab	kutib	'write'
CVCCVC	kattab	kuttib	'cause to write'
CVVCVC	ka:tab	ku:tib	'correspond'
tVCVVCVC	taka:tab	tuku:tib	'write each other'
nCVVCVC	nka:tab	nku:tib	'subscribe'
CtVCVC	ktatab	ktutib	'write'
stVCCVC	staktab	stuktib	'dictate'

Sometimes, morphs neither introduce new nor remove existing segments. Instead, they are realized as a change of phonetic properties or an alteration of prosodic shape.

Ablaut refers to vowel alternations inherited from Indo-European. It is a pure example of vowel modification as a morphological process. Examples are strong verbs in Germanic languages (e.g. swim—swam—swum). In *Icelandic* this process is still more common and more regular than in most other Germanic languages (Sproat 1992: 62):

(2.17) *Stem*   *Past sing.*   *Past pl.*   *PPP*
        /biːt/   /beit/   /bit/   /bit/   'to bite'
        /riːf/   /reif/   /rif/   /rif/   'to tear'

Umlaut has its origin in a phonological process, whereby root vowels were assimilated to a high-front suffix vowel. When this suffix vowel was lost later on, the change in the root vowel became the sole remaining mark of the morphological feature originally signalled by the suffix. In *German* noun plural may be marked by umlaut (sometimes in combination with a suffix), i.e. the stem vowel feature *back* is changed to *front*:

(2.18) *Singular*   *Plural*
        Mutter /mʊtɐ/   Mütter /mʏtɐ/   'mother'
        Garten /ɡartən/   Gärten /ɡɛrtən/   'garden'
        Hof /hoːf/   Höfe /høːfə/   'yard'

Altering the prosody can also realize a morpheme. **Tone modification** can signal certain morphological features. In *Ngbaka* (Congo) tense-aspect contrasts are expressed by four different tonal variants (Nida 1949):

(2.19) *Low*   *Mid*   *Low-high*   *High*
        /à/   /ā/   /ǎ/   /á/   'put more than one thing'
        /kpòlò/   /kpōlō/   /kpòló/   /kpóló/   'return'
        /ɓìlì/   /ɓīlī/   /ɓìlí/   /ɓílí/   'cut'

A morpheme may be realized by a **stress shift**. *English* noun–verb derivation sometimes uses a pattern where stress is shifted from the first to the second syllable:

(2.20) *Noun*   *Verb*
        éxport   expórt
        récord   recórd
        cónvict   convíct

Suppletion is a process of total modification occurring sporadically and idiosyncratically within inflectional paradigms. It is usually associated with forms that are used very frequently, for example *went*, the past tense of *to go*, and the forms of *to be*: *am, are, is, was*, and *were*.

Sometimes a morphological operation has no phonological expression whatsoever. Examples are found in many languages. *English* noun-to-verb derivation is often not explicitly marked:

(2.21) man   The <u>man</u> smiled.   <u>Man</u> the boats.
        house   He buys a <u>house</u>.   They <u>house</u> in a cave.

A possible analysis is to assume a **zero morph** which attaches to the noun to form a verb: book+$\emptyset_V$. Another possibility is to assume two independent lexical items disregarding any morphological relationship.

2.5 THE STRUCTURE OF WORDS: MORPHOTACTICS

Somehow morphs must be put together to form words. A word grammar determines the way this has to be done. This part of morphology is called **morphotactics**. As we have seen, the most usual way is simple concatenation. Let's have a look at the constraints involved. What are the conditions governing the ordering of morphemes in *pseudohospitalization*?

(2.22) *hospitalationizepseudo, *pseudoizehospitalation
(2.23) *pseudohospitalationize

In (2.22) an obvious restriction is violated: *pseudo-* is a prefix and must appear ahead of the stem, *-ize* and *-ation* are suffixes and must appear after the stem. The violation in (2.23) is less obvious. In addition to the pure ordering requirements there are also rules governing to which types of stems an affix may attach: *-ize* attaches to nouns and produces verbs, *-ation* attaches to verbs and produces nouns.

One possibility for describing the word-formation process is to assume a functor-argument structure. Affixes are functors that pose restrictions on their (single) argument. That way a binary tree is constructed. Prefixes induce right branching and suffixes left branching.

The functor *pseudo-* takes a noun to form a noun, *-ize* a noun to form a verb, and *-ation* a verb to form a noun. This description renders two different possible structures for *pseudohospitalization*, the one given in Fig. 2.1 and a second one where *pseudo-* combines directly with *hospital* first. We may or may not accept this ambiguity. To avoid the second reading we could state a lexical constraint that a word with the head *pseudo-* cannot serve as an argument anymore.

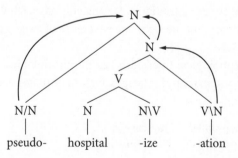

Fig. 2.1 **The internal structure of the word** *pseudohospitalization*

2.5.1 Constraints on affixes

Affixes attach to specific categories only. This is an example for a syntactic restriction. Restrictions may also be of a phonological, semantic, or purely lexical nature. A semantic restriction on the English adjectival prefix *un-* prevents its attachment to an adjective that already has a negative meaning:

(2.24) unhappy   *unsad
        unhealthy   *unill
        unclean   *undirty

The fact that in English some suffixes may only attach to words of Latin origin (cf. section 2.3.2) is an example for a lexical restriction.

2.5.2 Morphological vs. phonological structure

In some cases there is a mismatch between the phonological and the morphological structure of a word. One example is comparative formation with the suffix *-er* in English. Roughly, there is a phonological rule that prevents attaching this suffix to words that consist of more than two syllables:

(2.25) tall   taller
        happy   happier
        competent   *competenter
        elegant   *eleganter

If we want to stick to the above rule *unrulier* has to be explained with a structure where the prefix *un-* is attached to *rulier*. But, from a morphological point of view, the adjective *ruly* does not exist, only the negative form *unruly*. This implies that the suffix *-er* is attached to *unruly*. We end up with an obvious mismatch!

    A **clitic** is a syntactically separate word phonologically realized as an affix. The phenomenon is quite common across languages.

- English auxiliaries have contracted forms that function as affixes:
  he shall return → *he'll return*
- German prepositions can combine with the definite article:
  an dem Tisch → *am Tisch*
  in das Haus → *ins Haus*
- Italian personal pronouns can be attached to the verb. In this process the ordering of constituents is also altered:
  ce ne facciamo → *facciamocene*

2.6   THE INFLUENCE OF PHONOLOGY

Morphotactics is responsible for governing the rules for the combination of morphs into larger entities. One could assume that this is all a system needs to know to break down words into their component morphemes. But there is another aspect that makes things more complicated: Phonological rules may apply and change the shape of morphs. To deal with these changes and their underlying reasons is the area of **morphophonology**.

Most applications of computational morphology deal with text rather than speech. But written language is rarely a true phonemic description. For some languages, e.g. Finnish, Spanish, or Turkish, orthography is a good approximation for a phonetic transcription. English, on the other hand, has very poor correspondence between writing and pronunciation. As a result, we often deal with orthography rather than phonology. A good example is English plural rules (cf. section 2.8.1).

By and large, words are composed by concatenating morphs. Sometimes this concatenation process will induce a phonological change in the vicinity of the morph boundary.

Assimilation is a process where the two segments at a morph boundary influence each other, resulting in some feature change that makes them more similar. Take, for example, the English prefix *in-* where the *n* changes to *m* before labials:

(2.26)   <in+feasible>   →   infeasible
<in+mature>   →   immature
<in+probable>   →   improbable
<in+secure>   →   insecure

Other possibilities are **epenthesis** (insertion) and **elision** (deletion) of a segment under certain (phonological) conditions. Take for example English plural formation:

(2.27)   <door+s>   →   doors
<dish+s>   →   dishes
<bliss+s>   →   blisses
<match+s>   →   matches

In this case the rule requires the insertion of an /ə/ between /s/, /z/, /S/, or /Z/ and another /s/. On the other hand, the *German* suffix *−st* loses its starting segment /s/ when attached to stems ending in /s/:

(2.28)   <leb+st>   →   lebst
<sag+st>   →   sagst
<ras+st>   →   rast
<trotz+st>   →   trotzt

The change is not purely phonologically motivated. The same condition, namely two adjoining /s/, leads to either the epenthesis of /ə/, or the elision of the second /s/.[1]

Some morphophonological processes work long-distance. Most common are harmony rules. **Vowel harmony** is a phonological process where the leftmost (in rare cases the rightmost) vowel in a word influences all the following (preceding) vowels. It occurs in Finno-Ugric, Turkic, and many African languages. An example of Turkish vowel harmony is presented in section 1.2.

2.7 APPLICATIONS OF COMPUTATIONAL MORPHOLOGY

For **hyphenation** segmenting words correctly into their morphs is a prerequisite. The major problem is spurious segmentations. **Grapheme-to-phoneme conversion** for text to speech needs to resolve ambiguities in the translation of characters into phonemes. In the word *hothouse* we need to know the morph structure <hot+house> for correctly pronouncing the *th* sequence as /th/ instead of the usual /θ/ or /ð/.

Spelling correction is another low-level application. Comparing input against a list of word forms does not work well. The list will never contain all occurring words and enlarging the list has the negative side effect of including obscure words that will match with typos thus preventing their detection. Most current systems use a root lexicon, plus a relatively small set of affixes and simple rules to cover morphotactics.

Stemmers are used in information retrieval (see Chapter 29) to reduce as many related words and word forms as possible to a common canonical form—not necessarily the base form—which can then be used in the retrieval process. The main requirement is—as in all the above tasks—robustness.

In Chinese, Japanese, or Korean, words in a sentence are not separated by blanks or punctuation marks. Morphological analysis is used to perform the task of automatic word separation.

Written Japanese is a combination of kanji, the morphemic Chinese characters used for open-class morphemes, and the syllabic kana characters mainly used for closed-class morphemes (although in principle all Japanese words can be written exclusively in kana). Since there are several thousand kanji characters, many Japanese text input systems use kana–kanji conversion. The whole text is typed in kana and the relevant portions are subsequently converted to kanji. This mapping from kana

---

[1] The notion of insertion or deletion is purely descriptive. Phonological theory may explain the underlying processes completely differently. Nonetheless, this is the view most often taken by work in computational morphology.

to kanji is quite ambiguous. A combination of statistical and morphological methods is applied to solve the task.

An obvious application of computational morphology can be seen in systems based on parsing and/or generating utterances in written or spoken form. These range from message and information extraction to dialogue systems and machine translation. For many current applications, only inflectional morphology is considered.

In a parser, morphological analysis of words is an important prerequisite for syntactic analysis. Properties of a word the parser needs to know are its part-of-speech category and the morphosyntactic information encoded in the particular word form. Another important task is **lemmatization**, i.e. finding the corresponding dictionary form for a given input word, because for many applications a lemma lexicon is used to provide more detailed syntactic (e.g, valency) and semantic information for deep analysis. In generation, on the other hand, the task is to produce the correct word form from the base form plus the relevant set of morphosyntactic features.

At the moment most available speech recognition systems make use of full-form lexicons and perform their analysis on a word basis. Increasing demands on the lexicon size on the one hand and the need to limit the necessary training time on the other hand will make morph-based recognition systems more attractive.

2.8   Computational Morphology

The most basic task in computational morphology is to take a string of characters or phonemes as input and deliver an analysis as output. The input string (2.29) can be mapped to the string of underlying morphemes (2.30) or the morphosyntactic interpretation (2.31).

(2.29) incompatibilities
(2.30) in+con+patible+ity+s
(2.31) incompatibility+NounPlural

The simplest way to achieve the mapping from (2.29) to (2.31) is the **full-form lexicon**, i.e. a long list of pairs where each left side represents a word form and the right side its interpretation. Advantages are simplicity and applicability to all possible phenomena, disadvantages are redundancy and inability to cope with forms not contained in the lexicon.

Lemma lexicons reduce redundancy. A **lemma** is a canonical form—usually the base form—taken as the representative for all the different forms of a paradigm.[2] An

---

[2] This is also the approach taken in printed dictionaries.

interpretation algorithm relates every form to its lemma plus delivering a morpho-syntactic interpretation. As a default, forms are expected to be string concatenations of lemma and affixes. Affixes must be stored in a separate repository together with the relevant morphotactic information about how they may combine with other forms. Interpretation simply means finding a sequence of affixes and a base form that conforms to morphotactics. For different reasons a given word form may not conform to this simple picture:

- With very frequently used words we find suppletion.

One needs some exception-handling mechanism to cope with suppletion. A possible solution is to have secondary entries where you store suppleted forms together with their morphosyntactic information. These secondary forms are then linked to the corresponding primary form, i.e. the lemma.

- Morphs are realized in a non-concatenative way, e.g. tense of strong verbs in English: *give–gave–given*.

In languages like English, where these phenomena affect only a fairly small and closed set of words, such forms can be treated like suppletion. Alternatively, some exception-handling mechanism (usually developed ad hoc and language specific) is applied.

- Phonological rules may change the shape of a word form, e.g. English suffixes starting with *s* may not directly follow stems ending in a sibilant: *dish–dishes*.

If morphophonological processes in a language are few and local the lemma lexicon approach can still be successful. In our example it suffices to assume two plural endings: *-s* and *-es*. For all base forms it must be specified whether the former or the latter of the two endings may be attached.

Apart from the obvious limitations with regard to the treatment of morphophonological rules on a more general scale the approach has some other inherent restrictions:

- The algorithm is geared towards analysis. For generation purposes, one needs a completely different algorithm and data.
- Interpretation algorithms are language specific because they encode both the basic concatenation algorithm and the specific exception-handling mechanism.
- The approach was developed for morphosyntactic analysis. An extension to handle more generally the segmenting of word forms into morphs is difficult to achieve.

2.8.1 Finite-state morphology

Because most morphological phenomena can be described with regular expressions the use of finite-state techniques for morphological components is common. In particular, when morphotactics is seen as a simple concatenation of morphs it can straightforwardly be described by finite automata.

However, it was not so obvious how to describe non-concatenative phenomena (e.g. vowel harmony, root-and-template morphology, reduplication) and morphophonology in such a framework.

2.8.1.1 *Two-level morphology*

Two-level morphology explicitly takes care of morphophonology. The mechanism derives from the ideas developed in generative phonology (cf. Chomsky and Halle 1968). There, the derivation of a word form from its lexical structure is performed by the successive application of phonological rules creating a multi-step process involving several intermediate levels of representation. Such an approach may be suited for generation but leads to problems if applied to analysis. Since the ordering of rule application influences the result it is difficult to reverse the process.

Several proposals were made on how to overcome these problems. Two-level morphology (Koskenniemi 1984) is the most successful attempt. It has the further advantages of being non-directional (applicable to analysis and generation) and language independent (because of its purely declarative specification of language-specific data). Two-level morphology has since been implemented in a number of different systems and applied to a wide range of natural languages.

2.8.1.1.1 *Two-level rules*

As the name suggests, two levels suffice to describe the phonology (or orthography) of a natural language. On the surface level words appear just as they are pronounced (or written) in ordinary language (with the important exception of the null character). On the lexical level, the alphabet includes special symbols—so-called **diacritics**—which are mainly used to represent features that are not phonemes (or graphemes) but nevertheless constitute necessary phonological information. The diacritics '+' and '#' are used to indicate morph and word boundary respectively.

A set of pairs of lexical and surface characters—written as lexical character–colon–surface character, e.g. *a:a, +:0*—constitutes possible mappings. Pairs with no attached rules are applied by default. For all other pairs the attached rules restrict their application to a certain phonological context. Rules function as constraints on the mapping between surface and lexical form of morphs. They are applied in parallel and not one after the other as in generative phonology. Since no ordering of the rules is involved this is a completely declarative way of description.

A rule consists of the following parts:

- The **substitution** indicates the affected character pair.
- **left** and **right context** are regular expressions that define the phonological conditions for the substitution.
- **operators** define the status of the rule: the **context restriction operator** ⇐ makes

the substitution of the lexical character obligatory in the context defined by that rule (other phonological contexts are not affected). The **surface coercion operator** $\Rightarrow$ restricts the substitution of the lexical character to exactly this context (it may not occur anywhere else). The $\Leftrightarrow$ is a combination of the former two, i.e. the substitution must take place in this and only this context. The fourth operator $/\Leftarrow$ states prohibitions, i.e. the substitution may not take place in this context.

The following rule specifies that a lexical morph boundary (indicated by '+') between a *sibilant* on the left side and an *s* on the right side must correspond to surface level *e*. By convention a pair with identical lexical and surface character may be denoted by just a single character. Curly brackets indicate a set of alternatives, square brackets a sequence.

(2.32)   *a.* +:e $\Leftarrow$ { s x z [{ s c} h] } : _ s ;

The rule covers some of the cases where *e* is inserted between stem and an inflectional affix starting with *s* (plural, 3rd person, superlative) in English. By default, the morph boundary will map to null, but in the given specific context it maps to *e*. (2.32*a*) makes no statements about other contexts. The following examples demonstrate the application of this rule (vertical bars denote a default pairing, numbers the application of the corresponding rule):

(2.33)   #b l i s s+s#   #f o x+s#   #d i s h+s#   #w a t ch+s#
            | | | | | | 1 | | | | | | | 1 | | | | | | | | 1 | | | | | | | | 1 | |
            0 b l i s s e s 0   0 f o x e s 0   0 d i s h e s 0   0 w a t c h e s 0

(2.32*a*) does not capture all the cases where *e* epenthesis occurs. For example, the forms *spies*, *shelves*, or *potatoes* are not covered. A more complete rule is:

(2.32)   *b.* +:e $\Leftrightarrow$ { s x z [{ s c} h:h] :v [C y:] [C o]} _ s ;

Rule (2.32*b*) defines all the contexts where '+' maps to *e* (because of the $\Leftrightarrow$ operator). It makes use of some additional writing conventions. A colon followed by a character denotes the set of all pairs with that surface character. Accordingly, a character followed by a colon means the set of all pairs with that lexical character. The C stands for the set of English consonants, the V for the vowels. To cope with the *spies* example we need another rule which licenses the mapping from *y* to *i*.

(2.34)   y:i $\Leftrightarrow$ C _ { +:e [+: e] } ;
            V C$^+$ _ +: C ;

Rule (2.34) specifies two distinct contexts. If either of them is satisfied the substitution must occur, i.e. contexts are OR-connected. The '+' operator in the second context indicates *at least one occurrence* of the preceding sign (accordingly, the operator '*' has the reading *arbitrarily many occurrences*). Jointly with rule (2.35) for the mapping from 'f' to 'v' rule (2.32) also takes care of forms like *shelves* and *potatoes*:

(2.35) f:v ⇐ {e l}_+: s ;
        V _ e +: s ;

#spy+s#	#toy+s#	#shelf+s#	#wife+s#	#potato+s#
‖‖21‖‖	‖‖‖‖‖‖	‖‖‖31‖‖	‖‖3‖‖‖	‖‖‖‖‖1‖‖
0spies0	0toy0s0	0shelves0	0wive0s0	0potatoes0

A given pair of lexical and surface strings can only map if they are of equal length. There is no possibility of omitting or inserting a character in one of the levels. On the other hand, elision and epenthesis are common phonological phenomena. To cope with these, the null character (written as 0) is included in both the surface and the lexical alphabet. The null character is taken to be contained in the surface string for the purpose of mapping lexical to surface string and vice versa but it does not show up in the output or input of the system. Diacritics are mapped to the null character by default. Any other mapping of a diacritic has to be licensed by a rule.

Assumption of the explicit null character is essential for processing. A mapping between a lexical and a surface string presupposes that for every position a character pair exists. This implies that both strings are of equal length (nulls are considered as characters in this respect). Rules can either be directly interpreted or compiled into finite-state transducers. The use of finite-state machinery allows for very efficient implementation. For a more in-depth discussion of implementational aspects consult Chapter 18 or Beesley and Karttunen (2001).

One subtle difference between direct rule interpretation and transducers shows in the repeated application of the same rule to one string. The transducer implicitly extends the phonological context to the whole string. It must therefore explicitly take care of an overlapping of right and left contexts (e.g. in (2.32) the pair s:s constitutes both a left and right context). With direct interpretation a new instance of the rule is activated every time the left context is found in the string and overlapping need not be treated explicitly.

2.8.1.1.2 *The continuation lexicon*

A partitioned lexicon of morphs (or words) takes care of word formation by affixation. The lexicon consists of (non-disjunctive) sublexicons, so-called continuation classes. Morphs that can start a word are stored in the so-called *init lexicon*. For every morph, a set of legal continuation classes is specified. This set defines the sublexicons that must be searched for continuations. The whole process is equivalent to stepping through a finite automaton. A successful match can be taken as a move from some state x of the automaton to some other state y. Lexical entries can be thought of as arcs of the automaton: a sublexicon is a collection of arcs having a common *from* state.

The lexicon in two-level morphology serves two purposes: one is to describe which combinations of morphs are legal words of the language, the other one is to act as a filter whenever a surface word form is to be mapped to a lexical form. Its use for the second task is crucial because otherwise there would be no way to limit the insertion of the null character.

For fast access, lexicons are organized as letter tries (Fredkin 1960). A trie is well suited for an incremental (letter-by-letter) search because at every node in the trie exactly those continuations leading to legal morphs are available. Every node in the trie represents the sequence of characters associated with the path leading to that node. With nodes representing a legal morph their continuation classes are stored. In recognition, search starts at the root of the trie. Each proposed character is matched against the lexicon. Only a legal continuation at that node in the tier may be considered as a possible mapping.

Recent implementations collapse the lexicon and the two-level rules into a single, large transducer, resulting in a very compact and efficient system (cf. Chapter 18).

2.8.1.2 *Related formalisms*

For a more elegant description of phonological (or orthographic) changes affecting sequences of characters Black et al. (1987) propose a rule format consisting of a surface string (LHS for *left-hand side*) and a lexical string (RHS for *right-hand side*) of equal length separated by an operator. Surface-to-lexical rules ($\Rightarrow$) request the existence of a partition of the surface string where each part is the LHS of a rule and the lexical string the concatenation of the corresponding RHSs. Lexical-to-surface rules ($\Leftarrow$) request that any substring of a lexical string which equals an RHS of a rule must correspond to the surface string of the LHS of the same rule. The following rules are equivalent to rule (2.32*a*).

(2.36) ses $\Rightarrow$ s+s   ses $\Leftarrow$ s+s   shes $\Rightarrow$ sh+s   shes $\Leftarrow$ sh+s
       xes $\Rightarrow$ x+s   xes $\Leftarrow$ x+s   zes $\Rightarrow$ z+s   zes $\Leftarrow$ z+s
       ches $\Rightarrow$ ch+s   ches $\Leftarrow$ ch+s

These rules collapse context and substitution into one undistinguishable unit. Instead of regular expressions only strings are allowed. Because surface-to-lexical rules may not overlap, two different changes that happen to occur close to each other must be captured in a single rule. Also, long-distance phenomena like vowel harmony cannot be described in this scheme. As a remedy, Ruessink (1989) reintroduces contexts. Both LHS and RHS may come with a left and right context. They may also be of different length, doing away with the null character. Though Ruessink gives no account of the complexity of his algorithm one can suspect that it is in general less constrained than the original system.

An inherently difficult problem for two-level morphology is the root-and-template morphology of Semitic languages. One solution is the introduction of multi-tape formalisms as first described in the seminal paper by Kay (1987). The best-documented current system is SEMHE (Kiraz 1996), based on Ruessink's formalism with the extension of using three lexical tapes: one for the root, one for the vowel pattern, and one for the template.

Another extension to the formalism is realized in X2MorF (Trost 1992). In the standard system, morphologically motivated phenomena like umlaut must be described by introducing pseudosegmental material in the lexical level (see section 2.8.3). In X2MorF an additional morphological context is available to describe such phenomena more naturally.

2.8.2 Alternative formalisms

Alternative proposals for morphological systems include so-called paradigmatic morphology (Calder 1989) and the DATR system (Evans and Gazdar 1996). Common to both is the idea of introducing some default mechanism which makes it possible to define a hierarchically structured lexicon where general information is stored at a very high level. This information can be overwritten lower in the hierarchy. Both systems seem to be more concerned with morphosyntax than with morphophonology. It is an open question whether these approaches could somehow be combined with two-level rules.

2.8.3 Examples

Finnish vowels are classified into *back*, *front*, and *neutral*. According to vowel harmony all vowels in a word must be either back or front (disregarding neutral vowels).

(2.37) $V = \{a, o, u, ä, ö, y, e, i\}$
   $Vb = \{a, o, u\} \; Vf = \{ä, ö, y\}$
   [1] $\{A:a|O:o|U:u\} \Rightarrow =:Vb: =: (-Vf)^* \_ \, ;$
   [2] $\{A:ä|O:ö|U:ü\} \Rightarrow \{\#|=:Vf\} =: (Vb)^* \_ \, ;$

```
#taivas+tA#      #puhelin+tA#       #syy+tA#
||||||||| 1|     ||||||||||| 1|     ||||| 2|
0taivas0ta0      0puhelintAa0       0syy0tä 0
```

The phonological process of final devoicing in *German* works on syllable structure. Voiced consonants in syllable-final position are devoiced, e.g. the root /raːd/ (wheel) is realized as /raːt/ in the singular and as /reːdə/ in the plural). This phenomenon is not reflected by orthography.

(2.38) $Cx:Cy \Rightarrow \_ \, \#:0 \, ;$
   where Cx in (b d g)
      Cy in (p t k) matched;

```
#lo:b#    #ra:d#    #we:g#    #we:g+e#
||| 1|    ||| 1|    ||| 1|    |||  ||||
0lo:p0    0ra:t0    0we:k0    0we:g0e0
```

While the original linguistic motivation behind two-level morphology was genera-tive phonology, and two-level rules were designed to describe morphophonology, the mechanism can also deal with purely morphological phenomena.

German umlaut is used to mark—among other morphosyntactic features—plu-ral.

(2.39)   V={a, ä, e, i, o, ö, u, ü, A:a, A:ä, O:o, O:ö, U:u, U:ü}
         {A:ä | O:ö | U:ü} ⇒ _ ?* $:0;

All stem vowels eligible for umlaut are realized at the lexical level by a vowel under-specified for the back/front distinction. A pseudo-ending $ triggers the rule applica-tion, thus realizing the umlaut. In all other cases the default pairing is used. This way a morphological property is described as a morphophonological process. The ?* signifies zero or more occurrences of anything.

(2.40)   #mUt t e r+$#   #gAr t en+$#   #hOf+$e#
         | | 1| | | | | | | | | | 1| | | | | | | | | | 1| | | | |
         0müt t e r000   0gär t en000   0höf00e0

A (simplified) example from *Tagalog* shows how two-level rules can be used to describe reduplication and infixation. Rule [1] (see 2.41 below) captures infix inser-tion: On the lexical level, the prefix X is assumed. While X is not realized on the sur-face, it triggers the insertion of -*in*- between initial consonant and following vowel.

(2.41)   V={a, i, u, E}
         C={p t k b d g m n N s l r w y R}
         [1] X:0 ⇒ _ +:0 C 0:i 0:n V:V

         #X+p00 i l i #   #X+t00a h i #
         | 1| | | | | | | | | 1| | | | | | | |
         000p i n i l i 0   000t i n a h i 0

Rules [2] and [3] (2.42) cause the reduplication of the first (open) syllable: the R copies the initial consonant, the E the following vowel. The rules also take care of the case where the infix is inserted as well:

(2.42)   [2]   R:Cx ⇒ _ (0:i 0:n) E:V +:0 :Cx;
                     where Cx in (p p:m t t:n k K: N);
         [3]   E:Vx ⇒ _R:C (0:i 0:n) _ +:0 C Vx;
                     where Vx in (a i u);

         #RE+p i l i #   #RE+t a h i #
         | 23| | | | | | | 23| | | | | |
         0p i 0p i l i 0   0t a 0t a h i 0

         #X+R00E+p i l i #   #X+R00E+t a h i #
         | 1| 2| | 3| | | | | | | 1| 2| | 3| | | | | |
         000p i n i 0p i l i 0   000t i n a 0t a h i 0

FURTHER READING AND RELEVANT RESOURCES

Morphology and Computation (Sproat 1992) gives a concise introduction into morphology with examples from various languages and a good overview of applications of computational morphology. On the methodological side it concentrates on finite-state morphology. *Computational Morphology* (Ritchie et al. 1992) provides a more in-depth description of finite-state morphology but concentrates exclusively on English. An up-to-date description of finite-state technology can be found in Beesley and Karttunen (2001). The *Handbook of Morphology* (Spencer and Zwicky 1998) offers an excellent overview of morphology with examples from diverse languages.

To get some hands-on experience with morpological processing connect to *RXRC Europe* at http://www.rxrc.xerox.com/research/mltt/ and *Lingsoft* at http://www. lingsoft.fi/. A free downloadable version of two-level morphology is available from *SIL* at http://www.sil.org/pckimmo.

REFERENCES

Beesley, K. R. and L. Karttunen. 2003. *Finite-State Morphology*. Palo Alto, Calif.: CSLI Publications.

Black, A. W., G. D. Ritchie, S. G. Pulman, and G. J. Russell. 1987. 'Formalisms for morphographemic description', *Proceedings of the 3rd Meeting of the European Chapter of the Association for Computational Linguistics (ACL '87)* (Copenhagen), 11–18.

Calder, J. 1989. 'Paradigmatic Morphology'. *Proceedings of the 4th Meeting of the European Chapter of the Association for Computational Linguistics (ACL '89)* (Manchester), 58–65.

Chomsky, N. and M. Halle. 1968. *The Sound Pattern of English*. New York: Harper and Row.

Evans R. and G. Gazdar. 1996. 'DATR: a language for lexical knowledge representation'. *Computational Linguistics*, 22(2), 167–216.

Fredkin, E. 1960. 'Trie Memory'. *Communications of the ACM*, 3, 490–9.

Fromkin, V. and R. Rodman. 1997. *An Introduction to Language*. 6th edn, Orlando, Fla.: Harcourt, Brace, Jovanovich.

Kay, M. 1987. 'Nonconcatenative finite-state morphology', *Proceedings of the 3rd Meeting of the European Chapter of the Association for Computational Linguistics (ACL '87)* (Copenhagen), 2–10.

Kiparsky, P. 1987. *The phonology of reduplication*. Manuscript. Stanford University.

Kiraz, G. A. 1996. 'SEMHE: a generalized two-level system', *Proceedings of the 34th Meeting of the Association for Computational Linguistics (ACL '96)* (Los Altos, Calif.), 159–66.

Koskenniemi, K. 1984. 'A general computational model for word-form recognition and production', *Proceedings of the 10th International Conference on Computational Linguistics (COLING '84)* (Stanford, Calif.), 178–81.

Nash, D. 1980. *Topics in Warlpiri grammar*. Ph.D. Thesis, MIT, Cambridge, Mass.

Nida, E. 1949. *Morphology: The Descriptive Analysis of Words*. Ann Arbor: University of Michigan Press.

Ritchie, G. D., G. J. Russel, A. W. Black, and S. G. Pulman. 1992. *Computational Morphology*. Cambridge, Mass.: MIT Press.

Rose, S. 2001. 'Triple take: Tigre and the case of internal reduplication'. In R. Hayward, J. Ouhalla, and D. Perrett (eds.), *Studies in Afroasiatic Grammar*. Amsterdam: Benjamins.

Ruessink, H. 1989. *Two-level formalisms*. Working Papers in Natural Language Processing 5, Rijksuniversiteit Utrecht.

Spencer, A. and A. Zwicky (eds.). 1998. *The Handbook of Morphology*. Oxford: Blackwell.

Sproat, R. W. 1992. *Morphology and Computation*. Cambridge, Mass.: MIT Press.

Trost, H. 1992. 'X2MORPH: a morphological component based on augmented two-level morphology'. *Proceedings of the 12th International Joint Conference on Artificial Intelligence*. San Mateo, Calif.: Morgan Kaufmann, 1024–30.

CHAPTER 3

LEXICOGRAPHY

PATRICK HANKS

ABSTRACT

This chapter provides an overview of computational lexicography in two senses: (1) the function of the lexicon in computer programs; and (2) the use of computational techniques in compiling new dictionaries. The chapter begins with the historical background of lexicography. Next, it discusses the particular challenges of using human dictionaries for computational purposes. It goes on to examine the ways that computational techniques have changed the task of compiling new dictionaries; in these sections, special attention is paid to the links between meaning and use. In the chapter's final sections, future directions and sources for further reading are presented.

3.1 INTRODUCTION

An inventory of words is an essential component of programs for a wide variety of natural language processing applications, including information retrieval, machine translation, speech recognition, speech synthesis, and message understanding. Some of these inventories contain information about syntactic patterns and complementations associated with individual lexical items (see Chapter 4); some index the inflected forms of a lemma to the base form (see Chapter 2); some include definitions; some provide semantic links to an ontology and hierarchies between the various lexical items (see Chapters 13 and 25). Some are derived from existing human-user dictionaries, as discussed below. None are completely comprehensive; none are perfect. Even where a machine-readable lexicon is available, a lot of computational effort may need to go into 'tuning' the lexicon for particular applications. Sometimes, an off-the-peg lexicon is deemed to be more trouble than it is worth, and a required lexicon may be constructed automatically by induction from texts (see Chapter 21).

At the same time, the craft of lexicography has been revolutionized by the introduction of computer technology. On the one hand, new techniques are being used for compiling dictionaries and word lists of various kinds; on the other, new insights are obtained by computational analysis of language in use.

3.1.1 Definitions

In this chapter, two meanings of the term 'computational lexicography' are distinguished:

1. Restructuring and exploiting human dictionaries for computational purposes.
2. Using computational techniques to compile new dictionaries.

The focus is on computational lexicography in English. A comprehensive survey of computational lexicography in all the languages of the world is beyond the scope of this chapter. Lexicography in many of the world's neglected languages is now being undertaken in many research centres; the work is often computer assisted and associated with a machine-readable product.

3.2 HISTORICAL BACKGROUND

Until recently, the only reason anyone ever had for compiling a dictionary was to create an artefact for other human beings to use. Up to the Renaissance, dictionaries were either bilingual tools for use by translators, interpreters, and travellers, or Latin and Greek word lists for students and scholars. As living languages and cultures became more complex, vocabularies expanded and people began to compile dictionaries of 'hard words' in their own language–learned words which ordinary people might not understand. The earliest example in English is Robert Cawdrey's *Table Alphabeticall . . . of Hard Usuall Words . . . for the Benefit of Gentlewomen and Other Unskillful Per-*

sons (1604). It was not until the eighteenth century that lexicographers set themselves the objective of collecting and defining *all* the words in a language. For English, this culminated in Samuel Johnson's *Dictionary of the English Language* (1755), containing not only definitions but also illustrative citations from 'the best authors'.

Johnson's was the standard dictionary of English until the end of the nineteenth century, but already in 1857 Richard Chenevix Trench presented a paper to the Philological Society in London, 'On some deficiencies in our English dictionaries', in which he described lexicographers as 'the inventory clerks of the language'. This paper played a large part in motivating the Philological Society's *New English Dictionary on Historical Principles*, alias *The Oxford English Dictionary* (1884–1928).

3.2.1 Deficiencies

Many of the deficiencies that characterized nineteenth-century dictionaries still beset lexicography today, though sometimes in new forms, and they are of computational relevance. They arise from problems of both practice and principle. Chief among them are the following.

3.2.1.1 *Omissions and oversights*

It is literally impossible to compile an exhaustive inventory of the vocabulary of a living language. Trench noted many omissions and oversights in the dictionaries of his day, but the creative nature of the lexicon means that every day new words are created ad hoc and, in most but not all cases, immediately discarded. It is impossible for the inventorist to know which neologisms are going to catch on and which not. Murray deliberately omitted the neologism *appendicitis* from the first edition of *OED*. An American dictionary of the 1950s deliberately omitted the slang term *brainwash*. The first edition of *Collins English Dictionary* (1979) omitted *ayatollah*. In their day, each of these terms was considered too obscure, informal, or jargonistic to merit inclusion, though hindsight proved the judgement to be an error. That said, almost all today's machine-readable dictionaries offer a very high degree of coverage of the vocabulary of ordinary non-specialist texts—well over 99.9 per cent of the words (as opposed to the names). Lexical creativity is peripheral, not central, in ordinary discourse.

3.2.1.2 *Coverage of names*

Coverage of names is a perennial problem. Some dictionaries, on principle, do not include any entries for names; for example, they contain an entry for *English* (because it is classified as a word, not a name), but not for *England*. Other dictionaries contain a selection of names that are judged to be culturally relevant, such as *Shakespeare*, *New York*, *Muhammad Ali*, and *China*. Very few brand names and business names are found in dictionaries: *Hoover* and *Thermos flask* are judged to have become part of the common vocabulary, but no dictionary includes brand names such as *Malteser* or *Pepsi*, whatever their cultural relevance. No dictionary makes any attempt to include all the names found in a daily newspaper. However, names can be just as important as words in decoding text meaning. In Hanks (1997), discussing the role of immediate-context analysis in activating different meanings, I cited an example from the British National Corpus: in the sentence 'Auchinleck checked Rommel' selection of the meaning 'cause to pause' for *check* depends crucially on the military status of the subject and object as generals of opposing armies. If Auchinleck had been Rommel's batman, or a customs inspector, or a doctor, a different sense of *check* would have been activated.

3.2.1.3 *Ghosts*

Ghost words and ghost senses constantly creep in, evading the vigilance of lexicographers despite their best efforts. Crystal (1997: 111) mentions *commemorable* and *liquescency* as examples of words that have probably never been used outside the dictionaries in which they appear. He goes on to cite *Dord*, glossed as 'density', a ghost word that originated in the 1930s as a misreading of the abbreviation *D or d* (i.e. capital or lower-case d), which does indeed mean 'density'.

3.2.1.4 *Differentiating senses*

No generally agreed criteria exist for what counts as a sense, or for how to distinguish one sense from another. In most large dictionaries, it might be said that minor contextual variations are erected into major sense distinctions. In an influential paper, Fillmore (1975) argued against 'checklist theories of meaning', and proposed that words have meaning by virtue of resemblance to a prototype. The same paper also proposed the existence of 'frames' as systems of linguistic choices, drawing on the work of Marvin Minsky (1975) among others. These two proposals have been enormously influential. Wierzbicka (1993) argues that lexicographers should 'seek the invariant', of which (she asserts) there is rarely more than one per word. This, so far, they have failed to do; nor is it certain that it could be done with useful practical results. Nevertheless Wierzbicka's exhortation is a useful antidote to the tendency towards the endless multiplication of entities (or, to put it more kindly, drawing of superfine sense distinctions) that is characteristic of much currently available lexicography.

3.2.2 Usability of the lexicon

In the emergent United States, the indefatigable Noah Webster published his *American Dictionary of the English Language* (1828), a work which paid particular attention to American English, which was already beginning to differ from standard British English, although its definitions owe more to Johnson than its compiler liked to admit. Johnson, Murray, and Webster all compiled their dictionaries on 'historical principles'. That is, they trace the semantic development of words by putting the oldest meanings first. This is a practice still followed by many modern dictionaries. It is of great value for cultural and literary historians, but at best an unnecessary distraction and at worse a potential source of confusion in computational applications. For purposes of computational linguistics, if word meaning is in question at all, it is more important to have an inventory that says that a *camera* is a device for taking photographs than to know that, before the invention of photography, the word denoted 'a small room' and 'the treasury of the papal curia'.

The earliest comprehensive dictionary to make a serious attempt to put modern meaning first was Funk and Wagnall's (1898). Unfortunately, the great Funk and Wagnall's dictionaries of the early twentieth century no longer exist in any recognizable form. Current American large dictionaries that claim to put modern meanings first are *The Random House Dictionary* (1964, 1996), the second edition of which is available on CD-ROM, and *The American Heritage Dictionary* (1969; 4th edn. 2000). A British counterpart is *Collins English Dictionary* (1979; 4th edn. 1999).

Because they not only put modern meanings first, but also contain fuller syntactic information (including, in some cases, more or less sophisticated indications of **subcategorization** and **selectional preferences**), dictionaries for foreign learners are popular among computational researchers and tool builders. The pioneering work in this class was A. S. Hornby's *Oxford Advanced Learner's Dictionary of Current English* (*OALDCE*; 1948). The sixth edition (2000) has been fully revised, taking account of corpus evidence from the British National Corpus.

3.2.3 Machine-readable dictionaries (MRDs)

Most such dictionaries are available in **machine-readable** form, and research rights can sometimes be negotiated with publishers. To overcome problems of commercial sensitivity, in some cases older editions are licensed. Probably the most widely cited dictionary in computational applications is the *Longman Dictionary of Contemporary English* (*LDOCE*; 1978; http://www.longman-elt.com/dictionaries). The latest edition of *LDOCE* is available on CD-ROM. Like *OALDCE*, it has been revised using evidence from the British National Corpus. It also devotes considerable attention to spoken English. The electronic database of *LDOCE*, offered under specified conditions for NLP research, contains semantic domains and other information not present in the published text.

3.2.4 Corpus-based dictionaries

In 1987, with the publication of the COBUILD dictionary (an acronym for 'Collins Birmingham University International Language Database', 1987, 1995), a new development in lexicography emerged: the **corpus-based dictionary**. The word 'corpus' is nowadays a fashionable buzzword designating any of a wide variety of text collections (see Chapter 24). In the sense most relevant to lexicography, a corpus is a collection in machine-readable form of whole texts or large continuous extracts from texts. Such a collection provides a more *statistically valid* base for computational processing and study of contemporary English than a collection of citations or quotations. A corpus can be used to study words in use, but only indirectly to study word meanings. COBUILD is more intimately connected with its corpus than any other dictionary. It offers a highly interactive and informative website (http://titania.cobuild.collins.co. uk). Unlike the British National Corpus, which maintains its balance by being static, the so-called 'Bank of English' is dynamic: a so-called '**monitor corpus**', constantly growing. At the time of writing it consists of over 330 million words of running text. This provides Collins lexicographers with a magnificent resource for studying new words and meanings.

A recent addition to the stock of major corpus-based dictionaries is the *Cambridge International Dictionary of English* (*CIDE*; 1995; http://dictionary.cambridge.org), which has a number of interesting features, including associated data modules for NLP such as lists of verb complementation patterns, semantic classifications of nouns, and semantic domain categories.

In 1998, Oxford University Press published *The New Oxford Dictionary of English* (*NODE*), a dictionary for native speakers of English (as opposed to foreign learners) which draws both on the citation files of the large historical *Oxford English Dictionary*, collected by traditional methods, and on new corpus resources, in particular the British National Corpus of 100 million words of text. Use of a corpus enables lexicographers to make more confident generalizations about common, everyday meanings, while citation files provide a wealth of quotations to support rare, interesting, new, and unusual words and uses.

The biggest word list in a one-volume English dictionary is to be found in *Chambers English Dictionary*. This magnificent ragbag of curiosities achieves its vaunted 215,000 references by including a great deal of archaic Scottish and other dialect vocabulary (e.g. '**giz** or **jiz** (*Scot*) a wig') and obsolete literary forms (e.g. '**graste** (*Spenser*) pa p of grace'), of more interest to Scrabble players than to serious computational linguists.

The foregoing paragraphs mention the main 'flagship' dictionaries likely to be of interest to computational linguists. Each of the flagship publications is associated with a family of other lexical reference works, for example thesauri, dictionaries of idioms, dictionaries of phrasal verbs, dictionaries for business English, and smaller derivative works.

Section 3.5 of this chapter discusses corpus-based lexicography in Britain in more detail. No dictionaries based on serious large-scale corpus research have yet been prepared in the United States, although the *American Heritage Dictionary* made some use of the pioneering Brown Corpus of the 1960s (1 million words; see Francis and Kučera 1982), and an American edition of *NODE*, called the *New Oxford American Dictionary* (*NOAD*) was published in 2001. From a lexicographical point of view, a large corpus is an indispensable tool of the trade for serious compilation of paper dictionaries and computational lexicons alike. Studying the patterns of actual usage of words in a balanced and representative selection of texts such as the British National Corpus (www.hcu.ox.ac.uk/BNC; see Aston and Burnard 1998) or the forthcoming American National Corpus (see Ide and Macleod 2001) provides an essential antidote to the distortions created by introspective reporting of the lexicon, typical of older dictionaries.

3.3 Restructuring and Exploiting Human Dictionaries for Computational Purposes

All humans—foreign learners, native speakers, translators, and technical specialists alike—share certain attributes that are not shared by computers. Typically, humans are very tolerant of minor variation, whereas a computer process may be thrown by it. For example, the first edition of the *Oxford English Dictionary* (*OED*) contains innumerable minor variations that the nineteenth century compilers were unaware of or considered unimportant. To take a simple example, 'Shakes.', 'Shak.', and 'Shakesp.' are among the abbreviations used for 'Shakespeare'. When *OED* was prepared for publication in machine-readable form, at first on CD-ROM, and now on line (http://www.oed.com/), the editors spent much time and effort *standardizing* the text in order to ensure that user searches would produce comprehensive results as well as being swift, efficient, and robust. Imposing standardization has been a major concern for making dictionaries **machine tractable**. At the more complex end of the spectrum, it is clearly desirable to impose standardization in definition writing, so that, for example, the definitions for all edible marine fish would be retrievable by searching for a single defining phrase. This involves standardization of innumerable variations such as 'eatable fish', 'strong-tasting fish', 'edible sea fish', 'edible flatfish', 'marine fish with oily flesh', etc. Such tasks present a potentially infinite series of challenges for the standardizer. Attempts to devise short cuts or automatic procedures using resources such as a machine-readable thesaurus can lead to unfortunate consequences, such as equating the meaning of 'shaking hands' with 'shaking fists'.

Early work in creating MRDs generally involved converting typesetters' tapes into a database format. Unbelievably large quantities of typographical instructions had to be stripped out, leaving just a few that could be converted into logical **field delimiters**. Nowadays, new dictionaries are routinely set up from the outset as structured files or databases, from which typesetters' files are derived. However, the vast size and cost of dictionaries, their long gestation periods, and the great length of their marketing lives mean that there are still quite a few electronic dinosaurs lumbering about, containing valuable information in text but encrusted with typographic details.

The earliest MRD was the computerization at SDC (Systems Development Corporation), of *Webster's 7th New Collegiate Dictionary* (Olney 1967; Revard 1968), which was keyboarded from the printed text. The choice of text still seems surprising, in view of the historical principles which determine the order of definitions in this dictionary and the complete absence of any clues linking meanings to use, other than basic part-of-speech classes. However, the project leaders presumably took the view that one dictionary is as good as any other, or else that the market leader for human use (selling over a million copies a year) must be good for computer applications. Among other things, the SDC group explored word frequencies in definitions, postulating a privileged semantic status for certain frequent terms such as 'substance, cause, thing', and 'kind', akin to the semantic primitives of Wierzbicka and Wilks, or the 'semantic parts of speech' of Jackendoff. Revard later wrote that, in an ideal world, lexicographic definers would 'mark every . . . semantic relation wherever it occurs between senses defined in the dictionary' (Revard 1973).

Among the most comprehensive analyses of a machine-readable dictionary for lexicographic purposes is the work on *LDOCE* carried out under the direction of Yorick Wilks at New Mexico State University, and subsequently the University of Sheffield. The electronic database of *LDOCE* contains information going far beyond what appears in the published text, for example a systematic account of semantic domain. This work is reported in Wilks, Slator, and Guthrie (1996), which also includes a comprehensive survey of other work on making dictionaries machine tractable. An earlier survey volume is Boguraev and Briscoe (1989), a collection of nine essays describing work in the 1980s to extract semantic and syntactic information from dictionaries, in particular *LDOCE*. A more recent collection of relevant papers is Guo (1995).

The information encoded in large lexicons is widely used in algorithms for procedures such as sense coercion for unknown words (see, for example, Pustejovsky 1993) and word-sense disambiguation. Stevenson and Wilks (2001 and this volume, Chapter 13), for example, report a word-sense disambiguation algorithm trained on a large dictionary-based vocabulary, applying principles of preference semantics to a combination of several different knowledge sources, including part-of-speech tagger, shallow parser, semantic domain tagger (using *LDOCE*'s semantic codes), and semantically tagged corpus. It seems inevitable that a large lexicon of known facts is a prerequisite for determining unknown facts in text processing, for example choosing between senses of a word in a dictionary or assigning a semantic role to an unknown word. For computational applications such as these, dictionaries intended for human use are essential but not ideal. They are essential because they provide a reliable inventory. The most striking disadvantages of using currently available human dictionaries for computational purposes are:

- human dictionaries tend to make very fine semantic distinctions, which are not always computationally tractable and which, in many cases, make no practical difference to the interpretation or processing. It is hard for an algorithm to distinguish between an important and a trivial sense distinction;
- different senses of a word are not clearly, explicitly, and systematically associated with different syntagmatic patterns;
- information about comparative frequency of different words and senses is not given. (Recent editions of British learners' dictionaries have begun to do this for words in a broad-brush-stroke impressionistic fashion, but not for senses.)

Despite these drawbacks, a machine-readable version of a human dictionary is a great deal better than nothing, providing an inventory of all the words that are in ordinary conventional use, and a wealth of data that can be mined with successful results, given sufficient ingenuity and patience.

3.4 DICTIONARY STRUCTURE

Dictionaries are more highly structured than almost any other type of text. Nowadays, the norm is to follow the TEI (text-encoding initiative; www.uic.edu/orgs/tei) for SGML- and HTML-compatible mark-up.

The **tag set** for an entry in the *New Oxford Dictionary of English* may be regarded as typical. A simplified version of the basic structure is set out below, although it should be noted that *NODE* uses many additional, optional tags for various different kinds of information. The main tag set, with nesting (embedding) as shown, is as follows:

⟨se⟩   standard entry, *or*
⟨ee⟩   encyclopedic entry, *embedding*:
      ⟨hw⟩ headword
      ⟨pr ⟩ pronunciation
      ⟨s1 ⟩ sense level 1 (part of speech)
        ⟨ps⟩ part of speech

⟨s2 num=n⟩ sense level 2, with number attribute, *embedding*:

⟨df⟩ definition

⟨ms⟩ meaning extension

⟨ex⟩ example of usage (taken from the British National Corpus or the *Oxford English Dictionary* citation files)

⟨et⟩ etymology

⟨drv⟩ derivative form, *embedding*:

⟨ps⟩ part of speech

Additional tags are used for optional and occasional information, for example technical scientific nomenclature, grammatical subcategorization, significant collocations within ⟨ex⟩ examples, and usage notes. This tag set is derived from the even more elaborate tag set designed in the 1980s for the *OED*. Tagged, consistently structured dictionary texts can be searched and processed by algorithms of the kind designed by Tompa (1992) and his colleagues at the University of Waterloo. This software was designed with the computerized *OED* in mind, but it has a much wider range of applicability, to machine-readable texts of all kinds. The two principal components of this software are PAT, a full-text search system offering a powerful range of search options, and LECTOR, a text display facility. PAT allows users to construct combinations of results using Boolean expressions or proximity conditions. Depending on the text structure, search conditions can be specified within certain fields or regions, some of which are predefined, while others may be made up ad hoc by the user. For example, a user may wish to find all definitions containing the word 'structure' in entries for words beginning with R. PAT enables rapid text searches and retrieval within specified fields of specified groups of entries.

3.5 USING COMPUTATIONAL TECHNIQUES TO COMPILE NEW DICTIONARIES

Lexicographers were quick to seize on the benefits of computers in compiling and typesetting new dictionaries. As long ago as 1964, the *Random House Dictionary of the English Language* was set up as an electronic database, so that different technical senses could be dealt with in sets, regardless of alphabetical order, by relevant experts, thus greatly improving the *consistency of treatment*. Clearly, consistency of treatment in a dictionary benefits from compilation of entries for domain-related and semantically related words together as sets, without regard to where in the alphabet they happen to fall. This is now standard practice in the compilation of all new dictionaries (as opposed to revised editions and derivative or shortened versions, which usually proceed alphabetically).

3.5.1 Challenges of corpus-based lexicography

Corpus-based lexicography raised a whole new raft of issues, affecting the selection, arrangement, and definition of the lexical inventory. For example, there may be plentiful evidence for a verbal adjective, e.g. *extenuating*, while the base form (*extenuate*) is rare or non-existent. Should there be an entry for the base form, the verbal adjective, or both? Should the idealized lemma or paradigm set always be allowed to prevail over observed data?

The evidence of a large general corpus can help to identify the most common modern meaning of a word, but it must be treated with caution. Frequency alone is not enough. Corpus lexicographers also need to look at the **distribution**: does the word occur in many different texts, only in a particular domain, or only in a single author? For an idiosyncrasy, even if repeated many times, is still an idiosyncrasy.

Another trap is the **failure-to-find fallacy**. Failure to find a particular word or sense in a corpus does not mean that that sense does not exist. It may exist in a register or domain that is inadequately represented in the corpus. On the other hand, it might be argued that a word, phrase, or sense that does not occur in a balanced corpus of 100 million words (let alone 300 or 400 million words), containing a broad selection of text types, cannot be very important—or, rather, can only be of importance in a highly restricted domain.

Corpus lexicographers invoke criteria such as **generalizability** to identify the 'core meaning' of a word. So, for example, the expression *to shake one's head* is far more common in the British National Corpus than *to shake a physical object*, but the latter sense is still identified as the core meaning and placed first because the range of possible direct objects is so much wider. Core meanings have wider ranges of normal phraseology than derivative, pragmatic, metaphoric, and idiomatic senses.

Identifying the 'literal' modern meaning of a word is often far from straightforward. A sense whose status is that of a conventionalized metaphor may be more common than the so-called literal sense. Literal meanings are constantly on the move: today's metaphor may be tomorrow's literal meaning. Thus, *torrents of abuse* and *torrents of verbiage* may be more common in a large corpus of modern English than *torrents* denoting violently rushing mountain streams, but most English speakers would agree that the latter is nevertheless the literal meaning. It is often difficult to know how far to modify historical principles in describing modern English. For example, the oldest meaning of *check* is the chess sense, closely followed by 'cause to pause or suffer a setback', originally a metaphor based on chess. From this developed the 'inspect' sense, which is by far the most frequent sense today. Which of these senses should be classified as the literal meaning of the verb *check*?

3.5.2 Corpus-based revision

In the 1990s, British dictionary publishers, especially publishers of foreign learners' dictionaries, invested substantially in revising their dictionaries to conform better with corpus evidence, both for the word list and for the meaning and use of words. Corpus-driven revision can involve wholesale rewriting and restructuring of definitions, seeking levels of generalization that conform with the evidence. This in turn might affect the view of semantic hierarchies or ontologies derived from or associated with machine-readable dictionaries, though to the best of my knowledge no systematic comparison has been carried out. For more on ontologies, see Chapter 25.

3.5.3 WordNet

A revolutionary development of the 1990s was WordNet (see Fellbaum 1998; http: //www.cogsci.princeton.edu/~wn/), an on-line reference system combining the design of a dictionary and a thesaurus with the rich potential of an ontological database. Instead of being arranged in alphabetical order, words are stored in a database with hierarchical properties and links, such that *oak* and *ash* are subsumed under *tree*. Fourteen different senses of *hand* are distinguished, each with its own set of links. WordNet's design was inspired by psycholinguistic theories of human lexical memory. English nouns, verbs, adjectives, and adverbs are organized into synonym sets, each representing one underlying lexical concept. Different relations link the synonym sets.

It has to be said, however, that, while WordNet's design is new and ground-breaking, its lexicography is often disappointing, owing virtually nothing to corpus linguistics and far too much to traditional dictionaries on historical principles. So, for example, the first sense for the verb *fan* is glossed as 'strike out a batter, in baseball' and sense 4 is 'separate from chaff; of grain'. It cannot be claimed that either of these senses is central to general contemporary usage. The gloss at sense 3, 'agitate the air', is technically deficient, in that it fails to indicate that this is normally a transitive verb with a selectional preference for a direct object denoting a person (or a person's face or body). A systematic revised edition of WordNet, taking account of current advances in lexicographic methodology and resources, would be highly desirable. The present situation, in which different groups of researchers make their own adjustments on a piecemeal basis, is far from satisfactory.

In 1996, a European initiative, EuroWordNet, was set up to build a semantic net linking other European languages to the original English WordNet. EuroWordNet aims to be a standard for the semantic tagging of texts and an interlingua for multilingual systems of information retrieval and machine translation. The user can look up a term in Dutch and get synonyms in English, Spanish, or Italian. EuroWordNet could well turn out to be a strategically significant language tool in enabling everyday communication and commerce to take place in the diverse languages of Europe. It must be noted, however, that the theoretical assumptions underlying WordNet are not universally accepted. The psychological reality of hierarchically organized ontologies is controversial. Many words, inconveniently, do not fit neatly into an ontological hierarchy at all, while others fit equally well (or badly) at many places.

The single most important feature of the WordNet projects, like that of many more traditional research projects, is **coverage**. Unlike most other institutionally funded research projects, WordNet says something about everything. And, unlike commercial projects, it is free.

For a more detailed account of WordNet see Chapter 25.

3.6 LINKING MEANING AND USE

A serious problem for computer applications is that dictionaries compiled for human users focus on giving lists of meanings for each entry, without saying much about how one meaning may be distinguished from another in text. They assume a decoding application for the dictionary, in which ordinary human common sense can be invoked to pick out the relevant meaning from a list of competing choices. Computers, on the other hand, do not have common sense. Many computer applications need to know how words are used and, ideally, what textual clues distinguish one sense from another. On this subject, dictionaries are largely silent. Learners' dictionaries offer syntactic patterns, but these are at a clausal level, without any more delicate distinction between different semantic classes of direct object.

Choueka and Luisgnan (1985) were among the first to describe the essentials of choosing an appropriate meaning by reference to the immediate **co-text**. This is a technique that has been widely employed and developed since, but is still a subject on which further research is needed. Part of the problem is distinguishing signal from noise, while another is **lexical variability**. It is clear that there are statistically significant associations between words (see Church and Hanks 1989; Church et al. 1994), but it is not easy to see how to establish that, for purposes of choosing the right sense of *shake*, *earthquake* and *explosion* may be equated, while *hand* and *fist* may not. Corpus lexicographers often cite the words of J. R. Firth (1957): 'You shall know a word by the company it keeps.' Much modern research is devoted to finding out exactly what company our words do keep. This work is still in its infancy. Establishing the **norms and variations** of phraseology and **collocation** in a language will continue to be important components of many lexicographic projects for years to come. In 1999 a European Society for Phraseology (Europhras; www.europhras.unizh.ch) was founded, with the specific objective of promoting the study of phraseology, with relevant results for future lexicography.

COBUILD's innovative defining style expresses links between meaning and use by encoding the target word in its most typical phraseology (e.g. 'when a horse *gallops*, it runs very fast so that all four legs are off the ground at the same time') as the first part of the definition (see Hanks 1987). COBUILD does this impressionistically and informally, in a way designed for human users (foreign learners), not computers, but in principle a project to express similar information in a formal, computer-tractable, way is entirely conceivable. The editor-in-chief of COBUILD, John Sinclair, briefed his editorial team: 'Every distinction in meaning is associated with a distinction in form.' A great deal of research is still required to determine exactly what counts as a distinction in meaning, what counts as a distinction in form, and what is the nature of the association. The immediate local co-text of a word is often but not always sufficient to determine which aspects of the word's meaning are active in that text. For further discussion, see Hanks (1996, 2000).

The Japanese Electronic Dictionary Research Institute (http://www.iijnet.or.jp/edr/) has developed a series of eleven linked on-line dictionaries for advanced processing of natural language by computers. Subdictionaries include a concept dictionary, word dictionaries, and bilingual dictionaries (English–Japanese). The *EDR Electronic Dictionary* is aimed at establishing an infrastructure for knowledge information processing.

3.7 EXPLORING THE FUTURE

Until recently, innovation has been very much the exception rather than the rule in lexicography. Lexicography characteristically aims at breadth, not depth, and most of the lexicographic projects funded by the publishing industry have been required, for commercial reasons, to reach a very wide popular audience. Unlike most researchers, teams of lexicographers are obliged by the nature of their undertaking to say something about everything, even if they have nothing to say. These and other constraints mean that the style and presentation of most dictionaries tends to be very conservative, reflecting eighteenth-century concepts of meaning and definition for example. The main exception to this rule among published dictionaries is COBUILD.

In recent years, a number of research projects have explored possible new approaches to capturing, explaining, defining, or processing word meaning and use. Such studies may not yet cover the entire vocabulary comprehensively, but they have begun to explore new methodologies based on recent research in philosophy of language, cognitive science, computational linguistics, and other fields, along with new resources, in particular corpora. They point the way towards more comprehensive future developments. Some of the most important of these projects are mentioned in this section.

The European Community's Research and Development Service (www.cordis.lu/) provides information on research projects funded by the EC. Of particular relevance was the Information Technologies programme of 1994–8 (named *Esprit*; see http://www.cordis.lu/esprit/src/). This sought, with an emphasis on commercial relevance, to favour research in the languages of Central Europe, the Baltic States, the Mediterranean region, and the states of the former Soviet Union, designed to bring the information society to everyone, including speakers of minority languages.

A major theme in the EC's 'Fifth Framework' (1998–2002) is the development of 'Information Society technology' (IST; www.cordis.lu/ist/). There was disappointingly little provision for lexicographic research in this framework. Probably the most important such project is Defi at the University of Liège, which explores how to use the immediate context of a word in a text to select the right translation.

In the 'Fourth Framework' lexicographically relevant projects were funded such as DELIS, COMPASS, SPARKLE, and EAGLES, all of which are described on the Cordis website.

HECTOR. The HECTOR project (Atkins 1993; Hanks 1994) was a fifteen-month experimental collaboration between a computing research laboratory (the Systems Research Center of Digital Equipment Corporation) and a publisher (Oxford University Press). Approximately 1,400 words were studied in detail. Among the objectives were:

1. To provide a 'guinea-pig' project for software engineers developing large-scale corpus-handling software, search engines, graphical user interfaces, pointers, and writers' tools.
2. To categorize exhaustively, in terms of dictionary senses, all uses of the target words of a given general corpus.
3. To explore whether existing Oxford dictionaries such as the *Concise Oxford Dictionary* (*COD*), 8th edn. (1990) would benefit from corpus analysis or whether a new kind of dictionary was needed.
4. To develop the methodology of corpus analysis for lexicographical purposes.

Objectives (1), (3), and (4) were fulfilled. The SRC scientists went on to develop new search-engine technology, and the Oxford lexicographers went on to develop *NODE*, an entirely fresh look at the English language, which drew heavily on the British National Corpus for the organization of its entries, and from which *COD*, 10th edn, was derived. Interestingly, however, objective (2) proved to be much harder to fulfil. It was simply impossible to map *all* uses of the selected target words in the 18-million-word HECTOR corpus (a prototype of the 100-million-word British National

Corpus) onto the senses in the 8th edition of *COD*. This was not because *COD* was a bad dictionary, but rather because it focused on unusual senses rather than everyday ones and (like most dictionaries) made sense distinctions without specifying a decision procedure for distinguishing them. Even after a decision was made to create an entirely new, corpus-driven, customized HECTOR dictionary for the target words, the problems did not go away. For some perfectly normal-seeming uses of everyday words, it was impossible to decide between two or three dictionary senses, and yet there was no motivation to add a new sense. Rather, these uses seemed to activate senses only partially, or activated different components of two or three senses, rather than the whole of any one sense. This might suggest that the whole theoretical concept of word meaning needs to be reconsidered. For computational purposes, perhaps the folk notion of 'word meaning' needs to be replaced with something more practical from a processing point of view, e.g. the **presuppositions** and **entailments** associated with words in their **normal phraseological contexts**. It is all too easy for lexicographers to select examples that suit their purposes and to gloss over those that do not. The requirement to account for *all* corpus uses of the target words, including the ones that did not fit neatly anywhere, was a valuable discipline, unique to the HECTOR project.

Unfortunately, it never became possible to edit HECTOR for publication or to impose internal consistency or completeness on its entries. Nevertheless, in 1999, they were used as a benchmark for the Senseval project in word sense disambiguation (Kilgarriff 1998). For a fuller discussion of the word-sense disambiguation problem, see Chapter 13.

The generative lexicon. Recent work by Pustejovsky (1995) and his followers (see, e.g., Bouillon and Kanzaki 2001) on the '**generative lexicon**' addresses the problem of the multiplicity of word meaning: how we are able to generate an infinite number of senses for individual words given only finite means. Generative lexical theory deals, among other things, with the creative use of words in novel contexts, in a way that is simply beyond the scope of possibility in a finite, 'sense-enumerative' dictionary, but which seems ideally suited for dynamic processing by computer program. According to Pustejovsky, there are three aspects of the lexical structure of a word that impact the mapping of semantic information to syntax: an *argument structure*, an *event structure*, and a so-called *qualia structure*. Qualia for entities are:

formal: the basic category that distinguishes the term within a larger domain
constitutive: the relation between an object and its constituent parts
telic: its purpose and function
agentive: factors involved in its origin

In the generative lexicon, semantic types can constrain the meaning of other words. It has long been recognized that, for example, the verb *eat* imposes the interpretation [[FOOD]] on its direct object, regardless of how that direct object is actually realized.

Pustejovsky goes further, and shows how the sentence 'she enjoyed her coffee' entails an event type (namely *drinking*) and 'he enjoyed his book' entails a different event type (namely *reading*). The verb *enjoy* requires an event semantically as its direct object, so even though *coffee* is not an event, the semantics of a **prototypical** event type (*what do you do with coffee?—drink it*) are coerced by the verb *enjoy*. Different practical aspects of the implications of generative lexicon theory are currently being implemented by a team led by Pustejovsky himself and by others in the USA and elsewhere. The generative lexicon is no different from any other lexicographical project in this regard at least: coverage is key. It tries to say something about everything.

Framenet. Fillmore and Atkins (1992) describe another, equally exciting development in lexicon theory, subsequently put into development as Framenet (http://www.icsi.berkeley.edu/~framenet/). Framenet started by analysing verbs with similar meanings (e.g. verbs of movement), and showing how they are distinguished by the different semantic **case roles** of their arguments. Framenet is grounded in the theory of Frame Semantics, which starts with the assumption that in order to understand the meanings of the words in a language we must first have knowledge of the conceptual structures, or **semantic frames**, which provide the background and motivation for their existence in the language and for their use in discourse. Framenet is corpus-based and contrastive (e.g. it asks precisely what semantic features distinguish *creeping* from *crawling*). Its entries provide information, for each sense, about frame membership and the syntactic means by which each Frame Element is realized in the word's surrounding context. These entries summarize, as **valency patterns**, the range of combinatorial possibilities as attested in the corpus. From the point of view of natural language processing, developments such as Framenet and the generative lexicon seem to be the culmination of research in computational lexicography at the beginning of the twenty-first century. The potential for practical applications seems limitless. It is very much to be hoped that Framenet will be implemented comprehensively for the whole English lexicon (with the possible exception of domain-specific jargon), with resultant tools linking word senses to textual phraseology in a robust enough way to reduce the amount of lexical tuning needed to make a lexicon suitable for a wide variety of NLP applications.

FURTHER READING AND RELEVANT RESOURCES

Useful websites are Robert L. Beard's index of on-line dictionaries and multilingual resources (http://www.yourdictionary.com) and the Omnilex site (http://www.omnilex.com).

For European language resources, two associations are particularly relevant: ELRA (European Language Resources Association; www.icp.grenet.fr/ELRA) and TELRI

(Trans-European Language Resources Infrastructure; www.telri.de). ELRA, based in Luxembourg, promotes the creation and distribution of language resources for research, such as databases of recorded speech, text corpora, terminology collections, lexicons, and grammars. TELRI administers a research archive of computational tools and resources called TRACTOR. Both these associations organize seminars on language resources and corpus research. TELRI runs an annual series of seminars in different locations, with a focus on corpus research; ELRA runs workshops and LREC, a biennial conference on language resources and evaluation.

The most useful readings in computational lexicography are to be found in the proceedings of conferences and in specialist journals.

The Waterloo-OED conference: annually from 1984 to 1994, organized jointly by Oxford University Press and the University of Waterloo Centre for the New *OED* and Text Research, headed by Frank Tompa (Waterloo, Ontario, Canada N2L 3G1). The Proceedings contain accounts of most major developments in computational lexicography in this period, when seminal developments were taking place.

Complex: annual conference organized by the Hungarian Research Institute for Linguistics, Budapest (http://www.nytud.hu/). Proceedings edited by Franz Kiefer, Gabor Kiss, and Julia Pajsz, with many relevant papers.

Euralex: biennial conference of the European Association for Lexicography (www.ims.uni-stuttgart.de/euralex/). Proceedings contain occasional reports on significant computational developments.

International Journal of Lexicography (ed. R. Ilson (to 1997), A. Cowie (from 1998); Oxford University Press; www3.oup.co.uk/lexico/), quarterly. Occasional articles of computational relevance.

Dictionaries: the Journal of the Dictionary Society of North America (ed. William S. Chisholm (to 1999), M. Adams (from 2000); polyglot.lss.wisc.edu/dsna/); annual. Until recently, disappointingly few articles have been of computational relevance.

Other relevant collections of essays include those in Zernik (1991) and Atkins and Zampolli (1994).

The Oxford Text Archive (http://ota.ahds.ac.uk/) and the Linguistic Data Consortium at the University of Pennsylvania (http://www.ldc.upenn.edu/) both hold copies of a variety of machine-readable dictionaries, which are available for research use under specified conditions.

Some dictionary publishers are willing to make machine-readable versions of their dictionaries available for bona fide academic research, though great tenacity and diplomatic skill may be required to achieve agreement and delivery. Publishers' sensitivity about protecting commercial rights in their colossal, high-risk investments, along with the fact that negotiating the free gift of their products is not always among their highest priorities, can be perceived, usually erroneously, as hostility to research.

The *Oxford English Dictionary* is available on CD-ROM. The third edition is currently in preparation and has recently become available as work in progress on line through certain sites (http://www.oed.com/). This magnificent historical monument is a cultural keystone for the historical study of the English language. That does not, however, necessarily mean that it is suitable as a tool or benchmark for processing word meaning or distinguishing word senses computationally in modern English.

A broad overview of lexicography in English, including an evaluation of the impact of corpus evidence, may be found in Landau (2001).

With regard to lexicography in French, mention should be made of the *Trésor de la langue française*, with 114.7 million words of text and over 400,000 dictionary entries. This is now available on-line thanks to the ARTFL collection (American Research on the Treasury of the French Language; www.lib.uchicago.edu/efts/ARTFL) at the University of Chicago, in cooperation with Analyses et Traitements Informatiques du Lexique Français (ATILF) of the Centre National de la Recherche Scientifique (CNRS) in France. ARTFL also makes available on-line other important and historic French reference works, including Denis Diderot's massive *Encyclopédie* (1751–72).

ACKNOWLEDGEMENTS

I am grateful for discussion and comments on earlier drafts from Ken Litkowski, Yorick Wilks, and Mark Stevenson. And special thanks to Elaine Mar for help with finalization.

REFERENCES

Amsler, R. A. and J. S. White. 1979. *Development of a Computational Methodology for Deriving Natural Language Semantic Structures via Analysis of Machine-Readable Dictionaries.* Technical Report MCS77-01315, National Science Foundation. Washington.

Apresyan, Y., I. Mel'čuk, and A. K. Zholkowsky. 1969. 'Semantics and Lexicography: towards a new type of unilingual dictionary'. In F. Kiefer (ed.), *Studies in Syntax and Semantics.* Dordrecht: D. Reidel.

Aston, G. and L. Burnard. 1988. *The BNC Handbook.* Edinburgh: Edinburgh University Press.

Atkins, B. T. S. 1993. 'Tools for computer-aided lexicography: the Hector project'. In *Papers in Computational Lexicography: COMPLEX '93.* Budapest: Research Institute for Linguistics, Hungarian Academy of Sciences.

——J. Kegl, and B. Levin. 1988. 'Anatomy of a verb entry'. *International Journal of Lexicography,* 1(2), 84–126.

——and B. Levin. 1991. 'Admitting impediments'. In U. Zernik (ed.), *Lexical Acquisition: Exploiting On-Line Resources to Build a Lexicon.* Hillsdale, NJ: Lawrence Erlbaum Associates.

——and A. Zampolli (eds.). 1994. *Computational Approaches to the Lexicon.* New York: Oxford University Press.

Boguraev, B. and T. Briscoe. 1989. *Computational Lexicography for Natural Language Processing.* London: Longman.

Bouillon, P. and K. Kanzaki (eds.). 2001. *Proceedings of the 1st International Workshop on Generative Approaches to the Lexicon.* Geneva, Switzerland.

Choueka, Y. and S. Luisgnan. 1985. 'Disambiguation by short contexts'. *Computers and the Humanities*, 19, 147–57.

Church, K. W. and P. Hanks. 1990. 'Word association norms: mutual information, and lexicography'. *Computational Linguistics*, 16, 22–9.

——W. Gale, P. Hanks, D. Hindle, and R. Moon. 1994. 'Lexical substitutability'. In B.T. S. Atkins and A. Zampolli (eds.), *Computational Approaches to the Lexicon*. Oxford: Oxford University Press.

Crystal, D. 1997. *The Cambridge Encyclopedia of Language*. Cambridge: Cambridge University Press.

Fellbaum, C. (ed). 1998. *WordNet: An Electronic Lexical Database*. Cambridge, Mass.: MIT Press.

Fillmore, C. J. 1975. 'An alternative to checklist theories of meaning'. *Papers from the 1st Annual Meeting of the Berkeley Linguistics Society*, 123–32.

——and B.T. S. Atkins. 1992. 'Towards a frame-based lexicon'. In A. Lehrer and E. F. Kittay (eds.), *Frames, Fields, and Contrasts*. Hillsdale, NJ: Lawrence Erlbaum Associates.

Firth, J. R. 1957. 'A synopsis of linguistic theory 1930–55'. In *Studies in Linguistic Analysis*, Oxford: Philological Society.

Francis, W. N. and H. Kučera. 1982. *Frequency Analysis of English Usage*. Boston: Houghton Mifflin.

Guo, Cheng-Ming. 1995. *Machine Tractable Dictionaries: Design and Construction*. Norwood, NJ: Ablex Publishing.

Hanks, P. 1987. 'Definitions and explanations'. In J. M. Sinclair (ed.), *Looking Up*. London: Collins.

——1994. 'Linguistic norms and pragmatic explanations, or why lexicographers need prototype theory and vice versa'. In F. Kiefer, G. Kiss, and J. Pajzs (eds.), *Papers in Computational Lexicography: COMPLEX '94*. Budapest: Research Institute for Linguistics, Hungarian Academy of Sciences.

——1996. 'Contextual dependency and lexical sets'. *International Journal of Corpus Linguistics*, 1(1), 75–98.

——1997. 'Lexical sets: relevance and probability'. In B. Lewandowska-Tomaszczyk and M. Thelen (eds.), *Translation and Meaning, Part 4*. Maastricht: School of Translation and Interpreting.

——2000. 'Do word meanings exist?' *Computers and the Humanities*, 34, 205–15.

Hayes, B. 1999. 'The web of words'. *American Scientist*, 87, 108–12.

Ide, N. and C. Macleod. 2001. 'The American National Corpus: a standardized resource of American English'. *Proceedings of Corpus Linguistics 2001*. Lancaster, UK.

Jackendoff, R. 1990. *Semantic Structures*. Cambridge, Mass.: MIT Press.

Kilgarriff, A. 1993. 'Dictionary word sense distinctions: an inquiry into their nature'. *Computing and the Humanities*, 26, 356–87.

Landau, S. I. 2001. *Dictionaries: The Art and Craft of Lexicography*. 2nd edn. New York: Cambridge University Press.

Minsky, M. 1975. 'A framework for representing knowledge'. In P. H. Winston (ed.), *The Psychology of Computer Vision*. New York: McGraw-Hill.

Olney, J. 1967. 'Toward the development of computational aids for obtaining a formal semantic description of English'. SDC Technical Report, Santa Monica, Calif.

Pustejovsky, J. 1993. 'Type coercion and lexical selection'. *Semantics and the Lexicon*. Dordrecht: Kluwer, 73–96.

Pustejovsky, J. 1995. *The Generative Lexicon*. Cambridge, Mass.: MIT Press.

Resnik, P. 1997. 'Selectional preferences and word sense disambiguation'. *Proceedings of the SIGLEX Workshop 'Tagging Text with Lexical Semantics: What, Why, and How'*. Washington.

Revard, C. 1968. 'On the computability of certain monsters in Noah's ark'. SDC Technical Report, Santa Monica, Calif.

——1973. 'Towards a NUDE (New Universal Dictionary of English)'. In R. I. McDavid and A. R. Duckert (eds.), *Lexicography in English*. New York: New York Academy of Sciences.

Riloff, E. and W. Lehnert. 1993. 'Automatic dictionary construction for information extraction from text'. *Proceedings of the 9th IEEE Conference on Artificial Intelligence for Applications*, 93–9. Los Alamitos, Calif., USA.

Sinclair, J. 1987. *Looking Up: An Account of the Cobuild Project in Lexical Computing*. London: Collins ELT.

——1991. *Corpus, Concordance, Collocation*. Oxford: Oxford University Press.

Stevenson, M. and Y. Wilks. 2001. 'The interaction of knowledge sources in word sense disambiguation'. *Computational Linguistics*, 27(3), 321–49.

Tompa, F. W. 1992. *An Overview of Waterloo's Database Software for the OED*. University of Waterloo Centre for the New Oxford Dictionary and Text Research. Also published in T. R. Wooldridge (ed.), *Historical Dictionary Databases*, Toronto, Canada: University of Toronto Centre for Computing in the Humanities.

Trench, R. C. 1857. 'On some deficiencies in our English dictionaries'. *Proceedings of the Philological Society* (London).

Wierzbicka, A. 1985. *Lexicography and Conceptual Analysis*. Ann Arbor: Karoma.

——1987. *English Speech Act Verbs*. New York: Academic Press.

——1993. 'What are the uses of theoretical lexicography?' *Dictionaries: The Journal of the Dictionary Society of North America*, 14, 44–78.

Wilks, Y. A., B. M. Slator, and L. M. Guthrie. 1996. *Electric Words: Dictionaries, Computers, and Meanings*. Cambridge, Mass.: MIT Press

Zernik, U. (ed.). 1991. *Lexical Acquisition: Using On-line Resources to Build a Lexicon*. Hillsdale, NJ: Lawrence Erlbaum Associates.

DICTIONARIES

Note: dates cited are for first editions unless otherwise specified.

Cawdry, R. 1604. *A Table Alphabeticall . . . of Hard Usuall Words . . . for the Benefit of Gentlewomen and Other Unskillful Persons*.

Funk, I. K. and A. W. Wagnall (eds.). 1893. *A Standard Dictionary of the English Language*. New York: Funk and Wagnalls Company.

Gove, P. (ed.). 1963. *Webster's 7th New Collegiate Dictionary*. Springfield, Mass.: Merriam Webster.

Hanks, P. (ed.). 1979. *Collins English Dictionary*. London: Collins.

—— and J. Pearsall (eds.). 1998. *The New Oxford Dictionary of English*. Oxford: Oxford University Press.

Hornby, A. S. (ed.). 1948. *Oxford Advanced Learner's Dictionary of Current English*. Oxford: Oxford University Press.

Johnson, S. 1755. *Dictionary of the English Language*.

Morris, W. (ed.). 1969. *The American Heritage Dictionary*. Boston: Houghton Mifflin.

Murray, J., H. Bradley, A. Craigie, and C. T. Onions (eds.). 1884–1928. *A New English Dictionary on Historical Principles* (subsequently renamed *The Oxford English Dictionary*). Oxford: Oxford University Press.

Procter, P. (ed.). 1978. *Longman Dictionary of Contemporary English*. Harlow: Longman.

——(ed.). 1995. *The Cambridge International Dictionary of English*. Cambridge: Cambridge University Press.

Sinclair, J., P. Hanks, et al. (eds.). 1987. *Collins COBUILD English Language Dictionary*. London: Collins.

Stein, J., L. Urdang, et al. (eds). 1964. *The Random House Dictionary of the English Language*. New York: Random House.

Webster, Noah. 1828. *An American Dictionary of the English Language*.

CHAPTER 4

SYNTAX

RONALD M. KAPLAN

ABSTRACT

This chapter introduces some of the phenomena that theories of natural language syntax aim to account for and briefly discusses a few of the formal approaches to syntax that have figured prominently in computational research and implementation.

4.1 SYNTACTIC PHENOMENA

The fundamental problem of syntax is to characterize the relation between semantic **predicate–argument relations** and the superficial word and phrase configurations by which a language expresses them. The simple sentence in (4.1*a*) describes an event in which an act of visiting was performed by John and directed towards Mary. The predicate–argument relations for this sentence can be represented by a simple logical formula such as (4.1*b*). Here the predicate or action is indicated by the term outside the parentheses, the first parenthesized item indicates the actor, and the second parenthesized item indicates the individual acted-upon.

(4.1) *a.* John visited Mary.
     b. visit(John, Mary)

The examples in (4.2) illustrate the obvious fact that the particular English words together with the order they appear in determine the semantic relations:

(4.2) *a.* Bill visited Mary.
     b. Mary visited John.

The predicate–argument relations for these sentences might be represented by the formulas in (4.3), both of which are different from (4.1*b*).

(4.3) *a.* visit(Bill, Mary)
     b. visit(Mary, John)

Some strings of words are judged by native speakers as lying outside the bounds of ordinary English and have no conventional interpretation:

(4.4)   *Visited Mary John.

The asterisk prefixing this example is the standard notation used by syntacticians to mark that a string is unacceptable or uninterpretable. Strings of this sort are also often classified as **ungrammatical**.

If we assume a dictionary or lexicon that lists the **part-of-speech categories** (noun, verb, adjective, etc.) for individual words, then we can formulate some very simple rules for English syntax. The acceptability rule in (4.5) encodes the fact that the strings in (4.1) and (4.2) are grammatical sentences. The interpretation rules in (4.6) account for the predicate–argument relations in (4.1*b*) and (4.3).

(4.5) A sentence can consist of a noun-verb-noun sequence.

(4.6) *a.* A word listed as a verb denotes a predicate.
     b. The noun before the verb denotes the first argument (often the actor).
     c. The noun after the verb denotes the second argument (often the thing acted upon).

These rules for English are framed in terms of the **order** and **adjacency** properties of words in particular categories. But for other languages predicate argument relations can remain constant even when the order of words is varied. Japanese is a language that uses explicit **marking** to indicate how the words of a sentence map onto the predicate–argument relations it expresses. The sentences (4.7*a*) and (4.7*b*) both map onto the predicate–argument structure in (4.1*b*), while sentence (4.7*c*) with the marks switched around maps to the structure in (4.3*b*).

(4.7) *a.* John-ga Mary-o tazune-ta.
               visit-past
     b. Mary-o John-ga tazune-ta.
     c. Mary-ga John-o tazune-ta.

We see that the particle *ga* attaches to the first argument of the predicate and *o* marks the second argument, independent of the order in which the words appear. However, Japanese syntax is not completely order free: the verb comes at the end of the sentence, after all the nouns.

Rules based only on the immediate adjacency or markings of words do not easily extend to the patterns of more complicated sentences. In sentence (4.8), for instance, the actor/first argument is the man even though several words (including another noun) intervene between the noun *man* and the verb *visited* that conveys the predicate. The second argument is also a more complex expression, not just a single noun.

(4.8)   The man from the school visited the young girl.

There is no fixed upper bound to the length of the material that can intervene between the verb and the argument nouns. A well-formed and interpretable sentence can be formed, as in this example, by adding determiners and arbitrary numbers of adjectives and preposition-noun sequences to those already present. The adjacency-based rules in (4.5) and (4.6) would become quite complicated if conditions were added to correctly characterize all the patterns that express the same basic predicate–argument relations. Moreover, since the nouns before and after the verb admit of the same kinds of variations, these extra conditions would have to be stated separately for each of the arguments.

This kind of complexity can be avoided by observing that the intervening words in (4.8) are related to the nearby nouns in that they provide additional information about the entities participating in the described event. The contiguous sequences of related words thus group together to form **phrases** or **constituents**, as indicated by the grouping brackets in (4.9).

(4.9)   [The man from the school] visited [the young girl].

The phrases as a unit play the role of individual words in conveying the predicate–argument relations. The rules in (4.5) and (4.6) can be restated in terms of noun phrases instead of nouns, taking a noun phrase to consist of a noun grouped with its associated modifiers. Using the standard abbreviation of NP for noun phrase, we would say that an English sentence can be an NP-verb-NP sequence and that entire NPs, not just simple nouns, are interpreted as the arguments of the predicate:

(4.10)   *a.* A sentence can consist of an NP–verb–NP sequence.
         b. The NPs before and after the verb denote the first and second arguments, respectively.

Further rules are then necessary to say what sequences of phrases, categories, and words can make up a noun phrase, and how those subconstituents are interpreted to give an elaborated description of the entity that the noun phrase refers to. But the rules that specify the predicate–argument relations of a sentence need not take account of the many different ways that noun phrases can be realized.

Some sequences of words can be grouped into phrases in different ways, and this is one way in which the important syntactic phenomenon of **ambiguity** arises. Ambiguous strings can be interpreted as conveying more than one set of predicate–argument relations. The sentence in (4.11) illustrates this possibility:

(4.11)   The man from the school with the flag visited Mary.

Both interpretations of this sentence assert that a man visited Mary, but they differ as to whether the school has the flag or the man does. These two interpretations correspond to two different phrase groupings. One of them groups *the school* and *with the flag* into a single complex phrase, as indicated by the brackets in (4.12*a*). For the other, the prepositional phrase *with the flag* comes immediately after the phrase *from the school* but is not part of it. Rather, it is a subconstituent of the entire NP headed by *man*.

(4.12)   *a*. The man [from [the school with the flag]]
                from(man, school) with(school, flag)
          b. The man [from the school] [with the flag]
                from(man, school) with(man, flag)

The difference in meanings follows immediately from another simple mapping rule that interprets a prepositional phrase (a preposition followed by an NP) appearing inside an NP as a modifier of the head noun.

Ambiguity is the situation where one string has two or more predicate–argument interpretations. **Systematic paraphrase** is the complementary syntactic phenomenon in which the same predicate argument relations are conveyed by two or more strings that are related by general principles. English sentences in the passive voice and their active counterparts both express essentially the same predicate argument relations. Sentence (4.13) is the passive version of (4.1*a*) and also expresses the predicate–argument relations in (4.1*b*).

(4.13)   Mary was visited by John.

English actives and passives are related to each other in that the NP before the verb in the active appears in the passive at the end after the preposition *by*, and the NP after the active verb comes before the passive verb, which is accompanied by a form of the verb *to be*. In Japanese there is also a systematic relation between actives and passives, but this is not reflected by varying the order of words. Instead, the marks that indicate the predicate–argument relations are systematically modified: the word marked by *o* in the active is marked by *ga* in the passive, and the word marked by *o* is then marked by another particle *ni*. As in English, a different form of the verb appears in Japanese passives:

(4.14)   Mary-ga John-ni tazune-rare-ta.
                visit-passive-past

As discussed in Chapter 2, the words of a language often come in sets of related forms that express the same basic concept but convey different values for syntactic **features** such as number, person, and tense. Thus *boy* and *boys* have a common core of meaning (young and masculine), but the form with the plural suffix *s* is used when more than one such entity is being referred to. In phenomena of **agreement** or **concord** the features of one word or phrase must be consistent with the features of other words that they combine with. English requires agreement between the subject noun phrase and the verb of a finite clause and between the determiner and the noun of a noun phrase, as the contrasts in (4.15) illustrate:

(4.15)   *a.* Flying seems dangerous.
      b. *Flying seem dangerous.
      c. This boy is tall.
      b. *These boy is tall.

The starred sentences are ungrammatical because of the mismatch of agreement features.

Agreement is an example of a syntactic **dependency**, a correlation between items that appear at different positions in a sentence. Agreement sometimes plays a role in picking out the predicate–argument relations of what might otherwise be interpreted as ambiguous strings. Because the verb *seems* can take only a singular subject, sentence (4.16*a*) asserts that it is the act of flying the planes that is dangerous, not the planes as airborne objects; (4.16*b*) has the opposite interpretation. Since the subject's number is not distinctively encoded by English past-tense verbs, sentence (4.16*c*) admits of both interpretations.

(4.16)   *a.* Flying planes seems dangerous.
         seem(flying, dangerous)
      b. Flying planes seem dangerous.
         seem(planes, dangerous)
      c. Flying planes seemed dangerous.

Predicates differ according to the number and kind of phrases that they can combine with. This syntactic property is called the **valence** of the predicate. Intransitive verbs, for example, appear with only a single noun phrase, and that phrase denotes the only argument of the one-place predicate that the verb expresses. As shown in (4.17), a sentence with an intransitive verb is ungrammatical if it contains more than a single NP:

(4.17)   *a.* John fell.
         fell(John)
      b. *John fell the apple.

Transitive verbs, on the other hand, are two-place predicates that combine with two noun-phrase arguments:

(4.18)   *a.* John devoured the apple.
         devour(John, apple)
      b. *John devoured.
      c. *John devoured the apple Mary.

All the verbs with the same valence form a subset of the verbal part-of-speech category. Thus valency is often referred to as the property of **subcategorization**, and a valence specification is often called a **subcategorization frame**. Note that many verbs have several frames and thus can express different meanings when they appear in alternative contexts. The verb *eat* differs from *devour* in that the food NP is not required:

(4.19)   John ate.
          eat(John, something)

For this intransitive use of *eat* the unexpressed second argument is interpreted as denoting some unspecified substance appropriate for eating.

The frames for some predicates allow an argument to be expressed not by a noun phrase but by what would be regarded as a complete sentence if it is seen in isolation. A sentence contained as a part of another sentence is called an **embedded clause**. As illustrated in (4.20a), the predicate–argument relations of an embedded clause are determined by the same mapping rules that apply to simple sentences, and the proposition expressed by those relations then serves as the argument to the main predicate. The contrast between (4.20a) and (4.20b) shows that the possibility of taking an embedded clause is determined by the subcategorization frame of particular verbs.

(4.20) *a.* John believes that Mary likes Bill.
             believe(John, like(Mary, Bill))
        b. *John devours that Mary likes Bill.

Sentences can also be inserted into other sentences in the so-called relative clause construction. In this case the embedded sentence is associated with one of the noun-phrase arguments, and it is interpreted not as a separate argument of the main predicate but as a proposition that expresses additional properties of the entity that the noun phrase refers to. In this case the embedded clause has a form that differs systematically from the isolated sentence that would express those same properties. Sentence (4.21) asserts that the girl who left is also the girl that John visited, as indicated in the pair of predicate–argument relations. (The subscript notation signifies that the same girl is the argument of both propositions.)

(4.21)   The girl that John visited left.
          leave(girl$_1$)
          visit(John, girl$_1$)

The substring *John visited* is a fragment that does not express the required second argument of *visit*'s subcategorization frame, and it would be ungrammatical and would certainly not have the intended interpretation if it appeared in isolation. In the relative clause construction this fragment is understood as if an expression denoting the particular girl appeared in the normal location of the second argument, along the lines of (4.22a). Of course, the fragment is only understood that way: the sentence becomes ungrammatical if the string actually contains such an expression, as in (4.22b). The intransitive clause in (4.22c) shows that the embedded clause *must be* a fragment of a larger NP-containing sentence.

(4.22) *a.* The girl that John visited [*that girl*] left.
        b. *The girl that John visited that girl left
        c. *The girl that John fell left.

The examples in (4.21) and (4.22) show that the relative clause construction involves a correlation between the head NP and an argument position of the clause: the clause must be missing an otherwise required noun phrase, and the head NP must be interpretable as that missing argument. The rule that maps the NP and verb sequences of simple sentences into their predicate–argument relations must be modified or augmented to take account of these kinds of dependencies.

It is not sufficient to specify simply that an NP immediately in front of an embedded fragment can be interpreted as the missing argument. This is because the relative clause can be a complicated constituent which is itself made up of many clauses. If the main verb of the relative clause can take a sentential complement, like *believe*, then the missing-argument fragment can appear in that verb's embedded argument position, as in (4.23*a*). In general, the fragment can appear arbitrarily far to the right of its head NP, separated from it by many other words and phrases as in (4.23*b*), as long as all the intervening material can be analysed as a sequence of clauses each of which is an argument to a verb that permits embedded-clause arguments.

(4.23)   *a.* The girl that Jim believed that John visited left.
　　　　 b. The girl that Bill said that Jim believed that John visited left.

Because the NP that a relative clause modifies can be far away from the embedded-clause fragment where it is interpreted as an argument, the correlation between the head NP and the within-fragment argument position is called a **long-distance dependency**. Whereas most other syntactic phenomena can be characterized by elementary rules that operate over limited, local domains of words and phrases, long-distance dependencies are the result of some fundamentally iterative or recursive syntactic process that cuts across the normal partitioning of sentences into easily interpretable units. For this reason it has been a particular challenge to give a complete and accurate description of the various conditions that the intervening material of a long-distance dependency must satisfy, and long-distance dependencies are typically also a source of computational inefficiency in language processing programs.

4.2   SYNTACTIC DESCRIPTION AND SYNTACTIC REPRESENTATION

A major task of syntactic theory is to define an explicit notation for writing grammars that easily and naturally describes phenomena such as those we have listed above. An equally important task is to specify the elements and relations of the data structures that are assigned to represent the syntactic properties of individual sentences. Grammatical notations and syntactic representations go hand in hand, since the notation must make reference to the primitive elements and relations of a particular kind of representation.

A grammatical notation should be expressive enough to allow for all the variations that exist across all the languages of the world and also that occur across the different constructions within a particular language. But it should not be overly expressive: it should not have the power to characterize syntactic dependencies that are not attested by any human language. This consideration has a theoretical motivation, to the extent that the grammatical system is to be taken as a hypothesis about the universal properties common to all languages. But it is also motivated by practical computational concerns. The programs that implement more expressive systems are typically more complicated and also tend to require more computational resources—time and memory—when used to process particular sentences.

4.2.1 Regular grammars and finite-state machines

Chomsky's *Syntactic Structures*, published in 1957, presents an early and classic analysis of the expressive power of grammatical formalisms and their suitability for describing the syntactic phenomena of human languages. The most elementary restrictions on the order and adjacency of the words that make up a meaningful sentence can be described in the notation of **regular grammars** and implemented computationally as the equivalent **finite-state machines**. Finite-state systems, which are discussed in Chapter 18, can specify the set of words or part-of-speech categories that are possible at one position in a sentence as a function of the words or categories that appear earlier in the string. For example, the finite-state machine depicted as the state-transition diagram in (4.24) allows sentences that have a verb after an initial noun and a second noun following the N–V sequence. This is a formalization of the pattern specified informally in (4.5) above.

(4.24) *Start:*

The leftmost circle denotes the starting state of the machine, and the labels on the arrows indicate the categories in a string that permit transitions from one state to another. If there is a sequence of transitions from the start state that match against the category sequence of a given string and that lead to a double-circled 'final' state, that string is accepted as a sentence.

The transitions leaving a state determine exactly what the next set of words can be, and thus if two initial substrings of a sentence can be completed in two different ways, it must be the case that those initial substrings lead to different states, as shown in (4.25). This machine imposes the subject–verb agreement condition that initial (subject) nouns can only be followed by agreeing verbs. This is accomplished by dividing the nouns and verbs into singular and plural subclasses (N-sg and N-pl, V-sg and V-pl) and using these refined categories as transition labels.

(4.25)   *Start:*

Finite-state machines are limited in that they must contain a distinct state corresponding to every combination of dependencies that can cross a single position in a sentence. Any particular machine has a fixed number of states and therefore can represent a bounded number of dependency combinations. Chomsky observed that this limitation of finite-state systems makes them unsuitable for accurately describing human languages. Complete sentences can be embedded in other sentences, as we have seen, and an embedded sentence can itself contain complete sentences. Suppose there is a dependency (such as subject verb agreement) that must hold between the parts of a sentence that surround an embedded clause, and suppose that the embedded clause has a similar dependency, as illustrated in (4.26).

(4.26)   The fact that the men know John surprises Mary.

Two agreement dependencies are in play at the position between *men* and *know*, and more would stack up in sentences with deeper embeddings. In principle if not in practice, there is no finite bound on the depth of embedding that English permits. Thus, no matter how many states there are in a given finite-state machine, there is some grammatical sentence with more dependencies than those states can encode.

While finite-state machines are quite effective for describing phonological and morphological patterns (see Chapters 1 and 2), it is generally acknowledged that they can give only an approximate characterization of many syntactic phenomena. Even so, finite-state approximations may be good enough for practical applications such as information extraction (see Chapter 30) that are not very sensitive to the overall grammatical organization of sentences.

4.2.2 Context-free phrase-structure grammars

The nested dependencies illustrated in sentences like (4.26) are easy to account for with a grammatical system that can group a sequence of words into phrases. The agreement between *fact* and *surprises* is then seen as agreement between the entire singular noun phrase that happens to have a clause embedded within it, as indicated by the brackets in (4.27). The embedded dependencies do not interfere with the ones that hold at higher levels.

(4.27) [The fact that the men know John] surprises Mary.

The rules that specify the pattern of subconstituents that can make up a particular kind of phrase can be formalized as a collection of category-rewriting instructions in a **context-free grammar**. The context-free rule (4.28*a*) is a formalized version of (4.10*a*). The other rules in (4.28) provide a simple account of the sequence of words that appear in (4.27).

(4.28) *a*. S → NP V NP
     b. NP → N
     c. NP → Det N
     d. NP → NP that S

A string belongs to the language specified by a context-free grammar if it can be formed by a sequence of rewriting steps from an initial string consisting of a single category, in this case the category S for sentence. At each step a category in the string produced from earlier rule applications is selected, and a rule that has that category on the left side of the arrow is also chosen. A new string is produced by replacing the selected category by the string of symbols on the right side of the chosen rule. The string thus created is the input to the next step of the process. Since there is only one rule in (4.28) for rewriting the S category, the initial string will always be converted to NP V NP. There are three different ways of rewriting the NP category. Using rule (4.28*b*) to rewrite both NPs gives a simple N V N sequence. If finally the Ns are replaced by words in the noun part-of-speech category, the sentence *John visited Mary* (4.1*a* above) is one of the possible results. Using rule (4.28*d*) instead to rewrite the first NP produces the string NP *that* S, and further steps can expand this to the string Det N *that* Det N V N. This category sequence covers the words of the bracketed first NP in (4.27).

A sequence of rewriting steps starting at S and ending at a string of part-of-speech categories (or words in those categories) is called a **context-free derivation**. The derivations for a given context-free grammar not only specify the set of strings that make up its language, they also assign to each string the grouping structure to which phrase-based predicate–argument rules (such as 4.10*b*) can apply. The **phrase struc-**

(4.29)

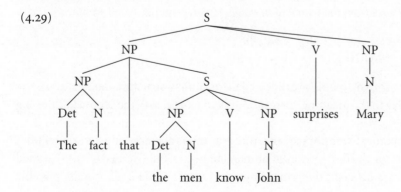

ture can be represented as a tree that records how categories are rewritten into strings of other categories. The phrase-structure tree assigned in this way to sentence (4.27) is shown in (4.29).

The daughter branches below a mother node show how the rules were applied to rewrite the mother category. This tree and the rules in (4.28) illustrate the possibility of **recursion** that context-free grammars provide for: the S inside the NP allows for embedded clauses that have all the grammatical properties of top-level sentences.

These categories and rules do not account for the subject–verb agreement dependencies of sentence (4.26), but context-free grammars differ from finite-state machines in that an unlimited number of dependencies of this type can be encoded with only a finite expansion of the grammar. We need only replace the NP, N, V, and Det categories with new categories that carry an additional indication of the number (singular or plural), and then introduce new rules as in (4.30) to keep track of the dependencies. The rules in (4.30a) permit two kinds of sentences, those with singular subject NPs that match singular verbs, and those with plural subject NPs that match plural verbs. Sentences with subject–verb mismatches cannot be derived. Moreover, the other rules in (4.30) ensure that the NP chosen at the S level is eventually realized by a noun with the proper number. The sg/pl subscripts on the second NPs in the two S rules indicate that either kind of NP is possible in that position.

$$(4.30) \quad a.\ S \rightarrow NP_{sg}\,V_{sg}\,NP_{sg/pl} \qquad S \rightarrow NP_{pl}\,V_{pl}\,NP_{sg/pl}$$
$$b.\ NP_{sg} \rightarrow N_{sg} \qquad NP_{pl} \rightarrow N_{pl}$$
$$c.\ NP_{sg} \rightarrow Det_{sg}\,N_{sg} \qquad NP_{pl} \rightarrow Det_{pl}\,N_{pl}$$
$$d.\ NP_{sg} \rightarrow NP_{sg}\,\text{that}\,S \qquad NP_{pl} \rightarrow NP_{pl}\,\text{that}\,S$$

With these refined rules the top-level S in tree (4.29) would expand into singular categories while the embedded S would expand into plural categories, and there would be no interaction between the two dependencies. Indeed, there would be no interaction between nested subject–verb dependencies no matter how many levels are created by recursive embedding of sentences.

Context-free grammars can provide a formal account of the alternative groupings of words into phrases that give rise to predicate–argument ambiguities. The additional rules in (4.31) allow for noun phrases that include prepositional-phrase modifiers as in *The man from the school with the flag* from sentence (4.11) above.

$$(4.31) \quad a.\ NP_{sg} \rightarrow NP_{sg}\,PP \qquad NP_{pl} \rightarrow NP_{pl}\,PP$$
$$b.\ PP \rightarrow Prep\,NP_{sg/pl}$$

The two derivations of this NP are reflected in the phrase-structure trees in (4.32). The man has the flag in the meaning corresponding to tree (4.32a); the school has the flag in (4.32b).

We see that context-free phrase-structure grammars are more effective than finite-state machines for the description of human languages, but Chomsky (1957) argued that they also are deficient in certain important ways. While it is formally possible

(4.32) *a.*

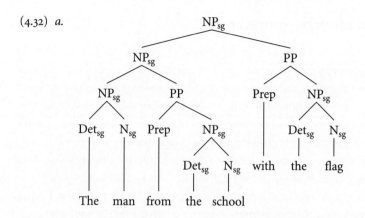

b.

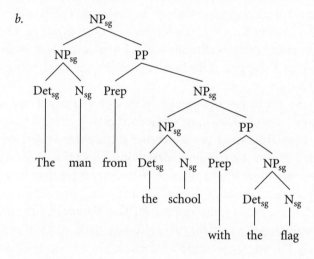

to treat subject–verb agreement by a finite elaboration of categories and rules, as in (4.30), the result is a complicated grammar that is difficult to create, understand, and maintain. The problem is compounded when dependencies involving other syntactic features, such as person or case, are taken into account, since there must be a set of categories and a collection of rewriting rules for each combination of feature values. Intuitively, these feature dependencies operate as a cross-classification that is orthogonal to the basic phrase-structure units of a sentence, but the context-free notation does not permit a succinct, factored characterization of their behaviour.

Another shortcoming of context-free grammars is the fact that they do not support a natural account of systematic paraphrases such as the relations between active sentences and their passive counterparts. The second NP of an English active and the first NP of a passive denote the same argument of the predicate. A context-free grammar can be defined to produce the phrase structures for both kinds of sentences, but the two different structures would have to key off different sets of predicate–argument mapping rules.

4.2.3 Transformational grammar

For these and other reasons, Chomsky argued that descriptive devices with more power than those of context-free phrase-structure grammars are required to give a satisfactory account of the syntactic phenomena of human languages. He proposed a framework called **Transformational Grammar** that combines a context-free phrase-structure grammar with another component of **transformations** that specify how trees of a given form can be transformed into other trees in a systematic way. The context-free grammar describes a phrase-structure tree (the **deep structure**) wherein the arguments of each predicate appear in canonical positions, typically the positions they would occupy in active declarative sentences. The deep structure is the starting point for a sequence of transformations each of which takes the tree from a previous step as input and produces a modified tree as its output. This modified tree can in turn become the input of the next transformation in the sequence. The tree produced by the last transformation is called the **surface structure**. The sentences of the language are the strings that appear at the bottom of all the surface structures that can be produced in this way.

In this framework the predicate–argument relations of a sentence are determined not by the arrangement of nodes in its surface structure tree but by the node configurations of the deep structure from which the surface tree is derived. The active–passive and other systematic paraphrase relations follow from the fact that the transformational rules produce from a given deep structure the surface structures that represent the alternative modes of expression. As an illustration, transformation (4.33) is a rough version of the passive rule for English. It has the effect of moving the NP (labelled 1) at the beginning of an active phrase structure to the end and prefixing it with the preposition *by*, moving the second NP (labelled 3) to the beginning, inserting the auxiliary verb *be*, and changing the main verb to its past participle form.

(4.33)   NP V NP $\Rightarrow$ 3 *be* 2+pastpart *by* 1
　　　　　1   2   3

Applying this rule to the deep structure (4.34*a*) produces the passive surface structure (4.34*b*). If this rule is not applied, a surface structure for the active sentence would be the final result.

(4.34) *a.*

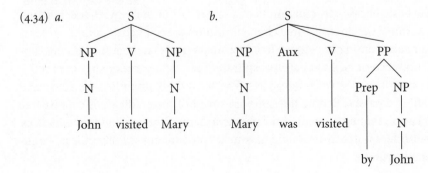

The active and passive have the same predicate–argument relations, as determined by their common deep structure. The deep structure is also the level at which predicate subcategorization frames are enforced. A transitive verb will be flanked by two NPs in deep structure even though those NPs might appear in quite different places (or perhaps not appear at all) in surface structure.

Transformations simplify the treatment of other phenomena that are difficult to handle with phrase-structure rules only. Feature dependencies that cross-classify the phrase structure can be implemented as transformations that copy information from one place to another place, for example, from the subject NP to the inflection on the adjacent verb. This guarantees the proper correlation of features in the surface structure and sentence. Transformations can also move information over large distances in the tree, thus accounting for the long-distance dependencies of relative clauses and questions discussed above.

The transformational framework provided reasonable descriptions of many syntactic phenomena, but subsequent research exposed several difficulties with the formalism. For example, the simplest specification of a rule aimed at operating on a phrase in one position would allow the rule to apply to phrases that were not the intended target. This could produce incorrect results. Without some restriction, the rule for topicalizing an English noun phrase by moving it to the front of the sentence would apply indiscriminately to noun phrases inside relative clauses, producing such ungrammatical strings as (4.35a). This could be derived by applying the transformation to the structure for the untopicalized sentence (4.35b).

(4.35) *a.* *John, the man who saw left.
         b. The man who saw John left.

As another example, the transformational idea of manipulating phrase structure was not very helpful in expressing generalizations across languages that encode information in very different ways from the phrasal configurations of languages like English. Thus, there is a universal notion that a passive sentence preserves the predicate–argument relations of the active but that it shifts the emphasis to the thing acted upon and away from the actor, but this alternation is not expressed as movement of phrases in languages such as Japanese where meaning is less strongly encoded in word order. The early transformational approach did not support one of the main goals of theoretical linguistics, the discovery and articulation of universal properties of human language.

Over the years, as solutions for these and other problems have been explored, Transformational Grammar has changed, sometimes dramatically, from Chomsky's original formulation. Some of the better-known and longer-lasting variants of the framework are Government Binding Theory, the Principles and Parameters framework, and, most recently, the Minimalist Program. All of these variants, however, retain the key features of the original architecture: phrase-structure trees represent basic syntactic properties, and transformations relating such trees figure in the description of various syntactic phenomena.

Apart from its problems as a system for syntactic description, Transformational Grammar did not have much appeal for computational linguists. Computational linguists are interested not merely in describing the form/meaning mapping in abstract terms, but in defining simple and efficient methods for finding the predicate–argument relations for a given sentence (**recognition** or **parsing**, discussed in Chapter 12) or finding the sentences that express a given meaning (**generation**, see Chapter 15). A transformational derivation provides a very indirect, multi-stage mapping between the meaning and form of a sentence. The transformations are set up so that they provide the correct surface structure for a given deep structure when they are applied in a prescribed order, but it is difficult if not impossible to apply them in the reverse order to find the deep structure (and hence the predicate–argument relations) of a given string. Transformational grammars therefore could not easily be used in practical language analysis systems, and they also could not serve as components of psychologically plausible models of human comprehension.

4.2.4 Augmented transition networks

Computational linguists, working outside of the transformational framework, devised other syntactic formalisms which were more amenable to computation but still had the expressive power to characterize a wide range of syntactic phenomena. The **Augmented Transition Network** (ATN) formalism, introduced by Woods (1970), was one of the earliest and most influential of these computationally motivated grammatical systems. It could be used to describe quite complicated linguistic dependencies, but it was organized in a very intuitive and easy-to-implement way. It became a standard component of computational systems in the 1970s and 1980s.

An ATN grammar consists of a set of finite-state transition networks, one for each of the phrasal categories (NP, S, etc.) that can appear in the surface structure of a sentence. The transitions in these networks can also be labelled with phrasal categories, and a phrasal transition in one network is allowed if there is an acceptable path through the separate network corresponding to the transition's label. Such a collection of networks, called a **recursive transition network** (RTN), is equivalent to but computationally somewhat more convenient than a standard context-free phrase-structure grammar. The ability to describe phenomena that are difficult or impossible to characterize with a context-free grammar comes from a set of operations that are attached to the transitions. These operations can store fragments of trees in named 'registers' and retrieve those fragments on subsequent transitions for comparison with the words and phrases later on in the string. By virtue of such comparisons, the system can enforce dependencies such as subject–verb agreement. Operations can also assemble the contents of registers to build deep-structure-like tree fragments that map directly to predicate–argument relations. The two networks in (4.36) give the general flavour of an ATN grammar in a somewhat informal notation.

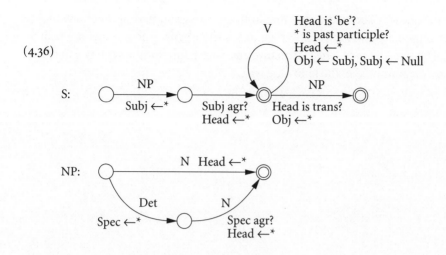

(4.36)

These networks trace out the surface structure of simple transitive and intransitive active sentences and also passive sentences that lack the *by*-marked agent NP. The first NP of the S is initially stored in the Subj register (Subj ← *) and checked for agreement with the first verb. If the first (Head) verb is the passive auxiliary *be* and it is followed by a past participle, the structure in the Subj register is moved to the Obj register and the Subj register is emptied. The initial NP of the passive thus ends up in the same register as the second NP of the active and will bear the same relation to the main predicate. The ATN characterizes the paraphrase relation of actives and passives in a one-step mapping rather than through a multi-stage transformational derivation: in effect, the deep structure is read directly from the transitions through the surface structure.

4.2.5 Constraint-based feature-structure grammars

Though much more successful than the Transformational Grammar approach, at least from the point of view of computational linguistics, the ATN also suffered from its own linguistic, computational, and mathematical inadequacies. Attempts to remedy these difficulties led to the development of a representation other than phrase-structure trees for encoding the underlying syntactic properties of sentences, the hierarchical attribute-value matrix or **feature structure**. This was proposed by Kaplan and Bresnan (1982) as the **functional structure** of **Lexical Functional Grammar** (LFG). Like the ATN, LFG also provides for a one-step mapping between the surface form of utterances and representations of their underlying grammatical properties. The surface form is represented by a standard phrase-structure tree, called the **constituent structure** or c-structure in LFG parlance. This encodes the linear order of words and their grouping into larger phrasal units. The deep grammatical properties are represented in the functional structure or f-structure. These are matrices of attributes and associated values that indicate how grammatical functions such as subject and object and grammatical features such as tense and number are realized for a particular sentence. The c-structure and f-structure for the sentence *John likes Mary* are diagrammed in the following way.

(4.37)

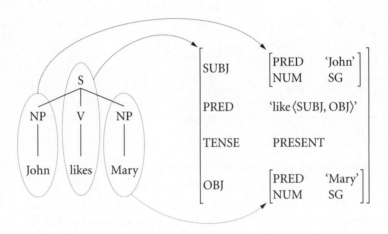

An ATN establishes the underlying representation through a particular left-to-right sequence of register operations, each one applying to the results of previous operations. LFG and other feature-structure grammars instead determine the appropriate structures as those that satisfy a system of constraints or conditions on the various combinations of features and values.

LFG starts from the basic architectural principle that particular phrases of the c-structure correspond to particular units of the f-structure, and that the words and phrases of a c-structure node carry information about the particular f-structure unit that the node corresponds to. The correspondences between nodes and f-structure units for this example are indicated by the dotted lines in (4.37). The figure shows that all the nodes in the first NP correspond to the subject f-structure unit, the S, V, and *likes* all correspond to the outermost f-structure, and the second NP nodes map to the object. The grammar imposes constraints on the f-structure units that correspond to c-structure phrases, and those constraints determine what properties (attributes and values) the f-structure must have. Thus an LFG grammar can be given a purely declarative (as opposed to a procedural, sequence-of-steps) interpretation: it allows corresponding pairs of c-structures and f-structures to be classified as grammatically correct or incorrect, although it does not explicitly prescribe a procedure for constructing one of those structures given the other.

An LFG grammar consists of an ordinary context-free phrase-structure grammar that describes completely the set of valid surface constituent structures. Rule (4.38*a*) indicates, for example, that a sentence S can consist of NP-V-NP sequence.

(4.38) *a.* S →   NP   V   NP
                (↑SUBJ)=↓   ↑=↓   (↑OBJ)=↓

   b. NP →   N
                  ↑=↓

The constraints on the f-structure units are specified by the annotations underneath the phrasal categories. The equation (↑SUBJ)=↓ specifies that an f-structure unit denoted by the symbol ↑ has a subject attribute, and the value of that attribute is the f-structure unit denoted by the symbol ↓. ↑ and ↓ are interpreted with respect to the correspondence that relates the c-structure nodes to f-structure units. The ↑ on the NP category refers to the f-structure unit that corresponds to the S-labelled mother of the NP node. The ↓ denotes the f-structure unit corresponding to the NP node itself. Taken as a whole, this equation asserts that the f-structure corresponding to the S node has a SUBJ attribute whose value is the f-structure corresponding to the NP node, or, less formally, that the first NP of a sentence is the subject. The dotted-line configuration satisfies this constraint. The ↑=↓ on the N and V nodes indicates that there is a single f-structure that those daughters and their respective mothers both correspond to, or, again less formally, that those daughters are the heads of their mother phrases.

Annotations of this sort can also be associated with lexical items, and these impose constraints on the syntactic features that must be found in the f-structures corresponding to the nodes under which those items appear. The following are some simple lexical entries:

(4.39) *John*: N (↑PRED)='John'
                  (↑NUM)=SG

    likes: V (↑PRED)='like⟨SUBJ, OBJ⟩'
                (↑TENSE)=PRESENT
                (↑SUBJ NUM)=SG

Note that the NUM feature of *John* is specified as singular, and so is the number of *like*'s SUBJ. Since *John* is the subject of this sentence, these equations impose consistent constraints on the same feature value. A plural subject with a singular verb would impose inconsistent constraints, and the sentence would be marked as ungrammatical. In this way, the constraints on the f-structure can enforce syntactic feature dependencies that would otherwise have to be encoded in complicated c-structure categories. The PRED equation in the entry for *likes* gives its subcategorization frame (its f-structure must have SUBJ and OBJ attributes) and also explicitly indicates that the SUBJ of the f-structure will be interpreted as the predicate's first argument and the OBJ as the second argument. LFG accounts for systematic paraphrases by means of alternative PRED features that specify systematically different mappings between grammatical functions and argument positions, for example, that the SUBJ maps to the second argument of a passive verb.

Other syntactic frameworks that are prominent in computational work also use hierarchical attribute-value structures as a primary syntactic representation. Feature structures are the only representation posited by **Head-Driven Phrase Structure Grammar** (HPSG) (Pollard and Sag 1994). In that framework, information about order and constituent grouping is encoded as attributes embedded in a special part of a more general feature structure rather than as a separate tree in a parallel config-uration, as in (4.37). The feature structures of HPSG are arranged in classes of differ-ent **types**, and the types themselves are arranged in a partially ordered inheritance structure. The **inheritance** relation is an important way of expressing theoretically significant syntactic generalizations. A supertype can have properties that are stated only once but are shared by all of its subtypes in the inheritance structure. Each of the subtypes may then have its own special properties. For example, transitives and intransitives are subtypes of the general class of verbs and share the properties of allowing a tense feature and agreeing with a subject. But they differ in their valence or subcategorization frames. LFG and HPSG have both been successful as linguistic theories, extending the range of phenomena that syntactic descriptions can account for, and also as platforms for developing new, efficient algorithms for syntactic processing.

The **PATR** system (Shieber et al. 1983) is another framework that makes uses of attribute-value structures. It is similar to LFG in associating equational constraints with phrase-structure rules and assigning to sentences both trees and feature struc-tures. PATR grammars have been used in several computational implementations but PATR, unlike LFG or HPSG, was not proposed as a linguistic theory and has not served as a basis for continuing linguistic research.

The feature structures of LFG and PATR grammars are consistent solutions to the system of equational constraints that are annotated to the rules that specify a phrase-structure tree. A **unification** operator on feature structures has become the standard way of solving such equational systems: it combines two feature structures into a third provided that none of the features have conflicting values. The unification oper-ator over typed feature structures plays a more significant theoretical role for HPSG. In that framework unification provides a definition for the correctness of an analysis, not just an implementation. LFG, PATR, and HPSG are often grouped together under the rubric of **unification-based grammars**.

4.2.6 Other syntactic frameworks

Finally, we mention briefly two other syntactic systems that are of linguistic and com-putational interest. **Generalized Phrase Structure Grammar** (GPSG) (Gazdar et al. 1985) is formally equivalent to context-free grammar and uses tree structures as its basic form of syntactic representation, but it uses a much more succinct notation to characterize the context-free rules that account for agreement and systematic paraphrase. Some syntactic phenomena, such as the so-called cross-serial dependencies of Dutch (Bresnan et al. 1982), lie beyond the mathematical power of any context-free system, and GPSG is not suitable for languages that exhibit those properties. **Tree-Adjoining Grammars** (TAGs) also stay closer to the tree representations of phrase-structure grammars and Transformational Grammar, but TAGs add an additional adjunction operation for combining phrases together. Adjunction provides a minimal increase to the expressive power of a context-free system that seems sufficient to nicely account for a wide range of syntactic dependencies. TAGs are discussed in detail in Chapter 26.

FURTHER READING AND RELEVANT RESOURCES

Chomsky's *Syntactic Structure* (1957) is a good place to start partly for its historical significance but also because it lays out many of the considerations of expressive and explanatory power that syntactic theories have been concerned with. A later book, *Aspects of the Theory of Syntax* (Chomsky 1965), is also the background for many later developments in the Transformational Grammar tradition, and it is a point of reference for many non-transformational theories. Sells (1985) gives an introductory summary of one of the later versions of transformational grammar, Government and Binding Theory, along with brief descriptions of LFG and GPSG. The papers in Webelhuth (1995) describe the concerns of more recent research in Government and Binding and Minimalism.

Augmented transition networks have been widely used in computational systems, but they have evolved very little, especially compared to Transformational Grammar, since Woods's (1970) original proposal. The ATN literature mostly describes applications in which ATNs have been embedded, with relatively little focus on their formal or linguistic properties. The most easily accessible descriptions of the ATN are found in textbooks on computational linguistics, for example, Gazdar and Mellish (1989).

In contrast to the ATN, the literatures for LFG and HPSG are broad and growing, with formal, linguistic, and computational issues all being explored. Bresnan (1982) contains an early collection of LFG papers while Dalrymple et al. (1995) is a collection of more recent papers with an emphasis on mathematical and computational issues. Bresnan (2000) and Dalrymple (2001) present the LFG approach in textbook form. The LFG website at http://www-lfg.stanford.edu/lfg includes a comprehensive LFG bibliography and links to a number of other LFG resources.

The basic properties of HPSG are set forth in Pollard and Sag (1994). The textbook by Sag and Wasow (1999) provides a general introduction to syntactic theory as seen from the vantage point of HPSG. Ongoing work in the HPSG framework is posted on the HPSG website at http://www.ling.ohio-state.edu/hpsg/. Sag and Wasow (1999) also includes an informative appendix that surveys many of the other syntactic frameworks that have not been mentioned in the present short chapter.

For a formal account of regular and context-free grammars, the reader is referred to Chapter 8 of this volume.

References

Bresnan, J. (ed.). 1982. *The Mental Representation of Grammatical Relations*. Cambridge, Mass.: MIT Press.

——R. Kaplan, S. Peters, and A. Zaenen. 1982. 'Cross-serial dependencies in Dutch'. *Linguistic Inquiry*, 13, 613–35.

——2000. *Lexical-Functional Syntax*. Oxford: Blackwell.

Chomsky, N. 1957. *Syntactic Structures*. The Hague: Mouton.

——1965. *Aspects of the Theory of Syntax*. Cambridge, Mass.: MIT Press.

Dalrymple, M. 2001. *Lexical Functional Grammar*. New York: Academic Press.

——R. Kaplan, J. Maxwell III, and A. Zaenen (eds.). 1995. *Formal Issues in Lexical-Functional grammar*. Stanford, Calif.: CSLI Publications.

Gazdar, G. and C. Mellish. 1989. *Natural Language Processing in Lisp/Pop-11/Prolog*. London: Addison-Wesley.

——E. Klein, G. Pullum, and I. Sag. 1985. *Generalized Phrase Structure Grammar*. Oxford: Blackwell.

Kaplan, R. and J. Bresnan. 1982. 'Lexical-functional grammar: a formal system for grammatical representation'. In Bresnan (1982), 173–281. Also appears in Dalrymple et al. (1995), 29–130.

Pollard, C. and I. Sag, 1994. *Head-Driven Phrase Structure Grammar*. Stanford, Calif.: Stanford University Press.

Sag, I. and T. Wasow. 1999. *Syntactic Theory: A Formal Introduction*. Stanford, Calif.: CSLI Publications.

Sells, P. 1989. *Lectures on Contemporary Syntactic Theories: An Introduction to Government-Binding Theory, Generalized Phrase Structure Grammar, and Lexical-Functional Grammar*. Stanford, Calif.: CSLI Publications.

Shieber, S., H. Uszkoreit, F. Pereira, J. Robinson, and M. Tyson. 1983. 'The formalism and implementation of PATR-II'. In B. Grosz and M. Stickel (eds.), *Research on Interactive Acquisition and Use of Knowledge*. SRI Final Report 1894, Menlo Park, Calif.: SRI International, 39–70.

Webelhuth, G. (ed.). 1995. *Government and Binding Theory and the Minimalist Program*. Oxford: Blackwell.

Woods, W. 1970. 'Transition network grammars for natural language analysis'. *Communications of the ACM*, 13(10), 591–606.

CHAPTER 5

SEMANTICS

SHALOM LAPPIN

ABSTRACT

Semantics is the study of linguistic meaning, where, in the case of a declarative sentence, sentential meaning is frequently taken to be a proposition which describes a possible state of affairs. Computational semantics is that area of computational linguistics that deals with linguistic meaning within a computational approach to natural language. A main focus of computational semantics is to model the way in which the meanings of phrases and sentences are computed systematically from the meanings of their syntactic constituents. This study can be factored into two main areas. The first is the representation of meanings. The second is the analysis of the way in which semantic representations of syntactically complex expressions are assembled from the meanings of their component parts. In seeking to clarify these issues three problems are considered. First, what is the nature of the interface between syntax and semantics? Second, how do we determine the precise nature of the general condition which is imposed by the requirement that a computational semantics define a systematic relation between the meaning of a sentence and the meanings of its constituents? Finally, what is the role of contextual and discourse factors in the interpretation of a sentence? These problems are central to the construction of a viable computational semantic system.

5.1 Introduction

Semantics is the study of linguistic meaning. In general terms, semanticists are concerned with modelling the way in which the meanings of lexical items contribute to the meanings of the phrases and sentences in which they appear.[1] In the case of a declarative sentence, sentential meaning is frequently taken to be a proposition, which describes a possible state of affairs. Computational semantics is that area of computational linguistics which deals with linguistic meaning within a computational approach to natural language. It shares many of the concerns of semantic theory and may apply some of its formal treatments of meaning. However, while semantic theory attempts to formalize the knowledge that speakers use in order to interpret the sentences of their language, computational semantics seeks to develop tractable procedures for representing and computing linguistic meaning as part of a computationally viable account of natural language.

A main focus of **computational semantics** is to model the way in which the meanings of phrases and sentences are computed systematically from the meanings of their syntactic constituents. It is possible to factor this study into two main questions. The first is, how should meanings be represented? The second is, how are the semantic representations of syntactically complex expressions assembled from the meanings of their component parts? The second question implies that a system for semantic interpretation will work in tandem with a procedure for representing and parsing the syntactic structure of an input string. Given the assumption that generating a semantic interpretation for a sentence involves constructing a representation on the basis of its syntactic structure, a central issue for any semantic theory is the nature of the interface between syntax and semantics. A second important problem is to determine the precise nature of the general condition which is imposed by the requirement that a computational semantics define a systematic relation between the meaning of a sentence and the meanings of its constituents. A third major concern that a theory of semantics must deal with is the role of contextual and discourse factors in the interpretation of a sentence.

In section 5.2 I will briefly compare two models of semantic representation which have been proposed in the literature and consider the way in which each of them deals with the **syntax–semantics interface**. In section 5.3 I will take up the contrast between the general approach to the syntax–semantics interface which is common to most systems of computational semantics, including the two discussed in section 5.2, on one hand, and an alternative view that characterizes Chomsky's derivational view

---

[1] For introductions to semantic theory see Chierchia and McConnell-Ginet (1990), and Lappin (2000a). For an overview of work in contemporary semantic theory see Lappin (1996). Blackburn and Bos (1999) provide a recent introduction to computational semantics.

of syntax on the other. Section 5.4 focuses on the possibility of using **underspecified representations** of meaning while still sustaining a systematic relation between the meaning of an expression and the meanings of its constituents. Finally, in section 5.5 I will briefly look at the move from static to **dynamic theories of meaning** that many computational semanticists have made in the past two decades in an attempt to model the interpretation of utterances in discourse and dialogue.

5.2 SEMANTIC REPRESENTATION

5.2.1 Translation into a higher-order logic

An influential approach to constructing a computational semantics for a language consists (primarily) in specifying a translation procedure for mapping each constituent in a syntactic parse tree into a corresponding expression in a system of **higher-order logic**.[2] This involves implementing Montague's (1974) programme for systematic translation of the syntactically disambiguated structures of a natural language into the expressions of IL (an Intensional Logic).[3] In Montague's framework, the expressions of IL are interpreted model theoretically. In an implemented computational semantics, it is possible to interpret the formulas and terms of IL relative to a database, which serves as the intended model of the natural language.

We can illustrate such a system with two simple examples. Assume that we have a grammar (implemented by a parser) which assigns the parse trees in (5.1*b*) and (5.2*b*) to the sentences in (5.1*a*) and (5.2*a*), respectively (where *PropNoun* is Proper Noun, *IV* intransitive verb, and *TV* transitive verb).

(5.1) *a.* John sings.

b.

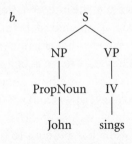

---

[2] Pereira and Shieber (1987) present a Definite Clause Grammar which assigns a syntactic parse tree to an input string and compositionally computes a semantic representation in the lambda calculus for the constituents of the parse tree.

[3] See Dowty, Wall, and Peters (1981) for an introduction to Montague semantics.

(5.2) *a.* Mary reads every book.

b.

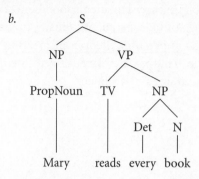

The semantic interpreter will first assign translations of the appropriate type to the lexical items at the terminal elements of the trees in (5.1*b*) and (5.2*b*). The proper names *John* and *Mary* are translated as the constants *john* and *mary*, respectively. The IV *sings* is paired with the one-place predicate $\lambda x[sings(x)]$ which is formed by λ-abstraction on the variable x. The argument to which the λ-term applies can be substituted for all occurrences of the variable bound by the λ-operator. So the proposition $\lambda x[sings(x)](john)$ is equivalent to $sings(john)$. The common noun *book* is also translated as a one-place predicate $\lambda x[book(x)]$. Quantified NPs are interpreted as **generalized quantifiers (GQs)** which correspond to sets of sets (or properties of properties).[4] *Every book* denotes the set of all sets that contain every book (the property of all properties true of every book). This set can be represented by a higher-order predicate term which holds of all predicates true of every book. The λ-term that expresses this predicate is $\lambda P[\forall x(book(x) \rightarrow P(x))]$. A quantificational determiner like *every* is mapped to a λ-term which, when applied to the predicate that translates its noun (or N′), yields the λ-term of the entire NP. *Every* goes to $\lambda Q[\lambda P[\forall x(Q(x) \rightarrow P(x))]]$. When this λ-term is applied to $\lambda x[book(x)]$ the result is $\lambda P[\forall x(book(x) \rightarrow P(x))]$. The TV *reads* corresponds to the two-place predicate $\lambda y[\lambda x[reads(x,y)]]$. However, we want to be able to combine the translation of *read* with the translation of *every book* to generate the one-place predicate $\lambda x[\forall y(book(y) \rightarrow reads(x,y))]$ as the intepretation of the VP *reads every book*. Therefore, we take the interpretation of a transitive verb to be a λ-term that denotes a function from a generalized quantifier (the denotation of an NP) to a suitable property term that provides the semantic value of the VP. Let Q' be a variable that takes GQs as values. Then the λ-term assigned to *reads* is $\lambda Q'[\lambda x[Q'(\lambda y[read(x,y)])]]$. When this λ-term is applied to the denotation of *every book* $(\lambda P[\forall w(book(w) \rightarrow P(w)))$, it yields $\lambda x[\forall w(book(w) \rightarrow read(x,w))]$ as the interpretation of the VP *reads every book*.

The semantic interpreter combines the translations of the lexical items to form the representations of the next higher constituents, where the combination generally consists of the application of a λ-term of one of the items to the translation of another.

---

[4] See Keenan (1996) and Keenan and Westerstahl (1997) for recent surveys of work in generalized quantifier theory.

This operation is repeated until a representation for the entire sentence is produced, as in (5.3*a*) and (5.3*b*).

(5.3) *a.*

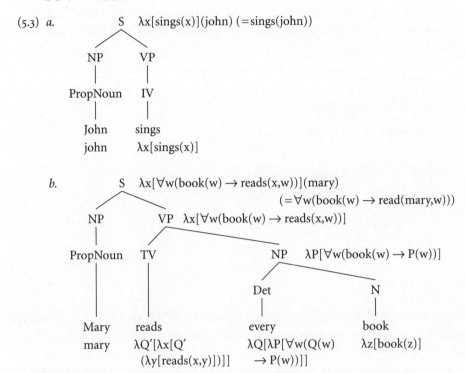

It is not difficult to add a procedure to the semantic interpreter which maps the **first-order** formulas derived from the representations of sentences into clausal normal forms which can be tested directly against a data base.[5] This second phase of translation and evaluation of the resulting normal forms relative to the data base corresponds to the interpretation of sentences in a model. The system described here generates a **compositional** interpretation of an expression which is computed entirely on the basis of the interpretations of its syntactic constituents.

5.2.2 Typed feature structures

Typed feature-structure grammars like Head-Driven Phrase Structure Grammar (HPSG) provide an alternative way of handling the syntax–semantics interface.[6]

---

[5] Pereira and Shieber (1987: appendix A.2) construct a simple query system along these lines. See Blackburn and Bos (1999) for model checkers for first-order formulas.

[6] Pollard and Sag (1994) provide the classic formulation of HPSG. For more recent versions of this framework see (among others) Sag (1997) and Bouma, Malouf, and Sag (2001). See Chapter 4 of this volume for additional background on typed feature-structure grammars.

They use directed graphs to represent all linguistic information as sequences of typed features which take values of specified kinds, where these values may themselves be feature structures. Consider, for example, the attribute-value matrix (**AVM**) in (5.4), which describes a (simplified) feature structure for the lexical entry of the transitive verb *reads*.[7]

(5.4)

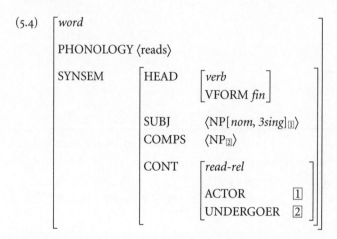

The SYNSEM (the top-level feature corresponding to the syntactic and semantic properties of the expression) takes as its value a feature structure that includes both syntactic and semantic features. The syntactic features identify *reads* as a finite verb which takes a third person singular subject and an NP (object) complement. The semantic feature CONT (CONTENT) gives the relation that *reads* denotes and the argument roles among which the relation holds. The index of the SUBJ NP is shared with the ACTOR role, and that of the COMPS (COMPLEMENTS) NP with the UNDERGOER to indicate that the CONT features of these NPs provide the values for these two role features. When the feature structure for an NP like *every book* is taken as the element of the list which is the value of the COMPS feature in (5.4), the result is a feature structure for the VP *reads every book*. Similarly, taking the feature structure for the NP *Mary* as the element of the list value for SUBJ (SUBJECT) in (5.4) yields the feature structure for the sentence *Mary reads every book*.

Pollard and Sag (1994: ch. 8), and Pollard and Yoo (1998), assign the quantificational NP *every book* the feature structure in (5.5) as the value of its CONT feature. The CONT of the determiner *every* contributes the basic form of this feature structure and the quantifier relation *forall*, while the noun *book* provides the value of the RELN (RELATION) in the NUCLEUS feature and the restricted INDEX ②, which

---

[7] See Pollard and Sag (1987, 1994) for the use of AVMs to represent typed feature structures in HPSG. Pollard and Sag (1994) base their treatment of semantic content on situation semantics. See Barwise and Perry (1983) for the original statement of this semantic theory.

(5.5)

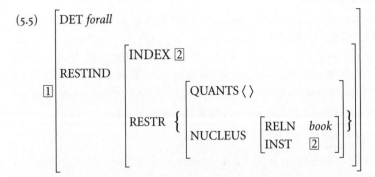

is analogous to a bound variable. The CONT feature in (5.5) is equivalent to the restricted quantifier $\forall x(book(x))$ in a first-order language.

The CONT value of a quantified NP like *every book* is added to the set that is the value of its QSTORE (quantifier storage) feature. It is inherited by the QSTORE features of successively higher phrases in which the NP is contained until it is retrieved in the feature structure of a containing sentence S. Retrieving a quantifier CONT from storage consists in taking it from the QSTORE set of a phrase immediately contained in S and adding it to the list of S's QUANTS feature, while not including it in S's QSTORE list.[8] QSTORE retrieval is illustrated in the abbreviated feature structure in (5.6).

(5.6)

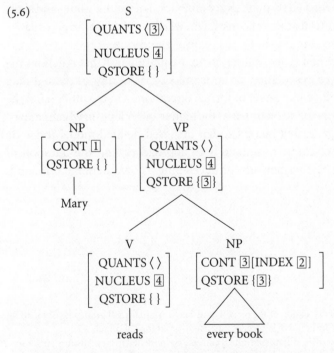

---

[8] This pattern of QSTORE feature inheritance and retrieval simulates the device of quantifier storage, originally proposed by Cooper (1983) and implemented by Pereira and Shieber (1987), and Pereira and Pollack (1991). I will discuss quantifier storage in section 5.4.

The CONTENT value of *every book* (indicated by [3]) is placed in QSTORE, inherited by the QSTORE of the VP and retrieved at S, where it is removed from QSTORE and assigned to QUANTS. The NUCLEUS value of the verb *reads*, which provides a CONT relation and its roles, is inherited by the VP and S. The QUANTS and NUCLEUS feature values of the entire S determine an interpretation of the sentence that corresponds directly to the first-order formula in (5.7).[9]

(5.7) $\forall x(book(x) \to read(mary,x))$

As in the case of the translations into higher-order logical formula discussed in section 5.2.1, it is possible to convert the CONT feature structures of sentences into normal forms that can be evaluated against a database. However, there is a significant difference between these two approaches to the syntax–semantics interface. In the first, the semantic interpretation of an expression is computed by mapping its syntactic representation into an expression in a logical language which is formally distinct from the grammatical structure that constitutes the input to the translation procedure. By contrast, in a typed feature-structure grammar all information about an expression is encoded in the same formal framework. The phonological, syntactic, and semantic properties of a sentence are expressed through a directed graph whose nodes are typed features and their values. Therefore, the syntactic and semantic representations of a sentence are constructed simultaneously as elements of the same formal object.[10] This is achieved through the combination of feature values and sharing of values among distinct features of constituent words and phrases in accordance with constraints on the feature graphs of each type of expression.

An obvious advantage of a typed feature-structure grammar is that it defines the syntactic and semantic representation of an expression as a fully integrated data structure which is computed by one set of formal operations. On the other hand the translation approach offers the attraction that the higher-order logic in which semantic representations are generated has a familiar and well-defined model-theoretic semantics. Researchers continue to pursue both approaches, and the question of which one provides the best framework for developing a computational semantics remains open.

---

[9] See Lappin (2000*a*) for a discussion of the representation of certain formal properties of meaning in natural language through translation of sentences into a first-order logical language.

[10] In fact, information concerning discourse context can also be modelled in typed feature structures. See Pollard and Sag (1994: 332–7) and Ginzburg and Sag (2000) for proposals on how to encode contextual and discourse information in HPSG. I will discuss this issue in section 5.5.

5.3   The Syntax–Semantics Interface

Although the two models of interpretation considered in section 5.2 offer different approaches to the relationship between syntactic and semantic representation, they share a common assumption concerning the architecture of the syntax–semantics interface. In both cases, the semantic representation of an expression is computed in parallel with its syntactic structure at each level of lexical and phrasal constituency. The translations into a higher-order logical language that are assigned to lexical items are combined through function-argument application at successively higher phrases to generate representations for each intermediate phrase structure until an interpretation is obtained for the highest sentence. Similarly, the CONT values of lexical and phrasal feature structures are systematically related to those of the phrases that immediately contain them by constraints that define the set of well-formed feature structures for specified lexical and phrasal types. Therefore, each unit of syntactic structure is (at least) a two-dimensional object that encodes both syntactic and semantic information.[11] Equivalently, each expression encodes a syntactic–semantic interface. I will refer to this general approach as the Parallel Correspondence Model (PCM) of the relation between syntax and semantics.

Taking a grammar to be a set of declarative conditions on well-formed structures, a grammar that conforms to the PCM provides a simultaneous recursive definition of well-formedness for both syntactic and semantic representations, where the specification of the lexical items is the base of the definition and the rules for phrasal types are its recursive clauses. From a procedural perspective, the PCM requires that a parser or generator compute the syntactic and semantic representations of a phrase stepwise and in tandem from its lexical items through each of its non-terminal constituents to its top level of structure.

Most theories of formal grammar have incorporated the PCM. Specifically Categorial Grammar, Generalized Phrase Structure Grammar (GPSG), HPSG, Lexical Functional Grammar (LFG), current versions of tree-adjoining grammar (TAG), tree-description grammar, dynamic syntax (DS), and the framework presented in Jackendoff (1997) take the PCM as a design feature of their respective treatments of the relation between syntax and semantics.[12]

---

[11] In HPSG an expression (sign) is a three-dimensional object, as it also includes phonological features. In fact, if we consider CONTEXT features to be a fourth dimension of information, then a sign is a four-dimensional entity.

[12] For an introduction to syntactic theory, see Chapter 3 of this volume. See Morrill (1994), Jacobson (1996), Moortgat (1996), and Steedman (1996) for different versions of Categorial Grammar. Gazdar et al. (1985) give a detailed exposition of GPSG. Kaplan and Bresnan (1982) present the classic model of LFG, and Chapter 4 of this volume gives an overview of LFG. Shieber and Schabes (1990) propose a theory of

The view of the syntax–semantics interface developed in Chomksy's (1981 and 1986) Government and Binding Theory, and subsequently in his (1995 and 1998) Minimalist Program, constitutes a marked exception to this pattern. In these frameworks a sentence is generated by a derivation, which is a sequence of (i) combinatorial operations that assemble lexical items and phrases into larger constituents, and (ii) (instances of) a movement operation that maps phrase structures into phrase structures. The output of a well-formed derivation is a pair of structures LF (logical form) and PF (phonetic form). The former is a syntactic structure that constitutes the input to procedures for semantic interpretation, and the latter is the representation which is converted into the sound pattern for the sentence. LF and PF are the only two interfaces with the modules of semantic and phonetic interpretation, respectively. As $\langle LF, PF \rangle$ is the end point of a derivation, this pair of interfaces for a sentence is only accessible after all of the syntactic operations that define its derivation have applied. I will refer to this approach as the Derivation Final Model (DFM) of interface. It treats the syntactic information of an expression as entirely insulated from semantic and phonological information until the end of a derivation, which produces the two interface levels.[13]

There are at least two reasons for preferring the PCM to the DFM. First, recent psycholinguistic work on sentence processing suggests that human parsing proceeds incrementally through the simultaneous application of syntactic, semantic, and phonological constraints to resolve syntactic ambiguity. Trueswell, Tanenhaus, and Garnsey (1994), and Tanenhaus and Trueswell (1995), for example, provide evidence that when subjects encounter ambiguous parse points in an input string, they invoke both semantic and syntactic conditions, as well as contextual and intonational factors, in selecting among possible alternative structures in first-pass parsing. The PCM is entirely compatible with a performance model in which non-syntactic constraints interact with syntactic conditions incrementally in the parsing of each level of constituent structure.[14] This sort of constraint interaction is built into its architecture. By contrast, a parser that operates in accordance with the DFM would require that the first-pass parse structure be built up solely on the basis of syntactic conditions, with semantic (as well as other) constraints consulted only on a second pass. Both the PCM and the DFM are schematic models of linguistic competence rather than performance. Therefore, psycholinguistic facts cannot provide direct support for

TAG (see Chapter 36 of this volume for an introduction to TAG) that implements the PCM. Kallmeyer (1997) describes a version of tree-description grammars that incorporates the PCM of the syntax–semantics interface. See Kempson, Meyer-Viol, and Gabbay (2000) for DS. Montague's (1974) PTQ is perhaps the earliest example of a theory of grammar that explicitly adopts the PCM.

[13] See Johnson and Lappin (1999) for a detailed comparison of the PCM and DFM, and arguments in support of the former.

[14] A performance model represents the way in which speakers actually apply their knowledge of grammar to produce and interpret sentences.

either of them. However, the fact that there is evidence for an incremental parallel constraint model of processing does offer important motivation for the PCM. A grammar that satisfies the PCM can be easily integrated into such a processing model while reconciling a DFM with the facts of incremental parallel processing poses obvious difficulties.

Second, in a PCM grammar semantic (and other types of) constraints can be invoked at the level of constituency where they hold, independently of the sentence in which these constituents are contained. In the DFM, on the other hand, these constraints are accessible only after a derivation has yielded the LF interface structure. From a procedural perspective, a PCM grammar can rule out a semantically ill-formed phrase as soon as it is encountered, but a DFM grammar must compute the complete derivation of the LF in which the phrase is contained before recognizing the phrase as semantically unacceptable. Therefore, the PCM offers a more efficient architecture for implementing constraint satisfaction. The following example illustrates this point.

When *meet* is used as an intransitive verb, it requires a subject NP that denotes a plural entity. As the well-formedness of (5.8*b*) indicates, this is a purely semantic constraint that cannot be reduced to grammatical number.

(5.8) *a*. The delegates met for an hour.
  b. The committee met for an hour.
  c. *The woman met for an hour.

Consider (5.9):

(5.9)   *John believes the woman to have met for an hour.

The sentence is ill formed because when *the woman*, a semantically singular NP, is taken as the subject of *to have met for an hour*, it violates the semantic selection constraint that the intransitive verb *met*, the head of the VP, imposes on its subject.

Two alternative analyses have been proposed for a VP of the form *believes the woman to have met*. Postal (1974) suggests a 'raising to object' account on which *the woman* is raised from the subject of the embedded clause *the woman to have met for an hour* to the position of the matrix object of *believes*. A variant of this approach is adopted in Pollard and Sag (1994), who take both *the woman* and the infinitival VP *to have met for an hour* as complements of *believes*. The SYNSEM value of the matrix object *the woman* is shared with the unrealized SUBJECT of the infinitival VP complement. Chomsky (1981) takes *the woman to have met for an hour* as a clausal complement of *believes*, where *believes* 'exceptionally' assigns Case to *the woman* as the embedded subject NP. Chomsky (1995) sustains a version of this approach. Regardless of which of these analyses one accepts, the contrast between the PCM and the DFM holds. On the former, it is possible to rule out the VP *believes the woman to have met for an hour* as soon as it is either encountered in parsing or constructed through the combinatorial operations of generation. Within the latter, it is necessary to complete the derivation of the matrix sentence before the semantic interpretations of the infinitival VP and its subject are available.

5.4 UNDERSPECIFIED REPRESENTATIONS AND NON-COMPOSITIONAL SEMANTICS

In section 5.1 I suggested that one of the main problems for computational semantics, and, in fact, for any semantic theory which represents meaning systematically, is to determine the precise nature of the relation between the meaning of a sentence and the meanings of its syntactic constituents. Frege (1892) proposes the **principle of compositionality** as a general condition on solutions to this problem. In a compositional semantic theory, the meaning of any expression is computable by a function on the meanings of its parts.

Montague's (1974) semantic theory satisfies the principle of compositionality in a particularly rigorous way. Montague characterizes the relation between the syntactic categories and the semantic types (types of semantic value) of a language as a **homomorphism**. This is a functional mapping from the domain of categories to the range of types which may assign the same type to several categories, as, for example, in the case of common nouns and VPs, both of which are mapped to the type one-place predicate (a function from individuals to truth values). Corresponding to every syntactic rule for generating an expression α of category C_0 from expressions $\beta_1, \ldots, \beta_k$ of categories $C_1, \ldots, C_k$, there is a semantic operation that computes α's semantic value from the values of $\beta_1, \ldots, \beta_k$. The value that the rule produces for α is of the required semantic type for C_0. These operations apply to expressions in disambiguated syntactic structures to yield unique semantic values. The translational semantics discussed in section 5.2 is a version of this system.

In compositional semantic theories the relation between the meaning of an expression and the meanings of its constituents is a function. However, it is possible to construct a non-compositional semantic theory in which this relation is systematic but not functional.[15] In such a theory an expression analysed by a single syntactic structure can be associated with a set of alternative interpretations rather than with a unique semantic value. Consider the quantifier scope ambiguity in (5.10).

(5.10)   Every student read a book.

---

[15] See Nerbonne (1996) for additional discussion of non-compositional representations of meaning within computational semantics. Zadrozny (1994) and Lappin and Zadrozny (1999) consider the status of compositionality as a condition on semantic theory.

If *every student* is taken as having wide scope relative to *a book*, then (5.10) asserts that every student is such that he or she read at least one book. When *a book* receives wide scope, the sentence is understood as stating that there is at least one book that every student read. In a compositional semantics, each scope interpretation is associated with a distinct syntactic structure. Montague (1974) obtains the narrow scope reading of *a book* by generating it *in situ* as the object NP and interpreting it in this position by a rule similar to that used to generate the translation of the VP *read every book* in (5.3*b*). When the translation of the subject NP *every student* is applied to the translation of this VP, the resulting formula is equivalent to (5.11).

(5.11) $\forall x(\text{student}(x) \rightarrow \exists y(\text{book}(y) \ \& \ \text{read}(x,y)))$

To derive the wide scope reading of *a book* Montague employs the syntactic operation of quantifying an NP from outside a sentence into the position of a pronoun. This involves generating *a book* outside the constituent structure for *every student read it*, where *it* is the pronominal counterpart of a free variable, and substituting the NP for the pronoun in the sentence. The semantic rule which corresponds to quantifying *a book* into the structure for *every student read it* yields an interpretation that is equivalent to (5.12).

(5.12) $\exists y(\text{book}(y) \ \& \ \forall x(\text{student}(x) \rightarrow \text{read}(x,y)))$

The operation of quantifier storage provides a non-compositional procedure for obtaining both scope readings. Let us assume that we are modelling quantifier storage within a typed feature-structure grammar, as we did in section 5.3. Then two feature structures are possible for (5.10).

(5.13) *a.*

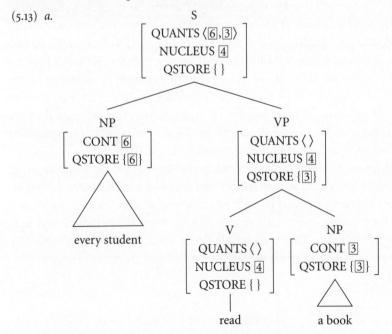

b.

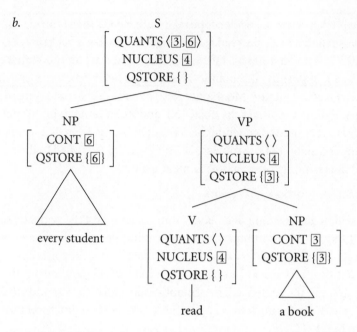

The value of the QSTORE feature is a set whose elements are unordered. The union of the QSTORE sets of the VP and the subject NP in (5.13a, b) is the set {$\boxed{3}$, $\boxed{6}$}. The elements of this set can be retrieved in any order to produce the ordered list which is the value of the QUANTS feature for the sentence. The two possible orders are given in (5.13a) and (5.13b), and these correspond to the scope readings in (5.11) and (5.12), respectively.

The QUANTS list is contained within the CONT feature, and so it is a component of the semantic representation of an expression. The relation between the value of the QUANTS feature of a phrase and the values of the QSTORES of its constituents is not, in general, functional. As (5.13a) and (5.13b) illustrate, distinct QUANTS lists can be obtained from the same QSTORE set QS by imposing alternative orderings on the elements of QS. Notice that the syntactic structure of the sentence remains constant for the two scope representations. Therefore, if quantifier scope is assigned through the device of storage, the semantic representation of a sentence containing quantified NPs is computed systematically but not necessarily compositionally.

In fact, this procedure for semantic interpretation can be generalized to an approach on which sentences are assigned underspecified representations containing parameters whose values can be defined in several distinct ways. Constraints apply to filter the possible combinations of values for the set of parameters in such a schematic representation. The interpretation of a sentence which is obtained by assigning values to the parameters in accordance with these conditions remains non-compositional.[16]

---

[16] Reyle (1993), Richter and Sailer (1997), Blackburn and Bos (1999), Crouch (1999), Copestake,

5.5 Dynamic Models of Interpretation

In the previous sections we have treated sentence meanings as determined in isolation from each other. This is not, in general, the way in which sentences are understood. In most cases we interpret a sentence within a discourse or dialogue sequence, where parts of its meaning are inherited from previous elements of the sequence. Recent theories of computational semantics have sought to model the way in which the incremental growth and modification of accessible information within a discourse or dialogue contributes to interpretation. This approach has caused a shift from a static to a dynamic view of sentence meaning.

The simple question–answer dialogue in 5.14 illustrates this perspective.

(5.14)   A: Who arrived? B: a student.

In order to construe B's response as a reply to A's question it is necessary to generate a propositional content for *a student* that corresponds to *A student arrived*. Ginzburg, Gregory, and Lappin (2001) propose a treatment of short answers within an HPSG framework that achieves this result. Their account is based upon Ginzburg and Sag (2000). A simplified version of the feature structure that they suggest for the CONT value of A's question in (5.14) is given in (5.15).

(5.15)

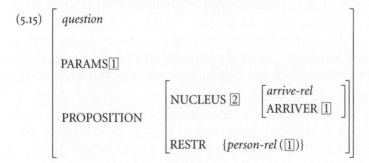

The value of the CONT feature for *Who arrived?* is of the type question, and its two highest features are PARAMS (PARAMETERS) and PROPOSITION. PARAMS shares its value ([1]) with the INDEX (an element of CONT) of the wh-phrase *who*. This INDEX is structure shared with the value of the ARRIVER role of the *arrive* relation in the NUCLEUS, and with the value of the RESTRICTION within PROPOSITION. The PARAMS feature is analogous to an abstraction operator that binds a variable within an open sentence corresponding to the value of PROPOSITION. (5.15) expresses the same content as the lambda expression $\lambda x[person(x)\ \&\ arrive(x)]$.

Flickinger, and Sag (1997), Pollard (1999), and Lappin (2000b) propose versions of the underspecified representation strategy to capture a variety of semantic phenomena.

The (abbreviated) feature structure of *who* is (5.16).

(5.16)
$$
\begin{bmatrix}
\text{CAT} & \text{NP [+nom]} \\
\\
\text{CONT} & \begin{bmatrix} \text{INDEX}\boxed{1} \\ \text{RESTR } \{person\text{-}rel\,(\boxed{1})\} \end{bmatrix} \\
\\
\text{STORE}\{\boxed{1}\}
\end{bmatrix}
$$

The INDEX value of *who*'s CONT feature is placed in storage and released at the level of the question as the latter's PARAMS value.

Ginzburg, Gregory, and Lappin (2001) treat *a student* in (5.14) as the non-head daughter (value of the NON-HD-DTRS feature) of a bare declarative clause. The CONT of this clause is a proposition, and the clause also has a CONTEXT feature, which in turn takes two features that are specified by previous contributions to the dialogue. One of these features is QUESTION-UNDER-DISCUSSION (QUD), which inherits its value from the CONT of the preceding question.[17] The second is SALI-ENT-UTTERANCE(SAL-UTT) whose value is identified with the feature structure of the wh-phrase in this question. The propositional CONT value for the entire bare declarative clause is determined by its QUD, SAL-UTT, and NON-HEAD-DTRS (the feature structure for *a student*) features in the way indicated in (5.17).

The QUD value for the bare declarative clause is identified with the CONT of the preceding question as represented in (5.15), and its SAL-UTT is 5.16, the feature structure of the wh-phrase of this question. The NUCLEUS of the propositional CONT of the entire bare declarative clause is obtained from the question in the QUD, and the RESTRICTION of this CONT is the union of the values of the RESTRICTION for the SAL-UTT (*who*) and for the NON-HD-DTR (*a student*). The CONT of the NON-HD-DTR *a student* is placed in storage (it is the value of the STORE feature), and it is retrieved as the value of the bare declarative clause's QUANTS feature. The propositional CONT of the clause in (5.17) is equivalent to the first-order formula in (5.18).

(5.18) $\exists x(student(x)\ \&\ person(x)\ \&\ arrive(x))$

Notice that the syntactic category feature CAT of the NON-HD-DTR is shared with that of the SAL-UTT. Therefore, the bare answer phrase must be of the same syntactic type as the wh-phrase in the question with which it is associated. This condition would block the question–answer sequence in (5.19), where the SAL-UTT is an NP while the NON-HD-DTR of the bare declarative clause is a PP (* indicates that the dialogue sequence is ill-formed).

---

[17] Actually, Ginzburg, Gregory, and Lappin (2001), following Ginzburg and Sag (2000), use MAXIMAL-QUESTION-UNDER-DISCUSSION (MAX-QUD), because a discourse context may contribute several subquestions. In (5.14) the context generated by B's utterance supplies only one question, and so for ease of exposition, I have reduced MAX-QUD to QUD.

(5.17)

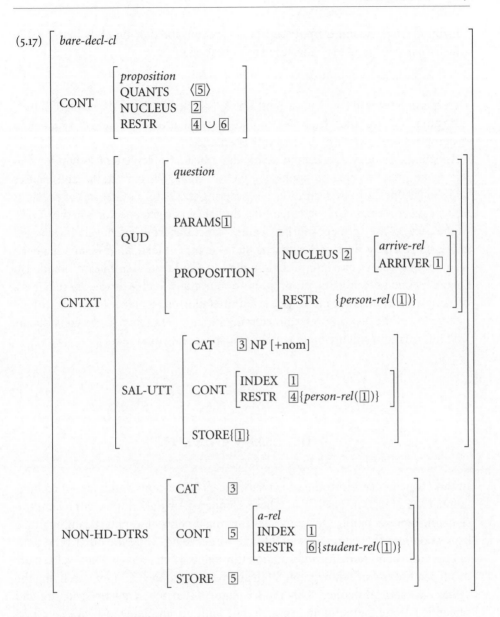

(5.19) *A: Who arrived? B: To a student.

Also the RESTRICTION features of the SAL-UTT and the NON-HD-DTR must be compatible, or it will not be possible to generate an interpretable propositional CONT for the bare answer. In (5.20) this requirement is violated, as the RESTR value of *a book* excludes the *person-rel* value of the RESTR feature for *who*.

(5.20) *A: Who arrived? B: a book.

Ginzburg, Gregory, and Lappin (2001) also account for sluicing cases like (5.21) in which a bare wh-phrase is understood as a question.

(5.21)   A: A student arrived. B: who?

Here it is necessary to construct a question CONT for *who* that is the result of substituting the CONT of the wh-phrase for that of the quantified NP subject *a student* in the propositional CONT of A's declarative sentence.

Ginzburg, Gregory, and Lappin (2001) describe an implemented system for dialogue interpretation that computes the CONT values for bare declarative clauses and sluiced questions by recording and ordering the feature structures of previous sentences in the sequence.[18] It then unifies the values of certain features in the CONT of the bare phrase with appropriate feature structures from previously interpreted expressions. The system uses syntactic and semantic information from a dialogue record to generate clausal interpretations for non-clausal phrases that are intended to be understood as expressing propositions or questions. Such a procedure requires a dynamic view of meaning on which the interpretation of a sentence is the result of the interaction of the lexically determined semantic content of its realized constituents with information built up incrementally from preceding utterances.

5.6 CONCLUSION

In this chapter I have introduced some of the basic concepts and issues of computational semantics. In particular, I have compared two alternative approaches to semantic representation. One translates the constituents of a syntactically analysed expression into the expressions of a higher-order logic, while the other represents both syntactic and semantic information through sequences of attribute-value pairs in a typed feature-structure graph. Both approaches use the PCM for specifying the syntax–semantics interface. This model requires that the syntactic structure and semantic representation of an expression be built up simultaneously at every level of constituency. It contrasts with the DFM on which the syntactic structure of a sentence is constructed prior to its semantic interpretation. I have argued that there is significant motivation for preferring the PCM to the DFM as an architecture for the syntax–semantics interface.

We have seen that it is possible to use underspecified semantic representations, like unordered sets of quantified NP interpretations in storage, in order to specify the

---

[18] This system combines Ginzburg and Sag's (2000) treatment of short answers and bare sluicing with some of the procedures for ellipsis resolution presented in Lappin and Gregory (1997).

meaning of an expression in terms of the meanings of its constituents through a relation which is not a function. Such representations permit us to compute the meaning of a sentence by means of procedures that are systematic but not compositional.

Finally, we moved from a static view that takes sentence meaning to be self-contained to a dynamic perspective on which the interpretation of a sentence depends upon the meanings of previous sentences in a discourse sequence. The dynamic approach requires the construction of a dialogue record in which the meanings of preceding sentences are accessible to the procedures that compute the interpretation of the current sentence in the sequence.

FURTHER READING AND RELEVANT RESOURCES

In addition to the sources cited in the text of the chapter, the following works provide useful background. The papers in Lappin (1996), and van Benthem and ter Meulen (1997), give an overview of current research in semantic theory. Lappin (2000*a*) offers a brief introduction to the history and central issues of formal semantics. For alternative theories of dynamic semantics the reader should consult Kamp (1981), Kamp and Reyle (1993), Groenendijk and Stokhof (1990, 1991), Groenendijk, Stokhof, and Veltman (1996), and Chierchia (1995). The FraCaS (Framework for Computational Semantics) Deliverables D1–D15 (1994–6) contain a comprehensive study of current issues in formal and computational semantics, as well as a review of the recent literature in these areas. These volumes are available from the Centre for Cognitive Science at the University of Edinburgh (www.cogsci.ed.ac.uk).

ACKNOWLEDGEMENTS

I am grateful to Christian Ebert and Ruslan Mitkov for helpful comments on earlier drafts of this chapter.

REFERENCES

Barwise, J. and J. Perry. 1983. *Situations and Attitudes*. Cambridge, Mass.: MIT Press.

Blackburn, P. and J. Bos. 1999. *Representation and inference for natural language*. MS. www.comsem.org/.

Bouma, G., R. Malouf, and I. A. Sag. 2001. 'Satisfying constraints on extraction and adjunction'. *Natural Language and Linguistic Theory*, 19, 1–65.

Chierchia, G. 1995. *Dynamics of Meaning*. Chicago: University of Chicago Press.

——and S. McConnell-Ginet. 1990. *Meaning and Grammar*. Cambridge, Mass.: MIT Press.

Chomsky, N. 1981. *Lectures on Government and Binding*. Dordrecht: Foris.

Chomsky, N. 1986. *Barriers*. Cambridge, Mass.: MIT Press.

——1995. *The Minimalist Program*. Cambridge, Mass.: MIT Press.

——1998. 'Minimalist inquiries: The framework'. MS. MIT.

Cooper, R. 1983. *Quantification and Syntactic Theory*. Dordrecht: Reidel.

Copestake A., D. Flickinger, and I. Sag. 1997. 'Minimal recursion semantics: an introduction'. MS. Stanford University.

Crouch, R. 1999. 'Ellipsis and glue languages'. In S. Lappin and E. Benmamoun (eds.), *Fragments: Studies in Ellipsis and Gapping*. Oxford: Oxford University Press, 32–67.

Dowty, D., R. Wall, and S. Peters. 1981. *Introduction to Montague Semantics*. Dordrecht: Reidel.

Frege, G. 1970. 'On sense and reference'. In Geach and Black (1970), 56–78. First pub. 1892.

Gazdar, G., E. Klein, G. Pullum, and I. A. Sag. 1985. *Generalized Phrase Structure Grammar*. Oxford: Blackwell.

Geach, P. and M. Black (eds.). 1970. *Translations from the Philosophical Writings of Gottlob Frege*. Oxford: Blackwell.

Ginzburg, J., H. Gregory, and S. Lappin. 2001. 'SHARDS: fragment resolution in dialogue'. In H. Bunt, I. van der Sluis, and E. Thijse (eds.), *Proceedings of the 4th International Workshop on Computational Semantics* (Tilburg), 156–72.

——and I. Sag. 2000. *Interrogative Investigations*. Stanford, Calif.: CSLI Publications.

Groenendijk, J. and M. Stokhof. 1990. 'Dynamic Montague Grammar'. In L. Kalman and L. Polos (eds.), *Papers from the Second Symposium on Logic and Grammar*, Budapest: Akademiai Kiado, 3–48.

————1991. 'Dynamic predicate logic'. *Linguistics and Philosophy*, 14, 39–100.

————and F. Veltman 1996. 'Anaphora, discourse, and modality'. In Lappin (1996), 179–213.

Jackendoff, R. 1997. *The Architecture of the Language Faculty*. Cambridge, Mass.: MIT Press.

Jacobson, P. 1996. 'The syntax–semantics interface in Categorial Grammar'. In Lappin (1996), 89–116.

Johnson, D. and S. Lappin. 1999. *Local Constraints vs. Economy*. Stanford, Calif.: CSLI Publications.

Kallmeyer, L. 1997. 'A syntax–semantics interface with synchronous tree description grammars'. In Kruiff, Morrill, and Oehrle (1997), 112–24.

Kamp, H. 1981. 'A theory of truth and semantic representation'. In J. Groenendijk, T. Janssen, and M. Stokhof (eds.), *Formal Methods in the Study of Language*. Amsterdam: Mathematical Center Tracts, 277–322.

——and U. Reyle. 1993. *From Discourse to Logic*. Dordrecht: Kluwer.

Kaplan, R. and J. Bresnan 1982. 'Lexical-functional grammar: a formal system for grammatical representation'. In J. Bresnan (ed.), *The Mental Representation of Grammatical Relations*. Cambridge, Mass.: MIT Press, 173–281.

Keenan, E. 1996. 'The semantics of determiners'. In Lappin (1996), 41–63.

——and D. Westerstahl 1997. 'Generalized quantifiers in linguistics and logic'. In van Benthem and ter Meulen (1997), 838–93.

Kempson, R., W. Meyer-Viol, and D. Gabbay. 2000. *Dynamic Syntax*. Oxford: Blackwell..

Kruiff, G.-J., G. Morrill, and R. Oehrle (eds.). 1997. *Proceedings of the Formal Grammar Workshop*. Aix-en-Provence: ESSLLI.

Lappin, S. (ed.). 1996. *The Handbook of Contemporary Semantic Theory*. Oxford: Blackwell.

——(2000a), 'An introduction to formal semantics'. In M. Aronoff and J. Rees Miller (eds.), *The Handbook of Linguistics*. Oxford: Blackwell, 369–93.

——(2000*b*), 'An intensional parametric semantics for vague quantifiers', *Linguistics and Philosophy*, 23, 599–620.

——and H. Gregory. 1997. 'A computational model of ellipsis'. In Kruiff, Morrill, and Oehrle (1997).

——and W. Zadrozny. 1999. 'Compositionality, synonymy, and the systematic representation of meaning'. MS. King's College, London and IBM. T. J. Watson Research Center, Hawthorne, NY.

Montague, R. 1974. 'The proper treatment of quantification in ordinary English'. In R. Montague, *Formal Philosophy*, ed. R. Thomason. New Haven: Yale University Press, 247–70.

Moortgat, M. 1996. 'Categorial type logics'. In van Benthem and ter Meulen (1996).

Morrill, G. 1994. *Type Logical Grammar*. Dordrecht: Kluwer.

Nerbonne, J. 1996. 'Computational semantics'. In Lappin (1996), 461–84.

Pereira, F. and M. Pollack. 1991. 'Incremental interpretation'. *Artificial Intelligence*, 50, 37–82.

——and S. Shieber. 1987. *Prolog and Natural-Language Analysis*. Stanford, Calif.: CSLI Publications.

Pollard, C. 1999. 'On "on": the syntax and combinatorial semantics of locative prepositions'. MS. Ohio State University.

——and I. A. Sag. 1987. *Information-Based Syntax and Semantics*. Stanford, Calif.: CSLI.

————1994. *Head-Driven Phrase Structure Grammar*. Chicago: CSLI Publications and University of Chicago Press.

——and E. J. Yoo. 1998. 'A unified theory of scope for quantifiers and wh-phrases'. *Journal of Linguistics*, 34, 415–44.

Postal, P. 1974. *On Raising*. Cambridge, Mass.: MIT Press.

Reyle, U. 1993. 'Dealing with ambiguities by underspecification: construction, representation and deduction'. *Journal of Semantics*, 10, 123–79.

Richter, F. and M. Sailer. 1997. *Underspecified semantics in HPSG*. MS. University of Tübingen.

Sag, I. A. 1997. 'English relative clause constructions'. *Journal of Linguistics*, 33, 431–83.

Shieber, S. and Y. Schabes. 1990. 'Synchronous tree-adjoining grammars'. *Proceedings of COLING*.

Steedman, M. 1996. *Surface Structure and Intepretation*. Cambridge, Mass.: MIT Press.

Tanenhaus, M. and J. Trueswell. 1995. 'Sentence comprehension'. In J. Miller and P. Elimas (eds)., *Speech, Language, and Communication: Handbook of Perception and Cognition*. San Diego: Academic Press, 217–62.

Trueswell, J., M. Tanenhaus, and S. Garnsey. 1994. 'Semantic influences on parsing: use of thematic role information in syntactic ambiguity'. *Journal of Memory and Language*, 33, 235–318.

van Benthem, J. and A. ter Meulen (eds.). 1997. *Handbook of Logic and Language*. Amsterdam: Elsevier.

Zadrozny, W. 1994. 'From compositional to systematic semantics'. *Linguistics and Philosophy*, 17, 329–42.

CHAPTER 6

DISCOURSE

ALLAN RAMSAY

ABSTRACT

When people use language, they produce and exchange sequences of connected sentences. The current chapter provides an overview of the devices that can be used to organize such extended discourses. Without such devices, which range from the use of explicit discourse connectives such as 'however' and 'moreover' to complex choices about the forms of referring expressions, large discourses become impossible to navigate.

6.1 DISCOURSE-LEVEL PHENOMENA

A **discourse** is an extended sequence of sentences produced by one or more people with the aim of conveying or exchanging information. Such extended sequences can be hard to follow: each sentence has to be understood and assimilated into a growing body of information, and this can only be done if the links between the current sentence and the previous discourse are clear. To take a simple example, consider the following short discourses:

(6.1) *a.* Arthur studied hard for the exam. He revised all the wrong things. He failed it.

      b. Arthur studied hard for the exam, but he revised all the wrong things, and hence he failed it.

      c. Arthur studied hard for the exam, and he revised all the wrong things, and yet he failed it.

(6.1*a*), (6.1*b*), and (6.1*c*) all report the same sequence of events. Arthur studied hard, he revised the wrong things, and he failed the exam. The only one that sounds right, however, is (6.1*b*). (6.1*a*) does not provide enough information for the hearer to work out the intended relations between the various sentences, and what (6.1*c*) says about them just does not seem to make sense. It seems as though in order to understand a discourse like this properly, we have to work out not just what events the speaker wants to bring to our attention, but also how he thinks they are related. In (6.1*a*) we are not given any information about these relationships. In (6.1*c*) the words 'and' and 'yet' are used to provide links between the component sentences. The trouble is that 'and' is a very neutral connective, and fails to express the fact that someone who studies hard for an exam would not normally be expected to revise the wrong things; and 'yet' suggests that the following sentence would normally conflict with the preceding one, whereas here it is clear that his choice of revision topic was a cause of his failure (as correctly indicated by the use of 'hence' in (6.1*b*)).

For larger discourses, it is often necessary to link not sentences but groups of sentences. In a chapter on discourse, for instance, it might be necessary to construct sections with headings like *Discourse Level Phenomena* and *Incremental Interpretation*, and then to break those sections into subsections and paragraphs. The links between these will typically be expressed at some length, with a chapter likely to begin with a summary explicitly explaining the links between the various sections, e.g. 'The chapter will introduce the theoretical background of anaphora and anaphora resolution and will look at the work done in the field over the last 35 years. In conclusion, future directions and issues that need further attention, will be discussed. Section 14.1 offers an introduction to anaphora and the concepts associated with it, . . .' The goal of the current chapter is to explore the various devices (choices of words and word order, forms of reference, use of explicit links) that are used to indicate the structure of an extended discourse and to explain the relationships between its parts, in other words to see how a discourse is broken into **segments** and how such segments are organized. The notion that discourses consisting of more than a single sentence are composed of related segments is not contentious: the aim of the current chapter is to explore the issues involved in identifying and relating them, where there is much less agreement.

6.2 INCREMENTAL INTERPRETATION

A discourse consists of a sequence of sentences produced by one or more people in order to convey or exchange information. There is surprisingly little difference, in terms of discourse structuring devices, between a discourse produced by a single speaker/author and one produced by several people in conversation or debate. The goals of such discourses vary considerably, but the mechanisms used for organizing them do not. Consider the following two examples:

(6.2) *a.* Sp1: Arthur studied hard for the exam, but he revised all the wrong things.
    b. Sp1: Arthur studied hard for the exam.
       Sp2: But he revised all the wrong things.

In (6.2*a*), Sp1 is reporting two facts of which he is aware, and is pointing out that the second one is unexpected in a context where the first is true. In (6.2*b*), Sp1 reports a single fact, and Sp2 reports another which is unexpected in a context where the one reported by Sp1 is true. The relationship between 'but he revised all the wrong things' and 'Arthur studied hard for the exam' is the same no matter who says each sentence. We will concentrate largely on single-speaker discourses in this chapter, and we will only look at cases involving several speakers where this makes a significant difference.

One reason why the number of speakers makes so little difference is that in any discourse there are multiple *participants*, with the person who is speaking at any given point having to bear the hearer's informational state in mind. For a discourse to work, the speaker and hearer must have very similar views of what it is about and how it is proceeding. It is tempting to say that discourses are underpinned by the participants' 'shared knowledge' or 'mutual knowledge', but these notions turn out to be very hard to work with. The problem is that you can only get very indirect information about what another person knows or believes. You can listen to what they say, and if you believe that they are telling the truth, or attempting to tell the truth, then you might be able to draw some conclusions about their beliefs (though even here, you could easily misunderstand them, so that although they were telling the truth as far as they knew it, your view of their beliefs could still be wrong). You can watch their behaviour: someone who puts mayonnaise in their coffee is likely to believe that what they are actually doing is putting cream in it, and if you see someone do this then you will probably draw the appropriate conclusions about their beliefs. And that is about it. It is unlikely that this is sufficient for obtaining anything which could reliably be referred to as shared or mutual knowledge.

It is clear, however, that participants in a discourse do have something in common. Consider the following:

(6.3)   Sp1: My husband bought me a Ferrari for Christmas.
        Sp2: I don't believe you.
        Sp1: He did, he really did.
        Sp2: Go on then, what colour is it?

Sp2 still does not believe that Sp1 has been given a Ferrari, so Sp1 and Sp2 cannot share the knowledge that it exists—if Sp2 believes that it does not, she can hardly know that it does. But if she does not believe it exists, how can she refer to it?

It seems safer to talk of each participant constructing a **discourse model**—an encapsulation of the events and objects mentioned in the discourse so far. If the discourse is progressing satisfactorily, the various models will be very similar. Furthermore, each participant will know that the others are constructing discourse models, and that they should all be similar. If there is some way of checking that they are not too divergent, then a set of individual models will serve to underpin a discourse in exactly the same way that mutual or shared knowledge would, without the problems that arise when you try to work out where such mutual knowledge could come from.

Discourse models have to be constructed incrementally. You cannot wait until the end of the discourse and then try to deal with it all at once—after all, in a conversation you may want to jump in even before the other person has finished their turn, and you can hardly decide to do this unless you are assimilating what they say as they go:

(6.4)   Martin: If you get to that point. Now move along about an inch
        Chris: To the right?
        Martin: to the right. Directly . . . horizontally across.
        (from the HCRC maptask corpus, dialogue 8, Anderson et al. 1991)

Chris could not possibly interrupt Martin at this point if he were not updating his view of what the discourse is about while Martin is speaking.

Interruptions of this kind can help the participants verify that their discourse models are reasonably similar. In situations where the participants are all present (either conversations or situations like lectures where only one person is talking, but everyone can see everyone else) there are various moves that the speaker *and hearers* can make to help with this task. The speaker can explicitly ask whether everything is alright—'you know what I mean', 'is that clear?', 'everybody happy?' More interestingly, the hearers will typically provide feedback to say that as far as they are concerned everything seems to be working: these 'back-channel cues' include things like making eye contact with the speaker and also making 'uh-huh' noises. So long as the speaker is receiving these, he will be reassured (possibly wrongly) that everything is proceeding satisfactorily. Hearers can indicate problems either by explicitly interrupting, or by choosing *not* to provide reassurance in this way.

In text, there is no opportunity for the hearer to respond, or choose not to respond, in this way. The author therefore has to be even more careful about providing enough information for the reader and writer to have a reasonable level of confidence that their discourse models are in step. We will see below that the way that referring expressions are constructed is particularly important in this respect.

6.3 REFERRING EXPRESSIONS AND DISCOURSE STRUCTURE

Discourses are generally *about* things. The various fragmentary discourses above are littered with references to objects which were either already known to the participants in the discourse, or were introduced in the discourse and then discussed further (for instance, the Ferrari in (6.3) was introduced in Sp1's first move, and explicitly referred to in Sp2's second one). Natural language provides a range of referring expressions for this task:

- **anaphors:** sometimes you want to refer to something which is mentioned in the current sentence. There are very specific reflexive pronouns ('himself', 'herself', ...) which are used for this purpose, and the rules that govern their use are driven very largely by syntactic constraints (Chomsky 1981; Pollard and Sag 1994).[1]
- **pronouns:** pronouns are used for referring to items that have been mentioned very recently, and which can be picked out on the basis of very simple characteristic properties.
- **definite NPs:** expressions like 'the man' or 'the pub in Maidenhead where we met your ex-husband' are often used for referring to entities which are known to all the discourse participants, and where furthermore all the participants know that the item in question fits the description provided. These expressions do not, however, behave entirely uniformly. 'Short' NPs, like 'the man', are rather like pronouns, in that they can only be successfully used in contexts where some man has been mentioned reasonably recently. Longer ones like the second example above, where the description fits exactly one item, can be used in almost any situation. Some definite NPs do not point to any particular object: in 'The first person to enter this room will get a nasty surprise,' the NP 'the first person to enter this room' does not refer to any particular individual. It can be hard to tell just on the basis of appearance whether a definite NP is being used referentially or not.

---

[1] There is scope for confusion here: the term 'anaphoric reference' is often used when referring expressions, of various kinds, are used for pointing at contextually salient items—see for instance Chapter 14 of this book. The referential properties of reflexive pronouns, however, seem to be governed by quite tight *syntactic* conditions: authors who are concerned with the specific characteristics of such reflexives tend to refer to these, and only these, as 'anaphors'.

- **referential aspect markers:** certain aspect markers seem to invite you to identify a particular time, in the same way that pronouns invite you to identify an individual. A simple past-tense sentence like 'He did the washing-up' can be interpreted in isolation; 'he was doing the washing-up', on the other hand, requires the hearer to work out when this took place.

In order to deal with these matters, there are two questions that need to be answered: (i) How do referring expressions work? (ii) Given that a single item could be referred to in several ways, what are the consequences of choosing one form rather than another? In particular, what are the consequences of choosing *not* to use a pronoun to refer to some highly salient item?

6.3.1 How do referring expressions work?

Every referring expression contains a description. For a pronoun like 'he', this description will be something like $male(X)\&salient(X)$, indicating that the item in question is male and has been recently mentioned. For a full NP like 'the tall man with a big nose' it will be more like $man(X)\&tall(X)\&\exists Y(nose(Y)\&big(Y)\&with(X,Y))$. The fact that pronouns always denote items that are contextually salient has to be marked as part of their semantics—'he' means 'the male individual who we are currently interested in'. Other definite NPs may happen to denote salient individuals, but this is not part of their meaning (and indeed, it is usually infelicitous to use a standard definite NP to refer to someone who is highly salient. It is better to say 'A man came into the room. He shouted a warning and then he pulled out a gun' than 'A man came into the room. The man shouted a warning and then the man pulled out a gun').

Such descriptions typically 'denote' items which are available in the discourse model—in other words, they point to something which is present in the discourse model. The dynamic semantic theories mentioned in Chapter 5 deal with this by building on Strawson's (1971) observation that a sentence like

(6.5) The present king of France is bald. (from Russell 1905)

is neither true nor false, but is instead 'inappropriate'. To formalize this notion, such theories take a meaning to be a relation between discourse states, or a function from discourse states to discourse states.[2]

---

[2] The terminology used differs from theory to theory—situation theory (Barwise and Perry 1983) talks of relations between situations, discourse representation theory (Kamp 1981; Kamp and Reyle 1993) talks of extending discourse representation structures, dynamic predicate logic (Groenendijk and Stokhof 1991) talks of extending models. To some extent these different terms reflect real differences between the theories, but the basic intuition is the same: an utterance is produced in a context, and the information available in that context is used for working out what follows from it.

In such theories, referring expressions are separated from the remainder of the interpretation, with the expectation that they will be dealt with before the utterance is assimilated into the discourse model. In classical DRT, this distinction is not as clear as it might be. According to Kamp and Reyle (1993), a 'discourse representation structure' (DRS) consists of a 'set of discourse referents' (corresponding to the set of individuals mentioned in the sentence being interpreted) and a set of 'conditions', which are propositions involving those referents. A DRS is taken to be true in a situation if the situation contains individuals which can be mapped onto the discourse referents in such a way as to make each of the conditions true. Thus the sentence

(6.6) Smith owns a book which Jones adores.

gives rise to the DRS in Fig. 6.1. This analysis shows that (6.6) would be true in a situation where there were people called Smith and Jones and a book which Smith owned and Jones adored. It fails, however, to capture the fact that the sentence is false if there is no such book, but meaningless or inappropriate in situations where there are no such people.

$$
\begin{array}{|c|}
\hline
X\ Y\ Z \\
\hline
\text{named}(X, \text{'Smith'}) \\
\text{named}(Y, \text{'Jones'}) \\
\text{book}(Z) \\
\text{owns}(X, Z) \\
\text{adores}(Y, Z) \\
\hline
\end{array}
$$

Fig. 6.1 DRT representation for (6.6)

Van der Sandt (1992) introduces 'presupposition triggers' to deal with these cases. A presupposition trigger is an embedded DRS which is explicitly marked, so that the DRS for (6.6) is as given in Fig. 6.2. We now have to find objects to make the α-marked

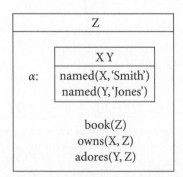

Fig. 6.2 Extended DRT representation for (6.6)

DRS true before we are allowed to even think about whether the sentence is true—if we cannot find suitable objects then we have to say that the sentence is uninterpretable in the current context.

Situation theory (Barwise and Perry 1983; Fenstad et al. 1987) deals with the matter by introducing 'situations' and 'situation-types'. A situation is simply a set of individuals and relations. If, for instance, a is a person called Elaine and b is a chair, then the situation s in which a is sitting on b at time t is specified as shown in Fig. 6.3.

$$\text{in } s\text{: at } t\text{: chair}(b); \text{yes}$$
$$\text{named('Elaine', } a); \text{yes}$$
$$\text{sitting-on}(a, b); \text{yes}$$

Fig. 6.3 A simple situation

The meaning $[\![U]\!]$ of an utterance U is then taken to be a relation between the situation u in which the utterance is produced,[3] the situation e which is being described, and some individual x. An utterance here may be a sentence or part of a sentence.

When someone assimilates an utterance, their task is to construct a new situation in which to interpret (or construct) the next utterance. This process of constructing a new situation from the old one corresponds to the development of a series of discourse models in section 6.2. In particular, the meaning of a definite NP such as 'the man' is the relation given in Fig. 6.4.

$$u[\![\text{'the man'}]\!]a, e \text{ iff. (i) } u \, [\![\text{'man'}]\!]a, e$$
$$\text{and (ii) there is at most one } b \text{ such that u } [\![\text{'man'}]\!]b, e$$

Fig. 6.4 The meaning of 'the man' in situation semantics

In other words, you can interpret the definite NP 'the man' in situations where there is exactly one man, and in these situations it denotes that man. The meaning of 'a man', on the other hand, is given by

$$u[\![\text{'a man'}]\!]a, e \text{ iff. } u[\![\text{'man'}]\!]a, e$$

Fig. 6.5 The meaning of 'a man' in situation semantics

So the definite NP places constraints on the situation u in which the phase is uttered, requiring it to contain exactly one man, whereas the meaning of the indefinite places constraints on the situation e being described, requiring it to contain at least one man.

---

[3] This situation contains a partial function c, called the 'speaker's connections', which connects referring expressions to individuals.

The meanings of complex phrases are built up from the meanings of their parts by showing how the interpretation of one constrains the utterance situation for the next. The meaning of a sentence made up of an NP and a simple intransitive VP, for instance, is given as follows:

$$u[\![S]\!]x, e \text{ iff. } u[\![NP]\!]a, e \text{ and } u[\![VP]\!]a, e$$

Fig. 6.6 Sentence meaning in situation semantics

If the NP is definite, then the sentence makes sense in utterance situations where there is some item *a* which satisfies the relevant description, and is true if the described situation fits the meaning of the VP with *a* playing the role specified for the subject of the VP; if the NP is indefinite, then the sentence makes sense in absolutely any utterance situation, and is true if the described situation contains some item *a* that satisfies the description and also makes the VP true.

Most dynamic theories of semantics deal with referring expressions in roughly this way. There are plenty of minor variations, and plenty of awkward cases, such as the use of definite NPs in ways that do not point to any particular individual (Kripke 1991) (as in 'He intends to marry the richest debutante in Dubuque' and 'The winner of this afternoon's race will be tested for drug abuse', where we know that there must be exactly one richest debutante in Dubuque (if there are any at all), and that there should be exactly one winner of the race; but we have no idea who they are). Nonetheless, it seems as though something along these lines is required for dealing with referring expressions.

6.3.2 Choices of referring expression

We can, then, refer to things that are available in the discourse model. In fact, we can generally refer to them in a number of ways:

(6.7) *a.* Sam arrived at the house. He had lost the key, and he knew Ruth would be furious. He rang the bell and waited despondently.

b. Sam arrived at the house. He had lost the key, and he knew Ruth would be furious. Sam rang the bell and waited despondently.

It seems as though we have a choice of how to refer to Sam in the final sentence—we can refer to him using 'he', as in (6.7*a*), or by using his name, as in (6.7*b*). Both are acceptable, *but they do not mean the same thing.* The choice of 'he' in (6.7*a*) indicates that the discourse is flowing smoothly, telling us about a single sequence of events which follow one after another after another. In (6.7*b*), on the other hand, it seems as though the decision to use his name rather than a simple pronoun marks a break in the story: we have been told about his situation, now we are about to find out what happened to him.

This break is also, of course, marked by the start of a new paragraph. This is very common: someone who has been referred to by the use of pronouns throughout one paragraph will very often be referred to by name at the start of the next, even though a pronoun would work perfectly well. In this situation, the use of the definite NP rather than a pronoun works in tandem with the typographical marker to indicate the start of a new segment of the discourse. In speech, there are no paragraph markers, and the use of a definite NP is a much stronger clue to the start of a new segment.

Planning referring expressions is a very delicate task. If you do not provide enough information to identify the item in question uniquely, then your hearer will not know what you mean (6.8a). If you provide more than is needed, your utterance will sound disfluent(6.8b).

(6.8)   a. *Mary bought a book by James Joyce and Susan bought a book by Barbara Cartland. John had already read the book.
  b. *Mary bought a book by James Joyce. John had already read the book by James Joyce.

Appelt (1985), Dale (1992), and Dale and Reiter (1995) discuss ways of computing referring expressions which provide just enough information to identify the required item, but not much has been said about *why* you should be careful not to provide more detail than is required.

If we consider the problem of keeping everyone's view of the discourse model more or less in step, it becomes clearer why minimal descriptions are desirable. Suppose that I say 'John had read the book.' We can construct a formal paraphrase of this as in Fig. 6.7.[4]

$$\exists A: \{instant(A)\&past(A)\}$$
$$\exists C: \{at(A, C)\}$$
$$\theta(C, agent, ref(\lambda D\,(named(D, John))))$$
$$\&\ read(C)\ \&\ \theta(C, object, ref(\lambda E(book(E))))$$

Fig. 6.7 'John read the book'

$ref(\lambda D(named(D,\ John)))$ and $ref(\lambda E(book(E)))$ here are the expressions which require to be anchored if the utterance is to be interpreted properly.[5] Chapter 5 discusses the role of such formal paraphrases in semantics: the example here is typical. Using θ-roles, or thematic roles, allows you to specify exactly how the various entitities mentioned in the utterance are involved in the reported event—agents are

---

[4] The notation $\exists x : \{R(x)\}\ P(x)$ in these paraphrases should be read as '$R(x)$ holds for some x such that $P(x)$ holds', and $\forall x : \{R(x)\}\ P(x)$ should be read as '$R(x)$ holds for every x such that $P(x)$ holds'. These formulae using 'restricted quantifiers' mean exactly the same as $\exists x(R(x)\ \&\ P(x))$ and $\forall x(R(x) \to P(x))$, whilst preserving some of the structure of the original English sentence.

[5] The use of the λ-calculus in semantics is discussed in Chapter 5, where its power as a means for combining the interpretations of parts of an utterance to obtain the meaning of a whole is considered at some length.

typically animate beings who intentionally bring the event about, actors are animate beings who bring events about without necessarily intending to do so, and so on. There is an extensive literature on the use of thematic roles. Fillmore (1968) used them in a discussion of various primarily syntactic phenomena, but his treatment was taken up enthusiastically by AI researchers looking for meaning representations, e.g. Bruce (1975). The idea that they are useful is extremely widespread, but there is little agreement about exactly how many such roles there are or what they signify. Dowty (1989, 1991) provides an insightful account of the issues involved.

If the hearer is to anchor $ref(\lambda E(book(E)))$ correctly, then the following must hold ($\Delta[H]$ denotes the hearer's discourse model, which we assume to be characterizable by a finite set of propositions), as in Fig. 6.8. This says that the hearer's view of the discourse model must support a proof that there is a book, but must only do so for one book (not that $\Delta[H]$ supports a proof that there is only one book, but that it only supports a proof of 'bookness' for one object. We can formalize the notion that there is only one such proof by using the deduction theorem to move between $\Delta[H] \vdash P$ ($\Delta[H]$ supports a proof of P) and $\Delta[H] \to P$ ($\Delta[H]$ implies P) (Ramsay 1999)).

$$\Delta[H] \to \exists X(book(X) \& \forall Y((\Delta[H] \to book(Y)) \to Y = X)$$

Fig. 6.8 Conditions on referring expressions

Now the more general the description D provided in the referring expression, the less likely it is that there will be only one item i for which $\Delta[H]$ supports a proof of $D(i)$. This means that by choosing very general descriptions—descriptions that provide minimal constraints on the objects that can satisfy them—you are sending out a strong message about your view of the discourse model. If I think that the word 'it' will suffice as a reference to some object, I am claiming that this is the only object for which my view of the discourse model supports a proof that it is both salient and neuter. I am thus making a very strong claim about the structure of my discourse model. If the discourse is proceeding smoothly, then this claim will also be true of your view. So making sure that your referring expressions say as little as possible about the entity you are trying to pick out provides your hearer with strong clues about your view of the discourse model, and hence provides him with good early warnings if his view has got out of step with yours.

6.4 Informational Structure

6.4.1 Theme and rheme

It has been widely noted that two sentences which report on identical circumstances can provide a different slant on what happened by making one item more or less prominent.

(6.9)   *a.* Ralph stole my bike.
        b. My bike was stolen by Ralph.

(6.10) a. I enjoyed the main course but I thought the dessert was awful.
        a. I enjoyed the main course but the dessert I thought was awful.

(6.11) a. I believe Betty is a fool.
        b. Betty, I believe, is a fool.

By moving things around, we can emphasize which entity the sentence is *about*. There are a number of mechanisms for doing this. You can simply passivize the sentence, as in (6.9), so that (6.9*a*) tells you what Ralph did, whereas (6.9*b*) tells you what happened to my bike. You can topicalize some item, so that the second part of (6.10*a*) is about what I thought, whereas the second part of (6.10*b*) is about the dessert. The syntactic processes underlying the relationship between (6.11*a*) and (6.11*b*) are less obvious, but it is equally clear that the effect is to switch attention from me to Betty.

Identifying which item a sentence is 'about' is fairly straightforward. Halliday (1985) defines the 'theme' of a sentence as its first phrase, with the 'rheme' being the remainder. So 'An old man sat on the bus' has 'an old man' as its theme, and 'On the bus sat an old man' has 'on the bus' as its theme. Any parser should be able to split a sentence into its theme and rheme. It is rather harder for a compositional approach to semantics to capture this distinction, since it requires you to treat things differently depending on where they appear. (It also seems very likely that the resulting formal paraphrases will be highly intensional, since the result will be that the interpretation of any sentence will be of the form *about(THEME, RHEME)*, where the semantic types of *THEME* and *RHEME* are unknown, but the consequences of *about(THEME, RHEME)* must include the fact that *RHEME* holds of *THEME*. It is hard to see how this can be accomplished without using some untyped intensional logic such as property theory (Turner 1987) or non-well-founded set theory (Aczel 1980; Aczel and Lunnon 1991). This is of some significance for computational treatments of language which want to *do* things with the theme and rheme, since reasoning with intensional logics is considerably more difficult than reasoning with propositional or first-order logics.)

The hardest thing of all, however, is to work out what the theme/rheme distinction signifies. If a computational system is to make any use of this notion, it must be able to do something using it which would not otherwise have been possible. Suppose, for instance, that (6.12) had the interpretation shown in Fig. 6.9.

(6.12)   A man kissed a woman.

Fig. 6.9 says that at some past time A there was a kissing event C involving some man D and some woman E in specified ways, and is exactly the kind of formal paraphrase discussed in Chapter 5.

$$\exists A : \{past(A)\}$$
$$\exists C : \{at(A, C)\}$$
$$\exists D : \{man(D)\}$$
$$\exists E : \{woman(E)\}$$
$$\theta(C, agent, D)\&kiss(C)\&\theta(C, object, E)$$

Fig. 6.9   Basic logical form for (6.12)

If we note that the theme of (6.12) is 'a man', then we can obtain a paraphrase that says that the sentence says something about this man, as in Fig. 6.10. This says that (6.12) is telling us something about some man D, and that what it is telling us is that he was involved as the agent in a past kissing event C involving some woman E. We can recover the consequences of the basic interpretation in Fig. 6.9 by using a meaning postulate that says that if $about(P, Q)$ is true then $Q.P$ is true, where $Q.P$ denotes the application of Q to P (so in the example P is the man and Q is the property of being involved in an appropriate kissing event: the topic:comment structure of (6.12) pulls these two apart, so that we know that we are being told something about a man, but then we have to put them back together to obtain the actual event report). This will immediately recover Fig. 6.9. It is, however, extremely unclear what can be done with Fig. 6.10 which was not possible on the basis of Fig. 6.9.

$$\exists A : \{past(A)\}$$
$$\exists C : \{at(A, C)\}$$
$$\exists D : \{man(D)\}$$
$$\exists E : \{woman(E)\}$$
$$about(\lambda F(F.D),$$
$$\lambda GG.\lambda H(\theta(C, agent, H))\&kiss(C)\&\theta(C, object, E))$$

Fig. 6.10   Logical form for (6.12) with theme and rheme marked

6.4.2   Topic and focus

There are other devices for achieving similar effects. If we consider intonation (or its typographical equivalents) then it is clear that sentences with the same words in the same order can be made to convey completely different messages:

(6.13)   *a.* I didn't steal your bike.
      b. I didn't steal your <u>bike</u>.
      c. I didn't steal <u>your</u> bike.
      d. I didn't <u>steal</u> your bike.

All of these have the same basic content—that I did not steal your bike. But (6.13*b*)–(6.13*d*) seem to carry an extra implication, that I stole something else of yours, or that I stole somebody else's bike, or that I did something else to your bike (Hajičová and Sgall 1984; Hajičová et al. 1986).

It seems as though the stress marker is used for dividing up the basic content into two parts, which are then consumed by the word 'not' to say something like: the basic proposition 'I stole your bike' is not true, but some other proposition, where some other expression has been substituted for the stressed phrase, is (interpretations where the meaning of the stressed part of an utterance is treated separately can be obtained compositionally, but as with the theme : rheme distinction, the fact that the semantic types of the components are unknown means that such interpretations must be couched in terms of intensional/higher-order logic (Pulman 1993; Ramsay 1994)).

There are other words that make similar use of stressed phrases (e.g. 'I only borrowed your bike' vs. 'I only *borrowed* your bike'). However, stress markers can also be used in situations where the sentence itself does not contain any such item.

(6.14)   *a.* She loves me.
      b. She loves *me*.
      c. She *loves* me.

All the examples in (6.14) report the fact that she loves me. But (6.14*b*) also says that it is *me* she loves, not you; and (6.14*c*) says that she does not hate me after all.

6.4.3 Presupposition

As noted in section 6.3, the correct use of referring expressions requires the speaker and hearer to each have some model of the discourse state which gets updated incrementally as the discourse proceeds. Referring expressions will not work unless each person's view of the discourse state supports a proof that there is something of the specified kind, and fails to support a proof that there is more than one such thing. Or so it seems:

(6.15)   *a.* The driver of the bus I came to work on must have been drunk.
      b. The driver of the spaceship I came to work on must have been drunk.

I can utter (6.15*a*) even if you know nothing about me or the way I get to work. Under those circumstances, the referring expressions 'the bus I came to work on' and 'the driver of the bus I came to work on' cause no problems, despite the fact that you cannot properly dereference them (since your discourse model will not contain a bus that I came to work on, and hence will not contain a driver of such a bus). (6.15b), on the other hand, sounds very odd. It seems that you will be prepared to 'accommodate' the existence of a bus that I came to work on, since this is quite a common way of getting to work (you can then cope with the driver of this bus, since common sense will tell you that any bus that brought me to work will indeed have a driver). You are less likely to do so for the spaceship that I came to work on because this is such an unlikely state of affairs.

Forcing the hearer to accommodate a referring expression in this way can be used for marking new information as uninteresting. Suppose I utter (6.15a) in circumstances where it is clear to both of us that the discourse model does not contain the fact I came to work by bus. Under these circumstances, you will accommodate this proposition; but at the same time you will also realize that I know you have accommodated it (and I will know that you have realized this).

You will only do this accommodation if the required proposition is unsurprising. So we see that after you have accommodated it, we will both know that it is (a) true and (b) unsurprising. In other words, by burying the fact that I came to work by bus in a referring expression, I have implicitly said that this information is not the core of what I want to say—after all, something which is marked as unsurprising is unlikely to be something that I really want to bring to your attention. (6.15a) is both more concise and better structured than

(6.15)   c. I came to work by bus. The driver must have been drunk.

There are a number of other ways of planting statements which assume that the discourse state supports some conclusion:

(6.16)   a. It was Dennis who stole it. [it-cleft]
         b. Whoever stole it must have got a big surprise. [headless relative clause]
         c. Martin regrets failing the exam. [lexical presupposition]
         d. Have you stopped beating your wife? [lexical presupposition]

Such 'presuppositions' can be used, just like the referring expressions in (6.15), to introduce new information whilst simultaneously marking it as being uninteresting. The examples in (6.16) have the same *content* as the ones in (6.17): but they sound much better, because the relative interest of the various components has been indicated by hiding the background information inside presuppositions.

(6.17)   a. Someone stole it, and that person was Dennis.
         b. Someone stole it, and they must have got a big surprise.
         c. Martin failed the exam, and he wishes he hadn't.
         d. Is it true that you used to beat your wife, but that you don't anymore?

Presuppositions have the curious property of making the same contribution to a sentence and to its exact opposite:

(6.18)   *a.* It was Dennis who stole it.
      b. It wasn't Dennis who stole it.
      c. He's stopped beating his wife.
      d. He hasn't stopped beating his wife.

(6.18*a*) and (6.18*b*) both presuppose that someone stole it, and (6.18*c*) and (6.18*d*) both presuppose that he used to beat her. This is hardly surprising, given what presuppositions are used for. Their primary function is to provide buried clues about what the speaker believes the discourse state to support, as happened with the provision of minimal descriptions in referring expressions in section 6.3.2; their secondary function is to provide background information buried inside an utterance. In both cases, they are supposed to denote some proposition without interrupting the main flow of the discourse. As such, it seems entirely reasonable for them to be treated outside the scope of any operators that govern the truth conditions of the embedding sentence.

There are, however, ways of blocking the presuppositional effects of these constructions:

(6.19)   *a.* If it was stolen then whoever stole it must have got a big surprise.
      b. No, Martin doesn't regret failing the exam, because actually he passed it.

(6.19*a*) is closely related to 'donkey sentences' such as

(6.20)   *a.* If a farmer owns a donkey he beats it.
      b. If there is a greatest prime number it must be odd.

The problem with (6.20*a*) is that there is nothing in the discourse state for 'he' or 'it' to refer to. You can utter (6.20*a*) without believing that there are any farmers or any donkeys, and certainly without any such individuals being present in the discourse state. For (6.20*b*), the situation is worse, since there certainly is *not* a greatest prime number. The key to these cases is that the conditional expression allows you to construct some sort of 'hypothetical' discourse state, and to deal with the presupposition/reference with respect to that state. I may not believe that it was stolen: but by contemplating the possibility that it was, I have made provision for the presupposition introduced by 'whoever stole it' in (6.19*a*), and likewise for the expectation that the discourse state contains a male individual and a neuter one in (6.20).

It is harder to see what is going on in (6.19*b*). Gazdar (1979) suggests that presuppositions should be regarded as 'defaults', to be taken into the discourse state so long as there is no reason why they should not be. Gazdar's proposal pre-dates the explosion of work on default logics which stemmed from Reiter (1980), McCarthy (1980), and Doyle (1970), and it is unclear how the default logic he proposes fits in with these later proposals. Nonetheless, his analysis does show why (6.19*b*) does not presuppose that Martin failed the exam, and it also hints at an alternative explanation of why (6.15*a*) is more acceptable than (6.15*b*) (namely that it is so unlikely that I would have travelled to work on a spaceship that this counts as grounds for rejecting the default).

6.4.4 Implicature

It is also possible to convey more than you say, simply by choosing your words carefully.

(6.21)   *a.* Some people left the party before midnight ($\rightarrow$ some of them didn't)
      b. I believe she loves me. ($\rightarrow$ I don't know that she does)
      c. Either you get up now or I won't take you to football. ($\rightarrow$ if you do get up I will take you)

In each of these cases, there is something stronger which the speaker could have said, but chose not to. Consider (6.21*b*). The speaker had a choice between saying 'I believe she loves me' and 'I know she loves me'. Both sentences are equally easy to say—they are, in Gazdar's (1979) terminology, 'expression alternatives'—but the speaker chose to say the weaker one. Why?

There is no reason to say less than you know (unless you are actively trying to deceive your hearer). If you want to convey some information to someone, you might as well give them everything you have. Suppose that Sp says 'I believe she loves me' to H, rather than saying 'I know she loves me'. Then H is entitled to assume that Sp was not in a position to say the stronger sentence, simply on the grounds that there is no point in saying less than you know. Crucially, however, Sp *would* know whether he knew that she loved him. So H is further entitled to assume that the second sentence is actually false—not just that Sp was not able to say 'I know she loves me', but that 'I don't know she loves me' is true.

This argument depends on the fact that (6.21*b*) concerns the speaker's own knowledge and belief, about which it is reasonable to suppose that he has fairly complete information. The same is true of (6.21*c*), where the speaker presumably knows that 'You will get up now and I won't take you to football' is false, since he knows what he will do under the relevant circumstances. In general, speakers know quite a lot about themselves. If a speaker says something weak about their own state of knowledge or about their own actions, their hearer can legitimately assume that any corresponding stronger expression alternative is false, since the speaker would (*a*) know that it was true if it was, and (*b*) say it if they knew it to be true.

Cases like (6.21*a*) are not so clearcut. Was Sp still at the party at midnight? If so, then he would indeed know whether everyone had left, and in that case H would again be entitled to infer from (6.21*a*) that some people had stayed later. If H knows that Sp left before midnight, then he is unlikely to draw this stronger conclusion. But if H does not know when Sp left, then he is likely to infer that some people did indeed stay on. The justification for this is that this pattern of reasoning is so entrenched that Sp should at least have the possibility of H's drawing this stronger conclusion in mind. If he does not want this to happen, then he can block it, by saying 'Some people, and possibly everyone, left the party before midnight'. Since Sp and H are both aware that H might leap to the stronger conclusion, and Sp chose *not* to stop him doing so, then Sp has, at least tacitly, said that he can.

This kind of argument depends heavily on reasoning about the participants' understanding of each other's knowledge and of the choices that are open to them. It may be better to think of this reasoning as being explicitly encoded in the rules of language use (Grice 1975), especially as computational treatments of knowledge and belief, which are based largely on Hintikka's (1962) observation that reasoning about knowledge and belief is in some ways similar to reasoning in modal logic, are as yet rather incomplete. This kind of reasoning about what the participants know and do not know (especially about their views of each other's knowledge) is crucial for understanding how dialogues work. The key to non-phatic use of language is that it enables you to exchange information about your current view of the world: how this works is discussed in much greater detail in Chapter 7 of this handbook.

6.5 DISCOURSE TREES

The discussion above shows a range of devices for structuring a discourse—for segmenting it, for indicating the speaker's attitude to each part of what he is saying, and so on. The question remains: what can we do with a discourse once we understand its structure which we could not have done otherwise?

6.5.1 Rhetorical structure theory

Mann and Thompson (1988) observe that extended discourses are made out of sequences of sentences *which are related to one another* (as noted in section 6.1). In order to understand a discourse properly, you have to understand these relations; and to generate a coherent discourse you have to specify them. It is, perhaps, more important for language generation systems to include a satisfactory treatment of the relations between parts of a discourse than it is for analysis systems. If an analysis system simply ignores all the discourse relations, it will probably still extract some useful information (an analysis system which ignored discourse relations would, for instance, correctly infer that Arthur studied hard, revised the wrong things, and failed the exam from each of the discourses in (6.1)). A generation system which failed to take these relations into account would be as likely to generate (6.1c) as (6.1b). It is therefore unsurprising that a great deal of work on discourse structure comes from people interested in generation—Mann and Thompson's work on 'Rhetorical structure theory' (RST) arises at least in part from Mann's (1983) earlier work on generation, and Dale's (1992) interest in constructing minimal referring expressions arises because of his awareness that if you generate over-elaborate referring expressions then your text will lack coherence.

RST provides a set of relations that can hold between pairs of sentences. Mann and Thompson (1988) discuss about twenty such relations, of which 'concession' is a good example. If P and Q are sentences such that the relation *concession*(P, Q) holds, then P describes some situation which is 'affirmed by the author' and Q describes some other situation which is 'apparently inconsistent with P but is also affirmed by the author'. In (6.1c), the use of 'yet' in the linked sentences 'he revised all the wrong things, and yet he failed it' indicates that 'he failed it' is a concession with respect to 'he revised all the wrong things'. The incoherence of (6.1c) then arises from the fact that these two are not in fact inconsistent.

There are a number of problems with RST, at least from a computational point of view. The most important is that the various relations are extremely difficult to formalize: the relation of 'background', for instance, is characterized by saying that *background*(P, Q) holds if Q facilitates the understanding of P. It is very unclear how you could make computational use of this notion. Furthermore, Mann (1999) notes that 'the set of relations is in principle open'. In other words, there may be relations between sentences which are not included in the given set, and which may indeed be entirely novel. It seems, in any case, that unless the relation between two sentences is explicitly marked by some term such as 'yet', 'hence', 'on the other hand', . . . then it is going to be extremely hard to determine what the connection between them is. Nonetheless, something like RST is required if our computational systems are going to extract all the information that is present in discourses that are presented to them and construct coherent discourses of their own.

6.5.2 Centering theory

Even if we cannot make use of all the information that is present, it is worth paying attention to the structure that rhetorical relations and some of the other devices described above impose on the discourse. In particular, in order to find out what some pronoun refers to it is essential to understand the dominance relations between sentences. Consider the following discourse (from Sidner 1983):

(6.22) Wilbur is a fine scientist and a thoughtful guy. He gave me a book$_i$ a while back which I really liked. It was on relativity theory and talks mostly about quarks. They are hard to imagine, because they indicate the need for elementary field theories of a complex nature. These theories are absolutely essential to all relativity research. Anyway, I got *it*$_i$ while I was working on the initial part of my research.

It is fairly easy to find the referent for 'it' in the last sentence of this discourse, despite the fact that its antecedent is quite some distance away. The key point here is that the discourse marker 'anyway' explicitly marks the end of a digression, indicating that the sentence containing it should be related to the sentence before the start of the digression. Exactly how this sentence can be found is rather unclear, but the notion that 'anyway' invites you to resume the discourse from some point at which it was interrupted suggests that discourses are tree shaped, rather than linear. The referent may have been last mentioned in a sentence which is some way back if you look at the discourse as a sequence; but this sentence is very close indeed to the current one if you think of the discourse as a tree.

Exactly how the cues described earlier in this chapter combine to show the structure of the discourse is still unclear—see Seville (1999) for an exploration of some possibilities. What is clear is that each utterance in a discourse makes various items available as potential referents. When you are faced with the task of choosing a referent for a pronoun, only those items which are offered as potential referents in accessible discourse states will be considered.

Grosz, Joshi, and Weinstein (1983, 1995) suggest that one of the links between a sentence and its predecessor[6] is through the relationship between the 'backward looking center' $C_b(U_n)$ of the current utterance U_n and the list $C_f(U_{n-1})$ of 'forward looking centers' of the previous one U_{n-1}. $C_b(U_n)$ corresponds roughly to the theme—Grosz, Joshi, and Weinstein (1995) talk of $C_b(U_n)$ being what U_n is 'about'—but it is not guaranteed to be the first phrase of U_n.

The forward-looking centers $C_f(U_n)$ of the utterance U_n are the items mentioned in U_n, ordered in some way which depends on a variety of factors such as the 'obliqueness' (Pollard and Sag 1994) of the role they are playing, their surface position in the sentence, and their own internal properties (e.g. pronouns might be ranked more highly than indefinite NPs). The backward-looking center of U_{n+1} is then taken to be the highest ranked member of $C_f(U_n)$ which is mentioned in U_{n+1}. This is slightly problematic unless we assume that U_n is the utterance that dominates U_{n+1} in the discourse tree, rather than the one that immediately precedes it: Hitzeman and Poesio (1998) quote the following extract from the *Guardian* in which the backward-looking center of (iv) comes from (i):

(6.23) (i) Joan Partington, aged 44 from Bolton, Lancashire, has six children. (ii) The eldest are [...]. (iii) A 13-year-old son has [...]. (iv) She was living [...]

In this case, nothing mentioned in (iv) appears in (ii) or (iii), so that if (iv) is to have a backward-looking center, as required by the theory, then the predecessor of (iv) must be (i).

Centering theory provides yet another way of tracking the structure of a discourse, by classifying the relations between connected utterances in terms of what happens to the backward-looking center:

---

[6] Remembering that the predecessor may *not* be the last sentence uttered: it is, rather, the immediate parent in the discourse tree.

- **Center continuation:** $C_b(U_{n+1})$ is the same as $C_b(U_n)$ and is the highest-ranked member of $C_f(U_{n+1})$ (and hence is likely to be $C_b(U_{n+2})$ as well).
- **Center retaining:** $C_b(U_{n+1})$ is the same as $C_b(U_n)$ but is not the highest-ranked member of $C_f(U_{n+1})$.
- **Center shifting:** $C_b(U_{n+1})$ is not the same as $C_b(U_n)$.

Clearly a discourse which consists of several center continuations followed by a center shift followed by several more center continuations (6.24a) will be more coherent than one which consists of nothing but center shifts (6.24b) (Strube and Hahn 1999 develop a more complex view of coherence based on cheap and expensive transition *pairs*, where 'Transition pairs hold for three immediately successive utterances').

(6.24)   *a.* David loved Elizabeth. He had known her for years. At one time he had disliked her. She, on the other hand, hated him. She had always thought he was a creep.

       b. David loved Elizabeth. She, on the other hand, hated him. He had known her for years. She had always thought he was a creep. At one time he had disliked her.

6.6 CONCLUSIONS

The relationships between the various devices summarized in this chapter are still very unclear. Are the notions of 'theme' and 'backward-looking center' different descriptions of the same phenomenon, or are they different phenomena which interact in subtle ways? Do RST and centering theory impose the same structure on a discourse or do they provide different views of it? Given that the decision not to use a pronoun can be used to mark the end of a discourse segment, should RST or centering theory pay more attention to the form which is used for referring expressions? There is evidently still plenty of work to be done.

Nonetheless, computational systems which aim to produce coherent extended discourses, or to take part in extended conversations, will have to pay attention to these issues. Systems which aim to understand such discourses can afford to be less careful about them, since it is possible to extract some information from a text even if you do not understand all its intricacies. Even so, an analysis system which does understand the significance of the various discourse structuring devices will get more out of a text than one that does not.

One major consequence of attempting to deal with these phenomena is that you inevitably end up working in a higher-order/intensional logic. Nearly all these devices express something about the speaker's attitude to what he has said—is it interesting, does it conflict with something that was said earlier, is it 'about' the same thing as the last utterance, …? These attitudes cannot in general be captured in a first-order framework. Progress in this area therefore depends, at least partly, in progress on the development of inference engines for the appropriate logics (Miller et al. 1991; Nadathur and Miller 1998; Ramsay 2001).

FURTHER READING AND RELEVANT RESOURCES

Textbooks on computational linguistics tend not to have very detailed sections dealing with the topics discussed in this chapter. The problem is that you cannot provide sensible treatments of this material until you have sound analyses of semantics (just as you cannot do semantics very well until you have a good syntactic framework, because the syntactic structure encodes so much of the meaning). Work in this area is thus still comparatively underdeveloped, and there is not yet a great deal of consensus about the right way forward. Grosz, Spärck Jones, and Webber (1986) contains a number of important early papers, and Allen (1995) has several useful sections, but most textbooks do not cover this material in any great depth. Walker, Joshi, and Prince (1998) provides a great deal of material about centering theory. The paper that introduced centering theory was only available as a hard-to-find technical report for many years, but is now available as Grosz, Joshi, and Weinstein (1995). Halliday (1985) is still probably the best place to look for a discussion of the theme : rheme distinction, and is also a good source for other insights into discourse structure, but there is no discussion of computational issues. Gazdar (1979) provides an excellent analysis of presupposition and implicature, bridging traditional philosophical discussions of these topics and trends in computational linguistics. The RST website (www.sil.org/linguistics/RST) is a comprehensive starting point for texts on rhetorical structure theory. There are, I am sure, plenty of other useful texts, but really the best thing to do in this area is to follow the original sources.

REFERENCES

Aczel, P. 1980. 'Frege structures and the notions of proposition, truth and set'. In J. Barwise (ed.), *The Kleene Symposium*. Amsterdam: North Holland, 31–9.

——and R. Lunnon. 1991. 'Universes and parameters'. In J. Barwise, J. M. Gawron, G. Plotkin, and S. Tutiya (eds.), *Situation Theory and its Applications*, ii. Stanford, Calif.: CSLI Publications.

Allen, J. 1995. *Natural Language Understanding*. Menlo Park, Calif.: Benjamin/Cummings.

Anderson, A., M. Bader, E. Bard, E. Boyle, G. M. Doherty, M., S. Garrod, S. Isard, J. Kowtko, J. McAllister, J. Miller, C. Sotillo, H. Thompson, and R. Weinert. 1991. 'The HCRC map task corpus'. *Language and Speech*, 34, 351–66.

Appelt, D. 1985. *Planning English Sentences*. Cambridge: Cambridge University Press.

Barwise, J. and J. Perry. 1983. *Situations and Attitudes*. Cambridge, Mass.: Bradford Books.

Bruce, B. 1975. 'Case systems for natural language'. *Artificial Intelligence*, 6, 327–60.

Chomsky, N. 1981. *Lectures on Government and Binding*. Dordrecht: Foris Publications.

Dale, R. 1992. *Generating Referring Expressions in a Domain of Objects and Processes*. Cambridge, Mass.: MIT Press.

——and E. Reiter. 1995. 'Computational interpretations of the Gricean maxims in the generation of referring expressions'. *Cognitive Science*, 19(2), 233–63.

Dowty, D. R. 1989. 'On the semantic content of the notion of "thematic role" '. In G. Chierchia, B. H. Partee, and R. Turner (eds.), *Properties, Types and Meaning*, ii: *Semantic Issues*. Dordrecht: Kluwer Academic Press, 69–130.

——1991. 'Thematic proto-roles and argument selection'. *Language*, 67, 547–619.

Doyle, J. 1970. 'A truth maintenance system'. *Artificial Intelligence*, 12(3), 231–72.

Fenstad, J. E., P.-K. Halvorsen, T. Langholm, and J. van Benthem. 1987. *Situations, Language and Logic*. Dordrecht: Kluwer Academic Publishers (SLAP-34).

Fillmore, C. 1968. 'The case for case'. In E. Bach and R. Harms (eds.), *Universals in Linguistic Theory*. Chicago: Holt, Rinehart and Winston, 1–90.

Gazdar, G. 1979. *Pragmatics: Implicature, Presupposition and Logical Form*. New York: Academic Press.

Grice, H. P. 1975. 'Logic and conversation'. In D. Davidson and G. Harman (eds.), *The Logic of Grammar*. Encino, Calif.: Dickenson.

Groenendijk, J. and M. Stokhof. 1991. 'Dynamic predicate logic'. *Linguistics and Philosophy*, 14, 39–100.

Grosz, B. J., A. Joshi, and S. Weinstein. 1983. 'Providing a unified account of definite noun phrases in discourse'. In *Proceedings of the 21st Annual Meeting of the Association for Computational Linguistics (ACL '83)* (Cambridge, Mass.), 44–50.

————1995. 'Centering: a framework for modeling the local coherence of discourse'. *Computational Linguistics*, 21(2), 175–204.

——K. Spärck Jones, and B. L. Webber (eds.). 1986. *Readings in Natural Language Processing*. Los Altos, Calif.: Morgan Kaufmann.

Hajičová, E. and P. Sgall. 1984. 'From topic and focus of a sentence to linking in a text'. In B. G. Bara and G. Guida (eds.), *Computational Models of Natural Language Processing*, Oxford: North-Holland, 151–63.

————and J. Vrbova. 1986. 'Topic, focus, and reference'. In E. Hajičová, J. Horecky, and M. Tesitelova (eds.), *Prague Studies in Mathematical Linguistics*, 9. Amsterdam: John Benjamins, 133–42.

Halliday, M. A. K. 1985. *An Introduction to Functional Grammar*. London: Arnold.

Hintikka, J. 1962. *Knowledge and Belief: An Introduction to the Two Notions*. New York: Cornell University Press.

Hitzeman, J. and M. Poesio. 1998. 'Long distance pronominalisation and global focus'. In *Proceedings of the 17th International Conference on Computational Linguistics (COLING '98/ACL '98)* (Montreal), 550–6.

Kamp, H. 1981. 'A theory of truth and semantic representation'. In J. Groenendijk, J. Janssen, and M. Stokhof (eds.), *Formal Methods in the Study of Language*. Dordrecht: Foris Publications, 277–322.

——and U. Reyle. 1993. *From Discourse to Logic: Introduction to Model Theoretic Semantics of Natural Language*. Dordrecht: Kluwer Academic Press.

Kripke, S. 1991. 'Speaker's reference and semantic reference'. In S. Davis (ed.), *Pragmatics: A Reader*. Oxford: Oxford University Press, 77–96. First pub. 1979.

McCarthy, J. 1980. 'Circumscription: a form of non-monotonic reasoning'. *Artificial Intelligence*, 13, 27–39.

Mann, W. C. 1983. 'An overview of the Penman text generation system'. *AAAI-83*, 261–5.

——1999. 'An introduction to rhetorical structure theory'. http://www.sil.org/linguistics/RST.

——and S. A. Thompson. 1988. 'Rhetorical structure theory: toward a functional theory of text organization'. *Text*, 8(3), 243–81.

Miller, D., G. Nadathur, F. Pfennig, and A. Scedrov. 1991. 'Uniform proofs as a foundation for logic programming'. *Annals of Pure and Applied Logic*, 51, 125–57.

Nadathur, G. and D. Miller. 1998. 'Higher-order logic programming'. In D. M. Gabbay, C. J. Hogger, and J. A. Robinson (eds.), *Handbook of Logic in Artificial Intelligence and Logic Programming*, v: *Logic Programming*, Oxford: Clarendon Press, 499–590.

Pollard, C. J. and I. A. Sag. 1994. *Head-Driven Phrase Structure Grammar*. Chicago: Chicago University Press.

Pulman, S. G. 1993. 'Higher order unification and the semantics of focus'. Technical Report, Cambridge Computer Laboratory, University of Cambridge.

Ramsay, A. M. 1994. 'Focus on "only", and "not"'. In Y. Wilks (ed.), *Proceedings of the 15th International Conference on Computational Linguistics (COLING '94)* (Kyoto), 881–5.

——1999. 'Does it make any sense? Updating = consistency checking'. In K. Turner (ed.), *The Semantics–Pragmatics Interface from Different Points of View*. London and Amsterdam: Elsevier.

——2001. 'Theorem proving for untyped constructive λ-calculus: implementation and application'. *Logic Journal of the Interest Group in Pure and Applied Logics*, 9(1), 89–106.

Reiter, R. 1980. 'A logic for default reasoning'. *Artificial Intelligence*, 13(1), 81–132.

Russell, B. 1905. 'On denoting'. *Mind*, 14, 470–93. Reprinted in D. Davidson and G. Harman, *Semantics of Natural Language*, Dordrecht: Reidel, 1977.

Seville, H. 1999. 'Experiments with discourse structure'. *3rd International Workshop on Computational Semantics* (Tilburg), 233–47.

Sidner, C. 1983. 'Focusing in the comprehension of definite anaphora'. In M. Brady and R. C. Berwick (eds.), *Computational Models of Discourse*. Cambridge, Mass.: MIT Press, 331–71. Reprinted in B. J. Grosz, K. Spärck Jones, and B. L. Webber (eds.), *Readings in Natural Language Processing*. Los Altos, Calif.: Morgan Kaufmann, 1986.

Strawson, P. F. 1971. 'Identifying reference and truth-values'. In D. D. Steinberg and L. A. Jakobovits (eds.), *Semantics: An Interdisciplinary Reader in Philosophy, Linguistics and Psychology*. Cambridge: Cambridge University Press, 86–99. First pub. 1964.

Strube, M. and U. Hahn. 1999. 'Functional centering: grounding referential coherence in information structure'. *Computational Linguistics*, 25(3), 309–44.

Turner, R. 1987. 'A theory of properties'. *Journal of Symbolic Logic*, 52(2), 455–72.

van der Sandt, R. 1992. 'Presupposition projection as anaphora resolution'. *Journal of Semantics*, 9, 333–77.

Walker, M. A., A. K. Joshi, and E. F. Prince (eds.). 1998. *Centering Theory in Discourse*. Oxford: Oxford University Press.

CHAPTER 7

PRAGMATICS AND DIALOGUE

GEOFFREY LEECH
MARTIN WEISSER

ABSTRACT

This chapter introduces the linguistic subdiscipline of pragmatics (the investigation of meaning in context) and shows how this is being applied to the development of spoken dialogue systems—currently perhaps the most important applications area for computational pragmatics. Sections 7.1–7.5.5 trace the history of pragmatics from its philosophical roots, and outline some key notions of theoretical pragmatics—speech acts, illocutionary force, the cooperative principle, implicature, relevance. Since pragmatics is concerned with meaning, most of its basic terms are conceptual: intention, belief, inference, and knowledge. Sections 7.6–7.9 turn to the application of pragmatics to dialogue modelling, especially the development of spoken dialogue systems intended to interact with human beings in task-oriented scenarios such as providing travel information. One major illustration of this is the application of speech act theory in the analysis and synthesis of service interactions in terms of dialogue acts (utterance units defined as having a functional role in the dialogue).

7.1 What is Pragmatics?

Thirty years ago, pragmatics was a fledgling branch of linguistics. In the 1970s it gained in importance, and remains an important subdiscipline within linguistics, with its own journals, handbooks, and international association.[1]

Only recently has pragmatics begun to be a major focus of research in computational linguistics, mainly because of its relevance to the development of **spoken dialogue systems** (SDSs), that is, computer systems designed to engage in purposeful dialogues with human beings. This chapter will focus on computational pragmatics in the context of spoken dialogue, although, on a more general level, pragmatics also applies to written language communication: for example, to the disambiguation of meaning (see Chapter 13) and the assignment of reference to personal pronouns such as *she* and *they* (see Chapter 14).

Pragmatics is the branch of linguistics which seeks to explain the meaning of linguistic messages in terms of their context of use. It is seen as distinct from semantics, which investigates meaning in a more abstract way, as part of the language system irrespective of wider context. In semantic terms an **utterance**[2] can therefore often be ambiguous, whereas the contextual setting in which the utterance occurs, combined with its intonation, would—in most cases—serve to disambiguate its function.

One way to differentiate pragmatics from semantics is to say that in pragmatics, meaning is a triadic relation: '*Sp* means *x* by *y*'; while in semantics meaning is a dyadic relation: '*y* means *x*.' This can be illustrated by the frequently quoted example of the utterance 'It's cold in here.' If we interpret this utterance on a purely semantic level, it simply states a *literal* or face-value meaning, i.e. the fact that the temperature in the place where the utterance has occurred is low. However, given the context that there are at least two people in the room at the time of the utterance and that the window is open, the same utterance can additionally take on a different meaning, depending on the context and the speaker's intention. For example, if the social relation between the interlocutors is appropriate, it can take the meaning that Sp wants H to close the window: in effect, it is a request. But the relationship between the two interlocutors is by no means the only personal factor that may influence the interpretation of the utterance. The willingness and ability of the hearer to cooperate with the speaker's request, for example, are amongst many other factors that can affect the meaning.

Pragmatics in general is concerned with questions such as:

---

[1] The International Pragmatics Association, with headquarters in Belgium, runs an annual international conference and publishes a quarterly journal, *Pragmatics*.

[2] The term *utterance* will be used here in the very general sense of 'a short piece of dialogue with a characterizable pragmatic function'.

- What does a listener suppose a speaker to intend to communicate by a given message? And how is this meaning decoded?
- What persons, entities, etc. does the message refer to?
- What background knowledge is needed to understand a given message?
- How do the beliefs of speaker and hearer interact in the interpretation of a given message, or of a given dialogue exchange?
- What is a relevant answer to a given question?

Pragmatics originated in philosophical thought (e.g. in the work of Charles Morris, J. L. Austin, John Searle, and H. P. Grice)[3] and may still show a tendency towards academic abstraction which makes it difficult to adapt to concrete computational applications. In the following sections, we will first give a brief overview of some of the theoretical constructs that form the basis of modern-day pragmatics. We will then go on to show how and why computational pragmatics differs from 'linguistic' pragmatics, and how pragmatics contributes to the computational analysis of dialogues, with particular respect to SDSs.

7.2 Speech Acts and Illocutionary Force

7.2.1 Speech acts

One of the philosophical foundations of pragmatics can be found in the notion of **illocutionary acts** (often simply called **speech acts**) as developed by J. L. Austin and J. R. Searle. The idea behind a speech act is that meaning can be explained in terms of action, rather than in terms of concepts like reference and truth conditions. Most philosophical approaches to language since Aristotle had always assumed that to make an utterance is almost by default to state something that can be specified as either true or false. Austin disputes this, saying that

One thing, however, that it will be most dangerous to do, and that we are very prone to do, is to take it that we somehow *know* that the primary or primitive use of sentences must be, because it ought to be, statemental or constative, in the philosopher's preferred sense of simply uttering something whose sole pretension is to be true or false and which is not liable to criticism in any other dimension.   (Austin 1962: 72)

---

[3] See Leech and Thomas (1990: 173–80) for a brief survey of the development of pragmatics.

He makes a distinction between the above-mentioned *constative* utterances and ones that he refers to as **performatives**, such as 'I apologize': utterances that do not state anything about the world, but rather constitute verbal actions. Such utterances may contain an overt *performative verb*, such as *apologize* above, or else the performance of an action may remain implicit. For example, a *request* such as 'Could you post this letter?' is an utterance which acts as an attempt to bring about some change through action by the addressee.

According to Austin, such utterances can be characterized in terms of three kinds of verbal act: locution, illocution, and perlocution. The notion of *locution* here is closest to the literal use of an utterance with a particular sense, whereas *illocution* relates to what the speaker (Sp) intends to perform, and *perlocution* relates to what is achieved—including uptake by the hearer (H).[4] Let us go back to our earlier example—the utterance 'It's cold in here'—to see how we can analyse it according to Austin's principles. The locution is simply the words used to form the utterance and the grammatical *form* of the utterance expressing a proposition. As for the **illocution- ary force** or intended meaning behind it, we can assume that, given the context of the open window, Sp wants to have H close the window, which would indicate that the illocution or pragmatic *function* is that of a directive (or request). The perlocutionary effect of the utterance is then twofold, depending on (*a*) whether H understands the utterance[5] of Sp and (*b*) if so, whether or not H is actually willing to comply with the request.

This simple example shows the different conceptual levels on which meaningful action works to explain the creating and disambiguation of meaning. It also illus- trates the key problem of relating pragmatic (or illocutionary) force to the syntax and semantics of an utterance. As we have just seen, syntactically the utterance appears to be a statement, but illocutionary force and perlocutionary effect realize it as a directive or request, showing an indirect relation between form and function, or between grammar and intended meaning. Perlocutionary effect has on the whole been neglected in academic pragmatics, since it lies strictly outside the domain of language and its interpretation. In computational pragmatics, however, it cannot be ignored, as it is the key to how one interlocutor responds to another in SDSs.

The perlocutionary component of the utterance also highlights the importance of mental constructs in pragmatics: both Sp and H have certain *beliefs* that affect their *intentions* or *goals* in an exchange, as well as the effect of utterances. We shall see in section 7.8.3 below how this affects issues in computational pragmatics.

---

[4] Following a common practice in pragmatics, we will refer to the speaker as Sp and the hearer as H. These terms Sp and H are here used in a deliberately general sense, to identify the originator(s) and addressee(s) of an utterance, whether in speech or in writing, and whether representing human or non- human agents.

[5] This description is slightly different from Austin's model, as he sees H's understanding of the mes- sage or *uptake* as part of the illocutionary act (see Austin 1962: 117).

Another aspect of Austin's theory is that certain conditions, which he terms **felicity conditions**, have to be fulfilled every time we perform a verbal action. For example:

(A.1)   There must exist an accepted conventional procedure having a certain conventional effect, that procedure to include the uttering of certain words by certain persons in certain circumstances, and further,

(A.2)   the particular persons and circumstances in a given case must be appropriate for the invocation of the particular procedure invoked.

(B.1)   The procedure must be executed by all participants both correctly and

(B.2)   completely.   (Austin 1962: 15–16)

As we see, Austin's understanding of verbal actions reflects the idea of explicitly achieving those actions according to convention rather than by **implication**.

In following Austin, Searle formalizes illocutionary acts as 'rule-governed intentional behaviour' (Searle 1969: 16) and claims that:

the semantic structure of a language may be regarded as a conventionalized realization of a series of sets of underlying constitutive rules , and that speech acts are acts characteristically performed by uttering expressions in accordance with these sets of constitutive rules. (Searle 1969: 37)

Four types of rules serve to define different illocutionary acts in different ways (see Searle 1969: 57, 62):

(7.1)   Propositional act   the propositional content
        Preparatory condition(s)   conditions that have to hold in order for the speech act to be possible, e.g. for something to have happened or be possible to happen or to be desirable
        Sincerity condition   beliefs or intentions of Sp
        Essential condition   what the speech act 'counts as' in illocutionary terms

He also proposes a typology for speech acts, here summarized according to Searle (1979):

(i)   *assertives* commit Sp to the truth of some proposition (e.g. stating, claiming, reporting, announcing);

(ii)   *directives* count as attempts to bring about some effect through the action of H (e.g. ordering, requesting, demanding, begging);

(iii) *commissives* commit Sp to some future action (e.g. promising, offering, swearing to do something);

(iv)   *expressives* count as the expression of some psychological state (e.g. thanking, apologizing, congratulating);

(v)   *declarations* are speech acts whose 'successful performance . . . brings about the correspondence between the propositional content and reality' (e.g. naming a ship, resigning, sentencing, dismissing, excommunicating, christening).

7.3 H.P. GRICE'S COOPERATIVE PRINCIPLE

Another of the major philosophical foundations of computational pragmatics is H. P. Grice's CP (**Cooperative Principle**), which holds that conversation takes place on the assumption (barring evidence to the contrary) that the interlocutors are being cooperative in contributing to the general goals of the conversation. The CP can be understood to apply to communication in general. It has four constituent subprinciples, which are expressed in the form of maxims to be followed by Sp (the following is a simplification of Grice 1975):

1. **Maxim of Quantity** (or informativeness): give the right amount of information;
2. **Maxim of Quality** (or truthfulness): try to make your contribution one that is true;
3. **Maxim of Relation**(or relevance): be relevant;
4. **Maxim of Manner**: avoid obscurity or ambiguity; be brief and orderly.

The crux of Grice's explanatory framework is that, since in general we can assume that the CP is being observed, apparent departures from the CP can be accounted for on that basis. An apparent breach of truthfulness, for example, may be due to wilful lying, or to a mistake—or it may be because Sp is trying to get a special point across, e.g. through metaphor or irony. The last case is said to be interpreted by **implicature**—or pragmatic implication (see section 6.4.4). An implicature is weaker than logical implication in that it is *defeasible*: that is, it can be rejected if other evidence contradicts it. From H's point of view, this is where **inference** (see section 7.5.4 below) plays a crucial role. Thus if H perceives that Sp is not expressing a literal or face-value meaning in accordance with the CP, H can assume that an alternative interpretation is intended. H therefore attempts to infer (from contextual information, the literal meaning of the utterance, and general principles of communication such as the CP) an interpretation that would make S's utterance rational and cooperative, and thus arrive at a conclusion about what Sp intended to communicate.

Here are examples of the four maxims at work.

1. *Maxim of Quantity*

If someone says

(7.2) Maggie ate some of the chocolate

it will generally be inferred that the speaker believes that:

(7.3) Maggie did not eat all of the chocolate.

The reasoning is that if Maggie had been noticed eating all the chocolate, the speaker would have been informative enough to say so. Note that (7.2) does not entail (7.3), because it is quite possible to truthfully assert the conjunction of (7.2) and (7.3):

(7.4)   Maggie ate some of the chocolate—in fact, she ate all of it.

2. *Maxim of Quality*
If someone says, talking about an expensive dental treatment,

(7.5)   That'll cost the earth

it will generally be assumed that the speaker is not telling the truth (because the proposition (7.5) is not believable). However, the message conveyed will be a proposition closely related to (7.5), in that (7.5) implies it:

(7.6)   That'll cost a very large amount.

3. *Maxim of Relation*
In the following exchange,

(7.7)   Child: Can I watch TV?
        Parent: It's bath time, Rosy.

the parent's reply apparently does not answer the child's question, and therefore breaks the Maxim of Relation. However, even a child can work out the missing part of the message: 'Because it's bath time, there is no time to watch TV, and therefore you cannot.'
4. *Maxim of Manner*
If someone, instead of (7.8), says (7.9):

(7.8)   Are you ready?

(7.9)   I am asking you whether you are ready or whether you are not ready.

it is obvious that the speaker is not choosing the quickest way of asking for the desired piece of information. This longwindedness will generally be assumed to convey an implicature—probably the implicature that the hearer is being unhelpful in withholding the information concerned.

7.4 COLLABORATION

Grice's idea of cooperation seems to be consistent with more recent research in both conversational analysis (CA) and linguistics that stresses the importance of interlocutors' interactive collaboration in constructing the meaning of exchanges between them (cf. Schegloff 1996; Ono and Thompson 1996). Ono and Thompson demonstrate how this kind of collaboration works even on the level of syntax, by giving examples of participants completing each other's sentences or recovering and repairing them. This clearly does not mean that the CP cannot be broken: there are many occasions where Sp and H do not cooperate in terms of the maxims, and indeed it is arguable that such concepts as informativeness, truthfulness, and relevance are matters of degree, rather than absolute quantities.

7.5   Conceptual Representations

From H's point of view, pragmatics deals with the communicative effects that an utterance can have, whether Sp intended them or not. However, communication takes place on the understanding that speaker and hearer share beliefs or assumptions. Therefore one of the key issues relevant to an understanding of pragmatics is what beliefs or assumptions both Sp and H need to bring into play when producing and interpreting an utterance. Pragmatics requires that propositional attitudes such as 'Sp intends x' and 'H assumes that y' be represented as part of Sp's or H's meaning.

7.5.1   Intentions or goals

On the part of Sp, there is usually at least one intention or goal behind the production of an utterance. This goal (or set of goals) underlies the illocutionary force of the utterance, for example whether it is intended to inform, to request, to thank, or to offer. However, while the intentions of a speaker may sometimes be relatively easy to understand, in some cases Sp may not manage to convey his or her intentions successfully to the hearer. Sperber and Wilson (1995: 34) cite the following potentially ambiguous example of a dialogue:

(7.10)   *Peter*: Do you want some coffee?
         Mary: Coffee would keep me awake.

As this example is presented, it is not clear whether Mary intends to accept Peter's offer, implying that coffee would enable her to stay awake a little longer, or whether she is refusing his offer because she would have trouble getting to sleep later on. Although this may be a constructed example and in real life Mary could (or would) disambiguate her reply by prefixing it with something like either 'Thanks' or 'No, thanks', it could conceivably occur in natural language and therefore presents a problem for interpretation. The intended meaning of Sp and the interpretative meaning of H may not correspond: that is, misunderstandings can (and often do) occur.

7.5.2 Beliefs and assumptions

Pragmatics is concerned with interlocutors' beliefs and assumptions about the world, and this includes beliefs about the other interlocutor(s), including *their* beliefs and intentions. For example, a speaker who makes a request will usually believe that there is a chance that H will comply with the request. In communication, there are *n*th order beliefs, just as there are *n*th order intentions. For example, a second-order belief is normally a belief about someone else's beliefs. A third-order belief can bring in the mutuality of beliefs between Sp and H, and potentially leads to infinite regress, e.g. Sp believes that H believes that Sp believes . . . The belief systems attributed to interactants in a dialogue are often complex, and cannot be ignored in computational pragmatics (see Ballim and Wilks 1991).

7.5.3 Knowledge

Knowledge can be seen as a specially privileged type of belief, a belief that is sanctioned by logic or authority or experience to be a fact. In pragmatic terms, knowledge may be shared by interlocutors, or else may be confined to one interlocutor or the other. *Mutual* or *shared* knowledge is often discussed as a key category in explaining communication—it is knowledge which is not only shared by the interlocutors, but known by each interlocutor to be shared by the other interlocutor. However, note that this so-called 'knowledge' is fallible, as there is ultimately no guarantee that both interlocutors actually do share the same knowledge. Hence it is better to think of 'assumed mutual knowledge' rather than 'mutual knowledge'. Sperber and Wilson (1995: 17–21, 40–2) think more realistically in terms of 'mutually manifest assumptions' which interlocutors share in a 'mutual cognitive environment'.

7.5.4 Inference

If *intention* is the key to meaning from the point of view of Sp, *inference* is a key concept from the point of view of H, the addressee. Inference is here understood as the use of reasoning to derive a new belief from a set of existing beliefs. Note that reasoning in pragmatics often deviates from classical deductive logic: it is more like the common-sense practical reasoning which human beings use in everyday situations. For example, we may conclude, noticing that the streets are wet, that it has been raining. The classical law of Modus Ponens here appears to apply in the reverse order (this example and the subsequent discussion are adapted from Bunt and Black 2000: 12–13):

(7.11)   If it has (recently) been raining, the street is wet

(7.12)   It has (recently) been raining

Therefore

(7.13)   The street is wet

In practical reasoning, conclusion (7.13) is our starting point, and in a classically invalid move, we derive from it premise (7.12), which may be characterized as the hypothesis we use to explain what we observe. There could, of course, be other explanations, such as flooding or burst water pipes, but rain is the most obvious one. This kind of reasoning has been formulated in terms of *abductive logic* (where the reasoner is 'permitted to assume additional premisses in order to reach a conclusion deductively'—ibid.). Another way of formulating it is in terms of *default logic*, using rules of the form: 'If p then q, unless there is evidence that not-q' (ibid.). In the case of wet streets, the hypothesis that it is raining is the default assumption we make in normal circumstances. This kind of logic can be readily applied to Grice's implicatures. For example, the assumptions of the CP (see section 7.3), that speakers are being truthful, informative, and relevant, is a useful default assumption which may nevertheless be invalidated by contrary evidence. Thus the addressee, while not having direct access to the intentions of Sp, can infer them from what Sp says, as well as from additional 'givens', notably contextual information and general principles of communication, especially the CP.

7.5.5   Relevance

The third maxim of the CP, 'be relevant', although vague in Grice's original formulation, has been formulated in detail and elevated to the major explanatory principle of pragmatics by Sperber and Wilson (1995), for whom it renders the other three maxims of Grice's CP unnecessary. Sperber and Wilson's **Principle of Relevance** (1995: 125) explicates the way the interpreter makes sense of what is said, by a trade-off between largeness of *contextual effects* and smallness of *processing effort*. By contextual effects is meant some addition to the addressee's set of assumptions ('fresh information') derived from the utterance in relation to its context. By processing effort is meant the amount of mental effort, notably in inference, the addressee has to expend in order to arrive at the interpretation. To revert to our stock example, 'It's cold in here' brings no contextual effects if it is interpreted as a mere remark about the low temperature, which is presumably already apparent to the addressee. Hence, in this case, the interpretation as a request to close the window will be more relevant in terms of contextual effects, but will be less relevant in so far as a less direct interpretation costs greater processing effort to figure out the meaning. Perhaps the request interpretation will win out, because the lack of contextual effects does not even justify the small processing effort needed to arrive at the bare assertion about temperature. In Grice's terms, this would be a breach of the Maxim of Quantity (the remark would be uninformative) leading to an implicature (Sp wants the window closed).[6]

An alternative formulation of *relevance* is that of Leech (1983: 94–6), who sees it as the contribution an utterance makes to the (assumed) goals of Sp (whose goals may include helping to satisfy the goals of H). Thus, in this case, H is able to arrive at the request meaning, by hypothesizing that Sp wishes to accomplish a goal: that of raising the temperature.

7.6 DIALOGUE IN COMPUTATIONAL PRAGMATICS

To understand how computational pragmatics relates to dialogue, we have first to ask the question: 'What makes computational pragmatics different from "theoretical" pragmatics?' This, in turn, invites the question: 'Why is the dialogue between two or more human interlocutors likely to be different from that between humans and computers?'

7.7 ORDINARY DIALOGUE

We may here term 'ordinary' dialogue the kind of dialogue that we as humans engage in every day, where two or more people communicate with one another, either face to face, by telephone or even in writing. This is the kind of dialogue that is normally the subject of the study of (linguistic) pragmatics, discourse analysis, and conversational analysis. Ordinary dialogue is essentially unrestricted in the range and complexity of topics and goals addressed, although constrained by such factors as the amount of knowledge or communicative ability the interlocutors bring to it. We can say that there is no restriction on a dialogue's *domain* (the kind of topic or subject matter it deals with) or *activity type* (the genre of activity to which the dialogue contributes).

Ordinary dialogue may also be *goal oriented*, i.e. intended to achieve certain pre-

---

[6] Note that this implicature is not arbitrary, but is derivable via some general assumption to the effect that 'If Sp mentions some unpleasant circumstance obvious to H, Sp probably wants some action performed to mitigate that circumstance'. Such a belief would help to explain other utterances such as 'Your coat's on the floor' or 'The TV's rather loud.'

determined aims, as in our example 'It's cold in here,' but most of it comes under the heading of 'casual conversation', where goals can be shifting and ill defined. Ordinary dialogue moreover typically involves *social interaction*, which is very different from the kind of interaction that we normally wish to have with a computer.

7.8 COMPUTATIONAL DIALOGUE

Dialogue involving computers differs in many respects from ordinary dialogue, as it is subject to a number of specific constraints, both of a technical and of an interactional nature. Here we mention two. First of all, almost all human communication with the computer is manifestly *task oriented*, i.e. goal restricted in seeking to achieve a practical outcome by definable procedures. Secondly, dialogue involving computers is usually highly restricted in *domain*. This severe domain restriction is not surprising, SDSs being among the most ambitious challenges that face computational linguistics. They integrate most of the components of natural language processing, including speech recognition, language understanding, information extraction, language generation, and speech synthesis. In addition to these, a *dialogue management* component is required to interpret the goals of incoming utterances and plan an appropriate response: this is where pragmatics has a key role. Without radical simplifications brought by domain restriction, combining and coordinating all these components would be well beyond current capabilities.

In this chapter, we confine our attention to SDSs which exhibit intelligence in the sense that they involve some kind of pragmatic processing, taking into account the goals and interpretations of utterances. Not all dialogues with computers are of this kind. A well-known exception to the task-driven nature of human–machine dialogue is the *conversational system* ELIZA (see Weizenbaum 1966). This was built in the 1960s to simulate human–computer conversation, and operated by mainly responding to keywords and patterns in the user input to ask seemingly intelligent questions or give non-committal answers like 'I'm sorry to hear that XXX' or 'Tell me more about your parents.' Different implementations of ELIZA can be found at http://128.2. 242.152/afs/cs/project/ai-repository/ai/areas/classics/eliza/0.html. ELIZA was innocent of pragmatics, as of all aspects of linguistic knowledge. More recently, conversational systems have been competitively entered for the Loebner Prize (http://www. loebner.net/Prizef/loebner-prize.html), offered every year to a computer system which is judged to come closest to passing the Turing Test, the test as to whether a computer system's observed (verbal) behaviour is indistinguishable from that of a human being. These, again, do not fall within the definition of SDSs considered here. (A more detailed treatment of SDSs is to be found in Chapter 34.)

7.8.1 Dialogue models and dialogue typology

To establish a typology of the dialogue models we are likely to encounter in computational analysis of dialogue, let us first look at the range of possibilities, i.e. establish what participants can be involved in a task-driven dialogue and in what way. The case that is most similar to the kind of ordinary pragmatics we discussed above is that of *human–human dialogue*, which can occur in two forms:

(a) *non-machine-mediated*: ordinary every-day human dialogue that is analysed using the computer.
(b) *machine-mediated*: a special type of dialogue between two or more people, which is monitored by the computer, so that the computer can offer assistance where the participants have trouble communicating in a lingua franca.

Type (*a*) is the kind of dialogue that computational linguists, as well as other linguists and conversational analysts, may analyse by extracting and modelling (aspects of) dialogue behaviour. For developing SDSs, such dialogue data may be recorded, transcribed, and analysed in order to provide the basis for a predictive model of human dialogue behaviour in task-oriented domains. For example, researchers may collect a **dialogue corpus** (see Chapter 24) of data from telephone call centres providing a public service, such as airline or train information and booking services, with a view to building an automated system to perform the same service. It is evident, however, that the human dialogue data so collected will differ in some respects from user dialogue behaviour when communicating with a computer system. For example, the data are likely to contain more socially appreciative utterances (such as 'Uh that's wonderful' and 'Okay thank you very much') than would occur in corresponding human–computer dialogue.

In type (*b*), the computer is used only in order to assist human–human communication to achieve a problem-solving task. A good example of this type of dialogue is the German VERBMOBIL system. Machine-mediated dialogue resembles non-mediated human–human dialogue in the way it is processed by computer (e.g. keeping track of keywords Sps use), yet in other ways it resembles our second main category, that of human–machine dialogue.

Human–machine dialogue is any kind of dialogue where a *user* communicates with a computer interface in order to achieve a set of aims. There are essentially two different kinds of human–machine dialogue:

(a) *simulated*: both participants are human, but one pretends to be a computer system. The computer interface is a 'sham'.
(b) *non-simulated*: genuine interaction between human and computer.

Type (*a*) is normally set up to investigate the behaviour of a user towards what he or she assumes to be a computer. This is an important means of *user modelling* since the behaviour of humans supposedly communicating with machines can be the best basis for human–computer dialogue modelling during system design. As such simulations recall the Wizard of Oz's deception in the Walt Disney movie, they are normally called **Wizard of Oz (WOZ) experiments** (see Gibbon, Moore, and Winski 1998: 581).

Type (*b*) is obviously the kind of human–machine dialogue which results from the implementation of fully-fledged SDSs. At present, such systems are relatively speaking in their infancy, but many are being developed as research prototypes, and a few have been commercially implemented. McTear (1999) provides an informative survey of the current state of the art, including working systems. As he explains (1999: 8), this technology is becoming important as 'it enables casual and naïve users to interact with complex computer applications in a natural way using speech'.

Having established which combinations are possible, we can now look at the different types of dialogue we are likely to encounter. We have already noted that, unlike ordinary dialogue, computational dialogue is so far only possible in *restricted domains*, i.e. with clearly delimited topics and vocabulary. So far, the domains covered in computational dialogue (with sample systems) include:

(*a*) travel information (SUNDIAL, ATIS, Philips Automatic Train Timetable Information System)
(*b*) transport (TRAINS)
(*c*) business appointments (VERBMOBIL)
(*d*) access to on-line information (SUN SpeechActs)
(*e*) repair and assembly (Circuit-Fix-It Shop)

Other domains under development include telebanking, directory enquiry services, and computer operating systems. The domain of a dialogue heavily influences the kind of vocabulary and background information the computer has to understand. For example, a travel information system needs to 'know' a large number of names of locations, whereas a telebanking application will have to 'be aware' of financial matters such as currencies, balances, and statements. A stored *knowledge base* will normally contain precise information about these specialized topics. Since existing computational SDSs are also *task driven*, the system is expected to perform one or more tasks and has to have some knowledge of how specific tasks are commonly performed. Systems are in general also *applications oriented*, i.e. they are not just there for the user to be able to have a conversation, but are designed to form a part of a specific application. This means that, to be commercially viable, they have to achieve a high level of accuracy in decoding and interpreting utterances, and in giving error-free responses.

The specific tasks to be performed by a system are closely bound to the domain in which they occur, e.g.:

(*a*) Negotiating appointments and travel planning (VERBMOBIL)
(*b*) Answering airline/travel enquiries (SUNDIAL, ATIS, Philips Automatic Train Timetable Information System)

(c) Developing plans for moving trains and cargo (TRAINS)

Additionally, SDSs can be categorized according to *activity types*:

(a) cooperative negotiation (VERBMOBIL)
(b) cooperative problem solving (TRAINS, Circuit-Fix-It Shop)
(c) information extraction (SUNDIAL, ATIS, Philips Automatic Train Timetable Information System)

Type (a) can normally occur only in systems where there are at least two human interlocutors and the computer present, although appointments can also be made by one human participant who gains access to a scheduler via a system such as the SUN SpeechActs system (see Martin et al. 1996). Types (b) and (c) are more typical of (single) human–computer interaction.

7.8.2 From speech acts to dialogue acts

It is not part of the task of this chapter to detail the various components of speech and language processing required for the decoding and encoding of components of a human–machine dialogue. They are dealt with in other chapters, for example Chapter 16 (speech recognition), Chapter 12 (parsing), Chapter 15 (natural language generation), and Chapter 17 (speech synthesis). Of primary relevance to this chapter, however, are the pragmatic levels of interpretation and generation of utterances, which may be roughly thought of as the computational linguist's adaptation of Searle's speech act theory. In computational pragmatics, however, the term more often used nowadays for such speech acts as REQUEST and ASSERTION is **dialogue acts**. Utterance interpretation, in terms of the identification of such pragmatic categories with their domain-associated content, is the key to the linguistic interpretation of incoming messages from the human users. Dialogue act interpretation, in such terms, has to depend substantially on the information derived from lower decoding levels, including phonic (including prosodic), lexical and syntactic decoding, although contextual information, in terms of what dialogue acts have preceded, also plays a major role.

We are here dealing with an area of computational linguistics which is still under development. Although dialogue acts are already being used in a number of systems with a certain degree of success, attempts are still being made to classify them to a higher degree, and to standardize them across a variety of different domains. Much effort is currently going into the compilation and annotation of corpora of dialogues (see Leech et al. 2000), so that these can act as *training* data for the development of automated systems. A common practice in dialogue research is to give parts of corpora, such as the corpora developed for the ATIS or TRAINS systems, to naive or expert subjects, who are then asked to *segment* them according to the functions of their individual parts (cf. Nakatani, Grosz, and Hirschberg 1995; Passonneau and

Litman 1996; Carletta et al. 1997). The resulting decomposition into *utterances* by a combination of *structural* and *functional* criteria (Leech et al. 2000)[7] determines both relations between the individual parts of the dialogue and their functional content. This can then lead to the development of improved dialogue (and dialogue management) models. The functional units—i.e. dialogue acts—differ from the speech acts occurring in everyday conversation, in that their scope is defined and potentially limited by the domain that they occur in, as well as their task orientation. Thus a model can often be built for a specific kind of dialogue with the help of relatively simple techniques such as the identification of keywords and phrases, and observing under which conditions and where within the task performance they have been used.

Some of the seminal work on dialogue acts has since 1996 been done by members of the Discourse Resource Initiative (DRI). The DRI consists of researchers in the fields of discourse and dialogue who have met at annual workshops in order to discuss their research and perform annotation exercises in order to develop and test new coding schemes (cf. Allen and Core 1997). An abridged annotation example from a recent workshop, held in May 1998 in Chiba, Japan, can be seen below:

1	A: so	ASSERT(?), DIRECTIVE, COMMISSIVE
2	we should meet again	ASSERT(?), DIRECTIVE, COMMISSIVE
3	how 'bout	DIRECTIVE, COMMISSIVE
4	how 'bout next week	DIRECTIVE, COMMISSIVE
5	what day are good for you	ABANDONED, INFO-REQUEST
6	what days are good for you	ABANDONED, INFO-REQUEST
7	B: actually next week I am on vacation	ASSERT, REJECT(3, 4), ANSWER(5, 6)
8	A: gosh	ACKNOWLEDGE(7), EXCLAIM
9	I guess we will have to meet the week after that	ASSERT, DIRECTIVE, COMMISSIVE, ACCEPT(7)
10	how 'bout Monday	DIRECTIVE, COMMISSIVE
11	B: Monday the tenth	INFO-REQUEST(?)
12	A: uh-huh	ANSWER(11)
13	B: well unfortunately my vacation runs through the fourteenth and I have plane tickets	ASSERT, REJECT(10–11)
14	I was planning on being on a beach in Acapulco about that point	ASSERT, REJECT(10–11), EXPLANATION(13)
15	A: well	? ACKNOWLEDGE(13–14)
16	when are you getting back	INFO-REQUEST

[7] Note that these utterance units are most often referred to as *segments* in the appropriate literature, but this term is avoided here, as it can lead to confusion with *segments* on the phonetic level.

In this extract, some of the labels have been expanded to make them more intelligible: e.g. INFO-REQ has become INFO-REQUEST. Some of the categories are clearly related to those of Searle (see section 7.2.1 above).

Dialogue acts can in principle be differentiated according to whether they actually contribute to the *task* itself or whether they serve a *task management* role, although this is not always an easy distinction to make. For example, stating or requesting new information is normally a direct contribution towards the performance of task goals, whereas clarifications, backchannels, or repairs can be seen as contributions towards the maintenance and management of the task. Other dialogue acts occur during certain phases of the dialogue, e.g. greetings at the beginning and closures towards the end. There is hence a need to recognize higher units of dialogue, to which dialogue acts contribute. In the VERBMOBIL scheme, a distinction is made between the following phases (Alexandersson et al. 1997: 10):

1. H – Hello
2. O – Opening
3. N – Negotiation
4. C – Closing
5. G – Goodbye

Dialogue acts of *greeting* and *introduce* are to be expected only in phases (1) and 5), *initiate* in (2) and *accept, reject* or *request* in (3) and (4).

From the system's point of view, the ongoing structure of the dialogue, in terms of dialogue acts or higher units, has to be monitored and controlled by the *dialogue manager*, to which we now turn.

7.8.3 Dialogue management models

As an SDS is subject to a large number of constraints, attempts have to be made to control the dialogue between system and user in as tight a way as possible, to enable the system to perform its tasks within those constraints and to pre-empt any misunderstandings.

In order to perform a specific task, it is not enough for either the system or the user to have access only to a kind of knowledge base of *domain knowledge*. Just as in the development of human conversation, the knowledge and intentions of both user and system need to be constantly augmented, i.e. a *dynamic context knowledge* and ongoing intentional structure (cf. Grosz and Sidner 1986: 187) need to be created. To keep track of these is the responsibility of the dialogue manager. Dialogue management models are based on the notion of a cooperative achievement of the task, and are of three main varieties: *dialogue grammars*, *plan-based approaches*, and *approaches based on the joint action model*.

Dialogue grammars are the oldest and simplest form of dialogue management. They assume that the task has a fixed structure of *finite states* representing dialogue acts (cf. Cohen 1998 and McTear 1999), and are usually arranged according to the conception of *adjacency pairs* (Sacks 1967–72) postulated in conversation analysis, e.g. questions followed by answers, etc. However, because of their relatively inflexible structure and the need for all structural options to be 'hard-coded', they are only suitable for small-scale systems and are rarely used these days. One additional problem with dialogue grammars is that the *initiative* rests solely with the system, i.e. the user is constrained in what he or she can say or has to say at any given time.

Plan-based systems are a more flexible way of dealing with the flexibility required of modern SDSs. The following description is from Litman and Allen (1990: 371):

Every plan has a *header*, a parameterized action description that names the plan. The *parameters of a plan* are the parameters in the header. ... Decompositions enable hierarchical planning. Although a plan may be usefully thought of as a single action at the level of description of the header, the plan may be decomposed into primitive (that is, executable) actions and other abstract action descriptions (that is, other plans). Such decompositions may be sequences of actions, sequences of subgoals to be achieved, or a mixture of both. ... Also associated with each plan is a set of applicability conditions called *constraints*. ... A library of *plan schemas* will be used to represent knowledge about typical speaker tasks. *Plan instantiations* are formed from such general schemas by giving values to the schema parameters.

Litman and Allen also make a distinction between *domain plans*, i.e. global domain-dependent task plans, and *discourse plans*, which are domain-independent 'meta-plans' that regulate the general flow of any dialogue (cf. the task management functions of dialogue acts mentioned above in section 7.8.2).

Approaches based on the *joint action model* (cf. Cohen 1998) are a relatively recent development. Even more than plan-based systems, they stress the collaborative effort participants engage in to achieve their aims. Like plan-based systems, they belong to the realm of *mixed-initiative* systems, where either the system or the user can take the initiative at any given time.

For more detail on *dialogue managers*, see section 34.3.2.6.

7.9 CONCLUSION

In spite of the inherent problems and complexities of the SDSs, intensive research and development in the area will doubtless lead to substantial advances in the next few years. Returning to the difference between academic and computational pragmatics, we ask how far academic approaches are now being reflected in the evolution of SDSs. Simpler approaches, emphasizing dialogue grammar, draw most clearly on rule-based conceptions of pragmatics, notably the speech act theory of Searle, which ironically lends itself more to the controlled nature of task-driven systems than to most ordinary dialogue. As the versatility of computational dialogue models increases, we are seeing a greater influence of theoretical approaches which emphasize the rational, cooperative basis of human–machine dialogue, with their philosophical roots in Grice's CP and related theory. As human–machine dialogue takes on more of the flexible characteristics of ordinary dialogue, the relevance of insights from academic pragmatics is likely to increase.

FURTHER READING AND RELEVANT RESOURCES

The classical texts Austin (1962), Searle (1969, 1980) and Grice (1975) are relatively easy and stimulating to read. On relevance, Sperber and Wilson (1995) has also attained classic status, although more demanding. In computational pragmatics, Ballim and Wilks (1991) deals with belief, and Bunt and Black (2000) with pragmatic reasoning. On SDSs, McTear (1999) and Leech et al. (2000) give surveys of the fast developing research and development scene.

Although there are no websites that specifically deal with the topic of computational pragmatics as a whole, below is a list of sites that provide comprehensive information on individual aspects, such as dialogue coding etc., involved in the study of computational pragmatics. These sites also include pointers to many other relevant sites.

Discourse Resource Initiative: http://www.georgetown.edu/luperfoy/Discourse-Treebank/dri-home.html. General discourse research and annotation with pointers to their annual workshop pages.

DAMSL (Dialog Act Markup in Several Layers): http://www.cs.rochester.edu/research/trains/annotation/RevisedManual/RevisedManual.html. An annotation scheme for dialogues.

EAGLES WP4 homepage: http://www.ling.lancs.ac.uk/eagles/. Survey and guidelines for the representation and annotation of dialogues.

MATE (Multilevel Annotation, Tools Engineering) project: http://mate.mip.ou.dk/. Survey and development of dialogue annotation schemes and tools.

TRINDI: http://www.ling.gu.se/research/projects/trindi/. Building a computational model of information revision in task-oriented and instructional dialogues and instructional texts.

VERBMOBIL project: http://www.dfki.uni-sb.de/verbmobil. Large-scale dialogue annotation and translation project.

REFERENCES

Alexandersson, J., B. Buschbeck-Wolf, T. Fujinami, E. Maier, N. Reithinger, B. Schmitz, and M. Siegel. 1997. *Dialogue acts in VERBMOBIL-2*. VM-Report 204 DFKI GmbH, Stuhlsatzen-hausweg 3, 66123 Saarbrücken.

Allen, J. and M. Core. 1997. *Draft of DAMSL: Dialog Act Markup in Several Layers*. Available from: http://www.cs.rochester.edu/u/trains/annotation/RevisedManual/ RevisedManual.html.

Austin, J. L. 1962. *How to Do Things with Words*. Oxford: Oxford University Press.

Ballim, A. and Y. Wilks. 1991. *Artificial Believers: The Ascription of Belief*. Hillsdale, NJ: Lawrence Erlbaum Associates.

Bernsen, N. O., H. Dybkjær, and L. Dybkjær. 1997. 'Elements of speech interaction'. *Proceedings of the 3rd Spoken Language Dialogue and Discourse Workshop* (Vienna), 28–45. http://www.mip.ou.dk/nis/publications/papers/hcm_paper/index.htm.

Bunt, H. 1989. 'Information dialogues as communicative action in relation to partner modelling and information processing'. In M. Taylor, F. Néel, and D. Bouwhuis (eds.), *The Structure of Multimodal Dialogue*. Amsterdam: North Holland Publishing Company, 47–71.

——and W. Black (eds.). 2001. *Abduction, Belief and Context in Dialogue: Studies in Computational Pragmatics*. Amsterdam: Benjamins.

Carletta, J., N. Dahlbäck, N. Reithinger, and M. Walker. 1997. *Standards for dialogue coding in natural language processing*. Seminar No. 9706, Report No. 167, Schloß Dagstuhl, internationales Begegnungs- und Forschungszentrum für Informatik.

Cohen, P. 1998. 'Dialogue modeling'. In Cole et al. (1998).

——J. Morgan, and M. Pollack (eds.). 1990. *Intentions in Communication*. Cambridge, Mass.: MIT Press.

Cole, R., J. Mariani, H. Uszkoreit, A. Zaenen, and V. Zue (eds.). 1998. *Survey of the State of the Art in Human Language Technology*. Cambridge: Cambridge University Press. On-line and postscript versions from: http://cslu.cse.ogi.edu/HLTsurvey/HLTsurvey.html.

Gibbon, D., R. Moore, and R. Winski. 1998. *Handbook of Standards and Resources for Spoken Language Systems*. Berlin: Mouton de Gruyter.

Grice, H. P. 1975. 'Logic and conversation'. In P. Cole and J. L. Morgan (eds.), *Syntax and Semantics*, iii: *Speech Acts*. New York: Academic Press, 41–58.

Grosz, B. and C. Sidner. 1986. 'Attention, intentions, and the structure of discourse'. *Computational Linguistics*, 12(3), 175–204.

Hirschberg, J. and C. J. Nakatani. 1994. 'A corpus-based study of repair cues in spontaneous speech'. *Journal of the Acoustical Society of America*, 3 (1995), 1603–16.

Hovy, E. H. and D. R. Scott. 1996. *Computational and Conversational Discourse: Burning Issues—An Interdisciplinary Approach*. NATO ASI Series, Series F: Computer and System Sciences, 151. Berlin: Springer-Verlag.

Leech, G. 1983. *Principles of Pragmatics*. London: Longman.

——and J. Thomas. 1990. 'Language, meaning and context: pragmatics'. In N. E. Collinge (ed.), *An Encyclopaedia of Language*. London: Routledge.

——M. Weisser, M. Grice, and A. Wilson. 2000. 'Survey and guidelines for the representation and annotation of dialogues'. In D. Gibbon, I. Mertins, and R. Moore (eds.), *Handbook of Multimodal and Spoken Dialogue Systems. Resources, Terminology and Product Evaluation*. Boston: Kluwer Academic Publishers, 1–101. First pub. 1998.

Levinson, S. 1983. *Pragmatics*. Cambridge: Cambridge University Press.

Litman, D. and J. Allen. 1990. 'Discourse processing and commonsense plans'. In Cohen, Morgan, and Pollack (1990).

McTear, M. F. 1999. *Spoken dialogue technology: enabling the user interface.* http://www. inlj. ulst.ac.uk/~cbdg23/survey/spoken_dialogue_technology.html.

Martin, P., F. Crabbe, S. Adams, E. Baatz, and N. Yankelovich. 1996. 'Speech acts: a spoken language framework'. *IEEE Computer*, July, 33–40.

Nakatani, C. J., B. J. Grosz, and J. Hirschberg. 1995. 'Discourse structure in spoken language: studies on speech corpora'. *Working Notes of the AAAI-95 Spring Symposium in Palo Alto, CA, on Empirical Methods in Discourse Interpretation*, 106–12.

Ono, T. and S. Thompson. 1993. 'Interaction and syntax in the structure of conversational discourse: collaboration, overlap, and syntactic dissociation'. In Hovy and Scott (1996). First pub. 1993.

Passonneau, R. and D. Litman. 1996. 'Empirical analysis of three dimensions of spoken discourse: segmentation, coherence, and linguistic devices'. In Hovy and Scott (1996). First pub. 1993.

Sacks, H. 1967–72. Unpublished lecture notes. University of California.

Schegloff, E. 1996. 'Issues of relevance for discourse analysis: contingency in action, interaction, and co-participant context'. In Hovy and Scott (1996). First pub. 1993.

Searle, J. R. 1969. *Speech Acts: An Essay in the Philosophy of Language.* Cambridge: Cambridge University Press.

——1980. *Expression and Meaning.* Cambridge: Cambridge University Press.

Sperber, D. and D. Wilson. 1995. *Relevance: Communication and Cognition*, 2nd edn. Oxford: Blackwell.

Thomas, J. 1995. *Meaning in Interaction: An Introduction to Pragmatics.* London: Longman.

Weizenbaum, J. 1966. 'ELIZA—a computer program for the study of natural language communication between man and machine'. *CACM*, 9, 36–43.

Worm, K. and C. Rupp. 1998. *Towards robust understanding of speech by combination of partial analyses.* VM-Report 222, Universität des Saarlandes, Saarbrücken.

CHAPTER 8

FORMAL GRAMMARS AND LANGUAGES

CARLOS MARTÍN-VIDE

ABSTRACT

This chapter introduces the preliminaries of classical formal language theory. The main classes of grammars as language-generating devices and automata as language-recognizing devices are outlined. In order to render the chapter accessible for readers without a mathematical background, a number of definitions and examples are offered and the basic results are presented without proofs.

8.1 LANGUAGES

8.1.1 Basic notions

An **alphabet** or *vocabulary V* is a finite set of letters. Multiple concatenations of letters from V result in V^*, an infinite set of **strings** or *words*. The *empty string* is denoted by λ^1 and contains no letters: it is the unit element of V^* under the concatenation operation. The *concatenation* of strings is an associative and non-commutative operation, which closes V^*, i.e.:

$$\text{for every } w, v \in V^*: wv \in V^*.$$

The *length* of a string, denoted by $|w|$, is the number of letters the string consists of. It is clear that:

- $|\lambda| = 0$,
- $|wv| = |w| + |v|$.

w is a *substring* or *subword* of v if and only if u_1, u_2 exist such that $v = u_1 w u_2$. Special cases of a substring include:

- if $w \neq \lambda$ and $w \neq v$, then w is a *proper substring* of v,
- if $u_1 = \lambda$, then w is a *prefix* or a *head*,
- if $u_2 = \lambda$, then w is a *suffix* or a *tail*.

The i-times *iterated concatenation* of w is illustrated in the following example:

(8.1) If $w = ab$, then $w^3 = (ab)^3 = ababab$.   ($w^0 = \lambda$.)

If $w = a_1 a_2 \ldots a_n$, then its *mirror image* $w^{-1} = a_n a_{n-1} \ldots a_1$. It is clear that:

$$(w^{-1})^{-1} = w, (w^{-1})^i = (w^i)^{-1} \text{ (for every } i \geq 0).$$

Any subset $L \subseteq V^*$ (including both $\varnothing$ and $\{\lambda\}$) is a **language**. The set V^+ is defined as follows: $V^+ = V^* - \{\lambda\}$.

The following *cardinality* (the number of elements a set contains) relations hold:

- V^* is denumerably infinite, i.e. $|V^*| = \aleph_0$ (the smallest transfinite number),
- $P(V^*)$ is nondenumerably infinite, i.e. $|P(V^*)| = 2^{\aleph_0}$ (also called $\aleph_1$).

We do not go deeper into the details of infinite sets here, which would require an extensive presentation.

Examples of languages include:

(8.2) $L = \{a, b, \lambda\}, L = \{a^i, b^i : i \geq 0\}, L = \{ww^{-1} : w \in V^*\}, L = \{a^{n^2} : n \geq 1\}, L = \{w : w \in \{a, b\}^+ \text{ and } |w|_a = |w|_b\}$ ($|w|_x$ denotes the number of occurrences of x in w).

8.1.2 Chomsky grammars: The Chomsky hierarchy

A (formal) **grammar** is a tuple $G = (N, T, S, P)$, where N, T are alphabets, with $N \cap T = \varnothing$, $S \in N$ and P is a finite set of pairs (w, v) such that $w, v \in (N \cup T)^*$ and w contains at least one letter from N. ((w, v) is usually written $w \to v$.) N is the *non-terminal*

---

[1] λ or ε are alternatively used to denote the empty string.

alphabet, T the *terminal alphabet, S* the *initial letter* or *axiom,* and *P* the set of *rewriting rules* or **productions**.

Given $G = (N, T, S, P)$ and $w, v \in (N \cup T)^*$, an *immediate* or *direct derivation* (in 1 step) $w \Rightarrow_G v$ holds if and only if:

(i) $u_1, u_2 \in (N \cup T)^*$ exist such that $w = u_1 \alpha u_2$ and $v = u_1 \beta u_2$, and
(ii) $\alpha \rightarrow \beta \in P$ exists.

Given $G = (N, T, S, P)$ and $w, v \in (N \cup T)^*$, a **derivation** $w \Rightarrow_G^* v$ holds if and only if either $w = v$ or $z \in (N \cup T)^*$ exists such that $w \Rightarrow_G^* z$ and $z \Rightarrow_G v$.

$\Rightarrow_G^*$ denotes the reflexive transitive closure and $\Rightarrow_G^+$ the transitive closure, respectively, of $\Rightarrow_G$.

The *language* generated by a grammar is defined by:

$$L(G) = \{w : S \Rightarrow_G^* w \text{ and } w \in T^*\}.$$

(8.3) Let $G = (N, T, S, P)$ be a grammar such that:
$N = \{S, A, B\}$,
$T = \{a, b\}$,
$P = \{S \rightarrow aB, S \rightarrow bA, A \rightarrow a, A \rightarrow aS, A \rightarrow bAA, B \rightarrow b, B \rightarrow bS, B \rightarrow aBB\}$.

The language generated by G is the following:

$$L(G) = \{w : w \in \{a, b\}^+ \text{ and } |w|_a = |w|_b\}.$$

(8.4) Let $G = (N, T, S, P)$ be a grammar such that:
$N = \{S, A, B\}$,
$T = \{a, b, c\}$,
$P = \{S \rightarrow abc, S \rightarrow aAbc, Ab \rightarrow bA, Ac \rightarrow Bbcc, bB \rightarrow Bb, aB \rightarrow aaA, aB \rightarrow aa\}$.

The language generated by G is the following:

$$L(G) = \{a^n b^n c^n : n \geq 1\}.$$

Grammars can be classified according to several criteria. The most widespread one is the form of their productions. According to it, a grammar is said to be of type:

- 0 (**phrase-structure grammar, RE**) if and only if there are no restrictions on the form of the productions: arbitrary strings are allowed on the left-hand side and the right-hand side of the rules.
- 1 (**context-sensitive grammar, CS**) if and only if every production is of the form:

$$u_1 A u_2 \rightarrow u_1 w u_2,$$

with $u_1, u_2, w \in (N \cup T)^*$, $A \in N$ and $w \neq \lambda$ (except possibly for the rule $S \rightarrow \lambda$, in which case S does not occur on any right-hand side of a rule).

- 2 (**context-free grammar, CF**) if and only if every production is of the form:

$$A \rightarrow w,$$

with $A \in N$, $w \in (N \cup T)^*$.

- 3 (*finite-state* or **regular grammar, REG**) if and only if every production is of any of the forms:

$$A \rightarrow wB,$$
$$A \rightarrow w,$$

with $A, B \in N$, $w \in T^*$.

A language is said to be of type i ($i = 0, 1, 2, 3$) if it is generated by a type i grammar. The family of type i languages is denoted by L_i.

One of the most important and early results in formal language theory is the so-called **Chomsky hierarchy** of languages: $L_3 \subset L_2 \subset L_1 \subset L_0$.

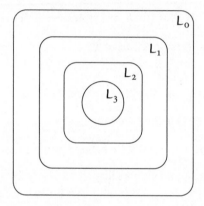

Note that every grammar generates a unique language. However, one language can be generated by several different grammars.

Two grammars are said to be:

- (*weakly*) *equivalent* if they generate the same string language,
- *strongly equivalent* if they generate both the same string language and the same tree language.

We shall see later that a context-free grammar generates not only a set of strings, but a set of trees too: each one of the trees is associated with a string and illustrates the way this string is derived in the grammar.

8.1.3 Operations on languages

Typical set-theoretic operations on languages include:

- *Union:* $L_1 \cup L_2 = \{w : w \in L_1 \text{ or } w \in L_2\}$.
- *Intersection:* $L_1 \cap L_2 = \{w : w \in L_1 \text{ and } w \in L_2\}$.

- *Difference*: $L_1 - L_2 = \{w : w \in L_1 \text{ and } w \notin L_2\}$.
- *Complement* of $L \subseteq V^*$ with respect to V^*: $\bar{L} = V^* - L$.

Specific language-theoretic operations on languages include:

- *Concatenation*: $L_1 L_2 = \{w_1 w_2 : w_1 \in L_1 \text{ and } w_2 \in L_2\}$.
- *Iteration*:

  $L^0 = \{\lambda\}$,

  $L^1 = L$,

  $L^2 = LL$,

  $\dots$

  $L^* = \bigcup_{i \geq 0} L^i$ (closure of the iteration: *Kleene star*),

  $L^+ = \bigcup_{i \geq 1} L^i$ (positive closure of the iteration: *Kleene plus*).

Note that L^+ equals L^* if $\lambda \in L$, and equals $L^* - \{\lambda\}$ if $\lambda \notin L$.

- *Mirror image*: $L^{-1} = \{w : w^{-1} \in L\}$.

Note that $(L^{-1})^{-1} = L$ and $(L^{-1})^i = (L^i)^{-1}$, for every $i \geq 0$.

- *Right quotient* of L_1 over L_2: $L_1 / L_2 = \{w : v \in L_2 \text{ exists such that } wv \in L_1\}$.
- *Right derivative* of L over v: $\partial_v^r L = L / \{v\} = \{w : wv \in L\}$.
- *Head* of $L \subseteq V^*$: $HEAD(L) = \{w \in V^* : v \in V^* \text{ exists such that } wv \in L\}$.

Note that for every $L : L \subseteq HEAD(L)$.

- *Left quotient* of L_1 over L_2: $L_2 \backslash L_1 = \{w : v \in L_2 \text{ exists such that } vw \in L_1\}$.
- *Left derivative* of L over v: $\partial_v^l L = \{v\} \backslash L = \{w : vw \in L\}$.
- *Tail* of $L \subseteq V^*$: $TAIL(L) = \{w \in V^* : v \in V^* \text{ exists such that } vw \in L\}$.

Note that for every $L : L \subseteq TAIL(L)$.

- *Morphism*: Given two alphabets V_1, V_2, a mapping $h : V^*_1 \rightarrow V^*_2$ is a morphism if and only if:

  (i) for every $w \in V_1^*$, $v \in V_2^*$ exists such that $v = h(w)$ and v is unique,
  (ii) for every $w, u \in V_1^*$: $h(wu) = h(w)h(u)$.

A morphism is called λ *free* if, for every $w \in V_1^*$, if $w \neq \lambda$ then $h(w) \neq \lambda$.

- *Morphic image*: $h(L) = \{v \in V_2^* : v = h(w), \text{ for some } w \in L\}$.
- A morphism is called an *isomorphism* if, for every $w, u \in V_1^*$, if $h(w) = h(u)$ then $w = u$.

(8.5) An isomorphism between $V_1 = \{0, 1, 2, \dots, 9\}$ and $V_2 = \{0, 1\}$ is the binary coded decimal representation of the integers:

$$h(0) = 0000, h(1) = 0001, \dots, h(9) = 1001.$$

Union, concatenation, and Kleene star are called *regular operations*.

Each of the language families L_i, for every $i \in \{0, 1, 2, 3\}$, is closed under regular operations.

A systematic study of the common properties of language families has led to the theory of abstract families of languages (AFLs). An *abstract family of languages* is a class of those languages that satisfy certain specified closure axioms. If one fixes an AFL, one can prove general theorems about all languages in the family.

A few simple closure properties are depicted next:

	REG	CF	CS	RE
union	+	+	+	+
intersection	+	−	+	+
complement	+	−	+	−
concatenation	+	+	+	+
Kleene star	+	+	+	+
intersection with regular languages	+	+	+	+
morphisms	+	+	−	+
left/right quotient	+	−	−	+
left/right quotient with regular languages	+	+	−	+
left/right derivative	+	+	+	+
mirror image	+	+	+	+

As an illustration, the union of two regular languages is always a regular language, but the intersection of two context-free languages is not always a context-free language.

8.2 GRAMMARS

8.2.1 Context-free grammars

For every CF grammar G an equivalent CF grammar G' can be found such that the right-hand sides of its productions are all different from λ except when $\lambda \in L(G)$. In this latter case, $S \to \lambda$ is the only rule with the right-hand side λ, but then S does not occur on any right-hand side of the rules. (This is also true for REG grammars.)

A grammar is said to be λ *free* if none of its rules has the right-hand side λ.

A CF grammar is said to be in *Chomsky normal form* (CNF) if each of its rules has either of the two following forms:

- $X \to a, X \in N, a \in T,$
- $X \to YZ, X, Y, Z \in N.$

For every λ-free CF grammar one can effectively (algorithmically) find an equivalent grammar in CNF.

8.2.2 Derivation trees

A very common and practical representation of the derivation process in a grammar (particularly, in a CF grammar) is a tree.

A **derivation tree** is defined as $T = (V, D)$, where V is a set of *nodes* or *vertices* and D is a *dominance* relation, which is a binary relation in V that satisfies:

(i) D is a weak order:
- (*a*) reflexive: for every $a \in V : aDa,$
- (*b*) antisymmetric: for every $a, b \in V$, if aDb and bDa, then $a = b,$
- (*c*) transitive: for every $a, b, c \in V$, if aDb and bDc, then $aDc.$
(ii) *root condition*: $r \in V$ exists such that for every $b \in V : rDb,$
(iii) *non-branching condition*: for every $a, a', b \in V$, if aDb and $a'Db$, then aDa' or $a'Da.$

Special cases of the dominance relation include, for every $a, b \in V$:

- *a strictly dominates b (aSDb)* if and only if aDb and $a \neq b$; so SD is a strict order in V:
    - (i) irreflexive: it is not the case that $aSDa,$
    - (ii) asymmetric: if $aSDb$, then it is not the case that $bSDa,$
    - (iii) transitive: if $aSDb$ and $bSDc$, then $aSDc.$
- *a immediately dominates b (aIDb)* if and only if $aSDb$ and no c exists such that $aSDc$ and $cSDb.$

The *degree* of a node b is defined as $deg(b) = |\{a \in V : bIDa\}|$. Consequences of this definition are:

- b is a *terminal node* or a *leaf* if and only if $deg(b) = 0,$
- b is a *unary node* if and only if $deg(b) = 1,$
- b is a *branching node* if and only if $deg(b) > 1,$
- T is an *n-ary derivation tree* if and only if all its non-terminal nodes are of degree $n.$

Two nodes a, b are *independent* of each other: $aINDb$ if and only if neither aDb nor $bDa.$

Some family relations among nodes include:

- a is a *mother node* of b: aMb if and only if $aIDb$,
- a is a *sister node* of b: aSb if and only if c exists such that cMa and cMb.

The mother relation has the following features:

(i) no $a \in V$ exists such that aMr,

(ii) if $b \neq r$, then it has just one mother node.

Given $T = (V, D)$, for every $b \in V$, a *derivation subtree* or a *constituent* is $T_b = (V_b, D_b)$, where $V_b = \{c \in V: bDc\}$ and $xD_b y$ if and only if $x \in V_b$ and $y \in V_b$ and xDy.

Given $T = (V, D)$, for every $a, b \in V$: a *c-commands* b (aCCb) if and only if:

(i) $aINDb$,

(ii) a branching node exists that strictly dominates a,

(iii) every branching node that strictly dominates a dominates b.

a *asymmetrically c-commands* b if and only if $aCCb$ and it is not the case that $bCCa$.

Given two derivation trees $T = (V, D)$, $T' = (V', D')$ and $h: V \rightarrow V'$:

- h *preserves* D if and only if for every $a, b \in V$: $aDb \rightarrow h(a)D'h(b)$.
- h is an *isomorphism* of T in T' $(T \approx T')$ if and only if h is a bijection and preserves D.

    (Note that a mapping $f: A \rightarrow B$ is a bijection if and only if:

    (i) f is one-to-one or injective: for every $x, y \in A$, if $x \neq y$ then $f(x) \neq f(y)$ or, equivalently, if $f(x) = f(y)$ then $x = y$,

    (ii) f is onto or exhaustive: for every $z \in B$, $x \in A$ exists such that $f(x) = z$.)

Any two isomorphic derivation trees share all their properties:

- $aSDb$ if and only if $h(a)SD'h(b)$,
- $aIDb$ if and only if $h(a)ID'h(b)$,
- $deg(a) = deg(h(a))$,
- $aCCb$ if and only if $h(a)CCh(b)$,
- a is the root of T if and only if $h(a)$ is the root of T',
- $depth(a) = depth\,(h(a))$,
    $(depth\,(a) = |\{b \in V: bDa\}| - 1.)$
- $height\,(T) = height\,(T')$.
    $(height\,(T) = max\,\{depth\,(a) : a \in V\}.)$

Once one has a $T = (V, D)$, one may enrich its definition to get a *labelled derivation tree* $T = (V, D, L)$, where (V, D) is a derivation tree and L is a mapping from V to a specified set of labels.

Given $T = (V, D, L)$ and $T' = (V', D', L')$, one says $T \approx T'$ if and only if:

(i) $h: V \rightarrow V'$ is a bijection,

(ii) h preserves D,

(iii) for every $a, b \in V$: $L(a) = L(b)$ if and only if $L'(h(a)) = L'(h(b))$.

A *terminally ordered derivation tree* is $T = (V, D, <)$, where (V, D) is a derivation tree and $<$ is a strict total (or linear) order on the terminal nodes of V, i.e. a relation that is:

(i) irreflexive: for every a terminal, it is not the case that $a < a$,

(ii) asymmetric: if $a < b$, then it is not the case that $b < a$,

(iii) transitive: if $a < b$ and $b < c$, then $a < c$,

(iv) connected: either $a < b$ or $b < a$.

Given $T = (V, D, <)$, for every $b, c, d, e \in V$: $b <' c$ (*b precedes c*) if and only if:

$$\text{if } bDd, d \text{ is terminal}, cDe \text{ and } e \text{ is terminal, then } d < e.$$

The following *exclusivity condition* completely orders a tree. Given $T = (V, D, <)$, for every $b, d \in V$, if $bINDd$, then either $b <' d$ or $d <' b$. Consequently, every two nodes of the tree must hold one, and only one, of the dominance and precedence relations.

8.2.3 More about context-free languages

A CF grammar is called *redundant* if it contains useless non-terminal letters. A non-terminal letter is *useless* if:

(i) either no terminal string is derivable from it: *inactive* or *dead* letter,

(ii) or it does not occur in any string derivable from S: *unreachable* letter.

For any CF grammar $G = (N, T, S, P)$:

- $A \in N$ is inactive if and only if the language generated by $G_A = (N, T, A, P)$ is empty.
- A is unreachable if and only if the language generated by $G_A^\lambda = ((N–\{A\})\cup T, \{A\},$ $S, P_1 \cup \{X \to \lambda : X \in (N-\{A\})\cup T\})$ (P_1 being the set of rules remaining after having removed from P the productions that have A on their left-hand sides) is $\{\lambda\}$.

A CF grammar is *non-redundant* or *reduced* if each of its non-terminal letters is both active and reachable.

For every CF grammar one can effectively (algorithmically) find an equivalent non-redundant grammar.

Given a CF grammar G, $w \in L(G)$ is an *ambiguous* string if and only if w has at least two derivation trees in G. G is said to be an *ambiguous* grammar if and only if some string in $L(G)$ exists that is ambiguous. L is an *inherently ambiguous* context-free language if and only if every CF grammar generating L is ambiguous.

An example of ambiguity is the following:

(8.6) Given $G = (\{S\}, \{a, +, *\}, S, \{S \to S+S, S \to S*S, S \to a\})$, $w = a*a+a$ has two different derivation trees in G:

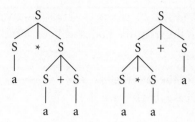

An example of inherent ambiguity is the following:

(8.7) Let $L = \{a^m b^m c^n : m, n \geq 1\} \cup \{a^m b^n c^n : m, n \geq 1\}$. Every CF grammar generating it will produce two different derivation trees for the strings of the form $a^n b^n c^n$ (which belong to both components of the language).

The *Bar-Hillel pumping lemma* for CF languages allows the proof that a language cannot be classed as CF on the basis of the structure of the strings:

for every $L \in CF$, $p, q \in N$ exist such that for every $z \in L$, if $|z| > p$, then $z = uvwxy$, where $u, v, w, x, y \in T^*$, $|vwx| \leq q$, $vx \neq \lambda$, and $uv^i wx^i y \in L$, for every $i \geq 0$.

Since not all languages satisfy the pumping lemma above, the following corollary is obvious.

There are non-context-free languages.

Examples of this include:

$\{a^n b^n c^n : n \geq 1\}$,
$\{a^{n^2} : n \geq 1\}$,
$\{a^n b^m c^n d^m : m, n \geq 1\}$.

8.2.4 Linear and regular languages

A CF grammar is called *linear* (LIN) if each production has either of the forms:

$A \rightarrow w, A \in N, w \in T^*$,
$A \rightarrow w_1 B w_2, A, B \in N, w_1, w_2 \in T^*$.

Further, it is called *left-linear* (LLIN) (respectively, *right-linear* (RLIN)) if w_1 (respectively, w_2) is λ in every rule of the second form.

Thus, the class of right-linear grammars exactly coincides with REG. Also, every LLIN grammar generates an REG language.

It is worthwhile checking whether all linear grammars generate languages in L_3. The answer is negative and the following is a counterexample:

(8.8) Consider the languages:

$L_1 = \{a^n b^n c^k : n \geq 1, k \geq 1\}$,

$L_2 = \{a^k b^n c^n : n \geq 1, k \geq 1\}$.

Both are generated by linear grammars. For instance, the first one by:

$$G = (\{S, A\}, \{a, b, c\}, S, P), P = \{S \rightarrow Sc, S \rightarrow Ac, A \rightarrow ab, A \rightarrow aAb\}.$$

However, regular grammars generating each one of them cannot be built. Since:

$$L_1 \cap L_2 = \{a^n b^n c^n : n \geq 1\} \notin CF$$

and it is known that CF ∩ REG = CF, one concludes that neither L_1 nor L_2 can be REG.

Every language in L_3 can be generated by a grammar having the following two types of productions: $X \rightarrow aY, X \rightarrow a$, with $X, Y \in N, a \in T$.

A CF grammar $G = (N, T, S, P)$ is said to be *self-embedding* if there exists an $A \in N$ such that $A \Rightarrow^* XAY$, for some $X, Y \in (N \cup T)^+$.

If a CF grammar is reduced and not self-embedding, then $L(G) \in L_3$.

Thus, self-embedding is the very characteristic feature of *CF* languages which separates them from smaller language classes. Since that feature (it is the case with relative sentences, for instance) does appear in natural languages (being the source for its recursiveness leading to an infinite set of sentences), it is obvious that a natural language cannot be smaller than a *CF* language.

A CF grammar is said to be in *Greibach normal form* (GNF) if each rule is of the form:

$$A \rightarrow aX, A \in N, a \in T, X \in N^*.$$

For every λ-free CF grammar one can find an equivalent grammar in GNF.

Given a finite alphabet V, a **regular expression** is inductively defined as follows:

(i) λ is a regular expression,
(ii) for every $a \in V, a$ is a regular expression,
(iii) if R is a regular expression, then so is R^*,
(iv) if Q, R are regular expressions, then so are QR and $Q \cup R$.

Every regular expression denotes an REG language. For example:

λ denotes $\{\lambda\}$,

a denotes $\{a\}$,

$a \cup b$ denotes $\{a, b\}$,

ab denotes $\{ab\}$,

a^* denotes $\{a\}^*$,

$(a \cup b)^*$ denotes $\{a, b\}^*$,

$(a \cup b)a^*$ denotes $\{a, b\}a^* = aa^* \cup ba^* = \{aa^*, ba^*\}$.

As well, every REG language is describable by a regular expression.

Every regular expression denotes a language in L_3 and, conversely, every language in L_3 is denoted by a regular expression.

A short list of valid equations for all regular expressions P, Q, R includes:

$P \cup (Q \cup R) = (P \cup Q) \cup R$,
$P(QR) = (PQ)R$,
$P \cup Q = Q \cup P$,
$P(Q \cup R) = PQ \cup PR$,
$(P \cup Q) R = PR \cup QR$,
$P^* = \lambda \cup PP^*$,
$\lambda P = P\lambda = P$,
$P^* = (\lambda \cup P)^*$.

The concept of a regular expression motivates the operation of *substitution* on languages. Given a finite alphabet V, let V_a denote an alphabet and $s(a) \subseteq V_a^*$ a language for each $a \in V$. For each string $w = a_1 a_2 \ldots a_n \in V^*$, the substitution is defined as the concatenation of the languages corresponding to the letters of w:

$$s(w) = s(a_1)s(a_2)\ldots s(a_n).$$

This definition is extended to any $L \subseteq V^*$ as follows:

$$s(L) = \{v : v \in s(w), \text{for some } w \in L\}.$$

The family L_3 is closed under substitution, i.e. the set of regular expressions is closed under substitution of a regular expression for each of its letters. Substitution can be regarded as the generalization of the notion of morphism.

As for CF languages, for both families LIN and REG there are necessary conditions in the form of pumping lemmata.

Pumping lemma for linear languages:

for every $L \in LIN$, $p, q \in N$ exist such that for every $z \in L$, if $|z| > p$ then $z = uvwxy$, where $u, v, w, x, y \in T^*$, $|uvxy| \le q$, $vx \ne \lambda$, and $uv^i wx^i y \in L$, for every $i \ge 0$.

Pumping lemma for regular languages:

for every $L \in REG$, $p, q \in N$ exist such that for every $z \in L$, if $|z| > p$ then $z = uvw$, where $u, v, w \in T^*$, $|uv| \le q$, $v \ne \lambda$, and $uv^i w \in L$, for every $i \ge 0$.

8.2.5 Semilinear, context-sensitive, and mildly context-sensitive languages

Whether or not natural languages are context-free sets of sentences was a much discussed issue in the 1980s. For details the reader is referred to the following papers: Gazdar (1981), Bresnan et al. (1982), Pullum and Gazdar (1982), Culy (1985), and Shieber (1985) (all of them were collected in Savitch et al. 1987).

Today, there is general agreement that natural languages are not context free. However, how large natural languages are continues to be a less simple matter. There are two main non-compatible views:

(i) Natural language forms a class of sentences that includes the context-free family but is larger than it (so still comfortably placed within the Chomsky hierarchy).

(ii) Natural language occupies a position eccentric with respect to that hierarchy, in such a way that it does not contain any whole family in the hierarchy but is spread along all of them.

The first view gave rise to a new family of languages, which is of a clear linguistic interest.

A family of *mildly context-sensitive languages* (MCS) is a family L such that:

(i) each language in L is semilinear,

(ii) for each language in L, the membership problem (whether or not a string belongs to the language) is solvable in deterministic polynomial time,

(iii) L contains the following three non-CF languages:
- $L = \{a^n b^n c^n : n \geq 0\}$: multiple agreements,
- $L = \{a^n b^m c^n d^m : n, m \geq 0\}$: crossed dependencies,
- $L = \{ww : w \in \{a, b\}^*\}$: duplications.

MCS is a linguistically-motivated family, both as it contains the above three languages, which are more or less agreed to represent structures that exist in natural languages, and as it enjoys good complexity conditions (i.e. fast processing), as stated by the deterministic polynomial time requirement.

In order to see what a semilinear language is, let us assume $V = \{a_1, a_2, \ldots, a_k\}$. N being the set of integers, the *Parikh mapping* of a string is:

$$\Psi : V^* \to \mathbb{N}^k$$
$$\Psi(w) = (|w|_{a_1}, |w|_{a_2}, \ldots, |w|_{a_k}), w \in V^*.$$

Given a language, its *Parikh set* is:

$$\Psi(L) = \{\Psi(w) : w \in L\}.$$

A *linear set* is a set $M \subseteq \mathbb{N}^k$ such that:

$$M = \{v_0 + \sum_{i=1}^{m} v_i x_i : x_i \in \mathbb{N}, \text{for some } v_0, v_1, \ldots, v_m \in \mathbb{N}^k\}.$$

A *semilinear set* is a finite union of linear sets. A *semilinear language* is an L such that $\Psi(L)$ is a semilinear set.

A phrase-structure grammar is called *length increasing* if, for every production $w \to v \in P$, one has $|w| \le |v|$. This is clear for every CS grammar. Moreover, every length-increasing grammar generates a CS language. The length-increasing property is, therefore, equivalent to context sensitivity with the sole exception of the rule $S \to \lambda$, which is needed only to derive λ.

A length-increasing grammar is said to be in *Kuroda normal form* (KNF) if each of its productions is of any of the following forms:

- $A \to a$,
- $A \to B$,
- $A \to BC$,
- $AB \to CD$,

  for A, B, C, D non-terminals and a terminal.

For every length-increasing grammar an equivalent grammar can be found in KNF.

Every λ-free CS language can be generated by a grammar in KNF.

A λ-free CS grammar is said to be in *Penttonen* or *one-sided normal form* (PNF) if each of its productions is of any of the following forms:

- $A \to a$,
- $A \to B$,
- $A \to BC$,
- $AB \to AC$,
- $AB \to BA$.

An example of a CS grammar generating a non-CF language is the following:

(8.9) Let $G = (N, T, S, P)$ be a grammar such that:
   $N = \{S, A_1, A_2, B_1, B_2, C_1, C_2\}$,
   $T = \{a, b, c\}$,
   $P = \{S \to A_1 B_1 C_1, {}^*A_1 \to a A_2 B_2, B_2 B_1 \to B_2 B_2, B_2 C_1 \to B_2 C_2 c, {}^*A_2 \to a A_1 B_1, B_1 B_2 \to B_1 B_1, B_1 C_2$
   $\to B_1 C_1 c, A_1 \to a, B_1 \to b, C_1 \to c, A_2 \to a, B_2 \to b, C_2 \to c\}$.

The generated language is:

$$L(G) = \{a^n b^n c^n : n \ge 1\} \notin CF.$$

As is easily seen, every application of the rules marked with $*$ sends a signal through the Bs to C_1 or C_2 on their right, which may be killed on its way or reach the Cs, where it deposits a c.

8.3 AUTOMATA

8.3.1 Finite automata

Grammars are generating devices which may simulate the productive (i.e. speaking) behaviour of speakers. Automata are recognizing devices which may simulate their receptive (i.e. hearing) behaviour. There are strong formal connections between grammar theory and automata theory.

A **finite automaton** (FA) is a tuple:

$$A = (Q, T, M, q_0, F),$$

with:

- Q a finite non-empty set of states,
- T a finite alphabet of input letters,
- M a transition function: $Q \times T \to Q$,
- $q_0 \in Q$ the initial state,
- $F \subseteq Q$ the set of final (accepting) states.

A *accepts* or *recognizes* a string if it enters a final state upon completion of the reading of the string.

(8.10) $A = (Q, T, M, q_0, F)$:
   $Q = \{q_0, q_1, q_2, q_3\}$,
   $T = \{a, b\}$,
   $F = \{q_0\}$,
   $M(q_0, a) = q_2, M(q_0, b) = q_1$,
   $M(q_1, a) = q_3, M(q_1, b) = q_0$,
   $M(q_2, a) = q_0, M(q_2, b) = q_3$,
   $M(q_3, a) = q_1, M(q_3, b) = q_2$.

The *transition table* and the *transition graph* for A are, respectively:

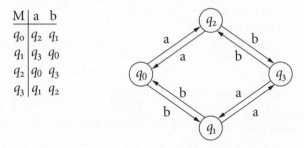

M	a	b
q_0	q_2	q_1
q_1	q_3	q_0
q_2	q_0	q_3
q_3	q_1	q_2

It can be easily checked that $L(A) = \{w \in \{a, b\}^* : |w|_a$ is even and $|w|_b$ is even$\}$.

If M is a one-valued function, the finite automaton is called *deterministic* (DFA).

Otherwise, it is called *non-deterministic* (NFA). In the first case, M contains exactly one transition with the same left-hand side. Note that the definition of M does not require M to be a total function, i.e. M may well not be defined for some combinations of a state and a letter.

The symbols $\vdash$ and $\vdash^*$ for transitions are, respectively, equivalent to the symbols $\Rightarrow$ and $\Rightarrow^*$ for derivations in grammars.

The *language* accepted by a finite automaton is:

$$L(A) = \{w \in T^*: q_0 w \vdash^* p, p \in F\}.$$

Note that $\lambda \in L(A)$ if and only if $q_0 \cap F \neq \emptyset$.

For every NFA an equivalent REG grammar can be found.

For every REG grammar an equivalent NFA can be found.

L_3 coincides with the family of languages accepted by NFAs.

The following question now arises: is there some language in L_3 that cannot be accepted by any DFA? The answer is negative in that the behaviour of an NFA can always be simulated by means of a DFA (with more states).

A number of important consequences for the languages in L_3 follow from the concept of an FA, among others:

- L_3 is a Boolean algebra,
- one can decide whether two REG grammars are equivalent, etc.

8.3.2 Pushdown automata

Pushdown automata are extensions of finite automata in that they have a memory added (see Fig. 8.1).

A **pushdown automaton** (PDA) is a tuple $A = (Z, Q, T, M, z_0, q_0, F)$, with:

- Z a finite alphabet of pushdown letters,
- Q a finite set of internal states,
- T a finite set of input letters,
- M the transition function:

$$Z \times Q \times (T \cup \#) \to P_{\text{fin}}(Z^* \times Q),$$

$(P_{\text{fin}}(Z^* \times Q)$ is the set of finite subsets of $Z^* \times Q)$

- $z_0 \in Z$ the initial letter,
- $q_0 \in Q$ the initial state,
- $F \subseteq Q$ a set of final or accepting states.

A *configuration* of a PDA is a string zq, where $z \in Z^*$ is the current contents of the pushdown store and $q \in Q$ is the present state of the control device.

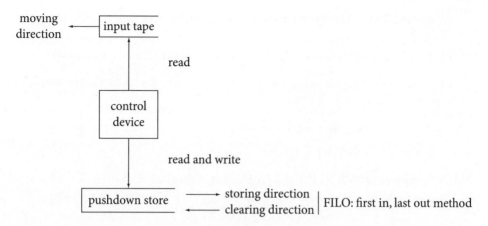

Fig. 8.1 A pushdown automaton

A *non-deterministic pushdown automaton* (NPDA) may reach a finite number of different new configurations from one configuration in one move:

$$M(z, q, a) = \{(w_1, p_1), (w_2, p_2), \ldots, (w_m, p_m)\},\, a \in T, w_i \in Z^*, p_i \in Q, 1 \le i \le m.$$

There may be λ-moves too, which make it possible for the PDA to change its configuration without reading any input.

For a string to be accepted, the three following conditions must hold:

 (i) the control device has read the whole string,
 (ii) the PDA has reached a final state,
 (iii) the pushdown store is empty.

Note that only the existence of at least one sequence of moves leading to an accepting configuration is required, while other sequences may lead to non-accepting ones.

(8.11) The language $L = \{a^n b^n: n \ge 1\}$ is accepted by the following PDA:
   $A = (\{z_0, a\}, \{q_0, q_1, q_2\}, \{a, b\}, M, z_0, q_0, \{q_2\}),$

with:

M	a	b	#
(z_0, q_0)	$(z_0 a, q_0)$	$\varnothing$	$\varnothing$
(a, q_0)	(aa, q_0)	(λ, q_1)	$\varnothing$
(z_0, q_1)	$\varnothing$	$\varnothing$	(λ, q_2)
(a, q_1)	$\varnothing$	(λ, q_1)	$\varnothing$
(z_0, q_2)	$\varnothing$	$\varnothing$	$\varnothing$
(a, q_2)	$\varnothing$	$\varnothing$	$\varnothing$

A PDA $A = (Z, Q, T, M, z_0, q_0, F)$ is said to be *deterministic* (DPDA) if and only if for every $(z, q) \in Z \times Q$:

(i) either $M(z, q, a)$ contains exactly one element, for every $a \in T$, while $M(z, q, \lambda)$ $= \varnothing$,

(ii) or $M(z, q, \lambda)$ contains exactly one element, while $M(z, q, a) = \varnothing$, for every $a \in T$.

The family of languages accepted by DPDAs is strictly contained in the family of languages accepted by NPDAs.

To illustrate this, let us observe the following:

(8.12) $L_1 = \{wcw^{-1} : w \in \{a, b\}^*\}, L_2 = \{ww^{-1} : w \in \{a, b\}^*\}.$

While L_1 belongs to both NPDA and DPDA, L_2 belongs only to NPDA.
The following results establish the relationship of NPDAs to *CF* languages.

NPDA = CF.

For every CF grammar an algorithm exists to transform it into an equivalent NPDA.

For every PDA an algorithm exists to transform it into an equivalent CF grammar.

Linear bounded automata are the class of accepting devices able to recognize *CS* languages.

Turing machines are the most powerful accepting devices, which are able to recognize any *RE* language. They are the foundation of computation theory and involve a lot of complexities which cannot be addressed here.

FURTHER READING AND RELEVANT RESOURCES

Partee, ter Meulen, and Wall (1990) is strongly recommended to enhance the mathematical background of readers with a grounding predominantly in linguistics. Brainerd (1971), Wall (1972), and Partee (1978) will be helpful references as well. Chapter 11.1 in Cole et al. (1997) discusses the main trends in integrating mathematical models with computational developments.

The most comprehensive and updated handbook of classical as well as nonclassical (which were not presented here) formal languages is Rozenberg and Salomaa (1997).

Extensively cited handbooks in classical formal language theory (with different levels of difficulty) include Aho and Ullman (1971–3), Davis, Sigal, and Weyuker (1994), Harrison (1978), Hopcroft and Ullman (1979), Révész (1991), Salomaa (1973), and Wood (1987). Other good books (not all of them having a completely general scope) are Brookshear (1989), Dassow and Păun (1989), Drobot (1989), Floyd and Beigel (1994), Gurari (1989), Howie (1991), Kelley (1995), Lewis and Papadimitriou

(1998), Linz (1990), McNaughton (1982), Moll, Arbib, and Kfoury (1988), and Sudkamp (1988).

Some of the developments in non-standard formal language theory can be found in Csuhaj-Varjú et al. (1994), Păun (1995, 1997), and Păun, Rozenberg, and Salomaa (1998).

The present state of the field is well covered in Martín-Vide and Mitrana (2001, 2002). For a less formal account of regular and context-free grammars, including natural language examples, see Chapter 4 of this volume.

The following references may be of help to the reader interested in learning more about linguistic applications of formal language theory: Kolb and Mönnich (1999), Levelt (1974), Manaster Ramer (1987), Martín-Vide (1994, 1998, 1999), Martín-Vide and Păun (2000), Miller (2000), Păun (1994), Savitch et al. (1987), Savitch and Zadrozny (1994), Sells, Shieber, and Wasow (1991), and Zadrozny, Manaster Ramer, and Moshier (1993).

References

Aho, A.V. and J. D. Ullman. 1971–3. *The Theory of Parsing, Translation and Compiling*, 2 vols. Englewood Cliffs, NJ: Prentice-Hall.

Brainerd, B. 1971. *Introduction to the Mathematics of Language Study*. New York: Elsevier.

Bresnan, J., R. M. Kaplan, S. Peters, and A. Zaenen. 1982. 'Cross-serial dependencies in Dutch'. *Linguistic Inquiry*, 13(4), 613–35.

Brookshear, J. G. 1989. *Theory of Computation: Formal Languages, Automata, and Complexity*. Redwood City, Calif.: Benjamin/Cummings.

Cole, R., J. Mariani, H. Uszkoreit, G. B. Varile, A. Zaenen, A. Zampolli, and V. Zue (eds.). 1997. *Survey of the State of the Art in Human Language Technology*. Cambridge: Cambridge University Press.

Csuhaj-Varjú, E., J. Dassow, J. Kelemen, and G. Păun. 1994. *Grammar Systems: A Grammatical Approach to Distribution and Cooperation*. London: Gordon and Breach.

Culy, C. 1985. 'The complexity of the vocabulary of Bambara'. *Linguistics and Philosophy*, 8, 345–51.

Dassow, J. and Gh. Păun. 1989. *Regulated Rewriting in Formal Language Theory*. Berlin: Springer.

Davis, M. D., R. Sigal, and E. J. Weyuker. 1994. *Computability, Complexity, and Languages: Fundamentals of Theoretical Computer Science*, 2nd edn. New York: Academic Press. First pub. 1983.

Drobot, V. 1989. *Formal Languages and Automata Theory*. Rockville, Md.: Computer Science Press.

Floyd, R. W. and R. Beigel. 1994. *The Language of Machines: An Introduction to Computability and Formal Languages*. Rockville, Md.: Computer Science Press.

Gazdar, G. 1981. 'Unbounded dependencies and coordinate structure'. *Linguistic Inquiry*, 12(2), 155–84.

Gurari, E. 1989. *An Introduction to the Theory of Computation*. New York: Computer Science Press.

Harrison, M. A. 1978. *Introduction to Formal Language Theory*. Reading, Mass.: Addison-Wesley.

Hopcroft, J. E. and J. D. Ullman. 1979. *Introduction to Automata Theory, Languages, and Computation* 2nd edn. Reading, Mass.: Addison-Wesley. First pub. 1969.

Howie, J. M. 1991. *Automata and Languages*. Oxford: Oxford University Press.

Kelley, D. 1995. *Automata and Formal Languages: An Introduction*. Englewood Cliffs, NJ: Prentice-Hall.

Kolb, H.-P. and U. Mönnich (eds.). 1999. *The Mathematics of Syntactic Structure: Trees and Their Logics*. Berlin: Mouton de Gruyter.

Levelt, W. J. M. 1974. *Formal Grammars in Linguistics and Psycholinguistics*, 3 vols. The Hague: Mouton.

Lewis, H. R. and C. H. Papadimitriou. 1998. *Elements of the Theory of Computation*, 2nd edn. Englewood Cliffs, NJ: Prentice-Hall. First pub. 1981.

Linz, P. 1996. *An Introduction to Formal Languages and Automata*, 2nd edn. Lexington, Mass.: D. C. Heath. First pub. 1990.

McNaughton, R. 1982. *Elementary Computability, Formal Languages, and Automata*. Englewood Cliffs, NJ: Prentice-Hall.

Manaster Ramer, A. (ed.). 1987. *Mathematics of Language*. Amsterdam: John Benjamins.

Martín-Vide, C. (ed.). 1994. *Current Issues in Mathematical Linguistics*. Amsterdam: North-Holland.

——(ed.). 1998. *Mathematical and Computational Analysis of Natural Language*. Amsterdam: John Benjamins.

——(ed.). 1999. *Issues in Mathematical Linguistics*. Amsterdam: John Benjamins.

——and V. Mitrana (eds.). 2001. *Where Mathematics, Computer Science, Linguistics and Biology Meet*. Dordrecht: Kluwer.

—— ——(eds.). 2002. *Grammars and Automata for String Processing: From Mathematics and Computer Science to Biology, and Back*. London: Taylor and Francis.

——and Gh. Păun (eds.). 2000. *Recent Topics in Mathematical and Computational Linguistics*. Bucharest: Editura Academiei Române.

Miller, P. 2000. *Strong Generative Capacity*. Stanford, Calif.: Center for the Study of Language and Information.

Moll, R. N., M. A. Arbib, and A. J. Kfoury. 1988. *An Introduction to Formal Language Theory*. Berlin: Springer.

Partee, B. H. 1978. *Foundations of Mathematics for Linguistics*. Harrisburg, Pa.: Greylock.

——A. G. B. ter Meulen, and R. E. Wall. 1990. *Mathematical Methods in Linguistics*. Dordrecht: Kluwer.

Păun, G. (ed.). 1994. *Mathematical Aspects of Natural and Formal Languages*. Singapore: World Scientific.

——(ed.). 1995. *Artificial Life: Grammatical Models*. Bucharest: Black Sea University Press.

——1997. *Marcus Contextual Grammars*. Dordrecht: Kluwer.

——G. Rozenberg, and A. Salomaa. 1998. *DNA Computing: New Computing Paradigms*. Berlin: Springer.

Pullum, G. K. and G. Gazdar. 1982. 'Natural languages and context-free languages'. *Linguistics and Philosophy*, 4, 471–504.

Révész, G. E. 1991. *Introduction to Formal Languages*, 2nd edn. New York: Dover. First pub. 1983.

Rozenberg, G. and A. Salomaa (eds.). 1997. *Handbook of Formal Languages*, 3 vols. Berlin: Springer.

Salomaa, A. 1973. *Formal Languages*. New York: Academic Press.

Savitch, W. J., E. W. Bach, W. Marsh, and G. Safran-Naveh (eds.). 1987. *The Formal Complexity of Natural Language*. Dordrecht: Reidel.

Savitch, W. J. and W. Zadrozny (eds.). 1994. *Mathematics of Language*. Linguistics and Philosophy, 17(6). Dordrecht: Kluwer.

Sells, P., S. M. Shieber, and T. Wasow (eds.). 1991. *Foundational Issues in Natural Language Processing*. Cambridge, Mass.: MIT Press.

Shieber, S. M. 1985. 'Evidence against the context-freeness of natural language'. *Linguistics and Philosophy*, 8, 333–43.

Sudkamp, T. A. 1988. *Languages and Machines*. Reading, Mass.: Addison-Wesley.

Wall, R. E. 1972. *Introduction to Mathematical Linguistics*. Englewood Cliffs, NJ: Prentice-Hall.

Wood, D. 1987. *Theory of Computation*. New York: John Wiley.

Zadrozny, W., A. Manaster Ramer, and M. A. Moshier (eds.). 1993. *Mathematics of Language*, Annals of Mathematics and Artificial Intelligence, 8(1–2). Basel: J. C. Baltzer.

CHAPTER 9

COMPLEXITY

BOB CARPENTER

ABSTRACT

We motivate the study of asymptotic complexity of problems and algorithms, introduce the mathematics of function growth, and then analyse examples of some standard problems and algorithms in natural language processing. We conclude with some reflections on the utility of complexity analysis both to understanding language complexity and to building practical natural language processing systems.

9.1 NOTIONS OF COMPLEXITY

For any computational problem we face, such as parsing a natural language sentence or determining the implications of a given utterance, we are interested in algorithms that can be used to solve the problem. For these algorithms, we are interested in how 'efficient' the algorithm is in terms of its run time or its use of memory or other system resources such as database accesses or network bandwidth. If the problem is important, we are usually interested in the complexity of the problem itself, as gauged by the efficiency of the best algorithm to solve the problem. We are also interested in how the algorithms fare as their input load gets higher; if a grammar intended for a fragment of English is extended to a wider domain, what impact will this have on the run time of the parser?

In addition to analysis at the algorithmic level, in practical situations we are faced with realizations of our algorithms on hardware, operating systems, programming languages, and compilers that have their own particular properties. An often overlooked, yet crucially important aspect of complexity analysis derives from the notions of benchmarking and profiling. A benchmark algorithm is often used to evaluate different hardware configurations, different compilers for a given programming language, or even a different way of organizing code at a fairly microscopic level. Often decisions on how to allocate memory and how to encode hash table keys, say as strings or as integers through a symbol table, will have a huge impact on the performance of a given algorithm in the field.

9.2 THE MATHEMATICS OF COMPLEXITY

9.2.1 Problems and algorithms

Computational problems are carried out over formal representations in terms of strings. A string is a sequence of elements drawn from a given finite alphabet. More formally, for a given finite set Σ, called an alphabet, we define $\Sigma^* = \{\sigma_1 \ldots \sigma_n \mid n \geq 0, \sigma_i \in \Sigma\}$ to be the set of strings over Σ. The length of a string $\sigma = \sigma_1 \ldots \sigma_n \in \Sigma^*$ is said to be n. (See Chapter 8 for more detail on alphabets and languages.)

For both generality and simplicty, we restrict our model to algorithms that compute functions $f: \Sigma^* \to \Sigma^*$ over strings. Technically, this does not restrict the power of our formalism, as all (discrete) computational problems can be directly encoded as string problems. For any such algorithm, we can measure a number of things about it. For an input $\sigma \in \Sigma^*$, we can measure the time required to compute $f(\sigma)$, or the maximum amount of memory used, the number of memory look-ups, the number of floating point operations carried out, the number of database accesses, the maximum number of applications that can run on a single computer, the maximum peak processor load, the number of cache misses, or any of a multitude of other measures of computational resources used. Typically we assume an idealized machine and count time in terms of the number of basic operations, because such measures are usually tightly correlated with real-world measures such as run time on a real machine.

9.2.2 Complexity measures

We consider discrete performance measures $c : \Sigma^* \to \mathsf{Int}$ that map strings into integers. As we said before, such functions can be used to measure many aspects of real-world or theoretical performance.

9.2.2.1 *Worst case complexity*

Because we are usually interested in running our algorithms on a number of inputs, we abstract away from individual input strings and measure complexity in terms of the length of the input. We are thus interested in complexity as a function of input length, which can be derived from performance on individual inputs by means of a cost function $f_c : \mathsf{Int} \to \mathsf{Int}$. This cost function is usually defined in terms of the **worst case complexity** of inputs by defining $f_c(n)$ to be the highest cost for any input of length n, or, more formally, by setting $f_c(n) = max_{\sigma_i \in \Sigma, 1 \le i \le n} f(\sigma_1 \dots \sigma_n)$. We assume that our cost functions are monotonic increasing, meaning that if $n \ge m$, then $f(n) \ge f(m)$.

9.2.2.2 *Average case complexity*

Worst case performance may not be indicative of real life algorithm performance over a number of inputs, because the worst cases might be rare. In order to define **average case complexity**, we need a probability distribution $p : \Sigma^* \to [\emptyset, 1]$ such that $\Sigma_{\sigma \in \Sigma^*} p(\sigma) = 1$. The probability of an input of length n is given by $Z(n) = \Sigma_{length(\sigma) = n} p(\sigma)$. We then define the average performance on an input of length n by taking a weighted average of the performance measure: $\Sigma_{length(\sigma) = n} p(\sigma) f_c(\sigma)/Z(n)$ (rounded up to the nearest integer). That is, we take averages based on the probability of inputs rather than just choosing the maximum. Average complexity tends to be difficult to derive analytically; thus it is typically estimated by benchmarking rather than being derived.

9.2.2.3 *Problem complexity*

The performance measures above are intended to measure algorithms. We can also measure the complexity of a problem, where a problem is a generic specification of functional (input/output) behaviour independent of algorithms. It thus measures the complexity of a task rather than its implementation.

For instance, we might have a sorting algorithm that takes n^2 comparisons to sort a list, and we might wonder if this is optimal. The notion of *problem complexity* is usually defined as the complexity (worst case or average case) of the best algorithm for the problem. (There are sorting algorithms like merge sort that use $n \log n$ comparisons in the worst case, which is in fact the worst case problem complexity of sorting in terms of comparisons.) It is rather difficult to get a handle on problem complexity, because we need to prove something about all algorithms that perform a task.

9.2.3 Formal languages

Any subset $L \subseteq \Sigma^*$ is said to be a formal language. The **decision problem** for L is to determine whether a string is an element of L or not. We can code algorithms for decision problems in terms of the characteristic function of L, which maps the elements of L to (a representation of) 1, and mapping other strings to (a representation of) ø. (See Chapter 8 for more detail on formal languages.)

9.2.4 Complexity classes

The basis of the mathematical theory of complexity is the asymptotic growth of a function up to a constant factor. Thus we set $g \leq f$ if and only if there exist integers k and m such that for all $n > m$, $k f(n) > g(n)$. The asymptotic component is that we only consider the operations of f and g on elements greater than m. The reason to be concerned with asymptotic growth when considering an algorithm is that any finite number of cases can be precompiled by an algorithm. (In practice, of course, precompilation is often limited by memory size.) The constant factor k equates all functions that grow within a linear bound of each other. We are only considering growth up to a constant factor because algorithms can, in general, be sped up by constant factors by composing several steps into one using precompilation; this is the content of the speed-up theorem (see Hopcroft and Ullman 1979). As usual, the practicality of these theoretical results is governed by other resources such as memory size and indexing scheme.

Note that $\leq$ is a partial (pre-)order; setting $f = g$ if and only if $f \leq g$ and $g \leq f$ defines an equivalence relation on functions. We set the asymptotic upper bound $O(f) = \{g \mid g \leq f\}$, the asymptotic lower bound to $\Omega(f) = \{g \mid f \leq g\}$, the asymptotic bound $\Theta(f) = \{g \mid g = f\} = O(f) \cap \Omega(f)$. Note that these classes contain functions on integers.

9.2.5 P: polynomial algorithms

The class **P** of algorithms which execute in polynomial time is defined by $\mathbf{P} = \cup_k O(n^k)$. Often a problem is said to be **tractable** if there is a polynomial algorithm to compute it, and is said to be *intractable* otherwise. Note that the exponential function $f(n) = k^n$ is not in P for any k.

9.2.6 NP: nondeterministic polynomial algorithms

Another well-known complexity class is **NP**, the class of **non-deterministic polynomial** decision problems. These problems have decision algorithms which run in polynomial time on a non-deterministic machine (see Cormen, Leiserson, and Rivest 1990 for precise definitions). A decision problem L is said to be **NP hard** if any other decision problem can be reduced to it by means of a polynomial correspondece; it is said to be **NP complete** if it is both **NP** hard and in **NP**. For example, Turing machine execution is **NP** hard but not **NP** complete. More formally, L is **NP** complete if for any problem $L' \in NP$, there exists an integer k and an algorithm f computing a function whose time complexity is in $O(n^k)$ such that $x \in L'$ if and only if $f(x) \in L$. The function f is essentially a coding of the problem L' into L; such codings can often be used to establish complexity results by reducing one problem to another. This is not so hard to establish at it may first appear; because there are dozens of well-known NP-complete problems, it is sufficient to reduce any one of them to the problem at hand in order to establish **NP** completeness for an algorithm in **NP**. See Barton, Berwick, and Ristad (1987) for a survey of **NP** completeness results in natural language processing.

9.3 COMPLEXITY OF REGULAR LANGUAGE PROBLEMS

We begin with a series of complexity analyses of problems involving the regular languages, an important class of languages which can be defined in terms of simple pattern matching via regular expressions or in terms of finite-state automata recognition. The analyses were chosen to illustrate important aspects of determinism, nondeterminism, and compilation.

9.3.1 Regular languages and finite-state automata

A finite-state automaton is a tuple $A = \langle Q, q_\emptyset, F, \delta, \Sigma \rangle$ such that Q is a finite set of states, $q_\emptyset$ is an initial state, F is a set of final states, $\delta \subseteq \Sigma \times Q \to Q$ is a transition relation, and Σ is the alphabet of symbols over which the automaton is defined. (See Chapter 8 for further details on finite-state automata.) We extend δ from symbols of the alphabet to strings by taking one step at a time. More formally, we assume δ^* is the least relation such that $\langle \varepsilon, q, q \rangle \in \delta^*$, and $\langle s\sigma, q, q' \rangle \in \delta^*$ if for some q'', $\langle s, q, q'' \rangle \in \delta$ and $\langle \sigma, q'', q' \rangle \in \delta^*$. A finite-state automaton is said to be *deterministic* if δ is a function on the first two arguments, that is, if $\langle s, q, q' \rangle, \langle s, q, q'' \rangle \in \delta$ entails $q' = q''$.

The language generated by A is the set of strings which lead the automaton from its initial state $q_\emptyset$ to a final state in F via the extended transition relation δ^*; thus the language generated by A is given by $L(A) = \{\sigma \mid \langle \sigma, q_0, q \rangle \in \delta^*, q \in F\}$. Any formal language generated by a finite-state automaton is said to be a *regular language*.

9.3.2 Determinism and non-determinism

It turns out that every regular language is generated by some deterministic finite-state automaton. More specifically, for any (possibly non-deterministic) automaton A, we can construct a deterministic automaton $\mathcal{D}(A)$ that recognizes the same language. The intuition behind this construction is that states in $\mathcal{D}(A)$ correspond to sets of possible states in A, representing the potential non-determinism at the state level. Note that if Q is finite, then so is the set 2^Q of all of its subsets. More formally, if $A = \langle Q, q_0, F, \delta, \Sigma \rangle$ is a finite-state automaton, we can **determinize** it to produce a deterministic automaton $\mathcal{D}(A) = \langle 2^Q - \varnothing, \{q_0\}, \{Q' | Q' \subseteq Q, Q' \cap F \neq \varnothing\}, \delta' \rangle$, where $\delta'(s, Q) = \{q' \mid q \in Q, \langle s, q, q' \rangle \in \delta\}$. The intuition given above can easily be expanded into a formal proof that the language of A is the same as that of $\mathcal{D}(A)$, or in symbols, $L(A) = L(\mathcal{D}(A))$. See Hopcroft and Ullman (1979) for a detailed proof.

9.3.3 Complexity of regular languages and automata

Eliminating non-determinism can have a significant impact on complexity. The potential states reached in a non-deterministic algorithm can be tracked at run time or precompiled in order to bound the complexity of the decision problem for regular languages. But, as we will see, the resulting asymptotic complexities of these approaches reveal subtle differences.

First, assume we have a deterministic finite-state automaton A. Then we can write an algorithm to recognize whether or not a string is in the language generated by A that is linear, that is, in $O(n)$. The algorithm keeps track of the current state and a pointer indicating the portion of the string remaining to process. It is initialized with the start state and the input string. Then for each symbol in the input string, $\delta(s, q)$ is computed from the current state q. If $\delta(s, q)$ is ever undefined during the computation, ø is returned. If, after all of the input is consumed, the resulting state is a final state, then 1 is returned, otherwise ø is returned. The number of steps is clearly linear in the length of the input string as only one computation of δ is required. Because we know that, for every regular language, there is a deterministic finite-state automaton that generates it, we know that the decision problem for any regular language is at most linear in complexity. This being only a worst case analysis, it is not surprising that some decision problems are easier; for instance, the language of strings that start with 'a' can be recognized in constant time with an appropriate encoding.

9.3.4 The universal finite-state recognition problem

In addition to the decision problem given by a particular automaton A, we might be interested in an algorithm that takes as input both an automaton and a string. Such an algorithm is said to be *universal* for finite-state recognition. We can assume that the input coding of the automaton can be converted into a directly indexed, pointer-based representation in linear time.

9.3.5   The deterministic case

We conclude that the universal, deterministic finite-state recognition problem is linear in time. This well-behaved run-time and universal problem complexity go a long way to explain the attractiveness of finite-state automata.

9.3.6   The non-deterministic case

Universal recognition for non-deterministic finite-state automata appears more complex. We cannot immediately deduce linear complexity, because the compilation given above involves a potentially exponential number of states in the deterministic automaton $D(A)$. The best we can do by using the precompilation given above is conclude that the problem is in $O(n2^m)$, where n is the input string length and m is the number of states in the input automaton. Of course, the growth in n is linear; once 2^m steps are expended in the determinization, the recognition is easy. But this means that the growth for the algorithm as a whole, including both string and automaton, is exponential.

Perhaps surprisingly, the universal recognition problem for non-deterministic finite-state automata can be bounded much more tightly. Suppose we design a variant of the deterministic algorithm that keeps track of a set of states rather than a single state at each point. Then the transition on a single input symbol will require each member of the set to be considered (at most m), and each possible resulting state to be considered (at most m), thus requiring as much as m^2 steps. Because we have these m^2 steps carried out for each symbol in the input, the overall complexity is bounded by $O(nm^2)$, a significant reduction in complexity for the universal problem from the precompiliation approach. But note that for a particular problem, precompilation is often the preferred approach, because it is guaranteed to produce an efficient run time if there is sufficient memory available to store and access the edges efficiently.

9.3.7   Linearity versus finite-stateness

It is tempting to reason that, because of the generality of finite-state automata and their linear run time, any language that can be recognized in linear time must be finite state. But this is simply not so. Consider the language $\{a^n b^n \mid n \geq \emptyset\}$ of all strings consisting of a sequence of as followed by an equal number of bs. Recognition is obviously linear because we simply count the as as we see them and then count the bs as we see them and see if the counts are the same, returning false if we ever encounter an a after a b. This language is a classic example of a non-regular language, although it is context free. But consider $\{a^n b^n c^n \mid n \geq \emptyset\}$, which also has a recognition problem in $O(n)$. This language is not even context free. This illustrates how the complexity hierarchy cuts across the Chomsky hierarchy of formal languages. Every regular language has a linear decision problem, but not conversely. (See Chapter 8 for further discussion of the Chomsky hierarchy and the particular language $a^n b^n$.)

9.3.8 Applicability of finite-state methods

It is important to note that finite-state methods can be used for any task for which the amount of memory needed at run time can be bounded. If the bound is high enough, virtually any reasonable application can be coded with finitely many states. The trade-off, in practical terms, is that the precompilation of a deterministic automaton or the run time computation of transitions may be more costly in real terms than a direct implementation. It should also be noted in this context that, in real terms, a very efficient finite-state library (such as the regular expression matching provided in Perl), which can be optimized independently of applications, may sway the argument for or against finite-state methods. Similarly, integration with other finite-state automata, as in speech recognition applications, may force a designer to restrict solutions to those that can be fairly easily modelled by finite-state automata.

9.4 COMPLEXITY OF CONTEXT-FREE LANGUAGE PROBLEMS

In this section, we consider the context-free languages and the complexity of their recognition problem. Context-free languages are significantly more complex than regular languages and require dynamic programming methods to efficiently handle the inherent recursion.

9.4.1 Context-free grammars

A context-free grammar is a tuple $G = \langle C, s, W, R, L \rangle$ where C is a finite set of categories, $s \in C$ is the distinguished start symbol, W is a finite set of words, $R \subseteq C \times C^*$ is a set of grammar rules, and $L \subseteq C \times W$ is a lexicon. We write $c \to w$ if $\langle c, w \rangle \in L$ and call it a lexical entry, and we write $c_\emptyset \to c_1 \ldots c_n$ if $\langle c_\emptyset, \langle c_1, \ldots, c_n \rangle \rangle \in R$ and call it a grammar rule. Each grammar rule has an arity, given by n; a rule $\langle c_\emptyset, \langle \, \rangle \rangle$ is said to be a nullary rule (also called an empty category by some linguists), a rule $\langle c_\emptyset, \langle c_1 \rangle \rangle$ is called a unary rule, and so on. (See Chapter 8 for an equivalent definition of context-free grammars.)

We define the languages generated by a grammar for each category. The languages $L(G, c)$ generated by a grammar G for categories $c \in C$ are defined by mutual recursion as the least such that $w \in L(G, c)$ if $c \to w \in L$, and $L(G, c_1) \cdots L(G, c_n) \subseteq L(G, c_\emptyset)$ if $c_\emptyset \to c_1 \cdots c_n \in R$ (note that $n \geq \emptyset$). The context-free language generated by G is taken to be $L(G) = L(G, s)$, where s is the distinguished start symbol of G.

9.4.2 The number of parse trees

The set of parse trees for a grammar G can be defined for the set of categories by mutual recursion. We define the set $T(G, c)$ to be the set of parse trees of category c as the least set such that $\langle c, w \rangle \in T(G, c)$ if $c \to w$, and such that $\langle c, \langle T_1, \ldots, T_n \rangle \rangle \in T(G, c)$ if $c \to c_1 \ldots c_n$ and $T_i \in T(G, c_i)$ for $1 \leq i \leq n$.

Clearly if a string is in the language of a category then there is a parse tree which yields that category, because the definition of parse tree matches the recursive definition of the members of the language. But there can be surprisingly many parse trees for a string in the language. Consider a grammar for noun compounds, with one lexical entry $NP \to thing$ and one rule $NP \to NP\ NP$ with a distinguished symbol NP. This may be a trivial grammar, but consider the sequence $thing^n$ of n instances of the word $thing$. Every possible way of breaking the string $thing^n$ in two corresponds to a valid parse tree, itself with as many ways of being derived as it has ways of being broken down. This kind of multiplication of subproblem combinatorics is indicative of exponential problems. In this case, the number of parse trees for $thing^n$ is given by the function $f(n)$, which we can define recursively. For $n = 1$ we set $f(1) = 1$, and for $n > 1$ we set $\sum_{k=1}^{n-1} f(k) f(n - k)$. The case for 1 holds because there is but a single derivation in this case. For $n > 1$, we have a derivation for each break point corresponding to the k in the summation for each way of analysing each half of the break, given by $f(k)$ and $f(n-k)$. The function f that solves this recurrence gives the sequence of Catalan numbers, which we can bound from below, noting that it is in $\Omega(4^n/n^{3/2})$ (see Cormen, Leiserson, and Rivest 1990).

9.4.3 Search-based context-free recognition

A number of simple search-based parsing algorithms are in wide use. These include examples that are bottom up, such as shift-reduce parsers, and those that are top-down, such as recursive descent parsers, or those that combine both strategies, as in left-corner parsers. All of these parsers have worst case complexity proportional to the number of possible parse trees, which can grow as quickly as the Catalan numbers, even for some simple fixed grammars, such as the one for compounding given above. On the bright side, these parsers have the advantage of only using an amount of memory that is linear in the input length.

9.4.4 Top-down recognition

For illustration, we will take the case of a simple recursive descent left-to-right parser. This is the strategy used in standard versions of Prolog for evaluating definite-clause grammars, for instance. The algorithm is straightforward, and involves keeping track of a derivation state, which is a sequence of categories that are sought and a position in the input string. The sequence of steps involved in parsing [S [NP [Det *the*] [N *kid*]] [VP [IV *ran*]]] starts from S/*the, kid, ran*, assuming that S is the start symbol. The representation consists of the symbols being sought, initially just the start symbol, and the remaining portion of the string. The algorithm is non-deterministic and can move from one state to the next by rewriting the first category on the list using one of the rules or by a lexical entry to consume the first word on the input list. The parse above would proceed to NP, VP/*the, kid, ran* by rewriting S using the rule S → NP VP. We now need to find an NP followed by a VP from the input string. We next rewrite the NP using the rule NP → Det N to yield Det, N, VP/*the, kid, ran*. We can now perform two lexical rewritings, first of Det → *the* and then of N → *kid*, yielding configurations N, VP/*kid, ran* and VP/*ran*. We then use a unary rule VP → IV to derive IV/*ran* and then finally use a lexical rewrite of IV → *ran* to get the final result. If there are alternative rules that have the same left-hand side, then any of the rules may be used. Typically this is implemented by backtracking. Although backtracking is built into languages such as Prolog, it can be implemented in functional or declarative languages by simply maintaining a stack of alternatives to be evaluated. In practice, storing these alternatives can be done with a pointer into a list of productions for a given category, or it can be implemented directly in the underlying language's function call stack. The number of pointers needed is then bounded by the number of productions employed, which must be linear in the input string. Thus the space requirements are linear in the input string. But this reasoning assumes that there is no left recursion in the grammar. For instance, the rule VP → VP PP is left recursive, as is the sequence of rules $A → B\,C$ and $B → A\,D$. A grammar is said to be left-recursive if the graph constructed from the grammar in the following manner is cyclic. The graph consists of a node for each category and an edge $\langle A, B \rangle$ from category A to category B for each rule of the form $A \rightarrow B \cdots$ in the grammar. The problem is that such left recursion can lead to infinite loops. In practice, we can either precompile grammars to eliminate left recursion (see Chapter 8 for further information on Greibach normal form, which converts any grammar into one without left recursion that generates the same context-free language). It is also evident why the time requirements follow the number of possible derivations; each state in the derivation corresponds to a possible derivation. For instance, if we have an input string σs for $\sigma \in \Sigma^*, s \in \Sigma$, and suppose that σ has exponentially many derivations and that σs is not in the language, then this parsing algorithm will cycle through all analyses for σ before it is able to conclude that σs is ungrammatical.

9.4.5 Deterministic grammar recognition in linear time and space

If we further restrict the grammars to be non-ambiguous under some conditions, we can reduce parsing time and space to linear. This is the basis of the practical parsing strategies LR, LL, and their cousins. For instance, LL is a top-down strategy similar to what we described above. A grammar is said to be an $LL(k)$-grammar if k symbols of lookahead combined with the top-down parsing methodology given above, is enough to uniquely determine which production must be applied. This obviously reduces both time and space to linear, but imposes a serious restriction in that only a single analysis can be returned. (This is the basis for so-called Marcus parsing; see Marcus 1980.)

9.4.6 Memoization of well-formed substrings

Maintaining polynomial time complexity while relaxing the requirement on deterministic grammars requires balancing the exponential number of derivations with the need to construct a representation that produces them all in polynomial time and thus in polynomial space (of course, space bounds can never grow faster than time bounds). This can be achieved through dynamic programming by the memoization of intermediate analyses. We take a bottom-up approach, but a top-down method is also possible (see Earley 1970). The algorithm we provide involves the basic functionality to efficiently store a set of categories from position m to position n. The number of categories is bounded by the grammar size, so this operation will depend on the size of the grammar, but we can use mechanisms such as hashing to do it in linear expected time or bit vectors to do it in linear time. Whether we use these or other mechanisms often depends on extrinsic factors such as storing derivations, and which method is most practical will depend on the density of categories stored and the access profile. For simplicity, we will assume a grammar with only binary branching rules, though in practice we can either convert the grammar to binary branching (known as Chomsky normal form, see Chapter 8), or use a method that works directly on arbitrary context-free grammars (Earley 1970). The following bottom-up parsing algorithm for binary branching grammars has been independently attributed to Cocke, Kasami, and Younger (see Kasami 1965 and Younger 1967), and is known as CKY parsing. The input consists of a grammar and a string of tokens $a[1], \ldots, a[n]$. The output is a Boolean indicating whether the string is accepted by the grammar.

1. for position = 0 to n−1
       categories[position, position+1] = $\{c \mid c \rightarrow a[\text{position} + 1]\}$
2. for span = 2 to n
3.   for left = 0 to n-span
4.   for mid = 1 to span−1
5.   for $c0 \rightarrow c1 \; c2 \in$ Grammar
                   if ($c1 \in$ categories[left, left+mid]
                       AND $c2 \in$ categories[left+mid, left+span])
                   categories[left, left+span] += $c0$
     return (start∈categories[0, n])

There are five loops in this program, which provides a simple structure to analyse in terms of complexity. The first loop in line 1 is for lexical insertion and will take $O(n)$ steps. The outer loop beginning on line 2 proceeds by inspecting ever larger spans of the input and for each span, looping in line 3 over every left position that could start such a span. The inner loop at line 4 considers each possible cut point between the left position and the left position plus the span; then for every grammar rule, the categories found in the left side and those found on the right side are inspected to see if they match the rule, and if they do, the category on the left-hand side is added to the result. The three outer loops are each bounded by n, the length of the input string, whereas the inner loop is bounded by m, the number of rules in the grammar. The result is an algorithm that runs in $O(n + n^3 m) = O(n^3 m)$ time.

9.5 PROBABILISTIC GRAMMARS AND HEURISTIC SEARCH

Most contemporary applications are based on probablistic notions of grammars. The best-known variety are the probabilistic finite-state automata and the probabilistic context-free grammars. We will consider the context-free case. The basic idea is that a probability distribution over the rules for a given non-terminal is given to represent the conditional likelihood of the (top-down) expansion of a given terminal. Then we require that for each non-terminal C, that $\Sigma_{C\rightarrow\sigma}p(C\rightarrow\sigma\,|\,C)=1$. This provides a natural way to assign a probability to a given derivation as represented by a parse tree; simply multiply the probabilities on each rule. (In practice, taking logarithms and adding is more efficient because addition is faster than multiplication on most machines, and because of underflow problems arising from very small probabilities.)

With probabilistic grammars there are a number of things we are interested in computing. For instance, we might want to find the analysis as category c for a given string; or we might want to find the sum of the probabilities of all of the analyses for a given string $\sigma\in\Sigma^*$, allowing us to define a language model, which is a probability distribution over Σ^* defining a model of the likelihood of a given string in the language. Here the likelihood of a string is estimated by summing the likelihood estimates of all of the trees that generate it. Either of these computations can be carried out efficiently. For instance, using the CKY parsing algorithm, rather than storing a set of categories that have been found spanning each substring of the input string, we can keep track of a pair consisting of the category and the highest probability derived. If we are interested in the total probability for the string, then we simply add the probability associated with each derivation during the innermost loop. Adding probabilities does not add to the asymptotic complexity of context-free grammar parsing.

9.5.1 Pruning and approximation

For wide coverage probabilistic context-free grammars, such as those induced directly from the Penn Treebank (Marcus, Santorini, and Marcinkiewicz 1993), there are literally millions of analyses even for sentences of average length, which is greater than twenty words in the treebank. This makes it impractical with today's computational power to compute all of the parse trees for a given input string. Instead, pruning is applied in order to eliminate hypotheses of low likelihood. This is typically done using heuristics defined bottom up. We could restrict our pruning to hypotheses that are dominated by other hypotheses (as in A* search), but that leaves us with a cubic algorithm just as before (see Norvig 1992 for a description of A* search).

One popular pruning strategy is known as a *beam search*, where a derivation spanning a given substring of the input is only kept if its probability is within some fraction b, called the beam, of the best analysis found with that span. This comparison can either be made for each category or it can be made across categories. And various estimates can be used of the likelihood of an analysis spanning a given part of the input to be completed (which is computed exactly as the so-called outside score; see Pereira and Schabes 1992). In addition to a beam approach, often the number of results allowed at a given point in the computation is limited to some constant. The effect of this move is to remove some of the complexity arising from having a large grammar, making it possible to reduce the contribution of the grammar to a constant factor by slightly reorganizing the innermost loop. Instead of looping over the grammar rules, they can loop over the categories on either side of the split point and build results that they can produce. This loop is bounded by the constant limit on the number of derivations, not the size of the grammar. Using this kind of pruning does have its drawbacks, not the least of which is that pruning can remove a subderivation of the best derivation at some point; removing a derivation in the best-scoring analysis is known as a search error. The usual game is to make the beam as small as possible while keeping search errors at a tolerable level.

In addition to beams, statistical parsers often limit the number of analyses at a given stage to the best-scoring m. This is sometimes known as histogram pruning. An exact method must maintain some ordering on the scores by means of a priority queue, which costs an extra $O(\log m)$ per look-up (see Cormen, Leiserson, and Rivest 1990 for a disucssion of heap-based implementations of priority queues). Often a priority queue is approximated with bins, resulting in linear run-time, but admitting the possibility of both search errors and keeping more than the maximum m analyses; see Ortmanns, Ney, and Aubert (1997), for example. If we limit all the analyses ending at a given point to m and maintain that set with a heap-based priority queue, the parsing time is $O(n \log m)$, where m is the size of the bin and n is the length of the input string. This is the reason that Collins's parser runs in real time over the Penn treebank (Collins 1997).

9.6 PARALLEL PROCESSING

The CKY approach to parsing is interesting because it illustrates the way in which parallel processing can be used to speed up computations, in theory at least. We will assume a parallel processing architecture where the processors can all address a shared memory, from which they can read and write concurrently (the so-called CRCW architecture). In practice, writes need to be synchronized and can lead to a small overhead. We then simply note that the two outside loops in the CKY algorithm can be executed in parallel.

For instance, suppose we had n processors for an input of length n. Then we could use one for each position in the inner loop over the midpoint to split the current span being considered. Each of the split points is independent in the sense that the results do not feed into each other and once an analysis is found, it does not go away, so all writing after initialization is to a Boolean true value. Using n processors for the inner loop in parallel, the computation time is reduced to a constant—there is simply no looping. This reduces the overall input time to $O(n^2)$. This provides an example of what is known as a work-efficient parallel algorithm. Using n processors brings processing time down from n^3 to n^2. Note that we can also parallelize the second innermost loop, which is over the left positions. Again, all derivations are independent. We can thus parallelize both inner loops with n^2 processors, and the resulting run time will be $O(n)$; another work-efficient result. What is perhaps more surprising, and beyond the scope of this survey, is that with n^6 processors, partial evaluation and combination can be used to reduce the processing time to $O(\log n)$ (Sikkel and Nijholt 1991); this is not work efficient, because $n^6 \log n$ grows faster than n^3.

9.7 ABBREVIATION AND NP COMPLETENESS

The last theoretical topic we consider is that of NP completeness. Many simple models of natural language phenomena, such as free word order, agreement, and non-deterministic finite-state transduction, wind up being NP complete. But most of the analyses of NP completeness put forward in the literature have been for universal problems, and the NP completeness results from having the ability to make the grammar larger.

The analysis we consider is that of ID/LP grammars (Gazdar et al. 1985). These grammars factor a context-free grammar into immediate dominance rules and linear precedence constraints. Formally, an ID/LP grammar is defined by a set of terminals and non-terminals as in a context-free grammar, and the notion of lexicon remains unchanged. The difference arises in the rule component. Instead of specifying a rule such as $A \to B_1 \ldots B_n$ where the right-hand side categories form a sequence, the rules are of the form $A \to \{B_1, \ldots, B_n\}$ where the right-hand side elements form a multi-set (roughly, a multiset can be viewed as either a set that allows repetitions, or a sequence that allows permutation). In addition to a collection of immediate dominance rules, there is a reflexive, anti-symmetric linear precedence relation < over the non-terminals. We can think of this grammar as inducing a context-free grammar in the following way. For each rule $A \to \{B_1, \ldots, B_n\}_m$, and each permutation $p : \{1, \ldots, n\} \to \{1, \ldots, n\}$ (a permutation is a one-one, onto function) such that $n < m$ in the numerical ordering implies that $B_{p(n)} \not< B_{p(m)}$ in the LP ordering, assume the context-free rule $A \to B_{p(1)} \ldots B_{p(n)}$. It is crucial to note here that the ID/LP formalism and the context-free grammar formalism generate exactly the same class of languages, namely the context-free languages.

It turns out that the universal recognition problem for this grammar formalism is NP complete, in contrast to that for ordinary context-free grammars, which is polynomial. The proof of NP completeness proceeds in two parts. First, we must prove that the recognition problem is in NP; that is, prove that there exists a non-deterministic polynomial algorithm that decides the universal grammatical problem. This is fairly straightforward; we simply use the existing parsing algorithm, but non-deterministically choose an ordering of the right-hand side of an ID rule and then check that it does not violate any LP constraints, the latter being a deterministic polynomial operation. The second step in the proof is to demonstrate a polynomial encoding of a problem known to be NP complete in terms of ID/LP grammaticality. To this end Barton, Berwick, and Ristad (1987) provide a reduction of the vertex covering problem, which is an NP complete problem.

It is widely believed, though not yet proven, that the class P of polynomially recognizable languages is a proper subset of the NP complete languages; that is, there will not be a polynomial algorithm to solve an NP complete problem (otherwise every NP complete problem would have a polynomial decision problem by the polynomial reduction to the NP complete problem that is shown to have one). So must we conclude that ID/LP parsing is intractable, but CFG parsing is tractable? Technically, in terms of the definition, the answer is a clear 'yes'. But it is crucial to note that this complexity is for the universal problem. Every given grammar will still have a polynomial parser for the language-specific decision problem. Furthermore, we could simply conclude that the ID/LP formalism provides a more terse encoding of a context-free grammar; so terse that the equivalent context-free grammar is at least exponentially larger. But we might conclude this is a good thing if in fact the language being specified is the one in which we are interested in. For that language, we can expand the ID/LP grammar to a context-free grammar, and then perhaps even transform the resulting context-free grammar for further optimizations. The point here is that you can view an NP complete problem as providing a particularly efficient encoding of information; so efficient that all known algorithms to decode it at run time are exponential.

9.8 Practical Efficiency

Theoretical complexity concerns can help to drive the decision as to which algorithm to use. But they should not be used to the exclusion of real-world measures. After all, if our goals are not purely theoretical, the practical goal is to solve some real problem on real hardware with a real compiler.

In practice, nothing beats a realistic set of benchmark tests and profiling in a real compiler. But developing realistic benchmark tests is difficult and also contentious. If there are groups of people who have slightly different needs, different benchmarks may be called for. And in practice, it is often difficult to test two approaches, because of the nasty little detail of implementation. It is simply possible to have a good implementation of a bad algorithm beat a bad implementation of a good algorithm. So a practical comparison of two competing algorithms is fraught with peril. For instance, consider the conclusion of Covington (1993) that chart-parsing was less efficient in practice than search-based methods. The problem here is that he chose an incredibly inefficient method in Prolog of representing analyses that have already been found, and then he tested on inputs that were very short and grammars that were very small.

A few years ago, after reading Covington's conclusions, I set out to build implementations of these algorithms that were as efficient as I could manage. What I found is rather typical, and is reported in Table 9.1, which shows run times versus input length

Table 9.1.

Input		PARSER		
|n|	CKY	LC	SR	TD
4	4	0	2	0
7	6	0	6	
10			52	0
13	18	0	402	
16	26	7	3184	0
19			15870	
22	49	80		10
25		295		
28	79	1113		90
31		4270		305
34	122	16330		1100
37	150	62520		3810
40				13585
43	211			48875
49	290			
55	394			
64	590			
73	753			
82	1172			
94	1722			

for a CKY parser, a left-corner parser, a shift-reduce parser, and a simple recursive descent top-down parser. (The top-down version has an unfair advantage, because it can be implemented directly as a definite clause grammar; see O'Keefe 1990 for information on definite clause grammars.) The inputs were of the form 'PN TV Det N (P Det N)^{k}' with the usual grammar (VP $\rightarrow$ VP PP, N $\rightarrow$ N PP, VP $\rightarrow$ TV NP, NP $\rightarrow$ Det N, and S $\rightarrow$ NP VP).

On short inputs, or with grammars and inputs with little ambiguity, the search-based parsers were far faster than ones that computed well-formed substring tables. On the other hand, with more ambiguous grammars such as those represented by compounding, my computer could not complete a search-based parse for longer inputs than those listed, but the dynamic programming methods were still highly efficient.

So what we should conclude is not that one algorithm is better than the other, but, if we trust my coding, that each would be used in different situations. If we need a small memory footprint, have short inputs, or grammars with little ambiguity, the search-based methods clearly dominate. If we have more memory and need to process longer inputs in more ambiguous grammars, dynamic programming is necessary. When probabilistic grammars are added to the mix, all bets are off again, and search algorithms should be re-evaluated relative to dynamic programming algorithms.

In practice, simple unfolding of loops often has a profound influence on efficiency, especially if it facilitates last call optimization. A quick tour through O'Keefe (1990) or Norvig (1992), or pretty much any reasonable book on compiler design, will have examples. It is this notion of unfolding that underlies the speed-up theorem we mentioned earlier. The trick for constant speed-up is simply to unfold things that would take two operations into one step; the program gets a lot bigger, and in practice the loss of code locality in cache will often overwhelm any gains from unfolding code. Similarly, folding, as in continuation passing techniques (again, see Norvig 1992 or O'Keefe 1990), can often improve performance if some computation can be done lazily, or on demand, rather than eagerly before it is needed; if the computation turns out to never be needed, the savings can be substantial for this methodology.

For those who want to hone their real-world programming skills, I can highly recommend the following books, which cover profiling, benchmarking, testing and what you can do to improve efficiency: Hunt and Thomas (1999) and Bentley (1999).

Another often overlooked factor of complexity is the combination of run time plus programmer effort. If it takes four hours to write a shell script that automates a task you have to do only twice, which would have taken an hour to do by hand, you have lost time and effort. Especially in experimental contexts where real-time performance is not crucial, it is worth trying to estimate the combined programming effort plus run time.

I can think of no better conclusion than to cite the following well-known advice to beginning programmers:

It is easier to optimize working code than it is to debug optimized code.

In the real world, optimization is often traded off against flexibility and reusability. Optimization should only be undertaken when there is a bottleneck indicated by profiling.

FURTHER READING AND RELEVANT RESOURCES

For a true understanding of complexity, it is best to read a serious algorithms book, such as Cormen, Leiserson, and Rivest (1990). For NP completeness, Barton, Berwick, and Ristad (1987) has examples, analyses, and further references. For a more practical guide to efficiency in simple programs, it is hard to beat Bentley (1999).

REFERENCES

Barton, G. E., R. C. Berwick, and E. S. Ristad. 1987. *Computational Complexity and Natural Language*. Cambridge, Mass.: MIT Press.

Bentley, J. L. 1999. *Programming Pearls*, 2nd. edn. Reading, Mass.: Addison-Wesley.

Carpenter, B. 1995. 'Compiling CFG parsers in Prolog'. http://www.colloquial.com/carp/Publications/prologparsers.html.

Collins, M. 1997. 'Three generative, lexicalized models for statistical parsing'. *Proceedings of the 35th Annual Meeting of the Association for Computational Linguistics* (Madrid), 16–31.

Cormen, T. H., C. E. Leiserson, and R. L. Rivest. 1990. *Introduction to Algorithms*. Cambridge, Mass.: MIT Press.

Covington, M. A. 1993. *Natural Language Processing for Prolog Programmers*. Englewood Cliffs, NJ: Prentice Hall.

Earley, J. 1970. 'An efficient context-free parsing algorithm'. *Communications of the ACM*, 13, 94–102.

Gazdar, G., E. Klein, G. Pullum, and I. Sag. 1985. *Generalized Phrase Structure Grammar*. Oxford: Blackwell.

Hopcroft, J. and J. Ullman 1979. *Introduction to Automata Theory, Languages, and Computation*. Reading, Mass.: Addison-Wesley.

Hunt, A. and D. Thomas. 1999. *The Pragmatic Programmer*. Reading, Mass.: Addison-Wesley.

Kasami, T. 1965. An efficient recognition and syntax analysis algorithm for context-free languages. Technical report AFCRL-65-758. Air Force Cambridge Research Laboratory. Bedford, Mass.

Marcus, M. 1980. *A Theory of Syntactic Recognition for Natural Language*. Cambridge, Mass.: MIT Press.

——B. Santorini, and M. A. Marcinkiewicz. 1993. 'Building a large annotated corpus of English: the Penn Treebank'. *Computational Linguistics*, 19, 313–30.

Norvig, P. 1992. *Paradigms of Artificial Intelligence Programming*. San Mateo, Calif.: Morgan Kaufmann.

O'Keefe, R. 1990. *The Craft of Prolog*. Cambridge, Mass.: MIT Press.

Ortmanns, S., H. Ney, and X. Aubert. 1997. 'A word graph algorithm for large vocabulary continuous speech recognition'. *Computer, Speech and Language*, 11, 43–72.

Pereira, F. and Y. Schabes. 1992. 'Inside–outside reestimation from partially bracketed corpora'. *Proceedings of the 30th Annual Meeting of the Association for Computational Linguistics* (Newark, Del.), 128–35.

Sikkel, K. and A. Nijholt 1991. 'An efficient connectionist context-free parser'. *2nd International Workshop on Parsing Technologies* (Cancun), 117–26.

Younger, D. H. 1967. 'Recognition and parsing of context-free languages in time n^3'. *Information and Control*, 10, 189–208.

PART II

PROCESSES, METHODS, AND RESOURCES

TEXT SEGMENTATION

ANDREI MIKHEEV

ABSTRACT

Electronic text is essentially just a sequence of characters. Naturally, before any real text processing is to be done, text needs to be segmented at least into linguistic units such as words, punctuation, numbers, alphanumerics, etc. This process is called tokenization. Traditionally, most Natural Language Processing techniques require text to be segmented into sentences as well. In this chapter we describe major challenges for text tokenization and sentence splitting, and outline various computational approaches to tackle them in different languages.

10.1 INTRODUCTION

Text analysis and processing is normally described in terms of linguistic units such as words, syntactic groups, clauses, sentences, paragraphs, discourse segments, etc. However, electronic text is essentially just a sequence of characters some of which are content characters, such as letters of an alphabet, numbers, punctuation, etc., and others are control and formatting (typesetting) characters such as whitespace, newline, carriage return, etc. Naturally, before any real text processing is to be done, text (sequence of characters) needs to be segmented at least into linguistic units such as words, punctuation, numbers, alphanumerics, etc. This process is called **tokenization** and segmented units are called word tokens.

Tokenization is usually considered as a relatively easy and uninteresting part of text processing for languages like English and other **segmented languages**, where words are delimited by blank spaces and punctuation. However, even in these languages there are cases where tokens are written with no explicit boundaries between them, and sometimes what seem to be two tokens (i.e. delimited by a whitespace) in fact form one and vice versa. Ambiguous punctuation, hyphenated words, clitics, apostrophes, etc. largely contribute to the complexity of tokenization. A much more challenging issue is tokenization in **non-segmented languages** such as many Oriental languages. There tokens do not have explicit boundaries and are written directly adjacent to each other. This is further complicated by the fact that almost all characters in these languages can be one-character words by themselves but they can also join together to form multi-character words.

Traditionally, most natural language processing techniques are applied to sequences of word tokens bound by sentence boundaries and thus, require text to be segmented into sentences as well. Segmenting text into sentences (**sentence splitting**) in most cases is a simple matter—a period, an exclamation mark, or a question mark usually signal a sentence boundary. However, there are cases when a period denotes a decimal point or is a part of an abbreviation and thus it does not signal a sentence break. Furthermore, an abbreviation itself can be the last token in a sentence in which case its period acts at the same time as part of this abbreviation and as the end-of-sentence indicator (full stop). Therefore, segmentation of sentences can present some unexpected difficulties which need to be addressed.

Tokenization and sentence splitting can be described as 'low-level' text segmentation which is performed at the initial stages of text processing. These tasks are usually handled by relatively simple methods such as scripts of *regular expressions* written in perl or flex, but errors made at such an early stage are very likely to induce more errors at later stages of text processing and are therefore very dangerous. To address this problem a number of advanced methods which deal with specific tokenization challenges have been developed to complement standard **tokenizers**.

Other tasks can be described as 'high-level' text segmentation. **Intra-sentential segmentation** involves segmentation of linguistic groups such as named entities (Chapter 30), segmentation of noun groups and verb groups, which is also called syntactic chunking, splitting sentences into clauses, etc. **Inter-sentential segmentation** involves grouping of sentences and paragraphs into discourse topics which are also called text tiles. 'High-level' segmentation is much more linguistically motivated than 'low-level' segmentation, but it can usually be tackled by relatively shallow linguistic processing. While 'high-level' segmentation is an important area of text processing, it would require a separate chapter to do it justice. In the current chapter we will concentrate on the low-level tasks such as tokenization and sentence segmentation and at the end of this chapter we will point to relevant reading for the high-level tasks.

A detailed introduction to evaluation metrics, resources, and techniques is given in Chapter 22. Here we will briefly review some evaluation metrics and standard resources commonly used for text segmentation tasks.

Performance of text processing modules is traditionally measured in *precision*, which is the ratio of the correct answers to the produced answers, and *recall*, which is the ratio of the correct answers to the total expected answers. Thus, if out of a hundred sentence boundaries a system assigned just one and this happened to be correct, the precision of such system would be 100 per cent but its recall would be only 1 per cent. When a system always assigns all candidates, its precision and recall are the same and the performance is measured in *accuracy* (same as precision) or *error rate*, which is the difference between the accuracy and 100 per cent.

There are two corpora normally used for evaluation in a number of text processing tasks for English and in text segmentation tasks in particular: the *Brown corpus* and the *Wall Street Journal (WSJ)* corpus—both part of the Penn Treebank (Marcus, Santorini, and Marcinkiewicz 1993). The Brown corpus represents general English; it is composed of subsections ranging from journalistic and science domains to fiction and speech transcriptions. The *WSJ* corpus represents journalistic newswire style. Both these corpora contain over a million words. Words in both these corpora are tokenized and annotated with part-of-speech (POS) information. Text is also split into documents, paragraphs, and sentences. This gives all the necessary information for the evaluation of a tokenizer or a sentence segmentor provided that they are targeted to English.

10.2 WORD SEGMENTATION

The first step in the majority of text processing applications is to segment text into words. The term 'word', however, is ambiguous: a word from a language's vocabulary can occur many times in the text but it is still a single individual word of the language. So there is a distinction between words of vocabulary or **word types** and multiple occurrences of these words in the text which are called **word tokens**. This is why the process of segmenting word tokens in text is called tokenization. Although the distinction between word types and word tokens is important it is usual to refer to them both as 'words' wherever the context unambiguously implies the interpretation. Here we will follow this practice.

In all modern languages that use a Latin-, Cyrillic-, or Greek-based writing system, such as English and other European languages, word tokens are delimited by a blank space. Thus, for such languages, which are called segmented languages, token boundary identification is a somewhat trivial task since the majority of tokens are bound by explicit separators like spaces and punctuation. A simple program which replaces whitespaces with word boundaries and cuts off leading and trailing quotation marks, parentheses and punctuation already produces a reasonable performance. For instance, a sequence of characters *However, they were his 'best friends'* is tokenized into *However , they were his ' best friends '*. Although this simple strategy in general is very productive, there are still situations where tokens are written with no explicit boundaries between them. For instance, when a period follows a word it is usually a separate token and signals the end of the sentence. However, when a period follows an abbreviation it is part of it and should be grouped together with it. Hyphenated segments also present a case of ambiguity—sometimes a hyphen is part of a word segment as in *self-assessment, F-16, forty-two,* and sometimes it is not, as in *New York-based*. Numbers, alphanumerics and special format expressions (dates, measures), as well as language-specific rules for contracting words and phrases. also present a challenge for tokenization.

The majority of existing tokenizers signal token boundaries by whitespaces. Thus, if such a tokenizer finds two tokens directly adjacent to each other, as, for instance, when a word is followed by a comma, it inserts a whitespace between them. This approach has two potential problems. First, it is impossible to delete inserted mark-up and revert to the original text. The second problem comes from tokens which contain whitespaces in them, as, for instance, numeric expressions in French. In this case a general strategy is to replace token internal whitespaces with another character such as underscore.

A cleaner strategy for marking tokens in text is to apply a special mark-up language such as SGML or XML to delimit token boundaries. In this case added mark-up can be easily deleted to revert to the original text, whitespaces can be placed within token boundaries, and tokens can also be associated with attributes which contain information about their class. Here is an example of such tokenization mark-up:

(10.1)   <W c=w>It</W> <W c=w>was</W> <W c=p>'</W><W c=n>3</W><W c=p>'
</W><W c=p>.</W>

In this example tokens are wrapped into W elements and the attribute c indicates the class of a token: w—word, n—number, p—punctuation.

Traditionally, tokenization rules are written using *regular expressions* which describe how to match different types of tokens such as words, numerics, punctuation, etc. Here is an example of a regular expression which matches numbers like *33* or *7,000,000* or *734.78*:

(10.2)   [0–9][0–9]?[0–9]?(,?[0–9][0–9][0–9])*([.][0–9]+)?

Sometimes, however, it is easier to describe how to locate boundaries between tokens rather than how to recognize tokens themselves, thus in some systems tokenization rules describe contexts which require insertion of token boundaries. Regular expressions can be associated with actions as in the lexical scanners lex and flex, or they can be associated with rewrite rules as in transducers. For more expressive power regular expressions are sometimes supplemented with look-ahead and look-back capabilities.

A general problem in building a set of tokenization rules is rule ordering and interaction because often several rules can match text segments starting from the same position and then the question is which one should be preferred. The standard solution to this problem is to ensure that the longest match always wins in such a competition. For efficiency purposes, regular expressions are often compiled into *Finite-state automata* (Chapter 18). More advanced tokenization systems, e.g. LT TTT (Grover, Matheson, and Mikheev 2000) also provide facilities for composing complex regular expressions from simpler ones and for plug-in of decision-making modules when handling tokens with no explicit boundaries. Such modules can involve *lexical look-up*, analysis of the local context around an ambiguous token, construction of word lists from the documents, etc.

Tokenization in non-segmented languages, such as many Oriental languages, presents substantial challenges for computational analysis since tokens are directly attached to each other using pictogram characters or other native writing systems. Identifying token boundaries in such languages requires more sophisticated algorithms. The most commonly applied methods are lexical look-up of longest matching sequences, hidden Markov models, *n*-gram methods, and other statistical techniques (Chapter 19).

10.2.1 Abbreviations

In English and other Indo-European languages although a period is directly attached to the previous word, it is usually a separate token which signals the end of the sentence. However, when a period follows an abbreviation it is an integral part of this abbreviation and should be tokenized together with it. Unfortunately, universally accepted standards for many abbreviations and acronyms do not exist. Customary usage within a certain professional group often determines when to abbreviate and which abbreviation to use: for instance, when engineers smash concrete samples into cubic centimetres, they use the abbreviation 'cm3', while doctors use the abbreviation 'cc' when prescribing cubic centimetres of pain-killer. Although there have been attempts to compile comprehensive dictionaries of abbreviations, this task does not look feasible with each professional field developing its own abbreviations and acronyms.

The most widely adopted approach to the recognition of abbreviations is to maintain a list of known abbreviations. Thus during tokenization a word with a trailing period can be looked up in such a list and, if it is found there, it is tokenized as a single token, otherwise the period is tokenized as a separate token. Naturally, the accuracy of this approach depends on how well the list of abbreviations is tailored to the text under processing. First, as we have already pointed out, there will almost certainly be abbreviations in the text which are not included in the list. Second, some abbreviations in the list can coincide with common words and can thus trigger erroneous tokenization. For instance, 'in' can be an abbreviation for 'inches', 'no' can be an abbreviation for 'number', 'bus' can be an abbreviation for 'business', 'sun' can be an abbreviation for 'Sunday', etc.

To test the potential performance of the abbreviation list look-up approach Mikheev (2000) collected a list of the 270 most frequent abbreviations from the *New York Times* 1996 corpus. When this list was applied to a similar corpus (the *WSJ* corpus) the look-up method showed high precision (under 1 per cent error rate) but its recall was only 64 per cent. In other words this method managed to make decisions for two abbreviations out of three leaving the third one in an undecided state, but its decisions were almost always correct.

In order to increase the recall, a natural extension to the look-up method is to apply to the undecided cases some guessing heuristics which examine the surface lexical form of a word token. Single-word abbreviations are short and normally do not include vowels (Mr., Dr., kg.). Thus a word without vowels can be guessed to be an abbreviation unless it is written in all capital letters in which case it could be an acronym or a name (e.g. NHL). A single capital letter followed by a period is a very likely abbreviation. A span of single letters separated by periods forms an abbreviation too (e.g. Y.M.C.A.). On their own these heuristics managed to identify about 60 per cent of all abbreviations in the text (recall), but when they were applied together with the list look-up the combined method assigned about 97 per cent of abbreviations with high (above 99 per cent) precision.

Surface guessing heuristics in conjunction with a list of abbreviations is the most widely used strategy in modern tokenizers. However, they still miss about 3–5 per cent of abbreviations. For instance, if abbreviations like 'sec.' or 'Okla.' are not included in the list of abbreviations, the surface guessing rules will not discover them. Basically any short word followed by a period can act as an abbreviation, especially if this word is not included in the list of known common words for a language. To adopt tokenizers to new domains, methods which automatically extract abbreviations from a corpus have been proposed, e.g. Grefenstette and Tapanainen (1994). Such methods are based on the observation that although a short word which is followed by a period can potentially be an abbreviation, the same word when occurring in a different context can be unambiguously classified as an ordinary word if it is used without a trailing period, or it can be unambiguously classified as an abbreviation if it is used with a trailing period and is followed by a lower cased word or a comma.

Similar technique has been applied on the document rather than corpus level (Mikheev 2000). The main reason for restricting abbreviation discovery to a single document is that this can be done on-line and does not presuppose access to a corpus where the current document is essentially similar to other documents. This document-centred approach in the first pass through the document builds a list of unambiguous abbreviations and a list of unambiguous non-abbreviations. In the second pass it applies these lists to make decisions about ambiguous cases.

10.2.2 Hyphenated words

Hyphenated segments present a case of ambiguity for a tokenizer—sometimes a hyphen is part of a token, i.e. *self-assessment*, *F-16*, *forty-two* and sometimes it is not e.g. *New York-based*. Essentially, segmentation of hyphenated words answers a question 'One word or two?' This has crucial importance in almost all text processing applications. For instance, in document retrieval, documents are indexed using words they contain. Now, if 'Moscow-based' is the only mentioning of Moscow in a document and it is tokenized as a single token, then this document will never be retrieved by a query such as 'Moscow'. On the other hand if 'co-operation' is split as two separate tokens, then for a query such as 'operation' documents about 'cooperation' will be retrieved, which clearly is not what was intended by the query.

Segmentation of hyphenated words is task dependent. For instance, *part-of-speech taggers* (Chapter 11) usually treat hyphenated words as a single syntactic unit and therefore prefer them to be tokenized as single tokens. On the other hand *named entity recognition* (NER) systems (Chapter 30) attempt to split a named entity from the rest of a hyphenated fragment; e.g. in parsing the fragment 'Moscow-based' such a system needs 'Moscow' to be tokenized separately from 'based' to be able to tag it as a location.

Generally we can distinguish between 'true hyphens' and 'end-of-line hyphens'. **End-of-line hyphens** are used for splitting whole words into parts to perform justification of text during typesetting. Therefore they should be removed during tokenization because they are not part of the word but rather layouting instructions. **True hyphens**, on the other hand, are integral parts of complex tokens, e.g. *forty-seven*, and should therefore not be removed. Sometimes it is difficult to distinguish a true hyphen from an end-of-line hyphen when a hyphen occurs at the end of a line. Grefenstette and Tapanainen (1994) performed an experiment to estimate the error bound for the simplest approach of always joining two segments separated by a hyphen at the end of a line into a single token (and removing the hyphen). In this experiment the Brown corpus was processed by a typesetting program (nroff) which introduced end-of-line hyphens on 12 per cent of lines. The simple strategy of always joining word segments separated by end-of-line hyphens produced a 4.9 per cent error rate.

Accuracy in processing of end-of-line hyphens can be substantially increased by applying a lexical look-up approach: after both parts are concatenated (and the hyphen is removed), the compound token is checked as to whether it is listed in the lexicon and therefore represents a legitimate word of a language. Otherwise the hyphen is classified as a 'true hyphen' and is not removed. To deal with words unknown to the lexicon both parts are checked in the lexicon as to whether they exist as separate words, and if the result is negative, then the hyphen is removed. This strategy is relatively easy to incorporate into a tokenizer and it reduced the error rate from 4.9 per cent to 0.9 per cent. There have also been document- and corpus-centred approaches to hyphenated words. These approaches build a list of hyphenated and non-hyphenated tokens from the document or the entire corpus and resolve hyphenated words according to the frequency with which their parts have been seen to be used hyphenated and non-hyphenated.

Within the 'true hyphens' one can distinguish two general cases. The first are so-called *lexical hyphens*—hyphenated compound words which have made their way into the standard language vocabulary. For instance, certain prefixes (and less commonly suffixes) are often written hyphenated, e.g. co-, pre-, meta-, multi-, etc. There also exists a specialized form of prefix conjunctions, as in *pre- and post-processing*. Certain complex words such as *rock-n-roll* are standardly written hyphenated. Usually this sort of hyphenation is tackled by the lexical look-up approach. However, word hyphenation quite often depends on the stylistic preferences of the author of a document, and words which are hyphenated by one author are written without a hyphen by another, e.g. *cooperate* vs. *cooperate, mark-up* vs. *mark up*.

The more challenging case is *sententially determined hyphenation*, i.e. hyphenation which depends on the sentential context. Here hyphenated forms are created dynamically as a mechanism to prevent incorrect parsing of the phrase in which the words appear. There are several types of hyphenation in this class. One is created when a noun is modified by an 'ed'-verb to dynamically create an adjective, e.g. *case-based, computer-linked, hand-delivered*. Another case involves an entire expression when it is used as a modifier in a noun group, as in a *three-to-five-year direct marketing plan*. In treating these cases a lexical look-up strategy is not much help and normally such expressions are treated as a single token unless there is a need to recognize specific tokens, such as dates, measures, names, in which case they are handled by specialized subgrammars (section 10.2.3).

10.2.3 Numerical and special expressions

Email addresses, URLs, complex enumeration of items, telephone numbers, dates, time, measures, vehicle licence numbers, paper and book citations, etc. can produce a lot of confusion to a tokenizer because they usually involve rather complex alpha numerical and punctuation syntax. Such expressions, nevertheless, have a fairly regular internal form and are usually handled by specialized tokenizers which are called

preprocessors. For instance, expressions like *15/05/76, 6-JAN-76, 3:30pm, 123km/hr* can be handled by a standard tokenizer as single units but preferably they should be handled by specialized tokenizers which would, for instance, correctly parse 'pm' as a modifier to '3:30' where both *3:30pm* and *3:30 pm* should produce similar tokenization. Telephone numbers such as *+44 (0131) 647 8907* or *1 800 FREECAR* are normally treated by a general tokenizer as multi-token expressions while a specialized preprocessor would correctly tokenize them as single tokens.

The design of a preprocessor is more complex than the design of a standard tokenizer. Normally preprocessors operate with two kinds of resources: grammars and lists. The lists contain words grouped by categories such as month names (January, February, . . .), month names abbreviated (Jan, Feb, . . .), weekdays (Sunday, Monday, . . .), weekdays abbreviated (Sun, Mon, . . .), etc. The grammar specifies how words from the list file are used together with other characters to form expressions. For instance, a rule like

(10.3)   DATE = [0–3]?[0–9] >> [.-/] >> month-any >> [.-/] >> [0–9][0–9]([0–9][0–9])?

says that if two digits in the range are followed by delimiting punctuation such as a period, a dash or a slash, and then by a word which is listed under the category month-any which is then followed by delimiting punctuation and two or four digits, this is a date token. This covers expressions like *6-JAN-76, 15.FEBRUARY.1976, 15/02/1976*, etc. assuming the month-any list includes full month names, abbreviated month names, and month numbers.

Sometimes preprocessors do not only tokenize special expressions but also attempt to interpret and normalize them. For instance, *3pm* can be normalized as *15:00* and *31-Jan-92* can be normalized as *31.01.1992*. A number of specialized subgrammars have been developed which handle dates, times, measures, citations, etc. as part of named entity recognition systems (Chapter 30). Such subgrammars are usually applied before standard tokenization and eliminate a fair number of difficult tokenization cases.

10.2.4 Multilingual issues

Most of the Western European languages (e.g. English, French, German, Italian) have very similar tokenization rules: such rules process tokens bounded by explicit separators like spaces and punctuation. However, there are also language-specific rules which handle tokens with no explicit boundaries. For instance, in some Germanic languages (German, Danish, Norwegian, Swedish, Dutch), noun phrases are written without spaces between the words but still need to be broken up into their component parts during tokenization, e.g. *Professorentreffen* in German is constructed from two nouns *Professoren + Treffen*.

It is perfectly feasible to code language-specific tokenization rules for a single language tokenizer but it is an open research issue whether such tokenization rules can be compiled into a single tokenizer which would work across several languages.

Consider the apostrophe. An apostrophe often means that a word has been contracted. Apart from the fact that different languages have different rules for splitting or not splitting text segments with apostrophes, even within one language there are several ways of handling such segments. In English, with verb contractions the deleted vowel is the first character of the second word (e.g *they are* → *they're*) and the tokens should be split at the apostrophe: *they* + *'re*. With negation contraction the tokenization is different, since the apostrophe is inserted inside the negation (e.g *does not* → *doesn't*) and the token boundary is one character before the apostrophe: *does* + *n't*. In French, an apostrophe is inserted between a pronoun, a determiner, or a conjunction and the following word if it starts with a vowel. The deleted vowel is always the last character of the first word (e.g *le avion* → *l'avion*) and the tokens should be split after the apostrophe (*l'* + *avion*). An apostrophe also can signal contraction within a token (e.g. *Wolverhampton* → *W'hampton* or *petit* → *p'tit* in French), or it can be an integral part of a word (e.g *O'Brien*, *Gurkovitch'*) in which case no token splitting is performed.

Numerical expressions also have language-specific structure. For instance, the number written in English as *123,456.78* will be written as *123 456,78* in French. The French structure is more difficult to deal with, since it requires the grouping of two segments which are separated by a whitespace. One can imagine that there also exist cases in French when two numbers are separated by a whitespace but should not be grouped together. Much more dangerous is the application of the French specific number recognizer to English texts, which will most certainly produce the wrong tokenization.

10.2.5   Tokenization in oriental languages

Word segmentation presents a substantial challenge in non-segmented languages. Iconic (ideographic) languages, like Chinese and Japanese, do not use whitespaces to delimit words but still the text consists of distinctive characters (pictograms). The Mon-Khmer family of writing systems, including Thai, Lao, Khmer, and Burmese, and dozens of other South-east Asian languages, present even more serious problems for any kind of computational analysis. Apart from the challenge that whitespaces are not necessarily used to separate words, vowels appear before, over, under, or following consonants. Alphabetical order is typically consonant-vowel-consonant, regardless of the letters' actual arrangement. Therefore, not just word boundaries but even morphemes, i.e. word constituting parts, are highly ambiguous. There have not been many computational attempts to deal with Mon-Khmer languages and in this section we will concentrate on the better studied Chinese and Japanese.

In Chinese and Japanese almost all characters can be one-character words by themselves but they can join to form multi-character words. For instance, if we were to drop whitespaces from English writing, the segment *together* might be interpreted as a single token but could equally well be interpreted as three tokens following each other (*to get her*). Second, compounding is the predominant word-formation device in modern Chinese and Japanese. It is often difficult to tell whether a low-frequency compound is a word or phrase, and the lexicon can never exhaustively collect all low-frequency compounds. Third, proper names in Chinese (and sometimes in Japanese) are written with the same characters, which constitute normal words. For instance, if we were to drop whitespaces and capitalization from English writing, it would be equally difficult to decide whether *fairweather* is a proper name or two tokens. Finally, some specific morphological structures similar in spirit to ones described for the European languages (section 10.2.4) also need to be taken into consideration.

Word segmentation in Japanese is a bit simplified by the fact that there are three types of Japanese characters: *kanji*, *hiragana*, and *katakana*. Normally, changes in character type signal a token boundary, but using this heuristic alone gives only about 60 per cent accuracy. Typically, word segmentation in Japanese is performed by the combination of morphological analysis, lexical knowledge and grammar constraints, as in the well-known Japanese morphological processor Juman (Kurohashi and Nagao 1998). However, character sequences consisting solely of kanji (Chinese characters) are difficult to handle with morphological rules and grammar constraints, since they often consist of compound nouns which are very likely to be domain terms and not to be listed in the lexicon.

In general, typical segmentation algorithms for Chinese and Japanese rely either on pre-existing lexico-grammatical knowledge or on pre-segmented data from which a machine learning system extracts segmentation regularities. The most popular approach to segmenting words from sequences of Chinese characters is the 'longest match' approach. In this approach the lexicon is iteratively consulted to determine the longest sequence of characters which is then segmented as a single token. More sophisticated algorithms require longest match not for a single word but for several words in a row. One of the most popular statistical method is based on character n-grams where statistics about which n-grams of characters form a single token are applied together with the probability optimization over the entire sentence for all accepted n-grams. Usually such statistics are collected from a pre-segmented corpus and also involve a lexicon of known words for a language. Recently there have been a number of attempts to train statistical tokenizers for Chinese and Japanese from a corpus of unsegmented texts, e.g. Xianping, Pratt, and Smyth (1999).

Ponte and Croft (1996) conducted a number of experiments to compare statistical models which rely on a single word (character) with models which rely on n-grams of characters and concluded that single-word models often outperform bigram models. This is somewhat surprising since bigrams bring more information to the decision-making process and hence create a better language model. However, sometimes they do not perform as well as simpler single-word models because of sparseness of the bigrams. Many token bigrams do not occur in the training data and therefore are marked as improbable. Thus building a good language model should involve not only utilizing different knowledge sources but also applying a model which combines these knowledge sources together and is robust with respect to unseen and infrequent events.

10.3   SENTENCE SEGMENTATION

Segmenting text into sentences is an important aspect of developing many text processing applications—syntactic parsing, information extraction, machine translation, text alignment, document summarization, etc. Sentence splitting is in most cases a simple matter—a period, an exclamation mark, or a question mark usually signal a sentence boundary. However, there are cases when a period denotes a decimal point or is part of an abbreviation and thus does not signal a sentence break as discussed in section 10.2.1. Furthermore, an abbreviation itself can be the last token in a sentence in which case its period acts at the same time as part of the abbreviation and as the end-of-sentence indicator (full stop). Therefore, accurate sentence splitting, which is also called **sentence boundary disambiguation** (SBD), requires analysis of the local context around periods and other punctuation which might signal the end the of the sentence.

The first source of ambiguity in end-of-sentence marking is introduced by abbreviations: if we know that the word which precedes a period is *not* an abbreviation, then almost certainly this period denotes a sentence break. However, if this word is an abbreviation, then it is not that easy to make a clear decision. The second major source of information for approaching the SBD task comes from the word which follows the period or other sentence-splitting punctuation. In general, in English as well as in many other languages, when the following word is punctuation, a number, or a lower cased word, the abbreviation is not sentence terminal. When the following word is capitalized the situation is less clear. If this word is a capitalized common word, this signals the start of another sentence, but if this word is a proper name and the previous word is an abbreviation, then the situation is truly ambiguous. For example, in *He stopped to see Dr. White* . . . the abbreviation is sentence internal, and in *He stopped at Meadows Dr. White Falcon was still open.* the abbreviation is sentence terminal. Note that in these two sentences the abbreviation 'Dr.' stands for two different words: in the first case it stands for 'Doctor' and in the second for 'Drive'.

The performance of sentence-splitting algorithms depends, not surprisingly, on the proportion of abbreviations and proper names in the text and, hence, is domain and genre dependent: scientific, legal, and newswire texts tend to have a large proportion of abbreviations and are more difficult to handle than, for instance, general fiction. Speech transcripts present a separate issue since neither punctuation nor word capitalization is present.

The simplest and perhaps most popular algorithm for sentence boundary disambiguation is known as 'period-space-capital letter'. This algorithm marks all periods, question, and exclamation marks as sentence terminal if they are followed by at least one whitespace and a capital letter. This algorithm can also be extended to handle optional brackets and quotes in between the period and capital letter which can be encoded in a very simple regular expression [.?!] [( )'']+[A-Z]. However, the performance of this algorithm is not very good. It produces an error rate of about 6.5 per cent measured on the Brown corpus and the *WSJ*.

For better performance the 'period-space-capital letter' algorithm can be augmented with a list of abbreviations and a lexicon of known words as was done in the STYLE program (Cherry and Vesterman 1991). A list of abbreviations can be supplemented with guessing rules as described in section 10.2.1. A system can also maintain special lists for abbreviations which never end sentences e.g. 'Mr.', 'Prof.', and words which always start a new sentence if used capitalized after a period, e.g. 'The', 'This', 'He', 'However'. The exact performance of such system depends largely on the size of these lists and was measured to produce about 3–3.5 per cent error rate on the Brown corpus and the *WSJ*.

10.3.1 Rules vs. statistics

To improve on the performance of the 'period-space-capital letter' algorithm and its modifications one needs to build a system of significant complexity. There are two major classes of sentence boundary disambiguators: rule based and statistical.

Many sentence boundary disambiguators use manually built rules which are usually encoded in terms of regular expression grammars supplemented with lists of abbreviations, common words, proper names, etc. To put together a few rules is fast and easy, but to develop a good rule-based system is quite a labour-consuming enterprise. Also such systems are usually closely tailored to a particular corpus and are not easily portable across domains.

Automatically trainable software is generally seen as a way of producing systems quickly retrainable for a new corpus, domain, or even for another language. Thus, more recent SBD systems often employ machine learning techniques such as decision-tree classifiers, maximum entropy modelling, neural networks, etc. Machine learning systems treat the SBD task as a classification problem, using features such as word spelling, capitalization, suffix, or word class, found in the local context of potential sentence-breaking punctuation. There is, however, one drawback—the majority of developed machine learning approaches to the SBD task require labelled examples for *supervised training*. This implies an investment in the annotation phase.

Recently progress has been reported in the development of statistical systems which need only *unsupervised training*, i.e. they can be trained from unannotated raw texts. These systems exploit the fact that only a small proportion of periods are truly ambiguous, and therefore, many regularities can be learned from unambiguous usages. LTSTOP (Mikheev 2000) applied an unsupervisedly trained hidden Markov model part-of-speech tagger. Schmid (2000) applied automatic extraction of statistical information from raw unannotated corpora. The core of this system is language independent but for achieving best results it can be augmented with language-specific add-ons. For instance, for processing German this system applied specialized suffix analysis and for processing English it applied a strategy for capitalized word disambiguation.

Most machine learning and rule-based SBD systems produce an error rate in the range of 0.8–1.5 per cent measured on the Brown corpus and the *WSJ* while the most advanced systems cut this error rate almost by a factor of four.

10.3.2 Words vs. syntactic classes

Most of the existing SBD systems are word based. They employ only lexical information (word capitalization, spelling, suffix, etc.) of the word before and the word after a potential sentence boundary to predict whether a capitalized word token which follows a period is a proper name or is a common word. Usually this is implemented by applying a lexical look-up method where a word is assigned a category according to which word list it belongs to. This, however, is clearly an oversimplification. For instance, the word 'Black' is a frequent surname and at the same time it is a frequent common word, thus the lexical information is not very reliable in this case. But by employing local context one can more robustly predict that in the context 'Black described . . .' this word acts as a proper name and in the context 'Black umbrella . . .' this word acts as a common word.

It is almost impossible to robustly estimate contexts larger than a single focal word using word-based methods – even bigrams of words are too sparse. For instance, there are more than 50,000 distinct words in the Brown corpus, thus there are $2^{50,000}$ potential word bigrams, but only a tiny fraction of them can be observed in the corpus. This is why words are often grouped into semantic classes. This, however, requires large manual effort, is not scalable, and still covers only a fraction of the vocabulary. *Syntactic* context is much easier to estimate because the number of syntactic categories is much smaller than the number of distinct words. For instance, there are only about 40 part-of-speech (POS) tags in the Penn Treebank tag set, therefore there are only 2^{40} potential POS bigrams. For this reason syntactic approaches to sentence splitting produce systems which are highly portable across different corpora and require much fewer training data in development. However, syntactic information is not directly observable in the text and needs to be uncovered first. This leads to higher complexity of the system.

Palmer and Hearst (1997) described an approach which recognized the potential of the local syntactic context for the SBD problem. Their system, SATZ, utilized POS information associated with words in the local context of potential sentence-splitting punctuation. However, they found difficulty in applying a standard POS tagging framework for determining POS information: 'However, requiring a single part-of-speech assignment for each word introduces a processing circularity: because most part-of-speech taggers require predetermined sentence boundaries, the boundary disambiguation must be done before tagging. But if the disambiguation is done before tagging, no part-of-speech assignments are available for the boundary determination system' (Palmer and Hearst 1997). Instead of requiring a single disambiguated POS category for a word they operated with multiple POS categories a word can potentially take. Such information is usually listed in a lexicon. Mikheev (2000) proposed to treat periods similarly to other word categories during POS tagging. In this approach sentence boundaries are resolved by the tagging process itself, and therefore the above-mentioned circularity is avoided, leading to an improved accuracy and a tighter integration of text segmentation with higher-level text processing tasks.

10.3.3 Non-standard input

The previous sections described methods and systems which have been mostly applied to so-called standard input—when text is written in English, conforming to capitalization and punctuation rules (i.e. sentence-starting words and proper names are capitalized whereas other words are lower cased, sentence boundaries are marked with punctuation such as periods, question or exclamation marks, semicolons). Ironically, text in other languages can be seen as non-standard since most published research is concerned with English and most of the resources developed for the evaluation of SBD systems have been developed only for English. In fact, this is true not only for the SBD task but for the text processing field in general.

First let us consider English texts which are written in single-case letters, i.e. in all capitals. This is a more difficult task for an SBD system than a mixed-case text because capitalization is a very predictive feature. In handling single-case texts the main emphasis falls on classifying words into abbreviations and non-abbreviations.

The simplest strategy is to assign periods which follow non-abbreviations as full stops and periods which follow abbreviations as sentence internal, i.e. always classify a word which follows an abbreviation as non-sentence starting. This produces about 2 per cent error rate on the *WSJ* and about 0.5 per cent error rate on the Brown corpus. When a decision-tree learner was trained on single-case texts (Palmer and Hearst 1997), it came with just a single modification to this strategy: if the word which follows an abbreviation can be a pronoun, then there should be a sentence break before it. This slightly improved the error rate.

More difficult are texts such as transcripts from automatic speech recognizers (ASRs). Apart from the fact that no punctuation and capitalization is present in such texts, there are also a number of misrecognized words. Little work has been done in this area but recently it gained more interest from the research community. CYBER-PUNC (Beeferman, Berger, and Lafferty 1998) is a system which aims to insert end-of-sentence markers into speech transcripts. This system was designed to augment a standard trigram language model of a speech recognizer with information about sentence splitting. CYBERPUNC was evaluated on the *WSJ* corpus and achieved a precision of 75.6 per cent and recall of 65.6 per cent. This task, however, is difficult not only for computers. Some recent experiments (Stevenson and Gaizauskas 2000) to determine human performance on this task showed about 90 per cent precision and 75 per cent recall and substantial disagreement among human annotators.

Not much is known about systems and their evaluation for languages other than English. Schmid's system mentioned above was described as working very well for a German newspaper corpus but was not formally evaluated because no manually annotated German corpus was available. The SATZ system was trained and tested on a small German newspaper corpus and an equally small corpus of German news articles as well as on the Canadian Hansard corpus in French. This system achieved 1.3 per cent, 0.7 per cent, and 0.7 per cent error rates respectively which indicates that at least for these languages the difficulty of the task is quite similar to that for English. The only formal evaluation of a sentence-splitting system for Slavonic languages known to us was described in Tanev and Mitkov (2000). This system used nine main end-of-sentence rules with a list of abbreviations and achieved 92 per cent in precision and 99 per cent in recall measured on a text of 190 sentences.

FURTHER READING AND RELEVANT RESOURCES

Grefenstette and Tapanainen (1994) give a good overview of choices in developing practical multilingual tokenizers. A fairly comprehensive survey of different approaches to tokenization of Chinese can be found in Sproat et al. (1996). Sentence boundary disambiguation issues are discussed in detail in Palmer and Hearst (1997). Comprehensive text tokenization systems are described in Grover, Matheson, and Mikheev (2000) (LT TTT) and Aberdeen et al. (1995) (Alembic Workbench). These systems are also available for download through the Internet. The Proceedings of the 7th Message Understanding Conference (available on line at http://www. muc. saic. com/) contain descriptions of several named entity recognition systems with close attention to the tokenization and preprocessing tasks. In this chapter we did not survey high-level segmentation tasks but a description of a clause-splitting algorithm can be found in Orasan (2000). Recent experiments on using machine learning for clause-splitting were reported at an ACL 2001 workshop on computational natural language learning (Sang, Kim, and Dejean 2001). An entry point text-tiling algorithm can be found in Hearst (1997). Crowe (1996) presents a number of shallow text segmentation mechanisms to construct a flat discourse structure from news reports.

References

Aberdeen, J., J. Burger, D. Day, L. Hirschman, P. Robinson, and M. Vilain. 1995. 'Mitre: description of the alembic system used for MUC-6'. *Proceedings of the Sixth Message Understanding Conference (MUC-6)* (Columbia, Md.), San Mateo, Calif.: Morgan Kaufmann, 141–55.

Beeferman, D., A. Berger, and J. Lafferty. 1998. 'Cyberpunc: a lightweight punctuation annotation system for speech'. *Proceedings of the IEEE International Conference on Acoustics, Speech and Signal Processing* (Seattle), 689–92.

Cherry, L. L. and W. Vesterman. 1991. *Writing Tools: The STYLE and DICTION Programs.* Berkeley and Los Angeles: University of California, 4.3 bsd unix system documentation edition.

Crowe, J. 1996. 'Shallow techniques for the segmentation of news reports'. *Proceedings of the AISB Workshop on Language Engineering for Contents Analysis and Information Retrieval* (Brighton).

Grefenstette, G. and P. Tapanainen. 1994. 'What is a word, what is a sentence? Problems of tokenization'. *Proceedings of 3rd Conference on Computational Lexicography and Text Research (COMPLEX '94)* (Budapest), 79–87.

Grover, C., C. Matheson, and A. Mikheev. 2000. 'Lt ttt - a flexible tokenization tool'. *Proceedings of Second International Conference on Language Resources and Evaluation (LREC 2000)* (Athens), 67–75.

Hearst, M. 1997. 'Texttiling: segmenting text into multi-paragraph subtopic passages'. *Computational Linguistics*, 22(1), 33–64,

Kurohashi, S. and N. Nagao. 1998. *Japanese Morphological Analysis System JUMAN*, version 3.6 edition.

Marcus, M., B. Santorini, and M. A. Marcinkiewicz. 1993. 'Building a large annotated corpus of english: the Penn Treebank'. *Computational Linguistics*, 19(2), 313–29.

Mikheev, A. 2000. 'Tagging sentence boundaries'. *Proceedings of the 1st Meeting of the North American Chapter of the Association for Computational Linguistics (NAACL '2000)* (Seattle), 264–71.

Orasan, C. 2000. 'A hybrid method for clause splitting in unrestricted English texts'. *Proceedings of ACIDCA '2000, Corpora and Natural Language Processing* (Monastir), 129–34.

Palmer D. D. and M. A. Hearst. 1997. 'Adaptive multilingual sentence boundary disambiguation'. *Computational Linguistics*, 23(2), 241–69.

Ponte, J. M. and W. B. Croft. 1996. *USeg: A Retargetable Word Segmentation Procedure for Information Retrieval*. Technical Report TR96-2, University of Massachusetts.

Sang, E. F., T. Kim, and H. Dejean. 2001. 'Introduction to the CoNLL-2001 shared task: clause identification.' In W. Daelemans and R. Zajac (eds.), *Proceedings of the Computational Natural Language Learning Workshop (CoNLL-2001)* (Toulouse), 53–7.

Schmid, H. 2000. *Unsupervised Learning of Period Disambiguation for Tokenization. Internal Report*, IMS, University of Stuttgart.

Sproat, R., C. Shih, W. Gale, and N. Chang. 1996. 'A stochastic finite-state word-segmentation algorithm for Chinese'. *Computational Linguistics*, 22(3), 377–404.

Stevenson, A. and R. Gaizauskas. 2000. 'Experimenting on sentence boundary detection'. *Proceedings of the 6th Applied Natural Language Processing Conference* (Seattle), 84–9.

Tanev, H. and R. Mitkov. 2000. 'LINGUA: a robust architecture for text processing and anaphora resolution in Bulgarian'. *Proceedings of the International Conference on Machine Translation and Multilingual Applications (MT2000)* (Exeter), 20.1–20.8.

Xianping, G., W. Pratt, and P. Smyth. 1999. 'Discovering Chinese words from unsegmented text'. *Proceedings on the 22nd Annual International ACM SIGIR Conference on Research and Development in Information Retrieval (SIGIR 1999)* (Berkeley), 271–2.

CHAPTER 11

PART-OF-SPEECH TAGGING

ATRO VOUTILAINEN

ABSTRACT

This chapter outlines recently used methods for designing **part-of-speech taggers**, computer programs for assigning contextually appropriate grammatical descriptors to words in texts. First, the general architecture and task setting are described. A brief history of tagging follows, where some central approaches to tagging are described: (i) taggers based on handwritten local rules; (ii) taggers based on n-grams automatically derived from tagged text corpora; (iii) taggers based on hidden Markov models; (iv) taggers using automatically generated symbolic language models derived using methods from machine learning; (v) taggers based on handwritten global rules; and (vi) hybrid taggers, attempts to combine advantages of handwritten taggers and automatically generated taggers. Since statistical and machine-learning approaches are described in more detail in other chapters of this volume, while handwritten tagging rules are not, the remainder of this chapter describes the design of linguistic rule-based disambiguators in more detail.

11.1 Parts of Speech, Tagging

Let us start by examining the term 'part-of-speech tagging' (or 'POS tagging' for short).

Parts of speech have been recognized in linguistics for a long time (e.g. by Panini, Thrax, and Varro). Thrax (*c.*100 BC) distinguished between eight word classes, using mainly formal criteria: noun, verb, participle, article (including the relative pronoun), pronoun, preposition, adverb, conjunction. According to Schachter (1985), parts of speech seem to occur in every natural language, and the most valid criteria for parts of speech seem to be grammatical (rather than semantic): (i) syntactic distribution, (ii) syntactic function, and (iii) the morphological and syntactic classes that different parts of speech can be assigned to.

Tagging means automatic assignment of descriptors, or **tags**, to input tokens. Given the following input: *However, if two contiguous words are both unambiguous, the time-slice corresponding to those words will contain only a single state with non-zero probability.*, a POS tagger[1] produces the following output:

(11.1)   However_ADVwh , if_Cs two_Ncard contiguous_A words_Npl are_Vpres both_P
unambiguous_A , the_DET time-slice_N corresponding_ING to_PREP those_DET
words_Npl will_Vmod contain_Vinf only_ADV a_DET single_A state_N with_PREP
non-zero_N probability_N . <p>

Each word is flanked by a tag. *However* is analysed as a certain type of adverb; *if* as a subordinating conjunction; *two* as a cardinal numeral; *contiguous* as an adjective; etc.

In fact, parts of speech usually are only a part of the information that POS taggers produce. Inflectional and lexico-semantic information (e.g. the distinction between common and proper nouns) is also often produced. There are also several names for what we have called POS taggers: 'POS' can be replaced with 'morphological', 'word class', even 'lexical'.

11.2 Applications

POS taggers can be used for several purposes, for instance:

- More abstract levels of analysis benefit from reliable low-level information, e.g. parts of speech, so a good tagger can serve as a preprocessor.

---

[1] Known as EngCG-2, to be found on-line at http://www.conexor.fi/testing.html.

- Large tagged text corpora (e.g. British National Corpus; Bank of English corpus) are used as data for linguistic studies.
- Information technology applications, e.g. text indexing and retrieval, can benefit from POS information; e.g. nouns and adjectives are better candidates for good *index terms* than adverbs, verbs, or pronouns.
- Speech processing benefits from tagging. For instance, the pronoun *that* is pronounced differently from the conjunction *that*.

11.3 ARCHITECTURE

The architecture of many taggers is remarkably similar:

1. **Tokenization**: the input text is divided into tokens suitable for further analysis: punctuation marks, word-like units, and utterance boundaries (see Chapter 10 on segmentation).

2. **Ambiguity look-up** involves use of a lexicon and a guesser for tokens not represented in the lexicon.

- At its simplest, the lexicon can be a list of word forms and their possible parts of speech. More economic solutions are based on finite-state models, e.g. two-level morphology, where linguistic generalizations (e.g. about inflection and derivation) can be made more adequately.
- Guessers analyse remaining tokens. The design of guessers is often based on what is known about the lexicon. If, for instance, it is known that the lexicon contains all 'closed-class words' such as pronouns and articles, the guesser can safely propose only open-class analyses (e.g. noun and verb analyses).
- Used with a compiler/interpreter, the lexicon and guesser constitute a lexical (or morphological) analyser that should provide all reasonable analyses as alternatives for each token, e.g.

(11.2)   The_DET
          design_NVpres_Vinf_Vimp_Vsbj
          of_PREP
          guessers_Npl
          is_Vpres
          often_ADV
          based_EN_Vpast
          on_ADV_PREP
          what_Pwh_DET
          is_Vpres

known_EN
about_ADV_PREP
the_DET
lexicon_N
.

<p>

This kind of simple representation with alternative atomic tags is used in most POS taggers (the abbreviation EN stands for forms with past participle endings such as *walked, given*). However, more complex representations are also sometimes used, e.g. compound tags and lemmata, such as:

(11.3)   '<design>'
         'design' N NOM SG
         'design' V PRES -SG3
         'design' V INF
         'design' V IMP
         'design' V SUBJUNCTIVE
   '<of>'
         'of' PREP

3. **Ambiguity resolution** or **disambiguation** is the last major phase in tagging. Disambiguation is based on two information sources, both coded in the tagger's formal language model:

- information about the word itself, e.g. to the effect that the word form *tables* is more frequently used as a noun than as a verb.
- information about word/tag sequences (or contextual information): e.g. the model might prefer noun analyses over verb analyses if the preceding word is a preposition or article.

The design of the disambiguator's language model is the hardest subproblem in tagging: how to approximate the design of the optimal model that always identifies the correct analysis from among the competing alternatives.

11.4   EVALUATING TAGGER PERFORMANCE

A tagger's performance can be evaluated in many ways. Metrics such as tagger speed and memory consumption are easy to evaluate, but no longer very interesting because acceptable levels of performance (thousands of tens of thousands of words per second) have been reached by many.

What makes a crucial difference between taggers is their linguistic quality: (i) the informativeness and specifiability of the tag set the tagger should assign to input texts, and (ii) the degree of correctness, or accuracy, with which the tagger assigns the tags to input texts.

- Informativeness and specifiability of the tag set. Informativeness is not easy to measure; size of the tag set and amount of ambiguity present in the input are used as rough measures.

  Specifiability of the tag set means the degree to which different linguists trained to use the tag set uniformly use the tag set when independently manually tagging the same texts. For some tag sets, a maximum interjudge agreement of 95–7 per cent seems possible (Church 1992; Marcus, Santorini, and Marcinkiewicz 1993); for some others, a near-100 per cent agreement has been demonstrated (Voutilainen 1999). A high specifiability is obviously preferable; it simply means that the linguistic task of the tagger has been carefully specified, and this enables a more precise linguistic evaluation of tagger performance.

- Accuracy. A tagger's accuracy can be evaluated by comparing its output to a large and varied benchmark corpus, a version of the test text optimally selected and manually tagged (in the best case according to the double-blind method) by linguists not familiar with the design of the tagger. Of the metrics used, precision and recall are best known, but ambiguity and error rate are perhaps more intuitive. Ambiguity is the average number of analyses in the tagger's output; error rate is the percentage of words whose analysis is not present in the corresponding part of the benchmark corpus.

What finally decides which tagger to use is often its suitability for the intended application.

11.5 A SHORT HISTORY OF TAGGING

Automatic taggers have been made since the late 1950s, and the research has become intensive during the past two decades. Problems related to tokenization and lexical analysis have played a part, but resolution of ambiguity has been recognized as the most difficult subproblem in tagging.

1. The earliest disambiguators used hand-coded disambiguation rules, in the form of

- regular expressions compiled into finite-state automata that are intersected with lexically ambiguous sentence representations. Sentence readings accepted by all rule automata are proposed as analyses.

• ordered context-pattern rules that, depending on rule type, select an alternative word analysis as legitimate (by discarding all its alternatives), or discard a word analysis as illegitimate.

The first large-scale system, TAGGIT (Greene and Rubin 1971), was based on context-pattern rules. TAGGIT used a 71-item tag set and a disambiguation grammar of 3,300 rules. Together, these rules made about 77 per cent of all words in the million-word Brown University corpus unambiguous; the remaining 23 per cent of words remained to be resolved by human posteditors.

2. The next major advance took place in the late 1970s. The first effort in this new wave of data-driven statistical taggers was carried out as part of the annotation of the Lancaster-Oslo/Bergen corpus. For annotating this corpus, a system called CLAWS1 was developed at the University of Lancaster (Marshall 1983; Garside, Leech, and Sampson 1987).

Disambiguation in CLAWS is based on choosing the right word category on the basis of statistical corpus evidence. Use of handwritten linguistic rules was mostly abandoned. In the modular system, the disambiguation was carried out by a module (CHAINPROBS) that chooses the most likely tag (or tags) of an ambiguous word on the basis of the likelihood of occurrence in a given local context. The information basis of CHAINPROBS is a matrix of collocational probabilities derived from some 200,000 words of text from the Brown corpus annotated according to the CLAWS tag set. The matrix represents bigrams (sequences of two words). From a matrix of this kind, two kinds of probabilities can be calculated: lexical (the likelihood of word A representing category X) and contextual (the likelihood of word A representing category X in context Y). A probabilistic disambiguator should determine an optimal balance between lexical and contextual probabilities. The formula used in the final version of CLAWS1 is given in Marshall (1987).

Compared to its predecessors, CLAWS1 is surprisingly accurate: 96–7 per cent of all input words get the correct tag when the tagger is forced to produce only unambiguous analyses. If 14 per cent of words are allowed to remain ambiguous, 99 per cent of all words retain the correct tag as part of the surviving analyses (Johansson 1986).

In the wake of CLAWS1, many other n-gram taggers have been developed (e.g. Church 1988; DeRose 1988; Weischedel et al. 1993; Åström 1995 (for Swedish); Nagata 1994 (for Japanese)). Interestingly, the accuracy of even the more recent n-gram systems has not been significantly better than that of CLAWS1.

3. The CLAWS-type probabilistic method implements a kind of 'open' Markov model (Cutting et al. 1992) where the grammatical categories and their frequencies are given explicitly. Another popular probabilistic tagging method is based on hidden Markov models (HMM); 'hidden' because here state transitions (grammatical categories) are unobservable (Cutting et al. 1992). A claimed advantage of HMM

taggers is that only a lexicon and some untagged text is needed for training a tagger, i.e. taggers can be trained without tagged corpora. Further, the mathematical basis of HMMs is better understood; no ad hoc solutions are needed for combining N-gram statistics into tag or tag-sequence probabilities. HMMs also contain methods for estimating probabilities (e.g. on the basis of probability re-estimation from held-out data) for low-frequency phenomena, such as long-distance dependencies. For more on HMM see Chapter 19.

The goal in HMM is to automatically make as simple a language model as possible on the basis of language observations. The basic idea of learning from ambiguous data is actually quite straightforward. Consider the following ambiguous sample from English:

(11.4) the   ART
        man   N V
        is   V
        an   ART
        agent   N

.

In this sentence there is one ambiguous word: *man* is ambiguous due to N and V. Because we have no lexical or contextual probabilities in this ambiguous corpus, choosing between the alternative analyses of 'man' may seem problematic. However, on examining a larger sample of morphologically analysed ambiguous text it becomes evident that in certain configurations verb tags (V) occur seldom, while noun (N) tags are quite often found. For instance, consider *agent* in the same sample sentence: the lexicon gives only a noun reading for 'agent', which, like *man*, happens to follow a word labelled as an article ART. In this corpus, accepting a noun analysis next to an article analysis will not add to the complexity of the model because a noun occurs after an article many times in any case (e.g. in *the man*). In contrast, proposing a verb reading after an article will make the Markov model more complex than the data actually warrant. The simpler model is preferred, so the noun analysis of *man* will be selected as the more likely one.

As a consequence of one round of training an HMM on an untagged corpus, this 'training corpus' itself becomes less ambiguous, which enables the making of further generalizations. In this way, the model becomes more and more accurate, up to a certain number of iterations.

In practice, some (optionally arbitrary) initial tag transition probabilities are assigned to the initial HMM; the training cycles refine this initial setting using the Baum–Welch re-estimation algorithm (Baum 1972). An interesting property of HMM taggers is that they operate on sentence readings rather than fixed-length word sequences. In principle, HMM taggers can employ long-distance information; the size of the contextual 'window' is not limited to two or three words. Another attractive feature of HMM taggers is that linguistic information can also, to some extent, be coded as biases (by manipulating the lexicon, the tag set, and the initial tag probabilities).

HMM taggers have been made for several languages, e.g. English (Cutting et al. 1992); Swedish (Cutting 1994); Chinese (Chang and Chen 1993); Spanish, French (Chanod and Tapanainen 1995); German (Feldweg 1995).

4. Training taggers with open and hidden Markov models is a kind of machine learning (ML), but the term 'machine learning' in the field of POS tagging is usually reserved for data-driven automatically generated language models that are symbolic rather than statistical (for a detailed discussion of Machine Learning see Chapter 20 of this volume). An advantage of symbolic representations, e.g. rules, is that they (sometimes) are readily understandable to humans, while interpreting (and manually modifying) numeric statistical representations is very difficult for people.

Currently there is a lot of work on data-driven symbolic tagging. Perhaps the best-known strain, proposed by Hindle (1989) and further developed by Brill (1992, 1994, 1995) is based on generating ordered local rules and, on the basis of evidence from tagged training corpora, generating more specific rules for 'exceptions' to the rules written so far, and applying specific rules before general ones. Brill calls this strain of tagging 'transformation-based tagging'.

The rules used in systems of this kind are formally like those used in the early context-pattern grammars. Grammar training is based on (i) a correctly tagged corpus, (ii) a set of rule templates, and (iii) a set of ordered initial rules (best first) based on the templates. The initial state disambiguator is applied to the tagged corpus, and statistics are generated about the mispredictions produced by the initial rules. A number of predefined local rule templates are used for creating and testing new rules for rewriting the initial-state tagger's analyses into correct ones, and the template with the best correction rate is added to the ordered grammar.

In accuracy, systems of this kind compare with Markov taggers. A very fast implementation of Brill-style taggers, based on finite-state transducers, is presented by Roche and Schabes (1995).

5. In the 1980s, a common belief in the 'tagging community' was that the proper role of linguists was designing linguistic tasks and problems, such as grammatical representations (e.g. tag sets and guidelines for manually applying them); the automatic solutions to linguistic problems were best left to statisticians and computer scientists. The belief seemed well justified by the relative success of Markov-model and ML-based taggers as compared to early systems and grammars written by linguists: much better results were obtained, and very little linguistic work was needed for generating the language models used by these data-driven taggers.

In the early 1990s, this belief was questioned by a team of Finnish linguists who developed a framework known as Constraint Grammar (CG) and designed a rule-based handwritten system known as ENGCG for tagging and shallow parsing of English (Karlsson 1990; Voutilainen, Heikkilä, and Anttila 1992; Karlsson et al. 1995).

The CG rule formalism is very similar to that used in early systems from the 1960s and 1970s with pattern-action rules; the main difference is that CG has a more expressive context-pattern formalism (e.g. reference to words, tags, and simple patterns in local and long-range context). An early experiment and comparison with Markov taggers received considerable interest and scepticism from the research community. EngCG-2, a redevelopment of certain parts of ENGCG, was evaluated by Samuelsson and Voutilainen (1997), whose experiment shows that the error rate of EngCG-2 is an order of magnitude smaller than that of a state-of-the-art statistical tagger in similar circumstances.

6. Currently, solutions to tagging are more varied than a decade ago. New systems based on Markov models and ML techniques are being proposed for an increasing number of languages; the same holds for the 'artisanal' linguistic approach. Hybrid solutions have also been investigated, with the hypothesis that at least some typical error sources of data-driven systems can be stemmed with a reasonable amount of skilled linguistic rule-writing.

An early approach in this direction was to use reliable linguistic rules in the first stage for resolving some of the ambiguities; less reliable automatically generated language models are applied only for the remaining ambiguities.

Recently, methods of combining hand-coded and automatically generated models in a single architecture have been reported. An interesting piece of work in this vein is by Padro (1997), who reports use of the Energy Optimizing Function for more accurate tagging with constraint rules and statistics.

11.6 HANDWRITTEN DISAMBIGUATION GRAMMARS

Use of statistical and machine learning methods for NLP are described in detail in Chapters 19 and 20. This section outlines only the design of handwritten disambiguation grammars.

Why in the first place should one choose to write grammars by hand? Writing a good rule-based description is laborious and may even require some kind of skill not easily acquired. Further, relatively little work in this paradigm has been well documented, so a realistic assessment of the pros and cons of this approach remains to be made. In contrast, several data-driven methods have been used by many, and experiences have been reported in many papers: granted that there are adequate tagged training corpora available, a reasonably accurate data-driven tagger can be trained with minimal effort. Further, several data-driven taggers are freely available from the WWW as source code, so it is not even necessary to write the program code by oneself.

There are two major cons with data-driven taggers. First, despite numerous efforts it seems highly difficult to cut down the tagger's error rate below a few percentage points (which at the sentence level means that most text sentences become misanalysed at some point). Secondly, data-driven taggers seem to be better suited for the analysis of fixed-word-order poor-morphology languages like English; languages with a richer morphology and less fixed word order seem to be more problematic for approaches that rely on the presence of local fixed-word-class sequences. In the artisanal approach it seems possible to obtain error rates significantly lower than in the data-driven approach (see Chanod and Tapanainen 1995; Samuelsson and Voutilainen 1997), but the amount of work involved and degree of expertise required have not been well reported yet.

The linguistic approach has used two related formalisms: finite-state rules and somewhat less expressive pattern-action rules (or constraint rules). More experience has been obtained from the use of pattern-action rules, so our attention will be on them here.

Pattern-action rules contain two basic actions or operations: 'remove an alternative reading' and 'select a reading' (by removing all its alternatives). These operations are conditional: conditions on context (specified other words or tags in the sentence, usually in the near context) have to be satisfied, otherwise the rule leaves the ambiguous word intact. Consider a simple rule (in the CG-2 formalism documented by Tapanainen 1996):

(11.5)   REMOVE (ART)
                IF (1C (V)) ;

This rule removes article (ART) readings if the first word to the right is unambiguously (1C) a verb (V). A grammar typically contains many rules of this kind, even thousands. Rules can (and often do) interact: for instance, a rule can disambiguate a word, as a result of which another rule can disambiguate another word. Consider an ambiguous sample sentence:

(11.6) '<The>'
                'the' <*> <Def> DET CENTRAL ART SG/PL
        '<table>'
                'table' <Count> N NOM SG
                'table' <SVO> V PRES -SG3 VFIN
                'table' <SVO> V INF
                'table' <SVO> V IMP VFIN
                'table' <SVO> V SUBJUNCTIVE VFIN
        '<collapsed>'
                'collapse' <SVO> EN
                'collapse' <SVO> V PAST VFIN

'<.>'
      '.' <.> Pun
'<<p>>'
      '<p>' Lim

The grammar may contain a rule that requires the presence of a finite verb for every sentence by selecting the VFIN tag as correct if there are no other words with a VFIN tag anywhere to the left (NOT *–1) or to the right (NOT *1):

(11.7)   SELECT (VFIN)
        IF (NOT *–1 (VFIN))
          (NOT *1 (VFIN)) ;

   This rule will not become active in our sample input because two words contain finite verb readings. However, the grammar also contains the rule:

(11.8)   REMOVE (V)
        IF (-1C (ART)) ;

This rule removes verb readings if the first word to the left is an unambiguous article. This rule removes all verb readings of the word *table*, so *collapsed* alone remains ambiguous due to an EN reading and a finite verb reading (past tense to be more precise):

(11.9) '<The>'
          'the' <*> <Def> DET CENTRAL ART SG/PL
     '<table>'
          'table' <Count> N NOM SG
     '<collapsed>'
          'collapse' <SVO> EN
          'collapse' <SVO> V PAST VFIN
     '<.>'
          '.' <.> Pun
     '<<p>>'
          '<p>' Lim

Now the SELECT rule is able to do its job, so *collapsed* becomes correctly disambiguated as a past-tense verb.

   As the reader may have noticed, one of our sample rules contains a reference to unbounded context (the practical use of which is not easy for most data-driven tagging methods). One partial explanation for the promise of handwritten grammars is that reliable disambiguation can be done with well-motivated global rules that refer to linguistic phenomena beyond the scope of local sequences of a few words.

   Another typical feature of handwritten grammars is their lexicalization: many rules refer not only to tags but also to words (lemmata or even word forms). For instance, over 50 per cent of the rules in the ENGCG grammar contain a reference to a lemma (or a set of lemmata), most typically to closed-class words. The word form *that* alone, itself five ways ambiguous,

(11.10) '<that>'

> 'that' <NonMod> <**CLB> <Rel> PRON SG/PL
> 'that' DET CENTRAL DEM SG
> 'that' PRON DEM SG
> 'that' ADV AD-A>
> 'that' <**CLB> CS

is disambiguated with well over 100 word-specific constraints. It seems that the formalization of partial generalizations is an easy though uneconomic way of describing language for analysis purposes.

A third characteristic of constraint grammars is the use of rule order in the form of ordered subgrammars. One way of using ordered subgrammars is in terms of reliability of the constraints: less reliable constraints are grouped into separate subgrammars so that the more reliable ones can do a significant part of the analysis, so the less reliable rules are needed only as a fall-back to reach an acceptable level of unambiguity in the tagger's output.

To conclude this section: regardless of method selected, well-tagged training corpora are a valuable resource for testing and improving the language model. With a suitably varied and large corpus where the correct reading is marked, it is not so fatal if the grammarian happens to forget some grammatical phenomenon in the object language when designing a rule because the test corpus is likely to remind him or her about the oversight in any case.

FURTHER READING AND RELEVANT RESOURCES

Syntactic Wordclass Tagging, edited by Hans van Halteren (1999), is probably the most comprehensive introduction to tagging written so far, both from the implementer's and the user's point of view. High-quality conference papers can be found in conference proceedings organized by the Association for Computational Linguistics (e.g. ACL, EACL, ANLP). Also COLING proceedings are useful. The following repository of on-line papers may be useful too: http://arXiv.org/archive/cs/intro.html.

On-line tagger and other NLP demos are listed in many places, e.g. in http://www.ifi.unizh.ch/CL/InteractiveTools.html.

With search engines, more resources can be found easily.

REFERENCES

Åström, M. 1995. 'A probabilistic tagger for Swedish using the SUC tagset'. *Proceedings of the Conference on Lexicon + Text*, Lexicographica Series Maior (Tübingen).

Baum, L. 1972. 'An inequality and associated maximization technique in statistical estimation of probabilistic functions of Markov processes'. *Inequalities*, 3, 1–8.

Brill, E. 1992. 'A simple rule-based part of speech tagger'. In *Proceedings of the 3rd Conference on Applied Natural Language Processing*.

——1994. 'Some advances in transformation-based part-of-speech tagger'. *Proceedings of the National Condeference on Artificial Intelligence*.

——1995. 'Transformation-based error-driven learning and natural-language processing: a case study in part-of-speech tagging'. *Computational Linguistics*, 21(4).

Chang, C.-H. and C.-D. Chen. 1993. 'HMM-based part-of-speech tagging for Chinese corpora'. *Proceedings of the Workshop on Very Large Corpora, June 22, 1993* (Ohio).

Chanod, J.-P. and P. Tapanainen. 1995. 'Tagging French: comparing a statistical and a constraint-based method'. *Proceedings of the 7th Conference of the European Chapter of the Association for Computational Linguistics*.

Church, K. 1988. 'A stochastic parts program and noun phrase parser for unrestricted text'. *Proceedings of the 2nd Conference on Applied Natural Language Processing* (Austin, Tex.), 136–43.

——1992. 'Current practice in part of speech tagging and suggestions for the future'. In C. F. Simmons (ed.), *Sbornik praci: In Honor of Henry Kučera*, Michigan Slavic Studies, Michigan, 13–48.

Cutting, D. 1994. 'Porting a stochastic part-of-speech tagger to Swedish'. In R. Eklund (ed.), *Proceedings of '9:e Nordiska Datalingvistikdagarna'* Stockholm: Department of Linguistics, Computational Linguistics, Stockholm University.

——J. Kupiec, J. Pedersen, and P. Sibun. 1992. 'A practical part-of-speech tagger'. *Proceedings of the 3rd Conference on Applied Natural Language Processing*.

DeRose, S. 1988. 'Grammatical category disambiguation by statistical optimization'. *Computational Linguistics*, 14(1), 31–9.

Elworthy, D. 1994. 'Does Baum-Welch re-estimation help taggers?' *Proceedings of the 4th Conference on Applied Natural Language Processing* (Stuttgart).

Feldweg, H. 1995. 'Implementation and evaluation of a German HMM for POS disambiguation'. *Proceedings of the ACL SIGDAT Workshop* (Dublin).

Garside, R., G. Leech, and G. Sampson (eds.). 1987. *The Computational Analysis of English*. London: Longman.

Greene, B. and G. Rubin. 1971. *Automatic Grammatical Tagging of English*. Providence: Brown University.

Hindle, D. 1989. 'Acquiring disambiguation rules from text'. *Proceedings of the 27th Meeting of the Association for Computational Linguistics*.

Johansson, S. 1986. *The Tagged LOB Corpus: User's Manual*. Bergen: Norwegian Computing Centre for the Humanities.

Karlsson, F. 1990. 'Constraint grammar as a framework for parsing running text'. In H. Karlgren (ed.), *Papers Presented to the 13th International Conference on Computational Linguistics*, iii (Helsinki), 168–73.

——A. Voutilainen, J. Heikkilä, and A. Anttila (eds.). 1995. *Constraint Grammar. A Language-Independent System for Parsing Unrestricted Text*. Berlin: Mouton de Gruyter.

Marcus, M., B. Santorini, and M. A. Marcinkiewicz. 1993. 'Building a large annotated corpus of English: the Penn Treebank'. *Computational Linguistics*, 19(2), 313–30.

Marshall, I. 1983. 'Choice of grammatical word-class without global syntactic analysis: tagging words in the LOB corpus'. *Computers in the Humanities*, 17, 139–50.

——1987. 'Tag selection using probabilistic methods'. In Garside, Leech, and Sampson (1987).

Merialdo, B. 1994. 'Tagging English text with a probabilistic model'. *Computational Linguistics*, 20.

Nagata, M. 1994. 'A stochastic Japanese morphological analyser using a Forward-DP Backward-A*N-Best search algorithm'. *Proceedings of the 15th International Conference on Computational Linguistics* (Kyoto).

Padro, L. 1997. *A hybrid environment for syntax-semantic tagging*. Ph.D. thesis, Departament de Llenguatges i Sistemes Informatics, Universitat Politecnica de Catalunya, Barcelona.

Roche, E. and Y. Schabes. 1995. 'Deterministic part-of-speech tagging with finite-state transducers'. *Computational Linguistics*, 21(2).

Samuelsson, C. and A. Voutilainen. 1997. 'Comparing a linguistic and a stochastic tagger'. *Proceedings of the 35th Annual Meeting of the Association for Computational Linguistics and the 8th Conference of the European Chapter of the Association for Computational Linguistics (ACL-EACL-97)* (Madrid), 246–53.

Schachter, P. 1985. 'Part-of-speech systems'. In T. Shopen (ed.), *Language Typology and Syntactic Description*, i: *Clause Structure*. Cambridge: Cambridge University Press.

Tapanainen, P. 1996. *The Constraint Grammar Parser CG-2 Manual*. Helsinki: Department of General Linguistics, University of Helsinki.

van Halteren, Hans ed. 1999. *Syntactic Wordclass Tagging*. Dordrecht: Kluwer Academic Publishers.

Voutilainen, A. 1999. 'An experiment on the upper bound of interjudge agreement: the case of tagging'. *Proceedings of the 9th Conference of the European Chapter of the Association for Computational Linguistics* (Bergen).

——J. Heikkilä, and A. Anttila, 1992. *Constraint Grammar of English. A Performance-Oriented Introduction*. Publication No. 21. Helsinki: Department of General Linguistics, University of Helsinki.

Weischedel, R., M. Meteer, R. Schwartz, L. Ramshaw, and J. Palmuzzi, 1993. 'Coping with ambiguity and unknown words through probabilistic models'. *Computational Linguistics*, 19(2).

CHAPTER 12

PARSING

JOHN CARROLL

ABSTRACT

This chapter introduces key concepts and techniques for natural language (NL) parsing; that is, using a grammar to assign a (more or less detailed) syntactic analysis to a string of words, a lattice of word hypotheses output by a speech recognizer (Chapter 16), or similar. The level of detail required depends on the language processing task being performed and the particular approach to the task that is being pursued: so, for instance, resolution of anaphora, or extraction of terminology to support machine-assisted translation, might require only identification of basic phrase boundaries; shortening of sentences in automatic text summarization might need complete, but fairly undetailed parses; whereas processing of database queries expressed in natural language might require detailed parses capable of supporting semantic interpretation.

Section 12.1 describes approaches that produce 'shallow' analyses in which, for example, recursive constructions (such as multiple prepositional phrases) are not explicitly structured hierarchically; for these, finite-state processing techniques or relatively simple statistical models are often sufficient. Section 12.2 outlines approaches to parsing that analyse the input in terms of labelled dependencies between words. Producing hierarchical phrase structure requires grammars that have at least context-free (CF) power; section 12.3 describes two basic CF parsing algorithms that are widely used in parsing of NL. To support detailed semantic interpretation more powerful grammar formalisms are required, but these are usually still parsed using extensions of CF parsing algorithms. Such formalisms typically augment atomic categories—or completely encode categories—by attribute-value matrices, or feature structures, combining them with the unification operation. Section 12.4 covers unification-based parsing. (Tree grammars are an alternative, powerful class of grammar formalisms which are discussed in Chapter 26.)

A grammar will often assign more than one syntactic analysis to a given word string; disambiguation is therefore an important problem, and one that is often tackled by using statistical preferences over syntactic structure and lexical relationships as a proxy for inference over much less tractable semantic, pragmatic, and real-world knowledge (section 12.5). The chapter concludes (section 12.6) with a discussion of three important issues that have to be tackled in real-world applications of parsing: evaluation of parser accuracy, parser efficiency, and measurement of grammar/parser coverage.

12.1 SHALLOW PARSING

For some types of application, a shallow syntactic analysis is sufficient. One standard method is to partition the input into a sequence of non-overlapping units, or **chunks**, each a sequence of words labelled with a syntactic category and possibly a marking to indicate which word is the head of the chunk. For example, the sentence (12.1a) might be chunked as (12.1b).

(12.1)   a. Give me flight times after ten in the morning.
         b. $[_V$ Give $^H]$ $[_N$ me $^H]$ $[_N$ flight times $^H]$ $[_P$ after $^H]$ $[_N$ ten $^H]$ $[_P$ in $^H]$ $[_N$ the morning $^H]$

One approach uses collections of manually developed finite-state transducers (see Chapter 18) to insert noun and verb chunk boundaries and mark heads (e.g. Grefenstette 1999). Statistical techniques have also been used (e.g. Ramshaw and Marcus 1995), the chunker being trained on text that has been manually marked up with chunk annotations.

Chunking can be a first step in constructing recursive phrase-structure analyses. Abney (1996) uses a set of regular expressions over part-of-speech labels and lower-level chunks to successively build up larger chunks out of smaller ones, thus approximating a CF grammar to a given depth of recursion. Similarly, but in a statistical framework, Brants (1999) uses a Markov model (Chapter 19) for each layer of syntactic structure, the output from each lower layer being passed as input to the next higher one.

12.2 Dependency Parsing

In dependency grammar (Mel'čuk 1987), a syntactic analysis takes the form of a set of head-modifier dependency links between words, with each link labelled with the grammatical function (for example, *subject*, or *object*) of the modifying word with respect to the head. In this framework, (12.1*a*) might be analysed as in (12.2).

(12.2)

Give   me   flight   times   . . .

There is a straightforward correspondence between a 'projective' dependency analysis (one with no crossing links) and a constituent structure analysis, of the sort given by a CF grammar.

There are a number of successful approaches to parsing with dependency grammar. In the Link Grammar system (Grinberg, Lafferty, and Sleator 1995), each word in the lexicon has associated with it a set of possible link (or grammatical function) types, each marked with the direction in which the head is expected to be found. When parsing, all possible linkages are efficiently explored (subject to a 'no crossing links' constraint), with additional pruning of impossible linkages making the technique more practical for large grammars.

In the Functional Dependency Grammar system (Tapanainen and Järvinen 1997), the parser first labels each word with all its possible function types, and then proceeds to apply a collection of handwritten rules which introduce links between specific types in a given context, and perhaps also remove other function-type readings. One of the rules, for instance, might add a subject dependency between a noun and an immediately following finite verb, and remove any other possible functions for the noun. Finally, a further set of rules are applied to remove unlikely linkages, although some ambiguity may still be left at the end in cases where the grammar has insufficient information to be able to resolve it.

12.3 Context-Free Parsing

Context-free (CF) parsing algorithms form the basis for almost all approaches to parsing that build hierarchical phrase structure.

A large number of distinct parsing algorithms exist, differing along a number of dimensions. For example, some only record complete constituents, whereas others also store partial constituents (recording that a particular category has been found and that further ones must also be found in specified locations relative to it). Some algorithms build all sub-analyses possible for the input, whereas others attempt by various means to avoid producing analyses for constituents that could not contribute to a complete parse of a pre-specified category. The common factor between the algorithms described below is that they cope efficiently with ambiguity by not deriving the same sub-analysis by the same set of steps more than once; they do this by storing derived sub-analyses in a **well-formed substring table** (WFST), or **chart**, and retrieving entries from the table as needed, rather than recomputing them.[1] This is an instance of the general technique of *dynamic programming*, in which intermediate results are recorded for possible later reuse to avoid computations being repeated.

The following sections outline two well-known parsing algorithms (CKY, and bottom-up left corner) that have been used in full-scale, implemented parsing systems. Many more algorithms have been described in the parsing literature (see Further Reading below), each having their own particular advantages and disadvantages. Unfortunately, there are no analytical techniques that will determine which parsing technique will work best for a given grammar and expected type of input string. Therefore, the selection and refinement of a parsing technique for a grammar must be a purely empirical enterprise (see section 12.6).

Some algorithms were 'discovered' independently within two distinct traditions: the study of formal (programming) languages, and research in natural language processing. So, for example, the CKY algorithm (section 12.3.1) and a bottom-up passive chart parser (Kay 1986) perform essentially the same operations. Where appropriate we give both names.

The main form of presentation for the parsing algorithms in this chapter is graphical, as a set of steps each with conditions to be satisfied (such as the presence of a particular sub-analysis or a rule) before a further sub-analysis can be derived. This treatment abstracts away from details of datastructures and the order in which processing steps are carried out. However, some form of control over processing order is required to ensure that the parser does not attempt a computation that it has performed already. This is commonly achieved by either (i) choosing a strict, perhaps left-to-right, processing order in which all possible steps are immediately executed with each newly derived sub-analysis, with the next word not being processed until all other possible steps have been performed; or (ii) adding new steps that have yet to be performed to a queue, or **agenda**, and removing them in order, one at a time, to execute them. Agenda-based processing allows for flexible control strategies (such as 'head driven', or priority driven with respect to weights assigned to rules), since the

---

[1] We concentrate here on tabular, as opposed to backtracking, parsing algorithms, since only the former perform well enough with wide-coverage NL grammars.

agenda can be sorted with respect to any attribute of a sub-analysis and step to be performed.

12.3.1 CKY and bottom-up passive chart

The most basic tabular CF parsing algorithm is CKY (Kasami 1965; Younger 1967). Strictly, it requires that the grammar be expressed in Chomsky normal form (Chomsky 1959; see also Chapter 8 of this volume): rules must rewrite a non-terminal either as a single terminal symbol, or as two non-terminals.[2] Fig. 12.1 illustrates the operation of the algorithm; in keeping with NL parsing tradition (as opposed to that in the theoretical study of parsing algorithms), the terminal symbols are exactly the words w_j in the input string and we have a function *entries* to return their category symbols, instead of having unary-branching rules rewriting terminal symbols. First, the lexical entries for each word are found and recorded as constituents (the *initialize* step). Then, successively processing larger segments of the input, a new higher-level constituent is formed (*complete*) for every pair of contiguous constituents and a rule that can combine them. This process continues until all constituents that can be constructed have been. For example, one of the *complete* steps performed in analysing the example sentence (12.1a) might involve a rule $PP \rightarrow P\ NP$ being applied to the category P corresponding to *in* between positions six and seven of the input string, and NP (*the morning*) between seven and nine, producing a PP (prepositional phrase) between positions six and nine.

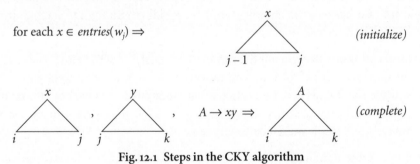

Fig. 12.1 Steps in the CKY algorithm

The CKY algorithm can be extended to work with any arbitrary CF grammar, without restriction on the numbers of daughters in rules. This variant is also known as the bottom-up passive chart parsing algorithm (Fig. 12.2). Since the grammar may now contain rules with empty right-hand sides, an additional initialization step (*initialize₂*) is required which creates constituents of the appropriate categories and

---

[2] An arbitrary CF grammar can be translated into Chomsky normal form with the help of additional, 'dummy' non-terminals.

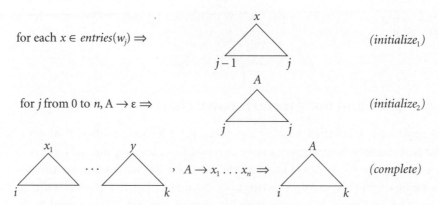

for each $x \in entries(w_j) \Rightarrow$ (initialize$_1$)

for j from 0 to n, $A \rightarrow \varepsilon \Rightarrow$ (initialize$_2$)

$A \rightarrow x_1 \ldots x_n \Rightarrow$ (complete)

Fig. 12.2 Steps in the extended CKY (bottom-up passive chart algorithm

of zero length at all positions $0 \ldots n$ relative to the input string. In the *complete* step a rule analyses all of its daughters in a single operation, with the proviso that all the constituents used must be contiguous. Thus, for the sentence (12.1*a*), the *complete* step might construct a VP (verb phrase) using the rule *VP → Vditrans NP NP* together with sub-analyses for *give* (a ditransitive verb), *me*, and *flight times . . . morning*.

The ambiguity inherent in natural language means that a given segment of the input string may end up being analysed as a constituent of a given category in several different ways. With any parsing algorithm, each of these different ways must be recorded, of course, but subsequent parsing steps must treat the set of analyses as a single entity, otherwise the computation becomes theoretically intractable. Tomita (1985) coined the terms:

- **local ambiguity packing** for the way in which analyses of the same type covering the same segment of the input are conceptually 'packed' into a single entity; and
- **subtree sharing** where if a particular sub-analysis forms part of two or more higher-level analyses then there is only a single representation of the sub-analysis, and this is shared between them.

The final representation produced by the parser is called a **parse forest** (see e.g. Billot and Lang 1989), and is produced quite naturally if each step records pointers to the constituents, rules, and words contributing to it. Fig. 12.3 shows a fragment of the parse forest that might be constructed for (12.1*a*). Each different combination of packed nodes gives rise to a distinct parse tree when the forest is unpacked.

For any CF grammar and any input string the computation of the parse forest is guaranteed to terminate since although in the (very) worst case for each segment of the string the parser will have to apply each rule in the grammar to every sequence of subtrees, there are only finitely many rules and string positions. In fact, with respect to a string of length n words, the CKY algorithm constructs the parse forest within a

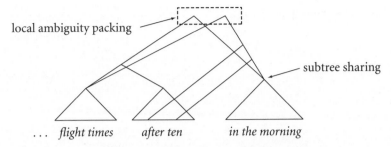

local ambiguity packing

subtree sharing

... *flight times*   *after ten*   *in the morning*

Fig. 12.3 A fragment of a parse forest

constant factor of n^3 operations at the most. The bottom-up passive chart algorithm performs within a constant factor of $n^{\rho+1}$ operations where ρ is the maximum number of daughters in a rule, because the algorithm (in the *complete* step) may repeatedly re-analyse in the same way subsequences of two or more constituents.

There can be an exponential (with respect to n) number of trees represented in the parse forest: for example, for English noun compounds analysed using a recursive binary-branching rule ($N \rightarrow N\ N$) the number of trees correlates with the Catalan series (Church and Patil 1982), with a three-word compound having two analyses, a four-word compound having five, five having fourteen, and so on. Cyclic grammars, in which sets of rules can apply recursively and indefinitely without consuming any input (for example a grammar containing the rule $N \rightarrow N$), do not present difficulties for parse forest construction, but in this case the forest might represent an infinite number of trees, so unpacking would fail to terminate.

If the process of matching rule daughters with sub-analyses is fast and categories are compact (as is indeed the case with an atomic-categoried CF grammar), and additionally rules are at most binary branching, a well-crafted implementation of the CKY algorithm can be competitive in throughput to more complex algorithms that attempt to limit the number of matching operations performed and entries in the WFST. Thus CKY is the algorithm of choice for use in statistical parsing with a CF grammar in conjunction with the *inside–outside* re-estimation algorithm (Chapter 19). CKY has also been used successfully in the LiLFeS system (Torisawa and Tsujii 1996), in an initial parsing phase with a very large **context-free backbone** grammar that approximates an HPSG, prior to applying the full set of feature-structure constraints.

12.3.2 Bottom-up left corner (bottom-up active chart)

The CKY and passive chart algorithms record only complete constituents. Thus they might attempt to match a particular constituent against the same rule daughter repeatedly in the course of trying to apply a rule, not taking advantage of the know-

Same as bottom-up passive chart   (initialize₁,
                                                                 (initialize₂)

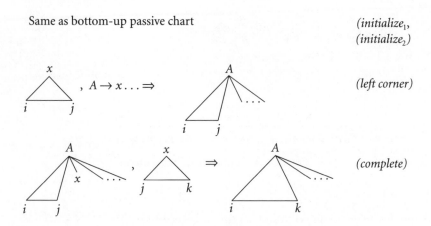

Fig. 12.4 Steps in the bottom-up left corner parsing algorithm

ledge that all previous attempts had succeeded or failed. Whereas matching a daughter against an existing constituent is a cheap operation in a CF parser with atomic
categories since it is merely an equality test, the procedure could be much more
expensive in a unification-based parser (section 12.4), for example. This potential
source of redundant computation is avoided by the bottom-up left corner parsing
algorithm (Fig. 12.4) since it explicitly records all partial constituents. In this algorithm the initialization steps for lexical entries and rules with empty right-hand sides
are the same as in the passive bottom-up parser. The difference is that application of
rules proceeds in stages, the first daughter of a rule being filled first, creating an **active
edge** or item,[3] and the remaining daughters being analysed one by one (the *complete*
step)[4] until a complete constituent, represented as a **passive edge**, is formed as the last
daughter is filled. So, in contrast to the passive chart algorithm, the *left corner* step
would take the rule *VP → Vditrans NP NP* and the lexical entry for *give* and create
an active edge looking for two noun phrases; two subsequent *complete* steps would
firstly create a second active edge, and then a passive edge representing a complete
verb phrase.

For best practical parsing performance, as few partial constituents should be created as possible. However, if the leftmost daughter of a rule is less constrained than
other daughters—in that it matches a wider range of constituents produced during a
parse—rule application would be better driven starting from one of the other daughters. In some types of grammar the appropriate daughter would be the syntactic head
of the rule, so the *left corner* step would be modified to start at the head of each rule,
complete would work bidirectionally on both sides of the head, and the parser would
then be 'head driven' (Kay 1989). Processing not now being strictly left to right means

---

[3] The term *active* refers to the fact that further constituents are still being sought to fill the remaining
daughters.
[4] The *complete* step is sometimes also called the *fundamental* step in chart parsing.

that more care is needed to ensure that steps are not duplicated or omitted. Similarly, when parsing output from a speech recognizer that associates with each word hypothesis a numeric score encoding the certainty with which it has been recognized correctly (see Chapter 16), processing could be initiated at the hypotheses with the highest scores, resulting in an **island parsing** strategy.

Bottom-up left/head corner parsing is used in a number of widely distributed grammar development/parsing systems, including ALE3.2 (Penn and Carpenter 1999), the Alvey NL Tools (Briscoe et al. 1987), the LKB (Copestake and Flickinger 2000), and PAGE (Kiefer et al. 1999). See Further Reading below for WWW references.

12.4 UNIFICATION-BASED PARSING

It is difficult to create and maintain an atomic-categoried grammar covering a substantial fragment of a language, since for a given type of syntactic dependency each possible combination of syntactic features requires a new rule to be written (see Chapter 4). However, CF parsing algorithms form the basis for parsing with more powerful and expressive grammar formalisms, such as Head-Driven Phrase Structure Grammar (HPSG; Pollard and Sag 1994) and Lexical Functional Grammar (LFG; Bresnan 2000). These formalisms make extensive use of attribute-value matrices, or feature structures, to encode linguistic information, combining them with the **unification** operation. For example, the result of unifying the feature structure (12.3a) with (12.3b) is (12.3c).

(12.3) *a.*

$$
\begin{bmatrix}
\text{SYN} & \begin{bmatrix}
\text{CAT } v \\
\text{AGR} & \begin{bmatrix}
\text{PER } 3 \\
\text{PLU } -
\end{bmatrix}
\end{bmatrix}
\end{bmatrix}
$$

b.

$$
\begin{bmatrix}
\text{PHON } helped \\
\text{SYN} & \begin{bmatrix}
\text{CAT } v \\
\text{VFORM } past
\end{bmatrix}
\end{bmatrix}
$$

c.

$$
\begin{bmatrix}
\text{PHON } helped \\[2ex]
\text{SYN} \quad
\begin{bmatrix}
\text{CAT } v \\[1ex]
\text{AGR} \quad
\begin{bmatrix}
\text{PER } 3 \\
\text{PLU } -
\end{bmatrix} \\[2ex]
\text{VFORM } past
\end{bmatrix}
\end{bmatrix}
$$

Unification would fail if, in this example, the value of the CAT feature in one of the input feature structures was not v. In contrast to the atomic, unstructured symbols of CF grammar, feature structures allow a grammar writer to conveniently cross-classify attributes of categories, and also leave attributes underspecified, as appropriate. Unification is used to communicate information introduced by lexical entries and grammar rules in order to validate proposed local and non-local syntactic dependencies (Chapter 4), and also in some grammar theories it is the mechanism through which semantic representations are constructed.

A key property of unification is that the order in which a set of unifications is performed does not affect the final result; therefore any parsing strategy valid for CF grammars is equally applicable to unification-based grammars. If each category is represented purely by a feature structure then the test for compatibility of categories is unification (rather than category symbol equality), and for local ambiguity packing one category must stand in a **subsumption** relationship to the other (see Oepen and Carroll 2000). On the other hand, the grammar may consist of a CF backbone augmented with feature structures, in which case parsing would be driven by the backbone and the appropriate unifications either carried out on each *complete* step, or after the full CF parse forest had been constructed (Maxwell and Kaplan 1993).

The most basic, efficient unification algorithm may end up destroying either or both of the two input feature structures in producing the output, so in a tabular parser additional bookkeeping is required to avoid this. Although a non-destructive version of unification can still be implemented efficiently, because (depending on the type of grammar) a high proportion of unifications may fail and each failure will still take some time before being detected, a parser may waste a lot of effort in ultimately unproductive computation. Malouf, Carroll, and Copestake (2000) discuss this issue and describe a number of techniques that can greatly improve parser throughput with large feature-based grammars.

12.5 Parse Disambiguation

Any grammar covering a substantial fragment of a language will find readings for sentences that would not have been intended by the original author. Some parsing systems have used manually developed heuristics for resolving particular types of ambiguity (for example 'prefer to attach prepositional phrases low'—i.e. to the most recent noun rather than a preceding verb); however, this approach is not entirely satisfactory since the heuristics would not be likely to cover the full range of ambiguities, and would also have to be recoded to work properly for a different language genre. An alternative approach, being investigated in a number of current research efforts, is for the parser automatically to learn to choose statistically plausible parses based on text that has been syntactically parsed by hand. This type of annotated text is called a **treebank**.

Data from the treebank is used to associate statistical preferences with a grammar to allow the analyses it produces to be disambiguated. The grammar may exist already, or it may itself be induced from the treebank. Although the latter approach is a simple and convenient way of obtaining a grammar, *treebank grammars* have the disadvantage that they cannot by themselves produce semantic predicate–argument structure since this information is not present in the original treebank; retrofitting it manually to the grammar would not be possible since in general the rules would not be sufficiently detailed. In contrast, manually developed grammars may produce more precise, detailed analyses that can support semantic interpretation—but at the cost of requiring an expert grammarian to develop the grammars.

A CF treebank grammar can be constructed by creating a production for each distinct local (one-level) tree in the treebank. The probability that a particular production should be applied can be estimated directly from the treebank by accumulating a frequency count for each rule and normalizing frequency counts so that the probabilities of each set of rules with the same mother category sum to one (Fig. 12.5). This results in a *Probabilistic CF Grammar* (PCFG). In PCFG, the probability of a parse tree is the product of the probabilities of the rules in the tree. The parser searches for and returns the parse with highest probability. Training on a 1-million-word treebank of English, Charniak (1996) shows that this method can give fairly accurate parses.

However, PCFG ignores the substantial influence on preferred readings exerted by syntactic context and word choice. For example, in English, right-branching syntactic structures are more prevalent than left-branching structures, but PCFG cannot capture this bias probabilistically. Nor can it model the fact that in the most plausible reading of (12.4a) the *after* prepositional phrase modifies *flight times*, whereas in (12.4b) the same type of prepositional phrase (but containing different words) modifies the main verb, *give*.

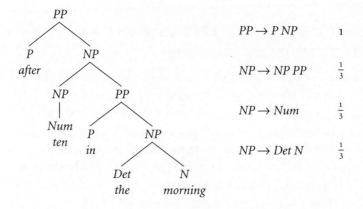

Fig. 12.5 Acquisition of PCFG rules and probabilities from a treebank parse

(12.4)   *a.* Give me flight times after ten in the morning.
         b. Give me flight times after availability checks.

Current research in parse disambiguation attempts to capture these types of preferences probabilistically. One approach (Collins 1996) is to acquire statistics from a
treebank on the likelihood that any particular pair of words stand in a head-modifier
relationship, given the syntactic category of the parse node that dominates them, their
relative ordering in the sentence, and the distance between them. These statistics are
then used to score, and thus choose between, potential parses. Another approach
(Bod 1998), which is able to model dependencies between arbitrary words, not just
lexical heads, constructs analyses of sentences out of segments of parse trees of
arbitrary shape and depth extracted from a treebank. Frequently occurring subtrees
would tend to encode significant dependencies between their constituent parts, and
so these would be more likely to appear in a parse than less frequent alternatives.

12.6 PRACTICAL ISSUES

12.6.1 Accuracy

Component-level evaluation (Chapter 22) of the accuracy of a parser should be
carried out with respect to a *gold standard* set of parses for some set of test inputs.
However, *exact* match of parser analyses against the gold standard is usually not

appropriate because (i) some apparent differences between analyses might not ultimately correspond to any real differences in meaning, and also (ii) the grammar might have been designed to analyse certain constructions differently from the standard. Carroll, Briscoe, and Sanfilippo (1998) survey various constituency- and dependency-based approaches to parser evaluation that have been proposed.

12.6.2 Efficiency

Computational complexity results for parsing algorithms are often not good indicators of the relative speeds of actual implementations of the algorithms with a particular NL grammar: implementational decisions and optimizations based on subtle properties of specific grammars can be more important (Chapter 9; also Carroll 1994). Indeed, despite the fact that unification-based parsing can be intractable in the worst case, a number of research groups working with wide-coverage unification-based grammars have observed relationships between length of sentence and parse time that are no more than quadratic. Although very long sentences could still take an excessive amount of processing time, this empirical relationship augurs well for practical processing of real language.

12.6.3 Coverage

Given that treebanks invariably contain a wide variety of local tree configurations with nodes whose syntactic category labels are only atomic, treebank grammars tend to both overgenerate and overaccept massively (that is, they return complete parses for ungrammatical input, and return too many parses for grammatical input, respectively). Any input usually receives some sort of parse, so coverage is not a problem. Gaps in coverage are often a problem for manually developed grammars, though, since they are typically much 'tighter'. Coverage—and also overgeneration and overacceptance—can be quantified with respect to a **test suite** (Oepen and Flickinger 1998). This is becoming increasingly important as a quality assurance measure as grammar coverage widens and parsing systems start to be deployed as modules in real-world applications (Chapters 27–38).

FURTHER READING AND RELEVANT RESOURCES

Jurafsky and Martin's (2000) textbook contains basic descriptions of various parsing techniques. Manning and Schütze (1999) give a general introduction to statistical parsing. Shieber, Schabes, and Pereira (1995) present a general deductive framework for expressing parsing algorithms, and in a similar vein Sikkel (1997) gives detailed specifications of a large number of parsing algorithms, relating them via abstract transformations. A special issue of the journal *Natural Language Engineering*, 6(1), 2000 contains a number of articles on recently developed techniques for efficient parsing with unification-based NL grammars.

The Association for Computational Linguistics (ACL) special interest group on parsing, SIGPARSE, organizes biennial workshops, under the title *International Workshop on Parsing Technologies*. The first such workshop was held in 1989. Links to on-line papers and abstracts, and references to books containing published versions of some of the papers, can be found at http://parlevink.cs.utwente.nl/sigparse/. Research specifically on statistical techniques for parsing is frequently published in the two series *Conferences on Empirical Methods in Natural Language Processing* and *Workshops on Very Large Corpora*, both sponsored by ACL/SIGDAT; see http://www.cs.jhu.edu/~yarowsky/sigdat.html. Parsing is usually also well represented at the major computational linguistics conferences.

The easiest way to gain practical experience with parsing with NL grammars is to obtain one of the number of publicly available grammar development/parsing systems. Most are supplied with at least one small and one more extensive grammar, together with one or more parsers using various algorithms. A few such systems are:

- ALE: http://www.sfs.nphil.uni-tuebingen.de/~gpenn/ale.html
- Alvey NL Tools: http://www.cl.cam.ac.uk/Research/NL/anlt.html
- HDrug: http://www.let.rug.nl/~vannoord/Hdrug/
- Link Grammar system: http://www.link.cs.cmu.edu/link/
- LKB: http://www-csli.stanford.edu/~aac/lkb.html
- MINIPAR: http://www.cs.umanitoba.ca/~lindek/minipar.htm

There is a collection of links to on-line demonstrations, including several parsers for English and German, at http://www.ifi.unizh.ch/CL/InteractiveTools.html.

References

Abney, S. 1996. 'Partial parsing via finite-state cascades'. *Natural Language Engineering*, 2(4), 337–44.

Billot, S. and B. Lang. 1989. 'The structure of shared forests in ambiguous parsing'. *Proceedings of the 27th Meeting of the Association for Computational Linguistics* (Vancouver), 143–51.

Bod, R. 1998. *Beyond Grammar: An Experience-Based Theory of Language*. Stanford, Calif.: CSLI Press.

Brants, T. 1999. 'Cascaded Markov models'. *Proceedings of the 9th Conference of the European Chapter of the Association for Computational Linguistics* (Bergen), 118–25.

Bresnan, J. 2000. *Lexical-Functional Syntax*. Oxford: Blackwell.

Briscoe, E., C. Grover, B. Boguraev, and J. Carroll. 1987. 'A formalism and environment for the development of a large grammar of English'. *Proceedings of the 10th International Joint Conference on Artificial Intelligence* (Milan), 703–8.

Carroll, J. 1994. 'Relating complexity to practical performance in parsing with wide-coverage unification grammars'. *Proceedings of the 32nd Annual Meeting of the Association for Computational Linguistics* (Las Cruces, N. Mex.), 287–94.

——E. Briscoe, and A. Sanfilippo. 1998. 'Parser evaluation: a survey and a new proposal'. *Proceedings of the 1st International Conference on Language Resources and Evaluation* (Granada), 447–54.

Charniak, E. 1996. 'Tree-bank grammars'. *Proceedings of the 13th National Conference on Artificial Intelligence* (Portland, Ore), 1031–6.

Chomsky, N. 1959. 'On certain formal properties of grammars'. *Information and Control*, 2(2), 137–67.

Church, K. and R. Patil. 1982. 'Coping with syntactic ambiguity or how to put the block in the box on the table'. *American Journal of Computational Linguistics*, 8(3–4), 139–49.

Collins, M. 1996. 'A new statistical parser based on bigram lexical dependencies'. *Proceedings of the 34th Annual Meeting of the Association for Computational Linguistics* (Santa Cruz, Calif.), 184–91.

Copestake, A. and D. Flickinger. 2000. 'An open source grammar development environment and broad-coverage English grammar using HPSG'. *Proceedings of the 2nd International Conference on Language Resources and Evaluation* (Athens), 591–600.

Grefenstette, G. 1999. 'Light parsing as finite-state filtering'. In A. Kornai (ed.), *Extended Finite State Models of Language*, Cambridge: Cambridge University Press, 86–94.

Grinberg, D., J. Lafferty, and D. Sleator. 1995. 'A robust parsing algorithm for link grammars'. *Proceedings of the 4th International Workshop on Parsing Technologies* (Prague), 111–25.

Jurafsky, D. and J. Martin. 2000. *Speech and Language Processing*. Englewood Cliffs, NJ: Prentice Hall.

Kasami, J. 1965. *An Efficient Recognition and Syntax Analysis Algorithm for Context-free Languages*. Report AFCRL-65-758, Air Force Cambridge Research Laboratory, Bedford, Mass.

Kay, M. 1986. 'Algorithm schemata and data structures in syntactic parsing'. In B. Grosz, K. Spärck Jones, and B. Webber (eds.), *Readings in Natural Language Processing*. San Mateo, Calif.: Morgan Kaufmann, 35–70.

——1989. 'Head-driven parsing'. *Proceedings of the 1st International Workshop on Parsing Technologies* (Pittsburgh), 52–62.

Kiefer, B., H.-U. Krieger, J. Carroll, and R. Malouf. 1999. 'A bag of useful techniques for efficient and robust parsing'. *Proceedings of the 37th Meeting of the Association for Computational Linguistics* (Baltimore), 473–80.

Malouf, R., J. Carroll, and A. Copestake. 2000. 'Efficient feature structure operations without compilation'. *Natural Language Engineering*, 6(1), 29–46.

Manning, C. and H. Schütze. 1999. *Foundations of Statistical Natural Language Processing*. Cambridge, Mass.: MIT Press.

Maxwell, J. III and R. Kaplan. 1993. 'The interface between phrasal and functional constraints'. *Computational Linguistics*, 19(4), 571–90.

Mel'čuk, I. 1987. *Dependency Syntax: Theory and Practice*. Albany, NY: SUNY Press.

Oepen, S. and J. Carroll. 2000. 'Ambiguity packing in constraint-based grammar—practical results'. *Proceedings of the 1st Conference of the North American Chapter of the Association for Computational Linguistics* (Seattle), 162–9.

Oepen, S. and D. Flickinger. 1998 'Towards systematic grammar profiling. Test suite technology ten years after'. *Computer Speech and Language*, 12(4), 411–36.

Penn, G. and B. Carpenter. 1999. 'ALE for speech: a translation prototype'. *Proceedings of the 6th Conference on Speech Communication and Technology (EUROSPEECH)* (Budapest), 947–50.

Pollard, C. and I. Sag. 1994. *Head-Driven Phrase Structure Grammar*. Chicago: University of Chicago Press.

Ramshaw, L. and M. Marcus. 1995. 'Text chunking using transformation-based learning'. *Proceedings of the 3rd Workshop on Very Large Corpora* (Cambridge, Mass.), 82–94.

Shieber, S., Y. Schabes, and F. Pereira. 1995. 'Principles and implementation of deductive parsing'. *Journal of Logic Programming*, 24(1–2), 3–36.

Sikkel, K. 1997. *Parsing Schemata: A Framework for Specification and Analysis of Parsing Algorithms*. Berlin: Springer-Verlag.

Tapanainen, P. and T. Järvinen. 1997. 'A non-projective dependency parser'. *Proceedings of the 5th ACL Conference on Applied Natural Language Processing* (Washington), 64–71.

Tomita, M. 1985. 'An efficient context-free parsing algorithm for natural languages'. *Proceedings of the 9th International Joint Conference on Artificial Intelligence* (Los Angeles), 756–64.

Torisawa, K., and J. Tsujii. 1996. 'Computing phrasal signs in HPSG prior to parsing'. *Proceedings of the 16th International Conference on Computational Linguistics (COLING)* (Copenhagen), 949–55.

Younger, D. 1967. 'Recognition and parsing of context-free languages in time n^3'. *Information and Control*, 10(2), 189–208.

WORD-SENSE DISAMBIGUATION

MARK STEVENSON

YORICK WILKS

ABSTRACT

Word-sense disambiguation is the process of identifying the meanings of words in context. We begin by discuss the origins of the problem in the earliest machine translation systems. The main approaches are described, including dictionary-based, connectionist, and statistical strategies. We conclude with a review of evaluation strategies for WSD and possible applications of the technology.

13.1 THE PROBLEM

It is commonplace that many words have multiple meanings; for example 'light' can mean 'not heavy' or 'illumination'. The particular meaning, or sense, a word bears on a particular occasion of use is, one conventionally says, determined by its context. It is clear which sense is in play in 'He turned on the light.' The process of deciding the senses of words in context is known as **word-sense disambiguation** (WSD, hereafter).

WSD has been a research area in natural language processing for almost as long as the field has existed. It was identified as a distinct task in relation to machine translation (MT) (see Chapters 27 and 28) over forty years ago (Yngve 1955). One of the first problems which was faced by these systems was that of word-sense ambiguity. It became rapidly apparent that semantic disambiguation at the lexical level was necessary for even trivial language understanding.

This review concentrates on some of the best-known approaches to the WSD problem, although space limitations have forced the omission of several important systems. We conclude with a brief discussion of possible areas of application for WSD technology.

13.2 EARLY APPROACHES

13.2.1 Preference semantics

Wilks (1972) made one of the earliest attempts to solve the WSD problem. He used hierarchically organized selectional constraints with complex semantic representations called formulas but, unlike Katz and Fodor (1963), whose constraints were necessary, preferences could be loosened within some overall numerical condition of satisfaction of preferences.

The system assumed that each sense in the lexicon had a formula associated with it which expresses its meaning. The system included a hierarchy of eighty semantic features which included items synonymous with HUMAN, WANT, ABSTRACT, MOVE, and so on. Adjective formulas contained the preferred semantic features of the noun they modified, verb formulas the preferred semantic features of the nouns they governed (the number depending upon the valency of the verb). Polysemy was represented by associating more than one possible formula with a word, and regular polysemy by an ability to modify the formulas of words in new contexts. Disambiguation was carried out by choosing a formula for each ambiguous word in a sentence so that the maximum number of preferences for a phrase or clause is satisfied. In this way it was possible to disambiguate all content words in a sentence simultaneously. In fact the ultimate aim of the **preference semantics** system was to construct a semantic representation for a text, and some form of WSD was a necessary substep of this more ambitious goal.

Wilks took his test examples from newspaper articles, believing that since these made sense to their authors the burden was on the system to provide an interpretation. He also argued that words are commonly used in novel ways which cannot be determined in advance and must be interpreted dynamically, using the preference mechanism. Wilks (1978) quotes two examples of the verb 'to drink', which normally prefers a subject with the ANIMATE feature:

(13.1)   The adder drank from the pool.

(13.2)   My car drinks gasoline.

In the first sentence 'adder' has two formulas associated with it: one for the 'calculator' sense which is marked as MACHINE and the other meaning 'snake' which is marked as ANIMATE. The second sense is chosen since this satisfies the verb's preferences and a representation of the sentence can be constructed. However, in the second sentence the subject, 'car', has no formula with the appropriate semantic feature and so, in order to process the text, the sentence is accepted as valid and a semantic representation constructed in which the subject of 'drink' has the MACHINE feature. It was intended that the extended usages discovered in this way would be added to the system's lexicon. Preference semantics was applied within a small English–French MT system (Wilks 1973).

13.2.2 Word expert parsing

Small (1980) provided an approach which was even more highly lexicalized than that of Wilks, with the lexicon being the source of all information in his system, rather than appearing in other rule-like structures, as in preference semantics, though, as with Wilks, a representation for the entire sentence would be built up from the representations of the individual words through the process of disambiguation. Small's approach was based on the assumption that 'human knowledge about language is organized primarily as knowledge about words rather than knowledge about rules' (Small and Riger 1982: 89). However, this view is rather unconventional and no attempt is made to support it with psycholinguistic evidence.

Small believed words are idiosyncratic to the extent that an individual *word expert*, essentially a hand-crafted disambiguator, should be constructed for each one. In Small's system word experts contain information which would be stored in the grammar, lexicon, parser, or knowledge base in a more conventional system. Small also believed that word experts should not be simple copies or adaptations of each other and should be constructed in a bottom-up first-principle fashion. The word experts themselves were extremely large: Small reported the word expert for 'throw' to be 'currently six pages long, but should be ten times that size' (Small and Riger 1982: 146). It should be borne in mind that the goal was to provide full semantic analyses for sentences, which is far more ambitious than WSD.

The size of word experts, the lack of a lexical hierarchy, and the high degree of lexicalization limited the applicability of Small's approach.

13.2.3 Polaroid words

Hirst (1987) created a system which was less lexicalized and more general than either
Small's or Wilks's. His system contained the modules found in a conventional NLP
system: a grammar, parser, lexicon, semantic interpreter, and a knowledge representation language. The disambiguation information and processes were distributed
across different parts of the system. Sentences entering the system would be translated to the knowledge representation language, and the information in them would
be added to the system's knowledge base, so that the whole system constituted a fully
working NLP system.

Dynamic interaction between the knowledge sources was achieved using a marker-
passing mechanism. This is a model where flags are passed around the knowledge
base and the result is obtained through a process of spreading activation, a symbolic
version of connectionist approaches (see section 13.4). Hirst calls this disambiguation method *polaroid words* since the final interpretation is revealed gradually, like a
polaroid photograph.

The approaches of Wilks, Small, and Hirst shared a lack of extensibility, given the
size of their lexicons (500 words in the case of preference semantics and unknown in
the other two). Each relied on manually-encoded disambiguation information. This
was dubbed the 'lexical bottleneck' (Briscoe 1991). Later systems attempted to avoid
this problem in two ways: first, by using existing dictionaries and ontologies as lexicons (see Chapters 3 and 25) and, secondly, by deriving disambiguation information
directly from corpora using statistical and machine learning techniques (see Chapters 19, 20, and 21). We now go on to discuss each of these developments.

13.3   DICTIONARY-BASED APPROACHES

13.3.1 Optimizing dictionary definition overlap

Lesk (1986) made one of the first attempts to use a **machine-readable dictionary**
(MRD) for WSD. He observed that dictionary definitions could be used to express the
way in which the choice of one sense in a text was dependent upon the senses chosen
for words close to it. He used the *Oxford Advanced Learners' Dictionary* (*OALD*)

(Hornby 1963), and chose the senses which share the most definition words with senses from neighbouring words. His motivating example was 'pine cone'; 'pine' has two major senses in the *OALD*, 'kind of evergreen tree with needle-shaped leaves' and 'waste away through sorrow or illness', while 'cone' has three: 'solid body which narrows at a point', 'something of this shape whether solid or hollow', and 'fruit of certain evergreen trees'. The correct senses have the words 'evergreen' and 'tree' in common in their *OALD* definitions.

Cowie, Guthrie, and Guthrie (1992) optimized Lesk's approach by using the **simulated annealing** algorithm to disambiguate all content words in a sentence. Simulated annealing is a numerical minimization algorithm first used in NLP for parsing by Sampson (1986). Cowie, Guthrie, and Guthrie's implementation of this proposal assigned senses from the machine-readable version of the *Longman Dictionary of Contemporary English* (*LDOCE*) (Procter 1978). Using a set of fifty example sentences from *LDOCE*, 47 per cent of words were correctly disambiguated to sense level and 72 per cent to the, more rough grained, homograph level compared to senses assigned by humans. This method certainly produces encouraging results—a high level of disambiguation to the homograph level over all content words in a text. However, it did not attempt to make use of all the information in the dictionary, concentrating only on the textual definitions.

13.3.2 Combining knowledge sources

Given the wide range of linguistic information available in machine-readable dictionaries, trying to combine them seems a natural approach. One of the first systems which used combinations of linguistic information was produced by McRoy (1992). Her system used a complex set of hand-created knowledge sources including a large lexicon, a concept hierarchy, and a library of collocations. Disambiguation was carried out by making use of several knowledge sources: syntactic tags, morphological information, semantic context (clusters), collocations and word associations, role-related expectations, and selectional restrictions. The knowledge sources were combined by adding their results. The individual knowledge sources assigned a numerical value, in the range −10 to +10, for each possible sense, with the exact value depending upon the strength or discriminatory value of the knowledge source.

This system was tested on a corpus of 25,000 words from the *Wall Street Journal* but McRoy did not compare the system's results against a manual annotation of the same text and so it is difficult to gauge the effectiveness of the system.

Ng and Lee (1996) used a machine learning algorithm to combine several knowledge sources including surrounding words, local collocates, and words in verb–object syntactic relation. This approach is described in detail in Chapter 20.

Harley and Glennon (1997) produced a sense tagger which used the *Cambridge*

International Dictionary of English (*CIDE*) (Procter 1995). This is a learners' dictionary which is quite similar to *LDOCE*. As this work was carried out within Cambridge University Press, teams of lexicographers were used to add information to the dictionary when it was found to be lacking for WSD. The tagger itself consisted of four tagging subprocesses (multi-word unit tagger, subject domain tagger, part-of-speech tagger, and selectional preference pattern tagger) combined using an additive weighting system similar to those used by computer chess systems. Harley and Glennon report 78 per cent correct tagging at the *CIDE* guideword level, which they equate to the *LDOCE* sense level, and 73 per cent at the sub-sense level compared to a hand-tagged corpus of 4,000 words.

Stevenson and Wilks (1999; Wilks and Stevenson 1998) analysed the sources of linguistic information available in one machine-readable dictionary (*LDOCE*), and argued that they are 'weak' in Newell's sense (Newell 1973). They noticed that many different sources of linguistic knowledge had been used for WSD but none had appeared more successful than any other and all were limited to some degree. They produced a sense tagger which used several of the information sources in *LDOCE* (part-of-speech codes, selectional restrictions, subject codes, and textual definitions) using a machine learning algorithm to combine their output (Daelemans et al. 1998). When tested against a specially created corpus, containing around 40,000 ambiguous tokens, it was found that 94 per cent were correctly disambiguated to the broad-grained homograph level and over 90 per cent to the finer-grained level of the *LDOCE* sense.

Stevenson and Wilks also analysed the interaction between the various knowledge sources, discovering that none of the individual knowledge sources could match the result of the overall tagger and that the tagger worked best when several of the knowledge sources worked well. This indicates that the different types of information cannot be notational variants of each other. It was also discovered that some knowledge sources are more applicable to certain parts of speech than others. (Part-of-speech classes are explained in Chapter 12.)

13.4 CONNECTIONIST APPROACHES

Some researchers have used connectionist techniques to perform WSD, often motivated by an interest in modelling the human disambiguation process.

Seidenberg et al. (1982) developed a model of lexical access, the STLB model, which postulated that all the meanings of an ambiguous word are accessed when it is read or heard, apart from the case when the ambiguity is between two nominal usages and there is a semantic priming effect. Cottrell (1984) implemented the STLB model within a manually created connectionist network using a spreading activation mechanism. When Cottrell tested this model he found that every possible meaning was accessed under all circumstances, even with ambiguity between meanings of the same semantic category, contrary to the STLB model. This led Cottrell to claim that multiple access, of possible senses, always occurs.

Waltz and Pollack (1985) independently developed a connectionist model of language processing based on psycholinguistic observations. Their approach was to carry out syntactic and semantic processing in parallel, rather than in a sequence of steps as was common in NLP systems. Their approach attempted to model comprehension errors demonstrated in semantic garden path sentences such as 'The astronomer married the star' (due to Charniak 1983). Readers usually report that such sentences are temporarily anomalous: that the first meaning for 'star' they entertain is 'celestial body' before they opt for the correct reading, 'celebrity'. This is usually explained by interactions of knowledge; there is a semantic priming effect from the word 'astronomer' which is initially stronger than the case-frame selection of the verb 'to marry'.

Waltz and Pollack's implemented model included forms of linguistic knowledge such as case frames, semantic priming, and syntactic preferences. By examining the relative activation of different nodes during the processing of semantic garden path sentences they found that the node representing the incorrect sense ('celestial body') was initially highly activated but that after several network cycles the correct sense dominated.

Ide and Véronis (1990) approached WSD by constructing large neural networks automatically from a machine-readable dictionary; *Collins English Dictionary* (*COLLINS*) (Hanks 1979). Their network consisted of word nodes and sense nodes. The word nodes were positively linked to different possible senses of that word in the dictionary, while the sense nodes were positively linked to the word nodes representing the words in the dictionary definition of that sense, and negatively linked to words in the definitions for other senses of the words. Disambiguation was carried out by activating the nodes which represented the words in the input sentence, the activation links then activated other nodes and activation cycles through the network using a feedback process. Once the network has stabilized the activated sense node for each word can be read off. This system produced 85 per cent correct disambiguation to the *COLLINS* homograph level (Véronis and Ide 1995), but over very small sentence samples.

13.5 STATISTICAL AND MACHINE LEARNING
APPROACHES

13.5.1 Learning the best disambiguation cue

One of the first applications of machine learning techniques to WSD was carried out by Brown et al. (1991). Although their system did not produce the level of results achieved by later systems using similar methods, their approach anticipated many of the features which became common in machine learning and statistical approaches.

Their algorithm carried out disambiguation for an English to French statistical MT system. It was trained on the Canadian Hansard, the proceedings of the Canadian Parliament, which is published as parallel French and English text. Different senses of the same source word may be translated differently: thus 'duty' is translated as 'droit' or 'impôt' when it means 'tax' and 'devoir' when it means 'obligation'. Usages like this which were translated into different words in French were used to define sense difference in the source language.

The algorithm was trained on sentence pairs which consisted of an English sentence and its French translation. Several different disambiguation cues were identified in the sentence pairs, such as: first noun to the left/right, second word to the left/right etc. The flip-flop algorithm (Nadas et al. 1991) was used to decide which of the cues was most important for each word by maximizing mutual information scores between words in the sentence pairs. This was one of the earliest attempts to empirically decide on the best disambiguation cues and made innovative use of bilingual corpora to provide disambiguated text, at the level required by the algorithm, without the cost of hand tagging.

The approach is even more impressive since it was tested on a concrete application: MT. In a small test set of 100 sentences, it was found that 45 per cent of the translations were acceptable when the sense disambiguation system was used, compared to 37 per cent when it was not. This was empirical proof that WSD does improve MT, which had been claimed for decades but never tested until this point.

13.5.2 Tagging with thesaurus categories

In some of the earliest WSD work, Mastermann in 1960 (described in Wilks 1972) used a simple algorithm on *Roget's Thesaurus* (Chapman 1977) to associate unique Roget head categories with words (thus resolving the ambiguity of words appearing under many heads) based on the repetition of categories associated with words in the same sentence. This early work was judged unsuccessful at the time. Yarowsky (1992) augmented this method with statistical models of the categories in the thesaurus expressed as 100 word-context windows in untagged text.

The training was carried out on an extremely large corpus, the electronic version of *Grolier's Encyclopaedia*, containing 10 million words. The statistical models for each Roget category were built by extracting all contexts which contain any of the words in that category. The models themselves were simple Naive Bayesian models of the type commonly used in information retrieval (Salton and McGill 1983; van Rijsbergen 1979). Salient words, those which distinguish these contexts from the rest of the corpus, were found, again using statistical techniques similar to those used in information retrieval. Disambiguation was carried out by examining the context of an ambiguous word in text and calculating the most likely of the possible categories using a probabilistic technique. This method was tested on twelve polysemous words, all used in the evaluation of previous WSD systems, and gave 92 per cent correct disambiguation. (A discussion of WSD on similar lexical structures can be found in Chapter 25.)

13.5.3 Two claims about senses

During the evaluation of a WSD algorithm which used Naive Bayesian classifiers Gale, Church, and Yarowsky (1992) noticed that the senses of words which occur in a text are extremely limited. They conducted a small experiment in which five subjects were each given a set of definitions for 9 ambiguous words and 82 pairs of concordance lines containing instances of those words. Of the concordance lines, 54 pairs were taken from the same discourse and the remainder from different texts (and hand checked to make sure they did not use the same sense). Fifty-one of the 54 pairs were judged to be the same sense by majority opinion, i.e. a 94 per cent probability that two instances of an ambiguous word will be used in the same sense in a given discourse. It was assumed that 60 per cent of words in text are unambiguous, so there is then a 98 per cent probability that two instances of any word in a discourse will be used in the same sense. They concluded that words have One Sense per Discourse, that is 'there is a very strong tendency (98 per cent) for multiple uses of a word to share the same sense in a well-written discourse' (Gale, Church, and Yarowsky 1992: 236).

Yarowsky followed this claim with another, the One Sense per Collocation claim: 'with a high probability an ambiguous word has only one sense in a given collocation' (Yarowsky 1993: 271). This claim was motivated by experiments where several different types of collocations are considered (first/second/third word to the left/right, first word of a certain part of speech to the left/right, and direct syntactic relationships such as verb/object, subject/verb, and adjective/noun pairs). It was found that a polysemous word was unlikely to occur in the same collocation with a different sense.

These are striking claims which have important implications for WSD algorithms. If the One Sense per Discourse claim is true, then WSD would be best carried out by gathering all occurrences of a word and performing a global disambiguation over the entire text. Local considerations, such as selectional restrictions, which have always been regarded as fundamental, would then seem to give way to simpler and more global considerations.

Krovetz (1998) commented that the definitions of 'sense' and 'discourse' are central to the testability of the One Sense per Discourse claim and conducted experiments which cast doubt upon its prevalence.

13.5.4 Clustering word usages

Yarowsky (1995) went on to present an unsupervised learning algorithm which made use of these constraints. This learns the disambiguation properties of a single word at a time, starting with seed definitions for the senses; these are used to classify some of the occurrences of that word in a training corpus. The algorithm then infers a classification scheme for the other occurrences of that word by generalizing from those examples. The One Sense per Discourse and One Sense per Collocation constraints are thus used to control the inference process. The actual disambiguation is carried out by generating a decision list (Rivest 1987), an ordered set of conjunctive rules which are tested in order until one is found that matches a particular instance and is used to classify it. The learning process is iterative: a decision list is used to tag the examples learned so far, then these tagged examples are generalized and a new decision list inferred from the text. Yarowsky suggests using dictionary definitions, defining collocates or most frequent collocates as the seed definitions of senses, and reports results ranging between 90 per cent and 96 per cent depending on the type of seed definition. It was shown that using the One Sense per Discourse property led the algorithm to produce better results than when it was not used. The One Sense per Collocation property was always used.

Schütze (1992, 1998) also used an agglomerative clustering algorithm to derive word senses from corpora. The clustering was carried out in *word space*, a real-valued vector space in which each word in the training corpus represents a dimension and the vectors represent co-occurrences with those words in the text. Sense discovery was carried out by using one of two clustering algorithms to infer senses from the corpus by grouping similar contexts in the training corpus. Disambiguation was carried out by mapping the ambiguous word's context into the word space and computing the cluster whose centroid is closest, using the cosine measure. Schütze (1992) reported that this system correctly disambiguated 89–97 per cent of ambiguous instances, depending on the word.

Some other approaches to WSD using machine learning techniques such as decision-tree, *rule-induction*, and *instance-based methods* are discussed in Chapter 20.

13.6 EVALUATION

Wilks and Stevenson (1998) pointed out that there are several different levels and types of WSD task, depending upon the proportion of words disambiguated and the sorts of annotation used. We have seen that different lexicons have been used, including MRDs such as *LDOCE*, *CIDE*, and WordNet as well as hand-crafted lexicons. Each pairing of WSD task and target lexicon requires a different evaluation corpus. A corpus annotated with one lexicon will not be useful in the evaluation of a system which assigns senses from another. These problems have led to a lack of comparative evaluation in this area. To date there have been two attempts to compare a set of supervised learning algorithms—Leacock, Towell, and Voorhees (1993), Mooney (1996)—and one recent evaluation exercise, **SENSEVAL** (Kilgarriff 1998), which we now describe.

SENSEVAL is an evaluation exercise organized along the lines of the (D)ARPA MUC and TREC competitions (see Harman 1995, 1996; MUC 1995, 1998). The exercise was first run in summer 1998 with seventeen participating systems classified into two broad categories: supervised and unsupervised. Supervised systems require sense-tagged training data training, with ten falling into this category, while unsupervised ones require no such information. HECTOR (Atkins 1993), a special sample lexicon created by Oxford University Press for this evaluation, was used to provide a set of senses. Participants were given training data which consisted of example contexts marked with the appropriate HECTOR sense in order to develop their entries. The evaluation was carried out by providing example contexts without the correct senses marked. The WSD systems then annotated those examples with the taggings being scored by the SENSEVAL organizer.

The first SENSEVAL was restricted to a sample of forty lexical items, the HECTOR dictionary and associated corpus being used to provide a set of senses. The evaluation was based on words chosen by randomly sampling the set of HECTOR words with sufficient corpus instances using a strategy described in Kilgarriff (1998). A special issue of the journal *Computers and the Humanities* (Kilgarriff and Palmer 2000) reports the results of this exercise.

SENSEVAL has recently (summer 2001) been repeated in an expanded form. The second exercise covered twelve languages and included over ninety systems from around thirty-five research sites. A significant change is the inclusion of an 'all words' task in which participating systems were required to disambiguate all content words in a text.

WSD has now joined the list of NLP subtasks amenable to statistical and corpus-based methods. So far it is the most 'semantic' of such tasks and the hardest to evaluate because the consensus about sense assignment to words in context by humans is less consistent than with other tasks; at one stage Kilgarriff (1993) suggested it could not be done consistently at all, although that view has been effectively refuted by the viability of the SENSEVAL competition.

13.7 APPLYING WSD

Although important, WSD is an 'intermediate' task in language processing: like part-of-speech tagging or syntactic analysis, it is unlikely that anyone other than linguists would be interested in its results for their own sake. 'Final' tasks produce results of use to those without a specific interest in language and often make use of 'intermediate' tasks. Examples of 'final' tasks are MT, information extraction (IE), and dialogue systems, all of which are described in Part III of this volume.

There are two 'final' tasks which would seem to benefit from access to reliable WSD technology: MT and information retrieval (IR). We have already discussed (section 13.5.1) experimental evidence showing that WSD can be beneficial for MT. However, there is less agreement over the usefulness of WSD for IR. It is intuitively plausible that WSD could help with IR: When searching for documents about flying animals we only want to find texts with the 'nocturnal creature' use of 'bat' (and not the 'sports equipment' sense). Krovetz and Croft (1992) (see also Krovetz 1997) manually disambiguated a standard test corpus and found that a perfect WSD engine would improve retrieval performance by only 2 per cent. Sanderson (1994) performed similar experiments in which ambiguity was artificially introduced into a test collection. It was found that performance improved only for queries containing less than five words. However, others have reported that WSD can help improve the performance of IR systems. This claim was first made by Schütze and Pedersen (1995), who reported substantial improvements in text retrieval performance of up to 14 per cent. Jing and Tzoukermann (1999) have also reported improvements of 8.6 per cent in retrieval performance. Their disambiguation algorithm computes the word-sense similarity in the local context of the query, the similarity of the lexical-occurrence information in the corpus, and the morphological relations between words (see Chapter 29).

WSD technology may also be useful for other NLP tasks. Yarowsky (1997) showed how it may be used by speech synthesis systems (see Chapter 17) to find the correct pronunciation of homophones such as 'lead' and 'live'. Connine (1990) showed that WSD may help in speech recognition (see Chapter 16) to identify the correct lexical item for words with identical phonetic renderings, such as 'base' and 'bass' or 'sealing' and 'ceiling'. WSD may also be applicable to other text processing problems discussed by Yarowsky (1994*a*, 1994*b*).

13.8 CONCLUSION

WSD is a long-standing and important problem in the field of language processing. Early attempts to solve the WSD problem suffered from a lack of coverage due to a lack of available lexical resources, the knowledge acquisition bottleneck. Two main methods for avoiding this problem have been used. First, the MRD movement has allowed access to large lexicons and knowledge bases and, secondly, empirical approaches have been used to extract data from corpora. Evaluation regimes for WSD algorithms were described, including the SENSEVAL exercise. Finally, possible applications for WSD technology were discussed.

FURTHER READING AND RELEVANT RESOURCES

The authors recommend three main books for those interested in WSD: *Electric Words* (Wilks, Slator, and Guthrie 1996) describes the application of MRDs to WSD in detail while Charniak's *Statistical Language Learning* (Charniak 1993) and *Foundations of Statistical Natural Language Processing* (Manning and Schütze 1999) each contain a chapter on statistical approaches to WSD.

For those interested in the latest research in the area we would recommend the following: the *Computational Linguistics* special issue on WSD (Ide and Véronis 1998), the special issue of *Computers and the Humanities* devoted to SENSEVAL (Kilgarriff and Palmer 2000), and the proceedings of the ANLP '97 workshop entitled *Lexical Semantic Tagging: Why, What and How?* (Light 1997), as well as papers in many recent NLP conferences. The SENSEVAL homepage contains useful information related to evaluation issues and both SENSEVAL exercises (http://www.itri.bton.ac.uk/events/senseval/).

Lexical resources are generally difficult to obtain and access to MRDs is very restricted. However, WordNet can be freely downloaded (http://www.cogsci.princeton.edu/~wn/). It is available in several formats and a corpus sense tagged with the lexicon, SEMCOR, is included as part of the package. Further linguistic resources relevant to WSD are available from the SIGLEX homepage (http://www.clres.com/siglex.html), the special interest group on the lexicon of the Association for Computational Linguistics. The Linguistic Data Consortium (http://www.ldc.upenn.edu) and the European Languages Resources Association (http://www.icp.grenet.fr/ELRA/home.html) websites also contain several useful lexical resources, although each requires subscription.

References

Atkins, S. 1993. 'Tools for computer-aided lexicography: the HECTOR project'. *Papers in Computational Lexicography (COMPLEX '93)* (Budapest), 1–60,

Briscoe, E. 1991. 'Lexical issues in natural language processing'. In E. Klein and F. Veltman (eds.), *Natural Language and Speech*. Berlin: Springer-Verlag, 36–68.

Brown, P., S. Della Pietra, V. Della Pietra, and R. Mercer. 1991. 'Word-sense disambiguation using statistical methods'. *Proceedings of the 29th Meeting of the Association for Computational Linguistics (ACL-91)* (Berkeley), 264–70,

Chapman, R. 1977. *Roget's International Thesaurus*, 4th edn. New York: Harper and Row.

Charniak, E. 1983. 'Passing markers: a theory of contextual influence in language comprehension'. *Cognitive Science*, 7, 171–90.

——1993. *Statistical Language Learning*. Cambridge, Mass.: MIT Press.

Connine, C. 1990. 'Effects of sentence context and lexical knowledge in speech processing'. In G. Altmann (ed.), *Cognitive Models in Speech Processing*. Cambridge, Mass.: MIT Press, 127–41.

Cottrell, G. 1984. 'A model of lexical access of ambiguous words'. *Proceedings of the National Conference on Artificial Intelligence (AAAI-84)* (Austin, Tex.), 61–7.

Cowie, J., L. Guthrie, and J. Guthrie. 1992. 'Lexical disambiguation using simulated annealing'. *Proceedings of the 14th International Conference on Computational Linguistics (COLING '92)* (Nantes), 359–65.

Daelemans, W., J. Zavrel, K. van der Sloot, and A. van den Bosch. 1998. *TiMBL: Tilburg memory based learner version 1.0*. ILK Technical Report 98-03.

Gale, W., K. Church, and D. Yarowsky. 1992. 'One sense per discourse'. *Proceedings of the DARPA Speech and Natural Language Workshop* (Harriman, NY), 233–7,

Hanks, P. 1979. *Collins English Dictionary*. London: Collins.

Harley, A. and D. Glennon. 1997. 'Sense tagging in action: combining different tests with additive weights'. *Proceedings of the SIGLEX Workshop 'Tagging Text with Lexical Semantics'* (Washington), 74–8.

Harman, D. (ed.). 1995. *Overview of the 3rd Text REtrieval Conference (TREC-3)*. Washington: National Institute of Standards and Technology (NIST) Special Publication 500-225, US Government Printing Office.

——(ed.), 1996. *Overview of the 4th Text REtrieval Conference (TREC-4)*. Washington: National Institute of Standards and Technology (NIST) Special Publication 500-236, US Government Printing Office.

Hirst, G. 1987. *Semantic Interpretation and the Resolution of Ambiguity*. Cambridge: Cambridge University Press.

Hornby, A. 1963. *The Advanced Learner's Dictionary of English*. Oxford: Oxford University Press.

Ide, N. and J. Véronis. 1990. 'Mapping dictionaries: a spreading activation approach'. *Proceedings of the 6th Annual Conference of the UW Centre for the New Oxford English Dictionary*, (Waterloo) 52–64.

——1998. 'Word sense disambiguation: the state of the art'. *Computational Linguistics*, 24(1), 1–40.

Jing, H. and E. Tzoukermann. 1999. 'Information retrieval based on context distance and morphology'. *Proceedings of the 22nd Annual International ACM SIGIR Conference on Research and Development in Information Retrieval (SIGIR '99)* (Seattle), 92–96.

Katz, J. and J. Fodor. 1964. 'The structure of a semantic theory'. In J. Katz and J. Fodor (eds.), *The Structure of Language*. New York: Prentice Hall, 479–518.

Kilgarriff, A. 1993. 'Dictionary word sense distinctions: an enquiry into their nature'. *Computers and the Humanities*, 26, 356–87.

——1998. 'SENSEVAL: an exercise in evaluating word sense disambiguation programs'. *Proceedings of the 1st International Cconference on Language Resources and Evaluation* (Granada), 581–5.

——and M. Palmer. 2000. 'Introduction to the Special Issue on SENSEVAL'. *Computers and the Humanities*, 34(1/2), 1–13.

Krovetz, R. 1997. 'Homonymy and polysemy in information retrieval'. In *35th Meeting of the Association for Computational Linguistics and the 8th Meeting of the European Chapter of the Association for Computational Linguistics (ACL/EACL '97)* (Madrid), 72–8.

——1998. 'More than one sense per discourse'. *Proceedings of SENSEVAL Workshop* (Herstmonceux Castle), 35–40.

——and W. B. Croft. 1992. 'Lexical ambiguity and information retrieval'. *ACM Transactions on Information Systems*, 10(2), 115–41.

Leacock, C., G. Towell, and E. Voorhees. 1993. 'Corpus-based statistical sense resolution'. *Proceedings of the ARPA Human Language Technology Workshop* (Plainsboro, NJ), 260–5.

Lesk, M. 1986. 'Automatic sense disambiguation using machine readable dictionaries: how to tell a pine cone from an ice cream cone'. *Proceedings of ACM SIGDOC Conference* (Toronto), 24–6.

Light, M. (ed.). 1997. *Proceedings of the SIGLEX Workshop 'Tagging Text with Lexical Semantics: Why, What and How?'* Association for Computational Linguistics.

McRoy, S. 1992. 'Using multiple knowledge sources for word sense disambiguation'. *Computational Linguistics*, 18(1), 1–30.

Manning, C. and H. Schütze. 1999. *Foundations of Statistical Natural Language Processing*. Cambridge, Mass.: MIT Press.

Mooney, R. 1996. 'Comparative experiments on disambiguating word senses: an illustration of the role of bias in machine learning'. *Proceedings of the Conference on Empirical Methods in Natural Language Processing* (Philadelphia), 82–91.

MUC. 1995. *Proceedings of the 6th Message Understanding Conference (MUC-6)*. San Mateo, Calif.: Morgan Kaufmann.

——1998. *Proceedings of the 7th Message Understanding Conference (MUC-7)*. San Mateo, Calif.: Morgan Kaufmann.

Nadas, A., D. Nahamoo, M. Picheny, and J. Powell. 1991. 'An iterative "flip-flop" approximation of the most informative split in the construction of decision trees'. *Proceedings of the IEEE International Conference on Acoustics, Speech and Signal Processing* (Toronto), 565–8.

Newell, A. 1973. 'Computer models of thought and language'. In R. Schank and K. Colby (eds.), *Artificial Intelligence and the Concept of Mind*. San Francisco: Freeman, 1–60.

Ng, H. and H. Lee. 1996. 'Integrating multiple knowledge sources to disambiguate word sense: an exemplar-based approach'. *Proceedings of the 34th Meeting of the Association for Computational Linguistics (ACL-96)* (Santa Cruz, Calif.), 40–7.

Procter, P. (ed.). 1978. *Longman Dictionary of Contemporary English*. London: Longman.

——(ed.). 1995. *Cambridge International Dictionary of English*. Cambridge: Cambridge University Press.

Rivest, R. 1987. 'Learning decision lists'. *Machine Learning*, 2(3), 229–46.

Salton, G. and M. McGill. 1983. *Introduction to Modern Information Retrieval*. New York: McGraw-Hill.

Sampson, G. 1986. 'A stochastic approach to parsing'. *Proceedings of the 11th International Conference on Computational Linguistics (COLING '86)* (Bonn), 151–5.

Sanderson, M. 1994. 'Word sense disambiguation and information retrieval'. *Proceedings of the 17th ACM SIGIR Conference* (Dublin), 142–51.

Schütze, H. 1992. 'Dimensions of meaning'. *Proceedings of Supercomputing '92* (Minneapolis), 787–96.

——1998. 'Automatic word sense discrimination'. *Computational Linguistics*, 24(1), 97–124.

——and J. Pedersen. 1995. 'Information retrieval based on word senses'. *Symposium on Document Analysis and Information Retrieval (SDAIR)* (Las Vegas, Nev.), 161–75.

Seidenberg, M., M. Tanenhaus, J. Leiman, and M. Bienkowski. 1982. 'Automatic access of the meanings of ambiguous words in context: some limitations of knowledge-based processing'. *Cognitive Psychology*, 14, 489–537.

Small, S. 1980. *Word expert parsing: a theory of distributed word-based natural language understanding*. Ph.D. Thesis, Department of Computer Science, University of Maryland.

——and C. Rieger. 1982. 'Parsing and comprehending with word experts (a theory and its realization)'. In W. Lehnert and M. Ringle (eds.), *Strategies for Natural Language Processing*. Hillsdale, NJ: Lawrence Erlbaum Associates.

Stevenson, M. and Y. Wilks. 1999. 'Combining weak knowledge sources for sense disambiguation'. *Proceedings of the 16th International Joint Conference on Artificial Intelligence* (Stockholm), 884–9.

van Rijsbergen, C. 1979. *Information Retrieval*. London: Butterworths.

Véronis, J. and N. Ide. 1995. 'Computational lexical semantics'. In P. Saint-Dizier and E. Viegas (eds.), *Large Neural Networks for the Resolution of Lexical Ambiguity*, Cambridge: Cambridge University Press, 251–69.

Waltz, D. and J. Pollack. 1985. 'Massively parallel parsing: a strongly interactive model of natural language interpretation'. *Cognitive Science*, 9, 51–74.

Wilks, Y. 1972. *Grammar, Meaning and the Machine Analysis of Language*. London: Routledge.

——1973. 'The Stanford MT project'. In R. Rustin (ed.), *Natural Language Processing*. New York: Algorithmics Press.

——1978. 'Making preferences more active'. *Artificial Intelligence*, 11(3), 197–223.

——B. Slator, and L. Guthrie. 1996. *Electric Words: Dictionaries, Computers and Meanings*. Cambridge, Mass.: MIT Press.

——and M. Stevenson. 1997. 'Sense tagging: semantic tagging with a lexicon'. *Proceedings of the SIGLEX Workshop 'Tagging Text with Lexical Semantics: What, Why and How?'*, (Washington), 47–51.

———1998. 'Word sense disambiguation using optimised combinations of knowledge sources'. *Proceedings of the 17th International Conference on Computational Linguistics and the 36th Annual Meeting of the Association for Computational Linguistics (COLING-ACL '98)* (Montreal), 1398–402.

Yarowsky, D. 1992. 'Word-sense disambiguation using statistical models of Roget's categories trained on large corpora'. *Proceedings of the 14th International Conference on Computational Linguistics (COLING '92)* (Nantes), 454–60.

——1993. 'One sense per collocation'. *Proceedings of the ARPA Human Language Technology Workshop* (Princeton), 266–71.

——1994*a*. 'A comparison of corpus-based techniques for restoring accents in Spanish and French text'. *Proceedings of the 2nd Annual Workshop on Very Large Text Corpora* (Las Cruces, N. Mex.), 19–32.

——1994*b*. 'Decision lists for lexical ambiguity resolution: application to accent restoration in Spanish and French'. *Proceedings of 32nd Annual Meeting of the Association for Computational Linguistics (ACL '94)* (Las Cruces, N. Mex.), 88–95.

——1995. 'Unsupervised word-sense disambiguation rivaling supervised methods'. *Proceedings of the 33rd Annual Meeting of the Association for Computational Linguistics (ACL '95)* (Cambridge, Mass.), 189–96.

——1997. 'Homograph disambiguation in text-to-speech synthesis'. In J. van Santen, R. Sproat, J. Olive, and J. Hirschberg (eds.), *Progress in Speech Synthesis*. New York: Springer-Verlag.

Yngve, V. 1955. 'Syntax and the problem of multiple meaning'. In W. Locke and D. Booth (eds.), *Machine Translation of Languages*. New York: Wiley.

ANAPHORA RESOLUTION

RUSLAN MITKOV

ABSTRACT

The chapter provides a theoretical background of anaphora and introduces the task of anaphora resolution. The importance of anaphora resolution in NLP is highlighted, and both early work and recent developments are outlined. Finally, issues that need further attention are discussed.

14.1 LINGUISTIC FUNDAMENTALS

14.1.1 Basic notions: anaphora and coreference

We define **anaphora** as the linguistic phenomenon of pointing back to a previously mentioned item in the text. The 'pointing back' word or phrase[1] is called an **anaphor**[2]

---

[1] The 'pointing back' word (phrase) is also called a *referring expression* if it has a referential function.

[2] As a matter of accuracy, note that *anaphora* is a linguistic phenomenon and not the plural of *anaphor* (the latter is the word/phrase pointing back), as it has been wrongly used in some papers on anaphora resolution so far.

and the entity to which it refers or for which it stands is its **antecedent**. When the anaphor refers to an antecedent and when both have the same referent in the real world, they are termed **coreferential**. Therefore **coreference** is the act of referring to the same referent in the real world.

Consider the following example from Huddleston (1984):

(14.1) *The Queen* is not here yet but *she* is expected to arrive in the next half an hour.

In this example, the pronoun *she* is an anaphor, *the Queen* is its antecedent, and *she* and *the Queen* are coreferential. Note that the antecedent is not the noun *Queen* but the noun phrase (NP) *the Queen*. The relation between the anaphor and the antecedent is not to be confused with that between the anaphor and its referent; in the example above the referent is *the Queen* as a person in the real world (e.g. Queen Elizabeth) whereas the antecedent is *the Queen* as a linguistic form.

A specific anaphor and more than one of the preceding (or following) noun phrases may be coreferential thus forming a **coreferential chain** of discourse entities which have the same referent. For instance in (14.2) *Sophia Loren, she, the actress,* and *her* are coreferential. Coreference partitions discourse into equivalence classes of coreferential chains and in (14.2) the following coreferential chains can be singled out: {Sophia Loren, she, the actress, her}, {Bono, the U2 singer}, {a thunderstorm}, and {a plane}.

(14.2) *Sophia Loren* says *she* will always be grateful to Bono. *The actress* revealed that the U2 singer helped *her* calm down during a thunderstorm while travelling on a plane.

Note that not all varieties of anaphora have a referring function, such as verb anaphora, for example.

(14.3) When Manchester United swooped to lure Ron Atkinson away from the Albion, it was inevitable that his midfield prodigy would *follow*, and in 1981 he *did*.

This sentence features the verb anaphor *did* which is a substitution for the antecedent *followed* but does not have a referring function and therefore we cannot speak of coreference between the two.

Also, the anaphor and the antecedent may refer but may still not be coreferential as in the case of identity-of sense anaphora.[3]

(14.4) The man who gave *his paycheque* to his wife was wiser than the man who gave *it* to his mistress.

as opposed to identity-of-reference anaphora

(14.5) This man gave *his paycheque* to his wife in January; in February he readily gave *it* again.

In (14.4) the anaphor *it* and the antecedent *his paycheque* are not coreferential whereas in (14.5) they are.

---

[3] In identity-of-sense anaphora, the anaphor and the antecedent do not correspond to the same referent in the real world but to ones of a similar description.

Bound anaphora is another example where the anaphor and the antecedent are not coreferential.

(14.6)   *Every participant* had to present *his* paper.

Anaphora normally operates within a document (e.g. article, chapter, book), whereas coreference can be taken to work across documents. We have seen that there are varieties of anaphora that do not involve coreference; it is also possible to have coreferential items that are not anaphoric, with *cross-document coreference* being an obvious example: two mentions of the same person in two different documents will be coreferential, but will not stand in an anaphoric relation.

14.1.2 Varieties of anaphora

The most widespread type of anaphora is **pronominal anaphora**. Pronominal anaphora can be exhibited by personal, possessive, or reflexive pronouns ('A knee jerked between *Ralph's* legs and *he* fell sideways busying *himself* with *his* pain as the fight rolled over *him.*') as well as by demonstrative pronouns ('*This* was more than he could cope with'). Relative pronouns are regarded as anaphoric too. Pronouns first and second person singular and plural are usually used in a deictic manner[4] ('*I* would like *you* to show me the way to San Marino') although their anaphoric function is not uncommon in reported speech or dialogues as with the use of *I* in the last sentence of (14.7).

Lexical noun phrase anaphors take the form of definite noun phrases, also called **definite descriptions**, and **proper names**. Although pronouns, definite descriptions, and proper names are all considered to be definite expressions, proper names and definite descriptions, unlike pronouns, can have a meaning independent of their antecedent. Furthermore, definite descriptions do more than just refer. They convey some additional information as in (14.7), where the reader can learn more about *Roy Keane* through the definite description *Alex Ferguson's No. 1 player*.

(14.7)   *Roy Keane* has warned Manchester United he may snub their pay deal. *United's skipper* is even hinting that unless the future Old Trafford Package meets *his* demands, *he* could quit the club in June 2000. *Irishman Keane*, 27, still has 17 months to run on *his* current £23,000-a-week contract and wants to commit *himself* to United for life. *Alex Ferguson's No. 1 player* confirmed: 'If it's not the contract *I* want, *I* won't sign'.

In this text, *Roy Keane* has been referred to by anaphoric pronouns (*he, his, himself, I*), but also by definite descriptions (*United's skipper, Alex Ferguson's No. 1 player*) and a

---

[4] Deictic refers to those words whose interpretation is derived from specific features of utterance (e.g. who is the speaker, who is the addressee, where and when the utterance takes place) and not from previously introduced words, as is the case with anaphors.

proper name (*Irishman Keane*). On the other hand, *Manchester United* is referred to by the definite description *the club* and by the proper name *United*.

Noun phrase anaphors may have the same head as their antecedents (*the chapter* and *this chapter*) but the relation between the referring expression and its antecedent may be that of synonymy (*a shop . . . the store*), generalization/hypernym (*a boutique . . . the shop*, also *Manchester United . . . the club* as in 14.7), or specialization/hyponym (*a shop . . . the boutique*, also *their pay deal . . . his current £23,000-a-week contract* as in 14.7).[5] Proper names usually refer to antecedents whose names they match in whole or in part (*Manchester United . . . United*) with exact repetitions not being uncommon.

According to the form of the anaphor, anaphora occurs as **verb anaphora** ('Stephanie *balked*, as *did* Mike.'), **adverb anaphora** ('We shall go to *McDonalds* and meet you *there*.') or **zero anaphora** ('*Amy* had made a special effort that night but Ø was disappointed with the results.'). In the last example Ø stands for the omitted anaphor *she*.

Nominal anaphora arises when a **referring expression**—pronoun, definite noun phrase or proper name—has a non-pronominal noun phrase as antecedent. This most important and frequently occurring class of anaphora has been researched and covered most extensively, and best understood, in the NLP literature. Broadly speaking, there are two types of nominal anaphora: *direct* and *indirect*. **Direct anaphora** links anaphors and antecedents by such relations as identity, synonymy, generalization, and specialization (see above). In contrast, **indirect anaphora** links anaphors and antecedents by relations such as part-of ('Although *the store* had only just opened, *the food hall* was busy and there were long queues at *the tills*.') or set membership ('Only a day after heated denials that *the Spice Girls* were splitting up, *Melanie C* declared she had already left the group.'). Resolution of indirect anaphora normally requires the use of domain or world knowledge. Indirect anaphora is also known as **associative** or **bridging** anaphora.[6] For more on the notions of anaphora and coreference and on the different varieties of anaphora see Hirst (1981); Mitkov (2002).

14.2 ANAPHORA RESOLUTION

14.2.1 Basic notions

The process of determining the antecedent of an anaphor is called **anaphora resolution**. In anaphora resolution the system has to determine the antecedent of the

---

[5] It should be noted that these are only the basic relationships between the anaphoric definite NP and the antecedent but not all.

[6] Note that some authors consider synonymy, generalization, and specialization as examples of indirect anaphora.

anaphor; for identity-of-reference nominal anaphora any preceding NP which is coreferential with the anaphor is considered as the correct antecedent. On the other hand, the objective of **coreference resolution** is to identify all coreferential chains. However, since the task of anaphora resolution is considered successful if any element of the anaphoric (coreferential) chain preceding the anaphor is identified, annotated corpora for automatic evaluation of anaphora systems require anaphoric (coreferential) chains and not only anaphor-closest antecedent pairs.

14.2.2 Sources of knowledge needed for anaphora resolution

The disambiguation of anaphors is a challenging task and considerable knowledge is required to support it—from low-level morphological and lexical information to high-level semantic and pragmatic rules.

In 'an easier scenario', some anaphors may be successfully resolved on the basis of lexical information such as gender and number. The fact that anaphors usually match (the heads of) their antecedents in gender and in number is often sufficient for the singling out of a unique NP candidate. Example:

(14.8)   *Christopher* slid over to the window and tried to force it open to throw out the sodden napkins. The window refused to budge no matter how hard *he* pushed and shoved.

Following the gender and number matching rule, the noun phrase *Christopher* is selected as an antecedent of the pronominal anaphor *he* because the remaining candidates *the window* and *the sodden napkins*[7] are discounted on the basis of a gender and number mismatch respectively.

Syntax knowledge is indispensable in anaphora resolution. In addition to providing information about the boundaries of the sentences, clauses, and other constituents (e.g. NP, PP), syntax plays an important role in the formulation of the different rules used in the resolution process. As an illustration, consider the simplified rule stipulating that an anaphoric NP is only coreferential with the subject NP of the same simple sentence when the anaphor is reflexive. This rule, which relies on syntactic information about (simple) sentence boundaries, along with information about the syntactic function of each word, would rule out *Jim* as antecedent of *him* in (14.10) and (14.11):

(14.9)   *Jim* is running the business for *himself*.

(14.10)   Jim is running the business for him.

(14.11)   John explained that Jim was running the business for him.

---

[7] Note that we are focusing on nominal anaphora, and only NPs preceding the anaphor are regarded as candidates for antecedents.

However important morphological, lexical, and syntax knowledge are, there are many cases where they alone cannot help to resolve anaphors. In the following example,

(14.12)   *The petrified kitten* refused to move from up the tree. *It* gazed beseechingly at the onlookers below.

gender or number agreement rules cannot eliminate either *the petrified kitten* or *the tree* as a potential antecedent, because both candidates are neuter. The selectional restrictions of the verb *to gaze* require that its agent (the subject in an active voice sentence) be animate here; semantic information on the animacy of *kitten* would be crucial.

Although the morphological, lexical, syntactic, and semantic criteria for the selection of an antecedent are very strong, they are not always sufficient to distinguish between a set of possible candidates. Moreover, they serve more as filters to eliminate unsuitable candidates than as proposers of the most likely candidate. In the case of antecedent ambiguity, it is the most salient element among the candidates for antecedent which is usually the front-runner. This most salient element is referred to in computational linguistics as the *focus* (Sidner 1979) or *center*[8] (Grosz, Joshi, and Weinstein 1995; see also Chapter 6 of this volume for a brief outline), although the terminology for this can be much more diverse (Hirst 1981).

As an illustration, neither machines nor humans would be confident in interpreting the anaphoric pronoun *it* in the sentence:

(14.13)   As Jane tried on the dress over her new skirt she ripped it.

However, if this sentence were part of a discourse segment[9] which would make it possible to identify the most salient element, the situation would be different:

(14.14)   Jane had begged George to buy her a fashionable dress for the party. Finally, George bought the nice dress but as Jane tried on the dress over her new skirt she ripped it.

In this example *dress* is the most salient entity and is the center of attention throughout the discourse segment.

The intuition behind theories of focus or center lies in the observation that discourse is normally structured around a central topic (object). This topic usually remains prominent for a few sentences before the focal point shifts to a new topic. The second key intuition has to do with the fact that the center of a sentence (or clause) is typically pronominalized.

Finally, an anaphora resolution system supplied with extensive morphological, lexical, syntactic, semantic, and discourse knowledge may still find itself helpless when confronted with examples such as:

---

[8] Center and focus are close, but not identical concepts. We refer the reader to Walker, Joshi, and Prince (1998) or Grosz, Joshi, and Weinstein (1995).

[9] Discourse segments are stretches of discourse in which the sentences are addressing the same topic (Allen 1995).

(14.15)   The soldiers shot at *the women* and *they* fell.

(14.16)   *The soldiers* shot at the women and *they* missed.

These examples show that real-world knowledge is often the crucial and most reliable factor in deciding on the antecedent.

14.2.3   The process of anaphora resolution

The automatic resolution of anaphors consists of the following main stages: (1) identification of anaphors, (2) location of the candidates for antecedents, and (3) selection of the antecedent from the set of candidates on the basis of anaphora resolution factors.

14.2.3.1   *Identification of anaphors*

In pronoun resolution only the anaphoric pronouns have to be processed further, therefore non-anaphoric occurrences of the pronoun *it* as in (14.17) have to be recognized by the program.

(14.17)   It must be stated that Oskar behaved impeccably.

When a pronoun *it* does not refer to anything specific, it is termed *pleonastic*. Therefore, grammatical information as to whether a certain word is a third person pronoun would not be sufficient: each occurrence of *it* has to be checked in order to find out if it is referential or not. Several algorithms for identification of pleonastic pronouns have been reported in the literature (Lappin and Leass 1994; Paice and Husk 1987; Evans 2001).

The search for anaphoric noun phrases can be even more problematic. Definite noun phrases are potentially anaphoric, often referring back to preceding noun phrases, as *The Queen* does in (14.18):

(14.18)   *Queen Elizabeth* attended the ceremony. *The Queen* delivered a speech.

It is important to bear in mind that not every definite noun phrase is necessarily anaphoric. Typical examples are definite descriptions which describe a specific, unique entity or definite descriptions used in a generic way. In (14.19) the NP *The Duchess of York* is not anaphoric and does not refer to *the Queen*.

(14.19)   The Queen attended the ceremony. The Duchess of York was there too.

Similarly to the automatic recognition of pleonastic pronouns, it is important for an anaphora resolution program to be able to identify those definite descriptions that are not anaphoric. Methods for identification of non-anaphoric definite descriptions have been developed by Bean and Riloff (1999), Vieira and Poesio (2000), and Muñoz (2001).

Finally, proper names are regarded as potentially anaphoric to preceding proper names that match in terms of first or last names (e.g. John White . . . John . . . Mr White).

14.2.3.2 *Location of the candidates for antecedents*

Once the anaphors have been detected, the program has to identify the possible candidates for their antecedents. The vast majority of systems only handle nominal anaphora since processing anaphors whose antecedents are verb phrases, clauses, sentences, or sequences of sentences is a more complicated task. Typically in such systems all noun phrases (NPs) preceding an anaphor within a certain search scope are initially regarded as candidates for antecedents.

The search scope takes different form depending on the *processing model* adopted and may vary in size depending on the *type of anaphor*. Since anaphoric relations often operate within/are limited to a discourse segment, the search scope is often set to the *discourse segment* which contains the anaphor. Anaphora resolution systems which have no means of identifying the discourse segment boundaries usually set the search scope to the *current and n preceding* sentences, with *n* depending on the type of the anaphor. For pronominal anaphors, the search scope is usually limited to the current and two or three preceding sentences. Definite noun phrases, however, can refer further back in the text and, for such anaphors, the search scope is normally longer. Approaches which search the current or the linearly preceding units to locate candidates for antecedents are referred to by Cristea et al. (2000) as *linear models*, as opposed to the *hierarchical models* which consider candidates from the current or the hierarchically preceding discourse units such as the discourse-VT model based on the Veins Theory (Cristea, Ide, and Lomary 1998). Cristea et al. (2000) show that, compared with linear models, the search scope of the discourse-VT model is smaller, which makes it computationally less expensive, and could be more accurate in picking out the potential candidates. However, the automatic identification of veins cannot be performed with satisfactory accuracy and therefore this model is not sufficiently attractive for practical anaphora resolution developments.

14.2.3.3 *The resolution algorithm: factors in anaphora resolution*

Once the anaphors have been detected, the program will attempt to resolve them by selecting their antecedents from the identified sets of candidates. The resolution rules based on the different sources of knowledge and used in the resolution process (constituting the anaphora resolution algorithm) are usually referred to as *anaphora resolution factors*. These factors can be *constraints* which eliminate certain noun phrases from the set of possible candidates. The factors can also be *preferences* which favour certain candidates over others. Constraints are considered to be obligatory conditions that are imposed on the relation between the anaphor and its antecedent. Therefore, their strength lies in discounting candidates that do satisfy these conditions; unlike preferences, they do not propose any candidates. Typical constraints in anaphora resolution are gender and number agreement,[10] c-command constraints,[11] and selectional restrictions.[12] Typical preferences are recency (the most recent candidate is more likely to be the antecedent), center preference (the center of the previous clause is the most likely candidate for antecedent), syntactic parallelism (candidates with the same syntactic function as the anaphor are the preferred antecedents), but it should be made clear that it is not difficult to find examples which demonstrate that the preferences are not absolute factors since very often they are overridden by semantic or real-world constraints. Approaches making use of syntax constraints such as Hobbs (1978) and Lappin and Leass (1994), or the knowledge-poor counterpart of the latter (Kennedy and Boguraev 1996), have been particularly successful and have received a great deal of attention, one of the reasons being that such constraints are good at filtering candidates for antecedent at intra-sentential (within the sentence) level.

As an illustration of how an anaphora resolution algorithm works, consider a simple model using the gender and number agreement constraint, the c-command constraint that a non-pronominal NP cannot corefer with an NP that c-commands it, and the center preference. First the constraints are applied and, if the antecedent still cannot be determined, the center preference is activated. We assume that analysis has taken place and we have all the necessary information about the morphological features of each word, the syntactical structure of the sentences, and the center of each clause, and that all anaphors have been identified.

(14.20)   How poignant that one of the television tributes paid to Jill Dando shows her interviewing people just before the funeral of Diana Princess of Wales. Some of the words she used to describe the late princess could equally have applied to her.

This discourse segment features four anaphors: *her* (first sentence), *she*, *the late princess*, and *her* (second sentences). The resolution takes place from left to right. Initially all noun phrases preceding the first anaphor *her* are considered potential candidates for antecedents: *one of the television tributes, television tributes*, and *Jill Dando*. The number agreement constraint discounts *television tributes*, whereas gender agreement rejects *one of the television tributes*, proposing *Jill Dando* unambiguously as the

---

[10]   However, Barlow (1998) and Mitkov (2002) point out that there are a number of exceptions.

[11]   A node A c-commands a node B if and only if (i) A does not dominate B, (ii) B does not dominate A, (iii) the first branching node dominating A also dominates B (Haegeman 1994). Therefore, in a tree generated by the rules S → AB, A → E, B → CD, C → F and D → G, A c-commands B, C, F, D, and G, B c-commands A and E, C c-commands D and G, and D c-commands C and F.

[12]   Mitkov (2002) shows that selectional restrictions differ in their degree of restriction.

antecedent of *her*. Next, the anaphor *she* has to be interpreted. The initial candidates are again all preceding NPs: *one of the television tributes, television tributes, Jill Dando, people, the funeral of Diana Princess of Wales, the funeral, Princess of Wales, some of the words, words*, but the gender and number filter eliminate all candidates but *Jill Dando* and *Diana Princess of Wales*. Now center preference is taken into account, proposing the center of the preceding clause *Jill Dando* as the antecedent. Due to gender and number mismatch, the anaphor *the late princess* can be resolved only to *Jill Dando* or *Diana Princess of Wales*.[13] Next, the c-command constraint is activated. Since *she* has been already instantiated to *Jill Dando*, and since *she* c-commands *the late princess*, coreference between *Jill Dando* and *the late princess* is impossible. Therefore, *Diana Princess of Wales* is the antecedent of *the late princess*. Finally, the anaphor *her* in the second sentence has to be resolved between *the late princess/Diana Princess of Wales* and *her/Jill Dando*. The center of the clause prior to the one containing the anaphor is *she* (*Jill Dando*), therefore *Jill Dando* is the preferred antecedent.

14.3 IMPORTANCE OF ANAPHORA RESOLUTION FOR NLP APPLICATIONS

Recent projects have increasingly demonstrated the importance of anaphora or coreference resolution in various NLP applications. In fact, the successful identification of anaphoric or coreferential links is vital to a number of applications such as machine translation, automatic abstracting, dialogue systems, question answering, and information extraction.

The interpretation of anaphora is crucial for the successful operation of a **machine translation** system (see Chapter 28). In particular, it is essential to resolve the anaphoric relation when translating into languages which mark the gender of pronouns. Unfortunately, the majority of MT systems developed in the 1970s and 1980s did not adequately address the problems of identifying the antecedents of anaphors in the source language and producing the anaphoric 'equivalents' in the target language. As a consequence, only a limited number of MT systems have been successful in translating discourse, rather than isolated sentences. One reason for this situation is that in

---

[13] Note that this model does not use any semantic knowledge or inferencing which could help find that *the late princess* refers to *Diana Princess of Wales* on the basis that the previous sentence reports her funeral; also, this model does not use any matching rule suggesting (not always correctly, however) that NPs with identical heads are coreferential and, therefore, cannot establish coreferential link between *the late princess* and *Diana Princess of Wales*.

addition to anaphora resolution itself being a very complicated task, translation adds a further dimension to the problem in that the reference to a discourse entity encoded by a source language anaphor by the speaker (or writer) has not only to be identified by the hearer (translator or translation system), but also re-encoded in a different language. This complexity is partly due to gender discrepancies across languages, to number discrepancies of words denoting the same concept, to discrepancies in gender inheritance of possessive pronouns, and to discrepancies in target language anaphor selection (Mitkov and Schmidt 1998).

Anaphora resolution in information extraction could be regarded as part of the coreference resolution task which takes the form of merging partial data objects about the same entities, entity relationships, and events described at different discourse positions. The importance of coreference resolution in **information extraction** (Chapter 30) has led to the inclusion of the coreference resolution task in the Message Understanding Conferences (MUC-6 and MUC-7). This in turn gave a considerable impetus to the development of coreference resolution algorithms and as a result several new systems emerged (Baldwin et al. 1995; Gaizauskas and Humphreys 1996; Kameyama 1997).

Researchers in **text summarization** (Chapter 32) are increasingly interested in anaphora resolution since techniques for extracting important sentences are more accurate if anaphoric references of indicative concepts are taken into account as well. More generally, coreference and coreferential chains have been extensively exploited for abstracting purposes. Baldwin and Morton (1998) describe a query-sensitive document summarization technique which extracts sentences containing phrases that corefer with expressions in the query. Azzam, Humphreys, and Gaizauskas (1999) use coreferential chains to produce abstracts by selecting a 'best' chain to represent the main topic of a text. The output is simply the concatenation of sentences from the original document which contain one or more expressions occurring in the selected coreferential chain. Boguraev and Kennedy (1997) employ their anaphora resolution algorithm (Kennedy and Boguraev 1996) in what they call 'content characterization' of technical documents.

It should be noted that *cross-document coreference resolution* has emerged as an important trend due to its role in **cross-document summarization**. Bagga and Baldwin (1998) describe an approach to cross-document coreference resolution which extracts all sentences containing expressions coreferential with a specific entity (e.g. *John Smith*) from each of several documents. In order to decide whether the documents discuss the same entity (i.e the same *John Smith*), the authors employ a threshold vector space similarity measure between the extracts.

Coreference resolution has proven to be helpful in **question answering** (Chapter 31). Morton (1999) retrieves answers to queries by establishing coreference links between entities or events in the query and those in the documents.[14] The sentences

---

[14] The coreference relationships that Morton's system supports are identity, part–whole, and synonymy.

in the searched documents are ranked according to the coreference relationships, and the highest ranked sentences are displayed to the user.

14.4 HISTORICAL OUTLINE AND RECENT DEVELOPMENTS

The early work on anaphora resolution typically relied on heuristical rules and did not exploit full analysis as in the case of Bobrow's system STUDENT or Winograd's SHRDLU, the latter being much more sophisticated and featuring a set of clever heuristics. However, it did not take long before the research evolved into the development of approaches benefiting from a variety of knowledge sources. For instance, Hobbs's naive approach (Hobbs 1978) was primarily based on syntax, whereas LUNAR and Wilks's approach exploited above all semantics. The late 1970s saw the first discourse-oriented work (Sidner 1979; Webber 1979); later approaches went even further, resorting to some form of real-world knowledge (Carter 1987; Carbonell and Brown 1988; Rich and LuperFoy 1988).

As with many NLP tasks, early work on anaphora resolution in the 1970s, and 1980s, was more theoretically oriented and rather ambitious in terms of the types of anaphora handled and the knowledge needed, which was difficult both to represent and process, and required considerable human input. Later in the 1990s the rising awareness of the formidable complexity of anaphora resolution, and the pressing need for working systems, encouraged more practical and down-to-earth research, often limiting the treatment of anaphora to a specific genre, but offering working and robust solutions in exchange. A number of successful proposals in the 1990s deliberately limited the extent to which they rely on domain and/or linguistic knowledge (Baldwin 1997; Dagan and Itai 1990; Harabagiu and Maiorano 1999; Kameyama 1997; Kennedy and Boguraev 1996; Mitkov 1996, 1998b; Nasukawa 1994) and reported promising results in knowledge-poor operational environments.

The drive towards knowledge-poor and robust approaches was further motivated by the emergence of cheaper and more reliable corpus-based NLP tools such as POS taggers and shallow parsers, alongside the increasing availability of corpora and other NLP resources (e.g. ontologies). In fact the availability of corpora, both raw and annotated with coreferential links, provided a strong impetus to anaphora resolution with regard to both training and evaluation. Corpora (especially when annotated) are an invaluable source not only for empirical research but also for automated learning methods (e.g. machine learning methods) aiming to develop new rules and approaches, and provide also an important resource for evaluation of the implemented approaches. From simple co-occurrence rules (Dagan and Itai 1990) through training decision trees to identify anaphor-antecedent pairs (Aone and Bennett 1995) to genetic algorithms to optimize the resolution factors (Orasan, Evans, and Mitkov 2000), the performance of more and more modern approaches depends on the availability of large suitable corpora.

While the shift towards knowledge-poorer strategies and the use of corpora represent the main trends of anaphora resolution in the 1990s, there are other significant highlights in recent anaphora resolution research. The inclusion of the coreference task in MUC-6 and MUC-7 gave a considerable impetus to the development of coreference resolution algorithms and systems (e.g. Baldwin et al. 1995; Gaizauskas and Humphreys 1996; Kameyama 1997). The last decade of the twentieth century saw a number of anaphora resolution projects for languages other than English such as French, German, Japanese, Spanish, and Portuguese. Against the background of a growing interest in multilingual NLP, multilingual anaphora/coreference resolution has gained considerable momentum in recent years (Aone and McKee 1993; Azzam, Humphreys, and Gaizauskas 1998; Harabagiu and Maiorano 2000; Mitkov and Barbu 2000; Mitkov and Stys 1997; Mitkov, Belguith, and Stys 1998; Palomar et al. 2001). Other milestones of recent research include the deployment of probabilistic and machine learning techniques (Aone and Bennett 1995; McCarthy and Lehnert 1995; Ge, Hale, and Charniak 1998; Kehler 1997; Cardie and Wagstaff 1999; Ng and Cardie 2002; Soon, Ng, and Lim 2001; see also Chapter 20), the continuing interest in centering, used either in original or revised form (Abraços and Lopes 1994; Hahn and Strube 1997; Strube and Hahn 1996; Tetreault 1999, 2001) and proposals related to the evaluation methodology in anaphora resolution (Mitkov 1998a, 2001a, 2001b; Byron 2001).

14.5 OUTSTANDING ISSUES IN ANAPHORA RESOLUTION

The last years have seen considerable advances in the field of anaphora resolution, but there are still a number of outstanding issues that either remain unsolved or need further attention and, as a consequence, represent major challenges to the further development of the field. A fundamental question that needs further investigation is how far the performance of anaphora resolution algorithms can go and what are the limitations of knowledge-poor methods. In particular, more research should be carried out into the factors influencing the performance of these algorithms. Another significant problem for automatic anaphora resolution systems is that the accuracy of the preprocessing is still too low and as a result the performance of such systems remains far from ideal. As a further consequence, only a few anaphora resolution systems operate in fully automatic mode: most of them rely on manual preprocessing or use pre-analysed corpora. One of the impediments for the evaluation or for the fuller utilization of machine learning techniques is the lack of widely available corpora annotated for anaphoric or coreferential links. More work towards the proposal of consistent and comprehensive evaluation is necessary; so is work in multilingual contexts.

Further Reading and Relevant Resources

For computational linguists embarking upon research in the field of anaphora resolution, I recommend as a primer Mitkov (2002), which includes a detailed description of the task of anaphora resolution and the work in the field so far. Graeme Hirst's book *Anaphora in Natural Language Understanding* (Hirst 1981), dated as it may seem (in that it does not cover developments in the 1980s and the 1990s), provides an excellent survey of the theoretical work on anaphora and also of the early computational approaches and is still very useful reading. Carter (1987) is another very useful book.

For an update on recent and latest works in anaphora resolution, the reader may wish to consult the Proceedings of the *ACL/EACL '97 Workshop on Operational Factors in Practical, Robust Anaphora Resolution*, the *ACL '99 Workshop on Coreference and its Applications*, as well as the *DAARC* (*Discourse Anaphora and Anaphor Resolution Colloquium*) conferences in 1996, 1998, 2000, and 2002, the 2002 *International Symposium on Reference Resolution for NLP*, and the *EACL'03 Workshop on the Computational Treatment of Anaphora*. The special issue on anaphora and ellipsis resolution of *Computational Linguistics* (2001) features recent research in the field. Also, a useful website with downloadable papers on anaphora resolution is http://www.wlv.ac.uk/~le1825/download.htm.

Among the approaches that have received a great deal of attention are those of Hobbs (1978); Brennan, Friedman, and Pollard (1987); Dagan and Itai (1990, 1991); Lappin and Leass (1994); Kennedy and Boguraev (1996); Mitkov (1996, 1998*b*); Baldwin (1997); and Ge, Hale, and Charniak (1998).

For demos on anaphora resolution, visit http://clg.wlv.ac.uk/resources/software.html.

References

Abraços, J. and J. G. Lopes. 1994. 'Extending DRT with a focusing mechanism for pronominal anaphora and ellipsis resolution'. *Proceedings of the 15th International Conference on Computational Linguistics* (*COLING '94*) (Kyoto), 1128–32.

Aone, C. and S. W. Bennett. 1995. 'Evaluating automated and manual acquisition of anaphora resolution strategies'. *Proceedings of the 33rd Annual Meeting of the ACL (ACL '95)* (Cambridge, Mass.), 122–9.

——and D. McKee. 1993. 'A language-independent anaphora resolution system for understanding multilingual texts'. *Proceedings of the 31st Annual Meeting of the ACL (ACL '93)* (Columbus, OH), 156–63.

Azzam, S., K. Humphreys, and R. Gaizauskas. 1998. 'Coreference resolution in a multilingual information extraction'. *Proceedings of the Workshop on Linguistic Coreference*. Granada, Spain.

————1999. 'Using coreference chains for text summarization'. *Proceedings of the ACL '99 Workshop on Coreference and its Applications* (College Park, Md.), 77–84.

Bagga, A. and B. Baldwin. 1998. 'Entity-based cross-document coreferencing using the vector space model'. *Proceedings of the 36th Annual Meeting of the Association for Computational Linguistics and of the 18th International Conference on Computational Linguistics (COLING '98/ACL '98)* (Montreal), 79–85.

Baldwin, B. 1997. 'CogNIAC: high precision coreference with limited knowledge and linguistic resources'. *Proceedings of the ACL '97/EACL '97 Workshop on Operational Factors in Practical, Robust Anaphora Resolution* (Madrid), 38–45.

——and T. S. Morton. 1998. 'Dynamic coreference-based summarization'. *Proceedings of the 3rd International Conference on Empirical Methods in Natural Language Processing (EMNLP-3)* (Granada), 1–6.

——J. Reynar, M. Collins, J. Eisner, A. Ratnaparki, J. Rosenzweig, A. Sarkar, and S. Bangalore. 1995. 'Description of the University of Pennsylvania system used for MUC-6'. *Proceedings of the 6th Message Understanding Conference (MUC-6)* (Columbia, Md.)

Barlow, M. 1998. 'Feature mismatches and anaphora resolution'. *Proceedings of the Discourse Anaphora and Anaphora Resolution Colloquium (DAARC '2)* (Lancaster), 34–41.

Bean, D. and E. Riloff. 1999. 'Corpus-based identification of non-anaphoric noun phrases'. *Proceedings of the 37th Annual Meeting of the Association for Computational Linguistics* (College Park, Md.), 373–80.

Bobrow, D. G. 1964. 'A qeustion-answering system for high school algebra word problems'. *AFIPS Conference Proceedings* 26, 591–614.

Boguraev, B. and C. Kennedy. 1997. 'Salience-based content characterisation of documents'. *Proceedings of the ACL '97/EACL '97 Workshop on Intelligent Scalable Text Summarisation* (Madrid), 3-9.

Brennan, S., M. Friedman, and C. Pollard. 1987. 'A centering approach to pronouns'. *Proceedings of the 25th Annual Meeting of the ACL (ACL '87)* (Stanford, Calif.), 155–62.

Byron, D. 2001. 'The uncommon denominator'. *Computational Linguistics*, 27(4), 569–77.

Carbonell, J. G. and R. D. Brown. 1988. 'Anaphora resolution: a multi-strategy approach'. *Proceedings of the 12 International Conference on Computational Linguistics (COLING '88)* (Budapest), 96–101.

Cardie, C. and K. Wagstaff. 1999. 'Noun phrase coreference as clustering'. *Proceedings of the 1999 Joint SIGDAT Conference on Empirical Methods in NLP and Very Large Corpora* (University of Maryland), 82–9.

Carter, D. M. 1987. *Interpreting Anaphora in Natural Language Texts*. Chichester: Ellis Horwood.

Cristea, D., N. Ide, and L. Lomary. 1998. 'Veins theory: a model of global discourse cohesion and coherence'. *Proceedings of the 36th Annual Meeting of the Association for Computational*

Linguistics and of the 18th International Conference on Computational Linguistics (COLING '98/ACL '98) (Montreal), 281–5.

————D. Marcu, and V. Tablan. 2000. 'An empirical investigation of the relation between discourse structure and coreference'. *Proceedings of the 19th International Conference on Computational Linguistics (COLING '2000)* (Saarbrücken), 208–14.

Dagan, I. and A. Itai. 1990. 'Automatic processing of large corpora for the resolution of anaphora references'. *Proceedings of the 13th International Conference on Computational Linguistics (COLING '90)* (Helsinki), iii, 1–3.

————1991. 'A statistical filter for resolving pronoun references'. In Y. A. Feldman and A. Bruckstein (eds.), *Artificial Intelligence and Computer Vision*. Amsterdam: Elsevier Science Publishers BV (North-Holland), 125–35.

Evans, R. 2001. 'Applying machine learning toward an automatic classification of it'. *Literary and Linguistic Computing*, 16(1), 45–57.

Gaizauskas, R. and K. Humphreys. 1996. 'Quantitative evaluation of coreference algorithms in an information extraction system'. Paper presented at the DAARC-1 conference, Lancaster, UK. Reprinted in S. P. Botley and A. M. McEnery (eds.), *Corpus-Based and Computational Approaches to Discourse Anaphora*. Amsterdam: John Benjamins, 2000, 143–67.

Ge, N., J. Hale, and E. Charniak. 1998. 'A statistical approach to anaphora resolution'. *Proceedings of the Workshop on Very Large Corpora* (Montreal), 161–70.

Grosz, B. J., A. Joshi, and S. Weinstein. 1995. 'Centering: a framework for modeling the local coherence of discourse'. *Computational Linguistics*, 21(2), 44–50.

Hahn, U. and M. Strube. 1997. 'Centering-in-the-large: computing referential discourse segments'. *Proceedings of the 35th Annual Meeting of the Association for Computational Linguistics (ACL '97)* (Madrid), 104–11.

Haegeman, L. 1994. *Introduction to Government and Binding Theory*. Oxford: Blackwell.

Harabagiu, S. and S. Maiorano. 1999. 'Knowledge-lean coreference resolution and its relation to textual cohesion and coherence'. *Proceedings of the ACL '99 Workshop on the Relation of Discourse/Dialogues Structure and Reference* (College Park, Md.), 29-38.

————2000. 'Multilingual coreference resolution'. *Proceedings of ANLP-NAACL2000*, (Seattle, Wa.) 142–9.

Hirst, G. 1981. *Anaphora in Natural Language Understanding*. Berlin: Springer Verlag.

Hobbs, J. R. 1978. 'Resolving pronoun references'. *Lingua*, 44, 311–38.

Huddleston, R. 1984. *Introduction to English Grammar*. Cambridge: Cambridge University Press.

Kameyama, M. 1997. 'Recognizing referential links: an information extraction perspective'. *Proceedings of the ACL '97/EACL '97 Workshop on Operational Factors in Practical, Robust Anaphora Resolution* (Madrid), 46–53.

Kehler, A. 1997. 'Probabilistic coreference in information extraction'. *Proceedings of the 2nd Conference on Empirical Methods in Natural Language Processing (EMNMLP-2)* (Providence), 163–73.

Kennedy, C. and B. Boguraev. 1996. 'Anaphora for everyone: pronominal anaphora resolution without a parser'. *Proceedings of the 16th International Conference on Computational Linguistics (COLING '96)* (Copenhagen), 113–18.

Lappin, S. and H. Leass. 1994. 'An algorithm for pronominal anaphora resolution'. *Computational Linguistics*, 20(4), 535–61.

McCarthy, J. and W. Lehnert. 1995. 'Using decision trees for coreference resolution'. *Proceedings of the 14th International Joint Conference on Artificial Intelligence (IJCAI)* (Montreal), 1050–5.

Mitkov, R. 1996. 'Pronoun resolution: the practical alternative'. Paper presented at the *Discourse Anaphora and Anaphor Resolution Colloquium (DAARC)*, Lancaster, UK. Also appeared in S. Botley and A. M. McEnery (eds.), *Corpus-Based and Computational Approaches to Discourse Anaphora*. Amsterdam: John Benjamins, 2000, 189–212.

——1998a. 'Evaluating anaphora resolution approaches'. *Proceedings of the Discourse Anaphora and Anaphora Resolution Colloquium (DAARC '2)* (Lancaster), 164–72.

——1998b. 'Robust pronoun resolution with limited knowledge'. *Proceedings of the 18th International Conference on Computational Linguistics (COLING '98/ACL '98)* (Montreal), 869–75.

——1999. 'Multilingual anaphora resolution'. *Machine Translation*, 14(3–4), 281–99.

——2001a. 'Outstanding issues in anaphora resolution'. In A. Gelbukh (ed.), *Computational Linguistics and Intelligent Text Processing*. Berlin: Springer, 110–25.

——2001b. 'Towards a more consistent and comprehensive evaluation of anaphora resolution algorithms and systems'. *Applied Artificial Intelligence: An International Journal*, 15, 253–76.

——2002. *Anaphora resolution*. London: Longman.

——and C. Barbu. 2000. 'Improving pronoun resolution in two languages by means of bilingual corpora'. *Proceedings of the Discourse, Anaphora and Reference Resolution Conference (DAARC 2000)* (Lancaster), 133–7.

——L. Belguith, and M. Stys. 1998. 'Multilingual robust anaphora resolution'. *Proceedings of the 3rd International Conference on Empirical Methods in Natural Language Processing (EMNLP-3)* (Granada), 7–16.

——and P. Schmidt. 1998. 'On the complexity of pronominal anaphora resolution in machine translation'. In C. Martín-Vide (ed.), *Mathematical and Computational Analysis of Natural Language*, Amsterdam: John Benjamins, 207–22.

——and M. Stys. 1997. 'Robust reference resolution with limited knowledge: high precision genre-specific approach for English and Polish'. *Proceedings of the International Conference 'Recent Advances in Natural Language Proceeding' (RANLP '97)* (Tzigov Chark), 74–81.

Morton, T. 1999. 'Using coreference for question answering'. *Proceedings of the ACL '99 Workshop on Coreference and its Applications* (College Park, Md.), 85–9.

Muñoz, R. 2001. *Tratamiento y resolución de las descripciones definidas y su aplicación en sistemas de extracción de información*. Ph.D. thesis, University of Alicante.

Nasukawa, T. 1994. 'Robust method of pronoun resolution using full-text information'. *Proceedings of the 15th International Conference on Computational Linguistics (COLING '94)* (Kyoto), 1157–63.

Ng, V. and C. Cardie. 2002. 'Improving machine learning approaches to coreference resolution'. *Proceedings of the 40th Annual Meeting of the Association for Computational Linguistics (ACL '02)* (Philadelphia, Pa.), 104–11.

Orasan, C., R. Evans, and R. Mitkov. 2000. 'Enhancing preference-based anaphora resolution with genetic algorithms', *Proceedings of NLP '2000* (Patras), 185–95.

Paice, C. and G. Husk. 1987. 'Towards the automatic recognition of anaphoric features in English text: the impersonal pronoun "it"'. *Computer Speech and Language*, 2, 109–32.

Palomar, M., A. Ferrández, L. Moreno, P. Martínez-Barco, J. Peral, M. Saiz-Noeda, and R. Muñoz. 2001. 'An algorithm for anaphora resolution in Spanish texts'. *Computational Linguistics*, 27(4), 545–67.

Rich, E. and S. LuperFoy. 1988. 'An architecture for anaphora resolution'. *Proceedings of the 2nd Conference on Applied Natural Language Processing (ANLP-2)* (Austin, Tex.), 18–24.

Sidner, C. 1979. *Toward a Computational Theory of Definite Anaphora Comprehension in English*. Technical Report No. AI-TR-537, Cambridge, Mass.: MIT Press.

Soon W. M., H. T. Ng, and D. C. Y. Lim. 2001. 'A machine learning approach to coreference resolution of noun phrases'. *Computational Linguistics*, 27(4), 521–44.

Strube, M. 1998. 'Never look back: an alternative to centering'. *Proceedings of the 18th International Conference on Computational Linguistics (COLING '98/ACL '98)* (Montreal), 1251–7.

——and U. Hahn. 1996. 'Functional centering'. *Proceedings of the 34th Annual Meeting of the Association for Computational Linguistics* (Santa Cruz, Calif.), 270–7.

Tetreault, J. R. 1999. 'Analysis of syntax-based pronoun resolution methods'. *Proceedings of the 37th Annual Meeting of the Association for Computational Linguistics (ACL '99)* (College Park, Md.), 602–5.

——2001. 'A corpus-based evaluation of centering and pronoun resolution'. *Computational Linguistics*, 27(4), 507–20.

Vieira, R. and M. Poesio. 2000. 'An empirically-based system for processing definite descriptions'. *Computational Linguistics*, 26(4), 525–79.

Walker, M., A. Joshi, and E. Prince. 1998. 'Centering in naturally occurring discourse: an overview'. In M. Walker, A. Joshi, and E. Prince (eds.), *Centering Theory in Discourse*, Oxford: Oxford University Press.

Webber, B. L. 1979. *A Formal Approach to Discourse Anaphora*. London: Garland Publishing.

Wilks, Y. 1973. *Preference semantics*. Stanford AI laboratory memo AIM-206. Stanford University.

Williams, S., M. Harvey, and K. Preston. 1996. 'Rule-based reference resolution for unrestricted text using part-of-speech tagging and noun phrase parsing'. *Proceedings of the International Colloquium on Discourse Anaphora and Anaphora Resolution (DAARC)* (Lancaster), 441–56.

Winograd, T. 1972. *Understanding Natural Language*. New York: Academic Press/Edinburgh: Edinburgh University Press.

Woods, W., R. Kaplan, and B. Nash-Webber. 1972. *The lunar sciences natural languages information system: final report*. Report 2378, Bolt Beranek and Newman Inc., Cambridge, Mass.

NATURAL LANGUAGE GENERATION

JOHN BATEMAN

MICHAEL ZOCK[1]

ABSTRACT

Communication via a natural language requires two fundamental skills, producing 'text' (written or spoken) and understanding it. This chapter introduces newcomers to the field of computational approaches to the former—**natural language generation** (henceforth NLG)—showing some of the theoretical and practical problems that linguists, computer scientists, and psychologists have encountered when trying to explain how language works in machines or in our minds.

[1] Authors in alphabetical order.

15.1 General Introduction: What is Natural Language Generation? (Cognitive, Linguistic, and Social Dimensions)

15.1.1 Natural Language Generation—a knowledge-intensive problem

Producing language is above all a social activity. We speak to solve problems, for others or for ourselves, and in order to do so we make certain choices under specific space, time, and situational constraints. The corresponding task of NLG therefore spans a wide spectrum: ranging from planning some action (verbal or not) to executing it (verbalization). Hence, information has to be mapped from some *non-linguistic* source (e.g. raw data from a knowledge base or scene) into some corresponding linguistic form (text in oral or written form) in order to fulfil some non-linguistic goal(s). This 'transformation' is neither direct nor straightforward, and bridging the gap between the non-linguistic 'scene' and its linguistic counterpart involves many decisions or choices: these include determination and structuring of *content* (i.e. choice of the message) and *rhetorical structure* at various levels (text, paragraph, sentence), choice of the appropriate *words* and *syntactic structures* (word order, morphology, and grammatical constructions), and determination of text layout (title, headers, footnotes, etc.) or acoustic patterns (prosody, pitch, intonation contour). Providing architectures in which all of these decisions can be made to coexist, while still allowing the production of natural sounding/reading texts within a reasonable amount of time, is one of the major challenges of NLG. A very simple, first view of this process and its stages is suggested in Fig. 15.1.

Another challenge is ascertaining just what the decisions involved in NLG are. NLG requires many kinds of expertise: *knowledge of the domain* (what to say, relevance), *knowledge of the language* (lexicon, grammar, semantics), *strategic rhetorical knowledge* (how to achieve communicative goals, text types, style), etc. Moreover, building successful NLG systems requires *engineering knowledge* (how to decompose, represent, and orchestrate the processing of all this information) as well as *knowledge* about the *habits* and *constraints* of the end user as an *information processor* (sociolinguistic and psychological factors).

While everybody speaks a language, not everybody speaks it equally well. There are substantial differences concerning its speed of learning, and its ease and success of use. How language works in our mind is still a mystery, and some consider the construction of NLG systems as a methodology for helping to unravel that mystery. Others see NLG as an approach to solving practical problems—such as contributing

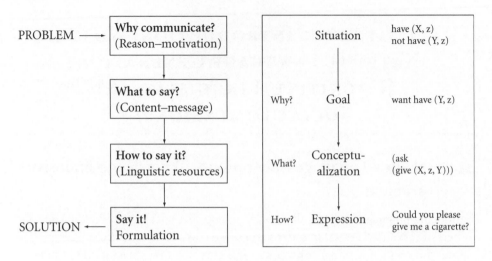

Fgure 15.1 NLG: a simple view

to the synthesis side of *machine translation* (cf. Chapters 27, 28), to *text summarization* (cf. Chapter 32), and to *multilingual* and *multimodal presentation of information* (cf. Chapters 36 and 38) in general. That our understanding of the process remains so poor is largely due to the *number*, the *diversity*, and the *interdependence* of the choices involved. While it is easy to understand the relationships between a glass falling and its breaking (causal relationship), it is not at all easy to understand the dependency relationships holding in heterarchically organized systems like biology, society, or natural language. In such systems, the consequences of a choice may be multiple, far reaching, and unpredictable. In this sense, there are many points in common between speaking a language well, hence communicating effectively, and being a good politician. In both cases one has to make the right choice at the right moment. Learning *what* the choices are, and *when* they should be made, is then a large part of the task of building NLG systems.

15.1.2 What is language? A functional perspective

Much of the complexity of NLG arises out of the fact that producing language is a knowledge-intensive, flexible, and highly context-sensitive process. This context sensitivity reveals itself best when we consider connected texts rather than isolated sentences. Consider the following example. Suppose you were to express the idea: [LEAVE (POPULATION, PLACE)]. It is instructive to watch what happens if one varies systematically the expression of the different concepts *leave*, *population*, and *place* by using either different *words* (*abandon, desert, leave, go away from* in the case of the verb, and *place* or *city* in the case of the noun), or different *grammatical resources*: e.g. a *definite description* ('the + N'), *possessives* ('yours', 'its'), etc. Concretely, consider the alternatives given in (15.1).

(15.1) 'X-town was a blooming city. Yet, when hooligans started to invade the place, [insert one of: (*a*)–(*e*) below]. The place was not livable any more.'

   (*a*) the *place* was abandoned by (its/the population)/them.

   (*b*) the *city* was abandoned by its/the population.

   (*c*) *it* was abandoned by its/the population.

   (*d*) its/the population abandoned the *city*.

   (*e*) its/the population abandoned *it*.

The interested reader may perform all the kinds of variations mentioned above and check to what extent they affect *grammaticality* (the sentence cannot be uttered or finished), *clarity* (some pronouns will create ambiguity), *cohesion*, and *rhetorical effect*. In particular, while all the candidate sentences we offer in (*a*)–(*e*) are basically well-formed, each one has a specific effect, and not all of them are equally felicitous. Some are ruled out by virtue of poor textual choices (e.g. in (a) '*the place*' is subopti-mal, since it immediately repeats a word), others because of highlighting the wrong element, or because of wrong assignment of the informational status (given–new) of some element (e.g. in (d) '*the city*' is marked as 'minimal' *new* information, while actu-ally it is known, i.e. *old* information). Probably the best option here is (*c*), since this preserves the given–new distribution appropriately, without introducing potentially ambiguous pronouns (see Chapter 14 for detailed discussion of anaphora).

Getting a text 'right' is therefore a major problem. Central here is the notion of the *effects* of individual linguistic choices—not only locally, but also globally for the text to which they are contributing. Both choices and effects have to be orchestrated so as to achieve collectively the speaker's overall goals. The notion of 'grammaticality', central to formal approaches of language (see, particularly, Chapters 4 and 8) is by no means sufficient and many other factors, such as social, discourse, and pragmatic constraints (Chapters 6 and 7), have to be taken into account in order to achieve *successful communication*. Many of these latter factors have traditionally been at the heart of **functional theories** of language (e.g. Halliday 1994), and this is one of the reasons why such theories have been used widely by the NLG community—far more widely than has been the case for natural language understanding.

15.1.3 Decomposing the NLG task: architectures for NLG

Architectures deal with the functional relations between components (dependencies, control of information flow) or the problem of *what* to process *when* (order). The sheer range of interdependencies found in language has motivated many different kinds of architecture (sequential, parallel, integrative, revision based, blackboard, connectionist). They have also led to differing conceptualizations of what NLG is, resulting in at least three kinds of definition:

1. NLG as a *mapping problem*
2. NLG as a *problem of choice*
3. NLG as a *planning problem*

All of these involve some decomposition of the problem space into different kinds of representational layers. The most common are those shown in Fig. 15.2, which divides the whole process into four broad tasks (macroplanning, microplanning, linguistic realization, presentation) and a series of subtasks. At the top of the figure there are recurring situational constraints and knowledge sources (e.g. dictionary, grammar) that can apply at various stages in processing; the boxes below represent the (sub)tasks at the various levels. These four main tasks may be described as follows:

- **Macroplanning**. Given some goal and knowledge sources (raw data), choose among them and organize them to build a text plan. This generally yields a tree composed of a set of leaves (messages to be expressed, generally sentences or clauses) and a set of nodes and arcs expressing the type of *rhetorical relation* (cause, sequence, etc.) and the textual status of the segment (*nucleus, satellite*: see below).

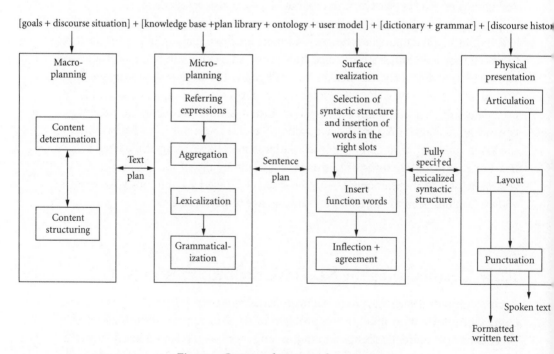

Fig. 15.2 Commonly assumed components

- **Microplanning.** Decide on how to describe any given event or entity, i.e. give enough information to allow its *discrimination from possible alternatives* (reference); group closely related material by *factoring out redundant elements* in order to build better integrated, more concise text (aggregation); and *select appropriate words* for expressing the chosen content and for achieving the necessary degree of cohesion (lexicalization, pronominalization, and choice of cue words). In practice (and perhaps in theory too), it is not possible to separate cleanly selection of lexical items and commitments to particular grammatical organizations.
- **Surface realization.** Impose selected *grammatical constructions* (entailing selection of syntactic functions: subject, direct object, etc.), *linear order* (constrained either by the grammar or by information status as a language requires), *part of speech* (noun, verb, etc.), *sentence complexity* (simple/compound), insert *function words* (e.g. prepositions), and determine the *final form* of the words (morphology).
- **Physical presentation.** Perform final *articulation*, *punctuation*, and *layout operations*.

15.2 CONTENT SELECTION AND DISCOURSE ORGANIZATION: MACROPLANNING

15.2.1 Content planning

Before starting to talk, one should have something to say. The crux of the problem is to find out how this 'something'—the conceptual input to be expressed by the surface generator—is determined. Obviously, given some topic, we will not say everything we know about it, neither will we present the messages in the order in which they come to mind; we have to make some choices and we have to perform certain rearrangements. But what guides these operations?

Suppose you had the task of writing a survey paper on NLG or a report on the weather. You could start from a knowledge base containing information (facts) on *authors*, *type of work*, *year*, etc. or *meteorological information* (numerical values). Since there is no point in mentioning all the facts, we have to filter out those that are relevant. *Relevance* here means to be sensitive to the writer's and reader's goals, their knowledge, preferences, and point of view. And, of course, there are still many other factors that have to be taken into account: for example external constraints like space (number of pages), time (deadline), mode (spoken vs. written), etc. Moreover, the knowledge to be expressed (message) may be in a form that is fairly remote from its corresponding linguistic expression (surface form). For example, the information may consist of raw, numerical data or qualitative representations. In both cases, data has first to be *interpreted* in order to specify its semantic value: e.g. a sequence of decreasing numeric values might be **semanticized** as *a drop, a decrease*, or *the falling of temperature*. Finally, although knowledge bases are generally structured, it is less often the case that this structure can be directly used for organizing a text. Data can be organized alphabetically or chronologically, but most types of texts exhibit other structures—their information is organized *topically* (e.g. for our survey paper task: deep generation, surface generation, lexical choice, etc.; or for the weather report: the state of the weather today, predictions about changes, statistics, etc.). This requires further information, either explicitly—via, for example, an *ontology* stating the components of an object or a task (Chapter 25) and some account of appropriate text structures—or implicitly, that is, via inference rules (which in that case are needed in addition to the knowledge base).

An important function of this organizational knowledge is to enable the text producer to select and structure information according to criteria not explicitly mentioned, for example, in our survey, according to *pioneering work, landmark systems*, etc. Such criteria then need to be operationalized before they can play a role in an NLG system: for example, one could define the notion of 'landmark' as work that has changed the framework within which a task is being carried out (e.g. the move from *schemata* to *RST* in discourse planning as discussed below), or as a paradigm shift that has since been adopted by the field, etc. This close link between *content selection* and *discourse structure* is a natural one: information is generally only relevant for a text given some particular communicative goals. For this reason, these two tasks are often addressed by the same component.

15.2.2 Text planning: the schema-based approach and the TEXT system

TEXT (McKeown 1985) was one of the first systems to automatically produce paragraph-length discourse. Having analysed a large number of texts and transcripts, McKeown noticed that, given some *communicative goal*, people tended to present the *same kind of information* in the *same order*. To capture these regularities, McKeown classified this information into **rhetorical predicates** and **schemata**. The former describe roughly the semantics of the text's building blocks; examples of predicates, their function, and illustrative clauses are shown in Fig. 15.3. The latter describe the legal combination of predicates to form patterns or text templates. Fig. 15.4(*a*) gives several possible decompositions of the *Identification* schema, using the notation for schema definition McKeown proposes. Fig. 15.4(*b*) then gives an example text; the connection between the sentences of the text and the responsible text schema

Name of predicate	Function	Example
Identification	identifies the object as a member of a class	*A catamaran is a kind of sailboat.*
Constituency	presents constituents of the entity	*A sailboat has sails and a mast.*
Illustration	provides an example	*The Titanic is a boat.*

Fig. 15.3 **Examples of rhetorical predicates**

elements are indicated by the sentence numbering. Schemata are thus both *organizational devices* (determining *what* to say *when*) and *rhetorical means*, i.e. discourse strategies for achieving some associated goals.

Once the *building blocks* and their *combinations* are known, simple text generation becomes fairly straightforward. Given a goal (define, describe, or compare), the system chooses a schema which stipulates in abstract terms *what* is to be said *when*. Whenever there are several options for continuing—for example, in the second sentence one could have used *analogy*, *constituency*, or *renaming* instead of the predicate *attributive* (cf. Fig. 15.4(*a*), schema B)—the system uses **focus rules** to pick the one that ties in best with the text produced so far. Coherence or text structure is thus achieved as a side effect of choosing a goal and filling its associated schema.

Not all information stipulated by the schema must appear in a final text; actually only schema parts (A) and (C) are compulsory. A given predicate may also be expanded and repeated. Optionality, repetition, and recursion (not illustrated in our example) make schemata very powerful, but they still have some recognized shortcomings—the most significant of which is the lack of connection between the components of an adopted schema and the goals of a text. The goals associated with a schema specify the role of the schema as a whole—i.e. why to use it—but they do

(A) Identification (<u>class</u> and <u>attribute</u> (1) /function)	(1) A *Hobie Cat* is a brand of *catamaran*, manufactured by the *Hobie Company*.
(B) {Analogy/Constituency/<u>Attributive</u> (2) /Renaming}*	(2) Its main attraction is that it's *cheap*.
(C) <u>Particular-illustration</u> (3) /Evidence +	(3) A *new one* goes for about $5000.
(D) {Amplification/Analogy/Attributive}	
(E) {Particular-illustration/Evidence}	

Fig. 15.4(*a*) **Identification schema**   Fig. 15.4(*b*) **Corresponding text**

Key: {} optionality; / alternative; * optional item which may appear o to n times; + item may appear 1 to n times. The underlined predicates are the ones that are actually used in the text produced (see 15.4*b*)

not specify the roles of its parts: why use a specific rhetorical predicate at a given moment? Hence, in case of failure (for example, the information given being considered as insufficient by the user), the system cannot recover in order to offer an alternative solution because there is no linking between schema-parts and subgoals for the text as a whole: the TEXT system will invariably produce the same answer, regardless of the user's expertise, informational needs, or problems.

15.2.3 Text planning and rhetorical structure theory

Rhetorical structure theory (RST) was adopted in NLG partly to overcome the problems of schemata and to provide a more flexible mechanism that links communicative goals and text structure more closely. According to RST (cf. Mann and Thompson 1987), any coherent text is decomposable into a recursive structure of text 'spans' (usually clauses): the relations between text spans construct, often implicit, propositions involving common rhetorically relevant predicates such as *cause, purpose, motivation*, and *enablement*; these relations generally divide a text span into at least two segments: one that is of most importance for the text—the **nucleus**—and others which have more a supportive role—the **satellites**. The existence of a single overarching rhetorical structure for a text then accounts for its perceived coherence. RST received its initial computational operationalizations in Hovy (1988) and Moore and Paris (1988) and has since been incorporated in a wide range of NLG systems. Probably the most widespread version of operationalized RST is that presented in Moore and Paris (1993).

RST in this form makes essential use of the *planning paradigm* from AI (Sacerdoti 1977). **Planning** here means basically *organizing actions rationally* in order to *achieve a goal*. Since most goals (problems) are complex, they have to be decomposed. High-level, global goals are thus refined to a point where the actions associated with them are primitive enough to be performed directly. Planning supposes three things: a *goal* (problem to be solved), a *plan library* (i.e. a set of plan operators each of which allows the achievement of a specified goal), and a *planning method* (algorithm). Each *plan operator* combines the following information: an *effect* (i.e. a state which holds true after the plan's execution, i.e. the goal); zero, one, or more *preconditions* (conditions which must be satisfied before the plan can be executed); and a *body* (i.e. a set of actions, which are the means for achieving the goal). Somewhat simplified, then, a hierarchical planner works by decomposing the top-level goal using plan operators whose effects match the goals given and whose preconditions are true. These plan operators may introduce further subgoals recursively.

Let us take an example. Suppose 'Ed' wanted to go to 'New York'. We assume that this can be represented in terms of a goal such as: [BE-AT(ACTOR, DESTINATION)], with the arguments instantiated as required for our particular case. Now, rather than building a plan that holds only for one specific problem, one generally appeals to a generic plan—e.g. a set of plans and solutions for a related body of problems. In Fig. 15.5, for example, we show a library of plan operators appropriate for the planning of trips for different people to go to different places. Given our present starting goal of wanting to get Ed to New York, the planner looks for operators to achieve this, i.e. operators whose effect fields match the goal. In our case the top-level goal can partially be achieved in a number of ways: for example via the TAKE-TRIP or the GET-ON operator; however, there are additional dependency relationships and states of affairs that need to be fulfilled and these restrict the ordering of applicability of the plan operators. Thus, we cannot take a trip unless we get on a train, etc. (cf. Fig. 15.5). Assuming that the text planner has got as far as proposing the taking of a trip, then the body of the operator is posted as a further subgoal: GET-ON. Associated with this further operator are two conditions, [BE-AT(ACTOR, TRAIN)] and [HAVE(ACTOR, TICKET)], which can be satisfied respectively via the GO-TO and BUY operators. The first one is unconditional, it can be directly achieved, while the second one decomposes into three actions: *go to the clerk*, *give him the money*, and *receive the ticket*. It is this last action that ensures that the traveller (actor) has finally what is needed to take the trip: the ticket (precondition of the GET-ON operator). The process terminates when all goals (regardless of their level) have been fulfilled, which means that all effects or preconditions hold true, either unconditionally—the action being primitive enough

Operator: TAKE-TRIP (ACTOR, TRAIN, DESTINATION)
Effect: be-at (actor, destination)
Precond.: destination (train, destination)+
           on-board (actor, train)
Body: • get-on (actor, train)

Operator: GET-ON (ACTOR, TRAIN)
Effect: on-board (actor, train)
Precond.: be-at (actor, train)
           have (actor, ticket (train))
Body: • buy (actor, clerk, ticket (train))
           • go-to (actor, train)

Operator: GO-TO (ACTOR, LOCATION)
Effect: be-at (actor, location)

Operator: BUY (ACTOR, RECIPIENT, OBJECT)
Effect: have (actor, object)+
Precond.: have (actor, price (object))+
Body: • go-to (actor, recipient)
           • give (actor, recipient, price (object))
           • give (recipient, actor, object)

Operator: GIVE (ACTOR, RECIPIENT, OBJECT)
Effect: have (recipient, object)
Precond.: have (actor, object)
           . . . .

+: Unconditionally true actions/states

Fig. 15.5 Plan library of action types

to dispense with any further action (see the GO-TO operator)—or because there is an operator allowing their realization. Fig. 15.6 shows the partially completed hierarchical plan for achieving the final goal.

Within operationalized RST, RST relations are modelled as plan operators and the effects are communicative goals. To illustrate this use of RST in text planning, we take a slightly adapted example from Vander Linden (2000). The application scenario is providing help or documentation for a computer program. Knowledge concerning user interactions with the program has been modelled, and help-information is to be automatically generated. Several NLG systems have been built for this kind of scenario. Suppose that a user would like to know how to save a file. For the NLG system to generate an appropriate text, it is first given a top-level communicative goal; in this case:

(COMPETENT H (DO-ACTION SAVING-A-FILE))

That is: achieve a state in which the hearer (H) is competent to do the action 'saving-a-file'. An RST-based hierarchical text planner then has to access information in the knowledge base and structure this into an appropriate text plan. Domain knowledge

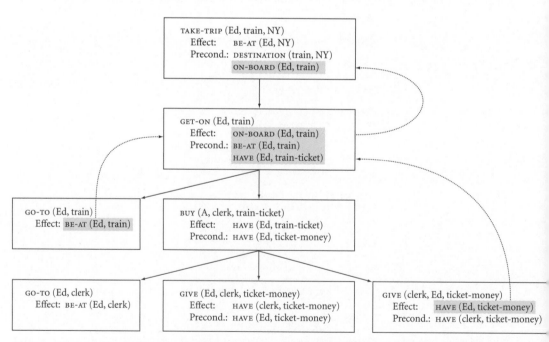

The three dotted arcs show that the effect of a given operator has to include satisfaction of the *precondition* of the field to which they point (hence they do not specify *dependency* relationships)

Fig. 15.6 A partial plan built to achieve the goal 'get to NY'

about the program to be documented is generally stored as a collection of goals and methods for achieving them. Thus, there will be a high-level goal 'save a file' and a sequence of actions corresponding to a method for it.

The simplest actions a hearer (H) is able to perform (*primitive planning actions*) are those expressed by individual messages associated with simple speech acts, such as 'inform', 'question', etc. When all goals have been expanded to plan steps involving primitive (and therefore directly achievable) subgoals, the planning process halts, as the text structure is then complete.

One plan operator that matches our example top-level goal is that given in Fig. 15.7(*a*): 'expand purpose.' In order to see if this operator may be applied, the preconditions/constraints must first be checked. To do this, the variable ?ACTION of the effect field is bound to the corresponding action in our top-level goal 'saving a file'; then the constraints slot specifies that this action must be decomposable into some substeps and that this sublist should not consist of a single action. If we assume that

Name:	Expand Purpose	**Name:**	Expand Sequence
Effect:	(COMPETENT H (DO-ACTION ?action))	**Effect:**	(COMPETENT H (DO-SEQUENCE ?actions))
Constraints	(& (c-get-all-substeps ?action ?subactions) (not (singular-list? ?subactions))	**Constraints:**	none
Nucleus	(competent H (do-sequence ?subactions))	**Nucleus:**	(rst-sequence (for each ?subaction in ?actions (competent H (do-action ?subaction))))
Satellite:	(((rst-purpose (inform Sp H (do ?action))) *required*))	**Satellite:**	none
(*a*) Plan Operator: Expand PURPOSE		(*b*) Plan Operator: Expand SEQUENCE	

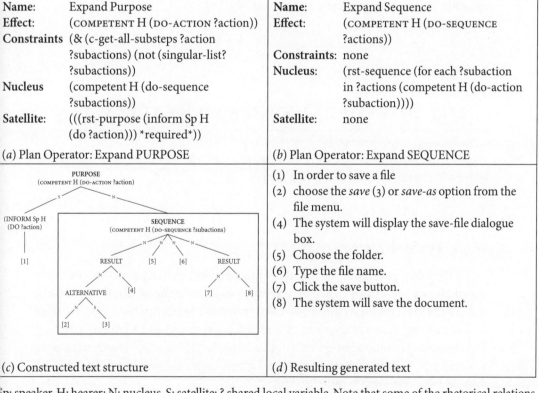

(*c*) Constructed text structure

(1) In order to save a file
(2) choose the *save* (3) or *save-as* option from the file menu.
(4) The system will display the save-file dialogue box.
(5) Choose the folder.
(6) Type the file name.
(7) Click the save button.
(8) The system will save the document.

(*d*) Resulting generated text

Sp: speaker, H: hearer; N: nucleus, S: satellite; ? shared local variable. Note that some of the rhetorical relations are 'multinuclear'--i.e., relate more than one nucleus

Fig. 15.7 Illustration of 2 plan operators, the resulting text plan (tree) and corresponding text

this is the case for our present example—saving a file will typically require several substeps—then the operator will apply. Note that this process not only checks constraints but also retrieves relevant information (via matching and binding), thereby combining content selection with its ordering. The subgoals specified in the nucleus and satellite slots are then posted and must both in turn be satisfied for planning as a whole to succeed. The satellite subgoal succeeds immediately, since it calls for the system, or speaker (Sp), to inform (a primitive act) the hearer (H) about some propositional content ('DO "save a file"'). Moreover, this entire content is embedded as a satellite under an RST 'purpose' relation, which then constrains its possible linguistic realizations; one possible realization of this branch of the text plan, provided by the surface generator on demand, is given in (1) in Fig. 15.7(d). The goal posted under the nucleus requires further expansion, however, and so the planning process continues (cf., e.g. Fig. 15.7(b): 'expand sequence'). The result of the process is a tree whose nodes represent the rhetorical relations (effect), and whose leaves represent the verbal material allowing their achievement. This result is then handed either to microplanning (e.g. for aggregation, which may eliminate redundancies) or to the surface generator directly. Fig. 15.7(c, d) show a final text plan constructed by the planning operators and a possible corresponding text.

15.3 Microplanning and Realization

We sketched above (section 15.1) some of the subtasks of microplanning; we will address here only one of these: *lexicalization*.

15.3.1 Lexicalization

Somewhere in a generation system, there must be information about the words that would allow us to express what we want to convey, their meanings, their syntactic constraints, etc. This kind of information is stored in a **lexicon**, whose precise organization can vary considerably (see, for examples and discussion, Chapters 3 and 25). Dictionaries are static knowledge, yet this latter has to be used: words have to be accessed and, in case of alternatives (synonyms), some selection has to be made. All this contributes to what is called *lexicalization*.

There are two broad views on lexicalization: one can conceive it either as conceptually driven (meaning) or as lexicon driven (see Fig. 15.8*a* and 15.8*b*). In the former view everything is given with the input (i.e. the message is complete), and the rela-

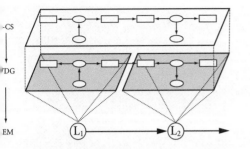 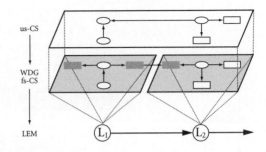

fs-CS: fully specified conceptual structure; us-CS: underspecified conceptual structure;
WDG: word definition graph; LEM: lemmata

Fig. 15.8(*a*) The lexicon as a resource for compacting a given conceptual chunk

Fig. 15.8(*b*) The lexicon as a resource for refining an underspecified message

tionship between the conceptual structure and the corresponding linguistic form is mediated via the lexicon: lexical items are selected provided that their underlying content covers parts of the conceptual input. The goal is to find sufficient mutually compatible lexical items so as to completely cover the input with minimal unwanted additional information. In the latter view, the message to be expressed is incomplete prior to lexicalization, the lexicon serving, among other things, to refine the initially underspecified message (for arguments in favour of this second view see Zock 1996). One begins with a skeleton plan (rough outline or gist) and fleshes it out progressively depending on communicative and speaker needs (for example, by providing further information necessary for establishing reference).

To illustrate the first view (conceptually driven lexicalization) we will use an adapted example taken from Zock (1996); suppose your goal were to find the most precise and economic way for expressing some content, let us say 'the fisherman rushed to the canoe'; the problem is to decide how to carve out the conceptual space so as to cover everything planned. We will show here only how the first two open-class words (*fisherman* and *rush*) are selected, suggesting by the direction link that more is to come. Lexicalization is performed in two steps. During the first only those words are selected that pertain to a given semantic field (for example, movement verbs). In the next step the lexicalizer selects from this pool the term that best expresses the intended meaning, i.e. the most specific term (maximal coverage). Thus we need to map the conceptual chunks (input) 'a man whose profession consists in catching and selling fish' and 'move fast on the ground' into their linguistic counterparts: *fisherman* and *rush*. The process is shown in Fig. 15.9; for more details see Nogier and Zock (1992) and Zock (1996); for a sophisticated proposal of what to do if one cannot find a complete covering, see Nicolov (1999). There are many open questions concerning how such a process may be controlled effectively when faced with more alternatives.

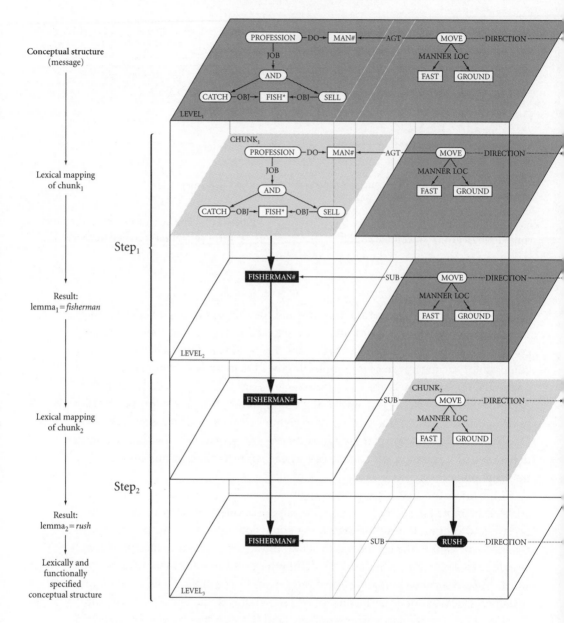

Fig. 15.9 Progressive lexical specification

15.3.2 Surface generation

The final stage of NLG consists in passing the results of the microplanner to the **surface generator** to produce strings of properly inflected words; while some surface generators produce simple text strings, others produce strings marked up with tags that can be interpreted for prosody control for spoken language, for punctuation, or for layout. Unlike in situations of theoretical grammar development, the primary task of a surface generator is certainly not to find all possible ways to express a given propositional content, but rather to find a way of expressing the given communicative content that is in line with the rules of the language, the speakers' goals, and, often most crucially, the rest of the text that has been generated so far and is to come (the co-*text*).

Surface generation is nevertheless the area of NLG that overlaps most with the traditional concerns of linguistics—particularly structural linguistics concerned with accounts of sentences (syntax: Chapter 4; semantics: Chapter 5). However, although nearly all linguistic theories have been implemented in trial generation and analysis systems, there are essentially three theoretical frameworks that have emerged as being particularly well suited to the needs of NLG. These are accounts based on systemic-functional grammars (SFG: Halliday 1994), tree-adjoining grammars (TAG: Danlos 2000), and Mel'čuk's meaning-text model (MTM: Mel'čuk 1988).

SFG has been adopted by those interested in the systematic representation, *functional motivation*, and consequences of the choice of particular linguistic resources—e.g. what impact do the selections of particular grammatical patterns (and hence indirectly of particular grammatical Subjects, Themes, etc.) have on the coherence and cohesion of a text? Systemic-functional grammars can also be viewed as 'feature-based' systems, since feature selection is their main operation for describing and choosing a linguistic unit. As a result, some systemically based generators are directly implemented using feature matching, or *unification*, as their main operation (e.g. FUF/SURGE: Elhadad and Robin 1997), others adopt special-purpose implementations—typically for the more efficient generation behaviour necessary when dealing with large-scale grammars (e.g. PENMAN: Mann and Matthiessen 1986; KPML: Bateman 1997).

TAG has typically been adopted by those who are seeking **incremental generation**—i.e. a generation architecture where information can be consumed by the available grammatical constructions of a language as soon as that information becomes available. To achieve this, TAGs place their main descriptive work on setting out extensive libraries of partial syntactic structures, which nowadays are increasingly indexed according to their so-called *lexical anchor*—that is, particular families of syntactic structures are linked with particular lexical items (cf. Chapter 26 and Harbusch, Finkler, and Schauder 1991)—and are organized hierarchically.

MTM has been adopted principally by researchers interested in issues of lexical variation (cf. Iordanskaja, Kittredge, and Polguère 1991) *and restricted lexical co-occurrence* (**collocations**). The latter are units where the form for expressing one part of the meaning (the *collocate*) depends on the other (the *base*), the one to which this meaning is applied. For example, suppose you wanted to express the idea that some entity has the property [SIZE-big]: surface generation here is complicated by the fact that lexicalization is not a local choice—depending on the lexeme selected for the entity being described, i.e. depending on the base (e.g. *man* vs. *mountain*), we may need to select different *collocates* (e.g. *tall* vs. *high* respectively). This is because it is not appropriate (in English) to say 'he is a high man' or 'this is a tall mountain'. Such collocational restrictions are widespread in all languages and are difficult, if not impossible, to 'predict' reliably on semantic grounds.

15.4 OPEN ISSUES AND PROBLEMS

Among the different open issues and problems, we will mention here only three: architectural, inferential and control.

(i) *Architectural.* Architectural decisions revolve around the problems of *order* (uni- vs. bi-directional); *completion* (one pass vs. several, revisions), *control* (central vs. distributed), etc. Many systems designers have—purely on engineering grounds (e.g. ease of implementation, speed of generation)—opted for a unidirectional flow of information between the modules (the **pipelined** view). This poses a number of problems; most prominently, there is a danger of not being able to find resources (e.g. words) to express the message planned. Hence, one reaches a deadlock; this is often discussed as one of the problems of the '**generation gap**' (Meteer 1992) between different levels of representation in NLG architectures. For a thorough discussion of architectures in general, see de Smedt, Horacek, and Zock (1996) and for attempts at architecture standardization take a look at Cahill et al. (1999) and the website mentioned below.

(ii) *Inferences.* Next to schemata and RST, **inference-driven generation** has been proposed to deal with the problem of content determination; for some pioneering work in this area, each very different from the others, see Cawsey (1991), Kölln (1997), Stone and Doran (1997). This is a particularly promising area; at the same time, it is known that one of the hardest problems of inferencing is to have good criteria for making the process stop.

(iii) *Control.* As the number of possibilities to express a given content grows, it becomes increasingly necessary to find good criteria for choosing among the alternatives. While it is relatively easy to find criteria and tests for deciding on well-formedness, it is a lot harder to settle the issue of adequacy. When should one use a grammatical resource, such as passive voice, a relative clause, etc.? What to do in case of conflict? When to stop? The problem of termination is a delicate issue in general: when is a text optimal? (ever?) And finally, what holds for the text in general, holds also for each of its components (what is a perfect input, the best organization, etc.). There is, therefore, still much to do both in the fundamental design of NLG systems and theory and in its practical application.

Further Reading and Relevant Resources

There are now several excellent introductory papers to NLG that take a more detailed view of both the tasks of NLG and the approaches that have attempted to deal with them; see, for example: Bateman (1998), Hovy (1996), Vander Linden (2000), and the many references cited there. In addition, for further pointers, descriptions of systems, etc., see Zock and Adorni (1996) and Reiter and Dale (2000). The latter include a particularly detailed comparison of the SFG, FUF, and MTM-syntactic approaches to surface generation. For more on grammars, see Teich (1998), while both Paiva (1998) and Gal et al. (1991) are good NLG sources for the practically minded. Reviews of the state of the art in approaches to text planning using rhetorical relations are given by Maybury (1990), Hovy (1993), and Paris (1993). They all make a very readable introduction to text planning and the latter shows well its control by *user-modelling*. For work on aggregation see Dalianis (1999). Two excellent survey articles covering work on lexical choice are Wanner (1996) and Stede (1999). In order to get a feel of the methods psychologists use at both the sentence and discourse level, Levelt (1989), Bock (1996), and Andriessen, de Smedt, and Zock (1996) can all be used as starting points.

For access to recent publications, reference lists, free software, or to know *who is who*, the best thing to start out with is the website of the ACL's Special Interest Group for Generation (SIGGEN); this can be accessed via the ACL pages at http://www.cs.columbia.edu/~acl/. There are also a number of freely available generation systems and generation grammars that can be used for hands-on exposure to the issues of NLG. The three most extensive are Elhadad's FUF/Surge system at http://www.cs.bgu.ac.il/fuf/index.htm, which includes a very wide-coverage generation grammar for English; the MTM-influenced syntactic generator RealPro at http://www.cogentex.com/technology/realpro/index.shtml; and the KPML multilingual generation system at http://purl.org/net/kpml, which includes an extensive grammar development environment for large-scale systemic-functional grammar work and teaching, introductory tutorials, as well as a growing range of generation grammars: e.g. grammars for English (very large), German, Dutch, Czech, Russian, Bulgarian, Spanish, French, and others. There are also several quite extensive on-line bibliographies including substantial NLG-related references—for example, several of the bibliographies under Alf-Christian Achilles's Collection of Computer Science Bibliographies at the University of Karlsruhe (http://liinwww.ira.uka.de/bibliography/index.html, subsection Artificial Intelligence) are worth bookmarking—particularly http://liinwww.ira.uka.de/bibliography/Ai/nlg.html (Kantrowitz) and http://liinwww.ira.uka.de/bibliography/Ai/bateman.html (Bateman). In addition, the following sites contain a variety of useful information about diverse aspects of NLG: the Reference Architectures for Generation (RAGS) project website describes an attempt to provide a general scheme for describing architectures for 'practical NLG' (http://www.itri.brighton.ac.uk/projects/rags); the Scottish and German NLG sites (http://

www.cogsci.ed.ac.uk/~jo/gen/snlg/nlg.html and http://www.ling.uni-potsdam.de/ ~stede/nlg-ger.htm respectively) have a variety of useful pointers to systems, literature, and researchers in their respective countries; and the RST site offers a wide range of information, both computational and linguistic, concerning all aspects of rhetorical structure theory and its application (http://www.sil.org/linguistics/RST). A range of papers are available on-line at http://www.iro.umontreal.ca/~scriptum/PublicationsMembres.html, and for pointers on AI in general http://www.norvig.com/ is very useful. Finally, we also maintain an almost complete list of NLG systems with linked bibliographical data and pointers to further web-based information at http: //purl.org/net/nlg-list—to which additions are welcome at any time!

REFERENCES

Adorni, G. and M. Zock (eds.). 1996. *Trends in Natural Language Generation: An Artificial Intelligence Perspective.* New York: Springer Verlag.

Andriessen, J., K. de Smedt, and M. Zock. 1996. 'Discourse planning: empirical research and computer models'. In T. Dijkstra and K. de Smedt (eds), *Computational Psycholinguistics: AI and Connectionist Models of Human Language Processing,* London: Taylor and Francis.

Bateman, J. 1997. 'Enabling technology for multilingual natural language generation: the KPML development environment'. *Journal of Natural Language Engineering,* 3(1), 15–55.

——1998. 'Automated discourse generation'. In A. Kent (ed.), *Encyclopedia of Library and Information Science,* New York: Marcel Dekker, Inc.

Bock, K. 1996. 'Language production: methods and methodologies'. *Psychonomic Bulletin and Review,* 3, 395–421.

Cahill, L., C. Doran, R. Evans, C. Mellish, D. Paiva, M. Reape, D. Scott, and N. Tipper. 1999. *Towards a reference architecture for natural language generation systems: the RAGS project.* Technical Report: ITRI-99-14, Brighton.

Cawsey, A. 1991. 'Using plausible inference rules in description planning'. *Proceedings of the 5th Conference of the European Chapter of the ACL* (Berlin), 119–24.

Cole, R., J. Mariani, H. Uszkoreit, G. B. Varile, A. Zaenen, A. Zampolli, and V. Zue. 1997. *Survey of the State of the Art in Human Language Technology.* Cambridge: Cambridge University Press.

Dalianis, H. 1999. 'Aggregation in natural language generation'. *Journal of Computational Intelligence,* 15(4).

Danlos, L. 2000, 'G-TAG: a lexicalized formalism for text generation inspired from tree adjoining grammar: TAG issues'. In A. Abeillé and O. Rambow (eds.), *Tree-Adjoining Grammars,* Stanford, Calif: CSLI, 343–70.

de Smedt, K., H. Horacek, and M. Zock. 1996. 'Some problems with current architectures in Natural Language Generation'. In: Adorni and Zock (1996), 17–46.

Elhadad, M. and J. Robin. 1997. *SURGE: a comprehensive plug-in syntactic realization component for text generation.* Technical Report, Computer Science Dept., Ben-Gurion University, Beer-Shiva, Israel.

Gal, A., G. Lapalme, P. Saint Dizier, and H. Somers. 1991. *PROLOG for Natural Language Processing.* Chichester: J. Wiley and Sons.

Halliday, M. A. K. 1994. *An Introduction to Functional Grammar*, London: Arnold.

Harbusch, K., W. Finkler, and A. Schauder. 1991. 'Incremental syntax generation with tree adjoining grammars'. In W. Brauer and D. Hernandez (eds.), *Verteilte Kuenstliche Intelligenz und kooperatives Arbeiten*, Berlin: Springer, 363–74.

Hovy, E. 1988. 'Planning coherent multisentential text'. *Proceedings of the 26th Annual Meeting of the ACL (ACL '88)* (Buffalo), 179–86.

——1993. 'Automated discourse generation using discourse structure relations'. *Artificial Intelligence*, 63, 341–85.

——1996. 'Language generation'. In Cole et al. (1997), 159–67.

Iordanskaja, L., R. Kittredge, and A. Polguère. 1991. 'Lexical selection and paraphrase in a meaning-text generation model'. In Paris et al. (1991), 293–312.

Kölln, M. 1997. 'Textproduktion als intentionaler, benutzerorientierter Prozess'. St. Augustin: Infix: DISKI, 158.

Levelt, W. 1989. *Speaking: From Intention to Articulation*. Cambridge, Mass.: MIT Press.

McDonald, D. 2000. 'Natural language generation'. In R. Dale, H. Moisl, and H. Somers (eds.), *A Handbook of Natural Language Processing Techniques*. New York: M. Dekker Inc., 147–79.

McKeown, K. 1985. 'Discourse strategies for generating natural-language text'. *Artificial Intelligence*, 27, 1–41.

Mann, W. and C. Matthiessen. 1986. 'Demonstration of the Nigel text generation computer program'. In J. Benson and W. Greaves (eds.), *Systemic Functional Approaches to Discourse*, Norwood, NJ: Ablex Publ. Company.

——and S. A. Thompson. 1987. 'Rhetorical structure theory: description and construction of text structures'. In G. Kempen (ed.), *Natural Language Generation: Recent Advances in Artificial Intelligence, Psychology, and Linguistics*. Dordrecht: Kluwer Academic Publishers, 85–96.

Maybury, M. 1990. *Planning multisentential English text using communicative acts*, Ph.D. thesis, University of Cambridge.

Mel'čuk, I. 1988. *Dependency Syntax: Theory and Practice*. New York: State University of New York Press.

Meteer, M. 1992. *Expressibility and the Problem of Efficient Text Planning*. London: Pinter.

Moore, J. D. and C. L. Paris. 1988. 'Constructing coherent texts using rhetorical relations'. *Proceedings of the 10th Annual Conference of the Cognitive Science Society (COGSCI-88)*, 199–204.

—— ——1993. 'Planning text for advisory dialogues: capturing intentional and rhetorical information'. *Computational Linguistics*, 19(4).

Nogier, J. F., and M. Zock. 1992. 'Lexical choice by pattern matching'. *Knowledge Based Systems*, 5(3), 200–12.

Nicolov, N. 1999. 'Approximate text generation from non-hierarchical representation in a declarative framework'. Ph.D. thesis, University of Edinburgh.

Paiva, D. 1998. *A survey of applied natural language generation systems*. Technical Report ITRI-98-03, Brighton. http://www.itri.brighton.ac.uk/techreports.

Paris, C. L. 1993. *User Modelling in Text Generation*. London: Frances Pinter.

——W. Swartout, and W. Mann (eds.). 1991. *Natural Language Generation in Artificial Intelligence and Computational Linguistics*. Boston: Kluwer Academic Publishers.

Reiter, E. and R. Dale. 2000. *Building Natural Language Generation Systems*. Cambridge: Cambridge University Press.

Sacerdoti, E. 1977. *A Structure for Plans and Behavior*. Amsterdam: North Holland.

Stede, M. 1999. *Lexical Semantics and Knowledge Representation in Multilingual Text Generation*. Dordrecht: Kluwer.

Stone, M. and C. Doran. 1997. 'Sentence planning as description using tree adjoining grammar'. *Proceedings of the 35th Annual Meeting of the Association for Computational Linguistics and the 8th Conference of the European Chapter of the Association for Computational Linguistics (ACL-EACL '97)* (Madrid), 198–205.

Teich, E. 1998. *Systemic Functional Grammar in Natural Language Generation: Linguistic Description and Computational Representation*. London: Cassell Academic Publishers.

Vander Linden, K. 2000. 'Natural language generation'. In D. Jurafsky and J. Martin (eds.), *Speech and Language Processing: An Introduction to Speech Recognition, Computational Linguistics and Natural Language Processing*. New Jersey: Prentice-Hall.

Wanner, M. 1996. 'Lexical choice in text generation and machine translation'. *Machine Translation*, 11(1–3), 3–35.

Zock, M. 1996. 'The power of words in message planning'. *Proceedings of the 16th International Conference on Computational Linguistics* (Copenhagen), 990–5.

——and G. Adorni. 1996. 'Introduction' to Adorni and Zock (1996), 1–16.

SPEECH RECOGNITION

LORI LAMEL

JEAN-LUC GAUVAIN

ABSTRACT

Speech recognition is concerned with converting the speech waveform, an acoustic signal, into a sequence of words. Today's most performant approaches are based on a statistical modellization of the speech signal. This chapter provides an overview of the main topics addressed in speech recognition, that is acoustic-phonetic modelling, lexical representation, language modelling, decoding, and model adaptation. The focus is on methods used in state-of-the-art speaker-independent, large-vocabulary continuous speech recognition (LVCSR). Primary application areas for such technology are dictation, spoken language dialogue, and transcription for information archival and retrieval systems. Some outstanding issues and directions of future research are discussed.

16.1 OVERVIEW

Speech recognition is principally concerned with the problem of transcribing the speech signal as a sequence of words. Today's best performing systems use statistical models (Chapter 19) of speech. From this point of view, speech is assumed to be generated by a **language model** which provides estimates of $Pr(w)$ for all word strings w

independently of the observed signal, and an **acoustic model** encoding the message w in the signal x, which is represented by a probability density function $f(x|w)$. The goal of speech recognition is to find the most likely word sequence given the observed acoustic signal. The speech decoding problem thus consists of maximizing the probability of w given the speech signal x, or equivalently, maximizing the product $Pr(w)$ $f(x|w)$.

The principles on which these systems are based have been known for many years now, and include the application of information theory to speech recognition (Bahl et al. 1976; Jelinek 1976), the use of a spectral representation of the speech signal (Dreyfus-Graf 1949; Dudley and Balashek 1958), the use of dynamic programming for decoding (Vintsyuk 1968), and the use of **context-dependent** acoustic models (Schwartz et al. 1984). Despite the fact that some of these techniques were proposed well over a decade ago, considerable progress has been made in recent years in part due to the availability of large speech and text corpora (Chapter 24), and improved processing power, which have allowed more complex models and algorithms to be

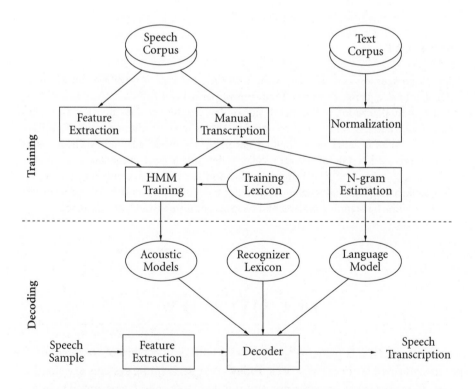

Fig. 16.1 System diagram of a generic speech recognizer based on statistical models, including training and decoding processes, and knowledge sources

implemented. Compared with the state-of-the-art technology a decade ago, advances in acoustic modelling have enabled reasonable performance to be obtained on various data types and acoustic conditions.

The main components of a generic speech recognition system are shown in Fig. 16.1. The elements shown are the main knowledge sources (speech and textual training materials and the pronunciation lexicon), the feature analysis (or parameterization), the acoustic and language models which are estimated in a training phase, and the decoder. The remaining sections of this chapter are devoted to discussing these main components.

16.2 ACOUSTIC PARAMETERIZATION AND MODELLING

Acoustic parameterization is concerned with the choice and optimization of acoustic features in order to reduce model complexity while trying to maintain the linguistic information relevant for speech recognition. Acoustic modelling must take into account different sources of variability present in the speech signal: those arising from the linguistic context and those associated with the non-linguistic context such as the speaker and the acoustic environment (e.g. background noise, music) and recording channel (e.g. direct microphone, telephone). Most state-of-the-art systems make use of **hidden Markov models** (HMM) for acoustic modelling, which consists of modelling the probability density function of a sequence of acoustic feature vectors. In this section common parameterizations are described, followed by a discussion of acoustic model estimation and adaptation.

16.2.1 Acoustic feature analysis

The first step of the acoustic feature analysis is digitization, where the continuous speech signal is converted into discrete samples. The most commonly used sampling rates are 16kHz and 10kHz for direct microphone input, and 8kHz for telephone signals. The next step is feature extraction (also called parameterization or front-end analysis), which has the goal of representing the audio signal in a more compact manner by trying to remove redundancy and reduce variability, while keeping the important linguistic information (Hunt 1996). Most recognition systems use short-time cepstral features based either on a Fourier transform or a linear prediction model.

Cepstral parameters are popular because they are a compact representation, and are less correlated than direct spectral components. This simplifies estimation of the HMM parameters by reducing the need for modelling the feature dependency. An inherent assumption is that although the speech signal is continually changing, due to physical constraints on the rate at which the articulators can move, the signal can be considered quasi-stationary for short periods (on the order of 10ms to 20ms).

The two most popular sets of features are cepstrum coefficients obtained with a Mel Frequency Cepstral (MFC) analysis (Davis and Mermelstein 1980) or with a Perceptual Linear Prediction (PLP) analysis (Hermansky 1990). In both cases a Mel scale short-term power spectrum is estimated on a fixed window (usually in the range of 20 to 30ms). In order to avoid spurious high-frequency components in the spectrum due to discontinuities caused by windowing the signal, it is common to use a tapered window such as a Hamming window. The window is then shifted (usually a third or a half the window size), and the next feature vector computed. The most commonly used offset is 10ms. The Mel scale approximates the frequency resolution of the human auditory system, being linear in the low-frequency range (below 1000 Hz) and logarithmic above 1000 Hz. The cepstral parameters are obtained by taking an inverse transform of the log of the filterbank parameters. In the case of the MFC coefficients, a cosine transform is applied to the log power spectrum, whereas a root-Linear Predictive Coding (LPC) analysis is used to obtain the PLP cepstrum coefficients. Both set of features have been used with success for LVCSR, but a PLP analysis has been found for some systems to be more robust in presence of background noise. The set of cepstral coefficients associated with a windowed portion of the signal is referred to as a **frame** or a **parameter vector**. Cepstral mean removal (subtraction of the mean from all input frames) is commonly used to reduce the dependency on the acoustic recording conditions. Computing the cepstral mean requires that all of the signal is available prior to processing, which is not the case for certain applications where processing needs to be synchronous with recording. In this case, a modified form of cepstral subtraction can be carried out where a running mean is computed from the n last frames (n is often chosen to be about 100, corresponding to 1s of speech). In order to capture the dynamic nature of the speech signal, it is common to augment the feature vector with 'delta' parameters. The delta parameters are computed by taking the first and second differences of the parameters in successive frames.

16.2.2 Acoustic models

Hidden Markov models are widely used to model the sequences of acoustic feature vectors (Rabiner and Juang 1986). These models are popular as they are performant and their parameters can be efficiently estimated using well-established techniques. They are used to model the production of speech feature vectors in two steps. First a Markov chain is used to generate a sequence of states, and second speech vectors are drawn using a probability density function (PDF) associated to each state. The Markov chain is described by the number of states and the transition probabilities between states.

The most widely used elementary acoustic units in LVCSR systems are phone based, where each **phone**[1] is represented by a Markov chain with a small number of states. While different topologies have been proposed, all make use of left-to-right state sequences in order to capture the spectral change across time. The most commonly used configurations have between three and five emitting states per model, where the number of states imposes a minimal time duration for the unit. Some configurations allow certain states to be skipped, so as to reduce the required minimal duration. The probability of an observation (i.e. a speech vector) is assumed to be dependent only on the state, which is known as a first-order Markov assumption.

Strictly speaking, given an n-state HMM with parameter vector λ, the HMM stochastic process is described by the following joint probability density function $f(\mathbf{x}, \mathbf{s} | \lambda)$ of the observed signal $\mathbf{x} = (x_1, \dots, x_T)$ and the unobserved state sequence $\mathbf{s} = (s_0, \dots, s_T)$,

$$(16.1) \quad f(\mathbf{x}, \mathbf{s} | \lambda) = \pi_{s_0} \prod_{t=1}^{T} a_{s_{t-1}, s_t} f(x_t | s_t)$$

where π_i is the initial probability of state i, a_{ij} is the transition probability from state i to state j, and $f(\cdot | s)$ is the emitting PDF associated with each state s. Fig. 16.2 shows a three-state HMM with the associated transition probabilities and observation PDFs.

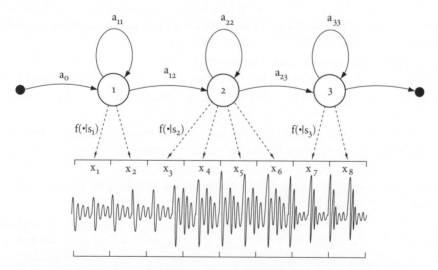

Fig. 16.2 A typical left-to-right 3-state phone HMM with no skip state (top) which generates feature vectors $(x_1 \dots x_n)$ representing speech segments

---

[1] Phones usually correspond to phonemes, but may also correspond to allophones such as flaps or glottal stop.

Phone-based models offer the advantage that recognition lexicons can be described using the elementary units of the given language, and thus benefit from many linguistic studies. It is of course possible to perform speech recognition without using a phonemic lexicon, either by use of 'word models' (as was the more commonly used approach ten years ago) or by a different mapping such as the fenones (Bahl et al. 1988). Compared with larger units (such as words, syllables, demisyllables), small subword units reduce the number of parameters, enable cross-word modelling, facilitate porting to new vocabularies and, most importantly, can be associated with back-off mechanisms to model rare contexts. Fenones offer the additional advantage of automatic training, but lack the ability to include a priori linguistic knowledge.

A given HMM can represent a phone without consideration of its neighbours (context-independent or monophone model) or a phone in a particular context (context-dependent model). The context may or may not include the position of the phone within the word (word-position dependent), and word-internal and cross-word contexts may be merged or considered as separate models. The use of cross-word contexts complicates decoding (see section 16.5). Different approaches are used to select the contextual units based on frequency or using clustering techniques or decision trees; and different context types have been investigated: single-phone contexts, triphones, generalized triphones, quadphones, and quinphones, with and without position dependency (within or cross-word). The model states are often clustered so as to reduce the model size, resulting in what are referred to as 'tied-state' models.

Acoustic model training consists of estimating the parameters of each HMM. For continuous density Gaussian mixture HMMs, this requires estimating the means and covariance matrices, the mixture weights, and the transition probabilities. The most popular approaches make use of the maximum likelihood criterion, ensuring the best match between the model and the training data (assuming that the size of the training data is sufficient to provide robust estimates).

Estimation of the model parameters is usually done with the expectation-maximization (EM) algorithm (Dempster, Laird, and Rubin 1977), which is an iterative procedure starting with an initial set of model parameters. The model states are then aligned to the training data sequences and the parameters are re-estimated based on this new alignment using the Baum–Welch re-estimation formulas (Baum et al. 1970; Liporace 1982; Juang 1985). This algorithm guarantees that the likelihood of the training data given the models increases at each iteration. In the alignment step a given speech frame can be assigned to multiple states (with probabilities summing to 1) using the forward-backward algorithm or to a single state (with probability 1) using the Viterbi algorithm (see Chapter 19). This second approach yields slightly lower likelihoods but in practice there is very little difference in accuracy especially when large amounts of data are available. It is important to note that the EM algorithm does not guarantee finding the true maximum likelihood parameter values, and even when the true maximum likelihood estimates are obtained they may not be the best ones for speech recognition. Therefore, some implementation details such as a proper initialization procedure and the use of constraints on the parameter values can be quite important.

Since the goal of training is to find the best model to account for the observed data, the performance of the recognizer is critically dependent upon the representativity of the training data. Some methods to reduce this dependency are discussed in the next subsection. Speaker independence is obtained by estimating the parameters of the acoustic models on large speech corpora containing data from a large speaker population. There are substantial differences in speech from male and female talkers arising from anatomical differences (on average females have a shorter vocal tract length resulting in higher formant frequencies, as well as a higher fundamental frequency) and social ones (female voice is often 'breathier' caused by incomplete closure of the vocal folds). It is thus common practice to use separate models for male and female speech in order to improve recognition performance, which in turn requires automatic identification of the gender.

16.2.3 Adaptation

In this section we discuss techniques that have been used with continuous density HMMs, although similar techniques have been developed for discrete and semi-continuous HMMs.

The performances of speech recognizers drop substantially when there is a mismatch between training and testing conditions. Several approaches can be used to minimize the effects of such a mismatch, so as to obtain a recognition accuracy as close as possible to that obtained under matched conditions. Acoustic model adaptation can be used to compensate mismatches between the training and testing conditions, such as those due to differences in acoustic environment, to microphones and transmission channels, or to particular speaker characteristics. The techniques are commonly referred to as noise compensation, channel adaptation, and speaker adaptation respectively. Since in general no prior knowledge of either the channel type, the background noise characteristics, or the speaker is available, adaptation is performed using only the test data in an unsupervised mode.

The same tools can be used in acoustic model training in order to compensate for sparse data, as in many cases only limited representative data are available. The basic idea is to use a small amount of representative data to adapt models trained on other large sources of data. Some typical uses are to build gender-dependent, speaker-specific, or task-specific models, or to use speaker adaptive training (SAT) to improve performance. When used for model adaption during training it is common to use the true transcription of the data, known as supervised adaptation.

Three commonly used schemes to adapt the parameters of an HMM can be distinguished: Bayesian adaptation (Gauvain and Lee 1994); adaptation based on linear transformations (Leggetter and Woodland 1995); and model composition techniques (Gales and Young 1995). Bayesian estimation can be seen as a way to incorporate prior knowledge into the training procedure by adding probabilistic constraints on the model parameters. The HMM parameters are still estimated with the EM algorithm but using maximum a posteriori (MAP) re-estimation formulas (Gauvain and Lee 1994). This leads to the so-called MAP adaptation technique where constraints on the HMM parameters are estimated based on parameters of an existing model. Speaker-independent acoustic models can serve as seed models for gender adaptation using the gender specific data. MAP adaptation can be used to adapt to any desired condition for which sufficient labelled training data are available. Linear transforms are powerful tools to perform unsupervised speaker and environmental adaptation. Usually these transformations are maximum likelihood trained and are applied to the HMM Gaussian means, but can also be applied to the Gaussian variance parameters. The maximum likelihood linear regression (MLLR) technique is very appropriate for unsupervised adaptation because the number of adaptation parameters can be very small. MLLR adaptation can be applied to both the test data and training data. Model composition is mostly used to compensate for additive noise by explicitly modelling the background noise (usually with a single Gaussian) and combining this model with the clean speech model. This approach has the advantage of directly modelling the noisy channel as opposed to the blind adaptation performed by the MLLR technique when applied to the same problem.

The chosen adaptation method depends on the type of mismatch and on the amount of available adaptation data. The adaptation data may be part of the training data, as in adaptation of acoustic seed models to a new corpus or a subset of the training material (gender, dialect, speaker, or acoustic condition specific), or can be the test data (i.e. the data to be transcribed). In the former case supervised adaptation techniques can be applied, as the reference transcription of the adaptation data may be readily available. In the latter case only unsupervised adaptation techniques can be applied.

16.3 Lexical and Pronunciation Modelling

The **lexicon** is the link between the acoustic-level representation and the word-sequence output by the speech recognizer. Lexical design entails two main parts: definition and selection of the vocabulary items and representation of each pronunciation entry using the basic acoustic units of the recognizer. Recognition performance is obviously related to lexical coverage, and the accuracy of the acoustic models is linked to the consistency of the pronunciations associated with each lexical entry.

The recognition vocabulary is usually selected to maximize lexical coverage for a given size lexicon. Since, on average, each out-of-vocabulary (OOV) word causes more than a single error (usually between 1.5 and 2 errors), it is important to judiciously select the recognition vocabulary. Word-list selection is discussed in section 16.4. Associated with each lexical entry are one or more pronunciations, described using the chosen elementary units (usually phonemes or phone-like units). This set of units is evidently language dependent. For example, some commonly used phone-set sizes are about 45 for English, 49 for German, 35 for French, and 26 for Spanish. In generating pronunciation base forms, most lexicons include standard pronunciations and do not explicitly represent **allophones**. This representation is chosen as most allophonic variants can be predicted by rules, and their use is optional. More importantly, there often is a continuum between different allophones of a given phoneme and the decision as to which occurred in any given utterance is subjective. By using a phonemic representation, no hard decision is imposed, and it is left to the acoustic models to represent the observed variants in the training data. While pronunciation lexicons are usually (at least partially) created manually, several approaches to learning and generating word pronunciations automatically have been investigated (Cohen 1989; Riley and Ljojle 1996).

There are a variety of words for which frequent alternative pronunciation variants are observed, and these variants are not due to allophonic differences such as the suffix *-ization* which can be pronounced with a diphthong (/ɑⁱ/) or a schwa (/ə/). Alternative pronunciations are also needed for homographs (words spelled the same, but pronounced differently) which reflect different parts of speech (verb or noun) such as *excuse, record, produce*. Some common three-syllable words such as *interest* and *company* are often pronounced with only two syllables. Fig. 16.3 shows two examples of the word *interest* by different speakers reading the same text prompt: '*In reaction to the news, interest rates plunged . . .*' The pronunciations are those chosen by the recognizer during segmentation using forced alignment. In the example on the left, the /t/ is deleted, and the /n/ is produced as a nasal flap. In the example on the right, the speaker pronounced the word with two syllables, without the optional vowel and producing a /tr/ cluster. Segmenting the training data without pronunciation variants is illustrated in the middle. Whereas no /t/ was observed in the first pronunciation example two /t/ segments had been aligned. An optimal alignment with a pronunciation dictionary including all required variants is shown on the bottom. Better alignment results in more accurate acoustic phone models. Careful lexical design improves speech recognition performance.

In speech from fast speakers or speakers with relaxed speaking styles it is common to observe poorly articulated (or skipped) unstressed syllables, particularly in long words with sequences of unstressed syllables. Although such long words are typically well recognized, often a nearby function word is deleted. To reduce these kinds of

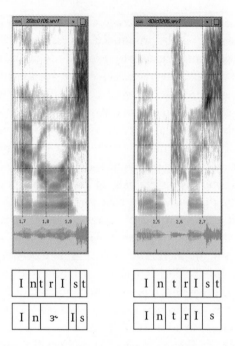

Fig. 16.3 Spectrograms of the word *interest* with pronunciation variants: /ɪnɜˈɪs/ (left) and /ɪntrɪs/ (right) taken from the WSJ corpus (sentences *20tc0106, 40lc0206*). The grid is *100ms* by *1kHz*. Segmentation of these utterances with a single pronunciation of *interest* /ɪntrɪst/ (middle) and with multiple variants /ɪntrɪst/ /ɪntrɪs/ /ɪnɜˈɪs/ (bottom).

errors, alternative pronunciations for long words such as *positioning* (/pəzɪʃənɪŋ/ or /pəzɪʃnɪŋ/) can be included in the lexicon allowing schwa deletion or syllabic consonants in unstressed syllables. Compound words have also been used as a way to represent reduced forms for common word sequences such as 'did you' pronounced as 'dija' or 'going to' pronounced as 'gonna'. Alternatively, such fluent speech effects can be modelled using phonological rules (Oshika et al. 1975). The principle behind the phonological rules is to modify the allowable phone sequences to take into account such variations. These rules are optionally applied during training and recognition. Using phonological rules during training results in better acoustic models, as they are less 'polluted' by wrong transcriptions. Their use during recognition reduces the number of mismatches. The same mechanism has been used to handle liaisons, *mute e*, and final consonant cluster reduction for French.

As speech recognition research has moved from read speech to spontaneous and conversational speech styles, the phone set has been expanded to include non-speech events. These can correspond to noises produced by the speaker (breath noise, coughing, sneezing, laughter, etc.) or can correspond to external sources (music, motor, tapping, etc).

16.4 Language Modelling

Language models (LMs) are used in speech recognition to estimate the probability of word sequences. Grammatical constraints can be described using a context-free grammars (for small to medium-size vocabulary tasks these are usually manually elaborated) or can be modelled stochastically, as is common for LVCSR. The most popular statistical methods are n-gram models, which attempt to capture the syntactic and semantic constraints by estimating the frequencies of sequences of n words (see also Chapter 19). The assumption is made that the probability of a given word string $(w_1, w_2, \ldots, w_k)$ can be approximated by $\Pi_{i=1}^{k} Pr(w_i | w_{i-n+1}, \ldots, w_{i-2}, w_{i-1})$, thereby reducing the word history to the preceding n–1 words. A **back-off** mechanism is generally used to smooth the estimates of the probabilities of rare n-grams by relying on a lower order n-gram when there are insufficient training data, and to provide a means of modelling unobserved word sequences (Katz 1987). While trigram LMs are the most widely used, higher-order (n>3) and word-class-based (counts are based on sets of words rather than individual lexical items) n-grams, and adapted LMs, are recent research areas aimed at improving LM accuracy.

Given a large text corpus it may seem relatively straightforward to construct n-gram language models. Most of the steps are pretty standard and make use of tools that count word and word sequence occurrences. The main differences arise in the choice of the vocabulary and in the definition of words, such as the treatment of compound words or acronyms, and the choice of the back-off strategy. There is, however, a significant amount of effort needed to process the texts before they can be used.

A common motivation for text normalization in all languages is to reduce lexical variability so as to increase the coverage for a fixed-size task vocabulary. Normalization decisions are generally language specific. Much of speech recognition research for American English has been supported by ARPA and has been based on text materials which were processed to remove upper/lower-case distinction and compounds. Thus, for instance, no lexical distinction is made between *Gates, gates* or *Green, green*. In the French *Le Monde* corpus, capitalization of proper names is distinctive, with different lexical entries for *Pierre, pierre* or *Roman, roman*.

The main conditioning steps are text mark-up and conversion. Text mark-up consists of tagging the texts (article, paragraph, and sentence markers) and garbage bracketing (which includes not only corrupted text materials, but all text material unsuitable for sentence-based language modelling, such as tables and lists). Numerical expressions are typically expanded to approximate the spoken form (*$150 → one hundred and fifty dollars*). Further semi-automatic processing is necessary to correct frequent errors inherent in the texts (such as obvious mispellings *milllion, officals*) or arising from processing with the distributed text processing tools. Some normalizations can be considered as 'decompounding' rules in that they modify the word boundaries and the total number of words. These concern the processing of ambiguous punctuation markers (such as hyphen and apostrophe), the processing of digit strings, and treatment of abbreviations and acronyms ($ABCD \rightarrow A. B. C. D.$). Another example is the treatment of numbers in German, where decompounding can be used in order to increase lexical coverage. The date 1991, which in standard German is written as *neunzehnhunderteinundneunzig*, can be represented by word sequence *neunzehn hundert ein und neunzig*. Other normalizations (such as sentence-initial capitalization and case distinction) keep the total number of words unchanged, but reduce graphemic variability. In general the choice is a compromise between producing an output close to the correct standard written form of the language and the lexical coverage, with the final choice of normalization being largely application driven.

Better language models can be obtained using texts transformed to be closer to observed reading styles, where the transformation rules and corresponding probabilities can be automatically derived by aligning prompt texts with the transcriptions of the acoustic data. For example, the word *hundred* followed by a number can be replaced by *hundred and* 50 per cent of the time; 50 per cent of the occurences of *one eighth* can be replaced by *an eighth*, and 15 per cent of *million dollars* are replaced with simply *million*.

In practice, the selection of words is done so as to minimize the system's OOV rate by including the most useful words. By useful we mean that the words are expected as an input to the recognizer, but also that the LM can be trained given the available text corpora. In order to meet the latter condition, it is common to choose the n most frequent words in the training data. This criterion does not, however, guarantee the usefulness of the lexicon, since no consideration of the expected input is made. Therefore it is common practice to use a set of additional development data to select a word list adapted to the expected test conditions.

There are the sometimes conflicting needs for sufficient amounts of text data to estimate LM parameters, and for ensuring that the data are representative of the task. It is also common that different types of LM training material are available in differing quantities. One easy way to combine training material from different sources is to train a language model per source and to interpolate them. The interpolation weights can be directly estimated on some development data with the EM algorithm. An alternative is to simply merge the n-gram counts and train a single language model on these counts. If some data sources are more representative than others for the task, the n-gram counts can be empirically weighted to minimize the perplexity on a set of development data. While this can be effective, it has to be done by trial and error and cannot easily be optimized. In addition, weighting the n-gram counts can pose problems in properly estimating the back-off coefficients.

The relevance of a language model is usually measured in terms of test-set perplexity defined as $Px = Pr(\text{text}|\text{LM})^{-\frac{1}{n}}$, where n is the number of words in the text. The perplexity is a measure of the average branching factor, i.e. the vocabulary size of a memoryless uniform language model with the same entropy as the language model under consideration.

16.5 DECODING

In this section we discuss the LVCSR decoding problem, which is the design of an efficient search algorithm to deal with the huge search space obtained by combining the acoustic and language models (Young and Bloothooft 1997; Aubert 2002). Strictly speaking, the aim of the decoder is to determine the word sequence with the highest likelihood given the lexicon and the acoustic and language models. In practice, however, it is common to search for the most likely HMM state sequence, i.e. the best path through a trellis (the search space) where each node associates an HMM state with given time. Since it is often prohibitive to exhaustively search for the best path, techniques have been developed to reduce the computational load by limiting the search to a small part of the search space. Even for research purposes, where real-time recognition is not needed, there is a limit on computing resources (memory and CPU time) above which the development process becomes too costly. The most commonly used approach for small and medium vocabulary sizes is the one-pass frame-synchronous Viterbi beam search which uses a dynamic programming algorithm. This basic strategy has been extended to deal with large vocabularies by adding features such as dynamic decoding, multi-pass search, and n-best rescoring.

Dynamic decoding can be combined with efficient pruning techniques in order to obtain a single-pass decoder that can provide the answer using all the available information (i.e. that in the models) in a single forward decoding pass over the speech signal. This kind of decoder is very attractive for real-time applications. Multi-pass decoding is used to progressively add knowledge sources in the decoding process and allows the complexity of the individual decoding passes to be reduced. For example, a first decoding pass can use a two-gram language model and simple acoustic models, and later passes can make use of three-gram and four-gram language models with more complex acoustic models. This multiple pass paradigm requires a proper interface between passes in order to avoid losing information and engendering search errors. Information is usually transmitted via word graphs, although some systems use n-best hypotheses (a list of the most likely word sequences with their respective scores). This approach is not well suited to real-time applications since no hypothesis can be returned until the entire utterance has been processed.

It can sometimes be difficult to add certain knowledge sources into the decoding process especially when they do not fit in the Markovian framework (i.e. short-distance dependency modelling). For example, this is the case when trying to use segmental information or to use grammatical information for long-term agreement. Such information can be more easily integrated in multi-pass systems by rescoring the recognizer hypotheses after applying the additional knowledge sources.

16.6 STATE-OF-THE-ART PERFORMANCE

The last decade has seen large performance improvements in speech recognition, particularly for large-vocabulary, speaker-independent, continuous speech. This progress has been substantially aided by the availability of large speech and text corpora and by significant increases in computer processing capabilities which have facilitated the implementation of more complex models and algorithms.[2] In this section we provide some illustrative results for different LVCSR tasks, but make no attempt to be exhaustive.

The commonly used metric for speech recognition performance is the 'word-error' rate (Chapter 22), which is a measure of the average number of errors taking into account three error types with respect to a reference transcription: *substitutions* (one word is replaced by another word), *insertions* (a word is hypothesized that was not in the reference) and *deletions* (a word is missed). The word-error rate is defined as $\frac{\#subs+\#ins+\#del}{\#reference\ words}$, and is typically computed after a dynamic programming alignment of the reference and hypothesized transcriptions. Note that given this definition the word error can be more than 100 per cent.

Three types of tasks can be considered: small vocabulary tasks, such as isolated command words, digits or digit strings; medium-size (1,000–3,000 words) vocabulary tasks such as are typically found in spoken dialogue systems (Chapter 35); and large-vocabulary tasks (typically 65k words). Another dimension is the speaking style, which can be read, prepared, spontaneous, or conversational. Very low error rates have been reported for small vocabulary tasks, below 1 per cent for digit strings, which has led to some commercial products, most notably in the telecommunications domain. For read speech tasks, the state of the art in speaker-independent continuous speech recognition in 1992 is exemplified by the Resource Management task (1,000 word vocabulary, word-pair grammar, 4 hours acoustic training data) with a word-error rate of 3 per cent. In 1995, on read newspaper texts (the *Wall Street Journal* task, 160 hours acoustic training data and 400 M words of language model texts) word-error rates around 8 per cent were obtained using a 65k word vocabulary. The word error with comparable systems was about 13 per cent for speech in the presence of noise, and 14 per cent on texts dictated by journalists. Progress is demonstrated by the presence of several commercial speaker-dependent continuous speech dictation systems for which comparable benchmarks are not publicly available. Substantially

---

[2] These advances can be clearly seen in the context of DARPA-supported benchmark evaluations. This framework, known in the community as the DARPA evaluation paradigm, has provided the training materials (transcribed audio and textual corpora for training acoustic and language models), test data, and a common evaluation framework. In recent years the data have been provided by the Linguistics Data Consortium (LDC) and the evaluations organized by the National Institute of Standards and Technology (NIST) in collaboration with representatives from the participating sites and other government agencies.

higher word-error rates, above 30–40 per cent, have been reported for the transcription of telephone conversational speech using the Switchboard and multilingual Callhome (Spanish, Arabic, Mandarin, Japanese, German) corpora. While most of the results given here are for American English, somewhat comparable results have been reported by various sites for British English and other languages including French and German.

A wide range of word-error rates have been reported for the speech recognition components of spoken dialogue systems (Chapters 7 and 35), ranging from under 5 per cent for simple travel information tasks using close-talking microphones to over 25 per cent for telephone-based information retrieval systems. It is quite difficult to compare results across systems and tasks as different as transcription conventions and text normalizations are often used.

Over the last few years there has been increasing interest in the transcription of radio and television broadcasts, often referred to as 'found speech'. This is a major step for the community in that the test data are taken from a real task, as opposed to consisting of data recorded for evaluation purposes. The transcription of such broadcasts presents new challenges as the signal is one continuous audio stream that contains segments of different acoustic and linguistic natures. Systems trained on 150 hours of acoustic data and 200 M words of commercial transcripts achieve word-error rates around 20 per cent on unrestricted broadcast news data. The peformance on studio-quality speech from announcers is comparable to that obtained on *WSJ* read speech data.

16.7 DISCUSSION AND PERSPECTIVES

Despite the numerous advances made over the last decade, speech recognition is far from a solved problem. Much of the recent progress in LVCSR has been fostered by the availability of large corpora for training and testing speech recognition and understanding technology. However, constructing corpora that are representative, complete, and yet at the same time not too big remains an open research area in spite of our collective experience. Recent efforts have been directed at developing generic recognition models and the use of unannotated data for training purposes, in order to reduce the reliance on manually annotated training corpora.

It has often been observed that there is a large difference in recognition performance for the same system between the best and worst speakers. Unsupervised adaption techniques do not necessarily reduce this difference, in fact, often they improve performance on good speakers more than on bad ones. Interspeaker differences are not only at the acoustic level, but also the phonological and word levels. Today's modelling techniques are not able to take into account speaker-specific lexical and phonological choices.

A wide range of potential applications can be envisioned based on transcriptions of broadcast data, particularly in light of the recent explosion of such media, which require automated processing for indexation and retrieval (Chapters 29, 30, and 32). Related spoken language technologies, such as speaker and language identification, which rely on the same modelling techniques, are clearly of interest for automated processing of large multilingual corpora. Important future research will address keeping vocabulary up to date, language model adaptation, automatic topic detection and labelling, and enriched transcriptions providing annotations for speaker turns, language, acoustic conditions, etc.

FURTHER READING AND RELEVANT RESOURCES

An excellent reference is *Corpus Based Methods in Language and Speech Processing*, edited by Young and Bloothooft (1997). This book provides an overview of currently used statistically based techniques, their basic principles and problems. A theoretical presentation of the fundamentals of the subject is given in the book *Statistical Methods for Speech Recognition* by Jelinek (1998). A general introductory tutorial on HMMs can be found in Rabiner and Juang (1986). For general speech processing reference, the classic book *Digital Processing of Speech Signals* (Rabiner and Schafer) remains relevant. A comprehensive discussion on signal representation can be found in chapter 1.3 of the *Survey of the State of the Art in Human Language Technology* (Cole et al. 1997; see also the website below). The most recent work in speech recognition can be found in the proceedings of major conferences (IEEE ICASSP, Eurospeech, and ICSLP) and workshops (most notably DARPA, ISCA ITRWs, IEEE ASRU), as well as the journals *Speech Communication* and *Computer Speech and Language*. In the latter journal a special issue in October 1998 was devoted to 'Evaluation in Language and Speech Technology'. A special issue on Spoken Language Processing was recently published in the Proceedings of the IEEE, August 2000.

Several websites of interest are:

- European Language Resources Association: http://www.icp.inpg.fr/ELRA/home.html.
- European Speech Communication Association: http://www.isca-speech.org.
- Linguistic Data Consortium: http://www.ldc.upenn.edu/.
- NIST Spoken Natural Language Processing: http://www.itl.nist.gov/div894/894.01.
- Survey of the State of the Art in Human Language Technology: http://cslu.cse.ogi.edu/HLTsurvey/HLTsurvey.html.

REFERENCES

Aubert, X. L. 2002. 'An overview of decoding techniques for large vocabulary continuous speech recognition'. *Computer, Speech and Language*, 16(1), 89–114.

Bahl, L. R., J. K. Baker, P. S. Cohen, N. R. Dixon, F. Jelinek, R. L. Mercer, and H. F. Silverman. 1976. 'Preliminary results on the performance of a system for the automatic recognition of continuous speech'. *Proceedings of the IEEE Conference on Acoustics Speech and Signal Processing (ICASSP-76)* (Philadelphia), 425–9.

——P. Brown, P. de Souza, R. L. Mercer, and M. Picheny. 1988. 'Acoustic Markov models used in the Tangora speech recognition system'. *Proceedings of the IEEE Conference on Acoustics Speech and Signal Processing (ICASSP '88)* (New York), i. 497–500.

Baum, L. E., T. Petrie, G. Soules, and N. Weiss. 1970. 'A maximization technique occurring in the statistical analysis of probabilistic functions of Markov chains'. *Annals of Mathematical Statistics*, 41, 164–71.

Cohen, M. 1989. *Phonological structures for speech recognition*. Ph.D. thesis, University of California, Berkeley.

Cole, R., J. Mariani, H. Uszkoreit, G. B. Varile, A. Zaenen, and V. Zue (eds.). 1997. *Survey of the State of the Art in Human Language Technology*. Cambridge: Cambridge University Press.

Davis, S. and P. Mermelstein. 1980. 'Comparison of parametric representations of monosyllabic word recognition in continuously spoken sentences'. *IEEE Transactions on Acoustics, Speech, and Signal Processing*, 28(4), 357–66.

Dempster, A. P., M. M. Laird, and D. B. Rubin. 1977. 'Maximum likelihood from incomplete data via the EM algorithm'. *Journal of the Royal Statistical Society Series B (methodological)*, 39, 1–38.

Dreyfus-Graf, J. 1949. 'Sonograph and sound mechanics'. *Journal of the Acoustic Society of America*, 22, 731.

Dudley, H. and S. Balashek. 1958. 'Automatic recognition of phonetic patterns in speech'. *Journal of the Acoustic Society of America*, 30, 721.

Gales, M. and S. Young. 1995. 'Robust speech recognition in additive and convolutional noise using parallel model combination'. *Computer Speech and Language*, 9(4), 289–307.

Gauvain, J. L. and C. H. Lee. 1994. 'Maximum *a posteriori* estimation for multivariate Gaussian mixture observations of Markov chains'. *IEEE Transactions on Speech and Audio Processing*, 2(2), 291–8.

Hermansky, H. 1990. 'Perceptual linear predictive (PLP) analysis of speech'. *Journal of the Acoustic Society of America*, 87(4), 1738–52.

Hunt, M. J. 1996. 'Signal representation'. In Cole et al. (eds.), *Survey of the State of the Art in Human Language Technology*, Cambridge: Cambridge University Press, 10–15. http://www.cse.ogi.edu/CSLU/HLTsurvey/ch1node2.html.

Jelinek, F. 1976. 'Continuous speech recognition by statistical methods'. *Proceedings of the IEEE*, 64(4), 532–56.

——1998. *Statistical Methods for Speech Recognition*. Cambridge, Mass.: MIT Press.

Juang, B.-H. 1985. 'Maximum-likelihood estimation for mixture multivariate stochastic observations of Markov chains', *AT&T Technical Journal*, 64(6), 1235–49.

Katz, S. M. 1987. 'Estimation of probabilities from sparse data for the language model component of a speech recognizer'. *IEEE Transactions on Acoustics, Speech, and Signal Processing*, 35(3), 400–1.

Leggetter, C. J. and P. C. Woodland. 1995. 'Maximum likelihood linear regression for speaker adaptation of continuous density hidden Markov models'. *Computer Speech and Language*, 9, 171–85.

Liporace, L. R. 1982. 'Maximum likelihood estimation for multivariate observations of Markov sources'. *IEEE Transactions on Information Theory*, 28(5), 729–34.

Oshika, B. T., V. W. Zue, R. V. Weeks, H. Neu, and J. Aurbach. 1975. 'The role of phonological rules in speech understanding research'. *IEEE Transactions on Acoustics, Speech, Signal Processing*, 23, 104–12.

Rabiner, L. R. 1989. 'A tutorial on hidden Markov models and selected applications in speech recognition. *Proceedings of the IEEE*, 77(2), 257–86.

——and B. H. Juang. 1986. 'An introduction to hidden Markov models'. *IEEE Acoustics Speech and Signal Processing ASSP Magazine*, 3(1), 4–16.

——and R. W. Schafer. 1978. *Digital Processing of Speech Signals*. Englewood Cliffs, NJ: Prentice-Hall.

Riley, M. D. and A. Ljojle. 1996. 'Automatic generation of detailed pronunciation lexicons'. In R. Dixon and T. Martin (eds.), *Automatic Speech and Speaker Recognition*, Dordrecht: Kluwer Academic.

Schwartz, R., Y. Chow, S. Roucos, M. Krasner, and J. Makhoul. 1984. 'Improved hidden Markov modelling of phonemes for continuous speech recognition'. *Proceedings of the IEEE International Conference on Acoustics Speech and Signal Processing (ICASSP '84)* (San Diego), iii, 35.6.1–35.6.4.

Vintsyuk, T. K. 1968. 'Speech discrimination by dynamic programming'. *Kibnernetika*, 4, 81.

Young, S. J. and G. Bloothooft (eds.). 1997. *Corpus-Based Methods in Language and Speech Processing*. Dordrecht: Kluwer Academic Publishers.

TEXT-TO-SPEECH SYNTHESIS

THIERRY DUTOIT
YANNIS STYLIANOU

ABSTRACT

This chapter gives an introduction to state-of-the-art text-to-speech (TTS) synthesis systems, showing both the natural language processing and (although with fewer details) the digital signal processing problems involved.

Section 17.1 gives a brief user-oriented description of a general TTS system and comments on its commercial applications. Section 17.2 gives a fairly general functional diagram of a modern TTS system and introduces its components. Section 17.3 briefly describes its morphosyntactic module. Section 17.4 examines why sentence-level phonetization cannot be achieved by a sequence of dictionary look-ups, and describes possible implementations of the phonetizer. Section 17.5 is devoted to prosody generation. It briefly outlines how intonation and duration can approximately be computed from text. Section 17.6 gives a conceptual introduction to the two main existing categories of techniques for waveform generation: (1) synthesis by rule and (2) concatenative synthesis.

17.1 INTRODUCTION

Text-to-speech (TTS) **synthesis** is the art of designing talking machines.

Speech sounds are inherently governed by the partial differential equations of fluid mechanics, applied in a dynamic case since our lung pressure, glottis tension, and vocal tract configuration evolve with time. These are controlled by our cortex, which takes advantage of the power of its parallel structure to extract the essence of the text read: its meaning. Even though, in the current state of the art, building a **text-to-speech synthesizer** on such intricate models is scientifically conceivable (intensive research on articulatory synthesis, neural networks, and semantic analysis provides evidence for it), it would result anyway in a machine with a very high degree of (possibly avoidable) complexity, which is not always compatible with economical criteria. After all, flies do not flap their wings!

On the other hand, producing speech automatically is not merely reduced to the playback of a sequence of prerecorded words: even though we write and think in terms of isolated words, we produce *continuous* speech, as a result of the coordinated and continuous action of a number of muscles. These articulatory movements are not produced independently of each other; they are frequently altered in a given context to minimize the effort needed to produce a sequence of articulatory movements. This effect is known as **coarticulation**. Coarticulatory phenomena are due to the fact that each articulator moves continuously from the realization of one phoneme to the next. They appear even in the most careful speech. In fact, they *are* speech. Thus, producing natural-sounding speech requires the ability to produce continuous, coarticulated speech.

There are numerous potential applications of TTS synthesis. Many of them are examined in Part III of this volume:

- TTS systems can play an important part in telecommunication services, by making it possible for users to access textual information over the telephone. Texts may range from simple messages, such as local cultural events not to be missed (cinemas, theatres, etc.), to emails, faxes, or information obtained from querying large databases. Queries to such information retrieval systems (see Chapter 29) can be put through the user's voice (with the help of a speech recognizer), or through the telephone keyboard (with touch-tone telephones). See Levinson, Olive, and Tschirgi (1993) for more details on these applications.
- TTS systems provide an invaluable aid to handicapped persons. With the help of an especially designed keyboard and a fast sentence-assembling program, synthetic speech can be produced in a few seconds by people with speech disorders. Blind people also widely benefit from TTS systems, which give them access to written information.
- TTS synthesis can also be helpful for language learning (see Chapter 37), provided the naturalness of the synthetic speech is sufficient. TTS has a part to play

in the design of attractive and educative *talking toys*.

- Because oral information is more efficient than written messages, TTS synthesis can advantageously be incorporated into measurement or control systems (as in cars or planes, for quickly drawing the attention of people to urgent problems). It also has its part to play in the use of portable electronics consumer products, such as mobile phones, palmtops, etc.

- In the long run, the development of high quality TTS systems is a necessary step (as is the improvement of speech recognizers) towards straightforward means of communication between man and machine (see chapters on natural language interfaces in part III, particularly Chapter 35 and Chapter 36) or between people speaking different languages (speech-to-speech translation, which requires speech recognition, translation, and speech synthesis: see Chapters 27, 28, and 38).

- Last but not least, TTS systems are helpful for pursuing fundamental and applied research on speech. As a matter of fact, TTS synthesizers possess a very interesting feature which makes them wonderful laboratory tools: they are completely under control, so that repeated experiments provide identical results (as is hardly the case with human beings).

17.2 TTS DESIGN

Fig. 17.1 introduces the functional diagram of a fairly general TTS synthesizer. It consists of a natural language processing module (NLP), capable of producing a phonetic transcription of the text read, together with the desired intonation and rhythm (often termed prosody), and a digital signal processing module (DSP), which transforms the symbolic information it receives into speech.

A preprocessing (or *text normalization*) module is necessary as a front end, since TTS systems should in principle be able to read any text, including numbers, abbreviations, acronyms, and idiomatics, in any format.[1] The preprocessor also performs the apparently trivial (but actually intricate) task of finding the end of sentences in the input text. It organizes the input sentences into manageable lists of word-like units and stores them in the internal data structure.[2]

[1] Although a preprocessor is absolutely necessary for real applications of TTS synthesis, we will not examine it here, due to a lack of space and given the limited scientific interest it conveys. More information can be found in Dutoit (1997: section 4.1) or Sproat (1998: chapter 3).

[2] In modern TTS systems, all modules exchange information via some *internal data structure* (most often, a multi-level data structure, in which several parallel descriptions of a sentence are stored with cross-level links; sometimes feature structures as used in unification grammars). More on this can be found in Dutoit (1997: chapter 3).

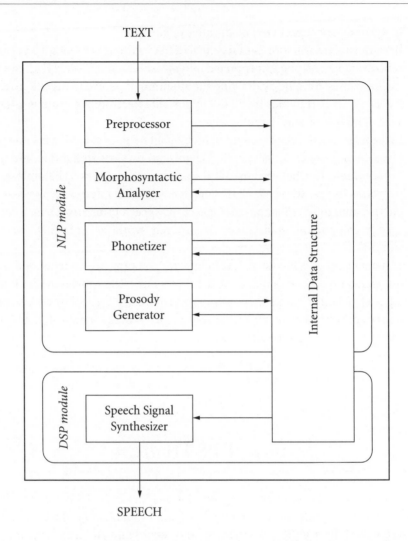

Fig. 17.1 The functional diagram of a fairly general text-to-speech conversion system

The NLP module includes a morphosyntactic analyser (section 17.3), which takes care of part-of-speech tagging and organizes the input sentence into syntactically related groups of words.

A phonetizer (section 17.4) and a prosody generator (section 17.5) provide the sequence of phonemes to be pronounced as well as their duration and intonation.

Once phonemes and prosody have been computed, the speech signal synthesizer (section 17.6) is in charge of producing speech samples which, when played via a digital-to-analogue converter, will hopefully be understood and, if possible, mistaken for real, human speech.

17.3 Morphosyntactic Analysis

Modern TTS systems cannot spare some form of morphosyntactic analysis, which is generally composed of:

- A morphological analysis module (see Chapter 2), the task of which is to propose all possible part-of-speech categories for each word taken individually, on the basis of its spelling. Inflected, derived, and compound words are decomposed into morphs by simple regular grammars exploiting lexicons of stems and affixes.
- A contextual analysis module considering words in their context, which allows the reduction of the list of possible part-of-speech categories for each word to a very restricted number of highly probable hypotheses, given the corresponding possible parts-of-speech of neighbouring words (see Chapter 11).
- Finally, a syntactic-prosodic parser, which finds the hierarchical organization of words into clause- and phrase-like constituents that more closely relates to its expected intonational structure (see section 17.5.1 for more details).

17.4 Automatic Phonetization

The phonetization (or *letter-to-sound*, LTS) module is responsible for the automatic determination of the phonetic transcription of the incoming text. At first sight, this task seems as simple as performing the equivalent of a sequence of dictionary look-ups. From a deeper examination, however, one quickly realizes that most words appear in genuine speech with several phonetic transcriptions, many of which are not even mentioned in pronunciation dictionaries. Namely:

1. Pronunciation dictionaries refer to word roots only. They do not explicitly account for morphological variations (i.e. plural, feminine, conjugations, especially for highly inflected languages, such as French), which therefore have to be dealt with by a specific component of phonology, called *morphophonology* (see Chapter 1).
2. Some words actually correspond to several entries in the dictionary, or more generally to several morphological decompositions, generally with different pronunciations. This is typically the case of heterophonic homographs, i.e. words that are pronounced differently even though they have the same spelling, as for *record* (/rekɔːd/ or /rɪkɔːd/), constitute by far the most tedious class of pronunciation ambiguities. Their correct pronunciation generally depends on

their part of speech and most frequently contrasts verbs and non-verbs, as for *contrast* (verb/noun) or *intimate* (verb/adjective). Pronunciation may also be based on syntactic features, as for *read* (present/past).

3. Words embedded into sentences are not pronounced as if they were isolated. Their pronunciation may be altered at word boundaries (as in the case of phonetic liaisons), or even inside words (due to rhythmic constraints, for instance)

4. Finally, not all words can be found in a phonetic dictionary: the pronunciation of new words and of many proper names has to be deduced from that of already known words.

Automatic phonetizers dealing with such problems can be implemented in many ways (Fig. 17.2), often roughly classified as *dictionary-based* and *rule-based* strategies, although many intermediate solutions exist.

Dictionary-based solutions consist of storing a maximum of phonological knowledge into a lexicon. Entries are sometimes restricted to morphemes, and the pronunciation of surface forms is accounted for by inflectional, derivational, and compounding morphophonemic rules which describe how the phonetic transcriptions of their morphemic constituents are modified when they are combined into words (see the introduction to morphology and morphophonology in Chapter 1). Morphemes that cannot be found in the lexicon are transcribed by rule. After a first phonemic transcription of each word has been obtained, some phonetic post-processing is generally applied, so as to account for coarticulation. This approach has been followed by the MITTALK system (Allen, Hunnicut, and Klatt 1987) from its very first day. A dictionary of up to 12,000 morphemes covered about 95 per cent of the input words. The AT&T Bell Laboratories TTS system followed the same guideline (Levinson, Olive, and Tschirgi 1993), with an augmented morpheme lexicon of 43,000 morphemes.

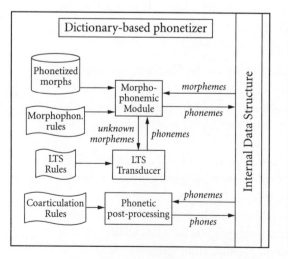
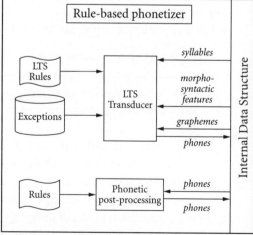

Fig. 17.2 **Dictionary-based (left) versus rule-based (right) phonetization**

A rather different strategy is adopted in rule-based transcription systems, which transfer most of the phonological competence of dictionaries into a set of letter-to-sound (or grapheme-to-phoneme) rules. In this case, only those words that are pronounced in such a particular way that they constitute a rule on their own are stored in an 'exceptions lexicon'. There has been recently a revival of corpus-based methods for automatically deriving phonetic decision trees (CARTs, see Chapter 20; see also Daelemans and van den Bosch 1997, for more details).

17.5 PROSODY GENERATION

The term *prosody* refers to certain properties of the speech signal which are related to audible changes in pitch, loudness, syllable length. Prosodic features have specific functions in speech communication (see Fig. 17.3). The most apparent effect of prosody is that of *focus* (see Chapter 6). There are certain pitch events which make a syllable stand out within the utterance, and indirectly the word or syntactic group it belongs to will be highlighted as an important or new component in the meaning of that utterance.

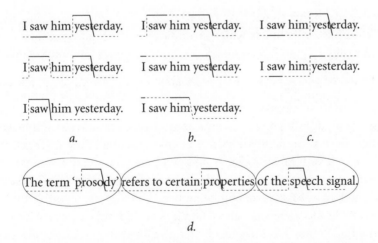

Fig. 17.3 Different kinds of information provided by intonation (lines indicate pitch movements; solid lines indicate stress)
a. Focus or given/new information;
b. Relationships between words (saw–yesterday; I–yesterday; I–him);
c. Finality (top) or continuation (bottom), as it appears on the last syllable;
d. Segmentation of the sentence into groups of syllables.

Although maybe less obvious, prosody has more systematic or general functions. Prosodic features create a segmentation of the speech chain into groups of syllables, or, put the other way round, they give rise to the grouping of syllables and words into larger chunks, termed *prosodic phrases*. Moreover, there are prosodic features which suggest relationships between such groups, indicating that two or more groups of syllables are linked in some way. This grouping effect is hierarchical, although not necessarily identical to the syntactic structuring of the utterance.

It is thus clear that the prosody we produce draws a lot from syntax, semantics, and pragmatics. This immediately raises a fundamental problem in TTS synthesis: how to produce natural-sounding intonation and rhythm, without having access to these high levels of linguistic information? The trade-off that is usually adopted when designing TTS systems is that of 'acceptably neutral' prosody, defined as the default intonation which might be used for an utterance out of context. The key idea is that the 'correct' syntactic structure, the one that precisely requires some semantic and pragmatic insight, is not essential for producing such acceptably neutral prosody. In other words, TTS systems focus on obtaining an acceptable segmentation of sentences and translate it into the continuation or finality marks of Fig. 17.3c. They often ignore the relationships or contrastive meaning of Fig. 17.3a and 17.3b, which require a high degree of linguistic sophistication.

17.5.1 Syntactic-prosodic parsing

Liberman and Church (1992) have reported on a very crude algorithm, termed the chinks 'n chunks algorithm, in which prosodic phrases are accounted for by the simple regular rule:

> *a prosodic phrase = a sequence of chinks followed by a sequence of chunks*

in which *chinks* and *chunks* belong to sets of words which basically correspond to the class of function and content words, respectively. The difference is that objective pronouns (like *him* or *them*) are seen as chunks (although they are function words) and that tensed verb forms (such as *produced*) are considered as chinks (although they are content words). The above rule simply states that prosodic phrases start with the first chink of a sequence of chinks, and end with the last chunk of the following sequence of chunks. Liberman and Church show that this approach produces efficient grouping in most cases, slightly better actually than the simpler decomposition into sequences of function and content words, as shown in the example below:

function words/content words	chinks/chunks
I asked	*I asked them*
them if they were going home	*if they were going home*

to Idaho
and they said yes
and anticipated
one more stop
before getting home

to Idaho
and they said yes
and anticipated one more stop
before getting home

Other, more sophisticated approaches include syntax-based expert systems as in the work of Traber (1993) or in that of Bachenko and Fitzpatrick (1990), and in automatic, corpus-based methods as with the *classification and regression tree* (CART) techniques of Hirschberg (1991).

17.5.2 Computing pitch values

The organization of words in terms of prosodic phrases is used to compute the duration of each phoneme (and of silences), as well as their intonation. This, however, is not straightforward. It requires the formalization of a lot of phonetic or phonological knowledge on prosody, which is either obtained from experts or automatically acquired from data with statistical methods.

Acoustic intonation models can be used to account for *F0* (i.e. intonation) curves with a limited number of *parameters*, a change of which makes it possible to browse a wide range of prosodic effects, governed by information provided by the syntactic-prosodic parser. Fujisaki's model (Fujisaki 1992), for instance, is based on the fundamental assumption that intonation curves, although continuous in time and frequency, originate in discrete events (triggered by the reader) that appear as a continuum given *physiological* mechanisms related to fundamental frequency control. Fujisaki distinguishes two types of discrete events, termed *phrase* and *accent* commands and respectively modelled as pulses and step functions. These commands drive critically damped second-order linear filters whose outputs are summed to yield *F0* values (see Fig. 17.4).

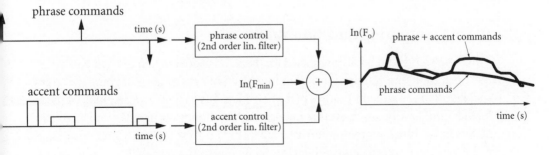

Fig. 17.4 Fujisaki's production model of intonation

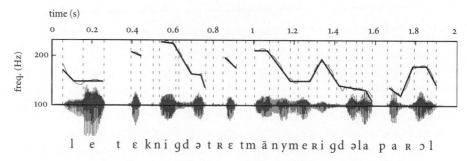

Fig. 17.5 A straight-line acoustic stylization of F0

F0 curves can also be expressed as sequences of target points, assuming that between these points, transitions are filled by an interpolation function (see Fig. 17.5). This approach is sometimes referred to as *acoustic stylization*.

Linguistic models of intonation are also used, as an intermediate between syntactic-prosodic parsing and an acoustic model. The so-called tone sequence theory is one such model. It describes melodic curves in terms of relative *tones*. Following the pioneering work of Pierrehumbert for American English, tones are defined as the phonological abstractions for the target points obtained after broad acoustic stylization. This theory has been more deeply formalized into the *ToBI (Tones and Break Indices)* transcription system (Silverman et al. 1992). Mertens (1990) developed a similar model for French.

How the *F0* curve is ultimately generated greatly depends on the type of prosodic model(s) chosen for its representation. Using Fujisaki's model, for example, the analysis of timing and amplitude of phrase and accent commands (as found in real speech) in terms of linguistic features can be performed with statistical tools (see Möebius, Paetzold, and Hess 1993). Several authors have also recently reported on the automatic derivation of *F0* curves from tone sequences, using statistical models (Black and Hunt 1996) or corpus-based prosodic unit selection (Malfrère, Dutoit, and Mertens 1998).

17.5.3 Computing duration values

Two main trends can be distinguished for duration modelling. In the first and by far most common one, durations are computed by first assigning an *intrinsic (i.e. average) duration* to segments (pauses being considered as particular segments), which is further modified by successively applying rules combining co-intrinsic and linguistic factors into additive or multiplicative factors (for a review, see van Santen 1993). In a second and more recent approach mainly facilitated by the availability of large speech corpora and of computational resources for generating and analysing these corpora, a very general duration model is proposed (such as CARTs). The model is automatically trained on a large amount of data, so as to minimize the difference between the durations predicted by the model and the durations observed on the data.

17.6 Speech Signal Synthesis

Current TTS systems employ two main categories of techniques for the speech signal generation: (1) *synthesis by rule* (formant-based and articulation-based rule systems) and (2) *concatenative synthesis*. The systems based on synthesis by rule techniques make use of a set of rules for generating simplified approximation to natural speech. On the other hand, systems based on concatenative synthesis attempt to synthesize speech by concatenating *acoustic units* (e.g. half-phonemes, phonemes, diphones, etc.) of natural speech.

17.6.1 Formant-based speech synthesis

This type of synthesizer uses the source-filter theory of speech production, where the speech signal is assumed to be obtained as the output of a time-varying linear system (vocal tract) excited by either random noise (for unvoiced sounds, e.g. /s/) or a quasi-periodic sequence of pulses (for voiced sounds, e.g. /ɪ/). The properties of the linear system are determined by the articulators during the production of various speech sounds. The articulators form different acoustical subcavities out of the vocal tract cavities, resulting in the creation of resonances (we refer to them as *formants*).

Suggested values of control parameters for the synthesis of basic phoneme patterns are usually presented in tabular form. As many as twenty to sixty control parameters may be varied as a function of time, serving as input to the waveform synthesizer. The control parameters are mostly related to formant and anti-formant frequencies and bandwidths, together with glottal waveforms. The synthesizer can be implemented as a cascade or a parallel connection of resonators (two-pole filters; one filter for each formant).

One of the crucial problems for synthesis of good quality is the transition from one pattern of parameters to another, as spoken phonemes are articulated in a context of adjacent phonemes. Allophone rules should also be added to the tables of the control parameters in order to permit context-conditioned modifications as well as various stress patterns. The large number of control parameters and rules needed by this type of synthesizer complicates the analysis stage, easily producing errors. For instance, formant frequencies and bandwidths are not easy to estimate from speech data. Because of the difficulty of precisely coordinating so many control parameters, the synthesis quality reveals typical buzziness problems (i.e. speech sounds metal-lic). Although high-quality synthetic speech can be obtained in case of hand-tuned control parameters for a given utterance and speaker, it is hard to match this quality using an automatic system.

Formant synthesizers are frequently used to create stimuli for experiments that explore the perception of speech. This is very useful in diverse areas such as hearing aid design, speech training, speech recognition, as well as in further refining the synthesis of speech. Another important application of formant synthesizers is their use as reading machines for visually challenged people, where a high speaking rate (about 600 words per minute) is needed without reducing the intelligibility of the utterance. Up to now, only formant synthesizers can provide these two features together. For further reading, see Klatt (1980), Allen, Hunnicut, and Klatt (1987).

17.6.2 Articulatory synthesizers

Articulatory synthesizers attempt to model the mechanical motions of the articulators and the resulting distributions of volume velocity and sound pressure in the lungs, larynx, and vocal and nasal tracts (Flanagan et al. 1975). In articulatory synthesis there is a need to develop dynamic models for the articulators (corresponding to many muscles, e.g. tongue, lips, and glottal muscles) as well as accurate measurements of vocal tract changes. An ideal articulatory synthesizer would need to combine and synchronize the articulators and then to generate and control the acoustic output of a three-dimensional model of the vocal tract (Sondhi and Schroeter 1997). This is a nontrivial task and requires control strategies incorporating considerable knowledge of the dynamic constraints of the system as well as resolving fundamental ambiguities of the acoustic to articulatory mapping. In addition, in order to develop a practical articulatory synthesizer capable of synthesizing speech in real time, approximations are required for the speech production models. Because of all these challenging tasks, and partly because of the unavailability of sufficient data on the motions of the articulators during speech production, the quality of the synthetic speech of current articulatory synthesizers cannot be characterized as natural. However, the strategies developed to control an articulatory synthesizer reveal many interesting aspects of the articulators and changes of the vocal tract during the production of natural speech.

17.6.3 Concatenative synthesizers

Concatenative speech synthesis puts together pieces (acoustic units) of natural (recorded) speech to synthesize an arbitrary utterance. This approach has resulted in significant advances in the quality of speech produced by speech synthesis systems. In contrast to the previously described synthesis methods, the concatenation of acoustic units avoids the difficult problem of modelling the way humans generate speech. However, it also introduces other problems: the type of acoustic units to use, the concatenation of acoustic units that have been recorded in different contexts, the modification of the prosody (intonation, duration) of these units, and the compression of the unit inventory using a speech coding technique.

Word-level concatenation is impractical because of the large amount of units that would have to be recorded. Also, the lack of coarticulation at word boundaries results in unnaturally connected speech. Syllables and phonemes seem to be linguistically appealing units. However, there are over 10,000 syllables in English and, while there are only 40 phonemes, their simple concatenation produces unnatural speech because it does not account for coarticulation. Units that are currently used in concatenative systems include **diphones** and half-syllables. A minimum inventory of about 1,000 diphones or half-syllables is required to synthesize unrestricted English text (Klatt 1987). Some diphone-based synthesizers also include multi-phone units of varying length to better represent highly coarticulated speech (such as in /r/ or /l/ contexts). In the half-syllable approach, highly coarticulated syllable-internal consonant clusters are treated as units. However, coarticulation across syllables in not treated very well. An extension of these strategies called *automatic unit selection* (Hunt and Black 1996) has recently been introduced. Given a phoneme stream and target prosody for an utterance, this algorithm selects an optimum set of acoustic units which best match the target specifications. While the technique tends to avoid as many concatenation points as possible (by selecting the largest available units in the inventory), it does not currently guarantee a minimum accepted speech quality. However, this is a very promising technique, which has good chances for dominating research in speech synthesis for many years to come.

For the concatenation, prosodic modification, and compression of acoustic units, speech models are usually used. Speech models provide a parametric form for acoustic units. The task of the speech model is to analyse the inventory of the acoustic units and then compress the inventory (using speech coding techniques), while maintaining a high quality of synthesized speech. During synthesis, the model has to have the ability to perform the following tasks in real time: concatenate an adequate sequence of parameters, adjust the parameters of the model so as to match the prosody of the concatenated segments to the prosody imposed by the language processing module, and finally smooth out concatenation points in order to produce the fewest possible audible discontinuities. Therefore, it is important to use speech models that allow easy and high-quality (without introducing artefacts) modification of the fundamental frequency, segmental duration, and spectral information (magnitude and phase spectrum).

There has been a considerable amount of research effort directed at the problem of speech representation for TTS. The advent of linear prediction (LP) has had its impact in speech coding as well as in speech synthesis (Markel and Gray 1976). However, the buzziness inherent in LP degrades perceived voice quality. Other synthesis techniques based on pitch synchronous waveform processing have been proposed such as the Time-Domain Pitch-Synchronous-Overlap-Add (TD-PSOLA) method (Moulines and Charpentier 1990). TD-PSOLA is currently one of the most popular concatenation methods. Although TD-PSOLA provides good-quality speech synthesis, it has limitations which are related to its non-parametric structure: spectral mismatch at segmental boundaries and tonal quality when prosodic modifications are applied on the concatenated acoustic units. An alternative method is the Multi-Band Resynthesis Overlap Add (MBROLA) method (Dutoit 1997: chapter 10) which tries to overcome the TD-PSOLA concatenation problems by using a specially edited inventory (obtained by resynthesizing the voiced parts of the original inventory with constant harmonic phases and constant pitch). Both TD-PSOLA and MBROLA have very low computational cost. Sinusoidal approaches (e.g. Macon 1996) and hybrid harmonic/stochastic representations (Stylianou 1998) have also been proposed for speech synthesis. These models are intrinsically more powerful than TD-PSOLA and MBROLA for compression, modification, and smoothing. However, they are also about ten times more computationally intensive than TD-PSOLA or MBROLA. For a formal comparison between different speech representations for text-to-speech, see Dutoit (1994) and Syrdal et al. (1998).

FURTHER READING AND RELEVANT RESOURCES

Most of the information presented in this chapter can be found with a lot more details in Dutoit (1997) and van Santen et al. (1997).

For more information on books, algorithms, tools, commercial systems, and conferences related to speech synthesis, see the inescapable speech FAQ: http://www-svr.eng.cam.ac.uk/comp.speech.

REFERENCES

Allen, J., S. Hunnicut, and D. H. Klatt. 1987. *From Text to Speech: The MITTALK System*, Cambridge: Cambridge University Press.

Bachenko, J. and E. Fitzpatrick. 1990. 'A computational grammar of discourse-neutral prosodic phrasing in English'. *Computational Linguistics*, 16, 155–67.

Black A. W. and A. J. Hunt. 1996. 'Generating Fo contours from ToBI labels using linear regression'. *Proceedings of the International Conference on Speech and Language Processing* (*ISCLP '96*) (Philadelphia), 1385–8.

Daelemans, W. and A. van den Bosch. 1997. 'Language-independent data-oriented grapheme-to-phoneme conversion.' In van Santen et al. (1997: 77–89).

Dutoit, T. 1994. 'High quality text-to-speech synthesis: a comparison of four candidate algorithms'. *Proceedings of the International Conference on Acoustics, Speech, and Signal Processing (ICASSP '94)* (Adelaide), 565–8.

——1997. *An Introduction to Text-to-Speech Synthesis*. Dordrecht: Kluwer Academic Publishers.

Flanagan, J. L., K. Ishizaka, and K. L. Shipley. 1975. 'Synthesis of speech from a dynamic model of the vocal cords and vocal tract'. *Bell System Technical Journal*, 54, 485–506.

Fujisaki, H. 1992. 'The role of quantitative modeling in the study of intonation'. *Proceedings of the International Symposium on Japanese Prosody* (Naza), 163–74.

Hirschberg, J. 1991. 'Using text analysis to predict intonational boundaries'. *Proceedings of the European Speech Communication and Technology (Eurospeech '91)* (Genova), 1275–8.

Hunt, A. J. and A. W. Black. 1996. 'Unit selection in a concatenative speech synthesis system using a large speech database'. *Proceedings of the International Conference on Acoustics, Speech, and Signal Processing (ICASSP '96)* (Atlanta), i. 373–6.

Klatt, D. H. 1980. 'Software for a cascade/parallel formant synthesizer'. *Journal of the Acoustical Society of America*, 67(3), 971–95.

——1987. 'Text-to-speech conversion'. *Journal of the Acoustical Society of America*, 82(3), 737–93.

Levinson, S. E., J. P. Olive, and J. S. Tschirgi. 1993. 'Speech synthesis in telecommunications'. *IEEE Communications Magazine*, 31, 46–53.

Liberman, M. J. and K. W. Church. 1992. 'Text analysis and word pronunciation in text-to-speech synthesis'. In S. Furui and M. M. Sondhi (eds.), *Advances in Speech Signal Processing*. New York: Dekker, 791–831.

Macon, M. W. 1996. *Speech synthesis based on sinusoidal modelling*, Ph.D. dissretation, Georgia Institute of Technology.

Malfrère, F., T. Dutoit, and P. Mertens. 1998. 'Automatic prosody generation using suprasegmental unit selection'. *Proceedings of the 3rd ESCA/IEEE International Workshop on Speech Synthesis* (Jenolan Caves), 323–8.

Markel, J. D. and A. H. Gray. 1976. *Linear Prediction of Speech*. New York: Springer Verlag.

Mertens, P. 1990. 'Intonation'. In C. Blanche-Benveniste et al. (eds.), *Le Français parlé*, Paris: Éditions du CNRS, 159–76.

Moëbius, B., M. Paetzold, and W. Hess. 1993. 'Analysis and synthesis of german F0 contours by means of Fujisaki's model'. *Speech Communication*, 13, 53–61.

Moulines, E. and F. Charpentier. 1990. 'Pitch synchronous waveform processing techniques for text-to-speech synthesis using diphones'. *Speech Communication*, 9, 5–6.

Silverman, K., M. Beckman, J. Pitrelli, M. Ostendorf, C. Whightman, P. Price, J. Pierrehumbert, and J. Hirschberg. 1992. 'ToBI: a standard for labeling English prosody'. *Proceedings of the International Conference on Spoken Language Processing (ICSLP '92)* (Alberta), 867–70.

Sondhi, M. M. and J. Schroeter. 1997. 'Speech production models and their digital implementations'. *The Digital Signal Processing Handbook*. New York: CRC and IEEE Press, 44-1–44-21.

Sproat, R. (ed). 1998. *Multilingual Text-to-Speech Synthesis*. Dordrecht: Kluwer Academic Publishers.

Stylianou, Y. 1998. 'Concatenative speech synthesis using a harmonic plus noise model'. *Proceedings of the 3rd ESCA Speech Synthesis Workshop* (Jenolan Caves), 261–6.

Syrdal, A., Y. Stylianou, L. Garisson, A. Conkie, and J. Schroeter. 1998. 'TD-PSOLA versus harmonic plus noise model in diphone based speech synthesis'. *Proceedings of the International Conference on Acoustics, Speech, and Signal Processing (ICASSP '98)* (Seattle), 273–6.

Traber, C. 1993. 'Syntactic processing and prosody control in the SVOX TTS system for German'. *Proceedings of the European Speech Communication and Technology Conference* (*Eurospeech '93*) (Berlin), iii. 2099–102.

van Santen, J. P. H. 1993. 'Timing in text-to-speech systems'. *Proceedings of the European Speech Communication and Technology Conference* (*Eurospeech '93*) (Berlin), 1397–404.

——R. Sproat, J. Olive, and J. Hirshberg, eds. 1997, *Progress in Speech Synthesis*. New York: Springer Verlag.

CHAPTER 18

FINITE-STATE TECHNOLOGY

LAURI KARTTUNEN

ABSTRACT

The chapter will introduce the basic concepts of **finite-state language processing**: *regular languages* and *relations, finite-state automata*, and *regular expressions*. The properties of finite-state automata will also be discussed.

18.1 INTRODUCTION

Many basic steps in language processing, ranging from tokenization (Karttunen et al. 1996), to phonological and morphological analysis (Koskenniemi 1983), disambiguation (Roche and Schabes 1997a), spelling correction (Oflazer 1996), and shallow parsing (Aït-Mokhtar and Chanod 1997), can be performed efficiently by means of finite-state transducers. Such transducers are generally compiled from regular expressions, a formal language for representing sets and relations. Although regular expressions and methods for compiling them into automata have been part of elementary computer science for decades (Hopcroft and Ullman 1979), the application of finite-state transducers to natural language processing has given rise to many extensions to the classical regular-expression calculus.

18.1.1 Basic notions and terminology

We assume that the reader is familiar with the basic concepts of set theory such as *set*, *ordered pair*, *relation*, the basic Boolean operations on sets such as *union*, *intersection*, and the common string operations such as *concatenation*. See Chapter 8 for the definition of some of these operations.

18.1.1.1 *Language*

The term **language** is used here in a general sense to refer to a set of strings of any kind. A *string* is a concatenation of zero or more *symbols*. In our examples, the symbols are in general single characters such as *a*, but we also admit user-defined multi-character symbols such as +*Noun*. Multi-character symbols are considered as atomic entities rather than as a concatenation of single-character strings. A string that contains no symbols at all, denoted ε, is called the *empty string*, with the language containing the empty string but no other strings known as the *empty-string language*. A language that contains no strings at all, not even the empty string, is called the *empty language* or *null language*. The language that contains every possible string of any length is called the *universal language*.

18.1.1.2 *Relation*

A set of ordered string pairs such as $\{\langle a, bb\rangle, \langle cd, \varepsilon\rangle\}$ is called a **relation**. We call the first member of a pair the *upper string* and the second member the *lower string*. A string-to-string relation is a mapping between two languages: the *upper language* and the *lower language*. They correspond to what is usually called the *domain* and the *range* of a relation. In this case, the upper language is $\{a, cd\}$ and the lower language is $\{bb, \varepsilon\}$. A relation such as $\{\langle a, a\rangle\}$ in which every pair contains the same string twice is called an *identity relation*. If a relation pairs every string with a string that has the same length, the relation is an *equal-length relation*. Every identity relation is obviously an equal-length relation.

18.1.1.3 *Network*

We consider finite-state automata as **networks**, directed graphs that consist of *states* and labelled *arcs*. A network contains a single *initial state*, also called the *start state*, and any number of *final states*. We represent states as circles and arcs as arrows. In our diagrams the start state is always the leftmost state and final states are marked by a double circle. Each state is the origin of zero or more arcs leading to some destination state. A sequence of arcs leading from the initial state to a final state is called a *path*. An arc may be labelled either by a single symbol such as *a* or a symbol pair such as *a:b* where *a* designates the symbol on the upper side of the arc and *b* the symbol on the lower side. If all the arcs of a network are labelled by a single symbol, the network is called a *simple automaton*; if at least one label is a symbol pair the network is a *transducer*. Unlike many introductory textbooks, we do not treat simple finite-state automata and transducers as different types of mathematical objects. Our presentation reflects closely the data structures in the Xerox implementation of finite-state networks. We hope it is as precise as but more approachable than a rigorous formal definition in terms of *n*-tuples of sets and functions.

18.1.2 Examples of finite-state languages and relations

In this section we give a few simple examples that illustrate some linguistic applications of finite-state networks. The following sections will describe how such networks can be constructed.

18.1.2.1 *A finite-state language*

Every path in a finite-state network encodes a string or an ordered pair of strings. The totality of paths in a network encodes a **finite-state language** or a **finite-state relation**. For example, the network in Fig. 18.1 encodes the language {*clear, clever, ear, ever, fat, fatter*}.

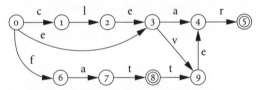

Fig. 18.1. A simple finite-state language

Each state in Fig. 18.1 has a number so that we can refer to them in describing the paths of the network. There is a path for each of the six words in the language. For example, the path ⟨0–e–3–v–9–e–4–r–5⟩ represents the word *ever*.

A finite-state network is a very efficient encoding for a word list because all words beginning and ending in the same way can share a part of the network and every path is distinct from every other path.

If the number of words in a language is finite, then the network that encodes it is acyclic; that is, no path in the network loops back onto itself. Such a network also provides a **perfect hash** function for the language (Lucchesi and Kowaltowski 1993), a function that assigns to each word a unique number in the range from 0 to *n*–1 where *n* is the number of paths in the network.

18.1.2.2 *A lexical transducer*

The network in Fig. 18.2 is an example of a **lexical transducer** (Karttunen, Kaplan, and Zaenen 1992). It encodes the relation {⟨*leaf+NN, leaf*⟩, ⟨*leaf+NNS, leaves*⟩, ⟨*left+JJ*, *left*⟩, ⟨*leave+NN, leave*⟩, ⟨*leave+NNS, leaves*⟩, ⟨*leave+VB, leave*⟩, ⟨*leave+VBZ, leaves*⟩, ⟨*leave+VBD, left*⟩}. The substrings beginning with + are multi-character symbols.

In order to make the diagrams less cluttered we often combine several arcs into a single multiply labelled arc. For example the arc from state 5 to 6 abbreviates four arcs that have the same origin and destination but a different label: +*NN:0*, +*NNN:s*, +*VB:0*, +*VBZ:s*. *0* is the epsilon symbol, standing for the empty string. Another important convention illustrated in Fig. 18.2 is that identity pairs such as *e:e* are represented as a single symbol *e*. Because of this convention, the network in Fig. 18.1 could also be interpreted as a transducer for the identity relation on the language.

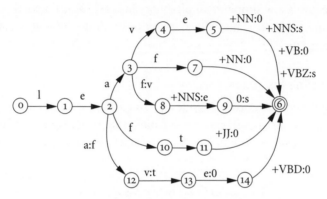

Fig. 18.2 A lexical transducer

The lower language of the lexical transducer in Fig. 18.2 consists of inflected surface forms *leaf, leave, leaves,* and *left*. The upper language consists of the corresponding lexical forms or lemmata, each containing a citation form of the word followed by a part-of-speech tag.

Lexical transducers can be used for analysis or for generation. For example, to find the analyses for the word *leaves*, one needs to locate the paths that contain the symbols *l, e, a, v, e,* and *s* on the lower side of the arc label. The network in Fig. 18.2 contains three such paths:

(18.1)   0 – l – 1 – e – 2 – a – 3 – v – 4 – e – 5 – +NNS:s – 6,
         0 – l – 1 – e – 2 – a – 3 – v – 4 – e – 5 – +VBZ:s – 6,
         0 – l – 1 – e – 2 – a – 3 – f:v – 8 – +NNS:e – 9 – 0:s – 6.

The result of the analysis is obtained by concatenating the symbols on the upper side of the paths: *leave+NNS, leave+VBZ,* and *leaf+NNS*.

The process of generating a surface form from a lemma, say *leave+VBD*, is the same as for analysis except that the input form is matched against the upper side arc labels and the output is produced from the opposite side of the successful path or paths. In the case at hand, there is only one matching path:

(18.2) $0 - l - 1 - e - 2 - a{:}f - 12 - v{:}t - 13 - e{:}0 - 14 - +VBD{:}0 - 6$

This path maps *leave+VBD* to *left*, and vice versa.

We use the term *apply* to describe the process of finding the path or paths that match a given input and returning the output. As the example above shows, a transducer can be applied *downward* or *upward*. There is no privileged input side. In the implementation described here, transducers are inherently bidirectional.

Lexical transducers provide a very efficient method for morphological analysis and generation. A comprehensive analyser for a language such as English, French, or German contains tens of thousands of states and hundreds of thousands of arcs, but it can be compressed to a relatively small size in the range of 500Kb~2MB.

18.1.2.3 *A rewrite rule*

A relation may contain an infinite number of ordered pairs. One example of such a relation is the mapping from all lower-case strings to the corresponding upper-case strings. This relation contains an infinite number of pairs such as ⟨*abc, ABC*⟩, ⟨*xyzzy, XYZZY*⟩, and so on. Fig. 18.3 sketches the corresponding network. The path that relates *xyzzy* to *XYZZY* cycles many times through the single state of the transducer. Fig. 18.4 shows it in linearized form.

The lower/upper-case relation may be thought of as the representation of a simple orthographical rule. In fact we may view all kinds of string-changing rules in this way, that is, as infinite string-to-string relations. The networks that represent phonological rewrite rules (Chomsky and Halle 1968), two-level rules (Koskenniemi 1983), or the GEN relation in Optimality Theory (Prince and Smolensky 1993) are of course in general more complex than the little transducer in Fig. 18.3.

Fig. 18.4 may also be interpreted in another way, that is, as representing the application of the upper/lower case rule to the string *xyzzy*. In fact, rule application is formally a **composition** of two relations; in this case, the identity relation on the string *xyzzy* and the upper/lower-case relation in Fig. 18.3.

a:A
b:B
c:C
... etc.

Fig. 18.3 The lower/upper case transducer

Fig. 18.4 A path in the lower/upper case transducer

18.1.2.4 *Composition*

A composition is an operation on two relations. If one relation contains the pair x, y and the other relation contains the pair $\langle y, z \rangle$, the relation resulting from composing the two will contain the pair $\langle x, z \rangle$. Composition brings together the 'outside' components of the two pairs and eliminates the common one in the middle. For example, the composition of $\{\langle leave+VBD, left \rangle\}$ with the lower/upper-case relation yields the relation $\{\langle leave+VBD, LEFT \rangle\}$.

Without going into too many technical details, it is useful to have a general idea of how composition is carried out when string-to-string relations are represented by finite-state networks. We can think of composition as a two-step procedure. First the paths of the two networks that have a matching string in the middle are lined up and merged, as shown in Fig. 18.5. For the sake of perspicuity, we show the upper and lower symbols explicitly on different sides of the arc except that zero, i.e. epsilon, is represented by a blank. We then eliminate the string *left* in the middle giving us the transducer in Fig. 18.6 that directly maps *leave+VBD* to *LEFT*.

Once we think of rule application as composition, we immediately see that a rule can be applied to several words, or even infinitely many words at the same time if the words are represented by a finite-state network. Lexical transducers are typically created by composing a set of transducers for orthographical rules with a transducer encoding the source lexicon. Two rule transducers can also be composed with one another to yield a single transducer that gives the same result as the successive application of the original rules. This is a fundamental insight in computational phonology (Johnson 1972; Kaplan and Kay 1981).

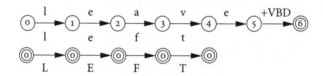

Fig. 18.5 Merging two paths

Fig. 18.6 The result of composition

18.2 REGULAR EXPRESSIONS

Finite-state networks can represent only a subset of all possible languages and relations; that is, only some languages are finite-state languages. One of the fundamental results of formal language theory (Kleene 1956) is the demonstration that finite-state languages are precisely the set of languages that can be described by a *regular expression*.

A regular expression *denotes* a set of strings (i.e. a language) or string pairs (i.e. a relation). It can be *compiled into* a finite-state network that compactly *encodes* the corresponding language or relation that may well be infinite.

The language of regular expressions includes the common set operators of Boolean logic and operators that are specific to strings such as concatenation. It follows from Kleene's theorem that for each of the regular-expression operators for finite-state languages there is a corresponding operation that applies to finite-state networks and produces a network for the resulting language. Any regular expression can in principle be compiled into a single network.

A set operation such as union has a corresponding operation on finite-state networks only if the set of regular relations and languages is *closed* under that operation. Closure means that if the sets to which the operation is applied are regular, the result is also regular, that is, encodable as a finite-state network.

Regular languages are closed with respect to all the common set operations including intersection and complementation (=negation). This follows directly from Kleene's proof. Regular relations are closed under concatenation, iteration, and union but in general not under intersection, complementation, or subtraction (Kaplan and Kay 1994; Roche and Schabes 1997c).

We can build a finite-state network for a complex language by first constructing a regular expression that describes the language in terms of set operations and then compiling that regular expression into a network. This is in general easier than constructing a complex network directly, and, in fact, it is the only practical way for all but the most trivial infinite languages and relations.

18.2.1 Basic regular-expression calculus

In the following definitions we use upper-case letters, A, B, etc., as variables over regular expressions. Lower case letters, *a*, *b*, etc., stand for symbols. The notation used in this section comes from the Xerox finite-state calculus (Karttunen et al. 1996; Beesley and Karttunen 2003).

The simplest regular expressions consist of single symbols or symbol pairs. An atomic expression such as *a* denotes the language consisting of the corresponding string, or alternatively, the corresponding identity relation. A symbol pair such as *a:b* denotes a relation, the cross-product of the two single string languages. There are two special symbols: 0, the epsilon symbol, which stands for the empty string and *?*, the any symbol, which represents the infinite set of symbols in some yet unknown alphabet. Consequently the regular expression 0 denotes the empty-string language and *?* the language of all single-symbol strings or the corresponding identity relation.

Complex regular expressions can be built from simpler ones by means of regular expression operators. The most common simple regular-expression operators are listed in Table 18.1. Most of them are 'classical', some are specific to the Xerox calculus. The component expressions may in general denote either languages or relations but in certain cases the subexpressions must be of a particular type. Regular relations in general are not closed under complementation, intersection, and subtraction. In other cases, such as cross-product, the restriction is inherent to how the operation is defined and the fact that we implement only two-level rather than *n*-level transducers.

The set of operators in Table 18.1 is somewhat redundant because some of them can easily be defined in terms of the others. For example, there is no particular need for the *contains* operator $ because the expression [?* A ?*] denotes the same language or relation as $A. Its purpose is to allow this commonly used construction to be expressed more concisely. The same applies to the *term complement* operator: \A is equivalent to [?–A].

Table 18.1 Common regular-expression operators

Expression	Operator name	Restriction
A*	zero or more	
A+	one or more	
$A	contains	
~A	complement (negation)	languages only
\A	term complement	languages only
A B	concatenation	
A|B	union	
A & B	intersection	languages only
A – B	subtraction	languages only
A .x. B	cross-product	languages only
A .o. B	composition	relations only

18.2.1.1 *Examples*

In order to understand the semantics of regular expressions it is useful to look at some simple examples in conjunction with the corresponding language or relation and the network that encodes it. A few minimal languages are shown in Table 18.2.

Table 18.2 Minimal languages

Expression	Language/relation	Network
0	The Empty-String Language	◎
?*	The Universal Language	◎ ? Sigma = {?}
~[?*]	The Empty Language	◯

The label *?* in the network for the Universal Language/Relation represents any *unknown* symbol. In order for it to be interpreted properly, the network must be associated with a list of 'known' symbols. This is called the *sigma* alphabet. In this case the sigma contains no other symbols. Consequently the *?* arc represents any symbol whatever.

The sigma alphabet includes every symbol that appears in the network either by itself or as a component of a symbol pair. The sigma alphabet may also contain symbols that do not appear in the network but are known because they were present in another network from which the current one was derived by some operation that eliminated all the arcs where the symbol occurred. For example, the language [\a]*, including all and only strings that do not contain *a*, is encoded by the same network as the Universal Language, but in the case of [\a]* the sigma includes both *?* and *a*. In that case, the *?* arc represents any symbol other than *a*.

18.2.2 Complex regular expressions

This section introduces two types of complex regular expressions that have many linguistic applications, **restriction** and **replacement**. Like the *contains* operator, these new constructs are definable in terms of more primitive expressions. Thus they do not extend the descriptive power of the regular-expression language but provide a higher level of abstraction that makes it easier to define complex languages and relations.

18.2.2.1 *Restriction*

The restriction operator is one of the two fundamental operators of two-level phono-logical rules (Koskenniemi 1983).

(18.3)   [$A \Rightarrow L \_ R$] denotes the language of strings that have the property that any string from
A that occurs as a substring is immediately preceded by a string from L and immedi-ately followed by a string from R.

The restriction expressed by [$A \Rightarrow L \_ R$] is that the substrings from A must appear in the *context* L _ R. For example, the language [$a \Rightarrow b\_ c$] includes all strings that contain no occurrence of *a* and all strings like *back-to-back* that completely satisfy the condition, but no strings such as *cab* or *pack*. A special *boundary* symbol, .#. indi-cates the beginning of a string in a left context and the end of the string in the right context. Any number of alternative contexts, separated by a comma, may be listed. For example, [$a \Rightarrow .\#. \_ , b \_$] allows *a* at the beginning of a string and after *b*.

In the general finite-state calculus described here, all the components of a restric-tion expression must denote languages, not relations. An expression that contains symbol pairs such as [$a{:}b \Rightarrow c{:}d \_ e{:}f$] is not allowed in the general calculus. Such expressions are, however, valid two-level rules. A compiler for two-level rules treats symbol pairs as atomic symbols (Karttunen and Beesley 1992; Karttunen 1993; Kaplan and Kay 1994) and only the final result may be viewed as a transducer. The compil-ation of two-level rules is a special application of the general calculus.

18.2.2.2 *Replacement*

Replacement expressions describe strings of one language in terms of how they dif-fer from the strings of another language. They can be used to create very complex string-to-string relations. Because the differences may depend on contexts and other parameters, the syntax of replacement expressions involves many operators and spe-cial constructs.

The family of replace operators is specific to the Xerox regular-expression calculus. In the original version, developed by Ronald M. Kaplan and Martin Kay in the early 1980s (Kaplan and Kay 1981, 1994), the goal was to model the application of phono-logical rewrite rules by finite-state transducers. Although the idea had been known before (Johnson 1972), Kaplan and Kay were the first to present a compilation algo-rithm for rewrite rules. The notation introduced in this section is based on Kaplan and Kay's work with extensions introduced by researchers at XRCE (Karttunen 1995, 1996; Kempe and Karttunen 1996).

We first give examples of simple unconditional replace expressions and then dis-cuss how the operation can be constrained by context and by other conditions.

(18.4)   [$A \rightarrow B$] denotes the relation in which each string of the universal language (the upper
language) is paired with all strings that are identical to it in every respect except that

every instance of *A* that occurs as a substring in the upper-language string is represented by a string from *B*.

For example, the transducer for [*a b c* → *d e*] applied downward to the upper-language inputs maps *de* to *de* and *abc* to *de*. In the opposite direction it maps *de* to both *de* and *abc*. Any number of multiple replacements may be done in parallel. [*a* → *b*, *b* → *a*] maps *abba* to *baab*.

(18.5) [*A* → *B* . . . *C*] denotes a relation in which each string of the upper-side universal language is paired with all strings that are identical to the original except that every instance of *A* in the upper-side string is represented by a copy that has a string from *B* as a prefix and a string from *C* as a suffix.

Expressions of the form *A* → *B* . . . *C* are typically used to mark instances of the language *A* in some special way. For example, the transducer for [*a* | *e* | *i* | *o* | *u* → %[. . . %]] maps *abide* to [*a*]*b*[*i*]*d*[*e*] enclosing each vowel in literal square brackets.

Both types of replace expressions can be constrained to apply only if the string to be replaced or its replacement appears in a certain context or contexts. Replacement contexts are specified in the same way as the contexts for restriction: *L _ R*, where *L* is the left context, *R* is the right context, and _ marks the site of the replacement.

The notion of context is self-evident in the case of restriction expressions because they denote simple languages. This is not the case for replacements that involve relations. The notation introduced below provides special symbols, | |, //, \\, and \/, to distinguish between four different ways of interpreting the context specification. The four expressions below all denote a relation that is like [*A* → *B*] except that the replacement of an original upper-side substring by a string from *B* is made only if the indicated additional constraint is fulfilled.

(18.6) [*A* → *B* | | *L _ R*] Every replaced substring in the upper language is immediately preceded by an upper-side string from *L* and followed by an upper-side string from *R*.

(18.7) [*A* → *B* // *L _ R*] Every replaced substring in the upper language is immediately followed by an upper-side string from *R*, and the lower-side replacement string is immediately preceded by a string from *L*.

(18.8) [*A* → *B* \\ *L _ R*] Every replaced substring in the upper language is immediately preceded by an upper-side string from *L*, and the lower-side replacement string is immediately followed by a string from *R*.

(18.9) [*A* → *B* \/ *L _ R*] Every lower-side replacement string is immediately preceded by a lower-side string from *L* and followed by a lower-side string from *R*.

In other words, in | | replacements both the left and right contexts are matched in the upper-language string. In the other variants, one or the other or both contexts are matched on the lower-side string adjacent to the replacement site. In practice, when writing phonologial/orthographical alternation rules, it is usually desirable to constrain a replacement by the original upper-side context. That is, most rules written in practice are | | rules. However, there are linguistic phenomena such as vowel harmony, tone spreading, and umlaut that are most naturally described in terms of a left-to-right or right-to-left process in which the result of a replacement itself serves as the context for another replacement.

Replacement relations described above are not necessarily one to one even if the replacement language contains just one string. The transducer compiled from $[a \mid a\,a \to b]$ maps the upper language aa to both b and bb. The transducer for $[a\,b \to x, b\,c \to y]$ gives two results, xc and ay, for the upper-language input string abc.

This non-determinism arises in two ways. First of all, possible replacements may overlap. We get a different result in the abc case depending on which of the two overlapping substrings is replaced. Secondly, there may be more than one possible replacement starting at the same point, as in the beginning of aa, where either a or aa could be replaced.

The family of **directed** replace operators (Karttunen 1996) eliminates this type of non-determinism by adding directionality and length constraints. Directionality means that the replacement sites are selected starting from the left or from the right, not allowing any overlaps. Whenever there are multiple candidate strings starting at a given location, the longest or the shortest one is selected. The four directed replace operators introduced below can be used in all types of replace expressions discussed above in place of $\to$.

(18.10) $[A @\to B]$ Replacement strings are selected from left to right. If more than one candidate string begins at a given location, the longest one is replaced.

(18.11) $[A \to@ B]$ Replacement strings are selected from right to left. If more than one candidate string begins at a given location, the longest one is replaced.

(18.12) $[A @> B]$ Replacement strings are selected from left to right. If more than one candidate string begins at a given location, the shortest one is replaced.

(18.13) $[A >@ B]$ Replacement strings are selected from right to left. If more than one candidate string begins at a given location, the shortest one is replaced.

The additional constraints attached to the directed replace operators guarantee that any upper-language input string is uniquely factorized into a sequence of substrings that belong either to A or to its complement language.

Transducers compiled from $@\to$ expressions are commonly used for text normalization, tokenization, and for 'chunking' regions of text that match a given pattern. For example $[[\text{``\textbackslash t''}\mid\text{``\textbackslash n''}\mid\text{`` ''}]+ @\to \text{``\textbackslash n''}]$ yields a transducer that greedily reduces a sequence of tabs, newlines, and spaces into a single newline character.

To give a simple example of chunking, let us assume that a noun phrase consists of an optional determiner, (d), any number of adjectives, a^*, and one or more nouns,

```
d a n n        v        a a n
– – – –                 – – –
[d a n n]      v        [a a n]
```

Fig. 18.7 Downward application of $[(d)a^*n+ @\to \%[\ldots\%]]$ to *dannvaan*

n+. The expression $[(d) a^* n+ @\rightarrow \%[\ldots \%]]$ compiles into a transducer that inserts brackets around maximal instances of the noun-phrase pattern. For example, it maps *dannvaan* into [*dann*]*v*[*aan*], as shown in Fig. 18.7.

Although the input string *dannvaan* contains many other instances of the noun phrase pattern, *dan*, *an*, *nn*, etc., the left-to-right and longest-match constraints pick out just the two maximal ones.

18.3 PROPERTIES OF FINITE-STATE NETWORKS

In this section we consider briefly the formal properties of finite-state automata. All the networks presented in this chapter have the three important properties defined in Table 18.3.

Table 18.3 Properties of networks

Epsilon free	There are no arcs labelled with the epsilon symbol.
Deterministic	No state has more than one outgoing arc with the same label.
Minimal	There is no other network with exactly the same paths that has fewer states.

If a network encodes a regular language and if it is epsilon free, deterministic, and minimal, the network is guaranteed to be the best encoding for that language in the sense that any other network for the same language has the same number of states and arcs and differs only with respect to the order of the arcs, which generally is irrelevant.

The situation is more complex in the case of regular relations. Even if a transducer is epsilon free, deterministic, and minimal in the sense of Table 18.3, there may still be another network with fewer states and arcs for the same relation. If the network has arcs labelled with a symbol pair that contains an epsilon on one side, these one-sided epsilons could be distributed differently, or perhaps even eliminated, and this might reduce the size of the network.

For example, the two networks in Fig. 18.8 encode the same relation, $\{\langle aa, a\rangle, \langle ab, ab\rangle\}$. They are both deterministic and minimal but one is smaller than the other due to a more optimal placement of the one-sided epsilon transition.

Fig. 18.8 [a:0 a | a b] vs. [a [a:0 | b]]

In the general case there is no way to determine whether a given transducer is the best encoding for an arbitrary relation.

For transducers, the intuitive notion of determinism makes sense only with respect to a given direction of application. But there are still two ways to think about determinism, as defined in Table 18.4.

Table 18.4 Properties of transducers

Functional	For any input there is at most one output
Sequential	No state has more than one arc with the same symbol on the input side

Although both transducers in Fig. 18.8 are in fact **functional**, i.e. unambiguous, in both directions, the one on the left is not **sequential** in either direction. When it is applied downward, to the string *aa*, there are two paths that have to be pursued initially, even though only one will succeed. The same is true in the other direction as well. In other words, there is local ambiguity at the start state because *a* may have to be deleted or retained. In this case, the ambiguity is resolved by the next input symbol one step later.

If the relation itself is unambiguous in the relevant direction and if all the ambiguities in the transducer resolve themselves within some fixed number of steps, the transducer is called **sequentiable**. That is, we can construct an equivalent sequential transducer in the same direction (Roche and Schabes 1997*c*; Mohri 1997). Fig. 18.9 shows the downward sequentialized version of the leftmost transducer in Fig. 18.8.

The sequentialization algorithm combines the locally ambiguous paths into a single path that does not produce any output until the ambiguity has been resolved.

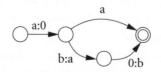

Fig. 18.9 Downward sequentialized version of [a:0 a | a b]

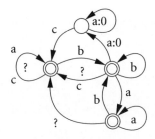

Fig. 18.10 Unsequentiable transducer [a+ @→ 0 || b _ c]

In the case at hand, the ambiguous path contains just one arc. When a b is seen the delayed a is produced as output and then the b itself in a one-sided epsilon transition. Otherwise, an a must follow, and in this case there is no delayed output. In effect, the local ambiguity is resolved with one symbol lookahead.

The network in Fig. 18.9 is sequential but only in the downward direction. Upward sequentialization produces the second network shown in Fig. 18.8, which clearly is the best encoding for this little relation.

Even if a transducer is functional, it may well be unsequentiable if the resolution of a local ambiguity requires an unbounded amount of look-ahead. For example, the simple transducer for [a+ @→ 0 || b _ c] in Fig. 18.10 cannot be sequentialized in either direction.

This transducer reduces any sequence of as that is preceded by a b to an epsilon or copies it to the output unchanged depending on whether the sequence of as is followed by a c. A sequential transducer would have to delay the decision until it reached the end of an arbitrarily long sequence of as. It is obviously impossible for any finite-state device to accumulate an unbounded amount of delayed output.

However, in such cases it is always possible to split the functional but unsequentiable transducer into a **bimachine** (Schützenberger 1961; Roche and Schabes 1997c; Laporte 1997). A bimachine for an unambiguous relation consists of two sequential transducers that are applied in a sequence. The first half of the bimachine processes the input from left to right; the second half of the bimachine processes the output of the first half from right to left. Although the application of a bimachine requires two passes, a bimachine is in general more efficient to apply than the original transducer because the two components of the bimachine are both sequential. There is no local ambiguity in either the left-to-right or the right-to-left half of the bimachine if the original transducer is unambiguous in the given direction of application. Fig. 18.11 shows a bimachine derived from the transducer in Fig. 18.10.

The left-to-right half of the bimachine in Fig. 18.11 is only concerned about the left context of the replacement. A string of as that is preceded by b is mapped to a string of a_1s, an auxiliary symbol to indicate that the left context has been matched. The right-to-left half of the bimachine maps each instance of the auxiliary symbol either to a or

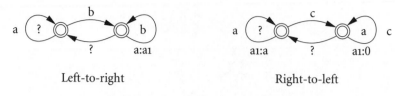

Left-to-right   Right-to-left

Fig. 18.11 Bimachine for [a+ @→ 0 || b _ c]

to an epsilon depending on whether it is preceded by *c* when the intermediate output
is processed from right-to-left. Fig. 18.12 illustrates the application of the bimachine
to three input strings, *aaa*, *baaa*, and *baaac*.

```
a a a           b a a a            b a a a c
- - -▶          - - - -▶           - - - - -▶
a a a           b a1 a1 a1         b a1 a1 a1 c
◀- - -          ◀- -- -- --        ◀- -- -- -- -
a a a           b a a a            b         c
```

Fig. 18.12 Application of a bimachine

The bimachine in Fig. 18.11 encodes exactly the same relation as the transducer in Fig.
18.10. The composition of the left-to-right half *L* of the bimachine with the reverse of
the right-to-left half *R* yields the original single transducer *T*. That is, *T* = [*L* .*o*. *R.r*]
when the auxiliary symbols introduced in the bimachine factorization are removed
from the sigma alphabet.

FURTHER READING AND RELEVANT RESOURCES

Two recent anthologies of papers on finite-state methods in language processing
(Roche and Schabes 1997*b*; Kornai 1999) contain many important papers on the
theory of finite-state automata and their application. The annual conference proceedings on the implementation of automata (Wood and Yu 1998; Champarnaud, Maurel,
and Ziadi 1999; Boldt and Jürgensen 2001; Yu and Păun 2001) are more computer-
science oriented but also contain many papers relevant for linguistic applications.

Some of the recent developments not covered in this chapter are *weighted* transducers (Pereira, Riley, and Sproat 1994; Pereira and Riley 1997) and *multitape* automata (Kiraz and Grimley-Evans 1999). Weighted finite-state transducers in which the
arc labels are annotated with numerical weights have been shown to be very useful
for speech processing applications. They can associate each output with a probability
score. Multitape automata, *n*-level transducers, provide a natural implementation for
linguistic models that make use of multiple tiers (Goldsmith 1990).

Another important issue not discussed here is the compilation of finite-state networks that approximate a language or a relation described by some more powerful formalism such as phrase-structure rules (Pereira and Wright 1997; Grimley-Evans 1997; Johnson 1998).

The compilation of regular expressions into transducers remains a very lively topic (Mohri and Sproat 1996; Grimley-Evans, Kiraz, and Pulman 1996; van Noord and Gerdemann 1999). Some websites such as http://www.xrce.xerox.com/research/mltt/ fst/ and http://odur.let.rug.nl/~vannoord/fsademo/ allow the user to compile regular expressions and view and apply the resulting automata. Van Noord's FSA Toolkit (written in Prolog) is available at http://odur.let.rug.nl/~vannoord/fsa/fsa.html. The AT&T FSM Library (written in C) for weighted automata (Mohri, Pereira, and Riley 1998) is available for non-commercial applications at http://www.research.att.com/ sw/tools/fsm/. The Beesley and Karttunen book includes a public version of the Xerox finite-state tools on a CD.

REFERENCES

Aït-Mokhtar, S. and J.-P. Chanod. 1997. 'Incremental finite-state parsing'. *Proceedings of the 5th Conference on Applied Natural Language Processing (ANLP '97)* (Washington), 72–9.

Beesley, K. R. and L. Karttunen. 2003. *Finite-State Morphology: Xerox Tools and Techniques.* Stanford, Calif.: CSLI Publications.

Boldt, O. and H. Jürgensen (eds.). 2001. *Automata Implementation.* Lecture Notes in Computer Science, 2214. Berlin: Springer Verlag.

Champarnaud, J.-M., D. Maurel, and D. Ziadi (eds.). 1999. *Automata Implementation.* Lecture Notes in Computer Science, 1660. Berlin: Springer Verlag.

Chomsky, N. and M. Halle. 1968. *The Sound Pattern of English.* New York: Harper and Row.

Goldsmith, J. 1990. *Autosegmental and Metrical Phonology.* Oxford: Oxford University Press.

Grimley-Evans, E. 1997. 'Approximating context-free grammars with a finite-state calculus'. *Proceedings of the 35th ACL Annual Meeting and the 8th EACL Conference (ACL-EACL '97)* (Madrid), 452–9. cmp-lg/9711002.

——G. A. Kiraz, and S. G. Pulman. 1996. 'Compiling a partition-based two-level formalism'. *Proceedings of the 16th International Conference on Computational Linguistics* (Copenhagen), 454–9. cmp-lg/9605001.

Hopcroft, J. E. and J. D. Ullman. 1979. *Introduction to Automata Theory, Languages, and Computation.* Reading, Mass.: Addison Wesley.

Johnson, C. D. 1972. *Formal Aspects of Phonological Description.* The Hague: Mouton.

Johnson, M. 1998. 'Finite state approximation of constraint-based grammars using left-corner grammar transforms'. *Proceedings of the 36th Annual Meeting of the ACL and the 17th International Conference of Computational Linguistics (COLING/ACL '98)* (Montreal), 619–23.

Kaplan, R. M. and M. Kay. 1981. 'Phonological rules and finite-state transducers'. In *Linguistic Society of America Meeting Handbook, 56th Annual Meeting* (New York). Abstract.

————1994. 'Regular models of phonological rule systems'. *Computational Linguistics,* 20(3), 331–78.

Karttunen, L. 1993. 'Finite-state constraints'. In J. Goldsmith (ed.), *The Last Phonological Rule.* Chicago: University of Chicago Press, 173–94.

——1995. 'The replace operator'. *Proceedings of the 33rd Annual Meeting of the Association for Computational Linguistics* (Cambridge, Mass.), 16–23. cmp-lg/9504032.

——1996. 'Directed replacement'. *Proceedings of the 34th Annual Meeting of the Association for Computational Linguistics* (Santa Cruz, Calif.), 108–15. cmp-lg/9606029.

——and K. R. Beesley. 1992. *Two-level rule compiler.* Technical Report ISTL-92-2, Xerox Palo Alto Research Center, Palo Alto, Calif.

——Kaplan, R. M. and A. Zaenen. 1992. 'Two-level morphology with composition'. *Proceedings of the 14th International Conference on Computational Linguistics* (Nantes), 141–8.

——Chanod, J.-P., G. Grefenstette, and A. Schiller. 1996. 'Regular expressions for language engineering'. *Journal of Natural Language Engineering*, 2(4), 305–28.

Kempe, A. and L. Karttunen. 1996. 'Parallel replacement in finite-state calculus'. *Proceedings of the 16th International Conference on Computational Linguistics* (Copenhagen), 622–7. cmp-lg/9607007.

Kiraz, G. A. and E. Grimley-Evans. 1998. 'Multi-tape automata for speech and language systems: a Prolog implementation'. In Wood and Yu (1998), 87–103.

Kleene, S. C. 1956. 'Representation of events in nerve nets and finite automata'. In C. E. Shannon and J. McCarthy (eds.), *Automata Studies.* Princeton: Princeton University Press, 3–42.

Kornai, A. (ed.). 1999. *Extented Finite State Models of Language.* Cambridge: Cambridge University Press.

Koskenniemi, K. 1983. *Two-level morphology: a general computational model for word-form recognition and production.* Publication 11, University of Helsinki. Helsinki: Department of General Linguistics.

Laporte, É. 1997. 'Rational transductions for phonetic conversion and phonology'. In Roche and Schabes (1997*b*), 407–29.

Lucchesi, C. L. and T. Kowaltowski. 1993. 'Applications of finite automata representing large vocabularies'. *Software: Practice and Experience*, 32(1), 15–30.

Mohri, M. 1997. 'Finite-state transducers in language and speech processing'. *Computational Linguistics*, 23(2), 269–311.

——F. C. N. Pereira, and M. Riley. 1998. 'Rational design for a weighted finite-state transducer library'. In Wood and Yu (1998), 144–58.

——and Sproat, R. 1996. 'An efficient compiler for weighted rewrite rules'. *Proceedings of the 34th Annual Meeting of the Association for Computational Linguistics (ACL '96)* (Santa Cruz, Calif.), 231–8.

Oflazer, K. 1996. 'Error-tolerant finite state recognition with applications to morphological analysis and spelling correction'. *Computational Linguistics*, 22(1), 73–90.

Pereira, F. C. N. and M. Riley. 1997. 'Speech recognition by composition of weighted finite automata'. In Roche and Schabes (1997*b*), 431–53.

————and Sproat, R. 1994. 'Weighted rational transductions and their application to human language processing'. In *ARPA Workshop on Human Langue Technology*, 249–54.

——and R. Wright. 1997. 'Finite-state approximation of phrase-structure grammars'. In Roche and Schabes (1997*b*: 149–73).

Prince, A. and P. Smolensky. 1993. *Optimality Theory: constraint interaction in generative grammar.* Technical Report, Rutgers University, Piscataway, NJ. RuCCS Technical Report 2. Rutgers Center for Cognitive Science.

Roche, E. and Schabes, Y. (1997*a*). 'Deterministic part-of-speech tagging with finite-state transducers'. In Roche and Schabes (1997*b*), 205–39.

——(eds.). 1997*b*. *Finite-State Language Processing*. Cambridge, Mass.: MIT Press.

——1997*c*. 'Introduction'. In Roche and Schabes (1997*b*), 1–65.

Schützenberger, M.-P. 1961. 'A remark on finite-transducers'. *Information and Control*, 4, 185–96.

van Noord, G. and D. Gerdemann. 2001. 'An extendible regular expression compiler for finite-state approaches in natural language processing'. In Boldt and Jürgensen (2001), 122–39.

Wood, D. and S. Yu (eds.). 1998. *Automata Implementation*. Lecture Notes in Computer Science, 1436. Berlin: Springer Verlag.

Yu, S. and A. Păun (eds.). 2001. *Implementation and Application of Automata*. Lecture Notes in Computer Science, 2088. Berlin: Springer Verlag.

CHAPTER 19

STATISTICAL METHODS

CHRISTER SAMUELSSON

ABSTRACT

Statistical methods now definitely belong to mainstream natural language processing. Here mathematical statistics is reviewed and applied to language modelling problems, leading up to hidden Markov and maximum entropy models. Further reading is suggested and some mathematical detail is provided.

19.1 INTRODUCTION

Data-driven methods for natural language processing have now become so popular that they must be considered mainstream approaches to computational linguistics. They have been successfully applied to virtually all tasks within this and neighbouring fields, including part-of-speech tagging (Chapter 11), syntactic parsing (Chapter 12), semantic interpretation (Chapter 13), lexical acquisition (Chapter 21), machine translation (Chapters 27 and 28), information retrieval (Chapter 29), and information extraction (Chapter 30), and also in language learning, such as automatic grammar induction and syntactic or semantic word clustering. A strongly contributing factor to this development is undoubtedly the increasing amount of available electronically stored data to which these methods can be applied; another factor might be a certain disenchantment with approaches relying exclusively on hand-crafted rules, due to their observed brittleness.

These methods constitute a heterogeneous collection of schemes and techniques that are to a widely varying degree anchored in mathematical statistics. The more statistically inclined ones tend to originate from speech recognition (Chapter 16), while the less so tend to come from machine learning (Chapter 20). We do not necessarily advocate statistical purism: all we can really extract from training data is frequency counts—and occasionally also what type of frequency counts to extract—so the choice of underlying model will be much more important than the details of how we let the data reshape and populate it. In addition to this, traditional machine-learning techniques or other data-driven approaches may prove more appropriate for a particular task at hand. Furthermore, there is a limit to the sophistication level achievable by any data-induced model due to the combinatorial increase in training data required as a function of model complexity; to take but two simple examples: the number of possible n-grams—sequences of n items—increases exponentially in n, as does the number of possible word classes as a function of the vocabulary size.

There is nonetheless considerable mileage to be gained by harnessing the power of mathematical statistics and we will here investigate some statistically well-founded methods. We will first carve out from the discipline of mathematical statistics the concepts, tools, and insights that we will need in the following, and then proceed to examine in some detail two very popular statistical models, namely hidden Markov models and maximum-entropy models, while applying them to linguistic tasks. A section on suggested further reading concludes the chapter.

19.2 MATHEMATICAL STATISTICS

The key ideas of mathematical statistics are actually very simple and intuitive, but tend to be buried in a sea of mathematical technicalities. If we are reasonably familiar with set theory, the first stumbling block will probably be the definitions of probability measure and probability distribution. The standard textbook definition of the former is:

> A **probability measure** P is a function from the set of subsets of the sample space Ω to the set of real numbers in $[0, 1]$ with the properties
>
> 1. $\forall_{A \subseteq \Omega} \, 0 \le P(A) \le 1$
> 2. $P(\Omega) = 1$
> 3. $A \cap B = \varnothing \Rightarrow P(A \cup B) = P(A) + P(B)$

The **sample space** Ω is simply the set of possible outcomes: the set of things that can possibly happen. A probability measure is then a way of distributing the total probability mass 1 over this set. If A is a subset of Ω, then $P(A)$ is the probability mass assigned to A. A more compact, but more abstract definition would be

> A **probability measure** is a positive Borel measure P on the sample space Ω, where $P(\Omega) = 1$. For any measurable set[1] $A \subseteq \Omega$, we call $P(A)$ the probability of A.

There is certainly a lot to be gained from knowing measure theory and abstract integration, but it requires a hefty investment of time and effort.[2]

For example, consider flipping a coin. The possible outcomes are *heads* and *tails* and they constitute the entire sample space. Since we want a simple mathematical model, we ignore other possibilities, such as the coin landing balancing on its side, the coin being snapped up mid-air by a bird, or an earthquake disrupting the entire experiment. The probability measure will distribute the total mass 1 over the two outcomes, for example assigning one half to each one. But perhaps the coin is a bit bent, and will tend to land on one side more often than on the other. We then assign probability p to one side, and the rest of the probability mass, i.e. $1-p$, to the other. Let us write q for $1-p$ to save some ink in the following.

Another classical example is that of throwing a die, which is the singular form of the word 'dice' and which denotes a kind of mechanical random generator used in games like Craps, Monopoly, and Fia-med-knuff. The die can show a face with 1 to 6 eyes, typically each with probability one sixth. Thus the sample space Ω is the set $\{1, 2, 3, 4, 5, 6\}$. Consider the event A of the outcome being odd and the event B of the outcome being greater than four. These events are subsets of Ω, namely $A=\{1, 3, 5\}$ and $B=\{5, 6\}$ respectively, and quite in general, events are subsets of the sample space. The joint event of both A and B is written $A \cap B$ or A, B; in our example, $A \cap B = \{5\}$. The probability of both A and B happening is the **joint probability** $P(A, B)$ of A and B. How does the joint event come about? Well, from a logical perspective, either first A happens, with probability $P(A)$, and then B happens, with probability $P(B|A)$, or vice versa:

$$P(A, B) = P(A) \cdot P(B \mid A) = P(B) \cdot P(A \mid B)$$

Here $P(B \mid A)$ is the **conditional probability** of B given A, which is defined as

$$P(B \mid A) = \frac{P(A,B)}{P(A)}$$

This is just a variant of the preceding formula, which can be reshuffled to yield **Bayes's** famous **inversion formula**:

$$P(B|A) = \frac{P(B)}{P(A)} \cdot P(A|B)$$

---

[1] You do not want to know about non-measurable sets.   [2] At least it did so for the author.

What happens if the fact that we know that A has happened does not affect the probability of B? In other words, if $P(B|A)=P(B)$? Well, we then have

$$P(B) = P(B \mid A) = \frac{P(A, B)}{P(A)}$$

or

$$P(A) \cdot P(B) = P(A, B)$$

This is the formal definition of independence between the events A and B:

Two events A and B are **independent** iff

$$P(A, B) = P(A) \cdot P(B)$$

In our example above of throwing a die, with $A=\{1,3,5\}$ and $B=\{5,6\}$, we have $A,B=\{5\}$. If the die is fair, then

$$P(A) = P(\{1, 3, 5\}) = 3 \cdot \frac{1}{6} = \frac{1}{2}$$

$$P(B) = P(\{5, 6\}) = 2 \cdot \frac{1}{6} = \frac{1}{3}$$

$$P(A) \cdot P(B) = \frac{1}{2} \cdot \frac{1}{3} = \frac{1}{6}$$

$$P(A, B) = P(\{5\}) = \frac{1}{6}$$

and we see that A and B are independent.

Random variables, also known as stochastic variables, will in the following prove trusty allies. However, they are typically introduced to us as follows:

A **random variable** X is a function from the sample space Ω to (some subset of) the set of real numbers R, i.e. $X : \Omega \mapsto R$.

This is a bad way to start off any relationship, and calling these functions *variables* adds to the confusion. To make things worse, probability distributions are then defined in terms of the measures of the inverse images of subsets of the real numbers:

The probability of the random variable X taking a value in some subset C of the real numbers R equals the measure P of the inverse image $X^{-1}(C)$ of this subset:

$$P(X \in C \subseteq R) = P(X^{-1}(C))$$

Although confusing, there is method to this madness: the probabilities are defined on the sample space Ω, but for technical reasons it makes sense to move over to the real numbers R to define the distribution function and establish a bunch of theoretical results. We will leave this issue here and take a more practical stance in the matter.

In practice, a random variable is an abstraction of a method for making an observation, and an outcome is an observation made using this method. The random variable is an abstraction in the sense that it abstracts over different experiments with the same mathematical properties, and these properties constitute the **probability distribution**. The most popular probability distributions have names; the biased coin-flipping experiment is an example of a **Bernoulli distribution** with parameter p. We realize that once we have stated that there are two possible outcomes, and that one of them has probability p, there is not really very much more to add. The other outcome must have probability $q = 1 - p$, and how we actually go about performing the experiment is of no further consequence from a mathematical point of view; the statement 'a Bernoulli distribution with parameter p' says it all. In doing so, we abstract over the sample space Ω, for example saying that 'heads' is 1 and 'tails' is 0, and forget that we are in fact flipping a coin.[3] In this ability to abstract over the actual experimental procedure lies the real power of random variables.

To completely characterize a random variable X, we simply need to specify what values it can take, and the probability of each one. Let the set of possible values X can take be Ω_X, which will be a subset of the real numbers.[4] For each $x \in \Omega_X$, we define the probability function $p(x)$ as the probability of X taking the value x:

$$p(x) = P(X = x)$$

The probabilities $p(x)$ have to be non-negative and sum to 1:

$$p(x) \geq 0$$

$$\sum_{x \in \Omega_X} p(x) = 1$$

For the Bernoulli distribution, we have

$$p(1) = p$$

$$p(0) = q = 1 - p$$

We can now calculate the probability of the random variable X taking a value in a set $C \subseteq \Omega_X$:

$$P(X \in C) = \sum_{x \in C} p(x)$$

This works fine in the case where the set of values Ω_X is discrete. If it is uncountable, we need to smear out the probability mass as a density, thus instead creating a **probability density function** $p(x)$. So rather than assigning a weight to each element in the set Ω_X in such a way that the weights sum to 1 weight unit, we need to specify the den-

---

[3] Actually, we just defined a function mapping the sample space {'heads','tails'} to the set {0,1} $\subset R$, in strict accordance with the formal definition of a random variable.

[4] The set Ω_X should not be confused with the sample space Ω. The set Ω_X is called the sample space of the random variable X and it is the image of Ω under X, written $\Omega_X = X(\Omega)$.

sity at each point in such a way that the entire set weighs exactly 1 weight unit. If we are familiar with calculus, we realize the analogous thing is to ensure that the integral of the density over the set equals 1 weight unit.

$$p(x) \geq 0$$

$$\int_{\Omega_X} p(x)\,dx = 1$$

The probability of the random variable X taking a value in a set $C \subseteq \Omega_X$ is now

$$P(X \in C) = \int_C p(x)\,dx$$

If we are familiar with abstract integration, we know that a sum is a special type of integral, and that this formula thus generalizes the previous one.

The same method allows us to calculate various statistical averages, or **expectation values**. Since X is numerical, we can calculate its expectation value $E[X]$

$$E[X] = \sum_{x \in \Omega_X} p(x) \cdot x \left(= \int_{\Omega_X} p(x) \cdot x\,dx \right)$$

which is often written μ, or the expectation value of $(X-\mu)^2$

$$E[(X-\mu)^2] = \sum_{x \in \Omega_X} p(x) \cdot (x-\mu)^2 \left(= \int_{\Omega_X} p(x) \cdot (x-\mu)^2\,dx \right)$$

which is known as the **variance** of X, often written σ^2. In fact, we can calculate the expectation value of any function $f(X)$ of X:

$$E[f(X)] = \sum_{x \in \Omega_X} p(x) \cdot f(x) \left(= \int_{\Omega_X} p(x) \cdot f(x)\,dx \right)$$

The last concept we need is that of entropy. The **entropy** $H[X]$ of a random variable X measures how difficult it is to predict its outcome, and one appropriate measure of this is the average bit length needed to report it. If we have n equally probable outcomes, we need to report a number from 1 to n, which requires $\log_2 n$ bits. If the distribution is biased, i.e. skewed, we can be clever and use fewer bits for more frequent outcomes and more bits for less frequent ones. It turns out that we then theoretically need $-\log_2 p$ bits to report an outcome with probability p. The average number of bits needed to report the outcome of the random variable X is thus the expectation value of $-\log_2 P(X)$:

$$H[X] = E[-\log_2 P(X)] = \sum_{x \in \Omega_X} -p(x) \cdot \log_2 p(x) \left(= \int_{\Omega_X} -p(x) \cdot \log_2 p(x)\,dx \right)$$

For the Bernoulli distribution, the entropy is

$$H[X] = -p \cdot \log_2 p - q \cdot \log_2 q$$

If all outcomes are equally probable, i.e. $p(x) = \frac{1}{n}$, we retrieve the result $\log_2 n$:

$$H[X] = \sum_{x \in \Omega_X} -p(x) \cdot \log_2 p(x) = \sum_{x \in \Omega_X} -\frac{1}{n} \cdot \log_2 \frac{1}{n} = n \cdot \frac{1}{n} \cdot \log_2 n = \log_2 n$$

This distribution is the hardest one to predict, since it is the least biased one, and it maximizes the entropy for a given number of outcomes n.

A **random** or **stochastic process** is simply a sequence of random variables, i.e. it is a recipe for making a sequence of observations. There is a bit more to be said about this from a formal perspective, but this is a rather informal treatment.

19.3 HIDDEN MARKOV MODELS

We typically think of a phrase, a sentence, or even a whole text as a sequence of words. Let's take the sentence as the basic unit, and take as an example sentence *John seeks a unicorn*. Assume that we have numbered the words of our vocabulary V from 1 to M and added the end-of-sentence marker # as word number 0, i.e. $V = \{w_0, w_1, \ldots, w_M\}$. Our example sentence would then look something like

$$w_0 \; w_{42} \; w_{123} \; w_2 \; w_{1067} \; w_0$$

if *John* is the 42nd word in our enumeration, *seeks* is the 123rd word, etc.

We now devise a method for making an experiment: let W_1 be the act of observing the first word of the sentence, whatever it may be, let W_2 be the act of observing the second word, etc. Then the quantities W_n for $n = 0, 1, 2, \ldots$ are random variables and the sequence $W_0, W_1, W_2, \ldots$ is a random process. The probability of the example sentence is the probability of the outcome of a random process:[5]

P(John seeks a unicorn)=

$$= P(W_0 = \#, W_1 = \textit{John}, W_2 = \textit{seeks}, \; W_3 = a, W_4 = \textit{unicorn}, W_5 = \#)$$

Let's generalize a bit and say that the first word is w_{k_1}, the second one is w_{k_2}, etc., and let's say that we have $N-1$ words, excluding the end-of-sentence markers. In our example $k_1 = 42$, $k_2 = 123$, etc., with $N = 5$. We are then, quite in general, faced with the problem of calculating the probability[6]

---

[5] Puritans would have us write

$$P(W_0 = 0, W_1 = 42, W_2 = 123, W_3 = 2, W_4 = 1067, W_5 = 0)$$

since the random variables really take numeric values, but we can view 'John' as a mnemonic name for 42, which makes the formulas much easier to understand.

[6] The first and last words, w_{k_0} and w_{k_N}, are #, i.e. w_0, which could be expressed as $k_0 = k_N = 0$.

$$P(W_0 = w_{k_0}, W_1 = w_{k_1}, \ldots, W_N = w_{k_N})$$

We use the definition of conditional probability

$$P(A, B) = P(A) \cdot P(B \mid A)$$

where A is $W_0 = w_{k_0}, \ldots, W_{N-1} = w_{k_{N-1}}$ and B is $W_N = w_{k_N}$, to establish

$$P(W_0 = w_{k_0}, \ldots, W_{N-1} = w_{k_{N-1}}, W_N = w_{k_N}) =$$

$$= P(W_0 = w_{k_0}, \ldots, W_{N-1} = w_{k_{N-1}}) \cdot P(W_N = w_{k_N} \mid W_0 = w_{k_0}, \ldots, W_{N-1} = w_{k_{N-1}})$$

Repeatedly applying this idea gives us[7]

$$P(W_0 = w_{k_0}, \ldots, W_N = w_{k_N}) = \prod_{n=0}^{N} P(W_n = w_{k_n} \mid W_0 = w_{k_0}, \ldots, W_{n-1} = w_{k_{n-1}})$$

So we simply break down this probability into the product of the probabilities of the outcome of the next random variable, given the outcomes of the previous ones.

Although this does look a bit like progress, we are now faced with the problem of determining $P(W_n = w_{k_n} \mid W_0 = w_{k_0}, \ldots, W_{n-1} = w_{k_{n-1}})$ for any sequence of words $w_{k_0}, \ldots, w_{k_n}$. To cope with this, we make the crucial assumption that

$$P(W_n = w_{k_n} \mid W_0 = w_{k_0}, \ldots, W_{n-1} = w_{k_{n-1}}) = P(W_n = w_{k_n} \mid W_{n-1} = w_{k_{n-1}})$$

We thus discard the entire process history, apart from the previous random variable outcome. A random process with this property is called a **Markov process**. We can view the outcome of the predecessor variable as the state in which the Markov process currently is, revealing that a Markov process corresponds to a probabilistic finite-state automaton. This is clearly a very naive model of natural language, but it does make the problem of calculating the probability of any sentence tractable: we simply multiply together the probability of each word given its predecessor.

$$P(W_0 = w_{k_0}, \ldots, W_N = w_{k_N}) = \prod_{n=0}^{N} P(W_n = w_{kn} \mid W_{n-1} = w_{k_{n-1}})$$

This is often called a **word bigram model**, and, however naive, this is the language model that virtually all speech recognizers use, and it has thus far proved nigh on impossible to substantially improve on it from a performance point of view.

We now instead apply this idea to part-of-speech (POS) tags. Let T_1 be the act of observing the POS tag of the first word, T_2 observing that of the second word, etc., and let's model this with a Markov process, i.e. with a tag bigram model:

$$P(T_0 = t_{j_0}, \ldots, T_N = t_{j_N}) = \prod_{n=0}^{N} P(T_n = t_{j_n} \mid T_{n-1} = t_{j_{n-1}})$$

Next, consider a somewhat strange way of producing a tagged sentence: first randomly select a POS tag based on the POS tag of the previous word, using a Markov

---

[7] For $n = 0$, the conditional probability reduces to $P(W_0 = \#)$, which equals 1.

process, then randomly select a word based solely on the current POS tag. This results in a so-called **Markov model**:

$$P(T_0=t_{j_0}, \ldots, T_N = t_{j_N}, W_0 = w_{k_0}, \ldots, W_N = w_{k_N}) =$$

$$= \prod_{n=0}^{N} P(T_n = t_{j_n} \mid T_{n-1} = t_{j_{n-1}}) \cdot P(W_n = w_{k_n} \mid T_n = t_{j_n})$$

The probabilities $P(T_n = t_j \mid T_{n-1} = t_i)$, here with $j = j_n$ and $i = j_{n-1}$, are often called **transition probabilities**, since they reflect the probability of transiting from the tag t_i to the tag t_j. The probabilities $P(W_n = w_k \mid T_n = t_j)$ are called **emission probabilities**, reflecting the probability of emitting the word w_k from the tag t_j.

Now assume that we can only observe the word sequence, not the tag sequence. This results in a **hidden Markov model** (**HMM**), since the tag variables are hidden; their outcomes cannot be observed. In HMM-based POS tagging, the goal is to find the most likely tag sequence for a given word sequence. We realize that

$$\underset{t_{j_0}, \ldots, t_{j_N}}{argmax} P(T_0 = t_{j_0}, \ldots, T_N = t_{j_N} \mid W_0 = w_{k_0}, \ldots, W_N = w_{k_N}) =$$

$$= \underset{t_{j_0}, \ldots, t_{j_N}}{argmax} P(T_0 = t_{j_0}, \ldots, T_N = t_{j_N}, W_0 = w_{k_0}, \ldots, W_N = w_{k_N})$$

since the word sequence $w_{k_0}, \ldots, w_{k_N}$ is given, and thus fixed. We know how to calculate the latter probability; in fact, we can utilize the correspondence with a probabilistic finite-state automaton to efficiently search for the most likely tag sequence, employing a version of dynamic programming known as **Viterbi search**; see Forney (1973). It hinges on the observation that the most likely tag sequence from the beginning of the sentence to the current word, ending with a particular POS tag, can be computed recursively from these quantities for the previous word and the transition and emission probabilities.[8]

To use our HMM-based tagger, we need to estimate the transition and emission probabilities. This can be done from frequency counts extracted from a tagged corpus, adding a measure of the black art of probability smoothing (see e.g. Jelinek and Mercer 1980; Katz 1987), or from unannotated text and an initial bias using some re-estimation procedure such as the Baum–Welch algorithm; see Baum (1972).

19.4 MAXIMUM-ENTROPY MODELS

We might perhaps be a bit disappointed by the simplistic HMM-based tagging model and harbour a wish to express correlations beyond the scope of tag n-gram models.

---

[8] See section 19.5.1 for the mathematical details of the Viterbi algorithm.

We could, for example, be inspired by the English Constraint Grammar Parser of Helsinki (Tapanainen 1996), and wish to build our own data-driven version of it. One simple, but highly effective, disambiguation rule that it employs is the following:

REMOVE (V)
   IF (*–1C DET BARRIER NPHEAD) ;

this means that if there is a known determiner somewhere to the left (the *–1C DET constraint) and no intervening words that are potential heads of the noun phrase (the BARRIER NPHEAD constraint), we should remove any verb reading of the current word (the REMOVE (V) action). It is impossible to express this rule using a hidden Markov model, due to the unbounded constraint *–1C DET, and we need a more flexible framework to accommodate it. Maximum-entropy modelling provides such a framework.

Schematically, let a grammar rule r_i be of the form

In context C_i, remove or select a particular reading x_i of a word.

In our probabilistic rendering of the grammar, we wish to calculate the probability of each reading x given any context y. Let X be the reading variable and Y be the context variable. The probabilistic model we are looking for consists of the distributions

$$P(X = x \mid Y = y)$$

To link this to the grammar rules, we introduce binary-valued features f_i that are triggered whenever rule r_i would apply, i.e. for reading x_i in context C_i:

$$f_i(x, y) = \begin{cases} 1 \text{ if } x = x_i \wedge y \in C_i \\ 0 \text{ otherwise} \end{cases}$$

For the example rule, this would be whenever there is a verb reading of the current word, i.e. $x = x_i$, and a known determiner somewhere to its left but no intervening candidate noun-phrase head, i.e. $y \in C_i$. If our original rule is any good, this would happen very seldom in annotated training data, since it recommends us to *remove* the verb reading in this context; if it had instead urged us to *select* the verb reading, we would expect this feature to be triggered relatively often.

The following two requirements sum up the philosophy underlying maximum-entropy modelling:

1. We want our probabilistic model to predict that the features f_i in average are triggered just as often as they were in the training data.
2. We do not want to impose any other bias into our model.

Let us write $p(x \mid y)$ for the sought distribution $P(X = x \mid Y = y)$, $p(x, y)$ for $P(X = x, Y = y)$, and $p(y)$ for $P(Y = y)$. Let the empirical distribution, i.e. the one observed in the training data, be $\tilde{p}(x, y)$ for the joint variable X, Y and $\tilde{p}(y)$ for Y. How often is the feature f_i on average triggered in the training data? This is the expectation value of the feature function f_i *under the empirical distribution* $\tilde{p}(x, y)$:

$$E_{\tilde{p}}[f_i(X,Y)]=\sum_{x,y}\tilde{p}(x,y)\cdot f_i(x,y)$$

How often does our model predict that this will on average happen? This is the expectation value of the feature function f_i *under our model distribution $p(x,y)$*:

$$E_p[f_i(X,Y)]=\sum_{x,y}p(x,y)\cdot f_i(x,y)$$

Since one needs very keen eyesight to distinguish $E_p[\ldots]$ and $E_{\tilde{p}}[\ldots]$, we will write $E[\ldots]$ for $E_p[\ldots]$ but retain $E_{\tilde{p}}[\ldots]$.

Unfortunately, our model defines the conditional distribution $p(x\,|\,y)$, rather than the joint distribution $p(x,y)$. However, using the definition of conditional probability, we realize that

$$p(x,y) = p(y)\cdot p(x\,|\,y)$$

so if we could just estimate $p(y)$, all would be fine, and to this end we use the empirical distribution $\tilde{p}(y)$:

$$E[f_i(X,Y)] \approx \sum_{x,y}\tilde{p}(y)\cdot p(x\,|\,y)\cdot f_i(x,y)$$

So the first requirement boils down to

$$\forall_i\, E[f_i(X,Y)]=E_{\tilde{p}}[f_i(X,Y)]$$

i.e.

$$\forall_i\sum_{x,y}\tilde{p}(y)\cdot p(x\,|\,y)\cdot f_i(x,y) = \sum_{x,y}\tilde{p}(x,y)\cdot f_i(x,y)$$

There are however infinitely many possible distributions $p(x\,|\,y)$ that satisfy these constraints, for example the empirical distribution

$$\tilde{p}(x\,|\,y) = \frac{\tilde{p}(x,y)}{\tilde{p}(y)}$$

To choose between these, we use our second requirement: we do not wish to introduce any additional bias. The way we interpret this is that we wish to maximize the entropy of the probability distributions, while satisfying the constraints derived from the first requirement. The rationale for this is that the least biased distribution is the one that is the hardest to predict, and we recall from the end of section 19.2 that this is the one with the highest entropy.

The two philosophical requirements thus result in the following constrained optimization problem:

$$\operatorname*{argmax}_{p(x|y)}\ H[X\,|\,Y]$$

$$\forall_{x,y} \; p(x \mid y) \geq 0$$

$$\forall_y \; \sum_x p(x \mid y) = 1$$

$$\forall_i \; E[f_i(X,Y)] = E_{\tilde{p}}[f_i(X,Y)]$$

The way to solve constrained optimization problems in general is to introduce so-called Lagrange multipliers, here $\lambda(y)$ and λ_i, and instead solve an unconstrained optimization problem:

$$\underset{p(x \mid y), \lambda(y), \lambda_i}{\text{argmax}} \; (H[X \mid Y] + \sum_y \lambda(y) \cdot (1 - \sum_x p(x \mid y)) + \sum_i \lambda_i \cdot (E[f_i(X,Y)] - E_{\tilde{p}}[f_i(X,Y)]))$$

It turns out that we then get a unique solution

$$p(x \mid y) = \frac{1}{Z(y)} \cdot \prod_i e^{\lambda_i \cdot f_i(x,y)} \geq 0$$

$$Z(y) = \sum_x \prod_i e^{\lambda_i \cdot f_i(x,y)}$$

which actually falls out rather directly from the equations. To determine the values of the multipliers λ_i, though, we need to resort to numerical methods.[9]

We note that each probability $p(x \mid y)$ consists of a product of a number of factors that are either e^{λ_i} if the feature f_i is triggered, or 1, if it is not. This is an example of a **Gibbs distribution**. Let's rename the factors e^{λ_i}, instead calling them α_i, and note that they are by necessity positive. Now, very small values of α_i will tend to push down the probability towards zero, corresponding to a remove action of the original rule r_i, while very large factors will push up the probability towards 1, corresponding to a select action.

However, the real strength of maximum-entropy modelling lies in combining evidence from several rules, each one of which alone might not be conclusive, but which taken together dramatically affect the probability. Thus, maximum-entropy modelling allows combining heterogeneous information sources to produce a uniform probabilistic model where each piece of information is formulated as a feature f_i. The framework ensures that the model distribution respects the empirical distribution in the sense that, on the training data, the model must predict each feature to be triggered just as often as it did. This forces the model to appropriately handle dependent information sources, e.g. when the same feature is accidentally included twice.

A special aspect of maximum-entropy modelling that has received much attention is that of automatically exploring the space of possible features to extract an appropriate feature set; see Della Pietra, Della Pietra, and Lafferty (1997).

---

[9] See section 19.5.2 for the mathematical details of solving the optimization problem.

19.5 SOME MATHEMATICAL DETAILS

We here present the mathematical details of the Viterbi algorithm and of solving the maximum-entropy equations. Some readers may wish to skip this section.

19.5.1 Viterbi search for hidden Markov models

We wish to find the most likely tag sequence $\hat{t}_0 \ldots \hat{t}_N$ for a given word sequence $w_{k_0} \ldots w_{k_N}$:

$$\hat{t}_0 \ldots \hat{t}_N = \underset{t_{j_0}, \ldots, t_{j_N}}{\mathrm{argmax}}\, P(T_0 = t_{j_0}, \ldots, T_N = t_{j_N}, W_0 = w_{k_0}, \ldots, W_N = w_{k_N})$$

Let $\delta_n(j)$ be the probability of the most likely tag sequence from word w_{k_0} to word w_{k_n} that ends with tag t_j, i.e.

$$\delta_n(j) = \max_{t_{j_0}, \ldots, t_{j_{n-1}}} P(T_0 = t_{j_0}, \ldots, T_{n-1} = t_{j_{n-1}}, T_n = t_j, W_0 = w_{k_0}, \ldots, W_n = w_{k_n})$$

and let $\iota_n(j)$ be the tag of word $w_{k_{n-1}}$ in this tag sequence. Then

$$\delta_0(0) = 1$$
$$\delta_0(j) = 0 \text{ for } j \neq 0$$
$$\hat{t}_N = \underset{i}{\mathrm{argmax}}\, \delta_N(i)$$

and for $n = 1, \ldots, N$

$$\delta_n(j) = \max_i \left(\delta_{n-1}(i) \cdot P(T_n = t_j \mid T_{n-1} = t_i) \cdot P(W_n = w_{k_n} \mid T_n = t_j)\right)$$

$$\iota_n(j) = \underset{i}{\mathrm{argmax}} \left(\delta_{n-1}(i) \cdot P(T_n = t_j \mid T_{n-1} = t_i) \cdot P(W_n = w_{k_n} \mid T_n = t_j)\right)$$

$$\hat{t}_{n-1} = \iota(\hat{t}_n)$$

which allows finding the most likely tag sequence in linear time in the sequence length N. Essentially the same algorithm allows calculating the probability of a given word sequence $w_{k_0} \ldots w_{k_N}$ in linear time:

$$\alpha_0(0) = 1$$

$$\alpha_0(j) = 0 \text{ ; for } j \neq 0$$

$$P(W_0 = w_{k_0}, \ldots, W_N = w_{k_N}) = \sum_i \alpha_N(i)$$

and for $n = 1, \ldots, N$

$$\alpha_n(j) = \sum_i \left(\alpha_{n-1}(i) \cdot P(T_n = t_j \mid T_{n-1} = t_i) \cdot P(W_n = w_{k_n} \mid T_n = t_j)\right)$$

19.5.2 The maximum-entropy equations

We wish to solve the optimization problem

$$\operatorname*{argmax}_{p(x\,|\,y),\lambda(y),\lambda_i} \left(H[X\,|\,Y] + \sum_y \lambda(y)\cdot\left(1-\sum_x p(x\,|\,y)\right) + \sum_i \lambda_i \cdot \left(E[f_i(X,Y)] - E_{\tilde{p}}[f_i(X,Y)] \right) \right)$$

We switch to the natural logarithm ln in $H[X\,|\,Y]$ and multiply the multipliers $\lambda(y)$ by $\tilde{p}(y)$, which does not affect the solution to the problem, and spell out the resulting object function $G(p(x\,|\,y),\lambda(y),\lambda_i)$:

$$G(p(x\,|\,y),\lambda(y),\lambda_i) =$$

$$= H[X\,|\,Y] + \sum_y \lambda(y)\cdot\tilde{p}(y)\cdot\left(1-\sum_x p(x\,|\,y)\right) + \sum_i \lambda_i\cdot\left(E[f_i(X,Y)] - E_{\tilde{p}}[f_i(X,Y)]\right) =$$

$$\sum_{x,y} -\tilde{p}(y)\cdot p(x\,|\,y)\cdot\ln p(x\,|\,y) + \sum_y \lambda(y)\cdot\tilde{p}(y)\cdot\left(1-\sum_x p(x\,|\,y)\right) +$$

$$+ \sum_i \lambda_i\cdot\left(\sum_{x,y}\tilde{p}(y)\cdot p(x\,|\,y)\cdot f_i(x,y) - \sum_{x,y}\tilde{p}(x,y)\cdot f_i(x,y)\right)$$

Since this is a smooth convex function of the parameters $p(x\,|\,y)$ that we are maximizing over, the maximum is obtained when its partial derivatives w.r.t. these parameters are zero:[10]

$$\frac{\partial}{\partial p(x\,|\,y)} G(p(x\,|\,y),\lambda(y),\lambda_i) =$$

$$-\tilde{p}(y)\cdot\ln p(x\,|\,y) - \tilde{p}(y) - \lambda(y)\cdot\tilde{p}(y) + \sum_i \lambda_i\cdot\tilde{p}(y)\cdot f_i(x,y) = 0$$

or

$$\tilde{p}(y)\cdot\ln p(x\,|\,y) = -\tilde{p}(y) - \lambda(y)\cdot\tilde{p}(y) + \sum_i \lambda_i\cdot\tilde{p}(y)\cdot f_i(x,y)$$

or

$$\ln p(x\,|\,y) = -1 - \lambda(y) + \sum_i \lambda_i\cdot f_i(x,y)$$

or

$$p(x\,|\,y) = e^{-1-\lambda(y)+\sum_i \lambda_i\cdot f_i(x,y)} = e^{-1-\lambda(y)}\cdot e^{\sum_i \lambda_i\cdot f_i(x,y)} = \frac{1}{Z(y)}\cdot\prod_i e^{\lambda_i\cdot f_i(x,y)}$$

Setting the partial derivatives w.r.t. the multipliers to zero simply yields the original constraints:

$$\frac{\partial}{\partial\lambda(y)} G(p(x\,|\,y),\lambda(y),\lambda_i) = \tilde{p}(y)\cdot\left(1-\sum_x p(x\,|\,y)\right) = 0$$

$$\frac{\partial}{\partial\lambda_i} G(p(x\,|\,y),\lambda(y),\lambda_i) = \sum_{x,y}\tilde{p}(y)\cdot p(x\,|\,y)\cdot f_i(x,y) - \sum_{x,y}\tilde{p}(x,y)\cdot f_i(x,y) = 0$$

---

[10] In any point where a smooth function has a (local) maximum, either the partial derivatives are all zero or the point is on the boundary. Conversely, if the smooth function is convex, then wherever all partial derivatives are zero, we have the (global) maximum.

or

$$\sum_x p(x|y) = 1$$

$$\sum_{x,y} \tilde{p}(y) \cdot p(x|y) \cdot f_i(x,y) = \sum_{x,y} \tilde{p}(x,y) \cdot f_i(x,y)$$

Recalling that $Z(y) = e^{1+\lambda(y)}$, the constraints $\frac{\partial G}{\partial \lambda(y)} = 0$ determine $\lambda(y)$:

$$\sum_x p(x|y) = \sum_x \frac{1}{Z(y)} \cdot \prod_i e^{\lambda_i \cdot f_i(x,y)} = 1$$

or

$$Z(y) = \sum_x \prod_i e^{\lambda_i \cdot f_i(x,y)}$$

The constraints $\frac{\partial G}{\partial \lambda_i} = 0$ are just the original constraints on f_i

$$E[f_i(X,Y)] = E_{\tilde{p}}[f_i(X,Y)]$$

and these determine the values of the only remaining unknown quantities, the λ_i multipliers. These equations can be solved using various numerical methods; a currently popular one is called **improved iterative scaling**:

1. $\forall_i \ \lambda_i := 0$
2. $\forall_i$ let $\Delta\lambda_i$ be the solution to

$$E[g_i(X,Y)] = E_{\tilde{p}}[f_i(X,Y)]$$

where

$$g_i(x,y) = f_i(x,y) \cdot e^{\Delta\lambda_i \cdot f_i(x,y)}$$
$$f(x,y) = \sum_j f_j(x,y)$$

i.e. the solution to

$$\sum_{x,y} \tilde{p}(y) \cdot p(x|y) \cdot f_i(x,y) \cdot e^{\Delta\lambda_i \cdot \Sigma_j f_j(x,y)} = \sum_{x,y} \tilde{p}(x,y) \cdot f_i(x,y)$$

3. $\forall_i \ \lambda_i := \lambda_i + \Delta\lambda_i$
4. If any λ_i has not converged, i.e. if $\Delta\lambda_i$ is not sufficiently close to zero, go to 2. Note that when $\Delta\lambda_i$ equals zero, then $g_i(x,y)$ equals $f_i(x,y)$ and the equations in Step 2 reduce to the original constraints on f_i, which in turn are satisfied if $\Delta\lambda_i = 0$ solve these equations.

FURTHER READING AND RELEVANT RESOURCES

There are a lot of good textbooks on mathematical statistics; we particularly like DeGroot (1975) and Mood, Greybill, and Boes (1974). A short, but comprehensive book on calculus is Rudin (1976). Entropy is just one of many useful tools from information theory, where Ash (1965) is a good textbook. We recommend Rabiner (1989) for an excellent tutorial on hidden Markov models for speech recognition and Berger, Della Pietra, and Della Pietra (1996) for maximum-entropy modelling, as applied to natural language processing. To date, three textbooks on statistical methods for computational linguistics have emerged, namely Charniak (1993), Manning and Schütze (1999), and Krenn and Samuelsson (1994–7). The latter has the advantage of being freely available on the World Wide Web. In the related field of speech recognition, we recommend Jelinek (1997).

HMM-based POS tagging was first proposed in Church (1988), while an approach using maximum-entropy modelling is given in Ratnaparki (1996). From a performance point of view, Samuelsson and Voutilainen (1997) is sobering reading. Probabilistic chart parsing is well described in Stolcke (1995) and probabilistic LR parsing in Briscoe and Carroll (1993), although the latter statistical model is flawed. Current mainstream probabilistic parsing evolved in Magerman (1995) and Collins (1997).

Yarowsky (1992) is a by now classic article on statistical word-sense disambiguation, but also check out Schütze (1992). A few different ways of using statistical methods in machine translation are presented in Brown et al. (1990), Wu (1995), and Alshawi (1996), respectively. Manning (1993) takes a statistical approach to learning lexical verb complement patterns and Samuelsson, Tapanainen, and Voutilainen (1996) to constraint-grammar induction.

ACKNOWLEDGEMENTS

The author wishes to thank Marc Dymetman, Eric Gaussier, Pierre Isabelle, and Åke Samuelsson for helpful comments and enlightening discussions.

REFERENCES

Alshawi, H. 1996. 'Head automata and bilingual tiling: translation with minimal representations'. In *Proceedings of the 34th Annual Meeting of the Association for Computational Linguistics* (Santa Cruz, Calif.), 167–76.

Ash, R. 1965. *Information Theory*. New York: John Wiley.

Baum, L. E. 1972. ' An inequality and associated maximization technique in statistical estimation of probabilistic functions of Markov processes'. *Inequalities*, 3, 1–8.

Berger, A., S. Della Pietra, and V. Della Pietra. 1996. 'A maximum entropy approach to natural language processing'. *Computational Linguistics*, 22(1), 39–71.

Briscoe, T. and J. Carroll. 1993. 'Generalized probabilistic LR parsing of natural language (corpora) with unification-based grammars'. *Computational Linguistics*, 19(1), 25–59.

Brown, P., J. Cocke, S. Della Pietra, V. Della Pietra, F. Jelinek, J. Lafferty, R. Mercer, and P. Roossin. 1990. 'A statistical approach to machine translation'. *Computational Linguistics* 16(2), 79–85.

Charniak, E. 1993. *Statistical Language Learning*. Cambridge, Mass.: MIT Press.

Church, K. 1988. 'A stochastic parts program and noun phrase parser for unrestricted text'. *Proceedings of the 2nd Conference on Applied Natural Language Processing* (Austin, Tex.), 136–43.

Collins, M. 1997. 'Three generative, lexicalized models for statistical parsing'. *Proceedings of the 35th Annual Meeting of the Association for Computational Linguistics* (Madrid), 16–23.

DeGroot, M. 1975. *Probability and Statistics*. Reading, Mass.: Addison-Wesley.

Della Pietra, S., V. Della Pietra, and J. Lafferty. 1997. 'Inducing features of random fields'. *IEEE PAMI*, 19(4), 380–93.

Forney, D. 1973. 'The Viterbi algorithm'. *Proceedings of the IEEE*, 61(3), 268–78.

Jelinek, F. 1990. 'Self-organizing language models for speech recognition'. *Readings in Speech Recognition*. San Mateo, Calif.: Morgan Kaufmann, 450–506.

——1997. *Statistical Methods for Speech Recognition*. Cambridge, Mass.: MIT Press.

——and R. Mercer. 1980. 'Interpolated estimation of Markov source parameters from sparse data'. In *Pattern Recognition in Practice*. Amsterdam: North Holland, 381–97.

Katz, S. 1987. 'Estimation of probabilities from sparse data for the language model component of a speech recognizer'. *IEEE Transactions on Acoustics, Speech, and Signal Processing*, 35(3), 400–1.

Krenn, B. and C. Samuelsson. 1996–7. *The Linguist's Guide to Statistics*. http://www.coli.uni-sb.de/~krenn.

Magerman, D. 1995. 'Statistical decision-tree models for parsing'. *Proceedings of the 33rd Annual Meeting of the Association for Computational Linguistics* (Cambridge, Mass.), 276–83.

Manning, C. 1993. 'Automatic acquisition of a large subcategorization dictionary from corpora'. *Proceedings of the 31st Annual Meeting of the Association for Computational Linguistics* (Columbus, Oh.), 235–42.

——and H. Schütze. 1999. *Foundations of Statistical Natural Language Processing*. Cambridge, Mass.: MIT Press.

Mood, A., F. Greybill, and D. Boes. 1974. *Introduction to the Theory of Statistics*. 3rd edn. New York: McGraw Hill.

Rabiner, L. 1989. 'A tutorial on hidden Markov models and selected applications in speech recognition'. *Proceedings of the IEEE*, 77(2), 257–95.

Ratnaparki, A. 1996. 'A maximum entropy model for part-of-speech tagging'. *Proceedings of the Conference on Empirical Methods in Natural Language Processing* (Philadelphia, Pa.), 257–95.

Rudin, W. 1976. *Principles of Mathematical Analysis*. New York: McGraw-Hill.

Samuelsson, C., P. Tapanainen, and A. Voutilainen. 1996. 'Inducing constraint grammars'. In *Grammatical Inference: Learning Syntax from Sentences*. Berlin: Springer Verlag, 146–55.

——and A. Voutilainen. 1997. 'Comparing a stochastic and a linguistic tagger'. In *Proceedings of the Joint 35th Annual Meeting of the Association for Computational Linguistics and 8th Conference of the European Chapter of the Association for Computational Linguistics* (Madrid), 246–53.

Schütze, H. 1992. 'Dimensions of meaning'. *Proceedings of Supercomputing '92* (Minneapolis, Minn.), 787–96.

Stolcke, A. 1995. 'An efficient probabilistic context-free parsing algorithm that computes prefix probabilities'. *Computational Linguistics*, 21(2), 165–202.

Tapanainen, P. 1996. *The Constraint Grammar Parser CG-2*. Publication 27. Helsinki: Department of General Linguistics, University of Helsinki.

Wu, D. 1995. 'Stochastic inversion transduction grammars, with application to segmentation, bracketing, and alignment of parallel corpora'. *Proceedings of the 14th International Joint Conference on Artificial Intelligence* (San Mateo, Calif.), 1328–35.

Yarowsky, D. 1992. 'Word-sense disambiguation using statistical models of Roget's categories trained on large corpora'. *Proceedings of the 14th International Conference on Computational Linguistics* (Nantes), 454–60.

CHAPTER 20

....

MACHINE LEARNING

....

RAYMOND J. MOONEY

ABSTRACT

This chapter introduces symbolic machine learning in which decision trees, rules, or case-based classifiers are induced from supervised training examples. It describes the representation of knowledge assumed by each of these approaches and reviews basic algorithms for inducing such representations from annotated training examples and using the acquired knowledge to classify future instances. These techniques can be applied to learn knowledge required for a variety of problems in computational linguistics ranging from part-of-speech tagging and syntactic parsing to word-sense disambiguation and anaphora resolution. Applications to a variety of these problems are reviewed.

20.1 INTRODUCTION

....

Broadly interpreted, **machine learning** is the study of computational systems that improve performance on some task with experience (Mitchell 1997; Langley 1996). However, the term is frequently used to refer specifically to methods that represent learned knowledge in a declarative, symbolic form as opposed to more numerically oriented statistical or neural-network training methods (see Chapter 19). In particular, it concerns methods which represent learned knowledge in the form of interpretable decision trees, logical rules, and stored instances. **Decision trees** are classification functions represented as trees in which the nodes are attribute tests, the branches are attribute values, and the leaves are class labels. Rules are implications in either propositional or predicate logic used to draw deductive inferences from data. A variety of algorithms exist for inducing knowledge in both of these forms from training examples. In contrast, instance-based (case-based, memory-based) methods simply remember past training instances and make a decision about a new case based on its similarity to specific past examples. This chapter reviews basic methods for each of these three approaches to symbolic machine learning. Specifically, we review top-down induction of decision trees, **rule induction** (including inductive logic programming), and nearest-neighbour **instance-based learning** methods.

As described in previous chapters, understanding natural language requires a large amount of knowledge about morphology, syntax, semantics, and pragmatics as well as general knowledge about the world. Acquiring and encoding all of this knowledge is one of the fundamental impediments to developing effective and robust language processing systems. Like the statistical methods described in the previous chapter, machine learning methods offer the promise of automating the acquisition of this knowledge from annotated or unannotated language corpora. A potential advantage of symbolic learning methods over statistical methods is that the acquired knowledge is represented in a form that is more easily interpreted by human developers and more similar to representations used in manually developed systems. Such interpretable knowledge potentially allows for greater scientific insight into linguistic phenomena, improvement of learned knowledge through human editing, and easier integration with manually developed systems. Each of the machine learning methods we review has been applied to a variety of problems in computational linguistics including morphological generation and analysis, part-of-speech tagging, syntactic parsing, word-sense disambiguation, semantic analysis, information extraction, and anaphora resolution. We briefly survey some of these applications and summarize the current state of the art in the application of symbolic machine learning to computational linguistics.

20.2 LEARNING FOR CATEGORIZATION

Most machine learning methods concern the task of categorizing examples described by a set of features. It is generally assumed that a fixed set of n discrete-valued or real-valued features, $\{f_1, \ldots, f_n\}$, are used to describe examples, and that the task is to assign an example to one of m disjoint categories $\{c_1, \ldots, c_m\}$. For example, consider the task of deciding which of the following three sense categories is the correct interpretation of the semantically ambiguous English noun *interest* given a full sentence in which it appears as context (see Chapter 13).

1. c_1: readiness to give attention
2. c_2: advantage, advancement, or favour
3. c_3: money paid for the use of money

The following might be a reasonable set of features for this problem:

- W+i: the word appearing i positions after *interest* for $i = 1, 2, 3$
- W−i: the word appearing i positions before *interest* for $i = 1, 2, 3$
- K_i: a binary-valued feature for a selected keyword for $1 = 1, \ldots, k$, where K_i is true if the ith keyword appears anywhere in the current sentence. Relevant keywords for interest might be, *attracted, expressed, payments, bank*, etc.

A learning system is given a set of supervised training examples for which the correct category is given. For example:

1. c_1: John expressed a strong interest in computers.
2. c_2: Acme Bank charges very high interest.
3. c_3: War in East Timor is not in the interest of the nation.

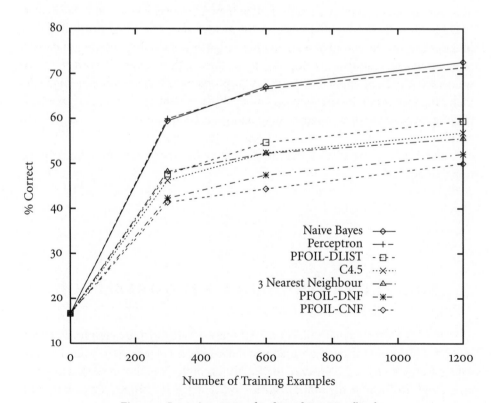

Fig. 20.1 **Learning curves for disambiguating 'line'**

In this case, the values of the relevant features must first be determined in a straight-forward manner from the text of the sentence. From these examples, the system must produce a procedure for accurately categorizing future examples.

Categorization systems are typically evaluated on the accuracy of their predictions as measured by the percentage of examples that are correctly classified. Experiments for estimating this accuracy for a particular task are performed by randomly splitting a representative set of labelled examples into two sets, a training set used to induce a classifier, and an independent and disjoint test set used to measure its classification accuracy. Averages over multiple splits of the data into training and test sets provide more accurate estimates and give information on the variation in performance across training and test samples. Since labelling large amounts of training data can be a time-consuming task, it is also useful to look at *learning curves* in which the accuracy is measured repeatedly as the size of the training set is increased, providing information on how well the system generalizes from various amounts of training data. Fig. 20.1 shows sample learning curves for a variety of systems on a related task of semantically disambiguating the word 'line' into one of six possible senses (Mooney 1996). Mitchell (1997) provides a basic introduction to machine learning including discussion on experimental evaluation.

20.3 Decision-Tree Induction

Decision trees are classification functions represented as trees in which the nodes are feature tests, the branches are feature values, and the leaves are class labels. An example is classified by starting at the root and recursively traversing the tree to a leaf by following the path dictated by its feature values. A sample tree for the *interest* problem is shown in Fig. 20.2. For simplicity, assume that all of the unseen extra branches for W+1 and W+2 are leaves labelled c_1. This tree can be paraphrased as follows: If the word *bank* appears anywhere in the sentence assign sense c_3; otherwise if the word following *interest* is *rate*, assign sense c_3, but if the following word is *of* and the word two before is *in* (as in . . . *in the interest of* . . .), then assign sense c_2; in all other cases assign sense c_1.

The goal of learning is to induce a decision tree that is consistent with the training data. Since there are many trees consistent with a given training set, most approaches follow 'Occam's razor' and try to induce the simplest tree according to some complexity measure such as the number of leaves, or the depth of the tree. Since computing a minimal tree according to such measures is an NP hard problem (i.e. a computational problem for which there is no known efficient, polynomial-time algorithm; see also

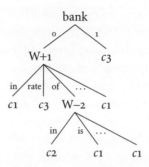

Fig 20.2 Sample decision tree for disambiguating *interest*

Chapter 9), most algorithms perform a fairly simple greedy search to efficiently find an approximately minimal tree. The standard approach is a divide-and-conquer algorithm that constructs the tree top down, first picking a feature for the root of the tree and then recursively creating subtrees for each value of the selected splitting feature. Pseudocode for such an algorithm is shown in Fig. 20.3.

The size of the constructed tree critically depends on the heuristic used to pick the splitting feature. A standard approach is to pick the feature that maximizes the expected reduction in the entropy, or disorder, of the data with respect to category (Quinlan 1986). The entropy of a set of data, S, with respect to category is defined as:

$$(20.1)\quad Entropy(S) = \sum_{i=1}^{m} -\frac{|S_i|}{|S|} \log_2 \frac{|S_i|}{|S|}$$

where S_i is the subset of S in category i ($1 \le i \le m$). The closer the data is to consisting purely of examples in a single category, the lower the entropy. A good splitting feature

---

InduceTree(*Examples, Features*)
    Create a node *Root* for the tree
    If all the examples are in the same category
        then return *Root* labelled with this category as a leaf.
    If features are empty
        then return *Root* labelled with the most common category in *Examples* as a leaf.
    Else pick the best splitting feature f_i and use it to label *Root*.
    For each possible value v_{ij} of f_i
        Add a branch to *Root* for the value v_{ij}.
        Let *Examples$_{ij}$* be the subset of *Examples* with value v_j for f_i.
        If *Examples$_{ij}$* is empty
            then below the branch add a leaf labelled with the most common category in *Examples*.
            else below the branch add the subtree InduceTree(*Examples$_{ij}$, Features* $- \{f_i\}$).
    Return *Root*.

Fig. 20.3 Decision-tree induction algorithm

fractions the data into subsets with low entropy. This is because the closer the subsets are to containing examples in only a single category, the closer they are to terminating in a leaf, and the smaller will be the resulting subtree. Therefore, the best split is selected as the feature, f_i, that results in the greatest *information gain* defined as:

$$(20.2) \quad Gain(S, f_i) = Entropy(S) - \sum_j \frac{|S_{ij}|}{|S|} Entropy(S_{ij})$$

where j ranges over the possible values v_{ij} of f_i, and S_{ij} is the subset of S with value v_{ij} for feature f_i. The expected entropy of the resulting subsets is computed by weighting their entropies by their relative size $|S_{ij}| / |S|$.

The resulting algorithm is computationally very efficient (linear in the number of examples) and in practice can quickly construct relatively small trees from large amounts of data. The basic algorithm has been enhanced to handle many practical problems that arise when processing real data, such as noisy data, missing feature values, and real-valued features (Quinlan 1993). Consequently, decision-tree methods are widely used in *data mining* applications where very large amounts of data need to be processed (Fayyad, Piatetsky-Shapiro, and Smyth 1996; see also Chapter 34). The most effective recent improvement to decision-tree algorithms has been methods for constructing multiple alternative decision trees from the same training data, and then classifying new instances based on a weighted vote of these multiple hypotheses (Quinlan 1993).

20.4 RULE INDUCTION

Classification functions can also be symbolically represented by a set of rules, or logical implications. This is equivalent to representing each category in *disjunctive normal form* (DNF), i.e. a disjunction of conjunctions of feature-value pairs, where each rule is a conjunction corresponding to a disjunct in the formula for a given category. For example, the decision tree in Fig. 20.2 can also be represented by the rules in Fig. 20.4, assuming that c_1 is the *default category* that is assigned if none of the rules apply.

$$bank \rightarrow c_3$$
$$\neg\, bank \wedge W+1 = in \rightarrow c_1$$
$$W+1 = rate \rightarrow c_3$$
$$\neg\, bank \wedge W+1 = of \wedge W-2 = in \rightarrow c_2$$

Fig. 20.4 Sample rules for disambiguating *interest*

InduceRules(*Examples, Features*)
  Let $S = \varnothing$
  For each category c_i do
      Let P be the subset of *Examples* in c_i.
      Let N be the subset of *Examples* not in c_i.
      Until P is empty do
          Let R = ConstructRule(P, N, *Features*)
          Let $S = S \cup \{R \rightarrow c_i\}$
          Let C be the subset of P covered by R.
          Let $P = P - C$
  Return S

Fig. 20.5 **Rule-induction covering algorithm**

Decision trees can be translated into a set of rules by creating a separate rule for each path from the root to a leaf in the tree (Quinlan 1993). However, rules can also be directly induced from training data using a variety of algorithms (Mitchell 1997; Langley 1996). The general goal is to construct the smallest rule set (the one with the least number of symbols) that is consistent with the training data. Again, the problem of learning the minimally complex hypothesis is NP hard, and therefore heuristic search is typically used to induce only an approximately minimal definition. The standard approach is to use a form of greedy set covering, where at each iteration, a new rule is learned that attempts to cover the largest set of examples of a particular category without covering examples of other categories. These examples are then removed, and additional rules are learned to cover the remaining examples of the category. Pseudocode for this process is shown in Fig. 20.5, where ConstructRule(P, N, *Features*) attempts to learn a conjunction covering as many of the positive examples in P as possible without covering any of the negative examples in N.

ConstructRule(P, N, *Features*)
  Let $A = \varnothing$
  Until N is empty do
      For each feature-value pair $f_i = v_{ij}$
          Let P_{ij} be the subset of P with value v_{ij} for feature f_i
          Let N_{ij} be the subset of N with value v_{ij} for feature f_i
      Given P, N, P_{ij}, and N_{ij}, pick the best specializing feature-value pair, $f_i = v_{ij}$
      Let $A = A \cup \{f_i = v_{ij}\}$
      Let $P = P_{ij}$
      Let $N = N_{ij}$
  Return the conjunction of feature-value pairs in A

Fig. 20.6 **Top-down rule construction algorithm**

There are two basic approaches to implementing ConstructRule. *Top-down* (*general-to-specific*) approaches start with the most general 'empty' rule (*True* $\rightarrow c_i$), and repeatedly specialize it until it no longer covers any of the negative examples in N. *Bottom-up* (*specific-to-general*) approaches start with a very specific rule whose antecedent consists of the complete description of one of the positive examples in P, and repeatedly generalize it until it begins covering negative examples in N. Since top-down approaches tend to construct simpler (more general) rules, they are generally more popular. Fig. 20.6 presents a top-down algorithm based on the approach used in the FOIL system (Quinlan 1993). At each step, a new condition, $f_i = v_{ij}$, is added to the rule and the examples that fail to satisfy this condition are removed. The best specializing feature-value pair is selected based on preferring to retain as many positive examples as possible while removing as many negatives as possible. A gain heuristic analogous to the one used in decision trees can be defined as follows:

$$(20.3) \quad Gain\,(f_i = v_{ij}, P, N) = |P_{ij}|(\log_2(\frac{|P_{ij}|}{|P_{ij}|+|N_{ij}|}) - \log_2(\frac{|P|}{|P|+|N|}))$$

where P_{ij} and N_{ij} are as defined in Fig. 20.6. The first term, $|P_{ij}|$, encourages coverage of a large number of positives and the second term encourages an increase in the *percentage* of covered examples that are positive (decrease in the percentage of covered examples that are negative).

This and similar rule-learning algorithms have been demonstrated to efficiently induce small and accurate rule sets from large amounts of realistic data. Like decision-tree methods, rule-learning algorithms have also been enhanced to handle noisy data and real-valued features (Clark and Niblett 1989; Cohen 1995). More significantly, they also have been extended to learn rules in first-order predicate logic, a much richer representation language. Predicate logic allows for quantified variables and relations and can represent concepts that are not expressible using examples described as feature vectors. For example, the following rules, written in Prolog syntax (where the conclusion appears first), define the relational concept of an uncle:

uncle(X, Y) :- brother(X, Z), parent(Z, Y).
uncle(X, Y) :- husband(X, Z), sister(Z, W), parent(W, Y).

The goal of *inductive logic programming* (ILP) or *relational learning* is to infer rules of this sort given a database of background facts and logical definitions of other relations (Lavrac and Dzeroski 1994). For example, an ILP system can learn the above rules for uncle (the *target predicate*) given a set of positive and negative examples of uncle relationships and a set of facts for the relations parent, brother, sister, and husband (the *background predicates*) for the members of a given extended family, such as:

uncle(Tom, Frank), uncle(Bob, John), $\neg$ uncle(Tom, Cindy), $\neg$ uncle(Bob, Tom)
parent(Bob, Frank), parent(Cindy, Frank), parent(Alice, John), parent(Tom, John),

brother(Tom, Cindy), sister(Cindy, Tom), husband(Tom, Alice), husband(Bob, Cindy).

Alternatively, logical definitions for brother and sister could be supplied and these relations could be inferred from a more complete set of facts about only the 'basic' predicates: parent, spouse, and gender.

The rule construction algorithm in Fig. 20.6 is actually a simplification of the method used in the FOIL ILP system (Quinlan 1990). In the case of predicate logic, FOIL starts with an empty rule for the target predicate $(P(X_1, \ldots, X_r) : -.)$ and repeatedly specializes it by adding conditions to the antecedent of the rule chosen from the space of all possible literals of the following forms:

- $Q_i(V_1, \ldots, V_r)$
- $not(Q_i(V_1, \ldots, V_r))$
- $X_i = X_j$
- $not(X_i = X_j)$

where Q_i are the background predicates, X_i are the existing variables used in the current rule, and $V_1, \ldots, V_r$ are a set of variables where at least one is an existing variable (one of the X_i) but the others can be newly introduced. A slight modification of the *Gain* heuristic in equation (20.3) is used to select the best literal.

ILP systems have been used to successfully acquire interesting and comprehensible rules for a number of realistic problems in engineering and molecular biology, such as determining the cancer-causing potential of various chemical structures (Bratko and Muggleton 1995). Unlike most methods which require 'feature engineering' to reformat examples into a fixed list of features, ILP methods can induce rules directly from unbounded data structures such as strings, stacks, and trees (which are easily represented in predicate logic). However, since they are searching a much larger space of possible rules in a more expressive language, they are computationally more demanding and therefore are currently restricted to processing a few thousand examples compared to the millions of examples that can be potentially handled by feature-based systems.

20.5 INSTANCE-BASED CATEGORIZATION

Unlike most approaches to learning for categorization, **instance-based learning** methods (also called *case-based* or *memory-based* methods) do not construct an abstract function definition, but rather categorize new examples based on their similarity to one or more specific training examples (Aha, Kibler, and Albert 1991; Stanfill and Waltz 1986). Training generally requires just storing the training examples in a database, although it may also require indexing the examples to allow for efficient retrieval. Categorizing new test instances is performed by determining the closest examples in the database according to some distance metric.

For real-valued features, the standard approach is to use Euclidian distance, where the distance between two examples is defined as:

$$(20.4) \quad d(x, y) = \sqrt{\sum_{i=1}^{n} (f_i(x) - f_i(y))^2}$$

where $f_i(x)$ is the value of the feature f_i for example x. For discrete-valued features, the difference, $(f_i(x) - f_i(y))$, is generally defined to be 1 if they have the same value for f_i and 0 otherwise (i.e. the *Hamming distance*). In order to compensate for differences in scale between different features, the values of all features are frequently rescaled to the interval $[0, 1]$. Intuitively, such distance measures are intended to measure the dissimilarity of two examples.

A standard algorithm for categorizing new instances is the *k nearest-neighbour* method (Cover and Hart 1967). The k closest examples to the test example according to the distance metric are found, and the example is assigned to the majority class for these examples. Pseudocode for this process is shown in Fig. 20.7. The reason for picking k examples instead of just the closest one is to make the method robust by basing decisions on more evidence than just one example, which could be noisy. To avoid ties, an odd value for k is normally used; typical values are 3 and 5.

KNN(*Example, TrainingExamples, k*)
   For each *TrainingExample* in *TrainingExamples*
     Compute d(*Example, TrainingExample*)
   Let *Neighbours* be the k *TrainingExamples* with the smallest value for d
   Let c be the most common category of the examples in *Neighbours*.
   Return c

Fig. 20.7 K nearest-neighbour categorization algorithm

The basic nearest-neighbour method has been enhanced with techniques for weighting features in order to emphasize attributes that are most useful for categorization, and for selecting a subset of examples for storage in order to reduce the memory requirements of retaining all training examples (Stanfill and Waltz 1986; Aha, Kibler, and Albert 1991; Cost and Salzberg 1993).

20.6 APPLICATIONS TO COMPUTATIONAL LINGUISTICS

Decision-tree learning, rule induction, and instance-based categorization have been applied to a range of problems in computational linguistics. This section surveys applications to a variety of problems in language processing starting with morphological and lexical problems and ending with discourse-level tasks.

20.6.1 Morphology

Symbolic learning has been applied to several problems in morphology (see Chapter 2). In particular, decision-tree and ILP methods have been applied to the problem of generating the past tense of an English verb, a task frequently studied in cognitive science and neural networks as a touchstone problem in language acquisition. In fact, there has been significant debate whether or not rule learning is an adequate cognitive model of how children learn this task (Rumelhart and McClelland 1986; Pinker and Prince 1988; MacWhinney and Leinbach 1991). Typically, the problem is studied in its phonetic form, in which a string of phonemes for the present tense is mapped to a string of phonemes for the past tense. The problem is interesting since one must learn the regular transformation of adding *ed*, as well as particular irregular patterns such as that illustrated by the examples *sing → sang, ring → rang,* and *spring → sprang.*

Decision-tree algorithms were applied to this task and found to significantly outperform previous neural-network models in terms of producing correct past-tense forms for independent test words (Ling and Marinov 1993; Ling 1994). In this study, verbs were restricted to fifteen phonemes encoded using the UNIBET ASCII standard, and fifteen separate trees were induced, one for producing each of the output phoneme positions using all fifteen of the input phonemes as features. Below is the encoding for the mapping *act → acted*, where underscore is used to represent a blank.

$$\&, k, t, \_, \_, \_, \_, \_, \_, \_, \_, \_, \_, \_, \_ \Rightarrow \&, k, t, I, d, \_, \_, \_, \_, \_, \_, \_, \_, \_, \_$$

ILP rule-learning algorithms have also been applied to this problem and shown to outperform decision trees (Mooney and Califf 1995). In this case, a definition for the predicate Past(X, Y), was learned for mapping an unbounded list of UNIBET phonemes to a corresponding list for the past tense (e.g. Past([&, k, t], [&, k, t, I, d])) using a predicate for appending lists as part of the background. A definition was learned in the form of a *decision list* in which rules are ordered and the first rule that applies is chosen. This allows first checking for exceptional cases and falling through to a default rule if none apply. The ILP system learns a very concise and comprehensible definition for the past-tense transformation using this approach. Similar ILP methods have also been applied to learning morphology in other European languages (Man-andhar, Dzeroski, and Erjavec 1998; Kazakov and Manandhar 1998).

20.6.2 Part-of-speech tagging

Tagging each word with its appropriate part of speech (POS) based on context is a use-ful first step in syntactic analysis (see Chapter 11). In addition to statistical methods that have been successfully applied to this task, decision-tree induction (Marquez, Padro, and Rodriguez 1999), rule induction (Brill 1995), and instance-based categor-ization (Dealemans et al. 1996) have also been successfully used to learn POS taggers.

The features used to determine the POS of a word generally include the POS tags in a window of two to three words on either side. Since during testing these tags must also be determined by the classifier, either only the previous tags are used, or an itera-tive procedure is used to repeatedly update all tags until convergence is reached. For known words, a dictionary provides a set of possible POS categories. For unknown words, all POS categories are possible but additional morphological features such as the last few characters of the word and whether or not it is capitalized are typically used as additional input features. Using such techniques, symbolic learning systems can obtain high accuracies similar to those obtained by other POS tagging methods, i.e. in the range of 96–7 per cent.

20.6.3 Word-sense disambiguation

As illustrated by the *interest* problem introduced earlier, machine learning methods can be applied to determining the sense of an ambiguous word based on context (see Chapter 13). As also illustrated by this example, a variety of features can be used as helpful cues for this task. In particular, *collocational* features that specify words that appear in specific locations a few words before or after the ambiguous word are useful features, as are binary features indicating the presence of particular words anywhere in the current or previous sentence. Other potentially useful features include the parts of speech of nearby words, and general syntactic information, such as whether an ambiguous noun appears as a subject, direct object, or indirect object.

Instance-based methods have been applied to disambiguating a variety of words using a combination of all of these types of features (Ng and Lee 1996). A feature-weighted version of nearest neighbour was used to disambiguate 121 different nouns and 70 verbs chosen for being both frequent and highly ambiguous. Fine-grained senses from WordNet were used, resulting in an average of 7.8 senses for the nouns and 12 senses for the verbs. The training set consisted of 192,800 instances of these words found in text sampled from the Brown corpus and the *Wall Street Journal* and labelled with correct senses. Testing on an independent set of 14,139 examples from the *Wall Street Journal* gave an accuracy of 68.6 per cent compared to an accuracy of 63.7 per cent from choosing the most common sense, a standard baseline for comparison. Since WordNet is known for making fine sense distinctions, these results may seem somewhat low. For some easier problems the results were more impressive, such as disambiguating *interest* into one of six fairly fine-grained senses with an accuracy of 90 per cent.

Decision-tree and rule induction have also been applied to sense disambiguation. Fig. 20.1 shows results for disambiguating the word *line* into one of six senses using only binary features representing the presence or absence of all known words in the current and previous sentence. Tree learning (C4.5), rule learning (PFOIL), and nearest neighbour perform comparably on this task and somewhat worse than simple neural-network (Perceptron) and statistical (Naive Bayes) methods. A more recent project presents results on learning decision trees to disambiguate all content words in a financial corpus with an average accuracy of 77 per cent (Paliouras, Karkaletsis, and Spyropoulos 1999).

20.6.4 Syntactic parsing

Perhaps the best-studied problem in computational linguistics is the syntactic analysis of sentences (see Chapters 4 and 12). In addition to statistical methods that have been successfully applied to this task, decision-tree induction (Magerman 1995; Hermjakob and Mooney 1997; Haruno, Shirai, and Ooyama 1999), rule induction (Brill 1993), and instance-based categorization (Cardie 1993; Argamon, Dagan, and Krymolowski 1998) have also been successfully employed to learn syntactic parsers.

One of the first learning methods applied to parsing the *Wall Street Journal* (*WSJ*) corpus of the Penn Treebank (Marcus, Santorini, and Marcinkiewicz 1993) employed statistical decision trees (Magerman 1995). Using a set of features describing the local syntactic context including the POS tags of nearby words and the node labels of neighbouring (previously constructed) constituents, decision trees were induced for determining the next parsing operation. Instead of growing the tree to completely fit the training data, *pruning* was used to create leaves for subsets that still contained a mixture of classes. These leaves were then labelled with class-probability distributions estimated from the subset of the training data reaching that leaf. During testing, the system performs a search for the highest probability parse, where the probability of a parse is estimated by the product of the probabilities of its individual parsing actions (as determined by the decision tree). After training on approximately 40,000 *WSJ* sentences and testing on 1,920 additional ones, the system obtained a *labelled precision* (percentage of constructed constituents that were correct) and *labelled recall* (percentage of correct constituents that were found) of 84 per cent.

20.6.5 Semantic parsing

Learning methods have also been applied to mapping sentences directly into logical form (see Chapter 5) by inducing a parser from training examples consisting of sentences paired with semantic representations. Below is a sample training pair from an application involving English queries about a database of US geography:

What is the capital of the state with the highest population?
answer(C, (capital(S, C), largest(P, (state(S), population(S, P)))))).

Unfortunately, since constructing useful semantic representations for sentences is very difficult unless restricted to a fairly specific application, there is a noticeable lack of large corpora annotated with detailed semantic representations.

However, ILP has been used to induce domain-specific semantic parsers written in Prolog from examples of natural language questions paired with logical Prolog queries (Zelle and Mooney 1996; Ng and Zelle 1997). In this project, parser induction is treated as a problem of learning rules to control the actions of a generic shift-reduce parser. During parsing, the current context is maintained in a stack and a buffer containing the remaining input. When parsing is complete, the stack contains the representation of the input sentence. There are three types of operators used to construct logical forms. One is the introduction onto the stack of a predicate needed in the sentence representation due to the appearance of a word or phrase at the front of the input buffer. A second type of operator unifies variables appearing in different stack items. Finally, an item on the stack may be embedded as an argument of another one. ILP is used to learn conditions under which each of these operators should be applied, using the complete stack and input buffer as context, so that the resulting parser deterministically produces the correct semantic output for all of the training examples.

This technique has been used to induce natural language interfaces to several database-query systems, such as the US geography application illustrated above. In one experiment using a corpus of 250 queries annotated with logical form, after training on 225 examples, the system was able to answer an average of 70 per cent of novel queries correctly compared to 57 per cent for an interface developed by a human programmer. Similar results were obtained for semantic parsing of other languages after translating the corpus into Spanish, Turkish, and Japanese (Thompson and Mooney 1999).

20.6.6 Information extraction

Information extraction is a form of shallow text processing that locates a specified set of relevant items in a natural language document (see Chapter 30). Fig. 20.8 shows an example of extracting values for a set of labelled slots from a job announcement

Posting from Newsgroup

Telecommunications. SOLARIS Systems Administrator. 38–44K. Immediate need

Leading telecommunications firm in need of an energetic individual to fill the following position in the Atlanta office:

SOLARIS SYSTEMS ADMINISTRATOR
Salary: 38–44K with full benefits
Location: Atlanta Georgia, no relocation assistance provided

Filled Template

computer_science_job
title: SOLARIS Systems Administrator
salary: 38–44K
state: Georgia
city: Atlanta
platform: SOLARIS
area: telecommunications

Fig 20.8 Information extraction example

posted to an Internet newsgroup. Information extraction systems require significant domain-specific knowledge and are time consuming and difficult to build by hand, making them a good application for machine learning.

A number of rule-induction methods have recently been applied to learning patterns for information extraction (Soderland 1999; Freitag 1998; Califf and Mooney 1999). Given training examples of texts paired with filled templates, such as that shown in Fig. 20.8, these systems learn pattern-matching rules for extracting the appropriate slot fillers from text. Some systems assume that the text has been preprocessed by a POS tagger or a syntactic parser, others use only patterns based on unprocessed text. Fig. 20.9 shows a sample rule constructed for extracting the transaction amount from a newswire article about corporate acquisition (Califf and Mooney 1999). This rule extracts the value *undisclosed* from phrases such as *sold to the bank for an undisclosed amount* or *paid Honeywell an undisclosed price*. The pre-filler pattern consists of two pattern elements: (1) a word whose POS is noun or proper noun, and (2) a list

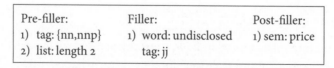

Pre-filler:	Filler:	Post-filler:
1) tag: {nn,nnp}	1) word: undisclosed	1) sem: price
2) list: length 2	tag: jj	

Fig. 20.9 Sample learned information-extraction rule

of at most two unconstrained words. The filler pattern requires the word *undisclosed* tagged as an adjective. The post-filler pattern requires a word in the WordNet semantic category *price*.

Such systems have acquired extraction rules for a variety of domains, including apartment ads, university web pages, seminar announcements, terrorist news stories, and job announcements. After training on a couple of hundred examples, such systems are generally able to learn rules as accurate as those resulting from a time-consuming human development effort. The standard metrics for evaluating information extraction are *precision*, the percentage of extracted fillers that are correct, and *recall*, the percentage of correct fillers that are successfully extracted. On most tasks that have been studied, current systems are generally able to achieve precisions in the mid-80 per cent range and recalls in the mid-60 per cent range.

20.6.7 Anaphora resolution

Resolving anaphora, or identifying multiple phrases that refer to the same entity, is another difficult language processing problem (see Chapter 14). Anaphora resolution can be treated as a categorization problem by classifying pairs of phrases as either coreferring or not. Given a corpus of texts tagged with coreferring phrases, positive examples can be generated as all coreferring phrase pairs and negative examples as all phrase pairs within the same document that are not marked as coreferring. Both decision-tree (Aone and Bennett 1995; McCarthy and Lehnert 1995) and instance-based methods (Cardie 1992) have been successfully applied to resolving various types of anaphora.

In particular, decision-tree induction has been used to construct systems for general noun-phrase coreference resolution. Examples are described using features of both of the individual phrases, such as the semantic and syntactic category of the head noun; as well as features describing the relationship between the two phrases, such as whether the first phrase precedes the second and whether the semantic class of the first phrase subsumes that of the second. In one experiment (Aone and Bennett 1995), after training on 1,971 anaphors from 295 texts and testing on 1,359 anaphors from an additional 200 texts, the learned decision tree obtained a precision (percentage of coreferences found that were correct) of 86.7 per cent and a recall (percentage of true coreferences that were found) of 69.7 per cent. These results were superior to those obtained using a previous, hand-built coreference procedure (precision 72.9 per cent, recall 66.5 per cent).

Soon, Ng, and Lim (2001) describe a C5-based decision-tree algorithm to coreference resolution of noun phrases in unrestricted text. The coreference resolution module is part of a larger coreference resolution system also featuring sentence segmentation, tokenization, morphological analysis, part-of-speech tagging, noun-phrase identification, named entity recognition, and semantic class determination (via WordNet). The feature vectors used for training and evaluation on MUC-6 and MUC-7 data consist of twelve features applied to NPs such as distance, string match, number agreement, semantic class agreement, and proper names. The authors also use cross-validation to obtain the learning parameters.

FURTHER READING AND RELEVANT RESOURCES

Introductory textbooks on machine learning include Mitchell (1997) and Langley (1996). Also useful is the collection of early papers assembled by Shavlik and Dietterich (1990). A recent special issue on natural language learning of the *Machine Learning* journal is presented by Cardie and Mooney (1999). An overview of the increasingly popular method of memory-based learning is to be found in Daelemans et al. (2001). Some websites with useful machine learning pointers are: http://www.aic.nrl.navy.mil/~aha/research/machine-learning.html and http://www. ai. univie.ac.at/oefai/ml/ml-resources.html. Also see the Association of Computational Linguistics' special interest group on Natural Language Learning at http://ilk.kub.nl/~signll/.

REFERENCES

Aha, D. W., D. F. Kibler, and M. K. Albert. 1991. 'Instance-based learning algorithms'. *Machine Learning*, 6(1), 37–66.

Aone, C. and S. W. Bennett. 1995. 'Evaluating automated and manual acquisition of anaphora resolution strategies'. *Proceedings of the 33rd Annual Meeting of the Association for Computational Linguistics (ACL '95)* (Cambridge, Mass.), 122–9.

Argamon, S., I. Dagan, and Y. Krymolowski. 1998. 'A memory-based approach to learning shallow natural language patterns'. *Proceedings of the 36th Annual Meeting of the Association for Computational Linguistics and COLING-98 (ACL/COLING-98)* (Montreal), 67–73.

Bratko, I. and S. Muggleton. 1995. 'Applications of inductive logic programming'. *Communications of the Association for Computing Machinery*, 38(11), 65–70.

Brill, E. 1993. 'Automatic grammar induction and parsing free text: a transformation-based approach'. *Proceedings of the 31st Annual Meeting of the Association for Computational Linguistics (ACL '93)* (Columbus, Oh.), 259–65.

——1995. 'Transformation-based error-driven learning and natural language processing: a case study in part-of-speech tagging'. *Computational Linguistics*, 21(4), 543–65.

Califf, M. E. and R. J. Mooney. 1999. 'Relational learning of pattern-match rules for information extraction'. *Proceedings of the 16th National Conference on Artificial Intelligence (AAAI '99)* (Orlando, Fla.), 328–34.

Cardie, C. 1992. 'Learning to disambiguate relative pronouns'. *Proceedings of the 10th National Conference on Artificial Intelligence (AAAI '92)* (San Jose, Calif.), 38–43.

——1993. 'A case-based apprach to knowledge acquisition for domain-specific sentence analysis'. *Proceedings of the 11th National Conference on Artificial Intelligence (AAAI '93)* (Washington), 798–803.

——and R. J. Mooney, 1999. 'Machine learning and natural language (introduction to special issue on natural language learning)'. *Machine Learning*, 34, 5–9.

Clark, P. and T. Niblett. 1989. 'The CN2 induction algorithm'. *Machine Learning*, 3, 261–84.

Cohen, W. W. 1995. 'Fast effective rule induction'. *Proceedings of the 12th International Conference on Machine Learning (ICML '95)* (San Francisco), 115–23.

Cost, S. and S. Salzberg. 1993. 'A weighted nearest neighbor algorithm for learning with symbolic features'. *Machine Learning*, 10(1), 57–78.

Cover, T. M. and P. E. Hart. 1967. 'Nearest neighbor pattern classification'. *IEEE Transactions on Information Theory*, 13, 21–7.

Daelemans, W., J. Zavrel, P. Berck, and S. Gillis. 1996. 'MBT: a memory-based part of speech tagger-generator'. *Proceedings of the 4th Workshop on Very Large Corpora* (Copenhagen), 14–27.

——K. van der Sloot, and A. van den Bosch. 2001. *TiMBL: Tilburg Memory Based Learner, version 4.0, Reference Guide*. ILK Technical report 01-04. http://ilk.kub.nl/papers/Timbl_4.1_Manual.ps.

Fayyad, U. M., G. Piatetsky-Shapiro, and P. Smyth. 1996. 'From data mining to knowledge discovery'. In U. M. Fayyad, G. Piatetsky-Shapiro, P. Smyth, and R. Uthurusamy (eds.), *Advances in Knowledge Discovery and Data Mining*. Cambridge, Mass.: MIT Press, 1–34.

Freitag, D. 1998. 'Toward general-purpose learning for information extraction'. *Proceedings of the 36th Annual Meeting of the Association for Computational Linguistics and COLING-98 (ACL/COLING '98)* (Montreal), 404–8.

Haruno, M., S. Shirai, and Y. Ooyama. 1999. 'Using decision trees to construct a practical parser'. *Machine Learning*, 34, 131–50.

Hermjakob, U. and R. J. Mooney. 1997. 'Learning parse and translation decisions from examples with rich context'. *Proceedings of the 35th Annual Meeting of the Association for Computational Linguistics (ACL '97)* (Madrid), 482–9.

Kazakov, D. and S. Manandhar. 1998. 'A hybrid approach to word segmentation'. *Proceedings of the 9th International Workshop on Inductive Logic Programming (ILP '99)* (Madison, Wis.), 125–34.

Langley, P. 1996. *Elements of Machine Learning*. San Francisco, Calif.: Morgan Kaufmann.

Lavrac, N. and S. Dzeroski. 1994. *Inductive Logic Programming: Techniques and Applications*. New York: Ellis Horwood.

Ling, C. X. 1994. 'Learning the past tense of English verbs: the symbolic pattern associator vs. connectionist models'. *Journal of Artificial Intelligence Research*, 1, 209–29.

——and M. Marinov. 1993. 'Answering the connectionist challenge: a symbolic model of learning the past tense of English verbs'. *Cognition*, 49(3), 235–90.

McCarthy, J. and W. Lehnert. 1995. 'Using decision trees for coreference resolution'. *Proceedings of the 14th Fourteenth International Joint Conference on Artificial Intelligence (IJCAI '95)* (Montreal), 1050–5.

MacWhinney, B. and J. Leinbach. 1991. 'Implementations are not conceptualizations: revising the verb model'. *Cognition*, 40, 291–6.

Magerman, D. M. 1995. 'Statistical decision-tree models for parsing'. *Proceedings of the 33rd Annual Meeting of the Association for Computational Linguistics (ACL '95)* (Cambridge, Mass.), 276–83.

Manandhar, S., S. Dzeroski, and T. Erjavec. 1998. 'Learning multilingual morphology with CLOG'. *Inductive Logic Programming: Proceedings of the 8th International Conference (ILP '98)* (Madison, Wis.), 135–44.

Marcus, M., B. Santorini, and M. Marcinkiewicz. 1993. 'Building a large annotated corpus of English: the Penn treebank'. *Computational Linguistics*, 19(2), 313–30.

Marquez, L., L. Padro, and H. Rodriguez. 1999. 'A machine learning approach to POS tagging'. *Machine Learning*, 39(1), 59–91.

Mitchell, T. 1997. *Machine Learning*. New York: McGraw-Hill.

Mooney, R. J. 1996. 'Comparative experiments on disambiguating word senses: An illustration of the role of bias in machine learning'. *Proceedings of the Conference on Empirical Methods in Natural Language Processing (EMNLP '96)* (Philadelphia), 82–91.

——and M. E. Califf. 1995. 'Induction of first-order decision lists: Results on learning the past tense of English verbs'. *Journal of Artificial Intelligence Research*, 3, 1–24.

Ng, H. T. and H. B. Lee. 1996. 'Integrating multiple knowledge sources to disambiguate word sense: an exemplar-based approach'. *Proceedings of the 34th Annual Meeting of the Association for Computational Linguistics (ACL '96)* (Santa Cruz, Calif.), 40–7.

——and J. Zelle. 1997. 'Corpus-based approaches to semantic interpretation in natural language processing'. *AI Magazine*, 18(4), 45–64.

Paliouras, G., V. Karkaletsis, and C. D. Spyropoulos. 1999. 'Learning rules for large vocabulary word sense disambiguation'. *Proceedings of the 16th International Joint Conference on Artificial Intelligence (IJCAI '99)* (Stockholm), 674–9.

Pinker, S. and A. Prince. 1988. 'On language and connectionism: analysis of a parallel distributed model of language acquisition'. In S. Pinker and J. A. Mehler (eds.), *Connections and Symbols*. Cambridge, Mass.: MIT Press, 73–193.

Quinlan, J. R. 1986. 'Induction of decision trees'. *Machine Learning*, 1(1), 81–106.

——1990. 'Learning logical definitions from relations'. *Machine Learning*, 5(3), 239–66.

——1993. *C4.5: Programs for Machine Learning*. San Mateo, Calif.: Morgan Kaufmann.

——1996. 'Bagging, boosting, and C4.5'. *Proceedings of the 13th National Conference on Artificial Intelligence (AAAI '96)* (Portland, Ore.), 725–30.

Rumelhart, D. E. and J. L. McClelland. 1986. 'On learning the past tense of English verbs'. In D. E. Rumelhart, and J. L. McClelland (eds.), *Parallel Distributed Processing*, vol. ii, Cambridge, Mass.: MIT Press, 216–71.

Shavlik, J. W. and T. G. Dietterich (eds.). 1990. *Readings in Machine Learning*. San Mateo, Calif.: Morgan Kaufmann.

Soderland, S. 1999. 'Learning information extraction rules for semi-structured and free text'. *Machine Learning*, 34, 233–72.

Soon, W. M., H. T. Ng, and C. Y. Lim. 2001. 'A machine learning approach to coreference resolution of noun phrases'. *Computational Linguistics*, 27(4), 521–44.

Stanfill, C. and D. L. Waltz. 1986. 'Toward memory-based reasoning'. *Communications of the Association for Computing Machinery*, 29, 1213–28.

Thompson, C. A. and R. J. Mooney. 1999. 'Automatic construction of semantic lexicons for learning natural language interfaces'. *Proceedings of the 16th National Conference on Artificial Intelligence (AAAI '99)* (Orlando, Fla.), 487–93.

Zelle, J. M. and R. J. Mooney. 1996. 'Learning to parse database queries using inductive logic programming'. *Proceedings of the 13th National Conference on Artificial Intelligence (AAAI '96)* (Portland, Ore.), 1050–5.

CHAPTER 21

LEXICAL KNOWLEDGE ACQUISITION

YUJI MATSUMOTO

ABSTRACT

The lexicon has gained a prominent role in providing linguistic knowledge for a variety of natural language processing (NLP) applications. While statistical natural language processing was a prevailing research topic in the last decade, advances in both grammatical theories and lexical semantics are another highlight of recent NLP research. A number of grammar formalisms are now 'lexicalized', with the field of Lexical Semantics growing in importance. A major part of automatic language learning is the acquisition of lexical knowledge, and it is essential to find ways to acquire and represent lexical knowledge for natural language processing by computers. This chapter gives an overview of the methods for automatic acquisition of various types of lexical knowledge from linguistic resources and, in particular, from corpora. The chapter summarizes the resources and the preliminary techniques for lexical knowledge acquisition. It also explains the types of lexical knowledge and the methods employed for their automatic acquisition.

21.1 BACKGROUND OF LEXICAL KNOWLEDGE ACQUISITION

Two main issues in natural language processing (NLP) are ambiguity and robustness. Ambiguity appears at every stage in language processing, the lexicon plays an important role in its resolution. Recent progress in statistical and theoretical approaches to NLP has highlighted the importance of lexical knowledge. The key to statistical natural language processing involves finding ways to incorporate lexical information with syntactic or semantic knowledge. It has become possible for statistical NLP to attain high performance in disambiguation only when statistical models exploit the lexical information properly. For example, high success rates in statistical parsing were achieved by means of lexical-level statistics (Collins 1996; Charniak 2000). On the other hand, a number of *lexicalized* grammar formalisms have been proposed such as Lexicalized Tree-Adjoining Grammar (Joshi 1998) and Head-Driven Phrase Structure Grammar (Pollard and Sag 1994; Sag and Wasow 1999). In such grammars, most of the grammatical contents are kept in the lexicon, and there exist only a small number of rules or patterns that govern the construction of proper linguistic forms.

Linguistic phenomena are typically subject to various exceptions, which hamper robust processing of language. Systems that cannot cope with exceptions are prone to failure when applied to new domains. In many cases, exceptions stem from mutual differences in lexical entries, and making the lexicon the main repository of linguistic information is essential to the modular development of NLP systems, not to mention their linguistic soundness.

Manual construction of the lexicon is tedious, time-consuming, and prone to errors and inconsistency. Furthermore, lexical information is changing over the time and domain of use. This means some automatic (or at least semi-automatic) acquisition of lexical knowledge is invaluable in maintaining a consistent lexicon with wide coverage and in keeping its contents up to date.

21.1.1 Forms of lexical knowledge

Since it is not easy to identify the precise form of lexical knowledge, most of the widely used lexical representations are simple and superficial. One form of lexical representation is a thesaurus. There are two types of thesauri. A **classification thesaurus** clusters words according to their semantic similarity. Clustering is usually hierarchical in that stratified clusters comprise a tree structure. In such a tree structure all the words are positioned at the leaf level. Words found in a finer cluster are assumed to be semantically more similar than those found in a wider cluster. In contrast, a **taxonomic thesaurus** arranges words in interior nodes as well, and the hierarchical relations between the nodes are usually defined with the hyponym–hypernym (or is-a) relation. An example of the former is *Roget's Thesaurus* (Chapman 1984), and examples of the latter are WordNet, CYC, and the EDR dictionary (Lenat, Miller, and Yokoi 1995). The definition and computation of word similarity measures for automatic construction of (domain-specific) thesauri are some of the main topics in lexical knowledge acquisition and are described in section 21.3.

Another type of important lexical knowledge is expressed in **subcategorization frames** (or case frames) of verbs. A subcategorization frame of a verb defines the set of syntactic constituents with which the verb can appear. Each of the syntactic constituents in a frame may be called a complement or a case slot. While a subcategorization frame usually specifies syntactic constraints on its complements, it is useful if it specifies semantic constraints as well. Such semantic constraints are referred to as **selectional restrictions** or **selectional preferences**. Acquisition of the subcategorization frames of verbs is described in section 21.4.

Other examples of lexical knowledge handled in recent literature include superficial or concrete **collocations** (see section 21.2) as well as much more detailed and sophisticated representations that are usually constrained by some linguistic theory and that are actively investigated in the field of lexical semantics. Lexical knowledge acquisition based on recent lexical semantics theories is discussed in section 21.5.

21.1.2 Resources and tools for lexical knowledge acquisition

The two main resources for lexical knowledge acquisition are **corpora** and **machine-readable dictionaries** (MRDs). Corpora can be classified according to different criteria and can be general or domain specific, monolingual or multilingual, either tagged or untagged. Corpora for use in lexical knowledge acquisition are in many cases *domain specific* since the acquired knowledge is usually aimed at some specific domain. Most of the research on lexical knowledge acquisition is based on monolingual corpora rather than bilingual or multilingual ones since monolingual corpora are widely available. Furthermore, the exploitation of multilingual corpora is more efficient if they are already aligned in some way (at sentence level or at phrase level). An additional problem is that large-scale aligned (or parallel) corpora are practically unavailable for most language pairs. Tagged corpora are linguistically analysed and annotated with labels for parts of speech (part-of-speech tags), for word senses in the case of ambiguous words, or for syntactic tree structures (treebanks). The best known and most extensively used tagged corpus is the Penn Treebank (Marcus, Santorini, and Marcinkiewicz 1993). Tagged corpora provide better exploitation opportunities than raw corpora, but their availability is limited.

While the availability of tagged corpora is generally scarce, there are certain NLP tools that are accurate enough to allow automatic annotation. By way of example, corpus-based POS taggers perform with accuracy reaching the high 90s, and up-to-date statistical parsers achieve bracketing accuracy of almost 90 per cent (Charniak 2000; Kudo and Matsumoto 2000). Thanks to such tools some grammatical relations such as subject–verb and verb–object relations can be extracted from an untagged corpus fairly reliably.

MRDs are another useful resource for lexical knowledge acquisition. The definition sentences in MRDs are written in a generally consistent manner and simple pattern-matching methods make it possible to identify the **headword** (**genus word**) which is in many cases a hypernym of the entry word. Extraction of taxonomic relations between words from MRDs has been intensively investigated for more than a decade. This type of work is summarized in section 21.6.

For more on dictionaries and corpora the reader is referred to Chapters 3, 24, and 25 of this Handbook.

21.1.3 Word co-occurrence and similarity

The corpus-based similarity measure between words is usually defined in terms of co-occurrence statistics. Though **co-occurrence** can be specified in a number of ways, the two main types of co-occurrence relations are the co-occurrence of words within a fixed distance (window) in a corpus, and the co-occurrence of words as a particular pattern of grammatical relations such as subject–verb and verb–object.

We will refer to the (direct) co-occurrence of the above types as first-order co-occurrence to distinguish it from what we call second-order (or indirect) co-occurrence. The latter represents a co-occurrence of a pair of words with a common expression. The idea behind first-order co-occurrence is that semantically related words tend to appear in some narrow contexts, whereas the idea behind second-order co-occurrence is that semantically similar words have the tendency to share similar contexts. For example, *beer* and *wine* are regarded as 'similar' because they are semantically related to the verb *drink* in that they frequently (and independently) appear as its object and thus share a common context.

Co-occurrence of a pair of words (or expressions) can be measured in many ways. The simplest measure is the *bare co-occurrence frequency*. Other more sophisticated co-occurrence measures for pairs of words are based on their co-occurrence frequencies and independent frequencies. A well-known measure of co-occurrence that was first used by Church and Hanks (1990) is *(pointwise) Mutual Information* defined as follows:

$$MI(x,y) = \log \frac{P(x,y)}{P(x)P(y)} = \log \frac{\frac{freq(x,y)}{N}}{\frac{freq(x)}{N}\frac{freq(y)}{N}} = \log \frac{freq(x,y)N}{freq(x)freq(y)}$$

Here $P(x,y)$ and *freq*(x,y) are the co-occurrence probability and frequency of two events x and y, $P(x)$ and *freq*(x) are the independent probability and frequency of x, and N is the total number of events.

A similar measure which is also widely used is the *Dice coefficient*:

$$Dice(x,y) = \frac{2P(x,y)}{P(x)+P(y)} = \frac{2 \times \frac{freq(x,y)}{N}}{\frac{freq(x)}{N} + \frac{freq(y)}{N}} = \frac{2\,freq(x,y)}{freq(x)+freq(y)}$$

Another well-known measure of co-occurrence is *log-likelihood ratio* (Dunning 1993), the detail of which we omit here.

Second-order co-occurrence is used to measure the semantic similarity between a pair of words. We usually use a number of words that provide the context for the pair, and then each word of the pair is represented as a **co-occurrence vector**, in which each component represents the first-order co-occurrence measure between the word and a certain word in the lexicon. Simple frequencies are often used for the first-order co-occurrence. Moreover, the values of the components in a vector are usually normalized to add up to 1 so that they can be seen as a probability distribution vector. The similarity measure based on this form of vectors is referred to as *distributional similarity*, and the similarity of two words is defined in terms of some similarity measure of two corresponding vectors. The representative similarity measures are *Cosine*, *Kullback–Leibler divergence* (or relative entropy), *Jensen–Shannon divergence* (or information radius), and *Jaccard's coefficient*, defined as follows:

$$Cosine(\vec{x},\vec{y}) = \frac{\vec{x}\cdot\vec{y}}{|\vec{x}|\times|\vec{y}|} = \frac{\sum_{i=1}^{n} x_i \times y_i}{\sqrt{\sum_{i=1}^{n} x_i^2} \times \sqrt{\sum_{i=1}^{n} y_i^2}}$$

$$KL(\vec{x}\ \vec{y}) = \sum_{i=1}^{n} x_i \log\frac{x_i}{y_i}$$

$$JS(\vec{x}\ \vec{y}) = \frac{1}{2}[KL(\vec{x}\ \frac{\vec{x}+\vec{y}}{2}) + KL(\vec{y}\ \frac{\vec{x}+\vec{y}}{2})]$$

$$Jaccard(\vec{x},\vec{y}) = \frac{|\{i : x_i > 0 \wedge y_i > 0\}|}{|\{i : x_i > 0 \vee y_i > 0\}|}$$

There are a number of other proposals for similarity measures. Comparison of distributional similarity is given in Dagan, Lee, and Pereira (1999) and Lee (1999). An interesting discussion on similarity is found in Lin (1998b).

21.2 LEXICAL COLLOCATION
AND ASSOCIATION

Lexical collocation and **association** refer to a group of words that co-occur more frequently than by chance, form a specific meaning all together, and do not keep the meaning when any one of the component words is replaced with its synonymous word. Here, we take the scope of collocation to be wider than usual so that it includes idioms, clichés, compounds, technical terms, fixed expressions specific to the domain of interest, and particular combinations of related words. We say *strong coffee*, but do not say *powerful coffee* or *mighty coffee*. Automatic extraction of collocations is quite important and useful since they are, by nature, unpredictable. Research in this field mainly uses first-order occurrence statistics to find correlations between words in a corpus.

The first systematic and influential work on extracting collocations from large text corpora is reported by Church and Hanks (1990), in which they make use of mutual information to evaluate the correlation between a pair of words. They define co-occurrence in several ways. When they take a window size of five words for co-occurrence and conduct experiments based on the 1987 AP corpus, interesting pairs of related words such as *doctors and nurses* and *doctors and treating* are extracted. When the co-occurrence is defined between a verb and its succeeding preposition, they could find many two-word verbs such as *set up* and *set off*. Furthermore, when the co-occurrence is defined between a specific verb (*drink* in their experiment) and the headword of its object by carrying out partial parsing, they find a lot of words for beverages such as *martinis, champagne*, and *coffee* with high mutual information values.

Calzolari and Bindi (1990) also propose to use Mutual Information (MI) for extracting lexical information from an Italian corpus. In addition to the use of Mutual Information for estimating the correlation of a pair of words, they use another measure, *dispersion*, which shows how the second word is distributed within the window under consideration. They report that dispersion is useful for finding the difference between fixed phrases and syntactic collocations in that the former shows a low dispersion value, which means that the second word appears almost at the same relative position, and the latter shows a high dispersion value, which means that the second word appears equally at the positions in the window. From their experiments, the following patterns are acquired from the corpus: proper nouns, titles, compounds, technical terms, idioms, modification relations between adjectives and nouns, verbs and their associated prepositions to form two-word verbs, nouns and their support verbs (like *take a bath*), and so on.

Xtract (Smadja 1993) aims at finding interesting collocations in corpora that are not necessarily restricted to pairs of words (bigrams). Smadja proposes a three-step algorithm to extract general collocations. In the first step, a target word is fixed and the frequency statistics of another word appearing within a five-word window in both directions are counted. Then two measures *strength* and *spread* are used to find candidate bigrams. The former is based on bare frequency to see the importance and the latter is based on the distribution in the window to evaluate the evidence of collocation. A word that has a biased distribution or that has some peak positions in its frequency distribution is picked up by the latter measure. The candidate bigrams are then extended to *n*-grams by adding the surrounding words or word classes that appear more frequently than some predetermined threshold. Although the idea is quite simple, it extracts very interesting expressions like the following:

(21.1)   the NYSE's a *composite index* of all its listed common stocks *VERB* *NUMBER* to *NUMBER*

This example is expanded from the original bigram *composite index*. Word classes are marked with asterisks, where *VERB* refers to the verb class that is actually generalized from *rise* and *fall*, and *NUMBER* refers to a numerical value.

Riloff and Shepherd (1997, 1999) use first-order co-occurrence statistics to acquire sets of words belonging to the same semantic category. The number of presumed semantic categories is not large since the intended application area is information extraction, where the important semantic categories are limited. They use noun–noun co-occurrence between the heads of closest noun phrases on the assumption that a word often appears near other members of the same semantic category in texts in such constructions as conjunctions, appositives, lists, and nominal compounds. For each semantic category they first prepare five seed words, typical words belonging to the category. Then, a ranked list of nouns according to the co-occurrence probability with the seed words is produced. Of them, the top five new words are added to the seed words, and the process is repeated for a fixed number of iterations. Roark and Charniak (1998) extend this method, parsing the corpus by means of an efficient statistical parser, limiting the constructions only to conjunctions, lists, and appositives, and taking the co-occurrence as that of head nouns within the constructions. They use log-likelihood statistics rather than simple probability. Through some experiments, they show that their improved method could extract useful words twice as accurately as the previous method.

21.3 LEXICAL SIMILARITY AND THESAURUS CONSTRUCTION

Semantically similar words tend to appear in similar contexts. The second-order co-occurrence statistics are often used as the basis of measuring the similarity of contexts in which a word appears.

Hindle (1990) forms the co-occurrence vector for a noun by using the Mutual Information between the noun and the verbs that take it as the head noun of their subject/object. Thus, an element in the vector is the MI value of the noun and a certain verb in the subject–verb or object–verb relation. To define the similarity between a pair of nouns, only the corresponding elements in the vectors that have the same sign (both positive or both negative) are taken into consideration. The similarity is calculated by adding the smaller absolute value of the corresponding elements in the vectors. This means that the more nouns have simultaneously positive or negative correlation with common verbs the larger the similarity between them. Hindle shows that classes of semantically similar nouns can be acquired automatically through this method. A similar approach is taken by Lin (1998a), where the author extracts various types of syntactic dependency relations as well as subject–verb and verb–object relations from corpora. This is done by a broad-coverage parser. Furthermore, only simultaneous positive elements in the co-occurrence vectors are taken into account. Then, instead of using the smaller value of the corresponding elements, he uses the sum of both of the MI values and normalizes the total sum by the sum of all positive elements in both vectors. Lin compares his measure not only with Hindle's method but with Cosine, Dice, and Jaccard measures and shows the advantage of his proposed method. Using the defined similarity measure, Lin was also able to extract semantically similar words for any target word. Though evaluation of acquired knowledge is usually a hard task, he proposed an interesting evaluation method. He first defines the similarity of words in *Roget's Thesaurus* and WordNet according to their positions in the structure, and then compares their similarity with the corpus-based similarity measures.

Information on the similarity between words or between word and word class helps to overcome the data sparseness problem. Low-frequency events in the training corpus which tend to be assigned low or zero probability can be estimated more properly when the information of similarity is available. Distributional similarity is widely used to estimate the probability of rare events by combining estimates of similar words. Class-based methods and similarity-based methods of probability estimation for NLP tasks are discussed in Brown et al. (1992) and Dagan, Marcus, and Markovitch (1993). An intensive comparison of distributional similarity measures is found in Dagan, Lee, and Pereira (1999) and Lee (1999).

Similarity-based clustering of words has another important application in automatic thesaurus construction. Thesauri may be constructed either in a top-down or bottom-up manner. While most of the research takes bottom-up approaches, Pereira, Tishby, and Lee (1993) take a top-down approach to construct a hierarchical clustering of nouns. The co-occurrence vector for nouns is represented by the verb–object relation, and Kullback–Leibler (KL) divergence is used as distributional similarity. A set of nouns are gradually clustered through an iterative procedure of minimizing the distortion of noun clusters from their centroid distribution and maximizing the entropy of class membership probabilities of clusters. This clustering is called *soft clustering* since a noun may belong to more than one cluster.

Bottom-up clustering (or *agglomerative clustering*) goes from the set of individual words and merges a pair of clusters at a time according to the similarity between them, where the similarity between the clusters is measured by their two most similar elements, by their two least similar elements, or by the group average between the clusters. Another merge criterion is to define and calculate a loss or gain function before and after merging a pair of clusters and to select the pair that gives the best result. Brown et al. (1992) take the difference of mutual information as the loss function to form noun clusters. Tokunaga, Iwayama, and Tanaka (1995) propose Hierarchical Bayesian Clustering, in which the merging criterion is the highest Bayesian posterior probability. They propose to construct a thesaurus for each grammatical relation, such as subject–verb and object–verb relations, since the selectional restriction varies according to the grammatical relation.

Another direction of thesaurus construction is to augment existing thesauri using the information obtained from corpora. The basic idea is straightforward. Using the distributional vectors of a new word and of classes in a thesaurus and also using some similarity measure, the new word is classified as belonging to the most appropriate class of the thesaurus (Uramoto 1996; Tokunaga et al. 1997). Hastings and Lytinen (1994) describe methods for finding the appropriate node in the hierarchy for unknown words. They claim that learning the appropriate hypothesis for nouns should go from general hypotheses to specific ones while that for verbs should go in the opposite direction.

Moldovan, Girju, and Rus (2000) propose a method to extend an existing thesaurus (WordNet) in a different way. Their aim is not to find the class for a word but to find new concepts for specific domains. They use pattern-matching and rule-based methods to identify expressions that come under a seed concept and to find semantic relations between concepts.

A direct pattern-matching method to extract the hyponymy (is-a) relation from corpora was first proposed by Hearst (1992). She identified several specific expressions in an untagged corpus that clearly indicate the hyponymy relation:

(21.2)   such NP_i as $\{NP_i,\}^*$ { or | and } NP_j

(21.3) NP_i {, $NP_j\}^*$ {,} { or | and } other NP_1

In both of the patterns, NP_i and NP_j are hyponyms of NP_1 (and NP_1 is a hypernym of NP_i and NP_j). An example of the latter pattern is 'Bruises, wounds, broken bones or other injuries'. Although it is difficult to find such a hierarchical conceptual relation using the similarity measures described so far, Hearst's method is quite effective for the task and applicable to many application areas. She also proposes a method to discover new useful patterns by observing the expressions in which a pair of words in the designated relation of interest appears in a corpus. Caraballo (1999) proposes an extended use of the technique. She first applies a bottom-up hierarchical clustering to nouns, where co-occurrence is based on conjunctions and appositives, and the similarity is calculated by the Cosine measure. Then, using Hearst's pattern-matching method, all the possible hypernym relations between nouns are marked. For each internal node in the cluster tree a word (or more than one word) is selected as the hypernym for the cluster based on the amount of evidence collected by the pattern-matching method.

21.4 SUBCATEGORIZATION FRAME ACQUISITION

A **subcategorization frame** of a verb is the set of syntactic constituents that the verb can take as its complements. Automatic acquisition of subcategorization frames has been intensively studied. Although most of the work is for extracting frames of *surface cases*, several attempts have been made to acquire *deep case frames*.

Brent (1991, 1993) takes a very cautious approach to extract five subcategorization patterns from large untagged corpora. To detect verbs and their complement nouns (subjects and objects) precisely, he only uses pronouns and proper nouns that appear in the complement position of a verb. He also applies a statistical filter to discard detection errors. This filter is based on binominal distribution and standard hypothesis testing. Though the recall of the result is very low (more than 90 per cent of existing data is not detected for three out of *five* patterns), the accuracy is very high (error rate is less than 2 per cent) and the atcquired patterns are quite reliable. Manning (1993) extends the method by using a POS tagger and a partial parser, and tries to collect as many candidates as detected by the system. He also extends the number of subcategorization patterns to nineteen. A similar method to Brent's is adopted and a statistical filter is used to discard adjuncts. He estimates two types of recall in the evaluation, both of which are calculated over some portion of the data since the estimation of true recall is very hard. One of the recall estimations is the proportion of patterns acquired to the patterns existing in the corpus. The other is the number of acquired patterns for some verbs compared with the number of patterns for the verbs described in the *Oxford Advanced Learner's Dictionary of Contemporary English*. The former is estimated to be 82 per cent and the latter 43 per cent. The accuracy is almost 90 per cent.

Selectional restrictions (or **selectional preferences**) are additional important information derived from subcategorization frames. Resnik (1992, 1996) proposes a method to acquire selectional preferences for complements as WordNet classes. The following formulas quantify *selectional preference strength* and *selectional association* respectively.

$$S(v) = KL(P(C|v) \quad P(C)) = \sum_{c \in C} P(c|v) \log \frac{P(c|v)}{P(c)}$$

$$A(v,c) = \frac{P(c|v) \log \frac{P(c|v)}{P(c)}}{S(v)}$$

A high value of the former shows that verb v strongly selects narrow classes of nouns. The latter identifies which classes of noun the verb actually prefers.

Li and Abe (1998) use the minimal description length (MDL) principle to identify the classes in a thesaurus that a verb selects for a particular case slot in its subcategorization frame. Their method is called a *tree-cut model* in that the selectional restriction is represented as a cut in a tree-structured thesaurus. A cut specifies the set of internal nodes in the tree that correspond to a set of semantic classes in the thesaurus. The best tree-cut model is determined by the trade-off between the description length of a particular cut and the description length of the data based on the classes selected by the cut. Similar approaches are taken by Haruno (1995) and Tanaka (1996).

Li and Abe (1999) also point out the importance of taking into account the dependency between complements (case slots) and propose an algorithm to detect the dependency as a dependency graph of random probability variables that correspond to the case slots. Utsuro and Matsumoto (1997) extend the association score to measure the subcategorization preference that takes into consideration the dependency between more than one case slot.

Riloff and Schmelzenbach (1998) propose automatic acquisition of conceptual case frames from texts of a specific domain. Syntactic patterns consisting of a passive or active verb and either a subject, an object, or a prepositional phrase are extracted. Then, for each type of pattern, a semantic profile is generated by replacing the head nouns by the corresponding semantic categories described in Riloff and Shepherd (1997, 1999). Semantic preferences are determined for each pattern by a simple statistical condition. Finally, by merging the patterns that share the same verb form, multi-slot case frames are obtained. The result is shown to be quite useful for information extraction tasks in which some specific information should be identified in a text. However, the dependency between the case slots is not taken into consideration. Furthermore, multiple usages of a verb (or verbal alternation patterns) are mixed up in the final representation.

21.5 LEXICAL SEMANTICS AND LEXICAL ACQUISITION

In the previous section, we focused on subcategorization frames of surface or grammatical cases such as subjects and objects. Verbs have deeper semantic structure where their arguments may be kept in some structured conceptual representation (Jackendoff 1990). Moreover, verbs in the same semantic class largely share syntactic alternation patterns (Levin 1993). Acquisition of such information is of great importance. Although the theory indicates that the syntactic alternation pattern of a verb is predictable from the semantic class to which the verb belongs, we can use the inverse of this for acquiring the semantic classes of verbs.

Zernik (1989) notes that semantically similar verbs share the same variation of syntactic realization, classifies the syntactic variation as lexical categories, and proposes a method of estimating the category for an unknown verb by observing its syntactic realization in a parsed corpus.

Dorr and Jones (1996) examine how the syntactic patterns of a verb can work to predict its semantic class. They use the semantic classes and sample sentences (both positive and negative samples) discussed in Levin's book (Levin 1993). They conduct two experiments to establish how the syntactic patterns obtained from sample sentences can predict the semantic classes of verbs. In the first experiment, for each verb they use all the sample sentences in which the verb appears, that is, word-sense distinction is disregarded and different usages of the verb are mixed up. In the second experiment, only the samples in one particular sense of a verb are used to predict its original semantic class. The results are very different. While only 6.3 per cent of verbs can uniquely identify their semantic class in the former experiment, 97.9 per cent of verbs correctly predict their class in the latter. Though the results look remarkable, the setting of their experiments is not realistic, since even in a very large corpus it is hardly imaginable that all possible syntactic patterns of a verb will occur. Moreover, information on negative examples is very difficult to obtain.

Oishi and Matsumoto (1995) first classify Japanese verbs into about forty semantic classes and describe lexical conceptual structure (LCS) representations (Jackendoff 1990), and possible alternation patterns for each of the classes. By collecting surface case patterns from a parsed corpus they try to identify the semantic class of the verb so as to estimate the thematic relation of the verb and its arguments. They report that the accuracy of the estimate is about 80 per cent. The same authors also suggest that knowledge of the lexical aspect of verbs can be predicted by observing the co-occurrence between a verb and its modifying adverbs (Oishi and Matsumoto 1997a).

Pustejovsky, Bergler, and Anick (1993) suggest that corpus analysis is effective for gradual acquisition of complex lexical representations like the Generative Lexicon (Pustejovsky 1995). They show that various types of expression, such as compounds, nouns with PP modifiers, and noun–verb co-occurrence, help to acquire the possible candidates for the TELIC and AGENTIVE in the QUALIA structure.

When we assume complex structure in lexical representation, we may think that acquisition of such lexicons from corpus analysis should be quite a difficult task. However, previous research, as outlined in this section, suggests that a clear representation of lexical structure may help or guide the acquisition process.

21.6 LEXICON ACQUISITION FROM
MACHINE-READABLE DICTIONARIES

Machine-readable dictionaries (MRDs) have been recognized as a valuable resource for constructing lexical knowledge bases for NLP tasks, and some pioneering work in extracting lexical knowledge from dictionaries was undertaken a couple of decades ago. The dictionary definition of a sense is in general described by a **genus term** followed by a set of differentiae to discriminate it from related senses. As a result of extracting the genus term, the identification of the hypernym appears straightforward.

An early work for constructing a taxonomy from a MRD is reported by Amsler (1981). He investigated the possibility of using definition sentences in a dictionary (*Merrian-Webster Pocket Dictionary*) to extract the genus terms and to construct a taxonomy of nouns and verbs. Though the analysis and disambiguation of the definition sentences are done manually, he points out a number of problems in this direction of research subsequently recognized by many other researchers.

1. Since the definition is written in natural language and disambiguation of the senses of genus terms is not easy, a tangled taxonomic hierarchy is usually obtained.
2. Genus terms at upper positions (such as *cause*, *thing*, and *class*) tend to form loops.
3. Some words in the definition appearing immediately before *of* such as *a type of* ... do not form genus terms. In such cases, the word appearing immediately after *of* tends to be the genus term.

Chodorow, Byrd, and Heidorn (1985) used a pattern-matching method on the *Webster 7th New Collegiate Dictionary* to extract genus terms from the definition sentences. By introducing several heuristic rules, they successfully identified those for verbs with almost 100 per cent accuracy. As for nouns, they propose very simple rules to identify the head nouns taking into account the *of* cases mentioned above, reporting about 98 per cent accuracy in extracting the genus terms.

Disambiguation of genus terms at upper positions is important in order to obtain a consistent taxonomy. Guthrie et al. (1990) describe how some dictionaries like *LDOCE* (*Longman Dictionary of Contemporary English*) provide box codes (semantic codes) and subject codes (area codes), and using such information is effective in disambiguating upper genus terms. Bruce and Guthrie (1992) extend this idea.

Lexical knowledge acquisition from MRDs is still not successful enough to construct useful lexical knowledge bases for NLP for several reasons. Ide and Véronis (1993) question (1) whether MRDs really contain information useful for NLP, and (2) whether this information is relatively easy to extract from MRDs. With regard to the first question, they point out that selection of a genus term in a definition sentence can be arbitrary. They are also ambiguous and easily form loops, since genus terms at the higher levels of the hierarchy tend to be too general. Furthermore, some of the information in dictionaries is insufficient and frequently lacks senses that appear in corpus usages. As for the second question, although genus term extraction is rather successful as reported in Chodorow, Byrd, and Heidorn (1985), the extracted terms are, in many cases, too general and are inappropriate as the direct hypernyms of the entry words. Moreover, their generality means that they often have multiple senses, making them semantically ambiguous. Though the above evidence may indicate that MRDs are not good resources for lexical knowledge acquisition, it does not lead to the conclusion that MRD analysis is wholly unsuitable for this task. It shows that combining information from five dictionaries reduces the percentage of problematic cases from 55–70 per cent to 5 per cent and suggests that a combination of information from MRDs and corpora is useful in improving the quality of the extracted information.

A number of researchers have attempted to combine information from distinct resources such as MRDs and thesauri. Rigau, Rodriguez, and Agirre (1998) propose a series of methods to assign WordNet semantic categories to the headwords in a dictionary. They identify some salient words to characterize semantic categories using selectional association (see the second formula for selectional association in section 21.4). They propose several simple filters to remove erroneous assignment, achieving very good accuracy (90 per cent to 100 per cent). Chen and Chang (1998) propose methods for linking MRD senses (*LDOCE*) with the semantic classes in a thesaurus (*LLOCE* or *Roget's*) and for clustering MRD senses into smaller top categories. Although their methods use very simple similarity measures (Dice for the former and *tf* × *idf* for the latter), they show very good performance. Kwong (1998) uses WordNet as a mediator between a dictionary (*LDOCE*) and a thesaurus (*Roget's*).

FURTHER READING AND RELEVANT RESOURCES

Manning and Schütze's (1999) textbook is a very good introduction to statistical natural language processing. The *Handbook of Natural Language Processing* edited by Dale, Moisl, and Somers (2000) includes a number of topics on empirical approaches to NLP. While this chapter deals only with monolingual lexical knowledge, bilingual lexical knowledge acquisition and a more detailed introduction to subcategorization frame acquisition are found in Matsumoto and Utsuro (2000).

A number of corpus data are obtainable either from the Linguistic Data Consortium (LDC) or from the European Language Resources Association (ELRA). WordNet is available from the Cognitive Science Laboratory at Princeton University. The Penn Treebank can be obtained from LDC.

LDC: http://www.ldc.upenn.edu/
ELRA: http://www.icp.grenet.fr/ELRA/home.html
WordNet: http://www.cogsci.princeton.edu/~wn

REFERENCES

Amsler, R. 1981. 'A taxonomy for English nouns and verbs'. *Proceedings of the 19th Annual Meeting of the Association for Computational Linguistics (ACL'81)* (Stanford, Calif.), 133–8.

Berland, M. and E. Charniak. 1999. 'Finding parts in very large corpora'. *Proceedings of the 37th Annual Meeting of the Association for Computational Linguistics (ACL '99)* (College Park, Md.), 57–64.

Brent, M. R. 1991. 'Automatic acquisition of subcategorization frames from untagged text'. *Proceedings of the 29th Annual Meeting of the Association for Computational Linguistics (ACL '91)* (Berkeley, Calif.), 209–14.

——1993. 'From grammar to lexicon: unsupervised learning of lexical syntax'. *Computational Linguistics*, 19(2), 243–62.

Brown P. F., V. J. Della Pietra, P. V. deSouza, J. C. Lai, and R. L. Mercer. 1992. 'Class-based n-gram models of natural language'. *Computational Linguistics*, 18(4), 467–79.

Bruce, R. and L. Guthrie. 1992. 'Genus disambiguation: a study in weighted preference'. *Proceedings of the 14th International Conference on Computational Linguistics (COLING '92)* (Nantes), 1187–91.

Calzolari, N. and R. Bindi. 1990. 'Acquisition of lexical information from a large textual Italian corpus'. *Proceedings of the 16th International Conference on Computational Linguistics (COLING '90)* (Helsinki), iii, 54–9.

Caraballo, S. A. 1999. 'Automatic construction of a hypernym-labelled noun hierarchy'. *Proceedings of the 37th Annual Meeting of the Association for Computational Linguistics (ACL '99)* (College Park, Md.), 120–6.

——and E. Charniak. 1999. 'Determining the specificity of nouns from text'. *Proceedings of the 1999 Joint SIGDAT Conference on Empirical Methods in Natural Language Processing and Very Large Corpora* (College Park, Md.), 63–70.

Chapman, L. R. 1984. *Roget's International Thesaurus*. 4th edn. New York: Harper & Row.

Charniak, E. 2000. 'Maximum-entropy inspired parser'. *Proceedings of 1st North American Meeting of Association for Computational Linguistics (NAACL 2000)* (Seattle), 132–9.

Chen, J. N. and J. S. Chang. 1998. 'Topical clustering of MRD senses based on information retrieval techniques'. *Computational Linguistics*, 24(1), 61–95.

Chodorow, M., R. Byrd, and G. Heidorn. 1985. 'Extracting semantic hierarchies from a large on-line dictionary'. *Proceedings of 23rd Annual Meeting of the Association for Computational Linguistics (ACL '85)* (Chicago), 299–304.

Church, K. and P. Hanks. 1990. 'Word association norms: mutual information, and lexicography'. *Computational Linguistics*, 16(1), 22–9.

Collins, M. J. 1996. 'A new statistical parser based on bigram lexical dependencies'. *Proceedings of the 34th Annual Meeting of the Association for Computational Linguistics (ACL '96)* (Santa Cruz, Calif.), 184–91.

Dagan I., S. Marcus, and S. Markovitch. 1993. 'Contextual word similarity and estimation from sparse data'. *Proceedings of the 31st Annual Meeting of the Association for Computational Linguistics* (*ACL '93*) (Columbus, Oh.), 164–71.

——L. Lee, and F. Pereira. 1999. 'Similarity-based models of cooccurrence probabilities'. *Machine Learning*, 34(1–3), 43–69.

Dale, R., H. Moisl, and H. Somers (eds.). 2000. *Handbook of Natural Language Processing*. New York: Marcel Dekker, Inc.

Dorr, B. J. 1997. 'Large-scale acquisition of LCS-based lexicons for foreign language tutoring'. *Proceedings of the 5th Conference on Applied Natural Language Processing* (*ANLP '97*) (Washington), 139–46.

——and D. Jones. 1996. 'Role of word-sense disambiguation in lexical acquisition: predicting semantics from syntactic cues'. *Proceedings of the 16th International Conference on Computational Linguistics* (*COLING '96*) (Copenhagen), 139–46.

——and M. B. Olsen 1997. 'Deriving verbal and compositional lexical aspect for NLP applications'. *Proceedings of 35th Annual Meeting of the Association for Computational Linguistics and 8th Conference of the European Chapter of the Association for Computational Linguistics* (*ACL/EACL '97*) (Madrid), 151–8.

Dunning, T. 1993. 'Accurate methods for statistics of surprise and coincidence'. *Computational Linguistics*, 19(1), 61–74.

Guthrie, L., B. M. Slator, Y. Wilks, and R. Bruce. 1990. 'Is there content in empty heads?' *Proceedings of the 13th International Conference on Computational Linguistics* (*COLING '90*) (Helsinki), 138–43.

Haruno, M. 1995. 'Verb case frame acquisition as data compression'. *Proceedings of the 5th International Workshop on Natural Language Understanding and Logic Programming* (Lisbon), 97–105.

Hastings, P. M. and S. L. Lytinen. 1994. 'The ups and downs of lexical acquisition'. *Proceedings of the 12th National Conference on Artificial Intelligence* (*AAAI '94*) (Seattle), 754–9.

Hearst, M. A. 1992. 'Automatic acquisition of hyponyms from large text corpora'. *Proceedings of the 14th International Conference on Computational Linguistics* (*COLING '92*) (Nantes), 539–45.

Hindle, D. 1990. 'Noun classification from predicate-argument structures'. *Proceedings of the 28th Annual Meeting of the Association for ComputationalLinguistics* (*ACL '90*) (Pittsburgh), 268–75.

Ide, N. and J. Véronis. 1993. 'Extracting knowledge bases from machine readable dictionaries: have we wasted our time?' *Proceedings of the 1st International Conference on Building and Sharing of Very Large-Scale Knowledge Bases* (Tokyo), 257–66.

Jackendoff, R. 1990. *Semantic Structures*. Cambridge, Mass.: MIT Press.

Joshi, A. 1998. 'Role of constrained computational systems in natural language processing'. *Artificial Intelligence*, 103(1–2), 117–32.

Kudo, T. and Y. Matsumoto. 2000. 'Japanese dependency structure analysis based on support vector machines'. *Proceedings of Joint SIGDAT Conference on Empirical Methods in Natural Language Processing and Very Large Corpora* (Hong Kong), 18–25.

Kwong, O. Y. 1998. 'Briding the gap between dictionary and thesaurus'. *Proceedings of the 36th Annual Meeting of the Association for Computational Linguistics and the 17th International Conference on Computational Linguistics* (*COLING-ACL '98*) (Montreal), 1487–9.

Lee, L. 1999. 'Measures of distributional similarity'. *Proceedings of the 37th Annual Meeting of the Association for Computational Linguistics* (*ACL '99*) (College Park, Md.), 25–32.

——and F. Pereira. 1999. 'Distributional similarity models; clustering vs. nearest neighbors'. *Proceedings of the 37th Annual Meeting of the Association for Computational Linguistics (ACL '99)* (College Park, Md.), 33–40.

Lenat, D. B., G. Miller, and T. Yokoi. 1995. 'CYC, WordNet, and EDR: critiques and responses'. *Communications of ACM*, 38(11), 45–8.

Levin, B. 1993. *English Verb Classes and Alternations: A Preliminary Investigation.* Chicago: The University Chicago Press.

Li, H. and N. Abe. 1998. 'Generalizing case frames using a thesaurus and the MDL principle'. *Computational Linguistics*, 24(2), 217–44.

————1999. 'Learning dependencies between case frame slots'. *Computational Linguistics*, 25(2), 283–91.

Lin, D. 1998a. 'Automatic retrieval and clustering of similar words'. *Proceedings of the 36th Annual Meeting of the Association for Computational Linguistics and 17th International Conference on Computational Linguistics (COLING-ACL '98)* (Montreal), 768–74.

——1998b. 'An information-theoretic definition of similarity'. *Proceedings of the 15th International Conference on Machine Learning (ICML '98)* (Madison, Wis.), 296–304.

Manning, C. D. 1993. 'Automatic acquisition of a large subcategorization dictionary from corpora'. *Proceedings of the 31st Annual Meeting of the Association for Computational Linguistics (ACL '93)* (Columbus, Oh.), 235–42.

——and H. Schütze. 1999. *Foundations of Statistical Natural Language Processing.* Cambridge, Mass.: MIT Press.

Marcus, M. P., B. Santorini, and M. A. Marcinkiewicz. 1993. 'Building a large annotated corpus of English: the Penn Treebank'. *Computational Linguistics*, 19(2), 313–30.

Matsumoto, Y. and T. Utsuro. 2000. 'Lexical knowledge acquisition'. Chapter 24 in Dale, Moisl, and Somers (2000), 563–610.

Moldovan, D., R. Girju, and V. Rus. 2000. 'Domain-specific knowledge acquisition from text'. *Proceedings of the 6th Applied Natural Language Processing (ANLP 2000)* (Seattle), 268–75.

Oishi, A. and Y. Matsumoto. 1995. 'A method for deep case acquisition based on surface case pattern analysis'. *Proceedings of the 3rd Natural Language Processing Pacific Rim Symposium (NLPRS '95)* (Seoul), 678–84.

—— ——1997a. 'Automatic extraction of aspectual information from a monolingual corpus'. *Proceedings of the 35th Annual Meeting of the Association for Computational Linguistics and 8th Conference of the European Chapter of the Association for Computational Linguistics (ACL/EACL '97)* (Madrid), 352–9.

—— ——1997b. 'Detecting the organization of semantic subclasses of Japanese verbs'. *International Journal of Corpus Linguistics*, 2(1), 65–89.

Pereira, F., N. Tishby, and L. Lee. 1993. 'Distributional clustering of English words'. *Proceedings of the 31st Annual Meeting of the Association for Computational Linguistics (ACL '93)* (Columbus, Oh.), 183–90.

Pollard, C. and I. A. Sag. 1994. *Head-Driven Phrase Structure Grammar.* Chicago: University of Chicago Press.

Pustejovsky, J., S. Bergler, and P. Anick. 1993. 'Lexical semantic techniques for corpus analysis'. *Computational Linguistics*, 19(2), 331–58.

——1995. *The Generative Lexicon.* Cambridge, Mass.: MIT Press.

Resnik, P. 1992. 'A class-based approach to lexical discovery'. *Proceedings of the 30th Annual Meeting of the Association for Computational Linguistics (ACL '92)* (Newark, Del.), 327–9.

Resnik, P. 1995. 'Using information content to evaluate semantic similarity in a taxonomy'. *Proceeding of the 14th International Joint Conference on Artificial Intelligence (IJCAI '95)* (Montreal), 448–53.

——1996. 'Selectional Constraints: An Information-theoretic model and its computational realization'. *Cognition*, 61(1–2), 127–59.

Rigau, G., H. Rodriguez, and E. Agirre. 1998. 'Building accurate semantic taxonomies from monolingual MRDs'. *Proceeding of the 36th Annual Meeting of the Association for Computational Linguistics and 17th International Conference on Computational Linguistics (COLING-ACL '98)* (Montreal), 1103–9.

Riloff, E. and M. Schmelzenbach. 1998. 'An empirical approach to conceptual case frame acquisition'. *Proceedings of the 6th Workshop on Very Large Corpora* (Montreal), 49–56.

——and J. Shepherd. 1997. 'A corpus-based approach for building semantic lexicons'. *Proceedings of the 2nd Conference on Empirical Methods in Natural Language Processing* (Providence), 117–24.

————1999. 'A corpus-based bootstrapping algorithm for semi-automated semantic lexicon construction'. *Natural Language Engineering*, 5(2), 147–56.

Roark, B. and E. Charniak. 1998. 'Noun-phrase co-occurrence statistics for semi-automatic semantic lexicon construction'. *Proceedings of the 36th Annual Meeting of the Association for Computational Linguistics and the 17th International Conference on Computational Linguistics (COLING-ACL '98)* (Montreal), 1110–16.

Sag, I. A. and T. Wasow. 1999. *Syntactic Theory*, CSLI Lecture Notes, 92, CSLI Publications. Stanford University.

Smadja, F. 1993. 'Retrieving collocations from text: Xtract'. *Computational Linguistics*, 19(1), 143–77.

Tanaka, H. 1996. 'Decision tree learning algorithm with structured attributes: application to verbal case frame acquisition'. *Proceedings of the 16th International Conference on Computational Linguistics (COLING '96)* (Copenhagen), 943–8.

Thompson, C. A. 1995. 'Acquisition of a lexicon from semantic representations of sentences'. *Proceedings of the 33nd Annual Meeting of the Association for Computational Linguistics (ACL '95)* (Cambridge, Mass.), 335–7.

——and R. J. Mooney. 1999. 'Automatic construction of semantic lexicons for learning natural language interfaces'. *Proceedings of the 16th National Conference on Artificial Intelligence and the 11th Conference on Innovative Applications of Artificial Intelligence Conference on Artificial Intelligence (AAAI/IAAI '99)* (Orlando, Fla.), 487–93.

Tokunaga, T., M. Iwayama, and H. Tanaka. 1995. 'Automatic thesaurus construction based on grammatical relation'. *Proceeding of the 14th International Joint Conference on Artificial Intelligence (IJCAI '95)* (Montreal), 1308–13.

——A. Fujii, M. Iwayama, N. Sakurai, and H. Tanaka. 1997. 'Extending a thesaurus by classifying words'. *Proceedings of the Workshop on Automatic Information Extraction and Building of Lexical Semantic Resources* (Madrid), 16–21.

Uramoto, N. 1996. 'Positioning unknown words in a thesaurus by using information extracted from a corpus'. *Proceedings of the 16th International Conference on Computational Linguistics (COLING '96)* (Copenhagen), 956–61.

Utsuro, T. and Y. Matsumoto. 1997. 'Learning probabilistic subcategorization preference by identifying case dependencies and optimal noun class generation level'. *Proceedings of the 5th Conference on Applied Natural Language Processing (ANLP '97)* (Washington), 364–71.

—————— and T. Miyata. 1998. 'General-to-specific model selection for subcategorization preference'. *Proceedings of the 36th Annual Meeting of the Association for Computational Linguistics and the 17th International Conference on Computational Linguistics (ACL/COLING '98)*
(Montreal), 1314–20.

Zernik, U. 1989. 'Lexicon acquisition: learning from corpus by capitalizing on lexical categories'. *Proceedings of the 11th International Joint Conference on Artificial Intelligence
(IJCAI '89)* (Detroit), 1556–62.

CHAPTER 22

··

EVALUATION

··

LYNETTE HIRSCHMAN
INDERJEET MANI

Abstract

This chapter reviews evaluation as it has been applied to natural language technology. There are multiple consumers of evaluation results, including funders, developers, and end users. The interests of these groups interact with the life cycle of advanced technology development to determine the kinds of evaluation that are appropriate at different stages of maturity. These range from **technology-based** evaluations in the early stages to **user-centred** evaluations[1] as the technology matures. The individual technologies also require different evaluation techniques, depending on their input and output. *Analysis* technologies map from language to some internal representation, such as labelled segments or an abstract meaning representation. *Output* technologies produce language as output, e.g. summarization, generation, and translation. Finally, *interactive* technologies allow the user and system to interact to achieve some goal. This article summarizes the techniques that have been used to evaluate these different technologies, and assesses their strengths and weaknesses.

[1] Technology-based evaluation is based on the performance of the underlying technology components, in terms of, e.g. speed, throughput, accuracy, while user-centred evaluation focuses on how the user interacts with the system.

22.1 INTRODUCTION

Evaluation has become an increasingly important topic as natural language (NL) technology matures into useful commercial products. Funders, researchers, and consumers want to know what the next goals are, how fast the field is progressing, how good the technology is, and how useful specific implementations and products are. To answer these questions, there has been significant investment in infrastructure to support evaluations, as well as exploratory research devoted to defining appropriate evaluation metrics.

The choice of evaluation method is intimately connected to the software life cycle of the emerging technologies. Fig. 22.1 shows four stages in the software life cycle, from research, to advanced prototype, to operational prototype, and finally to product. As the technology goes through these stages, the range of possible evaluations changes. In the early stages, developers (and research funders) are the major stakeholders. The technology is fragile, it is difficult to recruit real users for field testing, and evaluation is generally done on technology at the component level. As the application matures, it becomes possible to do situated tests of the technology and enlist feedback from 'realistic' users. Such tests can include embedding the technology in a larger system (**embedded-component evaluation**), as well as continued component-level evaluations. In the operational prototype stage, the application can support field studies, before it emerges into the product stage, where it will be judged on market performance, based on acceptance by real users. At all these points, evaluation feeds back into the development process, highlighting technology advances and areas that need improvement. This in turn can affect government and industry investment in particular technology areas.

The style of evaluation also depends on the inputs and outputs of the system. In the remaining discussion, we divide systems into three classes:

- *Analysis* systems that accept language input and produce an abstract representation or classification of that input, as in information extraction and retrieval systems, topic identification, or parsing;

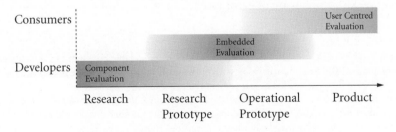

Fig. 22.1 Technology life cycle and evaluation

- Systems that produce *language output*, e.g. translation, generation, and summarization systems; and
- *Interactive* systems, where user and system exchange information through a multi-turn interaction to achieve a goal.

In *analysis* applications where a system accepts language input and produces an abstract representation of that input, component evaluation can be done by creating a set of 'correct' outputs (a **gold standard**) for some set of test inputs. It is often possible to define a (mostly) automated comparison process between system output and the gold standard, which computes a score or evaluation measure.

In applications that produce *language output*, the situation is more complicated, since there may be no unique 'correct' summary or translation for a given input. Language output systems can be evaluated for **quality** and **informativeness**[2] by various comparison methods; they can also be assessed for their impact on efficiency and acceptability in a task via embedded evaluation.

Finally, *interactive* systems are still more difficult, because the success of the system depends on both the human and the machine partner in the interaction. Evaluation requires human subjects and relies heavily on coarse-grained task-level metrics, expert judgements, and user feedback.

22.2 EVALUATION OF ANALYSIS COMPONENTS

For our purposes here, we define analysis components as those that take language as input and produce either a classification or an abstract representation of the input. These can be loosely grouped into four classes:

Segmentation including word segmentation (Palmer 2000; see also Chapter 10), sentence boundary detection (Palmer and Hearst 1997; Chapter 10), discourse segmentation for spoken dialogue (Passonneau and Litman 1997) and story segmentation for broadcast news (Fiscus et al. 1999). Metrics for segmentation are typically given in terms of **recall** vs. **precision** or **error rate**.[3]

---

[2] Quality is the extent to which a text is well formed, understandable, coherent, etc. to a native speaker of the language of the text. Informativeness is the extent to which a text conveys information content, usually related to the preservation of text content under some mapping.

[3] Precision is the number of correctly detected instances over the total number of instances detected. Recall is the number of correctly detected instances over the number that should have been detected. **Error rate** is generally defined as the number of insertions (false alarms) + deletions (missed instances) + substitutions, divided by the total number of true instances.

Tagging at different levels of linguistic description, including part-of-speech tagging (Chapter 11), morphological analysis (Chapter 2), name tagging (Chapter 30), word-sense tagging (Kilgariff 1998; Chapter 13), parsing at various levels from phrase to sentence (Black et al. 1991; Carroll, Briscoe, and Sanfilippo 1998; Chapter 12), and discourse tagging. Tagging is generally evaluated as mark-up on text; it consists of segmentation to find the correct unit, and classification to label it. Typical metrics are precision/recall, or error rate.

Information extraction, which extracts specific classes of information (entities, coreferring entities, relations, events) from text or audio into a structured form such as frames or database tables (Grishman and Sundheim 1996; Hirschman et al. 1999*a*; Chapter 30). Measures for these tasks include precision/recall, slot error rate, and for coreference, overlap of coreference equivalence classes (Vilain et al. 1995).

Document threading and ranking, for information retrieval and document routing applications. This includes topic classification and topic tracking (Fiscus et al. 1999), novel topic detection, and document ranking technologies (Salton and McGill 1983; Voorhees and Harman 1999). These operate across a collection of documents and return a list of relevant documents, generally ranked by score. Typical measures have been average precision/recall for information retrieval and cost functions based on recall vs. false alarms in topic detection and tracking.

22.2.1 Gold-standard-based measures

While the technologies listed above are very different, they have proved amenable to 'gold-standard'-based evaluation methods, consisting of the following stages:

- Definition of the evaluation task and an associated 'gold-standard' format for the answer keys, requiring:
  - Development of **annotation guidelines** that specify how and what to annotate for preparing training and test data with answer keys.
  - Development of tools to support the annotation process, especially comparison of annotations (a scoring tool).
  - Validation of the annotation process by computing **inter-annotator agreement**.
- Development of annotated training and test corpora.
- Release of the training and development test corpora, along with the task definition and the supporting annotation and evaluation tools, to allow developers to build systems to perform the task.
- Evaluation of the systems based on their processing of the (blind) test corpus to produce a set of system 'responses' which are scored automatically against the gold-standard answer keys.

- Interpretation of the system scores in relation to a baseline (default) system and a ceiling derived from human–human inter-annotator agreement, together with tests for statistical significance.

The Named Entity task provides a good example of this approach. The task is to tag text to identify proper names of persons, organizations, and locations, as well as certain numerical expressions (dates, times, percentages, money). The gold standard consists of text containing SGML mark-up indicating the named entities. This evaluation was run first as part of the Message Understanding Conferences (MUCs) (Grishman and Sundheim 1996), then extended to multiple languages (Merchant, Okurowski, and Chinchor 1998), and subsequently adapted for use on transcriptions of broadcast news speech data (Robinson et al. 1999). Each extension has required revisions to the task definition to accommodate the new data sources.

22.2.2   Feature-based metrics for analysis

There are a number of other methods for the evaluation of analysis components. The European community has established the EAGLES evaluation methodology (EAGLES 1996), and applied it to translators' aids, among other applications. The methodology is based on a consumer-report style model, where experts provide judgements rating features of the candidate systems. It derives some of its notions from ISO standards for 'quality characteristics to be used in the evaluation of software products', with a particular emphasis on functionality and usability. Checklists are constructed of critical features for different functional properties of components to be evaluated. The EAGLES methodology is clearly relevant to all stages of technology maturity.

22.2.3   Embedded-component evaluation

Once a component has reached the prototype stage, embedded evaluation can be useful. Different implementations or versions of a component can be compared by embedding them in a system and comparing the resulting system performance, assuming that interface standards exist to support plug-and-play experiments. This provides the opportunity to compare performance of different implementations within a larger context. For example, summarization systems have been embedded in a system supporting **relevance assessment** for information retrieval, in order to evaluate the effect of different summarization techniques on speed and accuracy of people's performance (Mani et al. 1998*b*).

Related to embedded evaluation are complex tasks that require integration of multiple components. An example of this is question answering (see Chapter 31). Performance on question answering has been evaluated in terms of a system's ability to provide answers to factual questions by locating the answer in a large (fixed) collection of documents (Voorhees and Tice 2000). Question answering has also been evaluated by having the system take a **reading comprehension** test (Hirschman et al. 1999*b*). For reading comprehension, the system is presented with a story and asked specific questions. The system must analyse the question, search the story for relevant information, and synthesize relevant information into an answer. The effectiveness of particular components (e.g. information extraction, question analysis, information retrieval, summarization) can be measured by the associated improvement in the score on the overall question-answering task.

Two issues not yet discussed are evaluations of **embeddability** and portability. Embeddability refers to the ease of integration of a component into a larger system and depends on interface standards. Portability refers to the ease of adapting or retargeting a system to a new task or a new language. These activities are associated with system development, and require the use of appropriate *software engineering* evaluation techniques, such as time, cost, and level of expertise required to develop a system performing at a given level.

22.2.4 Lessons learned

The previous sections have discussed gold-standard-based evaluations, feature-based evaluations, and evaluation by embedding components. The advantages of the gold-standard technology evaluations are that they are reproducible, they support creation of linguistic resources, and they can be used for machine learning experiments. The disadvantages are that task definition can be tricky, resulting in overly simple problems (those problems that humans can do quickly and reproducibly); significant resources are expended in infrastructure development; and finally, the results can be specific to the particular genre or corpus used for system development. For example, a statistical part-of-speech tagger trained on a newswire corpus may not do very well tagging questions, because the corpus has relatively few instances of questions.

Feature-based evaluations provide a good complement to corpus-based methods. They are relatively cheap to develop and easy to perform. They are independent of the corpus, so they can be adapted easily to different genres. The features are task or functionality based, in contrast to the data-derived approach used in gold-standard evaluations. As a result, the resources that are created are schematic and general, but not useful for certain kinds of machine learning.

Finally, the embedded component evaluations are especially useful because they encourage interface standards to facilitate plug-and-play experiments. On the negative side, component performance may be affected by the overall system implementation: for example, a statistical algorithm may work better when given noisy data from previous processing, while a hand-generated rule set might work better once clean data are available.

22.3 Evaluation of Output Technologies

The evaluation of output technologies such as text summarization, NL generation, and machine translation (MT) poses many interesting challenges. Such technologies can be evaluated in terms of **intrinsic measures** which test the system in itself, and **extrinsic measures** such as efficiency and acceptability in some task (Spärck Jones and Galliers 1996). These measures can be scored by humans or automatically scored in some cases.

22.3.1 Intrinsic measures

There are a number of different intrinsic methods of evaluating machine output. The output can be considered *by itself*, or it can be *compared against other outputs*, or it can be *evaluated against the input*. In all these cases, both the **quality** and **informativeness** of the output can be assessed.

22.3.1.1 *Quality*

The quality of machine output (e.g. the 'understandability' of a machine translation by a native speaker of the target language) can be judged based on a variety of measures. **Subjective grading** is often used to characterize various output disfluencies, e.g. lapses in grammaticality, style, word choice, presence of untranslated words, inappropriate rendering of proper names, presence of dangling anaphors, ravaging of structured environments like lists or tables, etc. (ALPAC 1966; Nagao, Tsujii, and Nakamura 1985; Minel, Nugier, and Piat 1997). Automatic scoring has a limited role to play here, given that tools such as readability measurements (based on word and sentence length) and grammar and style checkers result in extremely coarse assessments.

Overall, quality measures are somewhat independent of the informativeness (or accuracy) of the technology; for example, a summary could be beautifully written but remain an atrocious summary. In addition, quality measures involve implicit task-related criteria, which can confound the evaluation (Spärck Jones and Galliers 1996).

22.3.1.2 *Informativeness*

Evaluation against the input has been used to gauge the fidelity of the mapping performed by a component, namely whether it preserves the information in the source text, while adding no new information (ALPAC 1966). Note, however, that in the case of MT, a source text may have many natural translations, each of which could differ in several ways from the content of the source, in particular, when information that is usually left implicit in the source language needs to be made explicit in the target language. For example, when translating from Chinese or Japanese into English, pronouns, arguments, or definiteness information may be missing. A similar problem of missing or extraneous information would occur with a system that generated critical (evaluative) summaries such as book or movie reviews.

To carry out the evaluation against the input, it is possible to mark up the meaning of each sentence in the input document, with a subjective grading of the extent to which the output covers the propositions in the input (van Dijk 1979). However, such an effort can be prohibitively costly in terms of the extent of human annotation required and the delicacy of the grading involved. A more practical evaluation method involves subjective grading or automatic scoring as to the extent to which the text output covers information in the input document represented (e.g. in the case of summarization) in terms of an information extraction template (Paice and Jones 1993), a rhetorical structure for the text (Minel, Nugier, and Piat 1997), or even simply a list of highlighted phrases in the input (Mani et al. 1998).

Another way of measuring informativeness is *comparing against other outputs*, where such outputs can be produced by a system or a human. In particular, when human output is used as *reference output*, the informativeness measure can assess the accuracy of coverage of information in the reference output. A problem with reference output is its potential incompleteness: since different experts may not arrive at the same translation or summary of a given source, one would hardly expect a computer's version to coincide with a particular expert's. Research in text summarization has shown that different abstractors may produce very different summaries or extracts for a document (Rath, Resnick, and Savage 1961; Salton et al. 1997); however, there is some evidence that they tend to agree more on the most important sentences to include (Marcu 1999). Where there is disagreement, it is possible to pool multiple reference outputs.

Despite its problematic status, evaluation against reference output, in particular by subjective grading, has been a time-honoured tradition in text summarization and MT (Jordan, Dorr, and Benoit 1993; see also Chapter 32), and has also been used in NL generation (Lester and Porter 1997; Mani 2001). Automatic comparison of a summary against a pre-existing abstract (provided by the author or a professional abstractor) is a popular method in machine learning approaches to summarization (Mani and Bloedorn 1998). The unit of comparison is an obvious issue, with possible choices of passages, sentences, clauses, or phrases, e.g. NPs, clauses, VPs as used in the DARPA MT 'adequacy' evaluation (White 1995; Doyon, Taylor, and White 1998). Another important consideration in comparing against reference output has to do with experimental designs where a subject sees both a human and a machine output, i.e. a 'mixed' set, e.g. Lester and Porter (1997) for generation. Even if the subject is not told which is which, it may be patently obvious! In quality evaluations involving mixed sets, human translations are rated higher in clarity and machine translations lower than in non-mixed sets (Falkedal 1991).

In some cases, reference output is specified in terms of output examples in a test suite or corpus, as in Kukich (1983) and Robin (1994) for generation, and in numerous MT evaluations. In Robin's work, Robustness was defined as the percentage of output test sentences that could be covered without adding new linguistic and domain knowledge to the system, and Scalability measured the percentage of the knowledge base that consisted of new concepts that had to be added to cover the test sentences. Test suites, while especially useful to developers, are hard to construct, except in highly constrained domains where the varieties of constructions can be specified in advance. A potentially more attractive approach is to develop reference output for specific key semantic categories, such as person names (Hirschman et al. 2000), locations, time information, or task-specific nomenclature. Clearly, accurate performance on such tasks can result in more understandable (i.e. higher-quality) translations. Unlike the case of comparing a translated sentence against a reference translation, here there is a small set of possible correct answers. In such a scenario, it is possible to use alignment techniques between translated output and a set of reference answers to score the translation (Papineni et al. 2002).

22.3.2 Extrinsic measures

In addition to looking at the above intrinsic factors, it is often very useful to measure the impact of the output technology on the efficiencyof some task of interest to developers, funders, or users of the technology.

Post-edit measures (commonly used in MT) determine the amount of correction required to get a machine output to some acceptable state in terms of accuracy or intelligibility, e.g. by counting the number of word additions, deletions, and transpositions required. The acceptable state, in turn, may be determined with respect to the source, a reference output, or (in some cases) some implicit model of what is an appropriate output; it may vary greatly with the type of application (information versus dissemination) for which the machine output is intended.

For output consisting of manuals or instructional materials, efficiency can be measured in terms of *execution of instructions* by a subject reading the output, e.g. the assessment by Sinaico and Klare (1971) of LOGOS's English to Vietnamese MT system.

The *reading comprehension tests* discussed earlier can also be applied here, by having subjects read output and then answering questions, as in Orr and Small (1967) or White (1995) for MT, Morris, Kasper, and Adams (1992) for summarization, and Mittal (1993) for generation.

Evaluation in terms of efficiency of **relevance assessment** has been examined quite exhaustively for text summarization (Mani et al. 1998). In a relevance assessment task, a subject is presented with a document and a topic, and asked to determine the relevance of the document to the topic. The influence of the output technology on accuracy and time in the task is then studied. An issue in such an evaluation is the availability of documents covering a wide enough range of genres with ready-to-use relevance annotations.

22.3.3 Evaluation of mature output components

End-user **acceptability testing**, as indicated in section 22.1, is recommended for 'realistic' users; see for example Gervais (1980) for MT, Brandow, Mitze, and Rau (1994) for summarization. This testing can be accompanied, for mature products, by measures of *throughput* and *speed*, as well as *checklists* of questions. Feature-based metrics, discussed in section 22.2.2, are especially useful in assessing mature systems. In the case of MT, such metrics are also appropriate in assessing *tools* to aid the user to submit input in a variety of formats, to pre-edit and postedit text, to support lexicon update, incorporation of domain lexicons, and maintenance of term banks. Other capabilities which could be evaluated include tools to extend the system's linguistic coverage, support for error logging, handling of different, especially rarer, language pairs, extensibility to a new genre of text, and ability to translate updates to a text. (The latter becomes important, for example, in technical manuals for new versions for a product.)

In general, as a maturing NL system evolves through multiple versions, it is useful to perform **regression testing** to assess changes in accuracy over a test suite which the developer has not seen (Battelle 1977; Wilks and LATSEC 1979) for MT, and to measure extensibility and portability across changes in input and output test sets, e.g. the quantitative measures used by Robin (1994) for generation.

Finally, we turn to *cost* measures. For MT, Gervais (1980) and others have examined factors such as costs of MT system development and maintenance, as well as checking, reformatting, updating dictionaries, postediting text, printing, etc. Costs per page or word of MT and human translation are then compared.

22.4 EVALUATION OF INTERACTIVE SYSTEMS

Real applications involve users interacting with language processing systems to perform a task, such as machine-aided translation of on-line documents, web-based search, or telephone access to travel information. Evaluation of the interactive aspect of an application requires that the system and its user be evaluated as a team. The experimental design must account for **subject variability**, which necessitates running enough subjects to achieve statistically valid results, making evaluation costly. Typical metrics are time and cost to task completion, quality of solution, and user satisfaction. These coarse-grained task-level metrics provide little diagnostic information for system development. All these factors contribute to the difficulty of evaluating interactivity.

There have been a number of approaches to this problem. In the 1980s, research on NL database interfaces compared the use of NL versus menu-based interfaces (Whittaker and Walker 1989) and SQL (Jarke et al. 1985), scoring correctness of queries and answers, the number of queries, and time to completion, as well as the degree to which users were able to exploit specific NL features such as anaphora, ellipsis, and coordination.

Later work on the Air Travel Information System (ATIS) evaluation used component-based measures and provided useful insights on the importance of robust parsing and discourse processing (Hirschman 1994). However, these measures, based on the successful gold-standard measures for speech transcription and information extraction, used prerecorded training and test data. This evaluation paradigm precluded use of live human subjects and therefore did not provide measures of end-to-end or task-based performance.

More recently, the PARADISE framework (Walker et al. 1998) for spoken conversational interfaces provides a method for comparing performance across systems and across applications, while also providing more fine-grained diagnostics. The approach is to derive a performance function that models the variance in user satisfaction, measured by questionnaire. Contributors to the performance function include task success calculated using a Kappa statistic to normalize for variable **task difficulty**, and **dialogue cost**, measured as a function of time to completion, number of turns, and error repairs.

Polifroni et al. (1998) outline a novel approach for data collection and within-system evaluation for a conversational telephone interface to weather information. After initial development, the system was made available to users who call in for up-to-date weather information. The data was recorded, transcribed, and evaluated on a daily basis. This facilitated the cost-effective collection of large quantities of data, as well as supporting measures of system improvement over time. Reported metrics included word error, parse coverage, semantic correctness, and generation correctness. This approach is now being explored by the Communicator program for speech-enabled interfaces (Walker, Hirschmann, and Aberdeen 2000).

A different methodology has evolved in Europe (Bernsen, Dybkjær, and Dybkjær 1998; see also Chapters 7 and 35), based on extensive use of Wizard of Oz studies in the design of interactive systems. This method allows developers to determine, during the design phase, how users respond to various prompts, their likely vocabulary, and the kinds of constructions they use in different situations.

Evaluation of interactive systems is a challenge for any system that requires user interaction, such as collaboration systems, search engines, or agent-based systems. In addition, any system that offers alternative modalities (speech vs. pointing) or a combination of modalities, requires evaluation in terms of *human–computer interaction*, which has developed a whole suite of techniques for such evaluations.

There is an urgent need for research in this area, both to make subject-based experiments easier, cheaper, and more reusable, and to provide good diagnostic measures for system development.

22.5 CONCLUSION

Regardless of methodology, evaluation is a social activity. It creates a community that compares different techniques via shared evaluation criteria; it fosters creation of reusable resources and infrastructure; and it creates competition to produce better results. Evaluation has played a major role in the rapid progress of language analysis technologies over the past decade.

The evaluation of input technologies has progressed rapidly, using the gold-standard and feature-based methods. Evaluation of output and interactive NL systems is much more problematic, and requires additional research, particularly in developing cost-effective user-centred evaluations and repeatable evaluations for output technologies. Moreover, the critical software engineering issues of embeddability and portability will have major impact on the success of these technologies in the marketplace. In addition, a new challenge to evaluation comes from the increasingly accelerated technology life cycle, requiring ever quicker feedback cycles via evaluation. This in turn places tighter resource limits on the design of evaluations.

An examination of the history of NL evaluation shows that it has been and will continue to be a major driver of research progress. For these reasons, evaluation should be treated as a first-class research object, carried out in conjunction with the development of shared linguistic resources, tools, and supporting infrastructure.

FURTHER READING AND RELEVANT RESOURCES

Key resources in this area can be found in several publications and websites. The proceedings from the 1998, 2000, and 2001 LREC conferences (Language Resources and Evaluation Conferences: http://www.lrec-conf.org/) provide an excellent overview of language evaluation research. For earlier evaluations, there are proceedings published by Morgan Kaufmann from the Message Understanding Conferences, the DARPA Speech Recognition Workshops, Human Language Technology Workshops, and Broadcast News Workshops (http://www.mkp.com/books_catalog/). Both the Linguistic Data Consortium (http://www.ldc.upenn.edu/Catalog) and ELRA (European Language Resources Association at http://www.icp.grenet.fr) have catalogues of language resources and test suites. The NIST (US National Institute of Standards and Technology) homepage is a good source for evaluation tools and test suites: http://www.nist.gov/speech/tests. In addition to the short bibliography below, a more extensive and up-to-date bibliography and list of resources in this area is available at http://www.mitre.org/resources/centers/iime/nlp-evaluation.html.

References

ALPAC. 1966. *Language and machines: computers in translation and linguistics*. A report by the Automatic Language Processing Advisory Committee, Division of Behavioral Sciences, National Academy of Sciences, National Research Council, Publication 1416, Washington.

Battelle. 1977. *The evaluation and systems analysis of the SYSTRAN machine translation system*. RADC-TR-76-399 Final Technical Report, Battelle Columbus Laboratories, Rome Air Development Center, Air Force Systems Command, Griffis Air Force Base, New York.

Bernsen, N., H. Dybkjær, and L. Dybkjær. 1988. *Designing Interactive Speech Systems: From Ideas to First User Testing*. Berlin: Springer Verlag.

Black, E. , S. Abney, D. Flickinger, C. Gdaniec, R. Grishman, P. Harrison, D. Hindle, R. Ingria, F. Jelinek, J. Klavans, M. Liberman, M. Marcus, S. Roukos, B. Santorini, and T. Strzalkowski. 1991. 'A procedure for quantitatively comparing the syntactic coverage of English grammars'. *Proceedings of the February 1991 DARPA Speech and Natural Language Workshop*, San Mateo, Calif.: Morgan Kaufmann, 306–11.

Brandow, R., K. Mitze, and L. Rau. 1994. 'Automatic condensation of electronic publications by sentence selection'. *Information Processing and Management*, 31(5). Reprinted in Mani and Maybury (1999), 293–304.

Carroll, J., E. Briscoe, and A. Sanfilippo. 1998. 'Parser evaluation: a survey and a new proposal'. *Proceedings of the 1st International Conference on Language Resources and Evaluation* (Granada), 447–54.

Doyon, J., K. Taylor, and J. White. 1998. 'The DARPA machine translation methodology: past and present'. *Proceedings of the Workshop on Embedded MT Systems: Design, Construction, and Evaluation of Systems with an MT Component* (at AMTA 98) (Philadelphia).

EAGLES. 1996. *EAGLES: evaluation of natural language processing systems*. Final Report. EAGLES Document EAG-EWG-PR.2. http://issco.www.unige.ch/projects/ewg96/ewg96.html.

Falkedal, K. 1991. 'Evaluation methods for machine translation systems: an historical overview and critical account'. Report ISSCO, Université de Genève.

Fiscus, J., G. Doddington, J. Garofolo, and A. Martin. 1999. 'NIST'S 1998 topic detection and tracking evaluation'. *Proceedings of the DARPA Broadcast News Workshop* (San Francisco,), 19–24.

Gervais, A. 1980. *Évaluation du système-pilote de traduction automatique TAUM-AVIATION*. Rapport final, Bureau des Traductions, Secrétariat d'État, Ottawa.

Grishman, R. and B. Sundheim. 1996. 'Message Understanding Conference-6: A Brief History.' *Proceedings of the 16th International Conference on Computational Linguistics (COLING '96)* (Copenhagen), 466–71.

Hirschman, L. 1994. 'Roles of language processing in a spoken language interface'. *National Academy of Sciences Colloquium on Human–Machine Communication by Voice*, eds. D. B. Roe and J. G. Wilton, 217–37.

——E. Brown, N. Chinchor, L. Ferro, R. Grishman, P. Robinson, and B. Sundheim. 1999. 'EVENT99: event evaluation for broadcast news'. *Proceedings of the DARPA Speech and Language Technology Workshop* (San Francisco), 245–8.

——M. Light, E. Breck, and J. Burger. 1999. 'Deep read: a reading comprehension system'. *Proceedings of the 37th Annual Meeting of the Association for Computational Linguistics (ACL '99)* (College Park, Md.), 325–32.

——F. Reeder, J. D. Burger, and K. Miller. 2000. 'Name translation as a machine translation evaluation task'. *Workshop Proceedings for Evaluation of Machine Translation* (Athens), 54–8.

Jarke, M., J. Turner, E. Stohr, Y. Vassiliou, N. White, and K. Michielson. 1985. 'Field evaluation of natural language for data retrieval'. *IEEE Transactions on Software Engineering*, SE-11(1), 97–113.

Jordan, P., B. Dorr, and J. Benoit. 1993. 'A first-pass approach for evaluating machine translation systems'. *Machine Translation*, 8(1–2), 49–58.

Kilgariff, A. 1998. 'Gold standard datasets for evaluating word sense disambiguation programs'. *Computer Speech and Language*, 12(4), 453–72.

Kukich, K. 1983. *Knowledge-base report generation: a knowledge-engineering approach to natural language report generation*. Ph.D. thesis, University of Pittsburgh.

Lester, J. and B. Porter. 1997. 'Developing and empirically evaluating robust explanation generators: the KNIGHT experiments'. *Computational Linguistics*, 23(1), 65–102.

Mani, I. 2001. *Automatic Summarization*. Amsterdam: John Benjamins.

——and E. Bloedorn. 1998. 'Machine learning of generic and user-focused summarization'. *Proceedings of AAAI '98* (Madison, Wis), 821–6.

——and M. Maybury (eds.). 1999. *Advances in Automatic Text Summarization*. Cambridge, Mass.: MIT Press.

——T. Firmin, D. House, M. Chrzanowski, G. Klein, L. Hirschman, B. Sundheim, and L. Obrst. 1998. *The TIPSTER SUMMAC text summarization evaluation: final report*. MITRE Technical Report MTR 98W0000138, McLean, Va.: The MITRE Corporation.

Marcu, D. 1999. 'Discourse trees are good indicators of importance in text'. In Mani and Maybury (1999), 123–36.

Merchant, R., M. Okurowski, and N. Chinchor. 1998. 'The multi-lingual entity task (MET) overview'. *Advances in Text Processing: TIPSTER Program Phase II* (DARPA), 127–38.

Minel, J., S. Nugier, and G. Piat. 1997. 'How to appreciate the quality of automatic text summarization'. *Proceedings of the ACL/EACL '97 Workshop on Intelligent Scalable Text Summarization* (Madrid), 25–30.

Mittal, V. 1993. *Generating natural language descriptions with integrated text and examples*. Ph.D. thesis, University of Southern California.

Morris, A., G. Kasper, and D. Adams. 1992. 'The effects and limitations of automatic text condensing on reading comprehension performance'. *Information Systems Research*, 3(1). Reprinted in Mani and Maybury (1999), 305–24.

Nagao, M., J. Tsujii, and J. Nakamura. 1985. 'The Japanese government project for machine translation'. *Computational Linguistics*, 11, 91–110.

Orr, D. and V. Small. 1967. 'Comprehensibility of machine-aided translations of Russian scientific documents'. *Mechanical Translation and Computational Linguistics*, 10, 1–10.

Paice, C. and P. Jones. 1993. 'The identification of important concepts in highly structured technical papers'. *Proceedings of the 16th Annual International ACM SIGIR Conference on Research and Development in Information Retrieval (ACM-SIGIR '93)* (Pittsburgh, Pa), 69–78.

Palmer, D. 2000. 'Tokenisation and sentence segmentation'. In R. Dale, H. Moisl, and H. Somers (eds.), *Handbook of Natural Language Processing*. New York: Marcel Dekker, 11–35.

——and M. Hearst. 1997. 'Adaptive multilingual sentence boundary disambiguation'. *Computational Linguistics*, 23(2), 241–68.

Papineni, K., S. Roukos, T. Ward, J. Henderson, and F. Reeder. 2002. 'Corpus-based comprehensive and diagnostic MT evaluation: initial Arabic, Chinese, French, and Spanish results'. To appear in *Proceedings of the Human Language Technology Conference (HLT 2002)*.

Passonneau, R. and D. Litman. 1997. 'Discourse segmentation by human and automated means'. *Computational Linguistics*, 23(1), 103–40.

Polifroni, J., S. Seneff, J. Glass, and T. Hazen. 1998. 'Evaluation methodology for a telephone-based conversational system'. *Proceedings of the 1st International Conference on Language Resources and Evaluation* (Granada), 43–50.

Rath, G., A. Resnick, and T. Savage. 1961. 'The formation of abstracts by the selection of sentences'. *American Documentation*, 12(2). Reprinted in Mani and Maybury (1999), 287–92.

Robin, J. 1994. *Revision-based generation of natural language summaries providing historical background: corpus-based analysis, design and implementation*. Ph.D. thesis, Columbia University.

Robinson, P., E. Brown, J. Burger, N. Chinchor, A. Douthat, L. Ferro, and L. Hirschman. 1999. 'Overview: information extraction from broadcast news'. *Proceedings of the DARPA Speech and Language Technology Workshop*, San Francisco: Morgan Kaufmann, 27–30.

Salton, G. and M. McGill. 1983. *Introduction to Modern Information Retrieval*. New York: McGraw-Hill.

——A. Singhal, M. Mitra, and C. Buckley. 1997. 'Automatic text structuring and summarization'. *Information Processing and Management*, 33(2). Reprinted in Mani and Maybury (1999), 341–56.

Sinaico, W. and G. Klare. 1971. *Further experiments in language translation: readability of computer translations*. Institute for Defense Analyses, Arlington, Va.

Spärck Jones, K. and J. Galliers. 1996. *Evaluating Natural Language Processing Systems: An Analysis and Review*. Lecture Notes in Artificial Intelligence, 1083. Berlin: Springer Verlag.

van Dijk, T. A. 1979. 'Recalling and Summarizing Complex Discourse'. In W. Burchart and K. Hulker (eds.), *Text Processing*, Berlin: Walter de Gruyter, 11–35.

Vilain, M., J. Burger, J. Aberdeen, D. Connolly, and L. Hirschman. 1995. 'A model theoretic coreference scoring scheme'. *Proceedings of the 6th Message Understanding Conference*, San Mateo, Calif.: Morgan Kaufmann, 45–52.

Voorhees, E. and D. Harman. 1999. 'Overview of the seventh text retrieval conference (TREC-7)'. *Proceedings of the 7th Text REtrieval Conference (TREC 7)*, 1–24.

——and D. Tice. 2000. 'The TREC-8 question answering track report'. *Proceedings of the 8th Text REtrieval Conference (TREC 8)*, 83–106.

Walker, M., D. Litman, C. Kamm, and A. Abella. 1998. 'Evaluating spoken dialogue agents with PARADISE: two case studies'. *Computer Speech and Language*, 12(4), 317–48.

——L. Hirschman, and J. Aberdeen. 2000. 'Evaluation for DARPA communicator spoken dialogue systems'. *Proceedings of the 2nd International Conference on Language Resources and Evaluation (LREC 2000)* (Athens), 735–40.

White, J. 1995. 'Approaches to black-box MT evaluation'. *Proceedings of MT Summit V* (Luxembourg).

Whittaker, S. and M. Walker. 1989. *Comparing two user-oriented database query languages: a field study*. Technical Report HPL-ISC-89060, Hewlett Packard Laboratories, Bristol.

Wilks, Y. and LATSEC, Inc. 1979. 'Comparative translation quality analysis'. Final Report, Contract F33657-77-C-0695, LATSEC Inc.

CHAPTER 23

SUBLANGUAGES AND CONTROLLED LANGUAGES

RICHARD I. KITTREDGE

ABSTRACT

Restricted subsystems of language can arise *spontaneously* in a subject-matter domain where speech or writing is used for special purposes. Alternatively, language restrictions can be imposed by conscious design. This chapter introduces the phenomenon of *natural sublanguage* in the first case, and contrasts it with the increasingly important notion of *controlled language*, which applies in the second case. Many of the successful language processing applications which deal with language meaning are limited to naturally occurring sublanguages. We give examples of natural sublanguages and describe their key properties for automatic processing. One or more related sublanguages may serve as the basis for a controlled language, where standards are introduced to reduce ambiguity, limit complexity, and enforce uniform style.

23.1 COMPUTATIONAL LINGUISTICS IN LIMITED SEMANTIC DOMAINS

Many applications of natural language processing (NLP) focus on language as it is used in a restricted domain and recurrent situation. For example, the machine translation of Canadian weather forecasts has been a reality since 1977, when the University of Montreal's English–French system (TAUM-MÉTÉO) went into service. Today the volume of translation exceeds 20 million words per year, but the system's scope is limited to the vocabulary and telegraphic style of specific types of forecast. Similarly, text generation systems, when restricted to the domain of stock market summaries or economic data surveys, can produce very natural-sounding reports from numerical databases. Each such NLP application requires a grammar and lexicon of the *sublanguage* in question and takes advantage of the restrictions on the ways words are used in relation to one another in that specific domain and setting.

The following section introduces the concept of sublanguage, providing examples of naturally occurring sublanguages which illustrate the properties that computational linguists can exploit when designing and building applications. Special properties include restrictions on word usage (including word co-occurrences), sentence syntax and certain aspects of text structure. In extreme cases, they may also include rather bizarre sentence constructions, which would never show up in the standard form of a language. Sublanguage grammars incorporate the restrictions and other characteristic phenomena in a coherent way. Several examples are given in section 23.3 of NLP applications which exploit sublanguage grammars. Section 23.4 presents the notion of controlled language, in comparison and contrast with that of sublanguage. Section 23.5 summarizes some relationships between sublanguage and controlled language.

23.2 THE NOTION OF *NATURAL SUBLANGUAGE*

The term *language* can be applied equally well to a variety of semiotic systems including formal languages of mathematics, computer programming languages, systems for animal communication, and true human languages. The term **sublanguage** could therefore be used to refer to any proper subset of expressions in one of these languages which exhibits some systematic, i.e. 'language-like', behaviour. What we want to focus on here, however, is a very specific kind of human language usage that arises spontaneously in limited semantic domains. For this reason (and to emphasize the contrast with controlled language, discussed below) we may use the term *natural sublanguage*. For the remainder of this chapter, when we use the term *sublanguage*, we will always be referring to the natural variety.

Our definition of sublanguage has two parts. For a sublanguage to arise, there must be the following two preconditions:

- a community of speakers (i.e. 'experts') shares some specialized knowledge about a restricted semantic domain;
- the experts communicate about the restricted domain in a recurrent situation, or set of highly similar situations.

When the utterances (including writings) of domain experts show some systematic patterns that distinguish them from the language as a whole, then we say these utterances belong to a sublanguage. Among the systematic patterns that characterize a sublanguage are:

- usage of distinctive word classes in the sentence grammar which reflect domain semantics;
- consistency and completeness of the possible utterance set for expressing statements in the domain and situations;
- economy of expression.

The terms of this second part of our definition are still rather vague. Moreover, this definition leaves open the question of how much systematic behaviour (if this notion can be made precise) is required for a language subset to qualify as a sublanguage.

23.2.1 Two examples

Consider the following sample texts taken from two quite different natural sublanguages. Fig. 23.1 gives a short baseball game summary published in a Montreal newspaper. Despite the fact that this text is clearly in English, many English speakers

---

Redbirds gain split

The McGill Redbirds gained a wild split with the Concordia Stingers in Quebec university baseball action yesterday, winning the opener 23–3 behind Craig McFadzean's eight RBIs, but dropping the nightcap 10–9 in 12 innings. The Redbirds opened the campaign Saturday by sweeping Laval 10–4 and 12–5 in Sainte-Foy.

Fig. 23.1 Baseball game report (*Montreal Gazette*, 6 September 1999)

are unfamiliar with the meaning of terms such as *wild split, behind (somebody's) RBIs, dropping the nightcap,* and *sweep,* as they are used here.

North American sports fans have no difficulty in linking the *wild split* with the two games (the *opener* and the *nightcap*) whose scores are explicitly mentioned in the same sentence. The one-sided opening result, supported by the eight runs-batted-in (RBIs), set up an expectation of easy victory that was not met in the evening game, hence the *wild split*. Note the special usage of the verb *sweep* in the final sentence.

Now consider the text fragment given in Fig. 23.2, taken from a sublanguage of entomology, involving predation by Japanese hangingflies (order *mecoptera*) on arthropods. This second text represents a quite different kind of writing style, characteristic of the genre of field research articles in behavioural zoology.

'... There was no significant difference between the number of males (16 cases) and females (13 cases) hunting on 20–30 September (50% binomial test, P = 0.711). However, a significant difference was detected in the success rate of hunting (number of captures per number of contacts with prey) between males and females (43.8 versus 7.7 per cent, Fisher exact probability test, P= 0.038). Males swept hind legs over vegetation and grasped contacted prey (vegetation sweeping *sensu* Thornhill 1977, 1978). They repeated short flights (19 times during 30 min) to sweep the vegetation at the forest edge. Females, in contrast, usually grasped only those arthropods that came into the range of their prehensile tarsi while they were hanging. Males used vegetation sweeping more frequently than females. ...'

Fig. 23.2 Entomology research article fragment

The sublanguage of this article is obviously different in many ways from that of the baseball game report, but the two share one important lexical item, the verb *sweep*. Compare the usage of this verb:

(23.1)   The Redbirds opened the campaign ... by sweeping Laval 10–4 and 12–5.

(23.2) *a.* Males swept hind legs over vegetation ...
        b. They sweep the vegetation at the forest edge.

What matters for the computational linguist is not that the meaning of *sweep* is different in the two sublanguages, but rather that the syntactic pattern and semantic selection of the verb is quite different. In sports summaries the basic sentence pattern underlying the gerundive clause in (23.1) (i.e. for *The Redbirds swept Laval 10–4 and 12–5*) can be represented as

$$\langle \text{team-1} \rangle \; sweep \; \langle \text{team-2} \rangle \; \langle \text{string-of-scores} \rangle,$$

where ⟨team-1⟩ and ⟨team-2⟩ are names of baseball teams, and ⟨string-of-scores⟩ is a conjunction of at least two score expressions such as *10–4* or *18 to 3*, etc. When used in this syntactic pattern, only a team name, or a phrase referring to a particular team such as *the home team*, can be the subject or object of *sweep*.[1] No other kind of noun phrase is acceptable. If we examine a large sample of baseball game reports, we may find several distinct syntactic patterns for *sweep*, but in each case we see that these restrictions on *sweep* are very tight, and semantic in nature.

The usage of *sweep* in (23.2*a*) and (23.2*b*) follows two patterns, which represent two ways of paraphrasing the same content in this domain.[2] These are quite different from the patterns seen in (23.1):

⟨mecopteran_insect⟩ *sweep* ⟨body_part⟩ *over* ⟨vegetation⟩,
⟨mecopteran_insect⟩ *sweep* ⟨vegetation⟩ (**with** ⟨body part⟩).

Each expression in angular brackets stands for a class of possible nouns which can act as the head of a noun phrase at that position in an elementary sentence using the verb and the prepositions shown (e.g. *over* is required with the second object of *sweep*, when the first object denotes a body part; *with* introduces an optional second argument in the second pattern). As illustrated by (23.2*a*) and (23.2*b*), the verb *sweep* in our entomology sublanguage takes as subject only noun phrases denoting a certain class of insect predators. The possible direct objects of *sweep* in (23.2*a*) are likewise restricted to noun phrases denoting body parts of the same insect, and (in 23.2*b*) to noun phrases denoting vegetation found in the insect's environment.[3] Any other usage would be unacceptable (i.e. meaningless) and virtually 'ungrammatical' within this sublanguage. In fact, the author of the article makes it clear that he or she is using *sweep* in the technical sense introduced by another researcher ('*sensu* Thornhill').

This contrast between the different selectional restrictions of *sweep* in the two texts illustrates the most important fact about sublanguage, namely that **word co-occurrence** patterns (i.e. which nouns can be used as arguments of a given verb, and which nouns can be modified by a given adjective, etc.) are different in each sublanguage, and usually much more restricted than in the whole language. By stating these restrictions for each word in the lexicon, and stating the grammar in terms of classes of verbs, adjectives, and predicating nouns that have similar selections, we can characterize the elementary sentences which constitute the basic sublanguage information patterns. For example, one very frequent pattern in the baseball reporting sublanguage can be characterized:

⟨team-1⟩ ⟨defeat⟩ ⟨team-2⟩ ⟨score⟩, as in *The Cubs trounced the Yankees 10 to 3.*

---

[1] We leave aside other possible patterns for *sweep* in the same sublanguage, as in *The Cubs swept the series.*

[2] Paraphrastic alternations in English verb complementation patterns, including several for *sweep*, have been studied in detail by Levin (1993). Note, however, that the alternation given here is more specific with regard to the verb arguments required.

[3] The nominalization *vegetation sweeping* in Fig. 23.2 exhibits the same word-class selection as seen in (23.2*a*) and (23.2*b*). A detailed analysis might derive *vegetation sweeping* (*by X*) from (*X*) *sweeps vegetation.*

Sublanguages used in weather forecasting, financial reporting and sports summaries may have relatively simple grammars, statable in terms of a few very frequent elementary sentence patterns. Most sublanguages, however, use a wide range of word classes and sentence patterns. They may also present problems for grammatical description because texts include digressions outside the core domain. For detailed discussions of analysis methodology in complex sublanguages, see the readings at the end of this chapter.

23.2.2 Sublanguage contrasted with standard language

Most of the syntactic constructions we observe in typical sublanguages are quite recognizable ones, even if they admit very restricted classes of words. However, a few sublanguages exhibit unfamiliar syntax. For example, consider the following four 'sentences' of English:

(23.3)   Golds slumped.

(23.4)   Check reservoir full.

(23.5)   Knead and knead.

(23.6)   Becoming cooler tomorrow.

When submitted to a reasonably good and complete general-purpose parser of English, with access to a full on-line dictionary containing good semantic class information, sentences (23.3)–(23.6) would probably be rejected. In other words, they might well be considered ungrammatical according to standard English grammar. In sentence (23.3) the mass noun 'gold' takes a plural form and occurs as the subject of the verb 'slump', which normally takes a different type of subject. In sentence (23.4) the only possible verb is 'check' whose complement cannot be a sequence of the form Count-noun + Adjective. Sentence (23.5) is unusual at least in conjoining a normally transitive verb to a repetition of itself, without any object. Sentence (23.6) may have a clear meaning, but, as a sequence consisting of Gerund + Adjective + Adverb (with other possible lexical categories for each word), does not fit the pattern of a normal grammatical sentence. Despite their deviance from the normal patterns found in Standard English, each of these sentences is considered quite natural and 'grammatical' in its appropriate sublanguage. For example, (23.3) was found in a report on the financial securities market; (23.4) was observed among the maintenance instructions in an aircraft hydraulics manual; (23.5) comes from the middle of a bread recipe, and (23.6) is clearly from a weather forecast. We thus might be forced to conclude that none of these four sublanguages is, technically speaking, a subset of Standard English from the grammatical standpoint. Indeed, many general-purpose language analysis programs have broken down in relatively simple sublanguages. Experience shows that computational linguists should not expect that a 'domain-independent' grammar will be efficient or even adequate for any specific sublanguage.

Despite what has just been said about deviant examples, the vast majority of English sublanguages rely mostly on grammatical patterns that belong to Standard English. In fact, most of the unusual syntactic patterns found in sublanguages can be attributed to ellipsis of longer forms found in the standard language. For example, (23.4) can be seen as a shortened form of

(23.4′) Check that the reservoir is full.

The process of ellipsis that leads from (23.4′) to (23.4) can be broken into three separate steps (individual ellipsis operations on *that*-complementizer, article, and copula verb). Each individual ellipsis process is relatively common in English—it is only their simultaneous operation which produces an unusual sentence pattern.

In setting up the grammatical description of any sublanguage, it is important to start from a representative corpus of texts (see Chapter 24 on corpus methodology). Basing the description on texts from a single source may be sufficient for prototyping, or even building, a simple processing application to serve only that source, but does not normally give a good perspective on the full sublanguage, as used by a wider community. It must also be kept in mind that any corpus which aims to include extensive sublanguage material by taking whole texts will almost certainly contain segments of text that do not really belong to the target sublanguage. For example, stock market reports may contain reference to political events, described in clauses having quite unpredictable words and sentence patterns. A television weather forecaster may include comments about upcoming sporting events for conversational effect. Characterizing the 'core' sublanguage and dealing with extraneous material will depend on the degree of regularity observed, and the particular goals for language processing. (See the references at the end of this chapter for more detail.)

23.2.3 Sublanguage properties

Ideally, we should investigate both written and spoken sublanguages. However, much of what is known about sublanguage today is limited to written forms, possibly because it has been easier to capture and represent written language for description and processing. It may also be that written language tends to be more formal than spoken, so that sublanguage distinctions are easier to see in this mode. In any case, we can expect spoken sublanguages to share most of the properties of written ones.

We summarize here some of the known properties of sublanguages which are important for computational linguistics. Depending on the NLP application, some or all of these properties may be exploited in the design of the descriptive grammar, the lexicon, and the various stages of the processing algorithms:

- restricted lexicon (and possibly including special words not used elsewhere in the language);
- a relatively small number of distinct lexical classes (e.g. nouns or nominal phrases denoting ⟨body part⟩) which occur frequently in the major sentence patterns;
- restricted sentence syntax (e.g. some sentence patterns found in literature seem to be rare in scientific or technical writing: (?) *Often have we observed males sweeping vegetation with their hind legs*);
- deviant sentence syntax (e.g. the patterns of (23.3–23.6) are not usual in the standard language);
- restricted word co-occurrence patterns which reflect domain semantics (e.g. verbs take limited classes of subjects and objects; nouns have sharp word-class restrictions on their modifiers);
- restricted text grammar (e.g. stock market summaries typically begin with statements of the overall market trend, followed by statements about sectors of the market that support and go against the trend, followed by salient examples of stocks which support or counter the trend);
- different frequency of occurrence of words and syntax patterns from the norm for the whole language—each sublanguage has its own statistical profile, which can be used to help set up preferred interpretations for new texts.

23.2.4 Why study sublanguage?

The study of language processing in limited domains is important for several reasons. First, as implied above, building a successful NLP application for a sublanguage requires exploiting its grammatical and lexical restrictions, as well as allowing for any 'deviant' sentence types that may be perfectly acceptable for domain experts. A second and corollary reason is that, because of the limitations on vocabulary, syntax, and semantics in a sublanguage, it may be possible to carry out a relatively complete linguistic description, something well beyond the state of the art for any language as a whole. In this way sublanguages play the same role for computational linguistics as fruitflies (drosophilae) play for the study of genetics. In sublanguages one can study language systems which are microcosms (in many if not all respects) of the whole language. Just as drosophilae facilitate the study of genetics for biologists, sublanguages make natural language's information-carrying mechanisms more transparent to linguists and computer scientists.

Third, many computational linguists have also been attracted to limited domains as testing grounds for knowledge representation schemes. There may be some hope of representing a full range of concepts when the domain, situation, and resultant sublanguage are small and 'well-behaved'. A sublanguage processing system often presents an opportunity to integrate linguistic knowledge with non-linguistic domain knowledge, and hence to validate the descriptive adequacy and completeness of the representations. Indeed, and this is a fourth reason, a detailed analysis of a sublanguage provides one of the most reliable ways to set up classes of objects, their properties, and relations needed to describe the knowledge used in the corresponding domain. Remember, however, that a sublanguage grammar describes what is 'sayable' in the domain, and not what is true or false about the domain objects and relations.

Finally, a good appreciation of how sublanguages work is a prerequisite for any attempt to engineer a standard controlled language for one or more domains. We will see below that controlled languages (CLs) do not always have the tight single-domain restrictions one finds in true sublanguages. However, a CL standard is usually based on a specific type of text, which is used for one or more distinct, but similar, sublanguages. In other words, the motivation for setting up a controlled language usually comes from the need to introduce writing standards for an important family of pre-existing sublanguages.

23.2.5 Research issues concerning sublanguage

The phenomenon of sublanguage is still poorly understood, and requires further research to answer a number of basic questions. How, exactly, do sublanguages arise? What factors are most important in the formation of a new consensus about language usage among experts in a new domain? Are features from existing sublanguages borrowed into new ones? Can we account for (in terms of parameters of the text purpose) the special syntactic features we find in certain sublanguages, and the 'family resemblances' we find among some sublanguages which share the same text genre? For example, instructional texts ranging from aircraft maintenance manuals to cooking recipes in many languages use zero anaphora for repeated object noun phrases, and tend to delete definite articles, as shown in (23.7) and (23.8).

(23.7) Remove filter and rinse _ in benzene. (from an aircraft hydraulics manual)
(23.8) Remove roast from oven and cover _ with foil. (from a meat recipe)

Some of these research questions have practical importance, since we are often faced with the 'portability' of an NLP system from one domain to another, and the prospect of adapting the lexicon and grammar rules to the new sublanguage (cf. Hirschman 1986). Another research area deals with the following problem: many sublanguage texts refer to a core semantic domain but also allow reference to a broader context, with the result that the sublanguage as a whole is a composite or embedding of one linguistic system within another (Kittredge 1983).

23.3 Sublanguage Processing Applications

Following are a few examples of NLP applications which exploit sublanguage descriptions.

23.3.1 Machine translation

The best-known and most economically successful case of machine translation (MT, see Chapters 27 and 28) has been within a sublanguage, that is, embodied in the above-mentioned TAUM-MÉTÉO system for translation of English weather forecasts into French. Developed at the University of Montreal in 1974–5, this system took advantage of the fact that telegraphic-style forecasts use only a few basic sentence patterns, and a lexicon of fewer than a thousand words (not counting place names). Translation between English and French forecasting sublanguages can be formulated by relatively simple rules, even though parsing requires a sublanguage-specific grammar to handle elliptical structures such as:

(23.9) Becoming clear and cooler this evening with lows in the teens.

In the few cases where one English word can have more than one French translation (e.g. *heavy* rain gives *pluie abondante*, but *heavy fog* is rendered as *brouillard généralisé*), the English sublanguage categories provide semantic distinctions that dictate the correct choice. When the adjective *heavy* modifies an English noun denoting falling precipitation, its French translation is different than when it modifies a noun denoting suspended precipitation. *Rain* and *fog* fall into different sublanguage classes in English because their co-occurring verbs and adjectives are different (*rain ending*, but *fog lifting*, etc.). A detailed sublanguage grammar thus provides rich information about the lexical subclass and structural context of a word to help determine its correct translation.

Other systems for English–French sublanguage translation include TAUM-AVIATION (see Lehrberger 1982), for aircraft hydraulics manuals, and CRITTER (Isabelle, Dymetman, and Macklovitch 1988), for livestock market reports. Comparisons of linguistic features in several English and French sublanguages indicate a much stronger structural similarity between parallel (English and French) sublanguages than one sees among disparate sublanguages in the same language (Kittredge 1982, 1987).

23.3.2 Database extraction from text

One of the first applications of sublanguage processing was on medical and pharmaceutical texts at New York University (NYU). During the 1970s the NYU Linguistic String Project showed that physicians' summaries about test results and treatment of patients could be analysed with a sublanguage grammar to build a database of patient information. The NYU group developed the notion of **information format**, a tabular representation for texts in which the elementary sentences underlying each text sentence are aligned to show their structure in terms of sublanguage word classes (Sager 1978). Information formats were originally proposed by Harris (1952) for analysing scientific discourse, but the NYU work showed that the formats for medical report texts could be refined to build useful databases. This later led to the idea of generating report texts from relational databases in several domains (cf. Kittredge 1983).

23.3.3 Natural language generation

Natural sublanguages have proved to be an excellent testing ground for generating textual reports from databases (see Chapter 15 for a broad view of text generation). The ANA system (Kukich 1983) demonstrated that an important part of North American stock market summaries can be generated from twice-hourly price and share-volume data (i.e. from a database of numbers). The same data can also be summarized in French, using an equivalent French sublanguage grammar and lexicon (Contant 1985). The FoG[4] system, developed between 1985 and 1992, produces both English and French marine and public weather forecasts for the Canadian Environment service (Goldberg, Driedger, and Kittredge 1994). Other sublanguages for which bilingual generation has been demonstrated include reports on labour markets, retail trade, and the consumer price index (Iordanskaja et al. 1992). English reports have also been generated for basketball games (McKeown, Robin, and Kukich 1995), where historical information about players and teams is interspersed with statements about the game itself.

---

[4] FoG is an acronym for Forecast Generator.

23.3.4 Automated summarization and abstracting

One problem under active investigation today is how to produce summaries for texts (Chapter 32). In many cases the source text is written in a scientific or technical sublanguage. The increasing access to written articles through the Internet has increased the need for summarization in general and automatic abstracting in particular. The production of usable abstracts by automatic means is still a distant goal, which can be reached only through a better understanding of the sublanguages of the articles.

23.4 CONTROLLED LANGUAGE

23.4.1 What is a controlled language?

A **controlled language** (CL) is a restricted version of a natural language which has been engineered to meet a special purpose, most often that of writing technical documentation for non-native speakers of the document language. A typical CL uses a well-defined subset of a language's grammar and lexicon, but adds the terminology needed in a technical domain. Controlled languages have been used in language teaching since about 1930, but their recent success has come from making technical language more accessible to both non-experts and non-native speakers. The best-known example of a controlled language is AECMA[5] Simplified English, an internationally accepted norm for writing technical manuals in the aerospace industry. The AECMA standard, dating from a European initiative in 1979, has grown out of the collective experience over the past few decades of several large manufacturing companies, who aim to simplify technical documentation, either for reading in the original, or to facilitate automatic translation into the languages of their export markets.

Controlled languages have proved useful not only for aerospace and automotive product documentation, but also for telecommunications and software manuals, to cite the most important examples. There is a growing movement to apply CL standards to dialogue training materials for critically important personnel operating in multilingual contexts, such as border police and aircraft pilots. Now that various forms of Simplified English have gained wide acceptance, there is a surge in parallel work on French, German, Swedish, and other languages.

---

[5] AECMA is the French acronym for the European Association of Manufacturers of Aerospace Equipment.

There seem to be two different assumptions at work when a controlled language is designed. First, it is assumed that the technical jargon (sublanguage) and irregular writing of engineers and other domain experts needs to be clarified (e.g. disambiguated), standardized, and interpreted for all who are not native-speaking domain experts. Second, it is assumed that a text written in a regular subset of the language will be easier for non-native speakers to read. Thus a controlled language can be seen as the result of two operations on technical sublanguage, (1) paraphrasing technical texts into 'normal' standard language, and then (2) paraphrasing the normalized texts into a simpler form through use of a restricted set of words and structures.

It is by now well established that the clarifications and standardizations required by CL norms make the resulting text much more amenable to automatic translation, as well as to other forms of automatic processing, such as content analysis or document indexing for retrieval.

23.4.2 AECMA Simplified English

AECMA Simplified English is now used by most of the major manufacturers of aerospace equipment, and by many major airlines. The Simplified English Guide specifies three sources of words:

1. about 950 basic 'approved' words, which have well-defined non-technical meanings and selected parts of speech; these include all the important prepositions, articles, and conjunctions, as well as basic nouns, verbs, adjectives and adverbs;
2. an unlimited number of technical names, divided into twenty categories, which can be chosen by the user organization but used only as adjectives or nouns, in accordance with certain guidelines;
3. technical verbs to denote six categories of user-specified manufacturing processes, subject to strict rules of usage (e.g. *You must not use the -ing form of the verb*).

This Simplified English standard has about fifty-five rules governing word usage and sentence construction. Some of these are fairly precise (e.g. *You must break up noun clusters of four or more words by rewriting, hyphenating, or a combination of the two*). Among the precise rules are several regarding punctuation. Other rules are somewhat vague (e.g. *Keep to one topic per sentence*), or else express desirable writing goals (e.g. *Try to vary sentence lengths and constructions to keep the text interesting*). Most of the vague or goal-oriented guidelines can be seen as principles which apply to good expository writing in general.

23.4.3 Why use controlled languages?

Many manufacturing and service industries are using controlled languages to improve the quality and uniformity of their documentation. The clarity and freedom from ambiguity of CL texts leads to fewer errors, and hence to greater safety during the use and maintenance of products. Moreover, CL document users have fewer complaints and questions, which reduces product support costs. The relative simplicity and clarity of CL documents also reduces the need for translation. (For example, many aerospace workers around the world might not understand fully the manuals written by American engineers, but understand perfectly the documents produced by technical writers trained in AECMA Simplified English.) When translation is required, CL documents lend themselves more readily to human or computer-assisted translation, thanks to the elimination of ambiguity and complex syntax, and to the observance of uniform standards in vocabulary, abbreviations, etc.

23.4.4 Limitations of controlled languages

Controlled languages require a significant amount of effort to design and use correctly. Setting up a new controlled language, or adapting an existing standard for a new document producer, requires the intensive collaboration of domain experts (who can clarify the intended meanings), technical writers, and users. If sufficient care is not taken, there is a potential danger that document simplification will erase important nuances of meaning, or otherwise distort the intention of the expert writer. Several design iterations may be required to reach consensus among all parties involved in the document life cycle. Even when consensus is reached, it may take time to make all the required adjustments in the organization's business process.

Writing in a controlled language is an acquired skill for technical writers. The cost per page of writing and editing CL documentation may initially be substantially higher than for traditional documentation. Clearly, such investment is justified only when the user community is large and there are economic or other benefits of setting up and enforcing the standard. Whereas the aerospace industry has clearly seen the benefit of CL, smaller industries which deal in less critical products may not reap the same benefits. Nevertheless, no industry which produces documentation on a regular basis can afford to ignore CL. A detailed cost-benefit analysis may reveal that some, if not all, of the practices of CL make sense.

Many organizations using CL have experimented with CL-checking software to help technical writers ensure conformity to a particular standard. In practice, it has proved difficult for a computer to accurately detect all cases where a human author has deviated from CL prescriptions. Without full semantic analysis of each input sentence, many CL rules cannot be implemented (e.g. the prohibition against more than one idea per sentence). Moreover, as with spell checkers, CL checkers incorrectly flag a high number of suspected non-CL 'errors', which in fact are legitimate CL usage. (This is known as poor *precision*.) On the other hand, some non-conformance to implemented CL rules will, at least occasionally, escape detection by a CL checker (known as poor *recall*).

23.4.5 Current CL research and development issues

Most CL research and development has been driven by the application needs of the user industries. A major focus of current work is how to build better conformance checkers that can not only detect non-CL usage, but even propose possible corrections for approval by a human editor. The European SECC project of 1994–6 showed this to be possible and useful in certain situations, but more development is needed to improve both the precision and the recall of error detection. The SECC project also made progress in detecting and correcting typical non-native errors (occurring, for example, when French-speaking writers produce Simplified English documentation). Two more elusive goals, requiring further research, are: (1) reliable automatic correction of errors, and (2) the use of information from adjacent sentences to improve detection and correction of errors in a given sentence.

A few researchers are exploring new uses for controlled languages, for example, to aid large-scale collaborative work in knowledge acquisition. Others are trying to better understand the CL design principles that will allow CLs to have enough expressive coverage, and capture the sublanguage distinctions made by domain experts, without abandoning the need for simplicity and regularity. Pure research of this kind is taking place alongside investigation into practical issues of human factors in the CL production process.

23.5 RELATIONSHIPS BETWEEN SUBLANGUAGE AND CONTROLLED LANGUAGE

23.5.1 CL as a codification of one or more related sublanguages

There has been some confusion in computational linguistics between the notions of sublanguage and controlled language. In the mathematical sense, it could be argued that a CL is a kind of sublanguage, as a systematic subset of the standard language. However, a CL is clearly not a *natural* sublanguage in the sense described above. A CL is an attempt to standardize one or more related sublanguages into a form that will facilitate communication between (1) expert native speakers and (2) those who are either non-expert native speakers or expert non-natives (or perhaps both). The semantic material covered by a CL is often intended to mirror that of a sublanguage. Nevertheless, the AECMA Simplified English standard is clearly much broader in scope than any single sublanguage, since it allows instantiations of technical vocabulary from many separate subdomains of aerospace technology (with possibly conflicting word usage). The intention appears to be that in a given work context, the number of subdomains instantiated will be small and non-conflicting.

23.5.2 Contrasts between sublanguage and CL

The contrasts between sublanguage and controlled language are important from the theoretical point of view, and have practical consequences for the design of NLP systems. Recall that sublanguages are natural linguistic subsystems that arise spontaneously, and evolve over time by the tacit consensus of an expert community. Most sublanguages, especially those used in science writing, are like general language in having no limit on sentence length or syntactic complexity, so that in theory a sublanguage is an infinite set of sentences. In contrast, most CLs put an upper bound on sentence length (typically around twenty-five words), and also limit the recursive processes of syntax, so that the result is a finite set of sentences. This finitude of CLs, particularly the limitation on noun compounding, has made it possible to design efficient tools for CL analysis and translation.

23.5.3 Is there a better path from sublanguage to controlled language?

On the practical level, there is an important issue as to whether CLs, in their current form, can really achieve the goal of broader communication between native-speaking engineers and the less initiated. We have to assume that sublanguages have evolved in their present form for some reason. The 'best practice' of domain-expert writers is a sublanguage standard that may have merit as the basis of a CL. Despite the general success of CLs in industry, some evidence has been reported of dissatisfaction on the part of engineers with certain CL conventions such as restoration of ellipsis and reduction of terminology. Furthermore, problems of maintaining proper anaphoric reference sometimes arise, when CL editors attempt to shorten or simplify sublanguage sentences. At present, there are too few data on these situations, and very few detailed objective studies. Aside from these practical considerations, questions have been raised as to whether it is ethical to restrict the ability of writers to freely express themselves, and whether the constant effort to write to an 'unnatural' standard might not degrade some aspect of writers' linguistic competence over time.

One thing seems already clear—that the 'one-size-fits-all' mentality inherent in some CL standards is likely to be inadequate for the future. There are two reasons for this. First, the comprehension problems of non-native speakers are often different from those of non-expert native speakers. Moreover, there are important differences among the languages of non-natives (e.g. German speakers may be much more tolerant of English noun compounds, within the AECMA limit of length three, than French speakers, because of the presence of extensive compounding in German). Second, there are significant differences between the expertise levels of native speakers, which might be better served by allowing flexibility in applying certain CL rules.

One long-term solution to this problem is to use a better understanding of sublanguage rationale in the design of controlled languages, so that good writing practice can be enforced, while keeping desirable sublanguage features that are needed for economy of expression and for maintaining nuances of meaning. Given a sufficiently refined representation of the content of a sublanguage text, it should be possible, eventually, to rephrase the text on demand to fit the domain and language expertise of the reader/listener.

FURTHER READING AND RELEVANT RESOURCES

Two collections of articles on sublanguage (Kittredge and Lehrberger 1982; Grishman and Kittredge 1986) provide an overview of the field, with examples of sublanguage analysis for computational linguistics. See especially the articles on medical sublanguage and sublanguage methodology by N. Sager and by L. Hirschman in both volumes.

Several important articles on controlled language can be found in the proceedings of the three international Controlled Language Applications Workshops (CLAW-96, CLAW-98, CLAW-2000). Critiques of CLs can be found in Goyvaerts (1996) and Heald and Zajac (1996). For information about ordering proceedings from past CLAW workshops see http://www.controlled-language.org/. Information on AECMA Simplified English can be obtained at http://www.aecma.org/. For detailed work on a similar standard for French, see Barthe (1998); Lux (1998).

ACKNOWLEDGEMENTS

My sincere thanks go to Audrey Kittredge and to anonymous reviewers for comments which have improved the text. All remaining infelicities are my own. Permission from the Entomological Society of America to reprint the example in Fig. 23.2 is gratefully acknowledged.

References

Adriaens, G. 1994. 'The LRE SECC project: simplified English grammar and style correction in an MT framework'. *Proceedings of the Language Engineering Convention* (Paris), 1–8.

Barthe, K. 1998. 'GIFAS rationalised French: designing one controlled language to match another'. *Proceedings of the 2nd International Workshop on Controlled Language Applications (CLAW '98)* (Pittsburgh), 87–102.

Contant, C. 1985. *Génération automatique de texte: application au sous-langage boursier français*. MA thesis, Dept. of Linguistics, University of Montreal.

Goldberg, E., N. Driedger, and R. Kittredge. 1994. 'FoG: a new approach to the synthesis of weather forecast text'. *IEEE Expert*, 9(2), 45–53.

Goyvaerts, P. 1996. 'Controlled English, curse or blessing? A user's perspective'. *Proceedings of the 1st International Workshop on Controlled Language Applications (CLAW '96)* (Leuven), 137–42.

Grishman, R. and R. Kittredge (eds.). 1986. *Analyzing Language in Restricted Domains: Sublanguage Description and Processing*. Hillsdale, NJ: Lawrence Erlbaum Associates.

Harris, Z. 1952. 'Discourse analysis'. *Language*, 28, 1–30.

Heald, I. and R. Zajac. 1996. 'Syntactic and semantic problems in the use of a controlled language'. *Proceedings of the 1st International Workshop on Controlled Language Applications (CLAW '96)* (Leuven), 205–15.

Hirschman, L. 1986. 'Discovering sublanguage structures'. In Grishman and Kittredge (1986), 211–34.

Iordanskaja, L., M. Kim, R. Kittredge, B. Lavoie, and A. Polguère. 1992. 'Generation of extended bilingual statistical reports'. *Proceedings of the 14th International Conference on Computational Linguistics (COLING '92)* (Nantes), 1019–23.

Isabelle, P., M. Dymetman, and E. Macklovitch. 1988. 'CRITTER'. *Proceedings of the 12th International Conference on Computational Linguistics (COLING '88)* (Budapest), 261–6.

Kittredge, R. 1982. 'Variation and homogeneity of sublanguages'. In Kittredge and Lehrberger (1982), 107–37.

——1983. 'Semantic processing of texts in restricted sublanguages'. *Computers and Mathematics with Applications*, 9(1), 45–58.

——1987. 'The significance of sublanguage for automatic translation'. In S. Nirenburg (ed.), *Machine Translation*. Cambridge: Cambridge University Press, 59–67.

——and J. Lehrberger (eds.). 1982. *Sublanguage: Studies of Language in Restricted Semantic Domains*. Berlin: de Gruyter.

Kukich, K. 1983. 'The design of a knowledge-based report generator'. *Proceedings of the 21st Conference of the Association for Computational Linguistics* (Cambridge, Mass.), 145–50.

Lehrberger, J. 1982. 'Automatic translation and the concept of sublanguage'. In Kittredge and Lehrberger (1982), 81–106.

Levin, B. 1993. *English Verb Classes and Alternations*. Chicago: University of Chicago Press.

Lux, V. 1998. *Élaboration d'un français rationalisé étendu modulaire (FREM) pour les manuels de maintenance d'aéronefs*. Ph.D. thesis, Université de Paris 7.

McKeown, K., J. Robin, and K. Kukich. 1995. 'Generating concise natural language summaries'. *Information Processing and Management*, 31(5), 703–33.

Sager, N. 1978. 'Natural language information formatting: the automatic conversion of texts to a structured data base'. *Advances in Computers*, 17, 89–162.

CHAPTER 24

CORPUS LINGUISTICS

TONY McENERY

ABSTRACT

In this chapter the use of corpora in natural language processing is overviewed. After defining what a corpus is and briefly overviewing the history of corpus linguistics, the chapter focuses on corpus annotation. Following the review of corpus annotation, a brief survey of existing corpora is presented, taking into account the types of corpus annotation present in each corpus. The chapter concludes by considering the use of corpora, both annotated, and unannotated, in a range of natural language processing (NLP) systems.

24.1 INTRODUCTION

Corpus data are, for many applications, the raw fuel of NLP, and/or the testbed on which an NLP application is evaluated. In this chapter the history of corpus linguistics is briefly considered. Following on from this, corpus annotation is introduced as a prelude to a discussion of some of the uses of corpus data in NLP. But before any of this can be done, we need to ask: what is a corpus?

24.2 WHAT IS A CORPUS?

A **corpus** (pl. *corpora*, though *corpuses* is perfectly acceptable) is simply described as a large body of linguistic evidence typically composed of attested language use. One may contrast this form of linguistic evidence with sentences created not as a result of communication in context, but rather upon the basis of metalinguistic reflection upon language use, a type of data common in the generative approach to linguistics. Corpus data is not composed of the ruminations of theorists. It is composed of such varied material as everyday conversations (e.g. the spoken section of the British National Corpus[1]), radio news broadcasts (e.g. the IBM/Lancaster Spoken English Corpus), published writing (e.g. the majority of the written section of the British National Corpus) and the writing of young children (e.g. the Leverhulme Corpus of Children's Writing). Such data are collected together into corpora which may be used for a range of research purposes. Typically these corpora are machine readable—trying to exploit a paper-based linguistic resource or audio recording running into millions of words is impractical. So while corpora could be paper based, or even simply sound recordings, the view taken here is that corpora are machine readable.

In this chapter the focus will be upon the use of corpora in NLP. But it is worth noting that one of the immense benefits of corpus data is that they may be used for a wide range of purposes in a number of disciplines. Corpora have uses in both linguistics and NLP, and are of interest to researchers from other disciplines, such as literary stylistics (Short, Culpeper, and Semino 1996). Corpora are multifunctional resources.

With this stated, a slightly more refined definition of a corpus is needed than that which has been introduced so far. It has been established that a corpus is a collection of naturally occurring language data. But is any collection of language data, from three sentences to three million words of data, a corpus? The term corpus should properly only be applied to a well-organized collection of data, collected within the boundaries of a *sampling frame* designed to allow the exploration of a certain linguistic feature (or set of features) via the data collected. A sampling frame is of crucial importance in corpus design. Sampling is inescapable. Unless the object of study is a highly restricted sublanguage or a dead language, it is quite impossible to collect all of the utterances of a natural language together within one corpus. As a consequence, the corpus should aim for *balance and representativeness* within a specific sampling frame, in order to allow a particular variety of language to be studied or modelled. The best way to explain these terms is via an example. Imagine that a researcher has the task of developing a dialogue manager for a planned telephone ticket selling system and decides to construct a corpus to assist in this task. The sampling frame here is clear—the relevant data for the planned corpus would have to be drawn from tele-

---

[1] Details of all corpora mentioned in this chapter are given in 'Further Reading and Relevant Resources' below.

phone ticket sales. It would be quite inappropriate to sample the novels of Jane Austen or face-to-face spontaneous conversation in order to undertake the task of modelling telephone-based transactional dialogues. Within the domain of telephone ticket sales there may be a number of different types of tickets sold, each of which requires distinct questions to be asked. Consequently, we can argue that there are various linguistically distinct categories of ticket sales. So the corpus is balanced by including a wide range of types of telephone ticket sales conversations within it, with the types organized into coherent subparts (for example, train ticket sales, plane ticket sales, and theatre ticket sales). Finally, within each of these categories there may be little point in recording one conversation, or even the conversations of only one operator taking a call. If one records only one conversation it may be highly idiosyncratic. If one records only the calls taken by one operator, one cannot be sure that they are typical of all operators. Consequently, the corpus aims for representativeness by including within it a range of speakers, in order that idiosyncrasies may be averaged out.

24.2.1 Monolingual, comparable, and parallel corpora

So, a corpus is a body of machine-readable linguistic evidence, which is collected with reference to a sampling frame. There are important variations on this theme, however. So far the focus has been upon **monolingual corpora**—corpora representing one language. **Comparable corpora** are corpora where a series of monolingual corpora are collected for a range of languages, preferably using the same sampling frame and with similar balance and representativeness, to enable the study of those languages in contrast. **Parallel corpora** take a slightly different approach to the study of languages in contrast, gathering a corpus in one language, and then translations of that corpus data into one or more languages. Parallel and comparable corpora may appear rather similar when first encountered, but the data they are composed of are significantly different. If the main focus of a study is on contrastive linguistics, comparable corpora are preferable, as, for example, the process of translation may influence the forms of a translation, with features of the source language carried over into the target language (Schmied and Fink 2000). If the interest in using the corpus is to gain translation examples for an application such as example-based machine translation (see Chapter 28), then the parallel corpus, used in conjunction with a range of alignment techniques (Botley, McEnery, and Wilson 2000; Véronis 2000), offers just such data.

24.2.2 Spoken corpora

Whether the corpus is monolingual, comparable, or parallel, the corpus may also be composed of written language, spoken language, or both. With spoken language some important variations in corpus design come into play. The spoken corpus could in principle exist as a set of audio recordings only (for example, the Survey of English Dialects existed in this form for many years). At the other extreme, the original sound recordings of the corpus may not be available at all, and an orthographic transcription of the corpus could be the sole source of data (as is the case with the spoken section of the British National Corpus[2]). Both of these scenarios have drawbacks. If the corpus exists only as a sound recording, such data are difficult to exploit, even in digital form. It is currently problematic for a machine to search, say, for the word *apple* in a recording of spontaneous conversation in which a whole range of different speakers are represented. On the other hand, while an orthographic transcription is useful for retrieval purposes—retrieving word forms from a machine-readable corpus is typically a trivial computational task—many important acoustic features of the original data are lost, e.g. prosodic features, variations in pronunciation.[3] As a consequence of both of these problems, spoken corpora have been built which combine a transcription of the corpus data with the original sound recording, so that one is able to retrieve words from the transcription, but then also retrieve the original acoustic context of the production of the word via a process called time alignment (Roach and Arnfield 1995). Such corpora are now becoming increasingly common.

24.2.3 Research questions and corpora

The choice of corpus to be used in a study depends upon the research questions being asked of the corpus, or the applications one wishes to base upon the corpus. Yet whether the corpus is monolingual, comparable or parallel, within the sampling frame specified for the corpus, the corpus should be designed to be balanced and representative.[4] With this stated, let us now move to a brief overview of the history of corpus linguistics before introducing a further refinement to our definition of a corpus—the annotated versus the unannotated corpus.

---

[2] Some audio material for the BNC spoken corpus is available. Indeed, the entire set of recordings are lodged in the National Sound Archive in the UK. However, the recordings are not available for general use beyond the archive, and the sound files have not been time aligned against their transcriptions.

[3] One can, as will be seen later, transcribe speech using a phonemic transcription and annotate the transcription to show features such as stress, pitch, and intonation. Nonetheless, as the original data will almost certainly contain information lost in the process of transcription, and, crucially, the process of transcription and annotation also entails the imposition of an analysis, the need to consult the sound recording would still exist.

[4] There is another organizing principle upon which some corpora have been constructed, which emphasizes continued text collection through time with less of a focus on the features of corpus design outlined here. These corpora, called **monitor corpora**, are not numerous, but have been influential and are useful for diachronic studies of linguistic features which may change rapidly, such as lexis. Some, such as the Bank of English, are very large and used for a range of purposes. Readers interested in exploring the monitor corpus further are referred to Sinclair (1991).

24.3 A HISTORY OF CORPUS LINGUISTICS

Outlining a history of **corpus linguistics** is difficult. In its modern, computerized, form, the corpus has only existed since the late 1940s. The basic idea of using attested language use for the study of language clearly pre-dated this time, but the problem was that the gathering and use of large volumes of linguistic data in the pre-computer age was so difficult as to be almost impossible. There were notable examples of it being achieved via the deployment of vast workforces—Kaeding (1897) is a notable example of this. Yet in reality, corpus linguistics in the form that we know it today, where any PC user can, with relative ease, exploit corpora running into millions of words, is a very recent phenomenon.

The crucial link between computers and the manipulation of large bodies of linguistic evidence was forged by Bussa (1980) in the late 1940s. During the 1950s the first large project in the construction of comparable corpora was undertaken by Juilland (see, for example, Juilland and Chang-Rodriguez 1964), who also articulated clearly the concepts behind the ideas of the sampling frame, balance, and representativeness. English corpus linguistics took off in the late 1950s, with work in America on the Brown corpus (Francis 1979) and work in Britain on the Survey of English Usage (Quirk 1960). Work in English corpus linguistics in particular grew throughout the 1960s, 1970s, and 1980s, with significant milestones such as a corpus of transcribed spoken language (Svartvik and Quirk 1980), a corpus with manual encodings of parts-of-speech information (Francis 1979), and a corpus with reliable automated encodings of parts of speech (Garside, Leech, and Sampson 1987) being reached in this period. During the 1980s, the number of corpora available steadily grew as did the size of those corpora. This trend became clear in the 1990s, with corpora such as the British National Corpus and the Bank of English reaching vast sizes (100,000,000 words and 300,000,000 words of modern British English respectively) which would have been for all practical purposes impossible in the pre-electronic age. The other trend that became noticeable during the 1990s was the increasingly multilingual nature of corpus linguistics, with monolingual corpora becoming available for a range of languages, and parallel corpora coming into widespread use (McEnery and Oakes 1996; Botley, McEnery, and Wilson 2000; Véronis 2000).

In conjunction with this growth in corpus data, fuelled in part by expanding computing power, came a range of technical innovations. For example, schemes for systematically encoding corpus data came into being (Sperberg-McQueen and Burnard 1994), programs were written to allow the manipulation of ever larger data sets (e.g. Sara), and work began in earnest to represent the audio recording of a transcribed spoken corpus text in tandem with its transcription. The range of future developments in corpus linguistics is too numerous to mention in detail here (see McEnery and Wilson 2001 for a fuller discussion). What can be said, however, is that as personal computing technology develops yet further, we can expect that research questions not addressable with corpus data at this point of time will become possible, as new types of corpora are developed, and new programs to exploit these new corpora are written.

One area which has only been touched upon here, but which has been a major area of innovation in corpus linguistics in the past and which will undoubtedly remain so in the future, is corpus annotation. In the next section corpus annotation will be discussed in some depth, as it is an area where corpus linguistics and NLP often interact, as will be shown in section 24.6.

24.4 CORPUS ANNOTATION

24.4.1 What is corpus annotation?

McEnery and Wilson (1996: 24) describe annotated corpora as being 'enhanced with various types of linguistic information'. This enhancement is achieved by analysts, whether they be humans, computers, or a mixture of both, imposing a linguistic interpretation upon a corpus. Typically this analysis is encoded by reference to a specified range of features represented by textual mnemonics which are introduced into the corpus. These mnemonics seek to link sections of the text to units of linguistic analysis. So, for example, in the case of introducing a part-of-speech analysis to a text, textual mnemonics are generally placed in a one-to-one relationship with the words in the text.[5]

24.4.1.1 *Enrichment, interpretation, and imposition*

In essence corpus annotation is the enrichment of a corpus in order to aid the process of corpus exploitation. Note that enrichment of the corpus does not necessarily occur from the viewpoint of the expert human analyst—corpus annotation only makes explicit what is implicit, it does not introduce new information. For any level of linguistic information encoded explicitly in a corpus, the information that a linguist can extract from the corpus by means of a hand and eye analysis will hopefully differ little, except in terms of the speed of analysis, from that contained in the annotation. The enrichment is related to users who need linguistic analyses but are not in a position to provide them. This covers both humans who lack the metalinguistic ability to impose

---

[5] Note that there are exceptions to this general description. Multi-word units may be placed in a many-to-one relationship with a morphosyntactic tag. Similarly, enclitics in a text may force certain words to be placed in a one-to-many relationship with morphosyntactic annotations.

a meaningful linguistic analysis upon a text as well as computers, which may lack the ability to impose such analyses also.

Keywords in describing the process of corpus annotation are *imposition* and *interpretation*. Given any text, there are bound to be a plurality of analyses for any given level of interpretations that one may wish to undertake. This plurality arises from the fact that there is often an allowable degree of variation in linguistic analyses, arising in part at least from ambiguities in the data and fuzzy boundaries between categories of analysis in any given analytical scheme. **Corpus annotation** typically represents one of a variety of possible analyses, and imposes that consistently upon the corpus text.

24.4.2 What are the advantages of corpus annotation?

In the preceding sections, some idea of why we may wish to annotate a corpus has already emerged. In this section I want to detail four specific advantages of corpus annotation as a prelude to discussing the process of corpus annotation in the context of criticisms put forward against it to date. Key advantages of corpus annotation are *ease of exploitation, reusability, multi-functionality,* and *explicit analyses.*

24.4.2.1 *Ease of exploitation*

This is a point which we have considered briefly already. With an annotated corpus, the range and speed of corpus exploitation increases. Considering the range of exploitation, an annotated corpus can be used by a wider range of users than an unannotated corpus. For example, even if I cannot speak French, given an appropriately annotated corpus of French, I am capable of retrieving all of the nouns in a corpus of French. Similarly, even if a computer is not capable of parsing a sentence, given a parsed treebank and appropriate retrieval software, it can retrieve noun phrases from that corpus. Corpus annotation enables humans and machines to exploit and retrieve analyses of which they are not themselves capable.

Moving to the speed of corpus exploitation, even where a user is capable of undertaking the range of analyses encoded within an annotated corpus, they are able to exploit an analysis encoded within a corpus[6] swiftly and reliably.

24.4.2.2 *Reusability*

Annotated corpora also have the merit of allowing analyses to be exploited over and over again, as noted by Leech (1997: 5). Rather than an analysis being performed for a specific purpose and discarded, corpus annotation records an analysis. This analysis is then prone to reuse.

---

[6] Assuming that suitable, preferably annotation-aware, retrieval software is available.

24.4.2.3 *Multi-functionality*

An analysis originally annotated within a corpus may have been undertaken with one specific purpose in mind. When reused, however, the purpose of the corpus exploitation may be quite different from that originally envisaged. So as well as being reusable, corpus analyses can also be put to a wide range of uses.

24.4.2.4 *Explicit analyses*

A final advantage I would outline for corpus annotation is that it is an excellent means by which to make an analysis explicit. As well as promoting reuse, a corpus analysis stands as a clear objective record of the analysis imposed upon the corpus by the analyst/analysts responsible for the annotation. As we will see shortly, this clear benefit has actually been miscast as a drawback of corpus annotation in the past.

24.4.3 How corpus annotation is achieved

Corpus annotation may be achieved entirely automatically, by a semi-automated process, or entirely manually. To cover each in turn, some NLP tools, such as lemmatizers and part-of-speech taggers, are now so reliable for languages such as English, French, and Spanish[7] that we may consider a wholly automated approach to their annotation (see Chapter 11 for a more detailed review of part-of-speech tagging). While using wholly automated procedures does inevitably mean a rump of errors in a corpus, the error rates associated with taggers such as CLAWS (Garside, Leech, and Sampson 1987) are low, typically being reported at around 3 per cent. Where such a rate of error in analysis is acceptable, corpus annotation may proceed without human intervention.

More typically, however, NLP tools are not sufficiently accurate so as to allow fully automated annotation. Yet they may be sufficiently accurate that correcting the annotations introduced by them is faster than undertaking the annotation entirely by hand. This was the case in the construction of the Penn Treebank (Marcus, Santorini, and Marcinkiewicz 1993), where the constituent structure of the corpus was first annotated by a computer and then corrected by human analysts. Another scenario where a mixture of machine and human effort occurs is where NLP tools which are usually sufficiently accurate, such as part-of-speech taggers, are not sufficient because highly accurate annotation is required. This is the case, for example, in the core corpus of the British National Corpus. Here the core corpus (one million words of writ-

---

[7] See McEnery et al. (1997) for an account of a project which produced reliable English, French, and Spanish lemmatization and part-of-speech tagging.

ten English and one million words of spoken) was first automatically part-of-speech annotated, and then hand corrected by expert human analysts.

Pure manual annotation occurs where no NLP application is available to a user, or where the accuracy of available systems is not high enough to make the time invested in manual correction less than pure manual annotation. An example of purely manual annotation is in the construction of corpora encoding anaphoric and cataphoric references (Botley and McEnery 2000; Mitkov 2002). It should be noted that in real terms, considering the range of possible annotations we may want to introduce into corpus texts, most would have to be introduced manually or at best semi-manually.

24.4.4   Criticisms of corpus annotation

Two main criticisms of corpus annotation have surfaced over the past decade or so. I believe it is quite safe to dismiss both, but for purposes of clarity let us spell out the criticisms and counter them here.

24.4.4.1   *Corpus annotations produce impure corpora*

The first criticism to be levelled at corpus annotation was that it somehow sullied the unannotated corpus by the process of imposing an interpretation on the data. The points to be made against this are simple. First, in imposing one analysis, there is no constraint upon the user of the corpus to use that analysis—they may impose one of their own. The plurality of interpretations of a text is something that must be accepted from the outset. Secondly, just because we do not make a clear record of the interpretation we have imposed via annotation it does not disguise the fact that in using raw corpora interpretations still occur. The interpretations imposed by corpus annotations have the advantage that they are objectively recorded and open to scrutiny. The interpretations of those who choose not to annotate corpus data remain fundamentally more obscure than those recorded clearly in a corpus. Bearing these two points in mind, it is plain to see the fundamental weakness of this criticism of corpus annotation.

24.4.4.2   *Consistency versus accuracy*

The second criticism, presented by Sinclair (1992), is not a criticism of corpus annotation as such. Rather it is a criticism of two of the practices of corpus annotation we have just examined—manual and semi-automatic corpus annotation. The argument is subtle, and worth considering seriously. It is centred upon two related notions—accuracy and consistency. When a part-of-speech tagger annotates a text and is 97 per cent accurate, its analysis should be 100 per cent consistent, i.e. given the same set of decision-making conditions in two different parts of the corpus, the answer given is the same. This consistency for the machine derives from its impartial and unswerving application of a program. Can we expect the same consistency of analysis from human annotators? As we have discussed already, there is a plurality of analyses possible for any given annotation. Consequently, when human beings are imposing an interpretation upon a text, can we assume that their analysis is 100 per cent consistent? May it not be the case that they may produce analyses which, when viewed from several points of view, are highly accurate, but which, when viewed from one analytical viewpoint, are not as accurate? It may be the case that the annotation of a corpus may be deemed to be accurate, but simultaneously be highly inconsistent.

This argument is potentially quite damaging to the practice of corpus annotation, especially when we consider that most hand analyses are carried out by teams of annotators, hence amplifying the possibility of inconsistency. As a result of such arguments, experiments have been carried out by annotation teams around the world (Marcus, Santorini, and Marcinkiewicz 1993; Voutilainen and Järvinen 1995; Baker 1997) in order to examine the validity of this criticism. No study to date has supported Sinclair's argument. Indeed every study has shown that while the introduction of a human element to corpus annotation does mean a modest decline in the consistency of annotation within the corpus, this decline is more than offset by a related rise in the accuracy of the annotation. There is one important rider to add to this observation, however. All of the studies above, especially the studies of Baker (1997), have used teams of trained annotators—annotators who were well versed in the use of a particular annotation scheme, and who had long experience in working with lists of guidelines which helped their analyses to converge. It is almost certainly true, though as yet not validated experimentally, that, given a set of analysts with no guidelines to inform their annotation decisions and no experience of teamwork, Sinclair's criticism would undoubtedly be more relevant. As it is, there is no reason to assume that Sinclair's criticisms of human-aided annotation should colour one's view of corpora produced with the aid of human grammarians, such as the French, English, and Spanish CRATER corpora (McEnery et al. 1997).

24.5 What Corpora are in Existence?

An increasing variety of annotated corpora are currently in existence. It should come as no surprise to discover that the majority of annotated corpora involve part of speech and lemmatization, as these are procedures which can be undertaken largely automatically. Nonetheless, a growing number of hand-annotated corpora

Table 24.1 Corpus annotation

Annotation	Work undertaken to date
Lemmatization	Widespread, see for example McEnery et al. (1997).
Part of speech	Widespread, see for example Church (1988); McEnery et al. (1997).
Parsing	Increasingly common, for example, Black, Garside, and Leech (1993); Marcus, Santorini, and Marcinkiewicz (1993); Sampson (1995).
Semantic	Less work here, but annotated corpora are available, for example the Singapore Defence Science Organization corpus (Ng and Lee 1996).
Discoursal annotation	Work on annotation schemes developing rapidly, see Botley and McEnery (2000).
Pragmatic/stylistic	Again, work on annotation schemes getting under way, e.g. Short, Culpeper, and Semino (1996); Stiles (1992).
IE-oriented annotation	Aone and Bennett (1994); Gaizauskas et al. (1995).

are becoming available. Table 24.1 seeks to show something of the range of annotated corpora of written language in existence. For more detail on the range and use of corpus annotation, see McEnery and Wilson (1996)[8] and Garside, Leech, and McEnery (1997).

Having now established the philosophical and practical basis for corpus annotation, and having reviewed the range of annotations related to written corpora, I would like to conclude this chapter by reviewing the practical benefits related to the use of annotated corpora in one field, NLP.

24.6 THE EXPLOITATION OF CORPORA IN NLP

NLP is a rapidly developing area of study, which is producing working solutions to specified natural language processing problems. The application of annotated corpora

---

[8] Also see http://www.ling.lancs.ac.uk/monkey/ihe/linguistics/corpus2/2fra1.htm for some on-line examples of corpus annotation.

within NLP to date has resulted in advances in language processing—part-of-speech taggers, such as CLAWS, are an early example of how annotated corpora enabled the development of better language processing systems (see Garside, Leech, and Sampson 1987). Annotated corpora have allowed such developments to occur as they are unparalleled sources of quantitative data. To return to CLAWS, because the tagged Brown corpus was available, accurate transition probabilities could be extracted for use in the development of CLAWS. The benefits of this data are apparent when we compare the accuracy rate of CLAWS—around 97 per cent—to that of TAGGIT, used to develop the Brown corpus—around 77 per cent. This massive improvement can be attributed to the existence of annotated corpus data which enabled CLAWS to disambiguate between multiple potential part-of-speech tag assignments in context.

It is not simply part-of-speech tagging where quantitative data are of prime importance to disambiguation. Disambiguation is a key problem in a variety of areas such as anaphor resolution, parsing, and machine translation. It is beyond doubt that annotated corpora will have an important role to play in the development of NLP systems in the future, as can be seen from the burgeoning corpus-based NLP literature (LREC 2000).

Beyond the use of quantitative data derived from annotations as the basis of disambiguation in NLP systems, annotated corpora may also provide the raw fuel for various terminology extraction programs. Work has been developed in the area of automated terminology extraction which relies upon annotated corpora for its results (Daille 1995; Gausier 1995). So although disambiguation is an area where annotated corpora are having a key impact, there is ample scope for believing that they may be used in a wider variety of applications.

A further example of such an application may be called evidence-based learning. Until recently, language analysis programs almost exclusively relied on human intuition in the construction of their knowledge/rule base. Annotated corpora corrected/produced by humans, while still encoding human intuitions, situate those intuitions within a context where the computer can recover intuitions from use, and where humans can moderate their intuitions by application to real examples. Rather than having to rely on decontextualized intuitions, the computer can recover intuitions from practice. The difference between human experts producing opinions about what they do out of context and practice in context has long been understood in artificial intelligence—humans tend to be better at showing what they know rather than explaining what they know, so to speak. The construction of an annotated corpus, therefore, allows us to overcome this known problem in communicating expert knowledge to machines, while simultaneously providing testbeds against which intuitions about language may be tested. Where machine learning algorithms are the basis for an NLP application, it is fair to say that corpus data are essential. Without them machine learning-based approaches to NLP simply will not work.

Another role which is emerging for the annotated corpus is as an evaluation testbed for NLP programs. Evaluation of language processing systems can be problematic, where people are training systems with different analytical schemes and texts, and have different target analyses which the system is to be judged by. Using one annotated corpus as an agreed testbed for evaluation can greatly ease such problems, as it specifies the text type/types, analytical scheme, and results which the performance of a program is to be judged upon. This approach to the evaluation of systems has been adopted in the past, as reported by Black, Garside, and Leech (1993), for instance, and in the Message Understanding Conferences in the United States (Aone and Bennett 1994). The benefits of the approach are so evident, however, that the establishment of such testbed corpora is bound to become increasingly common in the very near future.

One final activity which annotated corpora allow is worthy of some coverage here. It is true that, at the moment, the range of annotations available is wider than the range of annotations which it is possible for a computer to introduce with a high degree of accuracy. Yet by the use of the annotations present in a hand-annotated corpus, a resource is developed that permits a computer, over the scope of the annotated corpus only, to act as if it could perform the analysis in question. In short, if we have a manually produced treebank, a computer can read the treebank and discover where the marked constituents are, rather than having to work it out for itself. The advantages of this are limited yet clear. Such a use of an annotated corpus may provide an economic means of evaluating whether the development of a certain NLP application is worthwhile—if somebody posits that the application of a parser of newspaper stories would be of use in some application, then by the use of a treebank of newspaper stories they can experiment the worth of their claim without actually producing a parser.

There are further uses of annotated corpora in NLP beyond those covered here. The range of uses covered, however, is more than sufficient to illustrate that annotated corpora, even though we can justify them on philosophical grounds, can more than be justified on practical grounds.

24.7 CONCLUSION

Corpora have played a useful role in the development of human language technology to date. In return, corpus linguistics has gained access to ever more sophisticated language processing systems. There is no reason to believe that this happy symbiosis will not continue—to the benefit of language engineers and corpus linguists alike—in the future.

Further Reading and Relevant Resources

There are now a number of introductions to corpus linguistics, each of which takes slightly different views on the topic. McEnery and Wilson (2001) take a view closest to that presented in this chapter. Kennedy (1999) is concerned largely with English corpus linguistics and the use of corpora in language pedagogy. Stubbs (1997) is written entirely from the viewpoint of neo-Firthian approaches to corpus linguistics, while Biber, Conrad, and Reppen (1998) is concerned mainly with the multi-feature multi-dimension approach to analysing corpus data established in Biber (1988).

For those readers interested in corpus annotation, Garside, Leech, and McEnery (1997) provides a comprehensive overview of corpus annotation practices to date.

Many references in this chapter will lead to papers where specific corpora are discussed. The corpora listed here are simply those explicitly referenced in this chapter. For each corpus a URL is given where further information can be found about each corpus.

This list by no means represents the full range of corpora available. For a better idea of the range of corpora available visit the website of the European Language Resources Association (http://www.icp.grenet.fr/ELRA/home.html) or the Linguistic Data Consortium (http://www.ldc.upenn.edu).

BritishNationalCorpus:http://www.comp.lancs.ac.uk/computing/research/ucrel/bnc.html; IBM/Lancaster Spoken English Corpus: http://midwich.reading.ac.uk/research/speechlab/marsec/marsec.html; Leverhulme Corpus of Children's Writing: http://www.ling.lancs.ac.uk/monkey/lever/intro.htm; Survey of English Dialects: http://www.xrefer.com/entry/444074.

References

Aone, C. and S. W. Bennett. 1994. 'Discourse tagging and discourse tagged multilingual corpora'. *Proceedings of the International Workshop on Sharable Natural Language Resources* (Nara), 71–7.

Baker, J. P. 1995. *The Evaluation of Mutliple Posteditors: Inter Rater Consistency in Correcting Automatically Tagged Data*, Unit for Computer Research on the English Language Technical Papers 7, Lancaster University.

——1997. 'Consistency and accuracy in correcting automatically-tagged corpora'. In Garside, Leech, and McEnery (1997), 243–50.

Biber, D. 1988. *Variation across speech and writing*. Cambridge: Cambridge University Press.

——S. Conrad, and R. Reppen. 1998. *Corpus Linguistics: Investigating Language Structure and Use*. Cambridge: Cambridge University Press.

Black, E., R. Garside, and G. Leech. 1993. *Statistically Driven Computer Grammars of English: The IBM/Lancaster Approach*. Amsterdam: Rodopi.

Botley, S. and A. M. McEnery (eds.). 2000. *Discourse Anaphora and Resolution*. Studies in Corpus Linguistics. Amsterdam: John Benjamins.

Botley, S., A. M. McEnery, and A. Wilson (eds.). 2000. *Multilingual Corpora in Teaching and Research*. Amsterdam: Rodopi.

Bussa, R. 1980. 'The annals of humanities computing: the index Thomisticus'. *Computers and the Humanities*, 14, 83–90.

Church, K. 1988. 'A stochatic parts program and noun phrase parser for unrestricted texts'. *Proceedings of the 2nd Annual Conference on Applied Natural Language Processing* (Austin, Tex.), 136–48.

Daille, B. 1995. *Combined Approach for Terminology Extraction: Lexical Statistics and Linguistic Filtering*. Unit for Computer Research on the English Language Technical Papers 5, Lancaster University.

Francis, W. 1979. 'Problems of assembling, describing and computerizing large corpora'. In H. Bergenholtz and B. Schader (eds.), *Empirische Textwissenschaft: Aufbau und Auswertung von Text Corpora*. Königstein: Scripter Verlag, 110–23.

Gaizauskas, R., T. Wakao, K. Humphreys, H. Cunningham, and Y. Wilks. 1995. 'Description of the LaSIE System as used for MUC-6'. *Proceedings of the 6th Message Understanding Conference (MUC-6)* (San Jose, Calif.), 207–20.

Garside, R., G. Leech, and A. M. McEnery. 1997. *Corpus Annotation*. London: Longman.

——and G. Sampson. 1987. *The Computational Analysis of English*. London: Longman.

Gausier, E. 1995. *Modèles statistiques et patrins morphosyntactiques pour l'extraction de lexiques bilingues*. Ph.D. thesis, University of Paris VII.

Juilland, A. and E. Chang-Rodriguez. 1964. *Frequency Dictionary of Spanish Words*. The Hague: Mouton.

Kaeding, J. 1897. *Häufigkeitswörterbuch der deutschen Sprache*. Steglitz: published by the author.

Kennedy, G. 1999. *Corpus Linguistics*. London: Longman.

Leech, G. 1997. 'Introducing corpus annotation'. In Garside, Leech, and McEnery (1997), 1–18.

LREC 2000. *Proceedings of the 2nd International Conference on Language Resources and Evaluation* (Athens).

McEnery, A. M. and M. P. Oakes. 1996. 'Sentence and word alignment in the CRATER project: methods and assessment'. In J. Thomas and M. Short (eds.), *Using Corpora for Language Research*. London: Longman, 211–31.

——and A. Wilson. 1996. *Corpus Linguistics*. Edinburgh: Edinburgh University Press.

————2001. *Corpus Linguistics*, 2nd edn. Edinburgh: Edinburgh University Press.

————F. Sanchez-Leon, and A. Nieto-Serano. 1997. 'Multilingual resources for European languages: contributions of the CRATER project'. *Literary and Linguistic Computing*, 12(4), 219–26.

Marcus, M., B. Santorini, and M. Marcinkiewicz. 1993. 'Building a large annotated corpus of English: the Penn Treebank'. *Computational Linguistics*, 19(2), 313–30.

Mitkov, R. 2002. *Anaphora Resolution*. London: Longman.

Nagao, M. 1984. 'A framework of a mechanical translation between Japanese and English by analogy principle'. In A. Elithorn and J. Banerji (eds.), *Artificial and Human Translation*. Brussels: Nato Publications, 173–80.

Ng, H. T. and H. B. Lee. 1996. 'Integrating multiple knowledge sources to disambiguate word sense: an exemplar-based approach'. *Proceedings of the 34th Annual Meeting of the Association for Computational Linguistics* (Santa Cruz, Calif.), 40–7.

Quirk, R. 1960. 'Towards a description of English usage'. *Transactions of the Philological Society*, 40–61.

Roach, P. and S. Arnfield. 1995. 'Linking prosodic transcription to the time dimension'. In G. Leech, G. Myers, and J. Thomas (eds.), *Spoken English on Computer: Transcription, Markup and Applications*. London: Longman, 149–60.

Sampson, G. 1995. *English for the Computer: The SUSANNE Corpus and Analytic Scheme*. Oxford: Clarendon Press.

Schmied, J. and B. Fink. 2000. 'Corpus-based contrastive lexicology: the case of English *with* and its German translation eqivalents'. In Botley, McEnery, and Wilson (eds.), 157–76.

Short, M., J. Culpeper, and E. Semino. 1996. 'Using a corpus for stylistics research: speech presentation'. In M. Short and J. Thomas (eds.), *Using Corpora for Language Research*. London: Longman.

Sinclair, J. 1991. *Corpus, Concordance, Collocation*. Oxford: Oxford University Press.

——1992. 'The automatic analysis of text corpora'. In J. Svartvik (ed.), *Directions in Corpus Linguistics: Proceedings of the Nobel Symposium 82, Stockholm*, The Hague: Mouton, 379–97.

Sperberg-McQueen, C. M. and L Burnard. 1993. *Guidelines for Electronic Text Encoding and Interchange*. Chicago: Text Encoding Initiative.

Stiles, W. B. 1992. *Describing Talk*. New York: Sage.

Stubbs, M. 1997. *Texts and Corpus Analysis*. Oxford: Blackwell.

Svartvik, J. and R. Quirk. 1980. *The London–Lund Corpus of Spoken English*. Lund: Lund University Press.

Véronis, J. 2000. *Parallel Text Processing*. Dordrecht: Kluwer.

Voutilanen, A. and T. Järvinen. 1995. 'Specifying a shallow grammatical representation for parsing purposes'. *Proceedings of the 7th Conference of the European Chapter of the Association for Computational Linguistics (EACL '95)* (Dublin), 210–14.

Wilson, A. and J. Thomas. 1997. 'Semantic annotation'. In Garside, Leech, and McEnery (1997), 53–65.

CHAPTER 25

ONTOLOGIES

PIEK VOSSEN

ABSTRACT

In this chapter we discuss ontologies and their role in natural language processing (NLP). First, the notion of ontology is explained from different paradigms and by reference to some common existing ontologies. Next, we discuss how ontologies are commonly used in NLP.

25.1 INTRODUCTION

To process information you need information. This information may be as trivial as a lexicon with part-of-speech information on the words of a language, or as sophisticated as a formal definition of our world knowledge. On the basis of knowledge we can derive properties, build up expectations, make inferences, and develop programs that take decisions. For example, the following classical examples get different interpretations of the *with*-phrase (as a modifier of the object or a manner adjunct of the main verb *saw*) based on our knowledge of the world:

(25.1)   I saw a man/star/molecule with a microscope/telescope/binoculars.

To analyse these sentences correctly and to see the possible interpretations you have to access knowledge on size, weight, shape, volume, purpose, etc. Whenever we store information to make such common-sense-like inferences, we tend to speak of an **ontology** or **knowledge base**. Whenever the stored information is more of a linguistic nature, such as part of speech, we tend to speak of a **lexicon**. Still, the difference between ontologies and lexicons is not clear-cut and there is often a large overlap in the information that they contain.

There is little agreement on what an ontology is. Different disciplines have worked on ontologies or knowledge bases from very different perspectives. In general, an ontology can be described as an inventory of the objects, processes, etc. in a domain, as well as a specification of (some of) the relations that hold among them. Gruber (1992) describes an ontology in a neutral way as 'the specification of a conceptualization', where many different conceptualizations are possible. We cannot give here a full overview of all the different approaches to ontologies. Our focus will be on the way ontologies can be used for natural language processing (NLP). In section 25.2, we therefore only briefly discuss different paradigms, provide some examples of ontologies and suggest some further readings. This will clarify the important notions. In section 25.3, we summarize ways in which ontologies are used in NLP tasks. The final section contains a discussion on future trends and further readings.

25.2 ONTOLOGIES FROM DIFFERENT PERSPECTIVES

Language is said to be inherently ambiguous. It is so because it relies upon the shared knowledge we have to fill in missing or distorted information. NLP is a technology that tries to decode the minimal, ambiguous, and implicit messages encoded in language, using only a fraction of all the background information that humans have. This makes clear what role knowledge structured in an ontology can play. Usually, semantic-based NLP technology is therefore not the same as complete natural language understanding, as we will see in section 25.3.

The relation between the words in language and the entities to which they refer is often complex. Many words can be used to refer to the same entities (e.g. *ship, vessel,* and *wreck* or *mother, sister, boss, wife, woman, granny*) and there are many entities for which we do not have a single word (e.g. *handbook of computational linguistics*). Nevertheless, defining words and defining the entities to which words refer is often done in the same way by referring to a general conceptual type that classifies them. We can thus schematically relate expressions and words to concepts and types, and these to entities that are seen as instances of types:

term or noun phrase	refers-to	a conceptual entity
conceptual entity	belongs-to	conceptual class or type
noun	names	class of concrete entities
		class of situations
		class of properties
verb	names	class of situations
adjective	names	class of properties
conceptual class or type	represents	generic concept in mind

We further see that nouns can be used to refer to concrete entities (e.g. *an eye*), but also to situations (e.g. *a view*) and properties (e.g. *the visibility*), whereas verbs and adjectives can be used to refer to events and properties only (e.g. *see*, *visible*). Several traditions that deal with the structuring of knowledge in ontologies can now be positioned in terms of their different focus on either words or concepts for different purposes:

(a) philosophical tradition: the categorization of entities as logical kinds and types;

(b) cognitive tradition: the categorization of entities as a function of human information processing and inferencing;

(c) artificial intelligence (AI) tradition: the categorization of entities as a function of machines to do information processing and inferencing;

(d) lexical semantics: the categorization of words in a lexicon as part of a linguistic theory;

(e) lexicography: the definition of words in a dictionary for human users;

(f) information science: the categorization of information into topics in order to retrieve it from, e.g., a library.

Each of these traditions has created different artefacts, which can be all seen as types of ontologies: formal ontologies (a), conceptual networks and frames (b) and (c), lexicons (d), dictionaries (e), and thesauri (f). For reasons of space, we discuss only the traditions that are most relevant for NLP: the philosophical tradition (section 25.2.1), the AI tradition (section 25.2.2), and the lexical semantic tradition (section 25.2.3). Lexicography is discussed in Chapter 3 and information science, insofar it is not covered by linguistic techniques, has a rather different scope. For the latter work, see Spärck Jones (1986) and specifically Fossket (1997) for an overview of thesauri in information science.

25.2.1 Philosophical tradition

The classical tradition, in which the world is defined in terms of categories on the basis of **genus** and **differentiae**, dates back to Aristotle. The genus is the category to which something belongs and the differentiae are the properties that uniquely distinguish the category members from their parent and from one another. While this method is too simplistic to deal with concepts in general, it does work well for certain types and classes, and it has become the traditional model for making some definitions in dictionaries:

> boy = male <u>child</u>;   woman = female <u>adult</u>
> girl = female <u>child</u>   child = young <u>human</u>
> man = male <u>adult</u>;   adult = grown-up <u>human</u>

From such definitions, we can automatically derive a hierarchical structure with features linked to nodes in the hierarchy, as is illustrated in Fig. 25.1. The nodes in the hierarchy in Fig. 25.1 are related by **subsumption**. Subsumption can be defined as a relation between two concepts c_1 and c_2 such that c_1 subsumes c_2 iff all properties that are true of c_1 are also true of c_2 but there is a set of properties true of c_2 (the differentiae) that are not necessarily true of c_1. According to this definition, *being an adult* subsumes *being a man*, because the property *adult* is true of both *adults* and *men* whereas *male* is not necessarily true of *adults* and is necessarily true for *men*. A network of *subtype* or *subsumption* relations as in Fig. 25.1 is also called a **taxonomy** or **hierarchy**. In a taxonomy, the subsumption relation is *transitive*. At each level, new distinguishing features are introduced and these can be inherited by default. Default inheritance exploits the class membership principle: members of a class share the properties that define the class (see Wittgenstein 1984 for his classical counter-argument: there is no property that is shared by *all games*, even though many games may share many properties). Because *boy* is a specific kind of *child* it thus should have all the properties of *child* (otherwise it could not be a member of the class). From this structure, we can thus infer that a *boy* has the features +*male* and −*adult*. Default values can be overwritten by specific subtypes: *penguins* are *birds* that cannot *fly*.

The structure in Fig. 25.1 is representative of many ontologies that are currently available in the world and it illustrates many aspects of ontologies that have been discussed in the past. The most common examples are taxonomies of plant and animal life.

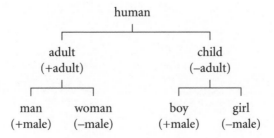

Fig. 25.1 Classical taxonomy tree

Recent formal concept hierarchies have become more complex, mainly because they allow multiple classifications and multiple inheritance. Instead of a tree structure, the result is a tangled network, or even a lattice of all possible permutations of features, as in Fig. 25.2, where the distinction *adult* and *male* are lifted to the same level as *human* so that they can be combined with non-human. The lattice structure has some advanced features. First, distinctions are systematically orthogonal (*male* and *adult*), unless they are introduced as mutually exclusive (+*male* versus –*male*). This leads to a systematic combination of compatible distinctions, representing all possible concepts (or *conceptualizations* in Gruber's sense) and an explicit encoding of incompatible feature combinations. The lattice structure in Fig. 25.2 is also more efficient than the tree structure in Fig. 25.1. For example, the distinction *male* is introduced only once in Fig. 25.2 but needs to be introduced at different nodes (below *child* and below *adult*) in the hierarchy in Fig. 25.1, with the risk of multiple divergent definitions. Finally, the lattice in Fig. 25.2 does not force you to order the introduction of distinctions at different levels, whereas the taxonomy in 25.1 does. The latter gives preference to the distinction *human* over *adult*, and to *adult* over *male*, but it is not clear why. We actually see that differences in ontologies can often be related to different (arbitrary) choices with respect to the introduction of the same features at different levels. Consequently, lattice structures can also be used to merge taxonomies with different but compatible structures, as is proposed by the ANSI Ad Hoc Group on Ontology Standards (see below). Sowa (1999) gives a more complete overview of ontologies in the philosophical and formal tradition.

Another difference is that the lattice structure in Fig. 25.2 introduces a (very) large number of internal nodes for feature combinations that have no natural human interpretation, and hence no lexical expression in many languages. Apparently, lexicalization in language does not obey the systematic rules of a lattice or a tree. Whereas the

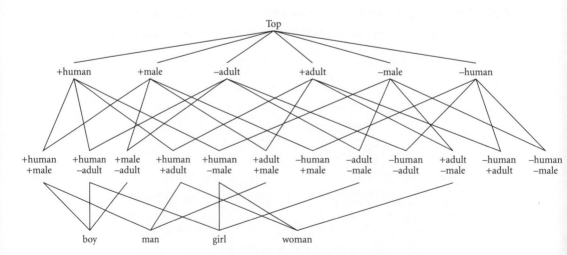

Fig. 25.2 Lattice structure with multiple classifications

lattice generates all logical concepts, language tends to lexicalize just those concepts that are efficient to support communication. Typically, formal ontologies are small, highly symmetric, and often developed top-down, whereas large-scale ontologies for NLP are often based on the less systematic lexicalization of concepts.

25.2.2 Cognitive and artificial intelligence traditions

Hierarchies have also been proposed as the basic structure of cognitive models of human knowledge. Collins and Quillian (1969) suggest that differences in response time to verify sentences such as 'a terrier is a dog' and 'a terrier is a mammal' are explained by assuming a hierarchy of so-called **is-a relations** between concepts: *terrier* **is-a** *dog* **is-a** *mammal*. Traversing more nodes in these so-called conceptual networks requires more processing and thus would lead to longer response times (see Smith and Medin 1981 for some criticism and for evidence for alternative models such as the prototype structures proposed by Rosch and Mervis 1975). Conceptual networks with associated features have frequently been used for structuring knowledge in artificial intelligence. Typical features that are associated with the nodes in these networks are *parts, functions*, and physical properties such as *colour*. In combination with inheritance via the *is-a* relations, these networks can be used as simple **knowledge representation systems**.

Gradually, semantic networks in artificial intelligence have evolved into more complex knowledge representation formalisms. Early work in knowledge representation focused equally on the **conceptual primitives** as on the actual representation formalism and mechanism. A classical example of content primitives is the conceptual dependency structure of Schank (1973). By combining primitive *acts* (e.g. GRASP, INGEST, TRANS) and *cases* (Agent, Instrument, Source, and Direction) complex concepts and propositions can be represented for instances of entities:

(25.2)   TRANS $\Leftrightarrow$ agent: John e_1
$\Leftrightarrow$ patient: book e_2
$\Leftrightarrow$ direction: table e_3

This example represents the conceptual scene of *putting a book on the table by John* regardless of the expression in language of this content.

With respect to knowledge representation formalisms and mechanisms, Brachman (1979) gives a historical overview how these early systems developed from loosely specified networks to complex frame specifications. Knowledge representation systems, of which KL-ONE is a well-known example (Brachman and Schmolze 1985), provide representation formalisms in which complex facts, relations, and properties can be expressed. Some knowledge representation systems support **description logics**, which have a more precise semantics, are more expressive, and support the implementation of functions such as constraints checking, querying, and automatic classification on the basis of descriptions (see Borgida 1995 for an overview). With the wild growth of knowledge representation formalisms there is also a tendency to standardize knowledge representation formalisms, to enable exchange of knowledge across systems, e.g. **Knowledge Interchange Format** or KIF (Genesereth 1991) and **Ontolingua** (Gruber 1992).

Although a knowledge representation formalism is important for a precise semantics and to enable inferencing about the knowledge that is expressed, it is of little use as long as there is no knowledge stored in the formalism. This is an extremely labour-intensive and complex task. Likewise, the above description logics are mostly used in small systems for specific domains, such as complex schemata for cars (Rychtyckyj 1996), software management (Devanbu et al. 1991), medicine (Rector et al. 1995), traffic control (Gaizauskas and Humphreys 1997). In all these cases, small ontologies are built manually and only occasionally extended with large-scale resources to add extensibility and robustness.

The best-known large ontology built in a formal knowledge representation language is Cyc (Lenat and Guha 1990). The Cyc knowledge base is a formalized representation of a vast quantity of fundamental human knowledge: facts, rules of thumb, and heuristics for reasoning about the objects and events of everyday life, stored in a formal representation language CycL. Cyc contains tens of thousands of concepts and hundreds of thousands of axioms (i.e. inter-concept relations and constraints). The concepts are not based on the words in natural language but created to support inferential reasoning. A lexicon for English is provided separately.

Ontologies in artificial intelligence systems, often called **Domain Models**, are designed and constructed for specific tasks and systems. The set of concepts and the structuring of these concepts are mainly determined by their purpose to enable decisions in an **information system**. Natural language vocabulary and logical divisions are not the main focus. It is not clear to what extent NLP technology, in its current form, needs such ontologies and their complex knowledge representation systems. Most of the properties and features that may play a role in doing general-purpose language analysis require only a fraction of the reasoning capacity provided by these systems. Currently for NLP, completeness in coverage is more important than richness of knowledge. To be able to process unlimited language, as is often required in Internet applications, large-scale vocabularies (both general level and domain specific) with very limited reasoning are preferred.

25.2.3 Linguistic traditions to lexical semantics

Whereas in cognitive models and AI, the focus is on the classes and types as categories that organize our mental knowledge and processing capacity, in linguistic approaches the focus has been on the meanings of words. We distinguish two main approaches in the linguistic tradition:

- **semantic features** or **meaning components**: words are associated with features that predict syntactic structures or behaviour;
- **lexical semantic networks**: words are defined in terms of relations to each other.

Feature approaches all have in common that a limited set of abstract semantic features (e.g. *animate/inanimate*) is used to describe certain linguistic phenomena (e.g. syntactic alternations (Levin 1993) or logical metonymy (Pustejovsky 1995)). These phenomena assume some sort of semantic typing in the lexicon. This semantic typing is limited in terms of the number of distinctions or features and does not require complex knowledge representation languages. Because they describe lexical phenomena, these features are not sufficient for complete common-sense inferencing. However, their focus on aspects relevant for structural phenomena of language still makes them useful for NLP.

Experimental NLP lexicons, as developed in ACQUILEX (Briscoe, Copestake, and de Paiva 1993), CORELEX (Buitelaar 1998), and DELIS (Heid et al. 1995), have implemented semantic features in HPSG-like specification formalisms such as Typed Feature Structures (Carpenter 1990; Pollard and Sag 1987; see also Chapter 9). A more recent example is the MikroKosmos lexical database (Mahesh and Nirenburg 1995*a*, 1995*b*). The ontology (4,500 concepts) and lexicons (7,000 entries in Spanish and English) in MikroKosmos are small but specifically designed for a machine translation system. Semantic classes and word senses are distinguished insofar as they select different translations. This means that the degree of **polysemy** (the number of senses per entry) in the MikroKosmos lexicon is much lower than in traditional dictionaries. The semantics is thus limited by the application.

Another high-level classification to be mentioned here is the PENMAN Upper Model (Bateman 1990; Bateman et al. 1994) which has been built from a language generation perspective (see Chapter 15). One of its key features was the methodology underlying its construction, according to which ontologies should be created by careful analysis of semantic distinctions as revealed through grammatical alternations in and across languages.

Typically, the focus of the above linguistic approaches is on verbs and not on nouns. This is different for the semantic network approach in lexical semantics, which focuses on nouns. In lexical semantic networks, words are defined in terms of relations to other words, without any reference to our cognitive understanding and reasoning. Cruse (1986) developed so-called **diagnostic frames** that evoke strong intuitions about semantic anomalies of sentences and can be used to elicit certain semantic relations between these words. For example:

(25.3) *a.* It's a *dog*, therefore it's an *animal*. ?It's an *animal*, therefore it's a *dog*.
        A $\Rightarrow$ B (unilateral entailment or hyponymy relation)
    b. It's a *violin*, therefore it's a *fiddle*. It's a *fiddle*, therefore it's a *violin*.
        A $\Leftrightarrow$ B (mutual entailment or synonymy relation)

Using the above system, Cruse defines a whole set of **lexical semantic relations**. Since all words in a language can be related to other words, the vocabulary of a language can also be seen as a huge semantic network. This network is a language-internal system. Each language has a different set of lexicalizations. For example, we have different *nails* on each *finger* and *toe* but we do not have different words for each *nail*, while in some languages even *fingers* and *toes* are lexicalized by the same word (e.g. *dedo* in Spanish and *dito* in Italian).

Amsler (1980), Briscoe and Boguraev (1989), and Wilks, Slator, and Guthrie (1996) describe many approaches to extract similar networks of lexicalized words from existing machine-readable dictionaries (see also Chapters 3 and 21). WordNet1.5, EuroWordNet, and EDR can be seen as the next generation of resources that define meanings in terms of relations to other meanings.

WordNet1.5 is a generic lexical semantic network developed at Princeton University (Miller et al. 1990; Fellbaum 1998) structured around the notion of **synsets**. Each synset comprises one or more word senses with the same part of speech that are considered to be synonyms in most contexts. Each synset represents a different concept. Semantic relations are expressed primarily between concepts. WordNet1.5 contains 91,591 synsets and 168,217 word senses or synonyms.

EuroWordNet (Vossen 1998) is a multilingual database containing several monolingual wordnets structured along the same lines as the Princeton WordNet1.5. The languages covered in EuroWordNet are English, Dutch, German, Spanish, French, Italian, Czech, and Estonian. In addition to the relations between the synsets of the separate languages, EuroWordNet contains an equivalence relation for each synset to the closest concept from an Inter-Lingual-Index (based on WordNet1.5 synsets) which allows cross-lingual comparison of words and relations. The size of the wordnets in EuroWordNet varies from 7,000 to 44,000 synsets and from 13,000 to 70,000 word senses per language.

The EDR database (Yokoi 1996) is one of the most complete large-scale lexical resources available. It combines rich bilingual (Japanese–English) and monolingual Japanese dictionaries (including details about syntactic and semantic subcategorization) with a WordNet-style organization of word senses into a hierarchy of concepts. The major repository of semantic information is the Concept Dictionary, which contains 400,000 concepts. The purpose of the Concept Dictionary is to describe, classify, and relate the concepts that are referred to in the word dictionaries, the bilingual dictionaries, and the co-occurrence dictionaries.

Despite the difference in starting point of lexical semantic networks, the overlap in concepts with most of the previous semantic networks in artificial intelligence is nevertheless quite large. Many systems therefore do not make a distinction between the conceptual level and the lexical level or have a direct mapping between the lexicon and the ontology (not surprisingly, most systems only deal with English words). This may have unexpected effects on the systems that exploit the hierarchies.

If the system's purpose is to manage substitution of words in text (for example, information retrieval or language generation), then we need something like a *word-*

net that precisely represents the relations between the lexicalized concepts of a language, and thus predicts how the same content can be paraphrased differently in a language. The lexicalizations in a language (and eventually also other more complex phrases and expressions) have to be the starting point for ontologies for paraphrasing content. If on the other hand the purpose of the semantic network is to manage semantic properties used for inference, then we may need a very different design (more like an ontology in artificial intelligence). Many words in a language may not be relevant for storing the relevant inferences and many concepts may be needed that are not lexicalized at all. Comparing the most important classes in the top level of Cyc with the most important top-level classes in WordNet1.5 makes this very clear. See Guarino (1998) and Vossen and Bloksma (1998) for further discussion.

25.3 THE USE OF ONTOLOGIES IN NLP

Most current NLP techniques hardly ever perform full natural language understanding. Nevertheless, they use knowledge in two ways:

- knowledge helps the system to make a structural analysis of language, e.g. to resolve PP attachments, correct spelling and syntax errors, improve speech recognition;
- knowledge is used to do partial understanding, e.g. query search in information retrieval, document classification, automatic summaries, word-sense disambiguation.

A structural analysis of the input text is often not an end-user application but a component technology that is used for some other purpose. The ontology can be used to filter out certain types of mistakes in the analysis or resolve structural ambiguity. This may involve a simple lexicon with semantic features that are encoded as constraints (e.g. the verb *eat* has selectional restrictions that require animate subjects and edible objects) or simple semantic hierarchies of hyponymy relations that are used in similarity measurements. For example, Agirre et al. (1998) describe a system for spelling correction based on semantic similarity of the misspelled word to other words in the document.

The second type of usage more directly relates to the content of the information rather than its structure. This means that the dependency on semantic resources and ontologies is higher, and that performance is more closely related to the quality of the ontology. In general, it is less clear how much semantics is needed to get the best performance. In principle, the most detailed and comprehensive semantic resource with the most complete inferencing component would give the best predictions and performance. However, there is no clear idea how such a resource can be built or exploited. Semantics-based NLP is limited by what is available. Most NLP-related applications therefore have used WordNet1.5.

We will look at a few of the above applications and briefly discuss the way in which they are used. The list should be seen merely as an illustration.

25.3.1 Information retrieval

In information retrieval (see Chapter 29), ontologies and wordnets are mostly used to expand a query by including with the user's query words other related terms so that queries will still match text that is formulated in alternative phrasings. The rephrasing capability is mostly limited to synonyms and hyponyms of the query words. Lee, Kim, and Lee (1993), Richardson and Smeaton (1995), Smeaton, Kelledy, and O'Donnell (1995), Smeaton and Quigly (1996), and Voorhees (1998) discuss this usage for WordNet1.5. Including an ontology significantly increases recall (i.e. more documents are found) but also leads to a decrease of precision (i.e. more wrong documents are retrieved), because of the ambiguity of the query words (see Chapter 29). In some cases, this is solved by having the user decide on the intended meanings of the words in the query before retrieval. Such a system is for example described in Guarino, Masolo, and Vetere (1998). See also on-line systems such as AskJeeves (www.ask.com) and Oingo (www.oingo.com).

The above-mentioned systems are all monolingual and for English. With Euro-WordNet the same technology can also be applied to other languages and across languages (see Chapter 38). Experiments on this usage are reported in Gonzalo et al. (1998), Vossen, Peters, and Gonzalo (1999), and Griot and de Loupy (1999).

Closely related to information retrieval are indexing and classification of documents (see Chapter 33). The difference is that there is no matching of queries to titles of text but that indices are extracted at compile time and organized hierarchically. For the hierarchical organization and clustering, an ontology can be used. This is demonstrated by Woods (1995), Stairmand and Black (1996), Scott and Matwin (1998), and Gomez-Hidalgo and de Buenaga Rodriguez (1997) using WordNet1.5.

25.3.2 Information extraction

Information extraction (see Chapter 30) is based on identification of entities and extraction of facts on these entities. The process is often guided by a predefined template that has to be filled. The semantics of the template can be linked to an ontology. The properties to be extracted are then based on the kind of entity that is differentiated and defined in the ontology. Although the ontologies are often limited in size and specialized for domains, systems can be made more robust by linking their domain ontologies to larger hierarchies. For the recognition of entities and facts, semantic networks, such as WordNet1.5, are used. Because of the information extraction systems' limited domains, the ambiguity problem mostly does not occur.

Gaizauskas and Humphreys (1997) describe the LaSIE information extraction system that attempts a fuller text analysis within the MUC domain of business news on new joint ventures. They translate text to quasi-logical form and construct a weak discourse model for filling templates. The system uses general world knowledge represented as a semantic net. The coverage of the system is extended using WordNet. Harabagiu and Moldovan (1997, 1998) describe an information extraction system (TextNet) that enriches WordNet and uses the result for further enrichment. Chai and Bierman (1997) describe a method for manually extracting graphical conceptual representations from text and generalizing these to more general rules, using WordNet1.5.

A more recent usage of WordNet, namely question-answering systems for unstructured text, is described in Chapter 31. In this case, questions are not answered relative to a fixed template or a closed domain model, but open questions are answered using more generic retrieval technology. The retrieval is however triggered by the specific types of questions that are distinguished (*who*, *what*, *where*), and more precise paragraph analysis to find the most likely passage. Extensive use of WordNet is described to find alternative phrasing and expressions of possible answers. Even though the actual performance comes closer to standard information extraction systems, the technology is more related to information retrieval.

25.3.3 Text summarization

Text summarization is based on the notions of textual relevance and lexical cohesion (see Chapters 14 and 32). Relevance is determined by the number of keywords in a sentence, and cohesion is computed by the connectivity of the relevant sentences in terms of overlapping content words. Such connectivity is usually based on overlap in words and word frequency, but many people have tried to improve this by using synonymy and hyponymy relations (mostly from WordNet1.5). Sentences in which different but related words are used can then still be connected: see Hirst and St-Onge (1998). Obviously, semantic ambiguity has to be resolved to be able to decide on such relatedness.

25.3.4 Semantic similarity and word-sense disambiguation

As suggested above, using semantic techniques to improve statistical and structural approaches to NLP is often hampered by the ambiguity problem. Although a semantic network or ontology may be a more precise level of representation of content than words or phrases (e.g. by indexing on the synset level in WordNet1.5 rather than at the word level), this also introduces a new problem, how to decide between different meanings of the words. Not surprisingly, many researchers have tried to develop word-sense disambiguation (WSD) systems as a component technique to enable other applications (see Chapter 13).

Most WSD systems employ a metric to measure semantic similarity measurement of concepts that occur in documents. The assumption is that words that belong to a similar class tend to co-occur in a single document, whereas other meanings of these words often do not belong to classes that are being discussed in the document. For example, *organ* is ambiguous between *body part* and *musical instrument*, and *bass* between *fish* and *musical instrument*. If *organ* occurs in a text with *bass* and *drums*, the shared *musical instrument* sense is more likely than the *fish* and *body part* meanings, for which there is less support. In other words, there will be a relative strong clustering of words around concepts in the sub-hierarchy of *musical instrument*, compared to the sub-hierarchies for other meanings such as *fish* and *body part*.

The implementations of this principle differ in details, e.g. role of depth of the hierarchy, frequency of the concepts in text, relative density of concepts in sub-hierarchies (how likely is a concept to occur in a sub-hierarchy anyway?), etc. Different techniques using WordNet1.5 are described in Li and Abe (1995); Fujii et al. (1997); Agirre and Rigau (1996); Resnik (1995, 1998); Leacock and Chodorow (1998).

Obviously, WSD heavily depends on the quality and the structure of the ontology that is being used. If related concepts are classified inconsistently (e.g. *dog* as a *pet* and *cat* as a *mammal*), or if hierarchies are shallow or have many tops (like verbs in Wordnet1.5), the clustering will fail. Another crucial aspect is the degree of sense differentiation in the resources. WordNet1.5 is known to have a very high number of senses, often not clearly distinguishable. This makes it much harder to select a single sense.

It is difficult to compare WSD systems that use other ontologies or resources. Yarowsky (1992) describes WSD technology using *Roget's Thesaurus* instead of Word-Net1.5. He reports high levels of success (over 90 per cent) but only chooses between rather general distinctions in that thesaurus. Something similar holds for Wilks, Slator, and Guthrie (1996), who use the homographs in the *Longman Dictionary of Contemporary English* (Procter 1978), and Segond et al. (1997), who use the lexicographer's file codes (twenty-five semantic clusters) in Wordnet1.5 to distinguish senses. Also the MikroKosmos group (Mahesh, Nirenburg, and Beale 1997) reports results above 90 per cent for the word-sense disambiguation capacity of the database. These high results are partly due to the richness of the data (e.g. the fact that the system can also use syntactic constraints to choose word senses) and partly to the small number of sense distinctions, since meanings in MikroKosmos are only differentiated to support machine translation.

The MikroKosmos approach is slightly different from the other systems. Word senses are disambiguated in smaller context using more information (selectional restriction). Similarly, Mihalcea and Moldovan (1999) describe a system that uses the glosses in WordNet1.5 to process isolated sentences. These knowledge-intensive approaches are not only relatively successful compared to the knowledge-poor approaches but can also be applied to smaller text fragments such as user queries in information retrieval. This indirectly follows from a study by Voorhees (1999). Crude statistical approaches that lemmatize words to stems regardless of their part of speech perform better than approaches that only use WordNet hypernym and synonym relations. The lemmatization would relate for example the verb *hammer* to the noun *hammer*, whereas these concepts are not related in WordNet (but would be related in richer ontologies such as MikroKosmos, EuroWordNet, and Cyc that also exploit other relations). The approaches that use semantic distance measurements via hyponymy and synonymy relations can therefore only be used for WSD if sufficient similar concepts recur, which they may do in larger text fragments but typically do not in isolated sentences or queries.

Further Reading and Relevant Resources

There is a tendency in NLP to move from morphosyntactic modelling and applications to semantics, where well known statistical or stochastic techniques can often easily be combined with semantic data. NLP is thus moving towards inferencing systems that exploit common-sense knowledge. On the other hand, we see that small-scale information systems can become more efficient when more general bits and pieces of information are (re-)used. The optimistic conclusion is then that the different paradigms are slowly merging.

Despite the lack of fundamental agreement about the organization, content, and size of ontologies in general, there is an ongoing discussion to standardize their content. The benefits of such a standardization effort are clear: (1) different disciplines can benefit from the same ontology, (2) existing ontologies or ontology fragments can be reused, (3) ontologies can be compared or evaluated. There have been two official initiatives to organize the standardization of the content of ontologies:

- **EAGLES** working group on lexical semantics that focuses on lexical semantic notions and resources for NLP (http://www.ilc.pi.cnr.it/EAGLES96/rep2/);
- **ANSI Ad Hoc Group on Ontology Standards**, with a focus on ontologies for artificial intelligence and formal ontologies but also on lexicon-based ontologies (http://www-ksl.stanford.edu/onto-std/).

Related to standardization is the issue of linking and, eventually, merging existing ontologies (Rigau and Agirre 1995; Hovy 1998; Peters et al. 1998). More papers on this issue can also be found at the EuroWordNet group (see URL below), which developed methods to compare and link wordnets across languages.

Further information on some major ontologies can be found at:

Cyc: http://www.cyc.com/
MikroKosmos http://crl.nmsu.edu/Research/Projects/mikro/index.html/
WordNet: http://www.cogsci.princeton.edu/~wn/w3wn.html/
EuroWordNet: http://www.hum.uva.nl/~ewn/
EDR: http://www.iijnet.or.jp/edr/
Generalized Upper Model: http://www.darmstadt.gmd.de/publish/komet/genum/
newUM.html/

It is also useful to check the Linguistic Data Consortium (LDC) and the European Language Resources Association (ELDA):

ELDA/ELRA: http://www.icp.grenet.fr/ELRA/home.html/
LDC: http://www.cis.upenn.edu/~ldc/ldc_catalog.html/

Brachman (1979) gives a good overview of the development of semantic networks from the early cognitive models to frame systems such as KL-ONE. Gruber (1992) discusses principles of ontologization and attempts to standardize existing ontologies and representations.

Wilks, Slator, and Guthrie (1996) give a very condensed but complete overview of approaches to (lexical) semantics and also how these relate to dictionaries and methods of extracting lexical databases from these dictionaries. Another survey of semantic notions, resources, and their usage in NLP is given in the EAGLES report on lexical semantics (Sanfilippo et al. 1999).

Fellbaum (1998) contains a description of WordNet in terms of history, content, and various ways in which it can be used, improved, and extended. Vossen (1998) describes the basic principles behind EuroWordNet and the usage in cross-lingual information retrieval.

Many papers on using wordnets can be found in proceedings of ACL and COLING and in journals such as *Computational Linguistics* and *Natural Language Engineering*. More specifically, two recent ACL workshops have been devoted to the usage of wordnets in NLP: ACL/EACL '97 in Madrid: *Workshop on Automatic Information Extraction and Building of Lexical Semantic Resources*; ACL/COLING '98 workshop in Montreal: *Workshop on Usage of WordNet for Natural Language Processing*. NAACL '01, Pittsburgh: *Workshop on WordNet and Other Lexical Resources Applications, Extensions and Customizations files*. ACL/EACL '01, Toulouse: *SENSEVAL workshop*. 1st Global WordNet Conference, Jan. 2002, Mysore, India. LREC-02, Las Palmas: Standardization of Wordnets and Wordnets for lesser-studied languages.

Acknowledgements

I am most grateful to Ed Hovy for his useful comments and suggestions on this chapter.

REFERENCES

Agirre, E. and G. Rigau. 1996. 'Word-sense disambiguation using conceptual density'. *Proceedings of the 16th International Conference on Computational Linguistics (COLING '96)* (Copenhagen), 16–22.

——K. Gojenola, K. Sarasola, and A. Voutilainen. 1998. 'Towards a single proposal in spelling correction'. *Proceedings of 17th International Conference on Computational Linguistics (COLING/ACL '98)* (Montreal), 22–8.

Amsler, R. A. 1980. *The structure of the* Merriam-Webster Pocket Dictionary. Ph.D. thesis, Texas University.

Bateman, J. A. 1990. 'Upper modelling: organizing knowledge for natural language processing'. *Proceedings of the 5th International Workshop on Natural Language Generation* (Pittsburgh). URL: http://www.darmstadt.gmd.de/publish/komet/papers/general-description.ps.

——R. T. Kasper, J. D. Moore, and R. A. Whitney. 1990. *A General Organization of Knowledge for Natural Language Processing: The PENMAN Upper Model.* Technical report, USC/ Information Sciences Institute, Marina del Rey, Calif.

Borgida, A. 1995. 'Description logics in data management'. *IEEE Transactions on Knowledge and Data Engineering,* 7(5), 671–782.

Brachman, R. 1979. 'On the epistemological status of semantic networks'. In N. Findler (ed.), *Associative Networks: Representation and Use of Knowledge by Computers.* New York: Academic Press, 191–215.

——and H. Levesque. 1985. *Readings in Knowledge Representation.* San Mateo, Calif.: Morgan Kaufmann.

——and J. Schmolze. 1985. 'An overview of the KL-ONE knowledge representation system'. *Cognitive Science,* 9, 171–216.

Briscoe, E. J. and B. Boguraev (eds.). 1989. *Computational Lexicography for Natural Language Processing.* London: Longman.

——A. Copestake, and V. de Paiva (eds.). 1993. *Default Inheritance in Unification Based Approaches to the Lexicon.* Cambridge: Cambridge University Press.

Buitelaar, P. 1998. *CoreLex: systematic polysemy and underspecification.* Ph.D. thesis, Brandeis University, Department of Computer Science.

Carpenter, R. 1990. 'Typed feature structures: inheritance, (in)equality and extensionality'. *Proceedings of the Workshop on Inheritance in Natural Language Processing* (Tilburg), 9–18.

Chai, J. and A. Bierman. 1997. 'The use of lexical semantics in information extraction'. *Proceedings of the ACL/EACL '97 Workshop on Automatic Information Extraction and Building of Lexical Semantic Resources* (Madrid), 61–70.

Collins, A. M. and M. R. Quillian. 1969. 'Retrieval time from semantic memory'. *Journal of Verbal Learning and Verbal Behavior,* 8, 240–8.

Copestake, A. 1992. *The Representation of Lexical Semantics Information.* Brighton: CSRP, University of Sussex.

Cruse, D. A. 1986. *Lexical Semantics.* Cambridge: Cambridge University Press.

Devanbu, P., R. Brachman, P. Selfridge, and B. Ballard. 1991. 'LaSSIE: a knowledge-based software information system'. *Communications of the ACM,* 34(5), 34–49.

Fellbaum, C. 1998. 'A semantic network of English verbs'. In C. Fellbaum (ed.), *WordNet: An Electronic Lexical Database.* Cambridge, Mass.: MIT Press, 69–104.

Fossket, D. J. 1997. 'Thesaurus'. In K. Spärck Jones and P. Willett (eds.), *Readings in Information Retrieval,* San Mateo, Calif.: Morgan Kaufmann, 111–34.

Fujii, A., T. Hasegawa, T. Tokunaga, and H. Tanaka. 1997. 'Integration of hand-crafted and statistical resources in measuring word similarity'. *Proceedings of the ACL/EACL '97 Workshop on Automatic Information Extraction and Building of Lexical Semantic Resources* (Madrid), 45–51.

Gaizauskas, R. and K. Humphreys. 1997. 'Using a semantic network for information extraction'. In *Natural Language Egnineering*, vol. iii, part 3/3. Cambridge: Cambridge University Press, 147–70.

Genesereth, M. R. 1991. 'Knowledge interchange format'. *Proceedings of the 2nd International Conference on Principles of Knowledge Representation and Reasoning* (Cambridge, Mass.), 599–600.

Gomez-Hidalgo, J. M. and M. de Buenaga Rodriguez. 1997. 'Integrating a lexical database and a training collection for text categorization'. *Proceedings of the ACL/EACL '97 Workshop on Automatic Information Extraction and Building of Lexical Semantic Resources* (Madrid), 39–44.

Gonzalo, J., F. Verdejo, I. Chugur, and J. Cigarrán. 1998. 'Indexing with WordNet synsets can improve text retrieval'. *Proceedings of the ACL/COLING Workshop on Usage of WordNet for Natural Language Processing* (Montreal), 38–44.

Griot, L. and C. de Loupy. 1999. *Demonstration of the WordNets.* Deliverable 2D015, EuroWordNet2, LE4-8328, University of Amsterdam, Amsterdam.

Gruber, T. R. 1992. *Ontolingua: a Mechanism to Support Portable Ontologies.* Report KSL, Stanford University, 91–66.

Guarino, N. 1998. 'Some ontological principles for designing upper level lexical resources'. *Proceedings of 1st International Conference on Language Resources and Evaluation* (Granada), 527–34.

——C. Masolo, and G. Vetere. 1998. *OntoSeek: Using Large Linguistic Ontologies for Accessing On-Line Yellow Pages and Product Catalogs.* Technical Report 02/98, LADSEB-CNR.

Harabagiu, S. M. and D. I. Moldovan. 1997. 'TextNet: a text-based intelligent system'. *Natural Language Engineering*, 3(2–3), 171–90.

————1998. 'Knowledge processing on an extended WordNet'. In C. Fellbaum (ed.), *WordNet: An Electronic Lexical Database.* Cambridge, Mass.: MIT Press, 379–406.

Heid, U., A. Alonge, S. Atkins, G. Bs, N. Calzolari, O. Corrazzari, C. Fillmore, K. Krueger, S. Schwenger, and M. Vliegen. 1995. *Lexicographic and Formal Description of the Lexical Classes of Perception and Speech Act Verbs.* Delis Deliverable D-III-1.

Hirst, G. and D. St-Onge. 1998. 'Lexical chains as representation of context for the detection and correction of malapropism'. In C. Fellbaum (ed.), *WordNet: An Electronic Lexical Database and Some of Its Applications.* Cambridge, Mass.: MIT Press, 305–32.

Hovy, E. 1998. 'Combining and standardizing large-scale, practical ontologies for machine translation and other uses'. *Proceedings of 1st International Conference on Language Resources and Evaluation* (Granada), 535–42.

Leacock, C. and M. Chodorow. 1998. 'Combining local context and WordNet similarity for word sense identification'. In C. Fellbaum (ed.), *WordNet: An Electronic Lecixal Database.* Cambridge, Mass.: MIT Press, 265–84.

Lee, J. H., M. H. Kim, and Y. J. Lee 1993. 'Information retrieval based on conceptual distance in IS-A hierarchies'. *Journal of Documentation*, 49(2), 188–207.

Lenat, D. B. and R. V. Guha. 1990. *Building Large Knowledge-Based Systems. Representation and Inference in the CYC Project.* Reading, Mass.: Addison Wesley.

Levin, B. 1993. *English Verb Classes and Alternations: A Preliminary Investigation*. Chicago: University of Chicago Press.

Li, H. and N. Abe. 1995. 'Generalizing case frames using a thesaurus and the MDL principle'. *Proceedings of the Conference on Recent Advances in Natural Language Processing (RANLP '95)* (Tzigov Chark, Bulgaria), 239–48.

Mahesh, K. and S. Nirenburg. 1995a. 'A situated ontology for practical NLP'. *Proceedings of the Workshop on Basic Ontological Issues in Knowledge Sharing, International Joint Conference on Artificial Intelligence (IJCAI '95)* (Montreal). http://citeseer.nj.nec.com/mahesh95situated.html.

———1995b. 'Semantic classification for practical natural language processing'. *Proceedings of the 6th ASIS SIG/CR Classification Research Workshop* (Chicago), 79–94.

———and S. Beale. 1997. 'If you have it: using full ontological knowledge for word sense disambiguation'. *Proceedings of the Conference on Recent Advances in Natural Language Processing (RANLP)* (Tzigov Chark, Bulgaria), 8–15.

Mihalcea, R. and D. Moldovan. 1995. 'A method for word sense disambiguation of unrestricted text'. *Proceedings of the 37th Annual Meeting of the Association for Computational Linguistics (ACL '99)*, (College Park, Md.), 152–8.

Miller, G. A., R. Beckwith, C. Fellbaum, D. Gross, and K. J. Miller. 1990. 'Introduction to Word-Net: an on-line lexical database'. *International Journal of Lexicography*, 3(4), 235–44.

Peters, W., P. Vossen, P. Diez-Orzas, and G. Adriaens. 1998. 'Cross-linguistic alignment of Word-nets with an inter-lingual-index'. In P. Vossen (ed.), *EuroWordNet: A Multilingual Database with Lexical Semantic Networks*. Dordrecht: Kluwer Academic Publishers, 221–51.

Pollard, C. and I. Sag. 1987. *Information-Based Syntax and Semantics*, i: *Fundamentals*. Lecture Notes 13. Stanford, Calif.: CSLI.

Procter, P. (ed.). 1978. *Longman Dictionary of Contemporary English*. Harlow: Longman.

Pustejovsky, J. 1995. *The Generative Lexicon*. Cambridge, Mass.: MIT Press.

Rector, A. L., S. K. Bechhofer, C. A. Goble, I. Horrocks, W. A. Nowlan, and W. D. Solomon. 1995. 'The GRAIL concept modelling language for medical terminology'. *Artifical Intelligence in Medicine*, 9, 139–71.

Resnik, P. 1995. 'Using information content to evaluate semantic similarity in a taxonomy'. *Proceedings of IJCAI*. http://xxx.lanl.gov/abs/cmp-lg/9511007.

———1998. 'WordNet and class-based probabilities'. In C. Fellbaum (ed.), *WordNet: An Electronic Lexical Database*. Cambridge, Mass.: MIT Press, 239–64.

Richardson, R. and A. Smeaton. 1995. 'Using WordNet in a knowledge-based approach to information retrieval'. *Proceedings of the BCS-IRSG Colloquium* (Crewe). http://www.compapp.dcu.ie/CA_Working_Papers/wp95.html#0395.html.

Rigau, G. and A. Agirre. 1995. 'Disambiguating bilingual nominal entries against WordNet', *Proceedings of the Workshop on the Computational Lexicon (ESSLLI)* (Barcelona), 71–82.

Rosch, E. and C. B. Mervis. 1975. 'Family resemblances: studies in the internal structure of categories'. In E. Hunt (ed.), *Cognitive Psychology*. New York: Academic Press, 573–603.

Rychtyckyj, N. 1996. 'DLMS: an evaluation of KL-ONE in the automobile industry'. *Knowledge Representation*, 588–96.

Sanfilippo, A., N. Calzolari, S. Ananiadou, R. Gaizauskas, P. Saint-Dizier, and P. Vossen (eds.). 1998. *EAGLES: Preliminary Recommendations on Semantic Encoding*. Interim Report.

Schank R. C. 1973. 'Identification of conceptualizations underlying natural language'. In R. C. Schank and K.M. Colby (eds.), *Computer Models of Thought and Language*. San Fransisco: Freeman and Company, 187–247.

Scott, S. and S. Matwin. 1998. 'Text classification using WordNet hypernyms'. *Proceedings of the ACL/COLING Workshop on Usage of WordNet for Natural Language Processing* (Montreal), 38–44.

Segond, F., A. Schiller, G. Grefenstette, and J. P. Chanod. 1997. 'An experiment in semantic tagging using hidden Markov model tagging'. *Proceedings of the ACL/EACL' 97 Workshop on Automatic Information Extraction and Building of Lexical Semantic Resources* (Madrid), 78–81.

Smeaton, A., F. Kelledy, and R. O'Donnell. 1995. 'Trec-4 experiments at Dublin city university: thresholding posting lists, query expansion with WordNet and pos tagging of Spanish'. *Proceedings of TREC-4.* (Gaithersburg, Md.), 373–90.

——and A. Quigley. 1996. 'Experiments on using semantic distances between words in image caption retrieval'. *Proceedings of the 19th International Conference on Research and Development in IR* (Zürich).

Smith, E. and D. Medin. 1981. *Categories and Concepts.* Cambridge Mass.: Harvard University Press.

Sowa, J. 1999. *Knowledge Representation: Logical, Philosophical, and Computational Foundations.* Boston: PWS Publishing Co.

Spärck Jones, K. 1986. *Synonymy and Semantic Classification.* Edinburgh: Edinburgh University Press.

Stairmand, M. and W. J. Black. 1997. 'Conceptual and contextual indexing using WordNet-derived lexical chains'. *Proceedings of BCS IRSG Colloquium 1997,* 47–65.

Voorhees, E. 1998. 'Using WordNet for text retrieval'. In C. Fellbaum (ed.), *WordNet: An Electronic Lecixal Database.* Cambridge, Mass.: MIT Press, 285–304.

——1999. 'Natural language processing and information retrieval'. In M. T. Pazienza (ed.), *Information Extraction: Towards Scalable, Adaptable Systems,* Berlin: Springer, 32–48.

Vossen, P. (ed.). 1998. *EuroWordNet: A Multilingual Database with Lexical Semantic Networks.* Dordrecht: Kluwer Academic Publishers.

——and L. Bloksma. 1998. 'Categories and classifications in EuroWordNet'. *Proceedings of 1st International Conference on Language Resources and Evaluation* (Granada), 399–408.

——W. Peters, and J. Gonzalo. 1999. 'Towards a universal index of meaning'. *Proceedings of the ACL '99 Siglex Workshop* (Baltimore), 81–90.

Wilks, Y. 1975. 'A preferential pattern seeking semantics for natural language inference'. *Artificial Intelligence,* 6, 53–74.

——B. M. Slator, and L. M. Guthrie. 1996. *Electric Words: Dictionaries, Computers and Meanings.* Cambridge, Mass.: MIT.

Wittgenstein, L. 1984. *Philosophische Untersuchungen.* Frankfurt: Suhrkamp.

Woods, W. A. 1997. *Conceptual indexing: a better way to organize knowledge.* A Sun Microsystems Laboratories, April 1997 Report: TR-97-61. Technical Reports, 901, Palo Alto, California 94303, USA.

Yarowsky, D. 1992. 'Word-sense disambiguation using statistical models of Roget's categories trained on large corpora'. *Proceedings of the 14th International Conference on Computational Linguistics (COLING '92)* (Nantes), 454–60.

Yokoi, T. 1996. 'The EDR electronic dictionary'. *Communications of the ACM,* 38(11), 42–4.

TREE-ADJOINING GRAMMARS

ARAVIND K. JOSHI

ABSTRACT

Each grammar formalism specifies a domain of locality, i.e. a domain over which various dependencies (syntactic and semantic) can be specified. It turns out that the various properties of a formalism (syntactic, semantic, computational, and even psycholinguistic) follow, to a large extent, from the initial specification of the domain of locality. In this chapter, as a case study, we will briefly explore the extended domain of locality provided by the Lexicalized Tree-Adjoining Grammar (LTAG) in the context of some linguistic, computational, and psycholinguistic properties. This extended domain is achieved by specifying the elementary objects as structured objects (trees or directed acyclic graphs) instead of strings and two universal combining operations. Using lexicalized elementary structured objects it is possible to study directly many aspects of strong generative capacity which are more relevant to the linguistic descriptions.

26.1 INTRODUCTION

Tree-adjoining grammar (TAG) is a formal tree rewriting system. TAG and **Lexicalized Tree-Adjoining Grammar** (LTAG) have been extensively studied with respect both to their formal properties and to their linguistic relevance. TAG and LTAG are formally equivalent; however, from the linguistic perspective LTAG is the system we will be concerned with in this chapter. We will often use these terms TAG and LTAG interchangeably.

The motivations for the study of LTAG are both linguistic and formal. The elementary objects manipulated by LTAG are structured objects (trees or directed acyclic graphs) and not strings. Using structured objects as the elementary objects of the formal system, it is possible to construct formalisms whose properties relate directly to the study of **strong generative capacity** (i.e. structural descriptions), which is more relevant to the linguistic descriptions than the **weak generative capacity** (sets of strings).

Each grammar formalism specifies a **domain of locality**, i.e. a domain over which various dependencies (syntactic and semantic) can be specified. It turns out that the various properties of a formalism (syntactic, semantic, computational, and even psycholinguistic) follow, to a large extent, from the initial specification of the domain of locality (see Chapter 4 for a comparison of grammar formalisms).

26.1.1 Domain of locality of CFGs

In a context-free grammar (CFG) the domain of locality is the one level tree corresponding to a rule in a CFG (Fig. 26.1). It is easily seen that the arguments of a predicate (for example, the two arguments of *likes*) are not in the same local domain. The two arguments are distributed over the two rules (two domains of locality)—$S \rightarrow NP\ VP$ and $VP \rightarrow V\ NP$. They can be brought together by introducing a rule $S \rightarrow NP\ V\ VP$. However, then the structure provided by the VP node is lost. We should also note here that not every rule (domain) in the CFG in (Fig. 26.1) is lexicalized. The four rules on

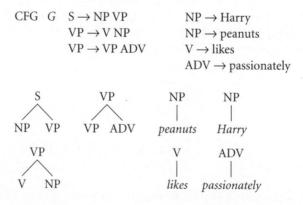

Fig. 26.1 Domain of locality of a context-free grammar

the right are lexicalized, i.e. they have a lexical anchor. The rules on the left are not lexicalized. The second and the third rules on the left are almost lexicalized, in the sense that they each have a preterminal category (V in the second rule and ADV in the third rule), i.e. by replacing V by *likes* and ADV by *passionately* these two rules will become lexicalized. However, the first rule on the left ($S \rightarrow NP\ VP$) cannot be lexicalized. Can a CFG be lexicalized, i.e. given a CFG, G, can we construct another CFG, G', such that every rule in G' is lexicalized and $T(G)$, the set of (sentential) trees (i.e. the tree language of G) is the same as the tree language $T(G')$ of G'? It can be shown that this is not the case (Joshi and Schabes 1997). Of course, if we require that only the string languages of G and G' be the same (i.e. they are weakly equivalent) then any CFG can be lexicalized. This follows from the fact that any CFG can be put in the Greibach normal form (see Linz 2001; see also Chapter 8 of this volume) where each rule is of the form $A \rightarrow w\ B_1\ B_2 \ldots B_n$, where w is a lexical item and the Bs are non-terminals. The lexicalization we are interested in requires the tree languages (i.e. the set of structural descriptions) to be the same, i.e. we are interested in the 'strong' lexicalization. To summarize, a CFG cannot be strongly lexicalized by a CFG. This follows from the fact that the domain of locality of CFG is a one-level tree corresponding to a rule in the grammar. Note that there are two issues we are concerned with here—lexicalization of each elementary domain and the encapsulation of the arguments of the lexical anchor in the elementary domain of locality. The second issue is independent of the first issue. From the mathematical point of view the first issue, i.e. the lexicalization of the elementary domains of locality, is the crucial one. We can obtain strong lexicalization without satisfying the requirement specified in the second issue (encapsulation of the arguments of the lexical anchor). Of course, from the linguistic point of view the second issue is very crucial. What this means is that among all possible strong lexicalizations we should choose only those that meet the requirements of the second issue. For our discussions in this chapter we will assume that we always make such a choice.

26.1.2 Lexicalization of CFGs

Now we can ask the following question. Can we strongly lexicalize a CFG by a grammar with a larger domain of locality? Fig. 26.2 and Fig. 26.3 show a tree substitution grammar where the elementary objects (building blocks) are the three trees in Fig. 26.3 and the combining operation is the **tree substitution** operation shown in Fig. 26.2. Note that each tree in the tree substitution grammar (TSG), G', is lexicalized, i.e. it has a **lexical anchor**. It is easily seen that G' indeed strongly lexicalizes G. However, TSGs fail to strongly lexicalize CFGs in general. We show this by an example. Consider the CFG, G, in Fig. 26.4 and a proposed TSG, G'. It is easily seen that although G and G' are weakly equivalent they are not strongly equivalent. In G',

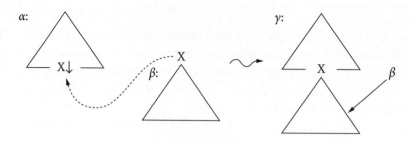

Fig. 26.2 Substitution

CFG *G*   S → NP VP   NP → Harry
           VP → V NP   NP → peanuts
                              V → likes

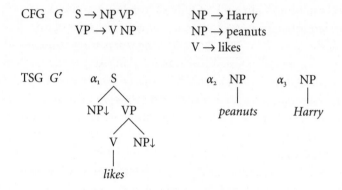

Fig. 26.3 Tree substitution grammar

suppose we start with the tree α_1, then by repeated substitutions of trees in G' (a node marked with a vertical arrow denotes a substitution site) we can grow the right side of α_1 as much as we want but we cannot grow the left side. Similarly for α_2 we can grow the left side as much as we want but not the right side. However, trees in G can grow on both sides. Hence, the TSG, G', cannot strongly lexicalize the CFG, G (Joshi and Schabes 1997).

CFG *G*   S → S S (non-lexical)
           S → a (lexical)

TSG *G'* α_1 S α_2 S α_3 S
             S   S↓   S↓   S   a
             a   a

Fig. 26.4 A tree-substitution grammar

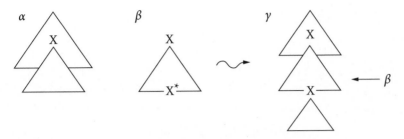

Fig. 26.5 Adjoining

We now introduce a new operation called **adjoining** as shown in Fig. 26.5. Adjoining involves splicing (inserting) one tree into another. More specifically, a tree β as shown in Fig. 26.5 is inserted (adjoined) into the tree α at the node X resulting in the tree γ. The tree β, called an **auxiliary tree**, has a special form. The root node is labelled with a non-terminal, say X, and on the frontier there is also a node labelled X called the foot node (marked with *). There could be other (terminal or non-terminal) nodes on the frontier of β; the non-terminal nodes will be marked as substitution sites (with a vertical arrow). Thus if there is another occurrence of X (other than the foot node marked with *) on the frontier of β it will be marked with the vertical arrow and that will be a substitution site. Given this specification, adjoining β to α at the node X in α is uniquely defined. Adjoining can also be seen as a pair of substitutions as follows: the subtree at X in α is detached, β is substituted at X, and the detached subtree is then substituted at the foot node of β. A tree substitution grammar when augmented with the adjoining operation is called a tree-adjoining grammar (lexicalized tree-adjoining grammar because each elementary tree is lexically anchored). In short, LTAG consists of a finite set of **elementary trees**, each lexicalized with at least one lexical anchor. The elementary trees are either initial or auxiliary trees. Auxiliary trees have been defined already. **Initial** trees are those for which all non-terminal nodes on the frontier are substitution nodes. It can be shown that any CFG can be strongly lexicalized by an LTAG (Joshi and Schabes 1997).

In Fig. 26.6 we show a TSG, G', augmented by the operation of adjoining, which strongly lexicalizes the CFG, G. Note that the LTAG looks the same as the TSG considered in Fig. 26.4. However, now trees α_1 and α_2 are auxiliary trees (marked with *) that can participate in adjoining. Since adjoining can insert a tree in the interior of another tree it is possible to grow both sides of the tree α_1 and tree α_2, which was not possible earlier with substitution alone. In summary, we have shown that by increasing the domain of locality we have achieved the following: (1) lexicalized each elementary domain, (2) introduced an operation of adjoining, which would not be possible without the increased domain of locality (note that with one-level trees as elementary domains adjoining becomes the same as substitution since there are no interior nodes to be operated upon), and (3) achieved strong lexicalization of CFGs.

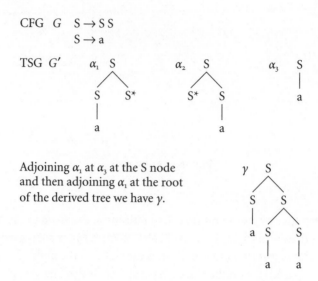

CFG G $S \to S\,S$
$S \to a$

Fig. 26.6 Adjoining arises out of lexicalization

26.1.3 Lexicalized tree-adjoining grammars

Rather than giving formal definitions for LTAG and derivations in LTAG we will give a simple example to illustrate some key aspects of LTAG. We show some elementary trees of a toy LTAG grammar of English. Fig. 26.7 shows two elementary trees for a verb such as *likes*. The tree α_1 is anchored on *likes* and encapsulates the two arguments of the verb. The tree α_2 corresponds to the object extraction construction. Since we need to encapsulate all the arguments of the verb in each elementary tree for *likes*, for the object extraction construction, for example, we need to make the elementary tree associated with *likes* large enough so that the extracted argument is in the same elementary domain. Thus, in principle, for each 'minimal' construction in which *likes*

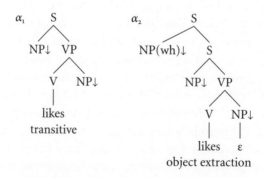

Fig. 26.7 LTAG: Elementary trees for *likes*

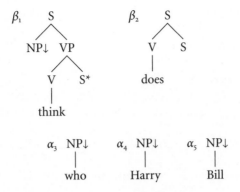

Fig. 26.8 LTAG: Sample elementary trees

can appear (for example, subject extraction, topicalization, subject relative, object relative, passive) there will be an elementary tree associated with that construction. By 'minimal' we mean when all recursion has been factored away. This factoring of recursion away from the domain over which the dependencies have to be specified is a crucial aspect of LTAGs as they are used in linguistic descriptions. This factoring allows all dependencies to be localized in the elementary domains. In this sense, there will, therefore, be no long-distance dependencies as such. They will all be local and will become long distance on account of the composition operations, especially adjoining.

Fig. 26.8 shows some additional trees. Trees α_3, α_4, and α_5 are initial trees and trees β_1 and β_2 are auxiliary trees with foot nodes marked with *. A derivation using the trees in Fig. 26.7 and Fig. 26.8 is shown in Fig. 26.9. The trees for *who* and *Harry* are substituted in the tree for *likes* at the respective *NP* nodes, the tree for *Bill* is substituted in the tree for *think* at the *NP* node, the tree for *does* is adjoined to the root node of the

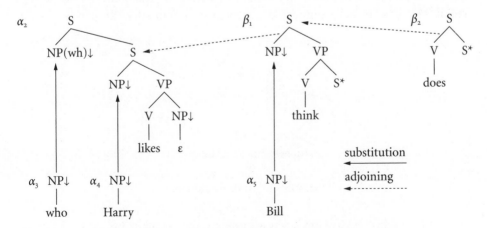

Fig. 26.9 LTAG derivation for *who does Bill think Harry likes*

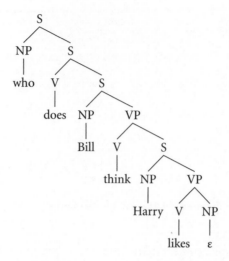

Fig. 26.10 LTAG derived tree for *who does Bill think Harry likes*

tree for *think* (adjoining at the root node is a special case of adjoining), and finally the derived auxiliary tree (after adjoining β_2 to β_1) is adjoined to the indicated interior S node of the tree α_2. This derivation results in the **derived tree** for *who does Bill think Harry likes* as shown in Fig. 26.10. Note that the dependency between *who* and the complement *NP* in α_2 (local to that tree) has been stretched in the derived tree in Fig. 26.10. This tree is the conventional tree associated with the sentence.

However, in LTAG there is also a **derivation tree**, the tree that records the history of composition of the elementary trees associated with the lexical items in the sentence. This derivation tree is shown in Fig. 26.11. The nodes of the tree are labelled by the tree labels such as α_2 together with the lexical anchor.[1] The derivation tree is the crucial derivation structure for LTAG. We can obviously build the derived tree from the derivation tree. For semantic computation the derivation tree (and not the derived tree) is the crucial object. Compositional semantics is defined on the derivation tree.

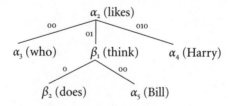

Fig. 26.11 LTAG derivation tree

---

[1] The derivation trees of LTAG have a close relationship to the dependency trees, although there are some crucial differences; however, the semantic dependencies are the same.

The idea is that for each elementary tree there is a semantic representation associated with it and these representations are composed using the derivation tree. Since the semantic representation for each elementary tree is directly associated with the tree there is no need to reproduce necessarily the internal hierarchy in the elementary tree in the semantic representation (Joshi and Vijay-Shanker 1999). This allows the so-called 'flat' semantic representation as well as helping in dealing with some non-compositional aspects as in the case of rigid and flexible idioms.

26.2 Some Important Properties of LTAG

The two key properties of LTAG are (1) extended domain of locality (EDL) (for example, as compared to CFG), which allows (2) factoring recursion from the domain of dependencies (FRD), thus making all dependencies local. All other properties of LTAG (mathematical, linguistic, and even psycholinguistic) follow from EDL and FRD. TAGs (LTAGs) belong to the so-called class of **mildly context-sensitive grammars** (Joshi 1985). Context-free languages (CFL) are properly contained in the class of languages of LTAG, which in turn are properly contained in the class of context-sensitive languages. There is a machine characterization of TAG (LTAG) called embedded pushdown automaton (EPDA) (Vijay-Shanker 1987), i.e. for every TAG language there is an EPDA which corresponds to this (and only this) language and the language accepted by any EPDA is a TAG language. EPDAs have been used to model some psycholinguistic phenomena, for example, processing crossed dependencies and nested dependencies have been discussed in Joshi (1990). With respect to formal properties, the class of TAG languages enjoys all the important properties of CFLs, including polynomial parsing (with complexity $O(n^6)$); see Chapters 8 and 9 for results concerning formal properties of other systems.

Large-scale wide-coverage grammars have been built using LTAG, the XTAG system (LTAG grammar and lexicon for English and a parser) being the largest so far (for further details see XTAG Research Group 2000). In the XTAG system, each node in each LTAG tree is decorated with two feature structures (top and bottom feature structures), in contrast to the CFG-based feature structure grammars. This is necessary because adjoining can augment a tree internally, while in a CFG-based grammar a tree can be augmented only at the frontier. It is possible to define adjoining and substitution (as it is done in the XTAG system) in terms of appropriate unifications of the top and bottom feature structures. Because of FRD (factoring recursion from the domain of dependencies), there is no recursion in the feature structures. Therefore, in principle, feature structures can be eliminated. However, they are crucial for linguistic descriptions. Constraints on substitution and adjoining are modelled via these feature structures (Vijay-Shanker 1987). This method of manipulating feature structures is a direct consequence of the extended domain of locality of LTAG.

26.3 AN ALTERNATIVE PERSPECTIVE ON ADJOINING

In adjoining we insert an auxiliary tree, say with root and foot nodes labelled with X in a tree at a node with label X. In Figs. 26.12 and 26.13 we present an alternative perspective on adjoining. The tree α which receives adjunction at X can be viewed as made up of two trees, the supertree at X and the subtree at X as shown in Fig. 26.12. Now, instead of the auxiliary tree β adjoined to the tree α at X we can view this composition as a wrapping operation—the supertree of α and the subtree of α are wrapped around the auxiliary tree β as shown in Fig. 26.13. The resulting tree γ is the same as before. Wrapping of the supertree at the root node of β is like adjoining at the root (a special case of adjoining) and the wrapping of the subtree at the foot note of β is like substitution. Hence, this wrapping operation can be described in terms of

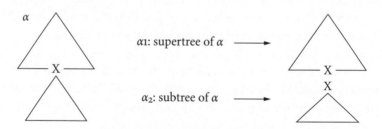

Fig. 26.12 Adjoining as wrapping 1

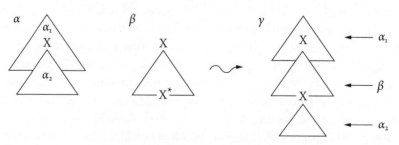

Fig. 26.13 Adjoining as wrapping 2

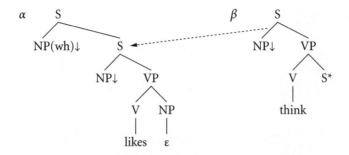

Fig. 26.14 Wrapping as substitution and adjunction 1

substitution and adjoining. This is clearly seen in the linguistic example in Figs. 26.14 and 26.15. The auxiliary tree β can be adjoined to the tree α at the indicated node in α as shown in Fig. 26.14. Alternatively, we can view this composition as adjoining the supertree α_1 (the *wh*-tree) at the root node of β and substitution of the subtree α_2 (the *likes* tree) at the foot node of β as shown in Fig. 26.15. The two ways of composing α and β are semantically coherent.

The wrapping perspective can be formalized in terms of the so-called **multi-component LTAGs** (MC-LTAGs). They are called multi-component because the elementary objects can be sets of trees; in our examples, we have two components (in which α was split). When we deal with multi-components we can violate the locality of the composition very quickly because the different components may be 'attached' (by adjoining or substitution) to different nodes of a tree and these nodes may or may not be part of an elementary tree depending on whether the tree receiving the multi-component attachments is an elementary or a derived tree. We obtain what are known as tree-local MC-LTAGs if we put the constraint that the tree receiving multi-component attachments must be an elementary tree. It is known that **tree-local MC-TAGs** are weakly equivalent to LTAGs; however they can give rise to structural descriptions not obtainable by LTAGs, i.e. they are more powerful than LTAG in the sense of strong

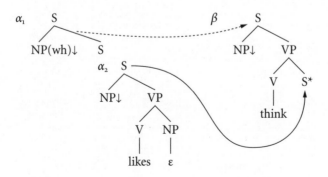

Fig. 26.15 Wrapping as substitution and adjunction 2

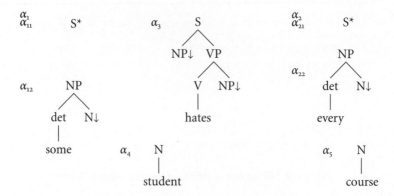

Fig. 26.16 Scope ambiguity: an example

generative capacity (Weir 1988). Thus the alternative perspective leads to greater strong generative capacity without increasing the weak generative capacity.

We will now present an example illustrating the use of this alternative perspective in characterizing the **scope ambiguity** in *some student hates every course* as shown in Figs. 26.16, 26.17, and 26.18 (Kallmeyer and Joshi 1999). In Fig. 26.16, we show a tree-local MC-LTAG for our example. The trees for *hates, student,* and *course* are standard LTAG trees. The trees for *some* and *every* are multi-component trees. For example, the tree α_1 for *every* has two components, α_{11} and α_{12}; one of the components α_{11} is a degenerate tree in this special case. The multi-component tree α_1 is lexically anchored by *some*; similarly for the tree α_2 for *every*. The main idea here is that the α_{12} component corresponds to the contribution of *some* to the predicate–argument structure of the tree for *hates* and the α_{11} component contributes to the scope structure. Similarly for the two components of α_2.

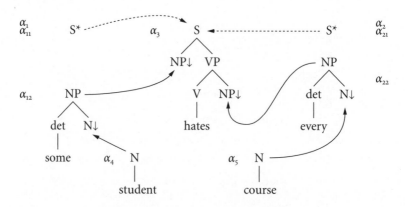

Fig. 26.17 Derivation with scope information

Fig. 26.17 shows the derivation. The main point to note here is that the two components of α_1 are attached (by substitution or adjoining) to α_3 at the appropriate nodes simultaneously. This composition is tree local as $\alpha3$ is an elementary tree. Similarly for the tree α_2. In this example, the two top components α_{11} and α_{21} are attached to the same node (the root node) of α_3.[2] This may give the impression that the composition is non-local because once α_1 is attached to α_3 we have a derived tree to which α_2 is attached. However, the two components, α_{11} and α_{21} are degenerate and it can be shown that in this case the composition of α_2 with α_3 (after α_1 has been composed with α_3) is still effectively tree local (Kallmeyer and Joshi 1999).

It is clear in this example that α_2 could have been attached to α_3 first and then α_1 attached to α_3. Fig. 26.18 shows the derivation tree for the derivation in Fig. 26.17. The numbers on the edges of the tree refer to the addresses of attachments, which are shown here for convenience. Note that both α_{11} and α_{21}, the scope information carrying components, are attached to α_3 at the same node. Thus they could be attached in any order (strictly speaking, α_1 and α_2 could be attached to α_3 in any order). Hence α_{11} will outscope α_{21} if α_{21} is attached first and then α_{11} and vice versa. The scope ambiguity is thus directly reflected in the derivation tree for *some student hates every course*. This is in contrast to all other approaches (which are essentially CFG based) where the scope ambiguity is represented at another level of representation. It is possible to represent in LTAG the scope ambiguity at the level of the derivation tree itself because of the alternative perspective on adjoining, which in turn is due to the extended domain of locality discussed earlier.

More recently, similar ideas have been explored in the context of other linguistic phenomena such as scrambling and clitic climbing, both with respect to linguistic coverage and certain psycholinguistic implications. A particularly interesting result is that all word-order variations up to two levels of embedding (i.e. three clauses in all) can be correctly described by tree-local MC-LTAGs, correctly in the sense of providing the appropriate structural descriptions. Beyond two levels of embedding not all patterns of word order variation will be correctly described (Joshi, Becker, and Rambow 2000; Kulick 2000).

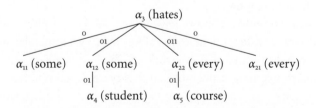

Fig. 26.18 Derivation tree with scope underspecification

[2] In general in a multi-component LTAG multiple adjunctions to the same node are not allowed as this violates the tree locality and also takes the system beyond LTAG. However, we are dealing here with a special case.

26.4 RELATIONSHIP TO OTHER SYSTEMS

Most modern formalisms, especially those that have been used in natural language processing, are lexicalized in a sense. The two important examples are LFG with its lexical rules (Kaplan and Bresnan 1983) and HPSG (Pollard and Sag 1994); see Chapter 4 for further discussion of LFG and HPSG. Both these sytems are basically CFG based, so a direct comparision is difficult. Since actual HPSG grammars are implicitly highly constrained, Kasper et al. (1995) have investigated the possibility of compiling HPSG into LTAG. It would be of great interest to try to translate LFG into an LTAG-like system by replacing the c-structures of LFG by LTAG structures and then mapping them into LTAG-like f-structures of LFG. The only early attempt along these lines is by Kameyama (unpublished work, 1984).

Categorial grammars, especially Combinatory Categorial Grammars (CCG) (Steedman 1997), are very closely related to LTAG. In fact under certain conditions they are weakly (but not strongly) equivalent to LTAG (Weir 1988). Categories assigned to lexical items in a categorial grammar framework do encapsulate the arguments of the lexical anchor. It is of interest to see how the basic insights of LTAG could be incorporated in a categorial framework. The idea is not to translate LTAG into a categorial grammar but rather to construct a categorial system with properties similar to LTAG. This is achieved by associating partial proof trees with lexical items. These partial proof trees are obtained by starting with the type assignment for a lexical item as specified by a categorial grammar and then 'unfolding' it by using certain categorial inference rules such as function application. This unfolding is done until the slots for the arguments of the lexical anchor are exposed. We thus have a finite collection of partial proof trees (lexicalized, of course) which serve as the building blocks of our system (analogous to the finite set of elementary trees in LTAG). These proof trees are then combined by universal categorial inference rules in terms of cuts. Informally speaking, the proof trees are hooked up by linking the conclusion nodes of one tree to the assumption nodes of another tree. Further discussion of such systems and their relationship to LTAG can be found in Joshi and Kulick (1997); Joshi, Kulick, and Kurtonina 1999).

Frank (2002) presents a comprehensive perspective on phrase-structure composition and syntactic dependencies in a TAG-based grammatical architecture and compares it to the minimalist framework of Chomsky, showing that a number of stipulative and problematic aspects of that theory can be eliminated.

FURTHER READING AND RELEVANT RESOURCES

A key aspect of such as TAG and LTAG from both the linguisitc and computational perspectives is the understanding of the notion of strong generative capacity of grammar formalisms. A comprehensive discussion of this topic can be found in a recent book on strong generative capacity by Miller (1999).

For details of the LTAG grammar for English and the associated parser please go to http://www.cis.upenn.edu/xtag/.

Resnik (1992) and Schabes (1992) discuss **stochastic LTAGs** and Srinivas and Joshi (1999) discuss supertagging, a technique for extending the statistical part-of-speech disambiguation techniques to the elementary trees of LTAG.

Finally, key ideas of LTAG have been extended to discourse structure by Webber et al. (1999).

References

Abeille, A. and M. Candito. 2000. 'FTAG: a lexicalized tree-adjoining grammar for French'. In A. Abeille and O. Rambow (eds.), *Tree-Adjoining Grammar*. Stanford, Calif.: CSLI, 305–30.

Frank, R. 2002. *Phrase Structure Composition and Syntactic Dependencies*. Cambridge, Mass.: MIT Press.

Joshi, A. K. 1985. 'Tree-adjoining grammars: how much context sensitivity is required to provide reasonable structural descriptions?' In D. Dowty, L. Karttunen, and A. Zwicky (eds.), *Natural Language Parsing*. Cambridge: Cambridge University Press, 206–50.

——1990. 'Processing crossed and nested dependencies: an automaton perspective on the psycholinguistic results'. *Language and Cognitive Processes*, 5, 1–27.

——T. Becker, and O. Rambow. 2000. 'Complexity of scrambling: a new twist to the competence–performance distinction'. In A. Abeille and O. Rambow (eds.), *Tree-Adjoining Grammars*, Stanford, Calif.: CSLI, 167–82.

——and S. Kulick. 1997. 'Partial proof trees as building blocks for a categorial grammar'. *Linguistics and Philosophy*, 20, 637–67.

——— and N. Kurtonina. 1999. 'Semantic composition for partial proof trees'. In *Proceedings of the 12th Amsterdam Colloquium* (Amsterdam), 169–74.

——L. S. Levy, and M. Takahashi. 1975. 'Tree adjunct grammars'. *Journal of Computer and System Sciences*, 10(1), 55–75.

——and Y. Schabes. 1997. 'Tree-adjoining grammars'. In G. Rosenberg and A. Salomaa (eds.), *Handbook of Formal Languages*, Berlin: Springer, 69–123.

——and K. Vijay-Shanker. 1999. 'Compositional semantics with lexicalized tree-adjoining grammar (LTAG): how much underspecification is necessary?' In H. C. Bunt and E. G. C. Thijsse (eds.), *Proceedings of the 3rd International Workshop on Computational Semantics (IWCS-3)* (Tilburg), 131–45.

Kallmeyer, L. and A. K. Joshi. 1999. 'Factoring predicate argument and scope semantics: underspecified semantics with LTAG'. In *Proceedings of the 12th Amsterdam Colloquium* (Amsterdam), 169–74.

Kaplan, R. and J. Bresnan. 1983. 'Lexical-functional grammar: a formal system of grammatical representation'. In J. Bresnan (ed.), *The Mental Representation of Grammatical Relations*. Cambridge, Mass.: MIT Press.

Kasper, R., B. Kiefer, K. Netter, and K. Vijay-Shanker. 1995. 'Compilation of HPSG toTAG'. *Proceedings of the 33rd Annual Meeting of the Association for Computational Linguisitcs (ACL '95)* (Cambridge, Mass.), 92–9.

Kulick, S. 2000. *Constrained non-locality: Long-distance dependencies in TAG*. Ph.D. thesis, University of Pennsylvania.

Linz, P. 2001. *An Introduction to Formal Languages and Automata*. Sudbury, Mass.: Jones and Bartlett Publishers.

Miller, P. H. 1999. *Strong Generative Capacity*. Stanford, Calif.: CSLI.

Pollard, C. and I. A. Sag. 1994. *Head-Driven Phrase Structure Grammar*. Chicago: Chicago University Press.

Resnik, P. 1992. 'Probabilistic tree-adjoining grammars as a framework for statistical natural language processing'. *Proceedings of the 14th International Conference on Computational Linguistics (COLING '92)* (Nantes), 418–24.

Schabes, Y. 1992. 'Stochastic lexicalized grammars'. *Proceedings of the 14th International Conference on Computational Linguistics (COLING '92)* (Nantes), 426–32.

Srinivas, B. and A. K. Joshi. 1998. 'Supertagging: an approach to almost parsing'. *Computational Linguistics*, 22, 1–29.

Steedman, M. 1996. *Surface Structure and Interpretation*. Cambridge, Mass.: MIT Press.

Vijay-Shanker, K. 1987. 'A study of tree-adjoining grammars'. Ph.D. thesis, University of Pennsylvania.

Webber, B., A. K. Joshi, A. Knott, and M. Stone. 1999. 'What are little texts made of? A structural and presuppositional account using lexicalized tag'. *Proceedings of the International Workshop on Levels of Representation in Discourse (LORID '99)* (Edinburgh), 151–6.

Weir, D. 1988. *Characterizing mildly context-sensitive grammar formalisms*. Ph.D. thesis, University of Pennsylvania.

XTAG Research Group 2000. *A lexicalized tree-adjoining grammar for English*. Technical Report 98-18, Institute for Research in Cognitive Science, Philadelphia.

PART III

APPLICATIONS

MACHINE TRANSLATION: GENERAL OVERVIEW

JOHN HUTCHINS

ABSTRACT

This chapter introduces the main concepts and methods used for machine translation systems from the beginnings of research in the 1950s until about 1990; it covers the main approaches of rule-based systems (direct, interlingua, transfer, knowledge based), and the principal translation tools; and it concludes with a brief historical sketch. (For methods since 1990 see Chapter 28.)

27.1 INTRODUCTION

The term **machine translation** (MT) refers to computerized systems responsible for the production of translations with or without human assistance. A distinction is commonly made between **human-aided** MT (HAMT) and **machine-aided human translation** (MAHT). The latter comprises computer-based **translation tools** which support translators by providing access to on-line dictionaries, remote terminology databanks, transmission and reception of texts, stores of previously translated texts ('translation memories'), and integrated resources, commonly referred to as **translator workstations** or translator workbenches. The term **computer-aided translation** (CAT) is sometimes used to cover all these computer-based translation systems.

In this chapter, we will cover first the main methods and problems of machine translation, then in more detail the main features of the rule-based approaches used until the late 1980s. After outlining the various types of translation aids developed up to 1990, we end with a brief survey of the historical development of MT and translation tools.

27.2 Principal Approaches and Methodologies

Although the ideal goal of MT systems may be to produce high-quality translation without human intervention at any stage, in practice this is not possible except in highly constrained situations (see below). In particular, if the reason for using an MT system is to produce translations of publishable quality, approximating what might be expected from a human translator, then the output must be revised (or, as it is known in MT circles, **post-edited**). It should be noted that in this respect MT does not differ from the output of most human translators, which is normally revised by a second translator before dissemination. However, the types of errors produced by MT systems do differ from those of human translators (incorrect prepositions, articles, pronouns, verb tenses, etc.). If the reason for using an MT system is simply to acquire some knowledge of the content of the original text, then the output may be left unedited or only lightly revised. This is frequently the case when the output is intended only for specialists familiar with the text subject. As a further example, unedited output might serve as a rough draft for a human translator, i.e. as a 'pre-translation', or for someone with some familiarity with the target language who needs a working basis for producing an original text.

The translation quality of MT systems may be improved by adjusting (editing or controlling) the input. One option is for input texts to be marked (**pre-edited**) to indicate prefixes, suffixes, word divisions, phrase and clause boundaries, or grammatical categories (e.g. to distinguish the noun *cónvict* and its homonymous verb *convíct*). More common (particularly in large installations) is the **control** of the vocabulary and of the grammatical structures of texts submitted for translation. In this way, the problems of ambiguity and of the selection of equivalents are reduced, in some cases eliminated. Although the costs of preliminary editing may be high, postediting is reduced considerably. Another option is for systems to be specifically designed for particular subject areas (**sublanguages**) or for the needs of specific users. In each case, they reduce the known deficiencies of full-scale general-purpose MT systems. (See Chapter 23 on sublanguages and controlled languages.)

MT systems can be designed either specifically for two particular languages, e.g. Russian and English (**bilingual** systems), or for more than a single pair of languages (**multilingual** systems). Bilingual systems may be designed to operate either in only one direction (unidirectional), e.g. from one **source language** (SL) into one **target language** (TL) only, or in both directions (bidirectional). Multilingual systems are usually designed to be bidirectional; but most bilingual systems are unidirectional.

In overall system design, there have been three basic types. The first (and historically oldest) type is generally referred to as the **direct translation** (or 'binary translation') approach: the MT system is designed in all details specifically for one particular pair of languages. Translation is direct from the source text to the target text, with as little syntactic or semantic analysis as necessary. The basic assumption is that the vocabulary and syntax of SL texts should not be analysed any more than strictly necessary for the resolution of SL ambiguities, for the correct identification of TL expressions, and for the specification of TL word order. In other words, SL analysis is oriented specifically to the production of representations uniquely appropriate for one particular TL. Typically, such systems consist of a single large bilingual dictionary and a single program for analysing and generating texts; such 'direct translation' systems are necessarily bilingual and normally unidirectional.

The second basic design strategy is the **interlingua** approach, which assumes that it is possible to convert SL texts into semantico-syntactic representations which are common to more than one language (but not necessarily 'universal' in any sense). From such interlingual representations texts are generated into other languages. Translation is thus in two stages: from SL to the interlingua and from the interlingua to the TL. Procedures for SL analysis are intended to be SL specific and not oriented to any particular TL; likewise programs for TL synthesis are TL specific and not designed for input from particular SLs. A common argument for the interlingua approach is economy of effort in a multilingual environment, i.e. an analysis program for a particular SL can be used for more than one TL, and a generation program for a particular TL can be used again. On the other hand, the complexity of the interlingua itself is greatly increased. Interlinguas may be based on a 'logical' artificial language, on a 'natural' auxiliary language (such as Esperanto), a set of semantic primitives common to all languages, or a supposedly 'universal' vocabulary.

The third basic strategy is the less ambitious **transfer** approach. Rather than operating in two stages via a single interlingual representation, there are three stages involving underlying (abstract) representations for both SL and TL texts. The first stage converts SL texts into abstract SL-oriented representations; the second stage converts these into equivalent TL-oriented representations; and the third generates the final TL texts. Whereas the interlingua approach necessarily requires complete resolution of all ambiguities in the SL text so that translation into any other language is possible, in the transfer approach only those ambiguities inherent in the language itself are tackled (e.g. homonyms and ambiguous syntactic structures). Problems of lexical differences between languages are dealt with in the second stage (transfer proper). 'Transfer' systems consist therefore typically of three types of dictionaries: SL dictionaries containing detailed morphological, grammatical, and semantic information; similar TL dictionaries; and a bilingual 'transfer' dictionary relating base SL forms and base TL forms. Likewise, 'transfer' systems have separate grammars for SL analysis, TL synthesis, and for the transformation of SL structures into equivalent TL forms.

Within the stages of analysis and synthesis, most MT systems exhibit clearly separated components involving different levels of linguistic description: morphology, syntax, and semantics. Hence, **analysis** may be divided into morphological analysis (identification of word endings, word compounds), syntactic analysis (identification of phrase structures, dependency, subordination, etc.), and semantic analysis (resolution of lexical and structural ambiguities); and **synthesis** (or **generation**) may likewise pass through stages of semantic synthesis (selection of appropriate compatible lexical and structural forms), syntactic synthesis (generation of required phrase and sentence structures), and morphological synthesis (generation of correct word forms). In 'transfer' systems, the **transfer** component may also have separate programs dealing with lexical transfer (selection of vocabulary equivalents) and with structural transfer (transformation into TL-appropriate structures). In some earlier forms of transfer systems, analysis did not involve a semantic stage; transfer was restricted to the conversion of syntactic structures, i.e. 'syntactic transfer'.

In many older systems, particularly those of the 'direct translation' type, the components of analysis, transfer, and synthesis were not always clearly separated. In some there was also a mixture of data (dictionary and grammar) and processing rules and routines. Later systems exhibited various degrees of **modularity**, so that system components, data, and programs can be adapted and changed with minimal damage to overall efficiency. A further development in more recent systems is the design of representations and processing rules for **reversibility**, i.e. the data and transformations used in the analysis of a particular language are applied in reverse when generating texts in that language.

The direct translation approach was typical of the 'first generation' of MT systems (from the 1950s to the mid-1970s). The interlingua and transfer-based systems were characteristic of the 'second generation' system (during the 1970s and 1980s). Both are based essentially on the specification of rules (for morphology, syntax, lexical selection, semantic analysis, and generation). They are thus now known generically as **rule-based systems**, distinguishing them from more recent corpus-based approaches (Chapter 28).

27.3 RULE-BASED SYSTEMS

The major problem for translation systems, whatever the particular strategy and methodology, concerns the resolution of lexical and structural ambiguities, both within languages (monolingual ambiguity) and between languages (bilingual ambiguity). The problems of monolingual disambiguation are not, of course, unique to translation; they are present in all natural language processing and are dealt with elsewhere in this volume.

Any monolingual ambiguity is a potential difficulty in translation since there may be more than one possible TL equivalent. Homographs and polysemes (English *cry*, French *voler*) must be resolved before translation (French *pleurer* or *crier*, English *fly* or *steal*); ambiguities of grammatical category (English *light* as noun, adjective, or verb, *face* as noun or verb) must likewise be resolved for choice between French *lumière*, *clair*, or *allumer*, and between *visage* or *confronter*, etc. Examples of monolingual structural ambiguities occur when a word or phrase can potentially modify more than one element of a sentence. In *old men and women*, the adjective *old* may refer only to *men* or to both *men* and *women* (French *vieux et femmes* or *vieux et vieilles*). In English, prepositional phrases can modify almost any preceding verb or noun phrase, e.g. (*a*) The *car was driven by the teacher at high speed*, (*b*) The *car was driven by the teacher with defective tyres*, and (*c*) The *car was driven by the teacher with red hair*. Lexical and structural ambiguities may and often do occur together: *He saw her shaking hands*, where *shaking* can be either an adjective ('hands which were shaking') or a gerundive verb ('that she was shaking hands').

Bilingual lexical ambiguities occur primarily when the TL has distinctions absent in the SL: English *river* can be French *rivière* or *fleuve*, German *Fluss* or *Strom*; English *eat* can be German *essen* or *fressen*; English *wall* can be French *mur* or *paroi*, German *Wand*, *Mauer*, or *Wall*. Even the apparently simple adjective *blue* can be problematic: in Russian a choice must be made between *sinii* (dark blue) and *goluboi* (light blue). A more extreme, but not uncommon, example is illustrated by the translation of the verb *wear* from English to Japanese; although there is a generic verb *kiru* it is normal to use the verb appropriate to the type of item worn: *haoru* (coat or jacket), *haku* (shoes or trousers), *kaburu* (hat), *hameru* (ring or gloves), *shimeru* (belt, tie, or scarf), *tsukeru* (brooch or clip), and *kakeru* (glasses or necklace).

Such choices can be circumvented by TL 'cover' words, i.e. selecting a single, most generally acceptable TL equivalent for a SL homograph, or by including phrases as dictionary items, e.g. for idioms (*wage war*), for compounds with specific TL equivalents which cannot be derived from components (*make away with* and *faire disparaître*, *look up* and *aufsuchen*), as well as for technical terms which have standardized translations (*plug connector* as *raccord de fiche*).

Bilingual structural differences can be either general (e.g. in English adjectives generally precede nouns but in French they usually follow); or they can be specific to particular structures, e.g. when translating the English verb *like* (*She likes to play tennis*) as a German adverb *gern* (*Sie spielt gern Tennis*); or they can be determined by particular lexical choices, e.g. an English simple verb (*trust*) rendered by a French circumlocution (*avoir confiance à*). Not uncommonly, structural differences combine with lexical differences, e.g. the translation of *know* into French or German, where choice of *connaître* (*kennen*) or *savoir* (*wissen*) affects both structure (*Je connais l'homme, Ich kenne den Mann*: *Je sais ce qu'il s'appelle, Ich weiss wie er heisst*) and the translation of other lexical items (*what* as *ce que* and *wie*).

The tools available are familiar from other fields of computational linguistics: the provision of dictionaries with lexical, grammatical, and translational information; the use of morphological and syntactic analysis to resolve monolingual ambiguities and to derive structural representations; the use of contextual information, of semantic features, of case markers, and of non-linguistic ('real world') information to resolve semantic ambiguities. The information required for resolution may be applied at any stage, during analysis of the SL text, during generation of the TL text, or at a transfer stage.

Dictionaries contain the information necessary for SL analysis (morphological variants, syntactic functions, semantic features, etc.) and for TL synthesis (translation equivalents, constraints on TL syntax and word formation, etc.). There may be a single bilingual dictionary, as in many older 'direct' systems, or, more commonly, there may be separate dictionaries for analysis (monolingual SL dictionary), transfer (bilingual SL–TL dictionary), and synthesis (monolingual TL dictionary). Dictionaries may contain entries either in full forms or in only base ('canonical' or root) uninflected forms, if these can be readily identified from inflected forms. In general, irregular forms are entered in full.

Morphological analysis is concerned with the identification of base forms from inflected forms, both regular (*fake*:*faked*) and irregular (*make*:*made*). It may also involve the recognition of derivational forms (e.g. English *-ly* as an adverb derived from an adjective, German *-heit* as a noun from an adjective). All MT systems have problems with 'unknown' words, primarily neologisms (common in scientific and technical literature), but also unanticipated combinations. If derivational elements can be correctly identified then some attempt can be made to translate, particularly in the case of 'international' prefixes and suffixes (e.g. French *demi-* and English *semi-*, French *-ique* and English *-ic*). Morphological analysis often includes the segmentation of compounds, e.g. in German. However, segmentation can be problematic, e.g. *extradition* might be analysed as either *extradit+ion* or *ex+tradition*, *cooperate* as either *co+operate* or *cooper+ate*. These would be resolvable by dictionary consultation, but sometimes alternative segmentations are equally valid (German *Wachtraum* could be *guard room* (*Wacht+Raum*) or *day dream* (*Wach+Traum*). (For more on morphological analysis see Chapter 2.)

As in other areas of computational linguistics, there have been three basic approaches to syntactic structure analysis. The first aims to identify legitimate sequences of grammatical categories, e.g. English article, adjective, noun. This approach led to the development of parsers based on *predictive analysis*, where a sequence of categories enables the prediction of a following category. The second approach aims to recognize groups of categories, e.g. as noun phrases, verb phrases, clauses, and ultimately sentences. These parsers are based on *phrase structure* or constituency grammar. The third approach aims to identify dependencies among categories, e.g. reflecting the fact that prepositions determine the case forms of German and Russian nouns. The basis for these parsers is *dependency grammar*. Each approach has its strengths and weaknesses, and systems often adopt an eclectic mixture of parsing techniques (see Chapter 12).

SL structures are transformed into equivalent TL structures by conversion rules, in the case of phrase structure or dependency trees by *tree transducers*, which may apply either unconditionally (e.g. English adjective+noun to French noun+adjective) or conditionally, triggered by specific lexical items (e.g. English *like* to German *gern*). Structural synthesis of TL sentences is similar: some syntax and morphology rules apply unconditionally (e.g. formation of English passives, case endings of German nouns after particular prepositions), others are conditional (irregular verb forms).

Semantic analysis concerns the resolution of problems remaining after morphological and syntactic analysis. While the latter can resolve problems of category ambiguity (e.g. whether a particular occurrence of *light* is a noun, a verb, or an adjective), semantic analysis must decide whether the homograph adjective *light* is being used to mean 'not heavy' or 'not dark'. Likewise semantic analysis is needed to resolve structural ambiguity (e.g. the *shaking hands* example), and any bilingual lexical differences (such as the *know* and *wear* examples). Two basic means are commonly employed. The first is the use of semantic features attached to dictionary items, e.g. the two senses of French *voler* may be distinguished by semantic features to indicate that in its 'flying' sense its subject (grammatical or logical) can be a 'bird' or a 'plane' and in its 'stealing' sense it may be a 'man'. Problems of structural ambiguity can also be resolved using semantic features: e.g. to avoid the mistranslation of *pregnant women and children* into French *femmes and enfants enceintes*, the features for *pregnant* might restrict its use to the modification of 'female' nouns and might exclude its attachment to 'young' nouns.

The second approach is through the identification of thematic (or 'deep' case) roles such as the agents, recipients, instruments, and locations of actions. Although languages differ in the expression of cases (English and French via prepositions and word order, German and Russian via grammatical noun case endings, Japanese via particles, etc.) and few surface markers are unambiguous (English *with* may express manner, attribute, or instrument), there is sufficient universality of underlying meanings and structures to encourage their widespread use in MT systems.

Semantic features and case roles may be adopted as **universals** in interlingua and transfer systems. Further steps towards interlingual representations have included the decomposition of lexical items into semantic 'primitives' (a basic set of components sufficient to distinguish meanings) and the analysis of structures into logical forms, e.g. in terms of predicates and arguments. A major difficulty with such analyses is the loss of surface information which may be essential to generate appropriate TL sentences: a logical analysis may disregard theme and rheme structure and may ignore differences of active and passive formation. The main problem for interlingua systems, however, is the treatment of bilingual lexical differences and specifically whether the interlingua should reflect every semantic difference in all languages involved, e.g. the Japanese *wear* distinctions even when translating between French and English.

A number of problems resist traditional linguistic treatment. The identification of the antecedent of a pronoun may well depend on (non-linguistic) knowledge of events or situations: The *soldiers killed the women. They were buried next day.* We know that the pronoun *they* does not refer to *soldiers* and must refer to *women* because we know that 'killing' implies 'death' and that 'death' is followed (normally) by 'burial'. This identification is crucial when translating into French where the pronoun must be *elles* and not *ils*. (For the treatment of anaphora see Chapter 14.)

Non-linguistic knowledge can be applied to many transfer problems, e.g. whether a *wall* is interior or exterior (*Wand* or *Mauer*), whether a *river* flows into the sea or not (*fleuve* versus *rivière*), whether the object modified is normally dark blue or light blue (*sinii* versus *goluboi*), etc. Such examples and many others are reasons for including **knowledge bases** in MT systems, either as adjuncts to traditional semantic analyses or as the basic mechanisms of lexical analysis and transfer.

Historically, rule-based MT systems have progressively introduced 'deeper' levels of analysis and transfer. Early word-for-word systems were restricted to bilingual dictionaries and simple morphology. Later 'direct' systems introduced syntactic analysis and synthesis. Phrase-structure and dependency analyses provided the basis for simple transfer systems with little semantic analysis ('syntactic transfer'). The addition of semantic features and case relations has led to the now more common type of 'semantico-syntactic' transfer system. The more extensive introduction of interlingual or quasi-universal items and structures characterizes 'advanced' transfer designs and, of course, interlingua systems. Finally, full conceptual-semantic analysis is a feature of **knowledge-based** interlingua systems based on or incorporating various AI techniques.

The characteristic feature of rule-based systems is the transformation ('transduction') of labelled tree representations, e.g. from a morphological tree into a syntactic tree, from a syntactic tree into a semantic tree, etc. Transduction rules require the satisfaction of precise conditions: a tree must have a specific structure and contain particular lexical items or particular (syntactic or semantic) features. In addition, every tree is tested by a 'grammar' for the acceptability of its structure at the level in question: morphological, syntactic, semantic, etc. Grammars and transduction rules specify the 'constraints' determining transfer from one level to another and hence, in the end, the transfer of a source language text to a target language text. Failure at any stage means failure of the whole process.

Since the mid-1980s there has emerged a widely accepted framework, embracing many variants of *unification* and *constraint-based* formalisms (see also Chapters 4 and 12). Instead of the large set of transduction rules devised only for very specific circumstances, these formalisms offer a restricted set of abstract rules and require conditions of application to be incorporated into lexical entries. For example, the translation of a sentence including *likely* (e.g. Th*e student is likely to work*) into a French equivalent with *probable* (*Il est probable que l'étudiant travaillera*) involves transformation of an English infinitival complement (*to work*) to a French subordinate clause (*que . . . travaillera*); the conditions for effecting the conversion are included in the feature sets of the lexical entries for *likely* and *probable*; no transduction rules specific for these constructions are required.

The main advantage of unification and constraint-based grammars is the simplification of the rules (and hence the computational processes) of analysis, transformation, and generation. Instead of a series of complex multi-level representations there are mono-stratal representations and/or simple lexical transfer; and the syntactic orientation which characterized previous transfer systems is replaced by lexicalist solutions. In addition, grammars are in principle *reversible*; the same formalism can in theory be applied in both analysis and synthesis.

27.4 TRANSLATION TOOLS

MT systems are not suitable for use by professional translators, who do not like to have to correct the irritatingly 'naive' mistakes made by computer programs. They prefer computer aids that are under their full control. Since the 1960s and 1970s translators have been using programs for accessing approved translations of subject terminology and for managing their own glossaries. An early computer-based aid was the provision of 'text-related glossaries', produced by matching individual words of a particular text against an existing bilingual terminology database. Next came facilities for on-line access to multilingual **termbanks**, and programs for **terminology management** by individual translators, essential with rapidly changing terminology in many scientific and technical fields and with the need for consistency in the translation of company and technical documentation.

The value of easy access to previous translations, either in whole or in part, has long been recognized by translators, particularly when dealing with repetitive texts or with updated versions of already translated documents (a frequent event in large organizations and companies). However, it is only since the end of the 1980s, with the increased availability of large electronic corpora of bilingual texts and of appropriate statistical methods for organizing and accessing them, that the **translation memory** has become an invaluable translation tool, and with it the integration of various translation tools (and MT systems) in the **translator workstation**, for producing good-quality machine-aided translations (see Chapter 28).

27.5 BRIEF HISTORICAL SKETCH

The use of computers for translation was first proposed in 1947 by Warren Weaver in correspondence with Norbert Wiener and in conversation with A. D. Booth, and in 1949 in his memorandum sent to American scientists. The next few years saw the beginning of research in the United States, the Soviet Union, and Western Europe. Projects were wide ranging: dictionary (lexicographic) work, 'direct translation' models, syntactic parsing, interlinguas, statistical analyses, dependency grammars, stratificational models, mathematical linguistics, etc.; and led to the beginnings of computational linguistics, artificial intelligence, formal linguistics, and non-numeric programming languages, etc.

However, the practical results were disappointing; by the mid-1960s there were few working translation systems, and the output quality was unsatisfactory. In 1966, a committee set up by US sponsors of research (ALPAC) concluded that there was little prospect of good-quality and/or cost-effective MT, and there were enough human translators to cope with demand. Many projects were ended, not just in the USA, but worldwide. However, in the next ten years there was a gradual revival in Europe and Canada; the turning point in 1976 was the *Météo* 'sublanguage' system (see Chapter 23), and the installation of the Systran system at the European Commission.

Research quickened in Europe and in Japan, a common framework being the multi-level (stratal) 'transfer' approach, e.g. in the Ariane system (Grenoble), the SUSY system (Saarbrücken), the Mu system (Kyoto), and the multi-national Eurotra project of the European Commission. During the 1980s, the 'interlingua' approach was investigated in the Netherlands (Rosetta and DLT) and at Carnegie-Mellon University—particularly notable for its knowledge-based approach.

During the 1980s, MT systems came into practical operation at numerous installations (particularly multinational corporations), invariably involving extensive pre-editing and postediting and/or the use of controlled language input. At the same time, systems for personal computers began to be marketed—Japanese computer companies such as Fujitsu, Hitachi, and NEC were major players.

At the end of the decade came the translator workstation, providing the human translator with facilities that genuinely increased productivity. Terminology control and improved text processing facilities had become familiar during the 1980s, but translation memories were the crucial development.

During the 1990s most research focused on corpora-based methods, and on combining them with traditional rule-based methods; at the cutting edge is the work on spoken language translation. In the marketplace, the situation has been transformed by low-cost (and low-quality) software for personal computers (mostly 'rule based'), by the demand for immediate 'less-than-perfect' translation on the Internet, and by the development of systems for cost-effective large-scale production of company documentation.

FURTHER READING AND RELEVANT RESOURCES

General introductions to machine translation have been provided by Arnold et al. (1994), Hutchins and Somers (1992), and in the collection edited by Newton (1992). For rule-based systems see the articles contained in King (1987), Nirenburg (1987), and Slocum (1988). The history of MT is covered by Hutchins (1986, 1995).

REFERENCES

Arnold, D., L. Balkan, R. Lee Humphreys, S. Meijer, and L. Sadler. 1994. *Machine Translation: An Introductory Guide.* Manchester: NCC Blackwell.

Hutchins, W. J. 1986. *Machine Translation: Past, Present, Future.* Chichester: Ellis Horwood.

——1995. 'Machine translation: a brief history'. In E. F. K. Koerner and R. E. Asher (eds.), *Concise History of the Language Sciences: From the Sumerians to the Cognitivists.* Oxford: Pergamon Press, 431–45.

——and H. L. Somers. 1992. *An Introduction to Machine Translation.* London: Academic Press.

King, M. (ed). 1987. *Machine Translation Today: The State of the Art.* Proceedings of the Third Lugano Tutorial, Lugano, 2–7 Apr. 1984. Edinburgh: Edinburgh University Press.

Newton, J. (ed). 1992. *Computers in Translation: A Practical Appraisal.* London: Routledge.

Nirenburg, S. (ed). 1987. *Machine Translation: Theoretical and Methodological Issues.* Cambridge: Cambridge University Press.

Slocum, J. (ed). 1988. *Machine Translation Systems.* Cambridge: Cambridge University Press.

CHAPTER 28

MACHINE TRANSLATION: LATEST DEVELOPMENTS

HAROLD SOMERS

ABSTRACT

The chapter reviews the current state of research, development, and use of machine translation (MT) systems. The empirical paradigms of example-based MT and statistical MT are described and contrasted with the traditional rule-based approach. Hybrid systems involving several approaches are discussed. Two recent developments within the rule-based paradigm are discussed, namely, anaphora resolution for MT and interlingua- and knowledge-based MT. As a major new application, spoken language MT is introduced. The prospect of MT systems for minority and less-developed languages is discussed, along with the use of MT on the Internet, notably for web-page translation. Finally, tools for translators are described, particularly those which exploit bilingual parallel corpora (translation memories, bilingual concordances), as well as translator-oriented word-processing tools.

28.1 Introduction

This chapter follows on naturally from the previous one, concentrating on the most recent research themes, and the current state of play in actual use of machine translation (MT) systems in the real world. The past ten years have been a very fruitful period for MT research and development on all fronts.

For basic research, the 1990s were marked by the emergence of a fairly new paradigm to challenge and eventually enrich the established methodologies. This was the so-called *empirical* approach, based on increasingly available amounts of 'raw data' in the form of **parallel corpora**, i.e. collections of texts and their translations. As we will describe below, these newly available data suggested to some researchers a way to approach the problems of MT which differed significantly from the traditional linguistic rule-based approaches. In parallel, several new ideas emerged under various names, notably **example-based MT** but also *analogy-based, memory-based,* and *case-based* MT, all having in common the use of a corpus or database of already translated examples, and involving a process of matching a new input against this database to extract suitable examples which are then recombined in an analogical manner to determine the correct translation.

A slightly different, but still corpus-based, approach has been called **statistical MT**: it is clearly example based in that it depends on a bilingual corpus, but the translation procedure depends on statistical modelling of the word order of the target language and of source–target word equivalences. There is thus a focus on the mathematical aspects of estimation of statistical parameters for the language models.

Not all the latest research in MT has been in this 'new' paradigm. Much work is continuing within the more traditional **rule-based** paradigm, often on new language pairs, sometimes attempting to address hitherto more difficult problems. Typical of this is work on **anaphora resolution** in the context of MT, and on the development of ontological knowledge in the context of **interlingua**-based MT. New directions in computational linguistics in general have found applications in MT, such as the development of *tree-adjoining grammars* (TAGs), which specify relationships between different representations, and so have a very clear application in transfer-based MT. Another is the lexicalist approach known as *Shake and Bake* MT which shuns explicit analysis and transfer rules in favour of a constraint- and unification-based approach.

An important new development for MT in the last decade has been the rapid progress that has been made towards developing **spoken-language** MT systems. Once thought simply too difficult, improved speech-analysis technology has been coupled with innovative design to produce a number of working systems, albeit still experimental, which suggest that this may be the new growth area for MT research.

Finally, we will mention arguably the most significant development to have influenced MT research, namely the *Internet* and the use of MT by web surfers. This originally seemed to take MT researchers a little by surprise, but the success of a number of MT systems which are available on the World Wide Web, usually free, has introduced an essentially new and unforeseen use for **low-quality MT**, as well as heightening awareness of MT for the general public. It has also introduced a number of new translation problems, however, which we will discuss below.

28.2 EMPIRICAL PARADIGMS

28.2.1 Example-based MT

Example-based MT (EBMT) was first proposed as long ago as 1981 (Nagao 1984), but was only developed from about 1990 onwards. The basic idea is to reuse examples of already existing translations as the basis for a new translation. In this respect it is similar to (and sometimes confused with) the translator's aid known as a **translation memory** (TM) (see below). Both EBMT and TM involve matching the input against a database of real examples, and identifying the closest matches. They differ in that in TM it is then up to the translator to decide what to do with the proposed matches, whereas in EBMT the automatic process continues by identifying corresponding translation fragments, and then recombining these to give the target text.

The process is thus broken down into three stages: matching (which EBMT and TM have in common), alignment, and recombination.

The *matching* stage can be implemented in a variety of ways, depending crucially on how the examples are stored in the first place. In early EBMT systems, examples were stored as fully annotated tree structures, with explicit links between the constituents in the two languages. The new input would be parsed, using the same grammar as the one used to build up the example database, and the resulting tree compared with the trees in the example database. Lexical differences are quantified using a hierarchical thesaurus. Since these trees were already aligned, all that remained was to cut and paste the partially overlapping tree structures in a fairly simple way. This arrangement works quite well, but the computational overhead is quite significant. In particular, the need for a traditional rule-based grammar with which to parse the input, and the need to align the tree structures (usually manually), meant that this approach to EBMT only really differs from traditional MT in the way it replaces the transfer stage, and so it is often referred to as *example-based transfer* rather than EBMT proper.

A more radical approach is to treat the examples, and the new input, just as strings of characters. The matching part of the process is then an example of *sequence comparison* found in many other computational applications, and for which several suitable algorithms exist. Again, a thesaurus can be used to quantify lexical substitutions, though other measures have also been used. Because there is no tree structure to rely on, the alignment and recombination phases become much more complex in this scenario.

In between these two extremes are approaches in which the examples are annotated to a greater or lesser degree. Quite widespread is the use of *POS tags* (see Chapter 11). Another approach is to combine several similar examples into a more general single example containing variables. Some systems use all of these approaches, so that the example set is a mixture of some very general cases which are effectively like the rules in rule-based MT, some partially generalized cases, and some literal examples.

One factor which applies in all of these cases is the *suitability* of examples. In the most purist of approaches to EBMT, the examples will be drawn from a real corpus of already existing translations. But such collections contain 'noise' in the form of *overlapping* or *contradictory* examples. Some researchers address this problem by eliminating troublesome examples, or changing them, or, in the extreme case, hand-picking or creating the examples manually. This approach has been criticized as repeating the major difficulty with rule-based MT, namely the reliance on hand-coded linguistic rules which are subject to human frailties such as inconsistency and whim.

The matching stage finds examples that are going to contribute to the translation on the basis of their similarity with the input. The next step is to identify which parts of the corresponding translation are to be reused, referred to as *alignment*. This will be straightforward if the examples are stored in a way that makes the links between the texts explicit, but otherwise it may involve some processing, perhaps using a bilingual dictionary, or comparison with other examples. This alignment stage is carried out by humans in the case of TM systems (see below), but must be automated for EBMT (see example (28.10–11) below). In some systems, the matching stage will identify several suitable examples each containing parts of the text to be translated. For instance, if we wanted to translate (28.1*a*) on the basis of retrieved examples (28.1*b, c*) (examples are from Sato and Nagao 1990), we would have to be able to identify which portions of the Japanese equivalents correspond to the underlined text in examples (28.1*b, c*).

(28.1)   *a.* He buys a book on international politics.
         b. <u>He buys a</u> notebook. *Kare wa nōto o kau.*
         c. I read <u>a book on international politics</u>. *Watashi wa kokusai seiji nitsuite kakareta hon o yomu.*

This brings us to the third stage, called *recombination*. Having identified which parts of the examples to reuse, we have to be sure that we are putting them together in a legitimate way. We can illustrate this by considering German, a language which has explicit case marking to distinguish subjects and objects. Suppose we want to translate (28.2*a*) on the basis of the examples (28.2*b, c*). The German text corresponding to the phrase *the handsome boy* is different in each example. We would have to know something about German grammar to know which alternative to choose.

(28.2) *a.* The handsome boy entered the room.

     b. The handsome boy ate his breakfast. *Der schöne Junge aß seinen Frühstück.*

     c. I saw the handsome boy. *Ich sah den schönen Jungen.*

28.2.2 Statistical MT

In its pure form, the statistics-based approach to MT makes use of no traditional linguistic data. The essence of the method is first to align phrases, word groups, and individual words of the parallel texts, and then to calculate the *probabilities* that any one word in a sentence of one language corresponds to a word or words in the translated sentence with which it is aligned in the other language. An essential feature is the availability of a suitable large bilingual corpus of reliable (authoritative) translations.

This approach is often seen as 'anti-linguistics' and is most closely associated with the IBM research group at Yorktown Heights, NY (Brown et al. 1990), who had had some success with non-linguistic approaches to speech recognition, and turned their attention to MT in the early 1990s. As already mentioned, the idea is to *model* the translation process in terms of statistical probabilities: to use their example, if we take the input sentence (28.3), then amongst the *possible* translations are (28.4*a*) and (28.4*b*).[1]

(28.3) President Lincoln was a good lawyer.

(28.4) *a. Le président Lincoln était un bon avocat.* ['President Lincoln was a good lawyer']

     b. Le matin je me brosse les dents. ['In the morning I brush my teeth']

What should emerge is that the probability that (28.4*a*) is a good translation is very high, while the probability for (28.4*b*) is very low. So for every sentence pair S and T there is a probability $P(T|S)$, i.e. the probability that T is the target sentence, given that S is the source. The translation procedure is a question of finding the best value for $P(T|S)$.[2]

This probability calculation depends on two other measures. The first is the probability that the words in S will 'give rise to' the words in T, the so-called *translation model*. The second is the probability that these words are correctly combined in the target language, which we could call the *(target)-language model*.

Probability that a given word in the source text is 'responsible' for a given word in the target text, $P(w_t|w_s)$, can be calculated on the basis of an **aligned corpus**. This is a laborious computation, but one which can be done once and for all for a given parallel corpus, looking at the relative distribution of all the words in the corpora. So for

---

[1] English translations shown in square brackets are for the benefit of readers, and are not part of the MT system.

[2] The original article presents this the other way round, modelling $P(S|T)$, and calculating the probability of the source sentence given the target. We prefer to describe the approach in a more intuitive manner, which is nevertheless faithful to the underlying approach.

example, it might appear from the corpus that the probability of the English word *the* being translated as *le* is 0.610, as *la* 0.178, and so on. An added complication in this calculation is the fact that word correspondences are not 1:1, the problem of *fertility*. For example, the English word *not* corresponds to *ne* and *pas* with probabilities of 0.469 and 0.460 respectively. The probability that *not* has a fertility value of 2 is quite high (0.758), so together this gives a good probability that *not* corresponds to *ne* . . . *pas*. For an interesting illustration of how this works consider the translation of the English word *hear*. The IBM group experimented with the English–French translations of the Hansard corpus of Canadian parliamentary proceedings. In this corpus, *hear* is translated as *bravo* with a probability of 0.992, but with fertility probabilities almost equally divided between 0 and 1. In other words, *hear* is only translated about half the time, but when it is, it comes out as *bravo*. This strange state of affairs is understandable when one considers how often in the corpus the English phrase *hear hear* is translated simply as *bravo*.

The translation model, then, gives us a 'bag' of the words most likely to be in the translation. The second part of the probability calculation must determine what is the best (i.e. most probable) arrangement of these words. This is the *(target)-language model*, which consists of probabilities of sequences of words, based on the model corpus. Bearing in mind that each source word is responsible for a number of possible target words, each with an associated probability, it becomes apparent that calculating the probabilities of all the possible sequences of all the possible target words is a huge task. Fortunately it can be simplified somewhat, since the probabilistic effect of sequence becomes infinitesimally small as the distance between the two words increases. It is sufficient therefore to calculate the probabilities of relatively short sequences of words, called *n*-grams, where *n* is the number of words in the sequence. Bigrams, for example are sets of word pairs, trigrams consist of three-word sequences. Yet even with this simplification, a large calculation is involved. So a useful starting point is to assume that the target-word sequence is the same as the source-word sequence. But we know that this is not generally true of language translation: there is often a degree of *distortion* of the target-language word order with respect to the source language. By allowing a certain amount of distortion, the search space can be limited, and probabilities of the most likely target sentences considered.

What is striking about this approach is the complete lack of linguistic 'knowledge' used in the process. If the system 'knows' that *la* and *table* go together, it is because it has seen this combination most often, not because it knows anything about gender agreement. When first reported, researchers using rule-based methods were surprised that the results were so acceptable: almost half the phrases translated either matched exactly the translations in the corpus, or expressed the same sense in slightly different words, or offered other equally legitimate translations. Nevertheless, as research progressed it became apparent that the possibilities of improving the performance of these systems were very limited. In particular, many of the errors made by the system could be corrected with the most minimal (and non-contentious) linguistic knowledge, such as notions of morphology, agreement, and so on. Subsequently, the IBM group made attempts to incorporate such linguistic knowledge—although remaining true to their empirical approach in that such information was always based on statistical observation—but the results were not very promising, and the group disbanded in the late 1990s.

28.2.3 Hybrid approaches

Neither the example-based nor the statistics-based approaches to MT have turned out to be demonstrably better than the rule-based approaches, though each has shown some promise in certain cases. As a result of this, a number of **hybrid systems** quickly emerged. Recognizing that some specific problems were particularly suited to an example-based approach, in some systems there is an example-based component which is activated specifically to deal with the kinds of problems that are difficult to capture in a rule-based approach. Other hybrid systems combine rule-based analysis and generation with example-based transfer. A third combination seems particularly suited to the thorny problem of spoken-language translation, where for example elements of the analysis part may rely more heavily on statistical analysis, while transfer and generation is more suited to a rule-based approach.

A rather different type of hybrid is the case of **multi-engine systems**. In this case, the source text is passed through a number of different MT systems, each using different techniques. One may be essentially lexicon based, another rule-based analysis and generation, a third example based or more purely statistical. In each case, built into the system will be a kind of scoring mechanism, by which the engine is able to evaluate for itself its 'confidence' in the output. For example, a rule-based engine may be able to reflect how sure it is of having been able to choose correctly between competing analyses. At the other end of the process is a kind of 'moderator' which will take the outputs of the various engines and compare them, choosing the highest scoring proposal, or confirming similar translations proposed by different engines, or perhaps even consolidating them by combining the best bits of each.

28.3 RULE-BASED APPROACHES TO MT

28.3.1 Anaphora resolution

The interpretation of **anaphora** (i.e. coreference especially, for example, pronouns, see Chapter 14) is crucial for the successful operation of MT. This is particularly evident when translating into languages which mark the gender of pronouns, or from languages which have *zero-anaphora* constructions into languages where the pronouns must be inserted. A further problem is that anaphoric reference often crosses a sentence boundary, whereas most MT systems are limited to the sentence as a translation unit. The problem is at its most acute when the system is used to translate conversational texts which are especially rich in anaphoric devices. In addition to anaphora resolution itself (i.e. the identification of links between anaphoric expressions and their antecedents) being a very complicated task, translation adds a further dimension to the problem in that the reference to a discourse entity encoded by a source-language anaphor by the speaker (or writer) has not only to be *identified* by the hearer (translator or translation system) but also *re-encoded* as a coreferential expression in a different language. For example, *elle* is used in French to refer to a grammatically feminine noun, for which the appropriate translation may be *it* rather than *she* as in (28.5).

(28.5)   *L'eau est claire mais elle est froide.*
          'The water is clear but it (*she) is cold.'

In recent years there has been a growth of research in this area, covering a number of languages including Japanese, German, French, Portuguese, Chinese, Spanish, Bulgarian, Italian, Russian, Polish, Arabic, Swedish, Turkish, Hindi, and Malayalam. Obvious techniques such as recognizing number (and gender) concord (e.g. in English *they* will usually be linked to a plural antecedent, *she* to a singular female one) can be supplemented by *heuristics* reflecting the most likely clues. For example, parallel structures often suggest a link as in (28.6), where at least *video recorder* and *red button* are possible antecedents for the pronoun *it* (and there may be others, from earlier sentences).

(28.6)   To turn on the video recorder, press the red button. To program *it*, press the 'Program' key.

Apart from heuristics like these, one way to resolve anaphora ambiguities is by better 'understanding' of the text. For example, in (28.7a), knowing whether video tapes or recorders are more likely to be rewound tells us which is the correct link for the pronoun, whereas in (28.7b) *it* refers to the machine.

(28.7)   a. Insert the video tape into the recorder, rewinding *it* if necessary.
          b. Insert the video tape into the recorder, after making sure that *it* is turned on.

Sometimes, pronouns refer to items only *implicit* in the text, in which case we need to understand the underlying situation, as in (28.8), where *it* refers to a not-mentioned meal or food.

(28.8)   We went to a restaurant last night. *It* was delicious.

These approaches imply the need for richer linguistic information in the system, which may be provided by incorporating *ontological knowledge bases* into systems. This is the theme of a second strand of research within the rule-based paradigm.

28.3.2 Interlingua-based MT

Dismissed in the 1980s as largely impractical, the notion of **interlingua**-based MT has undergone a revival in recent years. An example of this approach is the **knowledge-based MT** (KBMT) research based at Carnegie-Mellon University and NMSU. The *text-meaning representation* (TMR) in their multilingual MT system represents the result of analysis of a given input text in any one of the languages supported by the system, and serves as input to the generation process. The meaning of the input text—derived by analysis of its lexical, syntactic, semantic, and pragmatic information—is represented in the TMR as elements which must be interpreted in terms of an independently motivated model of the world (or *ontology*). The link between the ontology and the TMR is provided by the lexicon, where the meanings of most open-class lexical items are defined in terms of their mappings into ontological concepts and their resulting contributions to TMR structure. Information about the non-propositional components of text meaning—pragmatic and discourse-related phenomena such as speech acts, speaker attitudes and intentions, relations among text units, deictic references, etc.—is also derived from the lexicon, and becomes part of the TMR. The approach is made tractable by restricting the system to specific domains and by adopting the *controlled language* (see Chapter 23) approach to syntactic coverage.

The ontology at the heart of the system is a model that a particular speaker has about the world; this model is populated by *concepts*, organized in a particular hierarchy. The concepts in the ontology cover things (such as aeroplanes, ideas, or giraffes), events (e.g. buying, eating), as well as relations. The ontology is organized as a *taxonomy*, e.g. a concept such as HAMMER would be identified as a type of HAND-TOOL, with more specific types of hammer connected to HAMMER. As well as this basic IS-A-TYPE-OF link, other relations can be encoded in the ontology, such as HAS-AS-PART, IS-AN-OCCUPANT-OF, MANUFACTURED-BY, and so on, depending on the domain. The ontology can also be extended by associating frame-like information with concepts, such as COLOUR, SIZE, OWNER. Events in the ontology have associated case slots like AGENT and LOCATION, which in turn might have information about associated typical fillers.

The ontology, as mentioned above, is associated with a (multilingual) *lexicon*. Analysis and generation components are also of course necessary, but, as is usual in an interlingual system, no transfer component. Thus, the analyser can be used to generate a TMR for a text, and from this the target-language text can be generated directly. One implementation of this architecture translates Spanish news articles into English, but other languages are also covered.

28.4 SPOKEN-LANGUAGE MT

As recently as fifteen years ago, the task of MT applied to spoken language was thought too difficult for all but the most basic research. Recent developments in speech processing, coupled with new ideas about MT (EBMT and statistical approaches, as described above) have meant that **spoken-language translation** (SLT) is now a major research avenue within MT.

It might be thought that SLT was simply a matter of coupling a speech-to-text front-end and a text-to-speech back-end to a conventional text MT system, but this approach would be completely inadequate for all but the most formal types of spoken language. Spoken language is hugely different from written language, apart from the obvious difference of medium (sound vs. text), which involves an amount of pre-linguistic processing to isolate the speech signal from the surrounding background 'noise'. Among the problems particular to SLT, depending on the type of speech, are identifying and processing spoken-language phenomena such as hesitations and self-repairs (some of which actually serve a subconscious pragmatic function); correctly interpreting speech act phenomena and discourse functions; dealing with different accents, and mixed-language speech; much greater use of anaphora and ellipsis; ill-formed utterances, or rather, varied grammaticality of spoken language.

Interestingly, the field is dominated by one sort of SLT system, aimed at translating dialogues, and more particularly *cooperative dialogues*, for example between a travel-ler and a travel agent, where the dialogue partners collaborate towards a common goal, as opposed to *adversarial* dialogues, e.g. between business persons negotiating a contract. The implications of this apparently minor distinction are quite enormous, especially in terms of interpreting the pragmatic aspects of the dialogue. Other distinctions that might impinge on the design of an SLT system include

- whether it is face to face or telephonic;
- whether it has the possibility of *interactive disambiguation* and/or confirmation, and if so . . .
- whether this also is speech based (introducing the difficulty of identifying system–user *metadialogue*) or on a separate user interface;
- whether users are purely monolingual or may switch languages from time to time.

Almost all the SLT literature focuses on *dialogue translation*, with very little work as yet reported on what might be termed, by analogy with MT, *machine interpretation*, that is, simultaneous or consecutive translation of spoken language in the context of a meeting or a person addressing a group of people. Interestingly, this might prove to be a somewhat less difficult task than dialogue translation, apart from the exigencies of real-time processing of course, since the type of language that gets interpreted (by human interpreters) is usually much more formal than everyday dialogue, and closer in nature to the written language. Another application that does not yet seem to have attracted much attention is the SLT corollary of email translation, namely *voice-mail*, where there is also scope for translation. The problems would be similar to those involved in translation of other spoken messages, for example between emergency or security services across linguistic borders, e.g. in the Channel Tunnel.

28.5 DEVELOPMENT AND USE

28.5.1 MT for minority languages

A recent area of activity in MT and related fields cuts across the research, development, and use boundaries. This is the application of language technologies to less-favoured languages, generally (though perhaps misleadingly) termed *minority languages*. This term is misleading, because it refers not only to languages with small numbers of speakers, like Welsh, Breton, and so on, but also to languages which, because of the economic and geographic situation of their speakers, have not received much attention. Among these are languages with the most numerous speakers in the world: Urdu, Hindi, Cantonese, for example. These are of interest also in the 'West' as **non-indigenous minority languages** (NIMLs). These languages have not caught the attention of researchers and developers until now, for obvious, mainly economic, reasons: attention has been focused on European languages, plus Chinese (i.e. Mandarin), Japanese, Korean, Arabic. Now there is a small but growing area of activity to promote the development of MT, or at least related tools, for people using these minority languages. Fortunately, advances have been made at least regarding basic tools such as fonts and character sets, without which of course almost nothing of much use could be achieved. But beyond that there is a huge amount of work involved in building up grammars and lexicons, structured vocabularies, terminology, and so on for so many languages.

One approach that has been advocated is to look at research in **corpus linguistics**, where experiments have been reported in which linguistic information (word lists, rudimentary grammars, and even bilingual lexicons) can be extracted semi-automatically from mono- or bilingual text corpora. It remains to be seen to what extent these techniques, largely developed for European languages, can be extended to typologically varied languages; but at least the raw material, in the form of text corpora, is becoming more and more widely available, as the World Wide Web grows. It has been suggested that English is no longer a 'majority' language on the web, and the only impediment to the growth of linguistic diversity on the web seems to be the availability of computers, and, to a certain extent, standardization.

Related to this is research on rapid development of MT for new language pairs, perhaps within an existing computational framework. This has been supported largely by political motivations, whereby the language needs of the major powers fluctuate depending on sociological (and sometimes naturally occurring) events around the world. Researchers have been looking into methods which will enable language technology tools ranging from on-line dictionaries and phrase-books through to computer-aided translation and full MT systems to be developed quickly, to support aid workers, military and political advisers, and various other interested parties needing to work with speakers of a variety of languages.

28.5.2 Use of MT for WWW and chat rooms

One of the most important developments in the world of MT in recent years has been its ready availability both in the form of inexpensive software on sale in computer stores (or, in Japan at least, provided free as part of the operating system) and also, famously, on the web. First installed experimentally by CompuServe, *web-page translation*—in the form of the Systran system—is available via the AltaVista search engine at the touch of a button. Users can paste text into a translation window, or give the URL of the web page that they wish to see translated. Several other websites offer free translation using a variety of MT systems. Another recent innovation is *email translation*, and a 'translate' button on some *chat room* sites.

This increased visibility of MT has had a number of side effects. It has of course increased the general public's awareness of MT, in some cases clarifying its limits but also its benefits. Informal reports suggest that users are at first impressed, then disappointed as they realize its limitations, but finally pragmatic as they learn to get the best out of raw MT. One thing to notice is how using MT to translate the unrestricted (and sometimes poorly written) material that is found on web pages goes against the general recommendations for the use of MT that have been made over the last decade or so. There is certainly a need to *educate* the general public about the low quality of raw MT, and, importantly, *why* the quality is so low. Meanwhile, MT systems have to be adapted and improved so that the quality is raised a little. One particularly important way of doing this, and one which is starting to be addressed, is to tackle the problem of *proper name translation*. Fortunately, great strides have been made in the neighbouring field of information extraction towards the *named entity recognition task*, as it is termed (see Chapter 30), and there is evidence that similar techniques can be used to improve MT output so that proper names like *Bill Gates* or *Kanzler Kohl* are not translated as *Addition Barrières* or *Chancellor Cabbage*.

28.5.3 Tools for users

As well as research on MT itself, a lot of work has been done recently to develop computer-based tools for translators. Many of the most recent developments have been based on the growing availability of large bilingual corpora, i.e. collections of translated texts in machine-readable form.

A first priority with such corpora is to *align* them, i.e. to establish on a segment-by-segment basis (often paragraphs or sentences) which bits of text in one language correspond to which bits of text in the other. This is not always as straightforward as it may seem, especially when the two languages concerned are typologically very different (so that, for example, the notion of 'sentence' is not compatible), or when the translation is particularly 'free'; but for a lot of texts, this initial alignment is quite successful.

The **aligned bilingual corpus** can then be used as a resource on which can be based a number of tools for the translator. One of these, now widely used, is the **translation memory** (TM) already mentioned above. First proposed in the 1970s, the idea is that the translator can consult a database of previous translations, usually on a sentence-by-sentence basis, looking for anything similar enough to the current sentence to be translated, and can then use the retrieved example as a model. The key to the process is efficient storage of the sentences in the TM, and, most importantly, an efficient *matching* scheme. In current commercial TM systems, the matching is essentially based on character-string similarity, but one could envisage a more sophisticated method, incorporating linguistic 'knowledge' of inflection paradigms, synonyms, and even grammatical alternations. To exemplify, consider (28.9*a*). The example (28.9*b*) differs only in a few characters, and would be picked up by any currently available TM matcher. (28.9*c*) is superficially quite dissimilar, but is made up of words which are related to the words in (28.9*a*) as either grammatical alternatives or near synonyms. (28.9*d*) is very similar in meaning to (28.9*a*), but quite different in structure. Arguably, any of (28.9*b–d*) should be picked up by a sophisticated TM matcher.

(28.9) *a.* When the paper tray is empty, remove it and refill it with paper of the appropriate size.
      b. When the tray is empty, remove it and fill it with the appropriate paper.
      c. When the bulb remains unlit, remove it and replace it with a new bulb
      d. You have to remove the paper tray in order to refill it when it is empty.

As mentioned above, current TMs make no attempt to identify which parts of the translation correspond to the matched elements of the example: that is up to the translator to decide. For example, if (28.10) is the sentence to be translated, and the TM contains (28.11*a*) with its accompanying translation (28.11*b*), the TM may be able to highlight the differences between (28.10) and (28.11*a*), as we do here, but it is unable to identify which words in (28.11*b*) have to be changed.

(28.10)   The large paper tray can hold up to four hundred sheets of A4 paper.

(28.11) *a.* The <u>small</u> paper tray can hold up to <u>three</u> hundred sheets of <u>A5</u> paper.
       b. Die <u>kleine</u> Papierkassette fasst bis zu <u>dreihundert</u> Blatt in <u>A5</u>-Format.

Another useful tool based on aligned bilingual corpora is a **bilingual concordancer**. A concordancer in general is a software tool that allows the user to see how a word or phrase is used throughout a text. Sometimes called a *KWIC-index* (keyword in context), it is a tool that literature scholars have used for many years: for example, Fig. 28.1 shows a concordance of the word *curious* in Lewis Carroll's *Alice's Adventures in Wonderland*. A bilingual concordance gives the same sort of listing, but each line is linked to the corresponding translation. This enables the translator to see how a particular word—or more usefully a phrase or a technical term—has been translated before.

Another tool that has been discussed amongst researchers, but has not yet been developed commercially, might be called a *translator-friendly word-processor*. Here is

```
1          hed it off. * * * 'What a curious feeling!' said Alice; 'I must b
1          against herself, for this curious child was very fond of pretendi
2                              'Curiouser and curiouser!' cried Alice (
2                  'Curiouser and curiouser!' cried Alice (she was so muc
2          Eaglet, and several other curious creatures. Alice led the way,
4            — and yet—it's rather curious, you know, this sort of life!
6          eir heads. She felt very curious to know what it was all about,
6          out a cat! It's the most curious thing I ever saw in my life!' S
7          ht into it. 'That's very curious!' she thought. 'But everything'
7          hought. 'But everything's curious today. I think I may as well g
8          Alice thought this a very curious thing, and she went nearer to w
8          she had never seen such a curious croquet-ground in her life; it
8          seen, when she noticed a curious appearance in the air: it puzz
9          next, and so on.' 'What a curious plan!' exclaimed Alice. 'That's
10          : 'and I do so like that curious song about the whiting!' 'Oh,
10          th, and said 'That's very curious.' 'It's all about as curious a
10          ous.' 'It's all about as curious as it can be,' said the Gryphon
11          moment Alice felt a very curious sensation, which puzzled her a
11          er the list, feeling very curious to see what the next witness wo
12          ad!' 'Oh, I've had such a curious dream!' said Alice, and she tol
12          her, and said, 'It was a curious dream, dear, certainly: but no
```

Fig. 28.1 Concordance of the word *curious* in *Alice's Adventures in Wonderland*

envisaged software with the normal word-processing facilities enhanced to facilitate the sort of text editing 'moves' that a translator (or, perhaps, a translator working as a posteditor on some MT output) commonly makes. Simple things like transposing two words at the touch of a function key are easy to imagine, but the software could incorporate more linguistically sophisticated tools such as *grammar-conscious global replace*. Imagine you had a text in which the word *fog* had been translated as *brouillard* in French, but you decided *brume* was a better translation. Globally changing *brouillard* to *brume* is only half the job: *brouillard* is masculine, while *brume* is feminine, so some other changes (gender of adjectives and pronouns) may have to be made. A linguistically sophisticated word-processor could do it for you. Similarly, if you wanted to change *buy* to *purchase*, it would be nice if it could automatically change *buying* to *purchasing*, *bought* to *purchased*, etc. The translator-friendly word-processor could also search for 'false friends' (e.g. *librairie* as a translation of *library*) and other 'interference' errors, if the user is a competent but not fluent writer of the target language. Coming back to the idea of parallel text alignment, a similar tool could check the source and target texts to see if any of the source text had inadvertently been omitted in the translation. And the bilingual concordance tool can be used on the current translation texts to check for consistency of translation, e.g. of technical terms.

FURTHER READING AND RELEVANT RESOURCES

The field of MT is a fast-moving one. Latest research and developments are reported in the field's premier journal, *Machine Translation*, and at its conferences, the MT Summit, organized biannually by one of the three regional organizations which make up IAMT, the International Association for Machine Translation (namely AMTA, the Association for MT in the Americas; EAMT, the European Association for MT; and AAMT, the Asian Association for MT).

A comprehensive review of EBMT techniques appeared as Somers (1999). The IBM statistical MT system is described in Brown et al. (1990); a general overview of the approach appears in Knight (1997). A good example of a multi-engine system is PANGLOSS (Frederking et al. 1994)

Anaphora resolution in MT is the subject of a special issue of *Machine Translation* (Mitkov 1999).

KBMT research at Carnegie-Mellon is described in Nirenburg et al. (1992). Latest ideas on interlingua-based MT have been presented at a series of AMTA SIG-IL Workshops, the latest of which was at the MT Summit in Santiago de Compostela (Farwell and Helmreich 2001).

Spoken-language MT is represented by major research programmes such as VERBMOBIL (Wahlster 2000), SLT (Rayner et al. 2000), the C-Star consortium of several projects, and not a few others. A collection of articles on SLT is assembled in Krauwer (2000).

MT and other resources for minority languages was the subject of a workshop at LREC (LREC 2000), which includes a discussion by the present author of the particular case of NIMLs. Frederking et al. (2000) discuss DIPLOMAT, an example of a quickly developed ('rapid ramp-up') interactive MT system for Haitian Creole. Jones and Havrilla (1998) and Nirenburg and Raskin (1998) propose general approaches to this problem.

Possible uses of low-quality MT output were first discussed by Church and Hovy (1993). Systran's web-based MT system is described by Yang and Lange (forthcoming). Flournoy and Callison-Burch (2000) describe Amikai's chat-room translation system. Proper name recognition is discussed by Turcato et al. (2000) in connection with their TV closed-caption translation system.

Translation tools are the subject of Isabelle and Church (1998). Research involving aligned parallel bilingual texts has been copious in recent years. Overviews of the main issues are to be found in Manning and Schütze (1999:463 ff.); Véronis (2000); Wu (2000); Melamed (2001), among others. Hutchins (1998) gives a historical perspective of translators' tools, including the translation memory. Researchers at RALI in Montreal have developed a number of corpus-based translators' tools including the bilingual concordancer (Macklovitch, Simard, and Langlais 2000) and some of the other tools mentioned.

REFERENCES

Brown, P. F., J. Cocke, S. A. Della Pietra, V. J. Della Pietra, F. Jelinek, J. D. Lafferty, R. L. Mercer, and P. S. Roossin. 1990. 'A statistical approach to machine translation'. *Computational Linguistics*, 16(2), 79–85.

Church, K. W. and E. H. Hovy. 1993. 'Good applications for crummy machine translation'. *Machine Translation*, 8(4), 239–58.

Farwell, D. and S. Helmreich (eds.). 2001. *Proceedings of the 5th Workshop on Interlinguas and Interlingual Approaches to MT* (Summit VIII, Santiago de Compostela).

Flournoy, R. S. and C. Callison-Burch. 2000. 'Reconciling user expectations and translation technology to create a useful real-world application'. *Translating and the Computer 22: Proceedings of the 22nd International Conference on Translating and the Computer* (London).

Frederking, R., S. Nirenburg, D. Farwell, S. Helmreich, E. Hovy, K. Knight, S. Beale, C. Domashnev, D. Attardo, D. Grannes, and R. Brown. 1994. 'Integrating translations from multiple sources within the Pangloss Mark III machine translation system'. *Technology Partnerships for Crossing the Language Barrier: Proceedings of the 1st Conference of the Association for Machine Translation in the Americas* (Columbia, Md.), 73–80.

——A. Rudnicky, C. Hogan, and K. Lenzo. 2000. 'Interactive speech translation in the DIPLO-MAT Project'. *Machine Translation*, 15(1–2).

Hutchins, J., 1998. 'The origins of the translator's workstation'. *Machine Translation*, 13(4), 287–307.

Isabelle, P. and K. W. Church (eds.). 1998. 'New tools for human translators', special issue of *Machine Translation*, 13(1–2).

Jones, D. and R. Havrilla. 1998. 'Twisted pair grammar: support for rapid development of machine translation for low density languages'. In D. Farwell, L. Gerber, and E. Hovy (eds.), *Machine Translation and the Information Soup: Third Conference of the Association for Machine Translation in the Americas AMTA '98*. Berlin: Springer, 318–32.

Knight, K. 1997. 'Automating knowledge acquisition for machine translation'. *AI Magazine*, 18(1), 81–96.

Krauwer, S. (ed.). 2000. 'Spoken language translation', special issue of *Machine Translation*, 15(1–2).

LREC. 2000. *Proceedings of LREC 2000: The 2nd International Conference on Language Resources and Evaluation Workshop, Developing Language Resources for Minority Languages: Reusability and Strategic Priorities* (Athens).

Macklovitch E., M. Simard, and P. Langlais. 2000. 'TransSearch: a free translation memory on the world wide web'. *Proceedings of the 2nd International Conference on Language Resources and Evaluation (LREC)* (Athens), 1201–8.

Manning, C. D. and H. Schütze. 1999. *Foundations of Statistical Natural Language Processing*. Cambridge, Mass.: MIT Press.

Melamed, I. D. 2001. *Empirical Methods for Exploiting Parallel Texts*. Cambridge, Mass.: MIT Press.

Mitkov, R. (ed.). 1999. 'Anaphora resolution in machine translation', special issue of *Machine Translation*, 14(3–4).

Nagao, M. 1984. 'A framework of a mechanical translation between Japanese and English by analogy principle'. In A. Elithorn and R. Banerji (eds.), *Artificial and Human Intelligence*. Amsterdam: North-Holland, 173–80.

Nirenburg, S. and V. Raskin, 1998. 'Universal grammar and lexis for quick ramp-up of MT systems', *Proceedings of the 36th Annual Meeting of the Association for Computational Linguistics and 17th International Conference on Computational Linguistics (COLING-ACL '98)* (Montreal), 975–9.

——J. Carbonell, M. Tomita, and K. Goodman. 1992. *Machine Translation: A Knowledge-Based Approach*. San Mateo, Calif.: Morgan Kaufmann.

Rayner, M., D. Carter, P. Bouillon, V. Digalakis, and M. Wirén. 2000. *The Spoken Language Translator*. Cambridge: Cambridge University Press.

Sato, S. and M. Nagao. 1990. 'Toward memory-based translation'. *Proceedings of the 13th International Conference on Computational Linguistics (COLING '90)* (Helsinki), 247–52.

Somers, H. 1999. 'Review article: example-based machine translation'. *Machine Translation*, 14(2), 113–57.

Turcato, D., F. Popowich, P. McFetridge, D. Nicholson, and J. Toole 2000. 'Pre-processing closed captions for machine translation'. *Proceedings of ANLP/NAACL 2000 Workshop: Embedded Machine Translation Systems* (Seattle), 38–45.

Véronis, J. (ed.). 2000. *Parallel Text Processing: Alignment and Use of Translation Corpora*. Dordrecht: Kluwer Academic Press.

Wahlster, W. (ed.). 2000. *Verbmobil: Foundations of Speech-to-Speech Translation*. Berlin: Springer.

Wu, D. 2000. 'Alignment'. In R. Dale, H. Moisl, and H. Somers (eds.), *Handbook of Natural Language Processing*. New York: Marcel Dekker, Inc., 415–58.

Yang, J. and E. Lange. 2003. 'Going live on the Internet'. In H. Somers (ed.), *Computers and Translation: A Translator's Guide*. Amsterdam: John Benjamins.

INFORMATION RETRIEVAL

EVELYNE TZOUKERMANN

JUDITH L. KLAVANS

TOMEK STRZALKOWSKI

ABSTRACT

Broadly speaking, **information retrieval** (IR) refers to the science of finding objects in any media relevant to a user query. The focus of this chapter is on text retrieval, since our goal is to discuss the role of natural language in both query and document representation. Paradoxically, although texts are written in natural language, the use of computational linguistic techniques for information retrieval has been minimal. The primary techniques used for successful information retrieval have been statistical rather than symbolic in nature. Recently, however, the limits of these robust statistical techniques have been met. We review current research in integrating language-oriented methods with statistically based methods in information retrieval.

29.1 INTRODUCTION

Information retrieval consists of retrieving information from stored data through queries formulated by the user or through preformulated user profiles. This information can be in any medium or format, e.g. text, image, video, speech, databases, and often combines media. The field of IR has a well-established history, and has already reached an initial level of maturity that is deployed in industry and business. Recently, the need for effective information retrieval techniques has reached the public in an unprecedented way with the advent of the World Wide Web. Whereas in past years, IR was primarily required by subspecialities, such as business, law, and medicine, now users who simply want effective Internet searching are pushing the research community to solve information-finding needs. Increasing network transmission speed and capacity promise to bring even more impetus to this field. Finally, globalization adds yet another dimension to the need for powerful information retrieval across languages (see Chapter 38).

In this chapter, we first provide an overview of the basic approaches to IR. We give details on the components and technologies which have been used in standard systems. We then focus more specifically on the ways that natural language processing techniques have been utilized in different system components. Our discussion looks at impact on the morphological, lexical, syntactic, and semantic levels. We review both successes and failures, with an eye towards the future.

29.2 COMPONENTS OF INFORMATION RETRIEVAL SYSTEMS

The primary software components of an IR system for text consist of document processing, query processing, and then matching for retrieval techniques. Given a query or a statement of user needs, the goal of the system is to find a set of documents which fall within a definition of similarity or relevance.

29.2.1 Text types

The first stage in the information retrieval task is to determine the limits of the corpus over which subsequent processing will be performed. In the case of specialized corpora, document collection properties can affect performance (see Chapters 23 and 24). For example, a corpus of email messages has different properties from a corpus of transcribed speech. Furthermore, corpora could consist of single-subject documents, such as medicine or law, in which case the use of metadata as well as full text data can be helpful. This also holds for semi-structured text, such as memoranda or text associated with databases. Other collections could be selected based on user group, e.g. articles for medical providers across topics, or articles for patients. When highly heterogeneous corpora, such as web articles across sites, are to be processed, techniques geared towards generic documents are preferred. From the perspective of computational linguistics, key research areas include tailored processing for specific domains, user groups, genres, or other text characterisitics; complementary research includes dealing with widely heterogeneous text, coupled with image, sound, and video retrieval.

29.2.2 Document preprocessing

Classic models in IR consider that each document can be modelled by a set of indexed keywords. In principle, keywords give an indication of the document content. Before indexing, several text operations are performed in order to save space at indexing time. Among the main parts of speech (e.g. determiners, nouns, adjectives, verbs, adverbs, pronouns, etc.), content words, such as nouns, verbs, and adjectives, are the ones which carry most of the semantics, whereas function words such as prepositions, pronouns, and determiners have less impact on the determining of what an article is about (see Chapter 11). Thus, function words are often ignored when constructing representations. Furthermore, function words tend to be frequent, so eliminating them also contributes to efficiency, but researchers tend to disagree about the impact of keeping or removing them (see Riloff 1995). Among the document preprocessing tasks are: elimination of function words, stemming, which for English consists of stripping the end of words generally morphologically related to their common stem or root (see Chapter 2), the selection of index terms, and the representation of synonymic or taxonomic relations. Controversies about stemming techniques vis-à-vis collection types and language types still have not been resolved. In order to capture relationships between words (e.g. *walk, walks, walking* for English), stemming is applied. Stemming conflates morphologically related words to the same root, either by a traditional stemmer such as Porter's (Porter 1980) or Lovins's (1968), or by a linguistically based morphological analyser. The former tends to be efficient and robust but prone to error, whereas rule-based linguistic analysers tend to be more accurate.

Two main issues are at stake in using stemming. The first involves the concepts of **recall** and **precision**. Recall and precision are two independent metrics traditionally used to assess the performance of IR systems. Recall refers to the percentage of relevant documents that are classified as relevant, and precision refers to the percentage of documents classified as relevant which were correctly classified. In practice, most systems exhibit a trade-off between recall and precision: an improvement along one dimension typically forces a drop in performance along the other dimension. Depending on the target application, it may be desirable to buy high precision at the price of recall, or one may prefer to optimize recall and settle for low precision. A general IR controversy lies in the fact that while stemming increases recall, it has a negative effect on precision. Second, two main errors occur while stemming: understemming and overstemming (Paice 1996). Overstemming is caused by relating forms that are not in fact morphologically related, for example *magnesia, magnesian, magnet, magnetic,* etc. are conflated by Lovins's stemming algorithm (Lovins 1968) and reduced to one common stem *magnes.* On the other hand, understemming is the non-conflation of related words, such as *acquire, acquiring, acquired,* and *acquisition.* The first three are correctly related to *acquir,* but the stem for *acquisition* is *acquis.* Thus, *acquisition* and *acquire* are not modelled as related.

Different studies have shown inconsistent results of the effect of using stemmers. Harman (1991) showed that stemming provides no improvement over no stemming at all, and that different stemming algorithms do not affect performance. Krovetz (1993) showed that, with stemming, improvement ranges between 1.3 per cent and 45.3 per cent for different test collections and stemmers. Frakes and Baeza-Yates (1992) compare eight distinct studies and they all conclude that there are beneficial aspects of using stemming techniques. A large-scale analysis by Hull (1996) compared five algorithms for stemming: s-plural removal, Porter's, Lovins's, and two linguistic algorithms for inflectional and derivational morphology. The conclusion was that stemming always helped, but the improvements range from just 1 per cent to 3 per cent.

Once the index terms are determined for a document, it is clear that not all terms are relevant to the document content. In other words, if the same word appears in the 10,000 documents that form the collection, this index term is nearly useless in that it does not discriminate one document over another, and thus may not satisfy the user's request. On the other hand, if an index term appears only in five documents of the collection, it is very likely a discriminating term for a given query. Therefore, assigning a weight to index terms provides a discriminatory value. This observation forms the basis for the weighting schemes discussed below.

29.2.3   Building the document index

An inverted file, also called inverted index, is generally a two-column table in which words or keywords of the document appear next to the location of occurrence of these words in the document. The number, which identifies the word, marks the nth position of the character in a given document. For example, the following text in Table 29.1 is represented by the inverted index file, without stemming, shown in Table 29.2. Indexes of this type are built for each document in a collection, over large collections. Efficient search and retrieval can then take place over these indexes.

Table 29.1 Sample text for indexing

1	7	18	23	29	38	41	47	55	62
Video	technology	will	bring	patients	in	rural	clinics	closer	to

65	69	78	87	92	99	102	107
the	hospital	services	they	need.	It	will	soon

Table 29.2 Sample of inverted index file

Vocabulary	Occurrences
soon	107
will	18, 102
it	99
need	92
they	87
services	78
hospital	69
the	65
to	62
closer	55
clinics	47
rural	41
in	38
patients	29
bring	23
technology	7
video	1

29.2.4 Query processing and matching queries to documents

After the document index has been built, a query is processed in order to retrieve documents to fill the user's needs. In order to match a query representation to the index, and thus identify documents that are most relevant to that query, three statistical matching techniques are used for the bulk of IR systems, namely Boolean, vector space, or probabilistic.

In **Boolean systems**, queries are represented by keywords, connected with Boolean logical operators (e.g. 'and', 'or', 'not'). Due to the precise semantics of the Boolean representations which result in computational efficiency and speed, these systems are used by many commercial institutions, particularly the ones interested in biblio-graphic systems. Nevertheless, these models also suffer from their simplicity, in the sense that they retrieve documents based on binary decisions (i.e. the system decides if the document is relevant or not) as opposed to providing the user with a more graded answer. Another drawback of the Boolean systems is that although they have highly precise semantics, it is often not easy to translate a natural language query into a Boolean expression. In fact, users may have a hard time translating their complex information need into proper keywords and Boolean operators which will return the relevant documents (Belkin and Croft 1987).

In **vector space models**, documents and queries are represented in terms of vec-tors (Salton and Lesk 1968; Salton 1971). From a user's standpoint, the main difference between Boolean and vector space models resides at the retrieval level, providing a ranked set of documents corresponding better to degrees of relevance to the infor-mation need. In vector space models, non-binary weights are assigned to index terms in queries and documents. Eventually, these term weights are used to compute a degree of similarity between documents and queries, thus returning information that goes from full match to partial match to the user's request. Index term weight can be computed using many different techniques (Salton and McGill 1983). In the vector model, similarity is computed using $TF*IDF$ (Salton 1971; Salton and Lesk 1968). TF represents the **term frequency** and provides a measure of how well that term describes the document contents; this is the intra-document information. IDF, **inverse document frequency**, reflects inter-cluster dissimilarity. The premise is that terms which appear in many documents are not very useful for discriminating rele-vance and non-relevance. The advantages of the vector space model are that: (1) the term-weighting approach improves retrieval performance; and (2) the ranked docu-ments according to the degree of similarity permit a full to partial answer. The vector space model is simple, fast, and popular.

In **probabilistic models**, the approach to modelling queries and documents is based on probability theory. The probabilistic model was first instantiated by Rob-ertson and Spärck Jones (1976). Given an ideal answer set, it is possible to retrieve the closest set of documents. Therefore, one can think of the query as a way to specify the properties of an ideal answer set. The properties are characterized by the semantics of the index terms. However, properties of the ideal answer are not always known at query time and one needs to approximate the answer to the closest set of proper-ties. The main advantage of the probabilistic model is that documents are ranked in order of their probability to be relevant. The drawbacks are that: (1) the system has to guess an initial separation between relevant and non-relevant documents; and (2) the approach does not take into consideration the frequency at which index terms occur inside the document.

In addition to the three main categories of conceptual models, there are a number of alternative approaches. For example, some alternatives to Boolean systems are methods such as fuzzy set model and extended Boolean model, where ideas are borrowed from algebraic models such as vector space. There are many alternatives to probabilistic approaches, such as Bayesian networks, inference network models, belief network models, and many more. As for the vector space model, one alternative is the **Latent Semantic Indexing** (LSI) model, which introduces a way to think of the IR problem based on the theory of singular value decomposition. This is the only alternative model that we discuss in this chapter. The main idea of LSI (Deerwester et al. 1990) is to map each document and query vector into a lower dimensional space representing the most important features. LSI is a technique where queries and documents are projected into a space with latent semantic dimensions associated with concepts. Latent implies that these semantic associations are inherent in document structure. Singular value decomposition is a mathematical technique applied to a word-by-document matrix. This method permits better judgements on word similarity, based on word co-occurrence. As seen in the other models such as the Boolean one, reducing the content of documents and queries based on a set of index terms can lead to poor retrieval performance. Many unrelated documents can figure among the retrieved answer set, and the documents whose indexes are not connected with the keywords of the query will not be retrieved. In other words, the notion of keywords or keyword sets causes negative effects. In document matching, one can think of the notion of concept rather than the one of index terms. This allows the retrieval of documents where the concept encompasses a set of terms and not just direct match with the keywords. LSI addresses this very notion of concept relatedness where each document and query are mapped into a dimensional space associated with concepts. This dimensional space is lower and retrieval is better than in the large space of keyword based index terms.

29.3 THE IMPACT OF NATURAL LANGUAGE PROCESSING ON INFORMATION RETRIEVAL

Text information retrieval and NLP have in common the textual material on which operations are performed but the nature of these operations is quite different. IR is concerned with efficient access to large amount of stored texts. Speed of access and indexing models are a major concern. NLP is concerned with text analysis, representation, or generation, and thus deploys a different set of computational tools to achieve linguistic processing at the morphological, lexical, syntactic, and semantic and discourse levels. There has been a considerable amount of interest in including information from computational linguistic techniques in IR research, at many different levels. The key challenge in incorporating this information is that any module added to an already existing system must be robust and capable of handling megabytes of information without slowing down the overall system.

Due to the complex stages of IR systems outlined in the previous section, it is not obvious at exactly which level of the system the NLP contribution should be made. For example, should these techniques be used to process queries, documents, or to improve matching techniques? Even within each of these stages, there are substages. Since existing systems are grounded in statistical methods, adding in symbolic information at later stages is often difficult from an architecture or design point of view. Finally, it is not always clear how to evaluate the results since standard evaluation metrics are biased towards statistical rather than qualitative improvements.

29.3.1 A historical view

Some of the earliest attempts at using NLP in information retrieval were highly ambitious. For example, rather than using terms, which are more or less atomic objects, some researchers proposed representing concepts (entities, events, and other notable relations) as complex structures that need to be compared using sophisticated algorithms (e.g. tree matching). Notable attempts at using compound phrasal terms in indexing or retrieval include Dillon and Gray (1983); Spärck Jones and Tait (1984); Smeaton and van Rijsbergen (1988); Metzler and Haas (1989); Ruge (1991). These early approaches were not properly evaluated, primarily due to the lack of suitable test collections prior to the first Text Retrieval Conference (TREC) in 1992. Nonetheless, the results were generally discouraging, either because the expected gain in retrieval accuracy did not materialize, or because of the complexity of the task itself. It is interesting to see that these past attempts fell into one of the following two categories: either the application of an advanced NLP system to a small-scale task, e.g. COP (Metzler et al. 1989), or FERRET (Mauldin 1991), or the use of a relatively shallow NLP technique applied to a larger task, e.g. CLARIT (Evans and Lefferts 1995). One of the first large-scale experiments used a fast, approximate parser to process the 2 GByte TREC collection in order to extract indexing phrases and other structural terms (Strzalkowski and Vauthey 1992). Another example was the DR-LINK system (Liddy and Myaeng 1993), which attempted semantic analysis to improve both precision and recall.

Other techniques which use some shallow linguistic processing include **information extraction** (IE). IE is a technology that identifies references in text to entities, such as people, places, and organizations, as well as to events involving these entities, e.g. corporate mergers, personnel changes, terrorist acts, etc. (see Chapter 30). Although IE research has been successful over the last decade, particularly in the USA under the DARPA TIPSTER program (1991 to 1998), attempts at using advanced IE techniques to identify better-quality indexing terms or to produce more effective queries have largely failed. Thus, the application of IE for information retrieval has been limited. For example, indexing by named entities may be useful in some cases, but since many search queries are not about names at all, the overall effect has been negligible (Guthrie et al. 1996). Similarly, attempts at using IE techniques for automatic query expansion showed only modest gains in retrieval accuracy (Bear et al. 1997).

29.3.2 Current approaches: improving indexing using morphological, phrasal, and syntactic information

Many NLP applications in IR focus on how to use linguistic techniques to obtain better indexing terms: phrases, entities, concepts, etc., what has been referred to as linguistically motivated indexing (LMI) (Spärck Jones 1999). In NLP, a phrase refers to a syntactically well-formed unit, such as a noun phrase, a prepositional phrase, or a verb phrase. The most frequently used phrases for research are noun phrases since they tend to capture entities and concepts. On the other hand, terms can be collocational groupings of words but are not necessarily syntactically well formed, and thus do not qualify as phrases. Beyond that, the IR process itself remains fundamentally unchanged. Specifically, the relevance of a document is still determined by its degree of overlap with the query. With LMI installed, there are simply more terms to compare. We may note that this has been a practical, incremental approach, but perhaps too constrained. Buckley et al. (1995) reported that adding simple collocations to the term list can increase retrieval by 10 per cent, so there is strong evidence that using phrases could improve retrieval performance.

A very comprehensive evaluation of NLP in IR was achieved by Fagan (1987), who used phrases obtained through a syntactic parser and statistical means to index documents in five different test collections. In his work, Fagan showed that phrases could improve retrieval by 2 per cent to 23 per cent depending on the query.

There has also been a great deal of work on harnessing morphological and syntactic variants of multi-word indexing terms to improve the accuracy of indexing based on compounds (see Chapter 33). The original research by Spärck Jones and Tait (1984) proposed generating phrase variants at indexing time. In Jacquemin and Tzoukermann (1999) and Tzoukermann, Klavans, and Jacquemin (1997), a morphosyntactic generator is presented to provide multi-word variants for index terms as well as query expansion. A part-of-speech tagger, a derivational morphological system, and a shallow parser are parts of the system. The authors show that the expansion and the conflation of terms increase indexing coverage up to 30 per cent with precision of nearly 90 per cent for correct identification of related terms. This line of enquiry has also been explored by commercial information providers

(Zhou 1999; Thompson and Dozier 1999), particularly in the context of retrieval of legal or medical documents, where phrases and their variants often offer key cues to finding related cases. Other methods to identify phrases for indexing are discussed in Wacholder, Klavans, and Evans (2000).

Smeaton (Smeaton and van Rijsbergen 1988; Sheridan and Smeaton 1992) has been working at two levels, i.e. the syntactic level and the use of NLP resources in IR (Smeaton 1999). Syntactic analysis is used to generate term dependencies as well as to produce structured representations between document terms. This tree-structure analysis (TSA) was tested on a number of collections used in different information retrieval systems, such as SMART at Cornell University (Salton 1971), an LSI-based retrieval system at Bellcore (Deerwester et al. 1990), and INQUERY at the University of Massachusetts (Callan, Croft, and Harding 1992). The conclusion of these experiments reports that the use of TSAs did not contribute to improvement in retrieval. Rather, the simple use of *TF*IDF* gave better results than the syntactic representation.

A thorough evaluation of NLP contribution to indexing has been conducted by Strzalkowski (1997) and his group using the Stream Model design. The Stream Model has been conceived to facilitate optimization of various text representation methods, including complex linguistic processing. In their approach, alternative methods of document indexing were first applied to the documents in the collection, resulting in a set of parallel indexes called streams. Streams were built using a mixture of different indexing techniques, term extracting, and weighting strategies, and could be accessed using different search engines. A stream would then be a particular way of representing document content. For example, in a phrase stream each document would be indexed only with the phrases (or phrases of particular kind) that were identified in its text. For some experiments seven, eight, or more streams were produced. The final results were obtained by merging ranked lists of documents obtained from searching all streams with appropriately preprocessed queries, i.e. a phrase query would be run against the phrase stream, a query containing names would be run against the names stream, etc. The merging process weighted contributions from each stream using a combination that was found the most effective in training runs. This allowed for an easy combination of alternative retrieval and routing methods, creating a meta-search strategy which maximizes the contribution of each stream.

29.3.3 Current approaches using semantic information

Beyond syntactic variants, research continues to exploit information stored in various thesauri and ontologies, both in general-purpose lexical databases like Princeton's WordNet (Fellbaum 1998), as well as those developed specifically to categorize knowledge in certain domains of trade and science, e.g. UMLS (National Library of Medicine 1995), SNOMED (Côté et al. 1993). Specialized ontologies usually work well for the purpose they were created, for example, UMLS or its various subsets are routinely used for indexing formal medical documentation (Friedman et al. 1994). Word-Net, conceived and created at Princeton University, has been a widely used resource in generic IR tasks. Unfortunately, formal evaluations revealed that in most cases the impact of this knowledge on query expansion has been negligible (Voorhees 1993). This is rather surprising considering that WordNet encodes a substantial amount of knowledge about language and word-to-word correlations, although expansion by WordNet tends to bring in many ambiguous terms. One possible explanation is that this knowledge is not being fully utilized. In a typical study with thesauri, word-to-word relations are used to facilitate query-to-document matching on correlated but non-identical descriptors. Terms in the query are expanded with their synonyms, hyponyms, hypernyms, etc. in order to increase the likelihood of a positive match. Experimental results show that while a positive impact of such expansion is sometimes seen (e.g. 'car' is a synonym of 'automobile'), it is largely nullified by negative side effects, for example wrong-sense usage (e.g. Automobile Association), too broad or too narrow interpretation, etc. Often, there is no effect at all, when no correlated terms exist in the thesaurus. This lack of coverage is actually a thorny problem: domain- or subject-specific relations are frequently missing from general-purpose thesauri, even though those would appear to be the most useful to have around.

Several researchers have explored semantic disambiguation and some of them have experimented in IR (Krovetz and Croft 1992; Voorhees 1993; Sanderson 1994; Schütze and Pedersen 1995; Schütze 1998). Even though early results tended to show small and not significant improvements, as discussed in Chapter 13, recent research has shown more promise. For example, in Schütze and Pedersen (1995), the algorithm for word-sense disambiguation is based on vector representation and is applied to the vector space information retrieval model. The approach to word sense is context dependent as opposed to a fixed number of senses per word and results show an improvement of 7 to 14 per cent in an IR task. The problem of determining the relatedness between queries and documents is often tackled by measuring the word similarity between them. One important issue is then to identify semantically related words so that they can be considered as synonyms and treated as a single term in later computation. Jing and Tzoukermann (1999) improve retrieval performance by using semantic distance between words coupled with morphological relations. Their method computes relative semantic distance of words in contexts rather than determining the absolute sense of a word in a specific context. Words are correlated based on both their morphological relationship and their semantic distance, which is computed from local context (over a window of ten words) as well as lexical co-occurrence in a corpus. The semantic distance between words uses the local contexts of words within a single document as well as the lexical co-occurrence information in the set of documents to be retrieved. Using the standard vector space model, the method is evaluated on a subset of TREC-4 corpus and results show an improvement in precision of 8.6 per cent.

29.3.4 Outlook for the future

Why have these 'obvious' NLP techniques not thus far succeeded in improving IR to the degree that is useful in working systems? It seems that for what IR does, NLP techniques in their current implementations are either too weak to have a measurable impact (e.g. syntax, thesauri), or else are too expensive to be cost effective (e.g. information extraction, discourse analysis). In fact, Mitra et al. (1997) demonstrated that a well-executed term weighting scheme could largely outdo any performance gains that may be attributed to linguistic techniques. On the other hand, recent results with full-text query expansion techniques (Strzalkowski, Wang, and Wise 1998) suggest that a highly specific and sometimes redundant query is far more effective than any linguistically motivated indexing scheme. Similarly, there has been very little contribution in the area of **cross-language information retrieval**, i.e. the ability to query a collection written in several languages with a query in just one source language, and then to present information to users in a chosen language. Multilingual information access is further discussed in Chapter 38 of this book.

In full-text query expansion, either for monolingual search or multilingual search, a user query could be treated as a probe to obtain more data with which to build a better query, using text fragments or terms selected from some of the retrieved documents. This simple technique appears remarkably effective if the following conditions are met: (1) the text added to the query is indeed 'topical' and (2) it adds a new relevant aspect or relevant terms not already in the query. The problem is, of course, that these conditions have been hard to satisfy without a human in the loop. However, this may be where the advanced NLP methods can eventually make a difference.

Looking further ahead, we are likely to see a convergence of query manipulation approaches and advanced human–computer interaction at the core of the next generation of information retrieval systems, including sophisticated techniques for presentation of results to users. Information retrieval systems we have today were designed to facilitate self-service access to information, without having to involve a human librarian or a domain expert. This has made information easily accessible to everyone, but it also placed the burden of extracting the right content squarely upon the user and upon the system that processes user queries. In other words, it is no longer sufficient to know what question to ask, but now one has to know how to ask it, and moreover one has to decide if the answer is indeed acceptable. The self-service environment may be contrasted with one where a domain expert answers questions posed by students or customers. An expert is highly motivated and it is his or her job to help the customer quickly and efficiently. Clearly, a dialogue is a preferred form of interaction: both the caller and the expert negotiate an understanding of what needs and can be done, so that a consensus is reached and the right information is given out. This approach is significantly more efficient than the self-service IR paradigm, but it is also far more expensive, if human experts are to be used. On the other hand, an automated dialogue system, integrated with an efficient and accurate search engine, may be able to deliver the desired functionality, at least in some less complex cases. This requires significant advances in human–computer dialogue and sophisticated natural language processing technology at the core of this dialogue.

FURTHER READING, RELEVANT RESOURCES, AND RELATED TECHNOLOGIES

In recognition of the need to encourage research, several agencies in the United States sponsored extensive IR testing and comparison programs. One of the best known of these is the **Text Retrieval Conference (TREC)** (see http://trec.nist.gov/) which arose from the TIPSTER program (see http://www.itl.nist.gov/iaui/894.02/ related_projects/tipster_summac/) running from 1991 to 1998 and covering three technology areas: (1) document detection, (2) information extraction, and (3) summarization. The document detection track in TIPSTER emphasized the capability of a system to locate documents containing the type of information the user wants, either from a static collection or from a dynamic stream. The Text Retrieval Conference (TREC) was initiated in 1992 in the United States by the National Institute of Standards and Technology (NIST) and by the Defense Advanced Research Projects Agency (DARPA). The TREC program was initially started to develop measurement techniques for the document detection track of TIPSTER. As such, the focus was on processing large text collections in English. In later years, retrieval has been extended to Chinese, Japanese, and then to European languages. Extension to other languages such as Tamil and Malay may well continue to push the development of cross-language information retrieval even more. There are now numerous European organizations and institutions taking part in these benchmarks, such as **Cross-Language Evaluation Forum (CLEF)** (http://galileo.iei.pi.cnr.it/DELOS/CLEF/clef.html), and the international growth in cross-lingual and multilingual information retrieval is likely to increase further in the near term. The TIDES program (Translingual Information Detection, Extraction, and Summarization) of DARPA, started in 2000, has given a boost to new projects in multilingual information access, using both linguistic and non-linguistic methods for retrieval and presentation.

Two related technologies include text categorization and question answering. **Text categorization** refers to technologies to determine whether a document is a member of a given category. Categories can range from deciding domain (e.g. medical or legal domain), to genre (news vs. journal article), or to finer-grained categories (if medical news, cardiology vs. dermatology). The relationship between text categorization and NLP in IR relates to the use of phrases as a feature in categorization (see the Workshop on Learning for Text Categorization (AAAI-98) http://robotics.stanford.edu/ sahami/aaai98/program.html, as well as Joachims and Sebastiani 2001).

Question-answering (QA) systems involve techniques to search a document or document set for a specific answer to a given question. In this case, the answer may lie in a minor passage of an article, rather than being the major theme. In addition, the complexity of this task lies in returning only the relevant passage; thus QA is related to passage retrieval rather than full document retrieval (see Chapter 31 for a detailed discussion on QA).

References

Bear, J., D. Israel, J. Petit, and D. Martin. 1997. 'Using information extraction to improve document retrieval'. *Proceedings of the 6th Text REtrieval Conference (TREC-6)* (Washington), 367–77.

Belkin, N. J. and W. B. Croft. 1987. 'Retrieval techniques'. In M. Williams (ed.), *Annual Review of Information Science and Technology*. New York: Elsevier Science, 109–45.

Buckley, C., G. Salton, J. Allan, and A. Singhal. 1995. 'Automatic query expansion using SMART: TREC-3'. *Proceedings of the 3rd Text REtrieval Conference (TREC-3)* (Gaithersburg, Md.), 69–80.

Callan, J. P., W. B. Croft, and S. M. Harding. 1992. 'The INQUERY retrieval system'. *Proceedings of the 3rd International Conference on Database and Expert Systems Applications* (Valencia), 78–83.

Côté, A. R., D. J. Rothwell, R. S. Beckett, J. L. Palotay, and L. Brochu (eds.). 1993. *SNOMED International: The Systematized Nomenclature of Human and Veterinary Medicine*. Northfield, Ill.: College of American Pathologists.

Deerwester, S., S. T. Dumais, G. Furnas, T. K. Landauer, and R. Harshman. 1990. 'Indexing by latent semantic analysis'. *Journal of the American Society for Information Science*, 41(6), 391–407.

Dillon, M. and A. S. Gray. 1983. 'FASIT: a fully automatic syntactically based indexing system'. *Journal of the American Society for Information Science*, 34(2), 99–108.

Evans, D. A. and R. G. Lefferts. 1995. 'CLARIT-TREC experiments'. *Information Processing and Management*, 31(3), 385–95.

Fagan, J. L. 1987. 'Automatic phrase indexing for document retrieval: an examination of syntactic and non-syntactic methods'. *Proceedings of the 10th Annual International ACM SIGIR Conference on Research and Development in Information Retrieval (SIGIR '87)* (New Orleans), 97–101.

Fellbaum, C. 1998. 'The organization of verbs and verb concepts in a semantic net'. In P. St-Dizier (ed.), *Predicative Forms in Natural Language and Lexical Knowledge Bases*. Dordrecht: Kluwer, 93–109.

Frakes, W. and R. Baeza-Yates (eds.). 1992. *Information Retrieval: Data Structures and Algorithms*. Englewood Cliffs, NJ: Prentice Hall.

Friedman, C., P. O. Alderson, J. H. M. Austin, J. J. Cimino, and S. B. Johnson. 1994. 'A general natural language text processor for clinical radiology'. *Journal of the American Medical Informatics Association*, 1(2), 161–74.

Guthrie, L., F. Lin, T. Strzalkowski, and J. Wang. 1996. 'Integration of document detection and information extraction'. In *Advances in Text Processing: TIPSTER Program Phase II*. Plainsboro, NJ: Morgan Kaufmann, 167–78.

Harman, D. 1991. 'How effective is suffixing?' *Journal of the American Society for Information Science*, 42(1), 7–15.

Hull, D. A. 1996. 'Stemming algorithms: a case study for detailed evaluation'. *Journal of the American Society for Information Science*, 47(1), 70–84.

Jacquemin, C. and E. Tzoukermann. 1999. 'NLP for term variant extraction: synergy between morphology, lexicon and syntax'. In T. Strzalkowski (ed.), *Natural Language Information Retrieval*. Dordrecht: Kluwer, 25–70.

Jing, H. and E. Tzoukermann. 1999. 'Information retrieval based on context distance and morphology'. *Proceedings of the 22nd Annual International ACM SIGIR Conference on Research and Development in Information Retrieval (SIGIR '99)* (Seattle), 92–6.

Joachims, T. and F. Sebastiani (eds.). 2002. Special issue on automated text categorization. *Journal of Intelligent Information Systems*, 2.

Krovetz, R. 1993. 'Viewing morphology as an inference process'. *Proceedings of the 16th Annual International ACM SIGIR Conference on Research and Development in Information Retrieval (SIGIR '93)* (Pittsburgh), 191–202.

——and W. B. Croft. 1992. 'Lexical ambiguity and information retrieval'. *ACM Transactions on Information Systems*, 10(2), 115–41.

Liddy, D. E. and S. H. Myaeng. 1993. 'DR-LINK: a system update for TREC-2'. *Proceedings of the 2nd Text REtrieval Conference (TREC-2)*, (Gaithersburg, Md.), 85–100.

Lovins, J. B. 1968. 'Development of a stemming algorithm'. *Translation and Computational Linguistics*, 11(1), 22–31.

Mauldin, M. 1991. 'Retrieval performance in Ferret: a conceptual information retrieval system'. *Proceedings of the 14th Annual International ACM SIGIR Conference on Research and Development in Information Retrieval (SIGIR '91)* (Chicago), 347–55.

Metzler, D. P. and S. W. Haas. 1989. 'The constituent object parser: syntactic structure matching for information retrieval'. *ACM Transactions on Information Systems*, 7(3), 292–316.

——C. L. Cosic, and L. H. Wheeler. 1989. 'Constituent object parsing for information retrieval and similar text processing problems'. *Journal of the American Society for Information Science*, 40(6), 398–423.

Mitra, M., C. Buckley, A. Singhal, and C. Cardie. 1997. 'An analysis of statistical and syntactic phrases'. *Proceedings of RIAO-97 Conference* (Paris), 200–14.

National Library of Medicine. 1995. *UMLS Lexicon and Metathesaurus Manual and CD-ROM*. Bethesda, Md.

Paice, C. D. 1996. 'Method for evaluation of stemming algorithms based on error counting'. *Journal of the American Society for Information Science*, 47(8), 632–49.

Porter, M. F. 1980. 'An algorithm for suffix stripping'. *Program*, 14, 130–7.

Riloff, E. 1995. 'Little words can make a big difference for text classification'. *Proceedings of the 18th Annual International ACM SIGIR Conference on Research and Development in Information Retrieval (SIGIR '95)* (Seattle), 130–6.

Robertson, S. E. and K. Spärck Jones. 1976. 'Relevance weighting of search terms'. *Journal of the American Society for Information Science*, 27, 129–46.

Ruge, G. 1991. 'Experiments on linguistically based term associations'. *Proceedings of RIAO '91* (Barcelona), 2–5.

Salton, G. (ed.). 1971. The *SMART Retrieval System: Experiments in Automatic Document Processing*. Englewood Cliffs, NJ.: Prentice Hall.

——and M. E. Lesk. 1968. 'Computer evaluation of indexing and text processing'. *Journal of the ACM*, 15(1), 8–36.

Salton, G. and M. McGill. 1983. *Introduction to Modern Information Retrieval.* New York: McGraw Hill.

Sanderson, M. 1994. 'Word-sense disambiguation and information retrieval'. *Proceedings of the 17th Annual International ACM SIGIR Conference on Research and Development in Information Retrieval (SIGIR '94)* (Dublin), 142–51.

Schütze, H. 1998. 'Automatic word sense discrimination'. *Computational Linguistics*, 24(1), 97–124.

——and J. O. Pedersen. 1995. 'Information retrieval based on word senses'. *Symposium on Document Analysis and Information Retrieval (SDAIR)* (Las Vegas, Nev.), 161–75.

Sheridan, P. and A. F. Smeaton. 1992. 'The application of morpho-syntactic language processing to effective phrase matching'. *Information Processing and Management*, 28(3), 349–69.

Smeaton, A. F. 1999. 'Using NLP or NLP resources for information retrieval tasks'. In T. Strzalkowski (ed.), *Natural Language Information Retrieval.* Dordrecht: Kluwer, 99–109.

——and C. J. van Rijsbergen. 1988. 'Experiments in incorporating syntactic processing of user queries into a document retrieval strategy'. *Proceedings of the 11th Annual International ACM SIGIR Conference on Research and Development in Information Retrieval (SIGIR '88)* (Grenoble), 31–51.

Spärck Jones, K. 1999. 'What is the role for NLP in text retrieval'. In T. Strzalkowski (ed.), *Natural Language Information Retrieval.* Dordrecht: Kluwer, 1–21.

——and J. I. Tait. 1984. 'Automatic search term variant generation'. *Journal of Documentation*, 40(1), 50–66.

Strzalkowski, T. and B. Vauthey. 1992. 'Information retrieval using robust natural language processing'. *Proceedings of the 30th Annual Meeting of the Association for Computational Linguistics (ACL '92)* (Newark, Del.), 104–11.

——J. Wang, and B. Wise. 1998. 'Summarization-based query expansion in information retrieval'. *Proceedings of the 19th International Conference on Computational Linguistics and the 32nd Annual Meeting of the Association for Computational Linguistics* (Montreal), 1258–14.

——L. Guthrie, J. Karlgren, J. Leistensnider, F. Lin, J. Perez-Carballo, T. Straszheim, J. Wang, and J. Wilding. 1997. 'Natural language information retrieval: TREC-5 Report'. In D. Harman (ed.), *Proceedings of the 5th Text REtrieval Conference (TREC-5)* (Gaithersburg, Md.), 291–314.

Thompson, P. and C. Dozier. 1999. 'Name recognition and retrieval performance'. In T. Strzalkowski (ed.), *Natural Language Information Retrieval.* Dordrecht: Kluwer, 261–72.

Tzoukermann, E., J. L. Klavans, and C. Jacquemin. 1997. 'Effective use of natural language processing techniques for automatic conflation of multi-word terms: the role of derivational morphology, part of speech tagging, and shallow parsing'. *Proceedings of the 20th Annual International ACM SIGIR Conference on Research and Development in Information Retrieval (SIGIR '97)* (Philadelphia), 148–55.

Voorhees, E. 1993. 'Using WordNet to disambiguate words senses for text retrieval'. *Proceedings of the 16th Annual International ACM SIGIR Conference on Research and Development in Information Retrieval (SIGIR '93)* (Pittsburgh), 171–80.

Wacholder, N., J. L. Klavans, and D. K. Evans. 2000. 'Evaluation of automatically identified index terms for browsing electronic documents'. *Proceedings of ANLP-NAACL 2000* (Seattle), s. 1, 302–9.

Zhou, J. 1999. 'Phrasal terms in real-world IR applications'. In T. Strzalkowski (ed.), *Natural Language Information Retrieval.* Dordrecht: Kluwer, 215–57.

CHAPTER 30

INFORMATION EXTRACTION

RALPH GRISHMAN

ABSTRACT

Information extraction is the automatic identification of selected types of entities, relations, or events in free text. This chapter considers two types of extraction: extraction of
names and extraction of events. In each case, an approach to writing extraction rules is
presented. In addition, methods are described for learning extraction rules (or statistical
models) automatically from text corpora which have been annotated with information
about the names or the events they contain.

Information extraction (IE) is the automatic identification of selected types of
entities, relations, or events in free text. It covers a wide range of tasks, from finding all
the company names in a text, to finding all the murders, including who killed whom,
when, and where. Such capabilities are increasingly important for sifting through the
enormous volumes of on-line text for the specific information which is required.

This chapter will look at two of the more intensively studied IE tasks, that of **name
identification and classification**,[1] and that of **event extraction**.

---

[1] Also referred to as **named entity recognition**.

30.1 Name Identification and Classification

In conventional treatments of language structure, little attention is paid to proper names, addresses, quantity phrases, etc. Presentations of language analysis typically begin by looking words up in a dictionary and identifying them as nouns, verbs, adjectives, etc. In fact, however, most texts include lots of names, and if a system cannot identify these as linguistic units (and, for most tasks, identify their type), it will be hard pressed to produce a linguistic analysis of the text.

Different sorts of names predominate in different types of texts. Chemistry articles will contain names of chemicals. Biology articles will contain names of species, of proteins, of genes. General newspaper articles will include names of people, organizations, and locations (among others). We will use as our example this last task—finding people, organization, and location names—since it has been extensively studied by several groups.[2] The results of the name classification process are typically shown as an SGML mark-up of the text, using <NAME TYPE = xx> at the beginning of a name and </NAME> at the end. Thus the sentence

(30.1) Capt. Andrew Ahab was appointed vice president of the Great White Whale Company of Salem, Massachusetts.

would be annotated as

(30.2) Capt. <NAME TYPE=PERSON>Andrew Ahab</NAME> was appointed vice president of the <NAME TYPE=ORGANIZATION>Great White Whale Company </NAME> of <NAME TYPE=LOCATION>Salem</NAME>, <NAME TYPE= LOCATION>Massachusetts</NAME>.

30.1.1 Building a name tagger

The basic idea for such classification is quite simple: we write a large number of finite-state (regular) patterns (section 18.2), each of which captures and classifies some subset of names. The elements in these patterns would match specific tokens or classes of tokens with particular features. We use standard regular-expression notation, and in particular use the suffix '+' to match one or more instances of an element. For example, the pattern

capitalized-word+ 'Corp.'

---

[2] This task was used in several multi-site system evaluations, including Message Understanding Conferences 6 and 7 in the United States, and (with some extensions) the IREX evaluation in Japan.

finds all company names consisting of one or more capitalized words followed by 'Corp.' (Corporation). Such a sequence would be classified as an organization name. Similarly, the pattern

'Mr.' *capitalized-word+*

would match sequences beginning with Mr., which would be classified as person names. To build a complete classifier, we would assemble a program which tokenizes the text, and then, starting at each word of the text, tries to match all the patterns; if one succeeds, the sequence of words is classified and the process continues past the matched sequence. If several patterns match starting at a given point, rules must be included to choose a best match, typically by preferring the longest match and by assigning priorities to different rules.

Developing a high-quality classifier requires a systematic approach. Typically, this involves the preparation of a substantial corpus annotated by hand with names, and a program to compare the output of the classifier against the hand-annotated corpus. After a few basic patterns have been coded, this comparison process will point out other patterns which are helpful. For example, it may suggest that the pattern

capitalized-word+ ',' *number-below–100* ','

can be used to classify the capitalized words as a person name (as in the example 'Fred Smith, 42, was appointed chief dogcatcher.').

A high-performance system will need a set of word lists, including for example lists of well-known corporations ('IBM', 'Ford'), and lists of common first names ('Fred', 'Susan'). In addition, it should incorporate a mechanism for recognizing different aliases; for example, that 'Fred Smith' and 'Mr. Smith', appearing in the same article, probably refer to the same person. This can be useful in situations where some forms of a name cannot be unambiguously tagged. Thus 'Robert Smith Park' might refer to a person or a location (a park), but if the next sentence refers to 'Mr. Park' it is safe to say that 'Robert Smith Park' is a person.

30.1.2 Automated training

By systematically adding such patterns and features, it is possible to develop a high-performance name tagger.[3] However, this is a laborious process requiring a skilled system developer. As the need arises for taggers for multiple languages and multiple

---

[3] Several multi-site evaluations have been done for named entity taggers, applied to news text. The best-performing systems for English achieved an accuracy of about 96 per cent when trained and tested on news about a specific topic, and about 93 per cent when trained on news about one topic and tested on news about a different topic.

domains (with different name types), several groups have investigated the possibility of training such taggers automatically. In general, such approaches seek to learn statistical models or symbolic rules for the different classes of names, using a hand-annotated text corpus.

To see how such training could work, let us consider a simpler task, in which we only tag people's names. Each token will then be either: the start of a name, the middle of a name, the end of a name, the start and end of a one-token name, or not part of a name; stated as a word-tagging problem, each word w_i can be assigned one of these five tags tag_i. We can then create a simple probabilistic model for this task, in which we determine (based on the training corpus) the probability that any particular word should get one of these tags: $P(tag_i|w_i)$. For example, if w_i = 'John', there would be a significant probability that the token would be the start of a name or a one-token name, whereas if w_i = 'eat' both these probabilities would be (nearly) zero. Given a new sentence, we first compute the $P(tag_i)$ independently for each token. Then we search for the most probable consistent sequence of tags using a Viterbi search (see Chapter 19, sections 19.3, 19.5.1). This in turn determines how we shall tag the names in the sentence.

Having the probability of a tag depend only on the current word, however, is inadequate. As we noted earlier, the word 'Mr.' is a good clue that the following word is (or starts) a person's name; similarly, the word 'says' suggests that the previous word is (or ends) a person's name. This would lead us to a more detailed model, in which a tag probability depends on the preceding, current, and following words: $P(tag_i|w_{i-1},w_i,w_{i+1})$. However, completely training such a model is unrealistic: we will not see all combinations of three words in our training corpus (and in fact we might want to base our probabilities on even more information, requiring even more data). Different name taggers have taken different approaches to combining evidence without requiring enormous amounts of training data.

In a decision-tree name tagger, a sequence of tests—organized in a tree—are made at each token, and the results of these tests determine the probabilities of the various tags (Sekine, Grishman, and Shinnou 1998). These tests may involve the identity of the previous, current, or following word, or features such as capitalization. The tree is built automatically from the training corpus. In effect, the decision tree associates probabilities with conjunctions of conditions. However, not all possible conjoined conditions are included; rather, only those which appeared in the training corpus and had a significant effect on tag probabilities are selected. Once the probabilities are computed, the Viterbi algorithm is used to select the most probable sequence of tags.

A maximum-entropy (ME) model (Borthwick et al. 1998; Mikheev and Grover 1998) computes the individual contributions of each piece of evidence (e.g. the previous word, the current word) separately, and then combines them multiplicatively (section 19.4 of this volume). It thus assumes that they can contribute independently to the final probability. This can be valuable for name tagging if two clues appeared separately in the training data, but are later seen together. Suppose, for example, we have seen 'Mitkov' as a family name in the training data, and also (separately) several instances of the pattern '*person* says'. Then in our ME model the fact that the current word is 'Mitkov' and the fact that the next word is 'says' would both increase the probability that the current word is the end of a person's name. If we now encounter the phrase 'Mitkov says', both of these factors will contribute to the probability. In contrast, if we have not seen this combination in the training data, the decision-tree system will only be able to make use of one of these two facts; this has limited the performance of decision-tree systems.

In addition, it is possible to assist automated learning methods by writing special patterns to capture combinations of elements which might not be learned automatically, and making an instance of each pattern a new condition. This new condition would then be assigned the appropriate weight by the maximum-entropy method, along with the more conventional conditions. In this way, maximum entropy can be used as an automatically trained method, and then can be enhanced by manual pattern writing.

Hidden Markov models (HMMs) (section 19.3) have also been used successfully for name recognition (Bikel et al. 1997). The basic idea is to create separate statistical models of each type of name—a person name model, an organization name model, a location name model—as well as a model for word sequences which are not names. We then build a combined model, incorporating probabilities for moving from one language model (type of name) to another. Then, as in other probabilistic models, we use a Viterbi search to seek the most probable sequence of name labels.

All of these models require substantial amounts of annotated data for good performance. This has not been a major hurdle because name tags can be annotated quite rapidly, and most text has lots of examples of names. However, it is possible to build a tagger with modest performance with a minimal amount of hand tagging, using a bootstrapping approach. In this approach, one begins with a small set of known names and a large amount of (untagged) text. Name-internal features are identified from these known names, while occurrences of these names in the text are used to identify contextual clues. These clues can be used to find additional names, leading to a refinement of the clues in an iterative process (Strzalkowski and Wang 1996; Cucerzan and Yarowsky 1999; Collins and Singer 1999).

30.1.3 Using a name tagger

Most texts are replete with names. As a result, name tagging and classification is an important first step for most types of language analysis, such as event extraction (described below), parsing, and machine translation. In machine translation, the failure to recognize a sequence of words as a name, and the resulting attempt to translate the individual words, is a frequent source of translation errors.

Name recognition can be valuable for term-based document retrieval. In general, if a user's information request is a pair of words, we may look for each term separately in a sentence or document. However, if the pair is a name, we would require that the words appear consecutively in a document. A name recognizer can also be used to create a (partial) index for a document, since many of the important index terms will be names. Such an index will be particularly valuable if the names are classified into people, organizations, locations, etc. For example, one could create an index of all the companies mentioned in a day's news—a valuable feature for someone wishing to scan the news quickly.

30.2 Event Extraction

We now consider a more complex task: extracting all the instances of a particular type of relationship or event from text. For example, we may have a file of seminar announcements and want to build a table listing the speaker, title, date, time, and location of each seminar. This is fairly straightforward because most announcements cover a single talk, and the structure and format of such announcements is quite stylized (repetitive). As another example, we may want to scan newspaper articles and extract information on executives starting or leaving management positions. We will follow this latter example, which was the subject of a recent multi-site evaluation. If given the text

(30.3) Harriet Smith, vice president of Ford Motor Corp., has been appointed president of DaimlerChryslerToyota.

we would want to generate two database records:

```
Person: Harriet Smith
Position: vice president
Company: Ford Motor Corp.
Start/leave job: leave job
```

```
Person: Harriet Smith
Position: president
Company: DaimlerChryslerToyota
Start/leave job: start job
```

In IE terminology, we have produced two filled templates (database entries) from this text.

30.2.1 Event recognizers

How shall we go about this task? Mimicking the approach taken for name tagging, we can write a series of regular expressions specifically designed to capture the events of interest. Thus we may write a pattern

*capitalized-word+*₁ 'appointed' *capitalized-word+*₂ 'as' 'president'₃

and associate it with the template

```
Person: 2
Position: 3
Company: 1
Start/leave job: start job
```

Numbered items in the template would be filled with the words which match the associated numbered pattern elements. This pattern would handle a straightforward sentence like

(30.4) Ford appointed Harriet Smith as president.

However, it would not get us very far with real text, because the range of variation of possible sentences is so great. There are variations involving

- Company names: Abercrombie and Fitch appointed Harriet Smith as president.
- Company descriptors (and other company modifiers): IBM, the famous computer manufacturer, appointed Harriet Smith as president.
- Sentence modifiers: IBM unexpectedly appointed Harriet Smith yesterday as president.
- Tense: IBM has appointed/will appoint Harriet Smith as president.
- Clause structure: Harriet Smith was appointed president by IBM. Harriet Smith, who was appointed president by IBM, . . .
- Nominalization: IBM announced the appointment of Harriet Smith as president.
- Position names: IBM appointed Harriet Smith as executive vice president for networking.
- Conjunction: IBM declared a special dividend and appointed Harriet Smith as president.
- Anaphoric reference: IBM has made a major management shuffle; the company appointed Harriet Smith as president this week.
- Need for inference: Thomas J. Watson resigned as president of IBM, and Harriet Smith succeeded him.

In principle, each of these phenomena (except for anaphora and inference) can be handled by suitable additions to the event patterns, but the net result will be very complex patterns. This complexity can be reduced by recognizing that most of these problems reflect general linguistic phenomena, and should be attacked by general solutions.

30.2.2 Partial parsing

Some of these problems can be addressed by recognizing some types of constituents, and then stating the patterns in terms of these constituents. In particular, the examples above suggest that we should recognize at least names (of people and organizations), (some) noun phrases, and some sentence modifiers. Names can be recognized by a name tagger, as has been described above. While recognizing noun phrases in general is a difficult problem, a limited range of noun phrases can be recognized deterministically. In particular, noun groups (nouns with their left modifiers) can be recognized quite reliably, as well as some modifiers such as the apposition in the second example above. Noun group recognition is an example of partial or shallow parsing (section 12.1).

Variations in tense can be handled by recognizing 'appointed', 'has appointed', and 'will appoint' as instances of verb groups. These can also be recognized deterministically by straightforward patterns. In this way we have moved from a simple pattern matcher to a sequence or 'cascade' of pattern matchers, in which each stage of pattern matching generates constituent structure which can be used by the next stage (Appelt et al. 1993).

The action of a pattern would be to create a constituent which spanned one or more tokens; this constituent would have a *category* and one or more *features*. Patterns in stages after the first would include pattern elements which could match such constituents and test some of their features. The final stage of patterns would recognize events and generate event constituents whose features correspond to the database slots shown earlier.

A minimal system would have stages which create name, noun phrase, verb group, and event constituents. Names would have a *type* feature, with value *person*, *org*, or *location*. Noun phrases and verb groups would have a *head* feature, indicating the headword of the phrase; if the head is a name, we will use the type feature of the name. (Our simple system can afford to ignore noun and verb modifiers and tense information.) The stages would operate in sequence:

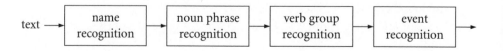

To see how this would work, consider a simple example:

(30.5) Ford Motor Company has appointed Harriet Smith, 45, as president.

Name tagging will produce the constituents (shown inside boxes):

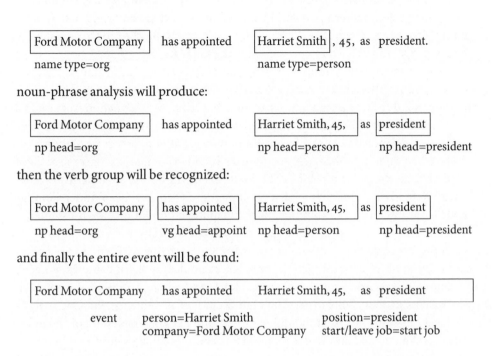

This is, in effect, a bottom-up parser, but one which operates deterministically and only produces partial syntactic analyses. We have restricted ourselves, in general, to constructs which can be identified unambiguously from local information. As a result, it can be more efficient than parsers which perform backtracking or follow multiple hypotheses.

30.2.3 Addressing other problems

Two approaches have been tried to handle variations in clause structure, so that active clauses, passive clauses, relative clauses, etc. can all be recognized without explicitly writing separate patterns for each variation. One approach extends the parsing a step further, to the level of clauses, and then produces a uniform structure for the different types of clauses. This would then be matched against patterns which explicitly specify syntactic roles such as subject and object. The difficulty with this approach is that clause structure cannot be analysed using syntactic information alone; semantic information has to be introduced into the parsing in order to make the correct attachment decisions. The alternative approach uses *metarules* which, given a pattern for a simple active clause, produce the patterns for other clause structures (passive, relative). For example, given the pattern *company* 'hired' *person*, it would produce the (passive) pattern *person* 'was' 'hired' 'by' *company*.

To handle anaphoric references we need to incorporate an anaphora resolution mechanism (see Chapter 14). A minimal resolution mechanism would take an anaphoric reference in a template ('it', 'the company'), search for the most recent item of the same type, and make the replacement in the template.

As shown by the last example, involving 'succeed', we also require some mechanism for performing inference, to handle situations where a management change cannot be understood from one sentence in isolation, but requires information from several sentences in the text. For most extraction systems, only a few inferences are performed, and these are handled by specialized rules, performed after reference resolution.

The techniques described here are quite restricted in comparison to some of those discussed elsewhere in this volume. There have been a number of attempts to use more powerful analysis techniques—what could be described as a 'deep understanding' model—for information extraction. Such an approach might include full-sentence syntactic analysis, generation of a general-purpose logical representation, and the use of theorem-proving or other general inference mechanisms. Particular examples can be found which warrant such an approach: examples involving complex syntactic structures, or requiring subtle inference. However, such approaches have not been very successful. Our ability to perform high-accuracy full-sentence syntactic analysis has been (at least until recently) quite limited, and our understanding of the inference mechanisms and knowledge required for general language understanding is still poor. So these deep understanding systems, while working well on selected difficult examples, have not performed very well in general.

The use (by most IE system developers) of simpler language analysis tools can be seen as an example of appropriate language engineering, where we select the tools suitable to the task. IE is a more restricted problem than general language understanding, and most cases can be handled through the use of simple, reliable language analysis, such as name and noun group recognizers. As more powerful high-accuracy tools become available, such as corpus-trained full-sentence analysers, it will be reasonable to incorporate them into IE systems.

30.2.4 Learning methods

For each new relation or event class to be extracted, a new extraction system has to be developed, with new patterns and possibly semantic classes and inference rules. Because this is a time-consuming task requiring considerable skill, there has been great interest in at least partially automating this process.

As in the case of name tagging, much of the research has been focused on creating systems automatically or semi-automatically from hand-annotated corpora. This typically involves creating extraction patterns from annotated examples, and then generalizing these patterns. For example, if given the sentence

(30.6) Newsweek reported that Frugal Footwear Inc. has appointed Neil Armstrong as executive vice president.

along with the desired output

person	Neil Armstrong
position	executive vice president
company	Frugal Footwear Inc.
start/leave job	start job

the system would begin by applying the three stages of syntactic analysis described above to identify the names, the noun phrases, and the verb groups in the sentence:

Newsweek	noun phrase	head = company
reported	verb group	head = report
that		
Frugal Footwear Inc.	noun phrase	head = company
has appointed	verb group	head = appoint
Neil Armstrong	noun phrase	head = person
as		
executive vice president	noun phrase	head = president

Suppose each constituent is mapped into a corresponding pattern element which matches a noun or verb group with that head, or to a literal pattern element:

noun phrase	head = company
verb group	head = report
'that'	
noun phrase	head = company
verb group	head = appoint
noun phrase	head = person
'as'	
noun phrase	head = president

In a semi-automated system, the user may be asked to review the generated pattern, either to accept or reject it, or to generalize it. For example, in the PET system (Yangarber and Grishman 1997) the user is able to delete irrelevant elements, to mark elements as optional, or to generalize noun phrases with respect to a semantic hierarchy. In this case, the user would delete the first three elements, deciding that 'Newsweek reported that' is not essential to filling the template. The user could also replace 'head = "president"' with 'head $\in$ positions', where *positions* is a word class of executive positions.

A more automated system may try to make these generalizations from multiple annotated examples. If the text also contains the sentence 'In other news, Costly Clogs Inc. has appointed Imelda Marcos yesterday as executive vice president.' such a system could build a pattern from each example and determine the minimum common pattern. If this pattern does not produce any 'false hits'—generate filled templates for sentences which should not produce templates—it can be accepted as a suitable generalization. Similarly, if the two examples differ in one position, and the two words are members of the same word class, one can merge the examples, generalizing to the word class, and check for false hits. Several pilot systems have been created which use such machine learning methods to build event extraction systems from annotated texts. These include both symbolic learning methods and methods for acquiring probabilistic rules. These learning methods are discussed in more detail in section 20.6.6.

Learning procedures can also be helpful in identifying examples to annotate. A straightforward approach is simply to annotate a large amount of consecutive text. This, however, is not efficient because a small number of patterns occur again and again; annotating them 100 times does not help the learning procedure learn these patterns any better. The goal in annotating a large amount of data is to find examples of less frequent patterns, and more generally to find examples which will help the learning process. 'Active learning' procedures can help in this effort. One way is by finding examples which 'almost match' a pattern. In the case illustrated above, we could look for patterns of the form *company __ person as president*, which could locate examples with other verbs such as 'name' or 'select'.

Approaches based on the distribution of patterns across documents have proven effective at finding relevant patterns with minimal user assistance. Riloff (1996) introduced a method in which documents are only marked as relevant or irrelevant to the extraction task. Word patterns which occur much more frequently in relevant documents proved to be good candidates for extraction patterns. Yangarber extended this to a bootstrapping method which does not require any corpus annotation. The user provides some initial patterns; these are used to find relevant documents, and then in turn more extraction patterns (Yangarber et al. 2000).

Automated learning procedures have proven effective in extraction from semi-structured text, such as classified ads, announcements, and other material with a regular, repetitive structure. For more complex extraction tasks on free text, where there is greater linguistic variation, they have had some success, but so far are not able to create complete extraction systems comparable in performance to manually developed systems.

30.2.5 Evaluation

US Government-sponsored evaluations have played a significant role in the development of this field, particularly in the United States (Cowie and Lehnert 1996; Grishman and Sundheim 1996). These evaluations, the Message Understanding Conferences (MUCs), have provided a regular assessment of the state of the art, and encouraged some of the developments in the field, such as the use of partial parsing and statistical training methods. The **named entity task**, introduced with MUC-6 in 1995, has set a model for similar evaluations in other languages.

As noted earlier, systems have achieved a high level of performance on the named entity task, and performance has also improved on somewhat more complex tasks, such as finding all the names and descriptions of a person or organization in a document. However, performance has not significantly improved to date on the MUC event extraction tasks, which in general have been significantly more complex than the example shown above.[4] This probably reflects the greater linguistic variation in event descriptions (requiring more patterns and better linguistic analysis) and the need for complex inferences for some of the cases.

30.2.6 Applications

There are many potential applications for event extraction: situations where information is currently extracted by hand from text, or where we would like to do some automatic analysis of the information in the text but need it first reduced to a structured database. For example, many manufacturers collect a brief written report each time a piece of equipment is repaired; they may want to analyse these reports to find patterns of failure. Business or international affairs analysts review many news reports to gather data on people, companies, and government activities; if some of this information can be reduced to tabular databases, it will be much easier to search. While some extraction systems have been implemented, their wider use at present is limited by the level of performance we can obtain, and the cost of moving systems to new tasks. Both of these may be improved by better semi-automated or automated learning procedures.

---

[4] The average of recall and precision in filling slots has remained at or below 60 per cent over a series of evaluations on different event types.

One area in which there has been long-standing interest in extraction has been the review of medical records (Sager et al. 1987). Hospitals produce very large amounts of patient data, and a significant portion of these is in text form. Medical research and monitoring of patient care require analysis of these data, in order to observe relationships between diagnosis and treatment, or between treatment and outcome, and this in turn has required a manual review of these textual data. Automatically transforming this text into standardized fields and categories based on medical criteria would greatly reduce the manual effort required; this is already feasible for specialized medical reports (Friedman et al. 1995).

FURTHER READING AND RELEVANT RESOURCES

The Proceedings of the Message Understanding Conferences contain descriptions of the wide variety of systems which participated. Proceedings of the last several conferences (prior to MUC-7) were distributed by Morgan Kaufmann Publishers; the proceedings of MUC-7 are available online (through the MUC website, http://www. itl. nist.gov/iaui/894.02/related_projects/muc). Cowie and Lehnert (1996) discuss some of the early applications of IE and the influence of the MUC conferences.

The Proceedings of the AAAI-99 Workshop on Machine Learning for Information Extraction contain a number of papers on trainable extraction systems, and are available online at http://www.isi.edu/~muslea/RISE/ML4IE. This site (http://www. isi.edu/~muslea/RISE) also contains links to a number of other extraction sites and resources for training extraction systems.

REFERENCES

Appelt, D., J. Hobbs, J. Bear, D. Israel, M. Kameyama, and M. Tyson. 1993. 'FASTUS: a finite-state processor for information extraction from real-world text'. *Proceedings of the 13th International Joint Conference on Artificial Intelligence (IJCAI '93)* (Chambéry), 1172–8.

Bikel, D. M., S. Miller, R. Schwartz, and R. Weischedel. 1997. 'Nymble: a high-performance learning name-finder'. *Proceedings of the 5th Conference on Applied Natural Language Processing* (Washington), 194–201.

Borthwick, A., J. Sterling, E. Agichtein, and R. Grishman. 1998. 'Exploiting diverse knowledge sources via maximum entropy in named entity recognition'. In *Proceedings of the 6th Workshop on Very Large Corpora* (Montreal), 152–60.

Collins, M. and Y. Singer. 1999. 'Unsupervised models for named entity classification'. *Proceedings of the 1999 Joint SIGDAT Conference on Empirical Methods in Natural Language Processing and Very Large Corpora* (College Park, Md.), 100–10.

Cowie, J. and W. Lehnert. 1996. 'Information extraction'. *Communications of the ACM*, 39(1), 80–91.

Cucerzan, S. and D. Yarowsky. 1999. 'Language independent named entity recognition combining morphological and contextual evidence'. *Proceedings of the 1999 Joint SIGDAT Conference on Empirical Methods in Natural Language Processing and Very Large Corpora* (College Park, Md.), 90–9.

Friedman, C., G. Hripcsak, W. DuMouchel, S. B. Johnson, and P. D. Clayton. 1995. 'Natural language processing in an operational clinical information system'. *Natural Language Engineering*, 1(1), 83–108.

Grishman, R. and B. Sundheim. 1996. 'Message Understanding Conference-6: a brief history'. *Proceedings of the 16th International Conference on Computational Linguistics (COLING '96)* (Copenhagen), 466–71.

Mikheev, A. and C. Grover. 1998. 'LTG: description of the NE recognition system as used for MUC-7'. *Proceedings of the 7th Message Understanding Conference (MUC-7)*. http://www.itl.nist.gov/iaui/894.02/related_projects/muc.

Riloff, E. 1996. 'Automatically generating extraction patterns from untagged text'. In *Proceedings of the 13th National Conference on Artificial Intelligence (AAAI '96)* (Portland, Ore.), 1044–9.

Sager, N., C. Friedman, and M. S. Lyman et al. 1987. *Medical Language Processing: Computer Management of Narrative Data*. Reading, Mass.: Addison-Wesley.

Sekine, S., R. Grishman, and H. Shinnou. 1998. 'A decision tree method for finding and classifying names in Japanese texts'. *Proceedings of the 6th Workshop on Very Large Corpora* (Montreal), 171–7.

Strzalkowski, T. and J. Wang. 1996. 'A self-learning universal concept spotter'. *Proceedings of the 16th International Conference on Computational Linguistics (COLING '96)* (Copenhagen), 931–6.

Yangarber, R. and R. Grishman. 1997. 'Customization of information extraction systems'. *Proceedings of the International Workshop on Lexically Driven Information Extraction* (Frascati).

——P. Tapanainen, and S. Huttunen. 2000. 'Automatic acquisition of domain knowledge for information extraction'. *Proceedings of the 18th International Conference on Computational Linguistics (COLING 2000)* (Saarbrücken), 940–6.

CHAPTER 31

QUESTION ANSWERING

SANDA HARABAGIU
DAN MOLDOVAN

ABSTRACT

Recently, a new trend in information processing from texts has emerged. Textual **Question Answering** (QA) aims at identifying the answer to a question in large collections of on-line documents. By providing a small set of exact answers to questions, QA takes a step closer to *information retrieval* rather than *document retrieval*, which, as detailed in Chapter 29, generates a list of relevant documents as a response to a user's query. Moreover, questions may be asked about virtually any topic, in contrast with the Information Extraction (IE) task presented in Chapter 30, which identifies textual information relevant only to a predefined set of events and entities. In open-domain QA systems, the finite-state technology and domain knowledge that made IE systems successful are replaced by a combination of (1) knowledge-based question processing, (2) new forms of text indexing, and (3) answer extraction that relies on empirical methods. In this chapter we review current research in integrating knowledge-based NLP methods with shallow processing techniques for QA.

31.1 INTRODUCTION

The process of providing a brief and precise answer to a question is profoundly different from the task of information retrieval (IR) or information extraction (IE). Current IR systems allow us to locate *relevant* documents that relate to a query, leaving it to the user to extract the answer from a ranked list of texts. In IR, relevant documents are identified by using one of the statistical techniques presented in Chapter 29 for matching the query against the document collection. In contrast, IE systems extract the information of interest, provided it has been presented in a predefined target representation, known as a *template*. IE systems generally operate on a set of documents deemed relevant to the extraction task. As presented in Chapter 30, IE systems are successful at populating templates when linguistic matching rules encode a wealth of domain knowledge for the extraction task. Although there is a coincidence between the output of IR systems and the input of IE systems, the immediate solution of combining IR and IE techniques for open-domain QA is impractical. First, such a solution would require extraction rules for all possible domains. Second, it would restrict the types of questions that may be asked to the forms of information modelled by extraction templates.

QA systems use IR methods to identify documents where the answer may lie as well as IE techniques to perform Named Entity recognition. However, successful QA systems encode complex natural language processing (NLP) techniques to capture the semantics of questions and to perform lexico-semantic unifications of questions and candidate answers. Since QA uses a multitude of syntactic, semantic, and pragmatic processing methods intensively, interest in the QA technology tends to stimulate NLP research and to bring natural language understanding to the forefront for researchers and systems developers.

31.2 POTENTIAL OF QUESTION-ANSWERING TECHNOLOGY

The need for answering questions is widespread, and because of this, the QA technology is about to play a major role in Information Technology for many years to come. The users may be casual questioners who ask simple factual questions; consumers who look for specific product features and prices; research analysts who are collecting market, finance, or business information; professional information analysts such as police detectives or law enforcement officials searching for very specific information requiring a great deal of expertise.

Depending on the form of processing questions and answers, QA systems may be broadly classified as **open-domain**, information-seeking QA systems or **canned** QA systems, based on predefined frequently asked questions (FAQ). In canned systems, a new question is first best matched against a set of predetermined questions for which answers are known. When there is a good match, a correct answer is provided. Companies like Ask Jeeves use this approach and their large customer base is a testimony to the acute need people have to find answers to their questions. These systems work better in restricted domains for which questions are easily anticipated.

(a)	Who was the first American in Space? Where is John Wayne airport? When did the neanderthal man live? How much did Mercury spend on advertising in 1993?	(b)	What will the US response be if Iran closes the Strait of Hormuz? What effects on the price of oil on the international market are likely to result from the terrorist attacks on Saudi facilities?

Fig. 31.1 Example of (a) factual questions and (b) expert questions

In contrast, open-domain QA systems aim at providing answers to questions from any domain by employing syntactic, semantic, and pragmatic language processing for discovering the answer in large on-line document collections. A difficulty in designing open-domain QA systems is the broad range of questions that systems need to handle. Questions may be asking for factual information, like the questions evaluated in the Text REtrieval Conference (TREC),[1] or may ask about complex events, facts, or situations. Factual questions are characterized by the ease of interpreting their semantics, mainly due to the presence of question stems such as *who* or *when*. Examples of factual questions from the TREC evaluations are presented in Fig. 31.1(a). As noted in Voorhees and Tice (2000), factual questions evaluated in TREC originated from a variety of sources, comprizing logs from the *excite.com* search engine or Microsoft's ENCARTA.

Other questions require reasoning on knowledge bases, collecting pieces of evidence from multiple documents, and then formulating answers by combining pieces of evidence. Examples of such questions were used in the evaluations of the DARPA High Performance Knowledge Bases (HPKB), and are presented in Fig. 31.1(b). In HPKB, as reported in Cohen et al. (1998), the evaluations were designed to address the reasoning aspects of questions about a specific expert field, i.e. international crises. From these examples one can see the complexity of question-answering systems,

---

[1] http://trec.nist.gov

requiring techniques that range from simple fact extraction to full understanding of text. Indeed, the QA technology is at the intersection of fields such as IR, IE, syntactico-semantic processing of texts and dialogues, discourse processing and reference resolution, abductive reasoning from texts and reasoning on knowledge bases, as well as knowledge acquisition by text mining.

31.3 A TAXONOMY OF QA SYSTEMS

As open-domain QA systems are presented with a broad range of questions, we believe that it is not sufficient to classify only the types of questions, since for the same question the answer may be easier or more difficult to extract depending on underlying document collection and on how the answer is phrased in the text. Thus instead of classifying question-processing techniques or answer-extraction techniques, we classify the the whole QA systems.

The taxonomy is based on three criteria that we consider important for building question-answering systems: (1) linguistic and knowledge resources, (2) natural language and document-processing techniques, and (3) reasoning and knowledge coercion methods. Typical linguistic resources for open-domain QA systems are lexico-semantic dictionaries such as WordNet (Fellbaum 1998), where content words are encoded along with their lexical information, e.g. their part of speech, and their possible semantic synonyms. WordNet can also be seen as a knowledge base, since ontological relations, like IS-A, span the synonym sets encoding noun and verb concepts. Additional expert knowledge bases provide the medium for building question contexts and matching them against text documents by using complex reasoning mechanisms, such as analogical reasoning.

The NLP techniques used in open-domain QA systems may range from simple lexical and semantic disambiguation of question stems to complex processing that combines syntactic and semantic features of the questions with pragmatic information derived from the context of candidate answers. Due to the complexity of such techniques, QA systems restrict the unification of questions with document paragraphs where the answer may lie, thus imposing different forms of document processing, ranging from simple, keyword-based indexing, similar to the models presented in Chapter 29, to conceptual indexing as introduced in Woods (1997).

Finally, the ability to justify the correctness of an answer by using lightweight abductions, as reported in Harabagiu, Pasca, and Maiorano (2000) is made possible by the reasoning and knowledge coercion capabilities of open-domain QA systems. The ability to use special-purpose reasoning techniques for providing answers distinguishes open-domain QA systems as well. We distinguish the following five classes of QA systems:

Class 1: QA systems capable of processing factual questions. The characteristic of these systems is that they extract the answer as a text snippet from one or several documents from the underlying collection. Typically, the answer is found verbatim in a text. QA systems evaluated in TREC (e.g. Abney, Collins, and Singhal 2000; Clarke et al. 2000; Ferret et al. 2000; Moldovan et al. 2000; Radev, Prager, and Samn 2000; or Srihari and Li 2000) belong to this category. They all rely on classifying the questions based on their stems (i.e. *who, where, how,* etc.) and on the category of the Named Entities (NE), such as Person, ORGANIZATION, or LOCATION standing for expressions like *Ulysses S. Grant, Bank of America,* or *Washington DC* respectively. When searching for answers, such systems are aware that an *author* is of the PERSON category, so they are able to combine in a novel way the semantics of Named Entities with the lexico-semantic classes provided by dictionaries such as WordNet. Since some names are very frequently mentioned in the document collection (e.g. *Washington DC*), these QA systems use a document processing that relies on the identification of paragraphs containing *all* the keywords extracted from the question, thus restricting the number of candidate answers. Typically, the answer is extracted by empirical methods that weight the presence and the distance of question keywords in the answer paragraph. Fig. 31.2 illustrates a factual question and its answer provided by a QA system of Class 1.

QUESTION: Who is the author of the book 'The Iron Lady : A Biography of Margaret Thatcher'?
ANSWER: THE IRON LADY ; A Biography of Margaret Thatcher by *Hugo Young* (Farrar , Straus & ; Giroux)
The central riddle revealed here is why , as a woman in a man's world , Margaret Thatcher evinces such an exclusionary attitude toward women

---

Fig. 31.2   **Answer provided to factual question**

The NLP techniques used by QA systems from Class 1 involve the recognition of complex nominals and appositive constructions as well as named entity recognition and identification of paraphrases.

Class 2: QA systems enabling simple reasoning mechanisms. The characteristic of this class is that the answer is found in a snippet of text, but simple forms of inference are necessary to connect the question with the answer. In this case the answer is detected using more elaborate ontologies or codifications of pragmatic knowledge and the answer extracted by reasoning on these forms of knowledge. Often world knowledge axioms are necessary to perform reasoning as simple paraphrases are not sufficient. WordNet is an excellent source of world axioms. The NLP methods

QUESTION: How did Socrates die?
ANSWER: Similarly, it was to refute the principle of retaliation that Socrates, who was sentenced to death for impiety and the corruption of the city's youth, chose to drink the poisonous hemlock, the state's method of inflicting death, rather than accepting the escape from prison that his friends had prepared.

Fig. 31.3 Answer provided to question requiring simple abduction

used encompass coreference resolution, abductive interpretation of paragraphs, and metonymic coercions. For example, the question illustrated in Fig. 31.2 is processed by allowing the abduction that drinking a poisonous beverage is a cause of death. In WordNet 1.6 the first sense of the noun *poison* is glossed as *any substance that causes injury or illness or death of a living organism*, thus providing evidence that the the collocation *poison hemlock* may be the cause of Socrates' death.

The question exemplified in Fig. 31.3 shows that the correct answer could not be extracted by only processing the morphological variations of the question keyword *die*, recognized in its nominalization *death*, since many other paragraphs from the collection contain information about the effects of Socrates's death on his friends without mentioning the manner of his death, which is explained by the abduction enabled by QA systems from Class 2. As detailed in Harabagiu, Pasca, and Maiorano (2000), QA systems from this class are capable of generating ad hoc axiomatic knowledge that participates in the abductive processes.

Class 3: QA systems enabling answer fusion from different documents. The characteristic of these systems is that they are able to extract partial information scattered throughout several documents and to formulate a comprehensive answer. The format of the answer dictates several levels of complexity of these QA systems. For example, on the more simple side are QA systems capable of answering list-questions, i.e. questions that ask for lists of answers extracted from various document sources. Fig. 31.4 represents a list-question and its corresponding answer. Far more complex is the processing of script-like questions (e.g. *How should I assemble a bicycle?*) or of template-questions (e.g. *What management successions occurred at IBM in the past year?*). Current state-of-the-art QA systems tackle only list-questions.

Open-domain QA systems capable of producing answer fusion require more advanced semantic processing of questions and name alias recognition capabilities. For example, such systems need to recognize *US* and *the United States* as referring to

QUESTION: Name three countries that banned beef imports from Britain in the 1990?
ANSWER: [France, West Germany, Luxembourg, Belgium]

Fig. 31.4 Answer provided to list-question

the same entity, thus avoiding unnecessary repetitions in the list-answer. Furthermore, these systems need to distinguish between separate entities bearing the same name, e.g. *Paris, France* and *Paris, TX*. As more complex forms of answer fusion are developed, such systems encode NLP techniques capable of summarizing information from multiple documents as well of extracting information from sets of relevant paragraphs.

Class 4: QA systems enabling analogical reasoning. The characteristic of these QA systems is their ability to answer speculative questions, similar to those listed in Fig. 31.5. Since it is reasonable to expect that the answer to such questions is not explicitly stated in any document, QA systems from this class decompose the question into queries that extract pieces of evidence, after which an answer is formulated using reasoning by analogy. The resources include ad hoc knowledge bases generated from mining textual documents clustered by the general topic of the question. Associated with these knowledge sources are case-based reasoning techniques as well as methods for temporal reasoning, spatial reasoning, and evidential reasoning.

QUESTION: Is the Fed going to raise interests at their next meeting?
QUESTION: Is the US out of recession?
QUESTION: Is the airline industry in trouble?

Fig. 31.5 Examples of speculative questions

Class 5: Interactive QA systems. The characteristic of these QA systems is the ability to ask questions in the context of the previous interactions with the user instead of asking questions in isolation. Fig. 31.6 illustrates the trace of the interaction between a user and a QA system from this class.

As reported in Harabagiu et al. (2001*b*), processing a list of questions posed in the same context imposes the resolution of several forms of reference. Unlike typical reference resolution algorithms that associate an anaphor with its referent, the reference imposed by context questions requires the association of an anaphor from the

---

Context QUESTION 1: Which museum in Florence was damaged by a major bomb
    explosion in 1993?
ANSWER: On June 20 , the Uffizi Gallery reopened it doors after the 1993 bombing.
Context QUESTION 2: On what day did this happen?
ANSWER: (Thursday) (May 27 1993)
Context QUESTION 3: Which galleries were involved?
ANSWER: One of the two main wings.
Context QUESTION 4: How many people were killed?
ANSWER: Five people were killed in the explosion.

Fig. 31.6 Question answering in context

current question with either (1) one of the previously asked question, (2) its answers, or (3) another anaphor used in a previous question.

Moreover, since dialogues enable the negotiation of the meaning of a question, processing questions in context determines question clarifications as well as the recognition of more complex taxonomies of questions and answers that can be extracted.

31.4 THE ARCHITECTURE OF QA SYSTEMS

A QA system normally comprises three modules: a *Question-Processing* module, a *Document-Processing* module, and an *Answer Extraction and Formulation* module. **Question processing** represents the set of techniques implemented in QA systems that enable the interpretation of the questions, and thus help identify its answer in the document collection. Unlike IR queries, composed of keywords and eventually operators such as AND, OR, or NEAR, natural language questions have an inherent semantic that humans understand and that needs to be processed by QA systems. The most important aspect of question semantics is represented by the **expected answer type**, i.e. the semantic category to which the answer must belong. For example, when asking *Who is best known for breaking the color line in baseball?*, the expected answer type is a PERSON, recognized also in a name such as Jackie Robinson.

The role of question processing is also to identify the question words that can be used to query the document index and thus to retrieve document paragraphs where the answer may lie. As illustrated in Fig. 31.7, the results of the *Question-Processing*

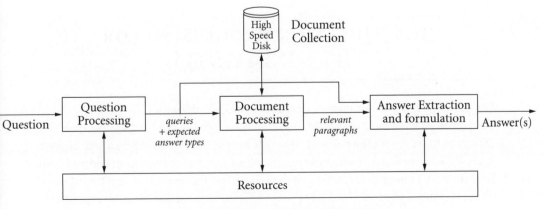

Fig. 31.7 Architecture of a typical QA system

module are passed to the *Document-Processing* module. **Document Processing** refers to the indexing model that enables the retrieval of *paragraphs* where the answer may lie. Some systems, e.g. Moldovan et al. (2000) and Clarke et al. (2000) require each retrieved paragraph to contain (*a*) all query keywords and (*b*) at least one word of the same semantic category as the expected answer type. Other systems, e.g. Ittycheriah et al. (2000), produce a question expansion before identifying relevant passages through a two-pass IR approach.

An important feature of *Document Processing* for QA comes from the evaluation of the quality of the paragraphs, as implemented in Moldovan et al. (2000). A quality metric, modelling the plausibility of a paragraph's containing the answer, is used to order the retrieved paragraphs. When the number of paragraphs having plausibility above a predefined threshold is too large or too low, we add/drop keywords and resume the paragraph retrieval. This loop generates a feedback retrieval context that enables only a reasonable number of paragraphs to be passed to the *Answer-Processing* module.

Answer Extraction is the process of identifying in a paragraph the text snippet representing the answer to a given question. The format of the answer is an important feature of the answer extraction, which influences the precision of the overall QA process. In the initial TREC evaluations, the answers could be returned either as a 50 byte-long string or as a 250 byte-long string, leaving it to the human to identify the exact answer in the text snippet. The 250 byte-long answers were more precise than the 50 byte-long answers by 10 per cent. However, the results reported in Pasca and Harabagiu (2001) show that the best criteria for obtaining more precise answers do not depend so much on the length of the answer, as on (1) the ability to assess the correctness of the answer and (2) exhaustive search for candidate answers by using lexico-semantic and morphological alternations of the keywords.

31.5 QUESTION PROCESSING FOR OPEN-DOMAIN QA

For processing a broad range of questions, an open-domain QA system needs to determine (1) what kind of information it looks for, or the *expected answer type*, and (2) where to search for the answers. Since the answer is represented by a text snippet, it should be contained in a text paragraph where most of the question concepts can be identified. Thus, the search for answers is based on the conjecture that the eventual answer is likely to be found in a text paragraph that (*a*) contains the most representative question concepts and (*b*) includes a textual concept of the same category as the expected answer. Since the current retrieval technology does not model semantic knowledge, most QA systems break down this search into a retrieval based on some question keywords and a filtering mechanism that retains only those passages containing the expected answer type. A way of identifying both the *question keywords* and the *expected answer type* is based on (1) the dependencies derived from the question parse, as reported in Harabagiu et al. (2001a), and on (2) the semantic categories associated with question stems like *who*, *what*, and *where*.

The need for a *dependency* model is motivated by the ambiguity of the most frequently used question stems, e.g. *what*, that can ask about virtually any category of concepts. Statistics from the TREC evaluations show that almost half of the questions used the *what* question stem, although they asked for a large number of different expected answer types. To resolve this ambiguity, a *dependency* model can be learned when mapping the parse trees into sets of binary relations between the headword of each constituent and its sibling-words. For example, the parse tree of TREC-8 question *What does the BMW company produce?* is represented in Fig. 31.8(*a*). For each possible constituent in a parse tree, rules first described in Magerman (1995) and Jelinek et al. (1994) identify the head-child and propagate the headword to its parent. For the parse from Fig. 31.8(*a*) the propagation is represented in Fig. 31.8(*b*). When the propagation is over, head-modifier relations are extracted, generating the dependency structure from Fig. 31.8(*c*), introduced as the *question semantic form* in Harabagiu, Pasca, and Maiorano (2000).

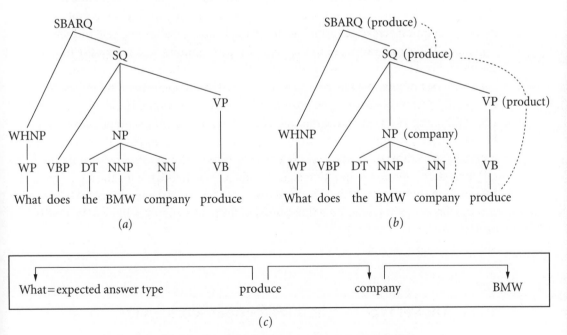

Fig. 31.8 (*a*) Parse of a question; (*b*) Dependency model determined by head-child propagation; (*c*) Question semantic form

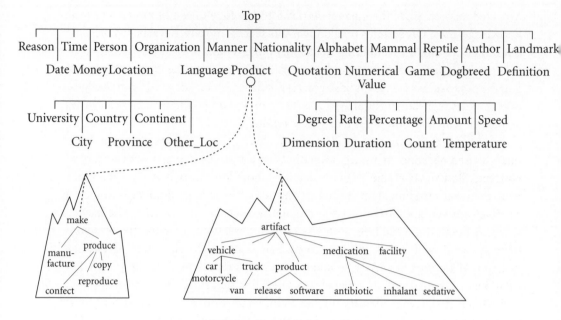

Fig. 31.9 Answer type taxonomy

To determine the answer type we use the word from the question semantic form that (1) is directly connected to the question stem; and (2) has the highest connectivity in the question semantic form. For the example illustrated in Fig. 31.8, this word is *produce*. We search this word in the **answer type taxonomy** and return the top of the hierarchy that contains it as the *expected answer type*. The answer type taxonomy is an ontology of possible answer types recognized by an open-domain QA system. Fig. 31.9 illustrates the answer type taxonomy reported in Pasca and Harabagiu (2001) whereas section 31.5.2 details the mechanisms for building an answer type taxonomy. For the question from Fig. 31.8, the word *produce* is found under the PRODUCT hierarchy, which becomes the expected answer type of the question, replacing the question stem *what* in the question semantic form. When looking for the answer to the question from Fig. 31.8, the paragraphs must contain at least one other PRODUCT concept like *car*, *motorcycle*, or a named entity of the type PRODUCT, like *BMW 333Xi* or *BMW Roaster*.

31.5.1 Answer type taxonomies for open-domain QA

An off-line taxonomy of answer types can be built by relying on vast lexico-semantic resources such as WordNet (Fellbaum 1998). The WordNet 1.6 database encodes more than 100,000 English nouns, verbs, adjectives, and adverbs organized in conceptual synonym sets, known as *synsets*. Moreover, the nouns and verbs are further organized in hierarchies by IS-A relations and classified into twenty-five noun categories and fifteen verb categories.

In building the answer type taxonomy, we followed three steps:

Step 1: For each semantic category of nouns or verbs we manually examined the most representative conceptual nodes and added them as tops of the ANSWER TYPE TAXONOMY. Moreover, we added open semantic categories corresponding to named entities. The tops of the ANSWER TYPE TAXONOMY are illustrated in Fig. 31.9. It can be noted that some of the tops (e.g. LOCATION or NUMERICAL VALUE) are further categorized, mostly because they subsume distinct semantic types corresponding to categories identified by our named entity recognizer.

Step 2: Since often the expected answer type is a named entity, a many-to-many mapping between the named entity categories and the tops of the ANSWER TYPE TAXONOMY is required. Fig. 31.10 illustrates some of the implemented mappings. For example, either an AMOUNT, a DURATION, or the SPEED are recognized as *Amount* expressions by a named entity recognizer, whereas concepts of type MONEY are identified either as *Money* or *Price* expressions by our named entity recognizer.

Step 3: Each leaf of the tops implemented in the ANSWER TYPE TAXONOMY is manually linked to one or several sub-hierarchies from WordNet. Fig. 31.9 illustrates only some of the hierarchies that generate an answer type classified as PERSON. Similar links are encoded for each leaf of the ANSWER TYPE TAXONOMY. These links connect abstract concepts, identified at *Step 1* with sub-hierarchies from WordNet, in which concepts are represented as synsets.

Currently, the ANSWER TYPE TAXONOMY presented in Pasca and Harabagiu (2001) encodes 8,707 English concepts, nouns, verbs, and adjectives, that help recognize the expected answer type of an open-domain natural language question. The vast majority of the concepts are nouns, since most of the leaves of the ANSWER TYPE TAXONOMY are connected to WordNet noun sub-hierarchies. Moreover, a

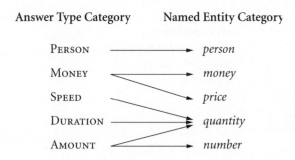

Fig. 31.10 Many-to-many mappings between named entities and
tops of the Answer Type Taxonomy

leaf from the ANSWER TYPE TAXONOMY may be connected simultaneously to (*a*) noun sub-hierarchies, (*b*) verb sub-hierarchies, or (*c*) adjectival satellites encoded in the WordNet database. For example the PRODUCT leaf from the ANSWER TYPE TAXONOMY is connected to both nouns from the sub-hierarchy synset {*artifact, artefact*} and verbs from the sub-hierarchy of {*manufacture, fabricate, construct*}.

Adjectival synsets and their WordNet satellites are connected through the VALUE-OF lexico-semantic relations encoded in WordNet. For example, *far, small,* and *tall* are connected to the DIMENSION leaf due to the fact that they are values of *distance, size,* and *stature or height,* respectively. Similarly *rich* is linked to MONEY and *many* to COUNT. The ANSWER TYPE TAXONOMY encodes 153 connections to WordNet sub-hierarchies, 130 of which link tops of the taxonomy to WordNet noun sub-hierarchies. Most of the tops are linked to one or two sub-hierarchies.

31.5.2 Keyword extraction for open-domain QA

The retrieval of the relevant paragraphs for an open-domain question is based on a keyword-based query. The process of extracting the query keywords is based on a set of empirical methods that extract content words from the question semantic form by giving precedence to (*a*) quoted expressions; (*b*) named entities; and (*c*) complex nominals. The list of possible keywords also contains all nouns and their adjectival modifiers as well as the main verbs from the question. Table 31.1 lists two questions from the TREC-8 evaluations together with their associated keywords. The table also illustrates the trace of keywords that were added or dropped until the paragraphs containing the answer were found. For question Q26, the paragraphs containing the answers could not be found before dropping many of the initial keywords. In contrast, the answer for question Q13 was found when the verb *rent* was added to the

Table 31.1 Examples of TREC-8 Question Keywords

Q13	*What is the name of the 'female' counterpart to El Nino, which results in cooling temperatures and very dry weather?*
Keywords	female El Nino dry weather cooling temperatures
	female El Nino dry weather cooling
	female El Nino dry weather
	female El Nino dry
	female El Nino
	female El
Q26	*How much could you rent a Volkswagen bug for in 1966?*
Keywords	Volkswagen bug
	Volkswagen bug rent

keyword-based query. This mechanism of adding/dropping keywords to optimize the plausibility of a paragraph's containing the answer was further enhanced by allowing lexico-semantic alienations of the keywords. As reported in Harabagiu et al. (2001*a*), the role of lexico-semantic feedbacks of the keywords was to bootstrap the precision of open-domain QA by enhancing the search space for candidate answers.

Keyword alternations can be classified according to the linguistic knowledge they rely upon:

1. Morphological Alternations. When lexical alternations are necessary because no answer has been found yet, the first keyword that is altered is determined by the question word that either prompted the expected answer type or is in the same semantic class as the expected answer type. For example, in the case of TREC question *Q209: Who invented the paper clip?*, the expected answer type is PERSON and so is the subject of the verb *invented*, lexicalized as the nominalization *inventor*. Moreover, since our retrieval mechanism does not stem keywords, all the inflections of the verb are also considered. Therefore, the initial query is expanded into:

QUERY(Q209):[paper AND clip AND (invented OR inventor OR invent OR invents)]

2. Lexical Alternations. WordNet encodes a wealth of semantic information that is easily mined. Seven types of semantic relations span concepts, enabling the retrieval of synonyms and other semantically related terms. Such alternations improve the recall of the answer paragraphs. For example, in the case of question *Q221: Who killed Martin Luther King?*, by considering the synonym of *killer*, the noun *assassin*, the QA system retrieved paragraphs with the correct answer. Similarly, for the TREC question *Q206: How far is the moon?*, since the adverb *far* is encoded in WordNet as being an attribute of *distance*, by adding this noun to the retrieval keywords, a correct answer is found.

3. Semantic Alternations and Paraphrases. We define as semantic alternations of a keyword those words or collocations from WordNet that (*a*) are not members of any WordNet synsets containing the original keyword; and (*b*) have a chain of Word-Net relations or bigram relations that connect them to the original keyword. These relations can be translated in axiomatic form and thus participate in the abductive backchaining from the answer to the question—to justify the answer. For example semantic alternations involving only WordNet relations were used in the case of TREC question *Q258: Where do lobsters like to live?* Since in WordNet the verb *prefer* has verb *like* as a hypernym, and moreover, its glossed definition is *liking better*, the query becomes:

QUERY(Q258):[lobsters AND (like OR prefer) AND live]

Sometimes multiple keywords are replaced by a semantic alternation. Sometimes these alternations are similar to the relations between multi-term paraphrases and single terms, at other times they simply are semantically related terms. In the case of question *Q210: How many dogs pull a sled in the Iditarod?*, since the definition of WordNet sense 2 of noun *harness* contains the bigram *pull cart* and both *sled* and *cart* are forms of *vehicles*, the alternation of the pair of keywords [*pull, slide*] is rendered by *harness*. Only when this feedback is received is the paragraph containing the correct answer retrieved. An alternative to keyword extraction and lexico-semantic alternations is to use predictive annotations, as reported in Radev, Prager, and Samn (2000). By using fifty semantic categories, called *QA-tokens*, the texts from the document collections are automatically annotated with these semantic categories, which are used in the indexing provided by document processing. More than 400 textual patterns are associated with the QA-tokens and enable their rapid identification in texts. By classifying any new question against the QA-tokens, only text passages annotated with the same QA-tokens are retrieved.

31.6 DOCUMENT PROCESSING FOR OPEN-DOMAIN QA

Finding the answer to a natural language question involves not only knowing *what* to look for (i.e. the expected answer type), but also *where* to look for the answer. The question is expressed with words that can be used in forming a query for an IR system, that returns sets of text passages, or *paragraphs* where the answer may lie. A very advanced form of retrieving candidate paragraphs is based on the usage of terminological variants for the document selection, as it was implemented in LIMSI's QUALC system (Ferret et al. 2000). This system uses high-level indexes comprising both terms and their variants. The variant recognition as well as the weighting of the matching between questions and documents are based on FAST (Jacquemin 1999)). Fast is a transformational shallow parser that recognizes term occurrences and their variants by combining their morphological family, as extracted from the CELEX database, with their semantic family, provided by WordNet synonyms.

An alternative form of retrieving relevant paragraphs that was implemented in the system reported in Pasca and Harabagiu (2001) is by using the ordered list of extracted keywords to perform a Boolean paragraph retrieval implementation that employs the SMART IR engine (Salton 1969). The well-known disadvantage of Boolean retrieval can be tackled by dropping some of the keywords when too few paragraphs are returned, or to add some keywords when too many meaningful paragraphs are found. An important observation that we made in our experiments, reported in Pasca and Harabagiu (2001), is that the ordering of the retrieved para-

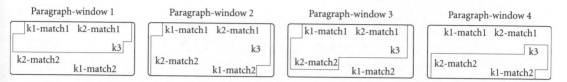

Fig. 31.11 Four answer windows defined on the same paragraph

graphs has significant effect on the overall performance of the Q/A system. To order the paragraphs we used a perceptron that employs four features.

The definition of these four features depends on the notion of **paragraph-window**. Paragraph-windows are determined by the need to consider separately each match of the same keyword in the same paragraph. For example, if we have a set of keywords $\{k_1, k_2, k_3, k_4\}$ and in a paragraph k_1 and k_2 are matched each twice, whereas k_3 is matched only once, and k_4 is not matched, we are going to have four different windows, represented in Fig. 31.11 and defined by the keywords: [k_1-$match_1$, k_2-$match_1, k_3$], [k_1-$match_2, k_2$-$match_1, k_3$], [k_1-$match_1, k_2$-$match_2, k_3$], and [k_1-$match_2$, k_2-$match_2, k_3$].

A window comprises all the text between the lowest positioned keyword in the window and the highest position keyword in the window. For each paragraph window we compute the following scores:

1. rel_{SWS} computes the number of words from the question that are recognized in the same sequence in the current paragraph-window.
2. rel_{DAW} represents the number of words that separate the most distant keywords in the window.
3. rel_{NMW} computes the number of unmatched keywords. This measure is identical for all windows from the same paragraph, but varies for windows from different paragraphs.

The formula employed by the perceptron that learns how to order paragraphs by their paragraph-window scores is:

$$ord_{pair} = q_{SWS} \times \Delta\, rel_{SWS} + q_{DAW} \times \Delta\, rel_{DAW} + q_{NMW} \times \Delta\, rel_{NMW} + threshold$$

We obtained the following values for the three weights: $q_{SWS} = 13.470984$; $q_{DAW} = -163.20379$; $q_{NMW} = -11.482971$ and the threshold has the value 72.88456. At testing time, when the relative order measure ord_{pair} is positive, the first paragraph precedes the second one, otherwise their order is reversed.

31.7 ANSWER EXTRACTION FOR OPEN-DOMAIN QA

Four different methods of extracting answers from relevant text passages have been developed.

Method 1: Multi-pass ranking of the text matching between the question and the candidate paragraphs. This method has been implemented in Srihari and Li (2000) by using initially a count of the unique keywords from the question in each sentence of the paragraph. The secondary ranking is provided by the order in which the keywords appear in the question whereas the third ranking is based on whether there is a match or a variant for the key verb of the question in any of the paragraph sentences.

Method 2: Optimization algorithms based on seven predictive variables that describe how likely the answer is to be found in a given span from the paragraph. This method was implemented by the *Ansel* and *Werlect* algorithms from the IBM system reported in Radev, Prager, and Samn (2000) The seven predictive variables are:

- f_1 = the position of the text span among all spans from the hit list of ten passages returned by document processing;
- f_2 = the position of the text span among all spans from the current passage;
- f_3 = the number of words in the span that do not appear in the query;
- f_4 = the position of the span type in the list of potential span types;
- f_5 = the average distance in words between the beginning of the span and the query words that appear in the passage;
- f_6 = the relevance of the annotated QA-term;
- f_7 = the position among all spans from the collection.

Method 3: Answer selection with Maximum Entropy. This method was used by the IBM system reported in Ittycheriah et al. (2000). For each window of three sentences from a passage five different distances were computed:

- *Matching words*, which is a TF-IDF[2] sum of the words that matched identically in the morphological space;
- The*saurus matching*, which is a TF-IDF sum of the words that matched when using semantic alternations provided by WordNet;
- *Mis-Match of Words*, representing the TF-IDF sum of the words that did not match;
- *Dispersion* counting the words in candidate sentences that occur between matching question words;

---

[2] The TF-IDF score was introduced in Chapter 29.

- *Cluster of words*, that counts the words in candidate sentences that occur adjacently both in the question and in the answer.

Each distance is weighted using a maximum entropy score before using them to select the most likely answers.

Method 4: Learning a comparison function between candidate paragraphs. This method was implemented in the system reported in Pasca and Harabagiu (2001). The comparison function is learned based on a perceptron model that was trained on the TREC-8 questions and applied to the TREC-9 questions during the evaluations. The learning technique is based on the observation that from the set of paragraphs, at least one paragraph may contain the correct answer. Typically, the cardinality of the set of paragraphs is between 500 and 3,000. Any sorting algorithm, e.g. *quicksort*, can order this set of paragraphs if a *comparison function* is provided. The goal of the TREC QA evaluations is to return five ordered text snippets that represent the most likely answers to a given question. Therefore we need to sort all the paragraphs and return the first five paragraphs from which the text snippets can be extracted.

To learn the comparison function, after experimenting with numerous possible features, the best results were obtained for the following seven features:

1. rel_{SP}: the number of question words matched in the same phrase as the concept of expected answer type;

2. rel_{SS}: the number of question words matched in the same sentence as the concept of expected answer type;

3. rel_{FP}: a flag set to 1 if the concept of expected answer type is followed by a punctuation sign, and set to 0 otherwise;

4. rel_{OCTW}: the number of question word matches separated from the concept of expected answer type by at most three words and one comma;

5. rel_{SWS}: the number of question words occurring in the same order in the answer text as in the question;

6. rel_{DTW}: the average distance from the concept of expected answer type to any of the question word matches;

7. rel_{NMW}: the number of question words matched in the answer text.

To train the perceptron we considered pairs of candidate answers. In the training phase, one of the paragraphs always contains the correct answer whereas its opponent is a paragraph returned by the multi-feedback retrieval. Given the pair of paragraphs (P_1, P_2), we compute $\Delta rel_{SP} = rel_{SP}^{P_1} - rel_{SP}^{P_2}$; $\Delta rel_{SS} = rel_{SS}^{P_1} - rel_{SS}^{P_2}$; $\Delta rel_{FP} = rel_{FP}^{P_1} - rel_{FP}^{P_2}$; $\Delta rel_{OCTW} = rel_{OCTW}^{P_1} - rel_{OCTW}^{P_2}$; $\Delta rel_{SWS} = rel_{SWS}^{P_1} - rel_{SWS}^{P_2}$; $\Delta rel_{DTW} = rel_{DTW}^{P_1} - rel_{DTW}^{P_2}$; and finally $\Delta rel_{NMW} = rel_{NMW}^{P_1} - rel_{NMW}^{P_2}$. The perceptron computes a relative comparison score, given by the formula:

$$rel_{pair} = w_{SWS} \times \Delta rel_{SWS} + w_{FP} \times \Delta rel_{FP} + w_{OCTW} \times \Delta rel_{OCTW} + w_{SP} \times \Delta rel_{SP} + w_{SS} \times \Delta rel_{SS} + w_{NMW} \times \Delta rel_{NMW} + w_{DTW} \times \Delta rel_{DTW} + threshold$$

The perceptron learns the seven weights as well as the value of the threshold used for future tests on the remaining 793 TREC-9 questions. We obtained the following values for the seven weights: w_{SWS} = 12.458484; w_{FP} = −4.411543; w_{OCTW} = 3.1648636; w_{SP} = 4.461322; w_{SS} = 22.148517; w_{NMW} = 42.286851; w_{DTW} = −49.9721809141. The learned value of the threshold is −15.0518481056. At the test phase, given any pair of paragraphs, when the value of the resulting rel_{pair} is positive, the comparison function selects the first paragraph, otherwise it chooses the second one. The extracted text snippet is then centred around the concepts of expected answer type.

31.8 HISTORICAL PERSPECTIVE

Mechanisms for open-domain QA were not discovered in a vacuum. Several theories for QA have been developed earlier in the context of NLP or cognitive sciences. First, we have the conceptual theory of question answering, proposed by Wendy Lehnert in Lehnert (1978) and implemented in the QUALM system with its associated question taxonomy. QUALM used thirteen conceptual categories to classify questions and to produce inferential analysis by using Shank's conceptual dependency, which constitutes a major departure from the IR point of view. Instead of indexing documents, the memory retrieval was achieved by content specification and a set of searching heuristics. The most influential contribution of QUALM to current research in open-domain QA is determined by the question taxonomy and its relation to the speech act theory based on quantitative research of interpersonal behaviour. The QUALM question taxonomy comprises categories such as *Enablement, Causal Antecedent,* or *Concept Completion.* This question taxonomy was further enhanced by Art Graesser to eighteen different categories by adding several new categories: a *Comparison* category, a *Definition* category, an *Example* category, and an *Interpretation* category. This taxonomy is presented in Graesser, Byrne, and Behren (1992).

For all the categories in his taxonomy, Graesser conducted a study of empirical completeness, showing that the taxonomy is able to accommodate virtually all enquiries that occur in a discourse. The study focused on three different contexts: (*a*) college students reading passages; (*b*) individuals using a computer, and (*c*) citizens asking questions in newspaper media. The study sessions spanned a variety of topics, including basic mathematics, statistics, research methods, a computer network, climate, agricultural products, and population density. However, Graesser's taxonomy was not implemented in a QA system, it was used only by humans to score the reliability of the taxonomy itself.

Other early QA systems that were developed as vehicles for NLP research were

STUDENT and SHRDLU, to solve high-school algebra problems and block-world problems, respectively, as reported in Winograd (1977). Similarly constrained by limited knowledge, LUNAR (Woods 1977) implemented 111 questions that operate on moon rock data. More recently, the MURAX system (Kupiec 1993) used an on-line encyclopedia as a source of answers for **closed-class questions**, which Kupiec defined as 'a question stated in natural language, which assumes some definite answer typified by a noun phrase rather than a procedural answer'.

Further Reading and Relevant Resources

Harabagiu et al. (2001*a*) sheds light on an important aspect of open-domain QA: question reformulation. Often a question has been posed before to the QA system and thus its extracted answer can be used again. To find such *cached questions*, we measure the similarity to the previously processed questions and, when a reformulation is identified, we consider all *question reformulations* and their corresponding answers. To classify questions in reformulation groups, we successively built a similarity matrix M. When a new question is posed, a new row and a new column is added to M, containing flags signifying whether the new question is similar to any of the previous questions. Fig. 31.12 represents the similarity matrix M for six questions that were successively posed to a QA system. Since question reformulations are transitive relations, if at step n questions Q_i and Q_j are found similar and Q_i already belongs to R, a reformulation class previously discovered (i.e. a group of at least two similar questions), then question Q_j is also included in R. Fig. 31.12 illustrates the transitive closures for reformulations at each of the five steps from the succession of six questions. Note that at step 4 no new similarities were found; thus Q_5 is not found similar to Q_4 at this step. However, at step 5, since Q_6 is found similar to both Q_4 and Q_5, Q_4 results similar to all the other questions but Q_3. Similarity measures between two questions are presented in Harabagiu et al. (2001*a*) and earlier in Burke et al. (1997).

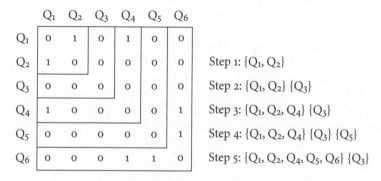

	Q_1	Q_2	Q_3	Q_4	Q_5	Q_6
Q_1	0	1	0	1	0	0
Q_2	1	0	0	0	0	0
Q_3	0	0	0	0	0	0
Q_4	1	0	0	0	0	1
Q_5	0	0	0	0	0	1
Q_6	0	0	0	1	1	0

Step 1: {Q_1, Q_2}
Step 2: {Q_1, Q_2} {Q_3}
Step 3: {Q_1, Q_2, Q_4} {Q_3}
Step 4: {Q_1, Q_2, Q_4} {Q_3} {Q_5}
Step 5: {Q_1, Q_2, Q_4, Q_5, Q_6} {Q_3}

Fig. 31.12 Building reformulation classes with a similarity matrix

A different way of performing open-domain QA is proposed in Mann (2001) by using *Mutual Information* as an estimator for correlation between the question class and the semantic tag that represents the expected answer type. A more promising approach is presented in Hermjacob (2001) since it proposes the construction of *question treebanks* in which semantic annotations enable enhanced matching of questions and answers. As first shown in Harabagiu, Pasca, and Maiorano (2000), the justification of answer correctness greatly improves the accuracy of QA systems. To enable justifications as abductive interpretations of the answers, axiomatic knowledge encoding pragmatic information needs to be translated from resources such as WordNet. Moldovan and Rus (2001) details a form of transforming the WordNet definitions into logical forms that participate in answer justification.

The reader is referred to the TREC proceedings (http://trec.nist.gov/pubs.html) for a detailed account of the question answering systems which participated at TREC-8, TREC-9, and TREC-10.

REFERENCES

Abney, S., M. Collins, and A. Singhal. 2000. 'Answer extraction'. *Proceedings of the 6th Applied Natural Language Processing Conference (ANLP 2000)* (Seattle), 296–301.

Burke, R. D., K. J. Hammond, V. A. Kulynkin, S. L. Lytien, N. Tomuro, and S. Shoenberg. 1997. *Question answering from frequently-asked question files: experiments with the FAQ finder system.* Technical Report TR-97-05. tUniversity of Chicago, Computer Science Department.

Cardie, C., V. Ng, D. Pierce, and C. Buckley. 2000. 'Examining the role of statistical and linguistic knowledge sources in a general-knowledge question answering system'. *Proceedings of the 6th Applied Natural Language Processing Conference (ANLP 2000)* (Seattle), 180–7.

Clarke, C. L., G. V. Cormak, D. I. E. Kisman, and T. R. Lynam. 2000. 'Question answering by passage selection'. *Proceedings of the Text Retrieval Conference (TREC-9)* (Gaithersburg, Md.), 65–76.

Cohen, P., R. Schrag, E. Jones, A. Pease, A. Lin, B. Starr, D. Gunning, and M. Burke. 1998. 'The DARPA high performance knowledge bases project'. *AI Magazine*, 18(4), 25–49.

Collins, M. 1996. 'A new statistical parser based on bigram lexical dependencies'. *Proceedings of the 34th Annual Meeting of the Association for Computational Linguistics (ACL '96)* (Santa Cruz, Calif.), 184–91.

Fellbaum, C. (ed). 1998. *WordNet: An Electronic Lexical Database.* Cambridge, Mass.: MIT Press.

Ferret, O., B. Grau, M. Hurault-Plantet, G. Illouz, C. Jacquemin, N. Masson, and P. Lecuyer. 2000. 'QALC: the question-answering system of LIMSI-CNRS'. *Proceedings of the Text Retrieval Conference (TREC-9)* (Gaithersburg, Md.), 316–26.

Gaizauskas, R. and K. Humphreys. 2000. 'A combined IR/NLP approach to question answering against large text collections'. *Proceedings of the 6th Content-Based Multimedia Information Access Conference (RIAO 2000)* (Paris), 1288–304.

Graesser, A. C., R. J. Byrne, and M. C. Behren. 1992. *Questions and Information Systems.* Hillsdale, NJ: Lawrence Erlbaum Associates.

Harabagiu, S., M. Pasca, and S. Maiorano. 2000. 'Experiments with open-domain textual question answering'. *Proceedings of the 18th International Conference on Computational Linguistics (COLING 2000)* (Saarbrücken), 292–8.

——D. Moldovan, M. Pasca, R. Mihalcea, M. Surdeanu, R. Bunescu, R. Girju, V. Rus, and P. Morarescu. 2001a. 'The role of lexico-semantic feedback in open-domain textual question-answering'. *Proceedings of the 39th Annual Meeting of the Association for Computational Linguistics (ACL 2001)* (Toulouse), 274–281.

—— —— —— —— —— —— —— —— ——2001b. 'Answering complex, list and context questions with LCC's question-answering server'. *Proceedings of the Text Retrieval Conference (TREC-10)*.

Hermjacob, U. 2001. 'Parsing and question classification for question answering'. *Proceedings of the ACL-2001 Workshop on Open-Domain Question Answering* (Toulouse), 17–22.

Hobbs, J., M. Stickel, D. Appelt, and P. Martin. 1993. 'Interpretation as abduction'. *Artificial Intelligence*, 63, 69–142.

Ittycheriah, A., M. Franz, W.-J. Zhu, and A. Ratnapakhi. 2000. 'IBM's statistical question-answering system'. *Proceedings of the Text Retrieval Conference (TREC-9)* (Gaithersburg, Md.), 229–37.

Jacquemin, C. 1999. 'Syntagmatic and paradigmatic representations of term variation'. *Proceedings of the 37th Annual Meeting of the Association for Computational Linguistics (ACL '99)* (College Park, Md.), 341–8.

Jelinek, F., J. Lafferty, D. Magerman, R. Mercer, A. Ratnaparkhi, and S. Roukos. 1994. 'Decision tree parsing using a hidden derivational model'. *Proceedings of the 1994 Human Language Technology Workshop* (Princeton), 272–7.

Katz, B. 1997. 'From sentence processing to information access on the World Wide Web'. *Proceedings of the AAAI Spring Symposium* (Stanford, Calif.), 77–86.

Kupiec, J. 1993. 'MURAX: a robust linguistic approach for question answering using an on-line encyclopedia'. *Proceedings of the 16th International ACM SIGIR Conference on Research and Development in Information Retrieval (SIGIR '93)* (Pittsburgh), 181–90.

Lehnert, W. 1978. *The Processing of Question Answering*. Hillsdale, NJ: Lawrence Erlbaum Associates.

Magerman, D. 1995. 'Statistical decision-tree models of parsing'. *Proceedings of the 33rd Annual Meeting of the Association for Computational Linguistics (ACL '95)* (Cambridge, Mass), 276–83.

Mann, G. 2001. 'A statistical method for short answer extraction'. *Proceedings of the ACL-2001 Workshop on Open-Domain Question Answering* (Toulouse), 23–30.

Moldovan, D. and V. Rus. 2001. 'Logic form transformation of WordNet and its applicability to question answering'. *Proceedings of the 39th Annual Meeting of the Association for Computational Linguistics (ACL 2001)* (Toulouse), 394–401.

——S. Harabagiu, M. Pasca, R. Mihalcea, R. Goodrum, R. Gîrju, and V. Rus. 2000. 'The structure and performance of an open-domain question answering system'. *Proceedings of the 38th Annual Meeting of the Association for Computational Linguistics (ACL 2000)* (Saarbrücken), 563–70.

Pasca, M., and S. Harabagiu. 2001. 'High performance question/answering'. *Proceedings of the 24th Annual International ACL SIGIR Conference on Research and Development in Information Retrieval (SIGIR 2001)* (Toulouse), 366–74.

Radev, D., J. Prager, and V. Samn. 2000. 'Ranking suspected answers to natural language questions using predictive annotation'. *Proceedings of the 6th Applied Natural Language Process-*

ing Conference (ANLP 2000) (Seattle), 150–7.

Salton, G. (ed.). 1969. The *SMART Retrieval System*. Englewood Cliffs, NJ: Prentice-Hall.

Srihari, R. and W. Li. 2000. 'A question answering system supported by information extraction'. *Proceedings of the 6th Applied Natural Language Processing Conference (ANLP 2000)* (Seattle), 166–72.

Voorhees, E. M. and D. Tice. 2000. 'Building a question answering test collection'. *Proceedings of the 23rd Annual International ACM SIGIR Conference on Research and Development in Information Retrieval (SIGIR 2000)* (Athens), 33–40.

Winograd, T. 1977. 'Five lectures on artificial intelligence'. In A. Zampolli (ed.), *Linguistic Structures Processing*, Fundamental Studies in Computer Science, 5. Amsterdam: North Holland, 399–520.

Woods, W. A. 1977. 'Lunar rocks in natural English: explorations in natural language question answering'. In A. Zampolli (ed.), *Linguistic Structures Processing*, Fundamental Studies in Computer Science, 5. Amsterdam: North Holland, 521–69.

——1997. *Conceptual Indexing: A Better Way to Organize Knowledge*. Technical Report of Sun Microsystems Inc.

CHAPTER 32

TEXT SUMMARIZATION

EDUARD HOVY

ABSTRACT

This chapter describes research and development on the automated creation of summaries of one or more texts. It presents an overview of the principal approaches in summarization, describes the design, implementation, and performance of various summarization systems, and reviews methods of evaluating summaries.

32.1 THE NATURE OF SUMMARIES

Early experimentation in the late 1950s and early 1960s suggested that text summarization by computer was feasible though not straightforward (Luhn 1959; Edmundson 1969). After a hiatus of some decades, progress in language processing, coupled with great increases of computer memory and speed, and the growing presence of on-line text—in corpora and especially on the web—renewed interest in automated text summarization.

Despite encouraging results, some fundamental questions remain unaddressed. For example, no one seems to know exactly what a **summary** is. In this chapter we use *summary* as a generic term and define it as follows:

(32.1)   **Definition**: a summary is a text that is produced from one or more texts, that contains a significant portion of the information in the original text(s), and that is no longer than half of the original text(s).

'Text' here includes multimedia documents, on-line documents, hypertexts, etc. Of the many types of summary that have been identified (Spärck Jones 1999; Hovy and Lin 1999), **indicative** summaries (that provide an idea of what the text is about without giving any content) and **informative** ones (that do provide some shortened version of the content) are often referenced. **Extracts** are summaries created by reusing portions (words, sentences, etc.) of the input text verbatim, while **abstracts** are created by re-generating the extracted content.

Section 32.2 outlines the principal approaches to automated text summarization in general. Section 32.3 reviews particular techniques used in several summarization systems. Problems unique to multi-document summarization are discussed in section 32.4. Finally, although the evaluation of summaries (and of summarization) is not yet well understood, we review approaches to evaluation in section 32.5.

32.2 THE STAGES OF AUTOMATED TEXT SUMMARIZATION

Researchers in automated text summarization have identified three distinct stages (Spärck Jones 1999; Hovy and Lin 1999; Mani and Maybury 1999). Most systems today embody the first stage only.

The first stage, *topic identification*, produces the simplest type of summary. (We define **topic** as a particular subject that we write about or discuss.) Whatever criterion of importance is used, once the system has identified the most important unit(s) (words, sentences, paragraphs, etc.), it can either simply list them (thereby creating an extract) or display them diagrammatically (thereby creating a schematic summary). Typically, topic identification is achieved using several complementary techniques. We discuss topic identification in section 32.3.1.

In many genres, humans' summaries reflect their own *interpretation*: fusion of concepts, evaluation, and other processing. This stage generally occurs after topic identification. Since the result is something new, not explicitly contained in the input, this stage requires that the system have access to knowledge separate from the input. Given the difficulty of building domain knowledge, few existing systems perform interpretation, and no system includes more than a small domain model. We discuss interpretation in section 32.3.2.

The results of interpretation are usually unreadable abstract representations, and even extracts are seldom coherent, due to dangling references, omitted discourse linkages, and repeated or omitted material. Systems therefore include a stage of *summary generation* to produce human-readable text. In the case of extracts, generation may simply mean 'smoothing' the extracted pieces into a coherent, densely phrased, text. We discuss generation in section 32.3.3.

32.3   REVIEW OF SUMMARIZATION METHODS

32.3.1   Stage 1: Topic identification

To perform this stage, almost all systems employ several independent modules. Each module assigns a score to each unit of input (word, sentence, or longer passage); then a combination module combines the scores for each unit to assign a single integrated score to it; finally, the system returns the n highest-scoring units, according to the summary length requested by the user.

An open issue is the size of the unit of text that is scored for extraction. Most systems focus on one sentence at a time. However, Fukushima, Ehara, and Shirai (1999) show that extracting subsentence-size units produces shorter summaries with more information. On the other hand, Strzalkowski et al. (1999) show that including certain sentences immediately adjacent to important sentences increases coherence—fewer dangling pronoun references, etc.

The performance of topic identification modules is usually measured using Recall and Precision scores (see section 32.5 and Chapter 22). Given an input text, a human's extract, and a system's extract, these scores quantify how closely the system's extract corresponds to the human's. For each unit, we let *correct* = the number of sentences extracted by the system and the human; *wrong* = the number of sentences extracted by the system but not by the human; and *missed* = the number of sentences extracted by the human but not by the system. Then

(32.2)   *Precision = correct / (correct + wrong)*
(32.3)   *Recall = correct / (correct + missed)*

so that Precision reflects how many of the system's extracted sentences were good, and Recall reflects how many good sentences the system missed.

Positional criteria. Thanks to regularities in the text structure of many genres, certain locations of the text (headings, titles, first paragraphs, etc.) tend to contain important information. The simple method of taking the lead (first paragraph) as summary often outperforms other methods, especially with newspaper articles

(Brandow, Mitze, and Rau 1995). Some variation of the **position method** appears in Baxendale (1958); Edmundson (1969); Donlan (1980); Kupiec, Pedersen, and Chen (1995); Teufel and Moens (1997); Strzalkowski et al. (1999); Kupiec et al. and Teufel and Moens both list this as the single best method, scoring around 33 per cent, for news, scientific, and technical articles.

In order to automatically determine the best positions, and to quantify their utility, Lin and Hovy (1997) define the genre- and domain-oriented Optimum Position Policy (OPP) as a ranked list of sentence positions that on average produce the highest yields for extracts, and describe an automated procedure to create OPPs given texts and extracts.

Cue phrase indicator criteria. Since in some genres certain words and phrases ('significant', 'in this paper we show') explicitly signal importance, sentences containing them should be extracted. Teufel and Moens (1997) report 54 per cent joint recall and precision, using a manually built list of 1,423 **cue phrases** in a genre of scientific texts. Each cue phrase has a (positive or negative) 'goodness score', also assigned manually. In Teufel and Moens (1999) they expand their method to argue that rather than single sentences, these cue phrases signal the nature of the multi-sentence rhetorical blocks of text in which they occur (such as Purpose/Problem, Background, Solution/Method, Conclusion/Claim).

Word and phrase frequency criteria. Luhn (1959) used Zipf's Law of word distribution (a few words occur very often, fewer words occur somewhat often, and many words occur infrequently) to develop the following extraction criterion: if a text contains some words unusually frequently, then sentences containing these words are probably important.

The systems of Luhn (1959), Edmundson (1969), Kupiec, Pedersen, and Chen (1995), Teufel and Moens (1999), Hovy and Lin (1999), and others employ various frequency measures, and report performance of between 15 per cent and 35 per cent recall and precision (using word frequency alone). But both Kupiec et al. and Teufel and Moens show that word frequency in combination with other measures is not always better. Witbrock and Mittal (1999) compute a statistical model describing the likelihood that each individual word in the text will appear in the summary, in the context of certain features (part-of-speech tag, word length, neighbouring words, average sentence length, etc.). The generality of this method (also across languages) makes it attractive for further study.

Query and title overlap criteria. A simple but useful method is to score each sentence by the number of desirable words it contains. Desirable words are, for example, those contained in the text's title or headings (Kupiec, Pedersen, and Chen 1995; Teufel and Moens 1997; Hovy and Lin 1999), or in the user's query, for a **query-based summary** (Buckley and Cardie 1997; Strzalkowski et al. 1999; Hovy and Lin 1999). The query method is a direct descendant of IR techniques (see Chapter 29).

Cohesive or lexical connectedness criteria. Words can be connected in various ways, including repetition, coreference, synonymy, and semantic association as expressed in thesauri. Sentences and paragraphs can then be scored based on the degree of connectedness of their words; more-connected sentences are assumed to be more important. This method yields performances ranging from 30 per cent (using a very strict measure of connectedness) to over 60 per cent, with Buckley and Cardie's use of sophisticated IR technology and Barzilay and Elhadad's lexical chains (Salton et al. 1997; Mitra, Singhal, and Buckley 1997; Mani and Bloedorn 1997; Buckley and Cardie 1997; Barzilay and Elhadad 1999). Mani and Bloedorn represent the text as a graph in which words are nodes and arcs represent adjacency, coreference, and lexical similarity.

Discourse structure criteria. A sophisticated variant of connectedness involves producing the underlying discourse structure of the text and scoring sentences by their discourse centrality, as shown in Marcu (1997, 1998). Using a GSAT-like algorithm to learn the optimal combination of scores from centrality, several of the above-mentioned measures, and scores based on the shape and content of the discourse tree, Marcu's (1998) system does almost as well as people for *Scientific American* texts.

Combination of various module scores. In all cases, researchers have found that no single method of scoring performs as well as humans do to create extracts. However, since different methods rely on different kinds of evidence, combining them improves scores significantly. Various methods of automatically finding a combination function have been tried; all seem to work, and there is no obvious best strategy.

In their landmark work, Kupiec, Pedersen, and Chen (1995) train a Bayesian classifier (see Chapter 19) by computing the probability that any sentence will be included in a summary, given the features paragraph position, cue phrase indicators, word frequency, upper-case words, and sentence length (since short sentences are generally not included in summaries). They find that, individually, the paragraph position feature gives 33 per cent precision, the cue phrase indicators 29 per cent (but when joined with the former, the two together give 42 per cent), and so on, with individual scores decreasing to 20 per cent and the combined five-feature score totalling 42 per cent.

Also using a Bayesian classifier, Aone et al. (1999) find that even within the single genre, different newspapers require different features to achieve the same performance.

Using SUMMARIST, Lin (1999) compares eighteen different features, a naive combination of them, and an optimal combination obtained using the machine learning algorithm C4.5 (Quinlan 1986). These features include most of the above mentioned, as well as features signalling the presence in each sentence of proper names, dates, quantities, pronouns, and quotes. The performances of the individual methods and the naive and learned combination functions are graphed in Fig. 32.1, showing extract length against f-score (joint recall and precision). As expected, the top scorer is the learned combination function. The second-best score is achieved by query term overlap (though in other topics the query method did not do as well). The third best score (up to the 20 per cent length) is achieved equally by word frequency, the lead method, and the naive combination function. The curves in general indicate that to be most

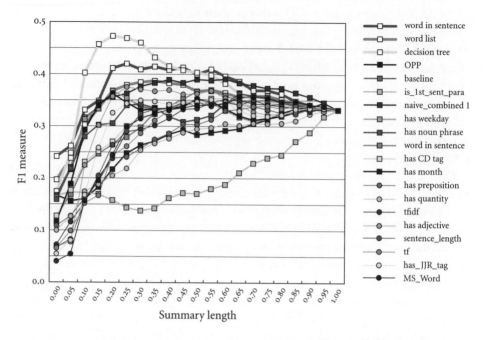

Fig. 32.1 Summary length vs. f-score for individual and combined methods
of scoring sentences in SUMMARIST

useful, summaries should not be longer than about 35 per cent and not shorter than
about 15 per cent; no 5 per cent summary achieved an f-score of over 0.25.

32.3.2 Stage 2: Interpretation or topic fusion

As described in section 32.2, the stage of *interpretation* is what distinguishes extract-
type summarization systems from abstract-type systems. During interpretation, the
topics identified as important are fused, represented in new terms, and expressed
using a new formulation, using concepts or words not found in the original text.

No system can perform interpretation without prior knowledge about the domain;
by definition, it must interpret the input in terms of something extraneous to the text.
But acquiring enough (and deep enough) prior domain knowledge is so difficult that
summarizers to date have only attempted it in a small way.

At first glance, the template representations used in information extraction (Chapter 30), or other interpretative structures in terms of which to represent stories for
summarization, hold some promise (DeJong 1978; Lehnert 1981; Rau and Jacobs
1991). But the difficulty of building such structures and filling them makes large-scale
summarization impractical at present.

Taking a more formal approach, Hahn and Reimer (1999) develop operators that condense knowledge representation structures in a terminological logic through conceptual abstraction (Chapter 5). To date, no parser has been built to produce the knowledge structures from text, and no generator to produce language from the results.

Taking a leaf from IR, Hovy and Lin (1999) use topic signatures—sets of words and relative strengths of association, each set related to a single headword—to perform topic fusion. By automatically constructing these signatures (using 30,000 texts from the *Wall Street Journal* and *TF∗IDF* to identify for each topic the set of words most relevant to it) they overcome the knowledge paucity problem. They use these topic signatures both during topic identification (to score sentences by signature overlap) and during topic interpretation (to substitute the signature head for the sentence(s) containing enough of its words). The effectiveness of signatures to perform interpretation has not yet been shown.

Interpretation remains blocked by the problem of domain knowledge acquisition. Before summarization systems can produce abstracts, this problem will have to be solved.

32.3.3 Stage 3: Summary generation

The third major stage of summarization is generation. When the summary content has been created through abstracting and/or information extraction, it exists within the computer in internal notation, and thus requires the techniques of natural language generation, namely text planning, sentence (micro-)planning, and sentence realization. For more on this topic see Chapter 15.

However, as mentioned in section 32.2, extract summaries require no generation stage. In this case, though, various dysfluencies tend to result when sentences (or other extracted units) are simply extracted and printed—whether they are printed in order of importance score or in text order. A process of 'smoothing' can be used to identify and repair typical dysfluencies, as first proposed in Hirst et al. (1997). The most typical dysfluencies that arise include repetition of clauses or NPs (where the repair is to aggregate the material into a conjunction), repetition of named entities (where the repair is to pronominalize), and inclusion of less important material such as parentheticals and discourse markers (where the repair is to eliminate them). In the context of summarization, Mani, Gates, and Bloedorn (1999) describe a summary revision program that takes as input simple extracts and produces shorter and more readable summaries.

Text compression is another promising approach. Knight and Marcu's (2000) prize-winning paper describes using the EM algorithm to train a system to compress the syntactic parse tree of a sentence in order to produce a single, shorter, one, with the idea of eventually shortening two sentences into one, three into two (or one), and so on. Banko, Mittal, and Witbrock (2000) train statistical models to create headlines for texts by extracting individual words and ordering them appropriately.

Jing and McKeown (1999) make the extract-summary point from the generation perspective. They argue that summaries are often constructed from the source document by a process of cut and paste—fragments of document sentences are combined into summary sentences—and hence that a summarizer need only identify the major fragments of sentences to include and then weave them together grammatically. To prove this claim, they train a hidden Markov model to identify where in the document each (fragment of each) summary sentence resides. Testing with 300 human-written abstracts of newspaper articles, Jing and McKeown determine that only 19 per cent of summary sentences do not have matching sentences in the document.

In an extreme case of cut and paste, Witbrock and Mittal (1999; see section 32.3.1) extract a set of words from the input document and then order the words into sentences using a bigram language model.

32.4 MULTI-DOCUMENT SUMMARIZATION

Summarizing a single text is difficult enough. But summarizing a collection of thematically related documents poses several additional challenges. In order to avoid repetitions, one has to identify and locate thematic overlaps. One also has to decide what to include of the remainder, to deal with potential inconsistencies between documents, and, when necessary, to arrange events from various sources along a single timeline. For these reasons, **multi-document summarization** is much less developed than its single-document cousin.

Various methods have been proposed to identify cross-document overlaps. SUMMONS (Radev 1999), a system that covers most aspects of multi-document summarization, takes an information extraction approach. Assuming that all input documents are parsed into templates (whose standardization makes comparison easier), SUMMONS clusters the templates according to their contents, and then applies rules to extract items of major import. In contrast, Barzilay, McKeown, and Elhadad (1999) parse each sentence into a syntactic dependency structure (a simple parse tree) using a robust parser and then match trees across documents, using paraphrase rules that alter the trees as needed.

To determine what additional material should be included, Carbonell, Geng, and Goldstein (1997) first identify the units most relevant to the user's query, using methods described in section 32.3.1, and then estimate the 'marginal relevance' of all remaining units using a measure called Maximum Marginal Relevance (MMR).

SUMMONS deals with cross-document overlaps and inconsistencies using a series of rules to order templates as the story unfolds, identify information updates (e.g. increasing death tolls), identify cross-template inconsistencies (decreasing death tolls), and finally produce appropriate phrases or data structures for the language generator.

Multi-document summarization poses interesting challenges beyond single documents (Goldstein et al. 2000; Fukumoto and Suzuki 2000; Kubota Ando et al. 2000). An important study (Marcu and Gerber 2001) show that for the newspaper article genre, even some very simple procedures provide essentially perfect results. For example, taking the first two or three paragraphs of the most recent text of a series of texts about an event provides a summary equally coherent and complete as that produced by human abstracters. Obviously, this cannot be true of more complex types of summary, such as biographies of people or descriptions of objects. Further research is required on all aspects of multi-document summarization before it can become a practical reality.

32.5 EVALUATING SUMMARIES

How can you evaluate the quality of a summary? The growing body of literature on this interesting question suggests that summaries are so task and genre specific and so user oriented that no single measurement covers all cases. In section 32.5.1 we describe a few evaluation studies and in section 32.5.2 we develop some theoretical background.

32.5.1 Previous evaluation studies

As discussed in Chapter 22, many NLP evaluators distinguish between black-box and glass-box evaluation. Taking a similar approach for summarization systems, Spärck Jones and Galliers (1996) define **intrinsic** evaluations as measuring output quality (only) and **extrinsic** as measuring user assistance in task performance (see also Chapter 22).

Most existing evaluations of summarization systems are intrinsic. Typically, the evaluators create a set of ideal summaries, one for each test text, and then compare the summarizer's output to it, measuring content overlap (often by sentence or phrase recall and precision, but sometimes by simple word overlap). Since there is no 'correct' summary, some evaluators use more than one ideal per test text, and average the score of the system across the set of ideals. Comparing system output to some ideal was performed by, for example, Edmundson (1969); Paice (1990); Ono, Sumita, and Miike (1994); Kupiec, Pedersen, and Chen (1995); Marcu (1997); Salton et al. (1997). To simplify evaluating extracts, Marcu (1999) and Goldstein et al. (1999) independently developed an automated method to create extracts corresponding to abstracts.

A second intrinsic method is to have evaluators rate systems' summaries according to some scale (readability; informativeness; fluency; coverage); see Brandow, Mitze, and Rau (1995) for one of the larger studies.

Extrinsic evaluation is easy to motivate; the major problem is to ensure that the metric applied correlates well with task performance efficiency. Examples of extrinsic evaluation can be found in Morris, Kasper, and Adams (1992) for GMAT testing, Miike et al. (1994) for news analysis, and Mani and Bloedorn (1997) for information retrieval.

The largest extrinsic evaluation to date is the TIPSTER-SUMMAC study (Firmin Hand and Sundheim 1998; Firmin and Chrzanowski 1999), involving some eighteen systems (research and commercial), in three tests. In the Categorization task testers classified a set of TREC texts and their summaries created by various systems. After classification, the agreement between the classifications of texts and their corresponding summaries is measured; the greater the agreement, the better the summary captures that which causes the full text to be classified as it is. In the Ad Hoc task, testers classified query-based summaries as Relevant or Not Relevant to the query. The agreement of texts and summaries classified in each category reflects the quality of the summary. Space constraints prohibit full discussion of the results; some interesting findings are that, for newspaper texts, all extraction systems performed equally well (and no better than the lead method) for generic summarization, and that IR methods produced the best query-based extracts. Still, despite the fact that all the systems performed extracts only, thereby simplifying much of the scoring process to IR-like recall and precision measures against human extracts, the wealth of material and the variations of analysis contained in Firmin and Chrzanowski (1999) underscore how little is still understood about summarization evaluation. This conclusion is strengthened in a fine paper by Donaway, Drummey, and Mather (2000) who show how summaries receive different scores with different measures, or when compared to different (but presumably equivalent) ideal summaries created by humans.

Recognizing these problems, Jing et al. (1998) compare several evaluation methods, intrinsic and extrinsic, on the same extracts. With regard to inter-human agreement, they find fairly high consistency in the news genre, as long as the summary (extract) length is fixed as relatively short (there is some evidence that other genres will deliver less consistency (Marcu 1997)). With regard to summary length, they find great variation. Comparing three systems, and comparing five humans, they show that the humans' ratings of systems, and the perceived ideal summary length, fluctuate as summaries become longer.

32.5.2 Two basic measures

Much of the complexity of summarization evaluation arises from the fact that it is difficult to specify what one really needs to measure, and why, without a clear formulation of what precisely the summary is trying to capture. We outline some general considerations here.

In general, to be a summary, the summary must obey two[1] requirements:

- it must be shorter than the original input text;
- it must contain the important information of the original (where importance is defined by the user), and not other, totally new, information.

One can define two measures to capture the extent to which a summary S conforms to these requirements with regard to a text T:

(32.4) **Compression Ratio:** $CR = (length\ S) / (length\ T)$
(32.5) **Retention Ratio:** $RR = (info\ in\ S) / (info\ in\ T)$

However we choose to measure the length and the information content, we can say that a good summary is one in which CR is small (tending to zero) while RR is large (tending to unity). We can characterize summarization systems by plotting the ratios of the summaries produced under varying conditions. For example, Fig. 32.2(a) shows a fairly normal growth curve: as the summary gets longer (grows along the x axis), it includes more information (grows also along the y axis), until it equals the original. Fig. 32.2(b) shows a more desirable situation: at some special point, the addition of just a little more text to the summary adds a disproportionately large amount of information. Fig. 32.2(c) shows another: quite early, most of the important material is included in the summary; as the length grows, the added material is less interesting. In both the latter cases, summarization is useful.

Measuring length. Measuring length is straightforward; one can count the number of words, letters, sentences, etc. For a given genre and register, there is a fairly good correlation among these metrics, in general.

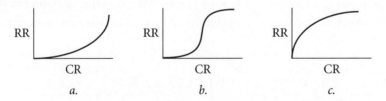

Fig. 32.2 Compression Ratio (CR) vs. Retention Ratio (RR)

---

[1] Ideally, it should also be a coherent, readable text, though a list of keywords or text fragments can constitute a degenerate summary. Readability is measured in several standard ways, for purposes of language learning, machine translation, and other NLP applications.

Measuring information content. Ideally, one wants to measure not information content, but *interesting* information content only. Although it is very difficult to define what constitutes *interestingness*, one can approximate measures of information content in several ways. We describe four here.

The *Expert Game.* Ask experts to underline and extract the most interesting or informative fragments of the text. Measure recall and precision of the system's summary against the human's extract, as outlined in section 32.3.1.

The *Classification Game.* Two variants of this extrinsic measure were implemented in the TIPSTER-SUMMAC evaluation (Firmin Hand and Sundheim 1998; Firmin and Chrzanowski 1999); see section 32.5.1.

The *Shannon Game.* In information theory (Shannon 1951), the amount of information contained in a message is measured by $-p \log p$, where p is, roughly speaking, the probability of the reader guessing the message (or each piece thereof, individually). To measure the information content of a summary S relative to that of its corresponding text T, assemble three sets of testers. Each tester must create T, guessing letter by letter. The first set reads T before starting, the second set reads S before starting, and the third set reads nothing, For each set, record the number of wrong guesses g_{wrong} and total guesses g_{total}, and compute the ratio $R = g_{wrong}/g_{total}$. The quality of S can be computed by comparing the three ratios. R_{none} quantifies how much a tester could guess from world knowledge (and should hence not be attributed to the summary), while R_T quantifies how much a tester still has to guess, even with 'perfect' prior knowledge. The closer R_S is to R_T, the better the summary.[2]

The *Question Game.* This measure approximates the information content of S by determining how well it allows readers to answer questions drawn up about T. Before starting, one or more people create a set of questions based on what they consider the principal content (author's view or query-based) of T. Then the testers answer these questions three times in succession: first without having read either S or T, second after having read S, and third after having read T. After each round, the number of questions answered correctly is tallied. The quality of S can be computed by comparing the three tallies, as above. The closer the testers' score for S is to their score for T, the better the summary. The TIPSTER-SUMMAC summarization evaluation (Firmin Hand and Sundheim 1998) contained a tryout of the Question Game.

Further Reading and Relevant Resources

Mani (2001) provides a thorough overview of the field, and Mani and Maybury (1999) provide a most useful collection of twenty-six papers about summarization, includ-

---

[2] In 1997, the author performed a small experiment using the Shannon Game, finding an order of magnitude difference between the three contrast sets.

ing many of the most influential. Recent workshop proceedings are Hovy and Radev (1998); Hahn et al. (2000); Goldstein and Lin (2001); DUC (2001) and DUC (2002). Useful URLs are at http://www.cs.columbia.edu/~radev/summarization/.

ACKNOWLEDGEMENTS

Thanks to Chin-Yew Lin, Daniel Marcu, Hao Liu, Mike Junk, Louke van Wensveen, Thérèse Firmin Hand, Sara Shelton, and Beth Sundheim.

REFERENCES

Aone, C., M. E. Okurowski, J. Gorlinsky, and B. Larsen. 1999. 'A scalable summarization system using robust NLP'. In Mani and Maybury (1999), 71–80.

Banko, M., V. O. Mittal, and M. J. Witbrock. 2000. 'Headline generation based on statistical translation'. *Proceedings of the 38th Annual Conference of the Association for Computational Linguistics (ACL 2000)* (Hong Kong), 318–25.

Barzilay, R. and M. Elhadad. 1999. 'Using lexical chains for text summarization'. In Mani and Maybury (1999), 111–21.

——K. R. McKeown, and M. Elhadad 1999. 'Information fusion in the context of multi-document summarization'. *Proceedings of the 37th Conference of the Association of Computational Linguistics (ACL '99)* (College Park, Md.), 550–7.

Baxendale, P. B. 1958. 'Machine-made index for technical literature: an experiment'. *IBM Journal*, 354–61.

Brandow, R., K. Mitze, and L. Rau. 1995. 'Automatic condensation of electronic publishing publications by sentence selection'. *Information Processing and Management* 31(5), 675–85. Also in Mani and Maybury (1999), 293–304.

Buckley, C. and C. Cardie. 1997. 'Using EMPIRE and SMART for high-precision IR and summarization'. *Proceedings of the TIPSTER Text Phase III 12-Month Workshop*. San Diego, USA.

Carbonell, J., Y. Geng, and J. Goldstein. 1997. 'Automated query-relevant summarization and diversity-based reranking'. *Proceedings of the IJCAI-97 Workshop on AI in Digital Libraries*. San Mateo, Calif.: Morgan Kaufmann, 12–19.

DeJong, G. J. 1978. *Fast skimming of news stories: the FRUMP system*. Ph.D. thesis, Yale University.

Donaway, R. L., K. W. Drummey, and L. A. Mather. 2000. 'A comparison of rankings produced by summarization evaluation measures'. *Proceedings of the NAACL Workshop on Text Summarization* (Seattle), 69–78.

Donlan, D. 1980. 'Locating main ideas in history textbooks'. *Journal of Reading*, 24, 135–40.

DUC. 2001. *Proceedings of the Document Understanding Conference (DUC) Workshop on Multi-Document Summarization Evaluation*, at the SIGIR-01 Conference. New Orleans, USA. http://www.itl.nist.gov/iad/894.02/projects/duc/index.html.

——2002. *Proceedings of the Document Understanding Conference (DUC) Workshop on Multi-Document Summarization Evaluation*, at the ACL-02 Conference. Philadelphia, USA.

Edmundson, H. P. 1969. 'New methods in automatic extraction'. *Journal of the ACM*, 16(2), 264–85. Also in Mani and Maybury (1999), 23–42.

Firmin, T. and M. J. Chrzanowski. 1999. 'An evaluation of text summarization systems'. In Mani and Maybury (1999), 325–35.

Firmin Hand, T. and B. Sundheim. 1998. 'TIPSTER-SUMMAC summarization evaluation'. *Proceedings of the TIPSTER Text Phase III Workshop*, Washington, DC.

Fukumoto, F. and Y. Suzuki. 2000. 'Extracting key paragraph based on topic and event detection: towards multi-document summarization'. *Proceedings of the NAACL Workshop on Text Summarization* (Seattle), 31–9.

Fukushima, T., T. Ehara, and K. Shirai. 1999. 'Partitioning long sentences for text summarization'. *Journal of the Society of Natural Language Processing of Japan*, 6(6), 131–47 (in Japanese).

Goldstein, J. and C.-Y. Lin (eds.). 2001. *Proceedings of the NAACL Workshop on Text Summarization*. Pittsburgh, USA.

——M. Kantrowitz, V. Mittal, and J. Carbonell. 1999. 'Summarizing text documents: sentence selection and evaluation metrics'. *Proceedings of the 22nd International ACM Conference on Research and Development in Information Retrieval (SIGIR '99)* (Berkeley), 121–8.

——V. Mittal, J. Carbonell, and M. Kantrowitz. 2000. 'Multi-document summarization by sentence extraction'. *Proceedings of the NAACL Workshop on Text Summarization* (Seattle), 40–8.

Hahn, U. and U. Reimer. 1999. 'Knowledge-based text summarization: salience and generalization operators for knowledge base abstraction'. In Mani and Maybury (1999), 215–32.

——C.-Y. Lin, I. Mani, and D. Radev (eds.). 2000. *Proceedings of the NAACL Workshop on Text Summarization* (Seattle).

Hirst, G., C. DiMarco, E. H. Hovy, and K. Parsons. 1997. 'Authoring and generating health-education documents that are tailored to the needs of the individual patient'. *Proceedings of the 6th International Conference on User Modelling (UM '97)* (Sardinia), 107–18. http://um.org.

Hovy, E. H. and C.-Y. Lin. 1999. 'Automating text summarization in SUMMARIST'. In Mani and Maybury (1999), 81–97.

——and D. Radev (eds.). 1998. *Proceedings of the AAAI Spring Symposium on Intelligent Text Summarization*. Stanford, Calif.: AAAI Press.

Jing, H. and K. R. McKeown. 1999. 'The decomposition of human-written summary sentences'. *Proceedings of the 22nd International ACM Conference on Research and Development in Information Retrieval (SIGIR-99)* (Berkeley), 129–36.

——R. Barzilay, K. McKeown, and M. Elhadad. 1998. 'Summarization evaluation methods: experiments and results'. In Hovy and Radev (1998), 60–8.

Knight, K. and D. Marcu. 2000. 'Statistics-based summarization—step one: sentence compression'. *Proceedings of the Conference of the American Association for Artificial Intelligence (AAAI)* (Austin, Tex.), 703–10.

Kubota Ando, R., B. K. Boguraev, R. J. Byrd, and M. S. Neff. 2000. 'Multi-document summarization by visualizing topical content'. *Proceedings of the NAACL Workshop on Text Summarization* (Seattle), 79–88.

Kupiec, J., J. Pedersen, and F. Chen. 1995. 'A trainable document summarizer'. *Proceedings of the 18th Annual International ACM Conference on Research and Development in Information Retrieval (SIGIR)* (Seattle), 68–73. Also in Mani and Maybury (1999), 55–60.

Lehnert, W. G. 1981. 'Plot units and narrative summarization'. *Cognitive Science*, 5(4). See also 'Plot units: a narrative summarization strategy', in Mani and Maybury (1999), 177–214.

Lin, C.-Y. 1999. 'Training a selection function for extraction'. *Proceedings of the 8th International Conference on Information and Knowledge Management (CIKM)* (Kansas City), 1–8.

——and E. H. Hovy. 1997. 'Identifying topics by position'. *Proceedings of the Applied Natural Language Processing Conference (ANLP '97)* (Washington), 283–90.

Luhn, H. P. 1959. 'The automatic creation of literature abstracts'. *IBM Journal of Research and Development*, 159–65. Also in Mani and Maybury (1999), 15–22.

Mani, I. 2001. *Automatic Summarization*. Amsterdam: John Benjamins.

——and E. Bloedorn. 1997. 'Multi-document summarization by graph search and matching'. *Proceedings of AAAI-97* (Providence), 622–8.

——B. Gates, and E. Bloedorn. 1999. 'Improving summaries by revising them'. *Proceedings of the 37th Conference of the Association of Computational Linguistics (ACL '99)* (College Park, Md.), 558–65.

——and M. Maybury (eds.). 1999. *Advances in Automatic Text Summarization*. Cambridge, Mass.: MIT Press.

Marcu, D. 1997. *The rhetorical parsing, summarization, and generation of natural language texts*. Ph.D. thesis, University of Toronto.

——1998. 'Improving summarization through rhetorical parsing tuning'. *Proceedings of the COLING-ACL'98 Workshop on Very Large Corpora* (Montreal), 10–16.

——1999. 'The automatic construction of large-scale corpora for summarization research'. *Proceedings of the 22nd International ACM Conference on Research and Development in Information Retrieval (SIGIR '99)* (Berkeley), 137–44.

——and L. Gerber. 2001. 'An inquiry into the nature of multidocument abstracts, extracts, and their evaluation'. *Proceedings of the Workshop on Text Summarization at the 2nd Conference of the North American Association of Computational Linguistics* (Pittsburgh), 1–8.

Miike, S., E. Itoh, K. Ono, and K. Sumita. 1994. 'A full-text retrieval system with dynamic abstract generation function'. *Proceedings of the 17th Annual International ACM Conference on Research and Development in Information Retrieval (SIGIR)*, 152–61.

Mitra, M., A. Singhal, and C. Buckley. 1997. 'Automatic text summarization by paragraph extraction'. *Proceedings of the Workshop on Intelligent Scalable Summarization at the ACL/ EACL Conference* (Madrid), 39–46.

Morris, A. G. Kasper, and D. Adams. 1992. 'The effects and limitations of automatic text condensing on reading comprehension performance'. *Information Systems Research*, 3(1), 17–35.

Ono, K., K. Sumita, and S. Miike. 1994. 'Abstract generation based on rhetorical structure extraction'. *Proceedings of the 15th International Conference on Computational Linguistics (COLING '94)* (Kyoto), i, 344–8.

Paice, C. D. 1990. 'Constructing literature abstracts by computer: techniques and prospects'. *Information Processing and Management*, 26(1), 171–86.

Quinlan, J. R. 1986. 'Induction of decision trees'. *Machine Learning*, 1, 81–106.

Radev, D. R. 1999. *Generating natural language summaries from multiple on-line source: language reuse and regeneration*. Ph.D. thesis, Columbia University.

Rau, L. S. and P. S. Jacobs. 1991. 'Creating segmented databases from free text for text retrieval'. *Proceedings of the 14th Annual ACM Conference on Research and Development in Information Retrieval (SIGIR)* (New York), 337–46.

Salton, G., A. Singhal, M. Mitra, and C. Buckley. 1997. 'Automatic text structuring and summarization'. *Information Processing and Management*, 33(2), 193–208. Also in Mani and Maybury (1999), 341–56.

Shannon, C. 1951. 'Prediction and entropy of printed English'. *Bell System Technical Journal*, Jan., 50–64.

Spärck Jones, K. 1999. 'Automatic summarizing: factors and directions'. In Mani and Maybury (1999), 1–13.

——and J. R. Galliers. 1996. *Evaluating Natural Language Processing Systems: An Analysis and Review*. New York: Springer.

Strzalkowski, T., G. Stein, J. Wang, and B. Wise. 1999. 'A robust practical text summarizer'. In Mani and Maybury (1999), 137–54.

Teufel, S. and M. Moens. 1997. 'Sentence extraction as a classification task'. *Proceedings of the ACL Workshop on Intelligent Text Summarization* (Madrid), 58–65.

————1999. 'Argumentative classification of extracted sentences as a first step toward flexible abstracting'. In Mani and Maybury (1999), 155–75.

Witbrock, M. and V. Mittal. 1999. 'Ultra-summarization: a statistical approach to generating highly condensed non-extractive summaries'. *Proceedings of the 22nd ACM Conference on Research and Development in Information Retrieval (SIGIR)* (Berkeley), 315–16.

CHAPTER 33

TERM EXTRACTION AND AUTOMATIC INDEXING

CHRISTIAN JACQUEMIN
DIDIER BOURIGAULT

ABSTRACT

Terms are pervasive in scientific and technical documents; their identification is a crucial issue for any application dealing with the analysis, understanding, generation, or translation of such documents. In particular, the ever-growing mass of specialized documentation available on-line, in industrial and governmental archives or in digital libraries, calls for advances in terminology processing for tasks such as information retrieval, cross-language querying, indexing of multimedia documents, translation aids, document routing and summarization, etc.

This chapter presents a new domain of research and development in natural language processing (NLP) that is concerned with the representation, acquisition, and recognition of terms.

33.1 BASIC NOTIONS

33.1.1 What is a term?

The definition of what constitutes a **term** proposed in **computational terminology** differs from the traditional notion of terms as elaborated by the Vienna School. The characterization of terms in a computational framework must take into account novel dimensions of termhood in the domain of terminological engineering and its applications.

33.1.1.1 *The classical view*

In the traditional sense, a term is considered as the linguistic label of a concept. This dominant approach to termhood stems from the General Theory of Terminology which was elaborated by E. Wüster in the late 1930s, with the Vienna Circle (Felber 1984). Born in the positivist movement during the inter-war period, the classical doctrine of terminology assumes that knowledge is organized into domains, each domain being equivalent to a network of concepts. In one domain, each concept is (ideally) associated with one term, which is its linguistic label. Such a concept-centred approach to terminology is well suited for normalization. It is however less suitable for computational term analysis.

33.1.1.2 *Problems with the applicability of the classical view*

To start with, the classical view assumes that experts in an area of knowledge have conceptual maps in their minds. This assumption is misleading and unproductive because experts cannot build a conceptual map from introspection. Terminologists constantly refer to textual data.

Secondly, the semi-automatic construction and exploitation of terminological resources gives rise to a wide variety of terminological data for the same field. There are as many types of resources as families of applications: thesauri for automatic indexing and information retrieval, structured index for hyper-documents, authority lists for computer-aided controlled writing, bilingual term lists for computer-aided translation, ontologies for industrial intelligence, structured keywords for digital libraries, etc.

The classical view of terminology cannot be successfully adapted to concrete applications.

33.1.1.3 *Terminological engineering*

According to a definition that is better suited to corpus-based terminology, a term is the *output* of a procedure of terminological analysis. A single word, such as *cell*, or a multi-word unit, such as *blood cell*, are terms because they have been manually selected as such. The decision process can involve a community of researchers or practitioners, a normalization institution, or even a single engineer or terminologist in charge of building a terminological resource for a specific purpose.

Building a terminological resource should be viewed as the *construction* of *an instance of* the terminological structures from a corpus. The resulting terminological database should be dually relevant:

- with regard to the corpus: it should be made of stable and domain-specific lexical items (see Chapter 24); and
- with regard to the application: it should contain units which are useful for the intended application in terms of economy, internal cohesion, and efficiency.

Thus, the construction of a thesaurus is an activity in the domain of linguistic engineering as outlined by Sager (1990: 10):

The theories underlying applied fields of study benefit from being application driven rather than following separate paths as terminological theory has been doing in recent years. By adopting the engineering approach of identifying problems and seeking solutions, significant advances have been made.

33.1.2 Linguistic work on terms in context

Recently, several linguists in terminology have focused on the notion of **rich contexts** which are involved in the detection of terms, relations between terms, or definitions and properties of terms (Condamines and Rebeyrolles 1998; Davidson et al. 1998; Pearson 1998). These works agree on the fact that tools for term acquisition should recognize and use terminological contexts.

In rich contexts relationships are established between terms. Connective phrases, such as *e.g.* or *called*, or formal or semi-formal definitions, such as *A configuration file is a family of source files* (Condamines and Rebeyrolles 1998), provide paraphrastic equivalents or synonyms of terms in texts. Thus, the hypothesis underlying the use of linguistically rich contexts is that the expression of terminological relationships in texts is made through cue words or structures. Such patterns are defined through linguistic studies with a genuine concern for the detailed observation of textual data. These patterns are then likely to be useful to the design of tools for computer-aided terminology.

33.1.3 Terms in thesauri

Among the terminological resources that can result from terminological investigation, thesauri are particularly interesting for computational applications such as NLP for specialized languages, automatic indexing, or automatic acquisition of terms and their relationships. For this reason, we briefly present the organization of a thesaurus in this section.

According to Sager (1990), the data used to describe terms can be classified into the following five categories: management data (numeric keys, record number, terminologist's name, date of coding, etc.), conceptual data (subject, scope, definition, related concepts and type of relation, etc.), linguistic data (lexical entries, synonymous entries, equivalents in other languages, variants, etc.), pragmatic data (usage restrictions, contextual data, etc.), and bibliographical data.

In order to illustrate the way in which a term can be documented in a thesaurus, we now turn to the description of the *Metathesaurus* in the *UMLS* project (see Table 33.1). The purpose of this project is to facilitate the information retrieval and the integration of all the linguistic data handled in the medical domain such as biomedical literature, clinical records, factual databanks, etc. The *Metathesaurus* is designed to help the processing of medical data by providing practitioners with an authority list of concepts. It is organized into concepts. Each concept is an abstract representation of linguistic utterances which are considered as synonymous in the medical domain. Each concept is linked to several terms (or to only one term in the case where the term

Table 33.1 **A sample concept in the *Metathesaurus* and associated terms and strings**

Concepts	Terms	Strings
C0004238 (preferred) *Atrial Fibrillation* *Atrial Fibrillations* *Auricular Fibrillation*	L0004238 (preferred) *Atrial Fibrillation* *Atrial Fibrillations*	S0016668 (preferred) *Atrial Fibrillation*
		S0016669 (plural variant) *Atrial Fibrillations*
	L0004327 (synonym) *Auricular Fibrillation* *Auricular Fibrillations*	S0016899 (preferred) *Auricular Fibrillation*
		S0016900 (plural variant) *Auricular Fibrillations*

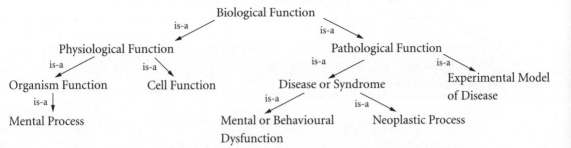

Fig. 33.1 Is-a relationships among types of concepts in the *Semantic network*

has no variant form). One of them is the preferred term. It corresponds to the usage most frequently observed in corpora. Terms are in turn linked to alternative strings (including graphical variants, lexical variants, translations in other languages). For each term, one of the strings is also considered as preferred.

The *Metathesaurus* also contains several types of semantic relationships between concepts. For instance, *Atrial Fibrillation* is a type of *Arrhythmia* and is therefore linked to it by an is-a link (see Chapter 25).

Since the major role of a thesaurus is to provide the user with details about the concepts it contains, the *Metathesaurus* associates several types of attributes with concepts. For instance, the concept *Atrial Fibrillation* shown in Table 33.1 has the semantic types *Pathologic Function* and *Finding* and the definition *Disorder of cardiac rhythm characterized by rapid, irregular atrial impulses and ineffective atrial contractions*. The semantic types associated with concepts are organized into a *Semantic network* of 134 types and 54 relationships (see Figs. 33.1 and 33.2).

Such a thesaurus can be used by a specialist in order to access information, control the quality of writing, get translation aids, etc. But, recently, thesauri have also proven to be useful resources in automatic text processing for the purpose of NLP and information retrieval. Conversely, NLP and knowledge engineering techniques are developed for the automatic construction of thesauri.

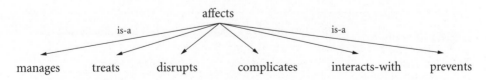

Fig. 33.2 Is-a relationships among types of relationships in the *Semantic network*

33.2 TERM-ORIENTED NLP

The two main areas of research involving terminology in NLP are term acquisition, the automatic discovery of new terms, and term recognition, the identification of known terms in text corpora.

33.2.1 Fields of activity in term-oriented NLP

The use of terms in NLP concerns either automatic processing, such as automatic translation (Chapter 27), information retrieval (Chapter 29), information extraction (Chapter 30) and knowledge management, or language planning, the description and the collection of terms in a given language and in a given area.

Basically, terms in NLP can be viewed as a particular type of lexical data. Contrary to general language lexicons, term bases contain mostly multi-word units and are prone to continuous evolutions: creation, modification, semantic shifts, neologisms, etc. Therefore, term databases need to be constantly rebuilt, maintained, and enriched in order to follow the thematic drifts in scientific and technical areas. Thus, a major domain of term-oriented NLP and term-oriented statistics is **term acquisition**. It is subdivided into two subfields, **initial term acquisition** and **term enrichment**, depending on whether or not initial terminological data are available. Both fields are described in section 33.2.2.

The use of terms in automatic text processing is closely related to **automatic indexing**, the association of documents with lists of words or phrases for the purpose of information access. The databases are constructed to be used for manual indexing, corporate knowledge representation, back-of-book indexing, etc. Since terms are condensed linguistic representations of major concepts in a field, they can be used as abstracted descriptors of the content of documents for automatic indexing. Indexing is called *controlled indexing* if it refers to an authority list of terms. It is called *free indexing* in the case where no preliminary terminological data are available.

To sum up, term-based NLP is divided as indicated by Table 33.2.

Table 33.2 The four main subdomains of term-based NLP

	Prior terminological data	No prior terminological data
Term discovery	*Term enrichment*	*Term acquisition*
Term recognition	*Controlled indexing*	*Free indexing*

33.2.2 Some milestones in term acquisition

There are basically two techniques for discovering **candidate terms** in corpora: symbolic approaches that rely on syntactic descriptions of terms—mainly noun phrases—and statistical approaches that exploit the fact that the words composing a term tend to be found recurringly close to each other more frequently than would occur just by chance (see Chapter 19).

33.2.2.1 *A grammar-based approach: TERMINO*

TERMINO (Lauriston 1994) is a seminal work in the domain of corpus-based terminology. It relies on the hypothesis that there are lexical and syntactic clues that can be used to detect terms in texts. The parsing module is divided in subcomponents. The sequence of operations that perform the extraction of terms from raw corpora is:

   (i) *Preprocessing.* Text filtering and removal of format characters.
  (ii) *Parsing and Term Extraction.*
      (*a*) Morphological analysis.
      (*b*) Noun phrase parsing.
      (*c*) Term generation.
 (iii) *Interactive Term Bank Construction and Management.* An additional tool provides a user-friendly interface for the construction of term banks from terms extracted in the preceding steps.

33.2.2.2 *A combination of patterns and learned selection restrictions: LEXTER*

Since LEXTER was developed in an applied environment, the tool is also accompanied by a visual interface for validating and organizing the candidate terms acquired from corpora. While TERMINO is based on generative grammar rules, LEXTER operates on a tagged corpus (see Chapter 11) with the help of lexico-syntactic patterns based on lexical elements and syntactic categories (Bourigault 1996).

   (i) *Maximal noun phrases.* The grammar of LEXTER is composed of transducers called *splitting rules* which indicate the most likely boundaries of noun phrases. For instance, a preposition following a past participle is a boundary. Thus *les clapets <u>situés sur</u> les tubes d'alimentation* (the valves *located on* the feeder pipes) is split into *les clapets* (the valves) and *les tubes d'alimentation* (the feeder pipes). This rule is applied unless the preposition is *de* (of) or unless the verb belongs to an exception list. The exception list is automatically acquired by the tool through an endogenous learning procedure which disambiguates problematic situations from unambiguous occurrences in the corpus.

(ii) *Decomposition into candidates.* The maximal noun phrases produced by the preceding step are then split into binary phrases made of a head and an expansion. These nominal chunks together with the maximal noun phrases are produced as output by LEXTER. The output phrases of the term extractor are intentionally called candidates in order to stress the crucial role of human validation as post-processing of the automatic acquisition. For instance, from a noun-preposition-adjective-noun structure such as *pylône à haute tension* (high voltage pylon), the candidate *haute tension* (high tension) is generated.

The candidate terms are then automatically organized into a network on the basis of shared lexical elements in similar syntactic positions. For example, the terms *vanne motorisée* (motorized gate), *vanne pneumatique* (pneumatic gate), and *vanne d'alimentation* (feeding gate) are linked together because they share the same head-word *vanne* (gate). The thus structured set of terms is finally entered into a database in order to be validated by an expert.

33.2.2.3 *A combination of syntactic patterns and statistical filters: ACABIT*

Since both TERMINO and LEXTER rely on lexico-syntactic analysis of the textual data, any occurrence—even if it appears only once in a corpus (a *hapax legomenon*)—is likely to be a candidate term. While this can be considered as an advantage in some situations (no occurrence will be missed), it may be desirable in other situations to rely on ranking techniques which sort candidates by decreasing order of termhood. This purpose is achieved in ACABIT through a hybrid technique that combines analytical filtering and statistical ranking (Daille 1996). The acquisition of candidate terms in ACABIT is performed in two steps:

(i) *Linguistic filtering.* As in LEXTER, the acquisition of candidate terms in ACABIT relies on finite-state transducers. Three main binary noun-phrase structures are considered for English (adjective-noun, noun-noun, and noun-preposition-noun) along with variation patterns such as coordination (*packet assembly/disassembly*), over-composition (*satellite transit network*), and syntactic modifications (*multiple satellite links*).

(ii) *Statistical ranking.* The candidates acquired in the preceding step are then sorted according to several statistical criteria such as *log-likelihood ratio* (Dunning 1993). The statistical measures for term ranking are complemented with a *measure of diversity* which indicates how frequently the head or argument words of a term combine with other words in the same configuration.

TERMS (Justeson and Katz 1995) is a tool developed for the acquisition of terminological data in English through the filtering of candidate structures by the following syntactic pattern, where A = adjective, N = noun, and P = preposition (see Chapter 18 on finite-state machines for more details on the syntax of regular expressions):

(33.1) $((A|N)^+ | (A|N)^* (N P) (A|N)^*) N$

While ACABIT and LEXTER take unambiguously tagged corpora as input, TERMS uses morphologically analysed corpora in which words may have several part-of-speech categories.

33.2.2.4 *A collocation extractor: Xtract*

In Xtract (Smadja 1993), a linguistic filter and a statistical measure are combined as in ACABIT and TERMS. The statistical measure (z-score) is applied to the corpus before syntactic filtering.

Contrary to ACABIT, Xtract is not focused on terms but on collocations, that is repeated associations of words. Only a subset of the collocations extracted by Xtract can be considered as candidate terms (e.g. *stock trader* or *last selloff*). Other structures are called grammatical associations and may correspond to compositional construction without terminological status such as *epic selloff* (for semantic reasons) or *investors awaited* (for syntactic reasons).

33.2.2.5 *A non-linguistic approach: ANA*

ANA (Enguehard and Pantera 1995) is at the opposite end of the term acquisition spectrum to TERMINO. ANA is a language-independent incremental tool for automatic term acquisition composed of two modules:

(i) *Familiarization module.* Three sets of words are defined at this step:

    (*a*) a *stop list* composed of the most frequent words,

    (*b*) a set of *seed terms* manually collected which contains some of the major concepts in the domain of a corpus,

    (*c*) a set of *scheme words* found inside co-occurrences of seed terms, which are mainly prepositions and determiners in the case of French.

(ii) *Discovery module.* The set of seed terms from the familiarization module serves as a bootstrap for the incremental process for term discovery. It relies on three schemes of acquisition which use the terms acquired up to the preceding step to acquire new candidates.

33.2.2.6 *A summary on monolingual term acquisition*

The major contrast between these approaches lies in the choice of whether or not to use a statistical filter. The tools without statistical filtering, such as LEXTER, assume that any occurrence in a document can be a good candidate even if it appears only once. Such tools generally provide the user with interactive facilities for the selection and the structuring of the candidates. In contrast, tools with a statistical ranking such as ACABIT are intended to be used in an environment in which it is preferable to offer an automatic pre-selection of the candidates.

33.2.3   Some milestones in monolingual term recognition and automatic indexing

The simplest way to index a document is to build an inverted file and to associate this document with each of the words that it contains. This bag-of-words technique has the major drawback of ignoring the linguistic structure of the words. In this section, we intend to focus on the NLP techniques used for extracting an index. Contrary to the bag-of-words approaches, NLP-based indexers preserve word order and dependency relationships between words. **Term recognition**—also called phrase indexing—is certainly the most prevalent technique in NLP for automatic indexing (see Chapter 29).

This section will first introduce shallow NLP-based indexing techniques such as text simplification and window-based keyword recognition. Then more sophisticated techniques such as dependency or transformation-based parsing will be presented.

33.2.3.1   *Text simplification: FASIT*

Automatic indexing with FASIT (Dillon and Gray 1983) consists of two steps: an index extraction through syntactic patterns and a conflation of the index through text simplification and stemming.

(i) *Tagging and pattern matching.* The first step in FASIT is a morphological analysis through suffix-based rules and exception lists for irregular suffixes. The analysed text is then matched against a set of syntactic patterns which describe index structures—mainly single or compound nouns with structures such as Noun, Noun-plural, Noun Noun, Proper-noun Proper-noun, etc.

(ii) *Index conflation.* The phrase indexes extracted at the preceding step are conflated through a classical text simplification technique composed of the following three steps:

    1. deletion of stop words such as prepositions, conjunctions, and general nouns,
    2. stemming,
    3. word reordering.

In addition, the bags of words produced by this technique are grouped if they share common words.

In LinkIt (Wacholder 1998), a system for the detection of significant topics in documents, major concepts are represented by noun phrases or named entities. As in FASIT, terms are grouped according to their lexical elements. LinkIt does not make use of statistical filtering but instead proposes a first organization of the terminological data.

33.2.3.2 *Disambiguated noun phrases: CLARIT*

The CLARIT system combines NLP techniques for morphological analysis (the initial system (Evans et al. 1991)) and shallow parsing and statistical filtering for compound noun disambiguation and decomposition (the latest version of the system).

First the text is morphologically analysed and unambiguously tagged. Then, a context-free parser builds candidate noun-phrase structures without considering structural ambiguities. For instance, *the redesigned R3000 chips from DEC* is analysed as $[the]_{Det} [redesigned\ R3000]_{PreMod} [chips]_{Head} [from\ DEC]_{PostMod}$ (PreMod and PostMod are pre- and post-modifiers). The candidates produced by the parser are then sorted according to statistical measures.

Subsequent work on the CLARIT system has focused on indexing refinement. In Evans and Zhai (1996), a corpus-based technique for structural disambiguation is proposed. Repeated associations of word pairs are used to select subcompounds from the ambiguous structures produced by the parser.

33.2.3.3 *Parsing for automatic indexing: TTP, COP, COPSY, etc.*

Several studies exploit parsers in order to extract noun phrases from documents. There are two main ways of expressing grammatical relations in a language: the constituency approach based on the generative paradigm and the dependency approach, which is the result of some linguistic constraints being satisfied in a given configuration.

(i) *Constituency*. The TTP parser (Strzalkowski 1995) produces parse trees of the sentences which may be incomplete. In the case where the input is ill formed or ungrammatical, the parser manages to parse the sentences through a skip-and-fit recovery procedure. The parse trees consist of a head and related arguments. For instance, *the former Soviet president* is analysed as

$$(33.2)\quad [_{NP} [_{N} president][_{T\_pos} the] [_{Adj} [former]] [_{Adj} [Soviet]]]$$

The TTP parser relies on a large and comprehensive grammar of the English language (drawn from the Linguistic String Grammar) and contains subcategorization extracted from the *Oxford Advanced Learners' Dictionary*. The TTP parser is certainly one of the most ambitious and most complete NLP modules for automatic indexing.

The phrases in the parse trees produced by the TTP parser are used to generate an index for the documents. An index is either composed of a head noun and one of its adjacent adjective modifiers, or a head noun and the head of its right adjunct, or the verb of a sentence and the headword of its subject or its object phrase.

Unlike the TTP parser, the Constituent Object Parser (COP) (Metzler et al. 1990) only relies on binary dependencies. Since the dominance relationship is assumed to be transitive, any n-ary dependency can be transformed into a binary tree of depth n

– 1. Through the COP, the utterance *small liberal arts college for scared junior* is analysed as follows:

(33.3)   [*[*small* *[*liberal* *[*arts* *college*]]] [*for* *[*scared* *junior*]]]

The starred branch in each binary subtree corresponds to the head and the non-starred one to the adjunct.

(ii) *Dependency*. The dependency-based approaches to NLP for automatic indexing, such as COPSY (Schwarz 1988), rely on a partial representation of dependencies—only noun phrases are analysed—and on an ambiguous representation—several competing crossing dependencies are generated. In COPSY, the analysis of *problems of fresh water storage and transport in containers or tanks* results in the following dependencies:

> *fresh → water*
> *water → storage → problem*   *water → transport → problem*
> *container → storage*   *container → transport*
> *tank → storage*   *tank → transport*

The dependencies are established on the basis of configurational properties combined with word categories.

Constraint Grammar is a dependency-based grammar (for more details on shallow parsing techniques, see Chapter 10 on segmentation and Chapter 12 on parsing which discusses partial parsing). It is used by two similar approaches to a dependency-based technique for automatic indexing in Sheridan and Smeaton (1992) and in NPTool described in Voutilainen (1993). In Sheridan and Smeaton (1992), the output of the Constraint Grammar is transformed into a partially ambiguous tree structure. In NPTool (Voutilainen 1993), the focus of the work is not automatic indexing but noun-phrase extraction, which can be however considered as some kind of automatic indexing procedure.

The dependency-based approach to language actually stems from earlier linguistic work such as Tesnière (1959). The automatic indexer (Debili 1982) developed in the framework of the SPIRIT system is based on Tesnière's notion of structural dependency. Words are included in a lattice of dependency relations as shown above in the presentation of COPSY. Even though Debili's approach was developed relatively early, approximately ten years earlier than the other approaches described in this section, it already contained most of the techniques that were used in later studies: morphological analysis, unambiguous tagging, extraction of dependencies through finite-state techniques, and resolution of ambiguity through endogenous learning. Another important feature of Debili's indexing technique is the extrapolation of words in term occurrences to their morphological family. Through this technique and through the morphological relationship between *afficher* (to post) and *affichage* ([a] posting), the utterance *affichage sur les murs* (posting on the walls) is related to *afficher sur les murs* (to post on the walls).

33.2.3.4 *Recognition of variation: FASTR*

Due to the high variability of terms, the recognition of variation appears to be a constant issue in NLP for automatic indexing and term acquisition. FASTR (Jacquemin 1999) is designed to recognize several types of term variants through transformations of reference terms.

The description of variations in FASTR relies on metarules which combine structural transformations and lexical relationships. Two main families of lexical relationships are used: morphological links as in Debili (1982) and semantic links such as synonymy or antonymy. For instance, FASTR can recognize that *malignancy in orbital tumours* is a variant of *malignant tumour*, because *malignancy* and *malignant* are morphologically related and *malignancy*$_{Noun}$ *in*$_{Prep}$ *orbital*$_{Adj}$ *tumours*$_{Noun}$ matches a predefined target pattern.

There are three basic types of variations:

- *syntactic variations* which involve only structural transformations,
- *morphosyntactic variations* which involve structural transformations and morphological relations, and
- *semantic variations* which involve only semantic relationships.

FASTR is designed for controlled indexing. It takes as input an authority list of terms transformed into computational data and generates candidate variants of these terms. The candidate variants are then paired with corpus sentences in order to retrieve actual variant occurrences.

An alternative approach to variant recognition is proposed in Spärck Jones and Tait (1984). It makes use of an explicit semantic representation of the base terms and their variants. Single words are labelled with semantic tags and semantic relations are added to the branches of the syntactic structures. Then variants are generated by transforming the semantico-syntactic representation of terms using paraphrase patterns. Similarly, Woods (1997) infers the semantic relationships between terms and variants using subsumption-based reasoning. This combines a semantic description of terms and a semantic lattice made of the single words contained in the terms and their variants.

33.2.4 Bilingual term acquisition

The programs for bilingual term acquisition generally operate in two steps: an acquisition step in which terms are acquired in each corpus and an alignment phase in which links are made between the terms in both languages.

In van der Eijk (1993) terms are extracted through part-of-speech tagging and selection of (Adj)*(Noun)$^+$ patterns. These candidate terms are then aligned by comparing local and global frequencies of co-occurrence.

The technique implemented in Termight (Dagan and Church 1994) is based on the alignment of their words through the Word-align program. For each occurrence of a source term, Termight identifies candidate translations as sequences of words aligned with any of the words in a source term.

The technique used by Gaussier (1998) relies on corpora aligned at the sentence level. Association probabilities between single words are calculated on the basis of bilingual co-occurrences of words in aligned sentences. Then these probabilities are used to find the French equivalents of English terms through a flow network model. The selected translations of the multi-word terms are those which correspond to the minimal cost flow in the graph.

Hull (1997) differs from Gaussier (1998) in that single-word alignment, term extraction and term alignment are three independent modules. Terms and words are aligned through a greedy algorithm (without backtracking) that scores the candidate bilingual pairs according to probabilistic data, chooses the highest scored pair, removes it from the pool, and repeatedly recomputes the scores and removes pairs until all the pairs are chosen.

33.3 RECENT ADVANCES AND PROSPECTS

Among the promising lines of research, the following issues should be highlighted:

- linguistic studies with a concern for specialized corpora and corpus investigation,
- construction of large-scale semantic and morphological resources for term and variant recognition,
- new hybrid solutions for term acquisition and recognition combining symbolic processing and machine learning techniques,
- semantic tagging and acquisition of semantic relationships from corpora,
- sophisticated techniques for corpus construction,
- combination of textual and structural information for the recognition of rich contexts such as expositive or paraphrastic contexts,
- enhanced term acquisition procedures: extraction of terms at the verb or adjective phrase level, combination of acquisition and recognition for term structuring, enhanced interfaces for expert validation ...

Further Reading and Relevant Resources

For a basic introduction to the various aspects of terminology, the textbook of Sager (1990) gives a very detailed presentation of the different facets of term analysis and processing. More recently, Pearson (1998) is an analysis of the contexts in which terms are encountered and which provide clues about semantic relationships between terms. For an update on recent works in computational terminology, the reader is referred to Bourigault, Jacquemin, and L'Homme (2001) and Jacquemin (2001).

Several useful websites contain details about research and applications of terminology. *Terminology Forum* (http://reimari.uwasa.fi/comm/termino/) contains principles and methods of terminological research and work. *Réseau International de Néologie et de Terminologie* (http://www.rint.org/) is a francophone non-governmental organization for the development of terminology. *TIA Special interest group* (http://www.biomath.jussieu.fr/TIA/) presents a research group in linguistics, NLP, and AI concerned with text-based acquisition of terminological resources. It also organizes conferences on computational terminology and knowledge engineering.

References

Bourigault, D. 1996. 'LEXTER: a natural language tool for terminology extraction'. *Proceedings of the 7th EURALEX International Congress* (Göteborg), 771–9.

——C. Jacquemin, and M.-C. L'Homme (eds.). 1998. *Proceedings of the COLING-ACL '98 1st International Workshop on Computational Terminology (COMPUTER '98)* (Montreal).

————(eds.). 2001. *Recent Advances in Computational Terminology*. Amsterdam: John Benjamins.

Condamines, A. and J. Rebeyrolles. 1998. 'CTKB: a corpus-based approach to a terminological knowledge base'. *Proceedings of the 1st Workshop on Computational Terminology (COMPUTERM '98)* (Montreal), 29–35.

Dagan, I. and K. W. Church. 1994. '*Termight*: identifying and translating technical terminology'. *Proceedings of the 4th Conference on Applied Natural Language Processing (ANLP '94)* (Stuttgart), 34–40.

Daille, B. 1996. 'Study and implementation of combined techniques for automatic extraction of terminology'. In J. L. Klavans and P. Resnik (eds.), The *Balancing Act: Combining Symbolic and Statistical Approaches to Language*. Cambridge, Mass.: MIT Press, 49–66.

Davidson, L., J. Kavanagh, K. Mackintosh, I. Meyer, and D. Skuce. 1998. 'Semi-automatic extraction of knowledge-rich contexts from corpora'. *Proceedings of the 1st Workshop on Computational Terminology (COMPUTERM '98)* (Montreal), 50–6.

Debili, F. 1982. *Analyse syntaxico-sémantique fondée sur une acquisition automatique de relations lexicales-sémantiques*. Thèse de doctorat d'état en sciences informatiques, University of Paris XI, Orsay.

Dillon, M. and A. S. Gray. 1983. 'FASIT: a fully automatic syntactically based indexing system'. *Journal of the American Society for Information Science*, 34(2), 99–108.

Dunning, T. 1993. 'Accurate methods for the statistics of surprise and coincidence'. *Computa-*

tional Linguistics, 19(1), 61–74.

Enguehard, C. and L. Pantera. 1995. 'Automatic natural acquisition of a terminology'. *Journal of Quantitative Linguistics*, 2(1), 27–32.

Evans, D. A. and C. Zhai. 1996. 'Noun-phrase analysis in unrestricted text for information retrieval'. *Proceedings of the 34th Annual Meeting of the Association for Computational Linguistics (ACL '96)* (Santa Cruz, Calif.), 17–24.

——K. Ginther-Webster, M. Hart, R. G. Lefferts, and I. A. Monarch. 1991. 'Automatic indexing using selective NLP and first-order thesauri'. *Proceedings of the Intelligent Multimedia Information Retrieval Systems and Management (RIAO '91)* (Barcelona), 624–43.

Felber, H. 1984. *Terminology Manual*. Paris: Unesco, International Information Center for Terminology (Infoterm).

Gaussier, É. 1998. 'Flow network models for word alignment and terminology extraction from bilingual corpora'. *Proceedings of the 36th Annual Meeting of the Association for Computational Linguistics and 17th International Conference on Computational Linguistics (COLING-ACL '98)* (Montreal), 444–50.

Hull, D. 1997. 'Automating the construction of bilingual terminology lexicons'. *Terminology*, 4(2), 225–44.

Jacquemin, C. 1999. 'Syntagmatic and paradigmatic representations of term variation'. *Proceedings of the 37th Annual Meeting of the Association for Computational Linguistics (ACL '99)* (College Park, Md.), 341–8.

——2001. *Spotting and Discovering Terms through NLP*. Cambridge, Mass.: MIT Press.

Justeson, J. S. and S. M. Katz. 1995. 'Technical terminology: some linguistic properties and an algorithm for identification in text'. *Natural Language Engineering*, 1(1), 9–27.

Lauriston, A. 1994. 'Automatic recognition of complex terms: problems and the TERMINO solution'. *Terminology*, 1(1), 147–70.

Metzler, D. P., S. W. Haas, C. L. Cosic, and C. A. Weise. 1990. 'Conjunction ellipsis, and other discontinuous constituents in the Constituent Object Parser'. *Information Processing and Management*, 26(1), 53–71.

Pearson, J. 1998. *Terms in Context*. Studies in Corpus Linguistics. Amsterdam: John Benjamins.

Sager, J. C. 1990. *A Practical Course in Terminology Processing*. Amsterdam: John Benjamins.

Schwarz, C. 1988. 'The TINA project: text content analysis at the Corporate Research Laboratories at Siemens'. *Proceedings of the Intelligent Multimedia Information Retrieval Systems and Management (RIAO '88)* (Cambridge, Mass.), 361–8.

Sheridan, P. and A. F Smeaton. 1992. 'The application of morpho-syntactic language processing to effective phrase matching'. *Information Processing and Management*, 28(3), 349–69.

Smadja, F. 1993. 'Retrieving collocations from text: Xtract'. *Computational Linguistics*, 19(1), 143–77.

Spärck Jones, K. and J. I. Tait. 1984. 'Linguistically motivated descriptive term selection'. *Proceedings of the 10th International Conference on Computational Linguistics (COLING '84)* (Stanford, Calif.), 287–90.

Strzalkowski, T. 1995. 'Natural language information retrieval'. *Information Processing and Management*, 31(3), 397–417.

Tesnière, L. 1959. *Éléments de syntaxe structurale*. Paris: Klincksieck. 5th edn., 1988.

van der Eijk, P. 1993. 'Automating the acquisition of bilingual terminology'. *Proceedings of the*

6th Conference of the European Chapter of the Association for Computational Linguistics (EACL '93) (Utrecht), 113–19.

Voutilainen, A. 1993. '*NPTool*: a detector of English noun phrases'. *Proceedings of the Workshop on Very Large Corpora: Academic and Industrial Perspectives* (Columbus, Oh.), 48–57.

Wacholder, N. 1998. 'Simplex NPs clustered by head: a method for identifying significant topics within a document'. *Proceedings of the COLING/ACL Workshop on the Computational Treatment of Nominals* (Montreal), 70–9.

Woods, W.A. 1997. *Conceptual indexing: a better way to organize knowledge.* Technical Report SMLI TR-97-61, Sun Microsystems Laboratories, Mountain View, Calif.

CHAPTER 34

TEXT DATA MINING[1]

MARTI A. HEARST

ABSTRACT

The possibilities for data mining from large text collections are virtually untapped. Text expresses a vast, rich range of information, but encodes this information in a form that is difficult to decipher automatically. Perhaps for this reason, there has been little work in text data mining to date, and most people who have talked about it have either conflated it with information retrieval or have not made use of text directly to discover heretofore unknown information. In this chapter I will first define data mining, information retrieval, and corpus-based computational linguistics, and then discuss the relationship of these to text data mining. The intent behind these contrasts is to draw attention to exciting new kinds of problems for computational linguists. I describe examples of what I consider to be real text data mining efforts and briefly outline our recent ideas about how to pursue exploratory data analysis over text.

[1] This chapter is reproduced with minor modifications from the paper Marti A. Hearst. 1999. 'Untangling text data mining'. *Proceedings of the 37th Annual Meeting of the Association for Computational Linguistics (ACL '99)*, 3–10. College Park, Md., USA (courtesy ACL).

34.1 INTRODUCTION

The nascent field of **text data mining** (TDM) has the peculiar distinction of having a name and a fair amount of hype but as yet almost no practitioners. I suspect this has happened because people assume TDM is a natural extension of the slightly less nascent field of **data mining** (DM), also known as knowledge discovery in databases (Fayyad and Uthurusamy 1999), and information archaeology (Brachman et al. 1993). Additionally, there are some disagreements about what actually constitutes data mining. It turns out that 'mining' is not a very good metaphor for what people in the field actually do. Mining implies extracting precious nuggets of ore from otherwise worthless rock. If data mining really followed this metaphor, it would mean that people were discovering new factoids within their inventory databases. However, in practice this is not really the case. Instead, data mining applications tend to be (semi)automated discovery of trends and patterns across very large data sets, usually for the purposes of decision making (Fayyad and Uthurusamy 1999; Fayyad 1997). Part of what I wish to argue here is that, in the case of text, it can be interesting to take the mining-for-nuggets metaphor seriously.

34.2 TDM vs. INFORMATION RETRIEVAL

It is important to differentiate between text data mining and information retrieval. The goal of information retrieval is to help users find documents that satisfy their information needs (Baeza-Yates and Ribeiro-Neto 1999). The standard procedure is akin to looking for needles in a needlestack—the problem is not so much that the desired information is not known, but rather that the desired information coexists with many other valid pieces of information. Just because a user is currently interested in NAFTA and not Furbies does not mean that all descriptions of Furbies are worthless. The problem is one of homing in on what is currently of interest to the user. As noted above, the goal of data mining is to discover or derive new information from data, finding patterns across data sets, and/or separating signal from noise. The fact that an information retrieval system can return a document that contains the information a user requested does not imply that a new discovery has been made: the information had to have already been known to the author of the text; otherwise the author could not have written it down.

I have observed that many people, when asked about text data mining, assume it should have something to do with 'making things easier to find on the web'. For example, the description of the KDD-97 panel on Data Mining and the Web stated:

Two challenges are predominant for data mining on the Web. The first goal is to help users in finding useful information on the Web and in discovering knowledge about a domain that is represented by a collection of Web-documents. The second goal is to analyse the transactions run in a Web-based system, be it to optimize the system or to find information about the clients using the system.

This search-centric view misses the point that we might actually want to treat the information in the web as a large knowledge base from which we can extract new, never-before encountered information (Craven et al. 1998).

On the other hand, the results of certain types of text processing can yield tools that indirectly aid in the information retrieval process. Examples include text clustering to create thematic overviews of text collections (Cutting et al. 1992; Chalmers and Chitson 1992; Rennison 1994; Wise et al. 1995; Lin, Soegeel, and Marchionini 1991; Chen et al. 1998), automatically generating term associations to aid in query expansion (Peat and Willett 1991; Voorhees 1994; Xu and Croft 1996), and using co-citation analysis to find general topics within a collection or identify central web pages (White and McCain 1989; Larson 1996; Kleinberg 1998).

Aside from providing tools to aid in the standard information retrieval process, I think text data mining can contribute along another dimension. In future I hope to see information retrieval systems supplemented with tools for exploratory data analysis. Our efforts in this direction are embodied in the LINDI project, described in section 34.5.3 below.

34.3 TDM AND COMPUTATIONAL LINGUISTICS

If we extrapolate from data mining (as practised) on numerical data to data mining from text collections, we discover that there already exists a field engaged in text data mining: corpus-based computational linguistics! **Empirical computational linguistics** computes statistics over large text collections in order to discover useful patterns. These patterns are used to inform algorithms for various subproblems within natural language processing, such as part-of-speech tagging, word-sense disambiguation, and bilingual dictionary creation (Armstrong 1994). It is certainly of interest to a computational linguist that the words 'prices, prescription, and patent' are highly likely to co-occur with the medical sense of 'drug' while 'abuse, paraphernalia, and illicit' are likely to co-occur with the illegal drug sense of this word (Church and Liberman 1991). However, the kinds of patterns found and used in computational linguistics are not likely to be what the business community hopes for when they use the term text data mining.

Within the computational linguistics framework, efforts in automatic augmentation of existing lexical structures seem to fit the data-mining-as-ore-extraction metaphor. Examples include automatic augmentation of WordNet relations (Fellbaum 1998) by identifying lexico-syntactic patterns that unambiguously indicate those relations (Hearst 1998), and automatic acquisition of subcategorization data from large text corpora (Manning 1993; see also Chapter 21 above). However, these serve the specific needs of computational linguistics and are not applicable to a broader audience.

34.4 TDM AND CATEGORY METADATA

Some researchers have claimed that text categorization should be considered text data mining. Although analogies can be found in the data mining literature (e.g. referring to classification of astronomical phenomena as data mining (Fayyad and Uthurusamy 1999)), I believe when applied to text categorization this is a misnomer. Text categorization is a boiling down of the specific content of a document into one (or more) of a set of predefined labels. This does not lead to discovery of new information; presumably the person who wrote the document knew what it was about. Rather, it produces a compact summary of something that is already known. However, there are two recent areas of inquiry that make use of text categorization and do seem to fit within the conceptual framework of discovery of trends and patterns within textual data for more general-purpose usage. One body of work uses text category labels (associated with Reuters newswire) to find 'unexpected patterns' among text articles (Feldman and Dagan 1995; Dagan, Feldman, and Hirsch 1996; Feldman, Kloesgen, and Zilberstein 1997). The main approach is to compare distributions of category assignments within subsets of the document collection. For instance, distributions of commodities in country C1 are compared against those of country C2 to see if interesting or unexpected trends can be found. Extending this idea, one country's export trends might be compared against those of a set of countries that are seen as an economic unit (such as the G-7). Another effort is that of the DARPA Topic Detection and Tracking initiative (Allan et al. 1998). While several of the tasks within this initiative are standard text analysis problems (such as categorization and segmentation), there is an interesting task called On-line New Event Detection, whose input is a stream of news stories in chronological order, and whose output is a yes/no decision for each story, made at the time the story arrives, indicating whether the story is the first reference to a newly occurring event. In other words, the system must detect the first instance of what will become a series of reports on some important topic. Although this can be viewed as a standard classification task (where the class is a binary assignment to the new-event class) it is more in the spirit of data mining, in that the focus is on discovery of the beginning of a new theme or trend. The reason I consider these examples—using multiple occurrences of text categories to detect trends or patterns—to be 'real' data mining is that they use text metadata to tell us something about the world, outside of the text collection itself. (However, since these applications use metadata associated with text documents, rather than the text directly, it is unclear if they should be considered text data mining or standard data mining.) The computational linguistics applications tell us how to improve language analysis, but they do not discover more widely usable information.

The various contrasts made above are summarized in Table 34.1.

Table 34.1 A classification of data mining and text data mining applications

	Finding patterns	Finding nuggets	
		Novel	Non-novel
Non-textual data	standard data mining	Logical inference	database queries
Textual data	computational linguistics	real TDM	information retrieval

34.5 TEXT DATA MINING AS EXPLORATORY DATA ANALYSIS

Another way to view text data mining is as a process of exploratory data analysis (Tukey 1977; Hoaglin, Mosteller, and Tukey 1983) that leads to the discovery of heretofore unknown information, or to answers to questions for which the answer is not currently known. Of course, it can be argued that the standard practice of reading textbooks, journal articles, and other documents helps researchers in the discovery of new information, since this is an integral part of the research process. However, the idea here is to use text for discovery in a more direct manner. Two examples are described below.

34.5.1 Using text to form hypotheses about disease

For more than a decade, Don Swanson has eloquently argued why it is plausible to expect new information to be derivable from text collections: experts can only read a small subset of what is published in their fields and are often unaware of developments in related fields. Thus it should be possible to find useful linkages between information in related literatures, if the authors of those literatures rarely refer to one another's work. Swanson has shown how chains of causal implication within the medical literature can lead to hypotheses for causes of rare diseases, some of which have received supporting experimental evidence (Swanson 1987, 1991; Swanson and Smalheiser 1994, 1997). For example, when investigating causes of migraine headaches, he extracted various pieces of evidence from titles of articles in the biomedical literature. Some of these clues can be paraphrased as follows:

- stress is associated with migraines
- stress can lead to loss of magnesium
- calcium channel blockers prevent some migraines
- magnesium is a natural calcium channel blocker
- spreading cortical depression is implicated in some migraines
- high levels of magnesium inhibit spreading cortical depression
- migraine patients have high platelet aggregability
- magnesium can suppress platelet aggregability

These clues suggest that magnesium deficiency may play a role in some kinds of migraine headache; a hypothesis which did not exist in the literature at the time Swanson found these links. The hypothesis has to be tested via non-textual means, but the important point is that a new, potentially plausible medical hypothesis was derived from a combination of text fragments and the explorer's medical expertise. (According to Swanson 1991, subsequent study found support for the magnesium–migraine hypothesis (Ramadan et al. 1989).)

This approach has been only partially automated. There is, of course, a potential for combinatorial explosion of potentially valid links. Beeferman (1998) has developed a flexible interface and analysis tool for exploring certain kinds of chains of links among lexical relations within WordNet.[3] However, sophisticated new algorithms are needed for helping in the pruning process, since a good pruning algorithm will want to take into account various kinds of semantic constraints. This may be an interesting area of investigation for computational linguists.

[3] See http://www.link.cs.cmu.edu/lexfn.

34.5.2 Using text to uncover social impact

Switching to an entirely different domain, consider a recent effort to determine the effects of publicly financed research on industrial advances (Narin, Hamilton, and Olivastro 1997). After years of preliminary studies and building special purpose tools, the authors found that the technology industry relies more heavily than ever on government-sponsored research results. The authors explored relationships among patent text and the published research literature, using a procedure which was reported as follows in Broad (1997):

The CHI Research team examined the science references on the front pages of American patents in two recent periods—1987 and 1988, as well as 1993 and 1994—looking at all the 397,660 patents issued. It found 242,000 identifiable science references and zeroed in on those published in the preceding 11 years, which turned out to be 80 percent of them. Searches of computer databases allowed the linking of 109,000 of these references to known journals and authors' addresses. After eliminating redundant citations to the same paper, as well as articles with no known American author, the study had a core collection of 45,000 papers. Armies of aides then fanned out to libraries to look up the papers and examine their closing lines, which often say who financed the research. That detective work revealed an extensive reliance on publicly financed science. . . . Further narrowing its focus, the study set aside patents given to schools and governments and zeroed in on those awarded to industry. For 2,841 patents issued in 1993 and 1994, it examined the peak year of literature references, 1988, and found 5,217 citations to science papers. Of these, it found that 73.3 percent had been written at public institutions—universities, government labs and other public agencies, both in the United States and abroad.

Thus a heterogeneous mix of operations was required to conduct a complex analysis over large text collections. These operations included:

1. Retrieval of articles from a particular collection (patents) within a particular date range.
2. Identification of the citation pool (articles cited by the patents).
3. Bracketing of this pool by date, creating a new subset of articles.
4. Computation of the percentage of articles that remain after bracketing.
5. Joining these results with those of other collections to identify the publishers of articles in the pool.
6. Elimination of redundant articles.
7. Elimination of articles based on an attribute type (author nationality).
8. Location of full-text versions of the articles.
9. Extraction of a special attribute from the full text (the acknowledgement of funding).
10. Classification of this attribute (by institution type).
11. Narrowing the set of articles to consider by an attribute (institution type).
12. Computation of statistics over one of the attributes (peak year)

13. Computation of the percentage of articles for which one attribute has been assigned another attribute type (whose citation attribute has a particular institution attribute).

Because all the data were not available on-line, much of the work had to be done by hand, and special-purpose tools were required to perform the operations.

34.5.3 The LINDI project

The objectives of the LINDI project[4] are to investigate how researchers can use large text collections in the discovery of new important information, and to build software systems to help support this process. The main tools for discovering new information are of two types: support for issuing sequences of queries and related operations across text collections, and tightly coupled statistical and visualization tools for the examination of associations among concepts that co-occur within the retrieved documents. Both sets of tools make use of attributes associated specifically with text collections and their metadata. Thus the broadening, narrowing, and linking of relations seen in the patent example should be tightly integrated with analysis and interpretation tools as needed in the biomedical example. Following St Amant (1996), the interaction paradigm is that of a mixed-initiative balance of control between user and system. The interaction is a cycle in which the system suggests hypotheses and strategies for investigating these hypotheses, and the user either uses or ignores these suggestions and decides on the next move. We are interested in an important problem in molecular biology, that of automating the discovery of the function of newly sequenced genes (Walker et al. 1998). Human genome researchers perform experiments in which they analyse co-expression of tens of thousands of novel and known genes simultaneously.[5] Given this huge collection of genetic information, the goal is to determine which of the novel genes are medically interesting, meaning that they are co-expressed with already understood genes which are known to be involved in disease. Our strategy is to explore the biomedical literature, trying to formulate plausible hypotheses about which genes are of interest.

Most information retrieval systems require the user to execute and keep track of tactical moves, often distracting from the thought-intensive aspects of the problem (Bates 1990). The LINDI interface provides a facility for users to build and so reuse sequences of query operations via a drag-and-drop interface. These allow the user to repeat the same sequence of actions for different queries. In the gene example, this allows the user to specify a sequence of operations to apply to one co-expressed

---

[4] LINDI: Linking Information for Novel Discovery and Insight.
[5] A gene g' co-expresses with gene g when both are found to be activated in the same cells at the same time with much more likelihood than chance.

gene, and then iterate this sequence over a list of other co-expressed genes that can be dragged onto the template. (The Visage interface (Derthick, Kolojejchick, and Roth 1997) implements this kind of functionality within its information-centric framework.) These include the following operations (see Fig. 34.1):

- Iteration of an operation over the items within a set. (This allows each item retrieved in a previous query to be used as a search term for a new query.)
- Transformation, i.e. applying an operation to an item and returning a transformed item (such as extracting a feature).

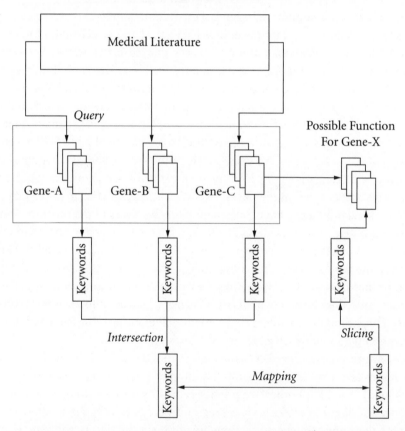

Fig. 34.1 A hypothetical sequence of operations for the exploration of gene function within a biomedical text collection, where the functions of genes A, B, and C are known, and commonalities are sought to hypothesize the function of the unknown gene. The mapping operation imposes a rank ordering on the selected keywords. The final operation is a selection of only those documents that contain at least one of the top-ranked keywords and that contain mentions of all three known genes.

- Ranking, i.e. applying an operation to a set of items and returning a (possibly) reordered set of items with the same cardinality.
- Selection, i.e. applying an operation to a set of items and returning a (possibly) reordered set of items with the same or smaller cardinality.
- Reduction, i.e. applying an operation to one or more sets of items to yield a singleton result (e.g. to compute percentages and averages).

This system will allow maintenance of several different types of history including history of commands issued, history of strategies employed, and history of hypotheses tested. For the history view, we plan to use a 'spreadsheet' layout (Hendry and Harper 1997) as well as a variation on a 'slide sorter' view which Visage uses for presentation creation but not for history retention (Roth et al. 1997). Since gene function discovery is a new area, there is not yet a known set of exploration strategies. So initially the system must help an expert user generate and record good exploration strategies. The user interface provides a mechanism for recording and modifying sequences of actions. These include facilities that refer to metadata structure, allowing, for example, query terms to be expanded by terms one level above or below them in a subject hierarchy. Once a successful set of strategies has been devised, they can be reused by other researchers and (with luck) by an automated version of the system. The intent is to build up enough strategies that the system will begin to be used as an assistant or adviser (St Amant 1996), ranking hypotheses according to projected importance and plausibility. Thus the emphasis of this system is to help automate the tedious parts of the text manipulation process and to integrate underlying computationally driven text analysis with human-guided decision making within exploratory data analysis over text.

FURTHER READING AND RELEVANT RESOURCES

This chapter was written in 1999, to accompany a keynote talk at the 37th Annual Meeting of the Association for Computational Linguistics. Since the date of writing, much more work has been done in the field of text data mining, and many more references have appeared; however, that new work is not reflected in this chapter.

For latest events/developments in the field, the reader is referred to the following Workshops:

IJCAI-2001 Workshop on Adaptive Text Extraction and Mining
http://www.smi.ucd.ie/ATEM2001/
KDD-2000 Workshop on Text Mining
http://www-2.cs.cmu.edu/~dunja/WshKDD2000.html
International Workshop on Text and Web Mining in conjunction with the 6th Pacific Rim International Conference on Artificial Intelligence (PRICAI 2000)
http://textmining.krdl.org.sg/cfp.html

Workshop on Text Mining (TextDM '2001)
http://www-ai.ijs.si/DunjaMladenic/TextDM01/

REFERENCES

Allan, J., J. Carbonell, G. Doddington, J. Yamron, and Y. Yang. 1998. 'Topic detection and track-ing pilot study: final report'. *Proceedings of the DARPA Broadcast News Transcription and Understanding Workshop* (Landsdowne, Va.), 194–218.

Armstrong, S. (ed.) 1994. *Using Large Corpora*. Cambridge, Mass.: MIT Press.

Baeza-Yates, R. and B. Ribeiro-Neto. 1999. *Modern information retrieval*. Ph.D. thesis. Addison-Wesley Longman Publishing Company.

Bates, M. J. 1990. 'The berry-picking search: user interface design'. In H. Thimbleby (ed.), *User Interface Design*. Reading, Mass.: Addison Wesley.

Beeferman, D. 1998. 'Lexical discovery with an enriched semantic network'. *Proceedings of the ACL/COLING Workshop on Applications of WordNet in Natural Language Processing Systems* (Montreal), 358–64.

Brachman, R. J., P. G. Selfridge, L. G. Terveen, B. Altman, A. Borgida, F. Halper, T. Kirk, A. Lazar, D. L. McGuinness, and L. A. Resnick. 1993. 'Integrated support for data archaeology'. *International Journal of Intelligent and Cooperative Information Systems*, 2(2), 159–85.

Broad, W. J. 1997. 'Study finds public science is pillar of industry'. *The New York Times*, 13 May.

Chalmers, M. and P. Chitson. 1992. 'Bead: exploration in information visualization'. *Proceedings of the 15th Annual International ACM/SIGIR Conference* (Copenhagen), 330–7.

Chen, H., A. L. Houston, R. R. Sewell, and B. R. Schatz. 1998. 'Internet browsing and searching: user evaluations of category map and concept space techniques'. *Journal of the American Society for Information Sciences (JASIS)*, 49(7).

Church, K. W. and M. Y. Liberman. 1991. 'A status report on the ACL/DCI'. *Proceedings of the 7th Annual Conference of the UW Centre for the New OED and Text Research: Using Corpora* (Oxford), 84–91.

Craven, M., D. DiPasquo, D. Freitag, A. McCallum, T. Mitchell, K. Nigam, and S. Slattery. 1998. 'Learning to extract symbolic knowledge from the World Wide Web'. *Proceedings of the 15th National Conference on Artificial Intelligence (AAAI '98)* (Madison), 509–16.

Cutting, D. R., J. O. Pedersen, D. Karger, and J. W. Tukey. 1992. 'Scatter/Gather: a cluster-based approach to browsing large document collections'. *Proceedings of the 15th Annual International ACM/SIGIR Conference* (Copenhagen), 318–29.

Dagan, I., R. Feldman, and H. Hirsh. 1996. 'Keyword-based browsing and analysis of large document sets'. *Proceedings of the 5th Annual Symposium on Document Analysis and Information Retrieval (SDAIR)* (Las Vegas, Nev.), 191–208.

Derthick, M., J. Kolojejchick, and S. F. Roth. 1997. 'An interactive visualization environment for data exploration'. *Proceedings of the 3rd Annual Conference on Knowledge Discovery and Data Mining (KDD '97)* (Newport Beach, Calif.), 2–9.

Fayyad, U. 1997. 'Editorial'. *Data Mining and Knowledge Discovery*, 1(1).

——and R. Uthurusamy, R. 1999. 'Data mining and knowledge discovery in databases: introduction to the special issue'. *Communications of the ACM*, 39(11).

Feldman, R. and I. Dagan. 1995. 'KDT: knowledge discovery in texts'. *Proceedings of the First*

Annual Conference on Knowledge Discovery and Data Mining (KDD '95) (Montreal), 112–17.

——W. Kloesgen, and A. Zilberstein. 1997. 'Visualization techniques to explore data mining results for document collections'. *Proceedings of the 3rd Annual Conference on Knowledge Discovery and Data Mining (KDD '97)* (Newport Beach, Calif.), 16–23.

Fellbaum, C. (ed.) 1998. *WordNet: An Electronic Lexical Database.* Cambridge, Mass.: MIT Press.

Hearst, M. A. 1998. 'Automated discovery of WordNet relations'. In Fellbaum (1998), 131–51.

Hendry, D. G. and D. J. Harper. 1997. 'An informal information-seeking environment'. *Journal of the American Society for Information Science*, 48(11), 1036–48.

Hoaglin, D. C., F. Mosteller, and J. W. Tukey. 1983. *Understanding Robust and Exploratory Data Analysis.* New York: John Wiley & Sons, Inc.

Kleinberg, J. 1998. 'Authoritative sources in a hyperlinked environment'. *Proceedings of the 9th ACM-SIAM Symposium on Discrete Algorithms*, 604–32.

Larson, R. R. 1996. 'Bibliometrics of the world web: an exploratory analysis of the intellectual structure of cyberspace'. *ASIS '96: Proceedings of the 1996 Annual ASIS Meeting.*

Lin, X., D. Soegeel, and G. Marchionini. 1991. 'A self-organizing semantic map for information retrieval'. *Proceedings of the 14th Annual International ACM/SIGIR Conference* (Chicago), 262–9.

Manning, C. D. 1993. 'Automatic acquisition of a large subcategorization dictionary from corpora'. *Proceedings of the 31st Annual Meeting of the Association for Computational Linguistics* (Columbus, Oh.), 235–42.

Narin, F., K. S. Hamilton, and D. Olivastro. 1997. 'The increasing linkage between US technology and public science'. *Research Policy*, 26(3), 317–30.

Peat, H. J. and P. Willett. 1991. 'The limitations of term co-occurrence data for query expansion in document retrieval systems'. *Journal of the American Society for Information Sciences (JASIS)*, 42(5), 378–83.

Ramadan, N. M., H. Halvorson, A. Vandelinde, and S. R. Levine. 1989. 'Low brain magnesium in migraine'. *Headache*, 29(7), 416–19.

Rennison, E. 1994. 'Galaxy of news: an approach to visualizing and understanding expansive news landscapes'. *Proceedings of UIST 94, ACM Symposium on User Interface Software and Technology* (New York), 3–12.

Roth, S. F., M. C. Chuah, S. Kerpedjiev, J. A. Kolojejchick, and P. Lucas. 1997. 'Towards an information visualization workspace: combining multiple means of expression'. *Human–Computer Interaction*, 12(1–2), 131–85.

St Amant, R. 1996. *A mixed-initiative planning approach to exploratory data.* Ph.D. thesis, University of Massachusetts, Amherst.

Swanson, D. R. 1987. 'Two medical literatures that are logically but not bibliographically connected'. *Journal of the American Society for Information Sciences (JASIS)*, 38(4), 228–33.

——1991. 'Complementary structures in disjoint science literatures'. *Proceedings of the 14th Annual International ACM/SIGIR Conference* (Chicago), 280–9.

——and N. R. Smalheiser. 1994. 'Assessing a gap in the biomedical literature: magnesium deficiency and neurologic disease'. *Neuroscience Research Communications*, 15, 1–9.

————1997. 'An interactive system for finding complementary literatures: a stimulus to scientific discovery'. *Artificial Intelligence*, 91, 183–203.

Tukey, J. W. 1977. *Exploratory Data Analysis.* Reading, Mass.: Addison Wesley.

Voorhees, E. M. 1994. 'Query expansion using lexical-semantic relations'. *Proceedings of the 17th Annual International ACM/SIGIR Conference* (Dublin), 61–9.

Walker, M. G., W. Volkmuth, E. Sprinzak, D. Hodgson, and T. Klingler. 1998. *Prostate Cancer Genes Identified by Genome-Scale Expression Analysis.* Technical Report (unnumbered), Incyte Pharmaceuticals, July.

White, H. D. and J. J. McCain. 1989. 'Bibliometrics'. *Annual Review of Information Science and Technology,* 24, 119–86.

Wise, J. A., J. J. Thomas, K. Pennock, D. Lantrip, M. Pottier, and A. Schur. 1995. 'Visualizing the non-visual: spatial analysis and interaction with information from text documents'. *Proceedings of the Information Visualization Symposium 95* (Atlanta), 51–8.

Xu, J. and W. B. Croft. 1996. 'Query expansion using local and global document analysis'. *SIGIR '96: Proceedings of the 19th Annual International ACM SIGIR Conference on Research and Development in Information Retrieval* (Zurich), 4–11.

CHAPTER 35

NATURAL LANGUAGE INTERACTION

ION ANDROUTSOPOULOS
MARIA ARETOULAKI

ABSTRACT

This chapter is an introduction to natural language interaction systems, that is, systems that allow their users to formulate requests in spoken or written natural language. The chapter introduces the central concepts of natural language interaction systems, focusing in turn on two of the most studied forms of these systems: natural language interfaces and spoken dialogue systems.

35.1 INTRODUCTION

This chapter is an introduction to **natural language interaction systems**, a term used here to refer to applications where users can formulate requests addressed to a computer in natural language. The user's requests may be spoken or written. They may be stand-alone sentences or parts of a dialogue. Furthermore, they may be analysed using shallow or deeper language processing. These options offer a range of choices to the system designer, different choices being more or less suitable to different applications.

The term **natural language interface** (NLI) has been used to refer mostly to natural language interaction systems where the user's requests are processed—more or less—as isolated sentences, often employing deep linguistic analysis. Systems of this kind have been studied extensively since the late 1960s, mainly in the context of database querying, and mostly with requests typed on a keyboard. More recently, attention has been shifting towards **spoken dialogue systems** (SDSs), where the user's requests are spoken and they are seen as parts of an evolving dialogue. SDSs typically place greater emphasis on the analysis of the overall dialogue and its relation to the user's intentions, often employing a more shallow analysis of individual sentences.

This chapter introduces the central concepts of natural language interaction systems, focusing in turn on NLIs and SDSs, as two of the most studied forms of these systems.

35.2 NATURAL LANGUAGE INTERFACES

Database querying constitutes the most studied form of NLIs (Perrault and Grosz 1988; Copestake and Spärck Jones 1990; Androutsopoulos, Ritchie, and Thanisch 1995; Androutsopoulos and Ritchie 2000). Typical database NLIs allow information to be retrieved from an underlying database by typing single-sentence queries, as in the following example where 'U:' and 'S:' mark user requests and system responses, respectively.

U: *Which customers have bought SmartCopiers?*
S: ABA France, QuickFly, Power Inc.
U: *How many SmartCopiers has each one bought?*
S: ABA France   15
   QuickFly   12
   Power Inc.   18
U: *Have any of them also bought QuickCams?*
S: Power Inc.

Although this section draws examples from database querying, most of the discussion also applies to other NLI applications, such as NLIs to operating systems (Wilensky et al. 1988), robots (Crangle and Suppes 1994), or virtual reality systems (Wauchope et al. 1997).

35.2.1 Basic NLI components

Fig. 35.1 sketches the typical NLI architecture. (We ignore for the moment speech input, assuming that the user types on a keyboard.) In most current NLIs, the user's requests are translated into a **meaning representation language** (MRL), usually some flavour of logic, with a subsequent phase translating the MRL expressions into a formalism supported by the underlying application (e.g. a database language). This arrangement has portability advantages. For example, it makes it easier to reuse the components that translate from natural language to MRL with different underlying applications.

The user's request first undergoes a pre-processing stage, which includes tokenization (Chapter 10), morphological analysis (Chapter 2), and lexicon look-up (Chapter

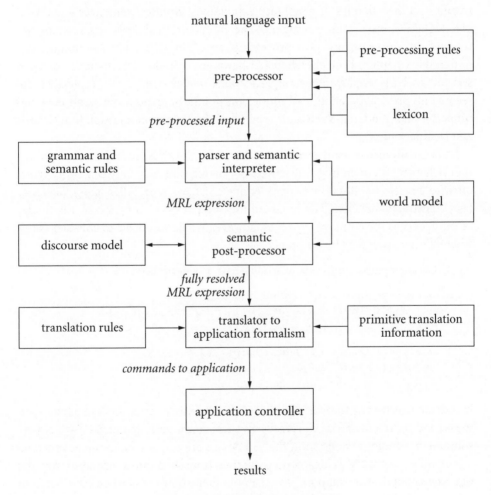

Fig. 35.1 Simplified NLI architecture

3). In database NLIs, proper names (e.g. *SmartCopier*) are very common. Name recognition and classification techniques (Chapter 30) can be used to identify them.

The pre-processed input is then parsed and analysed semantically (Chapters 4, 5, and 12), generating an MRL expression. In an MRL similar to first-order predicate logic, sentence (35.1) could be represented as (35.2). The '?' is an interrogative quantifier specifying which variable values are to be reported. Expression (35.2) requires all the names x_2 to be reported, such that x_2 is the name of a customer x_1, and x_1 has bought a SmartCopier x_3. To save space, here free variables are treated as existentially quantified. Tense and aspect issues are also ignored (Androutsopoulos, Ritchie, and Thanisch 1998; Androutsopoulos 2002).

(35.1)   Which customers have bought SmartCopiers?

(35.2) $?x_2 \, customer\_name\,(x_1, x_2) \wedge product\_name\,(x_3, SmartCopier) \wedge purchase\,(x_1, x_3)$

The resulting MRL expressions are often *underspecified* (Chapter 5), usually with respect to the semantics of anaphoric expressions, elliptical sentences (e.g. *What about QuickCams?*), and quantifiers. The underspecified MRL expressions are resolved during a semantic post-processing stage (Fig. 35.1); related techniques can be found in Chapter 14 and elsewhere (Alshawi 1992). Unlike SDSs, to be discussed in section 35.3, NLIs employ rather simple *discourse models* (Chapter 6). Typically, these record only previously mentioned entities, the point where they were mentioned, and properties like gender and semantic type, all useful for anaphora resolution (Barros and De Roeck 1994).

NLIs usually also consult a *world model*, which shows the ontology of the application (Chapter 25), including restrictions on the relationships between entity types, often called *selectional* or *sortal* restrictions (Alshawi 1992; Allen 1995). Sentence (35.3) illustrates their use. The intended meaning of (35.3) is (35.4), i.e. the holder of the licence is the employee. An NLI, however, would also have to consider (35.5), where the licence is held by the branch.

(35.3)   List all employees of Paris branches that have driving licences.

(35.4) $?x_2 \, employee\_name\,(x_1, x_2) \wedge branch\_name\,(x_3, x_4) \wedge$
$city\_name\,(x_5, 'Paris') \wedge works\_at\,(x_1, x_3) \wedge located\_in\,(x_3, x_5) \wedge$
$licence\,(x_6) \wedge for\_driving\,(x_6) \wedge has\,(x_1, x_6)$

(35.5) $?x_2 \, employee\_name(x_1, x_2) \wedge branch\_name(x_3, x_4) \wedge$
$city\_name\,(x_5, 'Paris') \wedge works\_at\,(x_1, x_3) \wedge located\_in\,(x_3, x_5) \wedge$
$licence\,(x_6) \wedge for\_driving\,(x_6) \wedge has(x_3, x_6)$

In order to reject (35.5), the world model would contain a restriction stating that when the second argument of *has* (x, y) is a driving licence, the first argument must be a person, and the ontology would show that employees are persons, but branches are not.

The fully resolved MRL expressions are then translated into a formalism that the underlying application supports, for example shell commands when interfacing to an operating system, or a sequence of API (application programming interface) calls when interfacing to other applications. In database NLIs, the target is usually the SQL database language. The translation from MRL to the underlying application formalism is often performed recursively. A ground mapping shows how MRL primitives (e.g. predicate functors) relate to concepts of the underlying application (e.g. database tables; this is the 'primitive translation information' of Fig. 35.1). Translation rules then specify how to translate more complex MRL expressions, possibly invoking recursively other rules to translate simpler MRL sub-expressions (Androutsopoulos and Ritchie 2000).

35.2.2 Other NLI components

Fully-fledged NLIs comprise additional components, not shown in Fig. 35.1. Some of these are listed below.

35.2.2.1 *Paraphraser*

NLIs often generate paraphrases of the user's utterances that reflect the system's interpretation of the utterances. This helps the users understand whether their requests have been interpreted correctly. When ambiguities arise, paraphrases of the candidate interpretations can also be presented, asking the user to select the most appropriate one. The paraphrases are produced from the MRL or application-formalism expressions by a component that uses generation methods. Related techniques can be found in Chapter 15 and elsewhere (De Roeck and Lowden 1986; Alshawi 1992).

35.2.2.2 *Response generator*

Most NLIs focus on the analysis of single-user utterances, without attempting to engage the users in dialogues. Hence, the planning of system responses is rather simple. In database NLIs, the system's response is usually a listing of the retrieved information, possibly after some post-processing (e.g. to remove internal keys or replace them with names).

More difficult is the generation of appropriate responses when the user's requests cannot be satisfied, in which case the cause of the failure must be explained (e.g. unknown word, syntax too complex). Particularly challenging are user requests that carry false presuppositions or do not express literally what the user wants to do. In the first question below, the system detects the false presupposition that ABA France has bought QuickCams, and generates an appropriate warning. To the second question, it does not reply with a single 'yes' (which would be the answer to the literal meaning of the question). It provides additional information, attempting to be more helpful.

U: *Has any customer bought more QuickCams than ABA France?*
S: ABA France hasn't bought any QuickCams.

U: *Has any customer bought more SmartCopiers than ABA France?*
S: Yes, Power Inc. has bought 18.

Responses of this kind are known as *cooperative*, and in the general case require a **user model** to represent the user's goals and beliefs (Chapter 7), a point that will be discussed further when presenting SDSs. In NLIs, however, relatively simple techniques often suffice (Kaplan 1982).

35.2.2.3 *Portability tools*

A significant amount of work on NLIs has been devoted to **portability**, i.e. the ability to reuse NLIs with different underlying applications (e.g. an operating system vs. a database) or in different domains (e.g. train ticket vs. payroll information). To achieve portability, NLI designers attempt to clearly separate those components that can be used across applications and domains from less portable ones, and to provide tools that allow the latter to be modified easily during a configuration phase (Grosz et al. 1987; Androutsopoulos, Ritchie, and Thanisch 1995; Androutsopoulos and Ritchie 2000).

35.2.3 The state of the art in NLIs

NLIs have been studied since the late 1960s (Woods, Kaplan, and Webber 1972), mainly for database querying. The current state of the art allows workable NLIs to be developed, and commercial database NLIs are available. The use of NLIs, however, is not as widespread as one might expect. This is usually attributed to the unclear linguistic capabilities of NLIs, the effort that is required to develop or configure an NLI, and the competition from graphical interfaces, which are often easier to configure and use (Whittaker and Stenton 1989; Bell and Rowe 1992; Dekleva 1994). These points are considered below.

Every NLI has a limited coverage of linguistic phenomena. The boundaries of this coverage, however, are usually unclear, and users often have trouble formulating requests that the system can interpret. They may have to rephrase their requests until (if ever) a form that the NLI can interpret is reached—a frustrating experience. The problem can be alleviated, but not solved completely, using **Wizard of Oz** experiments (Chapter 7) to tailor the system's coverage to the linguistic phenomena most likely to be found in user utterances, and robust parsing techniques to recover from parsing and interpretation failures. A related discussion on robust parsing can be found in section 35.3.2 below, Chapter 12, and elsewhere (Stallard and Bobrow 1993; Bates et al. 1994).

To bypass the linguistic coverage problem one can move from stand-alone requests to dialogues. Knowledge about the typical dialogue structure and the user's goals in a particular application domain can be used to fill in gaps left from the interpretation of the user's utterances, and to sustain the dialogue until the system has a clear view of the task to be performed. This is the approach that dialogue systems (to be discussed next) adopt, and it appears to be practical with tasks that require relatively few parameters to be specified (e.g. ticket booking, on-line banking). With less standardized tasks (e.g. ad hoc querying of sales databases for marketing analysis) and in contexts where lengthy interaction is undesirable, other solutions are needed. In applications where the requests are short, menu-based NLIs may be workable (Tennant et al. 1983). In that case, the requests are formulated by selecting words from dynamically updated menus that reflect the linguistic coverage of the system, clarifying its capabilities. Multimodal interaction, the ability to combine language with gestures and graphics (Chapter 36), is a promising alternative, as it leads to linguistically simpler utterances (Cohen et al. 1997) and it allows alternative modalities to compensate for language interpretation failures (McGee, Cohen, and Oviatt 1998).

In terms of development or configuration effort, it seems most likely that graphical interfaces will maintain the lead. This suggests that NLIs that incorporate speech functionality may be more viable commercially for applications where graphical interaction is impractical or impossible (e.g. in hands-busy environments, such as cars). We shall return to future applications of NLIs after discussing dialogue systems, in the context of which speech issues have been studied to a larger extent.

35.3 SPOKEN DIALOGUE SYSTEMS

Let us now turn to spoken dialogue systems (SDSs), focusing on non-simulated human–machine dialogues (cf. Chapter 7).

35.3.1 The idiosyncrasy of spoken language input

SDSs involve spoken—rather than written—input, which is most often ungrammatical, incomplete, or even unintelligible. To exemplify these points, here is a hypothetical dialogue with an SDS, where what the user says is contrasted to what the system actually 'understands'. Asterisks indicate one or more words that have not been recognized.

U: *ErmHelloErmWhatD'You–I'dLikeSomeInformationOnaFlightaFlighttoAthens*
   [* hello * what * you * information * flight * flight to aachen]

S: You want to fly to Aachen?

U: *EhNoNoNotAachenAthensAthensIsaidAachenWhereIsAachenAnyway*
     [* *no no nottingham aachen athens * aachen what is athens airways*]

S: You want to fly to Athens?

U: *YeahFinallyYouGotItIwantToLeaveFromGa–FromLondonGatwick*
     [*yes * gatwick i want * leave from * from london gatwick*]

S: You want to fly from London Gatwick?

The dialogue illustrates the difficulties involved in analysing **spontaneously spoken language**. With continuous speech (Chapter 16), the input is a stream of sounds that cannot be broken down into individual words without some prior knowledge of the language and context. There are no pauses to separate words, or punctuation to separate sentences. Here capital letters have only been used to help the reader identify the words.

Spontaneous utterances are also formed with limited time and cognitive resources, resulting in voiced gaps (*erm*), full or partial word repetitions (e.g. *a flight a flight, Ga– Gatwick*), false starts and self-repair (e.g. *what d'you– I'd like, from Ga– from London Gatwick*) (Levow 1998). **Elliptical sentences** (*not Aachen, Athens*) and anaphoric expressions (Chapter 14) are very frequent. Background noise may also be present (e.g. other people talking), and in telephone applications the channel quality will be lower and less predictable than with a good studio microphone. The occurrence of extralinguistic phenomena, such as coughing and chuckling, is also unavoidable. Moreover, in contrast to **speaker-dependent** systems, in most SDSs the majority of user accents cannot have been encountered before (see also Chapter 16).

35.3.2   The architecture of SDSs

Fig. 35.2 provides a simplified overview of the typical SDS architecture, based on an amalgamation of knowledge sources and processing modules found across several different SDSs (Bernsen, Dybkjær, and Dybkjær 1998; Flycht-Eriksson 1999; Gallwitz et al. 1998; ISDS '97; Smith and Hipp 1994; Veldhuijzen van Zanten 1996; Ward and Novick 1996; Young et al. 1989).

35.3.2.1   *Word recognizer*

The input speech signal is first processed by a *word recognizer*, which attempts to identify the words that were spoken on the basis of the words in the system's lexicon and predictions provided by other modules. (Related discussions can be found in Chapters 16 and 19.) The output of the recognizer is either a word chain or a word graph in the case of ambiguity. The following is an example of a user utterance and the corresponding word chain:

ErmHelloErmWhatD'You–I'dLikeSomeInformationOnaFlightaFlighttoAthens
[* *hello* * *what* * *you* * *information* * *flight* * *flight to athens*]

35.3.2.2 *Parser and semantic interpreter*

The word chain (or graph) is passed on to the *parser* (Chapter 12). As the input is usually elliptical and often ungrammatical (e.g. in the case of self-repair), parsing has to

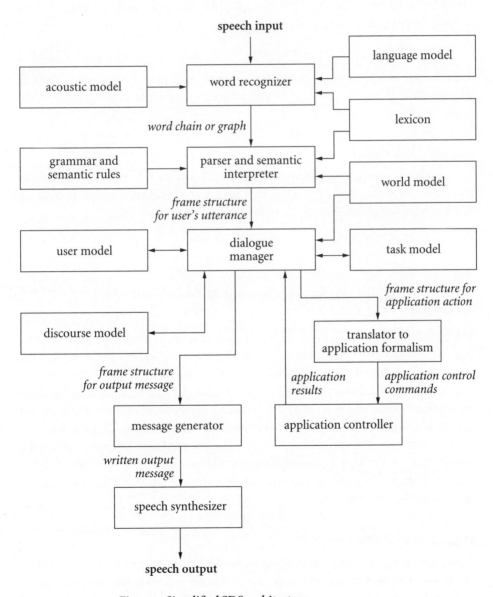

Fig. 35.2 Simplified SDS architecture

be performed on 'islands' of words or phrases that can be processed in isolation but cannot be combined to make up a full sentence. Syntactic processing can be carried out in conjunction with a targeted shallow semantic intepretation of the utterance in the limited context of the application domain. Thus, heuristics are used to extract *application parameters* (e.g. departure airport and time) and fill in some kind of a *frame structure* (e.g. attribute-value pairs), much as in information extraction (Chapter 30). This eliminates irrelevant material from the input signal (such as the reason of travel in a flight information system), and delivers only the essential information to the *dialogue manager* (Fig. 35.2). The example below shows a possible frame structure produced from the word chain above:

[[greeting:hello], [dest_airport:athens]]

As in the case of NLIs, a *world model* may be used during the semantic interpretation, for example showing the ontology of the application and sortal restrictions between entity types.

35.3.2.3 *Task model*

The **task model** contains knowledge about the tasks the user is likely to want to fulfil, especially the application parameters that need to be specified for each task. In an SDS for flight enquiries, the task model might include the following:

```
     search( [dep_date, dep_airport, dest_airport],
             [dep_time_range, arr_time_range],
             [flight_no, dep_time, arr_time])
  booking( [flight_no, dep_date, surname, initials], [], [status])
cancellation( [flight_no, dep_date, surname, initials], [], [status])
```

The simplistic task model above lists three possible tasks: searching for a suitable flight, booking a seat on a flight, and cancelling a booking. For the first task, the departure date, departure airport, and destination airport must always be specified, and the user may optionally specify a range for the departure or arrival time (all these are application parameters). The answer must report the flight number, and the exact departure and arrival times. In the booking and cancellation tasks, the flight number, departure date, passenger surname, and initials are needed, and the answer will report the status of the booking or cancellation. The SDS would exploit this task model to figure out which of the necessary application parameters have not been specified yet, and ask appropriate questions.

35.3.2.4 *User model*

A **user model** may also be present, which provides information about the user's interests and represents what the system assumes to be the current user's beliefs and goals. Related discussion can be found in Chapter 7 and elsewhere (Kobsa and Wahlster

1989). User models can be exploited, for example, to avoid reporting facts the user already knows, to identify information that is worth reporting even if it has not been explicitly requested, and to provide predictions about the next user utterance.

35.3.2.5 *Discourse model*

One of the main functions of the **discourse model** is to keep track of the *discourse history*. Apart from the entities that have been mentioned (useful for anaphora resolution purposes; see Chapter 14), the discourse history may show, for example, the dialogue acts (Chapter 7) associated with the user utterances and the system messages, along with related instantiations of application parameters. This is demonstrated in the following dialogue, where each utterance is followed by a discourse history entry (marked with '→') recording the dialogue act and the relevant application parameters.

    S: On which day do you want to fly?
    → system:[request:dep_date]
    U: *This Friday.*
    → user:[assert:[dep_date:25.05.2001]]
    S: Where do you want to fly to?
    → system:[request:dest_airport]
    U: *Athens.*
    → user:[assert:[dest_airport:athens]]

A history of the above type is useful, for example, when encountering elliptical user utterances (e.g. *Athens*), the meaning of which can be resolved only within the context of the previous dialogue exchange, a process known as **anchoring** (Alshawi 1992).

Apart from the discourse history, the discourse model often contains a representation of the typical *dialogue structure* in the particular application domain. To this effect, dialogue grammars (Chapter 7), often in the form of finite-state automata (FSAs; see Chapter 18) are used in many SDSs (Sutton et al. 1998). This is illustrated in Fig. 35.3, which shows an FSA model of a dialogue structure for flight enquiries. More elaborate discourse structures can be accommodated by employing statistical models (Nagata and Morimoto 1994; Reithinger et al. 1996) and machine learning techniques (Moeller 1997). The model of Fig. 35.3 accepts dialogues such as the following:

    S: This is the Flight Info System. Name your destination airport.
    U: *Athens.*
    S: Which airport are you flying from?
    U: *Gatwick.*
    S: Sorry, I didn't understand. Which airport are you flying from?
    U: *London Gatwick.*
    S: On which day do you want to fly?
    U: *Next Sunday.*

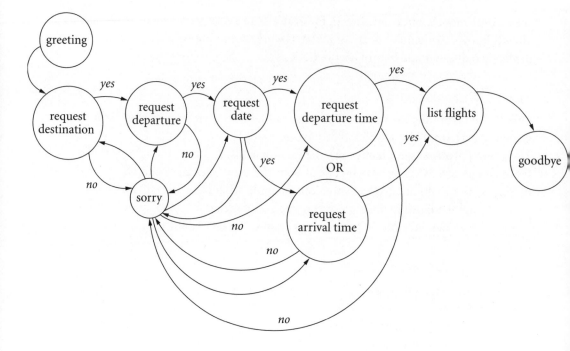

Fig. 35.3 Example FSA model of dialogue structure

S: What time do you want to leave?
U: *Say, around 10 am.*
S: The following two flights match your requirements: . . .
S: Thanks for ringing.

The 'yes'/'no' labels of Fig. 35.3 would in practice be tests, for example on the frame structures returned by the parsing and semantic interpretation, or on dialogue acts extracted from them, that would check if the user utterances contain the required information. (The absence of a label on an arc in Fig. 35.3 denotes an obligatory state transition. The OR signifies an alternative transition.) In some systems, each state has attached descriptions of messages to be generated whenever the state is entered. These may be canned texts (e.g. *Which airport are you flying from?*) or higher-level descriptions (e.g. system:[request:dep_airport]). States may also have attached predictions about the next possible user utterance, the idea being that at each dialogue state particular words or dialogue acts are more likely than others. These predictions can be exploited to improve the accuracy of the word recognizer and the parser.

35.3.2.6 *Dialogue manager*

The **dialogue manager** is the central module of a SDS. It exploits information provided by the world, task, user, and discourse models in order to:

- anchor the frame structure representations of a user utterance in the current context (e.g. resolving anaphora and elliptical sentences, extracting dialogue acts and parameter values),
- decide whether the system should generate a message, in which case a suitable representation of the message is passed to the message generator (Fig. 35.2),
- decide whether the underlying application (e.g. database system) should be asked to perform some action (e.g. retrieve information), in which case a suitable command is passed to the application, possibly after invoking a translation stage similar to that of section 35.2.1.

The dialogue manager may also be responsible for the coordination and communication of the various modules. In the simplest case, the dialogue manager invokes each module individually, feeding it with input data and collecting its results. In more advanced systems, a **blackboard** mechanism may be in place (Erman et al. 1981), allowing the various modules to exchange data more freely in order to have mutual constraints limit the search space at each stage (Young et al. 1989; Ward and Novick 1996).

The dialogue manager may be based on dialogue grammars, as discussed above, or on more elaborate approaches, possibly involving **plan recognition** (Chapter 7). McTear (1999) provides a survey of possible approaches. The exact functions of the dialogue manager vary across different SDSs. In some systems certain of the above-mentioned tasks (e.g. anchoring) may be carried out by separate modules.

35.3.2.7 *Message generator and speech synthesizer*

Whenever a message is to be communicated to the user, the dialogue manager outputs a representation of the message. This may be a canned text, possibly with additional intonation mark-up, that can be passed directly to the speech synthesizer (Chapter 17), or it may be a higher-level description of the goals to be achieved by communicating the message. In the latter case, a *message generator* is present, which produces the surface form (text) of the message, employing techniques such as those described in Chapter 15. (To save space, Fig. 35.2 does not show resources related to language generation and speech synthesis.)

35.3.3 Initiative and dialogue flexibility

Generally, it is desirable to let the user take the lead in the course of the dialogue, at least until there is a communication problem or additional information is needed. This is illustrated below, where the user specifies the departure airport, the destination, and a time range for the flight, without waiting to be asked. The system then takes the **initiative** to confirm the destination, probably because the speech recognition confidence for the corresponding word was low, and then it detects that the departure date has not been specified.

S: Hello. This is your Flight Info System.
U: *Hi, I'd like to find out about an evening flight from Gatwick to Athens please.*
S: Did you say Aachen?
U: *What? No, no, Athens.*
S: On which day do you want to fly to Athens?

Systems of this type, that allow the initiative to be shared between the user and the system, are said to support *mixed* or *variable initiative*. In contrast, SDSs based on *system initiative* guide the user at every step, usually asking questions and expecting answers to those particular questions. There is also a third case, *user initiative*-based applications, where the system never takes the lead. The NLIs of section 35.2 involve user initiative. Another example is the following subdialogue with the BT MAILSEC email handling SDS (Williams 1996):

U: *Do I have any messages from Peter?*
S: You have two messages from Peter Wyard.
U: *Do I have any from David?*

Selecting the appropriate initiative-sharing strategy requires a careful evaluation in the context of each application (Walker, Fromer, and Narayanan 1998; Haller and McRoy 1998/9). With dialogue managers based on plan recognition (Chapter 7), it is usually easier to support mixed initiative, with the cost of requiring elaborate inferencing to be performed in the course of the dialogue (Carberry 1990; Ferguson and Allen 1993; Smith and Hipp 1994; Traum 1996). To some degree, SDSs based on FSAs may be able to provide a similar effect by increasing the number of states and transitions, to model user utterances that do not answer directly system requests, jumps to previous topics, miscommunications, etc. FSA systems, however, still cannot avoid being rigid with respect to unpredictable situations, such as user-initiated counter-questions. Another problem with FSA systems is that their graph models become very difficult to design and maintain as the task complexity increases. This has instigated the development of generic dialogue-building tools, where short dialogue exchanges (e.g. subdialogues for specifying dates or credit card data) are saved as software libraries that can be reused in new applications (Baekgaard 1996; Aust and Schroeer 1998; Kölzer 1999).

35.3.4 Confirmation strategy

Equally important is the choice of **confirmation strategy**. It is often desirable to use *implicit confirmations*, at least when there have been no instances of misunderstanding:

U: *I'd like to find out about a flight from Gatwick to Athens please.*
S: On which day do you want to fly from London Gatwick to Athens?

This is much more natural than *explicitly* asking for a confirmation of each application parameter, for example after every user utterance (Danieli and Gerbino 1995):

U: *I'd like to find out about a flight from Gatwick to Athens please.*
S: Do you want to fly from London Gatwick?
U: *Yes.*
S: Do you want to go to Athens?
U: *Yes, yes*
S: On which day do you want to fly?

The other extreme of having no confirmations at all can sometimes be dangerous, because the system may misunderstand something and complete the task based on the wrong data. For some applications, it may be preferable to let the user select explicitly the confirmation (or initiative) strategy, as in '*Implicit confirmations please*'. (Litman and Shimei 1999). A more ambitious approach is to select the appropriate confirmation strategy automatically; for example, based on the confidence of the word recognizer or the parser (Smith 1997; Gallwitz et al. 1998).

35.3.5 The state of the art in SDSs

Research on dialogue-handling interaction systems can be traced back to ELIZA (Chapter 7), the keyboard-based system that pretended to be a consulting psychologist, scanning the user's input for specific patterns that would trigger canned responses. SHRDLU (Winograd 1972), a keyboard-based goal-driven system for problem-solving in a toy blocks world, can also be seen as an early dialogue-handling system. Putting aside attempts to recognize isolated words, HEARSAY (Erman et al. 1981) was one of the first spoken language understanding systems, which also pioneered the use of a blackboard (Engelmore and Morgan 1988; Ward and Novick 1996; Aberdeen et al. 1999) for the communication between the system modules (section 35.3.2.6).

Since then, great progress has been made and numerous experimental SDSs have appeared, including systems for transport information (Zue et al. 1994; Veldhuijzen van Zanten 1996; Gallwitz et al. 1998), voice email (Williams 1996; Walker, Fromer, and Narayanan 1998), planning and negotiation tasks (Traum 1996; LuperFoy 1996; Kipp, Alexandersson, and Reithinger 1999), telephone directory assistance, call centre automation and e-commerce (Minami et al. 1994; Vilnat 1996; Chu-Carroll and Carpenter 1998; Nugues et al. 1996), multimodal and multimedia systems (Zue 1994; Nugues et al. 1996; McGlashan 1996), computer-assisted instruction environments (LuperFoy 1996; Aberdeen et al. 1999), multilingual information retrieval (Aretoulaki et al. 1998), and many others. Several of these systems originate from research related to the DARPA ATIS project (Air Travel Information Systems), which funded bench-mark tests of different SDSs (Dahl 1995).

It seems likely that within the next two decades SDSs will become more common in real-life applications (Cole et al. 1995; Gibbon, Moore, and Winski 1997; Aust and Schroeer 1998; Bernsen, Dybkjær, and Dybkjær 1998). Further research, however, is still needed to develop, for example, more accurate speech recognizers, especially in noisy environments, reusable SDS components and system building tools (Baek-gaard 1996; Aust and Schroeer 1998; Sutton et al. 1998; Kölzer 1999), improved user modelling (Young et al. 1989; Cole et al. 1993; Ward and Novick 1994; Flycht-Eriksson 1999) and emotion detection (Gallwitz et al. 1998) in order to dynamically adapt dialogue strategies to user behaviour, standards for SDS evaluation (Danieli and Gerbino 1995; Walker et al. 1997; Walker et al. 1998; consult also Chapter 22), as well as flexible discourse models and techniques for the dynamic selection of initiative and confirmation strategies (Litman and Shimei 1999).

35.4 THE APPLICATIONS OF THE FUTURE

Sections 35.2 and 35.3 have pointed to several applications where NLIs and SDSs are being explored. We conclude this chapter with a discussion of more ambitious forms of natural language interaction that may become possible in the longer term.

Modern households and offices are flooded with increasingly sophisticated elec-tronic devices. Video recorders, microwave ovens, fax machines—to name just a few appliances—all offer an ever-increasing and overwhelming number of functionalities. Navigating through the labyrinth of features and options with buttons and menus is very cumbersome. SDSs may in the future provide a solution, spoken dialogues being a more natural—and thus intuitively easier and more user-friendly—way of interac-tion, whether mono- or multimodal (McGlashan 1996; Nugues et al. 1996). Ongoing efforts to establish API standards for household and office appliances will play a cru-cial role towards that direction, as they will provide a uniform interface for SDSs to control these appliances.

Hands-busy environments where devices need to be controlled (e.g. cars) may also benefit from natural language interaction systems, probably in the form of speech-enabled NLIs. There is also a variety of possible device-controlling applications for users with special needs, ranging from simple speech-sensitive light switches to dia-logue-based centralized home controllers. More conservative, but still challenging, are applications for accessing and navigating the World Wide Web using spontan-eous speech. Related research aims to give greater access to the blind and people who want to retrieve information from the web over the phone (Whalen and Patrick 1989; House 1995; Gallwitz et al. 1998; Boye et al. 1999).

FURTHER READING AND RELEVANT RESOURCES

Several surveys of database NLIs exist (Perrault and Grosz 1988; Copestake and Spärck Jones 1990; Androutsopoulos, Ritchie, and Thanisch 1995; Androutsopoulos and Ritchie 2000), and they constitute a useful starting point for readers wishing to learn more about NLIs. For more in-depth information on NLIs, readers are advised to consult Alshawi (1992), which provides a comprehensive description of a generic large-scale system that incorporates most of the modules of Fig. 35.1.

For SDSs, a good starting point is the book of Bernsen, Dybkjær, and Dybkjær (1998) and the handbook of Gibbon, Moore, and Winski (1997). McTear (1999) has written an extensive survey of the field; see also www.cs.cmu.edu/~aliceo/dialoglinks.html for a collection of publications from different research groups. Several specialized meetings on SDSs have been organized recently, and their proceedings constitute excellent overviews of the current approaches and applications (TWLT '96; ISDS '97; ISSD '98; KRPDS '99; SIGdial 2000). The special issue of *Speech Communication* on spoken dialogue (Shirai and Furui 1994) and the book of Smith and Hipp (1994) are also very useful sources of information. There is a special interest group on Discourse and Dialogue of the Association for Computational Linguistics; see www.sigdial.org. Related standards, resources, and best practice guidelines can be found at the web sites of the EAGLES project (http://coral.lili.uni-bielefeld.de/EAGLES), the DISC project (http://mate.nis.sdu.dk/isle and http://www.disc2.dk), and the VoiceXML Forum (http://www.voicexml.org). For those wishing to experiment with development tools for SDSs, we recommend the CSLU Speech Toolkit, available from cslu.cse.ogi.edu/toolkit, as a starting point.

REFERENCES

Aberdeen, J., S. Bayer, S. Caskey, L. Damianos, A. Goldschen, L. Hirschman, D. Loehr, and H. Trappe. 1999. 'Implementing practical dialogue systems with the DARPA communicator architecture'. *Proceedings of the IJCAI '99 Workshop on Knowledge and Reasoning in Practical Dialogue Systems* (Stockholm), 81–6.

Allen, J. F. 1995. *Natural Language Understanding*. Menlo Park, Calif.: Benjamin/Cummings.

Alshawi, H. (ed.). 1992. *The Core Language Engine*. Cambridge, Mass.: MIT Press.

Androutsopoulos, I. 2002. *Exploring Time, Tense and Aspect in Natural Language Database Interfaces*. Amsterdam: John Benjamins.

——and G. D. Ritchie. 2000. 'Database interfaces'. In R. Dale et al. (eds.), *Handbook of Natural Language Processing*. New York: Marcel Dekker, 209–40.

Androutsopoulos, I., G. D. Ritchie, and P. Thanisch. 1995. 'Natural language interfaces to databases: an introduction'. *Natural Language Engineering*, 1(1), 29–81.

————1998. 'Time, tense and aspect in natural language database interfaces'. *Natural Language Engineering*, 4(3), 229–76.

ANLP. 1994. *Proceedings of the 4th Conference on Applied Natural Language Processing* (Stuttgart).

——1997. *Proceedings of the 5th Conference on Applied Natural Language Processing* (Washington).

Aretoulaki, M., S. Harbeck, F. Gallwitz, E. Nöth, H. Niemann, J. Ivanecky, I. Ipsic, N. Pavesic, and V. Matousek. 1998. 'SQEL: a multilingual and multifunctional dialogue system'. In ICSLP '98 (1998), 855–8.

Aust, H. and O. Schroeer. 1998. 'Application development with the Philips dialog system'. In ISSD '98 (1998), 27–34.

Baekgaard, A. 1996. 'Dialogue management in a generic dialogue system'. In TWLT '96 (1996), 123–32.

Barros, F. A. and A. De Roeck. 1994. 'Resolving anaphora in a portable natural language front end to a database'. In ANLP (1994), 119–24.

Bates, M., R. Bobrow, R. Ingria, and D. Stallard. 1994. 'The Delphi natural language understanding system'. In ANLP (1994), 132–7.

Bell, J. E. and L. A. Rowe. 1992. 'An exploratory study of ad hoc query languages to databases'. *Proceedings of the 8th International Conference on Data Engineering* (Tempe, Ariz.), 606–13.

Bernsen, N. O., H. Dybkjær, and L. Dybkjær. 1998. *Designing Interactive Speech Systems: From First Ideas to User Testing*. Berlin: Springer-Verlag.

Boye, J., M. Wiren, M. Rayner, I. Lewin, D. Carter, and R. Becket. 1999. 'Language-processing strategies for mixed-initiative dialogues'. In KRPDS '99 (1999), 17–24.

Carberry, S. 1990. *Plan Recognition in Natural Language Dialogue*. Cambridge, Mass.: MIT Press.

Chu-Carroll, J. and B. Carpenter. 1998. 'Dialogue management in vector-based call routing'. In COLING-ACL (1998), 256–62.

Cohen, P. R., M. Johnston, D. McGee, S. Oviatt, and J. Pittman. 1997. 'QuickSet: multimodal interaction for simulation set-up and control'. In ANLP (1997), 20–4.

Cole, R. A., D. G. Novick, M. Fanty, S. Sutton, B. Hansen, and D. C. Burnett. 1993. 'Rapid prototyping of spoken language systems: the year 2000 Census project'. *Proceedings of the International Symposium on Spoken Dialogue* (Tokyo), 19–23.

——L. Hirschman, L. Atlas, M. Beckman, A. Bierman, M. Bush, J. Cohen, O. Garcia, B. Hanson, H. Hermansky, S. Levinson, K. McKeown, N. Morgan, D. Novick, M. Ostendorf, S. Oviatt, P. Price, H. Silverman, J. Spitz, A. Waibel, C. Weinstein, S. Zahorian, and V. Zue. 1995. 'The challenge of spoken language systems: research directions for the nineties'. *IEEE Transactions on Speech and Audio Processing*, 3(1), 1–21.

COLING-ACL 1998. *Proceedings of the 36th ACL Annual Meeting and the 17th International Conference on Computational Linguistics* (Montreal).

Copestake, A. and K. Spärck Jones. 1990. 'Natural language interfaces to databases'. *Knowledge Engineering Review*, 5(4), 225–49.

Crangle, C. and P. Suppes. 1994. *Language and Learning for Robots*. Stanford, Calif.: CSLI.

Dahl, D. A. (ed.). 1995. *Proceedings of the ARPA Workshop on Spoken Language Systems Technology* (Austin, Tex.).

Danieli, M. and E. Gerbino. 1995. 'Metrics for evaluating dialogue strategies in a spoken language system'. *Proceedings of the AAAI Symposium on Empirical Methods in Discourse Interpretation and Generation* (Stanford, Calif.), 34–9.

Dekleva, S. M. 1994. 'Is natural language querying practical?' *Data Base*, 24–36.

De Roeck, A. N. and B. G. T. Lowden. 1986. 'Generating English paraphrases from formal relational calculus expressions'. *Proceedings of the 11th International Conference on Computational Linguistics (COLING '86)* (Bonn), 581–3.

Engelmore, R. and T. Morgan (eds.). 1988. *Blackboard Systems*. Reading, Mass.: Addison-Wesley.

Erman, L. D., F. Hayes-Roth, V. R. Lesser, and D. R. Reddy. 1981. 'The Hearsay-II speech-understanding system: integrating knowledge to resolve uncertainty'. In B. L. Webber et al. (eds.), *Readings in Artificial Intelligence*. San Mateo, Calif.: Morgan Kaufmann.

Eurospeech 1997. *Proceedings of the 5th European Conference on Speech Communication and Technology* (Rhodes).

Ferguson, G. and J. F. Allen. 1993. 'Generic plan recognition for dialogue systems'. *Proceedings of the ARPA Workshop on Human Language Technology*, 171–6.

Flycht-Eriksson, A. 1999. 'A survey of knowledge sources in dialogue systems'. In KRPDS '99 (1999), 41–8.

Gallwitz, F., M. Aretoulaki, M. Boros, J. Haas, S. Harbeck, R. Huber, H. Niemann, and E. Nöth. 1998. 'The Erlangen spoken dialogue system EVAR: a state-of-the-art information retrieval system'. In ISSD '98 (1998), 19–26.

Gibbon, D., R. Moore, and R. Winski. 1997. *Handbook of Standards and Resources for Spoken Language Systems*. Berlin: Mouton de Gruyter.

Grosz, B. J., D. E. Appelt, P. A. Martin, and F. C. N. Pereira. 1987. 'TEAM: an experiment in the design of transportable natural-language interfaces'. *Artificial Intelligence*, 32, 173–243.

Haller, S. and S. McRoy (eds.). 1998/9. 'Computational models of mixed-initiative interaction', special issue of *User Modelling and User-Adapted Interaction*, 8–9.

House, D. 1995. *Spoken-language access to multimedia (SLAM): a multimodal interface to the world-wide web*. Master's thesis, Oregon Graduate Institute.

ICSLP '98. 1998. *Proceedings of the 5th International Conference On Spoken Language Processing* (Sydney).

ISDS '97. 1997. *Proceedings of the ACL Workshop 'Interactive Spoken Dialog Systems: Bringing Speech and NLP Together'* (Madrid).

ISSD '98. 1998. *Proceedings of 1998 International Symposium on Spoken Dialogue* (Sydney).

Kaplan, S. J. 1982. 'Cooperative responses from a portable natural language data base query system'. *Artificial Intelligence*, 19, 165–87.

Kipp, M., J. Alexandersson, and N. Reithinger. 1999. 'Understanding spontaneous negotiation dialogue'. In KRPDS '99 (1999), 57–64.

Kobsa, A. and W. Wahlster (eds.). 1989. *User Models in Dialog Systems*. Berlin: Springer.

Kölzer, A. 1999. 'Universal dialogue specification for conversational systems'. In KRPDS '99 (1999), 65–72.

KRPDS '99. 1999. *Proceedings of the IJCAI '99 Workshop on Knowledge and Reasoning in Practical Dialogue Systems* (Stockholm).

Levow, G. A. 1998. 'Characterizing and recognizing spoken corrections in human-computer dialogue'. In COLING-ACL (1998), 736–42.

Litman, D. J. and P. Shimei. 1999. 'Empirically evaluating an adaptable spoken dialogue system'. *Proceedings of the 7th International Conference on User Modelling* (Banff), 55–64.

LuperFoy, S. 1996. 'Tutoring versus training: a spoken language dialogue manager for instructional systems'. In TWLT '96 (1996), 45–9.

McGee, D. R., P. R. Cohen, and S. Oviatt. 1998. 'Confirmation in multimodal systems'. In COLING-ACL (1998), 823–9.

McGlashan, S. 1996. 'Towards multimodal dialogue management'. In TWLT '96 (1996), 13–22.

McTear, M. F. 1999. *Spoken dialogue technology: enabling the conversational user interface.* www.infj.ulst.ac.uk/~cbdg23/survey/spoken_dialogue_technology.html.

Minami, Y., K. Shikano, S. Takahashi, T. Yamada, O. Yoshioka, and S. Furui. 1994. 'Large-vocabulary continuous speech recognition algorithm applied to a multi-modal telephone directory assistance system'. In Shirai and Furui (1994), 301–10).

Moeller, J. U. 1997. 'DIA-MOLE: an unsupervised learning approach to adaptive dialogue models for spoken dialogue systems'. In Eurospeech (1997), 2271–4.

Nagata, M. and T. Morimoto. 1994. 'First steps towards statistical modelling of dialogue to predict the speech act type of the next utterance'. In Shirai and Furui (1994), 193–203.

Nugues, P., Ch. Godereaux, P.-O. El Guedj, and F. Revolta. 1996. 'A conversational agent to navigate in virtual worlds'. In TWLT '96 (1996), 23–33.

Perrault, C. R. and B. J. Grosz. 1988. 'Natural language interfaces'. In H. E. Shrobe (ed.), *Exploring Artificial Intelligence.* San Mateo, Calif.: Morgan Kaufmann.

Reithinger, N., R. Engel, M. Kipp, and M. Klesen. 1996. 'Predicting dialogue acts for a speech-to-speech translation system'. *Proceedings of 4th International Conference on Spoken Language Processing* (Philadelphia), 654–7.

Shirai, K. and S. Furui (eds.). 1994. 'Spoken dialogue' (special issue). *Speech Communication,* 15(3–4).

SIGdial. 2000. *Proceedings of the 1st SIGdial Workshop on Discourse and Dialogue* (Hong Kong).

Smith, R. W. 1997. 'An evaluation of strategies for selective utterance verification for spoken natural language dialog'. In ANLP (1997), 41–8.

——and D. R. Hipp. 1994. *Spoken Natural Language Dialog Systems: A Practical Approach.* New York: Oxford University Press.

Stallard, D. and R. Bobrow. 1993. 'The semantic linker: a new fragment combining method'. *Proceedings of the ARPA Workshop on Human Language Technology* (Princeton), 37–42.

Sutton, S., R. Cole, J. de Villiers, J. Schalkwyk, P. Vermeulen, M. Macon, Y.-H. Yan, E. Kaiser, B. Rundle, K. Shobaki, P. Hosom, A. Kain, J. Wouters, D. Massaro, and M. Cohen. 1998. 'Universal speech tools: the CSLU toolkit'. In ICSLP (1998), 3221–4.

Tennant, H. R., K. M. Ross, M. Saenz, C. W. Thompson, and J. R. Miller. 1983. 'Menu-based natural language understanding'. *Proceedings of the 21st ACL Annual Meeting* (Cambridge, Mass.), 151–8.

Traum, D. R. 1996. 'Conversational agency: the TRAINS-93 dialogue manager'. In TWLT '96 (1996), 1–11.

TWLT '96. 1996. *Dialogue Management in Natural Language Systems: 11th Twente Workshop on Language Technology* (Enschede).

Veldhuijzen van Zanten, G. V. 1996. 'Pragmatic interpretation and dialogue management in spoken-language systems'. In TWLT '96 (1996), 81–8.

Vilnat, A. 1996. 'Which processes to manage human–machine dialog?'. In TWLT '96 (1996), 35–44.

Walker, D.J., D. J. Litman, C.A. Kamm, and A. Abella. 1997. 'PARADISE: a framework for evaluating spoken dialogue agents'. *Proceedings of the 35th ACL Annual Meeting and the 8th EACL Conference* (Madrid), 271–80.

Walker, M. A., J. C. Fromer, and S. Narayanan. 1998. 'Learning optimal dialogue strategies: a case study of a spoken dialogue agent for Email'. In COLING-ACL (1998), 1345–51.

Ward, K. and D. G. Novick. 1996. 'On the need for a theory of integration of knowledge sources for spoken language understanding'. *Proceedings of the AAAI Workshop on the Integration of Natural Language and Speech Processing* (Seattle), 23–30.

Wauchope, K., S. Everett, D. Perzanowski, and E. Marsh. 1997. 'Natural language in four spatial interfaces'. In ANLP (1997), 8–11.

Whalen, T. and A. Patrick. 1989. 'Conversational hypertext: information access through natural language dialogues with computers'. *Proceedings of the Conference on Human Factors in Computing Systems* (Austin, Tex.), 289–92.

Whittaker, S. and P. Stenton. 1989. 'User studies and the design of natural language systems'. *Proceedings of the 4th EACL Conference* (Manchester), 116–23.

Wilensky, R., D. Chin, M. Luria, J. Martin, J. Mayfield, and D. Wu. 1988. 'The Berkeley UNIX consultant project'. *Computational Linguistics*, 14, 35–84.

Williams, S. 1996. 'Dialogue management in a mixed-initiative, cooperative, spoken language system'. In TWLT '96 (1996), 199–208.

Winograd, T. 1972. *Understanding Natural Language*. New York: Academic Press.

Woods, W. A., R. M. Kaplan, and B. N. Webber. 1972. *The Lunar Sciences Natural Language Information System: Final Report*. Report 2378, BBN, Cambridge, Mass.

Young, S. R., A. G. Hauptmann, W. H. Ward, E. T. Smith, and P. Werner. 1989. 'High-level knowledge sources in usable speech recognition systems'. *Communications of ACM*, 32, 183–94.

Zue, V. 1994. 'Toward systems that understand spoken language'. *IEEE Expert*, 9(1), 51–9.

——S. Seneff, J. Polifroni, M. Phillips, C. Pao, D. Goodine, D. Goddeau, and J. Glass. 1994. 'PEGASUS: a spoken dialogue interface for on-line air travel planning'. In Shirai and Furui (1994), 331–40.

NATURAL LANGUAGE IN MULTIMODAL AND MULTIMEDIA SYSTEMS

ELISABETH ANDRÉ

ABSTRACT

Recent years have witnessed a rapid growth in the development of multimedia applications. Improving technology and tools enable the creation of large multimedia archives and the development of completely new styles of interaction. This chapter provides a survey of multimedia applications in which natural language plays a significant role. It addresses the following three issues: (1) How to integrate multimedia input including spoken or typed language in a synergistic manner. (2) How to combine natural language with other media in order to generate more effective output. And (3) how to make use of natural language technology in order to enable better access to multimedia archives. The chapter pleads for a generalization of techniques developed for natural language processing to help overcome some of the deficiencies of current multimedia technology.

36.1 INTRODUCTION

Multimedia applications are finding their way into nearly every area of our daily life, such as education, entertainment, business, and transport. A walk through any computer fair shows that many manufacturers have already enriched their product lines with multimedia technology. The place of natural language as one of the most important means of communication makes natural language technologies integral parts of multimedia interfaces. An apparent advantage of natural language is its great expressive power. Imagine, for instance, the difficulties I would encounter if I had to provide this survey relying entirely on non-verbal media. Being one of the most familiar means of human interaction, natural language can significantly reduce the training effort required to enable communication with machines. On the other hand, the coverage of current natural language dialogue systems is still strongly limited. This fact is aggravated by the lack of robust speech recognizers. The integration of non-verbal media often improves the usability and acceptability of natural language components as they can help compensate for the deficiencies of current natural language technology. In fact, recent empirical studies by Oviatt (1999) show that properly designed multimedia systems have a higher degree of stability and robustness than those that are based on speech input only. From a linguistic point of view, multimedia systems are interesting because communication by language is a specialized form of communication in general. Theories of natural language processing have reached sufficiently high levels of maturity that it is now time to investigate how they can be applied to other media, such as graphics, or pointing gestures.

The objective of this chapter is to investigate the use of natural language in the context of a multimedia environment. To start with, we shall clarify the basic terminology. The terms **medium** and **modality**, especially, have been a constant cause of confusion due to the fact that they are used differently in various disciplines. In this chapter, we adopt Maybury's distinction between **medium**, **mode**, and **code** (see Maybury 1999). The term **mode** or **modality** is used to refer to different kinds of perceptible entities (e.g. visual, auditory, haptic, and olfactory) while the term **medium** relates to the carrier of information (e.g. paper or CD-ROM), different kinds of physical devices (e.g. screens, loudspeakers, microphones, and printers) and information types (e.g. graphics, text, and video). Finally, the term **code** refers to the particular means of encoding information (e.g. sign languages and pictorial languages).

Multimedia/multimodal systems are then systems that are able to *analyse* and/or *generate* multimedia/multimodal information or provide support in *accessing* digital libraries of multiple media.

Multimodal input analysis starts from low-level sensing of the single modes relying on interaction devices, such as speech and gesture recognizers and eye trackers. The next step is the transformation of sensory data into representation formats of a higher level of abstraction. In order to exploit the full potential of multiple input modes, input analysis should not handle the single modes independent of each other, but fuse them into a common representation format that supports the resolution of ambiguities and accounts for the compensation of errors. This process is called **modality integration** or **input fusion**. Conventional multimodal systems usually do not maintain explicit representations of the user's input and handle mode integration only in a rudimentary manner. In section 36.2, we will show how the generalization of techniques and representation formalisms developed for the analysis of natural language can help to overcome some of these problems.

Multimedia generation refers to the activity of producing output in different media. It can be decomposed into the following subtasks: the **selection** and **organization of information**, the **allocation of media**, and **content-specific media encoding**. As we do not obtain coherent presentations by simply merging verbalization and visualization results into multimedia output, the generated media objects have to be tailored to each other in such a way that they complement each other in a synergistic manner. This process is called **media coordination**. While the automatic production of material is rarely addressed in the multimedia community, a considerable amount of research effort has been directed towards the automatic generation of natural language. Section 36.3 surveys techniques for building automated multimedia presentation systems drawing upon lessons learned during the development of natural language generators.

Multimedia access to digital data is facilitated by methods for document classification and analysis, techniques to condense and aggregate the retrieved information, as well as appropriate user interfaces to support search tasks. Most contemporary multimedia retrieval systems do not aim at a deeper analysis of the underlying information, but restrict themselves to classifying and segmenting static images and videos. In section 36.4, we argue that the integration of natural language technology can lead to a qualitative improvement of existing methods for document classification and analysis.

36.2 ANALYSIS OF MULTIMODAL/ MULTIMEDIA INPUT INCLUDING LANGUAGE

Based on the observation that human–human communication is multimodal, a number of researchers have investigated the usage of multiple input devices for man–machine interaction. The first systems in this area accept written or spoken natural language input in combination with pointing gestures. Examples include

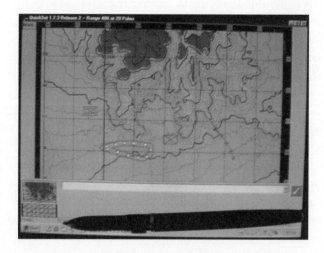

Fig. 36.1 QuickSet user interface (Figure used with Permission of OGI)

'Put-That-There' (Bolt 1980) and CUBRICON (Neal and Shapiro 1991) that operate on maps, and XTRA (Allgayer et al. 1989), an expert system for tax forms. One of the limitations of these early systems is the fact that they only allow for a limited set of deictic gestures in combination with language. In contrast, Koons, Sparrell, and Thorisson (1993) developed two prototype systems which are able to analyse simultaneous input from hand gestures, gaze, and speech. The first system allows for interaction with a two-dimensional map. The second system enables users to manipulate objects in a three-dimensional blocks world and includes not only deictic, but also iconic and pantomimic gestures. In QuickSet (Cohen et al. 1997), the user interacts with a map by drawing directly on the map displayed on a wireless hand-held and simultaneously uttering commands via speech. Drawing gestures in QuickSet include: map symbols, editing gestures, and spatial features (see Fig. 36.1). Similar interaction styles are supported by the Map-based Tourist Information System described in Cheyer and Julia (1995).

36.2.1 Natural language technology as a basis for multimodal analysis

Most systems rely on different components for the low-level analysis of the single modes, such as eye trackers, and speech and gesture recognizers, and make use of one or several mode integrators to come up with a comprehensive interpretation of the multimodal input. This approach raises two questions: how should the results of low-level analysis be represented in order to support the integration of the single modalities? How far should we process one input stream before integrating the results of other modality analysis processes? On the one hand, it does not make sense to merge gesture data and voice data on the level of pixels and phonemes. On the other hand, ambiguities of one modality should be resolved as early as possible by considering accompanying modalities.

CUBRICON and XTRA rely on parsers that were originally developed for the analysis of natural language: CUBRICON uses an augmented transition network (ATN) parser, XTRA a unification-based chart parser. To employ such parsers for the analysis of pointing gestures accompanied by natural language, additional grammatical categories, such as 'deictic', have been introduced. However, both parsers just map deictic gestures onto the corresponding categories, and additional gesture analysers are necessary in order to get to a more fine-grained representation of the non-verbal input. Since no uniform grammar formalism is used for the fusion of modalities, the integration of additional modes is relatively difficult.

In contrast to this, Koons and colleagues propose frames as a uniform representation format for speech, gestures, and gaze. For natural language input, a parse tree is created first and then transformed into a system of connected frames that represent the categories and properties of the single tokens as well as timing information. Frames with timing information are also created for eye and hand motion. Extracted features for motions of the eye include fixations, saccades, and blinks, while gestures are characterized by posture, orientation, and motion. Even though Koons and colleagues present a uniform representation formalism, their approach is still lacking a declarative method for modality integration.

Johnston and colleagues (1997) propose an approach to modality integration for the QuickSet system that is based on unification over typed feature structures. The basic idea is to build up a common semantic representation of the multimodal input by unifying feature structures which represent the semantic contributions of the single modalities. For instance, the system might derive a partial interpretation for a spoken natural language reference which indicates that the location of the referent is of type 'point'. In this case, only unification with gestures of type 'point' will succeed. Their approach also allows for the compensation of errors in speech recognition by gesture and vice versa (see Oviatt 1999). For instance, QuickSet may select speech recognition alternatives on the basis of gesture recognition and discard wrong hypotheses.

One limitation of the original unification-based approach as described in Johnston et al. (1997) lies in the fact that it can only handle combinations of single spoken phrases with single gestures. In order to account for a broader range of multimodal combinations, Johnston (1998) later combines the unification-based approach with a generalized chart parser that enables the integration of multiple elements which are distributed across two or three spatial dimensions, a temporal and an acoustic dimension.

36.2.2 Integration of modalities

In the ideal case, multimodal systems should not just accept input in multiple modalities, but also support a large variety of mode combinations. This requires sophisticated methods for modality integration.

An important prerequisite for modality integration is the explicit representation of the multimodal context. For instance, the interpretation of a pointing gesture often depends on the syntax and semantics of the accompanying natural language utterance. In 'Is this number <pointing gesture> correct?', only referents of type 'number' can be considered as candidates for the pointing gesture. The (semantic) case frame indicated by the main verb of a sentence is another source of information that can be used to disambiguate a referent since it usually provides constraints on the fillers of the frame slots. For instance, in 'Can I add my travel expenses here <pointing gesture>?', the semantics of *add* requires a field in a form where the user can input information.

A fundamental problem of most systems is that there is no declarative formalism for the formulation of integration constraints. A noteworthy exception is the approach used in QuickSet which clearly separates the statements of the multimedia grammar from the mechanisms of parsing (cf. Johnston 1998). This approach enables not only the declarative formulation of type constraints, such as 'the location of a flood zone should be an area', but also the specification of spatial and temporal constraints, such as 'two regions should be a limited distance apart' and 'the time of speech must either overlap with or start within four seconds of the time of the gesture'. The basis for the temporal constraints is empirical studies by Oviatt, DeAngelie, and Kuhn (1997).

36.3 GENERATION OF MULTIMEDIA OUTPUT INCLUDING LANGUAGE

In many situations, information is only presented efficiently through a particular media combination. Multimedia presentation systems take advantage of both the individual strength of each media and the fact that several media can be employed in parallel. Most systems combine spoken or written language with static or dynamic graphics, including bar charts and tables, such as SAGE (Roth, Mattis, and Mesnard 1991) and MAGIC (Dalal et al. 1996), maps, such as AIMI (Maybury 1991) and CUBRICON (Neal and Shapiro 1991) and depictions of three-dimensional objects, such as COMET (Feiner and McKeown 1991), WIP (Wahlster et al. 1993), and PPP (André, Rist, and Müller 1999). There are also systems which integrate natural language with hypertext. ALFRESCO (Stock, Strapparava, and Zancanaro 1997) generates text with entry points to an underlying pre-existing hypermedia network while PEA (Moore and Swartout 1990), ILEX (Knott et al. 1996), and PEBA-II (Dale and Milosavljevic 1996) make use of a hypertext-style interface to present the generated text.

36.3.1 Natural language technology as a basis for multimedia generation

Encouraged by progress achieved in natural language generation (see Chapter 15 for an introductory overview), several researchers had tried to generalize the underlying concepts and methods in such a way that they can be used in the broader context of multimedia generation.

A number of multimedia presentation systems make use of a notion of schemata (see Chapter 15) based on the original proposal by McKeown (1985) for text generation. Schemata describe standard patterns of discourse by means of rhetorical predicates which reflect the relationships between the parts of a multimedia presentation. Examples of systems using a schema-based approach are COMET (Feiner and McKeown 1991) and an earlier prototype of SAGE (Roth, Mattis, and Mesnard 1991). SAGE only relies on schemata to organize the textual parts of a multimedia presentation which makes the handling of structural dependencies between different media more difficult. Unlike SAGE, COMET employs schemata to determine the contents and the structure of the overall presentation. The result of this process is forwarded to a media coordinator which determines which generator should encode the selected information.

In the last few years, operator-based approaches similar to those used for text generation have become increasingly popular for multimedia presentation. Examples include AIMI (Maybury 1991), MAGIC (Dalal et al. 1996), WIP (Wahlster et al. 1993), PPP (André and Rist 1996), and a recent extension of SAGE (Kerpedjiev et al. 1997). The main idea behind these systems is to generalize communicative acts to multimedia acts and to formalize them as operators of a planning system. Starting from a presentation goal, the planner looks for operators whose effect subsumes the goal. If such an operator is found, all expressions in the body of the operator will be set up as new subgoals. The planning process terminates if all subgoals have been expanded to elementary generation tasks which are forwarded to the medium-specific generators. The result of the planning process is a hierarchically organized graph that reflects the discourse structure of the multimedia material (see Fig. 36.2 for a presentation plan generated by the WIP system).

An advantage of an operator-based approach is that additional information concerning media selection or the scheduling of a presentation can be easily incorporated and propagated during the content selection process. This method facilitates the

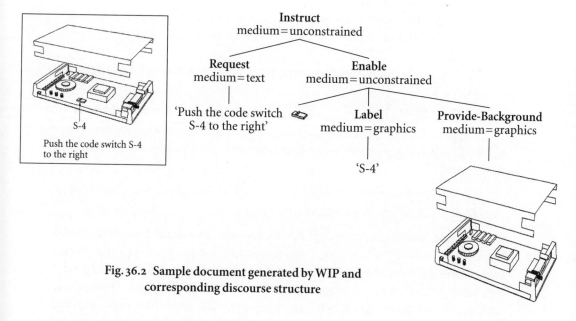

Fig. 36.2 **Sample document generated by WIP and corresponding discourse structure**

handling of dependencies, as medium selection can take place during content selection and not only afterwards, as is the case in COMET (cf. André and Rist 1995).

Operator-based approaches have also proven useful for the automated generation of hypertext. The basic idea is to refine certain parts of the discourse structure only on demand, namely if the user clicks on the corresponding hyperlink. Such an approach was used, for example, in PEA (Moore and Swartout 1990).

36.3.2 Media coordination

Multimedia presentation design involves more than just merging output in different media; it also requires a fine-grained coordination of different media. This includes distributing information onto different generators, tailoring the generation results to each other, and integrating them into a multimedia output.

36.3.2.1 *Media allocation*

The media allocation problem can be characterized as follows: given a set of data and a set of media, find a media combination which conveys all data effectively in a given situation. Earlier approaches rely on a classification of the input data, and map information types and communicative functions onto media classes by applying media allocation rules. Examples of media allocation rules are as follows (see André and Rist 1993):

1. Prefer graphics over text for spatial information (e.g. location, orientation, composition) unless accuracy is preferred over speed, in which case text is preferred.
2. Use text for quantitative information (such as most, some, any, exactly, and so on)
3. Present objects that are contrasted with each other in the same medium.

This approach can be generalized by mapping features of input data to features of media (e.g. static–dynamic, arbitrary–non-arbitrary). An example of such a mapping rule is:

> Data tuples, such as locations, are presented on planar media, such as graphs, tables, and maps. (Cf. Arens, Hovy, and Vossers 1993).

However, since media allocation depends not only on data and media features, media allocation rules have to incorporate context information as well. Arens and his colleagues (Arens, Hovy, and Vossers 1993) proposed representing all knowledge relevant to the media allocation process in And-Or- networks like those used by systemic functional linguists (see also Chapter 15) to represent grammars of various language in a uniform formalism. Presentations are designed by traversing the networks and collecting at each node features which instruct the generation modules how to build sentences, construct diagrams, and so on.

36.3.2.2 *Tailoring output in different media to each other*

To ensure the consistency and coherency of a multimedia document, the media-specific generators have to tailor their results to each other. An effective means of establishing coreferential links between different media is the generation of **cross-media referring expressions** that refer to document parts in other presentation media (cf. André and Rist 1994). Examples of cross-media referring expressions are 'the upper left corner of the picture' or 'Fig. x'. Another important task is the coordination of picture and sentence breaks (see Feiner and McKeown 1991). Constraints from graphics have to be considered when determining sentence size and the other way round. If we include too many objects in one graphics, the individual objects may be rendered too small to be recognizable. On the other hand, shortening a sentence may lead to ungrammatical text if obligatory case roles are left out. To support media coordination, the systems WIP and COMET rely on a common data structure which explicitly represents the design decisions of the single generators and allows for communication between them.

36.3.2.3 *Spatial and temporal coordination of the output*

Media coordination is also needed when integrating the individual generator results into a multimedia output. This includes the spatial arrangement of text blocks and graphics by means of a layout component. A purely geometrical treatment of the layout task would, however, lead to unsatisfactory results. Rather, layout has to be considered as an important carrier of meaning. To account for this, the WIP system maps coherence relations between presentation parts (such as sequence or contrast) onto geometrical and topological constraints (e.g. horizontal and vertical layout, alignment, and symmetry) and uses a finite domain constraint solver to determine an arrangement that is consistent with the structure of the underlying information (cf. Graf 1992).

If information is presented over time, layout design also includes the temporal coordination of output units. The PPP system generates a temporal schedule from a complex presentation goal to synchronize speech with the display of graphical elements and annotation labels. Basically, PPP relies on the WIP approach for presentation planning. However, in order to enable both the creation of multimedia objects and the generation of scripts for presenting the material to the user, the following extensions have become necessary (cf. André and Rist 1996): (1) the specification of qualitative and quantitative temporal constraints in the operators and (2) the development of a mechanism for building up presentation schedules. A similar mechanism is used in MAGIC that synchronizes spoken references to visual material with graphical highlighting.

36.4 LANGUAGE PROCESSING FOR ACCESSING MULTIMEDIA DATA

Rapid progress in technology for the creation, processing, and storage of multimedia documents has opened up completely new possibilities for building up large multimedia archives. While the necessary infrastructure is already in place, we still need tools for making information accessible to users in a beneficial way. Methods for natural processing facilitate the access to multimedia information in at least three ways: (1) information can often be retrieved more easily from the audio or closed-caption streams; (2) natural language access to visual data is often much more convenient since it allows for a more efficient formulation of queries; and (3) natural language provides a good means of condensing and summarizing visual information.

36.4.1 NL-based video/image retrieval

Whereas it is still not feasible to analyse arbitrary visual data, a great deal of progress has been made in the analysis of spoken and written language. Based on the observation that a lot of information is encoded redundantly, a number of research projects rely on the linguistic sources (e.g. transcribed speech or closed captions) when analysing image/video material. Unlike the approaches discussed in section 36.2, systems for NL-based video/image retrieval do not aim at a complete syntactic and semantic analysis of the underlying information. Instead, they usually restrict themselves to tasks, such as image/video classification and video segmentation, employing standard techniques for shallow natural language processing, such as text-based information retrieval (see Chapter 29 for an introduction) and extraction (for an introduction, we refer to Appelt 1999 and Chapter 30).

Sable and Hatzivassiloglou (1999) show how information found in associated text sources can be used for effectively classifying photographs as indoor or outdoor. Their classifier is based on information retrieval measures of text similarity which they adapted to their particular task by evaluating several variants of the standard approach, such as limiting their analysis to targeted parts of the surrounding text or certain word classes. They could show that their text-based classification methods clearly outperform competing image-based approaches and nearly approach human accuracy.

Jones et al. (1997) combine speech recognition with information retrieval in order to analyse video mail. Since most images in their application just consist of 'talking heads', they exclusively focus on the linguistic channel. Even though the authors had to cope with a number of problems that do not exist in text-based retrieval systems, such as the unreliability of the available speech recognition technology, they could achieve a retrieval performance between 75 per cent and 95 per cent of the performance that can be achieved with transcribed text depending on the generality of the underlying language model.

Whereas the approaches mentioned above focus on the task of image/video classification and do not aim at a deeper analysis of the visual material, the Broadcast News Navigator (BNN) developed by MITRE performs a segmentation of videos into different topics (see Merlino, Morey, and Maybury 1997). Besides video and audio cues, such as scene and speaker changes, the system looks for discourse cues embedded in a broadcast's transcribed speech or closed caption streams. By making use of information extraction methods, such as token detection and named entity tagging, the system can recognize typical language patterns that indicate topic shifts, such as explicitly stated reporter welcomes. For instance, it tries to detect names of persons, organizations, and locations which frequently occur in speaker introductions, such as 'This is Britt Hume, CNN, Washington'.

36.4.2   NL access to image and video databases

Direct manipulation interfaces often require the user to access objects by a series of mouse operations. Even if the user knows the location of the objects he or she is looking for, this process may still cost a lot of time and effort. Natural language supports direct access to information and enables the efficient formulation of queries by using simple keywords or free-form text.

The vast majority of information systems allow the user to input some natural language keywords that refer to the contents of an image or a video. Such keywords may specify a subject matter, such as 'sports' (cf. Aho et al. 1997), but also subjective impressions, such as 'buzzing sound' (cf. Blum et al. 1997) or 'romantic image' (cf. Kato 1992). The Informedia system (Hauptmann and Witbrock 1997) also accepts free-form typed or spoken natural language, but relies on similar methods for query processing to the other systems. It simply eliminates all stop words from the user's query and starts an index-based search.

The ALFRESCO system (Stock, Strapparava, and Zancanaro 1997) combines the benefits of hypermedia-style interaction and natural language queries to provide the user with access to a database of frescos. An interesting feature of the system is that it enables the user to continuously shift between browsing and querying. For instance, if the user asks: 'Tell me something about Ambrogio Lorenzetti', the system comes up with a generated text that contains links to a hypertext. The user is then free to browse through the hypertext or to ask natural language follow-up questions.

Even though natural language offers a number of advantages for query formulation, it might be hard in some cases to specify heterogeneous multimedia information exclusively via verbal means. Therefore, some systems are investigating additional means of accessing information, such as visual or example-based querying.

36.4.3 NL summaries of multimedia information

One major problem associated with visual data is information overload. Natural language has the advantage that it permits the condensation of visual data at various levels of detail according to the application-specific demands. Indeed, a number of experiments performed by Merlino and Maybury showed that reducing the amount of information (e.g. presenting users just with a one-line summary of a video) significantly reduces performance time in information-seeking tasks, but leads to nearly the same accuracy (cf. Merlino and Maybury 1999).

The Columbia Digital News System (CDNS, Aho et al. 1997) provides summaries over multiple news articles by combining methods for text-based information extraction and text generation (see McKeown et al. 1998). The basic idea is to use an information extraction system to deliver template representations of the events mentioned in the articles. These templates are then transformed into natural language using various summarization techniques, such as the merge of templates or the aggregation of linguistic phrases (see Chapter 32 for a general overview of summarization techniques). The system does not summarize images, but makes use of image classification tools to select a representative sample of retrieved images that are relevant to the generated summary.

While BNN and CDNS only partially analyse image or video material and assume the existence of linguistic channels, systems such as VITRA-SOCCER, start from visual information and transform it into natural language (cf. Herzog and Wazinski 1994). Here, the basic idea is to construct a symbolic scene representation from a sequence of video images which is then transformed into conceptual units of a higher level of abstraction. This process includes the explicit representation of spatial configurations by means of spatial relations, the interpretation of objects' movements, and even the automatic recognition of presumed goals and plans of the observed agents. A similar approach has been taken to generate natural language descriptions for games of the RoboCup simulator league (cf. André et al. 2000).

36.5 Language in Inhabited Multimedia Environments

Recent years have seen a trend towards more intuitive interfaces which go far beyond the traditional user interfaces in which people interact via keyboard or computer mouse. Animated characters play an important role in such interfaces since they allow for the emulation of communication styles common in human–human communication (see Elliott and Brzezinski 1998 for an overview). Examples include life-like characters that guide users through media spaces, tutor agents in pedagogical environments, and embodied personalized information agents.

Fig. 36.3 shows a conversational agent currently under development at DFKI GmbH in the role of a receptionist. Cyberella^{TM} runs on an info-terminal within the DFKI entrance. Her task is to welcome visitors, business partners, and students to DFKI and to answer questions on a wide range of dialogue topics covering news, research projects, and people within DFKI.

Bringing a character like Cyberella to life is not just a challenge from the point of view of computer graphics and animation. To come across as socially believable, characters need to be realized as unique individuals with their own personality. According to their functional role in a dialogue, they must be able to exhibit a variety of conversational behaviours. In particular, they have to execute gestures that express emotions (e.g. happiness or anger), convey the communicative function of an utterance (e.g. warn the user by lifting an index finger), support referential acts (e.g. look at an object and point at it), regulate the interaction between the character and the user (e.g. establish eye contact with the user during communication), and articulate what is being said.

For research on natural language processing, this has the following consequences. First of all, the generation of language should not only be driven by the goal of information delivery, but also be influenced by social and psychological factors. In order to support the full bandwidth of human–human communication, conversational models have to encompass not only speech, but also intonation, facial expressions, gaze and, body gestures.

From a technical point of view, it makes no difference whether we plan presentation scripts for the display of static and dynamic media, or communicative acts to be executed by animated characters. Basically, we can rely on one of the temporal planners presented in section 36.3.2.3 if we extend the repertoire of plan operators by including operators which control a character's conversational behaviour. Such an approach has been used in the PPP system to determine high-level presentation acts

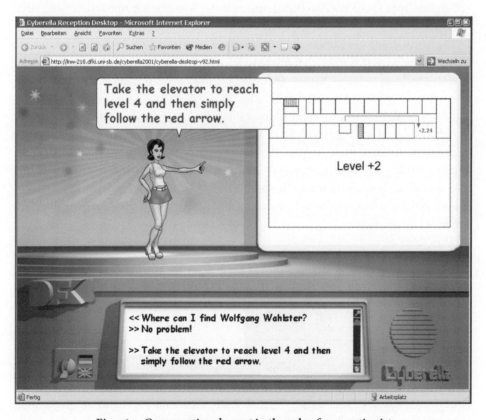

Fig. 36.3 Conversational agent in the role of a receptionist

for an animated presenter, the so-called PPP Persona. The planning approach also allows us to incorporate models of character's personality and emotions by treating them as an additional filter during the selection and instantiation of plan operators. For instance, we may define specific plan operators for characters of a certain personality and formulate constraints which restrict their applicability.

While planning techniques have proven to be useful for the specification of high-level conversational acts, the generation of immediate reactions and smooth animation sequences requires a method which is computationally less expensive. One solution is to precompile declarative behaviour specifications into finite-state machines (cf. Ball et al. 1997), which are also a suitable mechanism for synchronizing character behaviours. For instance, Cassell and colleagues (Cassell et al. 1994) use the so-called parallel transition networks (PaT-Nets) to encode facial and gestural coordination rules as simultaneously executing finite-state automata.

One of the most important communication channels is a character's face. To describe possible facial motions performable on a face, most systems rely on the facial action coding system (FACS, Ekman and Friesen 1978) or MPEG-4 facial animation parameters (FAPs). For instance, both Nagao and Takeuchi (1994) and Cassell and colleagues (1994) map FACS actions, such as Inner Brow Raiser, onto communicative functions, such as Punctuation, Question, Thinking, or Agreement.

The believability of a lifelike character depends on the quality of the output speech. Unfortunately, most lifelike characters today simply use the default intonation of a speech synthesizer (see Chapter 17 for an introduction to speech synthesis). The integration of natural language generation and speech synthesis technology offers a great potential for improvement, since a natural language generator may provide the knowledge of an utterance's form and structure that a speech synthesizer needs in order to produce good output. Prevost (1996) provides an example of such an approach: this work uses a Categorial Grammar to translate lexicalized logical forms into strings of words with intonational markings. Another noteworthy approach to speech synthesis is that adopted by Cahn (1990), which also addresses the affective impact of an utterance.

36.6 CONCLUSION

Multimedia systems pose significant challenges for natural language processing, which focuses on the analysis or generation of one input or output medium only. A key observation of this chapter is that methods for natural language processing may be extended in such a way that they become useful for the broader context of multimedia as well. While unification-based grammars have proven useful for media orchestration and analysis, text planning methods have successfully been applied to multimedia content selection and structuring. Work done in the area of multimedia information retrieval demonstrates that the integration of natural language methods, such as named entity recognition, enables a deeper analysis of the underlying multimedia information and thus leads to better search results.

The evolution of multimedia systems is evidence of the trend away from procedural approaches towards more declarative approaches, which maintain explicit representations of the syntax and semantics of multimedia input and output. While earlier systems make use of separate components for processing multiple media and are only able to integrate and coordinate media to a limited extent, more recent approaches are based on a unified view of language and rely on a common representation formalism for the single media. Unfortunately, a generic framework providing a bidirectional view of multimedia communication is currently not yet available. There has been an international initiative towards the development of a standard reference architecture for multimedia systems; however, it has been focusing on generation aspects only (cf. Bordegoni et al. 1997).

FURTHER READING AND RELEVANT RESOURCES

The original versions of many papers that have been discussed here can be found in Maybury (1993), Maybury (1997), and Maybury and Wahlster (1998). A more detailed overview on multimedia generation systems with a special focus on natural language is provided by André (2000). Cassell et al. (2000) contains a comprehensive collection of papers on embodied conversational agents. I also recommend the following special issues: Mc Kevitt (1994–6); Oviatt and Wahlster (1997); Rist (1998); and André (1999a). A useful website with conference announcements and downloadable information sources is the electronic colloquium on Intelligent User Interfaces of the Electronic Transactions of Articificial Intelligence (ETAI) (http://www.dfki.de/etai/colloqb.html).

ACKNOWLEDGEMENTS

This work has been supported by the BMBF under the contract 9701 0. I would like to thank Hamish Cunningham, Thierry Declerck, Michael Johnston, Peter Makumbi, Ruslan Mitkov, and Thomas Rist for their valuable comments and corrections of an earlier draft of this chapter.

REFERENCES

Aho, A. V., S. Chang, K. McKeown, D. R. Radev, J. R. Smith, and K. A. Zaman. 1997. 'Columbia digital news system: an environment for briefing and search over multimedia information'. *International Journal of Digital Libraries*, 1(4), 377–85.

Allgayer, J., K. Harbusch, A. Kobsa, C. Reddig, N. Reithinger, and D. Schmauks. 1989. 'XTRA: a natural-language access system to expert systems'. *International Journal of Man–Machine Studies*, 31, 161–95.

André, E. (ed.). 1999a. 'Animated Interface Agents', special double issue of *Applied Artificial Intelligence Journal*, 13(4–5).

——2000. 'The generation of multimedia presentations'. In R. Dale, H. Moisl, and H. Somers (eds.), *A Handbook of Natural Language Processing: Techniques and Applications for the Processing of Language as Text*. New York: Marcel Dekker Inc., 305–27.

——W. Finkler, W. Graf, T. Rist, A. Schauder, and W. Wahlster. 1993. 'WIP: the automatic synthesis of multimodal presentations'. In Maybury (1993), 75–93.

——and T. Rist. 1993. 'The design of illustrated documents as a planning task'. In Maybury (1993), 94–116.

————1994. 'Referring to world objects with text and pictures'. *Proceedings of the 15th International Conference on Computational Linguistics (Coling '94)* (Kyoto), 530–4.

————1995. 'Generating coherent presentations employing textual and visual material'. 'The Integration of Natural Language and Vision Processing', special issue of *Artificial Intelligence Review*, 9(2–3), 147–65.

————1996. 'Coping with temporal constraints in multimedia presentation planning'. *Proceedings of the 13th National Conference of the American Association on Artificial Intelligence (AAAI '96)* (Portland, Ore.), i. 142–7.

————and J. Müller. 1999. 'Employing AI methods to control the behavior of animated interface agents'. *Applied Artificial Intelligence Journal*, 13(4–5), 415–48.

——K. Binsted, K. Tanaka-Ishii, S. Luke, G. Herzog, and T. Rist. 2000. 'Three RoboCup simulation league commentator systems'. *AI Magazine*, 21(1), 57–66.

Appelt, D. 1999. 'An introduction to information extraction'. *AI Communications*, 12(3), 161–72.

Arens, Y., E. Hovy, and M. Vossers. 1993. 'Describing the presentational knowledge underlying multimedia instruction manuals'. In Maybury (1993), 280–306.

Ball, G., D. Ling, D. Kurlander, J. Miller, D. Pugh, T. Skelly, A. Stankosky, D. Thiel, M. van Dantzich, and T. Wax. 1997. 'Lifelike computer characters: the persona project at Microsoft'. In J. M. Bradshaw (ed.), *Software Agents*. Menlo Park, Calif.: AAAI Press, 191–222.

Blum, T., D. Keislaer, J. Wheaton, and E. Wold. 1997. 'Audio databases with content-based retrieval'. In Maybury (1993), 113–35.

Bolt, R. A. 1980. 'Put-That-There: voice and gesture at the graphics interface'. *Computer Graphics*, 14, 262–70.

Bordegoni, M., G. Faconti, S. Feiner, M. T. Maybury, T. Rist, S. Ruggieri, P. Trahanias, and M. Wilson. 1997. 'A standard reference model for intelligent multimedia presentation systems'. *Computer Standards and Interfaces: The International Journal on the Development and Application of Standards for Computers, Data Communications and Interfaces*, 18(6–7), 477–96.

Cahn, J. 1990. 'The generation of affect in synthesized speech'. *Journal of the American Voice I/O Society*, 8, 1–19.

Cassell, J., C. Pelachaud, N.I. Badler, M. Steedman, B. Achorn, T. Becket, B. Douville, S. Prevost, and M. Stone. 1994. 'Animated conversation: rule-based generation of facial expression, gesture and spoken intonation for multiple conversational agents'. *Proceedings of Siggraph '94* (Orlando, Fla.), 413–20.

——J. Sullivan, S. Prevost, and E. Churchill. 2000. *Embodied Conversational Agents*. Cambridge, Mass.: MIT Press.

Cheyer, A. and L. Julia. 1995. 'Multimodal maps: an agent based approach'. *Proceedings of the International Conference on Cooperative Multimodal Communication* (Eindhoven), 103–14.

Cohen, P. R., M. Johnston, D. McGee, and S. Oviatt. 1997. 'Quickset: multimodal interaction for distributed applications'. *Proceedings of the 5th International Multimedia Conference* (*Multimedia '97*) (Seattle), 31–40.

Dalal, M., S. Feiner, K. McKeown, S. Pan, M. Zhou, T. Hüllerer, J. Shaw, Y. Feng, and J. Fromer. 1996. 'Negotiation for automated generation of temporal multimedia presentations'. *Proceedings of the 4th International Multimedia Conference* (*Multimedia '96*) (Boston), 55–64.

Dale, R. and M. Milosavljevic. 1996. 'Authoring on demand: natural language generation in hypermedia documents'. *Proceedings of the First Australian Document Computing Symposium* (*ADCS '96*) (Melbourne), 20–1.

Ekman, P. and W. V. Friesen. 1978. *Facial Action Coding*. Palo Alto, Calif.: Consulting Psychologists Press Inc.

Elliott, C. and J. Brzezinski. 1998. 'Autonomous agents as synthetic characters'. *AI Magazine*, 19(2), 13–30.

Feiner, S. K. and K. R. McKeown. 1991. 'Automating the generation of coordinated multimedia explanations'. *IEEE Computer*, 24(10), 33–41.

Graf, W. 1992. 'Constraint-based graphical layout of multimodal presentations'. In M. F. Costabile, T. Catarci, and S. Levialdi (eds.), *Advanced Visual Interfaces: Proceedings of AVI '92* (Rome). Singapore: World Scientific Press, 365–85.

Hauptmann, A. G. and M. J. Witbrock. 1997. 'Informedia: news-on-demand multimedia information acquisition and retrieval'. In Maybury (1993), 214–39.

Herzog, G. and P. Wazinski. 1994. 'Visual translator: linking perceptions and natural language descriptions'. 'The Integration of Natural Language and Vision Processing', special issue of *Artificial Intelligence Review*, 8(2–3), 175–87.

Johnston, M. 1998. 'Unification-based multimodal parsing'. *Proceedings of the International Conference on Computational Linguistics and the 36th Annual Meeting of the Association for Computational Linguistics* (*COLING-ACL '98*) (Montreal), 624–30.

——P. R. Cohen, D. McGee, S. L. Oviatt, J. A. Pittman, and I. Smith. 1997. 'Unification-based multimodal integration'. *Proceedings of the International Conference on Computational Linguistics and the 35th Annual Meeting of the Association for Computational Linguistics* (*COLING-ACL '97*) (Madrid), 281–8.

Jones, G., J. Foote, K. Spärck Jones, and S. J. Young. 1997. 'The video mail retrieval project: experiences in retrieving spoken documents'. In Maybury (1993), 191–214.

Kato, T. 1992. 'Cognitive view mechanism for content-based multimedia information retrieval'. In R. Cooper (ed.), *Proceedings of the 1st International Workshop on Interfaces to Database Systems* (*IDS '92*), New York: Springer, 244–62.

Kerpedjiev, S., G. Carenini, S. F. Roth, and J. D. Moore. 1997. 'Integrating planning and task-based design for multimedia presentation'. *Proceedings of the 1997 International Conference on Intelligent User Interfaces* (Orlando, Fla.), 145–52.

Knott, A., C. Mellish, J. Oberlander, and M. O'Donnell. 1996. 'Sources of flexibility in dynamic hypertext generation'. *Proceedings of the 8th International Workshop on Natural Language Generation* (Brighton), 151–60.

Koons, D. B., C. J. Sparrell, and K. R. Thorisson. 1993. 'Integrating simultaneous input from speech, gaze, and hand gestures'. In Maybury (1993), 257–76.

McKeown, K. R. 1985. *Text Generation*. Cambridge: Cambridge University Press.

——S. Feiner, M. Dalal, and S. Chang. 1998. 'Generating multimedia briefings: coordinating language and illustration'. *AI Journal*, 103(1–2), 95–116.

Mc Kevitt, P. (ed.). 1994–6. 'The Integration of Natural Language and Vision Processing', special issues of *Artificial Intelligence Review*, 8(2–3, 4–5), 9(2–3, 5–6), 10(1–2, 3–4). Also available as vol. i (The BLUE book), vol. ii (The BLACK book), vol. iii (The GREEN book), and vol. iv (The GREEN book).

Maybury, M. T. 1991. 'Planning multimedia explanations using communicative acts'. *Proceedings of the 8th National Conference of the American Association on Artificial Intelligence (AAAI '91)* (Menlo Park, Calif.), 61–6.

——(ed.). 1993. *Intelligent Multimedia Interfaces*. Menlo Park, Calif.: AAAI Press.

——(ed.). 1997. *Intelligent Multimedia Information Retrieval*. Menlo Park, Calif.: MIT Press.

——1999. 'Multimedia interaction for the new millenium'. *Proceedings of Eurospeech 99* (Budapest), 357–64.

——and W. Wahlster (eds.). 1998. *Readings in Intelligent User Interfaces*. San Mateo, Calif.: Morgan Kaufmann Publishers.

Merlino, A. and M. T. Maybury. 1999. 'An empirical study of the optimal presentation of multimedia summaries of broadcast news'. In I. Mani and M. T. Maybury (eds.), *Automated Text Summarization*. Cambridge, Mass.: MIT Press, 391–401.

——D. Morey, and M. T. Maybury. 1997. 'Broadcast news navigation using story segmentation'. *ACM Multimedia 97*, 381–91.

Moore, J. D. and W. R. Swartout. 1990. 'Pointing: a way toward explanation dialogue'. *Proceedings of 7th National Conference of the American Association on Artificial Intelligence (AAAI '90)* (Menlo Park, Calif.), 457–64.

Nagao K. and A. Takeuchi. 1994. 'Social interaction: multimodal conversation with social agents'. *Proceedings of the 32nd Annual Meeting of the Association for Computational Linguistics (ACL '94)* (Las Cruces, N. Mex.), i. 22–8.

Neal, J. G. and S. C. Shapiro. 1991. 'Intelligent multi-media interface technology'. In J. W. Sullivan and S. W. Tyler (ed.), *Intelligent User Interfaces*. New York: ACM Press, 11–43.

Oviatt, S. L. 1999. 'Mutual disambiguation of recognition errors in a multimodal architecture'. *Proceedings of Conference on Human Factors in Computer Systems (CHI '99)* (Pittsburgh), 576–83.

——A. DeAngelie, and K. Kuhn. 1997. 'Integration and synchronization of input modes during multimodal human-computer interaction'. *Proceedings of Conference on Human Factors in Computer Systems (CHI '97)* (Atlanta), 415–22.

——and W. Wahlster (eds.). 1997. 'Multimodal Interfaces', special issue of *Human–Computer Interaction*, 12(1–2).

Prevost, S. 1996. 'An information structural approach to spoken language generation'. *Proceedings of the 34th Annual Meeting of the Association for Computational Linguistics (ACL '96)* (Santa Cruz, Calif.), 294–301.

Rist, T. (ed.). 1998. 'Intelligent Multimedia Presentation Systems', special issue of *Computer Standards & Interfaces*, 18(5–7).

Roth, S. F., J. Mattis, and X. Mesnard. 1991. 'Graphics and natural language as components of automatic explanation'. In J. W. Sullivan and S. W. Tyler (eds.), *Intelligent User Interfaces*. New York: ACM Press, 207–39.

Sable, C. and V. Hatzivassiloglou. 1999. 'Text-based approaches for the categorization of images'. *Proceedings of the 3rd European Conference on Research and Advanced Technology for Digital Libraries* (Paris), 19–38.

Searle, J. R. 1980. *Speech Acts: An Essay in the Philosophy of Language*. Cambridge: Cambridge University Press.

Stock, O., C. Strapparava, and M. Zancanaro. 1997. 'Explorations in an environment for natural language multimodal information access'. In Maybury (1993), 381–98.

Wahlster, W., E. André, W. Finkler, H.-J. Profitlich, and T. Rist. 1993. 'Plan-based integration of natural language and graphics generation'. *AI Journal*, 63, 387–427.

NATURAL LANGUAGE PROCESSING IN COMPUTER-ASSISTED LANGUAGE LEARNING

JOHN NERBONNE

ABSTRACT

This chapter examines the application of natural language processing to computer-assisted language learning including the history of work in this field over the last thirty-five years but with a focus on current developments and opportunities.

37.1 INTRODUCTION

This chapter focuses on applications of computational linguistics (CL) techniques to **computer-assisted language learning** (CALL). This always refers to programs designed to help people learn foreign languages, e.g. programs to help German high-school students learn French. CALL is a large field—much larger than computational linguistics—which no one can describe completely in a brief chapter. The focus of this chapter is therefore much narrower, namely just on those areas of CALL to which CL has been applied or might be. CL programs process natural languages such as English and Spanish, and the techniques are therefore often referred to as natural language processing (NLP).

To preview this chapter's contents, we note that NLP has been enlisted in several ways in CALL, e.g. to carry out the **alignment** of **bilingual texts** (see Chapter 24 on corpora) so that a learner who encounters an unknown word in French can seen how it was rendered in translation; to provide **lemmatized** access to corpora for advanced learners seeking subtleties unavailable in grammars and dictionaries (see Chapter 2 on morphology for an explanation of lemmatizing); to provide morphological analysis and subsequent dictionary access for words unknown to readers (Chapters 2, 18); and to parse user input and diagnose morphological and syntactic errors (Chapters 4, 12). Speech recognition has been used extensively in pronunciation training, and speech synthesis for single words (Chapters 16–17). The work on speech in CALL falls outside the scope of this chapter, but it is noted since we expect its use in CALL to enable further deployment of NLP, perhaps in parsing spoken input.

The chapter deliberately ignores two further areas which arguably involve language learning, first, software designed to diagnose and assist the verbally handicapped (Miller and Klee 1995; Perry 1995; Connolly 1997; Somers 1999), and second, programs for assistance in developing and polishing advanced writing skills. The first area seems genuinely extraneous (there is little overlap with CALL), and the second has attracted little interest from NLP practitioners even though it enjoys substantial attention in the larger CALL literature (Pennington 1999; Schultz 2000).

37.2 MOTIVATION

The traditional methods of learning and teaching foreign languages require a teacher to work 60 to 100 hours to bring an adult to a level at which she can function minimally with the foreign language (FSI 1973). By 'minimally functioning' we just mean being able to use short, pre-packaged phrases to communicate simple thoughts with long pauses and very foreign pronunciation. In general, progress beyond this level requires a great deal more time and energy, roughly doubling at each proficiency level (FSI 1973). Very high levels of fluency are normally unrealistic goals. Naturally, some learners *do* reach high levels of fluency, even near-native levels, but they have to arrange for extensive contact beyond language instruction.

CALL will be an attractive alternative whenever these teachers are unavailable (within reasonable travel), inconvenient (due to scheduling difficulties), or unaffordable. CALL can also be a useful supplement in all of these situations (i.e. when more extensive direct instruction might be contrasted). Looking ahead to the role we will suggest is most promising for NLP in CALL, we note that even extensive experience with a foreign language is of little didactic value if it is incomprehensible to the language learner. Unguided 'immersion' into a situation dominated by a foreign tongue does not result in proficiency. For learning to occur, learners must understand the language they are exposed to. A central role for CALL, especially when no teacher is available, is to provide comprehensible foreign-language material in spoken and written form; to help students understand foreign language material, e.g. to verify that inflections carry particular grammatical import; and to provide exercise and test material. Because the computer can process information, it can provide such verifying information much more extensively (and conveniently) than any static source could hope to. The section below on **lemmatization** (37.6.4) illustrates this in the greatest depth.

A standard question on CALL which is reflected in recurring comments to net lists (see the end of this chapter for a pointer to one of these) asks whether CALL has been proven superior to traditional methods of language learning and learning teaching. Naturally, there have been studies aimed at measuring differences, but it is important to note that this challenge misses the main features of CALL which make it an attractive alternative or supplement to traditional methods of language learning and learning teaching. Even if it were *worse* than traditional methods, CALL would be used extensively—human teachers are not available in the numbers and budget ranges needed.

37.2.1 Inflated expectations

This is emphatically not to say that CALL will ever provide all that its most wide-eyed admirers expect. Many potential primary users of NLP-enhanced CALL (learners) as well as secondary users (teachers and administrators) are unsophisticated in their expectations (Atwell 1998). Atwell (1999), while advocating increased user involvement in software development for English Language Teaching (ELT), illustrates how much deflation may be necessary:

> ... it turned out that one of the main things that English language teachers asked for was a 'conversation practice machine': a computer system with which a learner could 'chat' in ordinary English, to practise their everyday conversational skills. ... Another thing which ELT users seemed to want was an ability to correct errors and give guidance on the cause of errors in learners' conversations.   (Atwell 1999: 31–2)

It looks as if the simple Turing test is not sufficient: we need a machine which not only converses naturally, but which spots errors and diagnoses their causes for less fluent interlocutors! Teachers with some experience of CALL are naturally more sober. Levy (1997: ch. 5) reports on an extensive survey conducted under CALL practitioners at universities. As a whole, this group is guided most by availability and reliability of software (Levy 1997: 148–50).

37.2.2 Application sectors

Although we normally think of language education as a task for schools and universities, which it certainly is, there is an enormous need for language training outside of the schools. It is convenient to consider three distinct sorts of language learners and learning situations, as they differ in their interest for technical improvement and in their readiness to experiment, which in turn impacts on the assessment of application opportunities for CALL:

- **academic**. This group includes the schools and universities. Even though this is the group one most immediately thinks of in connection with language teaching and learning, it has well-known, peculiar difficulties, e.g. penurious budgets, uncertain hardware and software infrastructures, and teachers who feel pressed to meet regular responsibilities without assuming the extra challenges of trying new technologies.
- **industrial**. Government and private industry organize their own language courses, often at considerable expense. We group specialized language schools under this category as well, but with the reservation that their means are often more limited, since their pupils often pay the bills directly.
- **self-study**. There is a sizeable number of people who study languages without the benefit of formal instruction organized by their jobs or educational institutions. They have stimulated a surprisingly large market in what is sometimes disparagingly dubbed 'edutainment', but which proves that there is a mass market for CALL, as well.

Fox (1996: 9) estimated the multimedia market in Europe at 1.9 billion Euro in 1994, 28 per cent of which was educational. The CALL market is estimated as 20 per cent of the latter, or about 106 million Euro in 1994. The US market is more than twice the size of Europe's with a similar proportion devoted to education and language. A threefold growth by 1999 was predicted. This leads one to predict a one-billion Euro business area by 2000. Meanwhile the CALL business benefits like all of Information and Communication Technology (ICT) from steeply falling price/performance figures, and from large-scale commercial interest in the underlying technologies.

37.3 SECOND LANGUAGE LEARNING

In this section we turn to what is known about how people learn foreign languages, and how computers have been enlisted to help in this task, focusing first on how CALL *sans* NLP has progressed.

Applied linguistics studies **second language learning** and **foreign language learning**. Although the terms are used by some interchangeably, a distinction is often drawn. Foreign language learning normally takes place in classrooms and always takes place remote from extensive natural opportunity to use the foreign language. Second language learning occurs in a natural environment, normally in a country where the language is spoken. 'Second language learning' is often used as a cover term for the two situations, and that is the intention of this section's heading.

There are researchers who prefer the term second language *acquisition*, because 'acquisition' (as opposed to 'learning') emphasizes the degree to which automatic processes may play a role in the more natural situation when a language from the immediate environment is adopted.

Second and foreign language learning share an applied focus as scholarly fields: both consistently research not only how language learning normally proceeds, but also how it succeeds best. They seek to optimize learning, naturally with respect to the goals of language learners (e.g. scientific literature, tourism, or commerce), their (linguistic) backgrounds, and their age and educational level. Van Els et al. (1977) is an excellent reference on issues in this branch of applied linguistics, and Dulay, Burt, and Krashen (1982) a more theoretically oriented text on what research on second language learning acquisition reveals about underlying linguistic abilities and learning processing. Other texts can also be valuable (Larsen-Freeman and Long 1991; Ellis 1994).

37.3.1 The fundamental pedagogical principle

A principle on which the different schools agree is that the material to which learners are exposed must be comprehensible to the learners in order for learning to proceed optimally (Krashen 1981), cited often, *inter alia* by Widdowson (1990: 111). Krashen and others have gone on to postulate that the comprehensible input is the primary determinant in second language acquisition, dubbing this the 'fundamental pedagogical principle' in second language teaching. Krashen's idea is that comprehensible input triggers automatic processes which are ultimately responsible for successful language learning. There is an important qualification and an important restriction in scope. Krashen (1981: 66) explicitly qualifies his postulate that the comprehensible input determines second language acquisition, noting that 'conscious learning' (i.e.

morphology and 'easy' rules [scare quotes in original—J.N.]) does contribute to second language proficiency. The restriction in scope is implicit, but there is no suggestion that exposure to comprehensible input is sufficient for learning writing, even though many second-language learners do aspire to competence in writing.

Krashen's writings are clearly argued. He justifies the overarching postulate by showing how it makes sense first of the fact that understanding always precedes production—this is so because understanding is a prerequisite for production. The postulate also helps explain the variable speed of children vs. adults as language learners. Adults comprehend more initially because they make better use of non-linguistic cues etc., so they learn more quickly than children initially. The fact that children are ultimately more proficient is attributed to the adults' 'filtering' foreign input for emotional reasons. He reviews a series of studies on instruction and is able to generalize that the amount of comprehensible input was a determining, often confounding variable in these. Carter (1998: 208) makes the point that lots of vocabulary learning must take place without explicit teaching—since it is not taught. Krashen develops consequences of his ideas for the importance of reading (Krashen 1989), and the use of media and language laboratories, and the combination of language teaching with specialized subject matter (in some circumstances). Krashen has modified his original views to admit that a special 'weak interface' brokers the learning of second languages, and that this distinguishes it from learning first languages (Krashen 1985).

There are nonetheless important recent reactions to Krashen's emphases on automatic processes of acquisition. DeKeyser (1995) has shown that adult learners very definitely benefit from explicit instruction in grammar rules, claiming more strongly that adult learners basically do not learn to speak grammatically without explicitly being taught the rules. DeKeyser (2000) shows that the very few adults who appear to learn successfully without explicit instruction score high in analytical ability (which is irrelevant in children's success in foreign language acquisition). This suggests that they are exceptions precisely because they are capable of abstracting the rules themselves, to some extent. Norris and Ortega (2000) review dozens of studies over the last thirty years, and claim that Krashen had it exactly wrong, at least when it comes to adults' learning of grammar. Naturally, the range of potential CALL applications is broader if adults need explicit grammar instruction.

The applied linguistics community agrees further to a great degree on fundamentals such as holding the attention of learners, encouraging repetition, and aiming for varied practical exercise. There is less agreement on issues such as the value of formal grammatical tutoring (as just noted), the value of correcting errors, the time at which to encourage speaking, etc. See Larsen-Freeman and Long (1991) for more on the range of (conflicting) ideas current in language pedagogy. Under the circumstances it is wise for CALL developers not to embrace any theory too exclusively, but to remain consonant with different approaches (cf. Lantolf 1996).

It would seem straightforward that all that is known about second language learning ought to inform the development of CALL materials. It provides a modest amount of theory, and it suggests useful concepts and categories (natural learners vs. taught learners, reading/listening vs. writing/speaking), tests and means of evaluation, simple techniques, interdependencies between media, techniques, curricula, etc. But surprisingly, one respected recent book on CALL (Levy 1997) takes pains to consider alternative theoretical orientations for CALL. Levy's primary goal is to show that CALL should be regarded as a 'tool', in language learning rather than a 'tutor', or substitute for a teacher, and in general CALL practitioners have been receptive (Wolff 1999). But on the way to this goal, Levy considers psychology, linguistics, artificial intelligence, and other fields as candidates within which to locate CALL in an extended diatribe meant to establish that poor 'conceptualization' is hampering progress in the field.

There are no grounds to think that second language learning is fundamentally different when the computer is involved, however, and this suggests that CALL be viewed simply as technical innovation in second language learning. And Levy (1997: ch. 8) finally also comes to the sober—and, I believe, correct—view of CALL as an applied field that ought to pay more attention to the concrete success of its products and less to its theory and its ultimate place in the scientific scheme of things,[1] so perhaps the extended discussions in early chapters are intended to convince the unreflective.

37.4 CALL

CALL seeks to employ computers in order to improve language learning. CALL spans the range of activities in language pedagogy—hearing, speaking, reading, and writing—and draws from nearly all areas of ICT. Even if most CALL applications are automated language exercises, exploiting hypertext, simple database and network technology, and digital audio and video, one finds many others, including ingenious applications of everyday technology such as word-processing and email. Levy (1997), valuable for its survey of the surprisingly long history of CALL, reports on the field's extensive reflection on its proper relation to applied linguistics, computer science, and psychology, and his own astute view of its proper, technology-driven nature in the final chapters. There is no mention of opportunities for several common CL techniques, however, e.g. **alignment** software or software for **lemmatization**.

---

[1] On this point, Levy's view may be contrasted with Holland's (1995: p. vii–viii), who sees 'theory shaping technology'. Levy argues that effective CALL programs have seldom been developed with much direct inspiration from theory and that more practical inspiration has been crucial.

Although CALL employs the computer to assist in language teaching and in language self-study, it primarily uses non-language technology, as noted above. The basic ICT technologies used are as follows:

- **(simple) database technology** to record and present student work; and
- **digital audio and video** to vivify examples of language use (Rothenberg 1998);
- **hypertext** to provide varied access to exercises and explanatory material (Jager 1998);
- **network communication** to bring learners and teachers into easier contact (Hoffman 1996; Holliday 1998). An ingenious use of email is to put intermediate learners in symmetric contact—native English speakers learning Spanish with native Spanish speakers learning English (Appel and Mullen 2000a, 2000b).

We note this work to give an idea of the sorts of efforts which compete for development resources with NLP-informed CALL. As the introduction warned, this chapter will not discuss the non-NLP work. Cameron (1999b) is a good recent collection of articles on CALL which give a sense of the range of approaches that are used, current issues, evaluation techniques, etc. Several of its articles discuss CL techniques directly, however, and these figure below. Levy (1997) is a more reflective work, and indispensable for some of its comments on the history of the field.

37.4.1 History of CALL

CALL looks back on a long history of serious and widely interdisciplinary work. Levy (1997: ch. 2) reports *inter alia* on PLATO (Programmed Logic for Automatic Teaching Operations), a University of Illinois project begun in 1960, and TICCIT (Time-Shared Interactive Computer-Controlled Television), a Brigham Young University effort started in 1971. Both were sophisticated, featuring 'talk' facilities for exchanging typed messages; exercises for reading, writing, and listening; opportunities for instructors to modify material; and self-paced organization of materials. Evaluation of this early work noted that while the performance of students was good, the student retention rate was not. The systems were not popular with students, and this remains a caution to current work (Hamilton 1998). The 1983 Athena Language Project (ALP) started at MIT in 1983 and involved artificial intelligence tutoring techniques and multimedia to provide instruction in five European languages. In comparison to the earlier projects ALP focused more on communication as opposed to grammar, and it included games and puzzles (Murray 1995; Felshin 1995).

There is a new website at www.history-of-call.org with some presentational glitches (in Netscape as of March 2001) which contains many very useful pointers for those interested in the history of this technology.

37.5 NATURAL LANGUAGE PROCESSING

As earlier chapters have noted, NLP focuses on how computers can best process language—analyse, store, sort, and search it. It seems natural that NLP should be applied to the task of helping people learn language.

37.5.1 NLP from the CALL perspective

NLP offers a range of techniques for processing natural language; these are explored in earlier chapters. A few successful CALL programs make use of this language technology, but the great bulk do not (Zock 1996). Since CALL without NLP technology is successful, we must ask how (and whether) language technology can be applied to improve language learning and language teaching.

There are voices which urge caution in applying NLP to the CALL problem. Salaberry (1996: 12) assesses the suitability of language technology for CALL quite negatively, but not atypically:

> Linguistics has not been able to encode the complexity of natural language . . . That problem has been acknowledged by the most adamant proponents of Intelligent CALL [ICALL (J.N.)]. Holland (1995) lists the reasons that have prevented ICALL from becoming an alternative to CALL. The most important reason for this failure is that NLP (Natural Language Processing) programs—which underlie the development of ICALL—cannot account for the full complexity of natural human languages.[2]

Salaberry attributes the unpopularity of NLP methods in CALL to NLP's failure to produce systems for full-fledged intelligent dialogue in unrestricted form. The earlier chapters of this book should make it clear that many NLP techniques are extremely reliable and suitable for demanding, robust application (see Nerbonne, Jager, and van Essen 1998 for more extensive discussion of this negative perception of NLP among CALL developers, and see Salaberry 2000 for a thoughtful rejoinder). We note here only that the negative perception exists, and that, given that the great bulk of existing CALL programs and packages make little use of language technology (Zock 1996), one should not simply regard CALL programs by definition as applications of NLP.

To end this section on a more positive note, some language learning experts note the need for NLP techniques in CALL very clearly, if implicitly. John R. Allen developed CALL programs for over twenty-five years, and Allen (1996/7) presents his view of how CALL must develop, focusing on the issue of how we can fashion useful reaction to student input. Among other needs, he discusses clearly how simple

---

[2] Salaberry's reference to Holland (1995) is not accompanied by bibliographic information.

regular expressions will fail as specifications of syntactic patterns (p. 446), and he calls for better specification techniques of the sort that would be bread and butter to all NLPers. He further notes that CALL needs better techniques for recognizing parts of speech and morphological variants (p. 452), again calling for techniques which NLP can normally provide reliably. See section 37.6.4 for a discussion of NLP work in CALL which uses both part-of-speech tagging and lemmatization software. Allen is likewise clear about the need to incorporate intelligent tutoring schemes of the sort which Henry Hamburger and Kathleen McCoy have investigated most extensively (see section 37.6.6 for more on this work).

37.5.2 NLP interest in CALL

There has been regular and growing interest in the NLP community in the CALL application area.

Appelo and de Jong (1994) sparked the interest of a number of NLP researchers in CALL. Holland and Kaplan (1995) surveyed the state of the art in 1995, and Holland, Kaplan, and Sams (1995) survey lots of work which focuses on the question of how to use NLP in a pedagogically responsible way, and on using tutoring techniques from artificial intelligence (see section 37.6.6 below, as well). More recently, an Applied Natural Language Processing conference devoted a session to CALL (*Proceedings of the 5th Conference on Applied Natural Language Processing* 1997). The session was organized by Melissa Holland and Henry Hamburger, and it featured papers by researchers in NLP (Schoelles and Hamburger 1997; Nerbonne et al. 1997; Dorr 1997). In that same year Jager, Nerbonne, and van Essen (1998) organized a conference devoted to 'Language Teaching and Language Technology' whose Proceedings appeared in 1998. They explore especially the opportunities for language technology in CALL, and include several reports on CALL applications that exploit NLP, including **alignment** techniques (Paskaleva and Mihov 1998), **lemmatization** (Dokter and Nerbonne 1998; Roosmaa and Proszeky 1998), and **parsing** (van Heuven 1998; Murphy, Krüger, and Grieszl 1998). Schulze, Hamel, and Thompson (1999) is the collection of papers from a UMIST conference that was organized in 1998 (Schulze and Hamel 1998). Olsen (1999) presents the Proceedings of a joint workshop sponsored by the Association for Computational Linguistics and the International Association for Language Learning Technology. If the booming interest in the speech community is a good indication, we should see further growth in the NLP community's interest, too.[3]

---

[3] Bernstein et al. (2000) and other papers in that collection provide a good overview of work on speech in CALL.

37.6 CONTRIBUTING NLP TECHNOLOGIES

This section presents work in NLP which has sought to contribute to CALL. Many technologies have been enlisted in an effort to illustrate linguistic structures, make language comprehensible, provide varied exercise material, and spot and correct errors.

- **concordancing**. Concordance programs are by now so well known and widely available that one might hesitate to include them under NLP, but they are language processing programs, and they have inspired an enthusiastic group of advocates among language teaching professionals.
- **text alignment**. When alignment programs are applied to align bilingual texts, the resulting parallel texts offer a wealth of information to advanced language learners. There has been a stable market for bilingual texts in language instruction for decades. See Chapter 24.
- **speech recognition and synthesis**. Speech technology is applied to generate pronunciations, particularly pronunciations of isolated words. This relieves language learners of needing to understand pronunciation transcription systems. Speech recognition also is applied to check (and improve) pronunciation. See Chapters 16–17.
- **morphological processing**. Lemmatization, but also morphological generation, has been deployed to provide drill material for learners, to facilitate dictionary look-up of words (which is impossible in inflected languages without morphological analysis), and to make corpus access more flexible. See Chapters 2 and 18.
- **syntactic processing**. Syntactic generation may be employed to create exercise material, and parsing is employed both in order to clarify linguistic structure, and also in order to spot and diagnose errors in learners' output. See Chapters 4 and 12.

Machine translation (MT, see Chapters 27 and 28) has been argued to involve most of the language technology needed for CALL (Levin 1993) except perhaps error spotting and diagnosis, but we have noted the underlying techniques here rather than the analogy in application. MT indeed offers the application builder in CALL a great deal, but that is also because it is a very complex application.

The following sections focus, not on technologies, but rather on the sorts of tasks to which they are put in CALL.

37.6.1 Pronunciation

Speech technology is treated in Chapters 17–18, but as it is not the focus of this book, we recall here merely that the successful use of speech technology in CALL will generate more interest in NLP. In fact, there have been commercial products using speech technology in CALL for some time. Martin Rothenberg, known to phoneticians as the developer of the 'Rothenberg mask', a device for capturing air pressure information sensitively, is also the founder of Syracuse Language Systems, the world market leader in CALL products. If Rothenberg was early, he was not alone for long. DynEd and the Learning Company also offer pronunciation correction packages commercially (Aist 1999). Bernstein, De Jong, Pison, and Townshend (2000) measures the ability of a system marketed by Ordinate to score non-native pronounciations for quality, noting a high overall correlation with expert human graders ($r= 0.94$).

Speech is seeing an even stronger growth in interest in CALL than NLP. The forty-five contributed papers in Carlson et al. (1998) were devoted to speech technology applied to CALL, and EUROCALL 2000 included a special workshop on 'Integrating Speech Technology in Language Learning', the fifth in a series. Speech recognition was one of its focus areas (see the website listed below in 'Resources'). Holland (1999) reviews speech recognition in a range of CALL applications. Progress in this area will undoubtedly enable more NLP applications.

37.6.2 Corpora and CALL

In this section and the following, we examine the use of corpora in CALL (insofar as NLP is involved). Corpus-based CALL involves having students look into corpora in order to appreciate linguistic patterns and distinctions more elaborately, and it is argued to be of value to very advanced students. Language technology is already seen to contribute to language teaching as it uses corpora: concordancing and lemmatization have been applied to corpora in order to try to facilitate the use of corpora in CALL, and their added value is substantial.

There has been focused interest in using language corpora for CALL (Wichmann et al. 1997). Corpora are valued for providing access to authentic language use, unmediated by grammarians' theories, prescriptivists' tastes, pedagogy's traditions, or even lexicographers' limitations. It is very clear that corpora can only be useful for advanced students—beginners would simply understand nothing they saw.

There are moderate and extreme views on how corpora should best be utilized. The moderate view espouses the value of corpora, especially when accompanied by good search tools, for instructors and very advanced students—those for whom unabridged dictionaries and comprehensive grammars are insufficient as sources of information on nuances of meaning, common usage, or stylistic level. A more extreme view is often attributed to what Tim Johns has dubbed 'data-driven learning', which emphasizes the role of discovery in the language classroom, facilitated by tools for corpus analysis. Johns and King (1991: 2) find that 'the language learner is also, essentially, a research worker whose learning needs to be driven by access to linguistic data'.

Of course, a bare corpus is of reduced value to both teachers and students. If a corpus is to be used effectively, then it ought to be supplemented with at least two tools from language technology:

- **concordancing**. Concordance programs of the sort that find words in texts and present them perspicuously in context have inspired an enthusiastic group of advocates among language teaching professionals (Wichmann et al. 1997).

  ... pointing an accusing *finger* at governmental agencies ...
  ... who had injured one *finger* and sustained bruises ...
  ... arrested for giving the *finger* to an unsympathetic ...

- **lemmatization**. In inflected languages, such as French, Spanish, or Russian, the chance of finding any inflected form of a given lemma (i.e. searching for any form whatsoever) is one to two orders of magnitude greater than the chance of finding a particular inflected form. The chance can be even worse if the form is unfortunately chosen.

These tools should reduce the amount of preparation which instructors may need in order to make use of corpora effectively, a problem which Holmes (1999: 253–6) warns about. Holmes suggests that the apparent successes of corpora in CALL may be due to the enthusiasm of the innovators rather than the intrinsics of the activity or technique. He noticed no improvement in students' ability after their experiments with corpora (p. 256). This is not encouraging, but it should be clear that language learners need to invest a good deal of effort in corpora in order to obtain the information that might have been distilled into a brief dictionary entry or standard grammar explanation.

37.6.3 Bilingual corpora

The fundamental reason to explore bilingual texts in CALL is that they grant the language learner the same access to authentic language use, only now accompanied by convenient translation into a known language. This increases the chances, of course, that the foreign language corpus material will be comprehensible to learners, which, as noted above, is one of the prime requirements of all effective foreign language pedagogical material (Krashen 1982). The advantages of immediate access to genuine material thus accrue to language learners with access to bilingual texts, but now with the added advantage of comparison to a language they are assumed to know. Barlow (1996) illustrates these advantages by displaying the results of searches for English reflexives, on the one hand, and the English lexeme 'head', on the other. His examples show that French reflexive patterns mirror English only partially, sometimes using reflexive pronouns ('allowed himself': *s'est laissé*), but often omitting them ('buy themselves lunch': *acheter un déjeuner*), or using an impersonal construction ('enjoyed himself': *l'enchanta*), or, in some cases, using wholly different lexical material ('speaking for myself': *en mon nom*). The reflexive example is particularly striking in light of the extensive grammatical analyses that have been devoted to reflexive pronouns. Barlow's example suggests either that the rules put forward by such analyses fall short of providing adequate guidelines for language learners seeking full mastery of the language, or that the role of lexis is more extensive than often supposed. The example of English 'head' is of a sort more familiar to language learners: it is easy to find several common French equivalents, including *tête, chef,* and *directeur,* as well as to show that idiomatic uses show up frequently ('head on', 'keep one's head down').

Translation is often a course of study for advanced language learners, and Peters, Picchi, and Biagini (1996) note that as the goal of translation has shifted from formal linguistic equivalence to pragmatic equivalence, the bilingual corpus has risen in importance vis-à-vis the bilingual dictionary. The dictionary can never vie with extensive corpora in cataloguing and illustrating the sorts of correspondences found in translation. Danielsson and Ridings (1996*b*) report on an educational tool used in a training program for translators. It is based on Danielsson and Ridings's (1996*a*) parallel corpora work, and it is based on one million words which are aligned at the sentence level. Students of translation benefit from the abundance of material which they use to find unusual translation equivalences. To summarize this section: a number of researchers have begun experimenting with bilingual corpora in language learning situations, and they advocate more extensive experimentation. They adduce convincing reasons why bilingual corpora supply information that would otherwise be unavailable. They note unanimously that the use of bilingual corpora only makes sense if good software is available to support the sorts of searches which instructors and students wish to conduct. At the same time, we must note that the field is very young. Little has been reported on actual uses of bilingual corpora by students, and the (extensive) reports by instructors may be of interest more for their contributions to comparative grammar and descriptive linguistics than for their contributions to language pedagogy. There have been few attempts to evaluate the effect of the use of parallel, bilingual texts on language learning.

Bilingual corpora enjoy in some sense a special status since manually aligned and manually prepared texts have been used for decades in language teaching (even if they are not the object of current research interest in language teaching). Parallel texts show translation near originals, and they are a reasonable guarantee that textual material will be comprehensible, in accordance with Krashen's dictum, noted above. Of course, NLP can provide technology to support the use of bilingual texts.

- **text alignment**. Unaligned bilingual corpora offer little practical value to teachers and students. Once they are large enough for there to be a good chance of finding particular words or constructions, they are too large for simple search mechanisms to be effective (Nerbonne 2000).

Corpora are undeniably valuable to advanced learners, but in a user study with second-year students who were given automatic access to an on-line dictionary, a description of the grammatical function of inflectional morphemes, and examples of words from corpora, students made little use of the aligned, bilingual corpora (Dokter et al. 1998). Of course, they were not advanced enough to need to go beyond the dictionary, and they had been instructed that they would be asked about the content of a reading passage, which arguably did not promote an 'exploratory' attitude toward the software package. Dictionaries and brief grammars are efficient means for learners to acquire basic information about words and construction. They may be the language technology of the seventeenth century, but they have proven their worth.

37.6.4 Morphology

The idea of applying morphological analysis to aid learners or translators, although not new, has not been the subject of extensive experimentation. Goethals, Engels, and Leenders (1990) report on A.D.A.M. & E.V.E., a software package for advanced learners which generates practice material from a corpus of authentic texts. The exercises stimulate practice in different morphological forms and are generated in a way sensitive to frequency. Antworth (1992) applied morphological analysis software to create glossed text. But the focus was on technical realization, and the application was the formatting of interlinearly glossed texts for scholarly purposes. The example was Bloomfield's Tagalog texts. Kempen (1992) and Kempen and Dijkstra (1994) explore morphology as a means of recognizing and correcting spelling errors which seem to be triggered by morphological insensitivity. French has inflected forms which do not vary in pronunciation even though they are distinct in morphology and spelling, e.g. French *parler, parlais, parlait*, and *parlez* and Dutch final ⟨t⟩ and ⟨d⟩ are both pronounced [t] even though they differ in morphological significance.

The COMPASS project (Breidt and Feldweg 1997) focused on providing 'COMPrehsion ASSistance' to less than fully competent foreign language readers. Their motivation seems to have stemmed less from the situation in which language learning is essential and more from situations in which one must cope with foreign language. In addition, they focused especially on the problems of multi-word lexemes, examples such as English *call up* which has a specific meaning 'to telephone' but whose parts need not occur adjacently in text, such as *call someone or other up*.

GLOSSER assumed learners would have the task of understanding texts and would call on GLOSSER for information on the words in the text (Nerbonne, Dokter, and Smit 1998). Three sorts of information are provided, first a lemmatization of the inflected form, together with a brief indication of the grammatical significance of the morphology; second, the dictionary entry for the lemma; and third, examples of the word from corpora, some of which are bilingual. In order to improve the accuracy of the lemmatization, the text is labelled with part-of-speech (POS) tags (see Chapter 11) before it is subjected to morphological analysis (Bauer, Segond, and Zaenen 1995). The suitability of the NLP technology was assessed technically (Nerbonne and Dokter 1999) and from the perspective of users (Dokter and Nerbonne 1998). NLP improved the chances of students finding information in dictionaries (which is not always trivial in the case of morphological irregularity), and also improved the usefulness of corpora—lemma searches are much more effective than string searches—but it remains the case that GLOSSER's most valuable feature for users was that it made access to the dictionary fast (more than 100 times faster than learners' searches).

It is probably correct to view NLP's role in this sort of system more as a tool to be used when needed rather than as a supplying pedagogical content. GLOSSER supplies content about the grammatical meaning of morphology, but users were much more interested in the dictionaries. GLOSSER maintains a demonstration at www.let.rug.nl/~glosser (Nerbonne et al. 2001). The demonstrator is reduced in order to protect proprietary modules.

Surely the main reason for the success of this sort of use of NLP is that morphological processing is sufficiently mature to support nearly error-free lemmatization (in a random sample of 500 words we evaluated, there were no mistakes in lemmatization, and twelve faulty POS assignments). This functionality can be used to automate dictionary access, to explain the grammatical meaning of morphology, and to provide further examples of the word in use (perhaps in different forms). Second language learners look up words faster and more accurately using systems built on morphological processing. It is to be expected that this will improve their acquisition of vocabulary.

37.6.4.1 *The Ecology of NLP in CALL*

It is convenient to include here some discussion of some wider issues vis-à-vis the design of CALL programs which utilize NLP. These issues involve both the immediate context of use for the programs as well as the larger question of how these need to fit into complete curricula. Naturally different kinds of uses of NLP will prompt different questions, but we want to clarify that the use of NLP, the user interface, and the purpose of the CALL program are all of potential importance, and that there may well be research results in second language acquisition which can inform the particular deployment of NLP in CALL.

GLOSSER embedded NLP in a natural task, namely reading. The language ability targeted for improvement was vocabulary acquisition. The idea was that students who could read more (because GLOSSER made the texts more accessible) would tap into Krashen's automatic processes of acquisition. This meant that one should see vocabulary increase not just, and perhaps not even primarily, in the vocabulary that is looked up, but in the many words the learner has to process. The value of reading for vocabulary acquisition is widely supported by research in second-language acquisition. Carter (1998: 209) makes the stronger point that second language learners *cannot* learn sufficient vocabulary from vocabulary lists in textbooks—some sort of implicit acquisition must be taking place, and GLOSSER enables the learner to comprehend more easily than he otherwise would, providing the right sort of experience. Reading is seen to have a further advantage over vocabulary lists in that it introduces new vocabulary within a sensible context, even without the use of additional sources like dictionaries (Krantz 1991). Krantz (1991) emphasizes the importance of learning vocabulary words in context, and GLOSSER supports exactly that. The context provided by full text not only contributes to a better understanding of the possible uses of a specific word, but it also creates a framework in which words are more easily remembered (Mondria 1996).

A further perspective from second language acquisition is the extent to which programs exercise natural communication rather than mastery of grammar, and again from this *communicative* perspective it seems fair to rate GLOSSER as successful (Warschauer 1996). The choice of reading material is entirely up to the student and/or teacher, but it may include authentic materials, which Widdowson (1990) and others have argued improves the quality of learning by involving the learner more directly in the community in which the target language is spoken.

Hulstijn (1992) notes a further point of choice for second language learners who are acquiring vocabulary through reading, and that is whether they have immediate access to dictionary meanings or whether they try instead to infer meanings from texts (without using a dictionary). Hulstijn designed a series of experiments to measure vocabulary retention under these two conditions. With some qualifications, Hulstijn recommends that dictionary meanings *not* be made available immediately, but rather that students be encouraged to try to infer the meaning from context first. This was a recommendation we finally did not implement in GLOSSER, conceding that learners needed to learn to use the tool intelligently. It could make an interesting follow-up study. Several further variants were investigated, e.g. one which allowed students to leave notes in the texts as they read.

The purpose of the discussion here is not to praise GLOSSER's stance as pedagogically sound, but rather to signal to potential developers (or users) of NLP in CALL that the immediate pedagogical context of the NLP machinery is as important as the technology in evaluating how well an application can succeed. A clever setting for NLP can make up for potential problems: so Sanders and Sanders (1995) embed their dialogue system in a game about uncovering a spy ring. The context justifies their system's refusal to deal with some words, which learners are told are 'forbidden'. Levin and Sanders (1995) try to exploit sublanguages as a means of keeping processing within reasonable bounds of accuracy and efficiency. In their case the sublanguage was that of a first-year textbook that might have been used in the same course of instruction as their CALL system, and they present a lucid discussion of the options for systems whose linguistic coverage is less than perfect, finally opting for interactivity (to counter ambiguity) and some user preparation, the latter amounting to honest disclaimers regarding the possibility of errors.

This is also a convenient point at which to illustrate concretely another general point about CALL as an NLP application: the intended users (language learners) are intelligent and also undemanding. The users were intelligent in using the information GLOSSER provides: even though the program did occasionally make errors, e.g. 2.4 per cent of the POS categorizations were wrong, the users never stumbled over these. They are accustomed to using dictionaries and grammars, and they realize that the information these contain is not always relevant to the texts they have. The users were also undemanding: as experienced researchers in NLP realize immediately, GLOSSER suggests several further development paths, e.g. providing information about **multi-word lexemes** and attempting **sense disambiguation**. But since users are accustomed to dictionaries, that is the normal comparison, and there were never questions about why those improvements were not available. This suggests that CALL could be a more useful vehicle for practical experimentation in applications of NLP than it has been to date.

37.6.5 Grammar

Certainly most of the work in NLP-inspired CALL has been done on syntax. Michael Zock and his colleagues have developed systems which harness natural language **generation** (see Chapter 15) to walk language learners through exercises in sentence construction (Zock, Laroui, and Francopoulo 1989; Zock 1992; Zock 1994). The learners are made aware of the linguistic rules which underlie sentence construction, and in particular of the effects that some choices in expression have, e.g. the effect that the grammatical number of a clitic pronoun has on the form of the French participle in the perfect tenses

(37.1)   *Les filles! Qui est-ce qui les a aidées?*
         The girls! Who has helped them?

If the plural clitic pronoun *les* had a masculine antecedent, then the participle would need to have the form *aidés*. If the clitic were feminine singular the appropriate form of the verbal cluster would be *l'a aidée*, and if the clitic were masculine singular, then the cluster would be *l'a aidé*. Zock's systems clarify such dependencies to language learners in an interactive fashion.

Work on generation has also been applied to suggest games with language learners (Pasero and Sabatier 1998), e.g. the game of constructing a sentence from a list of words, and also in order to generate dialogue, e.g. in the microworlds tutorials which Hamburger (1995) and others have pursued.[4]

---

[4] See, however, Levin, and Evans (1995: 92) for a criticism of the microworlds approach. They question whether it will scale to useful size with a reasonable amount of work.

Furthermore, a good deal of work has been done using parsers and analysis trees to try to give students an idea of syntactic structure. Kempen (1999) presents a system for teaching students fundamental grammatical concepts as a *preparation* for foreign language study. The system is capable of providing different grammatical analyses— either dependency grammar style (see Chapter 4) or phrase-structure analyses (see Chapter 4), and Kempen goes on to suggest appealing graphical renditions of these analyses—families of friendly 'spooks' joining hands to indicate dependence, and multi-tiered 'temples' reflecting constituency.

Rypa and Feuerman (1995) try to support reading comprehension by providing analysis trees on demand. They focused on non-trivial grammatical points, and they use a Lexical-Functional Grammar (LFG, see Chapter 4) covering about 500 lexical entries, and a set of examples based on these. The most innovative aspect of their work involved the use of tree-based pattern matching in order to find examples of constructions satisfying a given description. Since they envisage that the system will be used by people naive about NLP, they needed to provide an interface to allow these users to specify what sorts of constructions they wish to find examples of.

Yet another use for syntactic analysis is suggested by Levin and Evans (1995), who present one of the most sophisticated systems exploiting NLP in CALL, ALICE-chan. Although it will be discussed here, it might also have figured in the section on morphology, and it performs error analysis as well (discussed in the following section). Like Rypa and Feuerman's (1995) work, it is based on LFG, which it uses to parse examples for students, to create grammar exercises from examples and further specifications, and to parse user input. The presentation suggests that the system attained the full coverage it targeted, i.e. the **sublanguage** covered in its chosen first-year Japanese text. This sort of approach—taking care that NLP work dovetails with the overall language curriculum—undoubtedly bears emulation.

Finally, there have been other uses of parsers which are harder to classify, but certainly interesting. For example, Loritz (1995) uses a parser to classify the constructions used by deaf learners of English. The resulting analysis shows where errors are made, but also what constructions are avoided or overused by learners.

The topic of spotting and classifying errors in learner input is peculiar to CALL and has been the focus of so much attention that we devote the next, separate section to it.

37.6.6 Error recognition and diagnosis

A central technical issue in NLP applied to CALL has been that of recognizing, diagnosing, and reacting to student errors. This is certainly a natural concern—learners will always make mistakes. It is also a central theme in CALL quite apart from NLP. Allen (1996/1997) writes almost exclusively on error recognition in programs for language drill in a paper he entitles 'Ten desiderata for CALL'—as if the question of responding to errors was all that CALL consisted of. It is useful to mention the paper because Allen is a language teaching expert, and he is emphatic about the recommendation that learners should *not* be corrected on every minor error. It is useful to set aside as a pedagogical question just which errors should be pointed out and what sort of feedback is appropriate. Collaboration with language teaching experts is recommended on that issue, and we can focus here on recognizing and diagnosing errors.

If a student using a CALL program is asked to answer a question about a picture, and if, in response to the question 'What do the children see?', she replies 'See dog', then errors have been made, and the program will need to note that (even if not every error results in a reaction to the student). If there is to be intelligent feedback, then the program needs to hypothesize a source of error, in this case probably the failure to appreciate the English grammatical requirements that subjects need to be expressed, and that singular count nouns normally appear with an article. (The answer would have been grammatical if the student had replied, 'They see a dog'.)

The first reaction of non-NLP experts on considering this problem is often to ask whether the error-spotting machinery found in grammar checkers might not be put to good use here. And CALL practitioners have experimented extensively with standard grammar checkers, of the sort developed in order to make recommendations to native speakers. Tschichold (1999) compares automatic grammar checkers systematically to the judgements of language teachers, and notes first that they are somewhat unreliable. Although they flag many more areas than expert humans, they often fail to spot problems, and what they flag as problems are a wide variety of errors, stylistic infelicities, and perfectly correct text. She concludes that automatic grammar checkers have only a modest role to play for (advanced) students who understand their limitations (see also Tschichold 1999). Of course, some of the technology that has gone into grammar checkers could be interesting for CALL, e.g. the heuristics which Jensen et al. (1993) introduce to complete structures when straightforward parsing fails.

The initial reaction of many NLP experts is that error recognition and classification might still be too difficult for existing technology. First, parsing often turns up multiple analyses, and some of these could make sense of the erroneous input. If the parser has access to a large dictionary, then it will note in the example above (*see dog*) that *see* can be a noun (*the bishop's see*) and postulate a noun-noun compound analysis. In longer sentences one often encounters thousands of possible analyses. Second, even where one can determine that there is no available analysis, so that an error must be present, it goes beyond the bounds of standard NLP to try to classify the error as to its cause. And in general there will be multiple plausible hypotheses about the source of the error. Third and finally, some NLP experts are sceptical of what sounds like a user-modelling issue. Didn't Spärck Jones (1991) show that user modelling is still technically ineffective, even in much simpler settings?

However, there is still reason for optimism in the CALL case. First, although ambiguity rises steeply as a function of sentence length (see Chapter 12), very short sentences (of six words and fewer) tend not to be syntactically ambiguous. Second, as Michaud and McCoy (2000) note, it is possible to add rules to existing grammars which explicitly cover the errors users make. Schneider and McCoy (1998) attribute this technique to Weischedel, Voge, and James (1978), and refer to it as *mal*-rules. And third, if this is a user-modelling issue, it is an issue of a limited sort—the model only needs to follow the language learners' progress in acquiring the various linguistic rules and constructs (Michaud and McCoy 2000). McCoy, Pennington, and Suri (1966) provide an extensive corpus analysis of errors made by deaf learners of English to support the claim that errors are (somewhat) predictable, which justifies the use of a user model incorporating at least the native language of learners (and its error tendencies in the second language).

Constraint relaxation would appear to provide an alternative to the *mal*-rule technique of recognizing and diagnosing errors, but projects which have set out to apply it seem to fall back on the use of special 'error rules' (Murphy, Krüger, and Grieszl 1998). Weinberg et al. (1995: 43) claim to use a variant of constraint relaxation to diagnose errors, spotting errors by 'modulating the exactness of the match between grammatical patterns and student input', but they do not provide technical details except to note (p. 42) that the parser is tuned to seek out particular errors, e.g. subject–verb agreement. Logically, constraint relaxation would appear to be similar to the use of *mal*-rules, but technically it seems to suffer more from problems of effective processing (ambiguity).

Menzel and Schröder (1999) report on a system which uses both *mal*-rules and constraint relaxation. It considers all possible associations of words, and arrives at its best considered result by a process of elimination. Non-eliminated analyses are ranked according to the severity of the violation which the *mal*-rule encodes or, alternatively, according to the strictness of the constraint violated. In addition to standard grammar rules, Menzel and Schrüder consider semantic and pragmatic violations, reasoning that language teachers do the same in understanding ill-formed expressions of students (pp. 26–7). They have analysed the ability of their implemented system to eliminate candidate analyses and arrive at a single indicated analysis and diagnosis. This is not the same as evaluating how well the system diagnoses, since it focuses on obtaining unique analyses, but the latter is a significant component of the sort of system needed.

DeSmedt (1995) reports that his grammar tutoring program was able to detect and correct 92.8 per cent of all errors with a false correction rate of only 1.1 per cent. He attributes this to an alternative parsing technique, more strongly driven by expectation, but his description of the parser makes it sound like a version of Earley parsing (DeSmedt 1995: 158–9), supplemented by techniques which find closest matches. The results are in any case impressive.

37.7 EVALUATION

As Holland and Kaplan (1995: 373 ff.) note, most of the work using NLP in CALL has not been evaluated carefully. They attribute this to the pressures of projects which have to show practical use, leaving little time for analysis. Goodfellow (1999) focuses on 'evaluation', and contains valuable remarks, but it studies a single system and shies from objective measures of performance. Some honourable exceptions to the trend of unevaluated work are noted above in the sections on Morphology and Grammar.

Both psycholinguist Brian MacWhinney and second language learning expert Nina Garrett identify large ranges of questions that need to be asked (MacWhinney 1995; Garrett 1995), even if one would hope that some of the issues MacWhinney raises could be obviated through the accumulated expertise of evaluation in (non-computer-assisted) second language learning (e.g. issues about which controls and comparisons should be most useful). Certainly projects should plan quantitative evaluation as part of their work.

37.8 CONSPECTUS AND PROSPECTUS

Whither research in NLP-inspired CALL?

Given the extensive industrial development of CALL packages, surely Cameron (1999a: 5) is sensible in advocating further cooperation for researchers. And Zock's (1998) plea for interdisciplinary collaboration with linguists and pedagogues bears repetition: many of the issues that arise in constructing and evaluating systems require the expertise of second language learning experts.

There are many reasons why NLP-based CALL ought to be an attractive area of research for NLP groups. As noted in section 37.2.2 above, there is genuine, substantial demand for language learning services that current supply is unlikely to be able to satisfy (at least not cheaply and generally). As sections 37.6.2–37.6.6 demonstrate, there is opportunity to apply a wide range of technologies. And, as noted in section 37.6.4 above, users are intelligent but undemanding—so that technologies which still function less than 100 per cent technically can provide a useful and appreciated service.

The opportunities for NLP collaboration with language learning experts should be optimal in view of their widespread positive reactive to Levy's (1997) book with its plea that the field should emphasize tools rather tutoring systems, and its conclusion that a practical focus would be salubrious for CALL.

All of these factors argue that a serious investment in this application area is promising, including the investment in serious evaluation, in incremental improvement, and the investment in collaborations needed to make use of all available expertise.

FURTHER READING AND RELEVANT RESOURCES

For computational linguists interested in CALL, the introduction in Cameron (1999b) and the other articles in that collection are probably the best starting place on CALL, and Holland, Kaplan, and Sams (1995) the only good collection on opportunities for NLP (and fortunately, it is very good). Cameron (1999b) contains excellent articles on several subfields of CALL, in particular on the use of speech technology (Aist), parsing (Kempen), grammar checking (Tschichold), corpora (Holmes), and intelligent tutoring systems (Hamburger). Although I was critical of some aspects of Levy (1997) above, it is strong on the history of the field and also the concerns of language educators. Pennington (1996) and Ellis (1994) are older, but contain further useful papers. Holland, Kaplan, and Sams (1995) is the only longer work with extensive presentation of the possibilities for NLP in CALL since Last (1989), now dated. The collections cited in section 37.5.2 comprise a great deal of what has been done recently in NLP applied to CALL.

There are several professional societies devoted to promoting computer-assisted language learning. CALICO, the Computer Assisted Language Instruction Consortium, is a professional organization with an emphasis on modern language teaching and learning. The oldest international group devoted to CALL, it sponsors an annual conference, several special interest groups, and a discussion list. See calico.org for a review site for software packages, and an on-line bibliography. CALICO also hosts CALICO-L, an active discussion list at the CALICO website.

EUROCALL, a large professional organization, has held regular conferences since 1988. It has published *ReCALL Journal* since 1989. See www.eurocall.org. IALLT, the International Association for Language Learning Technology, publishes the *IALL Journal of Language Learning Technologies*, which was the *Journal of Educational Techniques and Technologies* 1987–9, and earlier (1969–86) the *NALLD Journal*, i.e. newsletter of the National Association of Language Laboratory Directors. See iallt.org.

In addition to the journals published by the professional societies immediately above, there are several more journals devoted substantially to CALL and related topics. ALSIC, *Apprentissage des langues et systèmes d'information et de communication*, is a journal edited by Thierry Chanier with a French language focus and distinct tracks for research articles and reports on practice. LLT, *Language Learning and Technology*, is a refereed electronic journal first published in 1997 and available at llt.msu.edu. *System* is a journal on education technology which regularly carries CALL articles.

Syracuse Language Systems (see www.syrlang.com) is perhaps the leading company marketing CALL, and has been innovative in including speech and NLP technology. Agora (www.agoralang.com) maintains a hub of pointers to (mostly commercial) language learning products and services.

Finally, there are two interesting resources which are harder to classify. NTLL, 'New Technologies and Language Learning', is a Thematic Network Project (TNP) in the Area of Languages, coordinated by the Freie Universität Berlin. The TNP is closely affiliated with the European Language Council, an independent European association for the quantitative and qualitative improvement of knowledge of the languages and cultures of the European Union and beyond. See www.let.rug.nl/projects/tnp-ntll/. And History of CALL is a website with lots of pointers concerning the history of CALL, displayed with some infelicity in Netscape (in March 2001), but worthwhile for the content. See www.history-of-call.org/.

REFERENCES

Aist, G. 1999. 'Speech recognition in computer-assisted language learning'. In Cameron (1999*b*), 165–81.

Allen, J. R. 1996/7. 'Ten desiderata for computer-assisted language learning programms'. *Computers and the Humanties*, 30(6):441–55.

Antworth, E. L. 1992. 'Glossing text with the PC-KIMMO morphological parser'. *Computers and the Humanities*, 26(5–6), 389–98.

Appel, C. and T. Mullen. 2000*a*. 'A common gateway interface for tandem language learning'. In B. Strotmann (ed.), *Proceedings of the International Congress on Technology in Teaching, Jointly Organized by IATEFL Computer SIG, TESOL-Spain and Universidad Europea de Madrid, 20–22 Nov. 1998*, Universidad Europea: CEES Ediciones.

———2000*b*. 'Pedagogical considerations for a web-based tandem language learning environment'. *Computers and Education*, 34(3–4), 291–308.

Appelo, L. and F. M. de Jong (eds.). 1994. *Computer-Assisted Language Learning: Proceedings of the 7th Twente Workshop on Language Technology*. Twente: Parlevink.

Atwell, E. 1998. 'What can SALT offer the English teaching professional?' *English Teaching Professional*, 7, 46–7.

———1999. *The Language Machine: The Impact of Speech and Language Technologies on English Language Teaching*. London: British Council. http://www.comp.leeds.ac.uk/eric.

Barlow, M. 1996. 'Parallel texts in language teaching'. In S. Botley, J. Glass, and T. M. A. Wilson (eds.), *Proceedings of Teaching and Language Corpora*, UCREL Technical Papers, 9, 45–56.

Bauer, D., F. Segond, and A. Zaenen. 1995. 'Locolex: translation rolls off your tongue'. In *Conference Abstracts: ACH ALLC '95*. Santa Barbara, Calif., 6–8.

Bernstein, J., J. de Jong, D. Pison, and B. Townshend. 2000. 'Two experiments on automatic scoring of spoken language proficiency'. In *Integrating Speech Technology in the (Language) Learning and Assistive Interface*. Dundee: University of Abertay Dundee, 57–61. Prepublication of papers from the Workshop on Speech in CALL at EuroCALL 2000.

Breidt, E. and H. Feldweg. 1997. 'Accessing foreign languages with COMPASS'. Special issue on 'New Tools for Human Translators' of *Machine Translation*, 12(1–2), 153–74.

Cameron, K. 1999a. 'Introduction'. In Cameron (1999b).

——ed. 1999b. *Computer-Assisted Language Learning: Media, Design and Applications*. Lisse: Swets and Zeitlinger.

Carlson, R., C. Dunger, B. Granstrom, and A. Oster (eds.). 1998. *STiLL: Speech Technology in Language Learning*. Stockholm: ISCA.

Carter, R. 1998. *Vocabulary: Applied Linguistic Perspectives*. 2nd edn. London: Routledge. First edn. 1987.

Connolly, J. H. 1997. 'Quantifying target-realization differences'. *Clinical Linguistics and Phonetics*, 11, 267–98.

Danielsson, P. and D. Ridings. 1996a. *Parallel texts in Göteborg*. Research Reports from the Department of Swedish. University of Göteborg.

———1996b. 'Corpus and terminology: software for the translation program at Göteborg Universitet or getting the student to do the work'. In S. Botley, J. Glass, T. McEnery, and A. Wilson (eds.), *Proceedings of Teaching and Language Corpora*. Lancaster: University Centre for Computer Corpus Research on Language, 57–67.

DeKeyser, R. 1995. 'Learning second language grammar rules: an experiment with a miniature linguistic system'. *Studies in Second Language Acquisition*, 17(3), 379–410.

——2000. 'The robustness of critical period effects in second language acquisition'. *Studies in Second Language Acquisition*, 22(4), 499–533.

DeSmedt, W. 1995. 'Herr Kommissar: an ICALL conversation simulator for intermediate German'. In Holland, Kaplan, and Sams (1995), 153–74.

Dokter, D. and J. Nerbonne. 1998. 'A session with Glosser-RuG'. In Jager, Nerbonne, and van Essen (1998), 89–95.

———L. Schurcks-Grozeva, and P. Smit. 1998. 'Glosser-RuG: a user study'. In Jager, Nerbonne, and van Essen (1998), 169–78.

Dorr, B. 1997. 'Large-scale acquisition of LCS-based lexicons for foreign language tutoring'. *Proceedings of the 5th Conference on Applied Natural Language Processing* (Washington), 139–46.

Dulay, H., M. Burt, and S. Krashen. 1982. *Language Two*. Oxford: Oxford University Press.

Ellis, R. 1994. *The Study of Second-Language Acquisition*. Oxford: Oxford University Press.

Felshin, S. 1995. 'The Athena language learning project NLP system: a multilingual system for conversation-based language learning'. In Holland, Kaplan, and Sams (1995), 257–72.

Fox, D. 1996. 'Final market study report'. RECALL (LE 1615) D-28 Exlingua International & Linguistic Engineering of DG XIII (Luxemburg), Belfast.

FSI. 1973. 'Expected levels of absolute speaking proficiency in languages taught at the Foreign Service Institute'. Technical Report, Foreign Service Institute, School of Language Studies, Monterey, Calif.

Garrett, N. 1995. 'ICALL and second language acquisition'. In Holland, Kaplan, and Sams (1995), 345–58.

Goethals, M., L. Engels, and T. Leenders. 1990. 'Automated analysis of the vocabulary of English texts and generation of practice materials: from main frame to PC, the way to the teacher's electronic desk'. In M. Halliday, J. Gibbons, and H. Nicholas (eds.), *Learning, Keeping, and Using Language: Selected Papers from the Eighth World Congress of Applied Linguistics*. Amsterdam: John Benjamins, 231–68.

Goodfellow, R. 1999. 'Evaluating performance, approach and outcome'. In Cameron (1999b), 109–40.

Hamburger, H. 1995. 'Tutorial tools for language learning by two-medium dialogue'. In Holland, Kaplan, and Sams (1995), 183–99.

Hamilton, S. 1998. 'RECALL: some implications of learner as user in CALL'. In Jager, Nerbonne, and van Essen (1998), 200–8.

Hoffman, R. 1996. 'Computer networks: webs of communication for language teaching'. In Pennington (1996), 55–78.

Holland, V. M. 1995. 'The case for intelligent CALL'. In Holland, Kaplan, and Sams (1995), pp. vii–xvi.

——(ed.). 1999. 'Tutors that listen: speech recognition for language learning', special issue of *CALICO*, 16(3).

——and J. D. Kaplan. 1995. 'Natural language processing techniques in computer assisted language learning: status and instructional issues'. *Instructional Science*, 23, 351–80.

————and M. R. Sams (eds.). 1995. *Intelligent Language Tutors: Theory Shaping Technology*. Mahwah, NJ: Lawrence Erlbaum.

Holliday, L. 1998. 'The grammar of second language learners of English EMAIL messages'. In Jager, Nerbonne, and van Essen (1998), 136–45.

Holmes, G. 1999. 'Corpus CALL: corpora in language and literature'. In Cameron (1999*b*), 239–69.

Hulstijn, J. 1992. 'Retention of inferred and given word meanings: experiments in incidental vocabulary learning'. In P. J. L. Arnaud and H. Béjoint (eds.), *Vocabulary and Applied Linguistics*. London: Macmillan, 113–25.

Jager, S. 1998. 'Hologram: computer-assisted academic grammar learning'. In Jager, Nerbonne, and van Essen (1998), 82–8.

——J. Nerbonne, and A. van Essen (eds.). 1998. *Language Teaching and Language Technology*. Lisse: Swets and Zeitlinger.

Jensen, K., G. Heidorn, L. Miller, and Y. Ravin. 1993. 'Prose fitting and prose fixing'. In K. Jensen, G. Heidorn, and S. D. Richardson (eds.), *Natural Language Processing: The PNLP Approach*. Boston: Kluwer, 53–64.

Johns, T. and P. King. 1991. 'Should you be persuaded: two samples of data-driven learning materials'. In T. Johns and P. King (eds.), *Classroom Concordancing*. Birmingham: Birmingham University, 1–16. Also in *English Language Research Journal*, 4.

Kempen, G. 1992. 'Language technology and language instruction: computational diagnosis of word-level errors'. In M. L. Swartz and M. Yazdani (eds.), *Intelligent Tutoring Systems for Foreign Language Learning*. Berlin: Springer.

——1999. 'Visual grammar: multimedia for grammar and spelling instruction in primary education'. In Cameron (1999*b*), 223–38.

——and A. Dijkstra. 1994. 'Toward an integrated system for grammar, writing, and spelling instruction'. In Appelo and de Jong (1994).

Krantz, G. 1991. *Learning vocabulary in a foreign language*. Ph.D. thesis, Göteborg.

Krashen, S. D. 1982. 'The fundamental pedagogical principle in second-language teaching'. *Studia Linguistica* 35(1–2), 50–71.

——1985. *The Input Hypothesis*. London: Longman.

——1989. 'We acquire vocabulary and spelling by reading: additional evidence for the input hypothesis'. *Modern Language Journal*, 73(4), 440–64.

Lantolf, J. P. 1996. 'SLA theory building: "letting all the flowers bloom!"'. *Language Learning*, 46(4), 713–49.

Larsen-Freeman, D. and M. Long. 1991. *An Introduction to Second Language Acquisition Research*. London: Longman.

Last, R. 1989. *Artificial Intelligence Techniques in Language Learning*. Chichester: Horwood.

Levin, L. S. 1993. 'Translators' workstations and language learners' workstations'. In S. Nirenburg (ed.), *Progress in Machine Translation*. Amsterdam: IOS Press, 287–90.

——and D. A. Evans. 1995. 'ALICE-chan: a case study in ICALL theory and practice'. In Holland, Kaplan, and Sams (1995), 77–98.

Levy, M. 1997. *Computer-Assisted Language Learning: Context and Conceptualization*. Oxford: Oxford University Press.

Loritz, D. 1995. 'GPARS: a suite of grammar assessment systems'. In Holland, Kaplan, and Sams (1995), 121–34.

McCoy, K. F., C. A. Pennington, and L. Z. Suri. 1966. 'English error correction: a syntactic user model based on principled "Mal-Rule" scoring'. In *Proceedings of User-Modelling 1996, the Fifth International Conference on User Modelling* (Kailua-Kona, Hawaii), 59–66.

MacWhinney, B. 1995. 'Evaluating foreign language tutoring systems'. In Holland, Kaplan, and Sams (1995), 317–26.

Menzel, W. and I. Schröder. 1999. 'Error diagnosis for language learning systems'. *ReCALL* Spec. Publication, 20–30. Language Processing in CALL.

Michaud, L. and K. McCoy. 2000. 'Supporting intelligent tutoring in CALL by modelling the user's grammar'. *Proceedings of the 13th Annual International Florida Artificial Intelligence Research Symposium, Special Track on AI in Instructional Software* (Orlando, Fla.), 50–4. http://www.eecis.udel.edu/research/icicle/pubs/MichMcCooo.ps.

Miller, J. F. and T. Klee. 1995. 'Computational approaches to the analysis of language impairment'. In P. Fletcher and B. MacWhinney (eds.), *The Handbook of Child Language*. Oxford: Blackwell, 545–72.

Mondria, J.-A. 1996. *Vocabulaireverwerving in het vreemde-talenonderwijs: De effecten van context en raden op de retentie*. Ph.D. thesis, University of Groningen.

Murphy, M., A. Krüger, and A. Grieszl. 1998. 'RECALL—providing an individualized CALL environment'. In Jager, Nerbonne, and van Essen (1998), 62–73.

Murray, J. H. 1995. 'Lessons learned from the Athena language learning project: using natural language processing, graphics, speech, and interactive video for communication-based language learning'. In Holland, Kaplan, and Sams (1995), 243–56.

Nerbonne, J. 2000. 'Parallel texts in computer-assisted language learning'. In J. Veronis (ed.), *Parallel Text Processing*. Dordrecht: Kluwer, 354–69.

——and D. Dokter. 1999. 'An intelligent word-based language learning assistant'. *Traitement Automatique des Langages*, 40(1), 125–42. Special issue on multilingual processing edited by Remi Zajac.

————and P. Smit. 1998. 'Morphological processing and computer-assisted language learning'. *Computer-Assisted Language Learning*, 11(5), 421–37. Special issue on French edited by Michael Zock.

——S. Jager, and A. van Essen. 1998. 'Language teaching and language technology: an introduction'. In Jager, Nerbonne, and van Essen (1998), 1–10.

——L. Karttunen, E. Paskaleva, G. Prószéky, and T. Roosmaa. 1997. 'Reading more into foreign languages'. *Proceedings of the 5th Conference on Applied Natural Language* (Washington), 135–8.

——P. Kleiweg, P. Smit, E. Kuipers, and D. Dokter. 2001. 'A web-based foreign language assistant'. In *Essays in Language, Language Education, and the History of Linguistics in Honour of*

Arthur van Essen. Amsterdam: John Benjamins. http://www.let.rug.nl/~nerbonne/papers/ gloss-web/.

Norris, J. and L. Ortega. 2000. 'Effectiveness of L2 instruction: a research synthesis and quantitative meta-analysis'. *Language Learning*, 50(3), 417–528.

Olsen, M. B. (ed). 1999. *Computer-Mediated Language Assessment and Evaluation in Natural Language Processing.* College Park, Md.: ACL.

Pasero, R. and P. Sabatier. 1998. 'Linguistic games for language learning'. *Computer-Assisted Language Learning*, 11(5), 561–85. Special issue on French edited by Michael Zock.

Paskaleva, E. and S. Mihov. 1998. 'Second language acquisition from aligned corpora'. In Jager, Nerbonne, and van Essen (1998), 43–52.

Pennington, M. C. 1996. *The Power of Computer-Assisted Language Learning.* Houston: Athelstan.

——1999. 'The missing link in computer-assisted writing'. In Cameron (1999*b*), 271–93.

Perry, C. K. 1995. 'Review of phonological deviation analysis by computer (PDAC)'. *Child Language Teaching and Therapy*, 11, 331–40.

Peters, C., E. Picchi, and L. Biagini. 1996. 'Parallel and comparable bilingual corpora in language teaching and learning'. In S. Botley, J. Glass, and T. M. A. Wilson (eds.), *Proceedings of Teaching and Language Corpora*, UCREL Technical Papers, 9, 68–82.

Proceedings of the 5th Conference on Applied Natural Language Processing. 1997. Washington: Association for Computational Linguistics; with spec. section on CALL, 127–46.

Roosmaa, T. and G. Proszeky. 1998. 'GLOSSER: using language technology tools for reading texts in a foreign language'. In Jager, Nerbonne, and van Essen (1998), 101–7.

Rothenberg, M. 1998. 'The new face of distance learning in language instruction'. In Jager, Nerbonne, and van Essen (1998), 146–48.

Rypa, M. and K. Feuerman. 1995. 'CALLE: an exploratory environment for foreign language learning'. In Holland, Kaplan, and Sams (1995), 55–76.

Salaberry, M. R. 1996. 'A theoretical foundation for the development of pedagogical tasks in computer-mediated communication'. *CALICO Journal*, 14(1), 5–34.

——2000. 'Review of S. Jager, J. Nerbonne, and A. van Essen, *Language Teaching and Language Technology*'. *Language Learning and Technology* 4(1), 22–5. http://llt.msu.edu/.

Sanders, R. H. and A. F. Sanders. 1995. 'History of an AI spy game: Spion'. In Holland, Kaplan, and Sams (1995), 141–52.

Schneider, D. and K. McCoy. 1998. 'Recognizing syntactic errors in the writing of second language learners'. *Proceedings of the 36th Annual Meeting of the ACL and the 17th COLING* (Montreal), 1198–204.

Schoelles, M. and H. Hamburger. 1997. 'The NLP role in animated conversation for CALL'. *Proceedings of the 5th Conference on Applied Natural Language Processing* (Washington), 127–34.

Schultz, J.-M. 2000. 'Computers and collaborative writing in the foreign language classroom'. In M. Warschauer and R. Kern (eds.), *Network-Based Language Teaching: Concepts and Practice.* Cambridge: Cambridge University Press.

Schulze, M. and M.-J. Hamel. 1998. 'Conference Report on *Natural Language Processing in Computer-Assisted Language Learning*, Centre for Computational Linguistics, UMIST, 9 May 1998'. *ReCALL Journal*, 10(2), 55–6. http://www.eurocall.org/recall/.

————and J. Thompson (eds.). 1999. *Language Processing in CALL.* Hull: CTICML. *ReCALL* Special Publication (Proceedings of a one-day conference 'Natural Language Processing in Computer-Assisted Language Learning' held at UMIST, 9 May 1998, organized by the

Centre of Computational Linguistics, UMIST, in association with EUROCALL).

Somers, H. 1999. 'Aligning phonetic segments for children's articulation assessment'. *Computational Linguistics*, 25(2), 267–75.

Spärck Jones, K. 1991. 'Tailoring output to the user: what does user modelling in generation mean?' In C. Paris, W. Swartout, and W. Mann (eds.), *Natural Language Generation in Artificial Intelligence and Computational Linguistics*. Boston: Kluwer Academic, 201–25.

Tschichold, C. 1999. 'Grammar checking for CALL: strategies for improving foreign language grammar checkers'. In Cameron (1999b), 203–21.

van Els, T., G. Extra, C. van Os, and T. Bongaerts. 1977. *Handboek voor de Toegepaste Taalkunde*. Groningen: Wolters-Noordhof. English translation: *Applied Linguistics and the Learning and Teaching of Foreign Languages*. London: Edward Arnold.

van Heuven, V. 1998. 'COOL/CALP: computer-assisted learning to parse in Dutch'. In Jager, Nerbonne, and van Essen (1998), 74–81.

Warschauer, M. 1996. 'Computer-assisted language learning: an introduction'. In S. Fotos (ed.), *Multimedia Language Teaching*. Tokyo: Logos International, 3–20.

Weinberg, A., J. Garman, J. Martin, and P. Merlo. 1995. 'A principle-based parser for foreign language tutoring in German and Arabic'. In Holland, Kaplan, and Sams (1995), 23–44.

Weischedel, R., W. Voge, and M. James. 1978. 'An artificial intelligence approach to language instruction'. *Artificial Intelligence*, 10, 225–40.

Wichmann, A., S. Fligelstone, T. McEnery, and G. Knowles. 1997. *Teaching and Language Corpora*. New York: Addison-Wesley Longman.

Widdowson, H. 1990. *Aspects of Language Teaching*. Oxford: Oxford University Press.

Wolff, D. 1999. 'Review of M. Levy, *Computer-Assisted Language Learning: Context and Conceptualization*'. *System*, 27(1), 125–8.

Zock, M. 1992. 'SWIM or SINK: the problem of communicating thought'. In M. L. Swartz and M. Yazdani (eds.), *Bridge to International Communication: Intelligent Tutoring Systems for Foreign Language Learning*. Berlin: Springer, 235–47.

——1994. 'Language in action, or, learning a language by seeing it work'. In Appelo and de Jong (1994).

——1996. 'Computational linguistics and its use in the real world: the case of computer-assisted language learning'. *Proceedings of the 16th COLING* (Copenhagen), 1002–4.

——1998. 'Guest editorial introducing special issue on French'. *Computer-Assisted Language Learning*, 11(5), 467–74.

——A. Laroui, and G. Francopoulo. 1989. 'SWIM: a "natural" Interface for the scientifically minded language learner'. *Computers and the Humanities* 23, 411–22.

CHAPTER 38

MULTILINGUAL ON-LINE NATURAL LANGUAGE PROCESSING

GREGORY GREFENSTETTE

FRÉDÉRIQUE SEGOND

ABSTRACT

Beyond the theoretical linguistics search for language universals, there exist a number of practical linguistic problems concerning multilingual environments. Translation is the central problem and is discussed in Chapters 27 and 28. This chapter discusses a number of related multilingual NLP applications, many connected with using the Internet. In the current networked world, Internet users want to shop, interact in virtual communities, and find information without language being a barrier, with as much ease as they use a bank teller machine in any country today. It was initially thought that English would become the language of the web, but now we realize that the percentage of non-English websites is constantly increasing. In order to profit from worldwide sites, a number of multilingual tools and applications are being developed to remove language barriers while performing only part of the job of machine translation. This chapter presents a technical overview of the research and development being performed on four multilingual applications: language identification, terminology alignment, cross-language information retrieval and comprehension aids. **Language identification** techniques allow a computer to identify the language that a text is written in. This is a necessary first step in any fully automatic multilingual application. **Cross-language retrieval** applications allow a user to query in one language in order to access information written in a different language. Vital resources for these applications are **bilingual** and **multilingual dictionaries**. The coverage of these dictionaries can be enhanced by **bilingual alignment tools** that discover translations for new terms and expressions from parallel and comparable bilingual texts. **Comprehension aids** cover a wide range of tools that allow the user to understand text written in another language, without using the machinery of full automatic translation.

38.1 INTRODUCTION

One of the particularities about the web, distinguishing it from almost all other large corpora, is that it is inherently multilingual. This multilinguality seems to be growing as the Internet is used more and more for local communication needs (e.g. movie theatre times, announcement of concerts, school registration information, etc.). Local communication on the web is nonetheless globally visible, leading to the rather recent phenomena of end users being continually confronted with foreign language documents. This accidental exposure to information in foreign languages has revived interest and research in multilingual NLP and its applications. This chapter describes some multilingual NLP applications: language identification, bilingual terminology alignment, advanced look-up, and cross-language retrieval.

38.2 LANGUAGE IDENTIFICATION

The first step in applying any natural language processing technique is to identify the language of the input text. Subsequent techniques, including all those described in the other chapters of this book, are language dependent, using language-specific rules, resources, and methods, so that this identification step is an important part of any automatic language treatment system, especially one dealing with text retrieved through WWW search.

Identifying the language of a text from some of the text's attributes is a typical classification problem (Sneath and Sokal 1973). Luckily, it is a rather easy problem to solve; simple techniques work quite well. The two approaches to language identification that have been used are (i) using short words (e.g. articles, prepositions) as attributes (Ingle 1976), and (ii) using typical sequences of characters, often called *n*-grams, as attributes (Beesley 1988). Trigrams, sequences of three letters, are easy to calculate and store, and using them as attributes for identifying the language of a text is a little more robust, for short texts, than using characteristic words, since a given word may not appear in a text only a few words long.

Selecting either attribute, the method to be used to create a language identifier involves starting with a training set of texts identified by language. From this training set, one extracts short words (say, of five letters or less), or *n*-grams (sequences of three characters, for example). Tables 38.1 and 38.2 give the frequencies per million characters of short words and trigrams for a few European languages. These frequencies can be used to approximate probabilities to be used for classification. Given a new text to identify, the text is divided into *n*-grams or words and the estimated probabilities of the training set are used to predict in which language the new text is written.

This method can be extended to different character sets and to two-byte codes,[1] to create language identifiers which identify not only the language but the text encoding. Not many data need to be retained in order to perform well, and about 600 short words or 2,000 trigrams are sufficient for almost 100 per cent accuracy once the text to be identified contains twenty or more words (Grefenstette 1995).

Table 38.1 Most frequent short tokens and their frequency per million characters per language derived from the ECI Multilingual Corpus

English		French		German		Italian		Norwegian		Spanish	
11209	the	10726	de	6850	der	7014	di	6465	og	14626	de
6631	and	5581	la	4687	die	4045	e	6404	det	8159	la
5763	to	3954	le	3980	und	3313	il	4746	han	5915	que
5561	of	3930	à	2977	den	3006	che	4350	i	5724	el
5487	a	3563	et	2632	in	2943	la	3786	er	5347	en
3421	in	3295	des	1623	von	2541	a	3559	på	4786	y
3214	was	3277	les	1377	zu	2434	in	3306	til	3765	a
2313	his	2667	du	1371	dem	2165	per	3126	at	3149	los
2311	that	2505	en	1258	für	2013	del	2726	som	2914	del
2115	he	1588	un	1210	mit	1945	un	2657	var	2252	se

---

[1] http://www.unicode.org. Though the apparition of UNICODE compatible computer systems will make language identification easier, moving to UNICODE does not solve all identification problems, since many different languages are written using the same scripts. For example, many Amerindian languages have been transcribed using Latin characters.

Table 38.2 Most frequent trigrams and their frequency per million characters per language derived from the ECI Multilingual Corpus. The underscore represents a space or line break.

English		French		German		Italian		Norwegian		Spanish	
38426	he_	38676	es_	50040	en_	23293	to_	38994	et_	38732	de_
38122	the	28820	de_	38329	er_	20091	di_	38463	en_	27147	os_
20901	nd_	21451	ent	22824	der	17558	la_	32323	er_	23187	el_
20519	ed_	21072	nt_	18561	ie_	17549	re_	21849	an_	21758	la_
18417	and	18764	e_d	17946	ich	16137	ion	21286	de_	18463	que
16248	ing	17051	le_	17413	sch	16002	ent	18387	det	17409	as_
15295	to_	15803	ion	15596	ein	14525	e_d	17960	ar_	17303	ue_
15281	ng_	15491	s_d	14487	che	13930	le_	16538	og_	16530	en_
15192	er_	14888	e_l	14347	die	13885	o_d	15443	te_	15719	ent
14219	at_	14260	la_	14329	ch_	13297	ne_	14591	han	15645	es_

38.3 CROSS-LANGUAGE INFORMATION RETRIEVAL

Another result of the specifically multilingual characteristics of the WWW is a renewed interest in the area, first explored by Salton (1970), of cross-language information retrieval, which is defined as finding relevant documents in a second language using a query expressed in a first language. The yearly Text Retrieval Conference (TREC) has had a cross-lingual track since 1997. Fig. 38.1 gives a sample query in French, and part of the text of a relevant document in English. A cross-language retrieval system should find this document given this query.

Cross-language information retrieval (CLIR) shares many characteristics with both the fields of information retrieval and machine translation (see Chapter 29 and Chapters 27 and 28). With information retrieval, cross-language information retrieval researches robust language abstraction techniques which are domain independent. It tries to map the vocabulary used by the documents and the vocabulary used in the query to a space in which the computer can recognize similarity. But cross-language information retrieval is harder than monolingual information retrieval since it requires more than just simple orthographic comparisons. CLIR needs some way of mapping words in one language (the language of the query) to

<topic>
<num>
Number: CL10
<F-title>
Les voitures solaires
<F-desc>
Description: Des infor-
mations sur les voitures
solaires.
<F-narr>
Narrative: Un document
pertinent contiendra des
renseignements sur les
recherches et le développe-
ment des voitures solaires.
Les voitures solaires font
partie d'un effort pour
freiner l'exploitation de
carburants non renouve-
lables.
</topic>

<DOCNO> AP880921-0025 </DOCNO>
<HEAD>Congress Readying Final Action On
Energy Bill</HEAD>
<DATELINE>WASHINGTON(AP)<DATELINE>
<TEXT>
Congress is nearing final action on a plan designed
to reduce U.S. dependence on foreign oil, foster a
cleaner environment and cause motorists to say
fill-er-up—with corn, coal or natural gas.
By a voice vote, the Senate on Tuesday gave its
blessing to legislation its 64 co-sponsors hope will
promote commercial development and production of cars, trucks and buses that run on alternative fuels.
... Supporters say the United States has abundant
supplies of natural gas, the coal that is used to
produce methanol and the grains that are the roots
of ethanol.
Currently, methanol and ethanol are available
as fuels in some parts of the country, but most
vehicles experience problems if more than
5 percent to 10 percent is blended into gasoline.
All three alternative fuels produce less of the
carbon and other greenhouse pollutants that
scientists say are collecting in the atmosphere and
trapping heat from the sun.
Sen. Jack Danforth, R-Mo., who introduced similar
legislation in 1984 and cosponsored Rockefeller's
bill, said that 'the legislation is a grand slam for
energy independence ...'
'Increased use of alternative fuels will reduce our
dangerous dependence on foreign oil,' he said.
'Alternative fuels will help clean up our environment by reducing harmful auto emissions.'
</TEXT>

Fig. 38.1 French query (search topic) from TREC-6 (1997) and an English-language
newspaper article in the set of relevant documents for this query. A cross-language
information retrieval must find a way to represent both queries and the documents
so that they can be matched. Both documents and queries are divided into optional
fields using SGML-markings.

words in a different language (the language of the document) and this can rarely[2] be done without linguistic resources and linguistic processing such as lemmatization, term recognition, and bilingual dictionaries. Monolingual information retrieval is generally lightweight on language resources, whereas cross-language information retrieval is heavily dependent on linguistic transfer resources.

In terms of resources needed, cross-language information retrieval is then closer to machine translation. However, it is somewhat simpler in terms of the linguistic treatment required. Machine translation, as seen in Chapters 27 and 28, must solve deep parsing problems in order to produce correct translations. Cross-language information retrieval systems usually apply just enough syntactic effort to recognize multi-word terminological units, when they do not limit themselves to simple word-to-word translations.

38.3.1 The three problems of CLIR

After solving the language identification problem, there are three new substantial problems that a CLIR system must solve in order to use a query written in one language to find documents written in another. First, it must know how a term given in one language might be written in the target language. That is, what are the possible translations of each original query term? Secondly, it must decide how many of the possible translation alternatives should be kept. In this sense, CLIR has an easier job than machine translation, which must decide on one and only one way to translate a given input expression. But thirdly, can some of the translation possibilities be eliminated if there is more than one way to translate an input term? Information retrieval systems, in their bag-of-words approach, will give more importance to a term that contributes many query alternatives than to a term than contributes only one translation.

38.3.1.1 *Finding translations*

There are two solutions to finding translation terms. One solution involves using a bilingual dictionary which lists the possible translation terms (Hull and Grefenstette 1996). Another involves using parallel corpora of text (Sheridan and Ballerini 1996). Accessing dictionaries gives rise to a number of subsidiary problems: spelling variants (e.g. *trench coat* or *trenchcoat*), derivational variants (e.g. finding a translation for *electrostactically* if the dictionary contains an entry for *electrostatic*), coverage of

---

[2] Except for proper names transcribed in the same characters or a limited number of other cognates (e.g. pizza is written in the same way in most European languages), or to perform fuzzy matching of words from historically related languages (e.g. matching English *perfume* to French *parfum* by eliminating vowels *prfm*). There is no way, however, to know that an English word like *garbage* should be mapped to the French word *poubelle* or the Spanish word *basura* by simple orthographic manipulation.

vocabulary (Grefenstette 1998*b*) (e.g. the 1-million word Brown corpus contains the word *radiopasteurization* nine times, but this word rarely appears in translation dictionaries), treatment of proper names (Borkowski 1967) e.g. *Elstine* or *Yeltsin*.

An alternative to using a translation dictionary prepared for human users is to induce one from parallel corpora (Brown et al. 1990; Hiemstra, de Jong, and Kraaij 1997), using statistics based on the co-occurrence of words in aligned sentences. In this case, for each source language term, one derives a weighted list of translation candidates that can be used to generate a target language query (Nie et al. 1999). More complicated techniques, also requiring parallel corpora, involve reducing the bilingual term space to a much smaller one through Singular Value Decomposition (Landauer and Littman 1990; Evans et al. 1998).

The dictionary problem can be avoided altogether in the following way (Davis 1998), if one possesses a very large **bilingual corpus**. The original language query can be posed on original language documents, and relevant original language documents retrieved. The parallel, target language documents corresponding to the results of this first retrieval can then be collated into one huge bag of target language words that can serve as a new target language query without using an explicit translation dictionary.

38.3.1.2 *Pruning translation alternatives*

Once target language terms are found using a method such as the above, it is sometimes useful to eliminate some translations which would introduce noise into the query. For example, among the translations returned for the French word *voiture* in a common bilingual dictionary, we find archaic translations such as *carriage*. It is possible to leave such a word in place if one knows ahead of time that the corpus itself will act as a filter (Fluhr et al. 1998) since the odd translations will never appear in the target corpus. A more elaborate technique (Davis 1998) involves using a parallel corpus to do a first query using the original language query on original language documents, and then using the parallel target language documents to filter out query alternatives, only keeping those alternatives that appear in the highly ranked parallel target language documents. The retained translation terms then serve to create a new target language query on a new, unseen and monolingual, target language database.

If some rudimentary linguistic processing of the input query is performed, then words that are involved in a dependency relation can be translated as a pair, and the existence of the translation candidate can be tested in a target language corpus (Hull et al. 1997). Ballesteros and Croft (1998) show that with such filtering techniques cross-language queries can achieve almost 80 per cent of the average precision of monolingual queries.

38.3.1.3 *Weighting translation alternatives*

When more than one translation alternative is retained for an original term, the information retrieval system that will treat the target language query must account for this reduplication. Similar to the case of thesaurus expansion of queries in monolingual information retrieval (Salton 1972), if one original query word generates many different translations, its importance (represented by the sum of the weights that each alternative contributes during the document matching process) may be artificially inflated over words which only have one translation. Hull (1998) proposes a weighted Boolean retrieval technique that answers this problem.

Research in cross-language information retrieval has risen from the information retrieval community, using the same research models and evaluation methods: namely, long specific queries, and a pool of documents that are judged either relevant or not relevant to the query (with no in-between of 'somewhat relevant'). This means that techniques which generate many translation alternatives are preferable since co-occurrence of spurious translation candidates is less likely than co-occurrence of correct translations in the target language documents. These techniques are good for answering questions like 'I have this document here in language A, what documents are most similar in language B,' since the source language query will be the whole initial document. But for multilingual applications such as web browsing using short queries, it seems that what are needed more than anything are large collections of terminological expressions and their translations. The next section describes work in extracting and aligning terminology from multilingual parallel collections of documents.

38.4 MULTILINGUAL TERM ALIGNMENT

Whenever an application involves translations, it is useful to possess a list of terminological translations between the language pairs involved. Computer terminological databases can be purchased and some on-line databases exist. Research has been performed on extracting aligned words and terms from existing parallel multilingual corpora, which can often be found in large multinational organizations.

One way to perform terminology alignment is sketched below. First, given a parallel bilingual corpus, align paragraphs and sentences (Gale and Church 1993). Perform part-of-speech tagging on each corpus. For each aligned segment, create a matrix consisting of one line and one column for each adjective, adverb, noun, and verb in the source and target languages, and extract a list of phrases for each sentence using a shallow parsing method on each language side. Ideally, now, if we fill the matrix for each sentence with the expected word alignment frequencies, we could use the most likely word-by-word alignments to align the phrases from each language, thus extracting the multilingual term-to-term translations. But the expected alignment frequencies between the source words and the target words are unknown and must be estimated. There exists a classic algorithm in statistics, known as the Iterative Proportional Fitting Procedure (IPFP), for estimating missing values in a contingency table. Initially filling these cells with the frequencies with which source and target words co-occur or not in the corpus, we can alternatively renormalize the cell counts by the ratio of observed and estimated row and column sums. This procedure causes the estimated sums to gradually converge to their observed values. The cell counts after convergence provide valid estimates of the expected alignment counts. See Hull (1997) for details. This method produces bidirectional translation probabilities over the parallel corpus.

English: When electric/J arc/N welding/V on a vehicle/N, always disconnect/V the alternator/N wiring/V[N] to prevent/V the possibility/N of a surge/N of current/J[N] causing/V damage/N to the internal/J components/N of the alternator/N.

French: Lors de travaux/N de soudage/N à l'arc/N sur un véhicule/N, toujours débrancher/V le câblage/N de l'alternateur/N afin d'éviter/V de provoquer/V une décharge/N de courant/N susceptible/J d'endommager/V les éléments/N internes/J de l'alternateur/N.

Note: J=adjective, N=noun, V=verb. Correct tags are in brackets.

English: electric arc, welding, vehicle, disconnect, alternator, wiring, prevent, possibility, surge, current, causing, damage, internal components, alternator

French: travaux de soudage l'arc, véhicule, débrancher, le câblage de l'alternateur, éviter, provoquer, une décharge de courant susceptible d'endommager, les éléments internes de l'alternateur

alternator_N	alternateur_N	1.000	2	wire_V	câblage_N	0.214	-
vehicle_N	véhicule_N	0.900	-	cause_V	provoquer_V	0.169	[X]
disconnect_V	débrancher_V	0.737	-	damage_N	endommager_V	0.053	-
prevent_V	éviter_V	0.356	-	possibility_N	travail_N	0.013	[X]
internal_J	interne_J	0.310	-	surge_N	décharge_N	0.012	-
current_J	courant_N	0.250	-	arc_N	arc_N	0.011	-
weld_V	soudage_N	0.225	-				

(1)	travaux de soudage à l'arc	⇔	electric arc welding
(2)	véhicule	⇔	vehicle
(3)	débrancher	⇔	disconnect
(4)	câblage de l'alternateur	⇔	alternator wiring
(5)	éviter	⇔	prevent
(6)	décharge de courant susceptible	⇔	surge of current
(7)	provoquer	⇔	causing
(8)	endommager	⇔	damage
(9)	éléments internes de l'alternateur	⇔	internal components of the alternator

Fig. 38.2 Two sentences from a parallel corpus and their automatically aligned terms

Phrases from each language are then aligned using these translation probabilities. If the elements of a multi-word term all align to all the words of a source language term, then the two terms are returned. Partial matches can be used to break long terms apart or to glue short terms together. An example of this terminological extraction is given in Fig. 38.2. A French sentence aligned with an English sentence and the terms extracted are shown.

38.5 Multilingual Comprehension Assistants

The two main uses of the Internet, as a communication tool and as a means to access knowledge, confront ordinary users with the problem of understanding foreign language text. This exposure to multilingual information has spurred a non-professional demand for translation tools.

CompuServe reports that as soon as the automatic translation system they provide for email within the *Our world forum* community is broken, they receive millions of emails complaining. A study called HomeNet project (Kraut et al. 1996)[3] shows that the use of the Internet for personal/professional communication is more common than its use as a way to find information. There exist nowadays many international virtual communities and most websites offer visitors 'chatting places'. In all these, users are coming to expect multilingual tools to help them understand each other and to communicate better. A final example comes from the French company Canal+ which reports that, in their virtual Paris site, visitors who were not French and who communicated in English, whether or not it was their native language, were quickly rejected by the rest of the community, demonstrating the need for multilingual aids.

In the other major use of the Internet, knowledge mining, multilingual tools are also important. Contrary to initial fears, it seems that although today most of the information available on the web is in English, this will change (Nunberg 1996) together with the spreading of personal computers in the non-English-speaking countries. As a consequence, people will have access to more documents in more languages, increasing the need for multilingual tools to process them, to understand their content, to turn the information they contain into knowledge.

An alternative to machine translation (covered in Chapters 27 and 28) which can also satisfy users' demand for multilingual processing tools is covered by the class of

---

[3] http://homenet.andrew.cmu.edu/progress/index.html.

comprehension assistants. An example of such a comprehension assistant developed at the Xerox Research Centre Europe (XRCE) is described below.

38.5.1 LocoLex

Without going into implementations of commercial machine translation systems, multilingual resources can nonetheless be used in lightweight systems to ease and accelerate users' understanding of texts. Using HLT as far as it is reliable, we at XRCE decided to provide tools for users who have a working knowledge of a language and who might be able to figure out for themselves appropriate translations even in cases where full automatic translation might fail or require too many resources. Such tools are called *comprehension assistants* rather than *translation tools* because their goal is to help, to speed up users' comprehension of a text written in a foreign language, without necessarily providing them with a perfect translation. Typical users of such tools are those who navigate the Internet and who are looking for a quick, superficial understanding of their messages and documents irrespective of the language.

Building on work begun at PARC, XRCE started the comprehension assistant activity within the framework of the COMPASS European project, implementing an intelligent dictionary look-up (Bauer, Segond, and Zaenen 1995) called LocoLex. The difference between LocoLex and a simple dictionary look-up is that, when looking up a word in a simple electronic dictionary, users may have to hunt through a lot of irrelevant information to eventually find the translation of the word as it is used in a given sentence. Locolex uses part-of-speech tagging and idiom recognition to provide users with the translation relevant to the word in its particular context, facilitating and accelerating the process of comprehension.

Let's take a concrete example. Suppose that a native French speaker, with some knowledge of Italian, is using LocoLex while reading an Italian document about architecture. Reading the sentence *la scala a chiocciola conferisce eleganza all' intero sistema architettonico interno*,[4] the user sees the unfamiliar phrase *scala a chiocciola* and clicks on the word *chiocciola*. LocoLex retrieves the translation for the whole phrase *scala a chiocciola* (*spiral staircase*) and not only the translation for the word *chiocciola* (*snail*). In this case, the user may learn[5] that *chiocciola* was part of a longer multi-word expression (*scala a chiocciola*). It is important to note that, although the information usually stored in a dictionary is in a canonical form, LocoLex is able to

---

[4] 'The spiral staircase lends elegance to the whole internal architectural system.'

[5] In this way comprehension assistants may be seen as language learning tools in addition to multilingual NLP applications (see Chapter 37 for a complete discussion of computer-assisted language learning). LocoLex users could expand their vocabulary in a foreign language (in this case Italian) without the burden of looking into a paper dictionary for every other word.

recognize it even in its variant form, and to retrieve its translation out of the canonical form stored in the dictionary. Therefore not only should LocoLex find fixed patterns in the dictionary entry but it should also be able to derive all their possible variations from a generic phrase.

Suppose now that the user selects the word *sistema* in this sentence. *Sistema* can be both a noun (*system*) and a verb at the third or second person (*to put in order*). In this grammatical context, LocoLex prefers the noun interpretation and displays only the corresponding translations. These two examples illustrate how LocoLex differs from simple dictionary look-up. A simple dictionary look up system might not retrieve the phrase *scala a chiocciola*, simply by clicking on *chiocciola*, and by clicking on *sistema* users would get both the noun and the verb entries and would have to decide by themselves under which dictionary entry they should look.

LocoLex is not the first software tool to make use of machine-readable dictionaries; many applications in the past have stored and retrieved dictionary information. However, LocoLex illustrates how including more HLT in the task reduces noise by eliminating superfluous information and increases recall through the encoding of possible variations of items.

In order to build the LocoLex engine the following dictionary-specific tasks must be performed: (i) capture variation by rewriting multi-word expressions as regular expressions (Segond and Tapanainen 1995); (ii) build a finite-state machine (see Chapter 18) which compactly associates index numbers with dictionary entries. The LocoLex engine then employs several HLT components. Below is a brief summary of the look-up process when the user clicks on a word in the LocoLex environment:

- recognize and split the sentence string into words (tokenizer, see Grefenstette 1999 and Chapter 10);
- normalize each word to a standard form by changing cases and considering spelling variants (normalizer);
- identify each possible morphosyntactic usage of each word of the sentence and return the lexical form plus syntactic tags for each surface form (morphological analyser, see Chapter 2);
- disambiguate the most likely syntactic usage based on surrounding words (part-of-speech tagger, see Chapter 11);
- find relevant entries (including possible homographs or compounds) in the dictionary for the lexical form(s) chosen by the disambiguator (dictionary look-up);
- use the result of the morphological analysis and disambiguation to eliminate irrelevant sections (see also Chapter 13);
- process the regular expressions to see if they match the word's actual context in order to identify special or idiomatic usages (local grammars based on regular expressions);

- display to the user only the most appropriate translation based on the part of speech and surrounding context.

Let's see how these steps are applied to the example of when the user, using an English-to-French version of LocoLex, clicks on the word 'bore' in '... a village in Skenderaj in central Kosova which bore the brunt of Serb police and military operations.': first, through access to a lexicon, 'bore' is morphologically analysed to 'bore+Vb, bore+Nsg, bear+VpastT'. In this context, the part-of-speech disambiguator recognizes that the word is a verb, but since it cannot determine the tense, it does not know which of the verb forms to choose. Next, LocoLex retrieves the full dictionary entries for both verb forms, 'bore' and 'bear'. The entry for 'bore' also contains the noun interpretation, but this has been ruled out by the disambiguator. Within these entries, LocoLex checks for relevant multi-word expressions. Under the entry for 'bear', it finds a regular expression representing 'to bear the brunt of'. Since it finds this pattern in the sentence, it selects this idiomatic interpretation and returns to the user just the French translation *subir tout le poids de*.

In contrast, suppose the user had selected 'bore' out of context. A morphological analyser would return the same analyses, and, depending on the disambiguator, either the noun or verbs would be chosen. If the noun were chosen, a dictionary look-up program might return the French words *raseur/euse*, *barbe*, and *calibre*, reflecting different noun senses. If the verbs were chosen, the literal meanings *ennuyer* and *percer* for 'bore' and *porter*, *apporter*, *supporter*, *résister*, and *donner* for 'bear' might be returned.

LocoLex, as a comprehension assistant, bases its choices on purely syntactic grounds. When no multi-word expressions are present, LocoLex is not able to choose between the different meanings attached to a given part of speech for a given word. For instance LocoLex is not able to choose between $bank_{river}$ and $bank_{financial\ institution}$. In order to treat this problem of sense selection, a word-sense disambiguation module must be developed. Chapter 13 presents monolingual word-sense disambiguation. The next section describes a multilingual implementation of word-sense disambiguation as it has been integrated into a comprehension assistant.

38.5.2 Semantic module

In the XRCE semantic module, semantic disambiguation is performed by learning semantic disambiguation rules (Dini, Di Tomaso, and Segond 1999; Segond et al. 1999) from parsing a complete, full bilingual dictionary (Corréard and Grundy 1994). The system is an unsupervised rule-based semantic tagger which works on all input words. Semantic disambiguation rules are directly extracted from dictionary examples and their sense numberings. One may consider that sense distinctions and their corresponding examples, having been defined by lexicographers (see Chapter 3), provide a reliable linguistic source for constructing a database of semantic disambiguation rules. The system first builds a database of rules from the dictionary and from a separate ontology (see Chapter 25 for a discussion of ontologies). When applied to a new text the system returns as output a semantically tagged text.

To learn semantic disambiguation rules, the system uses, in addition to those mentioned for Locolex in the previous section, two more linguistic modules: (i) a shallow parser for English (XIFSP) (Ait-Mokhtar and Chanod 1997), and (ii) the English WordNet (Miller et al. 1990).

The general idea behind this system is to use electronic dictionaries as a large *semantically tagged corpus*, relying on the fact that when a phrase z is listed under the sense number n of a dictionary entry for the word w, a rule can reliably be created which stipulates that, in usages similar to z, the word y has the meaning x.

For instance, suppose that in the dictionary the entry for *shake* has four possible senses $shake_1$, $shake_2$, $shake_3$, and $shake_4$. Now suppose that the example *he shook the bag vigorously* is listed under the third sense $shake_3$, corresponding to the French translation *secouer*. XRCE's semantic disambiguation system treats this case as follows. First, the shallow parser extracts from the example the normalized syntactic functional relations: $SUBJ(he, shake)$, $DOBJ(shake, bag)$. These functional relations are then transformed into word-specific and WordNet sense-class pairs for deciding the sense of the target word, *shake*, sense $shake_3$. From the relation $DOBJ(shake, bag)$, the system extracts two rules:

1. 'bag' ISOBJ ($shake_1$; $shake_2$; $shake_3$; $shake_4$) $\rightarrow$ $shake_3$(secouer)
2. (6;18;23) ISOBJ ($shake_1$; $shake_2$; $shake_3$; $shake_4$) $\rightarrow$ $shake_3$(secouer)

The first, lexically based rule can be read as: if a verb can be read as being of sense $shake_1$, $shake_2$, $shake_3$, or $shake_4$, choose $shake_3$ if it has as an object the word *bag*. The second, generalized rule abstracts the word *bag* to the class of words having the same WordNet senses as the word *bag*,[6] and can be read as: if a verb can be read as being of sense $shake_1$, $shake_2$, $shake_3$, or $shake_4$, choose $shake_3$ if it has as an object a word associated with the WordNet classes 6 (artefact), 18 (person), or 23 (quantity). This generalization can be continued with any other ontology applicable to the syntactic relations extracted.

Just as these two rules are extracted from one syntactic relation, from one example associated with a translation sense, all dictionary examples are translated into semantic disambiguation rules and form a rule database covering the whole language, extending the LocoLex system described in the last section.

Many potential applications for comprehension assistants are attached to the use of Internet: companies can use such tools for doing on line customer support, provid-

---

[6] WordNet comes with a limited set of semantic sense tags that are independent of the senses used in the *Oxford-Hachette Dictionary*. The semantic disambiguation system described here is unique in using these two independent semantic resources.

ing their documentation on the web together with comprehension assistants, schools can use comprehension assistants to teach languages, virtual communities can use comprehension assistants to improve communication between users. Another domain where comprehension assistants turn out to be quite useful is that of digital libraries.

38.5.3 Augmenting digital libraries with comprehension assistants

In the domain of digital libraries, the Internet has been the catalyser of new technologies. Internet-accessible digital libraries contain a mixture of public and private information, free of charge or paying, and include books, reports, magazines, newspapers, video and sound recordings, scientific data. Digitizing the enormous quantity of paper-based information poses a significant challenge to digital library projects, as does the integration of this legacy of paper information with more recently acquired digital information, all stored on heterogeneous and distributed sources. Digital libraries require the pooling of know-how from different fields including networks, printers, scanners, graphical user interfaces, linguistic technologies, search and retrieval tools.

Xerox has developed a multilingual Digital Library project (Beltrametti et al. 1995) called *Callimaque* in which comprehension assistants are used. Callimaque offers wide access over the Internet to collections of 3,000 French documents showing the evolution of applied mathematics and computer science in France over the last forty years. Callimaque deals in an integrated fashion with document processing and production as well as information search and retrieval. It is based on the Xerox system XDOD (Xerox Document On Demand) which allows the scanning, archiving, and indexing of documents. XRCE has enriched Callimaque with comprehension assistants in order to help non-French-speaking persons to access this set of French documents. A reader who has little knowledge of the French language is able to: (i) formulate a query to search the XDOD database either in French or English and capture the linguistic variations of the multi-word expression they are looking for; and (ii) obtain a contextual translation from French to English on certain critical pieces of text such as the title or the abstract of a document. This multilingual service can be tested on-line at http://callimaque.imag.fr.

38.5.4 Conclusion

All the multilingual NLP applications described in this chapter can be integrated in different ways around and into existing intranets and extranets. They can be used to turn the web into a convivial place, reducing language barriers, opening the way for natural international user interaction on the multilingual web. As an example, they could help transform the web into a huge multilingual interactive encyclopedia. Italian members of the virtual community interested in history could ask directly 'chi é morto a Sant'Elena?' and get back documents about Napoleon in different languages, some known, some unknown to them. The language guesser would then be used to choose an appropriate version of a comprehension aid enabling them to browse a given text, to understand it, and to share remarks on this text with other community members, across languages. The WWW already promises to change international personal relations in unpredictable ways. The development of these multilingual NLP applications will facilitate this passage.

FURTHER READINGS AND RELEVANT RESOURCES

The URL http://www.xrce.xerox.com/competencies/content-analysis/tools/guesser. html leads to an on-line version of a language identifier. This language identifier was trained using data obtained through http://www.elsnet.org/resources/eciCorpus. html. The European Corpus Initiative produces inexpensive CD-ROMs with multilingual collections for research purposes. Their first collection contains 98 million words from twenty-seven (mainly European) languages.

The definitive on-line resource for cross-language information retrieval, including pointers to working systems, is Douglas Oard's pages: http://www.glue.umd.edu/ ~oard/research.html. Grefenstette (1998a) contains a review of techniques used in cross-language information retrieval and the National Institute for Standards and Techniques' website http://trec.nist.gov gives the latest articles describing the yearly TREC competition.

Multilingual terminology resources can be found at sites such as http://elda.fr/ cata/tabterm.html and at http://europa.int.eu/.

A bibliography of multilingual terminology extraction is maintained by Jean Véronis and Marie-Dominique Mahimon at http://www.up.univ-mrs.fr/~veronis/ biblios/ptp.htm. (See also Chapter 33.) Jean Véronis also coordinated an international exercise in evaluating parallel text alignment systems; see http://www.lpl.univ-aix.fr/ projects/arcade/ index-en.html. WordNet can be found at ftp://ftp.cogsci. princeton. edu/pub/wordnet/ README.

Multilingual and on-line communities can be found at such sites as *Paris, the Second World* http://www.2monde.com.

Some explanations about comprehension assistants and screen dumps can be found at http://www.sfs.nphil.uni-tuebingen.de/Compass/Info-en.html and http: //www.sfs.nphil.uni-tuebingen.de/Compass/Bild_1.GIF.

http://sunsite.berkeley.edu/Info/ and http://www.sics.se/diglib/resources.html are two digital libraries resources pages.

References

Aït-Mokhtar, S. and J.-P. Chanod. 1997. 'Subject and object dependency extraction using finite-state transducers'. *Proceedings of Workshop on Information Extraction and the Building of Lexical Semantic Resources for NLP Applications* (Madrid), 72–9.

Ballesteros, L. and W. B. Croft. 1998. 'Resolving ambiguity for cross-language retrieval'. In W. B. Croft, A. Moffat, C. van Rijsbergen, R. Wilkinson, and J. Zobel (eds.), *Proceedings of the 21st Annual International ACM SIGIR Conference on Research and Development in Information Retrieval* (Melbourne), 64–71.

Bauer, D., F. Segond, and A. Zaenen. 1995. 'Locolex: the translation rolls off your tongue'. *Proceedings of the ACH/ALLC '95* (Santa Barbara, Calif.), 6–8.

Beesley, K. R. 1988. 'Language identifier: a computer program for automatic natural-language identification of on-line text'. *Language at Crossroads: Proceedings of the 29th Annual Conference of the American Translators Association*, 47–54.

Beltrametti, M., L. Julliard, and F. Renzetti. 1995. 'Information retrieval and virtual libraries, the Callimaque model'. *CAIS '95 Conference* (Edmonton), 311–22.

Borkowski, C. 1967. 'An experimental system for the automatic identification of personal names and personal titles in newspaper texts'. *American Documentation*, 18, 131.

Brown, P. F., J. Cocke, S. A. Della Pietra, V. J. Della Pietra, F. Jelinek, J. D. Lafferty, R. L. Mercer, and P. S. Roossin. 1990. 'A statistical approach to language translation'. *Computational Linguistics*, 16(2), 79–85.

Corréard, M.-H. and V. Grundy (eds.). 1994. *The Oxford Hachette French Dictionary*. Oxford: Oxford University Press-Hachette.

Davis, M. W. 1998. 'On the effective use of large parallel corpora in cross-language text retrieval'. In Grefenstette (1998a), 11–22.

Dini, L., V. Di Tomaso, and F. Segond. 1999. Ginger ii: an example-driven word sense disambiguator. *Computers and the Humanities*, 121–6.

Evans, D. A., S. K. Handerson, I. A. Monarch, J. Pereiro, L. Delon, and W. R. Hersh. 1998. 'Mapping vocabularies using latent semantics'. In Grefenstette (1998a), 63–80.

Fluhr, C., D. Schmit, P. Ortet, F. Elkateb, K. Gurtner, and K. Radwan. 1998. 'Distributed crosslingual information retrieval'. In Grefenstette (1998a), 41–50.

Gale, W. and K. Church. 1993. 'A program for aligning sentences in bilingual corpora'. *Computational Linguistics*, 19(1), 75–102.

Grefenstette, G. 1995. 'Comparing two language identification schemes'. *Proceedings of the 3rd International Conference on the Statistical Analysis of Textual Data (JADT '95)* (Rome), 263–8.

——(ed.). 1998a. *Cross-Language Information Retrieval*. Dordrecht: Kluwer Academic Publishers.

——1998b. 'Evaluating the adequacy of a multilingual transfer dictionary for the cross language information retrieval'. In A. Rubio, N. Gallardo, R. Castro, and A. Tejada (eds.), *Proceedings of the 1st International Conference on Language Resource and Evaluation* (Granada), 755–8.

——1999. 'Tokenization'. In H. van Halteren (ed.), *Syntactic Wordclass Tagging*. Dordrecht: Kluwer Academic Publishers, 117–33.

Hiemstra, D., F. de Jong, and W. Kraaij. 1997. 'A domain specific lexicon acquisition tool for cross-language information retrieval'. In L. Deroye and C. Chrisment (eds.), *RIAO '97: Computer-Assisted Information Searching on the Internet* (Montreal), 217–32.

Hull, D. A. 1997. 'Automating the construction of bilingual terminology lexicons'. *Terminology*, 4(2), 225–44.

Hull, D. A. 1998. 'A weighted Boolean model for cross-language text retrieval'. In Grefenstette (1998a), 119–36.

——and G. Grefenstette. 1996. 'Querying across languages: a dictionary-based approach to multilingual information retrieval'. *Proceedings of the 19th ACM/SIGIR Conference* (Zurich), 49–57.

————B. M. Schulze, H. Schütze, and J. Pedersen. 1997. 'Xerox TREC-5 site report: routing, filtering, NLP, and Spanish tracks'. In D. Harman (ed.), *Proceedings of the 5th Text REtrieval Conference (TREC-5)* (Gaithersburg, Md.). Nist Special Publication, 500, 167–80.

Ingle, N. C. 1976. 'A language identification table'. *Incorporated Linguist*, 15(4), 98–101.

Kraut, R., W. Scherlis, T. Mukhopadhyay, J. Manning, and S. Kiesler. 1996. 'The HomeNet field trial of residential internet services'. *Communications of the ACM*, 39(55), 55–63.

Landauer, T. K. and M. L. Littman. 1990. 'Fully automatic cross-language document retrieval using latent semantic indexing'. *Proceedings of the 6th Annual Conference of the UW Centre for the New Oxford English Dictionary and Text Research*, Waterloo, Ont.: UW Centre for the New OED and Text Research, 31–8.

Miller, G. A., R. Beckwith, C. Fellbaum, D. Gross, and K. J. Miller. 1990. 'Introduction to Word-Net: an on-line lexical database'. *Journal of Lexicography*, 3(4), 235–44.

Nie, J.-Y., M. Simard, P. Isabelle, and R. Durand. 1999. 'Cross-language information retrieval based on parallel texts and automatic mining of parallel texts from the web'. In M. Hearst, F. Gey, and R. Tong. (eds.), *22nd International Conference on Research and Development in Information Retrieval*, Berkeley: SIGR '99, Association for Computational Machinery, 74–81.

Nunberg, G. 1996. *The Whole World Wired*. Commentary broadcast on 'Fresh Air', National Public Radio. http:// www.parc.xerox.com/istl/members/nunberg/wwwlg.html.

Salton, G. 1970. 'Automatic processing of foreign language documents'. *Journal of the American Society for Information Science*, 21, 187–94.

——1972. 'Comment on "query expansion by the addition of clustered terms for a document retrieval system"'. *Information Storage and Retrieval*, 8, 349.

Segond, F. and P. Tapanainen. 1995. *Using a finite-state based formalism to identify and generate multiword expressions*. Technical Report MLTT-019, Xerox Research Centre Europe, Grenoble.

——E. Aimelet, V. Lux, and C. Jean. 2000. 'Dictionary-driven semantic look-up'. *Computers and the Humanities*, 34(1, 2), 193–7.

Sheridan, P. and J. P. Ballerini. 1996. 'Experiments in multilingual information retrieval using the SPIDER system'. *Proceedings of the 19th Annual International ACM SIGIR Conference on Research and Development in Information Retrieval* (Zurich), 58–65. http://www-ir. inf. ethz.ch/Public-Web/sheridan/papers/SIGIR96.ps.

Sneath, P. H. A. and R. R. Sokal. 1973. *Numerical Taxonomy*. San Francisco: W. H. Freeman.

NOTES ON CONTRIBUTORS

Elisabeth André is a Full Professor of Computer Science at the University of Augsburg, Germany. Prior to that, she worked as a principal researcher at DFKI GmbH. She is Chair of the ACL Special Interest Group on Multimedia Language Processing (SIGMEDIA). Furthermore, she is on the editorial board of *Artificial Intelligence Communications* (AICOM), *Cognitive Processing* (*International Quarterly of Cognitive Science*), and the Universal Access to Information Society (UAIS). Elisabeth André is also the Area Editor for Intelligent User Interfaces of the *Electronic Transactions of Artificial Intelligence* (ETAI), and a member of the editorial board of *Computational Linguistics* for the period 2002–2004.

Ion Androutsopoulos is a Lecturer in the Department of Informatics at the Athens University of Economics and Business in Greece. He was previously an Associate Researcher at the Greek National Centre for Scientific Research 'Demokritos', and a Research Scientist at the Microsoft Research Institute, Macquarie University, Australia. Dr Androutsopoulos holds an M.Sc. and a Ph.D. in Artificial Intelligence from the University of Edinburgh. His current research interests include natural language interaction, information extraction, text classification, and natural language generation.

Maria Aretoulaki is head of Dialogue Development at Semantic Edge (formerly Interprice) in Germany, where she works on portable and extensible dialogue management for multimodal e-CRM applications. She has previously worked on telephone-based spoken dialogue systems at the University of Erlangen-Nuremberg, and at the Bavarian Research Centre for Knowledge-Based Systems, Forwiss, also in Germany. Her interests include connectionist approaches to pragmatics and discourse processing, an area she explored during her doctoral studies at UMIST, England.

John Bateman is Professor of Applied Linguistics at the University of Bremen, Germany. Since obtaining his Ph.D. from the Department of Artificial Intelligence at the University of Edinburgh in 1985, he has worked in natural language generation and functional linguistics, applying the latter to the former, on projects in Scotland, Japan, California, and Germany, as well as in a variety of European cooperations. His main research focuses are multilingual NLG, multimodal document design, discourse structure, and the application of all areas of systemic-functional linguistics.

Steven Bird is Associate Director of the Linguistic Data Consortium at the University of Pennsylvania. His current research focuses on formal and computational models for linguistic information, to support the description of the world's 6,800+ languages, including many languages that are endangered or unknown to science. Dr Bird conducted his doctoral and post-doctoral research within the Centre for Cognitive Science at University of Edinburgh (1987–94). From 1995 to 1997 he conducted linguistic fieldwork on the tone languages of Western Cameroon and helped develop several new writing systems. His undergraduate and postgraduate training were at the Department of Computer Science, University of Melbourne.

Didier Bourigault is a researcher at CNRS-ERSS (Toulouse, France). He has developed terminology extraction software (Lexter as well as Syntex) and acts as a consultant in the field of language engineering and computational terminology. He was also instrumental in the setting up and development of the TIA group, a French research group on computational terminology and knowledge engineering. Didier Bourigault has published at major conferences in computational linguistics (EACL, COLING, KAW) and co-edited a book on computational terminology published by John Benjamins in 2001.

John Carroll is a Reader in Computer Science and Artificial Intelligence at the University of Sussex, UK. He is involved in a number of collaborative research efforts in the areas of statistical techniques for robust parsing, automatic acquisition of lexical information from corpora, efficient unification-based parsing, and generation from logical form; he also works on applications of parsing technology.

Bob Carpenter works at SpeechWorks International, Inc., New York. He received his Ph.D. from the Centre for Cognitive Science at the University of Edinburgh and has been an Associate Professor of Computational Linguistics at Carnegie Mellon University, as well as a member of technical staff in the multimedia research group at Bell Laboratories. Dr Carpenter's research interests include spoken dialogue systems, user interfaces, parsing, and semantics.

Thierry Dutoit is a Professor in the Department of Electrical Engineering at the Faculté Polytechnique de Mons, Belgium where he obtained his Ph.D. in 1993. He worked for 16 months as a consultant for AT&T Labs Research in Murray Hill and Florham Park, NJ, in 1996 and 1998. Professor Dutoit is the author of two books and more than 60 reviewed papers on speech processing and text-to-speech synthesis, and is the coordinator of the MBROLA and EULER projects for free multilingual speech synthesis. His main interests are in speech synthesis and software engineering.

Jean-Luc Gauvain is a permanent CNRS researcher at LIMSI where he has been since 1983. He is head of the Spoken Language Processing Group. He received a doctorate in Electronics from the University of Paris XI in 1982. His research centres on speech recognition, language identification, audio indexing, and spoken language dialogue systems. He has over 160 publications and received the 1996 IEEE SPS Best Paper Award. He is a member of the IEEE Signal Processing Society's Speech Technical Committee.

Gregory Grefenstette is Principal Research Scientist at Clairvoyance Corporation, Pittsburgh, USA. He is the author of *Explorations in Automatic Thesaurus Discovery* (Kluwer, 1994) and editor of *Cross-Language Information Retrieval* (Kluwer, 1998). Gregory Grefenstette has published numerous papers on computational linguistics, information retrieval, and corpus analysis. He is currently working on very large lexicons.

Ralph Grishman is Professor of Computer Science at New York University and has been involved in research in natural language processing since 1969. He directs the Proteus Project (cs.nyu.edu/cs/projects/proteus), which conducts research in various areas of text analysis, including information extraction, lexicon construction, and syntactic and sublanguage analysis. He is a past president of the Association for Computational Linguistics, and author of *Computational Linguistics: An Introduction* (Cambridge University Press, 1986). He served as co-chair of the last two Message Understanding Conferences, where different types of information extraction were evaluated.

Patrick Hanks is chief lexical analyst at Lexeme/Lingomotors, Cambridge, MA. He is a visiting scholar at Brandeis University and the University of Sheffield. From 1990 to 2000 he was chief editor of current English dictionaries at Oxford University Press. He has worked on lexical analysis with computer scientists at AT&T, Bell Labs, Digital, and elsewhere, and has lectured and written extensively on the lexicon and names. In the 1980s he was editorial director of the Cobuild project in lexical computing, and in the 1970s he designed and edited the first edition of the *Collins English Dictionary* (1979).

Sanda Harabagiu is an Associate Professor and holds the Jonsson School Research Initiation Chair Professorship in the Department of Computer Science at the University of Texas at Dallas. Professor Harabagiu earned a second Ph.D. from the University of Southern California, Los Angeles in 1997, having gained her first from the University of Rome, Italy in 1994. She has held faculty positions at the University of Texas at Austin and Southern Methodist University. Dr Harabagiu was a recipient of an NSF CAREER award for studying reference resolution, and led the DARPA TIDES Roadmapping Committee on Question-Answering in 2000.

Marti Hearst is an Associate Professor in the School of Information Management and Systems at the University of California, Berkeley. Professor Hearst received her B.A., M.Sc., and Ph.D. degrees in Computer Science from the University of California at Berkeley. She was a Member of the Research Staff at Xerox PARC from 1994 to 1997. She is an Okawa Foundation Fellow, is on the editorial board of *ACM Transactions* *on Information Systems* and *ACM Transactions on Computer–Human Interaction*, and was formerly on the editorial board of *Computational Linguistics*. Her research interests are computational linguistics, human–computer interaction, and information retrieval.

Lynette Hirschman is Chief Scientist for the Information Technology Center at MITRE in Bedford, Mass. Dr Hirschman received her Ph.D. in formal linguistics from the University of Pennsylvania in 1972. She has worked in both text and spoken language processing, with a strong emphasis on evaluation. She was involved in the Message Understanding Conferences, and was the the organizer of the common data collection for the Air Travel Information System (ATIS) spoken language effort. Her current research interests include biolinguistics—the application of human language technology to bioinformatics—and reading comprehension tests as a vehicle for evaluation of language understanding systems.

Eduard Hovy heads the Natural Language Group at the Information Sciences Institute of the University of Southern California, and is a Research Associate Professor of the Computer Science Departments of USC and the University of Waterloo. His research focuses on text summarization, question answering, machine translation, and the semi-automated construction of large terminology banks. He is the author or co-editor of five books and over 100 articles. In 2001, Dr Hovy served as President of the Association for Computational Linguistics (ACL) and was elected President of the International Association of Machine Translation (IAMT).

John Hutchins is the author of several books and articles on linguistics, information retrieval and machine translation. Principal works include *Machine Translation: Past, Present, Future* (Ellis Horwood, 1986) and *Introduction to Machine Translation* with Harold Somers (Academic Press, 1992). He has been editor of *MT News International* (1991–1997), compiler of *Compendium of Translation Software* (2000), and editor of *Early Years in Machine Translation: Memoirs and Biographies of Pioneers* (John Benjamins, 2000). He is an active member of the European Association for Machine Translation (President since 1995) and the International Association for Machine Translation (President from 1999 to 2001).

Christian Jacquemin is a Professor in Computer Science at the University of Paris XI and head of the Research Group 'Language, Information, and Representation' at CNRS-LIMSI. He has published at major conferences in computational linguistics and information retrieval (ACL, COLING, ACM/SIGIR, RIAO). Professor Jacquemin was involved in the organization of workshops on compound analysis and computational terminology. He authored a book on natural language processing for term recognition published by MIT Press in 2001, and co-edited a book on computational terminology published by John Benjamins in 2001.

Aravind K. Joshi is the Henry Salvatori Professor of Computer and Cognitive Science and co-director of the Institute for Research in Cognitive Science at the University of Pennsylvania. Professor Joshi's current research focuses on the areas of computational linguistics, mathematical and processing models of language, and cognitive science. He is Fellow of IEEE, a Past President of ACL, a Founding Fellow of AAAI, and a Member of the National Academy of Engineering. He received the Research Excellence Award from IJCAI in 1997.

Ronald M. Kaplan is a Research Fellow at the Palo Alto Research Center (PARC) and leader of the linguistic research group. He is also a Consulting Professor of Linguistics at Stanford University. Among his contributions to computational linguistics are the Active Chart method for parsing context free languages, the basic mathematical and computational concepts of Finite State Morphology, the use of feature structures for syntactic representation, and the formalism of Lexical Functional Grammar. A Past President of the Association for Computational Linguistics, he received a Ph.D. in Social Psychology from Harvard University in 1975.

Lauri Karttunen is a Research Fellow at PARC. He received a Ph.D. in Linguistics from Indiana University in 1969. Dr Karttunen was at the University of Texas from 1969 to 1983, and worked mostly on semantics (discourse referents, presuppositions, and questions). His 1983 KIMMO system was an influential implementation of two-level morphology. At SRI 1984–7, he worked on unification and parsing. Since 1987, Dr Karttunen has contributed to finite-state technology and its applications to morphology and syntax at Xerox.

Martin Kay is Professor of Linguistics at Stanford University. He was educated at Cambridge University where he joined the Cambridge Language Research Unit, one of the earliest centres for research in what is now known as computational linguistics, in 1958. After three years at the Cambridge unit, he transferred to the Rand Corporation in Santa Monica, another early centre, eventually becoming head of Rand's research group in linguistics and translation before joining PARC in 1974. Professor Kay is a Past President of the Association for Computational Linguistics and has served for many years as Chairman of the International Committee on Computational Linguistics. He was awarded an Honorary Doctorate from the University of Gothenburg and is also an Honorary Professor at the University of Saarland.

Richard Kittredge is Professor of Linguistics at the University of Montreal, where he teaches formal and computational linguistics. He received a Ph.D. in Formal Linguistics from the University of Pennsylvania in 1969, and directed Montreal's TAUM project in machine translation during 1971–6. Currently Professor Kittredge serves on the editorial boards of the journal *Machine Translation*, and John Benjamins' book series on Natural Language Processing. Professor Kittredge is also affiliated with CoGenTex, Inc., a research and development company he founded in 1989, specializing in natural language generation, summarization, and translation.

Judith L. Klavans is Director of the Center for Information Access at Columbia University, an interdisciplinary research centre, the focus of which is to build research projects on networked information access. She joined Columbia after a decade at the IBM T. J. Watson Research Center working on language technologies. Prior to this, she had a fellowship as a researcher at MIT. In 1980, she received her Ph.D. in Theoretical Linguistics from University College London.

Lori Lamel joined LIMSI as a permanent CNRS researcher in October 1991. She received her Ph.D. in Electrical Engineering and Computer Science from the Massachusetts Institute of Technology (1988). Her research interests include speaker-independent, large vocabulary continuous speech recognition, acoustic-phonetics, lexical and phonological modelling, speaker/language identification, audio indexation and spoken language dialogue systems. She has over 140 publications, and is a member of the *Speech Communication* editorial board and the permanent council of ICSLP.

Shalom Lappin is Professor in the Department of Computer Science, King's College, London. His main research areas are computational linguistics, computational and formal semantics, and formal syntax. He has taught at SOAS, London and at the Universities of Tel Aviv, Haifa and Ottawa. From 1989 until 1993 he was a Research Staff Member in the Natural Language Group of the Computer Science Department at the IBM T. J. Watson Research Center, Yorktown Heights, NY. He is editor of the *Handbook of Contemporary Semantics Theory* (Blackwell, 1996), co-editor of *Fragments: Studies in Ellipsis and Gapping* (Oxford University Press, 1999), and associate editor of *Linguistics and Philosophy*. Together with David E. Johnson he co-authored *Local Constraints vs. Economy* (CSLI, 1999).

Geoffrey N. Leech is a Research Professor of English Linguistics at Lancaster University, UK. He is co-author of *A Comprehensive Grammar of the English Language* (Longman, 1985) and has also written books and articles in the areas of stylistics, semantics, and pragmatics, notably, *A Linguistic Guide to English Poetry* (Longman, 1969), *Semantics: The Study of Meaning* (Penguin, 2nd edn. 1981), and *Principles of Pragmatics* (Longman, 1983). In recent years, his research interests have focused on the computational analysis of English, using computer corpora. He was a member of the groups that compiled and annotated the Lancaster-Oslo-Bergen Corpus (LOB) and the British National Corpus (BNC).

Tony McEnery is Professor of Linguistics and English Language at Lancaster University, UK. He has worked on the construction and exploitation of a number of corpora, including the CRATER trilingual English/French/Spanish corpora and the EMILLE corpora of South Asian languages. He is the author of the book *Corpus Linguistics* with Andrew Wilson (Edinburgh University Press, 2001).

Inderjeet Mani is a Senior Principal Scientist at the MITRE Corporation in Reston, Virginia, and an adjunct faculty in Linguistics at Georgetown University. His books include a co-edited volume *Advances in Automatic Text Summarization* (MIT Press, 1999), and an authored book *Automatic Summarization* (John Benjamins, 2001). His work on evaluation includes assisting the US government with the TIPSTER SUM-MAC text summarization evaluation. In addition to text summarization, Dr Mani's current research includes temporal information processing, question-answering, and building ontologies. He also serves on the editorial board of *Computational Linguistics* (2002–4).

Carlos Martín-Vide is Professor at the Rovira i Virgili University, Tarragona, Spain, specializing in formal language theory and mathematical linguistics. He is editor of the recent volume *Where Mathematics, Computer Science, Linguistics and Biology Meet* with V. Mitrana (Kluwer, 2001). He has authored 175 papers in conference proceedings and journals. Carlos Martín-Vide is the editor-in-chief of the journal *Grammars* (Kluwer) and the chairman of the International Ph.D. School in Formal Languages and Applications.

Yuji Matsumoto is Professor of Computational Linguistics at Nara Institute of Science and Technology. He received his Bachelor, Master, and Ph.D. degrees of Engineering from Kyoto University. Professor Matsumoto's current research interests focus on knowledge acquisition and machine learning for natural language processing. Before joining Nara Institute of Science and Technology, Professor Matsumoto held positions at the Electrotechnical Laboratory, the Institute of New Generation Computer Technology, Imperial College of Science and Technology in London, and Kyoto University.

Andrei Mikheev is Chief Executive Officer of Infogistics Ltd. where he is leading the development of robust text processing applications. He is also a Senior Researcher at the Institute for Communicating and Collaborative Systems of the University of Edinburgh. Dr Mikheev started his research career in the Russian Academy of Sciences. His Ph.D. research was concerned with computational aspects of Russian morphology, syntactic parsing, and knowledge acquisition from corpora. Since joining the University of Edinburgh in 1993, Dr Mikheev has focused on applying machine learning methods to practical applications of language technology.

Ruslan Mitkov is Professor of Computational Linguistics and Language Engineering at the University of Wolverhampton, where he leads the Research Group in Computational Linguistics. His research has covered anaphora resolution, centering, machine translation, and automatic abstracting. Professor Mitkov is the author of the book *Anaphora Resolution* (Longman, 2002) and editor of the *Natural Language Processing* book series published by John Benjamins. He has served as Chair or a member of the Programme Committee of a number of NLP conferences. He was also recently guest editor of the journals *Machine Translation* and *Computational Linguistics* (with Branimir Boguraev and Shalom Lappin).

Dan Moldovan is Professor in the Department of Computer Science at the University of Texas at Dallas. Professor Moldovan earned a Ph.D. degree in Electrical

Engineering and Computer Science from Columbia University, New York, in 1978. He has held faculty positions at the University of Southern California and Southern Methodist University. Professor Moldovan's current research interests are in natural language processing, particularly in question-answering technology, knowledge acquisition, and knowledge bases. He has published over 150 research papers, one textbook, and several book chapters.

Raymond J. Mooney is Professor in the Department of Computer Sciences at the University of Texas at Austin. He received his Ph.D. in 1988 from the University of Illinois at Urbana/Champaign. Professor Mooney is the author of over 60 published papers in machine learning, and a former editor of *Machine Learning*. His current research focuses on natural language learning, including learning for semantic analysis, information extraction, text mining and recommender systems.

John Nerbonne is Professor of Computational Linguistics at the University of Groningen and Director of the Centre for Language and Cognition, Groningen. He earned advanced degrees in Computer Science and Linguistics at Ohio State University. Before joining the University of Groningen, Professor Nerbonne worked at Hewlett-Packard Labs and the German AI Center (Saarbrücken). He was coordinator of the GLOSSER project (1995–7), which applied mainly morphological analysis to computer assisted language learning. He is also the author of over 60 articles on computational linguistics. Professor Nerbonne is currently President of the International Association for Computational Linguistics (2002).

Allan Ramsay is Professor of Formal Linguistics in the Department of Computation at UMIST. Graduating in Logic and Mathematics at the University of Sussex in 1974, he took a masters in Logic at the University of London before returning to Sussex in 1980 to complete a Ph.D. concerned with using English as a programming language. Since that time, he has worked in research and held lecturing posts at Essex, Edinburgh, and Sussex, before taking up a Chair in Artificial Intelligence at University College Dublin, and then moving to UMIST.

Christer Samuelsson is Director of Natural Language Processing at Inzigo Research. He is a former Member of the Research Staff at Xerox Research Centre Europe and a former Member of Technical Staff at Bell Laboratories. He held a position at the University of Saarland after earning a doctoral degree at the Swedish Institute of Computer Science. Dr Samuelsson has applied machine-learning and statistical techniques to natural language processing, focusing on spoken language systems, parsing, and surface generation.

Frédérique Segond is in charge of e-learning projects at Xerox-NewStarts. She joined the Xerox Research Centre Europe in 1993 to work on computational linguistics and lead the Lexical Semantic project. Frédérique Segond received her Ph.D. in Applied Mathematics at the Ecole des Hautes Etudes en Sciences Sociales in Paris, implementing a categorical French grammar at IBM-France at the same time. After a post-doc at IBM Yorktown working on the links between syntax and semantics, Dr Segond was Maître de Conference at the Institut National des Telecommunications.

Harold Somers is Professor of Language Engineering and head of the Department of Language and Linguistics at UMIST, Manchester. Originally a linguist, he has more than 25 years' experience of computational linguistics research, specializing in MT. He is editor of *Machine Translation* and a member of the committee of the European Association for MT. His current research focuses on corpus-based methods, with a particular interest in developing resources for NIMLs (non-indigenous minority languages).

Mark Stevenson works at Reuters, London where he explores the business opportunities of NLP technology. His Ph.D. work focused on word–sense disambiguation and was supervised by Yorick Wilks. He has worked on and led various research projects funded by the European Union and UK research councils. His topics of investigation have included information extraction and retrieval, lexical and taxonomy adaptation, and speech recognition. In 2001/2002 he was on sabbatical as a visiting researcher at the Center for the Study of Language Information at Stanford University.

Tomek Strzalkowski is an Associate Professor of Computer Science at the University of Albany. His research interests include applications of natural language processing to information retrieval, automated summarization, open domain question answering, and natural language dialogue. Dr Strzalkowski is on the Programme Committee of the Text Retrieval Conference (TREC), where he is also co-Chair of the Question Answering track, and former Chair of the Natural Language track.

Yannis Stylianou is an Associate Professor of Computer Science at the University of Crete, Greece. After completing his Ph.D. at the École National Supérieure des Télécommunications (Telecom Paris) in 1996, he joined AT&T Labs Research, NJ, where he worked on Next Generation TTS and on speech coders. From February 2001 until February 2002, he was a Member of Technical Staff of Language Modelling and Research Department at Bell Labs, Murray Hill, NJ. His current interests are in various aspects of speech analysis for speech synthesis and coding.

Harald Trost is an Associate Professor at the University of Vienna and head of the Natural Language Group at the Austrian Research Institute for Artificial Intelligence. He has been active in the field of computational linguistics ever since his diploma thesis in the late 1970s. His research interest in computational morphology focuses on the treatment of non-concatenative phenomena within two-level morphology, the integration of morphology and syntax, and the morphology–speech interface.

Evelyne Tzoukermann is Research Staff Member at Bell-Labs, Lucent Technologies. After completing her Ph.D. at the University of Paris, she obtained a Fullbright fellowship to pursue a post-doctoral year at Brown University. Dr Tzoukermann spent two years at the IBM Watson Research Center as a visiting scientist. Her research interests include computational linguistics, information retrieval, and text-to-speech synthesis.

Piek Vossen is Chief Technical Officer at Irion Technologies, where he develops multilingual language technology and applications for many different languages. For more than 10 years, Dr Vossen worked on computational lexicons and multilingual semantic networks at the University of Amsterdam, as part of the EC projects Acquilex and Sift. More recently, he coordinated the EuroWordNet project, which resulted in a large-scale multilingual database with semantic networks in eight European languages. Dr Vossen has also worked as Senior Researcher at Sail Labs, Antwerp, Belgium.

Atro Voutilainen works at Conexor. He received his Ph.D. in 1994 from the University of Helsinki. Dr Voutilainen is best known for his work on word-class tagging (e.g. English Constraint Grammar), finite-state dependency parsing, and parser evaluation methodology. He has authored around 50 book chapters and articles in conference proceedings.

Martin Weisser received his Ph.D. in Phonetics/Corpus Linguistics from Lancaster University in 2001. He is currently involved in a project with Professor G. Leech dealing with the creation of a speech-act annotated corpus for dialogue systems (SPAAC) in the Department of Linguistics and Modern English Language at Lancaster University. His main interests include all aspects of spoken language, including automatic processing and markup, general linguistics, and accents and dialects.

Yorick Wilks is Professor of Computer Science at the University of Sheffield, and Director of the Institute of Language, Speech and Hearing. He has also been Director of the Computing Research Laboratory at New Mexico State University and Professor of Computer Science and Linguistics at the University of Essex. Professor Wilks received his doctorate from Cambridge University in 1968 for work investigating computer programs that understand written English. He has published numerous articles and five books in different areas of AI and NLP, the most recent being *Electric Words: Dictionaries, Computers and Meanings* with Brian Slator and Louise Guthrie (MIT Press, 1995).

Michael Zock is researcher at LIMSI (CNRS, France) and holds a Ph.D. in experimental psychology. Editor of five books, he initiated the European Workshop on Natural Language Generation (1987, Royaumont). Dr Zock's major research interests lie in the building of tools to support students learning to produce language. His recent work is devoted to the building of extensions to electronic dictionaries aiming to facilitate the access, memorization, and automation of words and syntactic structures, and to overcome the tip-of-the-tongue problem.

Glossary

abductive logic A type of logic that allows the reasoner to draw on additional premises or inferences not covered by traditional logic.

abstract A summary produced by re-generating the content extracted from the input text.

accept (noun) A type of speech or dialogue act whereby a dialogue participant signals acceptance, e.g. *Yes, please.*

acceptability testing Testing whether end-users find a system's performance acceptable given their needs.

acoustic model A model describing the probabilistic behaviour of the encoding of the linguistic information in a speech signal.

acoustic parameterization Selection of acoustic features which are used to reduce model complexity without losing relevant linguistic information.

activation In lexical processing, the extent to which some or all of a word's meaning potential is necessary for understanding that word when it is used.

active edge In parsing, a representation of a partially recognized constituent of a linguistic structure.

activity type In dialogue systems, the genre of activity to which the dialogue contributes.

adjacency pair A pair of speech acts or dialogue acts that can be assumed to always occur together or follow each other, e.g. questions followed by answers.

adjoining operation In tree-adjoining grammar, an operation of composition that adjoins an auxiliary tree to another tree (elementary or derived (non-elementary)) at a node in that tree.

adverb anaphora Anaphora where the anaphor is an adverb.

AECMA Simplified English An internationally accepted controlled language standard for writing technical manuals in the aerospace industry.

affix A bound morpheme realized as sequences of phonemes, which produce word forms in inflection and new words in derivation.

agenda A prioritized list of parser tasks still to be executed.

agent In a dialogue system, one of the participants in the dialogue, either the system or the user.

agreement A relationship between two elements of a sentence whereby the form of one element requires a corresponding form of the other.

aligned bilingual corpus A parallel corpus in which the correspondences (alignments) between the two texts are made explicit.

alignment Mapping the text segments (i.e. words, sentences, paragraphs) of a parallel text (written in two different languages) onto each other.

allomorph Any of the contextually determined realizations of a morpheme, for example the plural morpheme as *-s* in *cars* contrasted with its realization as *-es* in *buses.*

allophone Any of the various different realizations of a given phoneme in different phonetic contexts, such as the aspirated /t/ in *type*, as contrasted with the flapped /t/ in *butter*, or the final unreleased /t/ in *hot*.

alphabet Any finite set of letters.

ambiguity Situation wherein a word, phrase, or sentence conveys more than one meaning.

anaphor See **anaphora**.

anaphor resolution See **anaphora resolution**.

anaphora The linguistic phenomenon of pointing back to a previously mentioned item in the text. The pointing back word or phrase is called an *anaphor* (also called *referring expression* if it has a referential function) and the entity to which it refers or for which it stands is its *antecedent*.

anaphora resolution The process of determining the antecedent of an anaphor. Also referred to as **anaphor resolution**.

anchoring For a natural language interaction system, a process whereby an elliptical utterance or an ambiguous item is interpreted in the context of the previous dialogue exchange.

annotation The process of annotating specific linguistic features, relationships, or structures in a text (usually in a corpus).

annotation guidelines Instructions provided to humans for annotating linguistic features, relationships, or structures in text.

annotation scheme An adopted methodology prescribing how to encode linguistic features, relationships, or structures in text.

annotation tool A tool developed with a view to facilitating the application of a specific annotation scheme (or schemes), making the annotation process faster and more user-friendly.

answer extraction In question answering, the process of identifying in a paragraph the text snippet representing the answer to a given question.

answer type taxonomy The ontology of the semantic categories of possible answers in a question answering system.

antecedent See **anaphora**.

apologize (noun) A type of speech or dialogue act whereby a dialogue participant signals an apology, e.g. 'I'm sorry', 'I apologise sincerely . . .', etc.

associative anaphora See **indirect anaphora**.

attribute value matrix (AVM) A matrix of attributes and their values used to represent a typed feature structure graph.

automatic indexing Association of a document with linguistic descriptors that are expected to abstract the content of this document.

automatic scoring Scoring the performance of a system via a computer program.

autosegmental rules Procedures for converting one representation into another, by adding or removing association lines and autosegments.

auxiliary tree One of the two types of elementary trees in a TAG. In an auxiliary tree the root node of the tree and a designated foot node have the same label. An auxiliary tree enters a derivation via the operation of adjoining.

average case complexity The expected number of resources used to solve a problem of a given size.

back-off A mechanism for smoothing the estimates of the probabilities of rare events by relying on less specific models.

base form The part of a word that carries its meaning; it serves as the basis for all inflectional forms of the word.

Bayes's inversion formula A formula that relates the probability of an event A given an event B to the converse probability of event B given event A.

Bernoulli distribution A probability distribution modelling the experiment of flipping a biased coin.

bilingual alignment tools Tools that produce a bilingual dictionary from two parallel texts, one text being a translation of the other.

bilingual concordancer A tool for creating a concordance of terms together with their translations, as found in an aligned bilingual corpus.

bilingual corpus A collection of texts in which each text appears in two languages.

bilingual dictionary A dictionary that provides translations of words into another language.

bilingual system (i) An NLP system operating for two languages; (ii) a program for machine translation from one source language into one other target language, and not intended for any other pairs of languages. Compare **multilingual system**.

bimachine An encoding of a functional relation as a pair of sequential transducers. The first is applied to the input in the left-to-right direction; the second transducer applies to the output of the first in the opposite direction.

blackboard systems An architectural paradigm where the modules of a system communicate among themselves by way of a common data-holder, the blackboard, on which intermediate results of each module are visible to the other modules.

Boolean system In information retrieval, a system in which queries are represented by keywords, connected with Boolean logical operators (e.g. 'and', 'or', 'not').

bridging anaphora See **indirect anaphora**.

candidate term A term automatically acquired from a corpus of documents which is expected to be validated by an expert.

canned question answering Question answering performed by a system that provides answers based on matches with lists of predefined questions.

case-based learning See **exemplar-based learning**.

case role The semantic role that a noun or noun phrase plays in relation to a verb in a clause. For example, a clause containing a verb of movement will also include a noun phrase specifying some at least of the following: the *agent* (the mover), the *theme* (the thing moved), the *source* (where it came from), the *path* (what it moved along), the *goal* (where it went to), and the *manner* (how it moved). In the linguistics literature there is often a variety of different terms for what is essentially the same case role, e.g. *theme* is used as an alternative term for *patient* and *source* is also referred to as *from-loc*.

center The topically most prominent entity in an utterance.

centering A theory about discourse coherence based on the idea that each utterance features a topically most prominent entity called the center.

chart In parsing, a table storing completely and/or partially recognized constituents, in the form of passive and active edges.

Chomsky hierarchy A hierarchy of formal languages where the family of regular languages is a strict subclass of the family of context-free languages, which is a strict subclass of the family of context-sensitive languages, which is a strict subclass of the family of recursively denumerable languages.

chunk A sequence of words in text that constitutes a non-recursive, elementary grouping of a particular syntactic category (e.g. nominal, prepositional).

citation See **example**.

CLEF See **cross-language evaluation forum**.

coarticulation The influence of phonetic context on the pronunciation of a phoneme. Co-articulatory phenomena are due to the fact that each articulator moves continuously from the realization of one phoneme to the next so as to minimize the effort to produce each articulatory position.

collocation The phenomenon whereby particular lexical items occur predominantly, or with a high probability, with particular, identifiable other lexical items.

comparable corpora Two or more corpora representing data in different languages which have been collected using comparable sampling frames.

complementary distribution Mutually exclusive occurrence of a pair of speech sounds in different phonetic contexts. Compare **allophone**.

complexity A measure of the growth in resources (memory, time, bandwidth etc.) used by a program or required for a problem of a given size.

composition An operation on two relations. Composition is a common operator in regular expressions.

compounding The joining of two or more base forms to form a new word.

comprehension assistant/aid An interactive reading tool for foreign language texts providing a variety of services, from simple word lookup to contextual translations of words and phrases.

computational lexicography (i) Use of computers to assist in the compilation of dictionaries. (ii) use of existing dictionaries for a purpose for which they were not designed, namely applications in natural language processing by computer.

computational morphology The area of computational linguistics covering automatic morphological analysis and generation, typically through finite-state methods.

computational phonology The application of formal and computational techniques to the representation and processing of phonological information.

computational pragmatics The field of computational linguistics concerned with how theories and methods of pragmatics can be applied to the development of computer systems, particularly spoken dialogue systems.

computational semantics The area of computational linguistics that deals with linguistic meaning within a computational approach to natural language.

computational terminology The computer-assisted acquisition, maintenance, or exploitation of terminological data.

computer-aided instruction Any kind of learning in which an instructor uses a computer as a learning aid. The term emphasizes the role of the instructor and is therefore not favoured by those wishing to emphasize opportunities for learning that are less dependent on instruction.

computer-assisted language learning Any use of computers to provide language instruction or to support language learning.

concatenation An operation on two languages or relations. Concatenation is commonly represented by white space in regular expressions.

conceptual primitive A concept that is not further decomposed or defined in terms of more specific concepts.

concord See **agreement**.

concordance A list showing all the occurrences and contexts of a given word or phrase, as found in a corpus, typically in the form of a KWIC index.

confirmation strategy For a natural language interaction system, a procedure for determining whether the system requires explicit, implicit, or no confirmation of its interpretation of the user input.

constative Making a point or stating a truth; sometimes used synonymously with **declarative**.

constituent structure See **phrase structure**.

constraint A restriction imposed by a specific model or system (e.g. constraints imposed on the relation between the anaphor and the antecedent in an anaphora resolution model; constraints imposed on the participants by a conversational system etc.).

constraint relaxation A procedure in syntactic analysis in which violations of linguistic constraints are progressively tolerated; used for the analysis of texts which may contain errors.

context (i) In corpus linguistics and text linguistics, the parts of a text that surround a particular word or phrase, often providing clues to its meaning; (ii) in discourse analysis and pragmatics, the non-linguistic world situation in which a particular utterance is uttered, sometimes affecting its form and meaning; (iii) in phonetics, the speech sounds that surround a particular phoneme and affect its realization.

context-dependent model In speech recognition, a model that takes into account the neighbouring phones.

context-free backbone A partial, context-free representation of a grammar, without feature structure (or other) augmentation.

context-free grammar (formal definition) A type of grammar in which every production is of the form $A \rightarrow w$, A being a nonterminal letter and w being any string of nonterminal or terminal letters, including the empty string. The term 'letter' is used here in its broad sense in that it covers grammatical categories such as S, NP, VP etc. (informal definition) A system of rules that specify that single categories can be rewritten into sequences of words and other categories. The single categories can be rewritten without regard to their context, the words and phrases that surround them. Context-free grammars have the power to characterize nested dependencies.

context-sensitive grammar A type of grammar where every production is of the form $u_1 A u_2 \rightarrow u_1 w u_2$, where u_1, u_2, w are any strings, w is a non-empty string and A is a nonterminal letter. The term 'letter' is used here in its broad sense in that it covers grammatical categories such as S, NP, VP etc.

contextual effects In a dialogue system, the addition to the addressee's existing set of assumptions of new assumptions derived from the utterance in relation to its context. Compare **dynamic context knowledge**.

controlled language A restricted version of a natural language that has been engineered for a particular purpose, typically that of writing technical documentation for non-native or non-expert speakers of the document language. Controlled languages typically use a restricted vocabulary and a limited set of simple syntactic structures.

controlled language checker A software program that detects possible departures in word usage, syntax or style from a particular controlled language standard.

conversational system A dialogue system that simulates a conversation with a human agent, mainly by responding to key words and patterns in the user input.

co-operative principle A principle based upon the assumption expressed by the philosopher H. P. Grice that participants in a conversation are basically co-operative in contributing to the general goals of the conversation, and that any deviation from this behaviour is usually intended to convey an implication, unless a participant is simply lying. See also **maxim of manner, maxim of quality, maxim of quantity, and maxim of relation**.

core meaning The central, most important meaning of a polysemous word. The term is widely used in discussions of computational lexicography, often without a precise definition. In traditional lexicography, the core meaning is sometimes taken to be the oldest meaning, sometimes the most frequent meaning. In computational lexicography, the core meaning is sometimes defined as the conventional meaning that has the closest set of semantic links with the largest number of other, related meanings of the same word.

core sublanguage A highly regular component of a natural sublanguage characterized by text segments which (i) refer to the primary domain of interest and (ii) have a simpler grammar than that required for the whole sublanguage in which it is embedded (e.g. market activity clauses within a stock market report).

coreference The act of referring to the same referent in the real world.

coreference resolution The identification of all coreferential chains. Compare **coreferential chain**.

coreferential An anaphor and an antecedent are coreferential when they both have the same referent in the real world.

coreferential chain A specific anaphor and more than one of the preceding (or following) noun phrases may be coreferential, thus forming a coreferential chain of discourse entities which have the same referent.

corpus A body of linguistic data, usually naturally occurring data in machine readable form, especially one that has been gathered according to some principled sampling method.

corpus annotation See **annotation**.

corpus-based dictionary A dictionary based on analysis of a large collection of texts in machine-readable form, usually by a team of lexicographers using concordances and other interactive tools.

corpus-based lexicography Analysis of word meaning in the light of word behaviour as observed in a large corpus. Some modern lexicographers assert that corpus analysis is an essential prerequisite for balanced reporting of meaning and use in order to counteract distortions due to introspection and to traditional methods of lexical analysis. Compare **historical principles**.

corpus linguistics A computer-assisted methodology that addresses a range of questions in linguistics by empirical analysis of bodies of naturally occurring speech and writing.

cost measures Measures of the cost of developing, deploying, and maintaining a system, in terms of time and/or money.

co-text See **immediate-context analysis**.

coverage In lexicography, the extent to which a dictionary or lexicon has entries for all the words in the target language. Since the vocabulary of a natural language is a non-finite set, 100 per cent coverage is an impossible goal, hence compromises are necessary to achieve acceptable coverage.

cross-language evaluation forum (CLEF) European programme to build corpora and establish protocols for cross-language information retrieval evaluation benchmarks. CLEF evaluations are based on TREC procedures. See **TREC**.

cross-language information retrieval The task of retrieving documents that are relevant to a query but which are written in a different language from the query.

cross-media references References from one medium to document parts in other presentation media, such as 'the upper left corner of the picture' or 'Fig. x'.

cue phrase A phrase such as 'note that' or 'in conclusion' often indicating that the sentence containing it also contains particularly important information.

CYC A large proprietary knowledge base containing common sense knowledge, used for inferencing and other purposes.

data collection The collection of a corpus intended to be representative of the kinds of phenomena being studied.

data mining (Semi-) automated discovery of trends and patterns across very large datasets, usually for the purposes of decision making.

decision problem In the theory of formal languages, the problem of determining if a given string is in the language or not.

decision tree A tree data-structure used in machine learning for categorizing examples, generally acquired automatically through induction from a set of labelled training data.

deep structure A tree structure that represents the underlying grammatical relations in Transformational Grammar. In the deep structure a predicate and its arguments appear in canonical positions that make their meanings easy to determine, even though they may be transformed so as to appear in other configurations in actual sentences.

default logic A type of logic that assumes that there exists a default or prototypical assumption that a reasoner will always prefer to other assumptions.

default meaning A basic meaning of a polysemous term, which can be activated for computational use in the absence of any more detailed clues as to the correct meaning intended.

defeasible Possible to reject if there is evidence to the contrary.

definiendum A term (word or phrase) that is to be explained in a dictionary entry. See **entry**.

definition The explanation of the meaning of a term. Traditionally, definitions were assumed to state necessary and sufficient conditions for the correct use of a word, but modern lexicographers, following philosophers such as Wittgenstein and Putnam, object that a definition cannot set boundaries of this kind. For this reason, some lexicographers prefer to talk about the *sense* of a word rather than its definition. The term *explanation* is sometimes preferred to *definition* to describe what is actually said about the term.

derivation (i) In morphology, the production of new words—usually of a different part-of-speech category—by adding a bound morph to a base form; (ii) in formal languages, the transformation of a string into another string by means of the application of the rules in a grammar.

derivation tree The structure characterized by a set of nodes and a dominance relation between them.

derivative form A word that is derived from another word, for example, 'definitely' and 'definiteness' from 'definite'. Most dictionaries list derivative forms as subentries (often called *run-on entries*) within the main body of the entry if the semantic differences are negligible, but as separate headwords or main entries if there is a serious meaning difference. Thus, 'definiteness' is often found as a subentry, while 'definitely' is more often a separate main entry, because of its use to mean 'Yes'.

deterministic A network is deterministic if no state has more than one outgoing arc for any given label.

diagnostic frame Set of sentences that evoke strong intuitions about semantic anomalies and can be used to elicit certain semantic relations between words.

dialogue Communicative linguistic activity in which at least two speakers or agents participate.

dialogue act (i) A type of speech act that contributes towards achieving a specific sub-goal or goal in a dialogue. It may consist of a part of an utterance, a complete utterance or even a group of utterances; (ii) a stretch of speech that is normally identified by the criteria (a) that it is spoken by one person and (b) that it has an identifiable function. The term *utterance* is best avoided as it is used by different researchers for different purposes, and is liable to ambiguity.

dialogue corpus A corpus consisting of a collection of dialogues.

dialogue cost A measure of time or effort needed to carry out a dialogue interaction.

dialogue grammar A dialogue management model that assumes that dialogues have a fixed structure of finite states that represent dialogue acts, usually arranged according to the conception of adjacency pairs.

dialogue management Coordination of the different steps involved in the development of a dialogue, usually involving specific speech or dialogue acts that allow the participants (agents) to maintain coherence between different parts of the dialogue and to achieve its goal.

dialogue manager The central component in a spoken dialogue system which is responsible for coordinating the different levels of analysis the system has to perform and controlling the communication between the user and the system. It anchors the user input in context, selects the content of the next system message, and provides predictions about the next user utterance.

dictionary A collection of words and phrases with information about them. Traditional dictionaries contain explanations of spelling, pronunciation, inflection, word class (part of speech), word origins, word meaning, and word use. However, they do not provide much information about the relationships between meaning and use. A dictionary for computational purposes (often called a *lexicon*) rarely says anything about word origin, and may say nothing about meaning or pronunciation either.

differentiae The properties that uniquely distinguish the category members in an ontology from their parent and from one another.

diphone The acoustic piece of speech from the middle of one phoneme to the middle of the next phoneme.

direct anaphora Nominal anaphora where anaphors and antecedents are linked by relations such as identity ('a shop ... the shop'), synonymy ('a shop ... the store'), generalization ('a boutique ... the shop') and specialization ('a shop ... the boutique'). Compare **indirect anaphora**.

direct translation A method of machine translation, where analysis of source language, disambiguation of lexical items and changes of syntactic structures are restricted to those specifically required for a particular language pair.

directed graph A graph is a set of pairs of nodes (vertices), where each pair of nodes constitutes an edge of the graph. A directed graph is a graph whose pairs are ordered, and so for any pair of nodes a,b in the graph the edges <a,b> and <b,a> are distinct.

directed replacement In finite-state processing, a replacement relation that is constrained by directionality (left-to-right or right-to-left) and length of match (longest or shortest).

discourse An extended sequence of sentences produced by one or more people with the aim of conveying or exchanging information.

discourse model For a natural language interaction system, an encapsulation of the events and objects mentioned in the discourse so far and information as to how they relate to one another.

discourse plans In dialogue, task-independent behavioural patterns regulating exchanges between agents in general. Compare **domain plans**.

discourse segment Any separable part of a discourse. A discourse segment will typically be concerned with a sub-part of the topic covered by the discourse as a whole.

distinctive feature theory The theory that speech sounds are composed of a small number of features that contrast with one another, e.g. /b/ contrasts with /p/ by virtue of being voiced rather than unvoiced; /b/ contrasts with /v/ by virtue of being a plosive rather than a fricative; /b/ contrasts with /d/ by virtue of being a bilabial rather than a dental.

distribution The variety of different texts in a language or a corpus in which a particular word or phrase is used. Some terms tend to cluster in particular domains or text types.

document processing In question answering, the indexing model that enables the retrieval of paragraphs.

document ranking A method of organizing a collection of documents retrieved in response to a specific query, ranked by score, where a highly ranked document is more likely to be relevant to the topic than a lowered ranked document.

document threading The linking of several different documents on a related topic.

domain A distinct or specified area of language, dialogue, or discourse. Some words, phrases, and structures tend to be associated with particular domains (e.g. 'renal' is associated with the medical domain), while others have meanings that are domain-specific (e.g. 'treat', 'cure', and 'patient' have meanings that are particularly associated with the medical domain). Domain boundaries tend to be fuzzy, and the number of domains is non-finite. Domain is one of the variables that define types of dialogue, e.g. travel, transport, appointment scheduling etc.

domain knowledge In dialogue, the background knowledge of the relevant domain that agents engaging in a dialogue can be assumed to have before the dialogue begins. Compare **dynamic context knowledge**.

domain model An ontology describing a specific domain in an artificial intelligence system designed and constructed for a specific task or a specific system.

domain of locality A domain over which dependencies can be specified.

domain plans In dialogue, task-dependent behavioural patterns regulating exchanges between agents with respect to a particular domain. Compare **discourse plans**.

dynamic context knowledge Knowledge that is built up as a dialogue proceeds, as opposed to pre-existing domain knowledge. Compare **contextual effects**.

dynamic programming See **memoization**.

dynamic semantics A view of meaning which regards it as being concerned with changing whatever the current discourse model is.

EAGLES Acronym for **Expert Advisory Group on Language Engineering Standards**, a working group on standardization that focuses on lexical semantic notions and resources for NLP.

EDR Abbreviation for **electronic dictionary research**, a multilingual lexical semantic database for Japanese and English.

elementary tree One of a finite set of elementary trees in a tree-adjoining grammar, from which all other trees are derived by the operations of substitution and adjoining. These trees are elementary in the sense that they represent the minimal structure(s) associated with a lexical item, capturing syntactic and semantic dependencies associated with that item.

elliptical sentence A sentence that has missing grammatical constituents (e.g. no verb).

embeddability A measure of the ease with which a component can be embedded into a larger system.

embedded-component evaluation The evaluation of alternative components by embedding each of them into an end-to-end system and comparing the overall system performance for each version.

embedding (i) Inclusion of one linguistic element or structure within another; (ii) in lexicography, an aspect of dictionary structure in which one piece of information is contained within another. In many dictionaries, senses are embedded within a part-of-speech bloc (i.e. all the noun senses are grouped together, separately from all the verb senses). An example of usage may be embedded within a definition, or a definition of a subsense may be embedded within a definition of a major sense. Dictionaries are among the most intricately structured texts in the world: the entries in a major dictionary such as the *Oxford English Dictionary* (*OED*) contain up to nine levels of embedding.

emission probabilities The parameters of an HMM that express the probability of emitting any given observable signal from any given hidden state.

empirical computational linguistics Computing statistics over large text collections in order to discover useful patterns, which are used to inform algorithms for various subproblems within natural language processing, such as part-of-speech tagging, word–sense disambiguation, and bilingual dictionary creation.

empty language A language that contains no strings, not even the empty string.

end-of-line hyphen A hyphen used to split a whole word into two parts to perform justification of text during typesetting.

end-to-end testing Testing of a computer system with all of its components fully integrated.

entailment A logical consequence of a proposition. Many verbs and other predicators can be associated systematically with particular entailments and presuppositions: for example, 'abandoning' something 'presupposes' that you once had it and 'entails' that you no longer have it.

entropy The degree of disorder or randomness in a system, often taken as a measure of how difficult it is to predict the outcome of a random variable.

entry A word or phrase about which information is provided in a dictionary, or the word and phrase together with the information provided. An entry may consist of more than one word, e.g. 'fire engine' and 'take off', or a morpheme that is less than one word, e.g. 'multi-'. See also **definiendum**, **target word**.

equal-length relation A relation in which each string is paired with another string of the same length as the first.

error rate The number of errors created by a system performing a particular task or part of a task, sometimes defined as the sum of insertions, substitutions, and deletions divided by the total number of measured elements, when compared to a **gold standard**; typically used for word, tag, slot, or concept error rates.

etymology The linguistic origin of a word, often tracing it back to an ancient language of which records may or may not survive, such as Latin, Greek, Proto-Germanic, or Indo-European.

EuroWordNet Multilingual wordnet database for English, Spanish, Italian, French, German, Dutch, Czech, and Estonian.

event extraction The extraction of all the instances of a particular type of relationship or event from a text or group of texts.

example In lexicography, a phrase or sentence in a dictionary showing how a word is used. Traditional dictionaries often contained examples invented by the compilers, in some cases illustrating unusual but possible usage. Corpus-based dictionaries contain examples selected from or idealized from actual texts, often illustrating typical usage. Historical dictionaries such as the *OED* sometimes aim to include examples of the earliest known uses of a word or sense. Also called **citation**.

example-based MT A method of machine translation which uses examples of previously translated text as its model for translation.

exemplar-based learning An approach to machine learning that assigns new cases to the class of the most similar previously seen example. (See also **lazy learning** and **case-based learning**.)

expectation value The average outcome of a random variable; often written μ.

expected answer type The semantic category to which an answer must belong.

explanation See **definition**.

extract A summary produced by simply re-using parts (words, sentences, paragraphs etc.) of the original input text.

extrinsic evaluation See **intrinsic and extrinsic evaluation metrics**.

failure-to-find fallacy The mistaken assumption that, if something (such as a word or phrase) has not been found in a collection of data, it does not exist. Corpus analysts need to bear in mind that a term or linguistic structure not found in a particular corpus may nevertheless exist outside that corpus.

feature (i) In lexical semantics, a formal property of a word or phrase that marks it as similar to one set of words and phrases on a particular dimension and distinguishes it from other sets. A feature is usually indicated by naming the dimension (e.g. number or gender) and specifying the value (e.g. singular or plural); (ii) in phonetics, a particular aspect of the articulation of a speech sound. See **distinctive feature theory**; (iii) the term *feature* is used in a number of other areas of linguistics or computational linguistics to denote a property or attribute.

feature-based metrics A set of measurements of the effectiveness of a computational tool or system, based on the model of a consumer report, in which end users or expert evaluators provide judgements rating features of the candidate systems.

feature structure A representation of syntactic information in the form of a matrix that pairs the names of features with the values of those features for a particular word, phrase, or sentence. Hierarchical feature structures, where the feature values can themselves be feature structures, are used as the underlying syntactic representations in Lexical Functional Grammar (where they are called 'functional structures') and Head-Driven Phrase Structure Grammar.

felicity conditions A set of conditions that have to be fulfilled in order for a speech or dialogue act to become successful; a term devised by the philosopher J. L. Austin.

finite-state automaton A directed graph (= network) that consists of states and labelled arcs. A finite-state automaton contains a single initial state and any number of final states. If the arc labels are atomic symbols, the network represents a regular language; if the labels are symbol pairs, the network represents a regular relation. Each path (= succession of arcs) from the initial state to a final state encodes, depending on the labels, a string in the language or a pair of strings in the relation. A network that represents a finite-state language is sometimes called a simple automaton; a network that encodes a relation is called a finite-state transducer.

finite-state language A language (= set of strings) that can be represented by a finite-state automaton. See **regular expression**.

finite-state machine See **finite-state automaton**.

finite-state morphology Because most morphological phenomena can be described in terms of regular expressions, the use of finite-state techniques for morphological components is common. In particular, when morphotactics is seen as a simple concatenation of morphs, it can straightforwardly be described by finite automata. The most commonly used finite-state approach is **two-level morphology**.

finite-state network See **finite-state automaton**.

finite-state technology Tools and methods for creating and applying finite-state automata.

finite-state transducer A finite-state automaton that represents a regular relation. See **finite-state automaton**.

first-order logic Logic whose expressions include (i) logical constants for sentential connectives, (ii) quantifiers whose domains are sets of individuals, (iii) individual constants (names of individuals) and individual variables, and (iv) predicate constants that correspond to properties and relations of individuals. Such logics may also contain lambda operators that bind individual variables in open sentences to create predicate terms.

focus See **focusing**.

focus rules Rules that govern how a text may move elements in and out of focus.

focusing According to theories of focusing, discourse entities can be assigned differing focus statuses. These statuses then have consequences for the linguistic possibilities available for their expression as well as for preferences in interpretation. Two levels of focusing in discourse are commonly distinguished: *global* and *local* (or *immediate*). Entities that are most relevant and central throughout the discourse are considered globally focused, whereas those that are important just for a specific utterance are said to be *immediately* or *locally focused*.

foreign language learning Learning of a second or subsequent language in a country where that language is not spoken, i.e. in a situation without a great deal of natural interaction in the new language. Compare **second language learning**.

formal grammar A mathematical structure $G = (N,T,S,P)$, where N,T are disjoint finite alphabets, S is an axiom, and P is a finite set of rewriting rules.

formal language Any set of strings over an alphabet.

frame In speech recognition, set of acoustic parameters associated with a windowed portion of the signal. Also called **parameter vector**.

frame semantics The semantic theory of Charles Fillmore which deals systematically with the way in which different words in the same general semantic field differ in meaning by reason of some semantic or combinatorial feature.

functional A finite-state transducer is functional (= unambiguous) in a given direction of application just in case there is at most one output for any input string.

functional structure See **feature structure**.

functional theory Any theory of language that is centrally concerned with the role played by language in society and with explanation or motivations for the deployment of linguistic phenomena. Functional theory is very commonly employed in natural language generation systems, less so in natural language understanding.

functional utterance An utterance classified according to its functional content, rather than its structural or syntactic properties.

generalized quantifier (GQ) The semantic representation of a noun phrase as a set of sets (intensionally, as a property of properties). So for example, the GQs corresponding to (i) 'every student', (ii) 'some students', and (iii) 'Mary' are (i) 'the set of sets S such that S contains all students', (ii) 'the set of sets S such that S contains at least one student', and (iii) 'the set of sets M such that M contains Mary'. Given the GQ analysis of noun phrases, the sentence 'Every student is a liberal' is true if and only if the set of liberals is an element of the set of sets containing all students. This condition holds if and only if every student is a liberal. Corresponding truth conditions apply to predications involving the other GQs cited here.

generalized upper model An ontology provides a consistent conceptualization or modelling scheme for some area of knowledge. There are several proposals for so-called 'top ontologies': these are the most general concepts and organizations that serve to organize more specific areas. The generalized upper model is a top-ontology whose organization and content is motivated solely by grammatical distinctions made by the grammars of several natural languages. It has been used for natural language generation in a variety of languages and is also being experimented with for analysis. It provides a convenient semantic level of representation that is sufficiently close to grammar to allow ready mapping between semantic terms and grammatical terms, but is also sufficiently abstract to relate easily to domain and application knowledge.

generation (i) Automatic production of natural language texts by machine on the basis of some specified semantic, communicative, or syntactic input; (ii) in formal languages, the process of producing the strings that express a given set of meanings or grammatical relations.

generative lexicon A theory of meaning (based on the work of Pustejovsky) in which the meaning of an utterance is determined through interaction of the simple lexical semantic properties of the words used in such a way that novel meanings may be generated. For example, the verb 'enjoy' implies different activities depending on context: to 'enjoy a book' implies reading it, while to 'enjoy a meal' implies eating it. Similarly, according to context, the term 'book' may denote a physical object, or an abstract entity, or something that people read, or something that someone writes.

genus term A more general category or class to which something belongs as a subtype, e.g. 'bird' is the genus term for 'sparrow' and 'hawk'.

Gibbs distribution A log-linear probability distribution originating from statistical physics and used in maximum entropy modelling.

glossing Providing a rough word-by-word translation of a document.

goal In dialogue, the aim of a dialogue participant

goal-oriented In dialogue, pertaining to the achievement of a dialogue goal—as opposed to being purely conversational.

goal-restricted In dialogue, restricted to achieving the goal of the exchange between a human agent and a computer—as opposed to containing conversational elements.

gold standard For a given task, the set of 'correct' answers as created by one or more humans doing the task, used as a standard for evaluating the success of a computer system doing the task.

grammar (i) The whole system and structure of a language (or of languages in general), in particular syntax and morphology, or a systematic analysis of the structure of a particular language; (ii) in the theory of formal grammars, a generating device consisting of a finite nonterminal alphabet, a finite terminal alphabet, an axiom, and a finite set of productions.

grapheme-to-phoneme transformation See **phonetization**.

greeting A type of speech or dialogue act that contains a greeting, e.g. 'Hi', 'Hello', 'Good morning' etc.

half-syllable Half of a syllable; that is, either the syllable-initial portion up to the first half of the syllable nucleus, or the syllable-final portion starting from the second half of the syllable nucleus.

headword A word or phrase that is defined or explained in a dictionary.

heavy syllable A syllable that is not light, i.e. a syllable that has two vowels, or a single long vowel, or a final consonant. Compare **light syllable**.

hidden Markov model (HMM) A random process with hidden states and observable signals, fundamental to most speech recognition systems and many syntactic processing systems. In a Markov model, the states are observable, not hidden; in a Markov process there are no signals, only observable states.

hierarchy An ordered arrangement, typically of concepts in an ontology or other system, with the most general concept at the top and other concepts derived from it as subtypes.

higher-order logic Logic that, in addition to the expressions of first-order logic, contains (i) variables for predicates and other expressions which do not correspond to individuals, and (ii) quantifiers that bind these variables, and so range over objects which are of higher type than individuals. Such logics may contain lambda operators that bind higher-order variables to create higher-order function terms.

historical principles The traditional principles of scholarly lexicography, according to which the oldest meaning of a word (even if obsolete) is placed first, and subsequent meaning developments (including the modern meaning) are traced from it. Failure to appreciate the unstable nature of word meaning and the pervasive influence of historical principles has had a pernicious influence in computational linguistics, leading for example to the erroneous assumption that famous scholarly dictionaries such as the *OED* and Merriam Websters' *Collegiate* are suitable for use as look-up tables for the words and meanings of the modern English language. Compare **corpus-based lexicography**.

homograph Any of a group of two or more words that are spelled identically, even though the meaning and origin are different.

homomorphism Let $A = \langle A_1, f_1, \ldots, f_n \rangle$ and $B = \langle B_1, g_1, \ldots, g_n \rangle$ be algebras where A_1, B_1 are sets, and $f_1, \ldots, f_n$ and $g_1, \ldots, g_n$ are operations on the elements of A_1 and B_1, respectively. A and B are isomorphic iff there is a one-to-one correspondence between their operations, and a function $F: A_1 \to B_1$ such that (i) F is bijective (one-to-one and onto), and (ii) for all $a_1, \ldots, a_n$ in A_1 and all $i \leq n$, $g_i (F (a_1), \ldots, F(a_n)) = F(f_i(a_1, \ldots, a_n))$. A homomorphism $H: A \to B$ is onto and satisfies condition (ii), but it is not necessarily one-to-one. Therefore, in contrast to an isomorphism, H can be a many-to-one mapping of A_1 to B_1.

homophone Any of a group of two or more words that are pronounced identically, even though their spelling and meaning may be different.

human–computer interaction The interaction of people with computer systems, particularly in terms of the interface between a system and a human user.

human–human dialogue Dialogue between two or more human agents, which may or may not be computer-mediated.

human–machine dialogue Dialogue between one or more human agents and a computer system.

human scoring Evaluation of a system's performance by a human.

hybrid system In machine translation, a type of machine translation system that combines rule-based and corpus-based methods.

hypernym A word that has a more general meaning than another word with which it is in a hyponymy relation. Also called **superordinate**. For example, 'bird' is a hypernym of 'sparrow' and 'canary'.

hyponym A word that has a more restricted meaning than another word with which it is in a hyponymy relation. For example, 'sparrow' and 'canary' are hyponyms of 'bird'.

hyponymy relation Unilateral entailment relation between two word meanings, such that one is more general than the other.

illocution The part of an utterance that pertains to the intention of the speaker.

illocutionary act A verbal act by which the speaker of an utterance wants to achieve an effect on the hearer. Also called **speech act**, **dialogue act**.

illocutionary force The effect that a speech or dialogue act has on the hearer.

immediate-context analysis Analysis of the context in which a word is used, in order to find clues to the meaning. For example, in the sentence 'They toasted his memory', the direct object ('memory') identifies a different sense of 'toast' from the direct object in 'They toasted a sandwich'. Immediate-context analysis relates clause structure to statistical preferences. Compare **local grammar**.

implemented A theory or algorithm is said to be implemented if it has been formulated as a program that runs on a computer.

implication Any of various rhetorical devices used by a speaker to create a non-literal meaning. Compare **inference**.

implicature A pragmatic device that enables a hearer to interpret a speaker's use of implication due to the context in which an utterance occurs, on the basis of conversational principles such as Grice's cooperative principle.

incremental generation A particular form of system architecture in which information is passed from one component to the next as soon as it is available; components must therefore be able to work on partial inputs that are provided in unspecified orders.

independence (of events) Two events A and B are independent iff $P(A, B) = P(A).P(B)$

indeterminacy The tendency of linguistic items to resist facile pigeon-holing in ready-made categories. Very often the meaning of a word (other than a referring expression) is indeterminate. The part-of-speech class of certain words (e.g. 'enough', 'else') may also be regarded as indeterminate. Native speakers often disagree about whether certain sentences (typically those invented by linguists for testing purposes) are grammatically well formed or not: to this extent, therefore, syntax can also be indeterminate.

indicative summary A description of what a text is about without giving its content explicitly.

indirect anaphora Nominal anaphora in which anaphors and antecedents are linked by relations such as part-of ('the store ... the food hall ... the tills') or set membership ('the Spice Girls ... Melanie C'). Indirect anaphora is also known as **associative anaphora** or **bridging anaphora**. Compare **direct anaphora**.

inference A mechanism employed by a hearer to deduce non-literal meaning from an utterance. Compare **implication**.

inference-driven generation A language-generation architecture in which the generation process is based on logical deduction. Linguistic information is represented as a set of logical statements, together with a general deduction mechanism that is employed to generate strings. This contrasts with, for example, grammar-driven generation, where it is the grammar that determines what decisions are to be made and when.

inflection (i) The morphological process of adding inflections to base forms of words, as required by syntactic context; (ii) a linguistic element that is added to or alters the base form of a word, as required by particular syntactic contexts. Inflections change the grammatical function of a word but not the part-of-speech category. Typically, they express grammatical concepts such as number (e.g. English plural *-s* with nouns), tense (e.g. English *-ed* with verbs), or comparison (e.g. English *-er*, *-est* with adjectives). Most dictionaries for human use include only irregular inflections, taking the view that regular inflections should be described in a grammar rather than a lexicon. Dictionaries for computational use generally list all inflected forms.

information extraction The automatic identification of selected types of entities, relations, or events in text.

information format A tabular representation for texts in which the elementary sentences underlying each text sentence are aligned to show their structure in terms of sublanguage word classes.

information retrieval The science of finding objects in any media relevant to users' possible queries. For example, information retrieval over text takes a text query and retrieves documents relevant to that query; information retrieval over images might take a query in text or speech and retrieve images, or might take an image as query and retrieve related images.

information system Any system that takes decisions on the basis of a factual state in a world model, where the world model is defined in terms of ontological constraints, actual relations and properties.

informative summary A shortened version of the content of a text.

informativeness The extent to which a text conveys information content, usually related to the preservation of text content under some mapping.

initial tree One of the specified types of elementary trees in a TAG.

initiate (noun) A type of speech or dialogue act whereby a dialogue participant initiates an exchange of information or transaction with another participant: typically a request, suggestion, yes–no question, or wh-question.

initiative In the dialogue management of spoken dialogue systems, a control mechanism according to which what is or can be expressed in a dialogue at a given time depends on which agent in the dialogue currently holds, or is allowed to hold, the initiative: the user (**user initiative**), the system (**system initiative**), or both (**mixed** or **variable initiative**).

input fusion See **modality integration**.

instance-based learning A machine learning method that draws conclusions based on the similarity of an instance to one or more specific examples in a set of labelled training data.

integration The extent to which a component can fit together with other components so as to achieve end-to-end functionality.

intelligent computer-assisted language learning In most writers' views any use of computational linguistics (or intelligent tutoring) in an instructional application will allow it to qualify as 'intelligent'.

intention See **goal**.

interactive system A computer system whose response is dependent at each turn on input from a human 'partner'.

inter-annotator agreement In corpus annotation, the degree to which human annotators agree when performing a particular annotation task.

inter-sentential segmentation The process of grouping sentences and paragraphs into discourse topics.

interlingua A language-neutral text representation used in machine translation.

intervocalic Intervocalic consonant is a consonant between two vowels.

intra-sentential segmentation The process of segmenting linguistic groups within a sentence.

intrinsic and extrinsic evaluation metrics An **intrinsic metric** measures output quality as it stands; an **extrinsic metric** measures the usefulness of the output in helping the user perform a task.

intrinsic evaluation See **intrinsic and extrinsic evaluation metrics**.

introduce (noun) A type of speech or dialogue act whereby a dialogue participant introduces himself to the other, typically following a greeting, e.g. '(This is) XYZ speaking'.

inverse document frequency (idf) A measurement of the occurrence of a word within a collection of documents in inverse relation to the number of documents in the collection.

IPA Abbreviation for **International Phonetic Alphabet**, a writing system designed to make possible a one-to-one relationship between a speech sound and written symbol for any language in the world. Transcriptions of speech sounds in IPA may be **broad** (phonemic) or **narrow** (phonetic).

is-a **relation** A unilateral entailment relation between two concepts, such that one is a hyponym of the other.

island parsing Bi-directional processing of input, starting at one or more initial 'islands'.

joint action model A type of dialogue management model that stresses the collaborative effort that the user and the system make together in order to achieve a goal in a spoken dialogue system.

joint probability The probability of two or more events occurring.

KIF Abbreviation for **Knowledge Interchange Format**, a standardized knowledge representation formalism.

knowledge base A database containing knowledge representations that can support an information system or an NLP program or application.

knowledge-based machine translation A method of machine translation in which linguistic information is enriched by ontological knowledge about the domain so as to achieve a better quality of translation.

knowledge representation system A formally defined system to express relations and properties in a knowledge base and to enable operations such as inferencing, generalization, classification, and inheritance.

KWIC index An index of words or other items in a corpus, presented as **keyword in context**. The keyword is usually centred in each line of text, which is a specified selection of a certain amount of text, typically 50 characters to the left and 50 to the right of the key word.

lambda calculus A universal model of computation, used widely in semantics and computer science to model the functional behaviour of linguistic expressions. Any computation in a Turing machine can also be expressed in the lambda calculus.

lambda operator A binding operator that binds a variable, taking scope over an expression to make that operation a function. The resulting *lambda expression* can be *lambda reduced* by substituting variables with argument instances.

language (i) The system of communication used by human beings in general or a particular communicative system used by a particular community. A language may be natural (e.g. English or Bulgarian) or formal (e.g. a computer programming language or a logical system); (ii) in the theory of formal grammars and languages, any subset of the infinite set of strings over an alphabet.

language guesser See **language identification program**.

language identification program A program that identifies the language in which a text is written. Also called **language guesser**.

language model In statistical NLP, a model used to estimate the probability of word sequences.

latent semantic indexing In information retrieval, a technique whereby queries and documents are projected into a space with latent semantic dimensions associated with concepts, based on the theory of singular value decomposition.

lazy learning See **exemplar-based learning**.

lemma The canonical form of a word, usually the base form, taken as being representative of all the various forms of a morphological paradigm.

lemmatization The process of grouping the inflected forms of a word together under a base form, or of recovering the base form from an inflected form, e.g. grouping the inflected forms 'run', 'runs', 'running', 'ran' under the base form 'run'.

letter-to-sound transformation See **phonetization**.

lexical anchor The lexical item(s) associated with an elementary tree of a tree-adjoining grammar.

lexical entry A word or phrase in a lexicon, used as a peg on which to hang information about part of speech, subcategorization, meaning, pronunciation, links to related terms, and/or any of various other kinds of information.

lexical noun phrase anaphora Anaphora in which the anaphors are definite noun phrases (i.e. definite descriptions or proper names).

lexical semantic network A set of terms defined solely in terms of relations to each other.

lexical semantic relation Semantic relations between lexicalizations in a language.

lexical transducer A finite-state transducer for morphological analysis and generation. It maps inflected forms into the corresponding lexical forms (= lemmas), and vice versa.

lexical variability The property of words according to which a single word may be used with basically the same meaning in many different contexts, with different implications. For example, the verb *file* in *filing a story*, *filing a lawsuit*, and *filing a flight plan* has basically the same meaning ('place on record') but different implications.

lexicalization The process of generating an appropriate lexical item for given semantic content—typically a phase of the automatic text generation process.

lexicalized tree-adjoining grammar A tree-adjoining grammar where each elementary tree has at least one lexical anchor.

lexicography The compilation of an inventory of the lexicon of a language, typically including a statement about some or all of the following features with regard to each lexical entry: orthography, pronunciation, inflected forms, word class (part of speech), meaning(s) or translations, usage, phraseology, and history or origin.

lexicon (i) See dictionary; (ii) in speech recognition, see **pronunciation lexicon**.

light syllable A syllable that has a single short vowel and no following consonants. Compare **heavy syllable**.

local ambiguity packing The representation of a set of constituents of the same type covering the same segment of an input text as a single entity.

local grammar The syntagmatic properties of each individual word in a language. Compare **immediate-context analysis**.

locution In the terminology of J. L. Austin, the verbal act closest to the literal use and form of an utterance. Compare **illocution**, **perlocution**.

long-distance dependency Correlation between words or phrases that are separated by an unbounded amount of intervening material.

low-quality MT Translation produced by MT system at a standard well below that of human translation and perhaps barely intelligible without good knowledge of the subject matter.

machine learning The use of computing systems to improve the performance of a procedure or system automatically in the light of experience.

machine-readable dictionary (MRD) A dictionary (typically one originally compiled for human users) that is in the form of an electronic text. MRDs often contain additional information for NLP purposes which is not present in the paper version. A distinction is sometimes made between **machine-readable dictionaries** and **machine-tractable dictionaries**; the latter are in a logical form suitable for computational uses beyond the publisher's primary purpose of driving a typesetting machine.

machine-tractable dictionary See **machine-readable dictionary**.

machine translation (MT) The use of the computer with or without human assistance to translate texts between natural languages.

macroplanning The phase of automatic natural language production that determines overall text structure and content.

mal-rules Rules inappropriate to the true structure of a language, but which describe the systematic errors that learners make. They are used in some techniques for spotting and diagnosing learners' errors.

Markov model A random process with observable states and observable signals. In a hidden Markov model, the states are hidden, not observable; in a Markov process there are no signals, only observable states.

Markov process A type of random process with observable states; equivalent to a probabilistic finite-state automaton.

mature product A system or function that has a sufficiently high standard of performance and robustness so that it can be packaged and marketed as a product.

maxim of relation One of the sub-principles of Grice's co-operative principle, stating that participants in a dialogue should always be relevant in their contributions.

maxim of manner One of the sub-principles of Grice's co-operative principle, stating that participants in a dialogue should avoid obscurity or ambiguity, and be brief and orderly in their contributions.

maxim of quality One of the sub-principles of Grice's co-operative principle, stating that participants in a dialogue should try to make their contributions truthful.

maxim of quantity One of the sub-principles of Grice's co-operative principle, stating that participants in a dialogue should give the right amount of information, no more and no less.

meaning component An abstract semantic feature that is used to express a more systematic semantic property of a word, e.g. *causative, resultative* for verbs, *mass* or *countable* for nouns.

meaning potential The potential that a word has to make meanings in combination with other words, typically expressed as a set of components (not necessarily all mutually compatible), different combinations of which are activated in different contexts. Compare **generative lexicon**.

meaning representation language A formal language used to represent the essential meaning of sentences or utterances.

media coordination The process of tailoring different media to each other during a generation process, including subtasks such as media allocation, the generation of cross-media references, and the determination of spatial and temporal layout.

medium Any carrier of information, which may be a physical material (e.g. paper or CD-ROM), a physical device (e.g. screen, loudspeaker, microphone, or printer), or an information type (e.g. graphics, text, or video).

memoization Use by an algorithm of a procedure by which it keeps track of the solution to subproblems and re-uses them to solve larger problems. Also known as **dynamic programming**.

memory-based learning See **instance-based learning**.

microplanning The phase of automatic natural language generation that determines the precise form of sentences given communicative and contextual goals. Also called **sentence planning**.

mikroKosmos A proprietary multilingual lexical knowledge base, built for machine translation.

mildly context-sensitive grammars A class of grammars whose generative power lies between that of context-free grammars and context-sensitive grammars.

minimal finite-state automaton A finite-state automaton such that there is no automaton that contains the same paths and has fewer states.

mixed initiative A concept in spoken dialogue systems, allowing both the user and the system to take the initiative.

modality See **mode**.

modality integration The process of transforming input in different modalities into a common representation format. Also called **input fusion**.

mode In a multimedia system, any of the channels by which information is transmitted (e.g. visual, auditory, haptic, or olfactory).

model theory A theory of semantic interpretation that specifies meaning as a relation between the expressions of a language and appropriate types of entities defined in terms of the basic sets of objects of the model. Tarski (1936) provided the foundations of classical model theory by giving a recursive definition of the predicate 'true-in-L' for first-order languages L.

monitor corpus A corpus that enables diachronic research by continually growing over time. While a monitor corpus can operate with respect to an overall sampling frame, monitor corpora tend to de-emphasize the role of sampling frame specification in favour of a large volume of material which is continually supplemented over time.

monolingual corpus A corpus in which all of the texts belong to the same language.

monolingual dictionary A dictionary in which the definitions belong to the same language as the headwords.

morph The actual realization of an abstract morpheme as part of a word.

morpheme Any of the basic building blocks of morphology, defined as the smallest units in language to which a meaning may be assigned or, alternatively, as the minimal units of grammatical analysis. Morphemes are abstract entities expressing basic semantic or syntactic features.

morphology The internal structures and forms of words, or the branch of linguistics that studies these.

morphophonology The part of linguistics that is concerned with the influence of phonology on the realization of morphemes.

morphotactics The part of morphology that is concerned with identifying the structural constraints on the composition of morphs in word formation.

MT Abbreviation of **machine translation**.

MUC Abbreviation for **Message Understanding Conference**, any of a series of conferences organized by the US Government for the evaluation of information extraction systems.

multi-component TAG A tree-adjoining grammar in which the elementary objects are sets of trees.

multi-document summary A summary that describes the contents of more than one document.

multi-engine MT system An MT system where input is processed in parallel by different algorithms ('engines'—for example, traditional rule-based MT, EBMT, knowledge-based MT) and the output compared and reconciled to get the best possible result.

multi-word lexeme A group of words whose meaning is only understood when the words are taken together, e.g. 'call up', 'take [something] to heart', or 'get the message'. Also called **multi-word expression**.

multilingual dictionary A dictionary that provides translations of words in one language into two or more other languages.

multilingual system (i) An NLP system capable of operating in two or more languages; (ii) a machine translation program that translates from one source language into more than one target language. Compare **bilingual system**.

multimedia system A system that can analyse and/or generate information in several different media (e.g. text, sound, pictures) or provide support in accessing digital libraries of multiple media. Also called **multimodal system**.

multimodal system See **multimedia system**.

mutual knowledge Knowledge that all participants in a dialogue can be assumed to have a priori.

n-gram A sequence of n tokens.

name tagger A program for identifying and classifying names in text.

named entity recognition The automatic identification and classification of names in text.

named entity task The task of automatic identification and classification of names in text, as featured in MUC.

natural language generation The automatic production of natural language texts.

natural language interaction An exchange between a human and a computer system, in which the human is allowed to formulate requests in natural language, in spoken or written form, as stand-alone sentences or in the context of a dialogue, and the computer converts this input into machine-tractable form. Natural language interfaces and spoken dialogue systems are typical examples of such a communication situation.

natural language interaction system A computer system that enables a user to carry out various tasks (e.g. accessing information in a database or navigating virtual worlds) by formulating his/her requests in natural language.

natural language interface An aspect of a natural language interaction system in which the user's requests are processed more or less as isolated sentences. User requests are usually typed on a keyboard. Compare **spoken dialogue systems**.

natural sublanguage A sublanguage that has evolved spontaneously as a means of communication among domain experts in a recurrent situation or set of similar situations; characterized by the co-occurrence of distinctive word classes in the most frequent sentence types.

nesting See **embedding**.

network A directed graph that consists of states and labelled arcs. See **finite-state automaton**.

NLP Abbreviation for **natural language processing** (i.e. by computer).

nominal anaphora Anaphora that arises when a **referring expression**—pronoun, definite noun phrase, or proper name—has a non-pronominal noun phrase as antecedent. This most important and frequently occurring class of anaphora has been researched and covered most extensively, and is best understood in the NLP literature.

non-indigenous minority language A language spoken by a minority in a given location (e.g. migrants) and which is not local to that region. (It may indeed be a major language elsewhere on the planet.)

non-segmented language A language whose words are written directly adjacent to each other, without spaces or punctuation.

norm Any of the ways in which a word is ordinarily used (*norms of use*), associated with different standard meanings (*norms of belief*).

normal phraseological context The syntagmatic context in which a word is normally found. Corpus linguistics has demonstrated that ordinary usage is more patterned than previously believed, so that the normal phraseological contexts of a word can be computed probabilistically.

NP (non-deterministic polynomial) An algorithm is in the class NP if it can be computed in polynomial time with a non-deterministic Turing machine.

NP-complete A problem is NP-complete if it is both NP-hard and in NP.

NP-hard A problem is NP-hard if every other problem in NP can be reduced to it in polynomial time.

nucleus The most central node among a collection of nodes organized at a single level in a rhetorical structure tree as defined by rhetorical structure theory (RST). Non-nuclear nodes are called **satellites**.

Ontolingua A standardized knowledge representation formalism developed at Stanford University.

ontology An inventory of the objects or processes in a domain, together with a specification of some or all of the relations that hold among them, generally arranged as a hierarchy.

open-domain question answering Question answering that provides answers to questions regardless of the domain, and more importantly, without matching the questions against predetermined lists of questions.

operational prototype An early version of a system that provides end-to-end performance, but lacking the robustness, performance, or support expected from a commercial product.

overacceptance The error of returning too many parses for a grammatical input.

overgeneration The error of returning one or more complete parses for an ungrammatical input.

P (polynomial) An algorithm is in class P if it can be computed in polynomial time on a deterministic Turing machine (see **tractable**).

paradigm A set of words or other linguistic items that provide mutually exclusive choices in a particular syntactic role in a language. For example, the set of English determiners constitute a paradigm set: we can say 'a book' or 'his book', but not 'a his book'. One kind of paradigm consists of all the different inflected forms of a word, as set out in a morphological table. Another kind of paradigm consists of all the words having the same basic part of speech and meaning. For example, in the sentence 'He saw an X on the floor', X represents the paradigm set of all concrete nouns denoting visible objects.

paradigmatic Denoting the relationship that characterizes a group of words that form mutually exclusive choices in constructing a linguistically well-formed utterance. For example, all nouns are in paradigmatic relation with each other insofar as they compete for the role of head of a noun phrase. Compare **syntagmatic**.

parallel corpora Two or more corpora in which one corpus contains data produced by native speakers of a language while the other corpus/corpora have that original translated into another/a range of other languages.

parameter vector See **frame**.

paraphrase The situation in which two different strings express essentially the same predicate–argument relations, for example an active sentence and its passive counterpart.

parse forest A compact representation of a set of complete parses, typically using local ambiguity packing and subtree sharing.

parsing The process of determining the structure that a given grammar assigns to a particular string within its language.

part-of-speech Any of the basic grammatical classes of words, such as noun, verb, adjective, and preposition.

part-of-speech tag A label specifying a part of speech.

part-of-speech tagger A computer program for assigning labels for grammatical classes of words.

part-of-speech tagging Assigning labels for grammatical classes of words through a computer program.

passive edge In parsing a representation of a completely recognized constituent of a linguistic structure.

performative See performative verb.

performative verb A type of verb that allows the user to perform an action simply by uttering it, e.g. to name something, to make a promise, etc.

perlocution According to the philosopher J. L. Austin, the verbal act that relates to the effect of an utterance on the hearer. Compare **locution** and **illocution**.

phone An elementary unit of speech that generally corresponds to a phoneme, but may also correspond to an allophone.

phoneme Any of the perceptually distinct speech sounds that, together, constitute the sound system of a language. Two sounds that are in fact phonetically distinct (see **allophone**) may be perceived as identical in one language but as different phonemes in another language.

phonetics The study of speech sounds, including both the means of articulation (**articulatory phonetics**) and reception (**acoustic phonetics**).

phonetization Computation of the sequence of phonemes required to pronounce a word, phrase, or sentence. Alternative terms used are **letter-to-sound transformation**, or **grapheme-to-phoneme transformation**.

phonology The branch of linguistics that is concerned with the systematic study of the sounds used in language, their internal structure, and their composition into syllables, words, and phrases.

phrase A sequence of words that can be processed as a single unit in a text.

phrase structure A formal representation that indicates the hierarchical arrangement of phrases that make up a sentence, usually presented as a tree whose nodes are labelled with the categories (e.g. NP, VP) that the phrases belong to.

phrase-structure grammar A type of grammar where no restriction is imposed on the form of its productions.

pipeline generation architecture In language generation, a particular type of system architecture in which information is passed from one component to the next lower component without any feedback, interaction, or backtracking. A typical chain is goal setting, deep generation (content planning, content structuring), surface generation (word choice, syntactic structure), and articulation (generation of speech).

plan-based approach A type of dialogue management model that assumes that the cooperation between agents in a spoken dialogue system is regulated by a relatively fixed set of actions and goals, which are executed in a structured way.

plan library The knowledge component of a natural-language generation system, where information about the plans available for achieving particular communicative goals resides.

plan recognition In natural language interaction systems, the process whereby the system attempts to infer how what the users say relates to their goals, plans, and beliefs.

planning The process of trying to achieve specified goals by means of a set of actions. In computational language generation, the entire process is organized in such a way that, given some goal, executing the associated actions will lead to the achievement of that goal. There are various algorithms for carrying out planning developed within AI. The simplest is hierarchical top-down planning, which begins with a goal and then recursively seeks plan operators that fit the current situation, thus moving progressively towards the goal. In natural language generation, the goals typically correspond to speech and the actions to be performed correspond to linguistic utterances or propositions.

polysemy The phenomenon of words having multiple meanings.

portability The ease with which a system can be revised or adapted in order to work in a new domain or application area.

position method In text summarization, a method for identifying important sentences of a text based on their position (first sentence, first paragraph etc.), in texts with regular structure.

post-edit measure The cost (typically measured in numbers of keystrokes) required to edit machine output into a form acceptable to a human.

post-editing The processes of revising translations produced by a machine translation system.

pragmatics The branch of linguistics that deals with language use and meaning in context—as opposed to syntax and semantics, which deal more with the formal aspects of language.

pre-editing The processes of preparing texts for a machine translation system, by reducing ambiguities and simplifying syntactic structures, often involving the use of a controlled language.

precision The number of correct responses divided by the total number of actual responses.

predicate–argument relations The information that a sentence conveys about the action of an event (the predicate) and how the participants in the event (the arguments) relate to that action.

preference semantics A theory of language understanding (due to Wilks) which treats selectional restrictions as looser constraints which, when broken, can drive interpretation processes so as to preserve overall coherence.

pre-processor A software program that recognizes complex tokens such as dates, measures, telephone numbers etc.

primitive planning action The basic actions where hierarchical planning processes, as typically used in natural language generation systems, bottom out: the actions that can be directly executed, performed, or realized.

principle of compositionality The principle, originally stated by Frege, that the meaning of an expression E is computed as the value of a function whose arguments are the meanings of E's syntactic constituents. Therefore, the meaning of E is entirely determined by the meanings of its constituents.

principle of relevance A principle expressed by Sperber and Wilson on the basis of Grice's theory of conversational co-operation, explicating the way in which an interpreter makes sense of what is said, by a trade-off between largeness of contextual effects and smallness of processing effort.

probabilistic models In information retrieval, a series of methods that rely on the notion of guessing most likely events, or probabilities of events. Similarity is determined by probabilistic methods.

probability density function A function giving the density of probability mass at each point; the continuous counterpart of a probability function.

probability distribution A distribution that determines the mathematical properties of a random variable; it is the cumulative of the probability (density) function.

probability function A function that gives the probability mass at each point.

probability measure A function from a set of events, i.e. the subsets of the sample space, to the set of real numbers in [0,1].

problem complexity The complexity of the best algorithm for solving a problem.

processing effort The amount of effort that a language user has to make in order to interpret an utterance according to its context.

production A rewriting rule in a grammar.

pronominal anaphora Anaphora where the anaphors are personal, possessive, or reflexive pronouns.

pronunciation (i) The particular way in which a language user articulates the speech sounds of an utterance; (ii) in a human-user dictionary, a transcription of the standard pronunciation of a word in the International Phonetic Alphabet or some more or less regular form of spelling rewrite. Electronic dictionaries sometimes offer realization by a speech synthesizer of the pronunciation of a target word. Some speech synthesizers in turn utilize systematic phonetic transcriptions in a dictionary-like form.

prototype An idealized object or concept that represents the best example of its kind. Compare **norm**.

psycholinguistics The branch of linguistics concerned with the correlation between linguistic behaviour and the psychological processes thought to underline that behaviour.

pushdown automaton A recognizing device consisting of a finite alphabet of pushdown letters, a finite set of states, a finite alphabet of input letters, a transition function, an initial letter, an initial state and a finite set of final states.

qualia Plural noun (singular *quale*). In the generative lexicon theory of Pustejovsky, the semantic features that affect the relationship between a word's normal syntactic uses and its meaning. The basic qualia are the *formal* (what kind of thing is it?), the *constitutive* (what's it made of?), the *telic* (what's it for?), and the *agentive* (where or how did it originate?). For example, qualia of 'book' include formal=[[Physical Object]], constitutive=[[Paper]], telic=[[Reading]], and agentive=[[Writing]]. The sentence 'she enjoyed the book' activates the telic and implies 'she enjoyed *reading* the book'. The sentence 'she dropped the book' activates the formal and implies 'she dropped the *physical object* (book)'. The sentence 'George has finished the book' is ambiguous between telic and agentive: George may have been reading the book or writing it.

quantifier storage A computational procedure for placing the generalized quantifier representation of a quantified NP in a set (the quantifier store) that is associated with successively larger phrases in the sentence that contain the syntactic position of the stored NP. New GQs are added to the store as their NPs are encountered in the interpretation process. A GQ is released from the store and applied to the interpretation of a constituent that corresponds to a predicate in order to yield a scoped interpretation of the quantified NP. The store must be empty by the time the interpretation of the highest sentence is computed. Quantifier storage was first proposed by Cooper (1976) and (1983).

query-based summary Instead of summarizing the text from the author's perspective, a query-based summary focuses on some aspect of interest to the user, which the user enters as a query.

question answering (QA) The process of providing answer(s) to question(s) on large collections of on-line documents, using NLP techniques.

question processing Set of techniques implemented in QA systems that enable the interpretation of the questions.

random process A sequence of random variables.

random variable Formally, a function from the sample space to the set of real numbers R; informally, an abstraction of a method for making an observation.

rational expression See **regular expression**.

rational language See **regular expression**.

rational relation See **regular expression**.

reading comprehension A test method that requires the subject (or system) to read a document and answer questions based on the content of the document.

recall The number of correct responses divided by the total number of possibly correct responses.

recognition In the theory of formal grammars and languages, the process of determining whether a particular string belongs to the language (of a given grammar) accepted by a given automaton.

recording channel The means by which an audio signal is recorded (direct microphone, telephone, radio etc.).

reduction A mapping of one problem into another problem.

referring expression See **anaphora**.

regression testing Testing the effects of changes to a program on different data sets, so as to ensure that improvements made to address problems in one data set do not result in loss of performance on other data sets.

regular expression An expression that describes a set of strings (= a regular language) or a set of ordered pairs of strings (= a regular relation). Every language or relation described by a regular expression can be represented by a *finite-state automaton*. There are many regular expression formalisms. The most common operators are *concatenation, union, intersection, complement* (*=negation*), *iteration* and *composition*. Also called **rational expression**.

regular grammar A type of grammar where every production is of any of the forms $A \rightarrow wB$ or $A \rightarrow w$, where A, B are nonterminal letters and w is any terminal string.

regular language See **regular expression**.

regular relation See **regular expression**.

reject (noun) A type of speech or dialogue act whereby a dialogue participant rejects a proposal made by the other participant, e.g. 'No, thanks'.

relevance An important principle in pragmatics, according to which a hearer interprets a speaker's utterance, in part on the basis of its contextual impact. Relevance theory is largely based on Grice's **maxim of relation** and Sperber and Wilson's **principle of relevance**.

relevance assessment The act of determining whether information (e.g. a document or answer) is relevant to some information need (e.g. a request for information).

relevance theory See **principle of relevance**.

replacement An operation on pairs of strings that involves systematic substitutions, deletions, and insertions. Some regular expression formalisms include a replacement operator.

request (noun) A type of speech or dialogue act whereby a dialogue participant makes a request to the other participant. Requests can be further sub-divided into general requests, requests for information, request for directives etc.

research prototype A system put together for the purpose of demonstrating proof-of-concept or feasibility.

restriction In finite state processing, a language of strings that all satisfy a certain constraint. Some regular expression formalisms include a restriction operator.

reversibility The development of formalisms and representations which can be used (in principle) either for analysis or for generation of a specific language; or (in the case of machine translation) for the processes of translation between two languages in either direction.

rheme The part of a sentence that says something about the theme. Compare **theme**.

rhetorical predicate Any of the distinct kinds of rhetorical structures that may be employed for structuring texts, typically in natural language generation systems.

rhetorical structure theory (RST) A theory of text structure based on communicative goals. RST describes a text by labelling the role that each element or clause plays within the whole. A minimal text is a structured entity (schema), composed of three elements (clauses): a nucleus, a satellite (the former being more prominent than the latter), and a relation. Since schemata can be nested, the description of a text is formally speaking a tree.

rule-based machine translation Machine translation based on linguistic rule systems.

rule induction A machine learning method that automatically acquires knowledge in the form of rules through analysis of a set of labelled training data.

sample space A set of possible outcomes; a set of things that can possibly happen.

satellite Within any single level of structure in a rhetorical structure tree as defined by rhetorical structure theory (RST), one element may be singled out as being most important—the nucleus. The remaining elements are called satellites. They refer to text spans or nodes in the text structure that fulfil more of a supporting role for the text being described.

schema (plural *schemata*) A semi-fixed pattern of text structure. Schemata describe text as having particular constituents, which may have particular properties concerning further substructure, their linguistic realization, and the particular information that that part of a text is to contain. Schemata are commonly used in natural language generation for texts that are not as flexible as those planned using a model such as rhetorical structure theory.

scope ambiguity Ambiguity due to the interaction of two or more quantifiers.

second language acquisition The learning of a second or subsequent language. The term *acquisition* is preferred by people who wish to emphasize the role of unconscious, automatic processes in learning.

second language learning The learning of a second or subsequent language in a country where that language is spoken, i.e. in a situation where there is typically a great deal of natural interaction in the new language. Compare **foreign language learning**.

segment (i) (Verb) the act of splitting up a dialogue into utterance units; (ii) (noun) any of the subunits into which a text may be divided; (iii) (noun) a unit of sound in phonetics; (iv) (noun) an alternative term for **utterance unit**, best avoided as it can easily be confused with (ii) or (iii).

segmentation Determination of segment boundaries, typically by topic or 'story' for broadcast news.

segmented languages Languages that typically have delimiters (white space) between words.

selectional constraints The semantic limitations that a given word imposes on the choice of other words in a syntagmatic relation with it. For example, the verb 'sleep' normally applies only to animals and people. Also called **selectional restrictions**.

selectional preferences The set of words that co-occur typically or most often in a syntagmatic relation with a given word.

selectional restrictions See **selectional constraints**.

semantic feature Any of a set of meaning components that are assigned to a word to explain the syntactic structures in which it can occur.

semantic frame In the work of Fillmore and Atkins, the prototypical meaning and use of a group of words (for example, verbs of perception or verbs of motion), expressed in relation to the case roles of the verb's arguments and other frame elements. The meaning of individual verbs within a group is contrasted with that of others by differences in the frame elements, for example *manner* of motion in the *move* frame: *run* = fast, *creep* = slow.

semanticization The process of interpreting non-linguistic data or knowledge representation entities in linguistic semantic terms prior to expression using automatic natural language generation techniques.

semantics The study of linguistic meaning.

sentence boundary disambiguation See **sentence splitting**.

sentence splitting The process of identifying sentence boundaries.

sequentiable A finite-state transducer is sequentiable if it is functional (= unambiguous) in a given direction of application and if it can be converted into an equivalent sequential transducer.

sequential A finite-state transducer is sequential in a given direction of application just in case, for any symbol in the input alphabet, each state contains at most one matching arc.

shallow parsing Syntactic analysis of a text that recognizes only certain selected syntactic structures, e.g. a verb and its direct object, or a prepositional phrase independently of its attachment. Compare **chunk**.

shared knowledge See mutual knowledge.

simple automaton Finite-state automaton that represents a regular language or an identity relation; an automaton whose arcs are labelled by a single symbol. See **finite-state automaton**.

simulated annealing An optimization algorithm analogous to the physical process of strengthening metals by slow cooling. Although not guaranteed to find the optimal solution, simulated annealing has been shown to find solutions to NP-hard problems which cannot be significantly improved upon.

software life-cycle The evolution of a system's software from research through various prototyping phases to a product, which, typically, will then continue to undergo maintenance, including revisions and bug fixes.

sound system The network of phonemes and suprasegmental features that constitute the phonological inventory of a given language.

source language The language of the original text to be translated in a machine translation system.

speaker-dependent system A system for accepting spoken input that has to be trained on the voice of each new user.

speaker-independent system A system for accepting spoken input that does not need to be trained on the voice of each new user.

speech acts See **illocutionary act, dialogue act**.

speech recognition Transcription of the speech signal into a sequence of words.

spoken corpus A corpus that seeks to represent naturally occurring spoken language. While this could in principle be simply a collection of tape recordings, it is much more common to find that such material has been orthographically transcribed. It may also be that the material has been phonemically transcribed either in addition to, or instead of, an orthographic transcription, sometimes with suprasegmental markings.

spoken dialogue system A natural language interaction system where requests of the human user are spoken and are seen as parts of an evolving dialogue. Compared to natural language interfaces, spoken dialogue systems place greater emphasis on the analysis of the overall dialogue and its relation to the user's intentions, often employing a more shallow analysis of individual sentences.

spoken language MT Machine translation of speech, as opposed to (written) text.

spontaneous speech Speech that is formulated freely without the use of written cues or any careful preparation (e.g. ordinary conversation, face to face or on the phone).

statistical MT A method of machine translation in which the most probable translation is deduced on the basis of the statistics of patterns deduced from a parallel corpus.

stochastic process See **random process**.

stochastic TAG TAG associated with a probability model.

string Any sequence of letters from an alphabet, including numerals, punctuation marks, and spaces.

strong generative capacity The set of all structural descriptions characterized by a grammar.

subcategorization Grammatical classification of a word according to the classes of words it combines with in regular patterns. For example, verbs may be transitive or intransitive, and may in their direct object position require animates or inanimates.

subcategorization frame A pattern or template indicating which other types of words a given word regularly combines with, in specific positions. Compare **valence**.

subject variability The inherent differences of human subjects when performing a given task, whether due to experience, health, intelligence, background, or other factors.

subjective grading Grading the performance of a system by a human along a discrete scale.

sublanguage A proper subset of expressions in a natural or artificial language which exhibits some systematic, i.e. 'language-like' behaviour.

sublanguage grammar A characterization of the sentences of a sublanguage in terms of classes of words having similar co-occurrence (and hence similar domain reference) in a representative corpus. A sublanguage grammar may also be used to characterize text structure in terms of sentence types.

sublanguage information pattern A semantic interpretation of a pattern of word co-occurrence in a sublanguage.

subsumption (i) In parsing, a relation between two feature structures fs_1 and fs_2 such that fs_1 subsumes fs_2 iff the value of every feature in fs_1 subsumes the value of that feature in fs_2, and all paths that are reentrant in fs_1 are also reentrant in fs_2; (ii) in ontologies, a relation between two concepts c_1 and c_2 such that c_1 subsumes c_2 iff all properties that are true of c_1 are also true of c_2 but there is a set of properties true of c_2 that are not necessarily true of c_1.

subtree sharing Representing a sub-analysis only once even if it forms part of more than one higher level analysis.

summarization Condensing text in order to produce a summary of its information content in a manner sensitive to the application or user's needs.

summary A summary is a text that is produced from one or more texts, that contains a significant portion of the information in the original text(s), and that is no longer than half of the original text(s).

superordinate See **hypernym.**

surface form The form of a word as found in written text, e.g. 'sung' is one of the surface forms of 'sing'.

surface generator A generation component, or part of a generation component, that is responsible for turning a shallow semantic specification of some kind into a surface string.

surface structure In transformational grammar, a tree structure that represents the actual order of words and phrases in a sentence, as opposed to a deep structure which places the words and phrases in canonical positions. Surface structures are called **constituent structures** in lexical functional grammar.

synonym A lexical item that has the same meaning as another lexical item.

synset A set of one or more words that are considered to be synonyms in some or all contexts.

syntagmatic Denoting the relationship among words or other linguistic items that are put together in sequence to create linguistic structures. All the words in a well-formed sentence are in a syntagmatic relation with one another. Compare **paradigmatic.**

syntax The way that superficial word and phrase configurations of a language express meaningful predicate–argument relations.

syntax–semantics interface The level(s) of syntactic structure to which principles of semantic interpretation apply to generate a semantic representation.

TAG Abbreviation for **tree-adjoining grammar.**

tag A grammatical label, typically one attached to a word in context, expressing its part of speech and inflection, or in some cases semantic or other information.

tag set (i) The set of labels (which are usually part of a mark-up language) used to tag a text for computational processing. Compare **annotation**; (ii) the set of XML or other labels used to structure a dictionary entry systematically. Compare **embedding.**

tagging Assignment of tags to words or expressions in a text.

target language The language into which a text is (to be) translated in a machine translation system.

target word The headword or entry aimed at by a cross-reference in a dictionary or other reference work.

task difficulty The complexity of a given task, often expressed in terms of the number of choices a system must make, or the score that a system would get by chance—for example sorting into two bins has a 50 per cent success rate by chance, whereas sorting into ten bins has only a 10 per cent success rate by chance.

task-driven Denoting a type of dialogue in which the participants aim to solve a specific task, the nature of which is likely to influence the structure and content of the dialogue itself.

task management The act of maintaining communication between users in order to achieve a specific task.

task-oriented In dialogue, denoting a procedure or type of language that is geared towards achieving a specific task, rather than to maintain social interaction.

task success The correct completion of a task by a system.

taxonomy A network of transitive and disjunctive *subtype* or *subsumption* relations with the purpose of classifying.

teaching English as a foreign language Teaching English in a country where English is not normally spoken.

teaching English as a second language Teaching English in a country where English is normally spoken.

technology-based evaluation Evaluation based on the performance (speed, throughput, accuracy) of the underlying technology, rather than on how the user interacts with the system.

technology life-cycle The evolution from research through prototyping to development and product.

term A lexical unit, typically one validated for entry in an application-oriented terminological resource describing the vocabulary of a specialized subject field.

term acquisition Automatic discovery of previously unrecognized terms in corpora.

term frequency (tf) A measurement of the frequency of a word or term within a particular document. Term frequency reflects how well that term describes the document contents.

term recognition Automatic recognition of term and variant occurrences in corpora.

term spotting Extraction of occurrences of terms or variants from text documents.

terminology management The computer-based processes of creating, maintaining, and searching multilingual databases of terminology.

test suites A set of tests designed to cover a range of phenomena or tasks that a system must be able to perform; for example, for parsing, a system must demonstrate that it can handle coordination, comparatives, relative clauses, etc.

text categorization The process of making decisions about whether a document is a member of a given class or category, e.g. in news, sports vs. finance, or in literature, poetry vs. prose.

text compression Text compression is a technique by which sentences or sets of sentences are automatically merged and shortened by dropping out certain parts of them.

text data mining A process of exploratory data analysis using text that leads to the discovery of heretofore unknown information, or to answers to questions for which the answer is not currently known.

text retrieval conference (TREC) An ongoing series of conferences, started in 1991, focused on evaluating systems that retrieve information (as documents, partial documents, or smaller segments) in response to an information request.

text-to-speech synthesis The production of natural sounding speech automatically from a text in electronic format.

text-to-speech synthesizer A machine (hardware or software) designed to perform text-to-speech synthesis.

tf Abbreviation for **term frequency**.

theme The part of a sentence that identifies what the sentence is about. Compare **rheme**.

tokenization The process of segmenting text into linguistic units such as words, punctuation, numbers, alphanumerics etc.

tokenizer A software program that performs text tokenization and determines boundaries for individual tokens (words, numbers, punctuation) in text.

topic In text summarization, a particular subject that the text discusses.

topic identification Identification of the main topic (often from a list of previously defined topics) in a segment of text or recorded speech.

tractable A problem is said to be tractable if it can be computed in polynominal time on a deterministic Turing machine.

transducer Finite-state automaton that represents a regular non-identity relation, an automaton in which at least one arc label consists of a pair of non-identical symbols. See **finite-state automaton**.

transfer A stage of machine translation, intermediate between the analysis of a source language text and the generation of a target language text, in which lexical items and syntactic structures are converted from one language into another.

transfer system A type of machine translation program with three distinct stages of **analysis**, **transfer**, and **generation**, where (in principle) any of the analysis programs for a source language can be used together with any of the generation programs of a target language.

transformation Any of the rules that apply in a transformational grammar to convert the deep structure of a sentence into a corresponding surface structure. Transformations take phrase-structure trees as input and produce modified phrase-structure trees as output.

translation memory A translator's tool consisting of a database of previously translated texts together with software for retrieving the most similar examples for a given input. The translator can then use these examples as suggestions for how to translate a new text.

translation tool Computer-based system or program for the support of human translators, e.g. dictionaries, translation memory, terminology management.

translator workstation A computer system comprising a collection of translation tools for aiding human translators, typically including facilities for multilingual word processing and editing, for translation memory creation and use, for terminology management, and optionally for access to a machine translation system.

tree adjoining The operation of adjoining (inserting or splicing in) of another tree of a specified form at a given node of a tree.

tree-adjoining grammar A tree grammar with substitution and adjoining as the two composition operations.

treebank A syntactically analysed text corpus.

tree-local MC-TAG A multi-component lexicalized tree-adjoining grammar where a multicomponent tree set composes into an elementary tree only, where the elementary tree may be a singleton tree set or a component of another multi-component tree set.

tree substitution The operation of substituting a tree at the frontier node of another tree.

tree-substitution grammar A tree grammar with substitution as the only composition operation.

true hyphen A hyphen that is an integral part of a complex token.

Turing machine A general purpose computing device consisting of a finite-state controller and unbounded memory which is capable of representing any algorithm or, in other words, recognizing any recursively enumerable set.

two-level morphology Language-independent and non-directional method for morphological processing based on finite-state methods.

typed feature structure grammar A grammar that represents information about the syntactic, semantic, phonological, and (in some cases) pragmatic/contextual properties of a phrase as a graph whose nodes are features (or sets of features) of specified types. A feature at a given node in the graph takes the features (sets of features) at the nodes which it immediately dominates as its values.

underspecified semantics A semantic representation of a natural language expression that maintains any existing ambiguity (e.g. double meaning) and vagueness.

unification An operation that combines two input feature structures into a new output feature structure. The output structure contains all the features of the inputs; the unification fails if the input structures have conflicting values for some feature. Unification is a method commonly used for solving equational constraints in implementations of Lexical Functional Grammar, and it is used explicitly to specify grammatical constraints in Head Driven Phrase Structure Grammar.

universal language In the theory of formal languages and automata, the language that contains all strings of any length including the empty string.

universals Elements of a language (or representation) regarded as common to all (or most) natural languages, and therefore candidates for inclusion in an interlingua or transfer system of machine translation.

user A human agent involved in some form of communication or interaction with a computer system.

user-centred evaluation Evaluation focused on how well a user is able to interact with a system, measured for example by ease of use, learnability, utility, and cognitive load.

user modelling The act of producing a user profile with a representation of the user's overall goals, beliefs, preferences, and typical behaviour, for use in a spoken dialogue or general computer system.

user satisfaction The extent to which users are satisfied with the performance of a system, usually determined by a questionnaire or interview.

utterance A unit of spoken text, typically loosely defined and used. On the structural level utterances may correspond to phrases or sentences uttered by a speaker, whereas on the functional level they may correspond to dialogue acts.

valence The number and kinds of words and phrases a word can combine with in regular patterns. The valence of a word is often called its **subcategorization**.

variance The average quadratic deviation of the outcome of a random variable from its expectation value; often written σ^2.

vector space model In information retrieval, a method of finding documents which are similar to other documents or to a query. Similarity is defined as the cosine of the angle between a query vector and a document vector.

verb anaphora Anaphora where the anaphor is a verb, for example 'did' in 'Stephanie baulked, as did Mike'.

virtual community An on-line group of users who interact with each other via the internet.

Viterbi search A dynamic programming algorithm for finding the most likely hidden state sequence given an observed signal sequence.

weak generative capacity The set of strings of terminals generated by a generative grammar.

well-formed substring table See **chart**.

Wizard of Oz experiment A type of experimental dialogue scenario in which a human subject believes him-/herself to be communicating with a machine, when in fact the responses are made by a hidden human being. The purpose of a Wizard of Oz (WOZ) experiment is to find out as much as possible about how humans would behave in a human–machine dialogue situation.

word alignment The process of establishing the correspondences between words in different languages that are translations of each other in a bilingual forms of the same document.

word bigram model A Markov process whose parameters express the probability of any given word following any other given word.

word co-occurrence pattern Any of the recurrent syntagmatic relations among words in a language, in particular identification of the nouns that typically occur as subject or object of a given verb, or which nouns are typically modified by a given adjective; used to set up classes of words that have grammatical and semantic status in a sublanguage.

word history (i) The history of a word w_i in a sentence is the sequence of words $(w_1, w_2, \ldots, w_{i-1})$ preceding w_i; (ii) the etymology of a word, together with changes in its meaning over time.

WordNet A database based on the psycholinguistic theories of George Miller at Princeton University, consisting of a semantic network relating synsets to one another, where synsets are sets of synonyms in a language.

word–sense disambiguation The process of identifying the meanings of words in context.

word-token An occurrence in text of a word from a language vocabulary. Compare **word-type**.

word-type A word in a language vocabulary, as opposed to its specific occurrence in text. Compare **word-token**.

worst case complexity A complexity measure based on the most resource intensive case for a particular size.

zero anaphora Anaphora where an elliptically omitted word or expression acts as an anaphor as in '*Amy* had made a special effort that night but Ø was disappointed with the results' where Ø stands for the omitted anaphor *she*.

Index of Authors

Abe, N. 404, 405, 476
Aberdeen, J. 216, 424, 643
Abney, S. 234, 564
Abraços, J. 278
Aczel, P. 123
Adams, D. 422, 592
Adams, M. 65
Adorni, G. 301
Agirre, E. 408, 473, 476, 477
Aha, D. W. 385
Aho, A. V. (a) 174
Aho, A. V. (b) 661
Aist, G. 681, 692
Aït-Mokhtar, S. 339, 712
Albert, M. K. 385
Alexandersson, J. 152, 643
Allan, J. 619
Allen, J. (a) 133, 151, 153, 271, 632, 642
Allen, J. (b) 328, 334
Allen, J. R. 678, 688
Allgayer, J. 653
Alshawi, H. 373, 632, 633, 639, 645
Amsler, R. 407, 472
Anderson, S. R. 19
Andrade, E. d' 19
André, E. 655, 656, 657, 658, 659, 662, 665
Andriessen, J. 301
Androutsopoulos, I. 630, 632, 633, 634, 645
Anick, P. 406
Anttila, A. 226
Antworth, E. L. 684
Aone, C. 278, 391, 458, 460, 587
Appel, C. 677
Appelo, L. 679
Appelt, D. 121, 552, 660
Arbib, M. 175
Archangeli, D. 20
Arens, Y. 658
Aretoulaki, M. 643
Argamon, S. 388
Armstrong, S. 618
Arnfield, S. 451
Arnold, D. 511

Arvaniti, A. 20
Ash, R. 373
Aston, G. 54
Åström, M. 224
Atkins, B. 62, 65
Atkins, S. 259
Atwell, E. 672
Aubert, X. 191, 317
Aust, H. 642, 644
Austin, J. L. 138, 139, 140, 154
Azzam, S. 276, 278

Bachenko, J. 331
Baekgaard, A. 642, 644
Baeza-Yates, R. 532, 617
Bagga, A. 276
Bahl, L. R. 306, 310
Baker, J. 457
Balashek, S. 306
Baldwin, B. 276, 277, 278
Ball, G. 664
Ballerini, J. P. 704
Ballestros, L. 705
Ballim, A. 154
Banko, M. 590
Barbu, C. 278
Barlow, M. 274, 682
Barros, F. A. 632
Barthe, K. 446
Barton, G. E. 182, 193, 196
Barwise, J. 96, 117, 119
Barzilay, R. 587, 590
Bateman, J. 299, 301, 471
Bates, M. 634
Bates, M. J. 623
Bauer, D. 685, 709
Baum, L. E. 225, 310, 366
Baxendale, P. B. 586
Beale, S. 476
Bean, D. 273
Bear, J. 537
Beard, R. 64
Becker, T. 495

Beckman, M. E. 20
Beeferman, D. 216, 621
Beesley, K. R. 42, 46, 345, 348, 701
Behren, M. C. 578
Beigel, R. 174
Belkin, N. J. 534
Bell, J. E. 634
Beltrametti, M. 713
Bennett, S. 278, 391, 458, 460
Benoit, J. 421
Bentley, J. L. 195, 196
Berger, A. 216, 373
Bergler, S. 406
Bernsen, N. O. 424, 636, 644, 645
Bernstein, J. 679, 681
Berwick, R. C. 182, 193, 196
Biagini, L. 683
Biber, D. 461
Bierman, A. 475
Bikel, D. M. 549
Billot, S. 238
Bindi, R. 400
Bird, S. 20
Black, A. W. 43, 332, 335
Black, E. 417, 458, 460
Black, W. 154
Blackburn, P. 92, 95, 104
Blevins, J. 20
Bloch, B. 19
Bloedorn, E. 421, 587, 589, 592
Bloksma, L. 473
Bloothooft, G. 317, 320
Blum, T. 661
Bobrow, D. G. 277
Bobrow, R. 634
Bock, K. 301
Bod, R. 244
Boersma, P. 20
Boes, D. 372
Boguraev, B. 55, 274, 276, 277, 472
Boldt, O. 354
Bolt, R. A. 653
Booij, G. 19
Booth, A. D. 510
Bordegoni, M. 665
Borgida, A. 469
Borkowski, C. 705
Borthwick, A. 548
Bos, J. 92, 95, 104
Botley, S. 450, 452, 456, 458
Bouillon, P. 63
Bouma, G. 95
Bourigault, D. 605, 613
Boye, J. 645

Brachman, R. 469, 478
Brachman, R. J. 617
Brandow, R. 423, 586, 592
Brainerd, B. 174
Brants, T. 234
Bratko, I. 384
Breidt, E. 684
Brent, M. 404
Bresnan, J. 85, 88, 89, 99, 169, 241, 496
Brill, E. 226, 387, 388
Briscoe, E. 55, 241, 245, 252, 373, 417, 471, 472
Broad, W. J. 622
Broe, M. 20
Brookshear, J. 174
Brown, R. D. 277
Brown, P. 256, 373, 402, 403, 516, 526, 705
Bruce, B. 122
Bruce, R. 407
Brzezinski, J. 662
Buckley, C. 537, 586, 587
Buitelaar, P. 471
Bunt, H. 154
Burke, R. D. 580
Burnard, L. 54, 452
Burzio, L. 20
Burt, M. 674
Bussa, R. 452
Byrd, R. 407, 408
Byrne, R. J. 578
Byron, D. 278

Cahill, L. 300
Cahn, J. 664
Calder, J. 44
Califf, M. E. 386, 390
Callan, J. P. 538
Callison-Burch, C. 527
Calzolari, N. 400
Cameron, K. 677, 691, 692
Caraballo, S. 403
Carberry, S. 642
Carbonell, J. 277, 590
Cardie, C. 278, 388, 391, 392, 586, 587
Carletta, J. 151
Carlson, R. 681
Carpenter, B. 241, 471, 643
Carroll, J. 242, 245, 373, 417
Carson-Berndsen, J. 20
Carter, D. M. 277
Carter, R. 675, 685
Cassell, J. 664, 665
Cassidy, S. 20
Catford, J. C. 19
Cawsey, A. 300

Chai, J. 475
Chalmers, M. 618
Champarnaud, J. M. 354
Chang, C. H. 226
Chang, J. 408
Chang-Rodriguez, E. 452
Chanod, J. P. 226, 228, 339, 712
Chapman, R. 256, 397
Charniak, E. 243, 255, 261, 278, 373, 396, 398, 401
Charpentier, F. 336
Chen, C. D. 226
Chen, F. 586, 587, 592
Chen, H. 618
Chen, J. N. 408
Cherry, L. L. 213
Cheyer, A. 653
Chierchia, G. 92, 109
Chinchor, N. 418
Chisholm, W. S. 65
Chitson, P. 618
Chodorow, M. 407, 408, 476
Chomsky, N. 19, 40, 80, 82, 89, 92, 100, 101, 343
Choueka, Y. 60
Chrzanowski, M. J. 592, 594
Chu-Caroll, J. 643
Church, K. 60, 224, 239, 257, 330, 373, 398, 400, 458, 527, 612, 618, 706
Clark, J. 19
Clark, P. 383
Clarke, C. L. 564, 568
Cohen, M. 313
Cohen, P. 153, 562, 635, 653
Cohen, W. W. 383
Cole, R. 174, 320, 644
Coleman, J. 20
Collins, A. M. 469
Collins, M. 191, 244, 373, 396, 549, 564
Condamines, A. 601
Connell, B. 20
Connine, C. 261
Connolly, J. H. 671
Conrad, S. 461
Contant, C. 440
Cooper, R. 97
Copestake, A. 104, 241, 242, 471, 630, 635
Core, M. 151
Cormen, T. H. 181, 186, 191, 196
Corréard, M. H. 711
Cost, S. 385
Côté, A. R. 538
Cottrell, G. 255
Cover, T. M. 385
Covington, M. 194

Cowie, A. 65
Cowie, J. 253, 557, 558
Crangle, C. 630
Craven, M. 618
Cristea, D. 273
Croft, W. B. 211, 260, 534, 538, 539, 618, 705
Crouch, R. 104
Crowe, J. 217
Cruse, D. A. 471
Crystal, D. 51
Csuhaj-Varjú, E. 175
Cucerzan, S. 549
Culpeper, J. 449, 458
Culy, C. 169
Cutting, D. 224, 226, 618

Daelemans, W. 254, 329, 387, 392
Dagan, I. 277, 278, 388, 399, 402, 612, 619
Dahl, D. A. 644
Daille, B. 459, 606
Dalal, M. 655, 656
Dale, R. 121, 129, 301, 408, 656
Dalianis, H. 301
Dalrymple, M. 89
Danieli, M. 643, 644
Danielsson, P. 683
Danlos, L. 299
Dassow, J. 174
Davidson, L. 601
Davis, M. D. 174
Davis, M. W. 705
Davis, S. 308
DeAngelie, A. 655
Debili, F. 610, 611
de Buenaga Rodriguez, M. 474
de Jong, F. 679, 705
De Jong, J. 681
de Loupy, C. 474
de Paiva, V. 471
De Roeck, A. N. 632, 633
de Smedt, K. 300, 301
Deerwester, S. 535, 538
DeGroot, M. 372
Dejean, H. 217
deJong, G. J. 588
DeKeyser, R. 675
Dekleva, S. M. 634
Dempster, A. P. 310
Della Pietra, S. 235, 369, 373
Della Pietra, V. 235, 369, 373
DeRose, S. 224
Derthick, M. 624
deSmedt, W. 690
Devanbu, P. 470

Di Cristo, A. 19
Di Tomaso, V. 711
Diderot, D. 66
Dietterich, T. G. 392
Dijkstra, A. 684
Dillon, M. 536, 608
Dini, L. 711
Docherty, G. J. 20
Dokter, D. 679, 684, 685
Donaway, R. L. 592
Donlan, D. 586
Doran, C. 300
Dorr, B. 406, 421, 679
Doyle, J. 127
Doyon, J. 421
Dowty, D. 93, 122
Dozier, C. 538
Dreyfus-Graf, J. 306
Driedger, N. 440
Drobot, V. 174
Drummey, K. W. 592
Dudley, H. 306
Dulay, H. 674
Dunning, T. 399, 606
Dutoit, T. 325, 332, 336
Dybkjær, H. 424, 636, 644, 645
Dybkjær, L. 424, 636, 644, 645
Dymetman, M. 439
Dzeroski, S. 383, 387

Earley, J. 188, 189
Edmundson, H. P. 583, 586, 592
Ehara, T. 585
Eisner, J. 20
Ekman, P. 664
Elhadad, M. 299, 587, 590
Elliot, C. 662
Ellis, R. 674, 692
Ellison, M. 20
Engelmore, R. 643
Engels, L. 684
Enguehard, C. 607
Erjavec, T. 387
Erman, L. D. 641, 643
Evans, D. A. 536, 613, 687, 688, 705
Evans, D. K., 538
Evans, R. (a) 44
Evans, R. (b) 272, 278

Fagan, J. L. 537
Falkedal, K. 421
Farwell, D. 526
Fayyad, U. M. 381, 617, 619
Feiner, S. 655, 656, 658

Felber, H. 600
Feldman, R. 619
Feldweg, H. 226, 684
Fellbaum, C. 59, 472, 478, 538, 563, 570, 619
Felshin, S. 677
Fenstad, J. E. 119
Ferguson, G. 642
Ferret, O. 564, 574
Feuerman, K. 688
Fillmore, C. 50, 64, 122
Finkler, W. 299
Firmin, T. 592, 594
Firmin Hand, T. 592, 594
Firth, J. R. 19, 60
Fiscus, J. 416, 417
Fitzpatrick, E. 331
Flanagan, J. L. 334
Fleming, E. 20
Flickinger, D. 105, 241, 245
Flournoy, R. S. 527
Floyd, R. 174
Fluhr, C. 705
Flycht-Eriksson, A. 636, 644
Fodor, J. 250
Forney, D. 366
Fossket, D. 466
Fox, D. 673
Frakes, W. 532
Francis, W. N. 54, 452
Francopoulo, G. 687
Frank, R. 496
Frederking, R. 526, 527
Fredkin, E. 43
Frege, G. 102
Freitag, D. 390
Friedman, C. 539, 558
Friesen, W. V. 664
Frink, B. 450
Fromer, J. C. 642, 643
Fromkin, V. 31
Frost, R. 19
Fujii, A. 476
Fujisaki, H. 331
Fukumoto, F. 591
Fukushima, T. 585
Funk, I. K. 52
Furui, S. 645

Gabbay, D. 100
Gaizauskas, R. 276, 278, 458, 470, 475
Gal, A. 301
Gale, W. 257, 706
Gales, M. 312
Galliers, J. 420, 591

Gallwitz, F. 636, 643, 644, 645
Garnsey, S. 100
Garrett, N. 691
Garside, R. 224, 452, 455, 458, 459, 460, 461
Gates, B. 589
Gaussier, É. 459, 612
Gauvain, J. L. 311, 312
Gazdar, G. 44, 88, 89, 99, 127, 133, 169, 192
Ge, N. 278
Genesereth, R. M. 470
Geng, Y. 590
Gerber, L. 591
Gerbino, E. 643, 644
Gerdemann, D. 355
Gervais, A. 423
Gibbon, D. 149, 644, 645
Ginzburg, J. 98, 105, 106, 108
Glennon, D. 254
Goethals, M. 684
Goldberg, E. 440
Goldsmith, J. 19, 354
Goldstein, J. 590, 591, 592, 595
Gomez-Hidalgo, J. M. 474
Gonzalo, J. 474
Goodfellow, R. 691
Goyvaerts, P. 446
Graesser, A. C. 578
Graf, W. 659
Gray, A. H. 335
Gray, A. S. 536, 608
Greene, B. 224
Grefenstette, G. 206, 207, 216, 234, 701, 704, 705, 710, 714
Gregory, H. 105, 106, 108
Greybill, F. 372
Grice, H. P. 129, 138, 141, 142, 146, 154
Grieszl, A. 679, 690
Grimley-Evans, E. 354, 355
Grinberg, D. 235
Griot, L. 474
Grishman, R. 417, 418, 446, 548, 556, 557
Groenendijk, J. 109, 117
Grosz, B. 131, 133, 150, 152, 271, 630, 635
Grover, C. 205, 216, 548
Gruber, T. R. 465, 468, 470, 478
Grundy, V. 711
Guarino, N. 473, 474
Guha, R. H. 470
Guo, C. M. 55
Gurari, E. 174
Gurju, R. 403
Gussenhoven, C. 19
Guthrie, J. 253
Guthrie, L. 55, 253, 261, 407, 472, 476, 478

Haas, S. W. 536
Haegeman, L. 274
Hahn, U. 132, 278, 589, 595
Hajičová, E. 125
Hale, J. 278
Halle, M. 19, 40, 343
Haller, S. 642
Halliday, M. A. K. 123, 133, 287, 299
Hamburger, H. 679, 687, 692
Hamel, M. J. 679
Hamilton, K. S. 622
Hamilton, S. 677
Hammond, M. 19
Handke, J. 19
Hanks, P. 51, 60, 61, 62, 255, 398, 400
Hannicut, S. 328, 334
Harabagiu, S. 277, 278, 475, 563, 565, 566, 568, 569, 570, 571, 573, 574, 577, 579, 580
Harbusch, K. 299
Harding, S. M. 538
Harley, A. 254
Harman, D. 259, 417, 532
Harper, D. J. 625
Harrington, J. 20
Harris, Z. 440
Harrison, M. 174
Hart, P. E. 385
Haruno, M. 388, 405
Hastings, P. 403
Hatzivassiloglou, V. 660
Hauptmann, A. 661
Havrilla, T. 527
Hayes, B. 20
Heald, I. 446
Hearst, M. 215, 216, 217, 403, 416, 619
Heid, U. 471
Heidorn, G. 407, 408
Heikkilä, J. 226
Helmreich, S. 526
Hendry, D. G. 625
Hermansky, H. 306
Hermjacob, U. 388, 580
Herzog, G. 662
Hess, W. 332
Hiemstra, D. 705
Hindle, D. 226, 402
Hintikka, J. 129
Hipp, D. R. 636, 642, 645
Hirsch, H. 619
Hirschberg, J. 150, 331
Hirschman, L. 417, 419, 422, 424, 438, 446
Hirst, D. 20
Hirst, G. 252, 269, 271, 475, 589
Hitzeman, J. 131

Hoaglin, D. C. 620
Hobbs, J. 274, 277
Hockett, C. F. 19
Hoffman, R. 677
Holland, V. M. 676, 678, 679, 681, 691, 692
Holliday, L. 677
Holmes, G. 682, 692
Hopcroft, J. 174, 183, 339
Horacek, H. 300
Hornby, A. 52, 253
House, D. 645
Hovy, E. 292, 301, 527, 584, 586, 589, 595, 658
Howie, J. 174
Huddleston, R. 267
Hull, D. A. 532, 612, 704, 705, 706, 707
Hulstijn, J. 686
Humphreys, K. 276, 278, 470, 475
Hunt, A. 195
Hunt, A. J. 332, 335
Hunt, H. 154
Hunt, M. J. 307
Husk, G. 272
Hutchins, J. 511
Hyman, L. M. 20

Ide, N. 54, 255, 273, 407
Ilson, R. 65
Ingle, N. C. 701
Iordanskaja, L. 299, 440
Isabelle, P. 439, 527
Itai, A. 277, 278
Ittycheriah, A. 576
Iwayama, M. 403

Jackendoff, R. 55, 99, 406
Jacobs, H. 19
Jacobs, P. S. 588
Jacobson, P. 99
Jacquemin, C. 537, 574, 611, 613
Jager, S. 677, 678
James, M. 690
Jarke, M. 424
Järvinen, T. 235, 457
Jelinek, F. 306, 320, 366, 373, 569
Jensen, K. 689
Jing, H. 260, 539, 590, 592
Joachims, T. 541
Johansson, S. 224
Johns, T. 681
Johnson, C. D. 344, 348
Johnson, D. 100
Johnson, M. 355
Johnson, S. 50, 52
Johnson, W. 19

Johnston, M. 654, 655
Jones, D. 406, 527
Jones, G. 660
Jones, P. 421
Joos, M. 19
Jordan, P. 421
Joshi, A. 131, 133, 271, 396, 485, 486, 487, 491, 494, 495, 496
Juang, B. H. 308, 310, 320
Juilland, A. 452
Julia, L. 653
Jurafsky, D. 19, 245
Jürgensen, H. 354
Justeson, J. S. 606

Kaeding, J. 452
Kager, R. 20
Kallmeyer, L. 100, 494, 495
Kameyama, M. 276, 277, 278, 496
Kamp, H. 109, 117, 118
Kanzaki, K. 63
Kaplan, J. D. 679, 691, 692
Kaplan, R. 85, 99, 242, 341, 344, 345, 348, 496, 634
Kaplan, S. J. 634
Karkaletsis, V. 388
Karlsson, F. 226
Karttunen, L. 20, 42, 46, 339, 341, 345, 348, 350
Kasami, J. 237
Kasami, T. 189
Kasper, G. 422, 592
Kasper, R. 496
Katamba, F. 19
Kato, T. 661
Katz, L. 19
Katz, J. 250
Katz, S. M. 315, 366, 606
Kay, M. 43, 236, 240, 344, 345, 348
Kazakov, D. 387
Keating, P. A. 20
Keenan, E. 94
Kehler, A. 278
Kelledy, F. 474
Kelley, D. 174
Kempe, A. 348
Kempen, G. 684, 688, 692
Kempson, R. 100
Kennedy, C. 274, 276, 277
Kennedy, G. 461
Kenstowicz, M. 19, 20
Kerpedjiev, S. 656
Kfoury, A. 175
Kibler, D. F. 385
Kiefer, B. 241
Kiefer, F. 65

Kilgarriff, A. 63, 259, 417
Kim, M. H. 474
Kim, T. 217
King, M. 511
King, P. 681
Kingston, J. 20
Kiparsky, P. 31
Kipp, M. 643
Kiraz, G. 20, 43, 354, 355
Kiss, G. 65
Kisseberth, C. 20
Kittredge, R. 299, 439, 440, 446
Klare, G. 422
Klatt, D. 328, 334, 335
Klavans, J. 537, 538
Klee, T. 671
Kleene, S. C. 345
Klein, E. 20
Kleinberg, J. 618
Kloesgen, W. 619
Knight, K. 526, 589
Knott, A. 656
Kobsa, A. 638
Kölln, M. 300
Kolojejchick, J. 624
Kölzer, A. 642, 644
Koons, D. 653, 654
Kornai, A. 20, 354
Koskenniemi, K. 40, 339, 343, 348
Kowaltowski, T. 341
Kraaij, W. 705
Krantz, G. 686
Krashen, S. 674, 682
Kraut, R. 708
Krawer, S. 526
Krenn, B. 373
Kristoffersen, G. 19
Krovetz, R. 258, 260, 532, 539
Krüger, A. 679, 690
Krymolowski, Y. 388
Kubota Ando, R. 591
Kučera, H. 54
Kudo, T. 398
Kuhn, K. 655
Kukich, K. 422, 440
Kullick, S. 495, 496
Kupiec, J. 579, 586, 587, 592
Kurtonina, N. 496
Kwong, O. Y. 408

Labov, W. 19
Ladd, D. R. 20
Ladefoged, P. 19
Lafferty, J. 216, 235, 369

Laird, M. M. 310
Landau, S. I. 66
Landauer, T. K. 705
Lang, B. 238
Lange, E. 527
Langendoen, D. T. 20
Langlais, P. 527
Langley, P. 376, 382, 392
Lantolf, J. P. 675
Laport, É. 353
Lappin, S. 92, 98, 100, 102, 105, 106, 108, 109, 272, 274
Laroui, A. 687
Larsen-Freeman, D. 674, 675
Larson, R. R. 618
Last, R. 692
Lauriston, A. 605
Laver, J. 19
Lavrac, N. 383
Leacock, C. 259, 476
Lee, C. H. 311, 312
Lee, H. B. 253, 387, 458
Lee, J. H. 474
Lee, L. 399, 402
Lee, Y. J. 474
Leass, H. 272, 274
Leech, G. 138, 150, 151, 154, 224, 452, 453, 455, 458,
    459, 460, 461
Leenders, T. 684
Lefferts, R. G. 536
Leggetter, C. J. 312
Lehnert, W. 278, 391, 557, 558, 578, 588
Lehrberger, 439, 446
Leinbach, J. 386
Leiserson, C. E. 181, 186, 191, 196
Lenat, D. B. 397, 470
Lesk, M. 252, 534
Lester, J. 421
Levelt, W. J. 175, 301
Levin, B. 406, 434, 471
Levin, L. S. 680, 686, 687, 688
Levinson, S. E. 324, 328
Levow, G. A. 636
Levy, M. 673, 676, 677, 691, 692
Lewis, H. 174
L'Homme, M. C. 613
Li, H. 405, 476
Li, W. 564, 576
Liberman, M. Y. 20, 330, 618
Liddy, D. E. 536
Light, M. 261
Lim, C. Y. 391
Lim, D. C. Y. 278
Lin, C. Y. 584, 586, 587, 589
Lin, D. 399, 402

Lin, X. 618
Ling, C. X. 386
Linz, P. 175
Liporaz, L. R. 310
Litman, D. 151, 153, 416, 643, 644
Littman, M. L. 705
Ljojle, A. 313
Lomary, L. 273
Long, M. 674
Lopes, J. G. 278
Loritz, D. 688
Lovins, J. B. 532, 533
Lowden, B. G. T. 633
Lucchesi, C. L. 341
Luhn, H. P. 583, 586
Lunnon, R. 123
Luisgnan, S. 60
LuperFoy, S. 277, 643
Lux, V. 446
Lytinen, S. 403

McCain, J. J. 618
McCarthy, J. (a) 19
McCarthy, J. (b) 127
McCarthy, J. (c) 278, 393
McClelland, J. L. 386
McConnell-Ginet, S. 92
McCoy, K. 679, 690
McEnery, A. 450, 452, 453, 455, 456, 457, 458, 461
McGee, D. R. 635
McGill, M. 257, 417, 534
McGlashan, S. 643, 644
McKee, D. 278
McKeown, K. 290, 440, 590, 655, 656, 658, 661, 590
McKevitt, P. 665
Macklovitch, E. 439, 527
Macleod, C. 54
McNaughton, R. 175
Macon, M. W. 336
McRoy, S. 253, 642
McTear, M. F. 149, 153, 154, 641, 645
MacWhinney, B. 386, 691
Magerman, D. 373, 388, 569
Mahesh, K. 471, 476
Mahimon, M. D. 714
Maiorano, S. 277, 278, 563, 565, 569, 570, 580
Malfrère, F. 332
Malouf, R. 95, 242
Manandhar, S. 387
Manaster Ramer, A. 175
Mani, I. 418, 421, 422, 584, 587, 589, 592, 594
Mann, G. 580
Mann, W. C. 129, 130, 292, 299
Manning, C. 245, 263, 373, 404, 408, 527, 619

Marchionini, G. 618
Marcinkiewicz, M. 190, 203, 388, 397, 455, 457, 458
Marcu, D. 421, 587, 589, 591, 592
Marcus, M. 188, 190, 203, 234, 388, 397, 455, 457, 458
Marcus, S. 402
Marinov, M. 386
Markel, J. D. 335
Markovitch, S. 402
Marquez, L. 387
Marshall, I. 224
Martin, J. H. 19, 245
Martin, P. F. 150
Martín-Vide, C. 175
Masolo, C. 474
Mastermann, M. 256
Mateus, H. 19
Mather, L. A. 592
Matheson, C. 205, 216
Matsumoto, Y. 398, 405, 406, 408
Matthiessen, C. 299
Mattis, J. 655, 656
Matwin, S. 474
Mauldin, M. 536
Maurel, D. 354
Maybury, M. 301, 584, 594, 651, 655, 656, 660, 661, 665
Maxwell, J. III, 242
Medin, D. 469
Melamed, I. D. 527
Mel'čuk, I. 235, 299
Mellish, C. 89
Menzel, W. 690
Mercer, R. 366
Merchant, R. 418
Merlino, A. 660, 661
Mermelstein, P. 308
Mertens, P. 332
Mervis, C. B. 469
Mesnard, X. 655, 656
Meteer, M. 300
Metzler, D. P. 536, 609
Meyer-Viol, W. 100
Michaud, L. 690
Mihalcea, R. 476
Mihov, S. 679
Miike, S. 592
Mikheev, A. 205, 206, 214, 215, 216, 548
Miller, D. 133
Miller, G. 397, 472, 712
Miller, J. F. 671
Miller, P. 175, 497
Milosavljevic, M. 656
Minami, Y. 643
Minel, J. L. 420, 421

Minsky, M. 51
Mitchell, T. 376, 379, 382, 392
Mitkov, R. 216, 269, 274, 276, 277, 278, 456, 526
Mitra, M. 540, 587
Mitrana, V. 175
Mittal, V. 422, 586, 590
Mitze, K. 423, 586, 592
Möebius, B. 332
Moeller, J. U. 639
Moens, M. 586
Mohri, M. 352, 355
Moisl, H. 408
Moldovan, D. 403, 475, 476, 564, 568, 580
Moll, R. 175
Mondria, J. A. 686
Mönnich, U. 175
Montague, R. 93, 100, 102, 103,
Mood, A. 372
Mooney, R. 259, 379, 386, 388, 389, 390, 392
Moore, J. 292, 656, 657
Moore, R. 149, 644, 645
Moortgat, M. 99
Morey, D. 660
Morgan, T. 643
Morimoto, T. 639
Morrill, G. 99
Morris, A. 422, 592
Morris, C. 138
Morton, T. 276
Moshier, M. 175
Mosteller, F. 620
Moulines, E. 336
Muggleton, S. 384
Mullen, T. 677
Müller, J. 655
Muñoz, R. 273
Murphy, M. 679, 690
Murray, J. H. 677
Murrey, J. 52
Myaeng, S. H. 536

Nadas, A. 256
Nagao, K. 664
Nagao, M. 420, 515
Nagata, M. 224, 639
Nakamura, J. 420
Nakatani, C. 150
Narayanan, S. 642, 643
Narin, F. 622
Nash, D. 32
Nasukawa, T. 277
Nathadur, G. 133
Neal, J. G. 653, 655
Nerbonne, J. 102, 678, 679, 683, 684, 685

Newell, A. 254
Newton, J. 511
Ney, H. , 191
Ng, H. T. 253, 278, 387, 389, 391, 458
Niblett, T. 383
Nicolov, N. 297
Nida, E. 33
Nie, J. Y. 705
Nijholt, A. 192
Nirenburg, S. 471, 476, 511, 526, 527
Nogier, J. F. 297
Norris, J. 675
Norvig, P. 190, 195
Novick, D. G. 636, 641, 643, 644
Nugier, S. 420, 421
Nugues, P. 643, 644
Nunberg, G. 708

Oakes, M. 452
Oard, D. 714
Odden, D. 19
O'Donnell, R. 474
Oepen, S. 242, 245
Oflazer, K. 339
Oishi, A. 406
O'Keefe, R. 195
Okurowski, M. 418
Olivastro, D. 622
Olive, J. P. 324, 328
Olney, J. 55
Olsen, M. B. 679
Ono, K. 592
Ono, T. 142
Ooyama, Y. 388
Orasan, C. 217, 278
Orr, D. 422
Ortega, L. 675
Ortmanns, S. 191
Oshika, B. T. 314
Oviatt, S. L. 635, 651, 654, 655, 665

Padro, L. 227, 387
Paetzold, M. 332
Paice, C. D. 272, 421, 532, 592
Paiva, D. 301
Pajsz, J. 65
Paliouras, G. 388
Palmer, D. 215, 216, 416
Palmer, M. 259
Palomar, M. 278
Pantera, L. 607
Papadimitriou, C. 174
Papineni, K. 422
Paris, C. 292, 301

Partee, B. 174
Pasca, M. 563, 565, 569, 570, 571, 574, 577, 580
Pasero, R. 687
Paskaleva, E. 679
Passonneau, R. 150, 416
Patil, R. 239
Patrick, A. 645
Păun, A. 354
Păun, G. 174, 175
Peacock, C. 259
Pearson, J. 601, 613
Peat, H. J. 618
Pedersen, J. 260, 539, 586, 587, 592
Penn, G. 241
Pennington, M. C. 671, 692
Pereira, F. 93, 95, 97, 190, 246, 354, 355, 399, 402
Perrault, C. R. 630, 645
Perry, C. K. 671
Perry, J. 96, 117, 119
Peters, C. 683
Peters, S. 93
Peters, W. 474, 477
Piat, G. 420, 421
Piatetsky-Shapiro, G. 381
Picchi, E. 683
Pierrehumbert, J. 20
Pike, E. V. 20
Pike, K. L. 19, 20
Pinker, S. 386
Pison, D. 681
Poesio, M. 131, 273
Polguère, A. 299
Polifroni, J. 424
Pollack, J. 255
Pollack, M. 97
Pollard, C. 88, 89, 95, 96, 98, 101, 105, 131, 241, 396,
    471, 496
Ponte, J. M. 211
Porter, B. 421
Porter, M. F. 531, 532
Postal, P. 101
Prager, J. 564, 574, 576
Pratt, W. 211
Prevost, S. 664
Prince, A. S. 19, 20, 343, 386
Prince, E. 133, 271
Procter, P. 253, 254, 476
Proszeky, G. 679
Pulleyblank, D. 20
Pullum, G. 169
Pulman, S. G. 125, 355
Pustejovsky, J. 55, 63, 406, 471

Quigly, A. 474
Quillian, M. R. 469

Quinlan, J. R. 380, 381, 382, 383, 384, 587
Quirk, R. 452

Rabiner, L. R. 308, 320
Radev, D. 564, 574, 576, 590, 595
Ramadan, N. M. 621
Rambow, O. 495
Ramsey, A. 122, 125, 133
Ramshaw, L. 234
Raskin, V. 527
Rath, G. 421
Ratnaparki, A. 373
Rau, L. 423, 586, 588, 592
Rayner, M. 526
Rebeyrolles, J. 601
Rector, A. L. 470
Reimer, U. 589
Reiter, E. 121, 301
Reiter, R. 127
Reithinger, N. 639, 643
Rennison, E. 618
Reppen, R. 461
Resnick, A. 421
Resnik, P. 404, 476, 497
Revard, C. 55
Révész, G. 174
Reyle, U. 104, 109, 117, 118
Ribeiro-Neto, B. 617
Rich, E. 277
Richardson, R. 474
Richter, F. 104
Ridings, D. 683
Rigau, G. 408, 476, 477
Riger, C. 251
Riley, M. 313, 354, 355
Riloff, E. 273, 401, 405, 531, 556
Rist, T. 655, 656, 657, 658, 659, 665
Ristad, E. S. 182, 193, 196
Ritchie, G. D. 46, 630, 632, 633, 634, 645
Ritter, N. 20
Rivest, R. L. 181, 186, 191, 196, 258
Roach, P. 451
Roark, B. 401
Robertson, S. E. 534
Robin, J. 299, 422, 423, 440
Robinson, P. 418
Roca, A. 19
Roca, I. 19
Roche, E. 226, 339, 345, 352, 353, 354
Rodman, R. 31
Rodriguez, H. 387, 408
Roosmaa, T. 679
Rosch, E. 469
Roth, S. 655, 656
Roth, S. F. 624

Rothenberg, M. 677
Rowe, L. A. 634
Rozenberg, G. 174, 175
Rubach, J. 19
Rubin, D. B. 310
Rubin, G. 224
Rudin, W. 372
Ruessink, H. 43
Ruge, G. 536
Rumelhart, D. E. 386
Rus, V. 403, 580
Russel, B. 117
Rychtyckyj, N. 470
Rypa, M. 688

Sabatier, P. 687
Sable, C. 660
Sacerdoti, E. 292
Sacks, H. 153
Sag, I. 88, 89, 95, 96, 98, 101, 105, 106, 108, 131, 241,
    396, 471, 496
Sager, J. 601, 602, 613
Sager, N. 440, 446, 558
Sailer, M. 104
St Amant, R. 623, 625
St-Onge, D. 475
Salaberry, M. R. 678
Salomaa, A. 174, 175
Salton, G. 257, 417, 421, 534, 538, 574, 587, 592, 702,
    706
Salzberg, S. 385
Samn, V. 564, 574, 576
Sampson, G. 224, 452, 455, 458, 459
Sams, M. R. 692
Samuelsson, C. 227, 228, 373
Sanders, A. F. 686
Sanders, R. H. 686
Sanderson, M. 260, 539
Sanfilippo, A. 245, 417, 478
Sang, E. F. 217
Santorini, B. 190, 203, 388, 397, 455, 457, 458
Sato, S. 515
Savage, T. 421
Savitch, W. 169, 175
Schabes, Y. 99, 190, 226, 246, 339, 345, 352, 353, 354,
    485, 486, 487, 497
Schachter, P. 220
Schafer, R. W. 320
Schank, R. 469, 578
Schauder, A. 299
Schegloff, E. 142
Schmelzenbach, M. 405
Schmid, H. 214
Schmidt, P. 276

Schmied, J. 450
Schmolze, J. 469
Schneider, D. 690
Schoelles, M. 679
Schröder, I. 690
Schroeer, O. 642, 644
Schroeter, J. 334
Schultz, J. M. 671
Schulze, M. 679
Schütze, H. 245, 258, 260, 263, 373, 408, 527, 539
Schützenberger, M. P. 353
Schwartz, C. 610
Schwartz, R. 306
Scobbie, J. 20
Scott, S. 474
Searle, J. 138, 140, 152, 154
Sebastiani, F. 541
Segond, F. 476, 685, 709, 710, 711
Seidenberg, M. 255
Sekine, S. 548
Sells, P. 89, 175
Semino, E. 449, 458
Seville, H. 131
Sgall, P. 125
Shannon, C. 594
Shapiro, S. 653, 655
Shavlik, J. W. 392
Shepherd, J. 401, 405
Sheridan, P. 538, 610, 704
Shieber, S. 88, 93, 95, 97, 99, 169, 175, 246
Shimei, P. 643, 644
Shinnou, H. 548
Shirai, K. 585, 645
Shirai, S. 388
Short, M. 449, 458
Sidner, C. 130, 152, 271, 277
Sigal, R. 174
Sikkel, K. 192, 246
Silverman, K. 332
Simard, M. 527
Sinaico, W. 422
Sinclair, J. 61, 451, 456
Singer, Y. 549
Singhal, A. 564, 587
Siptár, P. 19
Slator, B. 55, 261, 472, 476, 478
Sleator, D. 235
Slenton, P. 634
Slocum, J. 511
Smadja, F. 400, 607
Smalheiser, N. R. 621
Small, S. 251, 252
Small, V. 422
Smeaton, A. F. 474, 536, 538, 610

Smit, P. 684
Smith, E. 469
Smith, R. W. 636, 642, 643, 645
Smolensky, P. 20, 343
Smyth, P. 211, 381
Sneath, P. H. A. 700
Soderland, S. 390
Soegeel, D. 618
Sokal, R. R. 700
Somers, H. 408, 511, 526, 671
Sondhi, M. M. 334
Soon, W. M. 278, 391
Sowa, J. 468
Spärck Jones, K. 133, 420, 466, 534, 536, 537, 584,
    591, 611, 630, 689
Sparrell, C. 653
Spencer, A. 46
Sperber, D. 143, 154
Sperberg-McQueen, C. M. 452
Sproat, R. 19, 20, 32, 46, 216, 325, 354, 355
Spyropoulos, C. D. 388
Srihari, R. 564, 576
Srivinas, B. 497
Stallard, D. 634
Stanfill, C. 385
Stede, M. 301
Steedman, M. 99, 496
Stevens, K. N. 19
Stevenson, M. 55, 254, 259
Stiles, W. B. 458
Stock, O. 656, 661
Stokhof, M. 109, 117
Stolcke, A. 373
Stone, M. 300
Strapparava, C. 656, 661
Strawson, P. F. 117
Strube, M. 132, 278
Strzalkowski, T. 536, 538, 540, 549, 585, 586, 609
Stubbs, M. 461
Stylianou, Y. 336
Stys, M. 278
Sudkamp, T. 175
Sumita, K. 592
Sundheim, B. 417, 418, 557, 592, 594
Suppes, P. 630
Sutton, S. 644
Suzuki, Y. 591
Svartik, J. 452
Swanson, D. 621
Swartout, W. 656, 657
Syrdal, A. 336

Tait, J. 536, 537, 611
Takeuchi, A. 664

Tanaka, H. 403, 405
Tanenhaus, M. 100
Tanev, H. 216
Tapanainen, P. 206, 207, 216, 226, 228, 235, 367, 373,
    710
Taylor, K. 421
Teich, E. 301
ter Meulen, A. 109, 174
Tesar, B. 20
Tesnière, L. 610
Tetreault, J. 278
Teufel, R. 586
Thanisch, P. 632, 634, 645
Thomas, D. 195
Thomas, J. 138
Thompson, C. A. 389
Thompson, J. 679
Thompson, P. 538
Thompson, S. A. 129, 130, 142, 292
Thorisson, K. 668
Tice, D. 419, 562
Tishby, N. 402
Tokunaga, T. 403
Tomita, M. 238
Tompa, F. W. 57, 65
Torisawa, K. 239
Towel, G. 259
Townshend, B. 693
Traber, C. 331
Traum, D. R. 642, 634
Trench, R. C. 50
Trost, H. 43
Trueswell, J. 100
Tschichold, C. 689, 692
Tschirgi, J. S. 324, 328
Tsujii, J. 239, 420
Tukey, J. W. 620
Turcato, D. 527
Türkenczy, M. 19
Turner, R. 123
Tzoukermann, E. 260, 537, 539

Ullman, J. 174, 183, 339
Uramoto, N. 403
Uthurusamy, R. 617, 619
Utsuro, T. 405, 408

van Benthem, J. 109
van Dijk, T. A. 421
van Els, T. 674
van Essen, A. 678
van Halteren, H. 230
van Heuven, V. 679
van Noord, G. 355

van Rijsbergen, C. J. 257, 536, 538
van Santen, J. P. H. 332, 336
van der Bosch, A. 329
van der Eijk, P. 611
van der Hulst, H. 20
van der Sandt, R. 118
Vander Linden, 294, 301
Vauthey, B. 536
Vaux, B. 19
Veldhuijzen van Zanten, G. V. 636, 643
Veltman, F. 109
Véronis, J. 255, 407, 450, 452, 527, 714
Vesterman, W. 213
Vetere, G. 474
Vieira, R. 273
Vijay-Shanker, K. 491, 492
Vilain, M. 417
Vilnat, A. 643
Vintsyuk, T. K. 306
Voge, W. 690
Vorhees, E. 259, 417, 419, 474, 477, 539, 562, 618
Vossen, P. 472, 473, 474, 478
Vossers, M. 658
Voutilainen, A. 226, 227, 228, 373, 457, 610

Wacholder, N. 538, 608
Wagnal, A. W. 52
Wagstaff, K. 278
Wahlster, W. 526, 638, 655, 656, 665
Walker, M. A. 133, 271, 424, 642, 643
Walker, M. G. 623
Wall, R. 93, 174
Walther, M. 20
Waltz, D. 255, 385
Wang, J. 540, 549
Wanner, L. 301
Ward, K. 636, 641, 643, 644
Wareham, T. 20
Warschauer, M. 686
Wasow, T. 89, 175, 396
Wauchope, K. 630
Wazinski, P. 662
Weaver, W. 510
Webber, B. 133, 277, 497, 634
Webelhuth, G. 89
Webster, N. 51, 52
Weinberg, A. 690
Weinstein, S. 131, 133, 271
Weir, D. 494, 496
Weischedel, R. 224, 690
Weizenbaum, J. 147
Westerstahl, D. 94
Weyuker, E. 174
Whalen, T. 645

White, H. D. 618
White, J. 421, 422
Whittaker, S. 424, 634
Wichmann, A. 681, 682
Widdowson, H. 674, 686
Wiener, N. 510
Wierzbicka, A. 51, 55
Wiese, R. 19
Wilensky, R. 630
Wilks, Y. 55, 154, 250, 251, 252, 254, 256, 259, 261, 277,
      423, 472, 476, 478
Willet, P. 618
Williams, S. 642, 643
Wilson, A. 450, 452, 453, 458, 461
Wilson, D. 143, 154
Winograd, T. 277, 579, 643
Winski, R. 149, 644, 645
Wise, B. 540
Wise, J. A. 618
Witbrock, M. 586, 590, 661
Wood, D. 174, 357
Woodland, P. C. 312
Woods, W. 84, 89, 277, 563, 579, 611, 634
Wright, R. 355
Wu, D. 373, 527
Wüster, E. 600

Xianping, G. 211
Xu, J. 618

Yalop, C. 19
Yang, J. 527
Yangarber, R. 556
Yarowsky, D. 256, 257, 258, 260, 261, 373, 476, 549
Yngve, V. 250
Yokoi, T. 397, 472
Young, S. 312, 317, 320, 636, 641, 644
Younger, D. 189, 237
Yu, S. 354

Zadrozny, W. 102, 175
Zaenen, A. 341, 685, 709
Zajac, R. 446
Zampolli, A. 65
Zancanaro, M. 656, 661
Zelle, J. 389
Zernik, U. 65, 406
Zhai, C. 609
Zhou, J. 537
Ziadi, D. 354
Zilberstein, A. 619
Zock, M. 297, 300, 301, 678, 687, 691
Zue, V. 643
Zwicky, A. 46

Subject Index

abductive logic 145
abductive reasoning 563
ablaut 32
abstract 584
ACABIT 606
acceptability testing 423
accuracy 203
accuracy of tagsets 223
acoustic models 308–11
acoustic parameterization 307
ACQUILEX 471
active edge 240
adjoining 487
adverb anaphora 269
AECMA simplified English 441, 442
affix 30
agenda 236
agglutinative language 28
agreement *see* concord
AIMI 655, 656
ALE 246
ALFRESCO 656, 661
aligned corpus 516, 524
alignment 671, 676, 679
allomorph 8, 26
allophone 4, 13, 313
ALPAC report 420
alphabet (in formal languages) 157
Alvey NL tools 246
ambiguity 72
ambiguity look-up 221
ambiguity resolution 222
ambisyllabicity 18
American Dictionary of English Language 51–2
American Heritage Dictionary 52, 54
American National Corpus 54
ANA 607
analogy-based machine translation 513; *see also*
    example-based machine translation
anaphor 116, 266
anaphora 266, 518
anaphora resolution 269–79, 391–2, 459, 513,
    518–20, 554

anaphora resolution factors 273–4, 278
annotated corpora 277, 554
annotation guidelines 417
answer extraction 568, 576–8
answer type taxonomy 570–2
antecedent 267
application programming interface 632
Ariane 510
assimilation 36
association 400
associative anaphora 269
assumption 144
Athena Language Project (ALP) 677
ATIS 150, 424, 644
attribute-value matrices 17
Augmented Transition Network (ATN) 84–5, 89
automated text summarization 584–95; *see also*
    text summarization
automatic downstep 11
automatic indexing 604, 608–11
automatic phonetization 327–9
autosegmental phonology 9–13
autosegmental rules 10
auxiliary tree 487
average case complexity 180

back-off mechanism 315
Bank of English corpus 53, 221, 451, 452
bare co-occurrence frequency 398
Bar-Hillel pumping lemma 166
base form 27
Baum–Welch re-estimation algorithm 225, 310
Bayesian adaptation 311
Bayesian classifier 587
Bayes's inversion formula 360
belief 144
Bernoulli distribution 362
bilingual alignment tool 700
bilingual concordancer 525
bilingual corpus (corpora) 682, 683, 705, 706
bilingual dictionary 618, 700
bilingual system 503
bilingual term acquisition 611–12

bilingual texts 671
bimachine 353
Boolean systems 534
bound morph 26
bridging anaphora 269
British National Corpus 51, 52, 53, 54, 62, 221, 449, 451, 452, 455, 461
Broadcast News Navigator 660
Brown corpus 54, 203, 213, 216, 224, 387, 459, 705

C4.5 388, 587
C5 391
Callimaque 713
Cambridge International Dictionary of English 53, 254
candidate term 605
canned question answering 562
case-based learning 384
case-based machine translation 513; *see also* example-based machine translation
case roles 64
categorial grammars 496, 664
c-command 274
CELEX 574
centering (theory) 130–2
Chambers English Dictionary 53
chart 236
Chomsky hierarchy 160, 185
Chomsky normal form 189, 237
chunk 234
chunker 234
circumfix 31
CKY parsing algorithm 189, 190, 191, 236–9
CLARIT 536, 609
classification and regression tree (CART) techniques 329, 331, 332
classification thesaurus 396
CLAWS 224, 455, 459
clitic 35
close-class question 579
clustering 402–3
coarticulation 18, 324
COBUILD dictionary 53, 61
code 651
Collins English Dictionary 50, 52, 255
collocation 60, 299, 397, 400
Columbia Digital News System 661
combinatory categorial grammars 496
COMET 655, 656, 657, 658
comparable corpora 450
COMPASS 684, 709
complementary distribution 4
complexity classes 181
complexity in NLP 178–96

complexity measures 179–80
composition 343, 344
compounding 29–30
comprehension aid 700; *see also* comprehension assistant
comprehension assistant 708–13
compression ratio 593
computational dialogue 147–53
computational lexicography 48, 49
computational morphology 25, 37–45, 680, 684–7
computational phonology 3, 16–19
computational semantics 92–109
computational terminology 600
computer-assisted language learning (CALL) 670–93
concatenation 158
conceptual primitive 469
concord 73
concordancing 680, 682
conditional downstep 11
conditional probability 360
constituent object parser (COP) 609
constituent structure 85
constraint-based feature-structure grammars 85–8
constraint grammar 226
context-dependent acoustic model 306
context-free backbone grammar 239
context-free derivation 79
context-free grammar 78–81, 159, 162–3
context-free parsers 235–6
context planning 289–90
context-sensitive grammar 159
continuous speech 324
contour tones 11
controlled indexing 604
controlled language 441–6, 502
co-occurrence 278, 398, 434, 535
co-occurrence vector 399
COP 536
COPSY 610
coreference resolution 270, 276, 278
coreference 267, 276
coreferential chain 267, 276
Corelex 471
corpus 397, 531, 449–50, 681
corpus annotation 453–7
corpus linguistics 448–61, 512
corpus-based dictionary 53–4
corpus-based lexicography 58
Cosine measure 402, 403
CRATER 457
CRITTER 439

cross-document coreference 268
cross-document coreference resolution 276
cross-document summarization 276; see also
    multi-document summarization
cross-language evaluation forum 541
cross-language information retrieval 540, 700,
    702–6
cross-media referring expression 658
c-structure see constituent structure
CUBRICON 653, 654, 655
cue phrase 586
Cyberella 662
CYBERPUNC 216
Cyc 397, 470, 473, 477, 478

DARPA 318, 421, 426, 537, 541, 562, 619, 644
data base extraction 440
data mining 381, 617
database technology 677
decision problem 180
decision tree 278, 376, 377, 548
decision-tree induction 379–81
decoding 317
deep structure 82
default logic 145
definite clause grammar 93, 187, 195
definite description 268
definite NP 116, 121
DELIS 471
dependency parsing 235
derivation (in formal languages) 159
derivation (in morphology) 29–30
Derivation Final Model 100
derivation tree 163–5, 490
description logics 469
deterministic finite-state automaton 182
diagnostic frame 471
dialogue 146–54
dialogue act 150
dialogue corpus 148
dialogue grammar 152, 153
dialogue management models 152
Dice coefficient 399, 402, 408
Dictionary of the English Language (Samuel
    Johnson) 50
differentiae 466
digital audio and video 677
digital library 713
DIPLOMAT 527
direct anaphora 269
direct translation 503
disambiguation 222
DISC 645
discourse 112–33

discourse knowledge 271
discourse model 115, 122, 632
discourse plans 153
discourse processing 563; see also discourse
    tagging
Discourse Resource Initiative (DRI) 151, 154
discourse segment 113, 271, 273
discourse segmentation 416; see also text
    segmentation
discourse structure 290
discourse tagging 417; see also discourse
    processing
document processing 530, 531, 568, 574
document ranking 417
document retrieval 560
document threading 417
domain model 470
domain of locality 484
DR-LINK 536
dynamic programming 236
dynamic theories of meaning 93
dynamic theories of semantics 120

EAGLES 154, 418, 477, 645
EDR Electronic Dictionary 61, 397, 472, 478
elementary tree 487
elision 36
ELIZA 147, 643
ELRA (European Language Resources
    Association) 65, 408, 426, 461, 478
email translation 523
embedded-component evaluation 415
emission probabilities 366
empirical computational linguistics 618
Encarta 562
end-of-line hyphen 207
ENGCG 226, 227
EngCG-2 220, 227
English constraint grammar parser 367
entropy 363
epenthesis 36
error diagnosis 688–90
error rate 203, 416, 417
error recognition 688–90
Eurotra 510
EuroWordNet 59, 472, 477, 478
evaluation 278, 414–26, 557
evaluation of interactive systems 416, 423–5
event extraction 545, 550–8
example-based machine translation 513, 514–16
expectation-maximization algorithm 310, 312
expectation value 363
expected answer type 567, 568
extra-metrical syllable 15

extract 584
extrinsic evaluation 591; *see also* extrinsic
    measures
extrinsic measures 420, 422–3; *see also* extrinsic
    evaluation

failure-to-find fallacy 58
FASIT 608
FAST 574
FASTR 611
feature geometry 13
feature structure 85
felicity conditions 140
FERRET 536
finite (state) automata 171–2, 182–5; *see also* finite-
    state machines
finite-state machines 16–17; 77–8; *see also* finite
    (state) automata
finite-state morphology 39–44
finite-state relation 341
finite-state technology 339–55
finite-state transducers 234
floating tone 12
focus 124–5, 291
foreign language learning 674
formal grammars 157–74
formal languages 157–74
frame vector *see* parameter vector
Framenet 64
free indexing 604
free morph 26
free variation 4
f-structure 85; *see also* functional structure
Functional Dependency Grammar (FDG) 235
functional structure 85; *see also* f-structure
functional theory 287

generalized phrase structure grammar
    (GPSG) 88
generalized quantifiers 94
generalized upper model 478
generation 84, 423, 687; *see also* natural language
    generation
generation gap 300
generative lexicon 63
generative phonology 6–9
genus 466
genus term 407; *see also* genus word
genus word 398; *see also* genus term
Gibbs distribution 369
GLOSSER 684, 685, 686, 687
gold standard 244, 416
government and binding theory 83, 89, 100
grapheme-to-phoneme conversion 37

Greibach normal form 167, 188
Grice's cooperative principle 141
Grolier's Encyclopaedia 257
guesser 221

Hamming distance 385
Hansard (corpus) 256, 517
head-driven phrase structure grammar
    (HPSG) 88, 89, 241, 396, 496
headword 398
HEARSAY 643
heavy syllable 14
HECTOR 62–3, 259
hidden Markov models (HMM) 205, 224, 307,
    310, 311, 364–6, 549, 590
hierarchy 467
high performance knowledge bases 562
higher-order logic 93
HMM tagger 225, 226
human-aided machine translation 501
hybrid system 518
hypertext 677
hyphenation 37

IBM/Lancaster Spoken English Corpus 449, 461
identity-of-reference anaphora 267
identity-of-sense anaphora 267
ILEX 656
illocutionary act 138
illocutionary force 138–9
image retrieval 659–60
implication 140
implicature 128–9, 141
incremental generation 299
independent evens 361
indicative summary 584
indirect anaphora 269
inference 141, 144–5
inflection 28–9
inflectional language 28
infix 31
Infomedia 661
information extraction 276, 389–90, 417, 474, 536,
    545–58, 560, 561, 563, 604
information format 440
information gain 381
information retrieval 474, 529–42, 560, 561, 563,
    604, 617, 618, 702
information theory 594
informative summary 584
informativeness 416, 420
informativeness of tag sets 223
inheritance relation 88
initial term acquisition 604

initial tree 487
INQUERY 538
instance-based categorization 377, 384–5; *see also* instance-based learning
instance-based learning 377, 384–5; *see also* instance-based categorization, case-based learning and memory-based learning
intelligent CALL 678
inter-annotator agreement 417
interlingua approach 503
interlingua-based MT 513, 520–1
international phonetic alphabet 4–6
inter-sentential segmentation 202
intervocalic consonant 14
intrinsic evaluation 591; *see also* intrinsic measures
intrinsic measures 420–2; *see also* intrinsic evaluation
inverse document frequency 534
inverted index 532
IREX 546
island parsing 241
isolating language 28
iterative proportional fitting procedure 707

Jaccard's coefficient 399, 402
Jensen–Shannon divergence 399
joint probability 360

KL-ONE 478
k-nearest neighbour 385
knowledge acquisition 563
knowledge base 465
knowledge-based (interlingua) MT system 508, 520
knowledge interchange format (KIF) 470
knowledge representation system 469
KPML 299
Kullback–Leibler divergence 399, 402
Kuroda normal form 170

Lancaster-Oslo/Bergen corpus 224
language identification 699, 700–2
language model 305, 315
large vocabulary continuous speech recognition (LVCSR) 315
LaSIE 475
latent semantic indexing 535
LDC (Linguistic Data Consortium) 318, 408, 426, 461, 478
LECTOR 57
lemma 38
lemma lexicon 38
lemmatization 38, 455, 672, 676, 678, 682

lemmatizer 455
letter-to-sound module 327
level tones 11
Leverhulme Corpus of Children's Writing 449, 461
lexical acquisition 405–6
lexical anchor 485
lexical functional grammar (LFG) 85, 88, 89, 241, 496, 688
lexical knowledge 270
lexical-level statistics 246
lexical look-up 205
lexical noun phrase anaphora 268
lexical semantic network 471
lexical semantic relation 471
lexical similarity 401–2, 535
lexical transducer 341–3
lexical tree-adjoining grammar 246
lexical variability 60
lexicalization 296–8
lexicalized tree-adjoining grammar 484, 488–91
lexicography 48–66
lexicon 221, 296, 312, 465
LEXTER 605
light syllable 14
LINDI 618, 623–5
linear bounded automata 174
linear grammar 166
linguistically motivated indexing 537
Link Grammar system 235, 246
LKB 246
local ambiguity parsing 238
LocoLex 709–11
log-likelihood ration 399, 606
long-distance dependency 76
Longman dictionary of contemporary English 52, 253, 407, 408
Longman lexicon of contemporary English 408
LTSTOP 214
LUNAR 579

machine-aided human translation 501
machine learning 226, 227, 278, 376–92
machine-readable dictionary 52, 252, 397, 398, 407
machine-tractable dictionary 54
machine translation 275, 325, 421, 422, 423, 439–40, 459, 501–11, 604, 680, 702, 704
macroplanning 288
MAGIC 655, 656, 659
Markov model 224, 227, 234, 366
Markov process 365
matching queries 533–5
MATE 154

maxim of manner 141, 142
maxim of quality 141, 142
maxim of quantity 141
maxim of relation 141, 142
maximum a posteriori (MAP) re-estimation
    formula 312
maximum-entropy equations 371–2
maximum-entropy models 366–9, 548, 576
maximum likelihood linear regression
    (MLLR) 312
meaning component 471
meaning representation language 631
meaning-text model 299
medium 651
memory-based learning 384
memory-based machine translation 513; see also
    example-based machine translation
Merrian-Webster Pocket Dictionary 407
Message Understanding Conference (MUC) 259,
    276, 278, 392, 418, 426, 460, 475, 546, 557, 558
metathesaurus 602, 603
Météo 431, 439, 510
microplanning 289
MikroKosmos 471, 476, 477, 478
mildly context-sensitive grammar 491
Minimalist Program 83, 89, 100
minority languages 522
MITTALK 328
modality 651
mode 651
monolingual corpus 450
monomorphemic words 26
monitor corpus 53, 451
morph 26
morpheme 26
morphological analysis 327, 417, 710, 711
morphology 25–47, 386–7, 684–7
morphophonology 36, 40, 327
morphosyntactic analysis 327
morphotactics 34–5
Mu 510
multi-component LTAG 493
multi-document summarization 590; see also
    cross-document summarization
multi-engine system 518
multilingual comprehension assistants 708–13
multilingual dictionary 700
multilingual system 503
multilingual term alignment 706
multimedia access 652
multimedia generation 652
multimodal input analysis 651
MURAX 579
mutual information 398, 400, 580

Naïve Bayesian classifiers 257, 388
name classification and identification 545,
    546–50; see also named entity recognition
name tagger 546–7
name tagging 417; see also named entity
    recognition
named entity recognition 207, 418, 524, 545,
    561, 632; see also name tagging and name
    classification and identification
named entity 564
named entity task 557
natural language generation 284–302, 440; see
    also generation
natural language interaction systems 629
natural language interface 630–5
network communication 677
*New English Dictionary on Historical
    Principles* 50
New Oxford American Dictionary 54
The New Oxford Dictionary of English 53
New York Times corpus 206
n-grams 205, 225, 401, 701
NIST 426, 541
nominal anaphora 269
non-compositional semantics 102–4
non-segmented languages 202, 205
nondeterministic polynomial algorithms 181
NP completeness 192–3
NP-hard problem 181
NPTool 610
nucleus 292

one sense per collocation claim 257
one sense per discourse claim 257, 258
onset maximization 14
Ontolingua 470
ontology 277, 290, 464–78
open-domain question answering 562
optimality theory 343
Oxford Advanced Learner's Dictionary 52, 252,
    404, 609
Oxford English Dictionary 50, 53, 54
Oxford-Hachette Dictionary 712

PANGLOSS 526
paradigm 27, 28
PARADISE 424
paragraph window 575
parallel corpora 450, 513, 706
parallel processing 191–2
parameter vector 308
Parikh mapping 169
Parikh set 169
parse disambiguation 243–4

parse forest 238
parser 233–48, 398, 637, 688
parsing 84, 233–48, 388, 417, 459, 679, 680
partial parsing 552–3; *see also* shallow parsing
part-of-speech 71, 203, 215, 220, 387, 466
part-of-speech tag 215, 387, 685
part-of-speech tagger 207, 215, 219, 220, 277, 387,
   398, 455, 710
part-of-speech tagging 219–30, 387, 417, 455, 459,
   618, 709
passive edge 240
PATR 88
PEA 656, 657
PEBA-II 656
PENMAN 299, 471
Penn Treebank 388, 397, 408, 455
Perceptron 388
perfect hash function 341
performative 139
phone 4, 309
phoneme 3–4
phonology 3–24
phonotactics 14
phrase structure 79, 80
phrase-structure grammar 89, 159
physical presentation 289
planning 292
PLATO 677
pleonastic pronoun 272
polaroid words 252
polynomial algorithms 181
polysemy 471
polysynthetic language 28
post-edit measures 422
post-edited 502
PPP 655, 656, 659
pragmatics 136–47
precision 203, 391, 416, 417, 531, 532, 585
predicate-argument relation 70, 71
pre-edited 502
preference semantics 250–1
prefix 31
preprocessor 209
presupposition 125–7
principles and parameters framework 83
probabilistic context-free grammar (PCFG) 189–
   90, 243
probabilistic model 548
probabilistic models 278, 534
probability density function 309, 362
probability distribution 362
probability measure 359, 360
problem complexity 180
pronominal anaphora 268

pronoun 116, 121
proper name 268
proper name translation 523, 705
prosodic hierarchy 13
prosody 9, 325
prosody generation 329–33
prosody generator 326
pruning 190–1, 388
pushdown automata 172–4

QUALC 574
quality 416, 420
QUALM 578
query-based summary 586
query processing 530, 533–5
question answering 276, 475, 541, 542, 560–80
question processing 567, 568–70
QuickSet 653, 654, 655

The Random House Dictionary 52
random process 364
random variable 361
reading comprehension 419
real-world knowledge 272
reasoning on data bases 563
recall 203, 391, 416, 417, 531, 532, 585
recursion 80
recursive transition network 84
reduplication 31–2
reference resolution 563, 566; *see also* anaphora
   resolution
referring expression 116–20, 121, 125, 205, 223, 266,
   269, 345–51
regression testing 423
regular grammar 77–8, 160
regular language 167–8, 182–5
relevance 145–6
relevance assessment 418, 422
replacement 347, 348–50
restriction 347, 348
retention ration 593
reversible MT system 504
rheme 123–4
rhetorical predicate 290
rhetorical structure theory 129–30, 292
rich contexts 601
Roget's Thesaurus 256, 397, 402, 408, 476
root 26, 27
root-and-template morphology 32
Rosetta 510
RST 290
rule-based MT system 504, 513
rule induction 377, 381–4

SAGE 655, 656
sample space 359
sampling frame 449
satellite 292
schemata 290
second language learning 674
segment 4
segmented languages 202
selectional preference 397, 404
selectional restriction 274, 397, 404, 476, 632
semantic disambiguation 711, 712; *see also*
　word sense disambiguation
semantic feature 471
semantic frames 64
semantic interpretation 638; *see also* semantic
　parsing and semantic processing
semantic knowledge 271
semantic parsing 389; *see also* semantic
　interpretation and semantic processing
semantic processing 563; *see also* semantic
　interpretation and semantic parsing
semantic similarity 475–7
semantically tagged corpus 712
semantics 91–109
SEMCOR 262
SENSEVAL 259
sentence boundary disambiguation 212
sentence segmentation 212, 416; *see also* sentence
　splitting
sentence splitting 202, 212; *see also* sentence
　segmentation
sequentiable transducer 352
SGML 204
shallow parser 277
shallow parsing 234, 712; *see also* partial parsing
SHRDLU 277, 579, 643
simulated annealing 253
SMART 538, 574
SNOMED 538
sound system 3
source language 503
specifiability of tagsets 223
speech acts 138–40
speech recognition 305–20, 636, 680
speech recognizer 216
speech signal synthesis 333–6
speech synthesis 680; *see also* speech signal
　synthesis
spelling correction 37
spoken corpus 450–1
spoken dialogue system 137, 630–44
spoken language machine translation 513,
　521–2
spontaneously spoken language 636

SQL 424
statistical machine translation 516–18
statistical methods 359–73
stem 27
stemmer 37, 532
stemming 531–2
stochastic lexicalized tree-adjoining
　grammar 497
stochastic process 364
strong generative capacity 484
stream model 538
story segmentation 416
STUDENT 277, 579
subcategorization 74, 609
subcategorization frame 74, 83, 397, 404
subject variability 424
subjective grading 420
sublanguage 431–9, 444–6, 503
subsumption 242, 467
subtree sharing 238
suffix 31
SUMMARIST 587
summarization 422, 441; *see also* text
　summarization
summary 583, 584
summary generation 589–91
SUMMONS 590, 591
SUNDIAL 149–50
suppletion 33
Survey of English Dialects 451, 461
SUSY 510
surface generation 298–300
surface generator 298
surface realization 289
surface structure 82
syllable canon 14
syllable structure 13–16
syllable weight 14
synset 472
syntactic analysis 233–48, 688; *see also* parsing
　or syntactic processing
syntactic dependency 74
syntactic feature 73
syntactic processing 563; *see also* parsing;
　syntactic analysis
syntax 70–89
syntax knowledge 270
syntax-semantics interface 92, 99–102
systemic-functional grammar 299
systemic paraphrase 73
Systran 510, 527

tag 220
tag set 56

tagged corpus 397
tagging 220
TAGGIT 224, 459
target language 503
task model 638
TAUM-AVIATION 439
TAUM-MÉTÉO 431, 439, 510
taxonomic thesaurus 396-7
taxonomy 467
taxonomy of QA systems 563-7
technology-based evaluation 415
term 600
term acquisition 604, 605-7
term alignment 706; see also multilingual term
    alignment
term discovery 604
term enrichment 604
term frequency 534
term recognition 604, 608-11
termbank 509
Termight 612
TERMINO 605
terminology management 509
TERMS 606
terrace tone language 11
test suite 245
TEXT 290
TextNet 475
text alignment 680, 683
text categorization 541, 619
text compression 589
text data mining 616-28; see also text mining
text mining 563; see also text data mining
text normalization 325
text planning 290-6
text segmentation 201-17; see also discourse
    segmentation
text summarization 276, 421, 422, 583-95; see also
    summarization
text-to-speech synthesis 323-36
text-to-speech synthesizer 324
TF*IDF 534, 538, 589
thematic roles 121, 122
theme 123-4
theory of distinctive features 5
thesaurus 402-3, 601-3
TICCIT 677
TIDES 541
TIPSTER 537, 541
TIPSTER-SUMMAC study 592
tokenization 201, 221
tokenizer 202
tone melody 12
topic 124-5, 584

topic classification 417
topic detection 417
topic detection and tracking initiative 619
topic fusion 588-9
topic identification 584, 585-8
topic tracking 417
transfer approach 503
transformational grammar 82-4, 89
transition probabilities 366
translation dictionary 705
translation memory 510, 514, 524
translation tool 501
translation workstation 502, 510
TREC 259, 536, 539, 541, 562, 564, 568, 573, 577, 578,
    580, 592, 702
TREC evaluation 572, 577
tree-adjoining grammar 89, 299, 483-97
tree-local MC-TAG 493
tree-structure analysis 538
tree substitution 485
treebank 243
TRINDI 154
true hyphen 207
TTP parser 609
TTS design 325-7
Turing machine 174
Turing test 673
two-level morphology 40-3
typed feature structure grammars 95-8
typed feature structures 95-8, 471

umlaut 33
UMLS 538, 539, 602
underlying form (of a word) 7
underspecified representation 93, 102-4
unification 88, 241
unification-based grammar 88
unification-based parsing 241-2
unvoiced consonants 5
user-centred evaluation 415
utterance 137

valence 74
valency patterns 64
variance 363
vector space models 534
verb anaphora 267, 269
VERMOBIL 149-50, 152, 154, 526
video retrieval 659-60
Viterbi algorithm 310, 366, 370, 548
Viterbi search 317, 366, 370
VITRA-SOCCER 662
vocabulary (in formal languages) 158
voiced consonants 5

voicing alternation 6
vowel harmony 9

Wall Street Journal corpus 203, 206, 213, 216, 319,
    387, 388, 589
weak generative capacity 484
web page translation 523
Webster's 7th New Collegiate Dictionary 55,
    407
well-formed substring Table 236
WIP 655, 656, 658, 659
Wizard of Oz experiments 149, 634
word biagram model 365
word expert parsing 251–2
word segmentation 203, 416
word sense disambiguation 249–62, 387–8, 475–7,
    618, 687, 711; *see also* word sense tagging and
    semantic disambiguation

word sense tagging 417; *see also* word sense
    disambiguation
word token 203
word type 203
WordNet 59–60, 387, 387, 388, 392, 402, 403, 404,
    408, 472, 473, 475, 476, 477, 478, 538, 539, 563,
    564, 565, 571, 573, 574, 580, 619, 621, 712, 714
world knowledge 466
worst case complexity 180

XDOD 713
XML 204
XTAG 491
XTRA 653, 654
Xtract 607

zero anaphora 269
Zipf's law 586t